Warman's

Antiques &
Collectibles
2008 Price Guide
41st Edition

Ellen T. Schroy
Edited by Tracy L. Schmidt

©2007 Krause Publications

Published by

700 East State Street • Iola, WI 54990-0001
715-445-2214 • 888-457-2873
www.krausebooks.com

Our toll-free number to place an order or obtain
a free catalog is (800) 258-0929.

As condition, regional fluctuations, and other factors influence market pricing, the prices
contained in this book are intended to serve only as a guide. The publisher recommends
users research price trends in their regions before buying and selling items.

Library of Congress Catalog Number: ISSN: 1076-1985

978-0-89689-497-6

Designed by Wendy Wendt and Marilyn McGrane

Edited by Tracy L. Schmidt

Printed in China

CONTENTS

DEDICATION

To Maeve Marguerite Phillips, remembered with love.

To all future generations of collectors who will continue our love of old treasures, including: Emily, Nicky, and Hope; Kenna and Aaron, Jonas, Lily Grace, and Lorraine.—Ellen S.

To Mom & Dad, Dan J. & Chris, Barb & Merlin H.-Thank you all for your guidance and friendship through the years. To Kyle B., you inspired many people with your strength and courage through the process of treating your cancer. Congratulations on your success.—Tracy

Introduction

WARMAN'S: SERVING THE TRADE FOR MORE THAN 50 YEARS

In 1994, *Warman's Antiques and Their Prices* became *Warman's Antiques and Collectibles Price Guide*. Individuals in the trade refer to this book simply as Warman's, a fitting tribute to E. G. Warman and the product he created. Warman's has been around for more than 50 years. We are proud as peacocks that Warman's continues to establish the standards for general antiques and collectibles price guides in 2008, just as it did in 1972 when its first rival appeared on the scene.

Warman's, the antiques and collectibles "bible," covers objects made between 1700 and the present. Because it reflects market trends, Warman's has added more and more 20th-century material to each edition. Remember, 1900 was more than 100 years ago—the distant past to the new generation of 20-something and 30-something collectors. The general "antiques" market consists of antiques

(for the purposes of this book, objects made before 1945), collectibles (objects of the post-World War II era that enjoy an established secondary market), and desirables (contemporary objects that are collected, but speculative in price). Although Warman's contains information on all three market segments, its greatest emphasis is on antiques and collectibles. In fact, this book is the essential field guide to the antiques and collectibles marketplace, which indicates that Warman's is much more than a list of object descriptions and prices. It is a basic guide to the field as a whole, providing you with the key information you need every time you encounter a new object or collecting category.

'Warman's is the Key'

Warman's provides the keys needed by auctioneers, collectors, dealers, and others to understand and deal with the complexities of the antiques and collectibles market. A price list is only one of many keys needed today. Warman's 41st edition contains histories, marks, reproductions and useful buying and collecting hints. Used properly, there are few doors these keys will not open. Warman's is designed to be your first key to the exciting world of antiques and collectibles. As you use the keys this book provides to advance further in your specialized collecting areas, Warman's hopes you will remember with fondness where you received your start. When you encounter items outside your area of specialty, remember Warman's remains your key to unlocking the information you need, just as it has in the past.

Scenic vase, etched and enameled, continuous frieze of pond scene, egrets in flight, polychrome and gilt, pale green and mauve ground, gilt signature Daum Nancy with Cross of Lorraine, c1890, 8-1/2", **$7,200.**
Photo courtesy of David Rago Auctions, Inc.

Organization

Listings: Objects are listed alphabetically. The major collecting areas have been compiled into in-

HOW DO YOU LIKE YOUR WARMAN'S®?

The editorial staff at Krause Publications would like to get your feedback and suggestions to further grow and improve *Warman's® Antiques & Collectibles*. Your feedback will make a difference. Please e-mail your responses to: tracy.schmidt@fwpubs.com.

dividual areas at the front of the book and have been color coded. The lisitngs contain some harder-to-find objects that are included to demonstrate market spread—useful information worth considering when you have not traded actively in a category recently. Each year as the market changes, we carefully review our categories—adding, dropping, and combining to provide the most comprehensive coverage possible. Warman's quick response to developing trends in the marketplace is one of the prime reasons for its continued leadership in the field.

History: Collectors and dealers enhance their appreciation of objects by knowing something about their history. We present a capsule history for each category. In many cases, this history contains collecting hints or other useful information.

References: Krause Publications also publishes other Warman's titles. Each concentrates on a specific collecting group, e.g., American pottery and porcelain, Americana and collectibles, glass, and jewelry. Several are second or subsequent editions. They have been included in each section. There are also several good publications collectors and dealers should be aware of to be knowledgeable about antiques and collectibles in general. Space does not permit listing all of the national and regional publications in the antiques and collectibles field; this is a sampling:

- **Antique & The Arts Weekly**, Bee Publishing Company, 5 Church Hill Road, Newton, CT 06470; http://www.thebee.com/aweb
- **Antique Review**, P.O. Box 538, Worthington, OH 43085
- **Antique Trader Weekly**, published by Krause Publications, Iola, WI 54990
- **AntiqueWeek**, P.O. Box 90, Knightstown, IN 46148; http://www.antiqueweek.com
- **Maine Antique Digest**, P.O. Box 358, Waldoboro, ME 04572; http:// www.maineantiquedigest.com
- **New England Antiques Journal**, 4 Church St., Ware, MA 01082

Reproductions: Reproductions are a major concern to all collectors and dealers. Throughout this edition, boxes will alert you to known reproductions and keys to recognizing them. Most reproductions are unmarked; the newness of their appearance is often the best clue to uncovering them. Specific objects known to be reproduced are marked within the listings with an asterisk (*). The information is designed to serve as a reminder of past reproductions and prevent you from buying them, believing them to be period. We strongly recommend subscribing to *Antique & Collectors Reproduction News,* a monthly online newsletter that reports on past and present reproductions, copycats, fantasics, and fakes. For the subscription price of $27, you will have a valuable library of information at your fingertips. The website is www.repronews.com and is well worth the investment.

Price notes

In assigning prices, we assume the object is in very good condition; if otherwise, we note this in our description. It would be ideal to suggest that mint, or unused, examples of all objects exist. The real-

Carousel horse, small, white painted cast zinc, painted orange bridal, leather saddle paint and leather losses, American, late 19th century, 27" h x 35" l, **$940.**
Photo courtesy of Skinner, Inc.

ity is that objects from the past were used, whether they are glass, china, dolls, or toys. Because of this, some normal wear must be expected. In fact, if an object such as a piece of furniture does not show wear, its origins may be more suspect than if it does show wear. Whenever possible, we have tried to provide a broad listing of prices within a category so you have a "feel" for the market. We emphasize the middle range of prices within a category, while also listing some objects of high and low value to show market spread. We do not use ranges because they tend to confuse, rather than help, the collector and dealer. How do you determine if your object is at the high or low end of the range? There is a high degree of flexibility in pricing in the antiques field. If you want to set ranges, add or subtract 10 percent from our prices.

Price research

Everyone asks, "Where do you get your prices?"

They come from many sources. First, we rely on auctions. Auction houses and auctioneers do not always command the highest prices. If they did, why do so many dealers buy from them? The key to understanding auction prices is to know when a price is high or low in the range. We think we do this and do it well. The 41st edition represents a concentrated effort to contact more regional auction houses, both large and small. The cooperation has been outstanding and has resulted in an ever-growing pool of auction prices and trends to help us determine the most up-to-date auction prices.

Second, we work closely with dealers. We screen our contacts to make certain they have full knowledge of the market. Dealers make their living from selling antiques; they cannot afford to have a price guide that is not in touch with the market. More than 50 antiques and collectibles magazines, newspapers, and journals come into our office regularly. They are excellent barometers of what is moving and what is not. We don't hesitate to call an advertiser and ask if his listed merchandise sold. When the editorial staff is doing fieldwork, we identify ourselves. Our conversations with dealers and collectors around the country have enhanced this book. Teams from Warman's are in the field at antiques shows, malls, flea markets, and auctions recording prices and taking photographs. Collectors work closely with us.

They are specialists whose devotion to research and accurate information is inspiring. Generally, they are not dealers. Whenever we have asked them for help, they have responded willingly and admirably.

Board of advisers

Our board of advisers is made up of specialists, both dealers and collectors, who feel a commitment to accurate information. You'll find their names listed in the front of the book. Several have authored a major reference work on their subject. Our esteemed board of advisers has increased in number and scope. Participants have all provided detailed information regarding the history and reference section of their particular area of expertise, as well as preparing price listings. Many have furnished photographs and even shared with us their thoughts on the state of the market. We are delighted to include those who are valuable members, officers, and founders of collectors' clubs. They are authors of books and articles, and many frequently lecture to groups about their specialties. Most of our advisers have been involved with antiques and collectibles for more than 20 years. Several are retired, and the antiques and collectibles business is a hobby that encompasses most of their free time. Others are a bit younger and either work full time or part time in the antiques and collectibles profession. One thing they all have in common is their enthusiasm for the antiques and collectibles marketplace. They are eager to share their knowledge with collectors. Many have developed wonderful friendships through their efforts and are enriched by them. If you wish to buy or sell an object in the field of expertise of any of our advisers, drop them a note along with an SASE. If time permits, they will respond.

Buyer's guide, not seller's guide

Warman's is designed to be a buyer's guide, suggesting what you would have to pay to purchase an object on the open market from a dealer or collector. It is not a seller's guide to prices. People frequently make this mistake. In doing so, they deceive themselves. If you have an object listed in this book and wish to sell it to a dealer, you should expect to receive approximately 50 percent of the listed value. If the object will not resell quickly, expect to receive even less. Private collectors may pay more, perhaps 70 to 80 percent of our listed price, if your object is something needed for their collection. If you have an extremely rare object or an object of exceptionally high value, these guidelines do not apply. Examine your piece as objectively as possible. As an antiques and collectibles appraiser, I spend a great deal of time telling people their treasures are not "rare" at all, but items readily available in the marketplace. In respect to buying and selling, a simple philosophy is that a good purchase occurs when the buyer and seller are happy with the price. Don't look back. Hindsight has little value in the antiques and collectibles field. Given time, things tend to balance out.

Always improving

Warman's is always trying to improve. Space is freely given to long price descriptions to help you understand what the piece looks like, and perhaps what's special about it. With this edition, we've arranged some old formats, Many times, identifying what you've got is the hardest part. Well, the first place to start is how big—grab that ruler and see what you can find that's a comparable size. You are still going to have to make a determination about what the object is made of, be it china, glass, porcelain, wood, or other materials. Use all your senses to discover what you've got. Ask questions about your object, who made it, and why, how was it used, where, and when. As you find answers to these questions, you'll be helping yourself figure out just what the treasure is all about.

Eager to hear from readers

At Warman's and Krause Publications, we're always eager to hear what you think about this book and how we can improve it. Write to either

> Ellen Schroy
> Warman's Editor
> 135 S. Main St.,
> Quakertown, PA 18951-1119
> schroy@voicenet.com

or

> Tracy Schmidt
> Krause Publications
> 700 E. State St.
> Iola, WI 54990
> tracy.schmidt@fwpubs.com

Ellrose bowl in stand, amber, fitted in a Webster quadruple-plate stand, undetermined association, Geo. Duncan and Sons, fourth quarter 19th century, 12" h, 9-1/4" d , $110.
Photo courtesy of Green Valley Auctions.

Clewell copper-clad vase, bottle shaped, good verdigris patina, incised Clewell/361, 10" x 4-1/2", sold at auction for $1,080.
Photo courtesy of David Rago Auctions, Inc.

Muller Freres, etched and enameled scenic vase, glass, wooded winter landscape, naturalistic colors, shaded mauve and amber ground, cameo signature, 4-1/4", **$1,200.**
Photo courtesy of David Rago Auctions, Inc.

Cabinet ewer, glass, etched amd enameled, applied handle and foot, Dutch landscape with blue windmills on white ground, engraved Daum Nancy with Cross of Lorraine, c1900, 3-1/2", **$1,080.**
Photo courtesy of David Rago Auctions, Inc.

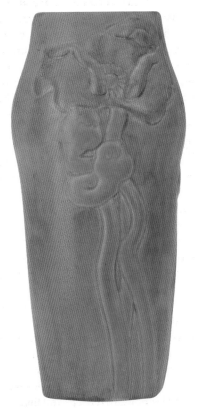

Van Briggle bulbous vase, ceramic, sharply embossed with purple poppies on bright green stems, mottled light blue-green ground, AA Van Briggle/1902/2D/III, 1902, 8" h x 4", sold at auction for **$31,200.**
Photo courtesy of David Rago Auctions, Inc.

Emile Galle, marqueterie-sur-verre butterfly vase, glass, four carved flying butterflies: mauve, white, yellow and black; mauve, amber and clear bubbled ground, engraved Emile Galle, c1900, 6-3/4" h, **$27,000.**
Photo courtesy of David Rago Auctions, Inc.

STATE OF THE MARKET
WARMAN'S ANTIQUES & COLLECTIBLES PRICE GUIDE
41ST EDITION

While there are some exciting changes to the format of this edition of Warman's that you are holding in your hands, some things are the same—including this segment giving my opinion of how the state of the antiques and collectibles market is presently faring. If you are a new reader to Warman's, you may be someone who's just coming into the antiques and collectibles marketplace and finding it a bit overwhelming. Congrats to you for picking up and reading this fine price guide. Hopefully it will help answer your questions and lead you to others than can help on your journey. If you are a collector, you know where to find the information you're searching for. If you are a seasoned Warman's reader, you probably can anticipate what I'm about to tell you, for you are one of those folks, be it a dealer or collector, or even causal visitor to the world of antiques and collectibles, who know how you feel about the current market.

Today is a great time to BUY BUY BUY! Why? The antiques market is cyclical and it looks like it's starting to rise again out of the valley it's been in for the past few years. And for those who are buying antiques as investments, you want to buy on the low side, enjoy your treasures, and if and when you sell them, sell them on the peak of the crest. As the market moves slightly higher, now is a great time to seriously think about investing in good quality pieces, buying the best you can afford. Today's marketplace is filled with terrific examples, some gleaned from private collections, others de-accessioned from major museums. It is the collector who has cash in his pocket at the moment who will be in a position to scoop up these treasures.

Many museums are now finding themselves to be in an unusual position. Many have showcases, closets, etc. filled to the brim with "things" donated during the past decades. As a museum continues to grow, perhaps re-define their collecting goals, they often decide that these boxes are filled with treasures they no longer need or will use. Often, they will quietly put these objects up for sale at auction or privately.

This gives collectors an excellent chance to purchase something that's "new" to the marketplace, plus may have an excellent provenance. The museum then also has a wonderful opportunity to take the cash generated from such a sale and go out and purchase examples that fit better into their collection. It is the savy dealer who can benefit from this side of the equation, by knowing what direction that particular museum may be heading with their collections and being able to offer them interesting examples.

As in real estate, the buzz word is "location, location, location"–to the antique collector it's "condition, condition, condition." While some antique treasures can be easily restored, others such as glass or textiles are very difficult to mend and return to a new-like condition. Some glass chips can be buffed or polished away, but a smashed vase is pretty worthless. A coverlet that has come apart at the seams can be re-stitched, but one that's been laundered and has simply worn away from use is probably beyond saving. Sadly, that example of a weaver's hard efforts may disappear from the collecting scene, perhaps to be replaced by another example, and hopefully not forgotten.

Today's modern collectors also have an edge collectors in the early years of accumulating antiques did not—we have the ability to tap into vast banks of knowledge, be it through the written word, through the generous nature of dealers' experiences, or through the internet. Many of the old timer collectors studiously wrote down their experiences, what they learned about their specialties. Today's collectors can and should be brave enough to buy some unattributed or unmarked examples, do the research on them just as the antiques market pioneers such as Edwin Warman or Hazel Weatherman did.

This is not the time to be a "penny collector"–only collecting one penny at a time and only searching for a penny with a particular date or mint mark –now is the time to be brave and buy that piece that has captured your heart. It is a perfect time to strike up a friendship with local auctioneers, museum curators, dealers, who can help direct you to what kinds of items may be coming up for sale in the

Hamm's Bear bank, unmarked, this example with raised letters, also found with decal, late 1950s, 12" h, **$400.**

Delaware bowl bride's basket, green, gilt dec, Meriden silver-plate frame, undetermined association, late 19th century, 5-1/2" h, bowl 7" h x 11-3/4", **$110.**
Photo courtesy of Green Valley Auctions.

Mickey Mouse Talkie Jector, electric phonograph/projector, 11 films (one not boxed), three records, Movie Jector Company, New York, early 1930s, machine 14" l, **$760.**
Photo courtesy of Skinner, Inc.

next few months. Do some reading, check out what other kinds of items have been included in collections of this type of item in the past, determine if there is something that has been missed by the earlier collectors, decide how you can make your own collecting even better and then act on it.

The excuses we've all used the past few seasons to avoid adding to our collections are slipping away –gas prices are dropping, the weather isn't as bad as had been predicted, the real estate market isn't so appealing, interest rates are rising. So the time is absolutely right to do just what the Greatest Generation did – hop in our cars and go out to seek objects from their childhoods. Treasure them, use them to decorate our homes, and marvel every day at the wonderful life we have now, thanks to their hard working efforts and the objects they choose to save so we can appreciate them too. It's the perfect time to make plans to meet friends and fellow collectors at a favorite antique show or mall, trade stories as you wander around and look for more examples to add to your collections. Like the bumper sticker on my car says "follow me to the greatest antiques show – Atlantique City" – hope to see you there!

ACKNOWLEDGMENTS

We at Warman's would like to thank the following people for their contributions to the new 41st edition of *Warman's Antiques & Collectibles Price Guide*:

Bill and Sliv Carlson; photographer Maurice Childs; Jerry Cohen; Jeff Evans; Alexandra Grais; Heritage Galleries & Auctioneers; Larry and Debbie Hicklin of Middle Tenessee Relics; photographer Paul Goodwin; Leigh Leshner; Cathy and Jamie Melton of Wytheville, Va.; Mark Moran; Karen O'Brien; Gerald and Louise Schleich of Lincoln Neb.; Carol Seman and Dan Eggent of Brecksville, Ohio; Majolica Auctions by Michael G. Strawser; Jim and Jan Van Hoven; the Wisconsin Veterans Museum, and Karen and Lorie Wuttke of Remember When Antiques, Delavan, Wis.

Sugar bowl, Hobbs, Brockunier & Co., no. 326, Window Swirl, colorless opalescent, colorless applied round finial to cover, late 19th century, 6-1/4" h, **$90.**
Photo courtesy of Green Valley Auctions.

Quimper Faïence vase, Breton Broderie motif, marked HB Quimper P.H., c1925, 12-1/2" h, **$235.**
Photo courtesy of Sloans & Kenyon Auctioneers and Appraisers.

Harvey Ellis mixed media drawing on paper, four men working in a foundry, framed, unmarked, c1903, **$29,375.**
Photo courtesy of David Rago Auctions, Inc.

Oil lamp, Wedgwood, Thomas Allen design, enamel decorated, ground earthenware body, panels of youths and sunflowers, metal mounted base and lamp fittings, impressed marks, Hink's patent insert, England, c1880, 13-1/4" h base, **$4,230.**
Photo courtesy of Skinner, Inc.

BOARD OF ADVISERS

Bob Armstrong
15 Monadnock Road
Worcester, MA 01609
(508) 799-0644
www.oldpuzzles.com
Puzzles

Al Bagdade
The Country Peasants
1325 N. State Parkway, Apt 15A
Chicago, IL 60610
(312) 397-1321
Quimper

James P. Bixler
Spirit Dancer Rare Books, LLC
P.O. Box 11
Cloudcroft, NM 88317
(505) 682-1387
www.SpiritDancerBooks.com
Coins

Ted Hake
Hake's Americana & Collectibles
   Auctions
P.O. Box 1444
York, PA 17405
(717) 848-1333
e-mail: auction@hakes.com
Disneyana, Political

Joan Hull
1376 Nevada
Huron, SD 57350
(605) 352-1685
Hull Pottery

David Irons
Irons Antiques
223 Covered Bridge Road
Northampton, PA 18067
(610) 262-9335
e-mail: Dave@ironsantiques.com
Irons

Michael Ivankovich
Auction Co.
P.O. Box 1536
Doylestown, PA 18901
(215) 345-6094
www.wnutting.com
Wallace Nutting,
Wallace Nutting
Look-Alikes

Ellen G. King
King's Antiques
359 Peaceful Valley Rd.
Hilliards, PA 16040-1926
(724) 894-2596
e-mail: ellenk2@earthlink.net
Flow Blue
Mulberry China

Michael Krumme
P.O. Box 48225
Los Angeles, CA 90048-0225
Paden City

Mark B. Ledenbach
P.O. Box 2421
Orangevale CA 95662
www.HalloweenCollector.com

Robert Levy
The Unique One
2802 Centre St.
Pennsauken, NJ 08109
(856) 663-2554
Antiqueslotmachines.com
e-mail: theuniqueone@worldnet.
   att.net
Coin-Operated Items

James S. Maxwell, Jr.
P.O. Box 367
Lampeter, PA 17537
(717) 464-5573
Banks, Mechanical

Suzanne Perrault
Perrault Rago Gallery
333 North Main Street
Lambertville, NJ 08530
phone: (609) 397-1802
fax: (609) 397-9377
email: suzanne@ragoarts.com
Ceramics

Bob Perzel
505 Rt. 579
Ringoes, NJ 08551
(908) 782-9361
Stangl Birds

Evalene Pulati
National Valentine Collectors Assoc.
P.O. Box 1404
Santa Ana, CA 92702
Valentines

David Rago
David Rago Auctions, Inc.
333 N. Main St.
Lambertville, NJ 08530
(609) 397-9374
www.ragoarts.com
Art Pottery
Arts & Crafts
Fulper
Greuby
Newcomb

Julie P. Robards
P.O. Box 117
Upper Jay, NY 12987
(518) 946-7753
Celluloid

Jerry Rosen
15 Hampden St.
Swampscott, MA 01907
Piano Babies

Susan Scott
882 Queen St. West
Toronto, Ontario Canada
M6K 1Q3
e-mail: SusanScottCA@aol.com
Chintz

George Sparacio
P.O. Box 791
Malaga, NJ 08328-0791
(856) 694-4167
e-mail: mrvesta1@aol.com
Match Safes

Henry A. Taron
Tradewinds Antiques
P.O. Box 249
Manchester By-The-Sea, MA
   01944-0249
(978) 526-4085
e-mail:
   taron@tradewindsantiques.com
Canes

Lewis S. Walters
143 Lincoln Lane
Berlin, NJ 08009
(856) 719-1513
e-mail: lew69@erols.com
Phonographs
Radios

CONTRIBUTING AUCTION HOUSES

Alderfer Auction Company
501 Fairgrounds Road
Hatfield, PA 19440
(215) 393-3000
www.alderferauction.com

American Bottle Auctions
2523 J Street Suite 203
Sacramento, CA 95816
(800) 806-7722
www.americanbottle.com

Bertoia Auctions
2141 DeMarco Drive,
Vineland, NJ 08360
(856) 692-1881
www.bertoiaauctions.com

Craftsman Auctions
(800) 448-7828
www.craftsman-auctions.com

David Rago Auctions, Inc.
333 N. Main St.
Lambertville, NJ 08530
(609) 397-9374
www.ragoarts.com

Dotta Auction Company, Inc.
330 W. Moorestown Road
Nazareth, PA 18064
(610) 759-7389
www.dottaauction.com

Early Auction Company, LLC.
123 Main St.
Milford, OH 45150
(513) 831-4833
www.earlyauctionco.com

Green Valley Auctions, Inc.
2259 Green Valley Lane
Mt. Crawford, VA 22841
(540) 434-4260
www.greenvalleyauctions.com

Hake's Americana & Collectibles Auctions
P.O. Box 1444
York, PA 17405
(717) 848-1333
www.hakes.com

Joy Luke Fine Arts Brokers & Auctioneers
300 East Grove Street
Bloomington, Illinois 61701
(309) 828-5533
www.joyluke.com

Lang's Sporting Collectibles
663 Pleasant Valley Road
Waterville, NY 13480
(315) 841-4623
www.langsauction.com

McMasters Harris Auction Co.
5855 John Glenn Hwy
P.O. Box 1755
Cambridge, Ohio 43725
(740) 432-7400
www.mcmastersharris.com

Webb three-color English cameo vase, bulbous stick form, citron with white, crimson carvings, lower part has four floral medallions with foliage, neck has Moorish paneled design, 9-1/2" h, sold at auction for **$27,000.**
Photo courtesy of The Early Auction Company.

Michael Ivankovich Auction Co.
P.O. Box 1536
Doylestown, PA 18901
(215) 345-6094
www.wnutting.com

Old Barn Auction
10040 St. Rt. 224 West
Findlay, OH 45840
Phone: (419) 422-8531
www.oldbarn.com

Pook and Pook, Inc. Auctioneers and Appraisers
463 East Lancaster Ave.
Downingtown, PA 19335
(610) 629-0695
www.pookandpook.com

Skinner Inc.
357 Main St.
Bolton, MA 01740
(978) 799-6241
www.skinnerinc.com

Sloans and Kenyon Auctioneers and Appraisers
7034 Wisconsin Ave.
Chevy Chase, MD 20815
(301) 634-2344
www.sloansandkenyon.com

Strawser Auctions
PO Box 332, 200 North Main
Wolcottville, IN 46795
(260) 854-2859
www.strawserauctions.com

Tradewinds Antiques
P.O. Box 249
Manchester By-The-Sea, MA
01944-0249
(978) 526-4085
www.tradewindsantiques.com

Wiederseim Associates, Inc.
P.O. Box 470
Chester Springs PA 19425
(610) 827-1910
www.wiederseim.com

ABBREVIATIONS

The following are standard abbreviations, which we have used throughout this edition of Warman's.

ABP	-	American Brilliant Period	ll	-	lower left
ADS	-	Autograph Document Signed	lr	-	lower right
adv	-	advertising	ls	-	low standard
ah	-	applied handle	LS	-	Letter Signed
ALS	-	Autograph Letter Signed	mfg	-	manufactured
AQS	-	Autograph Quotation Signed	MIB	-	mint in box
C	-	century	MOP	-	mother-of-pearl
c	-	circa	n/c	-	no closure
Cal.	-	caliber	ND	-	no date
circ	-	circular	NE	-	New England
cyl.	-	cylinder	No.	-	number
cov	-	cover	NRFB	-	never removed from box
CS	-	Card Signed	ns	-	no stopper
d	-	diameter or depth	r/c	-	reproduction closure
dec	-	decorated	o/c	-	original closure
dj	-	dust jacket	opal	-	opalescent
DQ	-	Diamond Quilted	orig	-	original
DS	-	Document Signed	os	-	orig stopper
ed	-	edition	oz	-	ounce
emb	-	embossed	pcs	-	pieces
ext.	-	exterior	pgs	-	pages
eyep.	-	eyepiece	PUG	-	printed under the glaze
Folio	-	12" x 16"	pr	-	pair
ftd	-	footed	PS	-	Photograph Signed
ga	-	gauge	pt	-	pint
gal	-	gallon	qt	-	quart
ground	-	background	RM	-	red mark
h	-	height	rect	-	rectangular
horiz.	-	horizontal	sgd	-	signed
hp	-	hand painted	S. N.	-	Serial Number
hs	-	high standard	SP	-	silver plated
illus	-	illustrated, illustration	SS	-	Sterling silver
imp	-	impressed	sq	-	square
int.	-	interior	TLS	-	Typed Letter Signed
irid	-	iridescent	unp	-	unpaged
IVT	-	inverted thumbprint	vert.	-	vertical
j	-	jewels	vol	-	volume
K	-	karat	w	-	width
l	-	length	yg	-	yellow gold
lb	-	pound	#	-	numbered
litho	-	lithograph			

Grading Condition. The following numbers represent the standard grading system used by dealers, collectors, and auctioneers:

C.10	Mint
C.9	Near Mint
C.8.5	Outstanding
C.8	Excellent
C.7.5	Fine+
C.7	Fine
C.6.5	Fine - (good)
C.6	Poor

Ceramics

STATE OF THE ASIAN CERAMICS MARKET

by Alexandra Grais
Sloans & Kenyon
Director of Asian Ceramics and Works of Art Department
Director of Antiquities, Islamic, Tribal,
and Pre-Columbian Art Departments

Collectors of Chinese ceramics have witnessed a skyrocketing market in the past few years. Western collectors are competing against Chinese collectors who seek to reclaim their heritage and are fueled by a growing Chinese economy. The flipside of the surging demand for Chinese ceramics is an increase in the past decade in the production of faked, deliberately copied, and artificially-aged Chinese ceramics

Imperial porcelains from the Ming (1368-1643) and Qing (1644-1911) dynasties as well as Chinese Export porcelain—porcelain produced exclusively for export to the Western market from the 17th through 19th centuries —are in demand with today's collectors of Chinese ceramics.

Ming Dynasty highlights sold at Sloans & Kenyon include a blue and white porcelain stem cup with dragon decoration ($11,210, sale 22/lot 107) and a 17th century blue and white porcelain figure of an official ($6,490, sale 21/lot 65).

Qing Dynasty highlights sold at Sloans & Kenyon include a pair of Wucai dragon and phoenix bowls bearing Daoguang underglazed blue seal mark and period ($14,160, sale 13, lot 367) a 32 in. pair of copper red and blue vases with dragon decoration $18,800 (sale 21, lot 73A); a 12 in. clair-de-lune (pale blueish-gray) cong vase ($6,136, sale 21, lot 51); a pair of blue and white saucers with flower-heads and scrolling foliage decoration ($5,900, sale 20, lot

132); seven blue and white dragon saucers, each depicting dragon chasing a flaming pearl ($4,720, sale 25, lot 108); and a blue and white reticulated perfumer with flower-head and scrolling foliage decoration ($3,304, sale 24, lot 112).

Chinese Export porcelain decorated with monograms, coats of arms and armorial crests or patterns such as "Tobacco Leaf" continues to be popular with Western collectors. Although of a lesser quality than Imperial porcelains, Chinese Export porcelain is highly sought after because of its historical value. Sloans & Kenyon's top lots included a Chinese Export porcelain crested cup and saucer, decorated with crest of the Ross family of Philadelphia ($4,248 sale 20, lot 150), a Chinese Export armorial blue and white open serving dish and American flag creamer ($4,425, sale 22, lot 119), and a Chinese Export Famille Rose "Tobacco Leaf" pattern platter, circa 1775-1785, ($4,366, sale 25, lot 184).

Large vases proved to be another popular collecting area in Chinese ceramics; top lots at Sloans & Kenyon include a 22 in. Famille Noire quadrangular vase painted with warriors on horseback ($11,800, sale 20, lot 93), a large (36 in.) 19th century Rose Mandarin vase with figural and floral decoration ($7,080, sale 25, lot 287), and a pair of 19th century Famille Verte vases ($2,714, sale 25, lot 177).

Contrary to other areas of collecting in Chinese ceramics, blue and white Canton porcelain has declined in popularity because of its abundance as well as the proliferation of inferior contemporary copies.

ABOUT MARKS

Chinese ceramics can be marked either with a reign mark and be of the period ("mark and period") or with retrospective marks. Chinese ceramics identified as "mark and period" were produced during the reign of an emperor **and** bear the emperor's reign mark; examples marked as such are more desirable and more valuable. Reign marks are read from top to bottom and right to left and begin with the Chinese character meaning "great" followed by the name of the dynasty, then the emperor's name, and end with the Chinese characters meaning "in the reign of."

Retrospective reign marks were used on Chinese ceramics not so much to deceive but rather to honor a previous emperor. For example, a Chinese Famille Rose peach charger ($5,900, sale 20, lot 183) has a Qianlong mark (1736-1795) yet was produced during the later Daoguang (1821-1850) period.

TIPS FOR NOVICES

• Chinese ceramics marked with Western characters were produced after the 1890s. Pieces marked with an iron red "Made in

China" were exported from China after 1920 while pieces marked "China" were exported from 1898-1920.

• Look for artificial aging at the base of pieces. Look for a brownish cast on a base where a piece has been placed in a kiln; for example, the rims of the bases of a 20th century pair of blue and white vases (sale 20, lot 147) are unnaturally brown. Compare this to the base of the two-centuries-older Famille Rose peach charger (above).

• Design elements and palettes may have been borrowed from earlier periods; many decorative 20th century pieces have the very same patterns as pieces several centuries older.

• Vases, and other vessels, are often drilled to house electrical wiring. Such modification can greatly diminish an object's value.

• Attend auction house exhibitions to handle Chinese ceramics first hand; take advantage of in-house specialists to learn more about the collecting area.

CHRONOLOGY
CHINESE DYNASTIES AND PERIODS

Neolithic period	6500-1700 BC	**Jin Dynasty**	1115-1234
Xia Dynasty	2100-1600 BC	**Yuan Dynasty**	1279-1368
Shang Dynasty	1600-1100 BC	**Ming Dynasty**	1368-1643
Zhou Dynasty	1100-256 BC	Hongwu	1368-1398
Western Zhou	1100-771 BC	Jianwen	1399-1402
Eastern Zhou	770-476 BC	Yongle	1403-1424
Spring & Autumn Period	770-256 BC	Hongxi	1425
Warring States Period	475-221 BC	Xuande	1426-1435
Qin Dynasty	221-206 BC	Zhengtong	1436-1449
Han Dynasty	206 BC -220 AD	Jingtai	1450-1456
Six Dynasties	220-581	Tianshun	1457-1464
Three Kingdoms	220-280	Chenghua	1465-1487
Jin Dynasty	265-420	Hongzhi	1488-1505
Western Jin	265-317	Zhengde	1506-1521
Eastern Jin	317-420	Jiajing	1522-1566
Southern Dynasties &		Longqing	1567-1572
Northern Dynasties	420-589	Wanli	1573-1619
Southern Dynasties		Taichang	1620
Liu Song	420-479	Tianqi	1621-1627
Southern Qi	479-502	Chongzhen	1628-1643
Liang	502-557	**Qing Dynasty**	1644-1911
Chen	557-589	Shunzhi	1644-1661
Northern Dynasties		Kangxi	1662-1722
Northern Wei	386-535	Yongzheng	1723-1735
Western Wei	535-557	Qianlong	1736-1795
Eastern Wei	534-549	Jiaqing	1796-1820
Northern Qi	549-577	Daoguang	1821-1850
Northern Zhou	557-581	Xianfeng	1851-1861
Sui Dynasty	581-618	Tongzhi	1862-1874
Tang Dynasty	618-906	Guangxu	1875-1908
Five Dynasties	907-960	Xuantong	1909-1912
Liao Dynasty	907-1125	**Republic of China**	1912-1949
Song Dynasty	960-1279	**Hongxian (Yuan Shi Kai)**	1915-1916
Northern Song	960-1127	**People's Republic of China**	1949
Southern Song	1128-1279		

RESOURCES
Magazines

Antique Trader, published by Krause Publications, Iola, WI.

Books

Antique Trader® American & European Art Pottery Price Guide, 2nd Ed., by Kyle Husfloen, Krause Publications, Iola, WI.

Antique Trader® Pottery & Porcelain Ceramics Price Guide, 5th Ed., by Kyle Husfloen, Krause Publications, Iola, WI.

Antique Trader® Stoneware and Blue & White Pottery Price Guide, by Kyle Husfloen, Krause Publications, Iola, WI.

Antique Trader® Teapots Price Guide, by Kyle Husfloen, Krause Publications, Iola, WI.

Collecting Lladró®, 2nd Ed., by Peggy Whiteneck, Krause Publications, Iola, WI.

Fiesta, A Warman's® Companion, by Mark F. Moran and Glen Victorey, Krause Publications, Iola, WI.

Luckey´s Hummel® Figurines & Plates, by Carl F. Luckey, updated by Dean Genth, 12th Ed., Krause Publications, Iola, WI.

McCoy Pottery, A Warman's® Companion, by Mark F. Moran, Krause Publications, Iola, WI.

Price Guide to Contemporary Collectibles and Limited Editions, 9th Ed., by Mary L. Sieber, Krause Publications, Iola, WI.

Roseville Pottery, A Warman's® Companion, by Mark F. Moran, Krause Publications, Iola, WI.

Warman's® American Pottery & Porcelain, 2nd Ed., by Susan and Al Bagdade, Krause Publications, Iola, WI.

Warman's® Cookie Jars, by Mark F. Moran, Krause Publications, Iola, WI.

Warman's® English & Continental Pottery & Porcelain, by Al Bagdade, Krause Publications, Iola, WI.

Warman's® Fiesta Ware, by Mark F. Moran, Krause Publications, Iola, WI.

Warman's® Flea Market Price Guide, by Ellen T. Schroy, Krause Publications, Iola, WI.

Warman's® Hull Pottery, by David Doyle, Krause Publications, Iola, WI.

Warman's® Hummel® Field Guide, by Carl F. Luckey, updated by Dean Genth, Krause Publications, Iola, WI.

Warman's® Majolica, by Mark F. Moran, Krause Publications, Iola, WI.

Warman's® McCoy Pottery, by Mark F. Moran, Krause Publications, Iola, WI.

Warman's® Red Wing Pottery, by Mark F. Moran, Krause Publications, Iola, WI.

Warman's® Roseville Pottery, by Mark F. Moran, Krause Publications, Iola, WI.

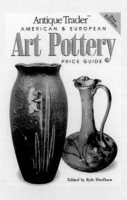

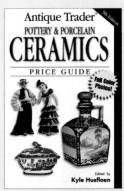

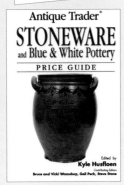

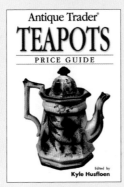

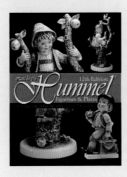

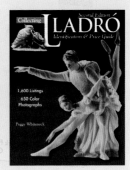

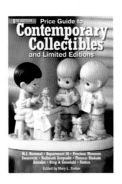

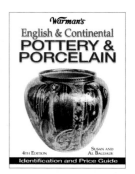

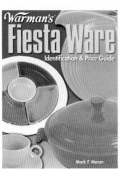

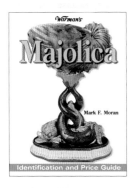

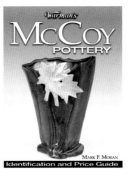

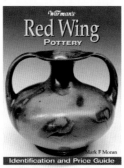

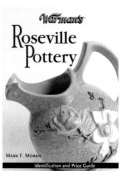

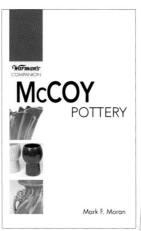

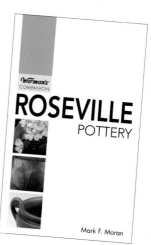

GALLERY

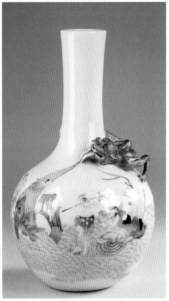

Famille Rose porcelain vase, Qianlong under glazed blue seal mark, 19th century, with applied dragon in high relief on shoulder above figure on waves and fish, 13" h, **$3,068.**

Famille Noire porcelain vase, Kangxi six character underglazed blue mark and period, quadrangular form painted to depict warriors on horseback, 22" h, **$11,800.**
Photo courtesy of Sloans & Kenyon Auctioneers and Appraisers.

Celadon glazed porcelain bottle vase, Chinese, Qianlong incised seal mark and probably of the period. The elongated neck bottle vase molded in low relief to depict two dragons confronting the flaming pearl of wisdom amidst swirling clouds and bat decoration, 11-1/2" h, **$4,130.**
Photo courtesy of Sloans & Kenyon Auctioneers and Appraisers.

Famille Rose porcelain vase, Guangxu six-character iron red mark, with bat decoration, 13" h, **$3,422.**
Photo courtesy of Sloans & Kenyon Auctioneers and Appraisers.

Pair Famille Verte porcelain vases, Kangxi six-character underglazed blue mark, 19th century, 19-7/8" h, **$2,714.**
Photo courtesy of Sloans & Kenyon Auctioneers and Appraisers.

Chinese blue and white porcelain bowl, Chenghua six-character underglazed blue mark, Kangxi period 1668-1722, painted to depict scholars in garden, 8" d, **$4,720.**
Photo courtesy of Sloans & Kenyon Auctioneers and Appraisers.

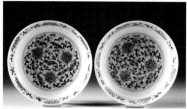

Pair Chinese blue and white porcelain saucers, Qianlong underglazed blue seal mark and of the period, painted with flower heads and scrolling foliate decoration, 6" d, **$5,900.**
Photo courtesy of Sloans & Kenyon Auctioneers and Appraisers.

Famille Rose porcelain vase, Qianlong mark, 10-1/2" h, **$5,015.**
Photo courtesy of Sloans & Kenyon Auctioneers and Appraisers.

Famille Rose porcelain vase, Jiaqing iron red seal mark and period, ovoid form, elongated neck, painted to depict bands with flower-heads and scrolling foliate, turquoise interior and foot, 8-1/2" h, **$5,015.**
Photo courtesy of Sloans & Kenyon Auctioneers and Appraisers.

Large Rose Mandarin porcelain vase, 19th century, figural and floral decoration, 36" h, **$7,080.**
Photo courtesy of Sloans & Kenyon Auctioneers and Appraisers.

Chinese blue and white porcelain figure of an official, Ming dynasty, 17th century, 13-1/4" x 7-1/4", **$6,490.**
Photo courtesy of Sloans & Kenyon Auctioneers and Appraisers.

Chinese blue and white porcelain reticulated perfumer, Jiaqing underglazed blue seal mark and of the period, flowerhead and scrolling foliate decoration, 1-3/4" x 4" x 1-1/4", **$3,304.**
Photo courtesy of Sloans & Kenyon Auctioneers and Appraisers.

Chinese Export Famille Rose porcelain "Tobacco Leaf" pattern platter, painted to depict a large blossom and smaller flowers and sprigs against and amidst an arrangement of larger overlapping pink leaves, underside of the scalloped rim painted with four iron red and underglazed blue sprays, c1775-1785, 11" x 8", **$4,336.**
Photo courtesy of Sloans & Kenyon Auctioneers and Appraisers.

Chinese Export porcelain crested cup and saucer, late 18th century, from a service made for the Ross family, Philadelphia, rim with gilt edge and cobalt band interrupted by crest of stylized wreath-in-hand and conforming banner inscribed with motto "Noblis Estria Leonis;" central sunburst medallion, saucer: 5-1/2" d cup: 2-3/4" h, **$4,248.**
Photo courtesy of Sloans & Kenyon Auctioneers and Appraisers.

AMERICAN HAND-PAINTED CHINA JEWELRY AND BUTTONS

History: The American china painting movement began in 1876, about the time the mass production of jewelry also occurred. Porcelain manufacturers and distributors offered a variety of porcelain shapes and settings for brooches, pendants, cuff links, and shirt-waist buttons. Thousands of artisans painted flowers, people, landscapes and conventions (geometric) motifs. The category of hand-painted porcelain jewelry comprises a unique category, separate from costume and fine jewelry. While the materials were inexpensive to produce, the painted decoration was a work of fine art.

Marks: American painted porcelain jewelry bears no factory marks, and is usually unsigned.

Notes: The quality of the artwork, the amount of detail, and technical excellence—not the amount of gilding—are the key pricing factors. Uncommon shapes also influence value.

Belt buckle brooch

Dec with white pansy, accented with white enamel, burnished gold ground, gold-plated bezel, 1900-1917, oval, 1-11/16" x 2-1/4" **$75**

Oval, dec with horse chestnuts, baby blue ground, gold-plated bezel, 1900-1917, 2" x 2-1/2" **$100**

Brooch

Crescent shape, dec with dark pink roses, burnished gold tips, brass bezel, 1900-20, 1-7/8" w **$45**

Cross-shape, dec with pink and ruby roses, polychrome ground, tips dec with raised paste dots, gold-plated bezel with tubular hinge, 1" x 1" **$80**

Diamond shape, dec with waterscape with water lilies, white enamel highlights, burnished with gold border, brass bezel, c1920-1940, 7/8" sq **$35**

Dec with Colonial dame, burnished gold rim, brass bezel, c1890-1910, 1" d **$40**

Dec with woman's portrait surrounded by forget-me-nots, ivory ground, white enamel highlights, framed by burnished gold, raised paste scrolls and dots, gold-plated bezel, oval, 1-1/4" x 1-7/8" **$80**

Dec with pink roses, burnished gold border, sgd "Albrecht," brass bezel, oval, 1-7/16" x 1-7/8" **$65**

Dec with Art Nouveau-style woman's head and neck, poppies in her hair, gold-plated bezel, oval, 1-1/4" x 1-7/8" **$90**

Dec with stained glass-like conventional design in polychrome colors and burnished gold, gold-plated bezel, oval, 1905-15, 1-1/2" x 2" **$65**

Dec with daisy, burnished gold border, brass bezel, c1900-10, 1-3/4" d **$45**

Dec with columbine and greenery, polychrome ground, burnished gold trim, gold-plated bezel, oval, 1-13/16" x 2-3/16" **$75**

Dec with pink roses and greenery on light blue and yellow, burnished gold ground, scrolls, and dots, sgd "E. GARDE," 1920s, gold-plated setting, 1-9/16" x 1-7/8" **$50**

Dec with a tropical landscape, burnished gold rim, sgd "OC" (Olive Commons, St. John's Island, FL, 1908-1920), gold-plated bezel, 1-11/16" x 2-1/8" **$105**

Dec with Art Nouveau-style poppies, burnished gold border, brass bezel, oval, 1856-1915, 2" x 1-5/8" **$75**

Dec with pink and ruby roses, solid dark blue ground, white enamel highlights, burnished gold border, brass bezel, c1940, oval, 2" x 1-1/2" **$65**

Dec with violets, burnished gold rim, brass bezel, 1900-1920, 2-1/16" d **$65**

Florida landscape in white on platinum ground, sterling silver bezel, rectangle, c1920-40, 1" x 3/4" **$75**

Horseshoe shape, dec with violets, burnished gold tips, brass bezel, 2-1/2" l..**$100**

Pink and ruby rose, leaves, polychrome ground, burnished gold rim, gold-plated bezels, 7/8" d, price for pr **$50**

Cuff buttons, pr, dec with lavender flowers, border of burnished gold dots and apple green jewels, burnished gold rims, c1890-1920, ovals, 3/4" x 1" **$40**

Dress set

Five pieces: belt buckle brooch, oval brass bezel, 2" x 2-5/8"; pr shirt waist buttons with shanks 1" d; pr shirt waist buttons with sew-through backs 1" d; dec with forget-me-nots, black green scalloped borders rimmed in burnished gold, c1900-17.....................................**$400**

Four pieces: shirt waist collar button, 3/4" d; three shirt waist buttons, 5/8" d; dec with pink roses, white enamel highlights, burnished gold rims, shank backs.......................**$60**

Flapper pin, dec with stylized woman, burnished gold border, brass bezel, oval, 1924-28, 1-5/8" x 2-1/8" **$75**

Hat pin, dec with four-leaf clover on burnished gold ground, brass bezel, 1900-20, 3/4" wide by 1" oval medallion, 6" l shaft..............................**$115**

Pendant

Dec with violets, burnished gold border, brass bezel, oval, c1880-1914, 1-5/8" x 2-1/8" **$60**

Dec with forget-me-nots, white enamel highlights, burnished gold rim, brass bezel, oval, c1900-20, 1-3/4" x 1-3/4" **$50**

Shirt-waist button

Set, with shanks, dec with maidenhair fern, pastel polychrome ground, burnished gold borders, two 7/8" d, three 5/8" d, price for five-pc set **$80**

With eye, dec with single daisy, burnished gold ground, 1-3/16" d...**$20**

With shank, dec with conventional floral design, burnished gold ground, 1-3/16" d **$35**

With shank, dec with violets entwined around burnished gold fancy letter "J," burnished gold border, sgd with illegible cipher, 7/8" sq..............**$20**

AMPHORA

History: The Amphora Porcelain Works was one of several pottery companies located in the Teplitz-Turn region of Bohemia in the late 19th and early 20th centuries. It is best known for art pottery, especially Art Nouveau and Art Deco pieces.

Marks: Several markings were used, including the name and location of the pottery and the Imperial mark, which included a crown. Prior to World War I, Bohemia was part of the Austro-Hungarian Empire, so the word "Austria" may appear as part of the mark. After World War I, the word "Czechoslovakia" may be part of the mark.

Additional Listings: Teplitz.

Center bowl, incised dec outlined in black, enameled blue-green and pink cabochons, mottled tan matte ground, four legs, circular base, 2-1/8" h **$200**

Ewer, pink, gold, and green floral dec, gold accents, salamander entwined handle, c1900, 14-1/2" h **$575**

Lamp base, stoneware, double handles ending in dragons, straw-colored glaze, China, T'ang period (618-920), drilled, 12-1/2" h **$650**

Umbrella stand, emb gleaners, stylized indigo trees, lustered amber glaze, stamped "Amphora (crown) Austria," restoration to base, 26-1/2" h, 15" d **$2,200**

Vase

Flattened spherical form, shoulder dec with alternating large and small moths in shades of blue, pink, and yellow, raised gilt outline, relief spider webs and enameled disk centers, gilt highlights on green and blue ground, imp "Amphora" in oval, printed "R. S. & K. Turn-Teplitz Bohemia" with maker's device on base, 6" h **$900**

Painted with portrait of Joan of Arc, eagle helmet, enameled garb, mkd "Amphora 1K" and red ink stamp mark, 6-1/4" h, 4" d **$2,600**

Pear shape, extended neck, two tri-part handles, mottled matte green and brown glaze, inscribed cipher, R. S. & K, Teplitz, Bohemia, crazing, base chip, c1900, 11-1/8" h **$1,035**

Three buttressed handles dec with naturalistic leafy rose vines, rose hip clusters, matte green rose on mottled brown round, gilt highlights, imp mark and stamp on base, 5-1/4" h **$250**

Wall plaque, Moorish man and woman in relief, red ground, gilt molded frames, marked "Amphora," 18-1/2" d, price for pr **$900**

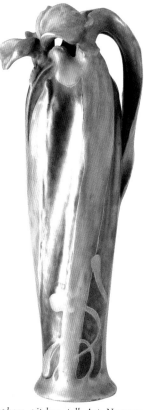

Amphora pitcher, tall Art Nouveau, modeled with pink, green, and gold Iris blossom, green leaves, lustered purple background, reglued spout petal, stamped AMPHORA 55/3683/Artist signed HE or TM, 18-1/2" x 7", **$3,000.**
Photo courtesy of David Rago Auctions, Inc.

ART POTTERY (GENERAL)

History: America's interest in art pottery can be traced to the Centennial Exposition in Philadelphia in 1877, where Europe's finest producers of decorative art displayed an impressive selection of their wares. America's artists rose to the challenge immediately, and by 1900, native artisans were winning gold medals for decorative ceramics here and abroad.

The Art Pottery "Movement" in America lasted from about 1880 until the first World War. During this time, more than 200 companies, in most states, produced decorative ceramics ranging from borderline production ware to intricately decorated, labor intensive artware establishing America as a decorative art powerhouse. Listed here is the work by various factories and studios, with pricing, from a number of these companies.

Additional Listings: See Clifton, Cowan, Dedham, Fulper, Grueby, Jugtown, Marblehead, Moorcroft, Newcomb, North Dakota School of Mines, Ohr, Paul Revere, Peters and Reed, Rookwood, Roseville, Van Briggle, Weller, and Zanesville.

Notes: Condition, design, size, execution, and glaze quality are the key considerations when buying art pottery. This category includes only companies not found elsewhere in this book.

Adviser: David Rago.

Amphora vase, applied pinecone decoration, 6-1/2" x 6", **$1,200.**
Photo courtesy of David Rago Auctions, Inc.

Arequipa ribbed vase, semi-sheer blue-gray glaze, red clay shows through, stamped AREQUIPA CALIFORNIA, 6" x 4", **$1,800.**

Photo courtesy of David Rago Auctions, Inc.

Arequipa floriform jardinière, closed-in rim, acanthus leaves, covered in matte blue gray glaze, brown clay shows through, stamped AREQUIPA CALIFORNIA 1325/24, 4-1/2" x 9", **$1,800.**

Photo courtesy of David Rago Auctions, Inc.

Jervis vase, enamel decoration, white goose in flight, indigo ground, incised JERVIS, 4" x 4", **$1,560.**

Photo courtesy of David Rago Auctions, Inc.

Jervis pitcher, enamel dec, cats and cattails, both front and back shown, polychrome on dark ground, 2" hairline, incised Jervis, 5" x 7", **$1,560.**

Photo courtesy of David Rago Auctions, Inc.

Arequipa

Bowl, closed-in, emb eucalyptus branches, matte green and dark blue glaze, stamped mark, incised "KH/11," 6-1/2" d, 2-1/4" h **$800**

Vase, baluster, purple and brown mottled semi-matte glaze, incised "Arequipa California/ 404/JG/JJ," 10-1/2" h, 7-1/2" d **$1,600**

Vase, baluster, carved foliate design, sheer green and turquoise glaze, incised "G.B. Arequipa California," 13-1/2" h, 6-1/4" d **$2,500**

Vessel, squat, carved swirls, matte green and indigo glaze, stamped "Arequipa California" with potter, 4-1/4" h, 4-1/4" d **$1,500**

Avon, Vance, vase, designed by Frederick Rhead, squeezebag stylized trees, orange and green ground, incised "Avon/WPTS.CO./174-1241," 5" d, 5-1/2" h.......................................**$920**

Bachelder, O. L., vase, bulbous, cobalt blue and teal sheer glossy glaze, incised "OLB/R," ink cipher, 5" h, 3-3/4" d..**$500**

Bennett, Edwin, vase, flat, Albion, painted squirrels on stonewall, pine bough above, "E. Bennett Pottery/1895/AHB/Albion," 1895, 8" h, 8-1/2" w **$2,400**

Bennett, John

Charger, dec with polychrome daisies and poppies enc within hearts, cobalt blue ground, black scroll design, sgd "J. Bennett/ 412 E24/NY/Oct 9/79," added inscription "Wed last 100 degs in shade," 14-1/2" d **$4,600**

Vase, bulbous, painted burgundy phlox and honeybee, ivory ground, minute rim fleck, marked "BENNETT/ W2E24/NJ/artist's cipher," 3-3/4" d, 7-1/2" h **$2,870**

Binns, Charles F., ovoid, amber, ochre, and chocolate brown hare's fur mirrored glaze, mkd "C.F.B. 1931," 7" d, 5-1/2" h **$3,250**

Cole, A. R., urn, hand-thrown, three fanciful twisted handles, mirror black glaze, unmarked, shallow scratches, 18-1/2" h, 9-1/2" d **$400**

Denaura, Denver, vase, squat top, small opening, molded poppies, matte green vellum glaze, stamped "Denaura/ Denver/169," 5-1/2" h, 5" d **$2,700**

Grand Feu, vase, corseted bulbous, purple and verdigris semi-matte crystalline glaze, stamped "Grand Feu Pottery, L.A. Cal, TT 154," 7" h, 4-1/4" d.......**$11,000**

Jervis, goblet, enameled green and white mistletoe, teal blue ground, vertical mark, few minute glaze flecks, 4" h, 3" d...................................**$2,000**

Kenton Hills, vase

Cylindrical, white prunts cov in mirrored umber glaze, incised "Hentschel" for William Hentschel, imp "KH/124," 4-3/4" d, 7-1/4" h **$775**

Four-sided, aventurine glaze, imp "KH/ 171," 6" d, 7-1/2" h..........**$650**

Norse, vase, applied salamander, verdigris and bronze glaze, stamped "Norse 25," 11-1/2" h, 7" d **$850**

Pewabic

Bookends, pr, emb animal, lustered blue and green glaze, stamped "Pewabic," repair to small edge chip, 4" w, 4-3/4" h **$415**

Miniature, vase, crackled turquoise glaze, blue plumes, sgd "Pewabic/ Detroit/PP," 2" h.......................**$265**

Plate, white crackleware, rim dec with squeezebag yellow and red roosters on green field, stamped "Pewabic," some loss of glaze, chips on back, 9-1/4" d **$920**

Vase, cylindrical with squatty base, mottled and lustered purple and turquoise glaze, paper label, hand written "Anne/ 1942," small glaze scale at rim, 3" d, 3-3/4" h **$265**

Vessel, bulbous, ribbed, glossy teal glaze, stamped "Pewabic/ Detroit," 5-1/4" d, 5-1/2" h **$520**

Pisgah Forest vase, tall, early Cameo Crystalline, pate-sur-pate painted, scene of sowers and reapers on green ground, over celadon crystalline ground, potter's mark/Stephen/1936, small rim chip, 5" hairline, 1936, 17" x 9", **$2,160.**
Photo courtesy of David Rago Auctions, Inc.

Teco vase, architectural, four full-height buttresses encasing urn, matte green and gunmetal glaze, stamped no., 10" h x 4-1/2", **$2,760.**
Photo courtesy of David Rago Auctions, Inc.

Teco vase, tall, three footed, lobed base, matte green glaze, two glaze rim nicks, no visible mark, 15-1/2" x 7-3/4", **$1,800.**
Photo courtesy of David Rago Auctions, Inc.

Pisgah Forest

Tea set, Cameo Ware, wagon and landscape dec, dark matte green ground, raised mark and date 1943, 5-1/4" h teapot **$950**

Vase, bulbous, white, blue, and yellow crystalline glaze, unmarked, 4-3/4" d, 6-1/4" h **$460**

Vessel, spherical, amber glaze, white and blue crystals, raised potter's mark and date 1947, 5" h, 5-3/4" d **$350**

Poillon, Clara, pitcher, bulbous, medium green glaze, incised CPI monogram, 5" d, 4-1/2" h **$365**

San Jose, charger, cuerda seca dec, polychrome wagon train scene, green semi-matte ground, unmarked, small rim fleck, 15-1/2" d **$435**

Robineau, Adelaide, vessel, hemispherical, café-au-lait and verdigris crystalline glaze, carved "AB/184/5," opposing lines to rim, 3" h, 4-1/4" d **$2,500**

Teco

Vase, buttressed handles, smooth matte green glaze, stamped "Teco," restored chip on handle, 11-1/4" h, 5" d **$1,300**

Vase, cylindrical, organic buttressed handles, matte buff glaze, stamped

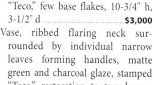

"Teco," few base flakes, 10-3/4" h, 3-1/2" d **$3,000**

Vase, ribbed flaring neck surrounded by individual narrow leaves forming handles, matte green and charcoal glaze, stamped "Teco," restoration to two leaves, rim touch-ups, 11-1/2" h, 4-1/2" d **$5,000**

Vessel, three handles, smooth matte green glaze, stamped "Teco," touch-up to rim bruise, 4-3/4" d, 3-1/4" h **$490**

Vessel, corseted, four handles, smooth matte green glaze with charcoal highlights, stamped "Teco," incised 172, restoration, 10" d, 14-1/2" h **$5,175**

Tiffany Pottery

Bud vase, emb tulips, Old Ivory glaze, incised "LCT," 7" h, 2-1/2" d .. **$4,250**

Lamp base, collar rim, brown and gunmetal flambé glaze, incised "LCT," 7" h, 8" d **$2,400**

Volkmar, pitcher, bulbous, collared neck, cucumber green matte glaze, incised illegible inscription, 4" d, 4-1/2" h **$265**

Walley, W. J., vase, bottle shape, sheer light green and gunmetal glaze, imp "W.J.W.," 6-1/2" h **$535**

Teco Art Noveau lamp base, M.P. White design, small spherical top, long buttresses, acanthus leaves, matte green glaze with charcoaled details, slight overfiring on one foot, stamped Teco, 18-1/2" x 7", **$11,750.**
Photo courtesy of David Rago Auctions, Inc.

AUSTRIAN WARE

History: More than 100 potteries were located in the Austro-Hungarian Empire in the late 19th and early 20th centuries. Although Carlsbad was the center of the industry, the factories spread as far as the modern-day Czech Republic.

Many of the factories were either owned or supported by Americans; hence, their wares were produced mainly for export to the United States.

Marks: Many wares do not have a factory mark but only the word "Austrian" in response to the 1891 law specifying that the country of origin had to be marked on imported products.

Additional Listings: Amphora, Royal Dux, and Royal Vienna.

Wheatley vase, four curled handles alternating with leaves, matte ochre glaze, WP and no., 12" x 6", **$3,000.**

Photo courtesy of David Rago Auctions, Inc.

Walrath

Cider set, pitcher, five cups, painted with cherries on green and brown ground, incised Walrath Pottery, orig Handicraft Guild label on pitcher, 6-1/2" x 8" pitcher **$4,250**

Vase, matte-painted green foliage trees, brown trunks, dark green ground, incised "Walrath Pottery," 6-3/4" h, 4-1/2" d..................**$4,250**

Wheatley

Lamp base, emb poppy pods, frothy matte green glaze, new hammered copper fittings, Japanese split-bamboo shade lined with new coral silk, stamped mark, 14" d, 23" h **$1,380**

Sand jar, high relief sculpted grape leaves and vines from rim, feathered medium green matte glaze, incised mark/722, several glaze nicks restored, 15" d, 24" h **$2,415**

Vase, bulbous, three climbing lizards, feathered medium matte green glaze, remnant of paper label, restoration to drill hole on side, 6-3/4" d, 12-1/4" h................**$1,380**

White, Denver

vase, squatty, smooth matte gold and green glaze, incised "Denver/1916," small bruise under rim, 6-1/2" d, 3-3/4" h................**$210**

Biscuit jar, cov, two handles, small pink roses dec, mkd "MZ Austria," 6-1/2" h..**$200**

Bowl, handles, marked "Imperial H&C Carlsbad Austria," numbers "2552" and "18," wear to gold edge, repaired chip, 14" d **$50**

Celery tray, scalloped border, pink roses, green leaves, gold trim, 12" l **$75**

Ewer, rococo gold scroll, hp pink and yellow wild roses, gold outlines, four ftd, 11-3/4" h, 6" d **$125**

Figural group, bronze, cold painted, realistically modeled as small songbird perched on wide leaf in front of tall iris flowers, twig base, late 19th/early 20th C, 13-1/2" w, 14-1/2" h **$1,840**

Luncheon plates

Carlsbad, "Austrian Plaque," oval, portrait of Pope Leo XIII, c1900, imp "Karl Knoll, Carlsbad," 7" h **$150**

Gilt, bead-molded shaped rim, body with cartouches of turquoise faux jewels on gilt ground, gilt scroll-work and quatrefoils with white jeweled points and mauve enameled centers, late 19th/early 20th C, set of 12, 9-3/8" d **$1,300**

Oyster plate, porcelain, shell-shaped wells to center, scalloped rim, blue and gilt enamel flowers, fish, and birds dec, 19th C, 9-7/8" d.........**$175**

Perfume set, orange cut glass finials, angular opaque black glass vessels, metal mounts, enameled fan motif, all imp "Austria" on metal, two acid-etched "Austria," 6-1/8" h atomizer, 5-3/8" h perfume, 5" h cov box, imperfections..**$500**

Pin tray, irregular scalloped shape, roses, green leaves, white ground, marked "Victoria Carlsbad Austria," 8-1/2" l.**$40**

Pokal, glass

Green, detailed enameled cavalier holding empty stein, c1890, 17-1/2" h **$400**

Green, detailed enameled scene of knight on horseback, colorful scrolled acanthus dec, c1890, 18-1/2" h...**$400**

Table lamp, attributed to Wiener Werkstatte, in the manner of Susi Singer, ceramic, ovoid, flanked by two mermaid figures in high relief, fish, octopus, and starfish in relief, glossy aqua, orange, white, and irid glazes, textured mottled green and brown ground, gilt highlights, four patinated metal dolphins on stepped metal base, 22-1/4" h...................**$375**

Trinket box, cov, oval, the gilt metal box stamped with continuous bands of anthemion and torches, porcelain set lid with printed scene of two classical beauties on cobalt blue ground, velveteen lining, early 20th C, 4-1/4" l..**$450**

Urn, rose bouquet, shaded ivory ground, marked "Carlsbad Austria," 14-1/2" h.......................................**$155**

Vase, charcoal gray iridescent pottery body relief-decorated with iridescent green branches, orange wash glaze int., Turn-Teplitz, Austria, numbered 3517, 7-1/4" d...............................**$825**

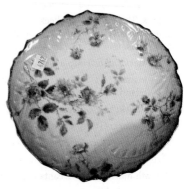

Austrian Ware plate, yellow and pink flowers, green leaves, brown twigs, gold trim, embossed swirls, **$25.**

BAVARIAN CHINA

History: Bavaria, Germany, was an important porcelain production center, similar to the Staffordshire district in England. The phrase "Bavarian China" refers to the products of companies operating in Bavaria, among which were Hutschenreuther, Thomas, and Zeh, Scherzer & Co. (Z. S. & Co.). Very little of the production from this area was imported into the United States prior to 1870.

Bavarian coffee set, coffeepot, two cups and saucers, white and pink shaded roses, green foliage, gold tracery and borders, marked, **$145.**

Bowl, ovoid, reticulated sides, beaded rim, center and sides painted with scenic roundels en grisaille, blue ribbon cartouches with gilt detailing, scenes titled on underside "Badenburg," "Apolloscumpeil," and "Schloss Nymphenburg," late 19th C, 7-3/8" l, 6" w **$325**

Celery tray, center with basket of fruit, luster edge, c1900, 11" l **$45**

Chocolate set, cov chocolate pot, six cups and saucers, shaded blue and white, large white leaves, pink, red, and white roses, crown mark **$295**

Creamer and sugar, purple and white pansy dec, marked "Meschendorf, Bavaria" **$65**

Cup and saucer, roses and foliage, gold handle **$30**

Dinner service, King Cedric, service for eight, plus two platters **$150**

Fish set, 13 plates, matching sauce boat, artist sgd **$295**

Pitcher, bulbous, blackberry dec, shaded ground, burnished gold lizard handle, sgd "D. Churchill," 9" h .. **$125**

Portrait vase, gold enameled flowers and leaves, hp portrait of Naomi, blue beehive mark and "TG Bavaria" mark, 10" h.................................. **$520**

Ramekin, underplate, ruffled, small red roses with green foliage, gold rim **$45**

Salt and pepper shakers, pr, pink apple blossom sprays, white ground, reticulated gold tops, pr **$35**

Shaving mug, hp, two colorful ducks at water's edge, mkd "J. & C Bavaria," 3-5/8" x 3-5/8" **$100**

Vase, hp, red poppies, gold enamel dec, marked "Classic Bavaria," 12" h .. **$260**

Bavarian dinner set, gilt edges, bread and butter plates, dinner plates, luncheon plates, finger bowls, soup bowls, teacups and saucers, platters, mkd "Bavaria," service for 11, **$300.**
Photo courtesy of David Rago Auctions, Inc.

BELLEEK

History: Belleek, a thin, ivory-colored, almost-iridescent porcelain, was first made in 1857 in county Fermanagh, Ireland. Production continued until World War I, was discontinued for a period of time, and then resumed. The Shamrock pattern is most familiar, but many patterns were made, including Limpet, Tridacna, and Grasses.

There is an Irish saying: If a newly married couple receives a gift of Belleek, their marriage will be blessed with lasting happiness.

Several American firms made a Belleek-type porcelain. The first was Ott and Brewer Co. of Trenton, New Jersey, in 1884, followed by Willets. Other firms producing this ware included The Ceramic Art Co. (1889), American Art China Works (1892), Columbian Art Co. (1893), and Lenox, Inc. (1904).

Marks: The European Belleek company used specific marks during given time periods, which makes it relatively easy to date a piece of Irish Belleek. Variations in mark color are important, as well as the symbols and words.

First mark: Black Harp, Hound, and Castle, 1863-1890.

Second mark: Black Harp, Hound, and Castle and the words "Co. Fermanagh, Ireland," 1891-1926.

Third mark: Black, "Deanta in Eirinn" added, 1926-1946.

Fourth mark: Green, same as third mark except for color, 1946-1955.

Fifth mark: Green, "R" inside a circle added, 1955-1965.

Sixth mark: Green, "Co. Fermanagh" omitted, 1965-March 1980.

Seventh mark: Gold, "Deanta in Eirinn" omitted, April 1980-Dec. 1992.

Eighth mark: Blue, Blue version of the second mark with "R" inside a circle added, Jan. 1993-present.

Additional Listings: Lenox.

Belleek American urn, spherical, two upright handles, four reticulated feet, red oriental poppies decoration, light wear to gilting around rim, red O&B crown stamp, 8" x 6", **$1,725.**
Photo courtesy of David Rago Auctions, Inc.

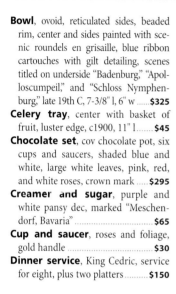

Belleek Irish porcelain openwork basket, floral details on rim and handles, mkd, 5" x 11" x 8-1/2", **$645.**
Photo courtesy of David Rago Auctions, Inc.

Belleek Irish cup and saucer, Nautilus shape, green handle, **$265.**

Belleek American beer set, 12" h beer pitcher with silver hinged lid, six mugs painted by Sturgis Laurence in the Delft style, different male characters drinking spirits, each signed "FWR Sturgis Laurence, Trenton, NJ, Dec 8 '94," 1894, **$2,200.**
Photo courtesy of David Rago Auctions, Inc.

American

Bowl
Double handles, ruffled rim, gilt trim and handles, gilt and rose-colored flowers dec, brown Willets mark, 7" d, 4-1/4" h............................**$275**
Green ext., wide gilt textured border, int. with hp floral design, artist sgd "MS" on base, brown Willets mark, 7-1/2" d **$100**

Candy dish, shell form, ivory ground, hp floral dec, ruffled gilt rim, marked "Columbia Art Co., Trenton, NJ," 8" x 6" **$80**

Chocolate pot, ivory ground, Art Deco rose design, pale green and yellow wide borders, gilt accents, green Lenox pallet mark, 10-1/4" h **$135**

Cider jug, hp, fruit dec, gilt handle, green Lenox pallet mark, 6" h **$50**

Cup and saucer, hp, pale pink and green beaded dec, gilt borders, brown Willets mark, 2" cup, 5-3/4" d saucer **$60**

Jug, hp, pale yellow ground, floral dec, gilt rim and handle, green CAC pallet mark, 5-1/2" h.............................**$110**

Mug, pink luster and enamel dec, continuous scene of drunken taverners, artist sgd "EMS '04," printed Ceramic Art Co. mark, Trenton, New Jersey, c1904, 4-1/2" h................**$150**

Pitcher, hp, white ground, geometric blue floral design, gilt trim, artist sgd "G. L. Urban," green Willets mark, 7" h..**$85**

Plate
Gilt foliate rim, blue enamel beads, red Willets mark, price for pr, 7-1/4" d **$45**
Swan, ivory, open back, green Lenox wreath mark, 8-1/2" h................**$90**

Salt, 1-1/2" d
Gilt, ruffled edge, marked "CAC," price for set of six......................**$45**
Pale green, hp pink enamel dec, artist sgd "E.S.M.," Lenox pallet mark, price for set of six....................**$135**

Tankard, hand painted, 5-3/4" h
Brown and blue painted ground, poppy dec, sgd "LM '06," green CAC pallet mark..............................**$135**
Multicolored ground, foliage dec, sgd "B.M.A.," brown Willets mark **$125**

Teapot, blue glazed ground, gilt dec, brown Willets mark, 6" h...........**$135**

Vase
Baluster, hp pine cone dec, artist sgd "A.E.G.," green Lenox pallet mark, 15" h **$450**
Cylindrical, hand painted, egrets in landscape, artist sgd "A.MacM.F.," printed mark, Trenton, NJ, c1900, 10" h **$215**

Irish

Basket, four strand, applied flowers, Belleek Co. Fermanagh Ireland pad mark, some repairs, petal missing, 6-1/2" x 4-1/2"...............................**$80**

Bread plate, Shamrock pattern, double handle, third green mark, 10-1/2" l, 9-1/4" w.........................**$80**

Bowl, Imperial Shell, modeled shell supported on shell adorned coral base, third black mark, c1930, 4-1/2" h.............**$565**

Butter dish, cov, Limpet pattern, first black mark, 6-1/2" d top, 8-1/2" d base **$475**

Cake plate, mask with grape leaves pattern, four looped handles, pale yellow edge, third black mark, 10-1/2" d **$155**

Compote, shell modeled dish, triangular base set with three dolphins, first black mark, c1880, dish restored, slight rim chips, 6-3/4" h **$470**

Creamer
Lifford pattern, third green mark, 3-1/4" h **$60**
Ribbon pattern, third green mark, 3-1/4" h **$40**
Cleary pattern, first green mark, 3-1/2" h **$50**
Rathmore pattern, third green mark, 4" h **$40**
Undine pattern, third black mark, 4-1/2" h **$55**

Creamer and sugar, 3-1/2" h creamer, 2" h sugar, Lotus pattern, third black mark, rim chip....................**$70**

Cream jug, Thorn Tea Ware, pale yellow relief dec, first mark, c1880, 5-1/2" h................................**$300**

Cup and saucer, Tea Ware, hexagon, pink tint, second black mark, early 20th C, 5-3/8" d saucer, price for pr **$460**

Figure

Pig, third green mark, 2-1/2" h **$90**

Harp, third green mark, 6" h **$70**

Flowerpot, naturalistically modeled shell body, applied flowers and foliage, second black mark, chips to leaves, c1900, 7" h......................**$940**

Font, Sacred Heart, cross form, shaped font, second green mark, 7" h.......**$50**

Lithophane, rect shape with arched top, modeled as two ladies with bird, no visible mark, mounted in electrified shadow box, 19th C, 5-1/2" l........**$715**

Mint tray, shell form, pink highlights on rim, brown mark, 8-1/2" l **$70**

Mustache cup and saucer, Tridacna, pink rim, first black mark, 2-1/2" h cup, 6" d saucer **$495**

Night light, figural, lighthouse, pierced cover and insert pot, modeled rocky base, second black mark, restored rim on insert pot, c1900, 10-3/4" h **$1,410**

Pitcher, Aberdeen, applied with flowers and leaves, second black mark, chips to leaves, c1900, 9" h **$300**

Plate, scalloped edge, woven, three strands, pad mark, 10-1/2" d **$200**

Spill vase

Owl, second green mark, 8" h **$55**

Shamrock, second green mark, 5" h **$50**

Shamrock Daisy, third green mark, 5-1/2" h.................................**$65**

Sugar bowl, Shell, pink tinted edge and coral, first black mark, c1880, foot-rim chips, 4" h **$575**

Swan, open back, yellow wings and head, brown mark, 4" h.................**$55**

Tea kettle, cov, Thorn Tea Ware, pale yellow relief dec, first mark, c1880, 7" h.....................................**$350**

Tea set

Grass tea ware, 4" h covered teapot; 3-3/4" h cov sugar bowl; cream jug; first black marks, c1880........**$1,175**

Tridacna, 5-1/2" h cov teapot; 4-1/4" h cov sugar bowl; 3-1/4" h cream jug; 3" h waste bowl, each with third black mark; 15-1/2" l rect tray with second black mark, c1920-30 ....**$1,120**

Tea urn, cov, gilt, bronze and enamel dec, China man finial, first black mark, c1880, cover with hairline and chip, stand missing, 6-1/2" h **$4,410**

Tray, Thorn tea ware, scalloped rim, molded floral border, web interior with central spider, second black mark, c1900, 14-1/2" sq **$1,175**

Vase

Cardium, shell form, coral and shell base, second black mark, 4-3/4" h, 5-3/4" d.................................**$80**

Coral, pink tinted coral and shell int., first black mark, c1880, 8" h.**$1,150**

Dolphin, first black mark, chip on tail, 8-1/4" h.................................**$775**

Six-sided pot, third green mark, 4-1/4" h.................................**$45**

Tree trunk with three lower and three upper vase spouts, applied with flowers and leaves, bird perched atop arched branches above another bird in nest, second black mark, c1900, chips to leaves, hairline repair to lower trunk, 12" h **$1,175**

Two scrolled and pierced handles, delicate applied bouquet of flowers, 1891 mark, 9" h, price for pr **$690**

BENNINGTON AND BENNINGTON-TYPE POTTERY

History: In 1845, Christopher Webber Fenton joined Julius Norton, his brother-in-law, in the manufacturing of stoneware pottery in Bennington, Vermont. Fenton sought to expand the company's products and glazes; Norton wanted to concentrate solely on stoneware. In 1847, Fenton broke away and established his own factory.

Fenton introduced to America the famous Rockingham glaze, developed in England and named after the Marquis of Rockingham. In 1849, he patented a flint enamel glaze, "Fenton's Enamel," which added flecks, spots, or streaks of color (usually blues, greens, yellows, and oranges) to the brown Rockingham glaze. Forms included candlesticks, coachman bottles, cow creamers, poodles, sugar bowls, and toby pitchers.

Fenton produced the little-known scroddled ware, commonly called lava or agate ware. Scroddled ware is composed of differently colored clays, which are mixed with cream-colored clay, molded, turned on a potter's wheel, coated with feldspar and flint, and fired. It was not produced in quantity, as there was little demand for it.

Fenton also introduced Parian ware to America. Parian was developed in England in 1842 and known as "Statuary ware." Parian is translucent porcelain that has no glaze and resembles marble. Bennington made the blue and white variety in the form of vases, cologne bottles, and trinkets.

The hound-handled pitcher is probably the best-known Bennington piece. Hound-handled pitchers were made by about 30 different potteries in more than 55 variations. Rockingham glaze was used by more than 150 potteries in 11 states, mainly in the Midwest, between 1830 and 1900.

Marks: Five different marks were used, with many variations. Only about 20 percent of the pieces carried any mark; some forms were almost always marked, others never. Marks include:

1849 mark (four variations) for flint enamel and Rockingham

E. Fenton's Works, 1845-1847, on Parian and occasionally on scroddled ware

U. S. Pottery Co., ribbon mark, 1852-1858, on Parian and blue and white porcelain

U. S. Pottery Co., lozenge mark, 1852-1858, on Parian

U. S. Pottery, oval mark, 1853- 1858, mainly on scroddled ware

Additional Listings: Stoneware.

Bennington inkwell, unsigned, five holes, formed column design, applied flint Bennington glaze, c1850, 3" d, 2" h, **$200.**
Photo courtesy of Bruce and Vicki Wassdorp.

Bennington stoneware jug, two gallons, ovoid, strap handle, ornate cobalt blue floral sprig dec, impressed maker's marks, "J.NORTON & CO BENNINGTON VT," 1839-43, 14" h, **$600.**
Photo courtesy of Skinner, Inc.

Bennington-type dog, seated, molded base, Rockingham glaze, 8" w, 11" h, **$350.**
Photo courtesy of Dotta Auction Co., Inc.

Bowl, shallow, brown and yellow Rockingham glaze, Fenton's 1849 mark, 7-1/8" d................................**$775**

Candlestick, flint enamel glaze, 8-1/4" h................................**$875**

Curtain tiebacks, pr, Barrett plate 200, one chipped, 1849-58, 4-1/2" l **$185**

Figure, poodle, standing, basket in mouth, Barrett plate 367, repairs to tail and hindquarters, 8-1/2" h, 9" l...**$2,500**

Flask, book, Barrett plate 411, flint enamel, title imp on spine, 1849-58 "Bennington Battle" on spine, brown and blue flint enamel glaze, 5-3/4" w, 2-5/8" d, 7-3/4" h..................**$3,300**
Titled "Hermit's Life & Suffering," 6" h **$980**
Titled "Ladies Companion," 7" h..**$690**

Flowerpot, molded shells, imp "Bennington Aug 16, 1877 Centennial," shallow flake, 3-1/8" h................**$200**

Jug, stoneware, cobalt blue leaf dec, imp mark "E. Norton & Co., Bennington, VT, 4," strap handle, stains, base flakes, 17-3/4" h...........................**$300**

Marble, blue, some wear, 1-1/2" d.**$90**

Paperweight, spaniel, 1849-58, Barrett plate 407, 3" h, 4-1/2" l.........**$815**

Picture frame, oval, Barrett plate VIII, chips and repairs, pr, 1948-58, 9-1/2" h...**$230**

Pitcher, hunting scene, Barrett plate 26, chips, 8" h................................**$175**

Spittoon, flint enamel glaze, rare 1849 mark, 9-1/2" d...........................**$450**

Sugar bowl, cov, Parian, blue and white, Repeated Oak Leaves pattern, raised grapevine dec on lid, 3-3/4" h........**$150**

Teapot, cov, flint enamel, Alternate Rib pattern, pierced pouring spout **$425**

Wash bowl and pitcher, flint enamel glaze..**$1,100**

Bennington-Type

Bank, chest of drawers shape, Rockingham glaze, Barrett plate 428, small chip to front top edge, 3-1/4" h, 3-3/4" l..**$150**

Creamer, figural, cow, Rockingham glaze, Barrett plate 378, chipped cov, repairs, 5-1/2" h, 6-3/4" l.............**$115**

Flask, boot, laced up one side, daubed Rockingham glaze, rare removable spout included, lip repaired, 7-1/4" l, 7" h..**$450**

Spittoon, scallop shell form, Rockingham glaze, 19th C, 8-1/2" d **$175**

Toby bottle, barrel, Rockingham glaze, rim and base chips, mid-19th C, 9" h................................**$175**

BISCUIT JARS

History: The biscuit or cracker jar was the forerunner of the cookie jar. Biscuit jars were made of various materials by leading glassworks and potteries of the late 19th and early 20th centuries.

Note: All items listed have silver-plated (SP) mountings unless otherwise noted.

Crown Milano
Jeweled body, starfish dec, rust and cream colored body, Mt. Washington, non- matching lid, 6" w....**$550**
Rect, raised gold tracery and large chrysanthemums, emb metal lid with seashell design, stamped "M.W. 4413," 10" h **$400**

Earthenware, Crown Ford, scenic dec, desert scene with figures and camels, 9" h **$200**

Nippon China, sq, white, multicolored floral bands, gold outlines and trim, 7-1/2" h, 4-1/2" w **$110**

Porcelain
Art Nouveau floral dec, silver plated lid and handle, 10" h **$230**

Blue flowers on molded panels, four-footed, 5-1/2" h........................**$125**
Crown Devon, molded panels, flowers dec, silver plated lid and handle, 10" h..**$145**
Fruit dec, minor rim chips, 7-1/2" h **$90**
German, cityscape panel dec, 7-1/2" h **$175**
Panels of small pink flowers, cobalt blue border, gilding, ftd, 7" h ..**$150**
Portrait panels and flowers, Tirchenreuth dec, 7" h **$175**
Roses and leaves dec, 7-1/2" h....**$120**
Scenic panels dec, blue beehive mark, silver plated lid and handle, 8" h **$175**

Unmarked, oriental landscape panels, silver plated lid and handle, 9" h $145

Pottery, blue morning glory flowers and leaves, silver plated lid and handle, 9" h $150

Royal Bayreuth, Poppy, blue mark $650

Wedgwood, jasper

Central dark blue ground bordered in light blue, applied white Muses in relief, banded laurel border, SP rim, handle and cover, imp mark, slight relief loss, c1900, 5-3/4" h $650

Central dark blue ground bordered in light blue ground, applied white classical relief, SP footrim, rim, handle and cover, imp mark, slight firing lines to relief, c1900, 6" h $600

Biscuit Jar, English, dark cobalt blue transfer of morning glories, brass lid with shaped finial, elaborately shaped handle, **$495.**

Green dip ground, applied white classical figure groups above acanthus leaves, SP rim, handle and cover, imp Wedgwood mark, footrim nick, late 19th C, 5" h $400

Biscuit Jar, Carlton Ware, Peony pattern, flowers decoration, silver-plated lid, **$295.**
Photo courtesy of Joy Luke Auctions.

Yellow ground, applied black relief of Muses below fruiting grapevine festoons terminating in lion masks with rings, grapevine border to foot, SP rim, handle and cover, imp mark, c1930, 5-3/4" h..............$800

BISQUE

History: Bisque or biscuit china is the name given to wares that have been fired once and have not been glazed.

Bisque figurines and busts, which were popular during the Victorian era, were used on fireplace mantels, dining room buffets, and end tables. Manufacturing was centered in the United States and Europe. By the mid-20th century, Japan was the principal source of bisque items, especially character-related items.

Bust, female holding flower, green ribbons in hair, Cybis #471, 12" h ...**$435**

Dish, cov, dog, brown, and white, green blanket, white and gilt basketweave base, 9" x 6-1/2" x 5-1/2"............**$500**

Figure

Hunters, dressed in Indian attire, riding on elephants, shooting attacking tigers, polychrome enameling, facing pair, 7-1/2" h..................**$350**

Woman seated in chair, Cybis #298, issued 1968, 11-1/2" h.............**$380**

Young man and woman, each with light green bicycling attire, holding metal bicycle, Heubach Brothers, Thuringia, Germany, early 20th C, 14" h, price for pr **$1,175**

Match holder, figural, Dutch girl, copper and gold trim **$45**

Planter, carriage, four wheels, pale blue and pink, white ground, gold dots, royal markings...................**$165**

Salt, figural, walnut, cream, branch base, matching spoon, 3" d..........**$75**

Wall plaque, light green, scrolled and pierced scallop, white relief figures in center, man playing mandolin, lady wearing hat, c1900, pr, 10-1/4" d **$275**

Bisque hen on nest with basketweave, naturalistic colors, English, 8-1/2" h, 9-1/2" l, **$275.**
Photo courtesy of Joy Luke Auctions.

Bisque figure, semi-nude child seated on a stone plinth, mold incised "H. Dopping," German, early 20th century, 17-5/8" h, **$250.**
Photo courtesy of Skinner, Inc.

Bisque box, covered, oval, two lambs on lid, applied coleslaw type grass and flowers, applied flowers on base, minor damage, 5" l, 4-1/2" h, **$95.**
Photo courtesy of Joy Luke Auctions.

BUFFALO POTTERY

History: Buffalo Pottery Co., Buffalo, New York, was chartered in 1901. The first kiln was fired in October 1903. Larkin Soap Company established Buffalo Pottery to produce premiums for its extensive mail-order business. Wares also were sold to the public by better department and jewelry stores. Elbert Hubbard and Frank Lloyd Wright, who designed the Larkin Administration Building in Buffalo in 1904, were two prominent names associated with the Larkin Company.

Early Buffalo Pottery production consisted mainly of semi-vitreous china dinner sets. Buffalo was the first pottery in the United States to produce successfully the Blue Willow pattern. Buffalo also made a line of hand-decorated, multicolored willow ware, called Gaudy Willow. Other early items include a series of game, fowl, and fish sets, pitchers, jugs, and a line of commemorative, historical, and advertising plates and mugs.

From 1908 to 1909 and again from 1921 to 1923, Buffalo Pottery produced the line for which it is most famous—Deldare Ware. The earliest of this olive green, semi-vitreous china displays hand-decorated scenes from English artist Cecil Aldin's *Fallowfield Hunt*. Hunt scenes were done only from 1908 to 1909. English village scenes also were characteristic of the ware and were used during both periods. Most pieces are artist signed.

In 1911, Buffalo Pottery produced Emerald Deldare, which used scenes from Goldsmith's *The Three Tours of Dr. Syntax* and an Art Nouveau-type border. Completely decorated Art Nouveau pieces also were made.

Abino, which was introduced in 1912, had a Deldare body and displayed scenes of sailboats, windmills, or the sea. Rust was the main color used, and all pieces were signed by the artist and numbered.

In 1915, the manufacturing process was modernized, giving the company the ability to produce vitrified china. Consequently, hotel and institutional ware became the main production items, with hand-decorated ware de-emphasized. The Buffalo firm became a leader in producing and designing the most-famous railroad, hotel, and restaurant patterns.

In the early 1920s, fine china was made for home use. Bluebird is one of the patterns from this era. In 1950, Buffalo made its first Christmas plate. These were given away to customers and employees primarily from 1950 to 1960. However, it is known that Hample Equipment Co. ordered some as late as 1962. The Christmas plates are very scarce in today's resale market.

The Buffalo China Company made "Buffalo Pottery" and "Buffalo China"—the difference being that one is semi-vitreous ware and the other vitrified. In 1956, the company was reorganized, and Buffalo China became the corporate name. Today, Buffalo China is owned by Oneida Silver Company.

Marks: Blue Willow pattern is marked "First Old Willow Ware Mfg. in America."

Buffalo pitcher, George Washington on horseback, blue and white decoration, some staining and crazing, 7-1/2" h, **$160.**
Photo courtesy of Joy Luke Auctions.

Abino Ware

Candlestick, sailing ships, 1913, 9" h **$475**
Pitcher, Portland Head Light, 7" h.. **$700**
Tankard, sailing scene, 10-1/2" h...**$900**

Advertising Ware

Jug, blue and green transfer print, inscribed "The Whaling City Souvenir of New Bedford, Mass," whaling motifs, staining, 6-1/4" h **$325**
Mug, Calumet Club, 4-1/2" h...........**$90**
Plate, Indian Head Pontiac, 9-3/4" d..**$55**
Platter, US Army Medical Dept., 1943, 13-1/2" l **$60**

Deldare

Calling card tray, street scene ...**$395**
Cereal bowl, Fallowfield Hunt, 6" d **$295**
Chop plate, Fallowfield Hunt, 14" d **$795**
Cup and saucer, street scene **$225**
Hair receiver, street scene **$465**

Jardinière, street scene **$975**
Mug
  Fallowfield Hunt, 3-1/2" h **$395**
  Three Pigeons, 4-1/2" h...............**$350**
Pitcher, The Great Controversy, sgd "W. Fozter," stamped mark, 12" h, 7" w **$320**
Powder jar, street scene **$395**
Punch cup, Fallowfield Hunt.......**$375**
Soup plate, street scene, 9" d **$425**
Tankard, Three Pigeons.............**$1,175**
Tea tile, Fallowfield Hunt............**$395**
Tea tray, street scene...................**$650**
Vase, King Fisher, green and white dec, olive ground, stamped mark, artist signature, 7-3/4" h, 6-1/2" d **$1,380**

Emerald Deldare

Creamer **$450**
Fruit bowl..................................**$1,450**
Mug, 4-1/2" h **$475**
Vase, stylized foliate motif, shades of green and white, olive ground, stamp mark, 8-1/2" h, 6-1/2" d **$810**

CANTON CHINA

History: Canton china is a type of Oriental porcelain made in the Canton region of China from the late 18th century to the present. It was produced largely for export. Canton china has a hand-decorated light- to dark-blue underglaze on white ground. Design motifs include houses, mountains, trees, boats, and bridges. A design similar to willow pattern is the most common.

Borders on early Canton feature a rain-and-cloud motif (a thick band of diagonal lines with a scalloped bottom). Later pieces usually have a straight-line border.

Early, c1790-1840, plates are very heavy and often have an unfinished bottom, while serving pieces have an overall "orange-peel" bottom. Early covered pieces, such as tureens, vegetable dishes, and sugars, have strawberry finials and twisted handles. Later ones have round finials and a straight, single handle.

Marks: The markings "Made in China" and "China" indicate wares that date after 1891.

Reproduction Alert. Several museum gift shops and private manufacturers are issuing reproductions of Canton china.

Bowl, cut corner, minor int. glaze imperfections, 19th C, 9-1/2" d .. **$900**

Box, cov, sq, domed top, cloud-and-rain border on lids, early 19th C, pr... **$6,270**

Coffeepot, mismatched cover, 7-1/4" h **$750**

Cup, cov, handle, repaired lid, 4" l, 3-1/2" h **$165**

Dish, leaf shape, 19th C, chips
6-3/4" l **$145**
8-1/2" l **$165**

Fruit basket
Minor chips, 9-1/4" d **$690**
Reticulated, with undertray, 10-1/2" l **$1,100**

Milk pitcher, very minor chips, 6-1/8" h **$575**

Miniature, tureen, underplate, 6-1/2" l, 5" w, 4" h **$300**

Plate, early, c1820-30
Bread and butter, 6" d **$65**
Dessert, 8" d **$95**
Dinner, set of six, one with rim chips, 19th C, 10-3/8" d, price for set **$360**
Lunch, 9" d **$115**
Salad, 7-1/2" d **$85**

Platter
Dark blue, finely detailed scene with figure inside pagoda, bridge, trees, mountains, small sailboat, basketweave design around rim, glaze flakes, 14" x 17" **$460**
Octagonal, oblong, China, small chip underside of rim, 19th C, 14-3/8" x 17-1/4" **$350**

Octagonal, oblong, China, minor glaze imperfections, 19th C, 14-3/4" x 18" **$450**

Octagonal, oblong, well and tree, Chinese Export, rim chip and glaze wear, 19th C, 17-1/4" x 20-1/4" **$390**

Salt, trench, chips, three-pc set, 3-3/4" l **$550**

Sauce boat, lobed, applied bifurcated handles, rim chips, one handle cracked, 6-7/8" w, 8" l, 3-3/8" h, price for pr **$850**

Serving dish, octagonal, 19th C, 15-1/4" x 18-1/4" **$650**

Shrimp dish, minor edge roughness, 10-1/4" d, pr **$690**

Tea caddy, cov, octagonal, 19th C, 5-1/2" h **$2,645**

Tray, lobed lozenge form, 19th C, 11-1/4" l, 8-1/4" w **$875**

Tureen, cov, stem finial, oval, ftd, hog snout handles, 14" l, 9-3/4" w, 7-3/4" h **$1,265**

Vegetable dish, cov, diamond shape, scalloped edges, fruit finial, orange peel glaze, unglazed bottom, 9-1/2" w, 8" d, 3-1/4" h **$225**

Canton teapot, Chinese, porcelain, blue and white, straight side, peach finial, entwined handle, medial horizontal rib, 19th century, 8-1/4" h, 5-1/4" d base, **$165.**
Photo courtesy of Green Valley Auctions.

Canton platter, Chinese, porcelain, blue and white, tree and well, octagonal, unmarked, 19th century, 2-1/4" h x 11-1/2" x 14-1/2", **$300.**
Photo courtesy of Green Valley Auctions.

Canton ewer, cylindrical shape with tapered neck, leaf ornaments, spout chips, China, 10-1/4" h, **$290.**
Photo courtesy of Skinner, Inc.

Capo-di-Monte plaques, pair, colored relief of Adam and Eve and The Adoration, conforming ebonized frames, mounted with gilt-bronze strapwork cartouche scrolls and marble medallions, blue crowned N marks, 20th century, 19-1/2" h, $1,065.
Photo courtesy of Sloans & Kenyon Auctioneers and Appraisers.

Capo-di-Monte basket, yellow, pink, and white roses, green foliage, tan basketweave base, marked with crown and "Capo-di-Monte, Made in Italy," $75.

Reproduction Alert. Many of the pieces in today's market are of recent vintage. Do not be fooled by the crown over the "N" mark; it also was copied.

CAPO-DI-MONTE

History: In 1743, King Charles of Naples established a soft-paste porcelain factory near Naples. The firm made figurines and dinnerware. In 1760, many of the workmen and most of the molds were moved to Buen Retiro, near Madrid, Spain. A new factory, which also made hard-paste porcelains, opened in Naples in 1771. In 1834, the Doccia factory in Florence purchased the molds and continued production in Italy.

Capo-di-Monte was copied heavily by other factories in Hungary, Germany, France, and Italy.

Box
Cov, angel relief top, relief band molded mythological figures on sides, beaded rims, blue crowned N mk **$145**
Cov, clover shape, cherubs at pursuits on cov, 4" w **$290**
Cov, gladiator in chariot on horse relief, cherub relief on sides, white, metal mts **$475**
Cov, multicolored, Italy mk, 8-1/2" l **$95**
Cov, round, domed lid molded with low relief figures of cherubs with flower baskets, sides similarly molded with cherubs at various artistic pursuits, gilt-metal rim mounts, int. painted with floral sprigs, late 19th C, 8" d, 4-1/4" h **$475**
Casket, molded opal body, cherubs in relief, detailed polychrome floral dec, gilt highlights, underglaze blue crown "N" mark, 19th C, 13" l, 8" w, 5-1/2" h **$2,400**
Creamer and sugar, mythological raised scene, dragon handles, claw feet, lion finial, 5-1/2" x 6" creamer, 6-1/4" x 6" cov sugar **$250**
Cup and saucer
Demitasse, mythical figure relief, pedestal and oil lamp, twisted gold and red feather handle, blue crowned N mk **$175**
Relief of frolicking cherubs, crown N mark **$195**
Dessert plate, four different polychrome armorials in center, molded polychrome and gilt classical figures on border, blue crowned N mks, set of four, 6" d **$425**
Dresser set, mythological raised scene, pair of 4" d, 7" h perfume bottles with figural stoppers, 5" d, 4" h cov powder jar, 30" l x 15" w tray **$500**
Ewer, polychrome, gold crown over blue dash mk **$375**
Ferner, oval, relief molded and enameled allegorical figures, full relief female mask at each end, 11" l **$120**

Figure, period gentleman, tan top hat, brown jacket, woman in black flowered dress, bonnet, circ base, crowned N mk, c1900, 14" h **$600**
Goblet shape, multicolored cherubs, flowers, and interwoven curls and swirls, Italy mk, 12" h **$390**
Lamp, table, figural Bacchus, female, and grapes, 25" h **$1,300**
Napkin ring, polychromed relief of frolicking cherubs, 1-1/2" d **$100**
Plate, each with Capo-di-Monte crest at top, pair of swans, pair of cranes, crimson, blue, yellow, and burnt-orange flowers on border, gold trim, minor wear, price for eight-pc set, 8-3/8" d **$1,100**
Snuffbox, hinged lid, cartouche shape, molded basketweave and flower-head ext., painted int. with court lady and page examining portrait of gentlemen, gold mountings, minor restoration, c1740, 3-1/4" d **$1,650**
Stein, lion-hunt scene, lion on lid, elephant-trunk handle, 7-1/2" h. **$400**
Table decoration, 8-3/4" h figural group of three female dancers on hexagonal base, 6-3/4" l four individual dancers, 6-1/4" l four kidney-shaped flower wells, gilt dec, 20th C, price for nine pcs **$365**
Urn, cov, ovoid, central-molded frieze of Nerieds and putti, molded floral garlands, gadroon upper section, acanthus-molded lower section, socle foot with putti, sq plinth base, applied ram's-head handles, domed cov, acorn finial, underglaze crowned N mark, minor chips and losses, 21-1/8" h, pr.....**$1,650**
Vase
Campana urn shape, relief of Roman mythological putti, satyrs, and goats, festooned ivy wreath, two horizontal gilt handles, swirl fluted pedestal on square base, gilt scrolling, blue crowned N mk, mid-19th century, 13-1/4" **$795**

CELADON

History: The term "celadon," meaning a pale grayish-green color, is derived from the theatrical character Celadon, who wore costumes of varying shades of grayish green in Honore d'Urfe's 17th-century pastoral romance, L'Astree. French Jesuits living in China used the name to refer to a specific type of Chinese porcelain.

Celadon divides into two types. Northern celadon, made during the Sung Dynasty up to the 1120s, has a gray-to-brownish body, relief decoration, and monochromatic olive-green glaze. Southern (Lung-ch'uan) celadon, made during the Sung Dynasty and much later, is paint-decorated with floral and other scenic designs and is found in forms that appeal to the European-and American-export market. Many of the southern pieces date from 1825 to 1885. A blue square with Chinese or pseudo-Chinese characters appears on pieces after 1850. Later pieces also have a larger and sparser decorative patterning.

Reproduction Alert.

Bowl

Cut corner shape, Rose Canton dec, hardwood stand, repaired, 9-1/2" d, 4-1/2" h **$385**

Exterior carved with lotus petals, China, 14th C, 6-1/4" d **$365**

Lung Chuan ware, interior with kylin and waves, China, 14th C, 15-1/4" d **$1,450**

Scalloped rim, dec with exotic birds, butterflies, and flowers, repairs and gilt losses to edge, 10-1/2" d **$245**

Sea green color, inlaid in Sangam technique with branches and sprigs of flowers, Korea, Koryo period, 12th/13th C, 7-1/2" d **$475**

Sea green color, inlaid in Sangam technique with clouds and phoenix, Korea, Koryo period, 12th C, 7-1/2" d **$875**

Wide flaring form, dark gray-green color, traces of three spurs on base, surface entirely glazed, Korea, Koryo period, 12th C, 5-3/4" d **$600**

Brush box, cov, dec in Rose Medallion palette, 7-1/2" w, 3-1/4" d, 2-1/2" h **$400**

Center dish, diamond shape, conforming foot, court scenes, central scene contained in vasiform device, Rose Canton pattern, China, gilt wear, 19th C, 11-1/4" l **$530**

Charger

Mandarin warrior, One Hundred Antiques border, China, 19th C, 10" d **$210**

Rose Medallion, court scene within medallion, Famille Rose border, minor glaze wear, 13-1/2" d **$725**

Ice cream tray, rect, flange handles, Rose Canton motif, China, minor gilt wear, 19th C, 7" x 13-1/4" **$600**

Incense burner, lid surmounted by Buddhist, lion base with lion mask feet, sea-green color, Korea, 12th C **$8,000**

Plate

Hexagonal, Lung Chuan ware, latticework center and floral rim, China, Ming period (15th-16th C), 11" d **$1,175**

River scene, butterfly and floral border, minor gilt and glaze wear, 10-1/4" d **$150**

Rose Canton dec, China, 19th C, 5-1/4" d **$90**

Rose Canton motif, bird and butterflies around tree peony, underglaze blue sq mark, wear, some in-painting, 10-1/4" h **$210**

Platter, oval, Rose Canton dec, 13-1/4" x 15-3/4" **$650**

Rice bowl, cov, underplate, dec with various animals, figures, and flowers, 7-1/2" d, 5-3/4" h **$390**

Sauce tureen, cov, undertray, gilt floriform finial, gilt handles, bird, butterfly, and floral motifs, China, minor edge wear, 19th C **$600**

Serving dish, cov, domed lid, single handle, Rose Canton dec, imperfections, 10" d, 6-1/2" h **$300**

Shrimp dish, bird, butterfly, and floral motif, China, minor glaze wear, 19th C, 10-1/4" x 9-3/4" **$650**

Soap dish, three part, figures in garden on lid, Rose Medallion border, minor edge wear, 4-1/8" l, 5-1/4" w, 2-1/2" h **$265**

Vase

Hexagonal paneled form, two handles, bird and floral dec, handle chip, gilt wear, 12-3/4" h **$385**

Maebyong form, carved floral sprigs on body and lotus petals at base, deep sea-green color, Korea, Koryo period, old repair to mouth, 12th/13th C, 10-3/4" h **$1,800**

*Celadon vase, porcelain, celadon crackled glaze over blue underglaze, Buddhist wheel designs in concentric circles on shoulder and lower body, Chinese, pieced wooden lid and base, 19th century, 9" x 7", **$1,000.***

Photo courtesy of David Rago Auctions, Inc.

*Celadon vase, carved, ovoid, peony dec, Chinese, 16th century, 6-1/2" h, **$497.***

Photo courtesy of Pook & Pook, Inc.

Chintz, Royal Winton, Evesham, stacking creamer, sugar and teapot, **$450.**

Chintz, Royal Winton, June, creamer and sugar on tray, **$225.**

Reproduction Alert. Both Royal Winton and James Kent reproduced some of their more popular patterns. Royal Winton is reproducing Welbeck, Florence, Summertime and Julia; in 1999 it added Joyce-Lynn, Marion, Majestic, Royalty and Richmond, Old Cottage Chintz and Stratford. The company added several new chintz patterns such as Blue Cottage and Christmas Chintz. James Kent reproduced Du Barry, Hydrangea, and Rosalynde, as well as creating several new colorways of old patterns. James Kent has discontinued the production of chintz ware. Elijah Cotton backstamp was purchased and as well as reproducing Rosetime chintz the factory has issued a number of new chintzes with the new backstamp. Wade recently produced three chintz patterns—Butterfly, Thistle and Sweet Pea. Two's Company and Godinger have also copied some of the Royal Winton patterns. Prices for vintage chintz seem to be rising again as new collectors have been attracted to the market but they are still well below the very high prices of the late 1990s. Inexperienced collectors often pay high prices for brand new pieces so check backstamps carefully.

CHINTZ CHINA

History: Chintz china has been produced since the 17th century. The brightly colored exotic patterns produced on fabric imported from India to England were then re-created on ceramics. Early chintz patterns were hand painted and featured large flowers, fantastical birds, and widely spaced patterns. The advent of transfer printing resulted in the development of chintz dishes, which could be produced cheaply enough to sell to the masses. By the 1830s, a number of Staffordshire potteries were producing chintzware for everyday use. These early patterns are now starting to attract the interest of some chintz collectors.

Collectors typically want the patterns dating from roughly 1920 until the 1950s although some of the earlier un-named Royal Winton patterns are starting to become popular with longtime collectors. In 1920, A.G. Richardson "Crown Ducal" produced a range of all-over-transfer chintz patterns that proved to be very popular in North America, particularly the East Coast. Florida was the most popular of the Crown Ducal patterns in North America for collectors, but Pink Chintz and Peony have become increasingly popular.

From the late 1920s until the mid-1950s, Royal Winton produced more than 80 chintz patterns. In some cases, the background color was varied and the name changed: Hazel, Spring, and Welbeck is the same pattern in different colorways. After World War II, Royal Winton created more than 15 new patterns, many of which were more modern looking with large flowers and rich dark burgundy, blue or black backgrounds—patterns such as May Festival, Spring Glory and Peony. These patterns have not been as popular with collectors as 1930s patterns, although other 1950s patterns such as Florence and Stratford have become almost as popular as Julia and Welbeck. Some of the more widely spaced patterns, like Victorian Rose and Cotswold, are now attracting collectors.

The 1930s were hard times in the potteries and factories struggled to survive. They copied any successful patterns from any other factories. James Kent Ltd. produced chintzes such as DuBarry, Apple Blossom and Rosalynde. The most popular pattern for collectors is the white Hydrangea, although Apple Blossom seems to be more and more sought after. Elijah Cotton "Lord Nelson" was another factory that produced large amounts of chintz. The workers at Elijah Cotton were never as skilled as the Grimwades' workers, and usually the handles and spouts of teapots and coffeepots were left undecorated. Collectors love the Nelson Ware stacking teapots, especially in Black Beauty and Green Tulip.

Although a number of factories produced bone china after World War II, only Shelley Pottery seems to be highly desired by today's collector.

By the late 1950s, young brides didn't want the dishes of their mothers and grandmothers, but preferred the clean lines of modern Scandinavian furniture and dishes. Chintz gradually died out by the early 1960s, and it was not until the 1990s that collectors began to search for the dishes their mothers had scorned.

Notes: A newsletter devoted to Chintz is available, *Crazed Collector*, P.O. Box 2635, Dublin, CA 94568, CrazedCollctr@aol.com, www.crazedcollector.net. For those who prefer online information, there is a free Chintz chat group: chintz-subscribe@yahoogroups.com.

Adviser: Susan Scott.

Warning. Before you buy chintz, ask whether it is new or vintage. Ask to see a photograph of the backstamps if not examining the piece in person. The "1995" on the RW backstamp refers to the year the company was bought, and not the year the chintz was made. Compare old and new backstamps on www.chintz.net.com or in Susan Scott's *Charlton Standard Catalogue of Chintz*, 3rd edition, New Chintz Section.

Elijah Cotton "Lord Nelson"

Bud vase, Marina pattern, 5" h **$65**
Creamer and sugar, Briar Rose pattern **$75**
Cup and saucer, Rosetime **$50**
Jug, Bute shape, Pansy pattern, 6" h ..**$150**
Plate, Briar Rose pattern, 8" **$50**
Sauceboat, undertray, Country Lane pattern **$95**
Teapot, stacking, totally patterned, Marina **$250**

Grimwades "Royal Winton"

Biscuit barrel, Rheims shape, Hazel pattern **$600**
Breakfast set, Somerset pattern **$700**
Bud vase, Royalty pattern **$115**
Candy dish, covered, Gordon shape, Cotswold pattern **$175**
Cake stand, three-tier Sweet Pea pattern **$195**
Coffeepot, Albans shape, Julia pattern **$400**
Cup and saucer, Chelsea pattern **$75**
Eggcup, footed, Bedale pattern **$90**
Hot water pot, Albans shape, Royalty pattern **$300**

Jug, Duval shape, Majestic pattern, 5" h **$175**
Plate, Ascot shape, Beeston pattern, 10" **$165**
Salt and pepper shakers on tray, Hazel pattern **$115**
Teapot
Albans shape, Esther pattern **$350**
Stacking, Pekin pattern **$225**
Stacking, Stratford pattern **$875**
Toast rack, Stafford shape, Summertime pattern **$200**
Tray, June Roses pattern, 10" Ascot shape **$175**

James Kent Ltd.

Coffeepot, Granville shape, Du Barry pattern **$300**
Dish
Octagonal, Milles Fleur pattern, 12" l **$95**
Ruffled, Chelsea Rose pattern, 12" x 8" **$75**
Plate
Crazy Paving pattern, 9" d **$95**
Hydrangea pattern, 10" d **$75**
Tray, Apple Blossom pattern, 8" by 5" **$55**
Teapot, Square Diamond shape, Mille Fleur pattern **$200**
Vase, Hydrangea pattern, 2" h **$105**

A. G. Richardson "Crown Ducal"

Cake plate, Peony pattern, 10" **$150**
Plate, Blue Chintz pattern, 9" sq **$65**
Sugar shaker, Primula pattern **$95**
Teapot, Georgian shape, Roseland pattern **$350**
Teapot and trivet, Primula pattern **$295**
Vase
Florida pattern, 8" h **$145**
Ivory Chintz pattern, 6" h **$125**

Shelley Potteries Ltd.

Biscuit barrel, Blue Pansy pattern **$235**
Cup and saucer
Henley shape, Countryside pattern **$165**
Henley shape, Summer Glory pattern **$125**
Miniature, Blue Pansy pattern ..**$1,860**
Oleander shape, Rock Garden pattern **$105**
Ripon shape, Briar Rose pattern **$160**
Plate, Oleander shape, Primrose pattern, 7" round **$50**
Teapot, Henley shape, Summer Glory pattern **$375**
Toast rack, 5 bar Melody pattern **$115**

CLIFTON POTTERY

History: The Clifton Art Pottery, Newark, New Jersey, was established by William A. Long, once associated with Lonhuda Pottery, and Fred Tschirner, a chemist.

Production consisted of two major lines: Crystal Patina, which resembled true porcelain with a subdued crystal-like glaze, and Indian Ware or Western Influence, an adaptation of the American Indians' unglazed and decorated pottery with a high-glazed black interior. Other lines included Robin's-Egg Blue and Tirrube. Robin's-Egg Blue is a variation of the crystal patina line, but in blue-green instead of straw-colored hues and with a less-prominent crushed-crystal effect in the glaze. Tirrube, which is often artist signed, features brightly colored, slip-decorated flowers on a terra-cotta ground.

Marks: Marks are incised or impressed. Early pieces may be dated and impressed with a shape number. Indian wares are identified by tribes.

Biscuit jar, cov, gray-brown ground, enameled running ostrich and stork, florals, bail handle, 7" h, 4-1/4" d ...**$300**
Bowl, Indian, black glazed dec, marked, minor rim flake, 9" d ...**$150**
Creamer, Crystal Patina, incised "Clifton," dated **$225**
Decanter, rose shading to deep rose, purple flowers, gilt butterfly on neck,

applied handle, marbleized rose and white stopper, 11-1/2" h **$150**
Jardinière, Four Mile Ruin, Arizona, incised and painted motif, buff and black on brown ground, imp mark and incised inscription, hairline to rim, 8-1/2" h, 11" d **$400**
Pedestal, Indian, unmarked, small chip to top and glaze, 20" h **$690**

Clifton crystal patina bottle-shaped vase, marked, dated, and stamped "164," 1906, 8-1/4" x 5-1/2", **$660.**
Photo courtesy of David Rago Auctions, Inc.

Sweetmeat jar, hp ducks and cranes, robin's egg blue ground, cow finial, 4" h................................**$375**

Teapot, brown and black geometric design, 6" h.................................**$200**

Vase
Angular handles, Crystal Patina, incised "Clifton," 10" h, 7" d **$450**
Bottle shape, Crystal Patina, incised "Clifton/158," 9-1/2" h, 4-1/2" d...**$350**
Bulbous, Indian, collared rim, geometric chain pattern, "Homolobi, #233," marked, few shallow scratches, 7-1/2" x 10"..........................**$925**
Bulbous, Indian, dark birds in flight, "Homolobi, #235," marked, 8" x 9"
....**$975**
Spherical, Crystal Patina, green and mirrored caramel glaze, sgd and dated 1906, 6-1/2" d, 5-1/2" h ...**$575**

Vessel
Gourd shape, Indian, swirl pattern, Arkansas, #216, marked, 5-1/4"..**$380**

Clifton Pottery, vase, Indian Ware, bulbous, tan, brown and terra cotta rounded panel design, incised "Clifton/231" and "Middle Mississippi Valley" around base, several glaze nicks around rim, 12-1/4" x 8-1/2", **$445.**
Photo courtesy of David Rago Auctions, Inc.

Clifton Pottery, Crystal patina squat covered teapot, squat two-handled organically shaped vase covered in matte green glaze, both marked, 6-1/4" h, **$300.**
Photo courtesy of David Rago Auctions, Inc.

CONTINENTAL CHINA AND PORCELAIN (GENERAL)

History: By 1700, porcelain factories existed in large numbers throughout Europe. In the mid-18th century, the German factories at Meissen and Nymphenburg were dominant. As the century ended, French potteries assumed the leadership role. The 1740s to the 1840s were the golden age of Continental china and porcelains.

Americans living in the last half of the 19th century eagerly sought the masterpieces of the European porcelain factories. In the early 20th century, this style of china and porcelain was considered "blue chip" by antiques collectors.

Additional Listings: French— Haviland, Limoges, Sarreguemines, and Sevres; German—Austrian Ware, Bavarian China, Dresden/Meissen, Rosenthal, Royal Bayreuth, Royal Bonn, Royal Rudolstadt, Royal Vienna, Schlegelmilch, and Villeroy and Boch; Italian—Capo-di-Monte.

French

Choisy, plate, earthenware transfer printed and hand enameled, each with different numbered scene relating to story of soldier's courtship and military life, naïve enamel accenting, mid-19th C, 8-1/4" d, price for set of 12..**$500**

Creil
Jug, transfer printed, canary ground, imp "CREIL"..........................**$300**
Pitcher, 10-3/4" h, glazed pottery, ewer-form, central beige band dec with trees, cream ground, imp "CREIL," 5-1/4" h....................**$420**

Faience
Bulb pot, sq, molded acanthus-capped scroll feet, conforming handles, front with scene of courting couple, verso landscape, each side with floral sprays, sq form insert, gilt highlights, attributed to Marseilles, last quarter 18th C, 3-1/8" d, pr...**$900**
Inkstand, figural, cartouche-shaped base molded with scrolls, front painted with harbor scene flanked by tower and knight-shaped inkpots, back sections support large figure of lion with raised paw resting on shield with armorial, 13-1/2" l.............**$650**
Plate, blue and white floral dec, foliate border, 9" d..............................**$115**

Paris porcelain coffee service, classical revival, white ground, green central medallions with flowers and figures, gilt trim, includes covered coffeepot 10-3/4", cream jug 6-3/4" h, sugar bowl 4-1/2" h, 10 coffee cans, 11 saucers, France, 19th century, **$380.**
Photo courtesy of Skinner, Inc.

Sugar caster, brightly polychrome scene of courting couple in landscape, floral sprays borders, dec band of fleur-de-lis border, pierced cov with conforming dec, early 19th C, 8-1/2" h **$450**

H.A. Balleroy Bros., attributed to, late 19th C, charger, 22-1/4" d, painted with scene of gentlemen studying drawings at trestle table, inscribed lower left "Le Portrait de L'Hote faience d'apres Brillouin par Pascault," gilt rim, mounted in 34" sq Aesthetic Movement gilt and copper frame with round inner surround **$1,100**

Lessore, Emile, platter, oval, earthenware, polychrome figural landscape with putti, artist signed, printed factory mark for Hautin and Boulenger, France, rim chip, c1855, 14-1/4" l **$450**

Paris

Cache pot, ovoid, apple-green ground, floral roundels in leaf surround, two gilt lion's head masks on sides, narrow undertray, late 19th C, 6" h **$115**

Candlesticks, pr, everted sconce, column-form standard, shaped base with man and woman among rocaille leaves, 9" h **$200**

Dessert plate, hand painted, four with flower centers, two with fruit centers, all with peach borders, gilt scrolls, maroon band at molded rim, late 19th C, 9-1/8" d **$750**

Lamp base, egg-shaped bodies, enamel dec multicolored floral sprays and gilt vines on lavender ground, drilled and electrified, late 19th C, 10-3/4" h, price for pr **$250**

Urn, gilding, hand-painted scene, two oval reserves, one with church near lake, other with courting couple, double handles with faintly molded heads, wear, lid missing, 10-5/8" h **$375**

Vase garniture, three vases, each with aqua ground, floral bouquet roundels in gilt surrounds, short scroll handles, domed foot molded with scallop shells, late 19th C, 8" h, 8-1/4" h, 9-1/2" h **$500**

Veilleuse, hand painted, small pot with black and pink bands, over enameled with gilt scrolls, short gilt spout, angular handle, octagonal pagoda-form stand hp with scenes titled "acqueduque de Buc," showing elevated aqueduct, and "a Bonnebose (Calvados)," showing village, base missing, 20th C, 4-1/2" h pot, 9" h overall.........**$475**

Samson & Co.

Character figure, three figures in masks and caps, two wielding swords, other dagger, bearded figure with guitar, each by vine-covered tree trunk, rect base, guilloche borders, 20th C, 6-3/8" to 7-5/8" h, price for four-pc set **$450**

Figure, Neptune, upraised hands standing on scallop shell, dolphin at feet, rocaille base encrusted with shells and seaweed, gilt accents, late 19th C, 12-1/4" h **$230**

Perfume bottle, figural, boy with vessel seated on dolphin, enamel detailing, boy's head as stopper, late 19th C, 2-7/8" l..................................**$230**

Unknown maker

Plate, centers painted with pastoral scenes, tooled gilt border, white ground, pink rim with three scenes within gilt cartouches, mid-19th C, 10" d, price for pr **$815**

Tray, painted in Oriental manner to resemble cloisonné, parrot and fish on turquoise ground gold geometric design, cast bronze frame with bamboo and scroll Oriental designs with trace of gilding, some areas of verdigris, unmarked, 12-3/4" x 18-1/2" **$575**

Germany

Böttger, tea cup and saucer, red stoneware, black lacquered ground, stylized

auricular handles, c1715, 3-1/8" h, 5-7/8" d saucer **$31,070**

Herend, dinner service, partial, Indian Basket pattern, puce dec on white ground, 10 dinner plates, six salad plates, five bread and butter plates, six bone dishes, five soup bowls, four serving trays of various size and form, gravy boat, four cups and six saucers, early 20th C............................**$1,450**

Hutschenreuther

Plaque, oval, Madonna and Child, giltwood frame, late 19th C, 5-1/8" x 6-7/8" **$600**

Westerwald tankard, blued glazed, cylindrical, inscribed reindeer and palmettes, hinged pewter lid, Germany, early 18th century, 8-1/2", **$560.**
Photo courtesy of Skinner, Inc.

Chocolate cup and saucer, handpainted porcelain, flared cup with beaded base, three paw feet, high scroll handle, titled street scene enamel decoration, pale lavender ground, German, mid-19th century, cup 4" h, saucer 5-3/4" w, **$323.**
Photo courtesy of Skinner, Inc.

Thuringian tankard, tin glazed earthenware, polychrome dec, spattered puce ground, central fancy horse flanked by trees and foliage, pewter foot and hinged lid, Germany, c1765, 7" h, **$1,295.**
Photo courtesy of Skinner, Inc.

Service plate, central dec, summer flowers within heavily gilt cavetto, rim worked with scrolling acanthus, textured ground, under-glaze green factory marks, minor rubbing, 12-pc set, 10-7/8" d **$1,600**

Vase, mehlem, detailed painted birds, irises, and foliage, bronze patinated handles and base, imp marks, "Franz Anton Mehlem Bonn," c1900, 13-1/2" h, price for pr **$1,380**

Nymphenburg

Dinner service, each hand painted in enamels and trimmed in gilt with cartouches of landscapes in blue bead pattern, titles on reverse, 12, 10" d dinner plates; 11, 8-1/4" d plates; 8-1/4" d cov soup tureen with undertray; two coffee cups and saucers; 12 tea cups; 16 saucers; 7-1/2" h cov water pitcher; 2-5/8" h cream jug; 3-5/8" h cov sugar bowl; 18-1/2" l oval tea tray; two 6-5/8" d cov vegetable dishes; two 7" h fruit coolers with inserts; 8-7/8" square serving dish; 10-3/4" l triangular serving dish;

two 9-1/2" d serving dishes; printed marks, mid-10th C **$28,200**

Vase, wide baluster form, enamel dec, continuous landscape scene, titled on underside "Vorfrohling in Oberbayorn," signed "R. Sieck," 20th C, 10-1/2" d **$750**

Unknown maker

Cup and saucer, bucket-shaped cup, cerulean blue band over horizontal gilt beaded band above landscape scene, short gilt acanthus scroll handle, three gilt paw feet, similarly beaded and gilded saucer, 3-5/8" h **$1,035**

Plaque, girl with candle, titled "Guten Nahct," oval, reeded giltwood frame, late 19th/early 20th C, 5" l **$1,035**

Italian

Pattarino, mask, Bacchus, finely molded, polychrome glaze, sprigged hair adjorned with applied grape clusters and vines, inscribed "Prof. E. Pattarino, Italy," 11-1/2" h **$2,645**

COOKIE JARS

History: Cookie jars, colorful and often whimsical, are popular with collectors. They were made by almost every manufacturer, in all types of materials. Figural character cookie jars are the most popular with collectors.

Cookie jars often were redesigned to reflect newer tastes. Hence, the same jar may be found in several different variations and these variations can affect the price.

Marks: Many cookie-jar shapes were manufactured by more than one company and, as a result, can be found with different marks. This often happened because of mergers or separations, e.g., Brush-McCoy, which became Nelson McCoy. Molds also were traded and sold among companies.

Woodsy Owl jar and bank, USA mark on jar, cold-painted details, 1970s, **$275.**

Abingdon Pottery

Bo Peep, No. 694D, 12" h **$425**
Choo Choo, No. 561D, 7-1/2" h **$120**
Daisy, No. 677, 8" h **$50**
Pumpkin, No. 674D, 8" h **$550**
Three Bears, No. 696D, 8-3/4" h **$245**
Windmill, No. 678, 10-1/2" h **$500**

Brayton Laguna Pottery

Partridges, Model No. V-12, 7-1/4" h **$200**
Provincial Lady, high-gloss white apron and scarf, red, green and yellow flowers and hearts, marked "Brayton Laguna Calif. K-27," 13" h **$455**
Swedish Maid, incised mark, 1941, 11" h **$600**

Hull Pottery

Barefoot Boy **$320**
Duck **$60**
Gingerbread Boy, blue and white trim **$400**
Gingerbread Man, 12" h............**$550**
Little Red Riding Hood, open basket, gold stars on apron..................**$375**

Metlox Pottery

Bear, blue sweater.......................**$100**
Chef Pierre................................**$100**
Pine Cone, gray squirrel finial, Model No. 509, 11" h **$115**
Rex Dinosaur, white....................**$120**
Tulip, yellow and green..............**$425**

Red Wing Pottery

French Chef, blue glaze..............**$250**
Grapes, yellow, marked "Red Wing USA," 10" h **$125**

Mickey Mouse on Birthday Cake, Japanese, impressed mark of conjoined letters (MR?), ink-stamped, "Copyright (symbol) Walt Disney Productions," 11" h, **$500.**

Herringbone Black Butler, rattan handle, ink-stamped, "Japan," Japanese, early 1950s, 8-3/4" h with handle down, **$2,500.**

Little Boy Blue, with rare red neckerchief, impressed mark, "K25 USA," Brush, mid-1950s, 10-1/4" h, **$800.**

Rooster, green glaze **$165**

Shawnee Pottery

Cinderella, unmarked **$125**

Dutch Boy, striped pants, marked "USA," 11" h.............................**$190**

Dutch Girl, marked "USA," 11-1/2" h **$175**

Great Northern Boy, marked "Great Northern USA 1025," 9-3/4" h.**$425**

Jo-Jo the Clown, marked "Shawnee USA, 12," 9" h **$300**

Little Chef......................................**$95**

Muggsy Dog, blue bow, gold trim and decals, marked "Patented Muggsy U.S.A.," 11-3/4" h **$850**

Smiley Pig, clover blossom dec, marked "Patented Smiley USA," 11-1/2" h **$550**

Winnie Pig, clover blossom dec, marked "Patented Winnie USA," 12" h **$575**

Stoneware, cobalt blue dec, unknown maker

Basketweave and Morning Glory,

marked "Put Your Fist In," 7-1/2" h **$625**

Flying Bird, 9" h.......................**$1,250**

Watt Pottery

Apple, No. 21, 7-1/2" h **$400**

Cookie Barrel, wood grain, 10-1/2" h **$50**

Goodies, No. 76, 6-1/2" h...........**$150**

Happy/Sad Face, No. 34, wooden lid **$165**

Starflower, No. 503, 8" h **$350**

Art Pottery, raspberry colored ground, white painted clematis and green leaves, signed M.R. Avon/65, 7" x 6-1/2", **$960.**
Photo courtesy of David Rago Auctions, Inc.

COPELAND AND SPODE

History: In 1749, Josiah Spode was apprenticed to Thomas Whieldon and in 1754 worked for William Banks in Stoke-on-Trent. In the early 1760s, Spode started his own pottery, making cream-colored earthenware and blue-printed whiteware. In 1770, he returned to Banks' factory as master, purchasing it in 1776.

Spode pioneered the use of steam-powered pottery-making machinery and mastered the art of transfer printing from copper plates. Spode opened a London shop in 1778 and sent William Copeland there about 1784. A number of larger London locations followed. At the turn of the century, Spode introduced bone china. In 1805, Josiah Spode II and William Copeland entered into a partnership for the London business. A series of partnerships between Josiah Spode II, Josiah Spode III and William Taylor Copeland resulted.

In 1833, Copeland acquired Spode's London operations and seven years later, the Stoke plants. William Taylor Copeland managed the business until his death in 1868. The firm remained in the hands of Copeland heirs. In 1923, the plant was electrified; other modernization followed.

In 1976, Spode merged with Worcester Royal Porcelain to become Royal Worcester Spode, Ltd.

Copeland Spode dinner set, transferware dec, floral and geometric pattern, gilt highlights, three cov dishes, large soup tureen, two large trays, gravy bowl, perforated plate, bowl, nine luncheon plates, 13, 10" d dinner plates, **$400.**
Photo courtesy of David Rago Auctions, Inc.

Copeland Spode dinner plate, red rose center, blue border with white floral decoration, gold rim, **$20.**

Bust, Una, by John Hancock, traces of printed verse on back, short socle, late 19th C, 11-1/2" h **$300**

Cabinet plate, artist sgd "Samuel Alcock," 1-3/4" jeweled border, intricate gold, beading, pearl and turquoise jeweling, c1889, 9-1/2" d..............**$750**

Coffee cup and saucer, 2-1/4" h cylindrical cup with allover maroon and gilt scrolled dec, 5" d saucer, retained by Tiffany & Co., late 19th C, price for set of 12........................**$325**

Dinner service

Indian Tree, service for 10, serving pcs, 46 pcs................................**$500**

Maritime Rose pattern, service for 12, serving pieces, some repairs **$1,100**

Figure, parian

Chastity, standing female figure modeled holding some lilies, impressed "J. Durham, sc," title and manufacturer, England, c1865, 25" h **$1,530**

Ophelia, standing female figure modeled clenching flowers in her cloak, impressed "W. Calder Marshall RA," publishing date and manufacture, England, missing a leaf of one floret, c1863, 16-1/2" h **$500**

Fish plate, artist sgd "H. C. Lea," four-part gold-swirled design, hp fly in each section, c1891, 9-3/4" d......**$175**

Jug, orange, teal green and gold dec, matte cream ground, ornate handle with two mythological characters, c1847 ....**$450**

Plate, blue and white, hunting scenes, 9-1/2" d...................................**$225**

Platter, Blue Willow pattern, oval, deep, shaped edge, marked "Copeland & Garrett/Late Spode," 18" x 23-1/4" d **$375**

Service plate, Brompton pattern, floral border, central design of birds and foliage, retailed by Wright, Tyndale & Van Roden, Inc., Philadelphia, marked "Rd. No. 608584," price for set of 10, 10-1/4" d **$335**

Spill vase, flared rim, pale lilac, gilt octagonal panels with portrait of bearded man, band of pearls on rims and bases, Spode, c1920, 4-3/4" h **$425**

Tea set, Blue Willow, retailed by Tiffany & Co., pattern registered January 1879, printed at rim with quotation from Robert Burns "Auld Lang Syne," 5" h cov hexagonal teapot, creamer, cov sugar, seven cups, six saucers, 20-3/4" d round tray with scalloped gilt rim, gilt handles, gilt foo dog lid finials, price for 17-pc set **$950**

Tray, black transfer, passion flowers, grape vines border, emb grapes, vines, and leaves on tab handles, c1900, 8-1/2" l..................................**$200**

Tureen, cov, white, gold and blue accents, marked "Spode New Stone," 13" w x 11" h **$1,470**

Urn, cov, Louis XVI style, cobalt blue ground, medallions on each side with bouquet of roses, majolica, repair to one handle, nick to one lid, pr, 15" h **$900**

Water pitcher, bulbous, tan acanthus leaf handle and spout, green field dec with white relief classical figures of dancing women, white relief banded floral garland dec at neck, marked "Rd. No. 180288," 8-1/4" h **$250**

DEDHAM POTTERY

History: Alexander W. Robertson established a pottery in Chelsea, Massachusetts, about 1866. After his brother, Hugh Cornwall Robertson, joined him in 1868, the firm was called A. W. & H. C. Robertson. Their father, James Robertson, joined his sons in 1872, and the name Chelsea Keramic Art Works Robertson and Sons was used.

The pottery's initial products were simple flower and bean pots, but the firm quickly expanded its output to include a wide variety of artistic pottery. It produced a very fine redware body used in classical forms, some with black backgrounds imitating ancient Greek and Apulian works. It experimented with underglaze slip decoration on vases. The Chelsea Keramic Art Works Pottery also produced high-glazed vases, pitchers and plaques with a buff clay body, with either sculpted or molded applied decoration.

James Robertson died in 1880 and Alexander moved to California in 1884, leaving Hugh C. Robertson alone in Chelsea, where his tireless experiments eventually yielded a stunning imitation of the prized Chinese Ming-era blood-red glaze. Hugh's vases with that glaze were marked with an impressed "CKAW." Creating these red-glazed vases was very expensive, and even though they received great critical acclaim, the company declared bankruptcy in 1889.

Recapitalized by a circle of Boston art patrons in 1891, Hugh started the Chelsea Pottery U.S., which produced gray crackle-glazed dinnerware with cobalt-blue decorations, the rabbit pattern being the most popular.

The business moved to new facilities in Dedham, Massachusetts, and began production in 1896 under the name Dedham Pottery. Hugh's son and grandson operated the business until it closed in 1943, by which time between 50 and 80 patterns had been produced, some very briefly.

Marks: The following marks help determine the approximate age of items:

• "Chelsea Keramic Art Works Robertson and Sons," impressed, 1874-1880

• "CKAW," impressed, 1875-1889

• "CPUS," impressed in a cloverleaf, 1891-1895

• Foreshortened rabbit only, impressed, 1894-1896

• Conventional rabbit with "Dedham Pottery" in square blue stamped mark along with one impressed foreshortened rabbit, 1896-1928

• Blue rabbit stamped mark with "registered" beneath, along with two impressed foreshortened rabbit marks, 1929-1943

Dedham pitcher, "Oak Block" style, blue registered stamp, 1.5 pints, 5.5", **$975.**
Photo courtesy of Jim Kaufman.

Dedham crackleware breakfast plate, Clockwise Rabbit pattern, bisque method, impressed stamp and hand incised "murtz C. W. whm," 8-1/2" d, **$960.**
Photo courtesy of David Rago Auctions, Inc.

Dedham crackleware shallow soup plate, Clockwise Rabbit pattern, KF monogram, with Dedham postcard, indigo and impressed stamps, 8-1/4" d, **$1,440.**
Photo courtesy of David Rago Auctions, Inc.

Dedham crackleware plate, Tapestry Lion design, indigo and impressed stamps, 8-1/4", **$2,040.**
Photo courtesy of David Rago Auctions, Inc.

Dedham crackleware crab plate, seaweed design, indigo stamp, 8-1/2" d, **$1,200.**
Photo courtesy of David Rago Auctions, Inc.

Dedham experimental vase, Hugh Robertson, incised Dedham Pottery/HCR/ ink DP10B, 8" x 6", **$2,400.**
Photo courtesy of David Rago Auctions, Inc.

Dedham experimental vase, bulbous, oxblood glaze, patch of green, by Hugh Robertson, incised Dedham Pottery HCR, 6" x 4", **$1,645.**
Photo courtesy of David Rago Auctions, Inc.

Reproduction Alert. Two companies make Dedham-like reproductions primarily utilizing the rabbit pattern, but always mark their work very differently from the original.

Bowl

Rabbit pattern, reg. stamp, 8-1/2" sq **$600**

Swan pattern, reg. stamp, 8-1/2" sq **$725**

Bowl, Poppy pattern, cut edge rim, Oriental-type, sloping poppies, registered blue ink stamp, "D" in red, minor glaze miss near base edge, 9-3/8" d, 3-3/4" h........ **$1,035**

Breakfast plate

Crab pattern, blue ink stamp, glaze imperfections, 8-3/4" d **$375**

Rabbit pattern, assembled set, marks include blue registered stamp, imp foreshortened rabbit, and 1931 stamp, set of six, one with rim chip, 8-3/4" d **$635**

Butter plate, Swan pattern, registered blue ink stamp, 4-3/8" d **$260**

Candlesticks, pr

Elephant pattern, reg. blue stamp **$525**

Rabbit pattern, reg. blue stamp.. **$32**

Creamer and sugar, Rabbit pattern, blue stamp and "1931" on creamer, blue registered stamp on sugar, 3-1/4" and 4" **$350**

Cup and saucer, Rabbit pattern, 3-7/8" d cup, 6" d saucers with rabbit borders, blue registered stamps, set of six **$700**

Knife rest, Rabbit form, blue reg. stamp **$575**

Paperweight, Rabbit form, blue reg. stamp **$495**

Pickle dish, Elephant pattern, blue reg. stamp, 10-1/2" l **$750**

Pitcher

Chickens pattern, blue stamp, 5-1/8" h.............................. **$2,300**

Rabbit pattern, 3-1/4" h **$175**

Rabbit pattern, blue stamp, 9" h ..**$700**

Style of 1850, blue reg. stamp **$975**

Turkey pattern, blue stamp, 7" h **$585**

Plate, 6" d

Clover pattern, reg. stamp **$625**

Iris pattern, blue stamp, Maude Davenport's "O" rebus **$280**

Rabbit pattern, registered blue ink stamp, set of four, foot chips on two **$290**

Plate, 6-1/8" d

Horse Chestnut pattern, one impressed rabbit mark **$150**

Magnolia pattern, blue ink stamp mark **$115**

Plate, Lobster pattern, registered blue ink stamp, two imp rabbits, 7-1/2" d....... **$290**

Plate, Rabbit pattern, glaze burst, 8-1/4" d **$125**

Plate, 8-1/2" d

Crab pattern, blue stamp **$550**

Elephant pattern, blue reg. stamp **$650**

Oriental Poppy, single rabbit and blue ink stamp mark, in-the-making glaze bursts **$265**

Rabbit pattern, blue stamp **$175**

Rabbit pattern, blue stamp, Maude Davenport's "O" rebus **$235**

Snow Tree pattern, blue stamp **$210**

Upside down dolphin, CPUS **$900**

Plate, 10" d

Dolphin pattern, blue reg. stamp **$875**

Elephant pattern, blue reg. stamp **$900**

Pine Apple pattern, CPUS **$775**

Turkey pattern, blue stamp, Maude Davenport's "O" rebus **$475**

Plate, Rabbit pattern, registered blue ink stamp, one imp rabbit, 10-1/4" d **$150**

Platter, Rabbit pattern, rect, blue ink stamp, two imp rabbits, 9-7/8" l, 6-3/8" w.................................. **$260**

Salt and pepper shakers, pr, Rabbit pattern, glaze miss, 3-1/2" h **$200**

Sherbet, two handles, Rabbit pattern, blue stamp **$350**

Tea cup and saucer

Azalea pattern, reg. stamp **$130**

Butterfly pattern, blue stamp...**$345**

Duck pattern, reg. stamp **$190**

Turtle pattern, reg. stamp **$680**

Water Lily pattern, reg. stamp...**$130**

Tea set, 8-1/2" h teapot, creamer, cov sugar, five 4" d cups, five saucers, waste bowl, small plate, Rabbit pattern, ink stamps on base, glaze voids and bubble bursts **$1,000**

Tea tile, Rabbit, round form with projections at ears and feet, white crackle glaze with outline of long-eared rabbit in blue, glaze missing to depict eyes against a blue-green ground, white clay body, base chip, 6-1/4" d................................. **$390**

Vase

Bulbous body, long neck, mottled green glossy glaze, incised "Dedham Pottery," William Robertson's initials, c1900, 9-1/4" h **$2,650**

Experimental, by Hugh Robertson, thick glossy emerald green glaze dripping over indigo, pink, brown, and green volcanic base, incised "Dedham Pottery HCR," 6-1/2" h, 4-1/2" d **$4,500**

Ovoid, mottled green glossy glaze, incised "Dedham Pottery" with Hugh Robertson's initials, c1900, 9-1/8" h **$2,500**

DELFTWARE

History: Delftware is pottery with a soft, red-clay body and tin-enamel glaze. The white, dense, opaque color came from adding tin ash to lead glaze. The first examples had blue designs on a white ground. Polychrome examples followed.

The name originally applied to pottery made in the region around Delft, Holland, beginning in the 16th century and ending in the late 18th century. The tin used came from the Cornish mines in England. By the 17th and 18th centuries, English potters in London, Bristol, and Liverpool were copying the glaze and designs. Some designs unique to English potters also developed.

In Germany and France, the ware is known as Faience, and in Italy as Majolica.

Reproduction Alert. Since the late 19th century, much Delft-type souvenir material has been produced to appeal to the foreign traveler. Don't confuse these modern pieces with the older examples.

Bowl, interior and exterior painted with polychrome orange, yellow, and blue flowers, hairline, late 18th C, 9" d, 3-3/4" h **$900**

Charger

Blue and white, foliate devices, chips, glass wear, restoration, 19th C, 13-5/8" d **$320**

Blue and white, foliate devices, Dutch, chips, glaze wear, 19th C, 13-1/8" d **$410**

Center branch with fruiting blossoms, two birds, conforming florals on wide rim, sgd "G. A. Kleynoven," c1655, 16-1/2" d **$2,250**

Floral design, building scene, manganese and blue, edge chips, 13" d... **$615**

Dish

Fluted oval, blue and white floral design, attributed to Lambeth, chips, 12-3/8" l **$440**

Molded rim, blue and white, stylized landscape and floral design, edge chips, 8-1/4" d **$315**

Flower brick, blue and white, Chinese figures in landscape, Dutch, chips, cracks, 18th C, 4-5/8" l, 2-1/2" h.................................... **$375**

Garniture, three bulbous 17-1/4" h cov urns, two octagonal tapered 12-3/4" h vases, polychrome dec foliage surrounding central blue figural panels, Dutch, late 18th/early 19th C **$8,625**

Inkwell, heart shape, blue and white floral dec, wear and edge chips, 4-1/2" h...................................... **$495**

Jar, blue and white, chips, pr, 5" h **$715**

Lamp base, octagonal bottle form with continuous blue and white Oriental figural landscape design, England, foot rim chips, drilled, 18th C **$690**

Model, tall case clock, blue dec white ground, panels of figural and architectural landscapes between scrolled foliate borders, slight glaze wear, 19th C, 17-1/2" h **$320**

Mug, blue and white, armorial surrounded by exotic landscape, palm trees, marked on base, Dutch, minor chips, glaze wear, 19th C, 6-3/8" h...................................... **$490**

Plate

Painted in polychrome manganese, blue, green and red with stylized flowers, few glaze chips around rims, late 18th C, 8-1/2" d **$950**

Tin-glazed earthenware, blue Chinoiserie motifs, manganese purple cracked-ice pattern border, England, chips, 18th C, 9-1/4" d **$295**

Tin glazed earthenware, central blue rosette, England, chips, 18th C, 7-7/8" d.................... **$125**

Tin glazed earthenware, flowers, bird in birdbath in center, minor damage, 8-7/8" d **$150**

Tin glazed earthenware, Oriental fence and chrysanthemum dec, yellow rim, axe and "X" mark, minor damage, 9" d **$150**

White tin glazed earthenware, two-tone blue flowers, wavy border, "6" mark, edge flakes, old repairs, 9-1/8" d.................... **$115**

Delftware, Lambeth, pair, blue and white lobed bowls, central landscapes, manganese, floral borders, rim chips, hairlines, England, mid-18th century, 8-5/8" d, **$1,175.**
Photo courtesy of Skinner, Inc.

Delftware plate, polychromed bird and floral decoration, English, 18th century, 8-7/8" d, **$500.**
Photo courtesy of Pook & Pook, Inc.

Delftware jar and cover, bulbous body, playful putto cartouches, 19th century, 14-1/4" h, **$472.**
Photo courtesy of Sloans & Kenyon Auctioneers and Appraisers.

Delft tile frieze, Dutch landscape with windmills, signed "Delft Blauw/Hand-painted/Made in Holland," framed, splintering to two edges of frame, 11-1/2" x 17-1/4", $245.
Photo courtesy of David Rago Auctions, Inc.

Posset pot, blue and white, birds among foliage, England, minor chips and cracks, 19th C, 4-3/4" h **$920**

Sauceboat, applied scrolled handles, fluted flaring lip, blue and white Oriental design, edge chips and hairline, later added yellow enamel rim, 8-1/4" l **$440**

Saucer, table ring, blue, iron-red, yellow and manganese bowl of flowers dec, 8-3/4" d **$825**

Strainer bowl, blue and white floral design, three short feet, chips, 9-1/8" d **$520**

Tankard, tin glazed earthenware, pewter mounts, polychrome floral sprays, "IK 1793," indistinct signature inscribed on pewter top, England, cracks, 18th C, 9" h **$400**

Tea caddy, blue and white floral dec, scalloped bottom edge, marked "MVS 1750," cork closure, wear, edge flakes, old filled in chip on lid, 5-7/8" h **$550**

Tile, Fazackerly, polychrome dec of floral bouquets, price for pr, one with edge nicks, other with edge flaking and chips, c1760, 5" sq .. **$350**

DRESDEN/MEISSEN

Meissen stemmed compote, reticulated basket with two handles, raised polychrome flowers, stem of two cherubs, signed with blue cross swords under glaze, minor flower restorations, 12" h, $775.
Photo courtesy of The Early Auction Company, LLC.

Dresden bowl, floral form, hand-painted floral decoration, hand-painted gilt design on border, impressed "D" mark, 10" d, 4" h, $135.
Photo courtesy of Alderfer Auction Co.

History: Augustus II, Elector of Saxony and King of Poland, founded the Royal Saxon Porcelain Manufactory in the Albrechtsburg, Meissen, in 1710. Johann Frederick Boettger, an alchemist, and Tschirnhaus, a nobleman, experimented with kaolin from the Dresden area to produce porcelain. By 1720, the factory produced a whiter hard-paste porcelain than that from the Far East. The factory experienced its golden age from the 1730s to the 1750s under the leadership of Samuel Stolzel, kiln master, and Johann Gregor Herold, enameler.

The Meissen factory was destroyed and looted by forces of Frederick the Great during the Seven Years' War (1756-1763). It was reopened, but never achieved its former greatness.

In the 19th century, the factory reissued some of its earlier forms. These later wares are called "Dresden" to differentiate them from the earlier examples. Further, there were several other porcelain factories in the Dresden region and their products also are grouped under the "Dresden" designation.

Marks: Many marks were used by the Meissen factory. The first was a pseudo-Oriental mark in a square. The famous crossed swords mark was adopted in 1724. A small dot between the hilts was used from 1763 to 1774, and a star between the hilts from 1774 to 1814. Two modern marks are swords with a hammer and sickle and swords with a crown.

Dresden

Cabinet vase, cylindrical, ruby, gold scrolling hand-painted scene of children playing, sgd "Dresden," 4-3/4" h **$800**

Compote, figural, shaped pierced oval bowl with applied florets, support stems mounted with two figures of children, printed marks, pr, late 19th/early 20th C, 14-1/4" h **$350**

Cup and saucer, hp medallion, marked "GLC Dresden" **$150**

Dessert plate in frame, set of four, 8" d printed and tinted plate, scenes of courting couples, insets, and floral sprigs, gilt details, early 20th C, 15-3/4" sq giltwood shadowbox frame **$175**

Figural group

Putti charting the heavens, putto seated at table, peering through telescope, another putto studying celestial globe, ovoid base, loss, crazing, late 19th/early 20th C, 5-3/4" h, 5-1/2" w **$375**

Two ladies, modeled as mischievous maidens in 18th C dress, ovoid base, early 20th C, 11" h **$460**

Loving cup, three handles, woodland scene with nymph, gold trim, 6-1/2" h **$475**

Plaque, molded relief of two partially nude women, flowing gowns, gilt florals, mounted in 22" x 16" glazed shadowbox frame, price for pr, mid 20th C, 13-1/2" x 11" **$435**

Portrait vase, front with oval roundel printed with portrait bust of 18th C lady, gilt floral surround, central band of beaded landscape cartouches and foliate scrolls, faux jeweled diapered ground, two short gilt flying-loop handles, 6" h **$635**

Urn, cov, domed lid with fruit finial, body with two gilt flying-loop handles, trumpet foot on sq base, rose Pompadour ground, painted scenes of courting couples and floral bouquets, price for pr, one damaged, late 19th/early 20th C, 14-1/2" h **$700**

Vase
Alternating panels of lowers and turquoise ground floral bouquets, minor damage, cov, pr, c1900, 14" h **$375**
Alternating panels of figures and yellow floral bouquets, Thieme factory, late 19th C, 13-1/4" h **$115**

Meissen

Basket, leaf form, entwined branch handle, gilt dec, over flowing polychrome porcelain blossoms, underglaze blue crossed swords mark, incised "Y5," some losses, c1847 .... **$1,725**

Cabinet plate, enameled center with cupid and female in wooded landscape, gilt dec pink and burgundy border, titled on reverse "Lei Wiedergut," 9-5/8" d **$490**

Chandelier, baluster-form shaft with hand-painted flower and leaf motifs, similar applied motifs on white ground, six S-scroll arms with conforming applied floral dec, candle cups, suspending tassels with applied floral bouquets, 23" h **$900**

Clock, Rococo style, clock face surrounded by applied floral dec, four fully molded figures representing four seasons, 18-3/4" h **$3,400**

Compote, stemmed, reticulated two handle basket, raised polychrome flowers, porcelain stem of two semi-nude cherubs, blue cross swords mark under glad, some restoration to flowers, 12" h **$775**

Cup and saucer, flower-filled basket dec **$90**

Demitasse cup and saucer set, six cups and saucers with different designs, including oriental dragons, phoenix birds, and assorted flowers, each with blue underglaze blue swords mark, faux alligator box with crossed swords mark, box worn and damaged, 18-1/4" w, 10-1/4" d, 3-3/4" h **$500**

Dessert service, partial, pink floral dec, gilt trim, five 8" d plates with pierced rims, two 11-1/2" h compotes with figures of boy and girl flower sellers in center of dish, pierced rims, 20th C **$1,850**

Dinner service, partial, Deutsche Blumen, molded New Dulong border, gilt highlights, two oval serving platters, circular platter, fish platter, 8-1/2" cov tureen with figural finial, two sauce boats with attached underplates, two serving spoons, sq serving dish, two small oval dishes, cov jam pot with attached underplate and spoon, 20 dinner plates, 11 teacups and saucers, nine salad plates, 10 bread plates, 10 soups, 74-pc set **$8,500**

Dish, cov, female blackamoor, beside covered dish with molded basketweave and rope edge, modeled on freeform oval base with applied florets, incised #328, 20th C, 6-5/8" h **$575**

Figure
Cockatoo, perched on tree stump, flower and leaves at base, early 20th C, 14-1/4" h **$2,300**
Continental woman holding basket of flowers, crossed swords mark, 5" h **$350**
Cupid dressed as blacksmith, heart on anvil, shell base, hand painted polychrome, gilt accents, underglaze blue crossed swords mark, 5" h **$875**
Five children at play with dog and lamb, hand painted polychrome, gilt accents, underglaze blue crossed swords mark, minor edge damage, repairs, 7" h, 5-3/4" d **$1,610**
Monkey band, all in 18th C dress, figure carrying drums, bagpiper, clarinet player, harpsichordist riding another monkey, conductor, ovoid gilt accented bases, losses, late 19th/early 20th C, 5" h to 5-3/4" h **$5,300**
Seated man holding basket of flowers and rooster, blue cross swords mark, 4-1/4" h **$450**
Young girl with basket of flowers, hand painted polychrome, gilt accents, underglaze blue crossed swords mark, 4-1/4" h............. **$675**

Mirror, oval, heavily applied with leaves and flowers, top adorned with two cherubs supporting floral garland, Germany, c1900, 9-1/2" l **$1,380**

Meissen figure, nymph with bow, porcelain, nude crouching figure holding unstrung bow, small domed base, 5-1/2" h, **$940.**
Photo courtesy of Skinner, Inc.

Nodder, Oriental gentleman, seated cross legged, nodding head, moving hands and tongue, white robe patterned with indianische blumen, gilt collar, blue slippers, underglaze blue crossed swords mark, incised "157," gilt painter's numerals "36," mid/late 19th C, 7-1/8" h **$5,750**

Plate, molded with four cartouches of bunches of fruit, shaped edge with C-scroll and wings, gilt dec, price for pr, late 19th C, 9" d **$250**

Stand, top painted and encrusted with flowers, pierced apron dec with floral garlands, scrolled legs, underglaze blue crossed swords mark, 5-1/2" d, 3" h.. **$250**

Tea set, partial, brown, pink, green, blue, gray, purple and orange enameled birds in center, dragons on rim, gilt accents, seven teacups, seven 6" d saucers, nine 7" plates, 23 pcs **$700**

Tray, oval, enameled floral sprays, gilt trim, 20th C, 17-3/8" l **$400**

Urn on pedestal, figural cartouches, scattered floral dec, two handles in form of pair of entwined snakes, mounted as lamps, pr, 21" h **$4,000**

Vase, cov
Facial form body, plinth of applied scrolled acanthus borders, similar dec domed lid with encrusted floral bouquets, bolted, crossed swords underglaze with star and numeral II, some losses, 13-1/2" h **$1,380**

Schnellball, thistle shaped bodies with domed lids, encrusted with small white flowerheads, applied with flowerhead spherules, branches and birds, lid with bird and branch finials, Meissen, price for pr, 20th C, 8-1/4" h **$7,100**

Vase, scrolled snake handles, cobalt blue ground, gold and silver floral dec, new gold trim to handles, 19th C, 15-1/2" h **$2,300**

Wall garniture, 12-5/8" w, 19" l two-light girandole in rococo-style frame topped by putto figure, two figures of children among flowers on sides, brackets for two serpentine candle arms, two 15-1/2" w, 15-3/4" h scenic plaques with center painted scenes of bustling harbor, similar styled frames, candle arm sockets, two 15-3/4" w, 15-3/4" h rococo-style three-light wall sconces, framed as rocaille scroll with three floral-encrusted serpentine candle arms, 19th C **$3,100**

Wine cooler, exterior boldly painted with sprays of deutsche Blumen, interior with fish, insects, and vegetation, gilt-edged scalloped rim set with two handles, underglaze blue crossed swords mark, 25" d, 9-1/2" h **$10,160**

Tobacco jar, blue and white, Indians and "Siville," older brass stepped lid, chips, 10" h **$1,870**

Vase, urn shape, ftd, cherub framed with applied fruit wreath, two figure centaurs on each side, mkd with hand painted rooster and "22," 18" h **$350**

Vase, cov, Delft blue and white, oval paneled sides with Chinese style dec alternating with female figures in courtyard setting, flowers and fence design, hexagonal form rim, foot and cov, cat finial, unidentified mark, Holland, rim damage, footrim chips, chips to cat's ears, typical edge flaking of tin glaze, 18th C, 23" h **$815**

Wall plaque, cartouche shape, blue enamel dec, windmill shoreline scene, Dutch, early 20th C, 23-1/2" l.................................. **$530**

Wall pocket, vasiform, ogee backplate, pierced grillwork, blue and white scenes of figures at harbor, scrollwork borders, applied flower buds on sides, price for pr, 20th C, 6-1/4" w, 4-1/2" d, 7" h **$350**

ENGLISH CHINA AND PORCELAIN (GENERAL)

English Caughley jug, molded cabbage leaves, mask spout, transfer-printed blue floral decoration, underglaze blue crescent mark, c1785, 8-1/2" h, **$800.**
Photo courtesy of Sloans & Kenyon Auctioneers and Appraisers.

English fish platter, center farm scene with pheasant and other game birds flying above, shaped floral border, marked "Brownfield & Son, Trademark, Woodland," registry diamond reads "Rd. No. 14058," **$125.**

History: By the 19th century, more than 1,000 china and porcelain manufacturers were scattered throughout England, with the majority of the factories located in the Staffordshire district.

By the 19th century, English china and porcelain had achieved a worldwide reputation for excellence. American stores imported large quantities for their customers. The special-production English pieces of the 18th and early 19th centuries held a position of great importance among early American antiques collectors.

Bow

Bowl, blue trailing vine, white ground, c1770, 4-1/2" d............................**$175**

Candlesticks, pr, two birds on flowering branches, dog and sheep on grassy base, wood stand, c1755 ....**$1,200**

Egg cup, two half-flower panels, powder blue ground, pseudo Oriental mark, c1760, 2-1/2" h.................**$900**

Plate, Turk's Cap Lily, dragonfly and moths, c1755, 9" d **$850**

Bradley Pottery

Jug, stoneware, applied in high relief with fruiting grapevine band above individually applied designs including windmill, cottage, manor house, farming implements, wheelbarrow and wagon, all surrounding central British coat of arms, impressed to one side of shoulder "MRS. ROBERTS" and "BARRELL INN" on other side, "BAGWORTH 1849" impressed below coat of arms, inscribed under the base "Made By John Bacon At Bradley Pottery 1849" inscribed under base, hairlines, rim chip, 15-3/4" h...**$1,300**

Chelsea

Candlesticks, pr, figural, draped putti, sitting on tree stump holding flower, scroll-molded base, encircled in puce, gilt, wax pan, 7-1/2" h **$850**

Cup and saucer, multicolored exotic birds, white ground, gold anchor mark, c1765 ....**$750**

Plate, multicolored floral design, scalloped rim, gold anchor mark, 8-1/2" d..**$475**

Davenport

Cup plate, Teaberry pattern, pink luster..**$40**

Jug, Jardiniere pattern, blue, orange, green, peach and gold, peach luster rim, c1805-20, 5-1/2" h **$450**

Plate, Oriental style design similar to Gaudy Welsh Grapes pattern, orange, blue, fuchsia, green and gilt, transfer labels on back, minor wear, set of four, 8-1/4" d.....................................**$350**

Serving bowl, cov, Chinoiserie Bridgeless pattern, internal bowl with steam holes, c1810, 7" w, 9-3/4" l **$700**

Tea service, Imari pattern, teapot, creamer, cov sugar, four cups and saucers, 18" l tray..........................**$850**

Derby

Beaker, two short shell-shaped handles, two painted landscape roundels in gilt borders, scenes titled "Near Spondon" and "Near Breadshall," both Derbyshire scenes, pale yellow ground, late 18th/early 19th C, 3-1/8" h........................**$1,265**

Dessert dishes, underglaze blue and iron red dec of trees and flowering vines, gilt enamel accenting, mid-19th C, two 9-3/4" l heart-shaped dishes; 11-1/4" l navette-shaped dish.......**$400**

Figure, pastoral, boy resting against tree stump playing bagpipe, black hat, bleu-do-roi jacket, gilt trim, yellow breeches, girl with green hat, bleu-du-roi bodice, pink skirt, white apron with iron-red flowerheads, gilt centers, leaves, scroll molded mound base, crown and incised iron-red D mark, pr, 8" h, 8-1/2" h.............**$2,200**

Jar, cov, octagonal, iron-red, bottle green and leaf green, alternating cobalt blue and white grounds, gilding, grotesque sea-serpent handles, now fitted as lamp with carved base, pr, 19th C, 22" h.....................**$10,000**

Plate, enamel dec, stylized Imari-type designs of birds in three, shaped molded rim, Bloor mark, price for set of seven, second quarter 19th C, 10-1/8" d....**$300**

Devon Art Pottery

Jug, pottery, slip dec, brown and yellow glazed sgraffito designs, late 19th C, 8-1/4" h.....................................**$1,530**

Earthenware

Stirrup mug, fox head, polychrome, small losses to ear tips, early 19th C, 5" l...**$715**

Flight, Barr & Barr

Crocus pot, D-form, molded columns and architrave, peach-ground panels, ruined abbey landscape reserve, gilding, 9" w, 4" d, 6-1/4" h.............**$2,400**

Pastille burner, cottage, four open chimneys, marked, c1815, 3-1/2" h **$425**

Tea service, gilt foliate, orange ground banded border, 9-1/2" h cov teapot (finial restoration), 7" l teapot stand, 4-3/4" h creamer, 4-1/2" h sugar bowl, 6-5/8" d waste bowl, two 8" deep dishes, 10 coffee cans, 11 teacups, 11 sau-

cers, minor chips to cups and saucers, incised "B" mark, light wear to gilt at rim throughout, c1792-1804.....**$1,320**

Grainger

Punch bowl, ext. enamel dec with large floral bouquets on either side of clipper ship titled above "City of Poonah," gilt inscription "Presented by Captain James Wilson to John Carr Esq. 1839," int. with central crest of stag, floral and foliate border in green, buff and gold, int. glaze stains, c1839, 13-5/8" d......................**$3,525**

Herculaneum

Jug, creamware, black transfer printed, obverse "Washington," oval design with medallion portrait on monument surmounted by wreath, birth and death dates below, flanked by eagle and grieving woman, upper ribbon inscribed "Washington in Glory," lower ribbon "America In Tears," reverse transfer of American sailing vessel, American eagle beneath spout, inscription "Herculaneum Pottery Liverpool," incised mark on base, imperfections, 10" h **$1,100**

Jackfield

Cheese dish, dome cover, black glaze, white, yellow, pink and blue flowers, gilding, 7-1/2" h.........................**$125**

Creamer, bulbous, emb grapes design, leaves, and tendrils, gilt highlights, three pr paw feet, ear-shaped handle, 4-1/4" h.......................................**$185**

Pitcher, applied handle, black, traces of enameling, bird, initials and "1763," wear, small flakes, 6-1/2" h **$125**

Sugar bowl, cov, scalloped SS rims, SS-mounted cov and ornate pierced finial, 4-1/2" h, 3-3/4" d **$250**

Lowestoft

Teapot, cov, fluted globular body, polychrome enamel dec Chinese figural courtyard scenes, cover with small chips, hairline to interior collar, 18th C, 5-1/4" h **$4,150**

Masons

Creamer, Oriental-style shape, marked "Mason's Patent Ironstone," 4" h...**$85**

Jug, octagonal, Hydra pattern, waisted straight neck, green-enameled handle, lion-head terminal, underglaze blue and iron-red flowers and vase, two imp marks and printed rounded crown mark, c1813-30, 8" h........**$320**

Derby Dr. Syntax figure, porcelain, enamel and gilt dec figure, Dr. Syntax riding piggyback on maiden, painted Stevenson & Hancock mark, England, late 19th century, 5-3/8" h, $410.
Photo courtesy of Skinner, Inc.

Platter, Double-Landscape pattern, Oriental motif, deep green and brick red, c1883, 13-1/2" x 10-3/4" **$265**

Potpourri vase, cov, hexagonal body, cobalt blue, large gold stylized peony blossom, chrysanthemums, prunus and butterflies, gold and blue dragon handles and knobs, trellis diaper-rim border, c1820-25, 25-1/4" h **$1,750**

New Hall

Bowl, Pattern 425, Window pattern, overglaze polychrome enamels, late 18th C, 5" d...............................**$350**

Coffeepot, cov, Pattern 425, Window pattern, pear shape, overglaze polychrome enamels, late 18th C, 9-5/8" h...............................**$1,950**

Dessert dishes, set of six, each with wide pale blue ground, floral and vine relief, gilt trim, polychrome enamel dec centers, 9-1/8" l oval with basket of fruit; five 9-1/4" l ovals with landscapes; four 7-7/8" strawberry shaped, each with gilt rim wear, c1825 ...**$940**

Dinner service, partial, landscape transfer dec, six shaped dishes, six plates, cup, two saucers, cov sauce tureen with ladle......................**$1,100**

Miniature, tea set, Pattern 2720, overglaze enamel floral bands, consisting of a 3-3/4" h cov teapot; 3-1/4" h cov sugar bowl; 2-3/8" h cream jug; four teacups with 2-3/4" d saucers, 19th C **$1,000**

Punch bowl, Pattern 425, Window pattern, overglaze polychrome enamel dec, late 18th C, 11-1/8" d **$1,800**

Teapot, cov, Pattern 425, Window pattern, oval shape, overglaze polychrome enamels, late 18th C, 5-1/4" h .. **$1,750**

Teapot stand, Pattern 425, Window pattern, overglaze polychrome enamels, late 18th C, 6-5/8" l **$750**

Tea service, partial

Pattern 264, gilt decorated with foliage, 6-1/2" h oval-shaped cov teapot and cover; 6-3/4" l oval teapot stand; 5-5/8" h oval shaped cov sugar bowl; 4" h cream jug; 4-3/4" cov tea canister; 7-7/8" d serving dish; 8-3/8" serving dish; eight 3-1/4" d tea bowls; 10 coffee cups; seven 5" d saucers, hairlines, late 18th C **$1,775**

Pattern 1064, polychrome enamel dec, two 5-3/4" h cov teapots; two 7-1/2" l teapot stands; two 3-5/8" h cream jugs; 4-1/2" h rect cov sugar bowl, 5" h oval cov sugar bowl, three 6-1/2" d bowls; three 7-7/8" d shallow bowls; nine coffee cups, three tea bowls, 17 assorted teacups, 29 assorted saucers, chips, hairlines on many pcs, early 19th C **$1,410**

Rockingham

Tea set, rococo-style, each with central pale buff band, enamel decorated landscape cartouche, gilt scrolled foliate trim, 10-1/2" l cov teapot with scrolled foliate handle and serpent-form spout, rim hairline, light gilt wear to spout and handle; 4-3/8" h creamer, slight chip to side of handle; 6" h cov sugar bowl; 7-1/8" d waste bowl, c1820 .... **$220**

Swansea

Tea set, floral pattern, underglaze blue, black transfer, gilt trim, 12 8" d plates; 11 each teacups, coffee cups, saucers; teapot; creamer; three trays; 7-1/2" d bowl, some professional repair, worn gilt, several pcs with chips and hairlines **$590**

Ralph Wood

Figure, pearlware

9-1/8" h shepherd and 8-3/4" h shepherdess, mounted to lamp bases, restoration, losses, 18th C **$1,000**

Seated herding couple, man playing pipe, lamb, goat, and dog at their feet, mounted to a lamp base, losses, restoration, 18th C, 11-1/2" h **$235**

Woods

Cup and saucer, handleless, Woods Rose **$65**

Dish, dark blue transfer of castle, imp "Wood," 8" l, 6" w **$165**

Jug, ovoid, cameos of Queen Caroline, pink luster ground, beaded edge, molded and painted floral border, c1820, 5-3/4" h **$425**

Plate, Woods Rose, scalloped edge, 9" d... **$125**

Stirrup cup, modeled hound's head, translucent shades of brown, c1760, 5-1/2" l...................................... **$2,200**

Whistle, modeled as seated sphinx, blue accents, oval green base, c1770, 3-7/8" h....................................... **$600**

Worcester, Chamberlain's, armorial

Sauce tureen, cov, stand, pr, finial in form of bull's head and crown, modeled on the crest of the Marquis of Abergavenny, painted Japan pattern of flowering Oriental plants, reserves painted with arms of Admiral Lord Nevill, Marquis of Abergavenny above the motto Ne Vile Velis; red script mark, c1813, 15" l, 10-1/2" h.... **$8,365**

Soup tureen, cov, stand, finial in form of bull's head and crown, modeled on the crest of the Marquis of Abergavenny, painted Japan pattern of flowering Oriental plants, reserves painted with arms of Admiral Lord Nevill, Marquis of Abergavenny above the motto Ne Vile Velis; red script mark, c1813, 15" l, 10-1/2" h........................ **$11,355**

Worcester, Dr. Wall

Cup and saucer, oriental design, flowers, mythical animals, oriental mark in underglaze blue............. **$950**

Plate, scalloped edge, Oriental design, flowers, mythical animals, oriental mark in underglaze blue, 7-1/2" d **$850**

ENGLISH SOFT PASTE

History: Between 1820 and 1860, a large number of potteries in England's Staffordshire district produced decorative wares with a soft earthenware (creamware) base and a plain white or yellow glazed ground.

Design or "stick" spatterware was created by a cut sponge (stamp), hand painting, or transfers. Blue was the predominant color. The earliest patterns were carefully arranged geometrics that generally covered the entire piece. Later pieces had a decorative border with a central motif, usually a tulip. In the 1850s, Elsmore and Foster developed the Holly Leaf pattern.

King's Rose features a large, cabbage-type rose in red, pale red, or pink. The pink rose often is called "Queen's Rose." Secondary colors are pastels—yellow, pink, and, occasionally, green. The borders vary: a solid band, vined, lined, or sectional. The King's Rose exists in an oyster motif.

Strawberry Chinaware comes in three types: strawberries and strawberry leaves (often called strawberry luster), green featherlike leaves with pink flowers (often called cut-strawberry, primrose, or old strawberry), and relief decoration. The first two types are characterized by rust-red moldings. Most pieces have a cream ground. Davenport was only one of the many potteries that made this ware.

Yellow-glazed earthenware (canary luster) has a canary yellow ground, a transfer design that is usually in black, and occasional luster decoration. The earliest pieces date from the 1780s and have a fine creamware base. A few hand-painted pieces are known. Not every piece has luster decoration.

Because the base material is soft paste, the ware is subject to cracking and chipping. Enamel colors and other types of decoration do not hold well. It is not unusual to see a piece with the decoration worn off.

Marks: Marked pieces are uncommon.

Additional Listings: Gaudy Dutch, Staffordshire Items.

English soft paste creamware charger, central urn, flowers, blue scalloped rim, early 19th century, 13-1/4" d, **$995.**
Photo courtesy of Pook & Pook, Inc.

English soft paste pearlware cup plate, octagonal, blue, yellow, and orange peafowl dec, 4" d, **$365.**
Photo courtesy of Pook & Pook, Inc.

English soft paste pearlware bowl, trailing vine exterior, landscape int., c1815, 9" d, **$995.**
Photo courtesy of Pook & Pook, Inc.

Basket, green trim, open sides, woven bottom, undertray with conforming pattern, reticulated border, green trim, hairline on basket side, wear on sides of underplate, 7-1/2" x 6-1/2", 9-1/2" x 7-1/2" undertray............ **$950**

Coffeepot, cov, pear shape, polychrome dec black transfer of Tea Party and Shepherd prints, leaf-molded spout, chips, restoration to body, attributed to Wedgwood, c1775, 10" h.............. **$350**

Jug, reeded lapped handle, emb floral applications, sides dec with red and green floral sprays, glaze wear, small rim nicks, 19th C, 5-1/8" h **$260**

Mug, Orange Institution, red transfer printed symbols with verse above "Holiness to the Lord" and verse below "May the Orange Institution stand as firm as the Oak and the Enemies fall off like the leaves in October," England, early 19th C, 3-1/3" h **$300**

Pitcher, two oval reserves with black transfer printed scenes of naval engagements, "The Wasp Boarding the Frolic," sgd "Bentley, Wear, and Bourne Engravers and Printers Shelton, Staffordshire," reverse depicting "The Constitution taking the Cyane and Livant," light green ground, luster embellishments, imperfections, 6-1/4" h.. **$2,760**

Plate, shaped edge, cutout floral design, unmarked, flakes on rim, price for pr, 9-1/2" d **$715**

Platter, oval, scallop dec rim, chips, restorations, 18" l, 14-1/2" w **$300**

Sugar bowl, int. with red and green enamel floral dec, purple luster and underglaze blue, ext. marked "Be

Canny with the Sugar" flanked by small flowers, 5-1/8" d, 2-3/4" h **$385**

Teapot
Flower knop, floral dec entwined reeded handle with touches of gilt, rim chip, restored spout, gilt loss, 19th C, 6-1/2" h **$230**
Molded acanthus spout, ribbed handle, small flakes, 4-3/4" h **$385**

King's Rose

Bowl, Rose, broken solid border, flakes, 7-3/4" d.................................... **$55**

Cup and saucer, handleless
Oyster pattern, hairline cracks **$40**
Rose, vine border........................ **$150**

Plate
Pink border, wear, 5-5/8" d **$55**
Scalloped border, four pcs, 9-3/4" d **$220**
Some flaking, 7-3/8" d **$90**
Vine border, three pcs, 8-1/4" d ... **$255**

Pitcher, dark red rose, blue and yellow flowers, green leaves, some wear, 5-5/8" h.................................... **$220**

Soup plate, broken solid border, scalloped edges, some flakes, three pcs, 9-1/2" d................................... **$360**

Teapot, broken solid border, some flakes, 5-3/4" h **$140**

Pearlware

Bowl
Black and brown slip-filled rouletted band at rim, field of rust with blue, black, and white scroddled dots, repaired, early 19th C, 4-3/4" d **$940**
Cream top band, rust, dark brown, and buff marbling, repaired, 8-1/2" d **$825**

English soft paste pearlware figure, crying boy in white smock, square base, chips, restoration to hands, late 18th/early 19th century, 8" h, **$350.**
Photo courtesy of Sloans & Kenyon Auctioneers and Appraisers.

Coffeepot, cov, baluster form, dome lid, ochre, green, brown and blue floral dec, imperfections, early 19th C, 13" h.......................... **$200**

Creamer, cup shape, straight sides, applied handle, light brown stripes, yellow band, gilt and light brown foliage band, slight bubbles to yellow, minor spout rim flake................ **$125**

Cup and saucer, handleless, black transfer scene of horse drawn chariot, flying putti set of six, 3-1/2" d cup, 5" d saucer **$525**

Figure
Sheep, brown, blue, and yellow ochre sponging, small edge flakes, 3" l **$275**
Squirrel, nut and collar with ring, polychrome, orange coat, attributed to Derby, minor wear and small flakes on base, 3-1/4" h........... **$635**

Famille Verte Yen Yen vase, porcelain, warrior decoration, 18" h, **$650.**
Photo courtesy of Sloans & Kenyon Auctioneers and Appraisers.

Famille Rose bowl, porcelain, floral decoration, Qianlong underglaze blue mark, 1736-1795, 7" d, **$2,950.**
Photo courtesy of Sloans & Kenyon Auctioneers and Appraisers.

Famille Rose vase, porcelain, copper red ground, floral decoration, gilt elephant head handles, Qianlong iron red seal mark, 9-1/2" h, **$825.**
Photo courtesy of Sloan's & Kenyon Auctioneers and Appraisers.

FAMILLE ROSE

History: Famille Rose is Chinese export enameled porcelain on which the pink color predominates. It was made primarily in the 18th and 19th centuries. Other porcelains in the same group are Famille Jaune (yellow), Famille Noire (black), and Famille Verte (green).

Decorations include courtyard and home scenes, birds, and insects. Secondary colors are yellow, green, blue, aubergine, and black.

Rose Canton, Rose Mandarin, and Rose Medallion are mid-to late-19th century Chinese-export wares, which are similar to Famille Rose.

Bowl, shallow, polychrome birds and butterflies, pink flowers, fruit, and vegetables, gilt rims, few rim chips, 8" d, price for set of six **$395**

Brush washer, sprays of peonies, cicada, and grasshopper on side, chi dragon in iron red and gold slithering around rim and peering into well, four-character mark in iron red on recessed base, "Jerentang Zhi," China, early 20th C, 2-7/8" h, 3-5/8" d **$1,035**

Cache pot, stand, 11" l, 7-1/4" w, 6" h, clusters of flowers on plain ground, 10-1/2" l, 7-1/2" w, 1-1/2" h stand, repaired, reglued foot.............**$1,100**

Charger, central figural dec, brocade border, 12" d **$265**

Dish, cov, figural dec, Qing dynasty, 11" d..**$200**

Figure
Cockerels, pr, 16" h.....................**$550**
Peacocks, pr, 13" h **$275**

Garden set, hexagonal, pictorial double panels, flanked and bordered by floral devices, blue ground, minor glaze loss, 19th C, 18-1/2" h **$1,100**

Jar, cov, baluster form, domed lid, ovoid finial, birds on rocky outcrop, flowering branches dec, early 20th C, price for pr, 19" h **$500**

Jardinierè, flowering branches dec, Jiaqing, 9-3/4" h...........................**$700**

Lamp base, made from ginger jar, pink, orange, and purple roses and other flowers, green foliage, on base, electrified, 12-1/2" h...................**$320**

Mug, Mandarin palette, Qianlong, 1790, 5" h **$425**

Plate, floral dec, ribbed body, Tongzhi mark, pr, 10" d **$275**

Platter, ogee form, export, China, 18th C, 19" l **$1,100**

Pot, cov, iron-red and gilt "JHS," cross, three swords in scalloped cartouche, "Jesus Hominum Salvator," phoenix standing on pierced rock among flowers and ducks, blue key fret base border, ruyi band on shoulder, iron-

red seal on base, six-character mark, "Daoguang," China, minor scratches, carved wooden lid, wear to gilding, c1821-50, 4-1/2" h **$700**

Tray, oval, multicolored center armorial crest, underglaze blue diaper and trefoil borders, reticulated rim, late 18th C, 8" l........................**$550**

Tureen, pink roses, polychrome butterflies, birds, fruits, and gourds in shades of orange, blue, green, yellow, foliage finial, twig handles, gilt accents, orange peel glaze, minor wear to gilt, hairline in base, 15-1/2" l, 10-1/2" h **$815**

Vase
Baluster, pr, 9-7/8" h...................**$450**
Birds and flowers dec, 19th C, 23-1/2" h **$450**
Diamond shape with flanged edges, landscapes and flowers, six-character Ch'ien Lung mark in red on the base, China, 19th C, 10-1/2" h **$1,120**
Flat pear shape with pointed sides, two raised panels outlined in iron-red and gold, molded horizontal lines on body, iron-red four-character mark on base, "Shen de Tang Zhi," China, 19th C, 5-1/4" h **$200**
Pair, flowering peony and butterflies, mkd on base in square "Hongxian Nian Zhi," Chinese, early 20th C, 9-1/4" h.............................**$1,750**
Underglaze blue with enameled landscape, early 20th C, 9" h **$1,000**

Vase, cov, shouldered ovoid, large cartouches with scenes of warriors on horseback, dignitaries holding court, molded fu-dog handles, conforming cartouches on lid, fu-dog finial, c1850-70, pr, 26" h...................**$2,400**

Water dropper, molded as lotus flowers, stem forming spout, inscribed in stems with commemorative inscriptions, Guangxu, China, pr, 7-1/8" l **$3,150**

Famille Rose lotus dish, porcelain, 18th century, 8-3/8" d, **$355.**
Photo courtesy of Sloans & Kenyon Auctioneers and Appraisers.

Famille Verte charger, porcelain, Kangxi period, 13-1/2", **$885.**
Photo courtesy of Sloans & Kenyon Auctioneers and Appraisers.

Famille Rose charger, porcelain, floral decoration, Yongzheng six-character underglaze mark, 14" d, **$1,180.**
Photo courtesy of Sloans & Kenyon Auctioneers and Appraisers.

Famille Verte

Bottle, porcelain, enameled flowering peonies and birds, Chinese, replaced wooden lids, 19th C, price for pr, 7-3/4" h **$1,495**

Figure, pair of cockerels, China, 19th C, 17" h **$1,880**

Ginger jar, cov, ovoid, foo dog beside sea reserve, floral and butterfly patterned ground, Kangxi, 10-1/2" h **$420**

Vase

High relief dec, warrior on horseback riding under pine tree in mountainous landscape, base with incised Qianlong four-character mark in sq reserve, China, 18th or 19th C, 9-1/8" h, 4-7/8" d **$425**

Dec with magpies flying among prunus trees, black ground, Rouleau, China, pr, 17-1/4" h **$1,920**

Famille Rose "Captain" tureen and cover, porcelain, medallion floral decoration, Qianlong period, 12-1/2" d, 9" h, **$3,305.**
Photo courtesy of Sloans & Kenyon Auctioneers and Appraisers.

Famille Rose plaque, lobed, enameled cicada perched on yellow flower, early 20th century, 9-1/8" l, 8" w, **$125.**

FIESTA

Vase, light green, 12″, **$1,200.**

Deep plate, red, **$65.**

Chop plate, rose, 13″, **$100.**

History: The Homer Laughlin China Company introduced Fiesta dinnerware in January 1936 at the Pottery and Glass Show in Pittsburgh, Pennsylvania. Frederick Rhead designed the pattern; Arthur Kraft and Bill Bensford molded it. Dr. A. V. Bleininger and H. W. Thiemecke developed the glazes.

The original five colors were red, dark blue, light green (with a trace of blue), brilliant yellow, and ivory. A vigorous marketing campaign took place between 1939 and 1943. In mid-1937, turquoise was added. Red was removed in 1943 because some of the chemicals used to produce it were essential to the war effort; it did not reappear until 1959. In 1951, light green, dark blue, and ivory were retired and forest green, rose, chartreuse, and gray were added to the line. Other color changes took place in the late 1950s, including the addition of a medium green.

Fiesta ware was redesigned in 1969 and discontinued about 1972. In 1986, Homer Laughlin China Company reintroduced Fiesta. The new china body shrinks more than the old semi-vitreous and ironstone pieces, thus making the new pieces slightly smaller than the earlier pieces. The modern colors are also different in tone or hue, e.g., the cobalt blue is darker than the old blue.

Color Guide

Color Name	Color palette	Years of Production
Red	Reddish-orange	1936-43, 1959-72
Blue	Cobalt blue	1936-51
Ivory	Creamy yellow-white	1936-51
Yellow	Golden yellow	1936-69
Green	Light green	1936-51
Turquoise	Sky blue	1937-69
Rose	Dark dusky rose	1951-59
Chartreuse	Yellow-green	1951-59
Forest green	Dark hunter green	1951-59
Gray	Light gray	1951-59
Medium green	Deep bright green	1959-69
Antique gold	Dark butterscotch	1969-72
Turf green	Olive green	1969-72
Cobalt blue	Very dark blue, almost black	1986-
Rose	Bubblegum pink	1986-
White	Pearly white	1986-
Black	High gloss black	1986-
Apricot	Peach-beige	1986-98
Turquoise	Greenish-blue	1988-
Yellow	Pale yellow	1987-2002
Periwinkle blue	Pastel gray-blue	1989-
Sea mist green	Pastel light green	1991-
Lilac	Pastel violet	1993-95
Persimmon	Coral	1995-
Sapphire (Bloomingdale's exclusive)	Blue	1996-97
Chartreuse	More yellow than green	1997-99
Pearl gray	Similar to vintage gray, more transparent	1999-2001
Juniper green	Dark blue-green	1999-2001
Cinnabar	Brown-maroon	2000-
Sunflower	Bright yellow	2001-
Plum	Rich purple	2002-
Shamrock	Grassy green	2002-
Tangerine	Bright orange	2003-

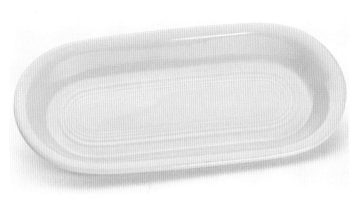

Utility tray, yellow, **$60.**

Demitasse coffeepot, light green, **$500.**

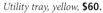

Reproduction Alert. Homer Laughlin has produced some new colors in their popular Fiesta pattern. It's important for collectors to understand when different colors were made.

Ashtray
Ivory	**$55**
Red	**$60**
Turquoise	**$50**
Yellow	**$48**

Bowl, green, 5-1/2" d ... **$60**
Cake plate, green ... **$1,950**
Candlesticks, pr, bulb
Cobalt blue	**$125**
Ivory	**$125**
Red	**$120**
Turquoise	**$110**

Candlesticks, pr, tripod, yellow ... **$550**
Carafe
Cobalt blue	**$495**
Ivory	**$385**

Casserole, cov, two handles, 10" d
Ivory	**$195**
Yellow	**$160**

Chop plate, gray, 13" d ... **$95**
Coffeepot
Cobalt blue	**$235**
Ivory	**$390**
Red	**$250**
Turquoise	**$250**
Yellow	**$185**

Compote, low, ftd, 12" d
Cobalt blue	**$175**
Ivory	**$165**
Red	**$185**
Yellow	**$165**

Creamer
Cobalt blue	**$35**
Ivory	**$30**
Red	**$65**
Yellow	**$30**

Creamer and sugar, figure-eight server, yellow creamer and sugar, cobalt blue gray ... **$315**
Cream soup bowl
Cobalt blue	**$60**
Ivory	**$55**
Red	**$65**
Turquoise	**$48**
Yellow	**$45**

Cup, ring handle
Cobalt blue	**$35**
Ivory	**$30**
Red	**$30**
Turquoise	**$25**
Yellow	**$25**

Demitasse cup, stick handle
Cobalt blue	**$75**
Ivory	**$80**
Red	**$85**
Turquoise	**$75**
Yellow	**$65**

Demitasse pot, cov, stick handle
Cobalt blue	**$650**
Ivory	**$535**
Red	**$575**
Turquoise	**$650**
Yellow	**$465**

Dessert bowl, 6" d
Cobalt blue	**$50**
Ivory	**$45**
Turquoise	**$40**
Yellow	**$40**

Egg cup
Cobalt blue	**$75**
Ivory	**$72**
Red	**$80**
Turquoise	**$55**
Yellow	**$70**

Fruit bowl, 5-1/2" d
Ivory	**$33**
Turquoise	**$25**
Yellow	**$25**

Fruit bowl, 11-3/4" d, cobalt blue ... **$485**
Gravy boat
Cobalt blue	**$75**
Ivory	**$65**
Red	**$85**
Turquoise	**$45**
Yellow	**$50**

Juice tumbler
Cobalt blue	**$40**
Rose	**$65**
Yellow	**$40**

Marmalade jar, cov
Cobalt blue	**$335**
Red	**$345**
Turquoise	**$325**
Yellow	**$250**

Mixing bowl
#1, red, 5" d	**$375**
#2, cobalt blue	**$195**
#2, yellow	**$140**
#4, green	**$195**
#5, ivory	**$275**
#7, ivory	**$580**

Mixing bowl lid, #1, red ... **$1,100**
Mug
Dark green	**$90**
Ivory, marked	**$125**
Rose	**$95**

Mustard, cov
Cobalt blue	**$325**
Turquoise	**$275**

Nappy, 8-1/2" d
Cobalt blue	**$55**
Red	**$55**
Turquoise	**$42**
Yellow	**$45**

Nappy, 9-1/2" d
Cobalt blue	**$65**
Ivory	**$65**
Red	**$70**
Turquoise	**$55**
Yellow	**$60**

Onion soup, cov, turquoise......$8,000

Pitcher, disk
Chartreuse........................$275
Turquoise $110

Pitcher, ice lip
Green $135
Turquoise $195

Plate, deep
Gray $42
Rose $42

Plate, 6" d
Dark green $15
Ivory $7
Light green.........................$9
Turquoise $8
Yellow $5

Plate, 7" d
Chartreuse.........................$12
Ivory $10
Light green.........................$9
Medium green $30
Rose $14
Turquoise $9

Plate, 9" d
Cobalt blue $15

Ivory $14
Red $15
Yellow $13

Plate, dinner, 10" d
Gray $42
Light green $28
Medium green $125
Red.................................$35
Turquoise $30

Platter, oval
Gray $35
Ivory $25
Red.................................$45

Relish
Ivory base and center, turquoise
inserts $285
Red, base and inserts $425

Salad bowl, large, ftd
Cobalt blue $375
Red.................................$460
Turquoise $335
Yellow $400

Salt and pepper shakers, pr
Red $24
Turquoise $135

Saucer
Light green..........................$5
Turquoise $5

Soup plate
Ivory $36
Turquoise $29

Sugar bowl, cov
Chartreuse.........................$65
Gray $75
Rose $75

Syrup
Green $450
Ivory $600
Red................................$695

Sweetmeat compote, high standard
Cobalt blue $95
Ivory $85
Red................................$100
Turquoise $125
Yellow $400

Teacup, flat bottom, cobalt blue $100

Teapot, cov
Cobalt blue, large.................$335
Red, large $245
Rose, medium $350

Tumbler, cobalt blue....................$75

Flow Blue Water Lily, Adams, milk pitcher, 1879 10", **$450.**

Flow Blue platter, "Scinde" by J. & G. Alcock, underglaze pattern name, impressed manufacturer mark, repaired chip, second quarter 19th century, 15-1/2" x 20-1/4", **$330.**
Photo courtesy of Green Valley Auctions.

FLOW BLUE

History: Flow blue, or flown blue, is the name applied to china of cobalt blue and white, whose color, when fired in a kiln, produced a flowing or blurred effect. The blue varies from dark royal cobalt blue to navy or steel blue. The flow may be very slight to a heavy blur, where the pattern cannot be easily recognized. The blue color does not permeate through the body of the china. The amount of flow on the back of a piece is determined by the position of the item in the sagger during firing.

Known patterns of flow blue were first produced around 1830 in the Staffordshire area of England. Credit is generally given to Josiah Wedgwood, who worked in that area. Many other potters followed, including Alcock, Davenport, Grindley, Johnson Brothers, Meakin, Meigh and New Wharf. They were attempting to imitate the blue and white wares brought back by the ship captains of the tea trade. Early flow blue, 1830s to 1870s, was usually of the pearl ware or ironstone variety. The later patterns, 1880s to 1900s, and the modern patterns after 1910, were of the more delicate semi-porcelains. Most flow blue was made in England but it was made in many other countries as well. Germany, Holland, France, Spain, Wales and Scotland are also known locations. Many patterns were made in the United States by several companies: Mercer, Warwick, Sterling and the Wheeling Pottery to name a few.

Adviser: Ellen G. King.

Abbey, Jones, 1900
Pitcher and wash basin $550
Teapot with lid..........................$295

Acacia, Unknown, 1845
Brush stroke razor box with lid..$250

Alaska, Grindley, 1891
Bone dish $85
Plate, 10".....................................$110

Albany, Grindley, 1891
Gravy boat.....................................$90
Plate, 10".......................................$85
Platter, 13-1/2" $175
Sauce tureen with lid, undertray
....$260
Shaving mug $145
Vegetable tureen with lid...........$250

Alton, Grindley, 1903
Platter, 18-1/2".......................$195
Amazone, Regout, 1890
Charger, 13-1/2"....................$225
Amhearst Japan, Unknown, 1850
Master salt..............................$150
Amoy, Davenport, 1844
Creamer.................................$325
Gravy boat.............................$225
Teacup and saucer..................$150
Anemone, B&S, 1891
Pitcher with dragon handle.......$350
Arabesque, Mayer, 1845
Platter, 15-1/2"......................$265
Arcadia, Wilkinsen, 1900
Rimmed soup bowl, 10-1/2".....$100
Argyle, Grindley, 1890
Butter pat..............................$55
Creamer and sugar with lid.......$750
Milk pitcher, 7".......................$250
Platter, 18".............................$395
Platter, 19".............................$475
Sauce tureen with lid................$295
Soup ladle..............................$225
Vegetable tureen with lid..........$350
Babes In Woods, Doulton, 1890
Mug.......................................$150
Vase, 6-1/2"...........................$110
Bamboo, Alcock, 1843
Teapot with lid........................$375
Basket, Unknown, 1860
Sugar with lid.........................$250
Toast rack..............................$750
Bentick, Cauldon, 1905
Plate, 10"..............................$65
Blackberry, Possil Pottery, Scotland, 1885
Teapot with lid........................$275
Blossom, Unknown, 1914
Cheese dish with lid.................$295
Platter, 12".............................$155
Vegetable tureen with lid..........$225
Bluebell, Ridgway, 1840
Relish dish..............................$225
Sauceboat..............................$195
Sauce tureen with lid and undertray
....$550
Blue Bird, Unknown, 1895
Razor box with lid....................$250
Blue Diamond, Wheeling, 1890
Chocolate pot with lid...............$355
Syrup with lid.........................$285
Brompton, Keeling, 1891
Teapot with lid........................$495
Brushstroke, Fig and Leaf, Unknown, 1840
Pitcher, copper lustre, 8"...........$350
Brushstroke, Tulip and Sprig, Walker, 1845
Mug.......................................$385
Plate, 10"..............................$275

Educational Alert. The Flow Blue International Collectors' Club, Inc. has been studying and discussing new versus reproduction flow blue and mulberry. There are still areas of personal judgment as yet undetermined. The general rule accepted has been "new" indicates recent or contemporary manufacture and "reproduction" is a copy of an older pattern. Problems arise when either of these fields is sold at "old" flow blue prices.

In an effort to help educate its membership, the club continues to inform of all known changes through its conventions, newsletters and the Web site: www.flowblue.org.

Warman's is working to those ends also. The following is a listing of "new" flow blue, produced since the 1960s.

Blossom: Ashworth Bros., Hanley, 1962. Washbowl and pitcher made for many years now, in several items.

Iris: by Dunn, Bennett, Burslem, has been reproduced in a full chamber set.

Romantic Flow Blue: Blakeney Pottery, 1970s. Resembles Watteau, but not exact. The old patterns never had the words "flow blue" written on them.

Touraine: by Stanley, by far the most prolific reproduction made recently, in 2002. Again, the "England" is missing from the mark, and it is made in China. Nearly the entire dinnerware set has been made and is being sold on the market.

Victoria Ware: mark is of lion and uniform, but has paper label "Made in China," 1990s. Made in various patterns and design, but the giveaway is the roughness on the bottoms, and much of it has a pea green background. Some of this line is also being made in Mulberry.

Vinranka: Upsala-Ekeby, Sweden, 1967-1968. Now discontinued and highly collectible, a full dinnerware set.

Waldorf: by New Wharf cups and saucers are out, but missing "England" from their mark and are made in China.

Floral pitchers (jugs) and teapots bearing a copied "T. Rathbone England" swan mark.

Williams-Sonoma and Cracker Barrel are also each releasing a vivid blue and white line. Both are made in China. One line is a simplified dahlia flower on white; the other has summer bouquets. Both are well made and readily available, just not old. The reproductions are more of a threat to collectors.

In all cases, regarding new pieces and reproductions, be aware of unglazed areas on the bottoms. The footpads are rough and just too white. The reproductions, particularly the Touraine, are heavier in weight, having a distinctive thick feel. The embossing isn't as crisp and the pieces are frequently slightly smaller in overall size than the originals.

Check the Flow Blue International Collectors' Club, Inc., Web site and also www.repronews.com. Join the club, study the books available, and always, always, KNOW your dealer! Good dealers guarantee their merchandise and protect their customers.

Flow Blue Marble, maker unknown, pitcher, mark Henry Farmer, 1845, **$495.**

Flow Blue tureen with ladle, "Hong Kong" by Charles Meigh, tureen and lid marked with manufacturer, ladle unmarked, second quarter 19th century light crazing, tureen 5-1/2" h, ladle 6-1/4" l, **$415.**
Photo courtesy of Green Valley Auctions.

Flow Blue teapot with lid, Blackberry, Possil Pottery, Scotland, 1885, **$275.**

Flow Blue creamer, "Hong Kong" by Charles Meigh, octagonal, unmarked, second quarter 19th century, 5-3/4" h, **$110.**
Photo courtesy of Green Valley Auctions.

Bryonia, Utzshneider, 1891
Creamer and sugar with lid $475
Teapot with lid $450
Calico, Warwick, 1900
Charger, 13-1/2" $325
Syrup with lid and underplate.... $475
Candia, Cauldon, 1860
Child's cup and saucer $65
Soup bowl, 9" $45
Carlton, Alcock, 1850
Fruit compote $455
Gravy boat, undertray $195
Carnation, Unknown, 1880
Mug $125
Cashmere, Ridgway, Morley, 1845
Platter, 14-3/4" $900
Sugar with lid $550
Soup tureen undertray $975
Cavendish, Keeling, 1891
Vase, 11-1/2" $375
Vase, 13" $425
Chapoo, Wedgwood, 1850
Honey dish $150
Pitcher, 7-1/2" $355
Vegetable tureen with lid $400
Chinese, Wedgwood, 1891
Cheese dish with lid $350
Chinese Japan, Ridgway, 1891
Biscuit jar with lid and handle ... $325
Teapot, lid and stand, polychromed
.... $275
Chintz, Dimmock, 1855
Pitcher and wash basin $850
Chusan, Clementson, 1830
Chestnut bowl with base............. $500
Child's sugar with lid................... $250
Creamer, 5" $175
Grandfather cup and saucer $150
Mug, 3-1/2" $125
Claremont Group, Hancock, 1850

Cheese dish with lid $450
Clemantis, Johnson Bros., 1910
Vegetable tureen with lid $225
Colonial, Meakin, 1890
Gravy boat and undertray........... $145
Platter, 16" $275
Vegetable tureen with lid $250
Conway, New Wharf, 1891
Waste bowl $150
Cotton Plant, Furnival, 1850
Plate, polychromed, 10" $175
Countess, Grindley, 1891
Creamer....................................... $135
Cracked Ice, Unknown, 1880
Cake plate with handles, 10-1/2"
.... $225
Inhaler.. $160
Invalid feeder $185
Dahlia, Challinor, 1850
Creamer....................................... $155
Vegetable bowl, open, 9-1/4" $185
Daisy Chain, Doulton, 1891
Pitcher, 8" $385
Delph, Warwick, 1900
Syrup with lid and underplate.... $285
Tray, 11-1/2" $195
Vegetable bowl, round, 10-1/2" .. $150
Denmark, Minton, 1900
Soup tureen with lid................... $250
Dresden, Unknown, 1860
Child's cup and saucer $55
Duchess, Wood & Sons, 1895
Pitcher and wash basin $800
Excelsior, Fell, 1850
Sugar with lid............................. $225
Fairy Villas, Adams, 1891
Butter dish with lid $245
Soup tureen with lid and undertray
.... $450
Fasan, Villeroy & Boch, 1860
Fish platter $800

Flow Blue platter, polychromed, Moyune, Ridgway, 1900, 16", **$475.**

Flow Blue platter, tree with well, "Whampoa" by Mellor and Vendeles, marked with pattern, second quarter 19th century, 15-3/4" x 19", **$495.**
Photo courtesy of Green Valley Auctions.

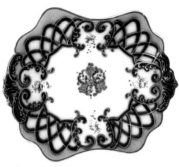

Flow Blue handled cake plate, poly-chromed, unknown, 1880, **$295.**

Flow Blue serving bowl, "Hong Kong" by Charles Meigh, hexagonal, marked with pattern, second quarter 19th century, 14" x 18", **$220.**
Photo courtesy of Green Valley Auctions.

Soup bowl, 9" $60
Flemsburg, Edward, 1865
  Teapot with lid $275
Fleur de Lis, Meakin, 1891
  Platter, 16" $225
  Soup bowl, 9" $45
  Waste bowl $150
Florida, Grindley, 1895
  Pitcher, 7-1/2" $400
  Platter, 14" $285
  Vegetable tureen with lid $350
Formosa, Mayer, 1840
  Plate, 7-1/2" $55
Gainesborough, Ridgway, 1900
  Cereal bowl, 7-1/2" $45
  Platter, 16" $325
Geneva, Doulton, 1895
  Waste bowl $185
Gironde, Grindley, 1890
  Creamer $110
  Cream soup $45
  Platter, 17-1/2" $275
  Soup tureen with lid $395
Glorie de Dijon, Doulton, 1891
  Cuspidor $275
Grace, Grindley, 1891
  Gravy boat $175
  Pitcher, 7-1/2" $300
  Platter, 14" $350
Hartwell, Meakin, 1900
  Butter dish with lid $155
Hindustan, Wood & Baggaley, 1884
  Water pitcher $200
Holland, Johnson Bros., 1891
  Butter dish with lid $250
  Teacup and saucer $95
  Vegetable tureen with lid $225
Hong Kong, Meigh, 1850
  Pitcher, inverted loop shape, 9" .. $350
  Platter, 14" $275
  Sauce tureen, lid, base, undertray .. $195
  Soup ladle with staple repair $325
  Vegetable tureen with lid $250
  Water pitcher $500
Hopberry, Unknown, 1840
  Child's creamer $195

Child's plate $50
Humphreys Clock, Unknown, 1898
  Chamber pot $150
Indian, Phillips, 1850
  Sugar with lid $155
  Teapot with lid $350
Indian Jar, Furnival, 1843
  Vegetable tureen with lid $255
Indian Stone, Walley, 1850
  Creamer $150
Iris, Doulton, 1850
  Creamer $155
  Stag pitcher $175
Ivy, Unknown, 1890
  Pitcher, 8" $225
  Soap dish with insert and lid $250
Japan, Dimmock, 1844
  Syrup pitcher with lid, green ground
  .... $1,500
Janette, Grindley, 1890
  Plate, 10" $90
  Teapot with lid $365
Jewel, Johnson Bros., 1900
  Bone dish, large $85
  Platter, 14" $225
Kinshaw, Challinor, 1855
  Shaving mug $250
Kremlin, Alcock, 1843
  Creamer, polychromed $325
La Belle, Wheeling, 1890
  Cracker jar with lid $355
  Chocolate pot with lid $685
  Charger, 10" $275
  Creamer, 5" $225
  Ice pitcher $2,400
  Pitcher, 7" $185
  Plate, 8" $130
  Plate, 10" $150
  Ribbon handled tray $450
  Round tray, 13" $250
  Sugar with lid, 5" $225
  Vegetable bowl, oval, 9" x 11" $165
  Water cooler $3,000
Ladas, Ridgway, 1895
  Gravy boat $135
  Plate, 9" $65

Rimmed soup bowl, 10" $55
Lancaster, New Wharf, 1890
  Oval bowl, 12" $250
  Vegetable tureen with lid $275
Linda, Maddock, 1898
  Egg cup $110
  Creamer $125
  Sauce tureen with lid $260
  Soup ladle $275
  Teacup and saucer $95
Lahore, Phillips, 1840
  Mitten relish $150
Lawrence, Bishop & Stonier, 1870
  Soup tureen with lid $325
Linton, Godwin, 1840
  Pancake dish with lid $250
Lorne, Grindley, 1900
  Pitcher, hot water $275
  Plate, 10-1/2" $100
Luneville, Meakin, 1891
  Platter, 18" $195
Maiden On A Rock, Unknown, 1880
  Jardeniere, 11" $500
Manilla, Podmore Walker, 1850
  Pitcher, 5-1/2" $250
  Pitcher, 7-1/2" $525
  Sauce tureen undertray $100
Marie, Grindley, 1895
  Oyster bowl $135
Marguerite, Grindley, 1890
  Creamer $225
  Fruit compote, 10" $450
  Sugar bowl with lid $225
  Teacup and saucer $95
  Well and tree platter $650
Melbourne, Grindley, 1890
  Bone dish $50
  Creamer, 4" $120
  Gravy boat with undertray $225
  Soup tureen with lid $400
Morning Glory, Ridgway, 1845
  Soup tureen, lid, undertray $500
Morning Glory, Unknown, 1840
  Coffee pot with lid $1,150
  Pitcher, henna accents, 10" $450

Moyune, Ridgway, 1900
Platter, polychromed, 16"............**$475**
Nankin, Edwards, 1850
Plate, 9-1/4"....................................**$85**
Teacup and saucer.......................**$100**
Waste bowl...................................**$125**
Normandy, Johnson Bros., 1890
Child's plate................................**$125**
Coffee cup and saucer.................**$175**
Sauce tureen underplate.............**$150**
Olympia, Grindley, 1895
Spooner.......................................**$135**
Oriental, Adams, 1840
Milk pitcher.................................**$275**
Oriental, Alcock, 1840
Plate, 9".......................................**$65**
Platter, 12"...................................**$175**
Soup bowl, 10-1/2".......................**$100**
Vegetable bowl, oval, 10".............**$150**
Oriental, Dimmock, 1850
Meat drainer................................**$375**
Oregon, Mayer, 1845
Creamer.......................................**$300**
Chamber pot................................**$350**
Mug...**$275**
Sugar with lid..............................**$260**
Tazza, stemmed...........................**$295**
Teapot with lid............................**$550**
Soup ladle....................................**$400**
Paisley, Mercer, 1890
Vegetable tureen with lid............**$265**
Pansy, Warwick, 1896
Cheese dish with lid....................**$235**
Chocolate cup..............................**$125**
Footed ferner...............................**$450**
Milk pitcher.................................**$300**
Syrup with lid, underplate..........**$250**
Tea tile..**$195**
Water pitcher...............................**$320**
Pelew, Challinor, 1840
Teapot with lid............................**$575**
Perak, Hancock, 1910
Vase, 9".......................................**$225**

Peonies, Unknown English, 1890
Square handled server, 12".........**$175**
Penang, Ridgway, 1850
Dessert set, polychromed, server, 8
plates.......................................**$950**
Phoenix, Unknown, 1845
Sauce tureen with lid, undertray
....**$250**
Pomeroy. Bishop & Stonier, 1910
Soup tureen with lid, undertray
....**$350**
Poppy, Grindley, 1895
Sauce tureen with lid, ladle, under-
tray..**$385**
Teapot with lid, sugar with lid, cream-
er...**$500**
Princess, T.R. & Co., 1898
Creamer.......................................**$225**
Soup tureen with lid, undertray.**$300**
Soup ladle....................................**$175**
Rock, Challinor, 1845
Vegetable tureen with lid............**$375**
Rose, Ridgway, 1900
Individual vegetable bowl............**$40**
Roseville, Maddock, 1885
Plate, 10".....................................**$90**
Soup bowl, 9"...............................**$65**
Scinde, Alcock, 1840
Creamer, 5-1/2"...........................**$275**
Gravy boat...................................**$250**
Sauce tureen with lid and undertray
....**$425**
Sauce ladle..................................**$600**
Soup bowl, 10-1/2".......................**$225**
Teapot with lid, gothic...............**$525**
Teacup (handled) and saucer.....**$165**
Vegetable bowl, open..................**$250**
Vegetable bowl, 11 x 8 octagon..**$325**
Shapoo, Boote, 1842
Sugar with lid..............................**$250**
Teapot with lid............................**$325**
Shell, Challinor, 1860
Platter, 12"...................................**$385**

Sugar with lid..............................$275
Teacup (handleless) and saucer.**$110**
Shell, Dimmock, 1844
Sugar bowl with lid......................**$225**
Waste bowl...................................**$175**
Sloe Blossom, Ridgway, 1835
Milk pitcher.................................**$375**
Mug...**$200**
Somerset, Grindley, 1900
Double handled sauce with attached
undertray.................................**$265**
St. Louis, Johnson Bros., 1890
Charger, 12".................................**$300**
Chowder tureen with lid.............**$325**
Soup bowl, 9"...............................**$55**
Teacup and saucer.......................**$100**
Spinach, Unknown, 1885
Teacup and saucer.......................**$95**
The Marquis, Grindley, 1850
Master berry bowl, four small dishes
....**$150**
Thistle, Burgess, Middle
Chocolate pot with lid, slight staining
....**$225**
Tivoli, Furnival, 1845
Sauce tureen with lid..................**$185**
Touraine, Alcock, 1898
Creamer.......................................**$150**
Pitcher, 7-3/4"..............................**$300**
Individual oval vegetable bowl.....**$95**
Plate, 6-1/2".................................**$45**
Touraine, Stanley, 1898
Cereal bowl..................................**$45**
Creamer, 5"..................................**$185**
Plate, 8-1/2".................................**$100**
Rimmed soup bowl, 10-1/2".......**$125**
Trilby, Wood & Sons, 1891
Bowl, round, open, 10"................**$145**
Toothbrush holder.......................**$125**
Turkey, Doulton, 1890
14 plates, 10", Well and Tree platter
....**$3600**
Turkey, France, 1898
12 plates, 10", platter, 17-1/2".....**$850**
Turkey, Wedgwood, 1880
Platter, 12" x 16".........................**$255**
Unknown, Davenport, 1845
Tazza, stemmed, polychromed...**$275**
Tea Caddy pair with lids.............**$575**
Unknown, Meakin, 1891
Pitcher, 12-1/2"...........................**$325**
Unknown polychromed, 1880
Handled cake plate......................**$295**
Fruit compote..............................**$450**
Wagon Wheel, Unknown, 1880
Child's mug..................................**$95**
Child's sugar bowl with lid.........**$125**
Watteau, Doulton, 1915
Demitasse cup and saucer...........**$85**
Waverly, Grindley, 1890
Bone dish....................................**$70**

Flow Blue fruit compote, Marguerite, Grindley, 1890, 10", **$450.**

FULPER POTTERY

History: The Fulper Pottery Company of Flemington, New Jersey, made stoneware pottery and utilitarian ware beginning in the early 1800s. It switched to the production of art pottery in 1909 and continued until about 1935.

The company's earliest artware was called the Vasekraft line (1910-1915), featuring intense glazine and rectilinear, Germanic forms. Its middle period (1915-1925) included some of the earlier shapes, but they also incorporated Oriental forms. Their glazing at this time was less consistent but more diverse. The last period (1925-1935) was characterized by watered-down Art Deco forms with relatively weak glazing.

Pieces were almost always molded, though careful hand glazing distinguished this pottery as one of the premier semi-commercial producers. Pieces from all periods are almost always marked.

Marks: A rectangular mark, FULPER, in a rectangle is known as the "ink mark" and dates from 1910-1915. The second mark, as shown, dates from 1915-1925; it was incised or in black ink. The final mark, FULPER, die-stamped, dates from about 1925 to 1935.

Adviser: David Rago.

Fulper temple jar, Mirrored Black glaze, vertical mark and paper label, light rim abrasion, 14" x 8-1/2", $1,440.
Photo courtesy of David Rago Auctions, Inc.

Bowl, flower holder, blue-green crystalline glaze, rect ink mark, 8" d, 5" h **$110**

Bud vase, baluster, Butterscotch flambé glaze, ink racetrack mark, 9" h **$275**

Chinese urn, two handles, Mirrored Black glaze, vertical mark, few short scratches, 9" h, 9" d **$1,400**

Doorstop, figural bulldog, amber, blue, purple crystalline glaze, unmarked, restoration to tip of ear and one toe, 8" x 10" **$600**

Effigy bowl
Copperdust Crystalline glaze int., Mirrored Black glaze ext., vertical mark, 10-1/4" d, 7-1/4" h **$1,400**
Mahogany and amber glaze int., indigo and matte beige ext., vertical mark, 10-1/2" d, 7-1/2" h **$700**

Ibis bowl, green and blue flambé over Copperdust Crystalline, ink racetrack mark, 10-1/2" d, 5-1/2" h **$815**

Jug, tall handle, Copperdust Crystalline glaze, vertical mark, 11-3/4" h, 7-3/4" d **$1,600**

Lamp, table
Mushroom-shaped lamp shade, covered in strong Leopard Skin Crystalline glaze, inset with leaded slag glass pieces, two orig sockets, rect ink mark on both pcs, hairline between two inset pcs, 15-1/4" d, 18-1/2" h **$5,750**
Mushroom-shaped shade covered in brown, celadon and blue glaze, inset with green and amber slag glass, on Cucumber Green matte base, rect ink mark on both, possibly married piece, 17" d, 21-1/2" h **$1,610**

Place card vases, covered in matte turquoise to gunmetal green flambé glaze, orig cardboard box which reads "For a dinner most select/These place card vases are quite correct/I know you like all things that's new/Hence I'm sending these to you, Fulper Co., Flemington, NJ," set of 12, 2-1/4" h **$1,600**

Urn
Hammered, frothy indigo and light blue glaze, incised racetrack mark, stilt-pull bruise, 11-3/4" d, 11-3/4" h **$865**
Two handles, fine Mirrored Green, Mahogany and Ivory flambé glazes, rect ink mark, 7-1/2" d, 12" h **$1,200**

Vase
Baluster, Cat's Eye flambé glaze, vertical mark, 16-1/2" h, 9" d **$1,600**
Bullet, frothy Leopard Skin Crystalline glaze, ink racetrack mark, two small opposing bursts at rim, grinding chips on base, 4-3/4" d, 7" h **$520**
Bulbous, double ribbon handles, textured surface, Mission Verde matte green glaze, vertical mark, 9" h, 8-3/4" d **$1,100**
Bulbous, floriform, emb panels, covered in exceptional mirrored Cat's Eye flambé glaze, raised racetrack mark, 11-1/2" h, 9" d **$2,990**
Bulbous, hammered texture, Mirrored Black, cobalt and blue crystalline flambé glaze, vertical mark, grinding chip, 12" h, 11-1/2" d **$2,200**
Bulbous, two handles, mottled gray

Fulper effigy bowl, three gargoyles, matte gray glaze, supporting bowl in Chinese blue flambé glaze, vertical mark, 7-1/2" x 11", $600.
Photo courtesy of David Rago Auctions, Inc.

Fulper vase, hammered texture, four small handles with Chinese Blue flambé glaze, vertical mark, 13" x 11-1/2", $2,350.
Photo courtesy of David Rago Auctions, Inc.

Fulper bud vase, pair of elephant head handles, mustard flambé glaze, small base restoration vertical mark, 5", $210.
Photo courtesy of David Rago Auctions, Inc.

and amber flambé glaze, vertical mark, 6-3/4" h, 7" d **$475**

Cattail, covered in Leopard Skin crystalline glaze, rect ink mark, rim minor burst bubble, 11-1/2" h, 7-3/4" d **$2,300**

Moss-to-Rose flambé glaze, vertical mark, 7-1/2" h, 6-1/4" d **$400**

Ovoid, light green crystalline glaze, vertical mark, 8" h, 5-1/4" d **$460**

Pillow, Cat's Eye flambé glaze, ink racetrack mark, 6-1/4" h, 5-3/4" w **$175**

Tear shape, gunmetal to Copperdust Crystalline flambé glaze, vertical mark, restoration to flat chip on foot ring, 13" h, 7-1/2" d **$1,900**

Vessel

Bulbous, four short handles, covered in Leopard Skin Crystalline glaze, incised racetrack mark, restoration to drill hole in bottom, 11-1/2" d, 13-1/4" h **$2,990**

Bulbous, three horn-shaped handles, ivory, blue and Mirror Black flambé glaze, vertical ink mark, 6" d, 6-1/2" h **$860**

Spherical, two buttressed handles, mirrored Cat's Eye flambé glaze, ink racetrack mark, 7-1/2" d, 6-1/4" h **$435**

Squatty, two angular handles, frothy blue flambé glaze, ink racetrack mark, restoration to one handle, 6" d, 5" h **$195**

GAUDY DUTCH

History: Gaudy Dutch is an opaque, soft-paste ware made between 1790 and 1825 in England's Staffordshire district.

The wares first were hand decorated in an underglaze blue and fired; then additional decorations were added over the glaze. The overglaze decoration is extensively worn on many of the antique pieces. Gaudy Dutch found a ready market in the Pennsylvania German community because it was inexpensive and extremely colorful. It had little appeal in England.

Marks: Marks of various potters, including the impressed marks of Riley and Wood, have been found on some pieces, although most are unmarked.

Gaudy Dutch plate, single rose pattern, 10" d, $975.
Photo courtesy of Pook & Pook, Inc.

Gaudy Dutch toddy plate, grape pattern, 6" d, $475.
Photo courtesy of Pook & Pook, Inc.

Reproduction Alert. Cup plates, bearing the impressed mark "CYBRIS," have been reproduced and are collectible in their own right. The Henry Ford Museum has issued pieces in the Single Rose pattern. They are porcelain, rather than soft paste.

Butterfly

Coffeepot, 11" h **$9,500**

Cup and saucer, handleless, minor enamel flakes, chips on table ring **$950**

Plate, 7-1/4" d **$645**

Sugar bowl, cov **$900**

Teapot, 5" h, squat baluster form **$2,400**

Carnation

Bowl, 6-1/4" d **$925**

Creamer, 4-3/4" h **$700**

Pitcher, 6" h **$675**

Plate, 9-3/4" d **$1,265**

Saucer, cobalt blue, orange, green and yellow, stains, hairline, minor flake on table ring, 5-1/2" d **$115**

Teapot, cov **$2,200**

Waste bowl **$675**

Dahlia

Bowl, 6-1/4" d **$1,800**

Plate, 8" d **$2,800**

Tea bowl and saucer **$8,000**

Double Rose

Bowl, 6-1/4" d **$545**

Creamer **$650**

Gravy boat **$950**

Plate, 8-1/4" d **$675**

Sugar bowl, cov **$750**

Tea bowl and saucer **$675**

Toddy plate, 4-1/2" d **$675**

Waste bowl, 6-1/2" d, 3" h **$850**

Dove

Creamer **$675**

Plate, very worn, scratches, stains, 8-1/8" d **$245**

Plate, 8-1/2" d **$770**

Tea bowl and saucer **$500**

Waste bowl **$650**

Flower Basket, plate, 6-1/2" d ... **$375**

Grape

Bowl, lustered rim, 6-1/2" d **$475**

Plate, cobalt blue, orange, green and yellow, minor stains, 8-1/4" d .. **$450**

Sugar bowl, cov **$675**

Tea bowl and saucer **$475**

Toddy plate, 5" d **$475**

Leaf, bowl, shallow, 11-1/2" d.... **$4,800**
No Name
Plate, 8-3/4" d **$17,000**
Teapot, cov **$16,000**
Oyster
Bowl, 5-1/2" d **$675**
Coffeepot, cov, 12" h.............. **$10,000**
Plate, 10" d **$1,550**
Soup plate, 8-1/2" d **$550**
Tea bowl and saucer.................. **$1,275**
Toddy plate, 5-1/2" d **$475**
Single Rose
Coffeepot, cov **$8,500**
Cup and saucer, handleless, minor
wear and stains........................ **$330**

Plate, 7-1/4" d **$550**
Plate, 10" d **$975**
Quill holder, cov **$2,500**
Sugar bowl, cov **$700**
Teapot, cov **$1,200**
Toddy plate, 5-1/4" d **$250**
Sunflower
Bowl, 6-1/2" d **$900**
Coffeepot, cov, 9-1/2" h............ **$6,500**
Cup and saucer, handleless, wear,
chips **$575**
Plate, 9-3/4" d **$825**
Urn
Creamer.................................... **$475**
Cup and saucer, handleless........ **$550**

Plate, 8-1/4" d **$910**
Plate, very worn, scratches, stains,
rim chips, 9-7/8" d **$225**
Sugar bowl, cov, round, tip and base
restored, 6-1/2" h.................... **$295**
Teapot **$895**
War Bonnet
Bowl, cov **$225**
Coffeepot, cov **$9,500**
Plate, pinpoint rim flake, minor wear,
8-1/8" d **$880**
Teapot, cov **$4,400**
Toddy plate, 4-1/2" d **$975**
Zinna, soup plate, impressed "Riley,"
10" d..................................... **$4,675**

GAUDY IRONSTONE

History: Gaudy Ironstone was made in England around 1850. Ironstone is an opaque, heavy-bodied earthenware which contains large proportions of flint and slag. Gaudy Ironstone is decorated in patterns and colors similar to those of Gaudy Welsh.

Marks: Most pieces are impressed "Ironstone" and bear a registry mark.

Biscuit jar, Rococo molded body, polychrome floral, Flow Blue accents, backstamp monogram for "F. J. Emery," Burslem, England, c1890, 7-1/2" h............................. **$195**
Bread plate, marked "Tunstall, England, by Enoch Wedgwood," 10-1/4" l, 5-1/4" w **$65**
Charger
Blue star design, orange-red flowers, blue green detail, wear, 10-7/8" d
.... **$150**
Center yellow daisy-shaped flower surrounded by orange-red flowers, tornado shaped blossoms, cobalt blue leaves, copper luster detail, imp "Emberton" on back, minor scratches, 12-1/8" d **$350**
Red Adams type roses, green leaves, blue feathers, red and yellow border, partial imp label, wear, 14-1/8" d, 2-5/8" h.................. **$250**
Stylized urn, large cobalt blue and orange-red flowers, small green leaves, copper luster highlights, price for pr, 11-3/8" d.............. **$435**
Coffeepot, cov, Strawberry pattern, 10" h.................................... **$650**
Creamer and sugar, fruit finial, Blackberry pattern, underglaze blue, yellow, and orange enamel and luster, wear, small flakes, int. chip on sugar, 6-3/4" h...................................... **$990**
Cup and saucer, handleless
Blackberry pattern, underglaze blue, yellow, and orange enamel and luster,

imp label or registry mark with "E. Walley," price for set of 10....... **$1,375**
Deep blue and orange flowers, pink and copper luster leaves........... **$225**
Jug, yellow, red, white, and blue tulips on sides, light blue pebble ground, luster trim, rim outlined, 7-1/2" h
.... **$350**
Pitcher, six-color floral dec, blue, green, burgundy, mauve, black, and yellow, molded serpent handle, dec has been enhanced, then reglazed, spider, 11" h **$320**
Plate
Morning Glories and Strawberries pattern, underglaze blue, polychrome enamel and luster trim, 6-1/4" d **$80**
Blackberry pattern, underglaze blue, yellow, and orange enamel and luster, some wear, set of seven, 9-1/2" d **$1,320**
Platter, recessed tree and well, cobalt blue floral dec, overglaze tomato red detail, imp "Mason's Patent Ironstone," wear, some flowers simply outlined, 18" x 14-1/2"....... **$250**
Soup plate, Blackberry pattern, underglaze blue, yellow, and orange enamel and luster, one imp "Elsmore & Forster, Tunstall," price for set of three, 9-7/8" d **$650**
Teapot, domed cov, floral finial, paneled body, blue flower, red and green strawberries, gilt highlights, c1850, 9-3/4" h................................. **$2,300**

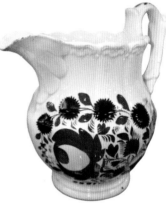

Gaudy Ironstone pitcher, large red rose, blue cornflowers, green leaves, embossed scrolls around top and handle, **$225.**

Gaudy Ironstone Strawberry pattern, left: covered sugar bowl with paneled sides, applied acanthus leaf handles, small interior rim chip, 8-1/2" h, **$575;** *right: pitcher, paneled sides, cracking in handle, discoloration on rim, small chip, 8-1/2" h,* **$850.**
Photo courtesy of Alderfer Auction Co.

Wash basin and pitcher, 14" d bowl, 13" h pitcher, hexagonal, blue morning glories and leaves, copper accents, hp red, green, and yellow berries, hairlines.................................. **$1,225**

GAUDY WELSH

History: Gaudy Welsh is a translucent porcelain that was originally made in the Swansea area of England from 1830 to 1845. Although the designs resemble Gaudy Dutch, the body texture and weight differ. One of the characteristics is the gold luster on top of the glaze. In 1890, Allerton made a similar ware from heavier opaque porcelain.

Marks: Allerton pieces usually bear an export mark.

Gaudy Welsh plate, underglaze cobalt blue floral design, **$75.**

Gaudy Welsh pitcher, green mark "Allertons, Est. 1831, Made in England," **$125.**
Photo courtesy of Dotta Auction Co., Inc.

Bethesda, pitcher, paneled form, scalloped rims, figural dragon handles, imp "Ironstone, China," some wear, price for pr, 6-3/8" h **$300**

Chinoiserie, teapot, c1830-40 ..... **$750**

Columbine
Bowl, ftd, underglaze blue and polychrome enamel floral dec, 10" d, 5-1/2" h **$400**
Plate, 5-1/2" d **$65**
Tea set, 17-pc set, c1810 .... **$625**

Conwys, jug, 9" h **$750**

Daisy and Chain
Creamer **$175**
Cup and saucer **$95**
Sugar, cov **$195**
Teapot, cov **$225**

Flower Basket
Bowl, 10-1/2" d **$190**
Mug, 4" h **$90**
Plate **$65**
Sugar, cov, luster trim **$195**

Grape
Bowl, 5-1/4" d **$50**
Cup and saucer **$75**
Mug, 2-1/2" h **$65**
Plate, 5-1/4" d **$65**

Grapevine Variant, miniature pitcher and bowl, 4-1/4" h pitcher, 4-1/2" d bowl, cobalt blue, orange, green and luster, scalloped edges **$250**

Oyster
Bowl, 6" d **$80**
Creamer, 3" h **$100**
Jug, c1820, 5-3/4" h **$85**
Soup plate, flange rim, 10" d **$85**

Primrose, plate, 8-1/4" d **$350**

Strawberry
Cup and saucer **$75**
Mug, 4-1/8" h **$125**
Plate, 8-1/4" d **$150**

Tulip
Bowl, 6-1/4" d **$50**
Cake plate, molded handles, 10" d **$120**
Creamer, 5-1/4" h **$125**
Plate, tea size **$95**
Tea cup and saucer, slight crazing in cup **$115**
Teapot, 7-1/4" h **$225**

Wagon Wheel
Cup and saucer **$75**
Pitcher, 8-1/2" h **$195**
Plate, 8-3/4" d **$85**
Platter **$125**

Gaudy Welsh tea set, tulip pattern, teapot, creamer, sugar, waste bowl, two serving plates, six 6" plates, six cups and saucers, teapot and sugar marked "BLAIRS/CHINA/ENGLAND," rest unmarked, late 19th century, teapot 7" h x 5" d, **$330.**
Photo courtesy of Green Valley Auctions.

GOUDA POTTERY

History: Gouda and the surrounding areas of Holland have been principal Dutch pottery centers for centuries. Originally, the potteries produced a simple utilitarian tin-glazed Delft-type earthenware and the famous clay smoker's pipes.

When pipe making declined in the early 1900s, the Gouda potteries turned to art pottery. Influenced by the Art Nouveau and Art Deco movements, artists expressed themselves with free-form and stylized designs in bold colors.

Gouda tray, scalloped, painted yellow flowers and cobalt blue medallions, stamped "Fanny Gouda," 10" x 13", **$195.**
Photo courtesy of David Rago Auctions, Inc.

Reproduction Alert. With the Art Nouveau and Art Deco revivals of recent years, modern reproductions of Gouda pottery currently are on the market. They are difficult to distinguish from the originals.

Bowl

Art Nouveau scrolled floral and foliage dec, shades of green, brown and blue, cracked white semi-matte glazed ground, black rooster mark on base, Arnhem factory, repairs to rim, c1910, 7" h **$100**

Dec with three clusters of flowers in symmetrical pattern, matte glaze, shades of orange, yellow and blue, black ground, blue painted maker's mark, c1927, 10-1/4" d, 2-1/2" h **$225**

Stylized floral design, matte glaze, yellow, orange, green and blue, black ground, black painted Regina marks, rim repair, c1927, 11-3/4" d, 2-3/4" h **$185**

Candlesticks and vase set, Art Nouveau style dec, matte glaze blue, orange, turquoise, brown and yellow, painted "Westland (house) Gouda Holland," date and artist's initials, pr 9-1/2" h candlesticks, 10-3/4" h vase **$400**

Candlesticks, pr, bulbed cup, ruffled rim drop pan, tall ribbed flared standard, Art Nouveau-style motif, high glaze, shades of blue, green, yellow and black, underglaze mark "Gouda Blauw (house)," date mark, artist's initials, and "Made in Holland, 872, 893," dec attributed to Franciscus Ijsselstein, base chip on one, c1926, 18" h.................................**$435**

Clock garniture, circular clock mouth with painted ceramic face supported by four ceramic arms on baluster-shaped body and flared base, candlesticks of similar form, all

dec with Art Nouveau-style flowers, glossy glaze pink, purple, blue, green and tan, sgd "Zuid Holland" and imp house and "R" on base, repairs to candlesticks, 20-1/2" h clock, 16-3/4" h pr candlesticks **$2,875**

Charger, multicolored flowers, rope border, black trim, 12" d **$150**

Compote, black ground, geometric design, multicolored scroll int., 7-5/8" **$175**

Ewer

Handle, floral and foliage design, high glaze, shades of purple, mauve, green, blue and taupe, base painted "Made in Zuid Holland (house)," and artist's initials, 7" h...........**$325**

Handle, stylized floral and foliage design, high glazes, shades of green, pink and purple on tan and brown ground, painted "Made in Zuid, Holland," 7-5/8" h...................**$350**

Incense burner, Roba, flowers and geometric designs, green ground, 8" h **$120**

Jug, Rosalie, cream ground, green handle, turquoise interior, marked "Rosalie, #5155," and "Zuid-Holland, Gouda," c1930, 5-3/4" d **$195**

Lamp base, flared rim, tapered oval form, butterfly design, matte glaze, shades of green, blue, gold, red and cream, base painted "380 Butterfly (tree, house) AJK Holland," c1920, 11-3/4" h.................................**$290**

Miniature, vase, floral and foliate design, high glaze, shades of green, purple, red, brown and black, 2-1/4" h....................................**$125**

Pitcher, stylized designs in shades of green, blue, rust and gold on black ground matte glaze, all with maker's marks, crazing, 1923, 8-1/4" h Henley **$275**

Plate, Unique Metallique, scalloped edge, deep blue-green ground, irid copper luster dec, 8-1/4" d **$350**

Shoe, floral and foliate design, high

Gouda vase, baluster shape, geometric dec, shades of blue, green, ochre on black ground, signed and numbered, **$250.**
Photo courtesy of David Rago Auctions, Inc.

glaze, shades of green, purple, red, brown and black, 4-7/8" h **$125**

Urn, stylized designs in shades of green, blue, rust and gold on black ground matte glaze, all with maker's marks, crazing, 1923, 8-1/8" h Gotton **$275**

Vase

Art Nouveau style, elongated neck, squat form, stylized flowers and leaves, high glaze, white, green and rust, taupe ground, painted "Holland Utrecht" on base, 6" h **$200**

Breetvelt double handles, all with stylized designs in shades of green, blue, rust and gold on black ground matte glaze, all with maker's marks, crazing, 9-3/4" h **$295**

Elongated neck on bulbous body, Art Nouveau stylized lilies, foliage, high glaze purple, green, yellow and black, base painted with wooden shoe "NB Faience du (illegible) Holland 504 Dec A," 13-1/4" h **$865**

Flared rim, ovoid form, stylized flowers and foliage, matte glaze, shades of yellow, green, blue, orange and brown, painted mark "Del Breetvelt (house) Zuid Holland Gouda," 10-3/4" h **$420**

Flared, stylized lily dec, high glaze, purple, brown, green, dark blue,

yellow and cream, painted mark "Made in Holland (house)," price for pr, c1898, 20-1/4" h **$575**

Raised rim, squatty form, flower blossoms dec, semi-matte glaze, yellow, brown, blue and cream, black ground, painted and paper labels, 4-1/2" h **$200**

Tapered oval, flowers and leaves, semi-matte glaze, gold, brown, turquoise, cream and black, painted maker's marks, 10-1/2" h **$200**

Two handles, bulbed neck flanked by arched handles on squatty body, tulip and foliate designs, high glaze

gray, green, yellow and brown tones, painted "Distel," distel factory, early 20th C, 7-3/4" h **$520**

Two handles, ftd, bulbous, brown, blue and green butterflies dec, crackled white matte ground, black stamped rooster mark on base, Arnhem factory, c1910, 7-1/4" h **$150**

Two handles, ovoid, ftd, floral and foliage design, high glaze, shades of purple, mauve, green, blue and taupe, base painted "Made in Zuid Holland (house)", and artist's initials, 10" h **$350**

Grueby vase, spherical, by Ruth Erickson, closed-in rim surrounded with tooled and applied full height green leaves on blue-gray ground, circular pottery stamp, paper label, incised "RE-D," 3-3/4" x 4-1/2", $22,000.
Photo courtesy of David Rago Auctions, Inc.

Grueby gourd-shaped vase, full height leaves under feathered matte green glaze, minor nicks to leaf edges, circular pottery stamp/ER, 8" h x 7", $7,800.
Photo courtesy of David Rago Auctions, Inc.

GRUEBY POTTERY

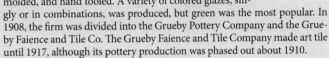

History: William Grueby was active in the ceramic industry for several years before he developed his own method of producing matte-glazed pottery and founded the Grueby Faience Company in Boston, Massachusetts, in 1897.

The art pottery was hand thrown in natural shapes, hand molded, and hand tooled. A variety of colored glazes, singly or in combinations, was produced, but green was the most popular. In 1908, the firm was divided into the Grueby Pottery Company and the Grueby Faience and Tile Co. The Grueby Faience and Tile Company made art tile until 1917, although its pottery production was phased out about 1910.

Minor damage is acceptable to most collectors of Grueby Pottery.

Adviser: David Rago.

Bowl, flaring, broad molded leaves, cucumber matte green ground, dec by Ruth Erickson, imp circular mark, incised "ER," two very short and shallow opposing lines, 9" d, 5-1/2" h **$1,900**

Jardinière, two-color three rows of curled leaves below nine light blue five-petaled flowers, oatmeal matte green glaze, stamped "Grueby Faience/174" and "EG," couple of minor flecks, 7-1/2" x 9" **$575**

Miniature vase, green-gray glaze, sgd "GRUEBY POTTERY BOSTON USA," in mold, 1899, 3" h **$600**

Paperweight, scarab, blue-gray glaze, sgd "GRUEBY FAIENCE Co. BOSTON. U.S.A.," c1905, 3" l **$650**

Planter, flaring, by Edith R. Felton, modeled leaves, closed-in rim, rich cucumber matte green glaze, circular Faience mark, ERF, three short tight lines at top, use scratches on interior, 4-1/2" h, 12" l **$1,100**

Tile, cuenca dec
Large oak tree against blue sky, puffy white clouds, #28 on reverse, 6" sq
....**$1,150**

"The Pines," polychrome cuenca, marked "FH," 6" sq **$1,485**

Yellow tulip on matte green ground, mounted in sterling silver trivet base by Karl Leinonen (Boston League of Arts & Crafts), tile unmarked, mount stamped "Sterling" and "L," very light abrasion to surface, 6-1/4" sq... **$2,990**

Vase

Bulbous, rolled rim, alternating rows of tight yellow bunds and broad leaves, rich medium to dark matte green ground, circular mark, 4" h, 4-1/4" d **$2,900**

Cylindrical neck, bulbous bottom, base dec with overlapping modeled leaves, medium green matte glaze, circular mark, 9-1/2" h, 6" d...**$2,300**

Five-sided neck, full height tooled and applied leaves alternating with ivory buds, leathery matte brown glaze, by Wilhemina Post, Grueby Pottery stamp mark and "WP/4/10," minute old bruise to one corner, 11-1/4" h, 5-1/2" d.................**$8,500**

Flaring rim, squat base, tooled and applied blossoms alternating with rounded, curled leaves, leathery matte green glaze, circular pottery stamp 187, 2" bruise to rim, 7-3/4" h, 7-3/4" d **$2,200**

Flat shoulder, tooled and applied rows of leaves, matte green glaze, shaved off mark, 3-1/2" h, 3" d **$2,600**

Ovoid, carved stylized leaves, medium matte green ground, imp circular mark, incised "MEJ," 7-1/4" h, 5-1/2" d **$1,500**

Ovoid, by Marie Seaman, green buds alternating with spade-shaped leaves, rich cucumber matte glaze, die-stamped faience mark, 28 MS, nicks to leaf edges, 11-1/2" h, 5-3/4" d **$3,500**

Tapering, crisply modeled with broad flat leaves, flowing ochre matte glaze, circular die-stamp mark, several small flakes to leaf edges, 7-1/4" h, 4-1/2" d...................**$4,500**

Grueby vessel, squat, two rows of footed and applied leaves, curdled rich matte green glaze, circular pottery stamp, artist signature, some scratches to glossy interior, provenance: from estate of Miriam Hubbard Roelofs, Elbert and Alice Hubbard's daughter, 3" x 5-1/2", **$2,400.**
Photo courtesy of David Rago Auctions, Inc.

Grueby, tall vase, tooled and applied full-height leaves, covered by thick, mottled purplish-brown glaze, small chip repair on rim and base, circular Faience stamp, 11-1/2" h x 5-1/2", **$2,520.**
Photo courtesy of David Rago Auctions, Inc.

Grueby vase, spherical, ribbed, covered in veined matte green glaze, small bottom chip, circular pottery mark, J.E., paper label, 6" x 7", **$2,350.**
Photo courtesy of David Rago Auctions, Inc.

Grueby tile, tall ship in ivory and brown, deep green ground, decorated in cuenca technique, encased in hammered copper mount, no visible mark, 6" sq , **$1,200.**
Photo courtesy of David Rago Auctions, Inc.

HALL CHINA COMPANY

History: Robert Hall founded the Hall China Company in 1903 in East Liverpool, Ohio. He died in 1904 and was succeeded by his son, Robert Taggart Hall. After years of experimentation, Robert T. Hall developed a leadless glaze in 1911, opening the way for production of glazed household products.

The Hall China Company made many types of kitchenware, refrigerator sets, and dinnerware in a wide variety of patterns. Some patterns were made exclusively for a particular retailer, such as Heather Rose for Sears.

One of the most popular patterns was Autumn Leaf, a premium designed by Arden Richards in 1933 for the exclusive use by the Jewel Tea Company. Still a Jewel Tea property, Autumn Leaf has not been listed in catalogs since 1978, has been produced on a replacement basis with the date stamped on the back.

Additional Listings: See *Warman's Americana & Collectibles* for more examples.

Cookie jar, cov

Autumn Leaf, Tootsie $265
Blue Blossom, Five-Band shape .. $275
Chinese Red, Five-Band shape ... $150
Gold Dot, Zeisel $95
Meadow Flower, Five-Band shape
.... $230
Owl, brown glaze $90
Red Poppy $50

Kitchen ware and advertising

Bean pot, New England, #1, Orange Poppy $80
Casserole, cov, Chinese Red, Sundial, #4, 8" w $65
Coffeepot, percolator, ducks and partridge dec $100
Cuspidor, green and white, 7-1/4" d, 4-1/4" h $90
Drip jar, Little Red Riding Hood, 4-1/2" h, 5" w $3,300
Jug, Primrose, rayed $20
Mixing bowl, nested set of three, pink, basketweave and floral dec, gold trim, 6" d, 7-1/2" d, 8-1/2" d $85
Mug, Braniff International Airlines, 4" h, 2" d $18
Refrigerator bowl, Addison Gray and Daffodil, ink stamped "GE Refrigerators, Hall Ovenware China, Made for General Electric," c1938 .... $12
Sauce boat, Quartermasters logo emb near handle on both sides, c1940, 10" l
.... $25

Patterns

Autumn Leaf
Bowl, 5-1/2" d $8
Coffeepot, electric $300
Cup and saucer $18
Juice reamer $250
Pepper shaker, gold trim, 4-1/4" h $20
Pie bird, 5" h $40
Plate, 8" d $15
Teapot, cov, automobile shape, 1993
.... $465
Tidbit tray, three tiers $125
Tumbler, frosted, 5-5/8" h, 2-3/4" d .. $45
Utensil holder, marked "Utensils," 7-1/4" h $275

Blue Bouquet
Bowl, 7" d, 3" h $30
Creamer, Boston $25
Cup and saucer $28
French baker, round $35
Platter, 13" l $35
Soup, flat $30
Spoon $100
Teapot, Aladdin infuser $165

Cameo Rose
Bowl, 5-1/4" d $3
Butter dish, 3/4 lb. $30
Casserole $25
Creamer and sugar $10
Cream soup, 6" d $7
Cup and saucer $9
Plate, 8" d $2.50
Teapot, cov, six-cup $35
Tidbit, three-tier $40

Gamebirds
Percolator, electric $140

Teapot, cov, two-cup size, ducks and pheasant $200

Mount Vernon
Coffeepot $125
Creamer $12
Cup $10
Fruit bowl $8
Gravy boat $20
Saucer $4
Soup bowl, flat, 8" d $17

Red Poppy
Bowl, 5-1/2" d $5
Cake plate $18
Casserole, cov $25
Coffeepot, cov $12
Creamer and sugar $15
Cup and saucer $8
French baker, fluted $15
Jug, Daniel, Radiance $28
Plate, 9" d $7
Salad bowl, 9" d $14
Teapot, New York $90

Silhouette
Bean pot $50
Bowl, 7-7/8" d $50
Coffeepot, cov $30
Mug $35
Pretzel jar $75
Trivet $125

Tulip
Bowl, oval, 10-1/4" l $36
Coffee maker, drip, Kadota, all china
.... $115
Condiment jar $165
Fruit bowl, 5-1/2" d $10
Mixing bowl, 6" d $27
Plate, luncheon, 9" d $16
Platter, oval, 13-1/4" l $42
Shakers, bulge-type, price for pr .. $110
Sugar, cov $25

Teapots

Camellia, gold roses, windshield, gold trim on handle, spout, rim, and finial, mkd "Hall 0698 6 cup made in USA"
.... $100
Chinese Red, donut, 9-1/2" w, 7-1/2" h
.... $500
Cleveland, turquoise and gold $165
Lipton Tea, off white stoneware, aluminum cozy, 9-1/2" l, 7-1/2" h $30

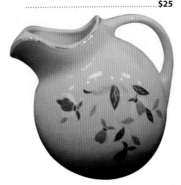

Hall pitcher, ball shape, Autumn Leaf, **$70.**

Teapot, squatty, deep maroon, silver trim, marked, **$85.**

HAMPSHIRE POTTERY

History: In 1871, James S. Taft founded the Hampshire Pottery Company in Keene, New Hampshire. Production began with redwares and stonewares, followed by majolica in 1879. A semi-porcelain, with the recognizable matte glazes plus the Royal Worcester glaze, was introduced in 1883.

Until World War I, the factory made an extensive line of utilitarian and art wares including souvenir items. After the war, the firm resumed operations, but made only hotel dinnerware and tiles. The company was dissolved in 1923.

Bowl, matte green glaze over foliate-forms, imp "Hampshire, M.O.," 5-1/2" d, 2-1/2" h **$320**

Chocolate pot, cream, holly dec, 9-1/2" h **$275**

Compote, ftd, two handles, Ivory pattern, light green highlights, cream ground, red decal mark, 13-1/4" d **$175**

Inkwell, round, large center well, three pen holes, 4-1/8" d, 2-3/4" h **$125**

Oil lamp, matte green glaze, price for pr, one handle restored, 3-1/2" x 7" **$485**

Stein, 1/2 liter, transfer printed scene of Pine Grove Springs resort, 7" h **$110**

Tankard, band of stylized dec, green matte glaze, imp "Hampshire," 7" h **$100**

Vase

Barrel shape, emb dandelions, feathered matte cobalt blue glaze, Hampshire Pottery 4 64, 6" h, 5-1/4" d **$950**

Bottle shape, imp leaves, feathered green glaze, blue-gray ground, Hampshire Pottery 124, 9-1/4" h, 6-1/2" d **$1,000**

Mottled drip glaze, soft clay and blue-green colors on slate blue ground, repeating leaf dec, incised pottery mark, "M" cipher, c1908, 8-3/4" h **$765**

Ovoid, full height leaves, frothy matte blue-green glaze, cobalt blue and apricot shoulder, Hampshire Pottery 98, 7" h, 4-1/2" d **$700**

Soft matte blue-green glaze, modeled leaf blades centered by buds and trailing stems, imp pottery mark and "M" cipher, numbered "33" c1908, 6-3/4" h.......................... **$765**

Thick matte green glaze, incised detail at rim, imp pottery mark, cipher, and number "76," spider hairline at base, possibly in the making, c1908, 4" h, 5-1/2" d.......................... **$325**

Wide mouth, glossy blue glaze, broad overlapping leaf dec, incised pottery mark and "M" cipher, Keene, New Hampshire, c1908, 8-1/4" h **$600**

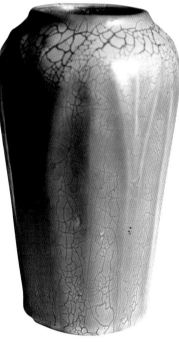

Hampshire vase, full-height buds alternating with leaves, covered in green and teal blue mottled matte glaze, stamped Hampshire Pottery, 6-1/4" x 4", **$765.**
Photo courtesy of David Rago Auctions, Inc.

Hampshire Pottery, Cadmon Robertson's artichoke bowl, matte green glaze, impressed mark, Emoretta Robertson tribute cipher and number 24, c1905, 3" h x 4-3/4" d, **$380.**
Photo courtesy of Skinner, Inc.

Hampshire vase, ovoid, full-height leaves, blue and green oatmealed glaze, stamped Hampshire Pottery 98, 7" x 5", **$880.**
Photo courtesy of David Rago Auctions, Inc.

HAVILAND CHINA

History: In 1842, American china importer David Haviland moved to Limoges, France, where he began manufacturing and decorating china specifically for the U.S. market. Haviland is synonymous with fine, white, translucent porcelain, although early hand-painted patterns were generally larger and darker colored on heavier whiteware blanks than were later ones.

David revolutionized French china factories by both manufacturing the whiteware blank and decorating it at the same site. In addition, Haviland and Company pioneered the use of decals in decorating china.

David's sons, Charles Edward and Theodore, split the company in 1892. In 1936, Theodore opened an American division, which still operates today. In 1941, Theodore bought out Charles Edward's heirs and recombined both companies under the original name of H. and Co. The Haviland family sold the firm in 1981.

Charles Field Haviland, cousin of Charles Edward and Theodore, worked for and then, after his marriage in 1857, ran the Casseaux Works until 1882. Items continued to carry his name as decorator until 1941.

Thousands of Haviland patterns were made, but not consistently named until after 1926. The similarities in many of the patterns makes identification difficult. Numbers assigned by Arlene Schleiger and illustrated in her books have become the identification standard.

Bone dish, hp, 8-1/4" l
  Crab dec **$60**
  Turtle dec **$65**
Bouillon cup and saucer, hp bluebirds, luster ground, gold rims, artist sgd "Poirer," green marks, price for set of 12 .... **$400**
Bowl, hp, yellow roses, 8" d **$35**
Butter dish, cov, Gold Band, marked "Theo Haviland" **$45**
Butter pat, sq, rounded corners, gold trim **$12**
Cake plate, gold handles and border, 10" d **$35**
Celery dish, scalloped edge, green flowers, pale pink scroll **$45**
Chocolate pot, cov, Countess pattern, green mark, c1893, 10-1/2" l **$475**
Cream soup, underplate, cranberry and blue scroll border **$30**
Creamer and sugar, small pink flowers, scalloped, gold trim **$65**
Cup and saucer, Etoile **$470**
Dinner set
  Forever Spring, service for five... **$165**
  Pink roses, 69 pcs **$500**

Violets, gold trim, service for 12, plus serving pcs **$1,295**
Game plate, hp, center scene of shore birds in natural setting, apple green edge, printed gold scrolled rim dec, artist sgd "B. Albert," Theodore Haviland & Co. blanks, price for set of 12, early 20th C, 9-1/4" d **$865**
Gravy boat, attached underplate
  Chantilly **$270**
  Monteray **$315**
  Schleiger #57 .... **$250**
Milk pitcher, pink flowers, green branches, underglaze green Haviland mark, red "Haviland & Co., Limoges for PDG, Indianapolis, Ind.," 8" h, 4-3/4" d **$450**
Oyster plate, five wells
  Rose dec, bright red roses, blue forget-me-nots, hp muscle scars, importer's mark "Warren & Wood, Providence, RI" **$700**
  Seascape, shellfish, aquatic plants, underglaze mark, CFH/GDM mark...... **$845**
  Seaweed, raised dec, underglaze green mark, importer's mark "J.

E. Caldwell Co., Philadelphia, PA," 8-3/4" d **$600**
Wave design, multicolored metallic dec, gold highlights and brushed rim, CFH/GDM mark **$725**
Oyster plate, six wells
  Floral transfers, hp muscle marks, gold trim, price for set of six, c1881-90 .... **$1,650**
  Hand brushed gold dec, white ground, five oyster wells, center sauce well, underglaze green mark, price for set of four **$760**
  Rose pattern, violet rim trim, price for set of six, c1877 .... **$1,350**
Pitcher, Rosalinde, 7-1/2" h **$280**
Plate, dinner
  Crowning Fashion, tan **$8**
  Golden Quail **$275**
Platter
  Chantilly **$275**
  Golden Quail **$350**
Relish dish, blue and pink flowers ... **$25**
Sandwich plate, Drop Rose pattern, 11-1/2" d **$275**
Teacup and saucer, small blue flowers, green leaves **$30**
Teapot, Portland **$250**
Tea set, rope and anchor pattern, transfer-printed, hand tinted blossoms, stamped "Haviland-Limoges" mark, restoration to lids, price for three-pc set, 8-1/2" d, 8" h teapot **$200**
Tureen, cov, pink roses, green ivy, 12" l, 6-1/2" h **$360**
Vase, tan, brown, pink and rose, two oval scenes of lady in large hat, baskets and flower garlands, Charles Field Haviland and GDA Limoges mark, 5-1/2" h, 3-5/8" d **$275**
Vegetable dish, open, Golden Quail, 9-1/2" x 7-1/2" **$435**

Haviland Limoges, seafood plates, hand painted in different marine patterns, each stamped "CFH/GDM," 7-1/2" square, price for set of 12, **$300.**
Photo courtesy of David Rago Auctions, Inc.

HOLT-HOWARD COLLECTIBLES

History: Three young entrepreneurs, Grant Holt and brothers John and Robert Howard, started Holt-Howard from their apartment in Manhattan, in 1949. All three of the partners were great salesmen, but Robert handled product development, while John managed sales; Grant was in charge of financial affairs and office management. By 1955, operations were large enough to move the company to Connecticut, but it still maintained its New York showroom and later added its final showroom in Los Angeles. Production facilities eventually expanded to Holt-Howard Canada; Holt-Howard West, Holt-Howard International.

The company's first successful product was the Angel-Abra, followed closely by its Christmas line. This early success spurred the partners to expand their wares. Their line of Christmas and kitchen-related giftware was popular with 1950s consumers. Probably the most famous line was Pixieware, which began production in 1958. Production of these whimsical pieces continued until 1962. Other lines, such as Cozy Kittens and Merry Mouse, brought even more smiles as they invaded homes in many forms. Three things that remained constant with all Holt-Howard products were a high quality of materials and workmanship, innovation, and good design.

The founders of this unique company sold their interests to General Housewares Corp. in 1968, where it became part of the giftware group. By 1974, the three original partners had left the firm. By 1990, what remained of Holt-Howard was sold to Kay Dee Designs of Rhode Island.

Holt-Howard pieces were marked with an ink-stamp. Many were also copyright dated. Some pieces were marked only with a foil sticker, especially the small pieces, where a stamp mark was too difficult. Four types of foil stickers have been identified.

Adviser: Walter Dworkin.

Chuckie's Cookie Jar, orange striping, black lettering, Pixie with green hair, **$45.**
Dworkin collection, photo by Brenner Lennon Photo Productions.

Christmas

Air freshener, Girl Christmas Tree **$65**
Ashtray, Snow Baby **$35**
Ashtray/cigarette holder, Starry-eyed Santa **$45**
Bells, Elf Girls, pr **$55**
Bottle opener, wooden
Santa **$28**
Snowman **$28**
Candle climbers, Ole Snowy, snowman, set **$48**
Candleholders
Camels **$38**
Carolers trio **$30**
Elf Girls, NOEL, set of four **$38**
Ermine Angels with snowflake rings, set **$48**
Green Holly Elf, pr **$35**
Madonna and Child **$25**
Naughty Choir Boy, set of two **$30**
Reindeer, pr **$38**
Santa driving car candleholders, traffic light candle rings, pr **$55**
Santa riding stagecoach, pr **$38**
Santas, NOEL, set of four **$90**
Snow Babies, igloo, set of two **$55**
Three Choir Boy **$60**
Three Snowmen **$50**

Totem Pole, Santa **$25**
Wee Three Kings, set of three **$60**
Cigarette holder with ashtrays, Santa King, stackable **$70**
Coffee mug, Green Holly Elf **$23**
Cookie jar, pop-up, Santa **$150**
Cookie jar/candy jar combination, Santa **$155**
Creamer and sugar
Reindeer **$48**
Winking Santas **$55**
Decanter and glasses, Santa King **$100**
Dish, divided, Green Holly Elf **$50**
Floral ring, Green Holly Elf **$48**
Head vase, My Fair Lady **$75**
Letter and pen holder, Santa **$55**
Napkin holder, Santa, 4" **$25**
Nutmeg shaker, Winking Santa **$55**
Pitcher and mug set, Winking Santa **$75**
Place card holders, Green Holly Elf, set of four **$40**
Planter
Camel **$40**
Elf Girl in Sleigh **$58**
Ermine Angel **$38**
Green Holly Elf, pr **$75**

Rudy's Cookie Jar, Santa hat, red stripes, black lettering, red and white scarf **$45.**
Dworkin collection, photo by Brenner Lennon Photo Productions.

Punch bowl set, punch bowl and eight mugs, Santa $145

Salt and pepper shakers, pr
Cloud Santa $38
Holly Girls, pr $23
Rock' N' Roll Santas, on springs... $75
Santa and Rudolph sleeping in bed
.... $105
Santa and snowman in NOEL candle-holder $95
Snow Babies $35

Server, divided tray, Santa King $60

Wall pocket
Green Holly Elf $65
Santa ornament $58

Cozy Kittens

Ashtray, with match holder $60
Bud vase, pr $95
Butter dish, cov $105
Condiment jar, Cat
Instant Coffee $190
Jam 'N' Jelly $180
Ketchup $180
Mustard $180
Cookie jar, pop-up $260
Cottage cheese crock $55
Creamer and sugar $295
Kitty catch clip $50
Letter holder/caddy $58
Match dandy $80
Memo minder $78
Meow milk pitcher $130
Meow mug $38
Meow oil and vinegar $195
Salt and pepper shakers, pr $20
Sewing kit, Merry Measure $80
Spice set of four, with rack $120
String holder $60
Sugar pour $85
Totem pole stacking seasons ... $70

Cows

Creamer and sugar $75
Milk glass, moo cow $32
Salt and pepper shakers, pr
Heads $38
Moveable tongues $38

Easter

Candelabra, three rabbits $65
Candle climbers, four-pc set
Feathered Chicks, cracked egg floral frog bases $78
Honey Bunnies, floral frog bases . $78
Candleholder
Totem pole, chicks $70
Totem pole, rabbits $50
Egg cups, Slick Chick, pr of egg cups with Chick salt and pepper shaker, four-pc set $50

Salt and pepper shakers with napkin holder, Winking Wabbits $60

Salt and pepper shakers, pr
Bunnies in baskets $35
Rabbit, pink and yellow $25

Jeeves, butler

Ashtray $65
Chip dish $80
Liquor decanter $165
Martini shaker set $185
Olives, condiment jar $135

Merry Mouse

Cocktail kibitzers, mice, set of six
.... $120
Coaster, ashtray, corner $55
Crock, "Stinky Cheese" $55
Desk pen pal $90
Match mouse $80
Salt and pepper shakers, pr $45

Minnie & Moby Mermaids

Ashtray, Moby $60
Cotton ball dispenser, Minnie.. $85
Matchbox holder, Moby $70
Pill box, Minnie & Moby $50
Planter, seahorse, Minnie & Moby, pr
.... $100 each
Powder jar, Minnie & Moby $60

Miscellaneous

Ashtray
Golfer Image $110
Li'l Old Lace $50
Bank, bobbing, Dandy Lion $135
Bud vase, Daisy Dorable $70
Candelabra, Li'l Old Lace, spiral.. $50
Candle climbers, Honey Bunnies, with bases, set $85
Candleholder, Market Piggy $28
Candle rings, Ballerina, with bases, set $58
Cookie jar, pop-up, Clown $225
Desk organizer, Market Piggy $78
Letter holder, Pheasant $60
Memo holder, Pheasant $60
Napkin doll, Sunbonnet Miss $75
Peepin' Tom & Tweetie Birds
Butter dish, cov $65
Candleholder/floral holder $40
Candle food-warmer set, three pcs
.... $65
Creamer, sugar and saccharin holder, 4-1/2" $85
Egg cups, thermal salt and pepper tops, 4" h $60
Salt and pepper shakers, set $30
Stackable condiment bowls, set of three $45

Pencil holder and sharpener, two-pc set
Chickadee $80
Cock-A-Doodle $85
Professor Perch $65
Planter, Doe & Fawn $35
Salt and pepper shakers, with napkin holder, Winking Wabbits $60
Salt and pepper shakers, pr
Bell Bottom Gobs (sailors) $55
Chattercoons, Peppy and Salty $38
Daisy Dorables, ponytail girls $40
Goose 'N' Golden Egg $35
Pink cat, white poodle $65
Rock 'N' Doll Kids, on springs $85
Tape dispenser
Chickadee $50
Pelican Pete $68
Tea maker, Tea Time Tillie $55

Pixiewares, 1958

Bottle bracelets
Bourbon $105
Gin $105
Scotch $105
Whiskey $105
Child's Pixie spoon
Carrot nose, flesh-colored Pixie . $145
Green head Pixie $145
Orange head Pixie $145
Yellow chicken beak Pixie $145
Condiment jar
Cherries $120
Cocktail Cherries $140
Cocktail Olives $130
Cocktail Onions $155
Instant Coffee $255
Jam 'N' Jelly $75
Ketchup $75
Mustard $75
Olives $100
Onions $145
L'il sugar and cream crock $155
Liquor decanter
"Devil Brew" $590
"300 Proof" $590
"Whisky" $590
Oil cruet, Sally $185
Oil cruet, Sam $185
Stacking seasons, shakers, set of four $180

Pixiewares, 1959

Ashtray Pixie
Blue stripe $160
Green stripe $160
Pink stripe $160
Red stripe $160
Condiment jar
Chili Sauce $365
Honey $725

Mayonnaise	$190
Relish	$225
Hanging planter, rare	$450

Party Pixies hors d'oeuvre dish

Green stripe boy pixie	$200
Orange stripe girl pixie, Australian	$475
Pink stripe girl pixie	$200

Salad dressing jar

Flat head, French Pixie	$140
Flat head, Italian Pixie	$140
Flat head, Russian Pixie	$140
Round head, French Pixie	$125
Round head, Italian Pixie	$125
Round head, Russian Pixie	$125
Salty & Peppy shakers	$350

Snack Pixie bowl

Berries	$750
Goo	$1,100
Ketchup Katie	$675
Mustard Max	$675
Nuts	$600
Onion Annie	$685
Oscar Olives	$575
Peanut Butter Pat	$675
Pickle Pete	$675
Tartar Tom	$850

Teapot candleholder hurricane vase, complete with glass globe

Blue stripe boy	$285
Pink stripe girl	$285

Towel hook

Brother	$150
Dad	$150
Mom	$150
Sister	$150

Red Rooster, "Coq Rouge"

Butter dish, cov	$65
Candleholders, pr	$30
Coffee mug	$14
Coffee server, 36 oz	$65
Cookie jar	$100
Creamer and sugar	$55
Dinner plate	$18
Electric coffee pot, six cups	$70
Mustard condiment jar	$60

Pitcher

12 oz	$45
32 oz	$60
48 oz	$75
Salt and pepper shakers, pr, 4-1/2"	$25
Snack tray	$18
Spoon rest	$25

Wooden

Canister set, four pcs	$145
Cigarette carton holder	$45
Recipe box	$70
Salt & pepper shakers, pr	$25

Tigers

Child's cup	$20
Cookie jar	$45
Napkin holder	$20
Salt and pepper shakers, pr	$23

The Holt-Howard style was popular with consumers. Several companies made products with a similar look. The above example is a Holt-Howard-like Lefton Russian Dressing, **$110.**
Dworkin collection, photo by Brenner Lennon Photo Productions.

Flirting Pixie Shakers, orange stripe, orange top, green hair; orange stripe, blue top, bow, for the pair **$40.**
Dworkin collection, photo by Brenner Lennon Photo Productions.

HULL POTTERY

History: In 1905, Addis E. Hull purchased the Acme Pottery Company, Crooksville, Ohio. In 1917, the A. E. Hull Pottery Company began making art pottery, novelties, stoneware and kitchenware, later including the famous Little Red Riding Hood line. Most items had a matte finish, with shades of pink and blue or brown predominating.

After a disastrous flood and fire in 1950, J. Brandon Hull reopened the factory in 1952 as the Hull Pottery Company. New, more-modern-style pieces, mostly with glossy finish, were produced. The company added dinnerware patterns, and glossy finished pottery. The company closed its doors in 1986.

Marks: Hull pottery molds and patterns are easily identified. Pre-1950 vases are marked "Hull USA" or "Hull Art USA" on the bottom. Many also retain their paper labels. Post-1950 pieces are marked "Hull" in large script or "HULL" in block letters.

Each pattern has a distinctive letter or number, e.g., Wildflower has a "W" and a number; Waterlily, "L" and number; Poppy, numbers in the 600s; Orchid, in the 300s. Early stoneware pieces are marked with an "H."

For more information about these marks and Hull Pottery patterns and history, consult Joan Hull's book, *Hull, The Heavenly Pottery,* 7th ed., 2000, and, *Hull, The Heavenly Pottery Shirt Pocket Price List,* 4th ed., 1999.

Additional Listings: See *Warman's Americana & Collectibles* for more examples.

Adviser: Joan Hull.

Pre-1950 Matte

Bowknot
B-4 vase, 6-1/2" h $250
B-7 cornucopia $325
B-12, basket, 10-1/2" h...............$750
B-17 candleholders, pr...............$225

Calla Lily
500-32 bowl $200
520-33, vase, 8" h........................$150

Dogwood (Wild Rose)
501, basket, 8-1/2" h...................$300
508 window box, 10-1/2"............$195
513, vase, 6-1/2" h.......................$125

Little Red Riding Hood
Creamer and sugar, side pour.....$400
Dresser or cracker jar..................$800
Lamp...$2,500

Hull, No. 414 Iris vase, 10-1/2", **$300.**

Salt and pepper shakers, pr, small..$120
Teapot, cov $395

Magnolia
3 vase, 8-1/2" h $125
9 vase, 10-1/2" h $200
14 pitcher, 4-3/4" h $75
20 floor vase, 15" $500

Open Rose/Camellia
106 pitcher, 13-1/2" h.................$650
119 vase, 8-1/2" h $175
127 vase, 4-3/4" h $75

Orchid
302 vase, 6" h $175
304 vase, 10-1/2" h $350
310 jardinière, 9-1/2" $450

Poppy
601 basket, 9" h...........................$800
610 pitcher, 13" $900
613 vase, 6-1/2" h $200

Rosella
R-2 vase, 5" h $35
R-6 vase, 6-1/2" h...........................$45
R-15 vase, 8-1/2" h $75

Tulip
101-33 vase, 9" h..........................$245
107-33 vase, 6" h..........................$125
109-33 pitcher, 8".........................$235

Waterlily
L-14, basket, 10-1/2" $350
L-16, vase, 12-1/2".......................$395

Wild Flower, No. Series
53 vase, 8-1/2" h $295
61 vase, 6-1/2" h $175
66 basket, 10-1/4" h...................$2,000
71 vase, 12" h $450

Woodland
W9 basket, 8-3/4" h......................$245
W11 flower pot and saucer, 5-1/2"..$175
W13 wall pocket, shell, 7-1/2" l...$195
W14 window box, 10-1/2" $200

Post 1950

Blossom Flite
T4 basket, 8-1/2" h $125
T13 pitcher, 12-1/2" h $150

Butterfly
B9 vase, 9" h $55
B13 basket, 8" h $150
B15 pitcher, 13-1/2" h $200

Continental
C29 vase, 12" h...............................$95
C55 basket, 12-1/2" $150
C62 candy dish, 8-1/4" $45

Ebb Tide
E-1 bud vase, 7" h $75
E-8 ashtray with mermaid $225
E-10 pitcher, 13" h $275

Parchment and Pine
S-3 basket, 6" h $95
S-11 and S-12 tea set $250
S-15 coffeepot, 8" h $175

Serenade
S1 vase, 6" h $55
S-15 fruit bowl, ftd, 11-1/2" d.....$125
S17 teapot, creamer and sugar ...$275

Sunglow
53 grease jar $60
82 wall pocket, whisk broom.........$75
85 vase, bird, 8-3/4" h $60

Tokay/Tuscany
3 pitcher, 8" h $95
8 vase, 10" h $150
10 cornucopia, 11" l........................$65

Tropicana
T53 vase, 8-1/2" h.........................$550
T55, basket, 12-3/4" h $750

Woodland (glossy)
W1 vase, 5-1/2" h $45
W15 vase, double, 8-1/2" h............$75
W19 console bowl, 14" d..............$100

Hull, C60 Continental vase, 15", **$90.**

Hull, No. 62 twin deer vase, 11-1/2" x 6-1/2", **$45.**

Hull, C87 Capri 12" ewer, **$125.**

Hull, F482 Imperial fish gurgling ewer, 11", **$90.**

Hull, No. 216 Granada vase, 9", **$65.**

Hull, No. 47 Mardi Gras vase. 9", **$90.**

Hum No. 6, Sensitive Hunter, **$170-$2,000.**

Hum No. 7, Merry Wanderer, **$330-$25,750.**

Hum No., 8 Book Worm, **$255-$850.**

HUMMEL ITEMS

History: Hummel items are the original creations of Berta Hummel, who was born in 1909 in Massing, Bavaria, Germany. At age 18, she was enrolled in the Academy of Fine Arts in Munich to further her mastery of drawing and the palette.

Berta entered the Convent of Siessen and became Sister Maria Innocentia in 1934. In this Franciscan cloister, she continued drawing and painting images of her childhood friends.

In 1935, W. Goebel Co. in Rodental, Germany, began producing Sister Maria Innocentia's sketches as three-dimensional bisque figurines. The Schmid Brothers of Randolph, Massachusetts, introduced the figurines to America and became Goebel's U.S. distributor.

In 1967, Goebel began distributing Hummel items in the U.S.A. Controversy developed between the two companies, the Hummel family, and the convent. Lawsuits and counter-suits ensued. The German courts finally effected a compromise: the convent held legal rights to all works produced by Sister Maria Innocentia from 1934 until her death in 1946 and licensed Goebel to reproduce these works; Schmid was to deal directly with the Hummel family for permission to reproduce any pre-convent art.

Marks: All authentic Hummel pieces bear both the signature "M. I. Hummel" and a Goebel trademark. Various trademarks were used to identify the year of production. For purposes of simplification the various trademarks have been abbreviated in the following list. Should you encounter any trouble interpreting the abbreviations, refer to the list below.

Trademark	Abbreviations	Dates
Crown	TMK-1	1934-1950
Full Bee	TMK-2	1940-1959
Stylized Bee	TMK-3	1958-1972
Three Line Mark	TMK-4	1964-1972
Last Bee	TMK-5	1972-1979
Missing Bee	TMK-6	1979-1991
Hummel Mark	TMK-7	1991-1999
Millennium Bee (Current)	TMK-8	2000-present

Additional Listings: See *Warman's Americana & Collectibles* for more examples.

Note: The first seventeen Hummels made are highly prized by collectors. We have included the first six to ten in this book with listings for all of the known marks.

All photos appear courtesy of Goebel of North America unless otherwise indicated.

The First Seventeen, Numbers Six to Ten

Hum 6: Sensitive Hunter
6/2/0, 4"
TMK-6	**$175-$180**
TMK-7	**$170-$175**
6, TMK-1, 4-3/4"	**$850-$1,000**

6/0, 4-3/4"
TMK-1	**$650-$800**
TMK-2	**$400-$500**

TMK-3	**$325-$350**
TMK-4	**$300-$325**
TMK-5	**$275-$300**
TMK-6	**$250-$275**
TMK-7	**$245-$250**
TMK-8	**$240**

6/I, 5-1/2"
TMK-1	**$850-$1,000**
TMK-2	**$500-$600**
TMK-3	**$375-$425**

TMK-4.............................$350-$375
TMK-5.............................$325-$350
TMK-6.............................$300-$325
6/II, 7-1/2"
TMK-1........................$1,500-$2,000
TMK-2.........................$955-$1,255
TMK-3...........................$550-$650
TMK-4...........................$475-$550
TMK-5...........................$425-$475
TMK-6...........................$350-$425
Hum 7: Merry Wanderer
7/0, 6-1/4"
TMK-1........................$750-$1000
TMK-2...........................$475-$650
TMK-3...........................$430-$455
TMK-4...........................$375-$410
TMK-5...........................$350-$370
TMK-6...........................$335-$340
TMK-7...........................$330-$335
TMK-8..................................$330
7/I, 7"
TMK-1......................$1,510-$1,750
  (double step base)
TMK-2......................$1,310-$1,500
  (double step base)
TMK-3......................$1,210-$1,300
  (double step base)
TMK-3...........................$600-$750
  (plain base)
TMK-4...........................$500-$600
TMK-5...........................$475-$500
TMK-6...........................$450-$475
TMK-7...........................$425-$450
7/II, 9-1/2"
TMK-1......................$3,000-$3,500
TMK-2......................$1,900-$2,750
TMK-3......................$1,700-$1,800
TMK-4......................$1,500-$1,700
TMK-5......................$1,250-$1,275
TMK-6......................$1,225-$1,250
TMK-7......................$1,200-$1,225
7/III, 11-1/4"
TMK-1......................$3,300-$4,000
TMK-2......................$2,500-$3,000
TMK-3......................$1,700-$2,000
TMK-4......................$1,400-$1,500
TMK-5......................$1,300-$1,350
TMK-6......................$1,250-$1,300
7/X, 32"
TMK-5....................$20,000-$25,750
TMK-6....................$15,000-$25,750
TMK-7....................$15,000-$25,750
TMK-8....................$15,000-$25,750
Hum 8: Book Worm
8, 4"
TMK-1...........................$700-$850
TMK-2...........................$425-$500
TMK-3...........................$350-$400
TMK-4...........................$325-$350
TMK-5...........................$290-$300
TMK-6...........................$270-$290

TMK-7.............................$255-$260
TMK-8..................................$255
Hum 9: Begging His Share
9, 5-1/2"
TMK-1...........................$750-$900
TMK-2...........................$450-$600
TMK-3, (hole)..................$400-$450
TMK-3, (without hole)......$350-$400
TMK-4...........................$325-$350
TMK-5...........................$300-$325
TMK-6...........................$290-$300
TMK-7...........................$280-$290
Hum 10: Flower Madonna
10/I, white, 9-1/2"
TMK-1...........................$500-$600
TMK-2...........................$300-$475
10/I, white, 8-1/4"
TMK-3...........................$275-$300
TMK-5...........................$230-$255
10/I, color, 9-1/2"
TMK-1...........................$800-$950
TMK-2...........................$700-$800
10/I, color, 8-1/4"
TMK-3...........................$575-$675
TMK-5...........................$500-$525
TMK-6...........................$475-$500
10/III, white, 13"
TMK-1...........................$450-$750
TMK-2, open halo.........$450-$650
TMK-2, closed halo........$450-$650
10/III white, 11-1/2"
TMK-3...........................$400-$470
TMK-5...........................$325-$350
TMK-6...........................$300-$325
10/III color, 13"
TMK-2, open halo.........$800-$900
TMK-2, closed halo........$800-$900
TMK-3...........................$600-$650
TMK-5...........................$525-$550
TMK-6...........................$500-$525

Bell, Annual
Anniversary Bell, Hum 730, 1985
............................$1,500-$2,000
Busy Student, Hum 710, 1988....$58
Farewell, Hum 701, 1979.............$25
Favorite Pet, Hum 713, 1991.......$58
Festival Harmony With Flute, Hum 781, 1995 ....$35
In Tune, Hum 703, 1981.............$38
Knit One, Hum 705, 1983.............$35
Latest News, Hum 711, 1989......$58
Let's Sing, Hum 700, 1978..........$38
Mountaineer, Hum 706, 1984 ....$35
She Loves Me, Hum 704, 1982....$35
Sing Along, Hum 708, 1986.........$58
Sweet Song, Hum 707, 1985.......$35
Thoughtful, Hum 702, 1980........$25
What's New?, Hum 712, 1990......$58
Whistler's Duet, Hum 714, 1992
....$58

With Loving Greetings, Hum 709, 1987 ....$58

Bell, Christmas
Angel With Flute, 1972.............$45
Angelic Gifts, 1987...................$48
Angelic Messenger, 1983.........$58
Angelic Procession, 1982...........$45
Cheerful Cherubs, 1988.............$53
Echoes Of Joy, Hum 784, 1998....$28
Gift From Heaven, 1984.............$45
Herald Angel, 1977...................$45
Nativity, 1973..........................$45
Parade Into Toyland, 1980.........$45
Sacred Journey, 1976................$45
Starlight Angel, 1979 ....$47

Cottages, Bavarian Village
Angel's Duet, 1996 ....$50
Bench & Pine Tree, **The/Set**, 1996
....$25
Christmas Mail, 1996................$50
Company's Coming, 1996...........$50
Sled & Pine Tree, **The/Set**, 1996
....$25
Village Bridge, **The**, 1996 ....$25
Winter's Comfort, 1996.............$50
Wishing Well, **The**, 1996 ....$25

Dolls and Plush
Anderl 1718.............................$150
Birthday Serenade/Boy, 1984
....$275
Birthday Serenade/Girl, 1984
....$275
Brieftrager 1720......................$175
Carnival, 1985...........................$275
Christl 1715.............................$150
Easter Greetings, 1985.............$275
Felix 1608.................................$175
Felix 1708.................................$175
Gretel 1501..............................$200
Gretel 1901, 1964.....................$160
Hansel 1504.............................$200
Hansel 1604.............................$175
Konditor 1723..........................$175
Lost Stocking 1926, 1964.........$125
Mariandl 1713..........................$150
Max 1506.................................$200
Merry Wanderer 1906, 1964....$125
On Secret Path 1928, 1964........$85
Peterle 1710.............................$150
School Boy 1910, 1964 ....$130
School Girl 1909, 1964 ....$130
Skihaserl 1722.........................$175
Valentine Gift Doll, Hum 524
....$200-$250
Visiting An Invalid 1927, 1964
....$130
Wanderbub 1507......................$200

Figurine, M.I. Hummel

Due to space constraints, a range of pricing has been provided. Please consult the 12th edition of *Luckey's Hummel® Figurines & Plates Identification and Price Guide* for individual pricing based upon trademark variations.

Accompanist, The, Hum 453, 1988 ....$140

Accordion Boy, Hum 185, 1947 ....$200-$750

Adoration With Bird, Hum 105, 1938 ....$7,000-$8,000

Angel Duet, Hum 261, 1968 ....$270-$850

Angel Lights, Candleholder, Hum 241 ....$300-$500

Angel With Accordion, Hum 238 B, 1967 ....$73-$125

Angel With Lute, Hum 238 A, 1967 ....$73-$125

Angel With Trumpet, Hum 238 C, 1967 ....$73-$125

Angel/Accordion, Candleholder, Hum 1/39/0 ....$80-$200

Angel/Accordion, Candleholder, Hum 111/39/0 ....$60-$200

Angel/Accordion, Candleholder, Hum 111/39/1 ....$200-$350

Angel/Lute, Candleholder, Hum 111/38/1 ....$200-$350

Angel/Trumpet, Candleholder, Hum 1/40/0 ....$73-$200

Angel/Trumpet, Candleholder, Hum 111/40/0 ....$60-$200

Angel/Trumpet, Candleholder, Hum 111/40/1 ....$200-$350

Angelic Conductor, Hum 2096/A, 2002 ....$135

Apple Tree Boy, Hum 142... $650-$950

Apple Tree Boy, Hum 142/3/0 ....$180-$550

Apple Tree Boy, Hum 142/I ....$350-$800

Apple Tree Boy, Candleholder, Hum 677 ....$200-$250

Apple Tree Boy/Girl-Bookends, Hum 252 A&B ....$300-$425

Apple Tree Girl, Hum 141 ...$650-$950

Apple Tree Girl, Hum 141/3/0 ....$180-$550

Apple Tree Girl, Candleholder, Hum 676 ....$200-$250

Ba-Bee-Ring, Hum 30/0 A&B ....$245-$700

Band Leader, Hum 129/4/0 ....$125-$140

Barnyard Hero, Hum 195/2/0 ....$205-$450

Barnyard Hero, Hum 195/I ....$350-$700

Chimney Sweep, Hum 12 $425-$800

Chimney Sweep, Hum 12/2/0 ....$145-$325

Christ Child, Hum 18 .... $165-$550

Christmas Gift, 1999 ....$95

Christmas Song, Hum 343/4/0, 1996 ....$135

Come Back Soon, Hum 545, 1995 ....$180-$500

Congratulations, Hum 17/0 ....$230-$750

Coquettes, Hum 179, 1948 ....$325-$1,100

Culprits, Hum 56 .... $900-$1,100

Culprits, Hum 56 A .... $365-$650

Dearly Beloved, Hum 2003, 1999 ....$200-$520

Delicious, Hum 435/3/0..... $170-$175

Doll Mother, Hum 67 .... $257-$900

Duet, Hum 130 .... $300-$1,000

Evening Prayer, Hum 495, 1991.. $135

Eventide (Rare), Hum 99 ....$3,000-$3,500

Eventide, Hum 99 .... $360-$1,250

Farewell, Hum 65............ $275-$1,000

Farewell, Hum 65/I .... $325-$1,000

Farewell, Hum 65/0 ..... $5,000-$8,000

Farm Boy, Hum 66............ $270-$900

Farm Boy/Goose Girl Bookends, Hum 60 A&B .... $400-$1,250

Favorite Pet, Hum 361 .. $335-$5,000

Feeding Time, Hum 199 ....$525-$1,000

Feeding Time, Hum 199/I.. $315-$575

Feeding Time, Hum 199/0 $250-$500

Festival Harmony (Flute), Hum 173/0 ....$350-$650

Festival Harmony (Mandolin), Hum 172 ....$1,000-$3,500

Festival Harmony (Mandolin), Hum 172/4/0 ....$135

Festival Harmony (Mandolin), Hum 172/II ....$450-$800

Festival Harmony (Mandolin), Hum 172/0 ....$350-$650

Flying Angel, Hum 366 .... $150-$275

Flying High, Hum 452, 1984 ....$175-$300

Follow The Leader, Hum 369 ....$1,390-$5,000

For Father, Hum 87 .... $270-$800

Forest Shrine, Hum 183 .. $595-$1,900

Free Flight, Hum 569, 1993 ....$215

Friend Or Foe, Hum 434, 1991 .. $275

Friends, Hum 136/I .... $240-$950

Girl With Doll, Hum 239B ....$73-$200

Girl With Nosegay, Hum 239A ....$73-$200

Girl With Sheet Of Music, Hum 389 ....$110-$275

Girl With Trumpet, Hum 391 ....$110-$275

Globe Trotter, Hum 79..... $200-$750

Going To Grandma's, Hum 52 ....$850-$1,600

Good Friends, Hum 182 ....$250-$750

Good Hunting, Hum 307 ....$300-$5,000

Goose Girl, Hum 47, 1996 ....$205-$1,300

Goose Girl, Hum 47........... $800-$900

Grandma's Girl, Hum 561, 1990 ....$185

Grandpa's Boy, Hum 562, 1990 ....$185

Guardian, The, Hum 455, 1991... $205

Guiding Angel, Hum 357 ....$110-$150

Happiness, Hum 86 .... $170-$500

Happy Days, Hum 150 ... $900-$1,600

Happy Days, Hum 150/2/0... $210-$400

Happy Pastime, Hum 69.. $190-$650

Happy Traveller, Hum 109/II ....$375-$900

Happy Traveller, Hum 109/0 ....$185-$350

Hear Ye, Hear Ye, Hum 15/2/0 ....$185-$190

Hear Ye, Hear Ye, Hum 15/I ....$280-$900

Hear Ye, Hear Ye, Hum 15/II ....$450-$1,500

Hear Ye, Hear Ye, Hum 15/0 ....$230-$750

Heavenly Angel, Hum 21/I ....$320-$1,000

Heavenly Angel, Hum 21/0 ....$160-$500

Heavenly Angel, Hum 21/0 1/2 ....$270-$850

Heavenly Lullaby, Hum 262 ....$270-$850

Hello, Hum 124 .... $450-$1,000

Hello, Hum 124/I .... $275-$1,000

Holy Water Font, Angel Cloud, Hum 206 ....$60-$500

Holy Water Font, Angel Duet, Hum 146 ....$60-$225

Holy Water Font, Angel Joyous News, Hum 241, 1955 .... $1,500-$2,000

Holy Water Font, Angel Joyous News, Hum 242, 1955 .... $1,500-$2,000

Holy Water Font, Angel Shrine, Hum 147 ....$68-$275

Holy Water Font, Angel Sitting, Hum 22 ....$68-$300

Home From Market, Hum 198 ....$375-$800

Home From Market, Hum 198/2/0 ....$190-$375

Home From Market, Hum 198/I ..... $240-$500

Horse Trainer, Hum 423, 1990 ..... $268-$280

Hosanna, Hum 480, 1989 ..... $140

I'll Protect Him, Hum 483, 1989 ..... $115

I'm Carefree, Hum 633, 1994 ..... $440-$1,000

I'm Here, Hum 478, 1989 ..... $145

In D Major, Hum 430, 1989 ..... $255

In The Meadow, Hum 459, 1987 ..... $255

Joyful, Hum 53 ..... $140-$450

Joyous News, Hum 27/3 ... $280-$2,000

Joyous News, Hum 27/I ... $250-$500

Joyous News, Hum 27/III $253

Jubilee, Hum 416, 1985 ..... $500-$600

Just Dozing, Hum 451, 1984 ..... $265

Just Resting, Hum 112 ... $700-$850

Just Resting, Hum 112/3/0 ..... $185 $550

Just Resting, Hum 112/I... $320-$800

Kindergartner, Hum 467, 1987... $255

Knit One, Purl One , Hum 432, 1983 ..... $160

Knitting Lesson, Hum 256 ..... $535-$1,150

Latest News, Hum 184 ..... $360-$1,100

Let's Play, Hum 2051/B, 1999 ..... $95

Let's Sing, Hum 110 ..... $325-$600

Let's Sing, Hum 110/0 ..... $160-$500

Letter To Santa Claus Prototype, Hum 340, 1956 ..... $15,000-$20,000

Letter To Santa, Hum 340 ..... $400-$1,000

Little Architect, The, Hum 410, 1978 ..... $3,000-$4,000

Little Band (On Base), Hum 392 ..... $275-$450

Little Bookkeeper, Hum 306 ..... $335-$1,500

Little Cellist, Hum 89 ... $1,250-$1,600

Little Cellist, Hum 89/I... $270-$850

Little Cellist, Hum 89/II... $450-$1,500

Little Fiddler, Hum 2/4/0 ... $130-$140

Little Fiddler, Hum 2/I ... $415-$1,500

Little Fiddler, Hum 2/II ..... $1,110-$3,500

Little Fiddler, Hum 2/III ..... $1,205-$4,000

Little Fiddler, Hum 2/0 ..... $325-$850

Little Gabriel, Hum 32, 1935 ..... $2,000-$2,500

Little Goat Herder, Hum 200 ..... $500-$850

Little Goat Herder, Hum 200/I ..... $270-$550

Little Hiker, Hum 16 ..... $450-$750

Little Hiker, Hum 16/I ..... $245-$700

Little Sweeper, Hum 171/4/0 .... $130

Little Sweeper, Hum 171/0 ..... $185

Little Tailor, Hum 308 ..... $305-$350

Little Thrifty, Bank, Hum 118 ..... $185-$650

Lost Sheep, Hum 68 ..... $350-$750

Lost Sheep, Hum 68/2/0 ... $160-$350

Lost Sheep, Hum 68/0 ..... $200-$450

Lost Stocking, Hum 374 . $185-$1,500

Madonna Holding Child, Hum 151, 1955 ..... $9,000-$12,000

March Winds, Hum 43 ..... $180-$600

Meditation, Hum 13 .. $4,000-$5,000

Message Of Love, Hum 2050/A, 1999 ..... $95

Mischief Maker, Hum 342 ..... $320-$1,000

Mountaineer, Hum 315 .. $250-$1,000

Old Man Reading Newspaper, Hum 181, 1948 ..... $15,000-$20,000

Old Woman Walking To Market, Hum 190, 1918 ... $15,000-$20,000

Ooh, My Tooth, Hum 533, 1995 ..... $145

Out Of Danger, Hum 56 B .. $345-$650

Out Of Danger, Table Lamp, Hum 44 B ..... $325-$650

Photographer, Hum 178 .. $335-$1,100

Pixie, Hum 768, 1995 ..... $145

Playmates, Hum 58 ..... $500-$1,050

Playmates, Hum 58/2/0 ... $185-$200

Postman, Hum 119/2/0 ..... $185

Postman, Hum 119/0 ..... $250

Puppy Love, Hum 1 ..... $305-$1,000

Ring Around The Rosie, Hum 348, 1957 ..... $3,200-$5,000

Run-A-Way, Hum 327 ..... $310-$325

Saint George, Hum 55 .. $350-$3,000

School Boy, Hum 82 ..... $625-$775

School Boy, Hum 82/2/0... $170-$600

School Boy, Hum 82/II .. $500-$1,600

School Boy, Hum 82/0 ..... $235-$775

School Girl, Hum 81 ..... $350-$750

School Girl, Hum 81/0 ..... $225-$700

Sensitive Hunter, Hum 6/2/0 ..... $170-$180

Sensitive Hunter, Hum 6/0 ..... $250-$800

Seraphim Soprano, Hum 2096/R, 2002 ..... $135

Serenade, Hum 85 ..... $775-$1,550

Serenade, Hum 85/4/0 ..... $130

Serenade, Hum 85/II ..... $500-$1,500

Serenade, Hum 85/0 ..... $160-$500

Shepherd Boy, Hum 395, 1996 ..... $280-$315

Shepherd's Boy, Hum 64 ..... $330-$900

Sing Along, Hum 433, 1987 ..... $330

Sing With Me, Hum 405, 1985 ..... $360-$4,000

Sister, Hum 98 ..... $325-$700

Sister, Hum 98/2/0 ..... $180-$250

Sister, Hum 98/0 ..... $230-$325

Soloist, Hum 135/4/0 ..... $135

Soloist, Hum 135/0 ..... $175

Spring Cheer, Hum 72 ..... $200-$650

Standing Boy, Plaque, Hum 168 ..... $200-$1,100

Standing Madonna With Child, Hum 247, 1955 ... $10,000-$15,000

Star Gazer, Hum 132 ..... $258-$800

Stitch In Time, Hum 255 ..... $325-$800

Stitch In Time, Hum 255/4/0 ..... $115-$140

Teacher's Pet, Hum 2125, 2002 ..... $175

Telling Her Secret, Hum 196 ..... $800-$1,500

To Market, Hum 49/3/0 ... $195-$650

Trumpet Boy, Hum 97 ..... $150-$525

Village Boy, Hum 51 ..... $900-$1,150

Wash Day, Hum 321 ..... $275-$1,000

Wash Day, Hum 321/I ..... $355-$365

Watchful Angel, Hum 194 ..... $385-$2,100

With Loving Greetings, Hum 309, 1983 ..... $220-$5,000

Wonder Of Christmas, Hum 2015 With Steiff Bear, 1999 ..... $575

Worship, Hum 84 ..... $475-$1,500

Hum No. 71/2/0 Stormy Weather, **$365-$380.**

Hum No. 9, Begging His Share, **$280-$900.**

Hum No. 10, Flower Madonna, **$230-$950.**

Hum No. 56/A Culprits, **$365-$650.**

Hummel, The Village Bakery, **$50.**

Hum No. 57/2/0 Chick Girl, **$185-$200.**

Hum No. 58/2/0 Playmates, **$185-$200.**

Hum No. 186 Sweet Music, **$250-$750.**

Hum No. 74 Little Gardener, **$150-$550.**

Hum No. 123 Max and Moritz, **$270-$800.**

Hum No. 127 Doctor, **$190-$650.**

Hum No. 131 Street Singer, **$245-$700.**

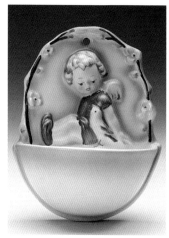

Hum No. 167 Holy Water Font, Angel With Bird, **$300-$325.**

Hum No. 170, The School Boys, stylized bee mark, 9-1/2" x 7-1/4", **$700.**
Photo courtesy of David Rago Auctions, Inc.

Hum No. 176/0 Happy Birthday, **$280-$500.**

Hum No. 152/A/0 Umbrella Boy, **$300.**

Hum No. 196 Telling Her Secret, **$800-$1,500.**

Hum No. 240, Little Drummer, **$185-$400.**

Hum No. 261, Angel Duet, **$270-$850.**

Hum No. 257/0, For Mother, **$255.**

Hum No. 311 Kiss Me, **$335-$550.**

Hum No. 355 Autumn Harvest, **$250-$3,000.**

Hum No. 364 Supreme Protection, **$3,000-$4,000.**

Hum No. 375/3/0 Morning Stroll, **$215.**

Hum No. 524 Valentine Gift Doll, **$200-$250.**

Hum No. 775 Christmas Bell 1989, **$28.**

Hum No. 776 Christmas Bell 1990, **$28.**

Hum No. 348, Ring Around the Rosey, stylized bee mark, 7-1/4" h, **$750.**

Photo courtesy of David Rago Auctions, Inc.

IMARI

History: Imari derives its name from a Japanese port city. Although Imari ware was manufactured in the 17th century, the pieces most commonly encountered are those made between 1770 and 1900.

Early Imari was decorated simply, quite unlike the later heavily decorated brocade pattern commonly associated with Imari. Most of the decorative patterns are an underglaze blue and overglaze "seal wax" red complimented by turquoise and yellow.

The Chinese copied Imari ware. The Japanese examples can be identified by grayer clay, thicker glaze, runny and darker blue, and deep red opaque hues.

The pattern and colors of Imari inspired many English and European potteries, such as Derby and Meissen, to adopt a similar style of decoration for their wares.

Imari porcelain charger, Japanese, floral decoration, Edo period, 13-1/4" d, **$1,770.**
Photo courtesy of Sloans & Kenyon Auctioneers and Appraisers.

Imari charger, Chinese, porcelain, floral decoration, Kangxi period, c1710, 11" d, **$1,120.**
Photo courtesy of Sloans & Kenyon Auctioneers and Appraisers.

Reproduction Alert. Reproductions abound, and many manufacturers continue to produce pieces in the traditional style.

Bottle vases, lobated form, underglaze blue with red, green, aubergine enamels and gilt, Japan, price for pr, late 19th C, 11" h **$775**

Bowl
Designs of dragons and auspicious emblems, set of 12, 19th C, 6" d **$400**
Gilt floral scrolling, heraldic emblems surrounding central dragon, six-character mark on base, 19th C, 13-3/4" d **$560**
Sq form with ribs, design of various flowers, Wan Li six-character mark on base, 19th C, 9" w ... **$120**

Charger
Fans with warriors and dragons dec, sgd "Koransha," late 19th C, 22" d **$1,645**
Hp, cinnabar red, underglaze dark blue, green and gilt, dragons in clouds circle border, leaves and clouds below, two phoenixes in center, ext. cov with blossoming vines, center base with cinnabar and gilt flower, glued repair to edge, gilt imperfections, 20-1/4" d, 4-3/4" h **$715**
Underglaze blue and enamel dec, central reserve of planter with flowers, grape and brocade borders, Japan, late 19th/early 20th C, 14-1/2" d........................... **$250**

Creamer and sugar, ovoid, dragon form handles, gilt and bright enamels, shaped reserves, dragon-like beasts, stylized animal medallions, brocade ground, high dome lid, knob, cipher mark of Mount Fuji, Fukagama Studio marks, Meiji period, 5-1/2" h creamer, 5-7/8" cov sugar **$500**

Dish
Central scene with fence and flowering tree dec, shaped cartouches enclosing flowers and hares on crackle blue ground at rim, gilt highlights, Meiji period, price for pr, 8-3/8" d **$650**
Gourd shape, flowering tree with checkered design in foreground, brown glaze on rim, underside with underglaze blue tendrils, Fuku mark on base, Japanese, pr, one with rim chip, 18th C, 6-3/4" l **$1,650**

Food box, three-section, ext. and lid with phoenix and floral design, underglaze blue, iron-red and gilt enamels, 19th C, 6" h.............. **$400**

Jar, cov, ribbed forms with shishi finials, Japan, price for pr, late 19th C, 26" h...................... **$2,000**

Jardinière, hexagonal, bulbous, short flared foot, alternating bijin figures and immortal symbols, stylized ground, 10" h............ **$250**

Luncheon set, partial, 12 8" d plates, four 10-1/4" oblong serving dishes, two boat-shaped serving dishes, sq serving dish, coffee can, Spode, 20 pcs, 19th C **$2,820**

Planter and stand, lobed form, floral dec, brocade patterns, Japan, late 19th C, 17" d, 43" h.......... **$460**

Plate
Brocade pattern, set of nine, 19th C, 9" d........................... **$470**
Reserves of dragons and flowers arranged around phoenix roundel, Japan, set of nine, 19th C, 8-1/2" d................................. **$470**

Sq, scalloped edge, central design of basket of flowers, 19th C, 17-1/4"............................... **$1,765**

Platter, alternating panels of figures and foliage, trellis work ground, Japanese, late 19th C, 18" d.... **$475**

Punch bowl, rubbed, c1870, 12" d **$1,650**

Teabowl and saucer, floriform, floral spray dec, gilt highlights on saucer, 5" d.............................. **$200**

Tea set, 6-1/8" h teapot; teapot stand; creamer; cov sugar; 8-1/4" d serving plate; two 7-3/4" d serving plates; two 6" d bowls; 16 5-3/8" d saucers; 11 coffee cans, 12 teacups, English, 48 pcs, early 19th C **$2,235**

Umbrella stand, allover hexagonal panels with gold pheasants and orange drawings, flowers and plants, orange, tomato red, yellow, green and cobalt blue, old shield shaped "U.S. Customs" label underneath, 25" h **$550**

Urn, tomato red, light green, mauve, and cobalt blue, dark gold details, floral panels on sides with pheasants and cranes, geometric band of dec around base, minor roughness around rim, 36-1/2" h **$2,100**

Vase, baluster, late Meiji period, c1900, 14-1/2" h **$775**

KPM plaque, hand painted, robed girl with sprig of flowers, raised gilt dec, titled "Carers Garland," signed lower right and stamped on reverse "Made in Germany," framed, 3-1/2" x 2-1/2", **$900.**
Photo courtesy of David Rago Auctions, Inc.

KPM plaque, "Fm Reiche der Tone," by A. Lesrel, French nobleman playing violin, gilt frame, KPM mark and scepter, Dresden mark with lamb, 4-3/4" x 7-1/2", **$1,800.**
Photo courtesy of The Early Auction Company, LLC.

KPM plaque, 11" x 9" portrait of mother and child, gold gilt frame with reticulated leaves, stamped KPM with scepter mark, 17" x 1'4" overall, **$2,900.**
Photo courtesy of The Early Auction Company, LLC.

KPM

History: The "KPM" mark has been used separately and in conjunction with other symbols by many German porcelain manufacturers, among which are the Königliche Porzellan Manufactur in Meissen, 1720s; Königliche Porzellan Manufactur in Berlin, 1832-1847; and Krister Porzellan Manufactur in Waldenburg, mid-19th century.

Collectors now use the term KPM to refer to the high-quality porcelain produced in the Berlin area in the 18th and 19th centuries.

Cheese board, rose and leaf garland border, pierce for hanging, marked **$48**

Cup and saucer, hunting scene, filigree, 19th C **$65**

Dinner service, partial, basketweave molded rim, enamel painted sepiatoned floral sprays, 10 6-3/4" d side plates, nine 9-1/2" d dinner plates, eight 8-3/8" d salad plates, 12" l oval platter, 13-5/8" l oval platter, 8" oblong dish, late 19th/early 20th C, price for 30-pc set **$520**

Figure, young man with cocked hat, long coat, trousers, and boots, young lady in Empire-style dress, fancy hat and fan, white ground, brown details, gold trim, round base, blue underglaze KPM mark, price for pr, 8-1/2" h, 3-1/2" d **$350**

Perfume bottle, rococo-cartouche form, sepia enamel dec of cherub in flight, floral bouquet, gilt detailing, gilt-metal and coral mounted stopper, late 19th C, 3-5/8" l **$230**

KPM three vases, assorted glazes, all with indigo stamps and numbers, tallest (13" h) with post-factory drilled bottom, price for three, **$2,200.**
Photo courtesy of David Rago Auctions, Inc.

Plaque
Monk tasting wine, ornate frame, imp on verso KPM and specter mark, c1900, 9-1/2" x 6-1/2" **$1,840**
First Snowfall, grandfather with two grandchildren standing in doorway, snowy foreground, 21" w, 18" h elaborate carved wood frame of scrolling acanthus, imp scepter mark and "KPM," artist sgd lower right "F. X. Thallmaier Munchen," 7-1/2" w, 10" h **$4,370**
Ruth, after painting by Bouguereau, late 19th C, 12-3/4" l, 7-7/8" w **$2,300**
Sistine Madonna, after Raphael, finely dec, period gilt frame, verso imp with scepter mark and "KPM," 10" w, 12" h **$1,955**
Titled "Entflohen," two young beauties seated in windswept wood, diaphanous gowns, floral headbands, anthemion and quatrefoil border, irid teal ground, 22-1/4" d giltwood and gesso frame, 13-3/4" d **$10,925**
Young beauty facing right, sgd "Grenier" lower left, verso imp "K.P.M" with scepter, c1900, ornate 14-1/2" frame, 5" x 7" **$2,300**

Punch bowl, cov, domed lid, Dionysian putto figural finial, enamel dec on one side with 18th C wigged gentleman at a drunken meeting of punch society, similar scene of gentleman at table to one side, vignette of couple outside village on other, floral bouquets and sprigs, imp basketweave rim, gilt edging, underglaze blue mark, late 19th C, 12" d, 14-1/2" h **$2,775**

Teapot, oval, medallion with floral dec, gilt ground, 6" h **$95**

Vase, baluster, two handles, hp multicolored florals, celery green ground, 8-1/2" h.. **$200**

LEEDS CHINA

History: The Leeds Pottery in Yorkshire, England, began production about 1758. Among its products was creamware that was competitive with that of Wedgwood. The original factory closed in 1820, but various subsequent owners continued until 1880. They made exceptional cream-colored wares, either plain, salt glazed, or painted with colored enamels, and glazed and unglazed redware.

Marks: Early wares are unmarked. Later pieces are marked "Leeds Pottery," sometimes followed by "Hartley-Green and Co." or the letters "LP."

Reproduction Alert. Reproductions have the same marks as the antique pieces.

Bowl, pearlware, shallow, molded basketwork, pierced loop, rim edged in cobalt blue, 18th C, 8" d **$225**

Charger, yellow urn with double handles and brown swag design holds cobalt blue, brown and yellow flowers, green foliage, blue line detail surrounding dec, scalloped blue feather edge, in-the-making separation along inner edge, minor glaze flakes, 14-3/8" d **$1,870**

Chop plate, blue and yellow brown polychrome flowers, green foliage, white ground, blue scalloped feather edge, wear, old chip beneath rim, 11-1/4" d **$825**

Creamer, yellow, brown and green tulip, umber and green sprig design on sides, dark brown stripe on rim and applied handle, flakes on table ring **$800**

Cup and saucer, handleless
Blue, yellow, green and goldenrod floral design, underglaze blue brushed crescent mark **$220**
Brown rim stripes, blue, green, shades of gold, and yellow floral swag, flakes, chips on saucer table ring, stains on cup **$150**

Cup plate
Octagonal, green feathered edge, 4-1/4" d **$200**
Round, green feathered edge, 4" d **$150**

Dish, leaf form, green feathered edge, imp "Rogers," 5-3/4" l **$225**

Egg cup, creamware, reticulated, 2-3/4" **$150**

Medallion, set of 12, black basalt, assorted subjects, shapes and sizes, impressed marks, England, late 19th C, 1-3/4" x 2-5/8" d **$530**

Miniature
Creamer and sugar, blue flower, green and brown buds, tooled handle on 2-3/4" h creamer, minor flake on 2-1/2" h sugar **$350**
Cup and saucer, handleless, pearlware, gold flower, green and brown leaves **$275**
Teapot, cov, yellow bands with green, orange, blue and brown sprigs, flakes, 4" h **$450**

Mug, multicolored polychrome floral dec, 5" h **$250**

Mustard pot, cov, pearlware, cobalt blue bands, minor rim chips, 18th C, 3-3/8" h **$425**

Pepper pot, green feathered edge, roughness, loss on rim and near holes, 4-1/2" h **$200**

Plate
Green feathered edge, patterned design, 8" d **$225**
Pearlware, central floral spray surrounded by trailing vine, brown, ochre, green and blue, feathered blue scalloped edge, 18th C, 10" d **$275**

Platter
Oval, blue feathered edge, 17-1/4" x 14" **$1,600**
Elongated octagonal form, green-feathered edge, rim wear, 19" x 14-1/4" **$525**

Sauceboat, underplate, 7-1/2" l, 3-3/4" h sauce boat, 6-1/2" x 5-1/4" underplate, green feathered edge, small crack on base, minor edge roughness **$335**

Teapot, cov, creamware, intertwined ribbed handle, molded floral ends and flower finial, polychrome enameled rose, 4-3/4" h **$3,025**

Tureen, cov, cov with pierced rim, melon finial, enamel dec, feather edge trim, floral sprays and wreaths, urn designs, slight edge nicks and enamel flaking, late 18th C, 8-1/2" h **$980**

Waste bowl, blue band, green, gold, mustard and black leaves, minor flakes on table ring, 4-1/4" d, 3" h **$110**

Leeds pearlware pipe, seated woman with cat, early 19th century, 4-3/4" h, 6-3/4" l, **$935.**
Photo courtesy of Pook & Pook, Inc.

Leeds plate, green scalloped edge, blue and yellow flowers, brown and green leaves, 8-3/4" d, **$575.**
Photo courtesy of Pook & Pook, Inc.

Lenox Belleek vase, porcelain, egg-shaped body, slender neck, trumpet foot, painted gypsy girl with tambourine and harp, gilt strapwork with rose spray on neck and foot, early 20th century, 18-7/8" h, **$820.**
Photo courtesy of Skinner, Inc.

Limoges occupational shaving mug, fireman on a hook and ladder fire truck, inscribed "E.H. & L. No 1," and "Newton J. Buck," 3-1/2" h, **$878.**
Photo courtesy of Pook & Pook, Inc.

LENOX CHINA

History: In 1889, Jonathan Cox and Walter Scott Lenox established The Ceramic Art Co. at Trenton, New Jersey. By 1906, Lenox formed his own company, Lenox, Inc. Using potters lured from Belleek, Lenox began making an American version of the famous Irish ware. The firm is still in business.

Marks: Older Lenox china has one of two marks: a green wreath or a palette. The palette mark appears on blanks supplied to amateurs who hand painted china as a hobby. The Lenox company currently uses a gold stamped mark.

Bouillon cup and saucer, Detroit Yacht Club, palette mark **$85**
Candlesticks, pr, Holiday, pillar, 7-1/2" h **$140**
Chocolate set, cov chocolate pot, six cups and saucers, Golden Wheat pattern, cobalt blue ground, 13-pc set. **$275**
Coffeepot, Lenox Legend **$170**
Cream soup, Tuxedo, green mark **$40**
Cup and saucer, Alden **$25**
Dinner plate, Montclair, two platinum bands, set of four **$195**
Dinner service
  Golden Wreath, service for 20, serving pcs, 138 pcs **$650**
  Imperial pattern, 12 each dinner plates, salad plates, bread plates, cups, saucers, one platter **$275**
Gravy boat and underplate
  Biltmore Hotel, New York City, Gorham silver plated lid, base mkd "2047 Lexon 12 oz," lid mkd "The Biltmore 1917 Gorham 02702 Electroplate," 7-1/4" d, 4-3/4" h **$165**
  Tuscany, bird and scroll dec, gold rim **$260**
Honey pot, ivory beehive, gold bee and trim, underplate, 5" h, 6-1/4" d **$85**

Jug, hp, grapes and leaves, shaded brown ground, sgd "G. Morley," 4" h **$250**
Perfume lamp, figural, Marie Antoinette, bisque finish, dated 1929, 9" h **$650**
Platter
  Castle Garden, coupe shape, gold trim, small **$200**
  Plum Blossoms, medium **$240**
Salt, creamy ivory ground, molded seashells and coral, green wreath mark, 3" d **$35**
Server, Holiday, oval, 16" x 11" **$155**
Shoe, white, bow trim **$190**
Tankard set, 14-1/2" h tankard, four 5-1/2" h steins, hp by W. Clayton, tippling Monk draining vintage bottle on tankard, different monk posed on each stein, ornate handles, shaded green grounds, wear to gilt at rim interiors **$995**
Teapot, Weatherly, coupe shape, platinum trim **$215**
Vase, corset shape, pink orchids dec by William Morley, green stamp mark, artist sgd, 11-3/4" h, 4-1/2" d **$850**
Vegetable dish, cov, Lenox Legend **$260**

LIMOGES

History: Limoges porcelain has been produced in Limoges, France, for more than a century by numerous factories, in addition to the famed Haviland.

Marks: One of the most frequently encountered marks is "T. & V. Limoges," on the wares made by Tressman and Vought. Other identifiable Limoges marks are "A. L." (A. Lanternier), "J. P. L." (J. Pouyat, Limoges), "M. R." (M. Reddon), "Elite," and "Coronet."

Bowl, ftd, hp, wild roses and leaves, sgd "J. E. Dodge, 1892," 4-1/2" h .. **$85**
Box, cov, cobalt blue and white ground, cupids on lid, pate-sur-pate dec, 4-1/4" sq **$195**

Cache pot, male and female pheasants on front, mountain scene on obverse, gold handles and four ball feet, 7-1/2" w, 9" h **$225**

Cake plate, ivory ground, brushed gold scalloped rim, gold medallion, marked "Limoges T & V," 11-1/2" d **$75**

Candy dish, ftd, two handles, silver overlay, white ground, c1920, 6-1/2" d **$95**

Chocolate pot, purple violets and green leaves, cream-colored ground, gold handle, spout, and base, sgd "Kelly JPL/France," 13" h **$350**

Creamer and sugar, cov, purple flowers, white ground, gold handle and trim, 3-1/4" h **$100**

Cup and saucer, hp, roses, gold trim, artist sgd **$75**

Dessert plates, Laviolette, gilt scalloped rim, printed green husk trim, center violet and grape sprays, retailed by Lewis Straus & Sons, New York, price for 12-pc set, late 19th/early 20th C, 8-1/4" d **$220**

Dresser set, pink flowers, pastel blue, green, and yellow ground, large tray, cov powder, cov rouge, pin tray, talc jar, pr candlesticks, seven-pc set **$425**

Figure, three girls, arms entwined, holding basket of flowers, books and purse, marked "C & V" and "L & L," 25" h, 13" w **$460**

Fish service, 22-3/4" platter, ten 9-1/4" plates, sgd "A. R. Bullock 1894" .. **$1,555**

Hair receiver, blue flowers and white butterflies, ivory ground, gold trim, marked "JPL".................................... **$80**

Lemonade pitcher, matching tray, water lily dec, sgd "Vignard Limoges" **$350**

Nappy, curved gold handle, gold scalloped edges, soft pink blossoms, blue-green ground, 6" d **$35**

Oyster plate, molded, scalloped edge, gilt rim, enamel dec of poppy sprays, raised gilt detailing, marked "A. Lanternier & Co., Limoges," price for set of eight, early 20th C, 9-1/4" d...... **$1,500**

Panel, enameled, Christ with crown of thorns, framed, 4-1/2" x 3-3/8" .. **$250**

Pitcher, platinum handle, platinum mistletoe berries and leaves, gray and pink ground, Art Deco style, marked "J. P. Limoges, Pouyat," 6" h, 5-1/8" d .. **$155**

Plaque, enameled, cavalier, after Meissonier, multicolored garb and banner, late 19th C, 7-5/8" x 4-1/2" **$460**

Plate
    Cavalier smoking pipe, marked "Coronet," 9-1/2" d **$90**
    Transfer scene of peacocks and flowers, hp border, 8" d **$290**

Punch bowl, hand painted grapes, marked "T & V Limoges France Depose," minor repairs, 14" d **$320**

Snuff box, cov, hp, wildflowers and gold tracery, pink ground, artist sgd, dated 1800 .... **$200**

Tankard set, five-pc set, hp, grape dec, gold and green ground, 14" h tankard, four mugs **$450**

Tea set, 9-1/2" h cov teapot, two 3" h cups, two 4-1/2" d saucers, 15" d tray, cream ground, floral dec, gold trim, red stamp "L. S. & S. Limoges France," green stamp "Limoges France" on two saucers, slight wear **$500**

Vase, hand painted, sgd "Florence Sladnick," 15" h **$350**

*Limoges punch bowl, grapes and leaves decoration, separate stand with four lion paw feet, 14-3/4" d, 9-3/4" h, **$700**.*

Photo courtesy of Joy Luke Auctions.

*Limoges vase, baluster form, enamel on copper, foil under iridescent glaze graduating from pale pink at neck to dark burgundy at foot, random splotches of yellow on shoulders, glaze on neck and shoulders rough with raised smooth globules giving effect of ice, foot signed "C. Faure, Limoges," restoration to edge of foot, 6" h, **$250**.*

Photo courtesy of Alderfer Auction Co.

*Limoges plaque, stag with hounds, gilt rim, green overglaze Flambeau mark, early 20th century, 9-3/4" d, **$110**.*

Photo courtesy of Green Valley Auctions.

LITHOPHANES

History: Lithophanes are highly translucent porcelain panels with impressed designs. The designs result from differences in the thickness of the plaque; thin parts transmit an abundance of light, while thicker parts represent shadows.

Lithophanes were first made by the Royal Berlin Porcelain Works in 1828. Other factories in Germany, France, and England later produced them. The majority of lithophanes on the market today were made between 1850 and 1900.

Candle shield, panel with scene of two country boys playing with goat, castle in background, 9" h **$275**

Fairy lamp, three panels, lady leaning out of tower, rural romantic scenes, 9" h **$1,250**

Lamp, colored umbrella style shade, four panels of outdoor Victorian scenes, bronze and slate standard, German, 20-3/4" h **$675**

Night lamp, sq, four scenes, irid green porcelain base, gold trim, electrified, 5-1/4" h **$650**

Panel
PPM, view of Paterson Falls, 3-1/4" x 5-1/4" **$190**
PR Sickle, scene of two women in doorway, dog, and two pigeons, sgd, #1320, 4-1/4" x 5" **$100**

Unmarked, Madonna and Child, 6" x 7-1/2" **$175**

Pitcher, puzzle type, Victorian scene, nude on bottom **$175**

Stein, regimental, half liter **$200**

Tea warmer, one-pc cylindrical panel, four seasonal landscapes with children, copper frame, finger grip and molded base, 5-7/8" h **$250**

LIVERPOOL CHINA

History: Liverpool is the name given to products made at several potteries in Liverpool, England, between 1750 and 1840. Seth and James Pennington and Richard Chaffers were among the early potters who made tin-enameled earthenware.

By the 1780s, tin-glazed earthenware gave way to cream-colored wares decorated with cobalt blue, enameled colors, and blue or black transfers.

Bubbles and frequent clouding under the foot rims characterize the Liverpool glaze. By 1800, about 80 potteries were working in the town producing not only creamware, but soft paste, soapstone and bone porcelain.

A transfer of the *Caroline* also was used on a Sunderland bowl about 1936 and reproduction mugs were made bearing the name "James Leech" and an eagle.

The reproduction pieces have a crackled glaze and often age cracks have been artificially produced. When compared to genuine pieces, reproductions are thicker and heavier and have weaker transfers, grayish color (not as crisp and black), ecru or gray body color instead of cream, and crazing that does not spiral upward.

Reproduction Alert. Reproduction Liverpool pieces date back to a black transfer-decorated jug made in the 1930s. The jugs vary in height from 8-1/2 to 11 inches. On one side is "The Shipwright's Arms"; on the other, the ship Caroline flying the American flag; and under the spout, a wreath with the words "James Leech."

Bowl, creamware
Black transfer printed, polychrome enamel dec, int. with American sailing vessel *Apollo*, border of military devices, ext. with nautical themes, coat of arms, vignette of lovers holding heart, above inscription "J. & S. Appleton," green, yellow, red, white and blue enamels, imperfections, 11-3/8" d **$5,875**
Black transfer printed, polychrome enamel dec, int. with British sailing ship, red, white, blue, gold and green enamels above inscription "James and Sarah Venn Bridgewater, 1796," rim dec with military devices, outside with vignettes of "Poor Jack," and "Billy's Farewell," sea creatures and mermaids, imperfections, 10-7/8" d **$560**

Cup and saucer, handleless, black transfer, bust of Washington and other gentleman on cup, "Washington, His Country's Father" on saucer, hairlines in cup **$330**

Jug, creamware
Black transfer printed and polychrome dec, obverse American Militia, oval scenic reserve with militiaman with flag, ships, and armament, surrounded by inscription, reverse with American sailing vessel above banner inscribed "Success to Trade," American eagle with Jefferson quote, red, blue, green and yellow enamels, yellow highlight around rim, minor imperfections, dated 1802 under spout, 8-3/4" h **$3,525**
Black transfer printed, "L. Insurgent and Constellation, Feb 10, 1799," depicting naval battle with American frigate on left, French frigate on right, inscription beneath each, reverse "Shipbuilding," oval wreath inscribed "Success to the Wooden Walls of America" beneath spout, imperfections, 8-3/4" h **$1,650**
Black transfer printed, obverse with

mortally wounded officer surrounded by his aides, successful sharpshooter waves his cap from background, reverse with British Man-of-War, beneath spout and rim dec with floral devices, imperfections, 10-1/2" h **$1,650**

Transfer printed, imperfections, obverse with Commodore Preble, reverse with Commodore Preble's Squadron Attacking the City of Tripoli Aug. 3, 1804, 9-1/8" h, 5" d **$2,185**

Transfer printed, obverse with compass and verse, reverse with The Sailors Adieu, minor imperfections, 7-1/4" h, 3-1/2" d **$750**

Transfer printed, obverse with Salem Shipyard and verse, reverse with transfer printed with polychrome enamels of Boston Frigate, transfer "LW" in cartouche above eagle and shield, imperfections, 10-1/4" h, 4-7/8" d **$4,890**

Transfer printed, obverse with ship *Massachusetts*, reverse with map of Newburyport Harbor with "Success to the Commerce of Newburyport" on other, gilt embellishments, circular reserve of Columbia, minor imperfections, 11-3/4" h, 6-5/8" d **$14,950**

Transfer printed, obverse with The Sailor's Return, reverse with

courting couple above verse "A Sailor's life's a pleasant life…" on other, motto reserve below spout "From Rocks & Sands and every ill…" imperfections, 8" h, 4" d **$550**

Transfer printed, obverse with three-masted ship, reverse with The Joiners Arms, eagle and shield below spout, repaired, 11-1/2" h, 5-3/4" d **$865**

Transfer printed, obverse with Washington, Liberty, and Franklin viewing map of early 19th C US, reverse with three-masted ship painted with polychrome enamels, eagle and shield, standing figure of Hope below spout, imperfections, 9" h, 4-3/4" d **$990**

Transfer printed and painted with polychrome enamels, imperfections, obverse with Hope, reverse with three-masted ship flying American flag, American eagle below spout with Jefferson quote, dated 1804, 9-1/4" h, 4-5/8" d **$3,740**

Transfer printed and painted with polychrome enamels, obverse with Boston Fusilier, reverse with "United We Stand, Divided We Fall," eagle and shield below spout, imperfections, 9-1/2" h, 4-1/2" d **$17,250**

Transfer printed and painted with

polychrome enamels, repaired, obverse with Proscribed Patriots, reverse with "Success to America whose Militia…," eagle and shield with Jefferson quote dated 1802 below spout, 10" h, 5" d **$3,220**

Jug, pearlware, black transfer printed, obverse with American eagle with ribbon in its beak, inscribed "E. Pluribus Unum," 15 scattered stars above its head, reverse with vignette of embracing couple, fleet of sailing vessels below spout, rim dec with scattered blossoms, black enamel highlights on rim, shoulder, and handle edges, minor imperfections, 6-1/4" h............................. **$1,120**

Plate, black transfer printed, ten are dec with sailing vessels, one inscribed "Returning Hopes" with lady waiting for return of her lover's ship, minor imperfections, price for 11 pc set, 10" d... **$1,570**

Sauceboat, oval, paneled sides, underglaze blue floral dec, attributed to Pennington & Part, c1780, 5-3/4" l **$460**

Tureen, cov, domed cov with oval handle, round base, black transfer dec on lid, int., and ext. depicting figure flanked by two coat-of-arm shields, two monograms "TF" and "BW" within oval, imperfections, 12-1/4" d, 9-1/2" h **$1,100**

Liverpool, Delftware blue and white bowl and cover, circular, loop handles with stripes, sides depict birds in floral gardens, pierced strainer to interior, restored bowl, glaze loss and flaking on rims, England, mid-18th century, 8-1/2" d, **$1,057.**
Photo courtesy of Skinner, Inc.

LLADRÓ PORCELAINS

History: Brothers Vicente, Jose, and Juan Lladró formally incorporated themselves as a company in 1953 and, by 1955, were selling their early porcelain creations in their own retail shop in Valencia, Spain. By 1958, they had acquired the land to build a small factory, probably not operational until the early 1960s. The factory underwent at least one major renovation and expansion, which went online in 1969, also the year of first export to the United States. Today, Lladró exports all over the globe. Management of the company has passed to the second generation of the Lladró family, with the aging founders in retirement.

Lladró is entirely handmade of fine porcelain, with many molds and artisans involved in the production of each item, and using traditional porcelain-making techniques that have changed little in the centuries since the famous Meissen manufactory of Germany first developed them. This intimate connection between artisan and product accounts for why the product is so expensive. Lladró is famous for its flowerwork, in which each stamen, petal, and leaf is separately applied, and items with flowerwork in mint condition command premium prices on the secondary market.

Oldest Lladró items found on today's secondary market would have been fired as early as the mid-1960s, and some of these made their way to the United States in tourist suitcases prior to 1969. Marks of these oldest items are impressed or etched into the porcelain base and include the word "Lladró" as well as the words "Made in Spain" and sometimes "España" (Spanish for "Spain"). The famous Lladró cobalt blue backstamp was first used in the late 1960s to early 1970s, with the accent missing, in this first mark, from the "o" in Lladró. The mark went through several minor changes throughout the 80s and 90s.

"Seconds" are sold at the factory in Spain and in the company's "outlet" stores in the U.S. Seconds are indicated by the scraping off of the logo flower in the backstamp. Serious collectors avoid these, as they are worth only a fraction of the value of a first-quality piece.

As Lladró has grown in popularity and value, the backstamp has also been counterfeited. Counterfeit marks have disproportionately large accent marks over the "o" and are a pale grayish purple in color rather than the deep cobalt blue of the genuine mark.

Other genuine Lladró and Lladró-affiliated brands have included NAO (which is still in production), Zaphir, and Golden Memories. Production of the latter two brands ceased more than a decade ago, but they are still seen on the secondary market. Each can be readily identified by its own unique backstamp. Although NAO is generally considered to be not as valuable as regular Lladró-marked pieces, its secondary market values have heated up as collectors seek a more affordable alternative to Lladró's expensive regular collection. NAO is also found with older, impressed marks.

Lladró has many Valencian competitors who are working "in the Lladró style," but such products have little or no following among serious collectors.

Lladró, "Grand Dame" 1568G/M, **$625.**
Photo courtesy of Lladró USA, Inc.

All photos appear courtesy of Lladró, USA, Inc.

"A" IS FOR AMY, L5145G/M, 1982 ....**$1,500**
"E" IS FOR ELLEN, L5146G, 1982 ....**$1,200**
"I" IS FOR IVY, L5147G, 1982 ....**$600**
"O" IS FOR OLIVIA, L5148G, 1982 ....**$450**
"U" IS FOR URSULA, L5149G, 1982 ....**$450**
ABRAHAM, L5169G, 1982 ....**$725**
ADMIRATION, L4907G/M, 1974 ....**$650**
AEROBICS FLOOR EXERCISE, L5335G, 1985 ....**$300**
AEROBICS PULL-UPS, L5334G, 1985 ....**$300**
AEROBICS SCISSOR FIGURE, L5336G, 1985 ....**$300**
AFGHAN, L1069G/M, 1969 ....**$625**
AFTER THE DANCE, L5092G, 1980 ....**$350**

AFTERNOON JAUNT, L5855G, 1992 ....**$550**
AFTERNOON PROMENADE, S7636G, 1995 ....**$350**
AFTERNOON TEA, L1428G/M, 1982 ....**$320**
AGGRESSIVE DUCK, L1288G/M, 1974 ....**$525**
ANDALUSIANS GROUP, L4647G, 1969 ....**$1,100**
ANGEL DREAMING, L4961M, 1977 ....**$185**
ANGEL PRAYING, N0010G, 1969 ..**$75**
ANGEL RECLINING, N0012G, 1969 ....**$75**
ANGEL WITH BABY, L4635G, 1969 ....**$165**
ANGEL WITH BABY, L4635M, 1969 ....**$250**
ANGEL WITH CLARINET, L1232G/M, 1972 ....**$450**
ANGEL WITH FLUTE, L1233G/M, 1972 ....**$450**

ANGEL WITH FLUTE, N0015G, 1969
....$80
ANGEL WITH LUTE, L1231G/M, 1972
....$450
ANGEL WITH LYRE, N0013G, 1969
....$80
ANGEL WITH MANDOLIN, N0016G,
1969 ....$80
ANGEL WITH TAMBOURINE,
N0011G, 1969 ....$75
ANGEL WONDERING, L4962M, 1977
....$275
ANGORA CAT, N0113M, 1970 ..... $90
ANTELOPE DRINKING, L5302G,
1985 ....$640
APPRECIATION, L1396G, 1982 $1,000
ARACELY WITH HER PET DUCK,
L5202G, 1984 ....$350
ARANJUEZ LITTLE LADY/LADY
WITH PARASOL, L4879G, 1974
....$375
ARTISTIC ENDEAVOR, L5234G, 1984
....$600
ARTISTS MODEL, L5417G/M, 1987
....$525
AT ATTENTION, L5407G, 1987 .... $350
AT THE BALL, L5398G, 1986 ......$700
AUGUST MOON, L5122G, 1982..$365
AUTUMN, L5218G/M, 1984 ....$220
AVOIDING THE GOOSE, L5033G,
1979 ....$400
AZTEC DANCER (GRES), L2143M,
1984 ....$600
AZTEC INDIAN (GRES), L2139M,
1984 ....$1,100
BABY DOLL, L5608G, 1989 ....$220
BABY JESUS, L4670G, 1969 ....$65
BABY JESUS, L4670M, 1969 ....$95
BABY ON FLOOR/LEARNING TO
CRAWL, L5101G, 1982...............$275
BABY WITH PACIFIER (TEETHING),
L5102G, 1982....................................$275
BABY'S OUTING, L4938G, 1976.$850
BACKSTAGE PREPARATION,
L5817G, 1991..................................$550
BACKSTAGE PREPARATION,
L5817M, 1991..................................$650
BALANCING ACT (SEAL), L5392G,
1986 ....$200
BALLERINA/WAITING BACKSTAGE,
L4559G/M, 1969 ....$500
BALLET FIRST STEP, L5094G, 1980
....$425
BALLET TRIO, L5235G, 1984 ... $1,775
BALLOON SELLER/BALLOONS FOR
SALE, L5141G, 1982.....................$310
BALTHASAR'S PAGE, L1516G, 1987
....$850
BARN OWL, L5421G, 1987...........$225
BARRISTER, THE, L4908G, 1974
....$450

BASKET OF CHICKS, N1070G, 1989
....$75
BASKET OF DAHLIAS, L1545M,
1988 ....$700
BASKET OF MARGARITAS, L1543M,
1988 ....$800
BASKET OF ROSES, L1073M, 1969
....$400
BASKET OF ROSES, L1544M, 1988
....$700
BEAGLE PUPPY (LYING), L1072G/M,
1969 ....$300
BEAGLE PUPPY (POUNCING),
L1070G/M, 1969................................$350
BEAGLE PUPPY (SITTING), L1071G/
M, 1969 ....$300
BEARLY LOVE, L1443G, 1983 .....$175
BEDTIME/SLEEPY TRIO, L5443G,
1987 ....$340
BETH, L1358G, 1978 ....$225
BIG PARTRIDGE (GRES), L2087,
1978 ....$375
BIKING IN THE COUNTRY, L5272G,
1985 ....$825
BILLY SOCCER PLAYER, L5135G,
1982 ....$600
BILLY THE BASEBALL PLAYER,
L5137G, 1982..................................$700
BILLY THE GOLFER, L5138G, 1982
....$950
BILLY THE SKIER, L5136G, 1982
....$850
BIRD, L1053G, 1969......................$250
BIRD, L1054G, 1969......................$250
BIRD ON CACTUS, L1303G, 1974
....$850
BLACK AND WHITE BUTTERFLY
NO. 5 (CAPRICHO), L1677M, 1989
....$200
BLACK BUTTERFLY NO. 3
(CAPRICHO), L1675M, 1989.....$200
BLESSED FAMILY, L1499G, 1986
....$400
BLUE BUTTERFLY NO. 9
(CAPRICHO), L1681M, 1989.....$275
BLUE CREEPER, L1302G, 1974....$675
BLUES, THE (BUST), L5600G, 1989
....$400
BOLIVIAN MOTHER, L4658, 1969
....$450
BONGO BEAT, L5157G, 1982 .....$250
BOWING CRANE, L1613G, 1989..$500
BOY & HIS BUNNY, L1507G/M, 1986
....$275
BOY BLOWING/KISSING, L4869G,
1974 ....$175
BOY BLOWING/KISSING, L4869M,
1974 ....$200
BOY FROM MADRID, L4898G/M,
1974 ....$175
BOY MEETS GIRL, L1188G, 1972..$425

BOY ON CAROUSEL HORSE, L1470G,
1985 ....$965
BOY POTTERY SELLER, L5080G,
1980 ....$600
BOY WITH CORNET (BUST), L1105G,
1971 ....$400
BOY WITH CYMBALS, L4613G/M,
1969 ....$350
BOY WITH DOG, L4522G/M, 1970
....$225
BOY WITH DOUBLE BASS, L4615G/
M, 1969 ....$400
BOY WITH DRUM, L4616G/M, 1969
....$350
BOY WITH GOAT (BUST), L2009,
1970 ....$900
BOY WITH GOAT, WHITE,, L2009.3,
1970 ....$800
BOY WITH GOAT/BOY WITH KID,
L4506G/M, 1969 ....$375
BOY WITH GUITAR, L4614G/M, 1969
....$400
BOY WITH LAMBS, L4509G, 1969
....$375
BOY WITH YACHT/YOUNG SAILOR,
L4810G, 1972...................................$215
BOY, BIG HAT N0182G, 1975 ......$150
BOY, BIG HAT N0182M, 1975......$200
BOYS PLAYING WITH GOAT,
L1129G, 1971.................................$2,500
BRIDE, THE, L5439G, 1987 ....$500
BRIDE, THE, L5439G/M, 1987 .....$500
BUDDHA, L1235G, 1972...............$700
BUDDING BLOSSOMS/FROM MY
GARDEN, L1416G, 1982.............$350
BUGLER, THE, L5406G, 1987......$370
BUTTERFLY GIRL/DAYDREAMING
NYMPH, L1402G/M, 1982.........$575
BUTTERFLY GIRL/PONDERING
NYMPH, L1403G/M, 1982.........$575
BUTTERFLY GIRL/SLEEPING NYMPH,
L1401G/M, 1982.............................$575
CADET CAPTAIN, L5404G, 1987 $370
CAFE DE PARIS, L1511G, 1987
....$3,000
CALF, L4680G, 1969 ....$110
CALF, L4680M, 1969 ....$175
CALIFORNIA POPPY W/BASE,
L5190M, 1984..................................$225
CAMEL (GRES), L2027, 1971 ...$2,000
CAN CAN, L5370G, 1986...........$1,200
CAREFREE ANGEL WITH FLUTE,
L1463G, 1985..................................$650
CAREFREE ANGEL WITH LYRE,
L1464G, 1985..................................$650
CARESS AND REST, L1246G/M,
1972 ....$325
CARMENCITA, L5373G, 1986......$250
CAT GIRL/KITTY, L5164G, 1982 .. $475
CAT, HEAD DOWN (EARLY,
RARE) L0008G/M, 1965 ....$150

Lladró, "Thoughts," 1272G, **$3,600.**
Photo courtesy of Lladró USA, Inc.

*Lladró, "Diana, Goddess of the Hunt,"
6269,* **$2,250.**
Photo courtesy of Lladró USA, Inc.

Lladró, "The Race," #1249G, **$2,350.**
Photo courtesy of Lladró USA, Inc.

CAT, HEAD UP (EARLY, RARE)
L0010G/M, 1965.........................**$150**
CENTAUR BOY, L1013G/M, 1969
....**$450**
CENTAUR GIRL, L1012G/M, 1969
....**$450**
CHARLIE THE TRAMP, L5233G, 1984
....**$900**
CHICK ON THE WATCH, L4630G,
1969 ....**$400**
CHILDREN AT PLAY, L5304, 1985
....**$500**
CHILDREN IN NIGHTSHIRTS,
L4874G, 1974.............................**$250**
CHILDREN IN NIGHTSHIRTS,
L4874M, 1974.............................**$350**
CHILDREN'S GAMES, L5379G, 1986
....**$675**
CHINESE BOY (GRES), L2153M,
1982 ....**$300**
CHINESE FARMER (GRES), L2068,
1977 ....**$1,000**
CHINESE GIRL (GRES), L2152M,
1982 ....**$300**
CHINESE NOBLEMAN, L4921G, 1974
....**$2,000**
CHINESE NOBLEWOMAN, L4916G,
1974 ....**$2,000**
CHRISTMAS CAROLS, L1239G, 1973
....**$750**
CHRYSANTHEMUM, L4990G, 1978
....**$350**
CHRYSANTHEMUM W/BASE,
L5189M, 1984.............................**$225**
CINDERELLA, L4828G, 1972........**$275**
CLEAN UP TIME, L4838G/M, 1973
....**$300**
CLOSING SCENE, L4935G, 1974
....**$550**

CLOSING SCENE, WHITE, L4935.30M,
1983 ....**$400**
CLOWN, L4618M, 1971.................**$450**
CLOWN WITH CLOCK, L5056G, 1980
....**$800**
CLOWN WITH CONCERTINA,
L1027G/M, 1969.........................**$800**
CLOWN WITH VIOLIN, L1126G, 1971
....**$2,000**
CLOWN'S HEAD (BUST), L5129G,
1982 ....**$500**
**COMFORTING BABY/MOTHER
KISSING CHILD (BUST)**, L1329M,
1976 ....**$1,200**
CONCERT VIOLINIST, L5330G, 1985
....**$475**
CONSIDERATION (BUST), L5355M,
1986 ....**$250**
COUNTRY GIRL N0522G/M, 1978
....**$100**
COUNTRY LADY, L1330, 1976....**$1,600**
COW WITH PIG, L4640G/M, 1969
....**$750**
CUPID (BLINDFOLDED), L4607G/M,
1969 ....**$400**
CURIOUS ANGEL, L4960M, 1977
....**$185**
DAHLIA W/BASE, L5180M, 1984
....**$150**
DALMATIAN (BEGGING), L1262G,
1974 ....**$400**
DALMATIAN (SITTING), L1260G,
1974 ....**$400**
DALMATIAN (TAIL IN AIR), L1261G,
1974 ....**$400**
DANCERS RESTING, L4992G, 1978
....**$750**
DANCING PARTNER, A, L5093G,
1980 ....**$380**

DANCING THE POLKA, L5252G,
1984 ....**$525**
DANTE, L5177G, 1982..................**$700**
DAUGHTERS/SISTERS, L5013G/M,
1978 ....**$850**
DEATH OF THE SWAN, L4855G/M,
1973 ....**$350**
DEATH OF THE SWAN, WHITE,
L4855.30M, 1983 ....**$250**
DEBUTANTE, THE, L1431G/M, 1982
....**$320**
DEEP IN THOUGHT, L5389G, 1986
....**$350**
DEER, L1064G/M, 1969.................**$395**
DEMURE CENTAUR GIRL, L5320G/
M, 1985 ....**$400**
DENTIST, L4762G, 1971...............**$550**
DERBY, L1344G, 1977................**$2,500**
DEVOTION, L1278G, 1974 ....**$450**
DIVERS (GRES), L2117, 1980...**$1,600**
DIVERS WITH CHICKEN (GRES),
L2116, 1980..............................**$1,400**
DOCTOR, L4602G, 1969...............**$400**
DOG (COLLIE), L1316G, 1974 .....**$500**
DOG (LLASA APSO), L4642G/M,
1969 ....**$500**
DOG AND CAT IN HARMONY,
N1048G, 1987 ....**$125**
DOG AND CAT/LITTLE FRISKIES,
L5032G, 1979.............................**$285**
DOG IN THE BASKET, L1128G, 1971
....**$450**
DOG PLAYING BASS FIDDLE,
L1154G, 1971.............................**$500**
DOG PLAYING BONGOS, L1156G,
1971 ....**$550**
DOG PLAYING GUITAR, L1152G,
1971 ....**$550**
DOG SINGER, L1155G, 1971 ....**$450**

DOGS BUST (GRES), L2067, 1977 ....$875

DON JUAN, L4609G, 1969 ....$715

DON QUIXOTE & SANCHO PANZA, L4998G, 1978 ....$2,800

DON QUIXOTE DREAMING (GRES), L2084, 1978 ....$1,900

DON QUIXOTE, L1030M, 1969 $1,550

DONKEY IN LOVE/DONKEY W/ DAISY, L4524G/M, 1969 ....$400

DONKEY, L4678M, 1969 ....$175

DONKEY, L4679G, 1969 ....$125

DORMOUSE, L4774G, 1971 ....$450

DOVE GROUP, L1335G, 1977 ...$1,500

DOVE, L1015G/M, 1969 ....$150

DOVE, L1016G/M, 1969 ....$225

DOVE N0060G, 1970 ....$50

DOVE N0062G, 1970 ....$50

DOVE N0063G, 1970 ....$50

DRESS REHEARSAL, L5497G, 1988 ....$450

DRESSING UP, L2119, 1980 ....$900

DRESSMAKER, L4700G/M, 1970 ...$450

DUCK JUMPING, L1265G, 1974 ...$110

DUCK, L1056G, 1969 ....$275

DUCK RUNNING, L1263G, 1974 ..$110

DUCKLINGS, L1307M, 1974 ....$175

DUCKS GROUP, N0006M, 1969 ....$75

DUTCH GIRL, L4860G/M, 1974 ...$335

EGYPTIAN CAT (GRES), L2130, 1983 ....$650

EGYPTIAN CAT (WHITE), L5154G/M, 1982 ....$650

ELEPHANT FAMILY, L4764G, 1971 ....$1,000

EMBROIDERER, L4865G, 1974 ..$725

ESKIMO BOY (GRES), L2007, 1970 ....$300

ESKIMO BOY (WHITE PARKA GRES), L2007.3, 1970 ....$300

ESKIMO BOY AND GIRL (GRES), L2138, 1971 ....$650

ESKIMO GIRL (GRES), L2008, 1970 ....$300

EXQUISITE SCENT/SCHOOLGIRL, L1313G, 1974 ....$650

FAIRY, L4595G/M, 1969 ....$200

FAWN HEAD (GRES), L2040, 1971 ....$575

FEEDING THE DUCKS, L4849G/M, 1973 ....$325

FEEDING TIME, L1277G/M, 1974 ....$400

FEMALE EQUESTRIAN, L4516M, 1969 ....$800

FEMALE TENNIS PLAYER, L1427M, 1982 ....$350

FISH A'PLENTY, L5172G, 1982 ..$435

FISH VENDOR, L2162, 1985 ....$275

FISHER BOY/GOING FISHING, L4809G/M, 1972 ....$175

FISHERMAN (BUST), L2108, 1978 ....$1,150

FLAPPER/LADY GRAND CASINO, L5175G, 1982 ....$450

FLOWER FOR MY LADY, A, L1513G, 1987 ....$1,500

FLOWER HARMONY, L1418G, 1982 ....$335

FLOWER HARVEST, L1286G, 1974 ....$535

FLOWER PEDDLER, L5029G, 1979 ....$1,550

FLOWER SONG (LLADRO MUSEUM), S7607G, 1988 ....$550

FLOWER VENDOR, L2160, 1985. $275

FLOWERS CHEST, L1572G, 1987 ....$1,200

FLOWERS IN POT, L5028G, 1980 ....$600

FLYING DUCK, L1264G, 1974 .....$110

FOLK DANCING, L5256G, 1984.. $500

FOREST BORN (DEER HEADS, GRES), L2191, 1990 ....$450

FORGOTTEN, L1502G/M, 1986.. $300

FOX AND CUB, L1065G/M, 1969 ....$425

FOXY, N366G, 1983 ....$150

FRIAR JUNIPER (GRES), L2138, 1984 ....$350

FRIDAY'S CHILD (BOY), L6019G, 1993 ....$285

FRIENDSHIP, L1230G/M, 1972.. $450

FRUIT VENDOR, 2161, 1985 ....$325

FULL OF MISCHIEF, L1395G, 1982 ....$1,000

GASPAR'S PAGE, L1514G, 1987. $550

GATHERING BUTTERFLIES, N0181G, 1975 ....$175

GATHERING BUTTERFLIES, N0181M, 1975 ....$200

GAYLE/LITTLE BALLET GIRL, L5109G, 1982 ....$350

GAZELLE, L5271G, 1985 ....$525

GAZELLE RESTING (GRES), L2048, 1971 ....$600

GEESE GROUP, L4549G/M, 1969 $250

GEISHA, L4807G/M, 1972 ....$550

GELSIE/LITTLE BALLET GIRL, L5108G, 1982 ....$350

GENTLEMAN EQUESTRIAN, L5329G, 1985 ....$500

GERMAN SHEPHERD W/PUP, L4731G, 1970 ....$950

GIRL AT THE FOUNTAIN, N0136G, 1971 ....$175

GIRL AT THE FOUNTAIN, N0136M, 1971 ....$200

GIRL CLOWN WITH TRUMPET, L5060G, 1980 ....$550

GIRL FROM THE FOUNTAIN, N0115G, 1970 ....$265

GIRL FROM THE FOUNTAIN, N0115M, 1970 ....$300

GIRL GATHERING FLOWERS, L1172G/M, 1971 ....$365

GIRL MANICURING, L1082G/M, 1969 ....$300

GIRL ON CAROUSEL HORSE, L1469G, 1985 ....$965

GIRL POTTERY SELLER, L5081G, 1980 ....$600

GIRL SHAMPOOING, L1148G/M, 1971 ....$300

GIRL SITTING UNDER TRELLIS, L5298G, 1985 ....$775

GIRL STANDING UNDER TRELLIS, L5297G, 1985 ....$800

GIRL WATERING/GROWING ROSES, L1354G, 1978 ....$625

GIRL WITH BASKET/SHEPHERDESS WITH DOG, L1034G/M, 1969 ...$235

GIRL WITH BONNET, L1147G/M, 1971 ....$300

GIRL WITH BRUSH, L1081G/M, 1969 ....$300

GIRL WITH CALF, 4513G/M, 1978 ....$550

GIRL WITH CALLA LILIES, L4650G, 1969 ....$170

GIRL WITH CATS, L1309M, 1974 ....$375

GIRL WITH COCKEREL/SHEPHERDESS W/BASKET, L4591G/M, 1969 ....$300

GIRL WITH DOLL, L1083G/M, 1969 ....$300

GIRL WITH DOLL, L1211G/M, 1972 ....$450

GIRL WITH DUCK, L1052G/M, 1969 ....$235

GIRL WITH DUCKS, N0026G/M, 1969 ....$150

GIRL WITH FLAX, N0089G, 1970 ....$175

GIRL WITH FLOWERS IN TOW, L5031G, 1979 ....$1,500

GIRL WITH FLOWERS, L1088G/M, 1969 ....$725

GIRL WITH GEESE, L1035G/M, 1969 ....$235

GIRL WITH GOOSE AND DOG, L4866G/M, 1974 ....$325

GIRL WITH GOOSE, L4815G/M, 1972 ....$335

GIRL WITH GOOSE, N0025G/M, 1969 ....$90

GIRL WITH LAMB, L1010G/M, 1969 ....$250

GIRL WITH LAMB, L4505G, 1969 ....$145

GIRL WITH LAMB, L4505M, 1969 ....$165

GIRL WITH LAMB, L4584G/M, 1969 ....$250

GIRL WITH LAMB/SHEPHERDESS, L4835G/M, 1972......................$295

GIRL WITH LILIES SITTING, L4972G, 1977 ....$180

GIRL WITH MANDOLIN, L1026G, 1969 ....$625

GIRL WITH MILK PAIL, L4682G/M, 1970 ....$325

GIRL WITH MOTHER'S SHOE, L1084G/M, 1969 ....$300

GIRL WITH PIG, L1011G, 1969....$125

GIRL WITH PIG, L1011M, 1969...$175

GIRL WITH PIGEONS, L4915G, 1974 ....$400

GIRL WITH PUPPIES, L1311G, 1974 ....$375

GIRL WITH RABBIT, N0003G/M, 1969 ....$75

GIRL WITH SLATE, N0117G, 1970 ....$110

GIRL WITH SLATE, N0117M, 1970 ....$135

GIRL WITH UMBRELLA AND GEESE, L4510G/M, 1969 ....$300

GIRL WITH WATER CARRIER (BUST), L2014, 1970................$1,000

GIRL WITH WATERING CAN/ BLOOMING ROSES, L1339G, 1977 ....$500

GIRLS IN THE SWING/SWINGING, L1366G, 1978........................$1,850

GOOSE (13"), N0052G, 1969 ......$100

GOOSE (13"), N0052M, 1969 ....$150

GOOSE (9"), N0053G, 1969........$100

GOOSE (9"), N0053M, 1969 ....$125

GOOSE-REDUCED (11-3/4"), N0054/2G, 1969 ....$75

GOOSE-REDUCED (8"), N0055/3G, 1969 ....$75

GOYA LADY/AMPARO, L5125G, 1982 ....$350

GRACEFUL DUO, L2073, 1977 .$1,700

GRACEFUL OFFERING, L5773G, 1991 ....$1,000

GRACEFUL SWAN, L5230G, 1984 ....$135

GREAT BUTTERFLY NO. 13 (CAPRICHO), L1685M, 1989.....$235

GREAT DANE, L1068G, 1969 .....$575

GREAT GRAY OWL, L5419G, 1987 ....$225

GRETEL/DUTCH GIRL HANDS AKIMBO, L5064G, 1980 ....$400

GROUP DISCUSSION, L1722, 1989 ....$1,700

GROUP OF MUSICIANS, L4617G/M, 1969 ....$550

GUARDIAN CHICK, L4629G, 1969 ....$400

GYMNAST BALANCING BALL, L5332G, 1985............................$350

GYMNAST EXERCISING WITH BALL, L5333G, 1985 ....$325

GYMNAST WITH RING, L5331G, 1985 ....$375

GYPSY WOMAN, L4919G, 1974 ....$1,300

HAMLET AND YORICK, L1254G, 1974 ....$1,300

HAPPY HARLEQUIN, L1247G/M, 1974 ....$1,000

HARLEQUIN "A", L5075G, 1980 ....$475

HARLEQUIN "B", L5076G, 1980 ....$400

HARLEQUIN "C", L5077G, 1980 ....$450

HARLEQUIN WITH DOVE, L1717, 1988 ....$1,000

HARLEQUIN WITH PUPPY, L1716, 1988 ....$1,250

HARVESTER, WOMAN, L4582G, 1969 ....$650

HATS OFF TO FUN, L5765G, 1991 ....$600

HAWAIIAN FLOWER VENDOR (GRES), L2154, 1985 ....$550

HEAD OF CONGOLESE WOMAN (GRES, BUST), L2148, 1984 ......$600

HEATHER, L1359G, 1978 ....$225

HEN, L1041G/M, 1969 ....$300

HERE COMES THE BRIDE, L1446G, 1983 ....$1,500

HIGH SOCIETY, L1430G/M, 1982 ....$700

HIKER, L5280G, 1985 ....$375

HINDU GODDESS, L1215G, 1972 ....$900

HORNED OWL, L5420G, 1987 .....$225

HORSE GROUP (2), L4655G/M, 1969 ....$785

HORSE HEADS (GRES), L3511, 1978 ....$650

HORSE, L4861G, 1974 ....$500

HORSE, L4863G, 1974 ....$500

HUNTERS, L1048G/M, 1969......$1,500

HUNTING DOG (EARLY/RARE), L308.13G, 1963 ....$2,000

I HOPE SHE DOES, L5450G, 1987 ....$375

ICE CREAM VENDOR, L5325G, 1985 ....$725

IDYLL, L1017G/M, 1969................$700

IN THE FOREST, N0092G, 1970 ..$200

IN THE GARDEN, L5416G/M, 1987 ....$425

IN THE MEADOW, L1508G/M, 1986 ....$300

INDIAN CHIEF (GRES, BUST), L2127, 1983 ....$700

INFANTILE CANDOR, L4963G, 1977 ....$1,200

INGRID, L5065G, 1980................$650

INNOCENCE W/BASE, GREEN, L3558M, 1984..........................$2,000

INNOCENCE W/BASE, RED, L3558.30M, 1984......................$2,000

JAPANESE CAMELLIA W/BASE, L5181M, 1984..........................$150

JOCKEY AND LADY, L5036G, 1979 ....$2,615

JOCKEY, L1341G, 1977................$500

JOCKEY, THE, L5089G, 1980....$1,200

JOSEFA FEEDING HER DUCK, L5201G, 1984............................$350

JULIA, L1361G, 1978 ....$225

KARENA/LITTLE BALLET GIRL, L5107G, 1982............................$350

KING BALTHASAR, L4675G, 1969 ....$125

KING BALTHASAR, L4675M, 1969 ....$175

KING GASPAR, L4674G, 1969.....$125

KING GASPAR, L4674M, 1969....$195

KING MELCHIOR, L4673G, 1969 ....$125

KING MELCHIOR, L4673M, 1969 ....$175

KING SOLOMON, L5168G, 1982 ....$900

KISSING DOVES, L1169M, 1971...$250

KISSING DOVES W/PLAQUE, L1170G, 1971............................$300

KIYOKO, L1450G, 1983 ....$600

KRISTINA, L5062G, 1980............$400

LA GIACONDA (BUST), L5337G, 1985 ....$550

LACTIFLORA PEONY W/BASE, L5185M, 1984............................$175

LADY AT DRESSING TABLE, L1242G, 1973 ....$3,200

LADY FROM MAJORCA, L5240G, 1984 ....$435

LADY MACBETH (GRES), L3518, 1980 ....$1,200

LADY WITH SHAWL, L4914G, 1974 ....$800

LADY WITH YOUNG HARLEQUIN, L4883G, 1974..........................$2,000

LADYBIRD AND NIGHTINGALE, L1227G, 1973............................$300

LAMB IN ARMS, N0120G, 1970 ....$175

LAMB IN ARMS, N0120M, 1970 ....$200

LANDAU CARRIAGE, THE, L1521G, 1987 ....$4,000

LANGUID CLOWN, L4924G, 1976 ....$1,200

LARGE PINK BUTTERFLY NO. 6 (CAPRICHO), L1678M, 1989.....**$185**
LATEST ADDITION (GRES VERSION), L2262, 1989.............**$600**
LAURA, L1360G, 1978.................**$225**
LAWYER, L1089G, 1971............**$900**
LAWYER, L1090G, 1971............**$900**
LETTERS TO DULCINEA (NUMBERED SERIES, GRES), L3509, 1978.............**$2,200**
LILY SOCCER PLAYER/GIRL SOCCER PLAYER, L5134G, 1982.....**$550**
LION, L5436G, 1987....................**$250**
LITTER OF KITTENS, N0104G/M, 1970.....................**$150**
LITTLE BIRD, L1301, 1974............**$650**
LITTLE BOY BLUE, N0521G/M, 1978.....................**$150**
LITTLE CONQUISTADOR, N1140G, 1991.....................**$115**
LITTLE DUCK, 4551G, 1969..........**$55**
LITTLE DUCK, 4551M, 1969..........**$75**
LITTLE DUCK, 4552G, 1969..........**$55**
LITTLE DUCK, 4552M, 1969.........**$200**
LITTLE DUCK, 4553G, 1969..........**$55**
LITTLE DUCK, 4553M, 1969.........**$150**
LITTLE DUCK, N0242M, 1979.......**$50**
LITTLE DUCK, N0243M, 1979.......**$50**
LITTLE DUCK, N0244M, 1979.......**$50**
LITTLE DUCK, N0245M, 1979.......**$50**
LITTLE DUCK/DUCKLING, N0369M, 1983.....................**$50**
LITTLE DUCK/DUCKLING, N0370M, 1983.....................**$50**
LITTLE EAGLE OWL (GRES), L2020, 1971.....................**$400**
LITTLE FLOWER JUG, L1222G, 1972.....................**$475**
LITTLE FLOWER SELLER, L5082G, 1980.....................**$2,800**
LITTLE GIRL FEEDING DOVES, N0382G, 1983.....................**$410**
LITTLE GIRL FEEDING DOVES, N0382M, 1982.....................**$450**
LITTLE GIRL W/GOAT/GETTING HER GOAT, L4812G, 1972.................**$450**
LITTLE JUG ROSE WITH FLOWERS, L1220G, 1972.....................**$475**
LITTLE RED RIDING HOOD, L4965G, 1977.....................**$550**
LITTLE SHEPHERD WITH GOAT, L4817G/M, 1972.........................**$475**
LONELY, L2076, 1978..................**$250**
LONG RABBIT (EARLY/RARE), 352.13G, 1965.....................**$800**
LOST IN THOUGHT, L2125, 1981.**$350**
LOST LOVE, L5128G/M, 1982......**$665**
LOVERS FROM VERONA, L1250G, 1974.....................**$1,200**
LOVERS IN THE PARK, L1274G/M, 1974.....................**$1,400**

MADAME BUTTERFLY, L4991G, 1978.....................**$350**
MAESTRO, MUSIC PLEASE!, L5196G, 1984.....................**$465**
MALLARD DUCK, L5288G, 1985.....................**$600**
MAN'S BEST FRIEND N0032G, 1969.....................**$175**
MARGARETTA/DUTCH GIRL WITH BRAIDS, L5063G, 1980.............**$400**
MARIKO W/BASE, L1421G, 1982.....................**$1,800**
MARY, L4671G, 1969.................**$85**
MARY, L4671M, 1969.................**$125**
MATERNAL ELEPHANT, L4765G, 1971.....................**$800**
MAYOR, L1728, 1981.................**$1,200**
MAYORESS (BUST), L1729, 1989.....................**$750**
MAYUMI, L1449G, 1983.............**$575**
MEDIEVAL COURTSHIP, L5300G, 1985.....................**$900**
MEDIEVAL LADY, L4928G, 1974.....................**$1,150**
MERMAID ON WAVE, L1347G, 1978.....................**$1,500**
MERMAIDS PLAYING, L1349G, 1978.....................**$2,500**
MIDWIFE, L5431G/M, 1987.........**$600**
MIGUEL DE CERVANTES, L5132G, 1982.....................**$1,400**
MILANESE LADY, L5323G, 1985...**$375**
MIME ANGEL, L4959M, 1977.....**$185**
MINIATURE BEGONIA W/BASE, L5188M, 1984.....................**$175**
MINIATURE BISON ATTACKING, L5313G, 1985.....................**$250**
MINIATURE BISON RESTING, L5312G, 1985.....................**$175**
MINIATURE CAT, L5308G, 1985.....................**$150**
MINIATURE COCKER SPANIEL, L5309G, 1985.....................**$200**
MINIATURE COCKER SPANIEL, L5310G, 1985.....................**$175**
MINIATURE DEER, L5314G, 1985.....................**$175**
MINIATURE DROMEDARY, L5315G, 1985.....................**$175**
MINIATURE FLOWER VASE, L1219G, 1972.....................**$475**
MINIATURE GIRAFFE, L5316G, 1985.....................**$225**
MINIATURE KITTEN, L5307G, 1985.....................**$225**
MINIATURE LAMB, L5317G, 1985.....................**$180**
MINIATURE POLAR BEAR, L5434G, 1987.....................**$150**
MINIATURE PUPPIES (3), L5311G, 1985.....................**$200**

MINIATURE SEAL FAMILY, L5318G, 1985.....................**$275**
MISS TERESA, L4999G, 1978..**$350**
MISS VALENCIA, L1422G, 1982.....................**$450**
MOMI, L1529G, 1987.................**$550**
MONK (GRES), L2060, 1977......**$175**
MONKEY, L5432G, 1987............**$325**
MONKEYS (GRES), L2000, 1970.....................**$650**
MOTHER AND CHILD, L4575G, 1969.....................**$300**
MOTHER AND CHILD, L4701G, 1970.....................**$325**
MOTHER WITH PUPS, L1257G, 1974.....................**$700**
MOTHER'S LOVE/YOUNG MOTHER (BUST, GRES), L3521, 1980...**$1,200**
MY GOODNESS, L1285G, 1974.....................**$450**
MY HUNGRY BROOD, L5074G, 1980.....................**$470**
MY PRECIOUS BUNDLE, L5123G/M, 1982.....................**$275**
NATURE'S BOUNTY, L1417G, 1982.....................**$400**
NAUGHTY DOG, L4982G, 1978..**$325**
NAUTICAL WATCH (BUST, GRES), L2134, 1984.....................**$725**
NIGHTINGALE PAIR, L1228G, 1972.....................**$650**
NOSTALGIA, L5071G, 1980.........**$360**
NOT SO FAST!, L1533G/M, 1987.....................**$325**
NUDE (FULL FIGURE), L4511M, 1969.....................**$650**
NUDE (TORSO), L4512M, 1969...**$500**
NUDE IN WHITE, L4511.3M, 1969.....................**$700**
NUDE WITH FAN (GRES), N1240, 1996.....................**$410**
NUDE WITH ROSE (GRES), L2079, 1978.....................**$800**
NUDE WITH ROSE (GRES), L3517.3, 1978.....................**$950**
NUNS, L2075, 1977.................**$275**
NURSE, L4603G, 1971.............**$400**
OBSTETRICIAN, L4763G/M, 1971.....................**$450**
OLD DOG, L1067G, 1969............**$625**
OLD FOLKS, L1033G/M, 1969..**$1,400**
OLYMPIC PUPPET, L4968G, 1977.....................**$900**
ON THE FARM, L1306G, 1974.....**$335**
ON THE LAKE, L5216G, 1984.....................**$1,000**
ON THE TOWN, L1452G, 1983....**$495**
ONE, TWO, THREE, L5426G, 1987.....................**$450**
ORCHESTRA CONDUCTOR, L4653G, 1969.....................**$875**

Lladró, "Halloween," 5067G, **$1,525.**
Photo courtesy of Lladró USA, Inc.

Lladró, "Kiyoko" 1450G, **$600.**
Photo courtesy of Lladró USA, Inc.

Lladró, "Wrath of Don Quixote,"
1343G, **$1,050.**
Photo courtesy of Lladró USA, Inc.

ORIENTAL GIRL/ORIENTAL FLOW-ER ARRANGER, L4840G/M, 1973
....$550

ORIENTAL SPRING, L4988G, 1978
....$350

ORIENTAL WOMAN (GRES), L2026, 1971 ....$450

OSTRICH (GRES), L2099, 1979 ...$650

OSTRICHES (EARLY/RARE), L297.13G, 1963 ....$2,000

OTHELLO, L3510 (GRES), 1978 .. **$1,050**

OWL (GRES), L2019, 1971 ....$400

PAINFUL BEAR, L5021G, 1978...**$825**

PAINFUL ELEPHANT, L5020G, 1978
....$850

PAINFUL GIRAFFE, L5019G, 1978
....$850

PAINFUL KANGAROO, L5023G, 1978 ....$900

PAINFUL LION, L5022G, 1978.....$850

PAINFUL MONKEY, L5018G, 1978
....$850

PAINTER, L4663G, 1969...............$900

PAN WITH CYMBALS, L1006G, 1969
....$550

PAN WITH PIPES, L1007G, 1969
....$550

PEKINESE SITTING, L4641G/M, 1969
....$450

PELUSA CLOWN, L1125G, 1971
....$1,500

PENSIVE CLOWN (BUST), L5130G, 1982 ....$500

PERUVIAN GROUP, L4610G, 1969
....$1,700

PET ME!, L5114G, 1982................$115

PHARMACIST, L4844G/M, 1973.. **$1,500**

PHYLLIS, L1356G, 1978 ....$225

PICKING FLOWERS, L1287G, 1974
....$475

PILAR, L5410G, 1987....................$375

PLANNING THE DAY, L5026G, 1980
....$275

PLATERO AND MARCELINO, L1181G, 1971 ....$400

PLAY WITH ME!, L5112G, 1982
....$100

PLAYFUL DOGS, L1367G, 1978 ..$725

PLAYFUL KITTENS, L5232G, 1984
....$325

PLAYFUL PIGLETS, L5228G, 1984..$200

PLAYING WITH DUCKS AT THE POND, L5303G, 1985 ....$725

PLEASANTRIES, L1440G, 1983 ... **$1,800**

POLAR BEAR OBSERVING (EARLY/RARE), L075G, 1966 ....$300

PONDERING, L5173G, 1982 ....$600

POODLE, L1259G/M, 1974 ....$475

POOR PUPPY, L5394G, 1986 ....$200

PRACTICE MAKES PERFECT, L5462G, 1988 ....$650

PRECOCIOUS COURTSHIP, L5072G, 1980 ....$700

PREDICTING THE FUTURE, L5191G, 1984 ....$450

PROFESSOR, L5208G, 1984 ....$600

PUPPY LOVE, L1127G, 1971.......$365

QUEST, THE, L5224G, 1984..........$330

QUIXOTE & THE WINDMILL, L1497G, 1986 ....**$2,200**

QUIXOTE ON GUARD/BRAVE KNIGHT, L1385G, 1978..............$800

RABBIT EATING (BROWN & WHITE), L4772G/M, 1971 ....$165

RABBIT EATING (GRAY & WHITE), L4773G/M, 1971.........................$165

RABBIT SCRATCHING (EARLY/RARE), 278.12G $700

RABBIT'S FOOD, L4826G/M, 1972
....$300

RACE, THE, L1249G, 1974.........**$2,200**

RAIN IN SPAIN, THE/UNDER THE RAIN, L2077, 1978 ....$525

RAM, L1046G, 1969......................$600

REACHING THE GOAL, L5546G, 1989 ....$325

READING, L5000G/M, 1978.........$325

REFLECTIONS OF HAMLET, L1455G, 1983 ....**$1,400**

REMINISCING, L1270G, 1974 .. **$1,400**

REVERENT MATADOR/LITTLE BOY BULLFIGHTER, L5115G, 1982... **$425**

REVERIE, L1398G, 1982.............**$1,100**

RHINO, L5437G, 1987 ....$300

RHUMBA, L5160G, 1982 ....$215

RIDE IN THE COUNTRY, L5354G, 1986 ....$500

ROARING TWENTIES, L5174G, 1982
....$400

ROMANCE, L4831G/M, 1972.... **$1,500**

ROMEO AND JULIET, L4750M, 1971
....**$1,450**

SAD HARLEQUIN, L4558G/M, 1969
....$625

SALLIE/LITTLE BALLET GIRL, L5104G, 1982..............................$300

SAMSON AND DELILAH, L5051G, 1980 ....**$1,600**

SANCHO PANZA, L1031G/M, 1969
....$600

SANTA CLAUS, L4904G, 1974 ...**$1,000**

SANTA CLAUS WITH TOYS, L4905G, 1974 ....**$1,200**

SATYR GROUP, L1008G, 1969 ....$975

SATYR WITH FROG (VERY RARE), L1093G, 1971 .... $750

SATYR WITH SNAIL (VERY RARE), L1092G, 1971 .... $750

SAYONARA, L4989G, 1978 .... $325

SCARECROW & THE LADY, L5385G, 1986 .... $725

SCAREDY CAT, L5091G, 1980 ... $115

SCHOOL CHUMS, L5237G, 1984 .... $525

SCHOOL MARM, L5209G, 1984 .. $825

SCOOTING, L5143G, 1982 .... $1,350

SCOTTISH LASS, L1315G, 1974 .. $2,800

SEA BREEZE/WINDBLOWN GIRL, L4922G, 1974 .... $400

SEA CAPTAIN, L4621G/M, 1969 . $325

SEA FEVER, L5166G/M, 1982 ..... $350

SEA HARVEST, L2142, 1984 .... $750

SEAMAN/HELMSMAN, THE, L1325M, 1976 .... $1,250

SEATED BALLERINA, L4504G/M, 1969 .... $350

SEATED HARLEQUIN, L4503G/M, 1969 .... $400

SEDAN CHAIR GROUP/HER LADY-SHIP, L5097G, 1980 .... $6,200

SEESAW, L1255G/M, 1974 .... $625

SEESAW, L4867G, 1974 .... $425

SETTER'S HEAD (GRES), L2045, 1971 .... $650

SEWING A TROUSSEAU/MED. LADY EMBROIDERER, L5126G, 1982 ... $550

SHARPENING CUTLERY, L5204G, 1984 .... $1,000

SHELLEY, L1357G, 1978 .... $225

SHEPHERD, L4659G, 1969 .... $325

SHEPHERD RESTING, L4571G/M, 1969 .... $450

SHEPHERD SLEEPING, L1104G, 1971 .... $2,000

SHEPHERD WITH LAMB, L4676G, 1969 .... $135

SHEPHERD WITH LAMB, L4676M, 1969 .... $225

SHEPHERDESS SLEEPING/SHEP-HERDESS W/LAMB (BUST, GRES) L 2005M, 1970 .... $700

SHEPHERDESS W/DUCKS/GIRL W/GEESE, L4568G/M, 1969 ..... $300

SHEPHERDESS WITH BASKET, L4678G, 1969 .... $135

SHEPHERDESS WITH BASKET, L4678M, 1969 .... $225

SHEPHERDESS WITH DOVE, L4660G/M, 1969 .... $300

SHEPHERDESS WITH GOATS, L1001G/M, 1969 .... $750

SHEPHERDESS WITH ROOSTER, L4677G, 1969 .... $125

SHEPHERDESS WITH ROOSTER, L4677M, 1969 .... $250

SHEPHERD'S REST, L1252G, 1974 .... $675

SHERIFF PUPPET, L4969G, 1977 . $650

SHORT EARED OWL, L5418G, 1987 .... $225

SIAMESE DANCER, L5593G, 1989 .... $525

SIDEWALK SERENADE, L5388G, 1986 .... $1,400

SINGING LESSON/CHOIR LESSON, L4973G, 1977 .... $1,350

SKIER PUPPET, L4970G, 1977 ..... $625

SLEEPY CHICK, L4632G, 1969 .... $400

SMALL DOG (PAPILLON), L4749G, 1971 .... $250

SMALL PARTRIDGE (GRES), L2088, 1978 .... $250

SOCCER PLAYER, L5200G, 1984 .... $450

SOCIALITE OF THE TWENTIES, L5283G/M, 1985 .... $370

SPANISH SOLDIER, L5255G, 1984 .... $500

SPECIAL MALE SOCCER PLAYER, L5200.30G, 1984 .... $600

SPRING BIRDS, L1368G, 1978 ... $2,700

ST. CRISTOBAL/ST. CHRISTOPHER, L5246G, 1984 .... $550

ST. FRANCIS (GRES), L2090M, 1978 .... $1,600

ST. JOSEPH, L4672G, 1969 .... $100

ST. JOSEPH, L4672M, 1969 .... $135

STEP IN TIME, A, L5158G, 1982 ... $250

STORYTIME, L5229G, 1984 .... $950

STUBBORN DONKEY, L5178G, 1982 .... $500

STUDENT FLUTE PLAYER, L4837G, 1973 .... $425

SUNNY DAY, A, L5003G/M, 1978 .... $425

SWAN, L4829G/M, 1972 .... $350

SWAN WITH WINGS SPREAD, L5231M, 1984 .... $250

SWAN, THE N1008G, 1987 .... $195

SWEET HARVEST, L5380G, 1986 .... $900

SWEETY/HONEY LICKERS, L1248G, 1974 .... $550

SWINGING/VICTORIAN GIRL ON SWING, L1297G, 1974 .... $1,850

TAKING A BOW, L5095G, 1980 ... $400

TEACHER WOMAN, L5048G, 1980 .... $625

TEACHER, THE (MALE), L4801G, 1972 .... $500

TEACHING THE GEESE (GRES), N0286, 1982 .... $275

TEACHING THE GEESE, N0286G, 1982 .... $220

TEACHING THE GEESE, N0286M, 1982 .... $250

TENNIS PLAYER PUPPET, L4966G, 1977 .... $550

THAI DANCER, L2069, 1977 .... $800

THOUGHTS, L1272G, 1974 .... $3,600

THREE PINK ROSES W/BASE, L5179M, 1984 .... $200

TORSO IN WHITE, L4512.3, 1969 . $600

TROUBADUOR, L4548G/M, 1969 . $800

TWO ELEPHANTS, L1151G, 1971 . $475

TWO HORSES, L4597M, 1969 .. $1,400

TWO WOMEN CARRYING WATER JUGS, L1014G/M, 1969 .... $850

TWO YELLOW ROSES W/BASE, L5183M, 1984 .... $150

UNDER THE WILLOW, L1346G, 1978 .... $2,200

VALENCIAN BOY, L1400G, 1982 ... $525

VALENCIANS GRP/VALENCIAN COUPLE-HORSEBACK, L4648G/M, 1969 .... $1,200

VETERINARIAN, L4825G/M, 1972 . $475

VIOLINIST AND GIRL, L1039G/M, 1969 .... $1,000

WAITING FOR SAILOR (GRES), L2129, 1983 .... $650

WAITING IN THE PARK, L1374G, 1978 .... $565

WAITING TO TEE OFF, L5301G, 1985 .... $315

WAKE UP KITTY (GRES), L2183, 1989 .... $335

WALK IN VERSAILLES, L5004, 1978 .... $1,000

WATCHING THE PIGS, L4892G, 1974 .... $1,200

WATER FROM THE WELL (GRES), N1253, 1997 .... $200

WATERING FLOWERS, L1376G, 1978 .... $950

WEARY BALLERINA, L5275G/M, 1985 .... $325

WEDDING DAY, L5274G, 1985 ... $435

WEDDING/MATRIMONY, L1404G, 1982 .... $585

WHITE CARNATION W/BASE, L5184M, 1984 .... $150

WILD FLOWER, L5030G, 1979 ... $750

WINTER WONDERLAND, L1429G, 1982 .... $2,350

WINTRY DAY, A, L3513, 1978 .... $800

WOMAN GOLFER/LADY GOLFER, L4851M, 1973 .... $400

WOMAN WITH BABY, L2091, 1978 .... $800

WOMAN/LADY WITH DOG, L4761G, 1971 .... $365

WOODCUTTER, L4656G, 1969 .... $650

WRATH OF DON QUIXOTE, L1343G/M, 1977 .... $1,050

YOUNG HARLEQUIN, L1229G/M, 1972 .... $575

LUSTER WARE

Luster ware creamer, copper luster, wide cream-colored band, two panels of rust transfer depicting woman listening to musician, band of magenta and rust leaf garland decoration on cream ground, small spout flake, 6-1/4" w spout to handle, 5-1/2" h, **$80.**
Photo courtesy of Alderfer Auction Co.

History: Lustering on a piece of pottery creates a metallic, sometimes iridescent, appearance. Josiah Wedgwood experimented with the technique in the 1790s. Between 1805 and 1840, lustered earthenware pieces were created in England by makers such as Adams, Bailey and Batkin, Copeland and Garrett, Wedgwood and Enoch Wood.

Luster decorations often were used in conjunction with enamels and transfers. Transfers used for luster decoration covered a wide range of public and domestic subjects. They frequently were accompanied by pious or sentimental doggerel, as well as phrases that reflected on the humors of everyday life.

Copper luster was created by the addition of a copper compound to the glaze. It was very popular in America during the 19th century, and collecting it became a fad from the 1920s to the 1950s. Today it has a limited market.

Using a gold mixture made pink luster. Silver luster pieces were first covered completely with a thin coating of a "steel luster" mixture, containing a small quantity of platinum oxide. An additional coating of platinum, worked in water, was then applied before firing.

Sunderland is a coarse type of cream-colored earthenware with a marbled or spotted pink luster decoration, which shades from pink to purple. A solution of gold compound applied to the white body developed the many shades of pink.

The development of electroplating in 1840 created a sharp decline in the demands for metal-surfaced earthenware.

Luster ware tea set, covered teapot, creamer and sugar, silver luster on white ground, England, **$125.**

Reproduction Alert. The market for copper luster has been softened by reproductions, especially creamers and the "polka" jug, which may fool new buyers. Reproductions are heavier in appearance and weight than the earlier pieces.

Canary

Child's mug, "A Present for Charles," pink luster trim, minor wear, 1-3/4" h..........................**$625**

Miniature, creamer, red and green flowers, pink luster accents and rim, pinpoint flake, 2-3/4" h..............**$850**

Pitcher, baluster form, low neck and spout, sides printed with scenes titled "Attempt before the guard...," On Guard, Single Stick, Staffordshire, c1810, 6-1/4" l, 6" h **$220**

Copper

Goblet, mauve and green colored band with floral dec around mid section, c1850, 3" d, 3-3/4" h **$85**

Pitcher, blue band with molded flower dec on both sides, copper luster bulbous base, 4" h **$50**

Teacup and saucer, turquoise blue background, copper luster floral band..**$65**

Vase, two handles, stag scene, 7-1/4" w, 6-1/2" h..**$70**

Pink

Child's mug, pink luster band, reddish hunter and dogs transfer, green highlighted foliate transfer, 2" h ...**$85**

Creamer, stylized flower band, pink luster highlights and rim, ftd, 4-3/8" h..**$75**

Cup and saucer, magenta transfers, Faith, Hope and Charity, applied green enamel highlights, pink luster line borders **$60**

Figure, dogs, white, luster gilt collar, cobalt blue base with gilt trim, Staffordshire, pr, 4-1/2" h **$620**

Pitcher, emb ribs, eagle, and flowers in pink and purple luster, 5-3/4" h ...**$150**

MAASTRICHT WARE

History: Petrus Regout founded the De Sphinx Pottery in 1836 in Maastricht, Holland. The firm specialized in transferprinted earthenwares. Other factories also were established in the area, many employing English workmen and adopting their techniques. Maastricht china was exported to the United States in competition with English products.

Bowl, red, green, and blue agate pattern, "Petrous Regout, Maastricht" and lion mark, 5-3/4" d.................**$35**

Cup and saucer, Oriental pattern, c1929, 3-1/4" d, 2" h cup...............**$25**

Pitcher, rooster with iris and leaves, red transfer, marked "Regout & Co.

Haan," 5" h.....................................**$75**

Plate

Rusty brown border, pink and yellow roses in center, Royal Sphinx mark, c1891, 7-1/2" d............................**$50**

Delft, blue and white windmill scene, Royal Sphinx mark, 10" d **$50**

Timor pattern, 8-1/4" d.................**$30**

Canton pattern, Geisha girls and man on walkway, marked "Canton, P. Regout Maastricht," c1836, 8-1/2" d..........**$40**

Platter, gaudy polychrome florals, red, yellow, and green white ground, 11-1/2" d..**$70**

MAJOLICA

History: Majolica, an opaque, tin-glazed pottery, has been produced in many countries for centuries. It was named after the Spanish Island of Majorca, where figuline—a potter's clay—is found. Today, however, the term "majolica" denotes a type of pottery made during the last half of the 19th century in Europe and America.

Majolica frequently depicts elements of nature: leaves, flowers, birds and fish. Designs were painted on the soft-clay body using vitreous colors and fired under a clear lead glaze to impart the rich color and brilliance characteristic of majolica.

Victorian decorative art philosophy dictated that the primary function of design was to attract the eye; usefulness was secondary. Majolica was a welcome and colorful change from the familiar blue and white wares, creamwares and white ironstone of the day.

Marks: Wedgwood, George Jones, Holdcraft and Minton were a few of the English majolica manufacturers who marked their wares. Most of their pieces can be identified through the English Registry mark and/or the potter-designer's mark. Sarreguemines in France and Villeroy and Boch in Baden, Germany, produced majolica that compared favorably with the finer English majolica. Most Continental pieces had an incised number on the base.

Although 600-plus American potteries produced majolica between 1850 and 1900, only a handful chose to identify their wares. Among these manufacturers were George Morely, Edwin Bennett, the Chesapeake Pottery Company, the New Milford-Wannoppee Pottery Company and the firm of Griffen, Smith and Hill. The others hoped their unmarked pieces would be taken for English examples.

Notes: Prices listed here are for pieces with good color and in mint condition. For less-than-perfect pieces, decrease value proportionately according to the degree of damage or restoration. Majolica images depicted appear courtesy of Michael Strawser Auction Group unless otherwise noted.

Reproduction Alert. Majolica-style pieces are a favorite of today's interior decorators. Many exact copies of period pieces are being manufactured. In addition, fantasy pieces incorporating late Victorian-era design motifs have entered the market and confused many novice collectors.

Modern majolica reproductions differ from period pieces in these ways: (1) modern reproductions tend to be lighter in weight than their Victorian ancestors; (2) the glaze on newer pieces may not be as rich or deeply colored as on period pieces; (3) new pieces usually have a plain white bottom, period pieces almost always have colored or mottled bases; (4) a bisque finish either inside or on the bottom generally means the piece is new; and (5) if the design prevents the piece from being functional—e.g., a lip of a pitcher that does not allow proper pouring—it is a new piece made primarily for decorative purposes.

Some reproductions bear old marks. Period marks found on modern pieces include (a) "Etruscan Majolica" (the mark of Griffen, Smith and Hill) and (b) a British registry mark.

Basket
Bird on branch, pink ribbon on handle, 10" x 6-1/2" **$250**
Yellow, angel faces on each side, 8" .. **$200**

Bread tray
Floral, butterflies, pastel colors, "Waste Not Want Not" **$250**
Geranium and basketweave, "Eat thy bread with thankfulness," 12-3/4" **$300**

Bud vase, Minton, yellow, green ribbon, triple holes, 6" **$450**

Butter pat
Cobalt blue, sunflower **$140**
Holdcroft, fan shape, bird in flight **$175**
Wedgwood, chrysanthemum **$150**

Cake stand
Etruscan, morning glory, 8-1/4" .. **$175**
George Jones, leaf on napkin, white ground, 9" w, 6" h **$450**
Wedgwood, green leaf, green ground, 8" d, 2-1/2" h **$125**

Candlestick, figural
Palmer Cox Brownie, 8-1/2" h **$250**

Wardle, water lily form, all green **$125**

Cheese keeper, cov
Bird on branch, yellow ground, ribbon and bow accents **$375**
George Jones, apple blossom and basketweave, 10" d **$1,900**
Mottled brown and green, wedge shape, florals, 12" l **$250**
Turquoise, blackberry and cow, 11-1/2" h **$700**

Compote, Wedgwood, double dolphin, nautilus shell top, 16" **$800**

Cup and saucer
Banks and Thorley, Basketweave and Bamboo, butterfly handle **$275**
Etruscan, bamboo **$125**
Lovebirds on branch, green and tan **$75**
Shell shape, pink, yellow and brown **$175**

Humidor, cov, figural
Clown head, yellow hat and collar, 6" h **$75**

Majolica, large Austrian Rococo Revival jardinière on stand, ovoid, scroll handles and feet, shaped rocaille rim with diaper cartouches, yellow and light blue ground, enamel dec with scattered bees, foliates and dragonflies, conforming waisted stand, late 19th century, 33" h, **$1,057.**
Photo courtesy of Skinner, Inc.

Majolica Rorstrand cachepot, hairline, rim and base chip, 8" h, 8-3/4" d, **$25.**

Majolica brown French oyster plate, 9-1/2" d, **$40.**

Majolica George Jones turquoise, water lily and iris pitcher, outstanding color and detail, Bacall Collection, 8-1/4" h, **$2,500.**

Majolica bird on branch, low cake stand, 8-3/4" d, **$60.**

Majolica, Wedgwood pedestal, Argenta ware "Corinthian," England, fluted column, relief neoclassical oval portrait pendants, fruiting grapevine garland, leopard masks, trophy drops, impressed mark, foot rim restoration, rim hairline, chip, c1878, 33-1/2", **$1,410.**
Photo courtesy of Skinner, Inc.

Man, night cape and pipe, 4-1/2" h **$75**
Oriental lady, hat, 5" h **$75**
Policeman, pot bellied, 10-1/2" h . **$150**
Sailor, hat and beard, 5" **$50**

Jardinière, Wardle, Bamboo and Fern, 8" **$550**

Match striker, Continental
Happy Hooligan, hat **$100**
Lady with tambourine, 10-1/2" .. **$100**
Man with violin, 12" **$125**
Monk, stein and brick barrels, 8" **$100**
Monkey, cobalt blue cape, 5-1/2" . **$125**

Mug
Etruscan, Water Lily **$250**
Samuel Lear, classical urn **$100**
Wedgwood, grape and vine **$150**
Mustache cup and saucer, Wild Rose and Rope **$250**

Oyster plate
French Orchies, blue and beige, 10" d **$150**
Minton, pink wells, 9" d **$450**
Russian, Imperial eagle, 9-1/2" d.. **$500**
Seaweed and Shell, cobalt blue center, 10" d **$375**

Pitcher
Bird and bird nest, 9" h **$225**
Gnarled tree trunk and florals, 8" h **$150**
Robin, mottled, 9-1/4" h **$100**
Stork in marsh, 11" h **$225**
Water lily, green and yellow, 8" h **$175**

Plate
Bellflowers, cobalt blue, 8-3/4" d ... **$225**
Bird and Fan, pebbles, cobalt blue, 9" d **$150**
Bird in flight, fern and cattail, white ground, 8-1/2" d **$125**
Blackberry and basketweave, brown, 9" d **$125**

Platter
Dragonfly and leaf, pink border, 11-1/2" l.................................. **$200**
Eureka, bird and fan, diamond shaped, 15-1/2" l...................... **$250**
Leaves and ferns, oval, greens and brown, 12"................................ **$250**

Sardine box, cov
English, green and brown mottled **$250**
Fielding, Fan and Scroll, attached underplate, blue and yellow **$500**
Wedgwood, boat shaped anchor finial **$550**

Server, Holdcroft, double leaf, squirrel handle, 13" **$675**

Spittoon, Etruscan, Pineapple, yellow and green **$500**

Syrup, pewter top
Holdcroft, Pond Lily, turquoise, 3-3/4" **$300**
Wedgwood, Caterer jug, turquoise and brown, 7-1/2" **$250**
Wedgwood, Doric, mottled cobalt blue and brown, 7-1/2" h **$125**

Teapot, cov
Basketweave and floral, pink and turquoise, pewter lid, 6-3/4" h **$275**
Bird and Bird's Nest, figural, brown and green, 9"........................... **$225**
Fielding, Fan and Scroll, insect, pebble ground, cream and purple, 7" **$275**
Pyramid shape, brown, yellow and green, 8-1/2" **$250**
Wild Rose, yellow pebble ground, white flowers, 5-1/2" **$225**

Tray, Minton, bird, oak leaf shape, 8" **$500**

Tureen, George Jones, mackerel on bed of ferns, 19"............................ **$4,250**

MARBLEHEAD POTTERY

History: This hand-thrown pottery was first made in 1905 as part of a therapeutic program introduced by Dr. J. Hall for the patients confined to a sanitarium located in Marblehead, Massachusetts. In 1916, production was removed from the hospital to another site. The factory continued under the directorship of Arthur E. Baggs until it closed in 1936.

Most pieces found today are glazed with a smooth, porous, even finish in a single color. The most desirable pieces have a conventional design in one or more subordinate colors.

Centerpiece bowl, flaring, incised lotus leaf design on ext., dark blue matte glaze, imp ship mark, 3-3/4" h, 8-1/4" d **$425**

Chamberstick, bright yellow matte glaze, imp ship mark, 4" h, 4-1/2" d **$275**

Flower pot, terra cotta glaze, imp ship mark, 5" d **$195**

Humidor, lightly modeled stylized dark blue flora, speckled sandy ground, rare large paper label, Arthur Baggs, marked "AEB and MHC/$5.00," 5" h, 4-1/4" d **$4,100**

Tile, cuerda seca, polychrome trees and house, matte gray ground, mounted in period frame, ship mark, remnant of paper label, restoration to Y-shaped crack, 6" sq **$1,725**

Tile frieze, two tiles, incised lake scene, matte yellow, browns and greens, imp mark, paper label, orig price tag on each, orig frame retaining sticker marked "o. 2-64 tiles Poplars with Reflections, Dec by A. E. Baggs, Price $10.00," minor edge nicks, kiln pops, from estate of Dr. Hall, founder of Marblehead Pottery, 7-1/2" sq tiles **$21,850**

Trivet, stylized flowers, matte blue, green, yellow and red, imp mark, paper label, remnant of price label, from estate of Dr. Hall, founder of Marblehead Pottery, 6" sq **$865**

Vase

Barrel shape, blue and gray band of flying geese, speckled gray ground, remnant of imp ship mark, drilled bottom, 6" d, 6-1/4" h **$4,025**

Beaker shape, brown gooseberry leaves, indigo branches, dark blue ground, imp ship mark, 5" d, 6" h **$1,955**

Bulbous, smooth indigo matte glaze, imp ship mark, 3-3/4" h.......... **$475**

Cabinet, tapering, designed by Arthur Baggs, dec by Hannah Tutt, incised chevron pattern, two-tone mottled matte green glaze, imp ship mark, artist's cipher, 2-3/4" d, 4-1/4" h **$5,350**

Curved rim, widening at base, mottled lavender semi-matte glaze, imp mark, c1915-36, 6" h **$650**

Fan shape, matte blue glaze, imp mark, paper label, 8" d, 6-1/4" h **$320**

Geometric, lightly tooled, stylized light brown trees, matte speckled sand-colored ground, imp ship mark, 4-1/4" d, 6-1/4" h **$4,750**

Vessel, squatty, incised and painted stylized pattern in dark green on lighter green ground, ship mark, incised "MT," 2-1/4" h, 4-1/2" d **$3,750**

Wall pocket, speckled gray ext., robin's egg blue int., unmarked, 5-1/4" w, 5" h **$295**

Marblehead trivet tile, blue bird amidst green foliage, red blossoms, light blue speckled ground, mounted in new Arts & Crafts frame, stamped ship mark and paper label, trivet 6-1/4" x 6-1/4", **$1,998.**
Photo courtesy of David Rago Auctions, Inc.

Marblehead vase, dark matte green speckled glaze, lightly incised, dark glazed geometric decoration, impressed ship mark on base, early 20th century, 5" h x 5" d, **$5,225.**
Photo courtesy of Green Valley Auctions.

Marblehead vase, bottle shape, incised swirls, green glossy glaze, ship mark, 8-1/2" x 5-1/2", **$1,080.**
Photo courtesy of David Rago Auctions, Inc.

Marblehead vessel, tapered, smooth grey-purple glaze, oval paper label, 3-1/2" d, **$265.**
Photo courtesy of David Rago Auctions, Inc.

Marblehead vase, four color, rim and seven tree trunks in caramel, blue-green leaves, darker brown outline, light caramel ground, artist initialed, 4-1/4" h, **$4,115.**
Photo courtesy of Skinner, Inc.

McCoy, large fan vase, also called "Blades of Grass," glossy black, McCoy USA mark, late 1950s, 10" h, **$200.**

MCCOY POTTERY

History: The J. W. McCoy Pottery Co. was established in Roseville, Ohio, in September 1899. The early McCoy company produced both stoneware and some art pottery lines, including Rosewood. In October 1911, three potteries merged, creating the Brush-McCoy Pottery Co. This firm continued to produce the original McCoy lines and added several new art lines. Much of the early pottery is not marked.

In 1910, Nelson McCoy and his father, J. W. McCoy, founded the Nelson McCoy Sanitary Stoneware Co. In 1925, the McCoy family sold their interest in the Brush-McCoy Pottery Co. and started to expand and improve the Nelson McCoy Co. The new company produced stoneware, earthenware specialties, and artware.

Marks: The Nelson McCoy Co. made most of the pottery marked "McCoy."

Additional Listings: See *Warman's Americana & Collectibles* for more examples.

Reproduction Alert. Unfortunately, Nelson McCoy never registered his McCoy trademark, a fact discovered by Roger Jensen of Tennessee. As a result, Jensen began using the McCoy mark on a series of ceramic reproductions made in the early 1990s. While the marks on these recently made pieces copy the original, Jensen made objects that were never produced by the Nelson McCoy Co. The best-known example is the Red Riding Hood cookie jar, originally designed by Hull, and also made by Regal China.

The McCoy fakes are a perfect example of how a mark on a piece can be deceptive. A mark alone is not proof that a piece is period or old. Knowing the proper marks and what was made in respect to forms, shapes and decorative motifs is critical in authenticating a pattern.

McCoy, strap pitcher in glossy burgundy, McCoy mark, late 1940s, **$80.**

McCoy, Ring Ware pitcher in glossy green, unmarked, 1920s, 9" h, **$90.**

McCoy, Hyacinth vase McCoy mark, early 1950s, 8" h, **$175.**

Bean pot, cov, Suburbia Ware, brown, blue lid....................$48

Cookie jar, cov
Aunt Jemima..........................$275
Bobby Baker............................$95
Bugs Bunny, cylinder, 1971-72 ....$185
Chef, "Cookies" on hat band........$85
Clown, bust, c1943 ....$95
Clown in Barrel, marked "McCoy USA," overall crazing, c1953-56 ....$145
Davy Crocket, c1956, 10" h........$325
Engine, black $175
Kangaroo with Joey, 12" h..........$525
Little Red Riding Hood, 10-1/2" h $650
Panda, upside down, Avon label in heart logo on paw....................$150
Rooster, shades of brown, light tan head, green highlights $225
Strawberry $125
Touring Car, marked "McCoy USA," c1962-64, 6-1/2" h....................$155

Creamer and sugar, Sunburst $120

Decanter set, Jupiter 60 Train, Central Pacific locomotive, c1969.....$350

Flower pot, saucer, hobnail and leaf $40

Hanging basket, Pine Cone Rustic $45

Jardinière, green, brown and gold, emb lion's heads and columns, 5-3/4" d, 5-1/4" d $45

Jardinière pedestal, Onyx glaze, sgd "Cusick," c1909, 16-1/4" h $400

Lamp base, cowboy boots, c1956, 14" h................................$150
Low bowl, turtle flower frog, polychrome squeezebag dec, swastikas on bowl, 9" d, 2-3/4" h $500

Planter
Brown, white drip dec, 7-1/2" l, 4-1/2" w, 3" h $20
Hunting Dog, No Fishing on sign, 12" l $275
Three large pink chrysanthemums, marked "McCoy," 8" h $155

Spoon rest, yellow, foliage, overall crazing, 1940s, 8" l......................$145

Strawberry jar, stoneware, 12" h $150

Tankard pitcher, Buccaneer, green, 8-1/2" h................................$135

Tea set, cov teapot, open creamer and sugar, Pinecone, c1946 .... **$350**

Umbrella stand, maroon, rose and yellow glaze, c1915, 11" d, 22" h ... **$795**

Valet, eagle **$75**

Vase

Bulbous, flaring rim, jeweled, pastel Squeezebag dec, green base, mkd "042," 8-3/4" h **$575**

Cornucopia, green, 7-1/4" h **$125**

Swan, white, gold trim, 9-1/2" h **$250**

Wall pocket

Bellows **$60**

Cuckoo Clock, brown, green, white, yellow bird **$225**

Fan, blue **$65**

Post Box, green **$70**

Sunflower, blue **$80**

Window box, Pine Cone Rustic ... **$40**

McCoy basket-weave horn of plenty wall pocket, McCoy USA mark, 1950s, 8", **$110.**

McCoy strawberry jar, McCoy USA mark, 1950s, **$125.**

McCoy barn jar with cow in door, McCoy USA mark, lid was easily damaged, 1960s, **$375.**

McCoy ivy jardinière in brown and green, unmarked, also found in a brighter glossy tan and green with matching pedestal, early 1950s, 8" h, **$400.**

METTLACH

History: In 1809, Jean Francis Boch established a pottery at Mettlach in Germany's Moselle Valley. His father had started a pottery at Septfontaines in 1767. Nicholas Villeroy began his pottery career at Wallerfanger in 1789.

In 1841, these three factories merged. They pioneered underglaze printing on earthenware, using transfers from copper plates, and also were among the first companies to use coal-fired kilns. Other factories were developed at Dresden, Wadgassen and Danischburg. Mettlach decorations include relief and etched designs, prints under the glaze, and cameos.

Marks: The castle and Mercury emblems are the two chief marks, although secondary marks are known. The base of each piece also displays a shape mark and usually a decorator's mark.

Additional Listings: Villeroy & Boch.

Note: Prices in this listing are for print-under-glaze pieces (PUG), unless otherwise specified.

Coaster, PUG, drinking scene, marked "Mettlach, Villeroy & Boch," 4-7/8" d **$150**

Jardinière, #2427, expanded bulbous body, fish and flower dec, imp castle mark and number, 16" w, 12" h **$1,100**

Loving cup, three handles, musicians dec, 7-3/8" w, 6-3/4" h **$185**

Plaque

#1044-1067, water wheel on side of building, sgd "F. Reiss," PUG, gold wear on edge, 17" d **$495**

#1168, Cavalier, threading and glaze, sgd "Warth," chip on rear hanging rim, 16-1/2" d **$465**

#2196, Stolzensels Castle on the Rhein, 17" d **$1,100**

#2442, classical scene of Trojan warriors in ship, cameo, white high relief, blue-gray ground, artist sgd "J. Stahl," some professional restoration, 18-1/4" d **$1,200**

Stein

#485, one liter, cameo relief with musicians and dancers, inlaid lid, 9-5/8" h **$365**

#1526, transfer and enameled, Student Society, Amico Pectus Hosti Frontem, roster on either side of crest, pewter lid, slight discoloration to int, dated 1902 .... **$465**

#1896, 1/4 liter, maiden on one side, cherub face on other, grape dec, pewter lift handle **$350**

#2028, 1/2 liter, etched, men in Gasthaus, inlaid lid **$550**

#2057, 1/2 liter, etched, festive dancing scene, inlaid lid **$325**

#2093, 1/2 liter, etched and glazed, suit of cards, inlaid lid **$700**

#2204, 1/2 liter, etched and relief, Prussian eagle, inlaid lid **$780**

#2580, 1/2 liter, etched, Die Kannenburg, conical inlay lid, knight in castle **$695**

#5001, 4.6 liter, faience type, coat of arms, pewter lid **$850**

Minton majolica tavern mug, tapering sides, mottled ground, tavern figures, England, 1862, 10 rim chips, hairlines, 8" h, $645.
Photo courtesy of Skinner, Inc.

Minton ewer, Oenochoe shape, white ground decorated with raised gilt and silver blossoms leaves, and butterfly, gilt trim, satyr mask handle, printed mark, 11" h, $325.
Photo courtesy of Skinner, Inc.

MINTON CHINA

History: In 1793, Thomas Minton joined other men to form a partnership and build a small pottery at Stoke-on-Trent, Staffordshire, England. Production began in 1798 with blueprinted earthenware, mostly in the Willow pattern. In 1798, cream-colored earthenware and bone china were introduced.

A wide range of styles and wares was produced. Minton introduced porcelain figures in 1826, Parian wares in 1846, encaustic tiles in the late 1840s, and Majolica wares in 1850. Many famous designers and artists in the English pottery industry worked for Minton.

In 1883, the modern company was formed and called Mintons Limited. The "s" was dropped in 1968. Minton still produces bone-china tablewares and some ornamental pieces.

Marks: Many early pieces are unmarked or have a Sevres-type marking. The "ermine" mark was used in the early 19th century. Date codes can be found on tableware and majolica. The mark used between 1873 and 1911 was a small globe with a crown on top and the word "Minton."

Bud vase and stand, majolica, amphora shape, double handled vase seated in tripod stand, molded ram's heads and hoof feet, impressed mark on base, England, glaze crazing, 1863, 6-7/8" h **$1,175**

Centerpiece, elongated parian vessel, molded scroll handles and feet, pierced rim, two brown reserves, white pate-sur-pate amorini, gilding, dec, attributed to Lawrence Birks, marked "Minton," retailer's marks of Thomas Goode & Co., Ltd., London, c1889, 16" l **$1,400**

Compote, majolica, figural, lobed oval dish and plinth, brown glaze on agate ks of two cherubs holding laurel wreaths, center lovebirds, impressed mark, c1863, 10-1/2" l **$2,415**

Dinner service, partial, Florentine pattern, 12 10-1/2" d dinner plates; 12 9" d luncheon plates; 12 2-3/8" h teacups; 11 saucers; 10 10-1/2" d soup plates; eight 8" d dessert plates; seven 2-5/8" h coffee cups; six 7" d side plates; five 4-5/8" bowls; three 13", 15", 17" l graduated serving platters; two 10-1/2" l cov serving dishes; two small oval dishes; two pickle dishes; two 5-5/8" d side plates; a sq cov serving dish; cov sugar; creamer; milk jug; sauce boat and undertray; 9-3/4" d serving bowl; open 12" l serving tureen; 15" l cov tureen, 108 pieces total, third quarter 19th C **$2,185**

Figure, putti, yellow basket and grape vine, professional repair at rim of basket, 1867, 10-1/2" h **$2,750**

Floor urn, majolica, Neo-Classical, turquoise, massive foliage handles, 35" h, 18" d **$12,650**

Garden set, earthenware, barrel form, central pierced band of entwined rings between blue printed bands of flowers, scrolled vines, imp mark, glaze wear, price for pr, 19th C, 17 3/4" h **$1,100**

Jardinière, majolica, ftd, bowl with swags of fruit terminating at lion masks, base molded with three partially draped male figures between cornucopia of fruits, impressed mark, England, restored, c1868, 21" h **$3,525**

Nut dish, majolica, leaf-molded dish with squirrel handle, imp mark, restored chips to ears, c1869, 9-3/4" l **$1,840**

Oyster plate, majolica
Mottled **$935**
Turquoise **$495**

Oyster server, four tiers, majolica, green and brown, white wells, turquoise finial, rim damage to six wells, mechanical turning mechanism missing **$3,575**

Plaque, framed, painted scene of Dutch man reading document by row of books, initials "HH" lower right, date mark for 1883, 11-1/2" sq **$290**

Plate, 9" d, hp, polychrome dec, garlands and swags on rims, marked "Mintons/England/Rd. No. 608547/73793/Pat. Apr 1st 1913," price for set of 12 .... **$225**

Portrait plate, Duchess de Berri Caroline, Princis Lambelle, Madame Mars, Madame Elizabeth, sgd "A.S.I.," names on reverse, price for set of four, 9" d.. **$350**

Sweetmeat dish, majolica, blue titmouse on branch, leaf-shaped dish, imp mark, 1888, 8" d **$675**

Tower pitcher, majolica, castle molded body with relief of dancing villagers in medieval dress, imp marks, chips to cov thumb rest, spout rim, c1873, 12-1/2" h **$1,035**

Vase, celadon green ground, five-spout, fan form, applied white floral relief, fish head feet, imp mark, foot rim chip, c1855, 6-1/4" h **$215**

Minton plate, enamel decoration, Oriental medallion of peony and prunus, sky blue ground, faint stamp, light wear to gild on rim, 1874, 9" d, **$700.**
Photo courtesy of David Rago Auctions, Inc.

Minton vase, designed by Louis Solon, two handles, trail-slip decoration of swags and medallions in bright polychrome, red ground, stamped "Minton Ltd. No. 1,8503," 11-1/2" x 5-1/4", **$900.**
Photo courtesy of David Rago Auctions, Inc.

MOCHA

History: Mocha decoration usually is found on utilitarian creamware and stoneware pieces and was produced through a simple chemical action. A color pigment of brown, blue, green or black was made acidic by an infusion of tobacco or hops. When the acidic colorant was applied in blobs to an alkaline ground, it reacted by spreading in feathery designs resembling sea plants. This type of decoration usually was supplemented with bands of light-colored slip.

Types of decoration vary greatly, from those done in a combination of motifs, such as Cat's Eye and Earthworm, to a plain pink mug decorated with green ribbed bands. Most forms of mocha are hollow, e.g., mugs, jugs, bowls and shakers.

English potters made the vast majority of the pieces. Collectors group the wares into three chronological periods: 1780-1820, 1820-1840 and 1840-1880.

Mocha mug, pearlware, applied strap handle with leaf terminals, blue bands, slip marbled dec, of white, light and dark brown, ochre ground, green reeded band, rim chip, crack, England, late 18th century, 6" h, **$1,175.**
Photo courtesy of Skinner, Inc.

Reproduction Alert.

Beaker, pearlware
Dark brown, medium brown and ochre marble decoration on rust field, thin lines of medium brown at rim and base, England, rim chips and glaze wear, early 19th C, 3" h...**$2,475**
Rust, dark brown, medium brown and white combed marble slip, England, early 19th C, 3" h **$2,820**

Bowl
Ochre band, black seaweed, crazing, stains, 6-7/8" d, 3-1/2" h **$275**
Aqua band, blue stripes, blue, brown and white earthworm design, faint imp label, stained, small edge flakes, 7-1/4" d, 3-1/4" h **$325**

Chamber pot, two-tone blue bands, black stripes, black and white earthworm, leaf handle, some wear and edge flakes, 8-3/4" d **$125**

Child's mug
Black banding with black and gray earthworm dec on green field, yellow glazed, extruded handle with foliate terminals, impressed partial maker's mark on bottom, England, chips to base edge, glaze wear to rim, early 19th C, 2-5/8" h **$2,990**
Pearlware, green glazed rouletted upper and lower bands flanking rust field with dark brown scroddled dots, with bisecting lines cut through slip to white body, applied handle, England, repaired, early 19th C, 2-1/2" h **$825**

Creamer, black and white checkered band on shoulder medium blue glaze, 5-1/4" h...**$215**

Cup, imp border above brown and white earthworm design, blue ground, imperfections, 19th C, 2-7/8" h .. **$375**

Mocha creamer, band of decoration in blue and brown on yellow body, hairlines, 4-1/2" h, **$200.**
Photo courtesy of Alderfer Auction Co.

Ink sander, pearlware, two rows of dark brown trailed slip "tendrils" on blue field, England, two small chips, early 19th C, 3-1/4" h **$1,175**

Jug, barrel-form, banded in blue and black, black, white and blue earthworm dec on ocher field, handles with foliate terminals, England, 5/8" rim chip, associated crack, 1/2" chip on spout, c1840, 7-1/2" h **$1,880**

Measure, tankard, blue, black and tan seaweed dec, one with applied white label "Imperial Pint," other with resist label "Quart," minor stains, wear, and crazing, three-pc set, 5", 6" and 6-1/4" h........................ **$440**

Milk pitcher, dark bluish-gray band, black stripes, emb band with green and black seaweed, leaf handle, wear and painted over spout flake, 4-5/8" h **$440**

Mug

Barrel-form, black mocha seaweed dec on ocher field between black and blue bands, extruded handles with foliate terminals, England, small chip on base edge, c1820, 3-7/8" h **$1,410**

Brown checkerboard design, 19th C, 3" h **$260**

Ftd, pink, blue and black marbling, England, five small hairlines on rim, 19th C, 3-1/2" h, 4-1/8" d **$360**

Quart, banded in dark brown and rust, two rows of blue, dark brown, rust and white earthworm flanked by upper and lower white rouletted bands, extruded handle with foliate terminals, England, circular and spider cracks in the base, three rim chips, early 19th C, 6" h **$1,765**

Mustard pot, cov

Creamware, blue banded lid with blue reeded band, cylindrical body with matching banding, dark brown, rust, gray and white earthworm pattern, extruded handle with foliate handles, creamware, England, chips to the lid, small crack to the body, discoloration, early 19th C, 2-1/2" h **$1,300**

Pearlware, lid with acorn finial, brown bands with dendritic seaweed on rust field, body decorated in the same manner, extruded handle with foliate terminals, England, finial repair, small rim and base chips, early 19th C, 3-1/2" h **$1,645**

Pearlware, lid with ball finial banded in dark brown and rust, matching banding on the body, unusual band of rust and dark brown slip in finely trailed diamond pattern, extruded handle with foliate terminals, England, crack in the handle, minor glaze wear, early 19th C, 3-1/2" h **$2,585**

Pitcher

Large band of dark brown seaweed and beaded diamonds on ochre ground between bands of dark brown and green stripes, imp chevron bands, 8-1/2" h, some minor glaze loss **$1,725**

Yellowware, brown bands, black seaweed, glaze flaking, three base chips **$5,250**

Portrait box, transfer and painted dec of Napoleon III and Empress Eugenie, 5" d.. **$150**

Salt, open, chocolate brown band, black seaweed dec, small chip on foot, 2-3/4" d, 1-3/4" h **$520**

Shaker

Blue band, black stripe, brown, black, and white earthworm dec, blue top, repair, 4-7/8" h.......................... **$330**

Tan bands, brown stripes, black seaweed dec, chips, 4-1/8" h **$220**

Tea canister, blue, black and white band on shoulder, white fluted band on bottom, medium blue glaze, 4" h.. **$125**

Teapot, oval shape, medium blue, fluted band on bottom, black and white checkered band on top, acorn finial, 5-7/8" h................................... **$500**

Waste bowl, amber band, black seaweed dec separated into five segments by squiggly lines, green molded lip band, stains and hairlines, 4-3/4" d **$275**

Mocha pint mug, pearlware, applied strap handle with leaf terminals, taupe band, brown, ocher and white earthworm dec, dark brown bands, white wavy lines, reeded green-glazed band, two hairlines, England, c1930, 4-7/8" h, **$1,410.**
Photo courtesy of Skinner, Inc.

MOORCROFT

History: William Moorcroft was first employed as a potter by James Macintyre & Co., Ltd., of Burslem in 1897. He established the Moorcroft pottery in 1913.

The majority of the art pottery wares were hand thrown, resulting in a great variation among similarly styled pieces. Color and marks are keys to determining age.

Walker, William's son, continued the business upon his father's death and made wares in the same style.

Marks: The company initially used an impressed mark, "Moorcroft, Burslem;" a signature mark, "W. Moorcroft" followed. Modern pieces are marked simply "Moorcroft," with export pieces also marked "Made in England."

Bowl, pansy dec, pale green ground, imp maker's mark, 3-5/8" d **$150**

Box, cov, pansy dec on lid, pale green ground, imp maker's mark, crazing, 4-3/4" l, 1-1/2" w, 1-3/4" h **$200**

Compote, Lily motif, yellow and green ground, 7-1/4" d **$150**

Ginger jar, cov, pomegranate dec, 11-1/2" h................................. **$525**

Jar, cov, Cornflower, ivory ground, coat of arms of Kings College, Oxford, c1911 .... **$1,450**

Lamp base, Anemone, 6-1/4" d, 11-1/4" h.................................. **$920**

Loving cup, Pomegranate pattern, stamped mark, minor rim fleck, 1914-16, 6" d, 5-1/2" h **$1,150**

Pitcher, Forget-Me-Not, c1902, 6-1/4" h **$1,350**

Plate, toadstool, blue ground, imp "Moorcroft Claremont," 7-1/4" d.............. **$600**

Vase

Eventide pattern, ovoid, squeezebag green trees, cobalt blue ground, stamped "Moorcroft/Made in England" and signature, rim chip, 2" line, 6-1/2" d, 15" h **$1,840**

Leaf & Berry, matte glaze, William's initials in blue, 7" h **$1,150**

Long narrow neck on bulbous base, green poppies, green ground, Moorcroft handmade pottery paper label, painted signature, imp mark, and "made in England," rim restoration, c1918, 12-3/8" h **$1,410**

Orchid, flambé, sgd by William in blue, imp "Potter to HM The Queen," 12" h **$4,350**

Pomegranate, vasiform, blue ground, red pomegranates, purple seeds, imp factory mark with facsimile signature, printed paper Royal Warrant label, 1928-49, 7-3/8" h **$500**

Moorcroft baluster vase, Pomegranate pattern, cobalt blue ground, ink signature, MADE IN ENGLAND, MOORCROFT, 12-1/2" x 6-1/2", **$1,060.**
Photo courtesy of David Rago Auctions, Inc.

Moorcroft vase, Eventide pattern, yellow background, sgd "W. Moorcroft," numbered RD0397964, extensive restoration, 7-3/4" d, 11-3/4" h, **$650.**
Photo courtesy of David Rago Auctions, Inc.

Moorcroft, Eventide biscuit jar, orig silvered cover and handle, glaze flake to rim, on edge of silver, MOORCROFT/ Signature/Made in England/hallmarks on silver, 6-1/2" x 5-1/2", **$2,040.**
Photo courtesy of David Rago Auctions, Inc.

Moorcroft plate, Pomegranate and Berry pattern, glossy cobalt blue ground, stamped "Made In England," ink signature, mounted in metal plate hanger, small plate ring chip, 8-1/2" d, **$175.**
Photo courtesy of David Rago Auctions, Inc.

MULBERRY CHINA

History: Mulberry china was made primarily in the Staffordshire district of England between 1830 and 1860. The ware often has a flowing effect similar to flow blue. It is the color of crushed mulberries, a dark purple, sometimes with a gray tinge or bordering almost on black. The potteries that manufactured flow blue also made Mulberry china, and, in fact, frequently made some patterns in both types of wares. To date, there are no known reproductions.

Educational Alert: The Flow Blue International Collectors' Club, Inc., has been discussing new versus reproduction mulberry and flow blue. There are still areas of personal judgment as yet undetermined. The general rule accepted has been "new" indicates recent or contemporary manufacture and "reproduction" is a copy of an older pattern. Problems arise when either of fields is sold at "old" mulberry prices.

In an effort to help educate its membership, the club continues to inform of all known changes through its conventions, newsletters and the Web site: www.flowblue.com.

Victoria Ware: Mark is of a lion and uniform, but has paper label "Made in China," 1990s. Made in various patterns and design, but the giveaway is the roughness on the bottoms, and much of it has a pea green background. Some of this line is also being made in flow blue.

Check the Flow Blue International Collectors' Club, Inc. Web site www.flowblue.org. Join the club, study the books available, and always, always, know your dealer! Good dealers guarantee their merchandise and protect their customers.

Adviser: Ellen G. King.

Mulberry sugar with lid, Corean, Podmore-Walker, 1849, **$255.**

Mulberry plate, Brushstroke, Strawberry, 1848, 9", **$125.**

Abbey, Adams, 1850
Platter, 15-3/4" $195
Alleghany, Goodfellow, 1840
Plate, 8"....................................... $85
Soup tureen with undertray $650
Athens, Adams, 1849
Child's sugar bowl with lid $120
Beauties of China, Venables, 1845
Creamer...................................... $100
Teapot with lid............................ $550
Berry, Ridgway, 1850
Cake plate with handles............. $135
Plate, 8"....................................... $75
Blackberry Lustre, Mellor Venables, 1849
Plate, 9"...................................... $120
Bochara, Edwards, 1847
10" Bowl $85
Bouquet, Wedgwood, 1846
Plate, 9"....................................... $65
Plate, charger, 12-1/2" $125
Sauce ladle.................................. $110
Brushstroke, Strawberry, Unknown, 1848
Plate, 9"....................................... $125
Bryonia, Utzshneider, 1890
Cake plate, stemmed, 14"............ $425
Demitasse cup and saucer $65
Dessert bowl, individual, 4"......... $30
Handled footed fruit bowl $275
Plate, 8"....................................... $45
Square fruit bowl, 9" $135
Teapot with lid............................ $325
Castle Scenery, Furnival, 1850
Plate, 8"....................................... $75
Coral, Challinor, 1845
Platter, 12-1/4" x 9-1/2"............... $175

Teacup (handleless) and saucer ... $95
Teapot with lid, polychromed shells
.... $275
Corea, Clementson, 1840
Plate, 8"....................................... $70
Platter, 16" x 12-1/2" $225
Vegetable tureen with lid........... $295
Corean, Podmore-Walker, 1849
Plate, 10".................................... $110
Platter, 14" $225
Sauce tureen with undertray $400
Sugar with lid.............................. $255
Teapot with lid............................ $450
Cyprus, Davenport, 1850
Punch cup $135
Shell relish, mask on handle....... $100
Flora, Hulme & Booth, 1851
Plate, 8"....................................... $45
Vegetable bowl, 9" $75
Flora, Walker, 1848
Cup plate $110
Handleless cup and saucer........... $85
Pitcher, 12"................................. $200
Plate, 8"....................................... $75
Floral, Unknown, 1850
Vase, polychromed, 10"............... $130
Floresque, Davenport, 1850
Soup tureen with lid and underplate
.... $650
Foliage, Walley, 1846
Plate, 9"....................................... $55
Plate, 10"..................................... $80
Genoa, Davenport, 1840
Platter, 13-3/4" $200
Hollyhock, Wedgwood, 1860
Green ground low tazza............. $145
Hong, Walker, 1848
Sauce boat, two handled $185

Hopberry, Meigh, 1845
Child's sugar with lid.................$110
Jardinere, U & C, 1860
Plate, 8"....................................$55
Jeddo, Adams, 1865
Handleless cup and saucer...........$80
Platter, 12-1/4"........................$225
Platter, 17-3/4"........................$300
Sauce tureen, lid, undertray......$275
Teapot with lid.........................$450
Vegetable bowl, 10", round........$150
Vegetable tureen with lid..........$255
Water pitcher...........................$350
Lily, Dimmock & Smith,1850
Pitcher....................................$125
Marble, Unknown, 1850
Milk pitcher.............................$145
Razor box with lid.....................$185
Marble, Wedgwood, 1850
Plate, 9"...................................$65
Platter, 15-1/2"........................$150
Toothbrush holder with lid........$110
Vegetable bowl, 9-1/2"...............$90
Medina, Furnivals, 1848
Plate, 9"...................................$75
Milan, South Wales Pottery, 1840
Platter, 14".............................$250
Montezuma, Goodwin, 1846
Plate, 9-1/2".............................$80
Moss and Sprig, maker unknown, 1845
Plate, 8"...................................$75
Neva, Challinor, 1847
Creamer..................................$125
Plate, 10"................................$155
Sugar with lid..........................$140
Ning Po, R. Hall, 1845
Cup plate..................................$55
Gravy boat.................................$85
Plate, 7-1/2".............................$60
Vegetable bowl, oval, 10"..........$150
Vegetable tureen with lid..........$200

Waste bowl................................$95
Pelew, Challinor, 1840
Creamer..................................$100
Grandfather's cup and saucer.....$135
Gravy boat...............................$110
Plate, 10"................................$125
Sugar bowl with lid...................$110
Teapot with lid, gothic shape......$300
Vegetable bowl, round, open, 12-1/2"
....$250
Peruvian, Wedgwood, 1849
Sugar bowl with lid, scroll handles
....$235
Teapot with lid, 16 panels...........$500
Peruvian Horse Hunt, Shaw, 1850
Vegetable bowl, octagonal.........$225
Phantasia Wreath, Furnival, 1855
Platter, poly cut corners, 16"......$250
Rhone Scenery, Mayer, 1850
Plate, 9"...................................$65
Plate, 10"..................................$80
Platter, 18".............................$255
Teacup and saucer......................$95
Teapot with lid.........................$275
Waste bowl..............................$100
Rose, Challinor, 1847
Plate, 8"...................................$90
Rose, Walker, 1846
Cup plate.................................$110
Plate, 9"...................................$80
Milk pitcher.............................$225
Waste bowl................................$70
Royal, Wood & Son, 1890
Plate, 9-3/4".............................$85
Teacup and saucer......................$65
Seaweed, Ridgway, 1840
Plate, 9"...................................$75
Teacup, handleless, with saucer.$135
Seville, Wood & Sons, 1890
Plate, 9-1/4".............................$50
Shanghae, Furnival, 1850
Sugar bowl with lid.....................$75

The Temple, Podmore-Walker, 1850
Creamer, 5-1/4".......................$195
Sugar bowl with lid...................$100
Tiger Lily, Furnivals, 1848
Punch bowl, pedestal, polychromed
flowers...................................$650
Tillenburg, Clementson, 1850
Plate, 10-1/4"............................$80
Tulip & Fern, maker unknown, 1840
Brushstroke pattern, mitten relish..$155
Ivy, maker unknown, 1850
Child's wash bowl and pitcher, poly-
chrome...................................$575
Vincennes, Alcock, 1860
Platter, octagonal, 15-1/4".........$200
Platter, 18".............................$350
Soup, 10-1/2"...........................$175
Wash basin..............................$325
Washington Vase, Podmore-Walker, 1850
Classic gothic creamer..............$135
Plate, 9"...................................$85
Platter, 18-1/4"........................$300
Sauce tureen with lid................$325
Teacup and saucer......................$95
Wash Pitcher...........................$285
Wreath, Furnival, 1850
Plate, 9-3/4".............................$95
Zinna, Bourne & Co., 1881
Creamer, 5"..............................$150
Plate, 9"...................................$95

Mulberry fruit bowl, handled and footed, Bryonia, Utzshneider, 1890, **$275.**

Mulberry vegetable tureen with lid, Corea, Clementson, 1840, **$295.**

Newcomb College bowl, carved by A. F. Simpson, wreath of white and yellow daffodils, blue ground, NC/JM/AFS/56/KV45, 1920, 3-1/4" x 6-1/2", **$1,800.**
Photo courtesy of David Rago Auctions, Inc.

NEWCOMB COLLEGE POTTERY

History: The Sophie Newcomb Memorial College, an adjunct of Tulane University in New Orleans, LA, was originated as a school to train local women in the decorative arts. While metalworking, painting and embroidery were among the classes taught, the production of fine, handcrafted art pottery remains its most popular and collectible pursuit.

Pottery was made by the Newcomb women for nearly 50 years, with earlier work being the rarest and most valuable. This is characterized by shiny finishes and broad, flat-painted and modeled designs. More common, though still quite valuable, are the matte glaze pieces, often depicting bayou scenes and native flora. All bear the impressed NC mark.

Adviser: David Rago.

Newcomb College cabinet vase, bayou scene against a pink sky, carved by Sadie Irvine, NC/SI/JM/KQ72/282, 1919, 3-1/2" x 4", **$2,880.**
Photo courtesy of David Rago Auctions, Inc.

Bud vase, tapered, high glaze, carved yellow jonquils, green leaves, blue ground, by Anna Frances Simpson, marked "NC/Q/FS/CQ52/JM," 1908, 9" h, 3-1/4" d **$6,900**

Cabinet vase, by Anna F. Simpson, 1926, blue live oak and Spanish moss, gray ground, high glaze, marked "NC/JH/PP56/15/AFS," 2" d, 4-1/2" h **$3,335**

Chocolate set, teal blue pine trees carved by A. F. Simpson, light blue and green glossy ground, two matching cups, four saucers, mkd "NC/AFS/JM/E112/B," some damage, 1911, 10-1/2" h, 6" d chocolate pot **$5,500**

Low bowl, carved pink irises, green leaves, medium blue matte ground, by A. F. Simpson, marked "NC/NF31/313/JM" and artist's cipher, couple of short, tight lines to rim, 1923, 9-1/4" d, 3-1/4" h **$1,610**

Vase
Bulbous, painted by Sara Levy, bright yellow blossom, green stems, pale ground, mkd "NC/S.B.L./JM/Q," c1903, 5-1/2" h, 3-1/2" d **$6,500**
Carved matte, by Sadie Irvine, pink and red loquat fruit and leaves around undulating rim, marked "NC/SK/JM/I47/NP47," small chips to foot ring, short tight line to rim, 1924, 4-1/2" d, 6-1/2" h **$1,150**

Vessel
Matte, squatty, by Sadie Irvine, sharply carved pink Japanese iris, green stems, around undulating top conforming to shape of blossoms, purple and blue ground, marked "NC/SI/JM/213?MV17," 1922, 6-1/2" d, 4-1/2" h **$3,220**
Organically shaped, by Marie De Hoa LeBlanc, three modeled ginkgo leaf handles, semi-matte olive green and gunmetal glaze, marked "NC/Q/JM/MHL," orig price tag, c1905, 7-1/2" d, 6" h **$5,175**

Newcomb College candlestick lamp, copper faceted clip on shade, pierced, embossed with arrowroot; base has carved and painted arrowroot, signed NC/MROBINSON/AV73/JM, Maude Robinson, 1906, 10-1/2" h x 5", **$6,600.**
Photo courtesy of David Rago Auctions, Inc.

Newcomb College transitional vase, bulbous, carved with wreath of white buds and green leaves, blue ground, May Morell, NC/MM/K/DM66, 1910, 5-1/2" x 5-1/4", **$2,820.**
Photo courtesy of David Rago Auctions, Inc.

Newcomb College charger, delft style, old Newcomb Chapel surrounded by border of oak leaves and Newcomb College Pottery logo/97. NC/M/S.E.B/APR97/JM26, 8-3/4", **$5,400.**
Photo courtesy of David Rago Auctions, Inc.

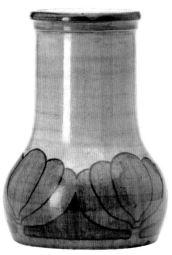

Newcomb College bulbous vase, stylized green foliage on light and dark blue background, painted by M.O. Delavigne, 1902, 6-1/4" x 4-1/2", **$3,120.**
Photo courtesy of David Rago Auctions, Inc.

Newcomb College vase, incised by Harriet Joor, ivory and yellow magnolia blossoms, green foliage, pale blue ground, NC/HJ/0024/JM, restoration to two rim chips, 1904, 11-3/4" x 7", **$20,000.**
Photo courtesy of David Rago Auctions, Inc.

Newcomb College vase, stylized trees in blue, unidentified artist, NC/N41/JM/U, 1902, 8" h x 5-3/4", **$7,800.**
Photo courtesy of David Rago Auctions, Inc.

NILOAK POTTERY

History: Niloak Pottery was made near Benton, Arkansas. Charles Dean Hyten experimented with native clay, trying to preserve its natural colors. By 1911, he perfected Mission Ware, a marbleized pottery in which the cream and brown colors predominate. The company name is the word "kaolin" spelled backward.

After a devastating fire, the pottery was rebuilt and named Eagle Pottery. This factory included enough space to add a novelty pottery line in 1929. Hyten left the pottery in 1941, and in 1946 operations ceased.

Marks: The early pieces were marked "Niloak." Eagle Pottery products usually were marked "Hywood-Niloak" until 1934, when the "Hywood" was dropped from the mark.

Additional Listings: See *Warman's Americana & Collectibles* for more examples, especially the novelty pieces.

Note: Prices listed here are for Mission Ware pieces.

Niloak Mission Ware vase, ovoid, marbleized clays, stamped "Niloak," spider line to base, 4" d, 8" h, **$115.**
Photo courtesy of David Rago Auctions, Inc.

Bowl, marbleized swirls, blue, tan, and brown, 4-1/2" d **$65**

Candlesticks, pr, marbleized swirls, blue, cream, terra cotta, and brown, 8" h **$250**

Flower pot, ruffled rim, green matte glaze, c1930 .... **$155**

Toothpick holder, marbleized swirls, tan and blue **$100**

Urn, marbleized swirls, brown and blue, 4-1/2" h **$45**

Vase
Applied twisted handles, Ozark Dawn glaze, c1930, 6" h **$120**

Early foil label, c1920-30, 3-1/4" h **$95**

Ozark Dawn glaze, c1930, 8-3/4" h, ... **$140**

Second art mark, c1925, 4-1/2" h **$75**

Starved rock mark, c1925, 4-1/2" h **$95**

Swirled colors, first art mark, c1910-24, 8-1/2" h **$230**

Swollen baluster with broad rim, brown, rose, blue, and cream, second art mark, 10-1/2" h **$500**

Niloak Mission Ware cordial set, four matching tumblers, all marbleized clay, paper labels and stamps, 12" h stoppered bottle, **$900.**
Photo courtesy of David Rago Auctions, Inc.

NIPPON CHINA, 1891-1921

Nippon urn, six-sided, hand-painted, scene of trees and lake, marked, some fading of gilt on handles, rim, and base, 14-3/4" h, **$395.**

Photo courtesy of David Rago Auctions, Inc.

History: Nippon, Japanese hand-painted porcelain, was made for export between 1891 and 1921. In 1891, when the McKinley Tariff Act proclaimed that all items of foreign manufacture be stamped with their country of origin, Japan chose to use "Nippon." In 1921, the United States decided the word "Nippon" was no longer acceptable and required all Japanese wares to be marked "Japan," ending the Nippon era.

Marks: There are more than 220 recorded Nippon backstamps or marks; the three most popular are the wreath, maple leaf, and rising sun. Wares with variations of all three marks are being reproduced today. A knowledgeable collector can easily spot the reproductions by the mark variances.

The majority of the marks are found in three different colors: green, blue, or magenta. Colors indicate the quality of the porcelain used: green for first-grade porcelain, blue for second-grade, and magenta for third-grade. Marks were applied by two methods: decal stickers under glaze and imprinting directly on the porcelain.

Reproduction Alert. Distinguishing old marks from new:

An old leaf mark approximately one-quarter-inch wide, has "Hand" with "Painted" below to the left of the stem and "NIPPO Box N" beneath. The newer mark has the identical lettering, but size is now one-half, rather than one-quarter, inch.

An old mark consisted of "Hand Painted" arched above a solid rising sun logo with "NIPPO Box N" in a straight line beneath. The modern fake mark has the same lettering pattern, but the central logo looks like a mound with a jagged line enclosing a blank space above it.

Basket, handle
Allover moriage dec, unmarked, 8-1/2" h **$375**
Hp roses, stippled gilt ground, unmarked, 7-1/2" h **$90**

Berry set, azalea dec, enameled and gilt floral borders, green M in wreath mark, 10-1/4" d master bowl, four 5" d individual bowls....................**$90**

Bowl
Ftd, grape dec, gilt borders, green M in wreath mark, 9-1/2" d **$175**
Hp, sailing ships with palm tree and ruins, three handles, green wreath mark, 8-1/2" d **$150**

Box, cov, floral dec, green maple leaf mark, 4-1/2" d..............................**$115**

Cake plate, lavender coastal scene, green and gilt borders, blue maple leaf mark, 10-1/2" d....................**$195**

Chocolate pot
Hp, cottage and lake scene, green wreath mark, 7-1/2" h.............**$260**
Hp, etched gold panels, jewel trim, green wreath mark, 9-1/2" h **$175**

Condensed milk jar, cov, underplate, pink roses, green leaves, gilt accents, unmarked **$295**

Humidor
Blown-out, reclining camel, jeweled saddle, green "M" in wreath mark, 6-1/2" h **$2,300**
Moriage trailings, partial "Imperial Nippon" mark, 7-1/2" h **$320**
Six panel sides, gilt trim, blue "maple leaf" mark, 5-1/2" h **$115**
Water lilies dec, tight hairline in base, unmarked, 5-1/2" h **$70**

Mayonnaise set, ftd bowl, matching underplate, ladle, delicate floral design, green M in wreath mark, blue mark on ladle................................**$80**

Nut dish, blown-out design, three ftd, green M in wreath mark, 7-1/4" d **$55**

Plate
Rose dec, raspberry and gilt border, blue maple leaf mark, 7-1/2" d **$220**
Scalloped edge, rose dec, gilt dec, blue maple leaf mark, 10" d **$250**

Portrait plate, raised gilt, enameled jeweled border, blue maple leaf mark, 9" d..**$835**

Portrait vase
Lacy gilt ground, blue maple leaf mark, 7" h **$435**

Two handles, portrait of Madame Lebrun, gilt tracery ground, drilled for lamp and later plugged, 9-3/4" h **$245**

Tankard, hp, gold dec rim and base, applied scrolled handle, blue maple leaf mark, minor gold loss, 13" h **$350**

Tea set, hp, powder blue background, swans dec, Paolownia flower mark **$325**

Toothpick holder, Woodland, white, green "M" in wreath mark, 2" h **$115**

Tray, hp, scenic center, medallions of roses at ends, green wreath mark, 8" l, 6-1/4" w................................**$150**

Urn
Scenic, enameled florals, blue maple leaf mark, bolted, lid missing, 11" h **$150**
Two handles, allover moriage dec, unmarked, 8-1/2" h..................**$150**

Vase
Coralene, six-ftd base, "Pat. Applied For" mark, 4-3/4" h **$230**
Four panels with cottage scene, concave shoulders, green "M" in wreath mark, 13" h **$700**
Four scenic panels in blown-out medallions, green "M" in wreath mark, bolted, 14-1/2" h........**$1,350**
Ring handles, floral dec, blue maple leaf mark, chip on one foot, 9-3/4" h **$150**
Snow scene, handles, "M" in wreath mark, minor gilt wear, 5" h .. **$260**
Two handles, moriage dec bird, blue maple leaf mark, minor professional rim repair, 7-1/2" h **$375**

Nippon vase, rose motif, base and rim gilt, green wreath mark, gilt wear, early 20th century, 9-1/4" h x 4-1/2" d, **$80.**
Photo courtesy of Green Valley Auctions.

Nippon vase, lakeshore motif, gilt dec, blue maple leaf design, minor gilt loss, late 19th/early 20th century, 8-1/2" h x 4-1/4" d, **$275.**
Photo courtesy of Green Valley Auctions.

Nippon vase, dragon decoration, small banding loss, c1900, 14-3/4", **$385.**
Photo courtesy of David Rago Auctions, Inc.

Nippon bowl, eight lobes, floral motif, gilt, blue maple leaf mark, late 19th/early 20th century, 3-3/4" h x 11-1/4" d , **$80.**
Photo courtesy of Green Valley Auctions.

NORITAKE CHINA

History: Morimura Brothers founded Noritake China in 1904 in Nagoya, Japan. The company made high-quality chinaware for export to the United States and also produced a line of china blanks for hand painting. In 1910, the company perfected a technique for the production of high-quality dinnerware and introduced streamlined production.

During the 1920s, the Larkin Company of Buffalo, New York, was a prime distributor of Noritake China. Larkin offered Azalea, Briarcliffe, Linden, Modjeska, Savoy, Sheridan, and Tree in the Meadow patterns as part of its premium line.

The factory was heavily damaged during World War II, and production was reduced. Between 1946 and 1948, the company sold its china under the "Rose China" mark, since the quality of production did not match the earlier Noritake China. Expansion in 1948 brought about the resumption of quality production and the use of the Noritake name once again.

Marks: There are close to 100 different marks for Noritake, the careful study of which can determine the date of production. Most pieces are marked "Noritake" with a wreath, "M," "N," or "Nippon." The use of the letter N was registered in 1953.

Bowl, fruit, Linden, 5-1/4" **$10**
Bowl, oval, Rosewin #6584 pattern, 10" l **$30**
Bowl, soup, rimmed, Sheridan, 7-3/4" **$14**
Bread and butter plate
 Azalea, 6-3/8" **$6**
 Briarcliffe, 6-1/2" **$8**
 Linden, 6-3/8" **$10**
 Modjeska, 6-3/8" **$8.50**
 Sheridan, 6-1/4" **$8**
Cake plate, handled, Linden, 10-1/2" **$41**
Cake set, desert scene with tent and man on camel, cobalt blue and gilt border, marked "Noritake/Made in Japan/Hand Painted," 11" d cake plate, six 6-1/4" serving plates **$770**
Candlesticks, pr, gold flowers and bird, blue luster ground, wreath with "M" mark, 8-1/4" h **$125**
Celery
 Azalea, 12-3/4" **$35**
 Linden, 13" **$40**
Coffee pot, small, lid, Rosewin, 6-3/8" **$45**
Console set, 11-3/4" d bowl, pr 8" h candlesticks, amber pearl center, 1"

Noritake Azalea pattern, lemon dish, ring handle, **$30.**

black rim with gold floral dec, green mark **$465**
Creamer
 Azalea **$27**
 Linden **$30**
 Sheridan, 8 oz **$25**
Creamer and sugar, Art Deco, pink Japanese lanterns, cobalt blue ground, basket type handle on sugar, wreath with "M" mark **$50**
Cup and saucer, Florola **$24**
Demitasse cup and saucer, Tree in the Meadow **$45**
Dinner set, floral motif, gold rimmed, 115-pc set **$375**
Egg cup, Azalea, 3-1/8" **$35**
Gravy boat, attached underplate, Briarcliffe **$38**
Gravy boat, Tree in the Meadow **$50**
Hair receiver, Art Deco, geometric designs, gold luster, wreath with "M" mark, 3-1/4" h, 3-1/2" w **$50**
Napkin ring, Art Deco man and woman, wreath with "M" mark, pr **$60**
Pitcher, Azalea, 28 oz **$195**
Place card holder, figural, bluebird with butterfly, gold luster, white stripes, wreath with "M" mark, pr **$35**
Plate, dinner
 Azalea, 9-7/8" **$24**
 Briarcliffe, 10" **$18**
 Linden, 10" **$15**
 Modjeska, 9-7/8" **$25**
 Sheridan, 10-1/2" **$19**
Plate, salad
 Briarcliffe, 7-1/2" **$10**
 Linden, 7-5/8" **$18**

Modjeska, 7-5/8" **$11**
 Rosewin, 8-1/4" **$10**
 Sheridan, 8-1/4" **$10**
Punch bowl set, 12" h two-part punch bowl with three-ftd base, six 2-3/4" h cups, peacock design, cobalt blue and gilt borders, blue ground ext., melon and blue interior, "M" in wreath mark **$600**
Relish
 Linden, 8-5/8" **$31**
 Rosewin, 9" **$17**
Salt, swan, white, orange luster, pr, 3" l **$25**
Salt and pepper shakers, pr, Tree in the Meadow, marked "Made in Japan" **$35**
Salt shaker, bulbous, Azalea **$21**
Serving platter, oval
 Briarcliffe, 11-3/4" **$50**
 Linden, 11-7/8" **$58**
 Linden, 13-3/4" **$80**
 Rosewin, 15-1/4" **$55**
 Sheridan, 13-7/8" **$38**
Teapot, lid, Azalea, 3 cup size **$150**
Tea tile, Tree in the Meadow, green mark, 5" w **$35**
Toothpick holder, Azalea **$80**
Vegetable bowl, cov, Magnificience, #9736 .... **$350**
Vegetable bowl, oval, Rosewin, 10" **$55**
Vegetable bowl, round, cov, Sheridan **$80**
Waffle set, handled serving plate, sugar shaker, Art Deco flowers, wreath with "M" mark **$50**
Wall pocket, butterfly, wreath with "M" mark **$75**

NORTH DAKOTA SCHOOL OF MINES

History: The North Dakota School of Mines was established in 1890. Earle J. Babcock, a chemistry instructor, was impressed with the high purity level of North Dakota potter's clay. In 1898, Babcock received funds to develop his finds. He tried to interest commercial potteries in the North Dakota clay, but had limited success.

In 1910, Babcock persuaded the school to establish a Ceramics Department. Margaret Cable, who studied under Charles Binns and Frederick H. Rhead, was appointed head. She remained until her retirement in 1949.

Decorative emphasis was placed on native themes, e.g., flowers and animals. Art Nouveau, Art Deco, and fairly plain pieces were made.

Marks: The pottery is marked with a cobalt blue underglaze circle of the words "University of North Dakota/Grand Forks, N.D./Made at School of Mines/N.D. Clay." Some early pieces are marked only "U.N.D." or "U.N.D./Grand Forks, N.D." Most pieces are numbered (they can be dated from University records) and signed by both the instructor and student. Cable-signed pieces are the most desirable.

North Dakota School of Mines vase, bulbous, decorated by Julia Mattson, band of leaping bison in matte green on brown ground, ink stamp "JM 111," 5" x 6", **$1,600.**

Photo courtesy of David Rago Auctions, Inc.

North Dakota School of Mines vase, bulbous, decorated by Julia Mattson, rodeo scenes in olive green and dark brown, circular ink stamp/JM/75, 7" x 4-3/4", **$1,400.**

Photo courtesy of David Rago Auctions, Inc.

North Dakota School of Mines vessel, squat, carved repeating owls under light to dark brown matte glaze, ink stamp "M.O.R. to KSR 34," 3" x 5-1/4", **$1,900.**

Photo courtesy of David Rago Auctions, Inc.

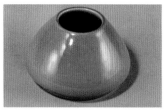

North Dakota School of Mines vase, conical, by Flora Huckfield and student, glossy celadon and brown glaze, circular ink stamp, incised "Huck and Le Masurier 2371," 3" x 5", **$235.**

Photo courtesy of David Rago Auctions, Inc.

Bowl, closed-in, incised birds of paradise and cornflowers, blue, ivory, and green, by L. Whiting, circular ink stamp, incised "L. Whiting," minor fleck at shoulder, 7-1/2" d, 4-1/4" h **$1,725**

Charger, carved by Margaret Cable, stylized turquoise flowers, terra cotta ground, incised "67/M Cable," stamped "Prarie Pottery Und Grand Forks," 8-1/4" d **$450**

Figure, Bentonite cowboy, brick-red, black, and gold glaze, incised "JJ/13/UND," Julia Mattson, 1913, 4-1/2" h, 3-1/4" w **$650**

Vase

Bulbous, carved narcissus, brown and umber matte glaze, by Margaret Cable, stamped circular mark, incised "M. Cable/223," 5-1/2" d, 7-1/2" h **$1,840**

Bulbous, emb cowboy scene, matte chocolate brown glaze, circular ink stamp, sgd "Flora Huckfield," titled "N. D. Rodeo," 5" d, 7-1/4" h **$1,500**

Bulbous, emb prairie roses, mottled green crystalline glaze, circular ink mark, incised "Steen-Huck-1100," Huckfield and Steen, 4-1/2" d, 5" h **$1,200**

Bulbous, polychrome painted band of pioneers and covered wagons, glossy brown ground, by Flora Huckfield, circular stamp mark/72/Huck, incised H?, 3-1/2" d, 5-1/2" h **$1,850**

By Woodward, green semi-matte glaze, circular ink stamp mark, 6" d **$200**

Carved daffodils, mahogany matte glaze, circular ink mark, incised "McCosh '48," 5-1/2" d, 8" h ...**$1,100**

Carved mocha brown narcissus, dark brown ground, ink stamp, incised "E. Cunningham/12/6/50," E. Cunningham, 1950, 5" h, 9" d **$1,000**

Conical, by Flora Huckfield and student, glossy celadon and brown glaze, circular ink stamp, incised "Huck" and "Le Masurier/2371," 5" d, 3" h.................................**$230**

Ovoid, carved sheaves of wheat, purple-brown matte glaze, ink stamped and incised "Huck 30/No. Dak. Wheat," F. Huckfield, 5-1/2" d, 10" h **$1,300**

Sq tapering, repeating scenes of farmer and horse-drawn plough, green and brown matte glaze, circular ink mark, incised "The Plowman/Huck/119," F. Huckfield, 6-1/4" d, 4-3/4" h **$1,200**

Vessel

Beaker shape, matte brown glaze, stamped and incised marks, small rim chip, c1915, 3-1/2" h, 3-1/2" d **$115**

Spherical, Covered Wagon, carved frieze of wagons and oxen, sandy brown matte glaze, circular ink mark, incised "M. Cable" and title, by Margaret Cable, 7" d, 6" h **$1,400**

Squatty, carved band of cowboys under terra cotta and brown matte glaze, by Julia Mattson, stamped circular mark, incised "Cowboy-54C/J Mattson," 5" d, 3-1/2" h **$980**

George Ohr pitcher, front and back shown, bisque fired, scroddled clay, hairline, nick and restoration to small rim chip, script signature, 3" x 6-1/4", **$2,160.**
Photo courtesy of David Rago Auctions, Inc.

George Ohr pitcher, bisque fired, marbleized clay, script signature, 4" x 4-1/2", **$4,500.**
Photo courtesy of David Rago Auctions, Inc.

George Ohr puzzle mug, rabbit handle, glossy amber glaze, stamped G.E. OHR BILOXI, 3-1/4" x 4-1/4", **$1,680.**
Photo courtesy of David Rago Auctions, Inc.

OHR POTTERY

History: Ohr pottery was produced by George E. Ohr in Biloxi, Mississippi. There is a discrepancy as to when he actually established his pottery; some say 1878, but Ohr's autobiography indicates 1883. In 1884, Ohr exhibited 600 pieces of his work, suggesting that he had been a potter for some time.

Ohr's techniques included twisting, crushing, folding, denting, and crinkling thin-walled clay into odd, grotesque, and, sometimes, graceful forms. His later pieces were often left unglazed.

In 1906, Ohr closed the pottery and stored more than 6,000 pieces as a legacy to his family. He had hoped the U.S. government would purchase it, but that never happened. The entire collection remained in storage until it was rediscovered in 1972.

Today Ohr is recognized as one of the leaders in the American art-pottery movement. Some greedy individuals have taken the later unglazed pieces and covered them with poor-quality glazes in hopes of making them more valuable. These pieces do not have stilt marks on the bottom.

Marks: Much of Ohr's early work was signed with an impressed stamp including his name and location in block letters. His later work was often marked with the flowing script designation "G. E. Ohr."

Bank, acorn shape, lustered brown and mirror black glaze, int. rattle, stamped "G.E.OHR/Biloxi, Miss," 2" d, 4" h **$1,100**

Candleholder, organic, pinched ribbon handle, in-body twist, ribbed base, yellow, green, and raspberry matte mottled glaze, small chip to base, script mark, 6-1/2" h, 4" d **$3,300**

Chalice, ovoid cup, flaring base, lustered black and umber glaze, script signature, restoration to cup, 3-1/4" d, 6" h **$805**

Demitasse cup, ext. with rare green, cobalt blue, and raspberry marbleized glaze, int. with sponged cobalt and raspberry volcanic glaze, die-stamped "G. E. Ohr, Biloxi, Miss," 2-1/2" h, 3-3/4" d **$1,500**

Jar, cov, spherical, gunmetal and green glaze dripping over mottled raspberry ground, shallow storage abrasion, die-stamped "G.E. OHR, Biloxi, Miss," 4-1/4" h, 5" d **$1,500**

Jug

Commemorative, molded form, wide mouth and angled handle, President on one side and Ohr's wife on other, decorative star and floral motifs, caramel-colored glaze, artist's mark imp on side and signature on base, 7-1/2" h **$3,820**

Flared cylindrical rim, pinched spout, bulbous body dimpled around middle, angled handle, dark brown matte glaze, imp "G. E. OHR, Biloxi, M…," 4-3/4" h **$4,350**

Mug

Cylindrical form, flared base and angled handle, mottled green on yellow glaze ext., yellow glaze and green flecks int., inscription around lower portion of mug reads "Heres your good health and your family's and may they all live long and prosper, J. Jefferson," base signed and dated "3-18-96," 6" h **$2,820**

Cylindrical waisted form, black mirror glaze, base sgd, c1900, 4-3/4" h **$1,175**

Mustache cup, hand built as a shirt cuff, ribbon handle, sponged blue glaze, die-stamped "GEO. E. OHR/BILOXI, MISS," 2-3/4" h, 4" d **$2,000**

Pitcher, pinched and folded bisque, scroddled terra cotta and buff clays, script sgd, two large sanded rim chips, 4" h, 5-1/4" d **$3,775**

Puzzle mug, mottled green, yellow, and brown glaze on exterior and interior, animal head carved into angled handle, three drinking holes along rim and 16 holes around upper body, base imp "G. E. OHR Biloxi Miss.," c1900, 3-1/2" h **$1,775**

Vase

Bottle shape, brown, green, and amber speckled lustered glaze, restoration to tiny rim chip, die-stamped

Ohr vessel, corseted, four-lobed rim, deep in-body twist, fine red, green, and blue leathery matted glaze, script signature, restoration to rim chips, 4-1/4" x 4-1/2", **$4,750.**
Photo courtesy of David Rago Auctions, Inc.

Ohr vase, bulbous, lobed rim, carved band, fine pink, green and cobalt blue mottled glaze, stamped "G.E. OHR, Biloxi, Miss," firing line to shoulder, 4-1/2" d, 5" h, **$9,750.**
Photo courtesy of David Rago Auctions, Inc.

Ohr vase, bulbous, ruffled rim, cobalt blue, pink, yellow and green flambé glaze, marked "5-1-1897, E. Dan Smith, 175 Mobile, Alabama," stamped "G.E. OHR, Biloxi, Miss," restoration to small rim chip, 4-1/2" d, 4-1/2" h, **$11,150.**
Photo courtesy of David Rago Auctions, Inc.

"G. E. OHR, Biloxi, Miss," 8-1/2" h **$1,200**

Bottle shape, mottled raspberry, purple, cobalt blue, and green satin glaze, small abrasion ring around widest part from years of storage at production site, die-stamped "G. E. OHR/Biloxi, Miss," 9-1/4" h ..**$2,500**

Cinched middle, folded rim, speckled brown and amber glaze, stamped "G. E. OHR/Biloxi, Miss," 4" d, 3-1/4" h **$3,220**

Cylindrical form expanding at base, caramel-colored glaze with green and black speckles, base incised "GEO E OHR, BILOXI MISS," 3-3/4" h **$2,585**

Tapered, asymmetrically folded rim, gunmetal and yellow glaze ext., bright orange int., marked "G.E.OHR/Biloxi, Miss," few minute rim flecks, 2-3/4" d, 5-1/4" h **$4,875**

Three-sectioned bottle form, glossy olive glaze, top and bottom sponged dark blue, center purple metallic glaze, die-stamped "G. E. OHR/Biloxi, Miss," 7" h...................**$1,200**

Vessel

Collared rim, bulbous base, mottled dark brown and gunmetal glaze, incised "Biloxi," 3" d, 4-1/2" h **$2,300**

Dimpled, squatty, floriform top, black-mirrored glaze sponged on amber ground, stamped "G. E. OHR/Biloxi, Miss," 4-1/2" d, 3" h **$4,025**

Ohr vase, baluster shape, top covered in indigo glaze over green and raspberry mottled base, mkd "G. E. OHR, Biloxi, Miss," 6-3/4" x 3", **$8,500.**
Photo courtesy of David Rago Auctions, Inc.

Ohr vase, bulbous, scalloped rim, floriform dimple on front, green, gunmetal, brown, and amber mottled glaze, mkd "G. E. OHR, Biloxi, Miss," small nicks to rim, 5-1/4" x 6", sold with handwritten letter from George Ohr with poem and signature by George and his six children, dated 1899, and period newspaper clipping concerning Ohr, **$27,500.**
Photo courtesy of David Rago Auctions, Inc.

Ohr cabinet vase, urn shape, pinched and folded rim, bulbous base, black-speckled green glaze, mkd "BILOXI, MISS, GEO. E. OHR," 3" x 3", **$8,000.**
Photo courtesy of David Rago Auctions, Inc.

George Ohr pitcher, dark brown gunmetal glaze, pinched and cut out handle, impressed "G.E. OHR, BILOXI," late 19th/early 20th century, 2-1/2" h x 7-1/2" w x 5-1/2" d, **$1,650.**
Photo courtesy of Green Valley Auctions.

Old Sleepy Eye pitcher, cobalt blue, white background, **$195.**

Reproduction Alert. Blue-and-white pitchers, crazed, weighted, and often with a stamp or the word "Ironstone" are the most common reproductions. The stein and salt bowl also have been made. Many reproductions come from Taiwan.

A line of fantasy items, new items which never existed as Old Sleepy Eye originals, includes an advertising pocket mirror with miniature flour-barrel label, small glass plates, fruit jars, toothpick holders, glass and pottery miniature pitchers, and salt and pepper shakers. One mill item has been made, a sack marked as though it were old, but of a size that could not possibly hold the amount of flour indicated.

OLD SLEEPY EYE

History: Sleepy Eye, a Sioux Indian chief who reportedly had a droopy eye, gave his name to Sleepy Eye, Minnesota, and one of its leading flour mills. In the early 1900s, Old Sleepy Eye Flour offered four Flemish-gray heavy stoneware premiums decorated in cobalt blue: a straight-sided butter crock, curved salt bowl, stein, and vase. The premiums were made by Weir Pottery Company, later to become Monmouth Pottery Company, and finally to emerge as the present-day Western Stoneware Company of Monmouth, Illinois.

Additional pottery and stoneware pieces also were issued. Forms included five sizes of pitchers (4, 5-1/2, 6-1/2, 8, and 9 inches), mugs, steins, sugar bowls, and tea tiles (hot plates). Most were cobalt blue on white, but other glaze hues, such as browns, golds, and greens, were used.

Old Sleepy Eye also issued many other items, including bakers' caps, lithographed barrel covers, beanies, fans, multicolored pillow tops, postcards, and trade cards. Regular production of Old Sleepy Eye stoneware ended in 1937.

In 1952, Western Stoneware Company made 22- and 40-ounce steins in chestnut brown glaze with a redesigned Indian's head. From 1961 to 1972, gift editions were made for the board of directors and others within the company. Beginning in 1973, Western Stoneware Company issued an annual limited edition stein for collectors.

Marks: The gift editions made in the 1960s and 1970s were dated and signed with a maple leaf mark. The annual limited edition steins are marked and dated.

Mill items

Advertising premium cards, full-color Indian lore illus, Old Sleepy Eye Indian character trademark, 10-pc set, 9-1/4" x 11-1/2" d.................**$875**

Cookbook, Sleepy Eye Milling Co., loaf of bread shape, portrait of chief **$150**

Label, egg crate, Sleepy Eye Brand, A. J. Pietrus & Sons Co., Sleepy Eye, MN, red, blue, and yellow, 9-1/4" x 11-1/2" d.......................................**$25**

Letter opener, bronze, Indian-head handle, marked "Sleepy Eye Milling Co., Sleepy Eye, MN"..................**$750**

Pinback button, "Old Sleepy Eye for Me," bust portrait of chief...........**$175**

Pottery and stoneware

Bowl, ftd, Bristol glaze, relief profile of Indian on one side, floral design on other, imp "X" on bottom, 4" h **$360**

Butter crock, cov, blue and gray salt glaze, relief and blue accented Indian profile on one side, trees and teepee on other side, imp "H" on bottom, surface rim chip, 4-3/4" h **$495**

Mug, marked "WS Co. Monmouth, Ill," 3-1/2" d, 4-3/4" h **$395**

Pitcher, #4, 7-3/4" h **$675**

Stein, Bristol glaze, relief and blue accented Indian profile on one side, trees and teepee on other side, 7-1/2" h **$470**

Tile, cobalt blue and white **$850**

ONION MEISSEN

History: The blue onion or bulb pattern is of Chinese origin and depicts peaches and pomegranates, not onions. It was first made in the 18th century by Meissen, hence the name Onion Meissen.

Factories in Europe, Japan, and elsewhere copied the pattern. Many still have the pattern in production, including the Meissen factory in Germany.

Marks: Many pieces are marked with a company's logo; after 1891, the country of origin is indicated on imported pieces.

Note: Prices given are for pieces produced between 1870 and 1930. Early Meissen examples bring a high premium.

Ashtray, blue crossed swords mark, 5" d...**$75**

Bowl, reticulated, blue crossed swords mark, 19th C, 8-1/2" d **$395**

Box, cov, round, rose finial, 4-1/2" d...**$80**

Bread plate, 6-1/2" d....................**$75**

Cake stand, 13-1/2" d, 4-1/2" h ..**$220**

Candlesticks, pr, 7" h **$90**

Creamer and sugar, gold edge, c1900 ....**$175**

Demitasse cup and saucer, c1890 ....**$95**

Fruit compote, circular, openwork bowl, five oval floral medallions, 9" h **$375**

Fruit knives, six-pc set.................. $75
Hot plate, handles........................ $125
Ladle, wooden handle.................. $115
Lamp, oil, frosted glass globular form
   shade, 22" h............................... $475
Plate, 10" d.................................... $100
Platter, crossed swords mark, 13" x 10"
   .... $295
Pot de creme................................ $65
Serving dish, floral design on handle,
   9-1/4" w, 11" l............................. $200
Tray, cartouche shape, gilt edge, 17" l
   .... $425
Vegetable dish, cov, sq, 10" w.... $150

Onion Meissen sardine box, covered, rectangular, fish finial, titled on front in plaque, marked, **$225.**

ORIENTAL CERAMICS

History: The Oriental pottery tradition has existed for thousands of years. By the 16th century, Chinese ceramic wares were being exported to India, Persia, and Egypt. During the Ming dynasty (1368-1643), earthenwares became more highly developed. The Ch'ien Lung period (1736-1795) of the Ch'ing dynasty marked the golden age of interchange with the West.

Trade between the Orient and the West began in the 16th century, when the Portuguese established Macao. The Dutch entered the trade early in the 17th century. With the establishment of the English East India Company, all of Europe sought Oriental influenced pottery and porcelain. Styles, shapes, and colors were developed to suit Western tastes, a tradition which continued until the late 19th century.

Fine Oriental ceramics continued to be made into the 20th century, and modern artists enjoy equal fame with older counterparts.

Additional Listings: Canton, Imari, Kutani, Orientalia, Rose Medallion, and Satsuma.

Bowl

Arita ware, crayfish and citron, floral sprigs on int., Japan, 19th C, 10" d
.... **$360**

Blue and white, central design of deer and pine tree, borders of rocks, tree peonies, and banana plats, ext. of foliate scrolling, five spur marks and fuku character on base, Japan, late 17th/early 18th C, 12" d **$4,410**

Blue and white, cranes enameled on int., Yongzheng mark, China, 3-7/8" d **$360**

Light brown glaze, six-character underglaze blue mark, Xuantong, China, 1909-1911, 5-3/4" d, 3-3/16" d
.... **$1,495**

Stoneware, hare's fur glaze, steep rounded sides, lustrous black glaze radiating off center with unglazed spot, exterior with heavy pooling of glaze towards unglazed base, China, possibly Song Dynasty (960-1279), area of raised glaze blob ground and smoothed, 4-1/2" d, 2-1/2" h **$450**

Thin body, int. with incised dragons among clouds, four-character mark, pale celadon glaze, China, 19th or 20th C, 9-1/8" l, 2-1/2" h.......... **$300**

Box, cov

Cov painted with dragon in famille rose enamels, turquoise ground, squiggly blue line pattern, int. with same pattern without dragon, China, imperfections to glaze, 19th C, 4-1/2" d, 2-1/2" h......... **$120**

Peach bloom glaze, Qianglong four-character underglaze blue mark within double circle, China, small rim chips, 19th or 20th C, 5-3/8" d..... **$150**

Brush pot, biscuit porcelain, cylindrical, relief landscape dec, Chen Lung six-character mark on base, Chinese, 18th or 19th C, 5" h, 2-1/4" d **$575**

Brush rest, robin's egg blue glaze, three wild animals perched on rock, turquoise glaze on underside, China, 18th or 19th C, 3-5/8" l, 2-1/8" h **$230**

Brush washer, peach-form, grayish celadon crackle glaze, some areas unglazed gray color base, China, possibly Ming Dynasty, 4-1/2" l, 3-3/8" w, 1-7/8" h........................ **$200**

Charger, blue and white, landscape with scholar on horseback being led over bridge, six-character Cheng Hua honorific mark on base, Japan, 19th C, 19-1/4" d **$765**

Vase, Chinese, finely painted in black and brown on biscuit ground, dragon among clouds, carp leaping waterfall, Xuande six-character mark on recessed base, 19th or 20th century, **$225.**

Chinese export charger, bird and floral polychrome decoration, scalloped rim, decorated on underside, 12" d, **$200.**
Photo courtesy of Alderfer Auction Co.

Cup

Quatrefoil lobed outline, turquoise glazed int., blue ground ext. with traces of gilt designs, slight flaring foot with iron red Jiaqing seal mark, China, 19th C, 3-3/4" l, 3-1/4" w, 2-3/4" h **$150**

Two medallions painted in rose enamel, underglaze blue ground, gilt highlights, border of flowers and geometric pattern inside rim, Kang Xi six-character mark on base, traces of gilt on rim, China, 18th or 19th C, 3" d, 1-1/2" h **$100**

Cup stand, Wucai dec, two dragons facing in opposite directions chasing flaming pearl, step-down base with underglaze blue band interspersed with iron red circles, deep recessed glazed base with four-character underglaze blue Yu Tang Jia Qi mark, two incised characters to left within double circle, China, 18th C or earlier, 5-5/8" d **$1,100**

Figure

Seated geisha, enveloped in kimono dec with maple leaves, Japanese, small loss to enamel, 19th C, 6-1/4" h **$325**

Sitting hound, mouth slightly open, brown glazed tongue, bell suspended from green glazed collar, China, 18th or 19th C, 6-3/4" h **$375**

Garden seat, painted underglaze blue dec, continuous band of peonies and ruyi designs around top and base, Chinese, hairline crack, 18th C, 9" d, 8" h **$925**

Incense burner

Ceramic, squat globular body tapering inwards and rising at neck, two loop handles at top of rim, thick black glaze thinning to brown around the rim, int. and base unglazed, three unglazed feet, China, firing cracks around feet, 19th C or earlier **$175**

Wucai style, painted underglaze blue and iron-red dragons on sides, band of waves, green and yellow enamels, elephant handles with attached ring, six-character underglaze blue Wanli mark on base, three feet, China, one foot chipped, cover missing, 18th C or earlier **$325**

Jar, cov, pr, bright turquoise ground, white slip dec of dragons among flowers and tendrils, cov with rose and yellow glazed peach finial, base with rose Hong Xian seal mark, China, wear to glaze on finials, early 20th C, 4-3/4" h, 5-1/4" d **$990**

Lamp base, 10-1/2" h double gourd vase, underglaze blue dec, outline painted flowers and horses conforming to raised molded panels, fluted paneled neck, China, 17th C, 23" h **$1,100**

Model, Tabarabune, painted overall with overglaze enamels, sides with birds flying over turbulent waves, waves and spray modeled in relief, int. with scene of people in garden landscape, two standing on side of large fish, dragon as figurehead, Japan, 19th C, 14-1/2" l, 6" h **$1,100**

Plaque, painted, scene of samurai protecting woman and child from pursuers, 14" x 12" **$400**

Plate

Finely painted overglaze dec of bird swooping over flowering peony, two medallions with precious things inset in fence of geometric designs, back with rect Kutani and artist's mark, Japan, Meiji period, 11-7/8" h **$530**

Round, side wall rising sharply, forming deep well, center with painted dragon among clouds within a circle, cavetto with interlocking band of ruyi, band of alternating triangles on outer border, foot rim painted with basketweave design, kiln grit on inside, underglaze blue mark on base, China, Ming Dynasty, 17th C, 7-5/8" d **$320**

Studio porcelain, painted with underglaze blue hydrangea with pink highlights, mkd on base, Japanese, c1900, 6-1/4" d **$120**

Platter

Octagonal oblong, gilt-starred cobalt blue oval centered with gilt floral spray, gilt and cobalt blue borders, Chinese Export, glaze and gilt wear to cavetto, late 18th C, 12-1/4" x 15-3/4" **$300**

Oval, blue Fitzhugh border, shield-shaped armorial and motto "SPES INFLEXIBILIS," (hope unbending), Chinese Export, Chien Lung, repaired, c1785, 17-1/2" l **$300**

Sake washer, underglaze blue scrolling tendrils, int. with landscape, Japanese, 19th C, 6" d, 3-1/2" h **$200**

Seal paste box, underglaze blue dec of dragon among clouds, stylized waves on bottom, Kang Xi four-character mark on base, China, 20th C, 2-1/8" d **$100**

Table screen, porcelain, underglaze blue dec, one side painted with flowers, other with mountainous landscape, flat spherical form with geometrical designs on border, Japanese, 19th C, 5-5/16" d, 5-1/2" h **$350**

Tazza, ceramic, in the style of Ogata Kenzan, thick black glaze, stylized flower wheels in bright enamels, Kenzan signature on side of bowl, Japanese, small rip chips, old repairs, 18th or 19th C, 6-1/2" d, 5" h **$500**

Vase

All-around painted landscape dec in grisaille colors, two openwork handles on sides of neck, base with four character Chien Lung mark, Chinese, early 20th C, 8-3/4" h **$1,725**

Baluster, blue and white continuous figural scene, Kangxi mark, China, 14-1/4" h **$1,195**

Bottle shape, coral red with a relief dragon with gilt accents, China, six-character Ch'ien Lung mark on base, but probably 19th C, 13-1/2" h **$3,200**

Blue and white dec of dragon, tiger, and pine tree, China, Transitional period (17th C), lines to base, 11-1/2" h **$1,410**

Blue and white, design of peonies and phoenixes, China, 19th C, 25-1/2" h **$450**

Carmine red glaze, incised feather-like spiral dec, interspersed with Buddhist precious things, two gilt stylized elephant handles with loose rings, Jurentang Zhi seal mark on base, China, Hongixan, wear to rim gilt, 1915-16, 7-7/16" h **$875**

Finely painted in black and brown on biscuit ground, dragon among clouds, carp leaping waterfall, dragon and clouds on neck, Xuande six-character mark on recessed base, China, 19th or 20th C, 9" h......**$300**

Flat bear shape tapering to rect neck, painted in iron red and overglaze enamels with chi dragons and sacred fungus, elephant handles top with ruyi design and key fret border on base, China, 19th C, 5-3/8" h **$425**

Hexagonal, painted in famille noire enamels, front and back panels with molded relief dec of cranes and gnarled tree trunk, elephant handles, China, 18th or 19th C, 10" h **$350**

Hexagonal, six panels with fluted ridges and aubergine glaze, yellow glazed flaring neck with chi dragon sculpted in relief in green and aubergine glaze, China, small foot rim chips, 18th C, 4-3/16" h **$135**

Hirado, underglaze blue dec of fishing boats moored near gnarled pine tree, flock of cranes flying on large flared neck, loose ring handles on sides, Japanese, old restoration, 18th or 19th C, 20-1/2" h, 10-3/8" d **$700**

Molded design of peony blossom, other peony flowers and foliage, underglaze blue mark of Makuzu Kozan within square, Japan, Meiji period (1868-1911), 8-1/2" h **$3,300**

Narrow slender form, tapering body unglazed towards base, mottled green and copper red glazes, underside revealing deep recessed glazed base with underglaze blue six-character Kan Xi mark, China, wooden stand, repairs, 18th C, 6-7/8" h **$260**

Painted famille verte enamels on yellow ground, two stylized dragon handles with aubergine glaze, China, 19th or 20th C, 6-5/8" h **$200**

Peach bloom glaze of celadon green running to deep red, Mei Ping, China, 19th C, 16" h **$1,100**

Shibayama, gold lacquer, diamond form, four sides dec with birds among flowering plants, mother-of-pearl, coral, and stained ivory, unsigned, Japanese, Meiji period, small rim chips, 6" h **$1,650**

Slender form, mottled copper red glaze with green splashes, heavy pooling of glaze towards base and partly ground, six-character underglaze blue Kang XI mark on slightly recessed base, China, 18th or 19th C, 5-1/4" h **$250**

Stoneware, double gourd, incised floral dec, beige-brown crackled glaze with distinct horizontal banding above base, China, several small fired cracks, glaze chips, 18th or 19th C, 12-3/4" h **$500**

Surface carved with lotus meanders under a mustard yellow glaze, Mei Ping, six character Ch'ien Lung mark and probably of the period, 7-1/2" h **$1,100**

Tall cylindrical neck with two raised rings, mottled green and copper red glaze, underglaze blue six-character Kan Xi mark, China 19th C, 7-7/16" h **$850**

Chinese export charger, underglaze blue and white floral decoration, thought to be Kang His, 16-3/4" d, **$875.**
Photo courtesy of Alderfer Auction Co.

Underglaze blue dec, band of stylized flowers around bulbous body, ruyi and artemesia leaf dec on shoulder and neck, Kan Xi six-character mark on base, China, 18th or 19th C, 8-3/4" h **$550**

Underglaze blue dec, three friends of winter, prunus, pine, and bamboo, Chinese, transitional period or late Ming, slight fritting to rim, 6" h **$750**

Woman and child in rock garden with overglaze enamels, base with sq seal "Jurentang Zhi," Chinese, small foot ring chip, early 20th C, 9" h **$900**

Water dropper, curved fish form, blue enamel glaze, Korean, price for pr, 19th C, 3-1/8" w **$300**

Whistle, modeled as child lying on tummy, pale celadon glaze, green, red, and black enamels, China, 17th or 18th C, 2-1/2" l, 1-1/2" h **$200**

Chinese bowl, blue and white, porcelain, floral decoration, Kangxi mark, 7-1/2" d, **$475.**
Photo courtesy of Sloans & Kenyon Auctioneers and Appraisers.

OWENS POTTERY

History: J. B. Owens began making pottery in 1885 near Roseville, Ohio. In 1891, he built a plant in Zanesville and in 1897, began producing art pottery. After 1907, most of the firm's production centered on tiles.

Owens Pottery, employing many of the same artists and designs as its two cross-town rivals, Roseville and Weller, can appear very similar to that of its competitors, e.g., Utopian (brown glaze), Lotus (light glaze), and Aqua Verde (green glaze).

There were a few techniques used exclusively at Owens. These included Red Flame ware (slip decoration under a high red glaze) and Mission (overglaze, slip decorations in mineral colors) depicting Spanish Missions. Other specialties included Opalesce (semi-gloss designs in lustered gold and orange) and Coralene (small beads affixed to the surface of the decorated vases).

Owens Soudaneze vase, white poppy, black ground, painted by Claude Leffler, impressed OWENS SOUDANEZE 220, CL, 8-3/4" x 5", **$900.**

Photo courtesy of David Rago Auctions, Inc.

Owens vase, matte green, banded geometric dec, impressed mark/218, 6-1/2" x 5-1/4", **$570.**

Photo courtesy of David Rago Auctions, Inc.

Bud vase, standard glaze, yellow roses, marked "#804," initials for Harry Robinson, 6-1/4" h, 2-1/2" w **$165**

Ewer, brown high glaze, cherry design, 10" h **$200**

Jug, standard glaze, ear of corn dec, marked and sgd "Tot Steele," 8" w, 4-1/2" w **$230**

Lamp base, Utopian, classically shaped, painted yellow daffodils, unmarked, drilled, some glaze bubbles to back, hairline around neck, 11-1/4" h, 5" d **$350**

Mug, standard glaze, cherries, marked "#830," sgd "Henry R. Robinson," hairlines to int., 7-1/2" h **$110**

Tankard, brown high glaze, Indian design, incised signature, restored, 7" h **$325**

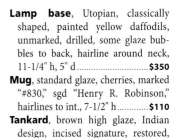

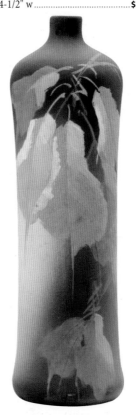

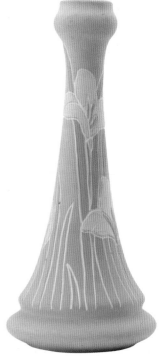

Owens vase, Coralene opalesce, painted bronzed flower, green ground, John Lessell, signed Lessell, 6" x 4", **$600.**

Photo courtesy of David Rago Auctions, Inc.

Owens vase, matte Utopia, autumn leaves, dark brown ground, by Cecil Excel, impressed Owens Utopian, painted sig, 14-1/2" x 4-1/2", **$450.**

Photo courtesy of David Rago Auctions, Inc.

Owens vase, tapered, incised irises, shaded ground, impressed Owensart, 13-1/2" x 6", **$780.**

Photo courtesy of David Rago Auctions, Inc.

PARIAN WARE

History: Parian ware is a creamy white, translucent porcelain that resembles marble. It originated in England in 1842 and was first called "statuary porcelain." Minton and Copeland have been credited with its development; Wedgwood also made it. In America, parian ware objects were manufactured by Christopher Fenton in Bennington, Vermont.

At first, parian ware was used only for figures and figural groups. By the 1850s, it became so popular that a vast range of items was manufactured.

Bust

Apollo, English, second half 19th C, 9-3/8" h **$295**

Beethoven, titled, mounted on waisted circular socle, England, second half 19th C, 20-3/4" h **$1,880**

Charles Dickens, printed quote from The Old Curiosity Shop on back, short socle, English, late 19th C, 10-1/2" h **$215**

Classical Woman, with impressed "RC" mark at shoulder, English, second half 19th C, 11-3/4" h..**$275**

Clytic, woman with Romanesque hair and draping bodice, with leaftip surround, England/France, late 19th/early 20th C, after the antique, 12" h **$300**

Maiden with ivy circlet, English, second half 19th C, 8-3/4" h **$250**

Peabody, mounted on waisted circular socle, raised title, England, c1870, 10-1/2" h **$250**

Creamer, 5" h, Tulip pattern, relief dec **$100**

Doll

Countess Dagmar, shoulder head, café au lait molded hair with side-swept wings to comb and curls in back, curls on forehead held by molded band, blue painted eyes, pierced ears, cloth body, brown leather arms, blue plaid wool dress, orig underwear, blue leather shoes, c1870, 18-1/2" h **$250**

Lady, bisque shoulder head, very pale coloring, center part blond hairstyle, 10 vertical curls, painted features, blue eyes, closed mouth, three sew holes, cloth body, kid arms, separate fingers, red cotton print jumper, white blouse with tucking and lace trim, leather slippers, Germany, c1870, 20" h....**$350**

Figure

Comedy modeled as woman adorned with flowers, seated on freeform rocky base, impressed year cipher, Minton, England, second half 19th C, 13-3/4" h **$1,200**

Lady with Lyre, modeled as draped woman, seated on rocky base, England, toe, finger, and lyre repair, c1870, 18-1/4" h **$765**

The Bather, scantily clad female figure modeled standing by tree stump, England, toe repair, footrim chip, c1870, 25-3/4" h **$1,300**

Una and Lion, unmarked, England, second half 19th C, 14-1/2" h **$1,115**

Vision of the Red Crosse Knight, John Rose & Co. later Coalport China, modeled by Josh Pitts, England, c1851, 18-3/4" h **$2,235**

Plaque, relief, angels, brass frames, orig German labels, Boston retailers label, pr, 6" d **$275**

Sculpture, nude riding back of lion, early registry marks, c1860 ....**$895**

Urn, cov, classical shape, allegorical scene in low relief, three Graces, temples, revelers, and centaur, fish scale pattern on pedestal base, double scrolled handles, fruit finial, base marked with crown with ribbon and "FB," 20" h **$250**

Vase, applied white monkey type figures, grape clusters at shoulders, blue ground, pr, c1850, 10" h.............**$265**

Parian ware figure, Homer, partially draped adult male and youth figures mounted atop oval base, England, c1870, 13-1/2" h, **$1,000.**

Photos courtesy of Skinner, Inc.

Parian ware figure, Milton, standing figure, modeled leaning on pedestal topped with stack of books, England, c1870, 14" h, **$600.**

PATE-SUR-PATE

History: Pate-sur-pate, paste-on-paste, is a 19th-century porcelain-decorating method featuring relief designs achieved by painting layers of thin pottery paste one on top of the other.

About 1880, Marc Solon and other Sevres artists, inspired by a Chinese celadon vase in the Ceramic Museum at Sevres, experimented with this process. Solon emigrated to England at the outbreak of the Franco-Prussian War and worked at Minton, where he perfected pate-sur-pate.

Box, cov, round, white female portrait, blue ground, Limoges, France, late 19th C, 5-3/4" d **$690**

Centerpiece, elongated parian vessel, molded scroll handles and feet, pierced rim, two brown reserves, white pate-sur-pate amorini, gilding, dec attributed to Lawrence Birks, marked "Minton," retailer's mark of Thomas Goode & Co., Ltd., London, c1889, 16" l **$1,400**

Dresser jar, ovoid, cobalt blue ground, lid with pate-sure-pate profile bust of classical woman, gilt banding, Meissen, Germany, early 20th C, 3-3/4" d **$1,955**

Lamp base, Chinoiserie-style, black ground moon flask with pate-sur-pate and blue-printed dec of village scenes, mounted on gilt-metal beaded and scroll ftd base, price for pr, 20th C, 10-1/4" h **$490**

Medallion, oval, blue ground, white relief cherub figure, unidentified factory mark on reverse, France, edge ground, 19th C, 2-3/8" x 3-3/8" **$320**

Plaque
Demi-lune shape, green ground, white slip, central figure of Venus holding mirror in each hand, fending off two groups of putti with their reflections, artist sgd Louis Solin, rosewood frame, 15" l **$9,200**

One with maiden and cupid spinning web, other with maiden seated on bench with whip in one hand, sunflowers stalked with humanistic snail on other, artist sgd "Louis Solin," both marked on back, framed, pr, 7-5/8" d **$2,500**

Victoria Ware, Wedgwood, rust ground, gilt florets, applied white figure of Adam, imp mark, rim chip, framed, c1880, 5-1/4" x 11-1/4" **$2,200**

Plate, deep brown ground, gilt trim, white dec of nude child behind net supported by two small trees, artist monogram sgd "Henry Saunders," printed and imp Moore Brothers factory marks, c1885, 9-1/8" d **$750**

Tile, sword wielding warrior on horseback, cobalt blue ground, sgd "Limo-

ges France" in gold script, mounted in antique frame, 7" l, 5" w **$220**

Urn, double handles, pedestal base, portrait medallion, pale green ground, ivory trim, gilt accents, 8" h **$250**

Vase
Brown ground, white slip dec of cherubs flying among foliage, gilt trim rings and stylized foliate band at necks, impressed George Jones marks, c1880, price for pr, one with slight glaze abrasion, 6" h **$5,000**

Cov, dark brown ground, white slip of partially draped female figure holding flowering branch, shaped tripod base, gilt dec at rim, artist sgd Louis Solin, printed and imp marks, rim cover damage, minor gilt wear, 1898, 13-3/4" h **$2,300**

Cov, deep green ground, circular panels dec in white slip, Psyche being carried heavenward by Mercury, maiden figures applied to shoulder, gilt trim, artist sgd Frederick Schenck, imp George Jones factory marks, cov damaged, hairlines to figures, light gilt wear, dated 1880, 16-1/2" h **$3,565**

PAUL REVERE POTTERY

Paul Revere Pottery pitcher, blue-gray matte glaze, frothy white glaze around rim, stamped "PAUL REVERE POTTERY," 4-1/2" d, 4-1/2" h, **$95.**
Photo courtesy of David Rago Auctions, Inc.

History: Paul Revere Pottery, Boston, was an outgrowth of a club known as The Saturday Evening Girls. The S.E.G. was composed of young female immigrants who met on Saturday nights to read and participate in craft projects, such as ceramics.

Regular pottery production began in 1908, and the name "Paul Revere" was adopted because the pottery was located near the Old North Church. In 1915, the firm moved to Brighton, Massachusetts. Known as the "Bowl Shop," the pottery grew steadily. In spite of popular acceptance and technical advancements, the pottery required continual subsidies. It finally closed in January 1942.

Items produced range from plain and decorated vases to tablewares to illustrated tiles. Many decorated wares were incised and glazed either in an Art Nouveau matte finish or an occasional high glaze.

Marks: In addition to an impressed mark, paper "Bowl Shop" labels were used prior to 1915. Pieces also can be found with a date and "P.R.P." or "S.E.G." painted on the base.

Bookends, pr, night scene of owls, ink marked "S.E.G./11-21," flat chip to one base, 1921, 4" h, 5" w **$1,300**

Bowl
Cuerda seca dec, band of white irises on bright yellow ground, mkd "S.E.G./4-16," restoration to chip, 4" h, 5" w **$900**

Cuerda seca dec, by Fannie Levine, white geese, bright yellow ground, 11-1/2" d, 5" h **$35,000**

Cake set, Tree pattern, black outline scene, blue sky, green trees, 10" d cake plate, six 8-1/2" d serving plates, each marked "J.G., S.E.G.," three dated 7/15, three dated 1/4/15, one dated 3/15, price for seven-pc set **$1,840**

Candle sconce, cuerda seca dec, mountainous landscape with trees and irises in foreground, mkd "SG/SEG/11-13," two tight lines from center edge, 7-3/4" h, 4-1/4" w **$4,250**

Cereal bowl, cuerda seca dec, white swans swimming on blue water, S.E.G./A70.5.11/AS, 5-1/2" d, 2-1/2" h **$1,000**

Child's breakfast set, dec with running rabbits, white, green, and blue, monogrammed "David His Mug," "His Bowl," "His Plate," potter's mark, two chips on mug, 3-1/2" h mug, 5-5/8" d bowl, and 7-3/4" d plate **$1,380**

Fruit set, green glaze with cream-colored border, incised and outlined in black, initialed "F. G." (Fanny Ginsburg) and "S. E. G." stylistic detail, large 8-1/4" d fruit bowl with artist's initials "I. G.," numbered "239.6.11," and "S. E. G."; and six 3-3/4" d smaller bowls with artist's initials "I. G.," sequentially numbered "196.6.11, 197.6.11, 198.6.11, 199.6.11, 200.6.11, 201.6.11" **$1,880**

Goblet, cuerda seca dec, band of white lotus, bright yellow ground, S.E.G./3.16/FL, 3-3/4" h **$850**

Humidor, cov, spherical, blue matte glaze, pink int., minute int. rim nick, sgd in slip "P.R.P. 3/36," 6-1/4" h, 5-3/4" d **$400**

Lamp base, ovoid, yellow glaze, reticulated wooden base, unmarked, 18-3/4" h **$230**

Mug, cuerda seca dec, three fishing boats, sails monogrammed "C.R.S.," green, brown, blue, and ivory, mkd "AM/224 412/S.E.G.," 6" h, 4-3/4" d **$2,300**

Pitcher
Ovoid, applied handle, charcoal gray glaze, partial imp potter's mark, painted "4 26," artist's initials L.S., three rim chips, c1926, 6-3/4" h ... **$70**
Ovoid, applied handle, green glaze, painted "J.M.D. June 17, 1920 S.E.G. 5-20," by Josephine M. Davis, handle repaired, 7-1/8" h **$115**

Plate
Cuerda seca dec, white and blue geese and water lilies, green matte ground, marked "S.E.G./6-17/AM," 8" d **$1,380**

Incised geese in mottled green on speckled blue ground, painted "S.E.G. 6-13," artist's initials "I.G.," c1913, 7-5/8" d **$490**
Incised white mice, celadon and brown band, ink mark "Dorothy Hopkins/Her Plate," 1911, 6-1/2" d **$1,300**

Ring tray, circular, blue-gray and green band of trees, blue-gray ground, marked "S.E.G./J.G.," 4" d **$275**

Teapot, brown and white wavy band of sailboats, yellow sky, restored, 1918, 4-1/2" h, 9" d **$700**

Tile, Washington Street, blue, white, green, and brown, marked "H.S. S4 9/1/10," edge chips, 3-3/4" sq **$420**

Trivet
Medallion of house against setting sun, blue-gray ground, imp P.R.P. mark, 1924, 4-1/4" d **$425**
Medallion of poplar trees in landscape, blue-green ground, imp P.R.P. mark, 1925, 5-1/2" d **$600**

Vase
Band of trees in blue and green glaze outlined in black, charcoal gray glazed body, imp pottery mark at center of base, dated "8-23," Brighton, MA, fine hairline at rim, 10-1/2" h **$1,300**
Ovoid, cuerda seca dec, band of green trees against blue sky, gunmetal black ground, 4-1/4" h, 4" d ...**$2,400**
Semi-matte ochre glaze, signed "P. R. P.," dated 1926, 9-1/4" h **$265**

Saturday Evening Girls bowl, blue rim and base, seven large cream-colored geese with incised black outline, brown hills on green ground, brown speckling, tight rim hairline, signed AH/5-14 SEG, c1914, 11-1/2" w x 5" h, **$4,700.**
Photo courtesy of Skinner, Inc.

Paul Revere bowl, flaring, decorated in cuerda seca technique, Revere on white horse, moonlit landscape, "The Midnight Ride of Paul Revere," "A Voice in the Darkness, A Knock at the Door, and a Word That Shall Echo Forever More," signed PRP/6-41/LS, 3" x 7-1/4" , **$8,815.**
Photo courtesy of David Rago Auctions, Inc.

Peters and Reed vase, Moss Aztec, jeweled, unmarked, c1925, few small chips to decoration, 9-1/2" d, 9" h, **$250.**
Photo courtesy of David Rago Auctions, Inc.

Peters and Reed vase, Chromal Ware, ovoid, unmarked, 4" d, 9-1/4" h, **$815.**
Photo courtesy of David Rago Auctions, Inc.

Reproduction Alert. In the 1950s American companies began importing bisque piano babies from Japan. Many of these were marked with paper labels. They are not true reproductions as they do not truly duplicate early styles, but collectors should be aware that they are also not vintage bisque piano babies just because they aren't marked. Generally these types of piano babies will have a different type of painting, especially around the eyes, and are usually not as detailed as the original piano babies. The quality of the bisque is usually inferior to that of genuine old bisque babies, and at times have the numbers on the base painted in red. Red mark numbers are not a sure sign of a reproduction as some antique piano babies were also marked in this way. Many reproductions also have a larger-bisque manufacturing hole in the bottom while older ones have a smaller hole. Because these Japanese bisque versions are from the 1950s and not the 1890s, their values should be considerably less than vintage German bisque piano babies.

PETERS AND REED POTTERY

History: J. D. Peters and Adam Reed founded their pottery company in South Zanesville, Ohio, in 1900. Common flowerpots, jardiniéres, and cooking wares comprised the majority of their early output. Occasionally, art pottery was attempted, but it was not until 1912 that their Moss Aztec line was introduced and widely accepted. Other art wares include Chromal, Landsun, Montene, Pereco, and Persian.

Peters retired in 1921 and Reed changed the name of the firm to Zane Pottery Company.

Marks: Marked pieces of Peters and Reed Pottery are unknown.

Peters and Reed vase, Moss Aztec, corseted, stylized flowers and leaves, unmarked, 4-1/4" d, 10-1/2" h, **$235.**
Photo courtesy of David Rago Auctions, Inc.

Bowl, closed-in rim, round tapering bowl, raised budding branches and berries in relief, matte green glaze, couple of chips on branch, 9" d, 3-1/4" h..**$175**

Doorstop, cat, yellow..................**$375**

Ewer, orange and yellow raised grapes dec, brown ground, 11" h.............**$50**

Jardinière, Moss Aztec, unmarked, few small chips to dec, c1925, 9-1/2" d, 9" h..............................**$200**

Mug, blended glaze........................**$40**

Pitcher, green and yellow raised fern leaves, gloss dark brown ground, 4" h **$65**

Vase, Moss Aztec, corseted, stylized flowers and leaves, 4-1/4" d, 10-1/2" h **$230**

PIANO BABIES

History: In the late 1900s, a well decorated home had a parlor, equipped with a piano, which usually was covered by a lovely shawl. To hold the shawl in place, piano babies were used. Piano babies are figures of babies, usually made of unglazed bisque. These "Piano Babies" range in size from three inches to over 20 inches. They were made in a variety of poses—sitting up, crawling, lying on their tummies, lying on their backs.

Most piano babies were produced in Germany and France. There were more than 15 factories in Germany that produced this type of bisqueware. Among them Hertwig and Co., Julius Heubach, Royal Rudolstadt, Simon and Halbig, Kling and Co, and Gerbruder Heubach, were the most prolific. Ger. Heubach produced most of his wares for export, between 1905 and 1918. Many of these manufacturers also made dolls and carried the artistry required for fine doll making to their piano baby creations.

Many of the piano babies found today were manufactured by the Heubach Brothers (1820-1945) in Germany, whose rising sun mark is well known. However, many pieces left factories with no mark. The Heubach factory is well known also for its pink-tinted bisque, used to create figurines and doll heads, In fact, this company made many of the same bisque babies but in different sizes. The Heubach babies are well known for their realistic facial features as well as their attention to minute details, such as intaglio eyes, small teeth looking out from lips, blond hair, blue eyes, etc.

Miniature babies made to sit on miniature pianos were introduced and became popular during the early part of the 20th century. Because they were so small, many of them were lost during the years making them highly desirable today.

Adviser: Jerry Rosen.

Piano Baby, two Bavarian babies, pair, 4-3/4" h, **$100.**

Piano Baby lying on back dressed in white gown with blue dotted collar hands touching raised foot, 5" t, 9" l, **$225.**

Piano Baby, baby playing with toes, white dressing gown with gold trim, 5-1/2" h, **$125.**

Baby boy, holding colorful ball, marked Heubach, 3" h.................**$300**

Baby in early walker, Heubach sunburst mark, 7" h...........................**$200**

Baby in white gown, blue ribbon with left hand in air, 6-3/4" h **$175**

Baby lying on back, touching toes, baby blue ribbon on top of gown, 4-1/2" h, 8" l.................................**$150**

Baby lying on side, sucking thumb, 4-1/2" h, 8" l................................**$150**

Baby sitting upright, egg on back, 6" h, 9" l **$250**

Boy blue knickers, eyeglasses, standing, 13" h **$355**

Boy in hat, feeding his kitty in his arms, 8" h **$300**

Boy in nightshirt, and black boots with arms at his side, 15" h......**$1,100**

Crawling baby, 3" h, 4-1/2" l **$125**

Crying face baby, sitting on potty, 8-1/2" h...**$380**

Dancing girl in blue dress, hands in air holding edge of skirt, Heubach blue marking, 6-1/2" h.................**$150**

Dutch boy and girl, 4" h...........**$100**

Girl with bonnet, holding basket, marked Germany 10379, 7" h.....**$250**

Girl with bonnet, holding edge of skirt in both hands, 12-1/2" h **$500**

Happy toddler girl, holding a pale green and gold beaded teacup, 15" h..**$355**

Heubach baby, raised leg, 6" h, 9" l
....**$105**

Heubach baby, with a long feeding bottle in hands, 9-1/2" **$450**

Heubach boy, hands holding white outfit, beige shoes, 8" h **$350**

Heubach boy and girl (separate pieces), elbows resting, hands on face, 7" h **$695**

Heubach incised mark boy, with puppies, one in each arm, 11-1/2" h......**$350**

Piano Baby with left hand on ear, white beaded gown, #8443 incised on back, 5" t, **$125.**

Piano Baby, grouping of miniature piano babies used to decorate miniature doll house pianos, 2"-3" h, **$35-$75.**

Piano Baby, Dutch girl sitting with hands in lap, blue and white gown, impressed Heubach mark, 6" h, **$150.**

Piano Baby, baby in blue outfit with arms and fingers pointing to mouth, 7-3/4" h , **$250.**

Heubach child, playful position laying on his side holding his foot in one paw with bear skin around head and back, marked, 3" across **$200**

Heubach girl, with hands on cheeks resting on log, marked, 3-1/2" h ...**$80**

Heubach little boy, holding egg in front of him on lap, 4-1/2" h **$140**

Heubach nude baby, in green dish, 5" h..**$625**

Nude position baby, unmarked Heubach, with hands and legs outstretched, number 87 on the bottom and an incised number 12, 5" h ...**$125**

Nude squatting baby, looking upwards, 4-1/2" t **$125**

Pouty nude baby, Heubach blue mark, 5" h.................................**$300**

Small baby, holding egg on stomach, 1-3/4" h **$80**

Twin piano baby girls, sitting up with original wigs, 5" h..............**$500**

Two boys, dressed in daddy's nightshirt, 7" h **$500**

Young Dutch boy and girl, standing back to back, 7" h.................**$150**

Pickard vase, tapered cylindrical form, double gilt handles, rim, and foot, bands below rim in iridescent blue and yellow, decorated with floral motifs, vertical bands of cobalt blue with white floral decoration, textured gold body, mark obscured by paper label inscribed "Pickard China, Arno vase, Eg. G. Linear," Edith Arno, early 1900s, 7-1/4" h, **$325.**

Photo courtesy of Alderfer Auction Co.

Pickard relish, embossed gold decoration, marked, **$65.**

PICKARD CHINA

History: The Pickard China Company was founded by Wilder Pickard in Chicago in 1897. Originally the company imported European china blanks, principally from the Havilands at Limoges, which were then hand painted. The firm presently is located in Antioch, Illinois.

Bowl

Autumn Blackberries, sgd "O. Goess" (Otto Goess), 1905-10 mark, 6" d **$200**

Red and white tulips, gold dec, Limoges blank, 10" d **$230**

Strawberries, white blossoms, and gooseberries dec, ftd, sgd "E. Challinor" (Edward Challinor), 1905-10 mark, 9-1/2" d, 4-1/2" h **$300**

Cabinet plate

Heavy gold enameled border, Limoges blank, 8-1/2" d...................**$175**

Lilies, gold background, artist sgd "Yeschek," 9" d **$100**

Celery set, two-handled oval dish, five matching salts, allover gold dec, 1925-30 mark..............................**$125**

Chocolate set, 12" h chocolate pot, creamer, cov sugar, 11" tray, sgd "F. Lind" (Frederick Lindner), Pickard and various French and German back stamps, c1903 ....**$1,495**

Claret set, claret jug, five tumblers, 11-1/2" d tray, Deserted Garden pattern, sgd "J. Nessy" (John Nessy), 1912-18 mark..........................**$2,600**

Coffee set, Modern Conventional pattern, coffee pot sgd "Hessler" (Robert Hessler), 1910-12 mark, eight cups and saucers sgd "Hess & RH" (Robert Hessler), 1912-18 mark **$1,450**

Creamer, Tulip Conventional, sgd "Tomash" (Rudolph Tomascheko), 1903-05 mark, 5-1/4" h **$400**

Creamer and sugar

Deserted Garden pattern, sgd "J. Nessy" (John Nessy), 1912-18 mark.......**$200**

White Poppies & Daisy, sgd, 1912-18 mark..**$250**

Demitasse cup and saucer

Gold Tracery Rose & Daisy pattern, green band, 1925-30 mark **$40**

Poppy pattern, sgd "LOH" (John Loh), price for pr, 1910-12.................**$325**

Lemonade pitcher

Encrusted Honeysuckle pattern, 1919-22 mark **$100**

Schoner Lemon pattern, sgd "Schoner" (Otto Schoner), 1903-05 mark **$1,700**

Match holder, Rose & Daisy pattern, allover gold, 1925-30 ....**$40**

Pin dish, violets dec.......................**$40**

Plate

Blackberries and leaves, sgd "Beitler" (Joseph Beitler), 1903-15, 8-1/2" d **$90**

Calla Lily pattern, sgd "Marker" (Curtis H. Marker), 1905-10 mark, 8-1/2" d **$225**

Florida Moonlight, sgd "E. Challinor" (Edward Challinor), 1912-18 mark, 8-3/4" d **$2,300**

Gibson Narcissus pattern, sgd "E. Gibson" (Edward Gibson), 1903-05 mark, 8-1/2" d **$300**

Lilium Ornatum pattern, sgd "Beulet" (F. Beulet), 1910-12 mark, 8-1/2" d **$100**

Yeschek Currants in Gold pattern, sgd "Blaha" (Joseph Blaha), 1905-10 mark, 9" d **$110**

Punch bowl, grape dec, sgd "Coufall" (John Anton Coufall) upper right, "T & V Limoges" and "Pickard" back stamps, c1905, 11" d...................**$895**

Tankard, red poppies, anonymous artist, "T & V Limoges" and "Pickard" back stamps, c1905, 10-1/4" h **$1,150**

Tea set, cov teapot, creamer, cov sugar, Carnation Garden pattern, each sgd

"Yeschek" (Joseph T. Yeschek), 1903-05 marks...................**$2,600**

Vase

Calla Lily pattern, sgd "Marker" (Curtis H. Marker), 1905-10 mark, 11" h **$550**

Carmen, red poppies, sgd "J. Kiefus" (Jacob Kiefus) lower right, "D & C France" and "Pickard" back stamps, c1905, 13-1/2" h **$595**

Golden Pheasant pattern, sgd "E. Challinor" (Edward Challinor), 1919-22 mark, 8" h...................**$500**

Scenic, sgd "E. Challinor" (Edward Challinor), 1912-18 mark, 8-1/4" h **$425**

PORTRAIT WARE

History: Plates, vases, and other articles with portraits on them were popular in the second half of the 19th century. Although male subjects, such as Napoleon or Louis XVI, were used, the ware usually depicts a beautiful, and often unidentified, woman.

A large number of English and Continental china manufacturers made portrait ware. Because most was hand painted, an artist's signature often is found.

Cabinet plate, classical woman and young girl, dark green border, set into 19" d bronze and gilt metal reticulated surround with six cartouches of cavorting cherubs, German, late 19th/early 20th C, 8-1/4" d **$560**

Charger, Elizabethan style figures, polychrome enamel and gilt dec, artist sgd "G. Sieves 79," impressed Worcester Royal Porcelain Works factory marks, England, price for pr, c1879, 18-3/4" d...................**$4,460**

Dresser box, cov, brass heart-shaped box, inlaid lid with hp portrait on ivory of women in formal dress, Florentine designs on box, portrait sgd "Brun," 4" l, 3-1/4" w, 1-1/2" h **$350**

Medallion, Le Pensee, sgd "Wagner," jeweled gilt bronze frame, 3-1/2" d **$975**

Plaque

Porcelain, partially nude beauty, sgd "Wagner," ornate 8-1/2" x 9-1/2" gilt shadow box frame, 3-1/2" x 2-3/4" **$1,035**

Woman in white gown, pink drape, outstretched hand with flowers, gilt bronze frame, putti and garlands, minor scratches, 6" x 4" **$725**

Plate

Empress Louise, central printed portrait, indistinctly titled and signed "L. Dgt," in gilt surround, paneled rim with scrolls, urns, and griffins, possibly Hutschenreuther, Bavaria, late 19th/early 20th C, 9-1/4" d **$115**

Dark haired mother and child, deep olive green border, gold tracery, marked "Royal Vienna," 9-1/2" d...................**$125**

Napoleon I, sgd "Wagner," cobalt blue and pale blue band, cornucopia and urn ornamentation, inscribed "Made for Mrs. John Doyle" verso, minor gilt loss, 9-1/2" d...................**$970**

Octagonal shape, hp portrait of Psyche, blue Vienna beehive mark, 9-3/4" d **$490**

Young woman with wreath of flowers in hair, marked "Royal Munich," 10" h **$115**

Young woman, gilt bronze-colored border, mounted in 15" x 17" walnut frame, German, 12" d **$300**

Tray, Napoleon I, standing, looking left, left hand behind back exposing dress sword and medals, background of fine furniture and papers, gilt garland border, dark blue-green ground, fitted frame, sgd "Reseh," marked "Vienna, FD, Austria," 9-1/2" sq...................**$1,320**

Portrait plaque, hand painted porcelain, young woman draped in gossamer thin veil, accompanied by cherubs with sprig of flowers, raised gilt decoration, stamped "Made in Germany," signed "Springtime, C. Viollemot," 4-1/2" x 7", **$1,400.**

Photo courtesy of David Rago Auctions, Inc.

Portrait Ware, cabinet plate, porcelain, enamel and gilt border, Royal Vienna Achilles and Thetis, c1900, 9-1/2" d, **$445.**

Photo courtesy of Sloans & Kenyon Auctioneers and Appraisers.

Portrait plaque, oval, depicting head and shoulders of maiden, Limoges, 19th century, 3-3/4" x 5", **$425.**

Photo courtesy of Sloans & Kenyon Auctioneers and Appraisers.

Portrait Ware, Knowles, Taylor & Knowles, Napoleon, dated 1901, 8" d, **$100.**

Photo courtesy of The Early Auction Company, LLC.

Urn, cov, double handles, "Mme de Montesson," central portrait of French woman wearing white wig, floral designs, reverse with floral dec, marked "2912, S-2," illegible ring mark, restored lid, 15-1/2" h **$275**

Vase

Bulbous, titled "Ariadne," sgd "Wagner," maroon ground, gilt floral dec, Austrian beehive mark, 4-3/4" h **$850**

Clementine, sgd "N. Kiesel," Art Nouveau form, green-brown mirrored ground, heavily gilt acanthus leaves

and vines, bearing mark of Richard Klemm, 8-1/2" h **$1,690**

Finely dec portrait of young man, natural colors, enameled bronze, tinted silver foil under sparkling crystal glaze, unmarked, attributed to Limoges, early 20th C, 7-1/2" h **$750**

Gold enamel framed portrait of Ruth, violet luster ground, blue beehive mark with "Germany" in script, 5-3/4" h **$435**

Hp portrait of young girl framed in gold enamel, violet luster ground, German, unmarked, 8" h **$375**

Woman holding yellow roses, opalescent ground in shades of green and purple, gilt floral design, Dresden, wear to gilding, 12" h **$1,570**

Young beauty with basket of flowers in garden setting, artist sgd "Garnet," base imp "Made in France," enamel on bronze, c1900, 6-1/2" h **$500**

Young beauty in red dress, red roses in hair, finely enameled on bronze, tinted silver foil cartouche against translucent emerald green ground, French, c1900, 7" h...................**$865**

Porcelain portrait plaque, handpainted portrait of young woman holding candle, Dresden, c1900, 9-1/4", **$920.**

Photo courtesy of Pook & Pook, Inc.

PRATT WARE

History: The earliest Pratt earthenware was made in the late 18th century by William Pratt, Lane Delph, Staffordshire, England. From 1810 to 1818, Felix and Robert Pratt, William's sons, ran their own firm, F. & R. Pratt, in Fenton in the Staffordshire district. Potters in Yorkshire, Liverpool, Sunderland, Tyneside, and Scotland copied the products.

The wares consisted of relief-molded jugs, commercial pots and tablewares with transfer decoration, commemorative pieces, and figures and figural groups of both people and animals.

Marks: Much of the early ware is unmarked. The mid-19th century wares bear several different marks in conjunction with the name Pratt, including "& Co."

Bank, figural, underglaze enamel dec center chimney house, male and female figure to either side, Yorkshire, damage to chimney and backside of roof, 19th C, 5" h **$275**

Cow creamer, sponge dec, milkmaid dressed in yellow, some edge damage, rebuilt ear, lid missing, 7" l **$350**

Cradle, pearlware
  Underglaze polychrome enamels, one molded with baby sleeping, repairs to hood and side of body, c1800, 4" l **$100**
  Underglaze polychrome enamels, oval form molded as hooded cradle with sleeping child, restored to lower body and under base, chip and hairline to hood, c1800, 7-3/4" l **$600**
  Underglaze polychrome enamel, restored chip, c1800, 5-1/4" l...**$100**

Cup plate, Dalmatian, white, black spots, 3-1/8" d..............................**$95**

Figure
  Gentleman feeding black bird, sitting on tree stump, chips, restorations, 10" h **$310**
  Lady with barrel, pitcher at her feet, chips, restorations, 9-3/4" h.....**$300**

Flask, pearlware, shell-form, underglaze polychrome enamels, slight glaze blemishes, c1800, 4-1/8" l............**$765**

Jar, cov, chromolithograph lid
  Rect, milkmaid, damage, undersized lid, 3-1/4" l **$150**
  Round, Albert Memorial, mis-matched base, stains, flakes, 4-1/8" d ... **$100**
  Round, Dangerous, ice skating man falling, stains, flakes, 4-1/4" d ...**$125**
  Round, Dr. Johnson, three men in parlor, flakes, 4" d....................**$150**
  Round, man reading the *Times*, stains, flakes, 4-1/8" d **$115**
  Round, mother and children playing hide and seek, stains, flakes, 4" d ..**$95**
  Round, shrimpers filling their nets, flakes and stains, 4-1/4" d **$165**

Jug, molded leaves at neck and base, raised and polychrome painted hunting scene on colored ground, c1800, 8" h..**$750**

Mug, colorful tavern scene transfer, 4" h
....**$95**

Pitcher
  Medium blue transfer scene on each side of "Swiss Cottage," by J. & W. Pratt, molded handle with man's face at end, stains, hairline, 12" h.......**$90**
  Molded figures on sides, leaves at rim and base, one side with Toby Philpots, other with classical warrior, green, gold, dark brown, and cobalt blue, flakes on base and handle, short hairline on spout, 5-5/8" h **$675**

Plaque, Louis XVI portrait, oval form, beaded border, polychrome enamels, rim nicks, glaze wear, c1793, 6-1/4" x 7-1/4"....................................**$900**

Plate, Haddon Hall, classical figure border, 9" d.................................**$120**

Pot lid, chromolithograph
  Dogs overturning kettle of fish, flakes, 4" d **$100**
  View of Windsor Castle, 6-1/2" d
....**$170**
  Village wedding, flakes, 4-1/8" d .. **$100**

Tea caddy, rect, raised figural panels front and back, fluted and yellow trimmed lid, blue, yellow, orange, and green dec, 6-1/4" h **$350**

Pratt ware "seasons" figures, two, polychrome dec, 9" h, 8-1/2" h, **$700,** *both.*
Photo courtesy of Pook & Pook, Inc.

Pratt ware pitcher, Duke of Cumberland, 18th century, 6-1/8" h, **$325.**
Photo courtesy of Pook & Pook, Inc.

Pratt ware miniature platter, oval, two alligators, braided rim, 19th century, 4-1/4" l, 3-1/2" w, **$527.**
Photo courtesy of Pook & Pook, Inc.

Precious Moments, Mother's Day, Thinking Of You Is What I Really Like To Do, *1993,* **$50.**

Precious Moments, Perfect Harmony, *521914, 1994,* **$33.**

PRECIOUS MOMENTS

History: Artist Sam Butcher's artwork was spotted by Enesco Corp. CEO Eugene Freedman at a booksellers' covention in 1975. At that time, Butcher and his business partner, Bill Biel, had a greeting card company. The characters depicted in Butcher's designs were teardrop-eyed children with inspiring messages. Freedman arranged to have a figurine created from one of Butcher's drawings by an Oriental sculptor, Yasuhei Fujioka.

Butcher liked the figurine and agreed to Enesco's creation of 20 others based on his artwork. He was very involved in the creation of the figurine line. The public embraced the original 21 figurines, which were released in 1978 and a collectible legacy was born.

Marks:

1981 Triangle	1989 Bow & Arrow	1997 Sword
1982 Hourglass	1990 Flame	1998 Glasses
1983 Fish	1991 Vessel	1999 Star
1984 Cross	1992 Clef	2000 Cracked Egg
1985 Dove	1993 Butterfly	2001 Sandal
1986 Olive Branch	1994 Trumpet	2002 Cross in Heart
1987 Cedar Tree	1995 Ship	2003 Crown
1988 Flower	1996 Heart	

Images appear courtesy of Enesco Group, Incorporated.

Additional Listings: See *Price Guide To Contemporary Collectibles and Limited Editions*, 9th edition by Mary L. Sieber, Krause Publications.

Advisor: Mary L. Sieber

Bell, Annual
God Sent His Love, 15873, 1985..**$38**
I'll Play My Drum For Him, E2358, 1982...**$50**
Let The Heavens Rejoice, E5622, 1980.....................................**$148**
Love Is The Best Gift Of All, 109835, 1987.................................**$33**
May Your Christmas Be Merry, 524182, 1990................................**$33**
Oh Holy Night, 522821, 1988.......**$38**
Once Upon A Holy Night, 523828, 1989...**$33**
Surrounded With Joy, E-0522, 1983...**$57**
Time To Wish/Merry Christmas, 115304, 1988................................**$38**
Wishing You A Cozy Christmas, 102318, 1985................................**$38**
Wishing You A Merry Christmas, E5393, 1984................................**$44**

Doll
Autumn's Praise, 408808, 1990..**$135**

Figurine, Precious Moments
3 Mini Nativity Houses/Palm Tree, E2387, 1982....................................**$54**
Animal Collection, Bunny, E 9267c, 1982...**$26**

Animal Collection, Dog, E 9267b, 1982...**$26**
Animal Collection, Kitty w/Bow, E 9267d, 1982.............................**$26**
Animal Collection, Lamb w/Bird E 9267e, 1982.............................**$26**
Animal Collection, Pig w/Patches E 9267f, 1982.............................**$26**
Animal Collection, Teddy Bear E 9267a, 1982.............................**$26**
Autumn's Praise Musical, 408751, 1984...**$114**
Baby Figurines Six Pc. Set, E 2852, 1983...**$165**
Baby's First Christmas, 15539, 1985 ....**$25**
Baby's First Christmas, 15547, 1985 ....**$25**
Baby's First Trip, 16012, 1985 ...**$258**
Be Not Weary In Well Doing, E 3111, 1979...............................**$127**
Bear Ye One Another's Burdens, E 5200, 1980...............................**$90**
Believe The Impossible, 109487, 1988...**$79**
Bless This House, E 7164, 1981 ..**$204**
Bless You Two, E 9255, 1982 ....**$47**
Blessed Are The Peacemakers, E 3107, 1979...............................**$87**
Blessed Are The Pure In Heart, E 3104, 1980...............................**$46**

Blessings From My House To Yours, E0503, 1983 ....**$76**
Bridesmaid, E2831, 1984 ....**$23**
Bringing God's Blessing To You, E0509, 1983................................**$79**
Bundles Of Joy, E 2374, 1982......**$89**
Bunny, Turtle & Lamb 3 Pc 102296, 1985...**$34**
But Love Goes On Forever, E 3115, 1979...**$68**
But Love Goes On Forever, E6118, 1981...**$95**
But Love Goes On Forever Plaque, E-0102, 1982................................**$88**
Camel, E2363, 1982 ....**$43**
Cheers To The Leader, 104035, 1986 ....**$68**
Christmas Is A Time To Share, E2802, 1979................................**$80**
Christmas Joy From Head To Toe, E2361, 1982................................**$72**
Christmastime Is For Sharing, E-0504, 1983................................**$81**
Clown Balancing Ball, 12238a, 1984 ....**$33**
Clown Bending Over Ball, 12238c, 1984...**$33**
Clown Holding Balloon, 12238b, 1984...**$33**
Clown Holding Flower Pot, 12238d, 1984...**$33**

Congratulations Princess, 106208, 1986 .... **$44**
Cow With Bell Figurine, E5638, 1980 .... **$43**
Crown Him Lord Of All, E2803, 1979 .... **$82**
Donkey Figurine, E5621, 1980 .... **$23**
Dropping In For Christmas, E2350, 1982 .... **$76**
Dropping Over For Christmas, E2375, 1982 .... **$88**
Easter's On Its Way, 521892, 1989 .... **$68**
End Is In Sight, The, E9253, 1982 .... **$98**
Especially For Ewe, E9282c, 1982 .... **$42**
First Noel, The, E2365, 1982 .... **$70**
First Noel, The, E2366, 1982 .... **$70**
For God So Loved The World, E5382, 1984 .... **$115**
Forgiving Is Forgetting, E9252, 1981 .... **$73**
Friends Never Drift Apart, 100250, 1985 .... **$60**
Get Into The Habit Of Prayer, 12203, 1984 .... **$44**
Goat Figurine, E2364, 1982 .... **$56**
God Bless America, 102938, 1985 .... **$48**
God Bless Our Home, 12319, 1984 .... **$69**
God Bless Our Years Together, 12440, 1984 .... **$204**
God Bless The Day We Found You, 100145, 1985 .... **$98**
God Bless The Day We Found You, 100153, 1985 .... **$91**
God Bless This Bride, E2832, 1983 .... **$52**
God Has Sent His Son, E-0507, 1983 .... **$79**
God Is Love, E5213, 1980 .... **$83**
God Is Love, Dear Valentine, E7153, 1981 .... **$43**
God Is Love, Dear Valentine, E7154, 1981 .... **$43**
God Is Watching Over You, E7163, 1981 .... **$89**
God Loveth A Cheerful Giver, E1378, 1979 .... **$850**
God Sends The Gift Of His Love, E6613, 1984 .... **$69**
God Sent His Love, 15881, 1985 .. **$30**
God Understands, E1379b, 1979..**$104**
God's Promises Are Sure, E9260, 1983 .... **$74**
God's Speed, E3112, 1979 .... **$82**
Hand That Rocks The Future, The, E3108, 1979 .... **$79**
He Leadeth Me, E1377a, 1979...**$105**

He Upholdeth Those Who Fall, E-0526, 1983 .... **$79**
He Watches Over Us All, E3105, 1979 .... **$74**
Heaven Bless You, 520934, 1989 .... **$70**
Heavenly Light, The, E5637, 1980 .... **$53**
His Burden Is Light, E1380g, 1979, ... **$108**
His Name Is Jesus, E5381, 1984 .... **$99**
His Sheep Am I, E7161, 1981 ..... **$80**
I Believe In Miracles, E7156, 1981 .... **$83**
If God Be For Us...Against Us, E9285, 1982 .... **$82**
I'll Play My Drum For Him, E2356, 1982 .... **$86**
I'll Play My Drum For Him, E2360, 1982 .... **$40**
I'll Play My Drum For Him, E5384, 1984 .... **$28**
I'm A Possibility, 100188, 1985 .. **$73**
I'm Sending You A White Christmas, E2829, 1984 .... **$70**
Isn't He Precious?, E5379, 1984... **$42**
Isn't He Wonderful, E5639, 1980 .... **$67**
Isn't He Wonderful, E5640, 1980.. **$68**
It Is Better To Give...To Receive, 12297, 1984 .... **$148**
It's No Yolk/I Say I Love You, 522104, 1990 .... **$81**
It's What's Inside That Counts, E3119, 1979 .... **$106**
Jesus Is Born, E2012, 1979........ **$118**
Jesus Is Born, E2801, 1979........ **$306**
Jesus Is The Answer, E1381, 1979 .... **$143**
Jesus Is The Light, E1373g, 1979 .... **$79**
Jesus Is The Light That Shines, E-0502, 1983 .... **$56**
Jesus Loves Me, E1372b, 1979... **$72**
Jesus Loves Me, E1372g, 1979... **$72**
Jesus Loves Me, E9278, 1982..... **$30**
Jesus Loves Me, E9279, 1982..... **$31**
Join In On The Blessings, E0104, 1984 .... **$40**
Joy To The World, E2343, 1982.. **$52**
Joy To The World, E2344, 1982.. **$95**
Joy To The World, E5378, 1984... **$54**
Let Heaven And Nature Sing, E2347, 1982 .... **$43**
Let Not The Sun Go Down... Wrath, E5203, 1980 .... **$149**
Let The Whole World Know, E7165, 1981 .... **$107**
Lord Bless You And Keep You, The, E3114, 1979 .... **$68**

Precious Moments, figurines from left to right, I'm So Glad That God Has Blessed Me With A Friend Like You, *523623, 1992,* **$85;** The Lord Giveth, And The Lord Taketh Away, *100226, 1986,* **$68;** A Friend Is Someone Who Cares, *520632, 1988,* **$70;** *and* Puppy Love Is From Above, *106798, 1987,* **$79.**

Lord Bless You And Keep You, The, E4720, 1980 .... **$43**
Lord Bless You And Keep You, The, E4721, 1980 .... **$54**
Lord Give Me Patience, E7159, 1981 .... **$56**
Love Beareth All Things, E7158, 1981 .... **$55**
Love Cannot Break/True Friendship, E4722, 1980 .... **$113**
Love Is Kind, E1379a, 1979 .... **$103**
Love Is Kind, E2847, 1983 .... **$43**
Love Is Patient, E9251, 1982...... **$79**
Love Is Sharing, E7162, 1981.... **$149**
Love Lifted Me, E1375a, 1979...**$106**
Love Lifted Me, E5201, 1980....... **$92**
Love Never Fails, 12300, 1984 .... **$50**
Love One Another, E1376, 1979.. **$79**
Loving Is Sharing, E3110b, 1979 .... **$94**
Loving Is Sharing, E3110g, 1979... **$68**
Make A Joyful Noise, E1374g, 1979 .... **$75**
May Your Birthday Be Gigantic, 15970, 1985 .... **$22**
May Your Christmas Be Blessed, E5376, 1984 .... **$70**
May Your Christmas Be Cozy, E2345, 1982 .... **$77**
May Your Christmas Be Delightful, 15482, 1985 .... **$55**
May Your Christmas Be Warm, E2348, 1982 .... **$109**
Mother Sew Dear, E3106, 1979... **$57**
My Guardian Angel, E5207, 1980 .... **$187**
Nativity Buildings & Tree, E2387, 1982 .... **$102**
Nativity Set Of 9 Pcs., E2800, 1979 .... **$158**
Nativity Wall, E5644 (Set Of 2), 1980 .... **$122**

Nobody's Perfect, E9268, 1982 .. **$262**

O Come All Ye Faithful, E2353, 1982 ....**$79**

O Worship The Lord, 102229, 1985 ....**$43**

Oh Worship The Lord, E5385, 1984 ....**$52**

Oh, Taste & See That The Lord Is Good, E9274, 1982 ....**$69**

Onward Christian Soldiers, E-0523, 1983 ....**$80**

Our First Christmas Together, E2377, 1982 ....**$80**

Part Of Me Wants To Be Good, 12149, 1984 ....**$75**

Peace Amid The Storm, E4723, 1980 ....**$83**

Peace On Earth, E2804, 1979 ....**$125**
Peace On Earth, E4725, 1981 ......**$80**
Peace On Earth, E9287, 1982 ....**$158**

Perfect Grandpa, The, E7160, 1981 ....**$67**

Praise The Lord Anyhow, E1374b, 1979 ....**$79**

Praise The Lord Anyhow, E9254, 1983 ....**$82**

Prayer Changes Things, E1375b, 1979 ....**$165**

Prayer Changes Things, E5214, 1980 ....**$121**

Precious Memories, E2828, 1983 ....**$88**

Prepare Ye The Way Of The Lord, E-0508, 1983 ....**$143**

Press On, E9265, 1983 ....**$78**

Purr-Fect Grandma, The, E3109, 1979 ....**$54**

Purr-Fect Grandma, The, E7242, 1982 ....**$83**

Purr-Fect Grandma, The, Thimble 13307, 1985 ....**$28**

Rejoice O Earth, E5636, 1980 ......**$53**

Rejoicing With You, E4724, 1980 ....**$74**

Serving The Lord, 100293, 1985...**$48**

Sharing Our Christmas Together, 102490, 1986 ....**$79**

Sharing Our Joy Together, E2834, 1982 ....**$55**

Sharing Our Season Together, E-0501, 1983 ....**$135**

Shepherd Of Love, 102261, 1985 ....**$29**

Silent Knight, E5642, 1980 ....**$360**

Silent Night, 15814, 1985 ....**$84**

Smile, God Loves You, E1373b, 1979 ....**$76**

Summer's Joy Musical, 408743, 1984 ....**$160**

Surrounded With Joy, E-0506, 1983 ....**$76**

Tell Me The Story Of Jesus, E2349, 1982 ....**$98**

Thank You For Coming To My Aide, E5202, 1980 ....**$122**

Thanking Him For You, E7155, 1981 ....**$51**

Thee I Love, E3116, 1979 ....**$99**

There Is Joy In Serving Jesus, E7157, 1981 ....**$57**

They Followed The Star, E5624, 1980 ....**$245**

They Followed The Star, E5641, 1980 ....**$196**

This Is Your Day To Shine, E2822, 1983 ....**$87**

Thou Art Mine, E3113, 1979 ....**$58**

To A Special Dad, E5212, 1980 ...**$50**

To A Very Special Mom, E2824, 1983 ....**$50**

To A Very Special Sister, E2825, 1983 ....**$56**

To God Be The Glory, E2823, 1983 ....**$94**

To My Favorite Paw, 100021, 1985 ....**$70**

To My Forever Friend, 100072, 1985 ....**$78**

To Some Bunny Special, E9282a, 1982 ....**$47**

To Thee W/Love, E3120, 1979 ......**$74**

Trust In The Lord, E9289, 1982 ...**$69**

Tubby's First Christmas, E-0511, 1983 ....**$40**

Unto Us A Child Is Born, E2013, 1979 ....**$102**

Voice Of Spring Musical, The, 408735, 1984 ....**$175**

Walking By Faith, E3117, 1979 ....**$93**

We Are God's Workmanship, E9258, 1982 ....**$44**

We Have Seen His Star, E2010, 1979 ....**$90**

Wee Three Kings, E5635, 1980 .....**$99**

We're In It Together, E9259, 1982 ....**$73**

Wishing You A Cozy Christmas, 102342, 1985 ....**$44**

Wishing You A Merry Christmas, E5383, 1984 ....**$41**

Wishing You A Yummy Christmas, 109754, 1986 ....**$57**

Worship The Lord, 100064, 1985...**$38**

You Are My Happiness, 526185, 1990 ....**$68**

You Can Fly, 12335, 1985 ....**$58**

You Can't Run Away From God, E-0525, 1983 ....**$108**

You Have Touched So Many Hearts, 527661, 1982 ....**$41**

You Have Touched So Many Hearts, E2821, 1984 ....**$56**

You're Worth Your Weight In Gold, E9282b, 1982 ....**$38**

Figurine, Family Christmas Scene

Christmas Fireplace, 524883, 1990 ....**$54**

God Gave His Best, 15806, 1985.. **$42**

Have A Beary Merry Christmas, 522856, 1989 ....**$41**

May You Have...Sweetest Christmas, 15776, 1985 ....**$43**

Sharing Our Christmas Together, 102490, 1986 ....**$79**

Story Of God's Love, The, 15784, 1985 ....**$50**

Tell Me A Story, 15792, 1985 ......**$32**

Figurine, Nativity

Come Let Us Adore Him, 104000 (Set Of 9), 1986..........................**$123**

Come Let Us Adore Him, 104523, 1986 ....**$396**

Come Let Us Adore Him, E2011, 1979 ....**$312**

Come Let Us Adore Him, E2395 (Set Of 11), 1982 ....**$135**

Come Let Us Adore Him, E2800 (Set Of 9), 1980..........................**$255**

Come Let Us Adore Him, E5619, 1980 ....**$42**

Plate, Christmas Collection

Come Let Us Adore Him, E5646, 1981 ....**$50**

Let Heaven And Nature Sing, E2347, 1982 ....**$43**

Unto Us A Child Is Born, E5395, 1984 ....**$43**

Wee Three Kings, E-0538, 1983.. **$44**

Plate, Christmas Love

I'm Sending You A White Christmas, 101834, 1986......................**$44**

May Your Christmas Be/Happy Home, 523003, 1989 ....**$44**

Merry Christmas Deer, 520284, 1988 ....**$54**

My Peace I Give To Thee, 102954, 1987 ....**$58**

Plate, Joy Of Christmas

Christmastime Is For Sharing, E-0505, 1983 ....**$70**

I'll Play My Drum For Him, E2357, 1982 ....**$58**

Tell Me The Story Of Jesus, 15237, 1984 ....**$70**

Wonder Of Christmas, The, E5396, 1984 ....**$44**

QUIMPER

Quimper, jug, "HenRiot Quimper C. Maillard" mk, **$300.**

Quimper, plate, "H R Quimper" mk, 9-1/2" d, **$225.**

History: Quimper faience, dating back to the 17th century, is named for Quimper, a French town where numerous potteries were located. Several mergers resulted in the evolution of two major houses—the Jules Henriot and Hubaudière-Bousquet factories.

The peasant design first appeared in the 1860s, and many variations exist. Florals and geometrics, equally popular, also were produced in large quantities. During the 1920s, the Hubaudière-Bousquet factory introduced the Odetta line, which utilized a stone body and Art Deco decorations.

The two major houses merged in 1968, the products retaining the individual characteristics and marks of the originals. The concern suffered from labor problems in the 1980s and was purchased by an American group.

Marks: The "HR" and "HR Quimper" marks are found on Henriot pieces prior to 1922. The "Henriot Quimper" mark was used after 1922. The "HB" mark covers a long time span. Numbers or dots and dashes were added for inventory purposes and are found on later pieces. Most marks are in blue or black. Pieces ordered by department stores, such as Macy's and Carson Pirie Scott, carry the store mark along with the factory mark, making them less desirable to collectors. A comprehensive list of marks is found in Bondhus's book.

Adviser: Al Bagdade.

Additional Terms:

A la touche border decor—single brush stroke to create floral

Breton Broderie decor—stylized blue and gold pattern inspired by a popular embroidery pattern often used on Breton costumes, dates from the Art Deco era.

Croisille—criss-cross pattern

Decor Riche border—acanthus leaves in two colors

Fleur-de-lys—the symbol of France

Basin, female peasant in center flanked by red and blue vert florals, blue and yellow striped inner border, pierced for hanging, "HenRiot Quimper France" mk, rim chips, 11-1/2" d, 3-3/4" h **$150**

Bell, figural female peasant, green and white coif, cobalt jacket and skirt, rose apron, unmkd, chips, 4-1/2" h **$300**

Bowl, male peasant in center red, yellow, green, and blue vert florals, red, blue, and green single stroke florals between yellow bands on border, wavy blue line on scalloped edge, unmkd, 10-1/8" d **$300**

Bread Tray, procession in center w/musicians, children watching, dk blue acanthus border w/crest of Brittany at top, gold edged lobed and indented rim, "HenRiot Quimper" mk, 20-1/4" 1 x 10-3/4" w **$900**

Cake Plate, frontal view of male peasant holding basket under arm, flanked by typical vert florals, inner red "s" chain, border of red, blue, yellow, and green sprigs and four blue dots, blue outlined shaped rim, blue sponged rope handles, "HR Quimper" mk, 11" H-H **$375**

Charger, Breton Broderie, female peasant holding skirt hem, male w/hands in pockets, ermine tail inner border, enameled yellow herringbone border w/four rosettes, irreg cobalt rim w/enameled beads, "HB Quimper" mk, 12-1/4" d **$2,000**

Clock, reverse heart shape, full figured male peasant smoking pipe, female peasant w/young girl in meadow, crest of Brittany in green and yellow wreath w/red ribbon and four blue dots at top, lg blue and yellow daisy and red and green single stroke florals and four blue dot designs on

sides between blue lines, HB Depose" mk, 6-7/8" h **$1,950**

Crepiere, oval, seated peasant woman w/basket in lap, standing peasant woman w/basket on arm, green decor riche or acanthus border, blue sponged underside, repairs, Porquier Beau, 13" 1 x 5-1/4" w **$2,950**

Cup and Saucer, oct, male peasant in panel, red, green, yellow, and blue scattered florals in other panels, blue dashes outlining vert borders between panels, scattered four blue dots, blue dash and yellow handle, "HenRiot Quimper" mk **$145**

Egg Dish, female peasant in center salt well, six blue dashed edged oval wells w/red and green sprigs in center, scattered sprigs and four blue dots between wells, blue line rim, "HB Quimper France" mk, 9-7/8" d **$225**

Quimper, creamer and cov sugar, "HenRiot Quimper France" mks, creamer 4-1/2" h, cov sugar 6-3/4" h, **$200.**

Figure

Male peasant, cobalt jacket, gold outlined lt blue vest, holding net over shoulder, blue walking stick, green oct base w/"COLAIK" on front, 9" h **$200**

Seated male peasant, playing horn, yellow edged green jacket, lt blue vest, brown hat, cream pantaloons, cobalt stockings, brown wooden shoes, seated on brown barrel, green mound base, "Porquier Beau Quimper" mk, 13-3/4" h.......... **$850**

Virgin Mary w/infant Christ, gold edged blue wrap, gold crown and cross at neck, "ST. MARIE" in circ base, "AP" mk, 10-1/2" h **$500**

Honey Pot, Cov, band of red and blue florals on undulating body, attached base w/band of blue half circles and dots, male peasant on cov, blue edged fan knob, "HR Quimper" mk, 4-1/2" h... **$375**

Inkstand, seated male peasant on base, cobalt acanthus designs, ovals of ermine tails at corners w/animal feet, crest of Quimper on horiz letter bar w/ cobalt acanthus and gold trim, molded gold waves and shell on backplate, molded shell on front, "HR Quimper" mk, 6-1/2" h x 8-3/4" w **$450**

Knife Rest, 3-1/8" l, male peasant, four blue dot designs on reverse, blue dashed between, blue diamond design on ends w/green splashes, "HB Quimper" mk.................................. **$70**

Pipe, female peasant on bowl w/sm red cabbage rose, blue acanthus design on top of stem, blue dashes on sides, orange dashes on under side, orange edge of bowl and stem, "HB Quimper" mk, 5" l **$650**

Pitcher, male peasant under spout, side vert panels of red, blue, and green zigzags and leaves, blue lined base and rims, blue dash handle, "HenRiot Quimper France" mk, 6" h **$295**

Plate

Bird, lg blue and yellow exotic, perched on red half sunflower, blue inner border stripes w/yellow outer stripes, unmkd, 8-5/8" d **$125**

Male peasant blowing horn in center, lt blue pantaloons, red vest, cobalt jacket, flanked by sm florals, border of blue, green, and yellow sprigs separated by four blue dot designs, indented shaped rim, "HB" mk, 9-3/4" d **$195**

Male peasant smoking pipe, frontal view, flanked by red, green, and blue florals, border of red, blue, and green floral bunches separated by four blue dot design, shaped rim, "HB" mk, 8-1/4" d **$250**

Sq w/cut corners, lg blue and white fleur de lys in center, smaller in each corner, blue chain rim, "HB Quimper" mk, 9" d **$125**

Porringer, male peasant in center, blue and yellow striped inner border, blue sponged handles, "HenRiot Quimper France" mk, 5-5/8" H-H **$50**

Soup Tureen, painted brown, yellow and orange seashells, green sea grass, black ground, four splayed feet, "Guy Trevoux," "HenRiot Quimper" mk, 7-1/2" h x 8" d **$495**

Sugar Bowl, cov, lump sugar, female peasant on side, red, blue, yellow, and red scattered florals, blue dot designs, blue sponged handles and knob, blue lined rims, "HenRiot Quimper" mk, 8" h, 10" H-H................................. **$195**

Tray, rect, group of peasant women and children w/produce in center, tent in bkd, blue acanthus border w/crest of Brittany, gold-orange rim, "blue HenRiot Quimper France" mk, 14-1/2" l x 12" w... **$2,500**

Trivet, center medallion of two male peasants playing horn and bagpipe, dk blue acanthus swirls on corners and lobed sides, gold lined edging, "HenRiot Quimper" mk, 1/2" sq x 2" h.......... **$475**

Vase

Bulbous body, flared neck, sq base, frontal view of male peasant flanked by red, yellow, and blue dot and single stroke florals, red edged cobalt coat, yellow pantaloons, yellow-brown boots, lg red and blue cabbage roses on reverse, blue zigzag and dot vert and horiz borders, blue dash gold edged scroll handles, ruffled and indented rim, "HenRiot Quimper France" mk, 8-1/4" h................... **$575**

Crescent shape, female peasant on front flanked by red, green, and blue florals, lg blue sunflower and scattered red and orange centered yellow flowers on reverse, club shaped base, yellow ground, "HenRiot Quimper" mk, 5-1/2" h....**$155**

Moon shape, w/green gargoyle handles, painted family scene on side w/children and house, lg pink and yellow florals, green foliage on reverse, green acanthus or scrolling sides, "PB Quimper" mk, 10" h x 13" w.......... **$4,800**

Teardrop shape, two male peasants playing instruments on front w/crest of Quimper on neck, lg pink and yellow cabbage roses on reverse, two blue, yellow, and green fancy scroll handles, blue acanthus band on neck w/band of half loops and dots, "HenRiot Quimper on front and base, 13" h **$895**

Wall Pocket

Dbl cone shape, male or female peasant on each cone, blue streaked base and top tabs, blue dash center loop, "HB Quimper France" mk, 5" h **$125**

Pleated fan shape and backplate, female peasant on front w/vert florals, blue crisscross left edge, band of florals on backplate w/four blue dots, blue sponged sides, "HenRiot Quimper France" mk, 10" h x 9-1/2" w..................................... **$225**

RED WING POTTERY

History: The Red Wing pottery category includes several potteries from Red Wing, Minnesota. In 1868, David Hallem started Red Wing Stoneware Co., the first pottery with stoneware as its primary product. The Minnesota Stoneware Co. started in 1883. The North Star Stoneware Co. was in business from 1892 to 1896.

The Red Wing Stoneware Co. and the Minnesota Stoneware Co. merged in 1892. The new company, the Red Wing Union Stoneware Co., made stoneware until 1920 when it introduced a pottery line that it continued until the 1940s. In 1936, the name was changed to Red Wing Potteries, Inc. During the 1930s, this firm introduced several popular patterns of hand-painted dinnerware, which were distributed through department stores, mail-order catalogs, and gift-stamp centers. Dinnerware production declined in the 1950s and was replaced with hotel and restaurant china in the early 1960s. The plant closed in 1967.

Marks: Red Wing Stoneware Co. was the first firm to mark pieces with a red wing stamped under the glaze. The North Star Stoneware Co. used a raised star and the words "Red Wing" as its mark.

Red Wing large cherry band pitcher with Marble Rock, Iowa, advertising, 9-1/2", **$1,000.**

Bean pot, cov, "It Pays to Trade with Shors & Alexander Pocahontas, IA" **$85**

Bowl
Brown shoulder, bottom mkd, 7" d **$45**
Greek Key, 6" d **$115**
Shoulder, mkd, 13" d **$175**
Sponge dec, cap shape, 7" d **$95**
Spongeband, 4" d **$275**
Spongeband, 9" d **$145**
Spongeband, "Merry Christmas from Weigolb & Nordby Stores, Mix With Us," 8" d **$125**

Butter churn, two gallons, 2" wing and oval mark **$250**

Butter crock
One gallon, "Polly Ann Boston Baked Beans" **$175**
Five lbs, "Goodhue County Co-operative Co.," minor nick on top edge **$95**
Three lbs, "Fresh Butter Model Dairy Inc." **$75**
Three lbs, "North American Creameries, Inc., Meadowbrook Butter" ..**$125**
Three lbs, "White & Mathers" adv **$200**

Casserole, spongeband, large **$125**
Casserole, cov, "Merry Christmas Hokah Co-Op Creamery," 8" d **$195**
Chicken water, half gallon, "Oak Leaf Simmon's Hardware Co." **$250**
Churn, four gallons
Oval mark and 4" wing **$175**
Oval over birch leaf, hairline in bottom **$145**

Salt glaze, lazy 8 and target dec **$375**

Churn lid, 5/6 gallon **$120**

Crock
Eight gallons, chip on base, oval mark and 6" wing **$75**
One gallon, 2" wing **$350**
Ten gallon, oval mark and 6" wing, "10" and oval in black ink **$125**
Two gallons, 4" wing mark **$90**
Three gallons, circle oval mark and 2" wing **$90**
Three gallon, "Potteries" oval, 2" wing **$65**
Twenty gallons, oval mark and 6" wing **$125**

Crock, salt glaze
Five gallons, birch leaf, Union label, chip on handle **$55**
Six gallons, leaf dec **$175**
Two gallons, target, bottom mkd ..**$100**
Ten gallons, leaf, front stamped "Minnesota Stoneware," hairline **$250**
Three gallons, tornado, front stamped "Red Wing Stoneware Company," large chip at bottom **$250**
Twenty lbs, butterfly, back stamped, hairlines **$175**

Crock lid
One-gallon size **$90**
Fifteen gallons, nick where wire handle enters lid **$65**
Two gallons **$225**

Custard, spongeband
Large, tight hairline **$65**
Small **$85**

Funeral vase, Brushware **$65**
Hotplate, Minnesota Centennial, 1958 ....**$45**

Jug
One-eighth pint, Michigan advertising **$225**
One gallon, ball top shoulders, bottom mkd **$95**
One gallon, brown top shoulders, "The Banner Liquor Store, Winona, Minn" **$175**
One gallon, brown top shoulders, wing mark **$195**
One gallon, "Fargo Creamery Supply House St. Paul, Minn" in oval, bottom marked **$150**
One gallon, tomato, brown top, wing mark **$395**
Five gallons, Imperial, shoulder, 4" wing and oval mark **$125**
Five gallon, shoulders, "Union" oval and 4" wing **$80**
Five gallons, shoulder, "The Mason House & Mineral Springs, Colfax Iowa," shield and Union label **$775**
Three gallons, shoulder, no oval mark, 2" wing **$35**

Koverwate
Fifteen gallons, mkd "15," small nick **$125**
Three gallons, "3" on side with instructions **$450**

Mug
Blue bands, "Certainly" **$150**
Blue bands, "Good Luck Malt Syrup," hairline **$135**

Red Wing ten-gallon crock with Washington advertising that includes crockery, **$1,500.**

Red Wing rare five-gallon white stoneware "beehive" two-handle jug with advertising, 17" h, **$4,000.**

Red Wing two-gallon white stoneware water cooler, small wing and bail handles, 11" h without lid; lid, 9" d, **$2,200.**

Red Wing six-gallon white stoneware churn with birch leaves called "elephant ears," 17-1/2" h, **$950.**

Blue bands, "I Came From Atlas Malt Products Co., Janesville, WI," hairline **$115**

Blue bands, "Souvenir West End Commercial Club, St. Paul June 21-26, 1909" **$185**

Spongeband **$575**

Nappy

Blue and white **$120**

Saffronware, "Compliments of C. A. Habergarten & Co., Waconia, Minn" **$195**

Pitcher

Blue mottled, large, minor bottom edge chips **$200**

Cherry band, large................. **$175**

Cherry band, small.................. **$195**

Spongeband, large **$195**

Sponge, mottled........................... **$165**

Spongeband, small **$335**

Refrigerator jar, small size, hairline **$65**

Salt shaker, Spongeband, white glaze **$120**

Sewer tile **$70**

Snuff jar, cov, North Star, Albany slip, minor chip under lid.................. **$125**

Spittoon, German-style, bottom edge chip **$375**

Thrashing jug, five gallons, beehive, six-sided spigot hole, oval mark and 4" wing............................. **$1,650**

Water cooler, five gallons, 4" wing mark **$350**

Red Wing two-gallon salt-glaze crock with strong cobalt decoration of "target with tail," marked on bottom, "Minnesota Stoneware Co. Red Wing, Minn.," c1890, **$475.**

Red Wing, two-gallon crock, with tilted birch leaves and oval stamp with "Minnesota Stoneware Company" (spelled out, commonly found as "Co."), 12" h with lid, otherwise unmarked, **$1,500.**

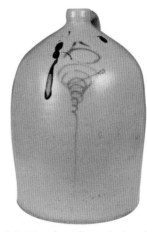

Red Wing five-gallon salt-glaze "beehive" jug with cobalt "tornado" decoration, with glaze drippings called "turkey droppings," unmarked, c1890, 17" h, **$2,900.**

Red Wing, Belle Kogan planter, called "The Nymphs," No. B2500, part of the "Deluxe Line," 16-1/2" w, 6-3/4" h, **$180.**

Red Wing, teapot, No. 260, early 1940s, 7-3/4" h, **$150.**

Red Wing, ashtray No. 54, Nokomis glaze, 4" w, **$600.**

Red Wing rare "dome top" jug, "bird jug," about 1-1/2 gallons, in Albany slip glaze, c1895, 9-1/4" h, **$150.**

Red Wing, Brushed Ware vase, No. 133, ink-stamped in a circle, "Red Wing Union Stoneware Co.—Red Wing, Minn," 8-1/4" h, **$175.**

Red Wing, ashtray, honoring the 1965 American League champion Minnesota Twins, 12-3/4" w, also marked, "Red Wing Potteries USA," **$90.**

Redware plate, sgraffito, showing Ben Franklin reading book, framed by Pennsylvania Dutch verse, dated 1779, 12" diameter, 2" deep, 19th century repair to glued crack, **$2,530.**
Photo courtesy of Bruce & Vicki Wassdorp.

Redware jar, incised rim, manganese splash dec, Pennsylvania, 19th century, 11" h, **$525.**
Photo courtesy of Pook & Pook, Inc.

REDWARE

History: The availability of clay, the same used to make bricks and roof tiles, accounted for the great production of red earthenware pottery in the American colonies. Redware pieces are mainly utilitarian—bowls, crocks, jugs, etc.

Lead-glazed redware retained its reddish color, but a variety of colored glazes were obtained by the addition of metals to the basic glaze. Streaks and mottled splotches in redware items resulted from impurities in the clay and/or uneven firing temperatures.

Slipware is the term used to describe redwares decorated by the application of slip, a semi-liquid paste made of clay. Slipwares were made in England, Germany, and elsewhere in Europe for decades before becoming popular in the Pennsylvania German region and other areas in colonial America.

Birdhouse, incised banding dec, finial with hanging hole, 8" d, 10-1/2" h **$470**

Bowl, mottled, orange glaze, unglazed exterior, attributed to Miller Pottery, minor chips, usage wear, 6-3/8" d, 1-1/2" h..**$440**

Crock
Molded rim, manganese brown int. glaze, 3-1/2" d, 2-1/2" h **$250**
Molded rim, red-orange and green glaze, 6" d, 4" h **$360**

Figure
Chicken on base, orange glaze, attributed to Jesiah Shorb, W. Manheim Twp, York County, Pennsylvania, restoration to front edge of base, 2" h, 2-1/4" l, 1-1/2" w...........**$1,320**
Dog carrying basket of fruit, green-orange glazing, base sgd "Ernst Beicher, the 8 1/3 Month 1862," provenance: possibly one of two known sgd examples, Eugene and Dorothy Elgin collection, Conestoga Auction, April 3, 2004, 5-1/2" h, 6-1/2" l, 2-3/4" w **$44,000**

Freestanding hound, yellow glazed, brown raised and incised ears and tail, attributed to Peter Bell, 5" l **$9,000**
Poodle, standing, yellow, green, and brown, coleslaw clay to front half of body, leads and raised head, stepped orange oval base, incised "Anton Audon Ruppert May 1869," 7-1/2" l, 8" w **$20,000**
Rooster on base, orange glaze, attributed to Jesiah Shorb, W. Manheim Twp, York County, Pennsylvania, restoration front edge of base, 2-5/8" h, 2-3/4" l, 1-1/2" w....**$1,485**
Seated begging dog on base, basket of fruit, incised fur, orange glaze, attributed to Jesiah Shorb, W. Manheim Twp, York County, Pennsylvania, 4-1/4" h, 2-3/4" l, 2-1/4" h **$7,150**
Seated begging dog on base, incised, dark glaze, circular banding imp at base, attributed to Elia Swartzbaugh, Jefferson, York County, Pennsylvania, 4-3/4" h, 3-1/2" l, 2" w..**$2,970**

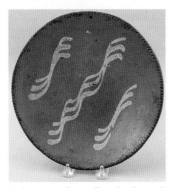

Redware pie plate, yellow slip dec, 19th century, 9-3/4" d, **$470.**
Photo courtesy of Pook & Pook, Inc.

Redware charger, yellow slip dec, 19th century, 12-1/2" d, **$760.**
Photo courtesy of Pook & Pook, Inc.

Redware charger, central slip rooster, Pennsylvania or German, 19th century, 13-1/2" d, **$410.**
Photo courtesy of Pook & Pook, Inc.

Seated dog, reddish-brown glaze, row incised circles at base, attr. Peter Bell, Shenandoah Valley, Waynesboro, Pennsylvania, 5" h **$8,500**

Seated squirrel on base, eating nut, orange glaze, attributed to Jesiah Shorb, W. Manheim Twp, York County, Pennsylvania, tail restoration, 3-1/2" h, 2-3/4" l, 2" w **$1,715**

Finger bowl, orange ground, brown sponge dec, molded base, incised banding to rim, chips, small rim restoration, 4" d, 1-3/4" h **$385**

Fireplace trivet, scalloped edges, four feet, unglazed, sgd "S. Hiney" on base, wear, 6-1/4" sq, 2-1/2" h **$635**

Flower pot, mottled green and brown glaze, rust ground, crimped rim, attached saucer, attributed to John Bell, 5-5/8" h **$275**

Inkwell, three inkwells, sander, two pen compartments, dark manganese glaze, PA, firing line on front, 8" l, 3-1/2" w, 3-3/4" h **$600**

Jar, cov, bear shape, button finial, orange-brown glaze, 7-5/8" h, 6" d **$1,045**

Jar, open

Barrel shaped, splotched dec, four ribbed and incised bands, dated "1766," 7-1/2" h **$5,000**

Bulbous, flared rim, incised banding, red-orange ground, black sponge-dripped highlights, 5-1/4" h, 5" d **$750**

Flared rim, sloped shoulder, brownish-green glaze with lighter spots and dark brown streaks, attributed to New England, minor wear to glaze on rim, late 18th/early 19th C, 7" h **$360**

Flared rim, three color slip dec of village, houses, pine trees, grass, festooned yellow slip border, found in Hanover, Pennsylvania, 6-3/4" h, 6" d **$9,350**

Ovoid, raised rim, lug handles, incised line on shoulder, brown streak deco, CT, minor shallow rim chips, early 19th C, 11" h **$1,530**

Jug

Applied handle, incised banding at center, brown manganese glaze, 5-3/4" d, 6-1/4" h **$200**

Bulbous, applied handle, brown manganese glaze, minor chips, 4-1/2" d, 5" h **$415**

Bulbous, applied handle, incised banding on shoulder, manganese glaze, glaze chips, 5-1/2" d, 6-1/2" h **$440**

Bulbous, applied handle, formed spout, brown manganese glaze, 6-1/2" d, 9" h **$220**

Bulbous, applied handle, molded spout, brown manganese glaze, 6" d, 7-1/8" h **$250**

Bulbous, applied handle, brown manganese glaze, 7" d, 8-3/4" h **$275**

Applied handle, brown manganese glaze, usage wear, base chips, 7-1/4" d, 8-1/4" h **$210**

Harvest, spout, mottled glaze, yellow and brown glaze, stamped "G. H. Baker" on side, ("G. H. Baker, Hamilton Twp, Adams County, PA," 9" d **$2,860**

Miniature

Jug, applied handle, brown and black mottled glaze, attributed to Jesiah Shorb, W. Manheim Twp, York County, Pennsylvania, handle broken and glued, 2-1/2" w, 3" h .. **$110**

Turk's head, brown-orange glaze, Pennsylvania, 3-3/4" d, 1-1/2" h **$715**

Pie plate, slip dec, orange base glaze int., three double slip squiggle lines, 8-5/8" d, 1-3/4" h **$1,375**

Plate

Orange ground glaze, green and black slip tulip dec, attributed to Dryville Pottery, some discoloration, 8-7/8" d, 1-1/2" h **$2,750**

Serrated rim, yellow slip dec of bird on branch, orange glaze, normal wear, 10-3/4" d, 1-3/4" h **$8,525**

Sgraffito dec, centralized flower, German text banding rim, orange ground, yellow, blue, and green highlights to flower, dated 1846, translation of rim inscription "The Star that Looks Down on the Flask has Destroyed the Luck of Many," minor chips on rim, 10-3/4" d, 1-3/4" h **$11,000**

Pot, incised bands at rim and base, brown glaze, 4-3/4" d, 3-7/8" h **$135**

Potter's brick, orange glaze, inscribed "Solomon Miller, Reading Township, Adams Co. May 28," back with date 186?, wear from use as door stop, 4-1/2" l, 3" w, 2" h **$715**

Salt, open, master, incised banding, brown and black glaze, inscribed "Made by Solomon Miller," Adams Co., Pennsylvania, 3-3/4" d, 2" h **$2,310**

Shaving mug, reddish-brown glazed slipware, brown splotched dots and lines, two bands of incised lines, c1805-25, small scuttle container **$3,300**

Redware covered crock, manganese splash and yellow slip dec, Pennsylvania, 19th century, 6-3/4" h, 10" d, **$820.**
Photo courtesy of Pook & Pook, Inc.

Redware crock, orange and brown glaze, attributed to Medinger, Pennsylvania, c1900, 10-1/4" h, **$820.**
Photo courtesy of Pook & Pook, Inc.

Redware crock, orange and green glaze, 19th century, 5-1/2" h, **$410.**
Photo courtesy of Pook & Pook, Inc.

Redware flower pot, attached undertray, green and brown glaze over cream ground, Shenandoah Valley, 19th century, 7-1/2" d, 8" h, **$2,900.**

Smoking pipe, orange and brown mottled glaze, 3-1/2" w, 3-1/2" h **$750**

Sugar bowl, cov
Open reticulated work on bowl and lid, rope twist handles, yellow-brown glaze, attributed to Jesiah Shorb, W. Manheim Twp, York County, Pennsylvania **$9,900**

Two applied handles, molded rim, red-brown glaze, drip manganese brown dec, zigzag banding on lid with finial, 6-1/2" w, 5-1/4" h **$1,595**

Vessel, tapered, incised banding, D-shaped cut-out handles, orange and green mottled glaze, Dover, York County, Pennsylvania, 7-3/4" d, 5-3/4" h **$880**

ROCKINGHAM AND ROCKINGHAM BROWN-GLAZED WARES

History: Rockingham ware can be divided into two categories. The first consists of the fine china and porcelain pieces made between 1826 and 1842 by the Rockingham Company of Swinton, Yorkshire, England, and its predecessor firms: Swinton, Bingley, Don, Leeds, and Brameld. The Bramelds developed the cadogan, a lidless teapot. Between 1826 and 1842, the Bramelds developed a quality soft-paste product with a warm, silky feel. Elaborate specialty pieces were made. By 1830, the company employed 600 workers and listed 400 designs for dessert sets and 1,000 designs for tea and coffee services in its catalog. Unable to meet its payroll, the company closed in 1842.

The second category of Rockingham ware includes pieces produced in the famous Rockingham brown glaze that became an intense and vivid purple-brown when fired. It had a dark, tortoiseshell appearance. The glaze was copied by many English and American potteries. American manufacturers that used Rockingham glaze include D. & J. Henderson of Jersey City, New Jersey; United States Pottery in Bennington, Vermont; potteries in East Liverpool, Ohio; and several potteries in Indiana and Illinois.

Additional Listings: Bennington and Bennington-Type Pottery.

Bowl, 9-1/2" d, 3-1/4" h **$65**

Casserole, cov, oval, fruit finial, applied handles, 12" l, 10-1/4" h **$275**

Creamer, cow-form, minor chips, 19th C, 6-3/4" h **$260**

Cuspidor, four sides, molded eagles, dark brown Rockingham glaze, 6-5/8", 4" h **$330**

Figure, molded seated spaniel, mottled brown glaze over yellow pottery, chips, flakes, 12-1/2" h **$615**

Flask, molded floral dec, band, 8" h ... **$45**

Flower pot, emb acanthus leaves, matching saucer, 10-1/4" h **$45**

Inkwell, shoe shape, 4-1/8" l **$60**

Mixing bowl, nested set of three, emb design **$95**

Pie plate, Rockingham glaze, 10" d .. **$80**

Pitcher, Revolutionary War battle scene with George Washington, 12" h .. **$2,750**

Plate, painted center with exotic bird in landscape, raised C-scroll border with gilt and painting, puce griffin and green number marks, 9" d **$650**

Potpourri vase, cov, two handles, pink ground borders with central

enamel dec floral bouquets, gilt foliage and trim, pierced neck, rim, and cov, printed griffin mark, slight gilt rim wear to vase, rim chips and hairline to cover, c1835, 11" h **$290**

Scent bottle, onion shape, applied garden flowers, gilt line rims, printed puce griffin mark, c1831-40, 6" h **$465**

Vase, flared, painted view of Larington Yorkshire, figures and sheep, wide gilt border, dark blue ground, restored, iron-red griffin and painted title, c1826-30, 4-3/8" h **$420**

Washboard, imperfections, 19th C, 24-1/4" h **$350**

Earthenware wall pocket, Rockingham glaze, wreath form, spaniel head, 8-3/4" d, **$470.**
Photo courtesy of Pook & Pook, Inc.

Rockingham mug, glaze, herringbone rim and foot, second half 19th century, 3-3/4" h, 4-1/8" d rim, **$55.**
Photo courtesy of Green Valley Auctions.

ROOKWOOD POTTERY

History: Mrs. Marie Longworth Nicholas Storer, Cincinnati, Ohio, founded Rookwood Pottery in 1880. The name of this outstanding American art pottery came from her family estate, "Rookwood," named for the rooks (crows) that inhabited the wooded grounds.

Though the Rookwood pottery filed for bankruptcy in 1941, it was soon reorganized under new management. Efforts at maintaining the pottery proved futile, and it was sold in 1956 and again in 1959. The pottery was moved to Starkville, Mississippi, in conjunction with the Herschede Clock Co. It finally ceased operating in 1967.

Rookwood wares changed with the times. The variety is endless, in part because of the creativity of the many talented artists responsible for great variations in glazes and designs.

Marks: There are five elements to the Rookwood marking system—the clay or body mark, the size mark, the decorator mark, the date mark, and the factory mark. The best way to date Rookwood art pottery is from factory marks.

From 1880 to 1882, the factory mark was the name "Rookwood" incised or painted on the base. Between 1881 and 1886, the firm name, address, and year appeared in an oval frame. Beginning in 1886, the impressed "RP" monogram appeared and a flame mark was added for each year until 1900. After 1900, a Roman numeral, indicating the last two digits of the year of production, was added at the bottom of the "RP" flame mark. This last mark is the one most often seen on Rookwood pieces in the antiques marketplace.

Rookwood vase, iris glaze, painted by Carl Schmidt, tapering, diaphanous white irises on black to pink shaded ground, flame mark/W/artist cipher, uncrazed, neatly drilled bottom, 1910, 9" x 5", **$5,000.**
Photo courtesy of David Rago Auctions, Inc.

Architectural tile, cuenca, tree landscape, blue, green, and tan matte glazes, mounted in Arts & Crafts frame, imp "Rookwood Faience," 17-1/2" sq **$3,450**

Bookend, elephant, semi-matte ivory glaze, production, 1920, flame mark/XX/244C, firing line to back, X'd for glaze drip, 6-1/4" w, 5-3/4" h **$145**

Bowl, Ombroso, carved and inlaid poppy pod dec around top, dec by Charles Todd, 1915, 6-1/2" d ... **$2,200**

Bud vase, bulbous, flowers on brown to gold ground, flame mark/III/745C/CCL, by Clara Lindeman, 1903, 5-1/4" h **$360**

Cabinet jug, by N. J. Hirschfeld, dec in Limoges-style, bamboo and butterfly, shaded brown, ivory, and blue-green ground, gilded details, stamped "Rookwood 1883 G 61," artist's cipher, 3-1/2" d, 4-1/2" h **$410**

Cabinet vase, Tiger Eye, flame mark obscured by glaze, two very minor grinding base chips, 3" d, 3" h **$350**

Chamberstick, Standard Glaze, painted by Jeannette Swing, yellow violets, flame mark, artist's cipher, 1894, 3" h **$350**

Charger, mauve and ochre galleon center, light blue splashed border, John Wareham, dated 1905, 12-1/2" d **$1,500**

Chocolate pot, standard glaze, oak leaves and across dec, shape #722, Lenore Ashbury, 1904, 10" h **$700**

Ewer, Standard glaze, painted by A. R. Valentein, branches of yellow cherry blossoms, flame mark/387A/S.A.R.V./I., minimal crazing, firing line to handle, 1890, 14" h, 8" d **$1,100**

Figure, woman's head, matte white glaze, flame mark/XXIV/2026, 1924, 7-1/2" d, 8" h **$365**

Flower boat, standard glaze, pansies dec, shape #3745, Matt A. Daly, 1890, 16" l **$900**

Flower frog, #2251, 1915 .... **$325**

Humidor, cov, round, Standard Glaze, portrait of American Indian, Pueblo Man, painted by Grace Young, dated 1901, 6" h **$3,750**

Jug, by Albert Humphrys, Limoges style, geese flying over bamboo thicket, stamped "ROOKWOOD 1882 A.H." with anchor, 1882, 3-1/2" d, 5-1/4" h **$490**

Pitcher
Flowers on green to gold ground, flame mark/I/657D/FH, artist's initials FH, 1901, 6" h **$270**
Flowers on blue to white ground, flame mark/VI/907F/EN, by Eliza Lawrence, 1906, 7" h **$300**

Rookwood vase, standard glaze, bronze overlay decorated by Kataro Shirayamadani, Japanese scene of fish and sea plants, flame mark/804C/Japanese cipher, 1898, 12-3/4" x 5", **$26,000.**
Photo courtesy of David Rago Auctions, Inc.

Rookwood urn, standard glaze, painted by Matt Daly, branches of yellow dogwood, gently tooled underglaze design encircling collar, flame mark/MAD/L/425/W, 1/2" glaze chip to base, possibly from manufacture, 1888, **$3,250.**
Photo courtesy of David Rago Auctions, Inc.

Rookwood vase, wax matte, painted by Kataro Shirayamadani, bulbous, orange and blue crocuses on shaded pastel ground, flame mark/XXXV/S/artist cipher, 1935, 6-1/2" x 3-3/4", **$1,200.**
Photo courtesy of David Rago Auctions, Inc.

Rookwood plaque, marine scenic vellum, by Carl Schmidt, "Morning in the Lagoon—Venice," sailboats in Venetian harbor, orig frame, flame mark, C. Schmidt, plaque 12" x 9", **$16,450.**
Photo courtesy of David Rago Auctions, Inc.

Rookwood vase, standard glaze, ovoid, painted by Kataro Shirayamadani, branches of yellow dogwood on yellow and amber ground, flame mark/531F/Japanese cipher, remnants of red crayon museum marks, 1886, 9-1/4" x 8-1/2", **$2,100.**
Photo courtesy of David Rago Auctions, Inc.

Rookwood jug, butterflies and leaves, cloudy sky, painted by Matt Daly, impressed mark/M.A.D., 1883, 6-3/4" x 7-1/2", **$480.**
Photo courtesy of David Rago Auctions, Inc.

Standard glaze, Kataro Shirayamadani, flowering tree branch, gold to brown ground, imp maker's and artist's mark on base, 1890, 9-1/2" h **$1,000**

Planter, incised stylized leaves, frothy brown-green matte glaze, flame mark/XI/180C, c1910, 8-3/4" h, 8-1/2" d **$500**

Plaque, scenic vellum

End of the Woods, view of trees and winter scene, frozen lake at twilight, painted by Elizabeth F. McDermott, 1910, 11-1/2" x 9" **$7,500**

Lake bordered by shade trees and mountain, painted by Ed Diers, orig frame, 1919, 14-1/2" x 9-1/2" **$10,000**

Meadow and trees, painted by L. Asbury, orig frame, 1922, 12" x 9-1/2" **$7,000**

Ombroso, pr of Rooks flanking bowl and reverse RP symbol, 1915, minor edge flakes, 7-1/2" x 3-1/2" **$6,000**

Penacock Lane, Concord, New Hampshire, view of lake through trees, sgd "ED," Rookwood flame mark and date on reverse, dec by Ed Diers, Cincinnati, Ohio, framed, crazing, 1916, 14-1/4" w, 8-3/4" h **$8,625**

Shade trees in foreground, lake and mountain in background, Arts & Crafts oak frame, 2" sq **$2,500**

The Morning Hour, Venetian sailboats, painted by Carl Schmidt, 9-1/2" x 11-1/2" **$6,500**

Teapot, cov, Turkish, frog fishing with pole and bobber on riverbank, painting attributed to Maria Longworth Nichols, dated 1833, 11" **$1,500**

Vase

Artist sgd with initials for W. E. Hentschel, olive brown mat glaze above emb green, blue, and light gray flowers, dated 1915, 7-3/8" h **$1,775**

Baluster, flowers on green to gold ground, flame mark/V/605E/GH, by Grace Hall, 1905, 5" h **$300**

Bottle shape, sea green, painted blue bells, black to celadon ground, Sally Toohey, flame mark/742D/ST/G, 1899, 12-1/2" h, 3-3/4" d **$5,500**

Bulbous, blue, turquoise, and magenta running glaze, flame mark/XXI/915F/LNL, by Elizabeth Lincoln, 1921, 4-3/4" h **$475**

Bulbous, flowers on brown to gold ground, flame mark/VII/654D/LEL, by Laura Lindeman, 1907, 5-1/4" h **$330**

Drip glaze, bulbous body, long neck, imp maker's mark and numbered "6363," 1949, 6" h **$300**

Iris glaze, decorated by Ed Diers, earth-tone underglaze color at neck shading to soft greens, mauve carnation with buds and trailing stems, marks include Rookwood logo, date, artist's monogram, "879D," paper label "133," crazing, c1904, 9-1/2" d **$1,530**

Rookwood loving cup, standard glaze, decorated by Grace Young, American Indian brave with illegible name beneath portrait, chased silver band, silver medallion of side, de-accessioned from Cincinnati Museum, flame mark/810/GY/title/Stanley Burt's red mark, Y-shaped line to interior of bottom foot ring, 1898, 6-3/4" x 8", **$6,000.**

Rookwood vase, vellum, bulbous, by Kataro Shirayamadani, brown crocus and green leaves on shaded yellow ground, flame mark/XXIV/S/X and artist's cipher, seconded mark for small black glaze spots, 1934, 4" d, 5-1/2" h, **$1,610.**

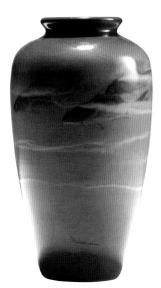

Rookwood vase, Iris glaze, fish swimming against celadon water, decorated by E.T. Hurley, flame mark/X/614E/W/E.T.H., 1910, 8" x 4-3/4", **$5,580.**

Iris glaze, painted by A. R. Valentien, two rooks on pine branch, shading from dark green to celadon to sky blue, flame mark/IV/S1766/A.R. Valentien, uncrazed, 1904, 15" h, 6-1/2" d **$22,500**

Iris glaze, possibly decorated by Rose Fechleimer, 1901, peach-colored underglaze shading to white near base, clusters of pendant flowers with wide green leaves and trailing stem, mkd with Rookwood logo, date, artist's monogram, incised "W" and "786C," paper label "257," crazing, 9-3/4" h **$1,530**

Iris glaze, diaphanous white poppies, pearl gray ground, painted by A. R. Valentien, flame mark/II/922B/A. R. Valentien, 1902, 10-3/4" h, 5-1/2" d **$2,100**

Jewel Porcelain, Oriental landscape with sailboats and prunus trees on three panels, painted by Arthur Conant, flame mark/XIX/2103/C, uncrazed, 1919, 5-1/4" h, 3-3/4" d **$4,500**

Later Tiger Eye, Empire Green, carved sea horse dec, by E. T. Hurley, 1923, 9-1/2" h **$3,500**

Matt, by O. G. Reed, pink roses with yellow centers, indigo-to-rose ground, flame mark/VI/907DD/O.G.R., 1906, 9-1/2" h, 3-3/4" d **$11,000**

Ovoid, flowers on blue to white ground, flame mark/VI/907F/EN, by Edith Nooan, 1906, 7" h **$800**

Scenic vellum, trees by lake, pink and blue sky, painted by Fred Rothenbusch, flame mark/XXIV/926B/FR, uncrazed, 1924, 11" h, 6" d ... **$6,500**

Scenic vellum, stark landscape at sunset, painted by Sally Coyne, flame mark/XII/SEC/951D/V/G, 1912, 9" h, 3-3/4" h **$3,500**

Scenic vellum, river landscape, blue and apricot sky, painted by E. T. Hurley, flame mark/XXI/892C/E.T.H., uncrazed, 1931, 9" h, 4-1/2" h **$2,700**

Standard glaze, bottle shape, painted by A. R. Valentien, orange nasturtium, flame mark/537B/A.R.V., shallow chip to int. of foot ring, 1897, 17-1/2" h, 11" d **$1,500**

Standard glaze, silver overlay of wild roses, poppies, and lily-of-the-valleys, painted nasturtiums, L. N. Lincoln, c1895, 8" h **$5,750**

Standard glaze, three handles, painted by Artus Van Briggle, woman's portrait, three champagne bottles, flame mark/659/W/AVB/L, 1893, 8" h, 10" d **$1,700**

Vellum glaze, Venetian harbor scene, Carl Schmidt signature stamp, dated 1922, 9-1/2" h **$3,450**

Vellum, bulbous, blue irises, purple ground, painted by Fred Rothenbusch, flame mark/VIII/1659/FR/V, 1908, 11-1/4" h, 5" d **$1,800**

Wax Matte, by Jens Jensen, stylized yellow, red, and purple flowers, pink ground, flame mark/XXIX/2303/artist's cipher, 1929, 6" d, 9-1/2" h **$1,610**

Rookwood paperweights, four production figural pieces, including fish, rabbit, cat, and dog, all marked, test 4-3/4" h, **$1,100.**

Rookwood Scenic Vellum plaque, winter landscape at dusk, painted by Fred Rothenbusch, mounted in original Arts & Crafts frame, flame mark/XII/FR, 1912, plaque 6" x 8", **$5,700.**

Rose Medallion garden seat, Chinese export, hexagonal, interior scenes, gardens, 19th century, 18" h, 10-1/2" w, **$1,755.**
Photo courtesy of Pook & Pook, Inc.

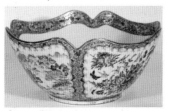

Rose Medallion bowl, scalloped rim, decorated with panels of birds and flowers, 10" d, **$475.**
Photo courtesy of Joy Luke Auctions.

Rose Medallion, covered jar, four gilt lion masks on shoulders, lion finial (damaged) on cover with stapled repair, body with various hairlines, wooden base, 9-1/2" d, 17" h, **$175.**
Photo courtesy of David Rago Auctions, Inc.

ROSE CANTON, ROSE MANDARIN, AND ROSE MEDALLION

History: The pink rose color has given its name to three related groups of Chinese export porcelain: Rose Mandarin, Rose Medallion, and Rose Canton.

Rose Mandarin, produced from the late 18th century to approximately 1840, derives its name from the Mandarin figure(s) found in garden scenes with women and children. The women often have gold decorations in their hair. Polychrome enamels and birds separate the scenes.

Rose Medallion, which originated in the early 19th century and was made through the early 20th century, has alternating panels of figures and birds and flowers. The elements are four in number, separated evenly around the center medallion. Peonies and foliage fill voids.

Rose Canton, introduced somewhat later than Rose Mandarin and produced through the first half of the 19th century, is similar to Rose Medallion except the figural panels are replaced by flowers. People are present only if the medallion partitions are absent. Some patterns have been named, e.g., Butterfly and Cabbage and Rooster. Rose Canton actually is a catchall term for any pink enamelware not fitting into the first two groups.

Reproduction Alert. Rose Medallion is still made, although the quality does not match the earlier examples.

Rose Canton

Brush pot, scenic, ladies, reticulated, gilt trim, 4-1/2" h........................**$275**

Charger, floral panels, 19th C, 13" d **$215**

Platter, enamel and gilt wear, 19th C, 16-1/2" l......................................**$200**

Puzzle teapot, Cadogan, painted birds and foliage, light blue ground, minor chips, late 19th C, 6" h.....**$150**

Umbrella jar, minor chips, 19th C, 24-1/4" h...**$805**

Urn, cov, minor chips, cracks, gilt wear, pr, 19-1/4" h **$2,990**

Vase, four panels of birds and butterflies, rocks and tree peonies, applied molded gilded serpents and animals at neck and shoulder, converted to electric lamp, slight wear, 14" h..**$320**

Rose Mandarin

Bowl, exterior with continuous courtyard scene, multiple figures including horse and groom, musician, checkers players, scholars, int. with mandarin panels surrounding gilt fretwork, alternating images of fans, scrolls, and vases, rose, bird, and butterfly border, gilt ground, gilt details, orange peel glaze, wooden base, 13-1/4" d, 5-1/2" h **$2,300**

Brush pot, continuous scene of empress on throne, surrounded by court ladies and maids, gilt trim, bright rose and butterfly border, small rim flakes and crow's foot in base, 5-3/8" d, 6-1/4" h **$230**

Creamer, continuous scene with figures indoors and in fenced yard, 100 Antiques border on int., gold accents, 3-1/2" h..............................**$200**

Cup and saucer, courtyard scenes in center, kissing carp border alternating with scrolls and other fish, wear **$350**

Dish, kidney shape, courtyard scenes, bird and flower borders, orange peel glaze, wear, 8-1/4" x 10-1/2" **$200**

Plate

Brilliant blue fretwork borders with pink flowers, flower baskets, dark mustard yellow irid ground, detailed center with women and children in courtyard, man brandishing sword at woman, minor wear, price for pr, 9-3/4" d **$500**

Courtyard scenes, bird and flower borders, 8-5/8" d......................**$200**

Detailed courtyard scene with fish pond, armored warrior with elaborate pheasant tail headdress, border of gourds, vases, and scrolls, gilt details, some wear, 10" d **$375**

Man and four women seated in courtyard overlooking lake, border of butterflies and birds with two reclining deer, minor wear, 7-3/4" d **$350**

Platter

26 children, courtiers with large necklaces, man holding scepter, kissing

carp border with alternating blue and green scrolls, dark gray silver oxide painted carp, faint orange peel glaze, minor wear, 14" x 17" **$1,955**

Court scene with 16 figures, borders with figures alternating with objects covered in Oriental calligraphy, gilt trim, orange peel glaze, 14-1/2" x 16-1/2"...............................**$2,100**

Multiple figures, scribe, and soldiers, border with birds chasing insects, butterflies, orange peel glaze, 10" x 13"...**$600**

Shrimp dish, bright butterflies, flowers, fruit on gilt border, gold trim and hair accents, orange peel glaze, minor wear, shallow rim flake, 10-1/8" x 10-1/4"..**$865**

Soup plate, armorial, one with garden scene, other with man holding baby with three women in courtyard, borders with multiple butterflies, birds, tree peonies, and bamboo trees, each with European dolphin above belt with "Avis La Fin," monogram "RAK," gilt trim and accents, two minor flakes, price for pr, 10" d.......... **$1,840**

Tray, oval, scalloped edge, gilt and rose border, gilt highlighted figures in center, one with gilt robe, orange peel glaze, flake on table ring, 9-1/2" x 11"...... **$250**

Tureen, cov, matching underplate, continuous courtyard scene, gild accents, pink roses and white trailing flowers borders, gilt finial and intertwined handles, well done professional restoration to lid and underplate, 7-3/4" l, 6" h...**$650**

Rose Medallion

Armorial plate, exotic birds, butterflies, marbleized textures, gold hair accents, hand painted orange armorial device in center with belt surrounding sword and laurel wreath, "Fides Praestantior Auro," slight wear, price for pr, 9-5/8" d...................**$600**

Basket and undertray, two handles, reticulated, China, chips, 19th C, 9-3/4" l, 7-1/4" w, 3-3/4" h.........**$325**

Boullion cup and saucer, cov, thinly potted, double handles................**$200**

Bowl, detailed panels with four figures and man at window alternating with roses and birds, wear, 10" d, 4" h...**$260**

Candlesticks, pr, China, one with a couple base edge repairs, 19th C, 7-1/4" h......................................**$600**

Charger

Celadon, court scene within shaped One Hundred Antiques border, textured ground, gilt wear to rim, 10-1/2" d **$275**

Celadon, court scene bordered with animals and floral trophies, textured ground, minor gilt wear, 13" d **$355**

Dish, scalloped rim, 19th C, 9-1/4" d **$275**

Lamp, chi dragons around neck, foo dog handles, mounted on pierced wood stand, China, late 19th C, 18" h vase **$760**

Plate

Alternating panels of men and women, birds and butterflies, faint gold dec, 8" d **$115**

Light blue, yellow, and pink reticulated border, 8-5/8" d **$120**

Alternating panels, gold trim, wear, 9-1/2" d **$90**

Platter

Oval, six alternating panels, orange peel glaze, faded colors, 12" x 15" **$115**

Six alternating panels, orange peel glaze, worn gilt trim, shallow rim flakes, 14" x 18-1/4" **$350**

Punch bowl

Chinese Export, 19th C, 13-1/2" d **$825**

Hp scenes, four with birds, fruits, clouds, and flowers, alternating with panels of village scenes, gilt rim and highlights, 24" d......**$3,680**

Saucer, figures dec, gilt, minor rim flakes, price for set of eight, 6-1/4" d **$250**

Serving dish, oval, shaped rim, celadon, mid-19th C, 10-3/4" l, 9-1/4" w, 1-3/4" h........................**$400**

Soup bowl, Mandarin scene, gilding, 8-1/4" d................................**$110**

Teapot, domed cov, squatty, gilt floral embellishments on handle and spout, 8" h................................**$765**

Tray, landscapes alternating with birds and flowers, hillside fort with multiple flakes, pagodas, fishing boats, orange peel glaze ext, 9-1/8" sq **$250**

Umbrella stand, cylindrical, China, 19th C

23-5/8" h, cylindrical form, repaired cracks **$400**

24-1/4" h................................**$1,880**

Vase

Four panels with matching mandarin courtyard scenes, scalloped edge rims, applied molded serpents and animals on neck and shoulder with worn gilding, birds and butterflies, wear, wooden stand, price for pr, 14" h **$700**

Truncated, mounted as a lamp, 19th C, 12" h **$400**

Vegetable tureen, cov, oval underplate, figures with gilt trim, blue bats under two intertwined handles, orange peel glaze on base, molded gilt finial, minor wear, 9-3/4" l, 8" h **$920**

Rose Mandarin, Chinese, bowl, porcelain, figural decoration, Qing Dynasty, Qialong period, 10" d, **$325.**
Photo courtesy of Sloans & Kenyon Auctioneers and Appraisers.

Rose Mandarin, vase, famille rose enamels, dragons, and foo dogs, 19th century, 25" h, **$2,470.**
Photo courtesy of Skinner, Inc.

ROSENTHAL

History: Rosenthal Porcelain Manufactory began operating at Selb, Bavaria, in 1880. Specialties were tablewares and figurines. The firm is still in operation.

Rosenthal pitcher, creamy ivory body, red rosebud decoration, green foliate, silvered base, marked, **$95.**

Rosenthal luncheon plates, painted with flowers, gold swag border, 9" d, price for set of 10, **$150.**
Photo courtesy of David Rago Auctions, Inc.

Box, cov, Studio Line, sgd "Peynet" **$175**

Cake plate, grape dec, scalloped ruffled edge, ruffled handles, 12" w **$75**

Candlestick, Art Deco woman holding candlestick, 9-1/2" h **$275**

Chocolate set, San Souci pattern, six cups and saucers, cov pot, creamer and sugar, marked "Selb Bavaria," c1880, 15-pc set **$425**

Creamer and sugar, pate-sur-pate type blue cherries dec **$115**

Cup and saucer, San Souci pattern, white **$20**

Demitasse cup and saucer, Marie pattern **$25**

Design page, hand rendered, each page showing transfer printed and hand-tinted designs, most numbered or named, some on graph paper, 10 pages, 6" w, 9-1/2" h **$230**

Figure

Band figure, male cello player, 5-1/4" h **$250**

Band figure, male clarinet player **$250**

Band figure, male tuba player **$285**

Man taking snuff, 8-1/2" h..........**$295**

Middle Eastern child with scimitar **$250**

Middle Eastern lantern lighter ...**$200**

Middle Eastern man with urn ...**$200**

Middle Eastern pipe smoker **$230**

Plaque, titled "Die Falknerin," sgd "Hans Makart," 9" x 7-1/2".......**$1,100**

Plate, girl and lamb dec, multicolored, 10" d...**$40**

Portrait plate, bust portrait of lady, pale yellow and white ground, faux green, turquoise, blue, and red hardstone jewels, 9-7/8" d **$350**

Vase, Hp, multicolored roses, 11" h **$125**

Rosenthal dinner set, prototype (never produced), red, blue edging, 13 each: dinner plates, dessert plates, mugs; 12 each: bowls, lunch plates, saucers; coffeepot, creamer, cov sugar, two serving platters, two bowls, **$550.**
Photo courtesy of David Rago Auctions, Inc.

ROSEVILLE POTTERY

History: In the late 1880s, a group of investors purchased the J. B. Owens Pottery in Roseville, Ohio, and made utilitarian stoneware items. In 1892, the firm was incorporated and joined by George F. Young, who became general manager. Four generations of Youngs controlled Roseville until the early 1950s.

A series of acquisitions began: Midland Pottery of Roseville in 1898, Clark Stoneware Plant in Zanesville (formerly used by Peters and Reed), and Muskingum Stoneware (Mosaic Tile Company) in Zanesville. In 1898, the offices also moved from Roseville to Zanesville.

In 1900, Roseville introduced Rozane, an art pottery. Rozane became a trade name to cover a large series of lines. The art lines were made in limited amounts after 1919.

The success of Roseville depended on its commercial lines, first developed by John J. Herald and Frederick Rhead in the first decades of the 1900s. In 1918, Frank Ferrell became art director and developed more than 80 lines of pottery. The economic depression of the 1930s brought more lines, including Pine Cone.

In the 1940s, a series of high-gloss glazes were tried in an attempt to revive certain lines. In 1952, Raymor dinnerware was produced. None of these changes brought economic success and in November 1954, Roseville was bought by the Mosaic Tile Company.

Roseville jardinière, experimental, colorful hand-carved grape leaves and branches on ivory ground, unmarked, few glaze flecks to decoration, 9" x 12-1/2", **$2,300.**
Photo courtesy of David Rago Auctions, Inc.

Roseville wall pocket, Baneda, green, foil sticker, 8-1/4" l, **$2,200.**
Photo courtesy of David Rago Auctions, Inc.

Basket
Gardenia, green, raised mark, No. 618-15" **$490**
Jonquil, pillow, unmarked, 10-1/2" d, 7-1/2" h **$750**
Ming Tree, white, raised mark, No. 585-14" **$425**
Poppy, green, raised mark, No. 347-10" **$350**
Vista, unmarked, 4-3/4" d, 6-3/4" h **$575**

Basket planter
Apple Blossom, green, asymmetrical rim, raised mark, No. 311-12 ....**$490**
Iris, spherical, pink, imp mark, No. 354-8 ....**$365**

Bookends, pr
Iris, book shape, blue, raised mark, No. 5, 5-1/4" w, 5-1/4" h **$290**
Water Lily, model no. 14, molded open book form, water lily blossoms in relief, walnut brown glaze, raised "Roseville U.S.A." mark, repair, 4-3/4" l, 5-1/4" d, 5-1/2" h **$200**

Bowl
Chloron, buttressed, unmarked, 4" x 8"...**$225**
Futura, "Aztec," faceted, unmarked, 4" x 8" **$325**
Futura, "Balloons," unmarked, touchups, 3-1/2" x 8-1/2" **$150**
Imperial II, emb snail-like designs around entire body, pale green dripping glaze over pink ground, unmarked **$2,000**
Mostique, two handles, bands of blue and white flowers, unmarked, 3" x 10"..**$350**

Bud vase
Orange blossoms, green ground, model no. 870, double reservoir, raised "Roseville U.S.A." mark, c1940, 6-1/4" h...........................**$100**
Pine Cone, blue, raised mark, minute flake on base, 5" d, 7-1/2" h **$400**

Candlesticks, pr
Blackberry, gold foil label, 4" d, 4-1/2" h **$690**
Imperial II, orange and green mottled glaze, unmarked, 3" x 4-1/4" ...**$350**
Sunflower, black paper label, 3-3/4" d, 4-1/4" h **$800**
Wisteria, brown, unmarked, 4-3/4" d, 4-3/4" h **$460**

Coffee set, cov coffeepot, cov teapot, creamer, cov sugar, Mock Orange, green, raised marks, 10-3/4" h coffeepot, minor spider lines to spout **$490**

Compote, Donatello, 7-1/2" d **$150**

Console bowl
Cremona, oval, pink, unmarked, 11" d, 2-1/4" h.............................**$95**
Ferella, ovoid, brown, black paper label, 13" l, 5-3/4" h **$815**

Roseville vase, Green Panel, ovoid base, flaring rim, RV ink mark, 10-1/4" x 5", **$1,320.**
Photo courtesy of David Rago Auctions, Inc.

Roseville Florentine vase, mold #233-10", "RV" rubber stamp mark, light crazing, early 20th century, 10-1/2" h x 4-3/4" d, **$100.**
Photo courtesy of Green Valley Auctions.

Roseville vase, Blue Falline, two large ear-shaped handles, unmarked, 6-1/4" x 6-1/4", **$660.**
Photo courtesy of David Rago Auctions, Inc.

Roseville vase, Sunflower, spherical, pin size rim fleck, 7-1/4" x 8-1/2", **$1,320.**
Photo courtesy of David Rago Auctions, Inc.

Roseville vase, Brown Wisteria, bottle shape, two-handled, unmarked, 9-1/4" x 5-3/4", **$480.**
Photo courtesy of David Rago Auctions, Inc.

Roseville vase, Blackberry, bulbous, two handled, unmarked, 12-1/2" x 8-1/2", **$1,200.**
Photo courtesy of David Rago Auctions, Inc.

Moderne, semi-matte ivory glaze, incised mark, No. 301-10 .... **$230**

Console set

Fuchsia, brown, imp marks, No. 1133-5 and No. 350-8" **$490**

Iris, pink, No. 360-10" oval center-bowl, pair of No. 1135-4-1/2 candle-sticks, imp marks **$375**

Thorn Apple, pink, low center bowl No. 307-6", pair of No. 1111 candle-sticks, imp marks **$290**

Cookie jar, cov

Clematis, No. 3-8, green ground .. **$550**

Magnolia, No. 2-8, tan ground ... **$450**

Water Lily, No. 1-8, gold shading to brown ground **$555**

Zephr Lily, No. 5-8, blue ground .. **$360**

Cornucopia vase

Pine Cone **$140**

White Rose **$95**

Ewer

Apple Blossom, green, raised mark, No. 318-15, minute fleck to body **$630**

Carnelian I, pink and gray glaze, RV ink mark, 7" d, 12-1/4" h **$345**

Freesia, green, raised mark, No. 21-15", two base chips **$290**

Gardenia, brown, raised mark, No. 618-15" **$490**

Mock Orange, No. 918-16, white blos-soms, green leaves, pink ground, 16" h **$310**

Pine Cone, brown, raised mark, No. 909-10" **$690**

Floor vase

Fuchsia, brown, raised mark, No. 905-18" **$750**

Pine Cone, brown, incised mark, No. 913-18", repair to rim and base **$815**

Vista, bulbous, 18" h, unmarked, sev-eral bruises and chips **$860**

Water Lily, green, raised mark, No. 85-18" **$630**

Flower pot and underplate, Iris, blue, raised marks, No. 648-5", 1" bruise to rim **$365**

Hanging basket, Mock Orange, white blossoms, green leaves **$375**

Jardinière

Baneda, pink, paper label, 4" x 5-1/2", small base nicks........................ **$250**

Cherry Blossom, pink, 6" x 8-1/2" **$500**

Jonquil, spherical, unmarked, 9" d, 6" h, small stilt-pull chips **$2,300**

Velmoss, broad leaves and buds, unmarked, 7" x 9-1/2" **$1,100**

Jardinière on stand

Freesia, No. 669, Delftware blue glaze, creamy yellow and white blossoms, raised "Roseville U.S.A." mark, stand marked "U.S.A.," c1945 .... **$500**

Freesia, No. 669-8, molded flo-rals, blue ground, base emb "Roseville, USA," 669-8, c1935 .... **$865**

Moss, green **$3,250**

Mostique **$900**

Lamp base, Imperial II, bulbous emb band around rim, dripping pale green over pink glaze, factory drilled **$1,400**

Roseville vase, Wisteria, blue ovoid body, molded flowers and relief leaves, stamped, paper label, 6" h, **$250.**
Photo courtesy of The Early Auction Company.

Roseville large Pauleo vase, brown, mottled olive, ochre, and red glaze, unmarked, 24" x 13-1/2", **$7,800.**
Photo courtesy of David Rago Auctions, Inc.

Roseville jardinière and pedestal set, Blackberry, two nicks at pedestal top, unmarked, 28" x 12", **$2,520.**
Photo courtesy of David Rago Auctions, Inc.

Low bowl

Blackberry, unmarked, minor glaze bubbles, 7-3/4" d, 3-1/4" h **$345**

Sunflower, low shoulder, unmarked, burst bubble on one leaf, 7-1/4" d, 4" h **$535**

Mug, Pine Cone, blue, imp mark, price for pr, No. 960-4" **$700**

Pitcher

Fuchsia, brown, imp mark, peppering to body, 8-1/2" d, 8" h **$400**

Pine Cone, No. 415, green glaze, brown, and cream tones, raised "Roseville, U.S.A." mark, c1931, 9-1/4" h **$750**

Rozane Olympic, Ulysees at the Table of Circe, signed and titled, restoration to 5" spider lines, 8-1/2" d, 7" h **$1,495**

White Rose, pink, raised mark, No. 1324, glaze drip around rim, 8" d, 7" h **$275**

Planter

Blackberry, faceted, unmarked, 9-3/4" d, 3-1/2" h **$435**

Florentine, brown, rect, few base chips, 11-1/4" l, 5-1/4" h **$290**

Lily, squeezebag dec with water lilies and waves, orig liner, unmarked, 6" x 7-1/2" **$800**

Persian, fitted liner, unmarked, abrasion to rim, 5" x 6-1/4" **$350**

Primrose, bulbous, pink, incised mark, No. 634-6", flecks to flowers and one handle **$85**

Wisteria, blue, unmarked, minor touch-ups, 6-1/4" x 8-3/4" **$475**

Planter bookends, pr, Columbine, blue, raised mark, 5" w, 5" d, 5-1/4" h **$260**

Sand jar, Primrose, blue, base chip and hairline, 15-3/4" h **$575**

Teapot, cov, Rozanne Della Robbia, hearts, cups, saucers, and Japanese fans dec, brown and celadon, Rozane Ware wafer, small lid nicks, 1" clay burst at rim **$1,355**

Tea set, cov teapot, creamer, cov sugar

Freesia, blue, raised marks **$415**

Snowberry, blue, raised marks...**$750**

White Rose, pink raised marks ..**$490**

Wincraft, brown, raised marks, minor flaws **$200**

Umbrella stand, Pine Cone, brown, raised mark, No. 777-20", minor scaling area at handle, 1" rim bruise **$2,070**

Urn

Baneda, bulbous, pink, black foil label, 7-3/4" d, 10-1/2" h **$1,355**

Carnelian I, pink and gray glaze, RV ink mark, 8-1/4" d, 9-1/2" h **$375**

Iris, bulbous, pink, imp mark, No. 928-12" **$460**

Moss, bulbous, buttressed base, incised mark, restorations to base and rim **$200**

Pine Cone, blue, imp mark, No. 912-15", restoration to rim chip **$2,185**

Velmoss, orange glaze, foil label, 8-1/4" x 6-3/4" **$675**

Roseville basket, Water Lily, brown, 382-12", raised mark, **$180.**
Photo courtesy of David Rago Auctions, Inc.

Roseville Jonquil vase, mold #621-4, first half 20th century, crazing, unmarked, 4-1/4" h x 3-1/2" d rim, **$100.**
Photo courtesy of Green Valley Auctions.

Roseville vase, two-handled Windsor, rim dec with branches of leaves, unmarked, 10-1/2" x 6-1/2", **$960.**
Photo courtesy of David Rago Auctions, Inc.

Roseville vase, "Lotus Leaf," spherical body, blue and green leaves, gray ground, trapezoidal base, two minor base edge flakes, unmarked, 7-3/4", **$645.**
Photo courtesy of David Rago Auctions, Inc.

Roseville Tourist bowl, painted with houses, woman driving car, chickens, unmarked, 3" x 6" d, **$840.**
Photo courtesy of David Rago Auctions, Inc.

Roseville pitcher, Pine Cone, blue, ice lip, pinhead size burst or fleck to rim, faint impressed mark, **$475.**
Photo courtesy of David Rago Auctions, Inc.

Vase

Baneda, bulbous, pink, foil label, 5-1/2" x 6-3/4" **$450**

Blackberry, black paper label, 6-1/2" x 5-3/4"...................................**$550**

Cherry Blossom, two handles, sq base, pink, unmarked, 8-1/2" x 5" **$700**

Earlam, tapering, ribbed, pink, unmarked, 8-1/2" x 6"..............**$450**

Falline, bulbous, blue, stepped neck, two handles, foil label, 7-1/4" x 6" **$2,300**

Ferella, bulbous, red, unmarked, 8-1/2" x 7", restoration to base **$850**

Ferella, flaring, brown, paper label, 5" x 7"......................................**$500**

Futura, conical form, three stepped rect devices on sides, round disk base, semi-gloss terra cotta, blue, and green glazes, unmarked, c1928, 8" h **$575**

Imperial II, bulbous, band of wave-like designs at rim, bright blue mottled glaze, paper label, tight 2" line from rim **$1,400**

Imperial II, flaring, mottled green and orange glaze, unmarked, 8-1/2" x 7" **$3,250**

Imperial II, tapering, ribbed bands around body, pale green and gray mottled glaze, unmarked, 5-1/2" x 3-3/4".....................................**$300**

Montacello, bulbous, brown, unmarked, 7-1/2" x 6-1/2".......**$500**

Morning Glory, pillow shape, two buttresses at base, unmarked, 7" x 3-3/4"....................................**$500**

Orion, cylindrical neck, red, unmarked, 7-1/2" x 4-3/4"......**$500**

Rozane Royal Dark, tapering, by Hester Pillsbury, painted yellow wild

Roseville vase, Blue Windsor, bulbous, two handled, ferns on sides, unmarked, 7-1/2", **$880.**
Photo courtesy of David Rago Auctions, Inc.

roses, Roxane Ware wafer, 7" d, 8-3/4" h **$475**

Rozane Woodland, corseted, enamel dec, white blossoms, green leaves, Rozane Ware/Woodland wafer, 3" d, 10" h......................**$575**

Sunflower, double handles, 9" h **$1,300**

Velmoss, spherical, unmarked, 6-1/2" x 8-1/2".....................................**$350**

Vista, bulbous, unmarked, 7-1/2" d, 17-1/2" h **$1,890**

Wisteria, blue, 10" h **$2,000**

Vessel

Imperial II, squat, yellow and green glaze over matte blue-gray ground, unmarked, 5-1/2" **$1,400**

Montacello, squat, green, unmarked, 4-1/2" x 5" **$300**

Sunflower, squat, unmarked, 4-1/4" x 7-1/2" **$700**

Wisteria, bulbous, blue, partial foil label, 6-3/4" x 8-1/2", tiny fleck to one leaf................................**$650**

Wisteria, squat, blue, unmarked, 4-1/2" x 6-1/2" **$450**

Wall pocket

Blackberry, flaring, unmarked, 7-3/4" l...................................**$1,610**

Cosmos, double, blue, unmarked, silver foil label **$630**

Earlham, unmarked, 6-1/2" l......**$920**

Imperial II, mottled green over lavender glaze, paper label, 6-1/2" x 6-1/2" **$800**

Moss, bucket, pink, unmarked, 10" l, 1/2" chip, small edge nick........**$520**

Pine Cone, triple, blue, raised mark, 9" l.......................................**$1,725**

Savona, blue, unmarked, 8-1/4" l **$630**

Silhouette, pink, ivy leaves, raised mark No. 766-8" **$290**

ROYAL BAYREUTH

History: In 1794, the Royal Bayreuth factory was founded in Tettau, Bavaria. Royal Bayreuth introduced its figural patterns in 1885. Designs of animals, people, fruits, and vegetables decorated a wide array of tablewares and inexpensive souvenir items.

Tapestry wares, in rose and other patterns, were made in the late 19th century. The surface of the piece feels and looks like woven cloth. Tapestry ware was made by covering the porcelain with a piece of fabric tightly stretched over the surface, decorating the fabric, glazing the piece, and firing.

Royal Bayreuth still manufactures dinnerware. It has not maintained production of earlier wares, particularly the figural items. Since thorough records are unavailable, it is difficult to verify the chronology of production.

Marks: The Royal Bayreuth crest used to mark the wares varied in design and color.

Royal Bayreuth Tapestry milk pitcher, pink rose columns, blue mark, signed "Morlerei/5289," early 20th century, 5" h, **$100.**
Photo courtesy of Green Valley Auctions.

Ashtray, elk................$225
Bell, musicians scene, man playing cello and mandolin..............$300
Candleholder, basset hound, dark body, unmarked..............$400
Creamer
Bird of Paradise $225
Cat, black and orange..............$200
Crow, brown bill $200
Duck..............$200
Eagle..............$300
Frog, green..............$225
Lamplighter, green..............$250
Pear..............$295
Robin..............$195
Water Buffalo, black and orange..............$225
Cup and saucer, yellow and gold, purple and red flowers, green leaves, white ground, green mark..........$80
Hatpin holder, courting couple, cutout base with gold dec, blue mark..............$400
Milk pitcher, butterfly..........$1,200
Miniature, pitcher, portrait..........$95
Portrait plate, Arab and camel, green back stamp, 9" d..........$125
Ring box, cov, pheasant scene, glossy finish..............$85
Salt and pepper shakers, pr, elk..............$165
Vase, peasant ladies and sheep scene, silver rim, three handles, blue mark, 3-1/2" h..............$60

Patterns
Conch Shell
Creamer, green, lobster handles...$125
Match holder, hanging..............$225
Sugar, cov, small flake..........$85

Corinthian
Creamer and sugar, classical figures, black ground..............$85
Pitcher, red ground, pinched spout, 12" h..............$225
Vase, conical, black, blue mark, 8-1/2" h..............$225
Devil and Cards
Ashtray..............$650
Creamer, blue mark, 4" h..........$175
Mug, large..............$295
Salt, master..............$325
Lobster
Ashtray, claw..............$145
Celery tray, figural, blue mark, 12-1/2" l..............$245
Pitcher, figural, orange-red, green handle, 7-3/4" h..............$175
Salt and pepper shakers, pr........$150
Nursery Rhyme
Bell, Jack and the Beanstalk........$425
Planter, Jack and the Beanstalk, round, orig liner..............$225
Plate, Little Jack Horner..............$125
Plate, Little Miss Muffet..............$100
Snow Babies
Bowl, 6" d..............$325
Creamer, gold trim..............$110
Jewelry box, cov..............$275
Milk pitcher, corset shape..........$185
Tea tile, blue mark, 6" sq..........$100
Sunbonnet Babies
Bell, babies sewing, unmarked...$425
Cake plate, babies washing, 10-1/4" d..............$400
Cup and saucer, babies fishing...$225
Dish, babies ironing, ruffled edge, blue mark, 8" d..............$175
Mustard pot, cov, babies sweeping, blue mark..............$395

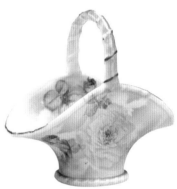

Royal Bayreuth Tapestry, basket, American Beauty rose, blue mark, gilt wear, early 20th century, 3-3/4" h, **$110.**
Photo courtesy of Green Valley Auctions.

Royal Bayreuth Tapestry, vase, white rose, blue mark, gilt wear, early 20th century, 5-1/4" h, **$110.**
Photo courtesy of Green Valley Auctions.

Royal Bayreuth Corinthian Ware bowl, porcelain, enameled black transfer figures, banded border, matte black ground, Bavaria, 20th century, 7-3/4" d, **$150.**
Photo courtesy of Skinner, Inc.

Royal Bayreuth toothpick holder, peasant musicians, blue mark, gilt wear, early 20th century, 3-1/4" h, **$88.**
Photo courtesy of Green Valley Auctions.

Nappy, Sunbonnet Babies, Wash Day, blue mark, 6" l **$230**
Plate, Sunbonnet Girls, pair, one washing, other sweeping **$290**
Tomato
Creamer and sugar, blue mark ...**$190**
Milk pitcher **$165**
Mustard, cov **$125**
Salt and pepper shakers, pr **$85**

Rose tapestry
Basket, reticulated, 5" h **$400**
Bell, American Beauty Rose, pink, 3" h **$500**

Boot **$550**
Bowl, pink and yellow roses, 10-1/2" d **$675**
Creamer **$250**
Dresser tray **$395**
Hairpin box, pink and white **$245**
Nut dish, three-color roses, gold feet, green mark, 3-1/4" d, 1-3/4" h **$175**
Pin tray, three-color roses **$195**
Plate, three-color roses, blue mark, 6" d **$150**
Salt and pepper shakers, pr, pink roses **$375**
Shoe, roses and figures dec **$550**

Tapestry, miscellaneous
Bowl, scenic, wheat, girl, and chickens, 9-1/2" d **$395**
Box, courting couple, multicolored, blue mark, 3-3/4" l, 2" w **$245**
Charger, scenic, boy and donkeys, 13" d **$300**
Dresser tray, goose girl **$495**
Hatpin holder, swimming swans and sunset, saucer base, blue mark **$250**

ROYAL BONN

Royal Bonn vase, tapered vasiform body, sinuous everted rim with short openwork loops, sinuous spreading base with openwork loops, glazed in maroon and green, body hand-painted with roses, gilt accenting, Franz Anton Mehlem Earthenware Factory, Bonn, Germany, early 20th century, 12-3/8" h, **$300.**
Photo courtesy of Skinner, Inc.

History: In 1836, Franz Anton Mehlem founded a Rhineland factory that produced earthenware and porcelain, including household, decorative, technical, and sanitary items.

The firm reproduced Hochst figures between 1887 and 1903. These figures, in both porcelain and earthenware, were made from the original molds from the defunct Prince-Electoral Mayence Manufactory in Hochst. The factory was purchased by Villeroy and Boch in 1921 and closed in 1931.

Marks: In 1890, the word "Royal" was added to the mark. All items made after 1890 include the "Royal Bonn" mark.

Console set, all over painted scenes on tapestry ground, gilt metal mounts, 14" l oval bowl, pr 13-1/2" h vases **$2,990**
Cup and saucer, relief luster bands, marked **$40**
Ewer, red and pink flowers, raised gold, fancy handle, 10-1/8" h **$75**
Portrait urn, cov, elaborate tooled gilt foliage dec, portrait of woman on one side, burgundy ground, sq plinth, underglaze blue beehive mark, c1900, 35" h..**$3,910**

Tea tile, hp, pink, yellow, and purple pansies, white ground, green border, marked "Bonn-Rhein," 7" d **$35**
Urn, cov, hp, multicolored flowers, green, and yellow ground, two gold handles, artist sgd, 13" h **$120**
Vase
Blue ground, gilt and enameled floral designs, scrolled handles, printed and imp marks, late 19th C, 18-3/4" h **$400**
Hp multicolored floral spray with raised gold dec, link handles, ftd, 20" h, 5" d..................................**$240**

ROYAL COPENHAGEN

History: Franz Mueller established a porcelain factory at Copenhagen in 1775. When bankruptcy threatened in 1779, the Danish king acquired ownership, appointing Mueller manager and selecting the name "Royal Copenhagen." The crown sold its interest in 1867; the company remains privately owned today.

Blue Fluted, Royal Copenhagen's most famous pattern, was created in 1780. It is of Chinese origin and comes in three styles: smooth edge, closed lace edge, and perforated lace edge (full lace). Many other factories copied it.

Flora Danica, named for a famous botanical work, was introduced in 1789 and remained exclusive to Royal Copenhagen. It is identified by its free-hand illustrations of plants and its hand-cut edges and perforations.

Marks: Royal Copenhagen porcelain is marked with three wavy lines, which signify ancient waterways, and a crown, added in 1889. Stoneware does not have the crown mark.

Royal Copenhagen figural, group of farmers, porcelain, man resting from scything, woman seated by harvest with lunchbox and jug, ovoid base, 17-1/4" h, **$705.**
Photo courtesy of Skinner, Inc.

Bowl, reticulated blue and white **$125**

Candlesticks, pr, blue floral design, white ground, bisque lion heads, floral garlands, 9" h **$160**

Cream soup, #1812 .... **$75**

Cup and saucer, 2-1/2" h cylindrical cup with angular handle, 5-1/2" d saucer with molded and gilded rim, hp floral specimen, 20th C.......... **$575**

Dish, reticulated blue and white... **$175**

Figure
  Girl knitting, No. 1314, 6-3/4" h. **$350**
  Dachshund, blue wave mark, 7-1/2" h, 11" l **$375**
  Nymph with Satyr, timid satyr kneeling at feet of nude female nymph, on naturalistic ovoid base, 20th C, 15-1/4" h **$1,100**

Fish plate, different fish swimming among marine plants, molded and gilt border, light green highlights, gilt dentil edge, crown circular mark,

10-pc set, 10" d **$8,250**

Inkwell, Blue Fluted pattern, matching tray **$150**

Pickle tray, Half Lace pattern, blue triple wave mark, 9" l **$70**

Plates, each with gilt serrated rim and central hp floral specimen, price for eight-pc set, two 7-5/8" d, six 10" d **$2,990**

Platter, #1556, 14-1/2" l **$140**

Salad bowl, Flora Danica, botanical specimen, molded gilt border, dentil edge, pink highlights, blue triple wave and green crown mark, 9-7/8" d **$825**

Soup tureen, cov, stand, Flora Danica, oval, enamel painted botanical specimens, twin handles, finial, factory marks, botanical identification, modern, 14-1/2" l **$5,750**

Tray, Blue Fluted pattern, 10" l **$65**

Vase, sage green and gray crackled glaze, 7" h **$150**

Royal Copenhagen plaque, oval, beaded rim surmounted by ribbon and bow decoration, depicting Fredensborg Castle, back marked "Prove," 5-3/4" w, 8" h, **$615.**
Photo courtesy of Alderfer Auction Co.

Royal Copenhagen figure, little girl and boy embracing puppy, **$85.**
Photo courtesy of Joy Luke Auctions.

Royal Copenhagen figures, left: girl mending sock, right: boy whittling stick, each **$75.**
Photo courtesy of Joy Luke Auctions.

Royal Copenhagen figure, milkmaid and cow, **$80.**
Photo courtesy of Joy Luke Auctions.

Royal Crown Derby vase, globular shape, cobalt ground, upturned scroll handles, raised gold Chinese lions, scrolled foliage, England, c1882, 6-3/4" h, **$265.**
Photo courtesy of Skinner, Inc.

Royal Crown Derby soup tureen, covered, stand, Kings pattern, oval, c1830, 10" x 17-1/2", **$2,300.**

ROYAL CROWN DERBY

History: Derby Crown Porcelain Co., established in 1875 in Derby, England, had no connection with earlier Derby factories which operated in the late 18th and early 19th centuries. In 1890, the company was appointed "Manufacturers of Porcelain to Her Majesty" (Queen Victoria) and since that date has been known as "Royal Crown Derby."

Most of these porcelains, both tableware and figural, were hand decorated. A variety of printing processes were used for additional adornment. Today, Royal Crown Derby is a part of Royal Doulton Tableware, Ltd.

Marks: Derby porcelains from 1878 to 1890 carry only the standard crown printed mark. After 1891, the mark includes the "Royal Crown Derby" wording. In the 20th century, "Made in England" and "English Bone China" were added to the mark.

Bottle, orig stopper, molded body, two handles, hp flowers, gold accents, 6" h **$150**

Candlesticks, pr, bone china, Imari pattern, paneled baluster form, bulbous toes, brass nozzle **$765**

Cup and saucer, Imari pattern, 20th C, 5" d saucer **$70**

Dessert service, Pattern 1128, Imari pattern, bone china, twelve 8-1/2" d dessert plates; twelve 6-1/2" d bowls; twelve teacups and saucers **$1,880**

Ewer, Oriental-style gold enameled dec, soft coral ground, handle, 6" h **$200**

Luncheon plates, dark Kelly green rim, gilt inner and outer rims, white faux jewelling applied to outer rim, price for set of 12, c1898, 9-1/8" d **$470**

Jug, Imari palette, pink round, gold trim, pr, c1885 .... **$750**

Mug, grapes and vines dec, blue and gold **$125**

Plate, Daisy pattern, blue transfer print, gilt details, price for set of 11, late 19th/early 20th C, 8" d **$260**

Soup plate, inner band of gold jewelling with wide rim of gilt quatrefoils, grapevine, and leaf sprays, some leaves accented with bronze tone, shaped beaded edge, retailed by Tiffany & Co., price for set of 18, early 20th C, 9-7/8" d **$5,750**

Tea and coffee service, bone china, Pattern 1128, Imari dec, 9" h ovoid coffeepot, 7-1/4" h teapot, creamer, cov sugar, modern **$950**

Urn, squatty, double reticulated handles and finials, birds, butterfly, and floral designs, ivory ground, gilt accents, marked "Bailey, Banks, and Biddle," dripped for lamp, finials replaced, restoration to one handle, price for pr, 12" h... **$1,325**

Vase

Enameled floral dec, gold encrusted lip, 7-1/2" h **$320**

Ovoid, narrow neck, flared rim, serpent handle, cobalt blue and ironred Imari type dec, gilt accents, hp floral panels, minor gilt loss, touchup, price for pr, 13" h **$925**

ROYAL DOULTON

History: Doulton pottery began in 1815 under the direction of John Doulton at the Doulton & Watts pottery in Lambeth, England. Early output was limited to salt-glazed industrial stoneware. After John Watts retired in 1854, the firm became Doulton and Company, and production was expanded to include hand-decorated stoneware such as figurines, vases, dinnerware, and flasks.

In 1878, John's son, Sir Henry Doulton, purchased Pinder Bourne & Co. in Burslem. The companies became Doulton & Co., Ltd. in 1882. Decorated porcelain was added to Doulton's earthenware production in 1884.

Most Doulton figurines were produced at the Burslem plants, where they were made continuously from 1890 until 1978. After a short interruption, a new line of Doulton figurines was introduced in 1979.

Dickens ware, in earthenware and porcelain, was introduced in 1908. The pieces were decorated with characters from Dickens' novels. Most of the line was withdrawn in the 1940s, except for plates, which continued to be made until 1974.

Character jugs, a 20th-century revival of early Toby models, were designed by Charles J. Noke for Doulton in the 1930s. Character jugs are limited to bust portraits, while Royal Doulton Toby jugs are full figured. The character jugs come in four sizes and feature fictional characters from Dickens, Shakespeare, and other English and American novelists, as well as historical heroes. Marks on both character and Toby jugs must be carefully identified to determine dates and values.

Doulton's Rouge Flambé (Veined Sung) is a high-glazed, strong-colored ware noted primarily for the fine modeling and exquisite colorings, especially in the animal items. The process used to produce the vibrant colors is a Doulton secret.

Production of stoneware at Lambeth ceased in 1956; production of porcelain continues today at Burslem.

Marks: Beginning in 1872, the "Royal Doulton" mark was used on all types of wares produced by the company.

Beginning in 1913, an "HN" number was assigned to each new Doulton figurine design. The "HN" numbers, which referred originally to Harry Nixon, a Doulton artist, were chronological until 1940, after which blocks of numbers were assigned to each modeler. From 1928 until 1954, a small number was placed to the right of the crown mark; this number added to 1927 gives the year of manufacture.

Royal Doulton pitcher, stoneware, carved by Frank Butler, stylized leaves, pods, and whiplash elements, brown and green glaze, floriform stamp/England/FAB/299, three tight firing lines to base, c1891-1902, 7" x 7", **$1,100.**
Photo courtesy of David Rago Auctions, Inc.

Animal

Alsatian, HN117	**$175**
Bull terrier, K14	**$325**
Dalmatian, HN114	**$250**
English bulldog, HN1074	**$175**
Salmon, flambé, printed mark, 12" h	**$435**
Tiger, flambé, printed mark, 14" l	**$375**

Biscuit jar, earthenware
Emb scrolled mold, polychrome florals, nickel silver mount, handle, and lid, green "Doulton Burslem England" backstamp, 6-1/2" h **$220**
Silver plated lid and handle, floral dec, Doulton Burslem mark, 9" h **$200**
Silver plated lid and handle, floral dec, Doulton Burslem mark, 9-1/2" h **$290**
Stoneware, enamel decorated geometric designs in relief, silver plated rim, handle and cover, imp Doulton Lambeth mark, 1882, 6-3/4" h...**$265**

Bowl, farm scene, rect, 1932 mark, 9" l, 7-1/2" w **$115**

Cabinet plate, pink and yellow roses painted in center, lower left artist sgd "W. Slater," raised gilt border and rim, turquoise faux jewel accents, early 20th C **$325**

Candlesticks, pr, Walton Ware, Battle of Hastings, cream color earthenware ground, stamped mark, small base chip on one, c1910, 6-1/2" h **$290**

Chambersticks, pr, Walton Ware, fishermen dec, ivory earthenware

ground, stamped mark, one of pair damaged, c1910, 2" h **$400**

Character jug, large
Cardinal.....................................**$150**
Poacher, D6781 ....**$350**

Character jug, miniature
Blacksmith **$50**
Pickwick....................................**$65**

Character jug, small
Pearly King...............................**$35**
Toby Philpots **$85**

Charger, hp, allover incised leaf, berry, and vine border, central fruits and leaves, attributed to Frank Bragwyn, printed mark, c1930, 12-5/8" d **$245**

Clock case, King's ware, night watchman, c1905.................................**$450**

Cuspidor, Isaac Walton ware, polychrome dec, transfer printed, fisherman on ext., verses on int. lip, printed mark, 7" h................................**$325**

Dinner service, Rondelay pattern, service for eight, platter, tea set, 60 pcs **$450**

Figure

Carolyn, HN 2112, 71/4" h, 3-1/2" d **$335**
Fair Lady, coral pink, HN2835 ...**$225**
King Charles I, dark brown gloves, black flora at boots, imp date 1919 ....**$1,312**
Orange Lady, HN1758.................**$245**
Queen Mother's 80th Birthday, HN464, 1980...........................**$750**
Priscilla, pantaloons showing beneath crinoline, HN1380, 1920-40 ....**$288**

Royal Doulton pitcher, stoneware, decorated in graffito by Hannah Barlow, mother cat surrounded by kittens, floriform stamp/HBB/AB/2280/MA/782, c1887-1891, 6-1/2" x 6-1/2", **$2,400.**
Photo courtesy of David Rago Auctions, Inc.

Royal Doulton Gibson Girl plate, titled "Some think she has remained in retirement too long, others are surprised she is out so soon," **$95.**
Photo courtesy of Dotta Auction Co., Inc.

Royal Doulton flambe vase, Sung Ware, lobed globular, England, signed and printed mark, no. 925, c1925, 7" h, **$590.**
Photo courtesy of Skinner, Inc.

Royal Doulton Toby jug, large size, Falstaff, marked on base, **$245.**

Royal Doulton Toby mug, large, pirate, green and yellow parrot for handle, black hat with white skull and crossbones, brown shirt, **$85.**

Royal Doulton figurine, Lorraine, brown hair, blue dress with white bow and top, blue shoes, raised hand, dog at feet, no HN3118, 7-3/4" h, **$99.**
Photo courtesy of Green Valley Auctions.

Royal Doulton figurine, Marguerite, blonde hair, holding bouquet of flowers, red dress, no. HN1946, 8" h, **$605.**
Photo courtesy of Green Valley Auctions.

Sandra, HN2275 .... **$200**
The Leisure Hour, HN2055 .... **$400**
Victorian Lady, HN1208, 1926-38 .... **$355**
Fish plate, swimming fish centers, pale yellow ground, gold bands and rims, sgd "J. Hallmark," 10-pc set, 9" d **$700**
Game plate, bone china, each with gilt trim lines and polychrome enamel painted with shore birds in landscapes, artist sgd "C. Holloway," titled and factory marked on reverse, retailed by Tiffany & Co., set of 12, c1925, 9-1/2" d **$1,300**
Humidor, Walton Ware, Battle of Hastings, cream color earthenware ground, stamped mark, c1910, 7-1/2" h **$365**
Inkstand, stoneware, tapered cylindrical form molded with floral sprays, blue, ochre, and brown glazes, silver mounts, Doulton Lambeth, hallmarked London, 1901, 3" h **$215**
Jardinière, Walton Ware, Battle of Hastings, cream color earthenware ground, stamped mark, c1910, 4-1/2" h... **$350**
Jug, Regency Coach, limited edition, printed marks, 20th C, 10-1/2" h ... **$930**
Loving cup
King George V and Queen Mary, 25-year reign anniversary, c1935, 10-1/4" d **$750**
Three Musketeers, limited edition, sgd "Noke, H. Fenton," orig certificate, 20th C, 9-3/4" h **$920**
Milk pitcher, sharkskin ground, cobalt blue flowers trimmed in gold, US patent, 7" h **$150**
Mug
Gladiator, #D6553, 4" h **$300**
St. John Falstaff, 8-1/4" h **$125**

Pitcher
Stoneware, dec by Florence Barlow, stippled ground with enameled pate-sur-pate design of birds in flight among marshy grass, incised artist monogram and imp Doulton Lambeth mark, c1884, 7-3/4" h **$1,000**
Walton Ware, fishermen dec, ivory earthenware ground, stamped mark, price for pr, one with bruise and restoration, c1910, 12-1/2" h **$400**
Plate, English Garden series, 8-1/2" d **$115**
Platter, Dr. Johnson at Bootham Bar-York, registered in Australia, 9" l, 7-1/2" w **$120**
Service plate, cream-colored ground, interior band of gilt anthemia, rim with gilt scrollwork over cream-colored ground, apple green reserves, gilt-shaped rim, price for 18-pc set, mold date mark 1910, 10-5/8" d **$5,465**
Spirits barrel, King's Ware, double, silver trim rings and cov, oak stand, c1909, 7" l **$1,200**
Sweet meat, sharkskin ground, applied flowers, silvered lid and handle, rosette mark artist sgd "Eleanor Tosen," 5" d, 3-1/2" h **$125**
Tankard, hinged pewter lid, incised frieze of herons among reeds, blue slip enamel, imp mark, sgd, c1875, 9-1/2" h **$1,600**
Teacup and saucer, cobalt blue, heavy gold dec **$120**
Tea set, Walton Ware, cov teapot with underplate, creamer, sugar bowl, Battle of Hastings, cream-colored earthenware ground, stamped mark, chip on spout, hairline on sugar lid **$365**

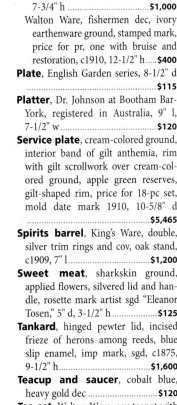

Tobacco jar, incised frieze of cattle, goats, and donkeys, imp mark, sgd, worn SP rim, handle and cover, dated 1880, 8" h **$995**

Toby jug
Beefeater, #D6206, 6" h **$85**
Winston Churchill, #8360 .... **$95**

Umbrella stand, stoneware, enamel dec, applied floral medallions within diamond formed panels, framed by button motifs, imp mark, glaze crazing, c1910, 23-1/2" h **$550**

Vase
Emb tapestry dec, enameled scrolls, imp mark, Slaters patent, price for pr, early 20th C, 11-3/4" h **$2,250**

Hannah Barlow dec, double handled, wide central panel with incised landscape and horses grazing by sleeping hound, enameled bands of scrolled leaves and stylized stiff leaves to borders, artist signed and imp Doulton Lambeth mark, 1882, 6-1/2" h **$1,765**

Titanium Ware, sq, hand painted enamel dec of birds below sunny sky, titled "Herring Gulls," artist signed Harry Allen, printed mark, c1925, 7-3/4" h...................... **$1,645**

Royal Doulton Lambeth vase, bulbous stick form, green blue and brown panels, stemmed flower dec, stamped with factory trademark, 5-1/4" h, **$100.**
Photo courtesy of The Early Auction Company, LLC.

ROYAL DUX

History: Royal Dux porcelain was made in Dux, Bohemia (now the Czech Republic), by E. Eichler at the Duxer Porzellan-Manufaktur, established in 1860. Many items were exported to the United States. By the turn of the century, Royal Dux figurines, vases, and accessories, especially those featuring Art-Nouveau designs, were captivating consumers.

Marks: A raised triangle with an acorn and the letter "E" plus "Dux, Bohemia" was used as a mark between 1900 and 1914.

Bowl, modeled as female tending a fishing net, oval shell-form bowl, imp mark, early 20th C, 17-1/2" l **$490**

Bust, female portrait, raised leaves and berries on base, Czechoslovakia, unmarked, chips, early 20th C, 14" h **$290**

Compote, figural, modeled as female atop shell-form bowl, another figure within the wave modeled freeform base, imp mark, early 20th C, 14-1/2" l **$750**

Figure
Flamenco dancer, cobalt blue and white glaze, gold trim, pink triangle mark, stamped, numbered, 15" x 9-1/2" x 4-1/2" **$1,250**

Pierrot serenading lover, perched on harvest moon, pre-war "E" mark, price for facing pair, 18" x 11" x 6" **$3,500**

Male and female European peasant, sgd on inner side of base, price for facing pr, 21" h......................... **$750**

Floor vase, date palm tree form, Middle Eastern woman and water urn on one, her suitor playing lute on other, matte finish flesh toned skin, cobalt blue clothing against white, gilt rims and highlights, ink labels "Royal Dux Bohemia" with acorn in triangle,

glued unstable repairs to man, price for pr, 36-1/2" h, 37-1/4" h....... **$5,225**

Tazza, figural, putti and classically draped woman supporting shell, price for pr, one with hairline in base, 19-1/2" h....................................... **$880**

Vase, Grecian, "E" mark, 11" h..... **$595**

Royal Dux figure, female bather, nude woman seated on rocky outcrop, drying her foot with gilt enameled cloth, oblong base, Czechoslovakia, early 20th century, 18-1/2" h, **$1,000.**
Photo courtesy of Skinner, Inc.

Royal Dux figurines, pr, male and female, European peasants, signed on base, 21" h, **$750.**
Photo courtesy of The Early Auction Company, LLC.

Royal Dux figure, shepherd and shepherdess, lady standing holding staff, man seated playing an instrument, naturalistic ovoid base, indistinct initials OAP?, man lacking item from hands, Czechoslovakia, early 20th century, 22" h, **$825.**
Photo courtesy of Skinner, Inc.

Royal Worcester ewer, white body, gold neck band and handle, multicolored floral decoration, crossed arrows mark, one of pair shown, **$400.**

Photo courtesy of Dotta Auction Co., Inc.

Royal Worcester lamp base, tripod, gilt floral decoration and satyr motif, damage to foot, 10" x 9" base, **$325.**

Photo courtesy of David Rago Auctions, Inc.

ROYAL WORCESTER

History: In 1751, the Worcester Porcelain Company, led by Dr. John Wall and William Davis, acquired the Bristol pottery of Benjamin Lund and moved it to Worcester. The first wares were painted blue under the glaze; soon thereafter decorating was accomplished by painting on the glaze in enamel colors. Among the most-famous 18th-century decorators were James Giles and Jefferys Hamet O'Neale. Transfer-print decoration was developed by the 1760s.

A series of partnerships took place after Davis' death in 1783: Flight (1783-1793); Flight & Barr (1793-1807); Barr, Flight, & Barr (1807-1813); and Flight, Barr, & Barr (1813-1840). In 1840, the factory was moved to Chamberlain & Co. in Diglis. Decorative wares were discontinued. In 1852, W. H. Kerr and R. W. Binns formed a new company and revived the production of ornamental wares.

In 1862, the firm became the Royal Worcester Porcelain Co. Among the key modelers of the late 19th century were James Hadley, his three sons, and George Owen, an expert with pierced clay pieces. Royal Worcester absorbed the Grainger factory in 1889 and the James Hadley factory in 1905. Modern designers include Dorothy Doughty and Doris Lindner.

Basket, flaring pierced sides mounted with floral heads, pine cone and floral cluster int., blue and white transfer dec, first period, mid-18th C, 8-1/2" d **$550**

Biscuit jar, cov, fluted body, raised spearhead borders surrounding enamel floral design, 7-1/4" h **$550**

Bowl, scalloped border, shell molded boy, fruit and floral spray, blue and white transfer dec, first period, mid-18th C, 10" d **$320**

Butter tub, cov, cylindrical, fully sculpted finial, painted floral sprays below geometric borders, first period, c1765, 4-1/4" d, 3-1/4" h **$450**

Demitasse cups and saucers, 4-3/8" d saucer, hand painted, painted fruits dec, gilt rims and handles, sgd "E. Townsend," retailed by the Goldsmiths and Silversmiths Company, c1936, orig boxed set includes set of six 4" l gold-washed silver spoons, London, 1931, maker's mark HJH **$3,820**

Dessert plate
Bone china, hand painted, center with peach stem and bluettes, sgd lower right "E. Townsend," gilt rocaille inner rim, seafoam green fluted outer rim, set of 12, c1941, 9-1/8" d **$900**
Bone china, hand painted, center with flowers, gilt rim, labeled "Designed by A. H. Williamson, Royal Worcester, Made in England," set of 12, 9-1/4" d **$375**

Ewer, pale pink powder horn shape, gold stag horn handle, minor chip, 9" h **$150**

Figure
Cairo water carrier, 1895, 8-3/4" h **$635**
Lady and gentleman, George III costumes, sgd "Hadley," pr, 7-3/4" h and 8-1/4" h **$1,100**
Welsh girl, shot enamel porcelain, sgd "Hadley," late-19th C, 6-1/2" h .. **$690**

Fish plates, bone china, hp fish, gilt lattice and foliage border, sgd "Harry Ayrton," printed marks, 13-pc set, c1930, 9-1/4" d **$2,300**

Fruit cooler, cylindrical, Royal Lily pattern, stylized floral reserve, stepped circular foot, first period, c1800, 6-1/4" h **$225**

Lamp base, baluster vase form, slender gilt neck, two short Moorish-style gilt handles, hand-painted scene of gilt shipwreck on shore by lighthouse, reverse with small scenic roundel, gilt guilloche foot, electrified, 13-3/4" h **$325**

Mustard pot, cylindrical, blue and white transfer, floral clusters, floral finial, first period, mid-18th C, 4" h **$325**

Pitcher
Cream, gold enamel dec, 5-3/4" h .. **$150**
Floral dec, gold handle, 6" h, 5" d ... **$230**
Indian elephant head handle, 5-3/4" h **$175**
Tri-corner shape, blue and white overlapping circles, gold enameled pouring lip, c1860, 5-3/4" h **$260**

Plate

Blind Earl pattern, raised rose spray, polychrome floral sprays, scalloped border, first period, mid-18th C, 7-3/4" d **$1,100**

Octagonal, landscape fan form reserves, cobalt blue ground, first period, pr, 18th C, 7" w **$350**

Salad bowl, leaf molded, three handles, printed mark, c1899, 9" d ..**$560**

Sauceboat, geometric band above foliate molded body, painted floral sprays, oval foot, first period, pr, c1765, 4-1/4" h **$275**

Service plate, hand painted, central roundel painted with dense spray of various flowers, sgd "E. Phillips," speckled green inner rim, gilt outer rim etched with laurel wreaths and husk swags, price for set of 12, c1921, 10-1/2" d.................................**$1,530**

Sweetmeat jar, molded swirl base, thistles dec, silverplate lid, bail, and handle, marked "RW" with crown, 6" d..**$200**

Tankard, cylindrical, blue and white transfer dec of parrot among fruit, first period, mid-18th C, 6" h **$325**

Teabowl and saucer, painted chinoisiere vignette, blue border, first period, c1865 ....**$185**

Teapot, cov, globular form body, fully sculpted blossom finial, domed top, painted floral sprays, first period, c1765, 6-1/2" h **$375**

Urn, cov, pierced dome top, globular body, painted floral sprays, basketweave molded base, early 20th C, 11-1/2" h **$195**

Vase, double handles, gilt and enamel dec, scene of birds by moonlit sky, printed mark, c1887, 9-5/8" h **$715**

Royal Worcester pitcher, hand-painted polychrome flowers, cream ground with gilded details, purple ink stamp, fully marked, 5-1/4" d, 6-1/2" h, **$150.**
Photo courtesy of David Rago Auctions, Inc.

SARREGUEMINES CHINA

History: Sarreguemines ware is a faience porcelain, i.e., tin-glazed earthenware. The factory that made it was established in Lorraine, France, in 1770, under the supervision of Utzschneider and Fabry. The factory was regarded as one of the three most prominent manufacturers of French faience. Most of the wares found today were made in the 19th century.

Marks: Later wares are impressed "Sarreguemines" and "Germany" as a result of changes in international boundaries.

Basket, quilted, green, heavy leopard skin crystallization, 9" h..............**$250**

Centerpiece, bowl with pierced ringlets to sides, supported by center stem flanked by sea nymphs either side, mounted atop circular base on four scrolled feet, polychrome dec, imp marks, chips, restorations, c1875, 14-3/4" h, 14-3/4" d **$900**

Cup and saucer, orange, majolica, crack to one cup, nicks, set of four **$200**

Dinnerware service, white china, multicolored scenes, six luncheon plates, six bread and butter plates, six demitasse cups, six porringers, two platters, divided dish.................**$150**

Face jug, majolica
Suspicious Eyes, #3320.............**$550**
Upward Eyes, #3257 ....**$500**

Garniture, Art Nouveau faience, pr of vases, shouldered trumpet form, shaped oval centerpiece bowl, each with wide gilt band of foliage within diamond borders centered by decorative medallion, verte ground, 10-3/4" h.................................**$350**

Plate, dec with music and characters from French children's songs, 12-pc set, 7-1/2" d **$375**

Tankard, cov, stoneware, continuous country scene of dancing and celebrating villagers, branch handle, pewter lid with porcelain medallion and painted polychrome coat of arms, dated 1869, 11" h **$325**

Urn, gilt metal mounted majolica, baluster form, cobalt blue glazed, mounted with the figure of a crowned lion holding sword, lion and mask handled sides, pierced foliate rim, raised on four scrolling foliate cast feet, imp "Majolica Sarreguemines," second half 19th C, 31-1/4" h **$1,800**

Sarreguemines fruit basket, white plate center with cobalt blue floral decoration, wirework frame, **$175.**

SATSUMA

History: Satsuma, named for a warlord who brought skilled Korean potters to Japan in the early 1600s, is a hand-crafted Japanese faience (tinglazed) pottery. It is finely crackled, has a cream, yellow-cream, or gray-cream color, and is decorated with raised enamels in floral, geometric, and figural motifs.

Figural satsuma was made specifically for export in the 19th century. Later satsuma, referred to as satsuma-style ware, is a Japanese porcelain also hand decorated in raised enamels. From 1912 to the present, satsuma-style ware has been mass produced. Much of the ware on today's market is of this later period.

Bowl
Lobed body, scalloped rim, overall flowering peonies and chrysanthemums in red and gold, mkd on base, Meiji period, slight wear to gilding, 12-1/4" d, 5-1/4" h ...**$2,000**
Scene of figures before Mount Fuji, sgd, late 19th C, 10" d **$470**

Cache pot, figural and landscape scene, 6-1/2" h **$120**

Censor
Ovoid, three cabriole legs, two shaped handles rising from shoulder, lid with large shishi seated on top, continual river landscape scene, patterned lappet border above, key fret border below, base sealed "Yabu Meizan," minor loss to one ear on shishi, 3-1/2" h.......................**$2,990**
Tapering rect form, lobed base, two squared handles, pierced domed lid, all-over dec or Arhats, Meiji period, 10-1/4" h **$635**

Cup and saucer, bird and floral motif, cobalt blue border, Kinkozan **$115**

Figure
God of Longevity, holding scroll, sgd, 4" h **$360**
Kannon, seated on rock throne holding lotus, repairs, 19th C, 12" h **$765**

Incense burner, two reserves, one with sparrows and flowers, other of Mijo shrine, borders of brocade patterns, butterflies caught in net, and hanging jewels, sgd "Kinkozan," Meiji period, 1868-1911, 5" d............**$5,500**

Jar, cov, two cartouche panels, one of Samurai, other with birds, insects, and flowers, one side ring missing, 4" d, 6" h **$230**

Koro, pierced lid, hexagonal, six bracket feet, each side with flowers blooming behind garden fences, domed lid, sgd with Shimazu mon, 3" h....**$2,185**

Miniature cup, interior painted with Bishamon and Hoi tei, ext. with dancing children, mille fleur borders, sgd with paulownia crest in gold, Meiji period, 1868-1911, 2" d..............**$980**

Plate
One Hundred Birds design, early 20th C, 9-1/4" d **$650**
Samurai design, monogram at top, sgd "Kinkozan" in gold on base, Meiji period (1868-1911), 10-1/2" d **$345**

Seal paste box, cobalt blue, gilt trim, reserve of children flying kites, sgd "Kozan," Meiji period, minor int. chip, 1868-1911, 5" d...................**$320**

Tea bowl, dec with butterflies, powdered gold ground, sgd "Kinkozan," Meiji period, 1868-1911, 4-3/4" d ..**$350**

Tea cup and saucer, colorful groups of flowerheads with scrolling gilt vines, minor gilt wear, sgd "Yabu Meizan," 1-3/4" h cup, 4-3/4" d saucer **$900**

Tea set, paneled designs of courtesans in courtyard settings, c1900, 6-1/2" h teapot, creamer, sugar, six cups and saucers, six 7-1/4" d plates..........**$290**

Tray, rounded form with indented edge, design of scrolls of birds, flowers, and women, cobalt ground with gold bamboo, sgd with imp seal "Kinkozan," Meiji period, 1868-1911, 11-1/2" d **$1,650**

Urn, dragon handles, geishas in landscape, 37-1/2" h **$295**

Vase
Basketweave design with panels of prunus blossoms, sgd "Taizan," 19th C, 12" h......................**$360**
Cylindrical form, slight neck, mythological scenes with brocade and floral borders, sgd "Hakuzan," Meiji period (1868-1911), 6-1/2" h **$2,235**
Double gourd earthenware body, enameled and gilt battle scenes, upper body with applied sinuous dragon, sgd, price for matched pair, 19th C, 12-3/4" h **$1,000**
Double handles, designs of dragons and various brocade patterns, sgd "Senzan," 7" x 6" **$1,410**
Double handles, blue ground, pheasants, butterflies, flowers, sgd "Taizan," Meiji period (1868-1911), 12" h **$530**
Samurai on horseback, fighting each other and tigers, price for pr, 4-7/8" h **$500**
Sq, blue and yellow panels, birds, flowers, and butterflies, sgd "Taizan," Meiji period (1868-1911), 12" h **$650**

Satsuma doll tea set, decorated with flowers: tray, teapot, lidded sugar, creamer, two cups and two saucers, **$65.**
Photo courtesy of Joy Luke Auctions.

Satsuma vase, ovoid form, scene having many figures, reverse with floral decoration, unmarked, crazed, 7" h, **$200.**
Photo courtesy of Alderfer Auction Co.

SCHLEGELMILCH PORCELAINS

History: Erdmann Schlegelmilch founded his porcelain factory in Suhl in the Thuringia region in 1861. Reinhold, his brother, established a porcelain factory at Tillowitz in Upper Silesia in 1869. In the 1860s, Prussia controlled Thuringia and Upper Silesia, both rich in the natural ingredients needed for porcelain.

By the late 19th century, an active export business was conducted with the United States and Canada due to a large supply of porcelain at reasonable costs achieved through industrialization and cheap labor.

The Suhl factory ceased production in 1920, unable to recover from the effects of World War I. The Tillowitz plant, located in an area of changing international boundaries, finally came under Polish socialist government control in 1956.

Marks: Both brothers marked their pieces with the "RSP" mark, a designation honoring Rudolph Schlegelmilch, their father. More than 30 mark variations have been discovered.

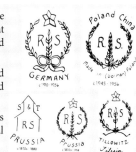

Reproduction Alert. Dorothy Hammond in her 1979 book, *Confusing Collectibles*, illustrates an R. S. Prussia decal that was available from a china-decorating supply company for $14 a sheet. This was the first of several fake R. S. Prussia reproduction marks that have caused confusion among collectors. Acquaint yourself with some of the subtle distinctions between fake and authentic marks as described in the following.

The period mark consists of a wreath that is open at the top. A five-pointed star sits in the opening. An "R" and an "S" flank a wreath twig in the center. The word "Prussia" is located beneath. In the period mark, the leg of the letter "P" extends down past the letter "r." In the reproduction mark, it does not. In the period mark, the letter "I" is dotted. It is dotted in some fake marks, but not in others.

The "R" and the "S" in the period mark are in a serif face and uniform in width. One fake mark uses a lettering style that utilizes a thin/thick letter body. The period mark has a period after the word "Prussia." Some fake marks fail to include it. Several fake marks do not include the word "Prussia" at all.

The period mark has a fine center line within each leaf of the wreath. Several fake marks do not.

R.S. Germany

Biscuit jar, cov, loop handles, roses dec, satin finish, gold knob, 6" h .. **$95**

Bonbon dish, pink carnations, gold dec, silver-gray ground, looped inside handle, 7-3/4" l, 4-1/2" w **$40**

Bowl
Emb floral mold, red steeple mark, 10-1/4" d **$100**
Lily mold, "S & T" steeple mark, 10-1/2" d **$165**

Bread plate, iris variant edge mold, blue and white, gold outlined petals and rim, multicolored center flowers, steeple mark.................................**$115**

Cake plate, deep yellow, two parrots on hanging leaf vine, open handles, green mark.................................**$235**

Celery tray, lily dec, gold rim, open handles, blue label, 11" l, 5-3/4" w **$120**

Chocolate pot, white rose florals, blue mark.......................................**$95**

Cup and saucer, plain mold, swan, blue water, mountain and brown castle background, RM...................**$225**

Demitasse cup and saucer, pink roses, gold-stenciled dec, satin finish, blue mark, 3" h **$90**

Dessert plate, yellow and cream roses, green and rich brown shaded ground, six-pc set, 6-1/2" d **$135**

Ewer, mold #640, green mark, 4-3/4" h **$75**

Hatpin holder, Art Deco mold, green mark, 4-1/2" h................................**$85**

Lemon plate, cutout handle shaped as colorful parrot, white ground, gold trim, artist sgd "B. Hunter" **$60**

Napkin ring, green, pink roses, white snowballs.....................................**$55**

Nut bowl, cream, yellow, roses, green scalloped edge, 5-1/4" d, 2-3/4" h **$65**

Pitcher, light blue, chrysanthemums, pink roses, gold trim, 5-3/4" h **$85**

Plate, allegorical scene, sgd "Kaufmann," green mark, 9-1/2" d **$90**

Powder box, cov, green poppies, green mark................................**$50**

Punch bowl, mahogany shading to pink, polychrome enameled flowers with gilt, imp fleur-de-lis mark with "J. S. Germany," 17-1/4" d, 8" h **$275**

Tea tile, peach and tan, greenish white snowballs, RM over faint blue mark **$165**

Schlegelmilch R.S. Prussia, flower form tea set: 8" h green and lavender teapot, 7-1/2" h lidded sugar, 7-1/2" h creamer, 7-1/2" h pink and green teapot, **$300.**
Photo courtesy of Joy Luke Auctions.

Toothpick holder, Art Deco mold, green mark, 2-3/4" h **$80**

Vase, crystalline glaze, orange and white, 6" h **$45**

R. S. Poland

Berry bowl, white and pale orange floral design, green leaves, small orange-gold border flowers, marked, 4-1/2" sq **$45**

Creamer, soft green, chain of violets, applied fleur-de-lis feet, RM **$110**

Dresser set, glossy, pink roses, pr 6-1/4" h candlesticks, 5" h hatpin holder, 13" x 9" tray **$425**

Flower holder, pheasants, brass frog insert **$675**

Vase
Large white and tan roses, shaded brown and green ground, 8-1/2" h, 4-3/4" d **$195**
White poppies, cream shaded to brown ground, pr, 12" h, 6-1/4" d **$750**

R. S. Prussia

Biscuit jar, cov
Clematis florals, red mark, 9" l **$225**
Mold #501, unmarked, 5-1/2" h **$115**
Mold #644, red roses, red mark, 7" h **$300**

Bowl, lily mold #29, ftd, red mark, 10-1/2" h..................................**$275**

Box, cov, rect, detailed floral and gilt highlights, sgd, 4-3/4" h, 1-1/2" h **$150**

Butter dish, cov, porcelain insert, cream and gold shading, pink roses, raised enamel, RM **$715**

Cake plate, reflecting lilies dec, red mark, 11" d................................**$165**

Celery dish, mold #207, rose dec, red mark, 12" l...............................**$85**

Chocolate pot, mold #501, rose dec, red mark, 9-1/2" h.......................**$150**

Creamer and sugar
Iris mold, Winter Portrait, red mark, very minor flake touch-up on creamer.....................................**$275**
Mold #605, red mark, sugar lid finial reattached **$125**
Pedestal form, florals, red mark **$185**

Dresser tray, mold #18, red mark, 11-3/4" l.................................**$165**

Ferner, mold 876, florals on purple and green ground, unsgd, 7" d **$165**

Hair receiver, green lilies of the valley, white ground, RM..................**$95**

Milk pitcher, Morning Glory mold, pink carnations dec, 5" h **$200**

Mustard, cov, mold #511, red mark, 3-1/4" h.................................**$50**

Plate
Floral mold, red mark, 8-3/4" d **$115**
Swans in lake, red mark, 9" d **$210**

Portrait bowl, mold #18, dice player variant, red mark, 5-1/2" d **$275**

Portrait plate, mold #32, Springtime, red mark, faint 1" hairline on back, 8-3/4" d...................................**$375**

Shaving mug, emb floral mold, 3-3/4" h...................................**$85**

Spoon holder, pink and white roses, 14" l....................................**$200**

Syrup, cov, underplate, green and yellow luster, pink flowers **$125**

Tankard
Ftd, mold #642, red mark, 10-3/4" h **$275**
Mold #643, reflecting water lilies, red mark, repaired, 14" h **$165**

Striped floral mold #525, red mark, small flake touch-up on lip, 13" h **$325**

Toothpick holder, green shadows, pink and white roses, jeweled, six feet, RM....................................**$250**

Vase, jeweled, rose floral dec, embedded opal jewels, sgd, 6-1/4" h **$275**

R. S. Suhl

Coffee set, coffeepot, creamer, sugar, six cups and saucers, figural scenes dec, some marked "Angelica Kauffmann," 9" h..............**$1,750**

Pin tray, round, Nightwatch, 4-1/2" d **$375**

Plate, cherubs dec, 6-3/4" d...........**$90**

Powder dish, cov, Nightwatch, green shading......................................**$425**

Vase, four pheasants, green mark, 8" h **$275**

R. S. Tillowitz

Bowl, slanted sides, open handles, four leaf-shaped feet, matte finish, pale green ground, roses and violets, gold flowered rim, marked, 7-3/4" d **$125**

Creamer and sugar, soft yellow and salmon roses **$65**

Plate, mixed floral spray, gold beading, emb rim, brown wing mark, 6-1/2" d **$120**

Relish tray, oval, hp, shaded green, white roses, green leaves, center handle, blue mark, 8" l **$45**

Tea set, stacking teapot, creamer, and sugar, yellow, rust, and blue flowers, gold trim, ivory ground, marked "Royal Silesia," green mark in wreath **$95**

Vase, pheasants, brown and yellow, two curved handles, 10" h **$125**

SEVRES

History: The principal patron of the French porcelain industry in early 18th-century France was Jeanne Antoinette Poisson, Marquise de Pompadour. She supported the Vincennes factory of Gilles and Robert Dubois and their successors in their attempt to make soft-paste porcelain in the 1740s. In 1753, she moved the porcelain operations to Sevres, near her home, Chateau de Bellevue.

The Sevres soft-paste formula used sand from Fontainebleau, salt, saltpeter, soda of alicante, powdered alabaster, clay, and soap. Many famous colors were developed, including a cobalt blue. Such famous decorators as Watteau, La Tour, and Boucher painted the wonderful scenic designs on the ware. In the 18th century, Sevres porcelain was the world's foremost diplomatic gift.

In 1769, kaolin was discovered in France, and a hard-paste formula was developed. The baroque gave way to rococo, a style favored by Jeanne du Barry, Louis XV's next mistress. Louis XVI took little interest in Sevres, and many factories began to turn out counterfeits. In 1876, the factory was moved to St. Cloud and was eventually nationalized.

Marks: Louis XV allowed the firm to use the "double L" in its marks.

Box, cov

Oval, cobalt blue ground, panels of putti dec, sgd "JB," chip on base, 2-1/2" l, 1-1/4" w, 1-1/2" h **$425**

Oval, hp, hinged lid, opalescent cranberry ground, gilt roses and scrolls, lid with painted scene of woman and putti, sgd "E. Carelle," int. dec with polychrome floral panels, 7" l, 4-1/2" w, 3-1/4" h **$650**

Bud vase, gilt ground, enamel Art Nouveau stylized leaf and flower design, printed mark, 6" h **$635**

Bust, Marie Antoinette, bisque bust, gilt highlights, cobalt blue ground, molded porcelain socle with central garland and monogram, 19th C, 13" h **$650**

Café au lait cup and saucer, ftd cup, cobalt blue enameled ground, gilt cagle roundel and torcheres, corresponding molded saucer, early 20th C, 6" h **$200**

Candelabra, pr, painted scenes of winged cherubs, Bleu-celeste ground, foliate gilt border, figural gilt bronze cherubs holding branches of three candle sockets, c1900, 18" h **$2,530**

Centerpiece, int. painted with scene of two lovers, Bleu-celeste ground, scrolled gilt border, bronze plinth, foliate gilt bronze handles, 19th C, 17-1/2" l, 13-1/2" h **$2,990**

Clock, emb metal case, five inset painted porcelain panels, three are scenic, frontal pc with young lovers, c1900, 17" h **$815**

Compote, int. painted with young beauty and cherub, sgd "Lote," Bleu-celeste ground, dec porcelain pedestal, bronze plinth, 19th C, 11-1/2" d, 9-1/2" h **$2,760**

Cup and saucer, cobalt blue ground, painted roundel depicting an 18th century couple playing with dog, gilt tooled surround, saucer with floral painted center, blue border with floral cartouches, late 19th C, 3" h cup **$815**

Dish, rim dec with flowers, reserve with portrait of lady, turquoise ground, gilt bronze stand with two handles cast with scrollwork, garlands of leaves and grapes, 19th C, 14" d, 7" h **$2,150**

Display tray, round, short gilt handles, cobalt blue rim with rocaille scrolls, center painted with scene of court-

Sevres wall plaque, portrait of two girls in skirts, gilt trim, signed "E. Furloud," underglaze blue Sevres mark, 17" d, **$1,300.**
Photo courtesy of The Early Auction Company, LLC.

ing couple, sgd E. Roy, early 20th C, 14-5/8" h **$400**

Ecuelle, cov, panel florals, bright enamels, raised gilt cartouches, pink ground, round matching stand, c1860, 8" d **$460**

Figure, pair in Elizabethian dress, royal blue ground, gold accents, early, 8-1/2" h **$640**

Inkwell, scene of winged cherub and florals against Bleu-celeste ground, foliage gilt borders, each ink receptacle supported by gilt bronze sphinx-like young beauty, 19th C, 11-1/2" l, 8-1/2" h **$1,150**

Lamp base, urn shape, cartouches painted with allegorical female depictions of Spring and Autumn, surrounded by cherubs, gilt enamel surrounds, cerulean blue ground, landscape cartouches recto, mounted with vine-wrapped reeded handles ending in Demetre masks, trumpet foot topped by turquoise molded beading, rect bronze base molded with swags, corners with swag centered patera, electrified, price for pr, late 19th C, 21-1/2" h **$7,650**

Mantel urns, pr, lidded teal blue tapered vases with horizontal gilt banding, oblong bases set with pair of kneeling bisque figures of semi-nude classical women, base chips, c1919, 18" h **$2,500**

Mantel vase, cov, painted with wide central band of courtiers on verandas in pastoral landscape, white and red faux jeweled borders, body with cobalt blue ground accented with gilt enameling, angular husk-draped ormolu handles, lids with inverted berry fini-

Sevres-style, pair of plates, each painted with scene of youths picking cherries, gilded accents, 16" d, **$1,800.**
Photo courtesy of David Rago Auctions, Inc.

als, price for pr, late 19th C, 19-1/2" h **$9,400**

Monteiths, pr, scalloped rim flanked by two scroll handles, floral garlands and blue ribbon dec, white ground, blue interlaced L's mark, 19th C, 12" w **$960**

Patch box, cov, shaped ovoid, green ground, hinged lid with hand painted scene of Napoleon on horseback, sgd lower right "Morin," 3-1/4" l **$250**

Plaque, 10-1/2" l, 9-5/8" w oval format, Marie Antoniette, mauve gown, blue celeste border with gilt scrollwork, late 19th C, 10-3/4" x 13-5/8" giltwood and crème painted frame **$550**

Portrait plate, Lobelia portrait, surrounded by wreath, cobalt blue band border with gilt dec including Napoleonic crest and crowns, mounted in shadow box frame, gilt loss, 9" d ... **$150**

Solitaire, 6-1/4" h teapot, cup and saucer, cov sugar, tray, gilt scrollwork, reserves dec with flowers or fetes galantes, turquoise ground, 19th C **$1,135**

Tray, six-sided oblong form, French allegorical park scene, ladies with parasols, Florentine gilt border, sgd "Bertien," 18-1/2" x 13" **$525**

Urn

Campana form, Napoleonic scenes painted reserves, green ground, sgd "L. Loreau," mounted on plastic base, fitted as lamp, 19" h **$1,195**

Light blue body, hp elephant lady framed with gold medallion, overall random amethyst leafy stemmed flowers, gold gilt emb foot, metal handled collar, blue trademark, metal stamped "France," 15" h **$950**

Sevres centerpiece bowl, cobalt, hand-painted courting scene, gilt bronze mounts, "F. Lacoste," 19th century, 6" h, 16-1/2" d, $995.

Photo courtesy of Pook & Pook, Inc.

Urn, cov
Dome cov, pine cone finial, neck dec with band of vitruvian scrolls and ram's heads, reserves dec with flowers, fluted socle and octagonal base, gilt metal mounts, 19th C, 14-1/2" h **$1,675**
Finely painted French garden scene by L. Bertren within gilt foliate cartouche, cobalt blue ground, winged anthropomorphic bronze handles, verso with pastoral cottage and stream scene, bronzed acorn finial

lid, mkd with Serves style cipher, c1900, 40-1/2" h **$10,120**
Vase, pink ground, oval cartouches with figural landscapes and ornaments, metal mount, pr, 11" h **$1,380**
Wine cooler, Louis XVI style, circular tapering form, top section with gilded ram's heads over reeded band, base dec with ribboned garlands and entwined laurel, multicolored, white ground, 10-1/4" h **$2,300**

SHAWNEE POTTERY

History: The Shawnee Pottery Co. was founded in 1937 in Zanesville, Ohio. The company acquired a 650,000-square-foot plant that had previously housed the American Encaustic Tiling Company. Shawnee produced as many as 100,000 pieces of pottery a day until 1961, when the plant closed.

Shawnee limited its production to kitchenware, decorative art pottery, and dinnerware. Distribution was primarily through jobbers and chain stores.

Marks: Shawnee can be marked "Shawnee," "Shawnee U.S.A.," "USA #-—," "Kenwood," or with character names, e.g., "Pat. Smiley" and "Pat. Winnie."

Shawnee cookie jar, Smiley Pig, green ruffled color, red roses and green leaves on hat, purse tucked under arm, $325.

Bank, bulldog **$50**
Basket, 9" l, 5-1/2" h at handle, turquoise glaze, relief flowers and leaves, USA 688 ....**$45**
Batter pitcher, Fern **$65**
Casserole, cov, Corn Queen, large **$40**
Cookie jar, cov
Cinderella, unmarked **$125**
Drum major, marked "USA 10," 10" h **$295**
Jo-Jo the Clown, marked "Shawnee USA, 12," 9" h **$300**
Little Chef **$75**
Owl **$110**
Creamer
Elephant **$25**
Puss n' Boots, green and yellow **$65**

Shawnee planter, mill scene, olive green glaze, marked "Shawnee, USA, 769," $65.

Smiley Pig, clover bud **$165**
Figure
Gazelle **$45**
Squirrel **$30**
Rabbit **$40**
Fruit bowl, Corn Queen **$25**
Mug, Corn King **$35**
Paperweight, Muggsy **$65**
Pitcher
Bo Peep, blue bonnet, yellow dress **$125**
Chanticleer **$75**
Planter
Gazelle **$25**
Horse with hat and cart **$20**
Locomotive, black **$60**
Mouse and cheese, pink and yellow **$25**
Wheelbarrow **$20**
Salt and pepper shakers, pr
Chanticleer, large, orig label **$45**
Dutch Boy and Girl, large **$55**
Milk cans **$30**
Mugsey, small **$65**
Puss n' Boots, small **$30**
Smiley, small **$30**
Watering cans **$28**
Teapot
Granny Ann, peach apron **$125**
Horseshoe, blue **$65**
Tom Tom, blue, red, and yellow **$175**
Utility jar, Corn King **$50**
Wall pocket, bird house **$25**

Spatterware Peafowl plate, red, peafowl in red, blue, and green, "Adams," 8-1/2" d, **$320.**
Photo courtesy of Pook & Pook, Inc.

Spatterware plate, paneled, red, green, and blue rainbow spatter, 9-1/4" d, **$1,150.**
Photo courtesy of Pook & Pook, Inc.

Spatterware plate, thistle dec, yellow, 19th century, 9-3/4" d, **$890.**
Photo courtesy of Pook & Pook, Inc.

SPATTERWARE

History: Spatterware generally was made of common earthenware, although occasionally creamware was used. The earliest English examples were made about 1780. The peak period of production was from 1810 to 1840. Firms known to have made spatterware are Adams, Barlow, and Harvey and Cotton.

The amount of spatter decoration varies from piece to piece. Some objects simply have decorated borders. These often were decorated with a brush, requiring several hundred touches per square inch to achieve the spatter effect. Other pieces have the entire surface covered with spatter.

Marks: Marked pieces are rare.

Notes: Collectors today focus on the patterns—Cannon, Castle, Fort, Peafowl, Rainbow, Rose, Thistle, Schoolhouse, etc. The decoration on flatware is in the center of the piece; on hollow ware, it occurs on both sides.

Aesthetics and the color of spatter are key to determining value. Blue and red are the most common colors; green, purple, and brown are in a middle group; black and yellow are scarce.

Like any soft paste, spatterware is easily broken or chipped. Prices in this listing are for pieces in very good to mint condition.

Spatterware plate, Stick spatter, blue cog flowers, green leaves, red petals, English, **$250.**
Photo courtesy of Wiederseim Associates, Inc.

Reproduction Alert. Cybis spatter is an increasingly collectible ware in its own right. The pieces, made by the Polishman Boleslaw Cybis in the 1940s, have an Adams-type peafowl design. Many contemporary craftsmen also are reproducing spatterware.

Bowl, Morning Glory flowers, red spatter, purple flowers, light overall crazing, small table rim chip, 5-1/2" d **$65**

Charger
Stick spatter, red, blue, green, and purple flowers, purple stick spatter border, 12-1/2" d **$125**
Stick spatter, red and blue flowers, green leaves, purple stick spatter buds, mkd "Adams, England," minor staining, 14-1/2" d **$100**

Creamer
Morning Glory, blue and green flower, red spatter, 3-3/4" h.............. **$2,750**
Peafowl, red, green, and blue, paneled, unusual squiggly branches, minor enamel flake in blue, 5-5/8" h **$770**
Rainbow Thumbprint, red, yellow, and blue peafowl, red, blue, and green spatter, damage and restoration, 4" h **$1,650**
Red and green cockscomb design, blue spatter, paneled, stains on foot, minor flakes, 5" h **$860**
Red and green rose, brown and black spatter, rim flake, 3-1/2" h **$650**
Cup, blue stick spatter looping pattern, red, green, and blue long tulip **$75**

Spatterware, Peafowl plate, blue, three-color bird, impressed "Adams," second half 19th century, 8-1/2" d, **$330.**
Photo courtesy of Green Valley Auctions.

Spatterware pitcher, Peafowl decoration, red spatter, 8" w, 7" h, **$775.**
Photo courtesy of Joy Luke Auctions.

Spatterware sugar bowl, Daisy and Bowtie, pink and blue, green daisies on lid, unmarked, second half 19th century, 5" h, 5" d rim, **$85.**
Photo courtesy of Green Valley Auctions.

Spatterware cup and saucer, Drape pattern, red and blue, 19th century, **$935.**
Photo courtesy of Pook & Pook, Inc.

Cup and saucer, handleless

Dark blue, green, and red pomegranate, yellow dots, blue spatter, light stains, crazed saucer **$800**

Light brown spatter, red and blue spray with green leaves, hairlines **$385**

Peafowl, light blue, mustard yellow, and green dec, red spatter, damage and repair to cup, flake and inpainting in saucer **$150**

Rainbow, Drape pattern, red, yellow, and green, small rim repair on cup, minor stains on saucer **$3,080**

Red, mustard, and green six-pointed star, stains on cup, foot chip **$925**

Red, yellow, green, and blue tulip dec, blue spatter, cup has stained area, filled-in flakes, hairline **$110**

Miniature, handleless cup and saucer

Blue spatter, blue, mauve, and green dahlia **$300**

Blue spatter, light green yellow, and red peafowl **$350**

Red spatter **$200**

Pitcher

Acorns, yellow and teal green, green and dark brown leaves, purple spatter, paneled, bubbles in brown and yellow, stains, rim repair, 8-1/2" h **$3,650**

Blue drape with bands on shoulder, rim, and handle, hairlines, some stains, in-the-making separation at handle, 4-3/4" h **$460**

Paneled sides, five-color rainbow spatter, handle cracked, 7-1/2" h **$5,500**

Plate

Black Beauty, black floral border, red, blue, and green floral center, transfer label "Wm. Adams & Co., Tunstall, England," 9-1/8" d **$150**

Blue border, blue, red, and green dahlia pattern, 8-3/8" d **$350**

Blue border, center red and green flower, light stains, 8-1/2" d **$150**

Blue flowers, red and blue flowers green leaves, 10-3/4" d **$150**

Peafowl, dark blue, green, and dark brown, long tail, red spatter, short hairline, in-the-making chip on table ring, 8-1/2" d **$715**

Peafowl, red, yellow, and green, blue spatter border, rim chips, 7-1/2" d **$110**

Rainbow, blue and reddish-purple, red Adams rose in center, stains, rim flake, 9-5/8" d **$450**

Rainbow, light red, blue, and yellow border, rim flake, 8-1/2" d **$3,300**

Rainbow, purple and black, bull's eye center, 9-1/2" d **$1,500**

Rainbow, red, blue, and green border, scalloped edge, imp "Adams," filled-in rim chip, 10-1/2" d **$385**

Rainbow, red, yellow, and blue spatter, few minor knife scratches, 8-5/8" d **$3,250**

Red border, red, blue, and green flowers, minor enamel imperfections, minor stains, 8-3/4" d **$110**

Platter

Dark brown eagle and shield transfer center, blue spatter border, octagonal, stains and hairline, 13-3/4" x 17-1/2" **$295**

Light blue borders, rect white center panel, oblong, scalloped corners, minor rim flakes, 12-3/8" d, 15-7/8" w **$220**

Peafowl, red, blue, and dark brown, appears to have been scoured, two hairlines, and flake on rim underside, 8-1/4" x 10-3/4" **$615**

Red and green rainbow border, large red and blue tulip with green and black foliage, imp anchor mark, restorations, hairline, 10-1/2" x 13-3/4" **$4,510**

Soup plate, blue border, red, green, and yellow stripes, floral center, 8-3/4" d **$195**

Sugar bowl, cov

Blue, green, and red designs, blue stripes, minor roughness on inside flange, 5" d, 5" h **$250**

Paneled, red schoolhouse, green spatter trees and grass, blue spatter, small crow's foot, restored handles, lid blue transfer replacement, 5-3/4" h **$715**

Teapot

Cockscomb, red and green design, blue spatter, hairlines in base, restored replaced lid, 7-5/8" h **$550**

Peafowl, blue, green, and red, red spatter, small flakes, 9" h **$1,400**

Rainbow, green and yellow with purple loops, black spots, stains, filled-in rim chip, restoration to handle, spout, and lid, 5" h **$5,060**

Waste bowl, brown, red, and black Fort pattern, blue spatter, hairline, 6-1/4" d, 3-1/2" h **$200**

STAFFORDSHIRE, HISTORICAL

History: The Staffordshire district of England is the center of the English pottery industry. There were 80 different potteries operating there in 1786, with the number increasing to 179 by 1802. The district includes Burslem, Cobridge, Etruria, Fenton, Foley, Hanley, Lane, Lane End, Longport, Shelton, Stoke, and Tunstall. Among the many famous potters were Adams, Davenport, Spode, Stevenson, Wedgwood, and Wood.

Notes: The view is the most critical element when establishing the value of historical Staffordshire; American collectors pay much less for non-American views. Dark blue pieces are favored; light views continue to remain under-priced. Among the forms, soup tureens have shown the largest price increases.

Prices listed here are for mint examples, unless otherwise noted. Reduce prices by 20 percent for a hidden chip, a faint hairline, or an invisible professional repair; by 35 percent for knife marks through the glaze and a visible professional repair; by 50 percent for worn glaze and major repairs.

The numbers in parentheses refer to items in the Armans' books, which constitute the most detailed list of American historical views and their forms.

Staffordshire commemorative jug, Caneware, molded body, relief, Brittania, figure riding shell pulled by seahorses, ship under spout, textured ground, 7", **$590.**
Photo courtesy of Skinner, Inc.

Adams

W.ADAMS&SONS   ADAMS

The Adams family has been associated with ceramics since the mid-17th century. In 1802, William Adams of Stoke-on-Trent produced American views.

In 1819, a fourth William Adams, son of William of Stoke, became a partner with his father and was later joined by his three brothers. The firm became William Adams & Sons. The father died in 1829 and William, the eldest son, became manager.

The company operated four potteries at Stoke and one at Tunstall. American views were produced at Tunstall in black, light blue, sepia, pink, and green in the 1830-40 period. William Adams died in 1865. All operations were moved to Tunstall. The firm continues today under the name of Wm. Adams & Sons, Ltd.

Bowl, English scenes with ruins, dark blue transfer, yellowed repair on back, 11" d, 2-1/2" h **$155**

Creamer, English scene, imp "Adams," dark blue, 5-3/8" d **$175**

Pitcher, Eagle, Scroll in Beak, blue and white transfer, illegible imp mark for William Adams, Stoke, glaze scratches, 1827-31, 5-3/4" h **$1,320**

Plate, Mitchell & Freeman's China and Glass Warehouse, Chatham St, Boston, blue and white transfer, imp marker's mark and printed title on reverse, 10-1/4" d...................................... **$500**

Teapot, Log Cabin, medallions of Gen. Harrison on border, pink (458) **$450**

Clews

From sketchy historical accounts that are available, it appears that James Clews took over the closed plant of A. Stevenson in 1819. His brother Ralph entered the business later. The firm continued until about 1836, when James Clews came to America to enter the pottery business at Troy, Indiana. The venture was a failure because of the lack of skilled workmen and the proper type of clay. He returned to England, but did not re-enter the pottery business.

Bowl, Landing of General Lafayette, ext. floral design, rim repair, 9" d **$410**

Cup plate, Landing of General Lafayette at Castle Garden, dark blue **$400**

Pitcher
Welcome General Lafayette the Nation's Guest and Our Country's Glory, blue and white transfer, handle repair, int. staining, 6" h .**$2,070**
States Border pattern, scenic country vista with mansion on hill, river in foreground, blue and white transfer dec, minor int. staining, 6-3/4" h **$980**

Staffordshire, Clews, plate, America and Independence, States border, imp mark, 10-1/2" d, **$825.**
Photo courtesy of Wiederseim Associates, Inc.

Staffordshire, unknown maker, coffeepot, dark blue transfer printed decoration, wide floral and scroll border, English landscape scene with old woman and seated man, rim chip, lid broken, 9" h, **$390.**
Photo courtesy of Alderfer Auction Co.

Staffordshire, Clews, plate, The Landing of General Lafayette at Castle Garden, impressed Clews mark, 10" d, $375.

Photo courtesy of Wiederseim Associates, Inc.

Staffordshire plate, view of Trenton Falls, impressed, "Wood & Sons," 19th century, 7-1/2" d, $380.

Photo courtesy of Pook & Pook, Inc.

Plate

America and Independence, States border, America wears Mason's apron, holds portrait of Washington, dark blue transfer, scalloped edge, imp "Clews, Warranted, Staffordshire," 10-1/2" d **$825**

Landing of General Lafayette, blue and white transfer, imp maker's mark for James and Ralph Clews, minor wear, c1819-36, 7-3/4" d **$500**

Landing of General Lafayette, imp "Clews," dark blue, very minor wear, 10" d **$375**

States series, America and Independence, fisherman with net, imp "Clews," dark blue, small rim flake, 10-5/8" d **$440**

Platter

Landing of General Lafayette at Castle Garden New York 16 August 1824, blue and white transfer, imp maker's mark, minor glaze scratches, 11-3/4" x 15-1/4" **$2,200**

States Border, center with vista of river with two swans, two men, rowboat on river bank, large country house surrounded by trees in background, blue and white transfer, imp maker's mark of James and Ralph Clews, Cobridge, glaze scratches, 1819-36 .... **$2,530**

Winter View of Pittsfield Massachusetts, blue and white transfer, imp maker's mark, glaze scratches, 14" x 16-1/2" **$3,450**

Soup plate

Picturesque Views, Pittsburgh, Pennsylvania, imp "Clews," steam ships with "Home, Nile, Larch," black transfer, chips on table ring, 10-1/2" d **$330**

Winter View of Pittsfield, Massachusetts, imp "Clews," dark blue, 10-3/8" d **$440**

Saucer, Landing of Gen. Lafayette, dark blue transfer, imp "Clews Warranted Staffordshire" **$275**

Toddy plate, Winter View of Pittsfield, Massachusetts, scalloped edge, medium blue transfer, imp "Clews Warranted Staffordshire," 5-3/4" d **$400**

J. & J. Jackson

J & J. JACKSON

Job and John Jackson began operations at the Churchyard Works, Burslem, about 1830. The works formerly were owned by the Wedgwood family. The firm produced transfer scenes in a variety of colors, such as black, light blue, pink, sepia, green, maroon, and mulberry. More than 40 different American views of Connecticut, Massachusetts, Pennsylvania, New York, and Ohio were issued. The firm is believed to have closed about 1844.

Deep dish, American Beauty Series, Yale College (493) **$125**

Plate, The President's House, Washington, purple transfer, 10-3/8" d **$275**

Platter, American Beauty Series
Iron Works at Saugerties (478), 12" l **$275**

View of Newburgh, black transfer (463), 17-1/2" l **$575**

Soup plate, American Beauty Series, Hartford, Connecticut, black transfer (476), 10" d **$150**

Thomas Mayer

In 1829, Thomas Mayer and his brothers, John and Joshua, purchased

Stubbs' Dale Hall Works of Burslem. They continued to produce a superior grade of ceramics.

Cream pitcher, Lafayette at Franklin's Tomb, dark blue, 4" h **$550**

Gravy tureen, Arms of the American States, CT, dark blue (498) **$3,800**

Plate, Arms of Rhode Island, blue and white transfer, eagle back stamp, minor glaze scratches, 1829, 8-1/2" d **$790**

Platter

Arms of the American States, New Jersey, dark blue (503), 19" l **$7,200**

Lafayette at Franklin's Tomb, dark blue, 8-1/4" l **$525**

Sugar bowl, cov, Lafayette at Franklin's Tomb, dark blue (510) **$850**

Mellor, Veneables & Co.

Little information is recorded on Mellor, Veneables & Co., except that it was listed as potters in Burslem in 1843. The company's Scenic Views with the Arms of the States Border does include the arms for New Hampshire. This state is missing from the Mayer series.

Plate, Tomb of Washington, Mt. Vernon, Arms of States border, 7-1/2" d **$125**

Platter

European view, light blue and white transfer, imp and printed maker's mark, hairline, light wear, c1843, 14-1/2" x 19-3/4" **$365**

Scenic Views, Arms of States border, Albany, light blue (516), 15" l .. **$265**

Sugar bowl, cov, Arms of States, Pennsylvania, dark blue **$350**

Teapot, Windsor pattern, dark blue, 9-1/2" h **$200**

J. & W. Ridgway and William Ridgway & Co.

John and William Ridgway, sons of Job Ridgway and nephews of George Ridgway, who owned Bell Bank Works and Cauldon Place Works, produced the popular Beauties of America series at the Cauldon plant. The partnership between the two brothers was dissolved in 1830. John remained at Cauldon.

William managed the Bell Bank Works until 1854. Two additional series were produced based upon the etchings of Bartlett's American Scenery. The first series had various borders including narrow lace. The second series is known as Catskill Moss. Beauties of America is in dark blue. The other series are found in light transfer colors of blue, pink, brown, black, and green.

Plate

American Scenery, Valley of the Shenandoah from Jefferson's Rock, brown (289), 7" d **$120**

Beauties of America, City Hall, New York, dark blue (260), 10" h **$225**

Platter

Beauties of America series, Alms House, New York, blue and white transfer, printed title, scratches, scattered minor staining, 12-3/4" x 16-1/2" **$1,265**

Catskill Moss, Boston and Bunker's Hill, imp "William Ridgway Son & Co," medium blue, minor chips, knife marks, edge wear, dated 1844, 19" l **$525**

Relish tray, Savannah Bank, Beauties of America Series, blue and white transfer, printed title, minor imperfections, c1814-30, 5-3/8" x 8-1/4"....**$750**

Soup plate, Octagon Church, Boston, imp "Ridgway," dark medium blue, 9-7/8" d...........................**$330**

Wash bowl, American Scenery, Albany (279) **$325**

Rogers

ROGERS

John Rogers and his brother George established a pottery near Longport in 1782. After George's death in 1815, John's son Spencer became a partner, and the firm operated under the name of John Rogers & Sons. John died in 1916. His son continued the use of the name until he dissolved the pottery in 1842.

Basket and undertray, Boston State House, blue and white transfer, imp marker's mark for John Rogers and Son, Longport, hairline cracks, 1815-50, 3" x 6-1/2" x 9-1/4" **$2,760**

Cup and saucer, Boston Harbor, dark blue.....................................**$650**

Cup plate, Boston Harbor, dark blue (441) **$1,400**

Deep dish, Boston State House, blue and white transfer, imp marker's mark for John Rogers and Son, Long-

Staffordshire plate, "Commodore Mac-Donough's Victory," blue and white, early 19th century, 10" d, **$365.**
Photo courtesy of Pook & Pook, Inc.

port, minor glaze scratches, 1815-42, 12-3/4" d..................................**$2,070**

Plate, The Canal at Buffalo, lace border, purple transfer, int. hairline, 9-5/8" d..**$55**

Platter, Boston State House, medium dark blue (442), 16-5/8" l..........**$1,000**

Sauce tureen, cov, undertray, Boston State House, blue and white transfer, imp maker's mark for John Rogers and Son, Longport, 1815-42 ....**$2,900**

Waste bowl, Boston Harbor, dark blue (441) **$850**

Stevenson

As early as the 17th century, the name Stevenson has been associated with the pottery industry. Andrew Stevenson of Cobridge introduced American scenes with the flower and scroll border. Ralph Stevenson, also of Cobridge, used a vine and leaf border on his dark blue historical views and a lace border on his series in light transfers.

The initials R. S. & W. indicate Ralph Stevenson and Williams are associated with the acorn and leaf border. It has been reported that Williams was Ralph's New York agent and the wares were produced by Ralph alone.

R.S.W.

Bowl

Capitol Washington, blue and white transfer, printed mark, Ralph Stevens and Williams, Cobridge, glaze imperfections, 1815-40, 11" d **$2,645**

Park Theater, New York, blue and white transfer, printed mark, Ralph Stevens and Williams, Cobridge, minute scratches, 1815-40, 8-3/4" d **$2,530**

Staffordshire, unknown maker, bowl, "A View Near Philadelphia," titled on back, 9-3/4" d, **$395.**
Photo courtesy of Wiederseim Associates, Inc.

Cup and saucer, New Orleans, floral and scroll border **$95**

Jug, dark blue print, 8-1/4" h........**$750**

Pitcher, Almshouse, Boston, reverse with Esplanade and Castle Garden, New York, blue and white transfer, unmarked, 10" h **$2,300**

Plate

Boston Hospital, blue and white transfer, stamped title, maker's initials, imp maker's mark, minor glaze scratches, 9" d **$350**

Catholic Cathedral, New York, floral and scroll border, dark blue (395), 6-1/2" d **$1,650**

Columbia College, portrait medallion of President Washington, inset View of the Aqueduct Bridge at Rochester, blue and white transfer, Ralph Stevens and Williams, Cobridge, minor scratches, 1815-40, 7-1/2" d **$8,625**

New York from Brooklyn Heights, printed title, imp maker's mark, A. Stevenson, Cobridge, 1808-29, 10-1/4" d **$900**

View of Governor's Island, printed title, imp maker's mark, A. Stevenson, Cobridge, 1808-29, 10-1/4" d **$950**

Welcome Lafayette the Nation's Guest, portrait medallion of President Washington, City Hotel, New York, inset "entrance to the Canal into the Hudson at Albany," blue and white transfer, Ralph Stevens and Williams, Cobridge, minor scratches, 1815-40, 8-1/2" d.................**$4,600**

Welcome LaFayette the Nation's Guest, Jefferson, Washington, Governor Clinton, Park Street Theater New York, vignette of View of Aqueduct Bridge at Little Falls, blue and white transfer, Ralph Stevens and Williams, Cobridge, minor scratches, 1815-40, 10" d.......**$3,740**

Platter

Battle of Bunker Hill, blue and white transfer, printed title, imp maker's mark, Ralph Stevenson, Cobridge, one scratch, 1815-40, 10-1/4" x 13" **$8,625**

New York Esplanade and Castle Garden, blue and white transfer, printed title, imp maker's mark, Ralph Stevenson, Cobridge, minor glaze scratches, 1815-40, 14-1/2" x 18-1/2"..**$5,750**

Troy from Mount Ida, by W. G. Wallogy, landscape scene, floral border, blue and white transfer, back stamped with American eagle, marked "A. Stevenson Warranted Staffordshire," 7-1/4" x 9-1/4" **$1,550**

Soup plate, View on the Road to Lake George, printed title, imp maker's mark, A. Stevenson, Cobridge, 1808-29, 9" d **$1,100**

Toddy plate, American Museum, New York, dark blue transfer, mkd "Scudder's American Museum, R.S.W.," impressed Stevenson, 4-7/8" d **$660**

Wash bowl, Riceborough, Georgia, lace border (388) **$375**

Stubbs

In 1790, Stubbs established a pottery works at Burslem, England. He operated it until 1829, when he retired and sold the pottery to the Mayer brothers. He probably produced his American views about 1825. Many of his scenes were from Boston, New York, New Jersey, and Philadelphia.

Gravy boat, Hoboken in New Jersey, Steven's House, blue and white transfer, printed title, Joseph Stubbs, Burslem, minor imperfections, 1790-1829, 4-1/4" h.........................**$550**

Pitcher, Boston State House, reverse with City Hall, New York, blue and white transfer, unmarked, small chip on handle, 6" h **$980**

Plate

City Hall, New York, floral and eagle border, medium blue transfer, unmarked, minor wear and small repair, 6-1/2" h..........................**$225**

Fair Mount near Philadelphia, floral border with eagles, medium blue transfer, imp "Stubbs," 10-1/4" h................**$475**

Upper Ferry Bridge of the River Schuylkill, blue and white transfer,

printed title, Joseph Stubbs, Burslem, imperfections, 1790-1829, 9" d **$950**

Platter

State House, Boston, blue and white transfer, printed title, marked "Joseph Stubbs, Burslem," minor scratches and crazing, 1790-1829, 12" x 14-3/4" **$1,265**

Mendenhall Ferry, blue and white transfer, printed title, minor glaze scratches, 13-3/4" x 16-3/4" ...**$2,185**

Upper Ferry Bridge over the River Schuylkill, well and tree, printed title on reverse, hairline, 15-1/2" x 18-3/4"...**$715**

Salt shaker, Hoboken in New Jersey, spread eagle border, dark blue (326) **$700**

Wash bowl and pitcher, Upper Ferry Bridge Over the River Schuylkill, 12-5/8" d bowl, 10" h pitcher, blue and white, printed title, Joseph Stubbs, Burslem, 1790-1829 ....**$1,840**

Unknown makers

Bowl, Franklin, scene of Ben flying kite, red transfer, minor wear, 11-1/8" d, 3-1/4" d...**$495**

Cup, handleless, dark blue transfer, Quadruped series, llama on both sides, floral border, scalloped rim **$115**

Fruit bowl, undertray, reticulated, blue and white transfer, figures, cows, and manors in rural landscape, floral borders, 10-1/2" l, 5" h **$765**

Jug, pearlware, brown transfer print, commemorating British Admiral Nelson, portrait, ship *Victory,* various nautical devices, orange enamel highlights on rim and edges of handle, minor imperfections, 6-3/4" h **$1,650**

Pitcher, dark blue transfer, View of the Erie Canal, floral borders, transfer slightly blurred, repairs, 5-7/8" h **$715**

Plate

City Hall, New York, dark blue transfer, minor wear, 9-3/4" d..........**$275**

Court House, Baltimore, blue and white transfer, fruit and flower border, printed title on reverse, light wear, hairline, 8-1/2" d **$470**

Exchange, Baltimore, blue and white transfer, fruit and floral border, printed title on reverse, 10" d..**$390**

Fulton's Steamboat, blue and white transfer, floral border, minor scratches and rim chips, 10-1/4"...........**$890**

Nahant Hotel near Boston, dark blue transfer, wear, chips on table ring, 8-3/4" d **$200**

The Dam and Waterworks, Philadelphia, blue and white transfer, fruit and flower border, printed title on reverse, 9-7/8" d **$650**

The Residence of the late Richard Jordon, New Jersey, brown, minor wear and stains, 9" d **$250**

View from Coenties-slip, scene of Great Fire, City New York, light blue transfer, wear, small edge flakes, 8" d **$385**

Platter, Sandusky, dark blue, very minor scratches, 16-5/8" l........**$8,525**

Saucer, scene of early railroad, engine and one car, floral border, dark blue, 5-7/8" d...................................**$275**

Teapot, The Residence of the Late Richard Jordan, New Jersey, brown transfer, small chip, stain and repair to lid, 8-1/4" h....................................**$715**

Tea service, partial, Mount Vernon the Seat of the Late Gen Washington, blue and white transfer, floral border, three teapots, creamer, three cov sugar bowls, waste bowl, 13 tea bowls, 12 saucers, some with printed titles, imperfections............................**$8,625**

Wood

Enoch Wood, sometimes referred to as the father of English pottery, began operating a pottery at Fountain Place, Burslem, in 1783. A cousin, Ralph Wood, was associated with him. In 1790, James Caldwell became a partner and the firm was known as Wood and Caldwell. In 1819, Wood and his sons took full control.

Enoch died in 1840. His sons continued under the name of Enoch Wood & Sons. The American views were first made in the mid-1820s and continued through the 1840s.

It is reported that the pottery produced more signed historical views than any other Staffordshire firm. Many of the views attributed to unknown makers probably came from the Woods.

Marks vary, although always include the name Wood. The establishment was sold to Messrs. Pinder, Bourne & Hope in 1846.

Creamer, horse-drawn sleigh, imp "Wood," dark blue, minor hairline in base, 5-3/4" h **$550**

Cup and saucer, handleless
Commodore MacDonnough's Victory, imp "Wood & Sons," dark blue, pinpoints on cup table ring.......... **$355**
Ship with American flag, Chancellor Livingston, imp "Wood & Sons" **$770**

Gravy boat, Catskill Mountains Hudson River, blue and white transfer, printed title, minor imperfections, 7-1/2" l.................................. **$650**

Pitcher and basin, Lafayette at Franklin's Tomb, floral and foliate borders, blue transfer dec, Burslem, England, repair on spout of pitcher, 1819-46, 4-1/2" d x 9-5/8" h pitcher, 12" d basin................................ **$1,410**

Plate
Boston State House, blue and white transfer, imp maker's mark, 1819-46, 8-1/2" d..................... **$325**
Commodore MacDonnough's Victory, shell border, blue transfer, printed titles on the front and impressed maker's marks on the reverse, c1819-46, 7-5/8" d.................. **$325**
Commodore MacDonnough's Victory, shell border, blue transfer, printed titles on the front and impressed maker's marks on the reverse, c1819-46, 9-1/8" d.................. **$300**
Commodore MacDonnough's Victory, shell border, blue transfer, printed titles on the front and impressed maker's marks on the reverse, c1819-46, 10-1/4" d................. **$300**
Constitution and Guerriere, imp

"Wood," dark blue minor scratches, 10-3/8" d **$1,760**
Cowes Harbour, blue and white transfer, shell border, imp maker's mark on reverse, light wear, 6-1/2" d **$245**
Dartmouth, ships in harbor, irregular shell border, medium blue transfer, unmarked, knife scratches, minor stains, 8-1/4" d........................ **$350**
East Cowes, Isle of Wright, shell border, blue and white transfer, 10-1/2" d **$765**
Mount Vernon, the Seat of the Late Gen'l Washington, blue and white transfer, imp maker's mark, 1819-46, 6-1/2" d **$850**
Pine Orchard House, Catskill Mountains, blue and white transfer, printed title, glaze scratches, 10-1/4" d **$575**
The Baltimore & Ohio Railroad, (incline), imp "Enoch Wood," dark blue, 9-1/4" d **$770**
The Baltimore & Ohio Railroad, (straight), imp "Wood," dark blue, minor scratches, 10-1/4" d **$825**
Transylvania University, Kentucky, shell border, dark blue, label with eagle and banner and "E Pluribus Unim," imp "Wood," 6-1/2" d .. **$775**
View of Liverpool, shell border, blue transfer, printed titles on the front and impressed maker's marks on the reverse, c1819-46, 10" d **$350**

Platter
Christianburg Danish Settlement on the Gold Coast, Africa, blue and

white transfer, imp maker's mark, minor glaze imperfections, 14-1/2" x 18-3/4"................................ **$3,220**
Highlands, Hudson River, blue and white transfer, printed title, imp maker's mark, Enoch Wood & Sons, Burslem, minor roughness, 1819-46, 10" x 12-3/4" **$3,335**
Lake George, State of New York, blue and white transfer, printed title, partial imp marker's mark, minor glaze imperfections, c1819-46, 12-3/4" x 16-1/2" **$2,585**

Sugar bowl, cov, Wadsworth Tower, blue and white transfer, scalloped shaped handles, minor imperfections, 7" d, 6" h **$265**

Tea service, partial, Wadsworth Tower, cov teapot, two large teacups, one large saucer, five teacups, six saucers, 15 plates, imperfections **$2,645**

Toddy plate, dark blue transfer, Catskill House, Hudson, imp "Wood," minor wear and stains, 6-1/2" d .. **$525**

Tureen, cov, Passaic Falls, State of New Jersey, blue and white transfer, repairs, glaze wear, 7" h **$200**

Undertray, Pass in the Catskill Mountains, blue and white transfer, imp maker's mark, printed title, repair to handle, 8-1/8" l **$200**

Waste bowl, Washington standing at Tomb, scroll in hand, blue and white transfer, unmarked, Enoch Wood & Sons, Burslem, minor imperfections, 1819-40, 6-1/4" d, 3-1/4" h **$750**

STAFFORDSHIRE ITEMS

History: A wide variety of ornamental pottery items originated in England's Staffordshire district, beginning in the 17th century and still continuing today. The height of production took place from 1820 to 1890.

Many collectors consider these naive pieces folk art. Most items were not made carefully; some even were made and decorated by children.

The types of objects are varied, e.g., animals, cottages, and figurines (chimney ornaments).

Note: The key to price is age and condition. As a general rule, the older the piece, the higher the price.

Reproduction Alert. Early Staffordshire figurines and hollowware forms were molded. Later examples were made using a slip-casting process. Slip casting leaves telltale signs that are easy to spot. Look in the interior. Hand molding created a smooth interior surface. Slip casting produces indentations that conform to the exterior design. Holes occur where handles meet the body of slip-cast pieces. There is no hole in a hand-molded piece.

A checkpoint on figurines is the firing or vent hole, which is a necessary feature on these forms. Early figurines had small holes; modern reproductions feature large holes often the size of a dime or quarter. Vent holes are found on the sides or hidden among the decoration in early Staffordshire figurines; most modern reproductions have them in the base.

These same tips can be used to spot modern reproductions of Flow Blue, Majolica, Old Sleepy Eye, Stoneware, Willow, and other ceramic pieces.

Staffordshire teapot and cover, black basalt, fruiting grapevines, wine barrel shape, England, 19th century, 4-3/4" h, **$350.**
Photo courtesy of Skinner, Inc.

Staffordshire, dog, closed legs, seated, green accents, unmarked, late 19th/ early 20th century, 12-3/4" h x 5" x 8-1/2" base, **$165.**
Photo courtesy of Green Valley Auctions.

Staffordshire, Beswick jug, no. 1214, polychrome dec, relief-molded design, impressed under base, foot band reads "ROMEO AND JULIET" and "FARE-WELL," first half 20th century, 8" h, 4"d rim, **$110.**
Photo courtesy of Green Valley Auctions.

Bank, cottage shape, repairs, 5-1/4" h **$195**

Bust, Empress Maria Theresa, England, lead glaze creamware, under-glaze translucent enamels, half bust mounted atop waisted socle, pierced hole to one shoulder factory made and apparently for holding additional ornament, slight glaze chip, late 18th C, 8-1/4" h **$1,175**

Cake stand, blue and white transfer, Wild Rose pattern, crazing, 12" d, 2-1/2" h **$400**

Candlestick, lead glazed creamware
Underglaze translucent brown, green, and blue enamels, molded tree form with applied foliage and shells, bird perched on branch, male figure standing on flat platform in center, restorations, late 18th C, 11-3/4" h **$650**

Underglaze translucent colors, free form tree with leaf molded sconce and applied florets, restorations, late 18th C, 11-1/4" h **$1,175**

Cheese dish, cov, figural, cow head, enamel and pink luster detailing, shaped undertray, 9-3/4" l, 7-1/2" h **$265**

Chimney piece
Castle with two towers, drummer, polychrome enamel dec, gilt, cole-slaw foliage, minor edge damage, 7-1/4" h **$215**
Multistoried house, coleslaw trim, pierced windows, topped with vining strawberries, some wear, hairlines, 9-1/8" h **$320**

Creamer, cow, blue and dark red splotch polychrome dec, pearl-ware, early 19th C, 7" l, 2-1/2" h **$235**

Cup and saucer, handleless, Gaudy floral design, blue, dark green, and gold, saucer imp "Clews Warranted Staffordshire," small rim flake on cup **$250**

Cup plate
Hand dec, polychrome floral wreath border, spring center, imp "TT," 3-3/4" d **$145**
Moral Maxim, red, two border reserves, 4-1/8" d **$125**
Moses and the Ten Commandments, red, floral and shell border, indiscernible imp mark, 4" d **$180**
Prunus Wreath, medium dark blue, imp "Rogers," 4" d **$165**
Sheltered Peasants, dark blue, flower and fruit border, mkd with title, 3-15/16" d **$110**

Two hunters, one seated, hunting dog, light blue, border with gun and bag, imp "D," 3-7/8" d **$100**

Figure, polychrome enamel dec
Antony and Cleopatra, reclining, silver lustered armor, England, possibly Wood and Caldwell, slight footrim chips, price for pr, early 19th C, 12" l **$2,585**
Charles Stewart Parnell, England, c1880, standing, holding shillelagh in one hand, flag bearing the Union Jack and Irish harp in other, raised title on base, Victorian, gilt wear, c1880, 13-7/8" h **$450**
Cow and calf with tree trunk vase, facing pair, Victorian, c1870, 10-7/8" h **$470**
Gordon-Cumming, modeled standing by dead lion, titled "The Lion Slayer," c1860, 16-1/2" h **$275**
King John Signing the Magna Carta, King John seated beneath tent, page to either side, Victorian, restored chip at tip of flag, pen chipped, c1865, 12-3/4" h **$300**
Male and female figures arm in arm, seated beneath arbor, Victorian, stained glaze, c1860, 13-3/4" h **$200**
Mary, standing, holding book, peasant garb, Victorian, c1860, 15-1/2" h **$200**
Napoleon III, standing, military uniform, holding cocked hat, base titled "Louis Napoleon," enamel and gilt dec, Victorian, c1855, 15-1/2" h **$200**
Prodigal's Return, two standing figures, raised title on base, gilt highlights, Victorian, c1880, 13-1/4" h **$360**
Scottish couple, matching green feathered caps, man wearing green and orange tartan, holding horn, woman holding basket, 9-1/4" h **$115**
Spaniels, seated, red and white, yellow collars, hairlines, pr, 7-5/8" h **$320**
Sportsman, orange jacket, mounted on horse, hairlines, 7" h **$350**
St. Patrick, standing, hand to heart, base titled, enamel and gilt dec, Victorian, c1860, 11-3/4" h **$215**
Templars, modeled as three officials, two women flanking bearded man, raised initials I.O.G.T. (International Order of Good Templars), Victorian, c1870, 11" h **$200**
The Lost Sheep, pearlware, shepherd wearing maroon coat, ochre striped

Staffordshire figures of William Wallace and Scottish lass, mounted as lamps, 19th century, 16-1/2", **$625.**
Photo courtesy of Sloans & Kenyon Auctioneers and Appraisers.

Staffordshire, Beswick jug, no. 1366, polychrome dec, relief-molded design, impressed under base, foot band reads "I AM A SPIRIT OF/NO COMMON RATE" and "A MIDSUMMER NIGHTS DREAM," first half 20th century, 8" h, 4" d rim, **$110.**
Photo courtesy of Green Valley Auctions.

vest and green breeches, carrying sheep with its legs tied to stick over his shoulder, rocky base and square plinth, England, small repair, 1750-85, 8-1/8" h **$530**

Turpin and King, titled bases, late Victorian, price for pr, 11" h.... **$400**

Victoria and Victor Emmanuel II, modeled standing figures, man in military attire with hound by his feet, woman in formal dress, base titled "Queen & King of Sardinia," gilt trim, Victorian, crazing, c1855, 13-3/4" h **$200**

Whippet holding rabbit in its mouth, Victorian, price for pr, one with leg damage, 10-3/4" h, second half 19th C **$425**

William Wallace, standing, holding shield in one hand, sword in other, raised title to base, Victorian, c1860, 14-3/4" h **$250**

Fruit basket and underplate, 12" l basket molded and reticulated with central guilloche band, 10" d underplate with matching rim, under-glaze blue and pink floral sprays, gilt accenting, mid-19th C **$235**

Hen on nest, polychrome, good color, minor edge wear and chips on inner flange of base, 10-1/2" l **$715**

Jar, cov, melon shape, alternating yellow and green stripes, cov with mold-ed leaf, lead glaze, hairline to cover, finial and rim chips, 18th C, 3-1/4" h **$4,315**

Jug, Fair Hebe, high relief, modeled as tree trunk, creamware, lead glaze, attributed to Yoyez, rim chip and repair, c1788, 8-1/2" h **$998**

Miniature, tea set, gaudy pink and green rose dec, 4-1/4" h teapot, creamer, sugar, waste bowl, two cups and saucers, few flakes, repairs **$425**

Mug, pearlware, black transfer print of Hope in landscape scene, silver luster highlights, minor imperfections, 3-3/4" h **$60**

Pitcher, mask, pink luster rim, glaze wear, hairline to spout, 4-7/8" h.... **$175**

Plate

New York, US, medium red, eagle and cornucopia mark, 5-7/8" d **$95**

Shannondale Springs, Virginia, US, medium red, eagle and cornucopia mark, 7-7/8" d **$70**

Platter, blue and white transfer, "The Italian Pattern," attributed to Spode, unmarked, glaze wear, scratches, early 19th C, 21" d **$575**

Sauce boat, fruit and flowers, molded feet and handle, dark blue, rim chips, 7-7/8" l.. **$330**

Stirrup cup, creamware, modeled as a stag and decorated in translucent brown and yellow enamels, lead glaze, England, restorations, 18th C, 4-3/4" l **$2,585**

Teapot, cov, black basalt, oval form, scalloped rim and classical reliefs centering columns with floral festoons, banded drapery on shoulder, incised brick banded lower body, unmarked, restored spout, early 19th C, 9-3/4" l **$360**

Toddy plate, multicolored view of thatched cottage at foot of hill, sur-mounted by castle ruins, sepia butterfly border, imp "P," 4-13/16" d.. **$90**

Tureen, cov, stoneware, white, salt glazed, oval, press molded dot and diaper, star and diaper and basket pattern, three grotesque mask and paw feet, England, rim line, repaired chips to two feet, c1760, 10-1/4" l **$2,350**

Vegetable dish, cov, domed cover with ornately molded knop and handles, blue transfer flowers, fruit, and shells, sq foot, Longport, England, minor nick to knop and cover rim, early 19th C, 10-3/4" d, 7-1/2" h **$1,410**

Waste bowl, Forget Me Not, red transfer, edge roughness, 5-5/8" d **$60**

Whistle, overglazed enamel dec, modeled as bird perched on tree trunk, applied florets, tail restored, c1820, 3-1/2" h **$420**

STAFFORDSHIRE, ROMANTIC

History: In the 1830s, two factors transformed the blue-and-white printed wares of the Staffordshire potters into what is now called "Romantic Staffordshire." Technical innovations expanded the range of transfer-printed colors to light blue, pink, purple, black, green, and brown. There was also a shift from historical to imaginary scenes with less printed detail and more white space, adding to the pastel effect.

Shapes from the 1830s are predominately rococo with rounded forms, scrolled handles, and floral finials. Over time, patterns and shapes became simpler and the earthenware bodies coarser. The late 1840s and 1850s saw angular gothic shapes and pieces with the weight and texture of ironstone.

The most dramatic post-1870 change was the impact of the craze for all things Japanese. Staffordshire designs adopted zigzag border elements and motifs such as bamboo, fans, and cranes. Brown printing dominated this style, sometimes with polychrome enamel highlights.

Marks: Wares are often marked with pattern or potter's names, but marking was inconsistent and many authentic, unmarked examples exist. The addition of "England" as a country of origin mark in 1891 helps to distinguish 20th-century wares made in the romantic style.

Caledonia, Williams Adams, 1830s
Plate, purple transfer, imp "Adams," 9-1/2" d **$60**
Platter, 17" l **$500**
Soup plate, two colors **$175**

Canova, Thomas Mayer, c1835; G. Phillips, c1840
Plate, 10-1/2" d **$95**
Pudding bowl, two colors **$200**
Vegetable, cov **$325**

Cheshire pattern, Burleigh Ware, cheese dish, cov, rect, sloped lid, underglaze blue ovoid finial, rect undertray, transfer printed green and blue, dish 9-1/4" l, 5" h **$115**

Columbia, W. Adams & Sons, 1850
Creamer **$115**
Cup and saucer **$65**
Cup plate **$65**
Plate, 10" d **$60**
Relish... **$65**

Dado, Ridgways, 1880s
Creamer, brown **$75**
Cup and saucer, polychrome **$80**
Plate, brown, 7-1/2" d **$35**

Dr. Syntax, James and Ralph Clews, Cobridge, 1819-36
Plate, Dr. Syntax Disputing his Bill with the Landlady, blue and white transfer, 10-1/2" d **$125**
Platter, Dr. Syntax Amused with Pat in the Pond, blue and white transfer, glaze scratches, scattered minor staining, 14-1/4" x 19" **$1,840**
Undertray, Death of Punch, Dr. Syntax literary series, blue and white transfer, crazing on reverse, 10" x 5-3/4" **$85**

Marmora, William Ridgway & Co., 1830s
Platter, 16-1/2" l **$325**
Sauce tureen, matching tray **$350**

Soup plate **$100**
Millenium, Ralph Stevenson & Son, 1830s, plate, 10-1/2" d **$145**
Palestine, William Adams, 1836
Creamer and sugar **$265**
Cup and saucer, two colors **$135**
Cup plate **$75**
Platter, 13" l **$325**
Vegetable, open, 12" l **$200**
Quadrupeds, John Hall, 1814-32
Plate, central medallion with lion, printed maker's mark, pattern mark in crown, price for pr, 10" d **$865**
Platter, Quadrupeds pattern, central cartouche of elephant, printed maker's mark, pattern mark in crown, minor surface imperfections, 14-3/4" x 19" **$4,315**
Shell pattern, Stubbs and Kent, Longport, 1828-30
Cream jug, blue and white transfer, unmarked, imperfections, 5" h **$1,200**
Milk pitcher, blue and white transfer, unmarked, imperfections, 7" h .. **$900**
Platter, oval, blue and white transfer, imp maker's mark, repaired rim chip, 18-1/2" l **$1,955**
Soup plate, blue and white transfer, imp maker's mark, wear, price for three, 10" d **$750**
Tea bowl and saucer, blue and white transfer, imp maker's mark, 2-1/2" h **$450**
Vegetable dish, oval, blue and white transfer, imp maker's mark, scratches, wear, 12-1/4" d, 2-1/2" h ... **$1,150**
Union, William Ridgway Son & Co., 1840s
Plate, 10-1/2" d **$70**
Platter, 15" l **$165**
Unknown pattern
Cup and Saucer, two dogs, flower and leaf border, imp maker's mark for James & Ralph Clews, Cobridge, minor light wear, 1817-34, 2-1/4" h, 5-3/4" h **$150**
Tea Set, partial, blue and white transfer
Bird in oval reverse, floral border, two teapots, creamer, small bowl, waste bowl, imperfections **$1,265**
Three figures in landscape, manor house in distance, teapot, creamer, and two cov sugar bowls **$1,610**
Venus, Podmore, Walker & Co., 1850s, plate, 7-1/2" d **$50**
Yorkshire, soup plate, light blue, slight glaze lines, 10" d **$200**

Romantic Staffordshire coffeepot, blue transfer decoration, Oriental-type scene, **$350.**
Photo courtesy of Dotta Auction Co., Inc.

STANGL POTTERY BIRDS

History: Stangl ceramic birds were produced from 1940 until the Stangl factory closed in 1978. The birds were produced at Stangl's Trenton plant and either decorated there or shipped to its Flemington, New Jersey, outlet for hand painting.

During World War II, the demand for these birds, and other types of Stangl pottery as well, was so great that 40 to 60 decorators could not keep up with the demand. Orders were contracted out to be decorated by individuals in their own homes. These orders then were returned for firing and finishing. Colors used to decorate these birds varied according to the artist.

Marks: As many as 10 different trademarks were used. Almost every bird is numbered; many are artist signed. However, the signatures are used only for dating purposes and add very little to the value of the birds.

Note: Several birds were reissued between 1972 and 1977. These reissues are dated on the bottom and are worth approximately the same as older birds, if well decorated.

3250, preening duck, natural colors $125
3273, rooster, 5-3/4" h $800
3274, penguin $500
3276, bluebird $90
3281, mother duck $600
3285, rooster, early blue green base, 4-1/2" h $100
3400, lovebird, old, wavy base $135
3400, lovebird, revised leaf base $75
3402, pair of orioles, revised ... $115
3402, pair of orioles, old $300
3404, pair of lovebirds, old $400
3404, pair of lovebirds, revised $125
3405, pair of cockatoos, revised, open base $150
3406, pair of kingfishers, blue $165
3407, owl $350
3430, duck, 22" $8,000
3431, duck, standing, brown $850
3432, rooster, 16" h $3,500
3443, flying duck, teal $250
3445, rooster, yellow $185
3446, hen, gray $300
3450, passenger pigeon $1,800
3451, William Ptarmigan $3,500
3453, mountain bluebird $1,500

3454, Key West quail dove, single wing up $275
3454, Key West quail dove, both wings up $1,800
3455, shoveler duck $2,000
3457, walking pheasant $3,500
3458, quail $2,000
3490, pair of redstarts $200
3492, cock pheasant $225
3518, pair of white-headed pigeons $950
3580, cockatoo, medium $150
3580, cockatoo, medium, white $600
3581, group of chickadees, black and white $300
3582, pair of green parakeets $225
3582, pair of blue parakeets $250
3584, cockatoo, large $275
3590, chat $165
3591, Brewers blackbird $160
3595, Bobolink $150
3596, gray cardinal $80
3597, Wilson warbler, yellow $55
3599, pair of hummingbirds $325
3625, Bird of Paradise, large, 13-1/2" h $2,500
3634, Allen hummingbird $90
3635, group of goldfinches $215

3717, pair of blue jays $3,500
3746, canary, rose flower $250
3749, scarlet tanager $425
3750, pair of western tanagers $500
3751, red-headed woodpecker, pink glossy $300
3752, pair of red-headed woodpeckers, red matte $550
3754, pair of white-winged crossbills, pink glossy $425
3755, audubon warbler $475
3756, pair of audubon warblers $600
3758, magpie jay $1,400
3810, blackpoll warber $185
3811, chestnut chickadee $145
3812, chestnut-sided warbler $150
3813, evening grosbeak $150
3814, blackthroated green warbler $165
3815, western bluebird $440
3848, golden crowned kinglet $125
3852, cliff swallow $170
3853, group of golden crowned kingfishers $780
3868, summer tanager $750
3921, yellow-headed verdin $1,700
3922, European finch $1,200
3924, yellow-throated warbler $680

Stangl fish hawk, osprey, impressed STANGL U.S.A./3459, 10" x 11", **$4,500.**
Photo courtesy of David Rago Auctions, Inc.

Stoneware crock, five gallon, "Butter," dated 1862, 13" h, 11-1/2" d, **$500.**
Photo courtesy of Pook & Pook, Inc.

Stoneware crock, 1-1/2 gallon, "S. Hemingway 132 Newark Ave. Jersey City," 8-1/4" h, **$295.**
Photo courtesy of Pook & Pook, Inc.

Stoneware crock, four gallon, "A.B. Wheeler & Co. Boston, Mass.," cobalt floral dec, 19th century, 11-1/4" h, 11-1/4" d, **$380.**
Photo courtesy of Pook & Pook, Inc.

Stoneware churn, salt glazed, galleried rim, applied handles, cobalt stenciled 6 capacity, stenciled and freehand dec, period wooden lid and dasher, second half 19th century, 18" h, 9-1/2" d rim, **$715.**
Photo courtesy of Green Valley Auctions.

STONEWARE

History: Made from dense kaolin and commonly salt-glazed, stonewares were hand-thrown and high-fired to produce a simple, bold, vitreous pottery. Stoneware crocks, jugs, and jars were made to store products and fill other utilitarian needs. These intended purposes dictated shape and design—solid, thick-walled forms with heavy rims, necks, and handles and with little or no embellishment. Any decorations were simple: brushed cobalt oxide, incised, slip trailed, stamped, or tooled.

Stoneware has been made for centuries. Early American settlers imported stoneware items at first. As English and European potters refined their earthenware, colonists began to produce their own wares. Two major North American traditions emerged based only on location or type of clay. North Jersey and parts of New York comprise the first area; the second was eastern Pennsylvania spreading westward and into Maryland, Virginia, and West Virginia. These two distinct geographical boundaries, style of decoration, and shape are discernible factors in classifying and dating early stoneware.

By the late 18th century, stoneware was manufactured in all sections of the country. This vigorous industry flourished during the 19th century until glass fruit jars appeared and the use of refrigeration became widespread. By 1910, commercial production of salt-glazed stoneware came to an end.

Stoneware bean pot, cobalt highlights, orig lid, "BOSTON BAKED BEANS" on side, White's Pottery, Utica, NY, late 19th century, 7" h, 5" d rim, **$110.**
Photo courtesy of Green Valley Auctions.

Advertising

Butter crock, 1 lb size, "Western Dairy Company Pasture Queen Butter, Chicago, Ill," hairline **$90**

Jug, J. Fisher, Lyons, New York, 1 gal, blue script on front "Collins & Jordan 351 Elk St Buffalo, NY," minor wear and staining from use, c1870, 10-1/2" h **$315**

Jug, unsigned, half gal, Bristol glaze, stenciled under glaze "This Jug Not To be Sold Registered," blue script "Hollander Bros., 1-3-5 Main St, Paterson, NJ," glaze flakes throughout, glaze chipping at spout, c1880, 9" h **$440**

Preserve jar, S. Hart, 3 gal, imp and blue accents, "Crawfords & Murdock, Dealers in Dry Goods Groceries, Clothing Crokery & Hardware, Pulaskie, NY," blue script "3" surrounded by brushed plumes below store mark, professional restoration to rim chip at front, c1875, 12-1/2" h **$385**

Rolling pin, cobalt blue wildflower dec, "John Quast & Son Furniture, Pianos-Undertaking, Buffalo Lake, Minn" **$665**

Rolling pin, "Mix with Us and Save Dough, H. D. Bryam & Son General Mdse & Drugs," blue bands **$485**

Stoneware crock, three gallon, double-sided cobalt floral dec, 19th century, 14", $350.
Photo courtesy of Pook & Pook, Inc.

Stoneware crock, unsigned, attributed to New York state, brushed and sponge blue horse design below gallon mark, c1870, 8" h, $4,400.
Photo courtesy of Bruce & Vicki Wassdorp.

Stoneware jar, salt glazed, five gallon, straight sided, applied handles, slip-trailed cobalt tobacco leaf dec, wire under rim supporting bail handles of a later date, hairline off rim, second half 19th century, 13" h, 12-1/2" rim, $193.
Photo courtesy of Green Valley Auctions.

Batter jug, Cowden and Wilcox, Harrisburg, Pennsylvania, scrolling floral dec, orig bail handle, tin spout, tin spout cover, 8-1/2" h...............**$7,000**

Batter pail
N. White & Co., Binghamton, blue brush accents at ears, handle, spout, and impressed name, orig bail handle, surface chip under spout, c1860, 8-1/2" h.........................**$415**

Unsigned, attributed to Whites, Utica, one gal, cobalt blue slip leaf below spout on front, orig bail handle, c1865, 9" h **$615**

Unsigned, attributed to White's, Utica, six quarts, imp "6," oak leaf design under spout, orig bale handle, short tight hairline, c1865, 6" h **$330**

Unsigned, attributed to Whites, Utica, six quarts, navy blue hollyhock dec, professional restoration to rim chips and lug handle, c1865, 10" h
....**$360**

Bottle
Imp and blue accented "B. F. Haley California Pop Beer 1889," glaze drip at shoulder to right of imp name, 10" h
....**$135**

Imp and blue accented "C. F. Washburn," minor crow's foot at shoulder, 9-1/2" h **$35**

Butter churn
H. M. Whitman, Havana, New York, five gal, dasher guide, top to bottom iris dec, blue at name and gallon designation, long in-body thru line that runs thru design on left side, c1860, 18" h **$2,200**

J Burger Jr, Rochester, New York, six gal, dotted bird on stump dec, blue accent at maker's mark, professional restoration, c1885, 20" h **$1,210**

J Norton & Co., Bennington, Vermont, six gal, orig dasher guide, flowering cornucopia of flowers, some very minor staining, 3" very tight lie on side, c1861, 19" h **$8,250**

Joshua J. German, Muskingum County, Ohio, five gal, imp "5" capacity mark, raised initials "JJG" hidden in the mark that was filled in with raised dots, incised owl, stenciled C. C. Rankin, (Newark, OH grocer), badly cracked, wide metal band and wire around rim to stabilize it, ex-Clark Garrett...........................**$4,800**

West Troy, New York, Pottery, six gal, stoneware guide, blue dec, bird perched in large tree stump, restoration to glaze flaking, c1880, 19" h
....**$1,020**

White & Wood, Binghamton, New York, five gal, dasher guide, top to bottom paddletail dec, double flower branch, fully filled bird's body, long surface chip at front worn smooth from use, c1885, 17-1/2" h
....**$8,800**

Whites, Utica, four gal, ribbed orchid dec, possible fire damage on left side, ear missing, c1865, 16" h
....**$330**

Cake crock, cov
J. & E Norton, Bennington, Vermont, c1855, two gal, dotted reclining deer with fences, pine tree, tree stump, ground cover, two extremely tight hairlines at back of right ear, 12" d, 7-1/2" h.....................**$18,700**

Salt glazed, stamped "John Bell, Waynesboro" under lid and handle, 8" d, 4-3/4" h.........................**$3,850**

Stoneware crock, blue stenciled decoration, E.J. Miller & Co., Alexandria, VA, late 19th century, 11-1/2" h, $472.
Photo courtesy of Sloans & Kenyon Auctioneers and Appraisers.

Stoneware crock, Cowden & Wilcox, Harrisburg, PA, cobalt blue leaf decoration, 8-1/2" d, 7-1/2" h, $225.
Photo courtesy of Joy Luke Auctions.

Stoneware jug, two gallon, "A.B. Wheeler & Co. 69 Broad Street Boston, Mass.," cobalt dec, 19th century, 14" h, **$410.**
Photo courtesy of Pook & Pook, Inc.

Stoneware jug, three gallon, cobalt inscription "C.N. Guerlice 334 Warren St. Hudson N.Y.," New York, 19th century, 16" h, **$410.**
Photo courtesy of Pook & Pook, Inc.

Stoneware jug, three gallon, cobalt bird decoration, 15", **$470.**
Photo courtesy of Pook & Pook, Inc.

Salt glazed, applied handles, stamped under handle, cobalt blue floral dec, attributed to Peter Hermann, Baltimore, 13" d, 7-1/2" h **$1,925**

Canning jar, unsigned, 1 gal, four wide accent stripes across front, stack mark, glaze burns on left side, c1850, 9-1/2" h **$110**

Chicken waterer, unsigned, probably Pennsylvania origin, 1 gal, imp "I" at shoulder, brushed blue accents at button top and inner and out rim of watering hole, c1840, 11" h **$415**

Cream pot

Brady & Ryan, Ellenville, New York, 6 quarts, singing bird on dotted branch, imp "6" below maker's name, extensive glaze flaking at rim and spots on back, c1885, 8-1/2" h **$180**

Roberts, Binghamton, New York, 1 gal, bird on branch, ext. rim chip on back, c1860, 7-1/2" h **$770**

T. Harrington Lyons, two gal, brushed wreath surrounding gallon designation, couple of minor surface chips at rim in back, c1865, 10-1/2" h **$330**

Crock, cov

Four gal, straight sided, two handles, "No. 4" stamped on side, copious cobalt blue floral dec, line repair on side **$2,420**

Three gal, floral cobalt blue banding, "No. 3" stamped on side, two handles, 11" d, 14-1/2" h **$1,155**

Crock

Brady & Ryan, Ellenville, New York, two gal, singing bird on plume, professional restoration, c1885, 9" h **$550**

D. Mooney, Ithaca, NY, pail shape, brushed blue dec, somewhat overglazed in the firing, c1862, 8" h **$330**

E & L P Norton, Bennington, VT, three gal, bird on plume dec, small stone ping in design, c1880, 10-1/2" h **$360**

F. B. Norton & Co., Worcester, Mass, three gal, chicken pecking corn design, blue at maker's mark and imp gallon designation, thick blue cobalt application, c1870, 10-1/2" h ... **$3,850**

J. Clark & Co., Troy, two gal, ovoid, simple brushed design, blue at deeply imp maker's mark, blue accents under ears, couple of surface chips at rim, c1826, 9-1/2" h **$360**

J Fisher Lyons NY, five gal, "Lyons" in artistic script across front, some surface roughness at rim, age spider line, c1880, 13" h **$275**

Lyons, two gal, double tulip dec, blue accents at name and ears, stained from use, c1860, 9" h **$165**

N. A. White & Son, Utica, NY, five gal, flying bird dec, floral wreath, artistically shaded tail feathers, professional restoration, c1870, 12-1/2" h **$3,960**

N York Corlears Hook Commeraws, two gal, ovoid, applied open handles, deep incised and blue accented clamshell swag design all along shoulder, deep signature impression, stack mark and kiln burn on one side, minor surface wear at base, c1805............................ **$5,390**

Paul Cushman, Albany, approx 1-1/2 gal, brush blue accents, deeply impressed name, blue accent at handles, three petal lightly brushed flower on back, deeply tooled diamond and leaf pattern all around extended rim, cinnamon clay color in the making, c1807, 9-1/2" h **$2,530**

Paul Cushman Stoneware Factory, 1 gal, deeply impressed unusual maker's mark, blue handles, large stone ping thru name, restoration to full-length hairline on back, c1807, 11" h **$1,980**

Salt glazed, attributed to Pfaltzgraff, York, PA, bulbous, flared rim, incised banding at top, cobalt blue dec tulip, int. brown glaze, small line at top rim, 4-3/4" d, 4-3/4" h **$3,960**

Three gal, Eagle Pottery, eagle stencil **$1,765**

Three gal, ovoid, freehand dec of cat-like face **$19,000**

Three gal, America, early 19th C, salt glazed, cylindrical form, brown

Albany slip interior, applied lug handles, impressed cow motif filled with cobalt blue, 10" h **$900**

Three gal, Wedding Proposal, NY **$10,450**

Troy, NY, Pottery, four gal, large dotted and stylized leaf and floral design, some glaze flakes, c1870, 11" h **$360**

Two gal, B. C. Milburn, Alexandra, VA, sunflower and flourishes **$3,520**

Unsigned, attributed to Crolius, NY, three gal, ovoid, thick blue draped design all around shoulder, blue accents at open handles, overall stained from use, old age cracks, c1800, 13" h **$500**

Unsigned, attributed to Macquoid & Co. Pottery Works, New York City, 1 gal, Victorian style woman's profile on front, minor staining, 3" tight hairline, c1870, 7" h **$4,620**

Weston & Gregg, Ellenville, NY, six gal, large bird on detailed plume, blue accent at deeply imp maker's mark, Y-shaped through line extending along bottom, c1869, 12-1/2" h **$1,155**

Whites, Utica, three gal, standing stag among ground cover, dry glaze in the making, c1865, 10-1/2" h **$3,190**

Face jug, black man, caricatured features, imperfections, 6-1/2" h.. **$4,600**

Flask, unsigned, brushed blue tree dec, design repeated on both sides, incised reeded accents at neck, minor surface wear at base, stack mark, c1810, 6-1/2" h **$2,630**

Jar

Attributed to New York or New Jersey, salt-glazed, wide-mouth ovoid, applied open loop handles, cobalt blue inscriptions around shoulder, (some indistinct) "Mark PBH N???29 1797," minor chips, c1797, 9-1/4" h **$3,100**

N. Clark & Co., Lyons, one gal, ovoid, stoneware lid, brush blue lollipop flower, blue accents at ears and maker's mark, minor surface chip, 10-1/2" h **$690**

Jug

America, imp "2" below top, cobalt blue bird with high comb and long bill perched on large leaf, light staining, early 19th C, 13" h **$420**

America, salt glazed, ovoid, applied strap handle, cobalt blue stylized head of an animal, minor base chip, early 19th C, 13-5/8" h **$1,100**

America, salt-glazed, ovoid, applied strap handle, cobalt blue "1833," few minor rim chips, 1833, 15-3/8" h **$600**

Humiston & Stockwell, S. Amboy, New Jersey, three gal, ovoid, large brushed flower design, pin head size flake at top of lip, stack mark on side, c1830, 15" h **$1,890**

J. Clark & Co., Troy, two gal, brushed blue flower dec, blue at marker's mark, stack mark at top, c1827, 14-1/2" h **$220**

J & E Norton, Bennington, Vermont, two gal, peacock dec, minor stone ping at back near handle, c1855, 14" h **$4,950**

J & E Norton, Bennington, Vermont, three gal, compote of flowers, thick glassy cobalt, professional restoration, some staining from use, c1855, 16" h **$550**

J Fisher & Co, Lyons, New York, two gal, bee stinger dec, minor glaze burning, large glaze drips at shoulder and back, c1880, 13-1/2" h **$180**

N. A. White & Son, Utica, New York, two gal, paddletail bird, ribbed wings, head, and beak, kiln burn, stone ping, c1870, 14" h **$1,595**

N. Clark Jr., Athens, New York, five gal, double handled, brushed blue bird with dotted wing perched on flowering branch, blue at maker's mark, very tight jagged hairlines extend down from rim and thru pottery's mark, c1850, 18-1/2" h **$935**

Lyons, two gal, large brushed leaf design, some over glazing at shoulder, c1865, 13-1/2" h **$165**

S Hart Fulton, three gal, signature double love birds, staining from use, long J-shaped glued crack on back, c1875, 13-1/2" h............. **$500**

W. Hart, Ogdensburgh, four gal, horse-head design, blue at name, minor stone pings in the making, c1860, 16" h **$17,325**

Whites, Binghamton, two gal, dotted double poppy dec, professional restoration to tight line, c1860, 12-1/2" h **$275**

Whites, Utica, one gal, long tailed bird, blue at maker's mark, very tight lie in handle, short clay separation line at base, c1865, 11-1/2" h **$880**

Keg, unmarked, ovoid, incised bands, painted cobalt blue pinwheels, stars,

and leaves, molded relief dec of man's head, ex-Clark Garrett, 13-3/4" h **$10,000**

Milk pitcher, unsigned, Shenandoah Valley origin, attributed to Remmey factory, three gal, brushed blue floral design fills entire front, professional restoration to handle, partially replaced, c1850, 17" h **$1,210**

Mug, Shenandoah Valley, incised banding, single cobalt blue flower and leaves on each side, bottom initialed "L. B.," attributed to Levi Dice Bell, 4-1/2" h, 4-1/4" d **$2,090**

Pitcher

J. Burger, Rochester, New York, 1 gal, blue accents at handle and imp name, bow tie dec, c1880, 11" h **$615**

Ovoid, applied handle, brushed cobalt blue flower with long leaves, three flourishes around rim at handle, interior with grown glaze, hairline at base, 7" h.............................. **$675**

Unsigned, attributed to Lyons, New York, factory, 1 gal, wreath surrounding floral design, blue accent at handle, cobalt blue has bled because of heavy application by potter, surface chip at spout may be in the making, c1860, 10-1/2" h ..**$330**

Whites, Binghamton, incised line around middle, raised rim, cobalt blue polka dot floral dec, 10" h **$615**

Plaque, emb with Daniel and the lion, 5" x 6" **$1,800**

Preserve jar

1-1/2 gal, J. Norton & Co., Bennington, Vermont, stylized flower design, blue at deeply imp maker's mark, c1861, 11" h **$2,420**

1-1/2 gal, Little West, 12th St. N. Pottery Works, double dropping flower design, two short clay separation lines at rim probably occurred in making, c1870, 10" h **$495**

1-1/2 gal, unknown maker, military general, orig lid **$18,700**

Two gal, A. O. Whittemore, Havana, New York, squat, blue flower design, blue "2" and blue at maker's mark, couple of short hairlines, c1870, 10" h **$310**

Two gal, Brady & Ryan, Ellenville, New York, fitted stoneware lid, bushy tailed bird on dotted plume dec in bright blue, surface chip on lid, mottled clay color in the making, c1885, 12" h **$470**

Stoneware jar, salt glazed, three gallons, ovoid form, applied handles, incised rings below squared rim, heavy beaded foot, freehand cobalt dec of a monument flying the American flag, floral dec on sides, reverse has capacity mark above floral dec, depicts either Washington Monument at Fell's Point, MD, or pre-construction image of Washington Monument in D.C., several chips, body wear, tight base hairline, second quarter 19th century, 14" h, 7-5/8" d rim, 8" d base, **$6,050.**

Photo courtesy of Green Valley Auctions.

Stoneware butter churn, five gallons, New York Stoneware Co., Fort Edward, New York, bull's eye stylized flower design, c1880, 17-1/2" h, **$330.**

Photo courtesy of Bruce & Vicki Wassdorp.

Two gal, F. Stetzenmeyer & G. Goetzman, Rochester, New York, blue dec ribbed leaf and flower bud design, long glaze spider on side, c1857, 11" h **$990**

Two gal, Harrington & Burger, Rochester, bowed wreath design, script blue in center of wreath, blue at name, int. short clay separation line at rim occurred in making, c1853, 11" h **$330**

Two gal, J & E Norton, Bennington, Vermont, peacock on stump design, short clay separation lines that occurring in the making, c1855..........**$635**

Two gal, John Burger, Rochester, orig stoneware lid, triple fern design surrounds large "2," minor crow's foot glaze spider on side, c1865, 11-1/2" h **$580**

Two gal, N. Clark & Co., Rochester, New York, stoneware lid, finely executed floral design, int. lime staining, couple of surface chips at rim, stone ping on side, c1850, 11-1/2" d **$1,760**

Two gal, T. Harrington Lyons, bull's eye wreath design, two blue "2"s, light blue at maker's mark, professional restoration to surface chips around rim and full-length hairline at back, c1850 ....**$415**

Two gal, W. Hart Ogendsburg, orig lid, signature horse head design, cinnamon clay color, dry glaze in the making, chips, surface wear, staining from use, hairline at rim at back, c1860 ....**$3,300**

Three gal, Cortland, brushed plume design, blue accent at name, minor surface chips from use, c1850, 12" h **$165**

Stoneware cake crock, four gallons, unsigned, attributed to New York state, bold flower and leaf decoration, some staining from use, 2" clay separation in the base that occurred in the making, c1870, 9-1/2" h, **$275.**

Photo courtesy of Bruce & Vicki Wassdorp.

Three gal, J & F Norton, Bennington, antlered and spotted deer in landscape with trees and fences, ex-Clark Garrett, surface edge chip to handle **$16,000**

Three gal, N. A. White & Son, Utica, New York, wide paddletail bird, very minor design fry to thick blue, c1868, 13-1/2" h **$3,520**

Four gal, Buffalo, New York, rooster, orig lid, few hairline cracks, c1870 ....**$34,100**

Five gal, freehand dec of Colonial-era soldier, long coat, broad rimmed hat, holding riffle, handle, 15-3/4" h **$14,000**

Five gal, freehand dec of standing woman in long dress, tulips on either side, circled "V" **$9,000**

Five gal, freehand dec of woman holding garment, standing between two trees above standing peacock and two more trees, 15-3/4" h **$19,000**

Water cooler

Gates City, patented May 25, 1886, six quarts, stoneware lid, orig spigot, cobalt blue bird dec, 11" h **$935**

Henry Dilts, Ohio, 12 gal, two handles, elaborate tree emblem and Masonic compass, incised "12," ex-Clark Garrett, handles and some lip missing **$11,000**

J & E Norton, Bennington, Vermont, six gal, barrel shape, incised and blue accented horizontal lines frame dotted centerpiece floral design, additional blue dotted accents at bung hole, X-shaped spider line to left of design, c1855, 15-1/2" h **$1,760**

Somerset Potters Works, three gal, elaborate incised double bird dec, blue accents at ears, maker's mark, blue dabs and brush blue leaf designs at rim and front, brushed, potted, double flower design on back, kiln burn on front, glued crack, chip out of bung hole frame that may have occurred during the making, c1870, 15" h **$3,960**

Whimsy, slice of watermelon, orig paint, ex-Clark Garrett, c1900, 7" l **$5,500**

Whistle, figural, Rockingham glaze, c1870

Bird, chips in glaze, 1-1/2" h **$90**

Owl on stump, 3-1/2" h...............**$220**

Seated poodle, 3-3/4" h...............**$250**

TEAPOTS

History: The origins of the teapot have been traced to China in the late 16th century. Early Yixing teapots were no bigger than the tiny cups previously used for drinking tea. By the 17th century, tea had spread to civilized nations of the world. The first recorded advertisement for tea in London is dated 1658 and called a "China drink…call Tcha, by other Nations Tay, alias Tee…" Although coffee houses were already established, they began to add tea to their selections.

From the very first teapots, figural shapes have always been a favorite with tea drinkers. The Victorian era saw a change from more utilitarian teapots toward beautiful, floral, and Rococo designs, yet figural pots continued to be manufactured.

Early American manufacturers mimicked Oriental and British designs. While the new land demanded sturdy teapots in the unsettled land, potteries were established steadily in the Eastern states. Rockingham teapots were produced by many companies, deriving this term from British companies manufacturing a strong, shiny brown glaze on heavy pottery. The best known is from the Bennington, Vermont, potteries.

By the 1800s and the turn-of-the-century, many pottery companies were well established in the U. S., producing a lighter dinnerware and china including teapots. Figural teapots from this era are highly desired by collectors, while others concentrate on collecting all known patterns produced by a company.

The last 20 years have seen a renewed interest in teapots and collectors desire not only older examples, but also high-priced, specialty manufactured teapots or individual artist creations commanding hundreds of dollars.

Teapot, Copeland, earthenware, hexagonal, underglaze blue and burnt orange Imari-style dec, Robert Burns quotation on rim, foo dog finial, mid-19th century, 6" h, **$264.**
Photo courtesy of Skinner, Inc.

Teapot, Chinese blue and white, porcelain, fan-shaped reserves with branches, blue ground, Yongzheng period, 1723-1735, **$770.**
Photo courtesy of Sloans & Kenyon Auctioneers and Appraisers.

Reproduction Alert. Teapots and other ware with a blurry mark of a shield and two animals, ironstone, celadon-colored body background, and a design made to look like flow blue, are new products, possibly from China. Yixing teapots have been reproduced or made in similar styles for centuries.

Basalt, black, oval form, scalloped rim and classical relief centering columns with floral festoons, banded drapery on shoulder, incised brick banded lower body, unmarked, England, restored spout, early 19th C, 9-3/4" l **$360**

Cloisonné, panel with butterflies and flowers, Chinese, late 19th C **$450**

Earthenware, brown and green speckled ext., matching lid, c1880, 7" h.. **$420**

Flow blue, Scinde pattern, Alcock, octagonal, 8-1/2" h **$950**

Graniteware, large teapot with pewter handle, lid and spout, Manning Bowman & Co. Manufacturers, called Perfection Granite Ironware, West Meriden, Connecticut **$325**

Ironstone, Mason's Ironstone, Vista pattern, red and white scenic dec, matching trivet **$195**

Majolica, fish, multicolored, Minton, no mark, late 1800s **$2,000**

Pratt, pearlware, underglaze polychrome enamels on oval forms molded with ribbed bodies and central medallions of classical reliefs, swan finial, slight flake and line to cover, chipped spout, 6" h **$450**

Rockingham glaze, brown glaze, tree trunk form body, molded fruiting vines, branch handle, twig finial, imp Wedgwood, England, mark, chip to cover collar, c1870, 4-3/8" h ... **$520**

Silver, Hester Bateman, London, oval, domed lid with beaded rim, engraved bands, body with engraved bands and central cartouche, wood ear handle and finial, approx 13 troy oz, 1786, 5-3/4" h..................................... **$3,450**

Wedgwood, Rosso Antico, Egyptian, applied black basalt hieroglyphs, crocodile finial, imp mark, slight chips to rim and spout, early 19th C, 7-1/4" l.................................... **$1,100**

Yang-Tz-u, enameled, hexagonal, bright polychrome painted mountainous landscapes on each panel, imitation famille rose and jaune dec top and borders, Chinese export, professional repairs on spout, lid, and handle, 19th C, 8-1/4" h **$250**

Teapot, Meissen, ovoid, short griffin's head spout, angular handle ending in shell, enamel dec with scattered foliates, flower bud finial on lid, 18th/19th century, 4-5/8", **$590.**
Photo courtesy of Skinner, Inc.

Teapot and cover, Wedgwood, dark blue Jasper dip, England, cylindrical shape, applied white classical relief and foliate borders, impressed mark, early 19th century, 4-1/2" h, **$528.**
Photo courtesy of Skinner, Inc.

Terra-cotta wall relief, three-dimensional head, green and blue matte glazes, incised signature of G. Staindl, 15-1/2" x 10-1/2" x 2-1/2", $235.
Photo courtesy of David Rago Auctions, Inc.

TERRA-COTTA WARE

History: Terra-cotta is ware made of hard, semi-fired ceramic. The color of the pottery ranges from a light orange-brown to a deep brownish red. It is usually unglazed, but some pieces are partially glazed and have incised, carved, or slip designs. Utilitarian objects, as well as statuettes and large architectural pieces, were made. Fine early Chinese terra-cotta pieces recently have sold for substantial prices.

Architectural element, foo lion, scribed character on sides, fish scale design on bodies, small saddles carry filled bags, flat base, price for pr, base and edge chips, 22" w, 22" h **$425**

Bowl, glazed, 6" d, 2" h **$30**

Bust, good detail, dark red patina, hollow interior, firing separation noticeable from underside, nose restored, 10-1/2" w, 10" h **$125**

Figure
Aphrodite, dressed in tunic, open back, South Italian, third century B.C., 7-1/2" h **$345**
St. Joseph, wearing long loose robes, black hat, polychrome dec, Spanish, 19th C, 11" h **$600**
Reclining male figure with dog, inscribed "Claude Janin," 18-3/4" l **$400**

Pedestal, price for pr, 7" sq top, 24" h **$400**

Planter, garland and mask motif, 10-1/4" h **$100**

Portrait plaque, Benjamin Franklin, circular shape, self-framed with raised title "B. Franklin Americain" surrounding portrait in relief, sgd "Nini" (for Jean Baptiste Nini) dated 1777, unidentified impressed fleur-de-lis mark, France, mounted in ebonized wood frame, shallow rim nicks, 4-1/2" d **$1,410**

Statue, Minera, woman in draped toga, grape and cable head dress, holding wine cup, 55" h **$2,000**

Urn, molded putti and foliage dec, green glaze, waisted neck, two handles, circular base, 29-1/2" h **$395**

Water pitcher, base chip, c1810, 13" h **$325**

TILES

History: The use of decorated tiles peaked during the latter part of the 19th century. More than 100 companies in England alone were producing tiles by 1880. By 1890, companies had opened in Belgium, France, Australia, Germany, and the United States.

Tiles were not used only as fireplace adornments. Many were installed into furniture, such as washstands, hall stands, and folding screens. Since tiles were easily cleaned and, hence, hygienic, they were installed on the floors and walls of entry halls, hospitals, butcher shops, or any place where sanitation was a concern.

Note: Condition is an important factor in determining price. A cracked, badly scuffed and scratched, or heavily chipped tile has very little value. Slight chipping around the outer edges of a tile is, at times, considered acceptable by collectors, especially if a frame can cover these chips.

It is not uncommon for the highly glazed surface of some tiles to have become crazed. Crazing is not considered detrimental as long as it does not detract from the overall appearance of the tile.

Art pottery, landscape with birds and moose in foreground, dark green high gloss glaze, 6" h, 12" w **$175**

Arts & Crafts, framed, scene of salt marsh landscape, blues, greens, and white, c1907, 10" x 5-1/2" **$2,100**

Batchelder, beige bisque clay with blue engobe, stamped "Batchelder/ Los Angeles," 6" h, 18" l
Bouquet of flowers and birds, slight abrasion to surface **$375**
California desert landscape, abrasion to a few spots **$850**

California Art, scene of California courtyard with fountain, restored color and varnish, imp mark, mounted in Arts & Crafts frame, 8" h, 12" l ... **$1,600**

Cambridge Art Tile, Covington, Kentucky, 6" x 18"
Goddess and Cherub, amber, pr .. **$250**
Night and Morning, pr **$500**

Claycraft
Five tile faience panel, molded landscape of Mediterranean houses by sea, marks hidden by contemporary Arts & Crafts frame, 13-1/4" h, 35" l **$2,400**

Horizontal, English thatched roof cottage next to foot bridge, semi-matte polychrome, mounted in period ebonized Arts and Crafts frame, covered stamp mark, 6" x 12" **$1,610**
Molded lone tree rising over ocean, matte polychrome glazes, stamped "Claycraft," mounted in new Arts & Crafts frame, 7-3/4" x 4" **$815**

Grueby, mottled matte green glaze, mustard yellow blossom, ftd copper frame, raised indecipherable mark on base, 6-1/4" sq **$1,100**

Greuby tile, frieze of ivory horses, blue sky, dec in Cuenca technique, tile designed by Addison LeBoutillier, professional restoration lower right side, signed K.C., 6" sq, **$2,640.**
Photo courtesy of David Rago Auctions, Inc.

Claycraft tile, pirates on deck of tall ship, sun or moon in distance, matte polychrome, mounted in fine arts frame, light abrasion, minor nicks, a few flat chips to back edges, stamped Claycraft, 11-3/4" x 15-3/4" , **$1,175.**
Photo courtesy of David Rago Auctions, Inc.

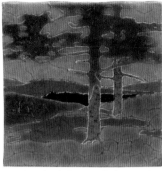

Greuby tile, "The Pines," decorated in cuenca technique, glazed sides, artist-signed RD, 6" sq, **$3,480.**
Photo courtesy of David Rago Auctions, Inc.

J. & J. G. Low, Chelsea, MA
Putti carrying grapes, blue, pr, 4-1/4" sq **$75**
Circular, yellow, minor edge nicks and glaze wear, 6" d **$35**
Woman wearing hood, brown, 6" sq **$95**

KPM, portrait of monk, titled "Hieronymous of Ferrara sends this image to the prophet to God," small nicks to corners, 5-3/4" x 3-3/8" **$245**

Lowe, Chelsea, Massachusetts, architectural, glossy taupe glaze, including forty-eight undecorated bricks, thirty-four scroll and leaf pattern, two pairs of framed tiles, one depicting winged dragon, the other warriors faces in mottled cream-color and brown glossy glazes, some with pottery marks, late 19th/early 20th C **$360**

Marblehead, ships, blue and white, pr, 4-5/8" sq **$125**

Minton China Works
Aesops Fables, Fox and Crow, black and white, 6" sq **$75**

Rob Roy, Waverly Tales, brown and cream, 8" sq **$95**

Minton Hollins & Co.
Morning, blue and white, 8" sq .. **$100**
Urn and floral relief, green ground, 6" sq **$45**

Moravian
Autumn, young man picking apples, basket at his feet, stamped "MR," made for Old Wicker Art School, Detroit, Michigan, custom made wrought iron museum stand, 1920s, 18" d, 1-1/2" h **$5,750**
Tempus, Father Time, blue and ivory glaze, red clay showing through, unmarked, small glaze flake on one edge, 10" x 7-1/4" **$1,150**

Mosaic Tile Co., Zanesville, Ohio
Fortune and the Boy, polychrome, 6" sq **$80**
Delft windmill, blue and white, framed, 8" sq **$55**

Pardee, C.,
Chick and griffin, blue-green matte, 4-1/4" sq **$175**

Portrait of Grover Cleveland, gray-lavender, 6" sq **$125**

Providential Tile Works, Trenton, New Jersey, round, stove type, hole in center, flowered **$20**

Rookwood Faience, emb pink, ochre, and green geometric floral pattern, Arts & Crafts frame, stamped "RP," chips to corners, 8" h **$325**

Sherwin & Cotton
Dog head, brown, artist sgd, 6" sq **$100**
Quiltmaker and Ledger, orange, pr, 6" x 12" **$145**

Trent, 6" sq, head of Michelangelo, sea green glaze, sgd by Isaac Broome, imp mark **$115**

U.S. Encaustic Tile Works, Indianapolis, IN, panel, Dawn, green, framed, 6" x 18" **$150**

Wedgwood, England
Calendar, November, boy at seashore, peacock blue, 6" sq **$95**
Tally Ho, man riding horse, blue and white, 8" sq **$85**

TOBY JUGS

History: Toby jugs are drinking vessels that usually depict a full-figured, robust, genial drinking man. They originated in England in the late 18th century. The term "Toby" probably is related to the character Uncle Toby from Tristram Shandy by Laurence Sterne.

Reproduction Alert. During the last 100 years or more, Tobies have been copiously reproduced by many potteries in the United States and England.

Bennington type, standing, 9-1/2" h **$175**

Delft, man seated on barrel, green hat, green and black sponged coat, blue and yellow pants, old cork stopper, 19th C, 11-1/4" h **$365**

Toby jug, Yorkshire, Pratt palette, sponged hat int and base, molded caryatid handle, old restoration on hat brim, England, early 19th century, 7-3/4" h, **$560.**
Photo courtesy of Skinner, Inc.

Toby jug, Staffordshire, pearlware, translucent polychrome enamels, seated figure holding ale jug in one hand and cup in the other, England, 18th century, 6-3/8" h, **$1,175.**
Photo courtesy of Skinner, Inc.

Toby jug, Staffordshire, pearlware, polychrome enamel, seated figure holding ale jug, England, early 19th century, 8-3/4" h, **$765.**
Photo courtesy of Skinner, Inc.

Toby jug, Staffordshire, creamware, translucent enamel dec., seated figure holding redware ale jug, England, c1800, 9-7/8", **$1,175.**
Photo courtesy of Skinner, Inc.

Luster ware, blue coat, spotted vest, 19th C, 6-1/2" h **$175**

Minton, majolica, Quaker man and woman, polychrome dec, imp mark, pr, 11-1/4" h **$4,600**

Portobello pottery, standing, spatter enamel dec, orig cov, c1840, 10" h **$275**

Pratt
Hearty Good Fellow, blue jacket, yellow-green vest, blue and yellow striped pants, blue and ochre sponged base and handle, stopper missing, slight glaze wear, c1770-80, 10-3/4" h **$1,500**
Pearlware glaze, typical blue, brown, and ochre palette, hat inset, small chips, 9-1/4" h............**$425**

Royal Doulton
Sam Weller, #d6265, "A" mark, 4-1/2" h **$190**
Stoneware, blue coat, double XX, Harry Simson, 6-1/2" h............**$395**
The Fortune Teller, 2-3/4" h........**$500**

Winston Churchill, DT6171, 9" h ...**$175**
Shaker, polychrome dec, standing figure, yellow hat, blue coat, and red breeches with pink luster highlights, England, 19th C, 5" h **$150**
Shorter Son, Ltd., England, Long John Silver, 9-3/4" h....................**$375**
Staffordshire
Cobalt blue coat, red breeches, gilt accented vest, standing on green sponged ground, minor wear to gilding, 9-7/8" h........................**$300**
Martha Gunn, translucent brown and ochre glazes, pearl body, brim repaired at hairline, 9-1/4" h....**$1,265**
Pearlware, seated figure, sponged blue jacket, ochre buttons, ochre and lavender speckled vest and trousers, brown hair and hat, green glazed base, shallow flake inside hat rim, attributed to Ralph Wood, c1770-80, 9" h **$1,950**
Seated, holding jug in one hand, glass in other, cobalt blue jacket, plaid

vest, orange trousers, yellow hat, c1850, 5-1/4" h, 4-1/4" h..........**$235**
Whieldon, pearlware, seated figure, yellow greatcoat, green vest, blue trousers, holding brown jug in left hand, raises foaming glass of ale towards mouth, lid missing, c1770-80, 9-1/2" h................**$1,600**

Wilkinson
Field Marshall Haig, modeled by Sir Francis Carruthers Gould, titled "Push and Go," printed marks, c1917, 10-3/4" h **$460**
Marshall Joffre, modeled by Sir Francis Carruthers Gould, titled "75mm Ce que joffre," printed mark, hat brim restored, c1918, 10" h **$345**
Winston Churchill, multicolored, designed by Clarice Cliff, black printed marks, number and facsimile signature, c1940, 11-3/4" h.............**$825**
Yorkshire-Type, caryatid form handle, Pratt palette dec, sponged base and hat brim int., 7-3/4" h..........**$750**

VAN BRIGGLE POTTERY

Reproduction Alert. Van Briggle Pottery still is made today. These modern pieces often are mistaken for older examples. Among the glazes used are Moonglo (off white), Turquoise Ming, Russet, and Midnight (black).

History: Artus Van Briggle, born in 1869, was a talented Ohio artist. He joined Rookwood in 1887 and studied in Paris under Rookwood's sponsorship from 1893 until 1896. In 1899, he moved to Colorado for his health and established his own pottery in Colorado Springs in 1901.

The Art Nouveau schools he had seen in France heavily influenced Van Briggle's work. He produced a great variety of matte-glazed wares in this style. Colors varied.

Artus died in 1904. Anne Van Briggle continued the pottery until 1912.

Marks: The "AA" mark, a date, and "Van Briggle" were incised on all pieces prior to 1907 and on some pieces into the 1920s. After 1920, "Colorado Springs, Colorado" or an abbreviation was added. Dated pieces are the most desirable.

Van Briggle vase, small, abstract floral design, covered in frothy matte blue glaze, 1908-1911, AA Van Briggle Colo. Spgs/654, 4" x 4-1/4", $840.
Photo courtesy of David Rago Auctions, Inc.

Van Briggle vessel, flat shoulder, yellow and light green matte glaze, marked, 1908-1911, 4", $350.
Photo courtesy of David Rago Auctions, Inc.

Van Briggle vase, embossed blossoms, unusual lavender to chartreuse matte glaze, marked, 1" line from rim, 1908-1911, 3-3/4", $250.
Photo courtesy of David Rago Auctions, Inc.

Advertising plaque, green and blue matte glaze, emb "VAN BRIGGLE POTTERY/COLORADO CLAY," 1/3" corner chip, few smaller edge chips, 11-1/2" l, 5-3/4" h **$2,300**

Bowl, spade-shaped leaves, frothy green and purple matte glaze, robin's egg blue ground, buff clay showing through, mkd "AA Van Briggle/Colo Spgs/737," 2-1/2" hairline from rim, 1908-11, 5" x 10" **$1,690**

Cabinet vase, emb flowers in curved panels, covered in dark teal matte glaze, incised AA/Van Briggle/190?/186, with XXII/IV/33188 in ink, 1904, 2-1/2" d, 4-1/4" h **$1,610**

Chamberstick, molded-leaf shape, hood over candle socket, green glaze, 5-1/2" h **$115**

Figure, female nude holding shell, matte Persian blue glaze, incised "Van Briggle," 7" h **$250**

Lamp base, emb stylized florals under maroon glaze with blue over-spray, orig factory fittings, incised varnished bottom with logo, name, and Colorado Sprgs, c1920, 9" h **$115**

Low bowl

Dragonfly, closed-in rim, four molded dragonflies around rim, deep mulberry matte glaze, incised cipher, incised Van Briggle U.S.A., c1922-29, 8-3/4" d, 2-3/4" h **$350**

Mug, feathered matte green over blue glaze, overfired, burst bubbles, crack in handle, 1908-11, 6" h **$175**

Shape no. "689," emb arrow root design, under matte green glaze, incised with logo, varnished bottom, Colo Sprgs, c1920, 6-1/2" h **$260**

Night light, figural, stylized owl, bulb cavity, light refracting glass eyes, turquoise blue matte glaze, unsgd, 8-1/2" h **$425**

Tile, six tile frieze, cuenca with stylized trees against blue sky, framed, 18" x 12" **$250**

Vase

Bulbous, crisply emb spade-shaped leaves, covered in mottled purple dripping over green matte glaze, incised AA/Van Briggle/Colo. Spgs./804/18/7, c1907-11, 3/4" rim bruise, 8-1/4" h, 2-3/4" d **$1,100**

Bulbous, crisply molded, spade-shaped leaves, sheer frothy light turquoise glaze, clay showing through, AA Van Briggle, 1908, 4-3/4" h, 4" d **$800**

Bulbous, cupped rim, two loop handles, emb leaves around base, covered in rare purple and green matte glaze, incised AA/Van Briggle/1903/III/232, 9" h, 6" d ... **$3,775**

Bulbous, emb panels of berries and leaves, covered in caramel, amber, and indigo matte glaze, incised AA/Van Briggle/1904/V/164, 8-1/2" h, 7" d **$6,900**

Bulbous, emb panels of stylized flowers and heart-shaped leaves in purple and green, matte blue ground, incised AA/Van Briggle/1905/?09/X, small glaze scale to one stem, 5-1/2" h, 5-1/4" d **$2,760**

Bulbous, emb poppy pods, rare dark blue-green leathery matte glaze, incised AA/Van Briggle/1903/III/18, 9" h, 6" d **$4,890**

Emb tulips, purple to periwinkle matte glaze, AA/Van Briggle/1903/II/141, 1903, 7-3/4" h, 3" d ... **$2,000**

Figural, Native American Indian with pottery vase, incised "Van Briggle Col. Spgs D.R.," 8" h **$360**

Van Briggle vase, bulbous, embossed trefoils under rich, feathery matte green glaze, AA/Van Briggle/Colo Springs/1906, some burst glaze bubbles from firing, 1906, 7" x 6-1/2", $2,400.
Photo courtesy of David Rago Auctions, Inc.

Van Briggle vessel, straight sides, embossed with tulips, covered in fine, frothy brownish-green matte glaze, red clay showing through, AA/VAN BRIGGLE/COLORADO SPRINGS/19??/06, 4-3/4" x 5", $1,600.
Photo courtesy of David Rago Auctions, Inc.

Van Briggle vase, embossed with poppy pods and foliage, purple and light green frothy glaze, AA Van Briggle/1903/III/173, 1903, 10" x 4-3/4", **$5,700.**
Photo courtesy of David Rago Auctions, Inc.

Van Briggle vase, tall vase, four short handles, embossed peacock feathers under Persian Rose glaze, AA1919, 1919, 13-1/2", **$1,320.**
Photo courtesy of David Rago Auctions, Inc.

Van Briggle vase, gourd shape, embossed with blossoms and leaves, matted raspberry glaze with touch of green, AA/Van Briggle/1903/III, 1903, 10" x 5-1/4", **$3,250.**
Photo courtesy of David Rago Auctions, Inc.

Incised and molded stylized flowers, under blue/gray glaze with turquoise over-spray, "dirty bottom" incised with logo, name, and date "20," c1920, 6" h..........................**$375**

Shape no. 833, molded stylized flowers, under brown glaze with green over-spray, dirty bottom with incised logo, name and Colo Sprgs, c1920, 5-1/2" h.........................**$230**

Squat, emb spade-shaped leaves, stylized blossoms, mustard and olive green dead matte glaze, 1904, AA/Van Briggle/1904/151, 4-3/4" h, 5-1/4" d **$1,300**

Tapering, emb peacock fathers, covered in charcoal and chartreuse matte glaze, incised AA/Van Briggle/1905/III/174, 11-1/4" h, 4" d **$5,750**

Tapering, emb tobacco leaves, covered in matte ochre and umber glaze, incised AA, die-stamped 1915 and 45, 10-1/4" h, 4-1/4" d..........**$1,380**

Vessel, bulbous, molded poppies, fine indigo and teal green frothy glaze, AA Van Briggle, Colo Spgs mark, 1908-11, 4-1/4" h, 5-1/2" d **$1,000**

VILLEROY & BOCH

Villeroy & Boch, stein, 1/2 litre, stoneware, dancing figures, King of Hops, #1909, pewter lid, **$100.**
Photo courtesy of Joy Luke Auctions.

History: Pierre Joseph Boch established a pottery near Luxembourg, Germany, in 1767. Jean Francis, his son, introduced the first coal-fired kiln in Europe and perfected a water-power-driven potter's wheel. Pierre's grandson, Eugene Boch, managed a pottery at Mettlach; Nicholas Villeroy also had a pottery nearby.

In 1841, the three potteries merged into the firm of Villeroy & Boch. Early production included a hard-paste earthenware comparable to English ironstone. The factory continues to use this hard-paste formula for its modern tablewares.

Beaker, quarter liter, couple at feast, multicolored, printed underglaze **$115**

Charger, gentleman on horseback, sgd "Stocke," 15-1/2" d **$600**

Dish, cov, triangular, orange and black dec, marked "Villeroy &

Boch, Mettlach," and "Made in Saar-Basin," molded "3865," c1880-1900 ....**$125**

Ewer, central frieze of festive beer hall, band playing while couples dance and drink, neck and foot with formal panels between leaf molded borders, subdued tones, imp shape number, production number and date codes, c1884, 17-3/4" h **$900**

Figure, Venus, scantily clad seated figure, ribbon tied headdress, left arm raised across chest, resting on rock, inscribed "Villeroy & Boch," damage to foot and base, 53" h **$1,900**

Platter, white basketweave ground, blue fish and aquatic plants dec, marked "Villeroy & Boch, Delphin, Mettlach, Ceschutzt," 9-1/4" l, 8" w **$110**

Stein, #2942, half liter, pewter lid, brown ground, beige earthenware cartouche "Braun ist meine Maid, Schaumt uber jeder-zeit," Jewish Star of David on reverse, marked "Villery

& Boch/Mettlach, 7 02" **$275**

Tray, metal gallery with geometric cutouts, ceramic base with border and stylized geometric pattern, white ground, soft gray high gloss glaze, blue accents, base marked, 11-1/4" d ... **$200**

Tureen, cov, Burgenland, dark pink transfer, white ground, marked "Mettlach, Made by Villeroy & Boch," 11" w **$195**

Vase, bulbous, cylindrical, deep cobalt blue glaze, splashes of drizzled white, three handled SP mount cast with leaves, berries, and blossoms, molded, pierced foot, vase imp "V" & "B," "S" monogram, numbered, price for pr, c1900, 15" h **$2,750**

Villeroy & Boch Jugendstil vase, large, four long buttresses, stylized mushrooms in blue-green and amber decorate band, V & B glaze stamp, 21-1/4" x 11", **$1,200.**
Photo courtesy of David Rago Auctions, Inc.

WEDGWOOD

History: In 1754, Josiah Wedgwood and Thomas Whieldon of Fenton Vivian, Staffordshire, England, became partners in a pottery enterprise. Their products included marbled, agate, tortoiseshell, green glaze, and Egyptian black wares. In 1759, Wedgwood opened his own pottery at the Ivy House works, Burslem. In 1764, he moved to the Brick House (Bell Works) at Burslem. The pottery concentrated on utilitarian pieces.

Between 1766 and 1769, Wedgwood built the famous works at Etruria. Among the most-renowned products of this plant were the Empress Catherina of Russia dinner service (1774) and the Portland Vase (1790s). The firm also made caneware, unglazed earthenwares (drabwares), piecrust wares, variegated and marbled wares, black basalt (developed in 1768), Queen's or creamware, and Jasperware (perfected in 1774).

Bone china was produced under the direction of Josiah Wedgwood II between 1812 and 1822 and revived in 1878. Moonlight luster was made from 1805 to 1815. Fairyland luster began in 1920. All luster production ended in 1932.

A museum was established at the Etruria pottery in 1906. When Wedgwood moved to its modern plant at Barlaston, North Staffordshire, the museum was expanded.

Wedgwood hedgehog crocus pot, black basalt, oval shape, pierced body, impressed mark, England, mid-19th century, slight tail chip, 6-1/2" h, **$645.**
Photo courtesy of Skinner, Inc.

Agate ware

Candleholder, surface agate, applied creamware drapery swags, black basalt base, wafer Wedgwood & Bentley mark, restored chip to socle, c1775, 6-1/2" h **$1,495**

Vase, cov, solid agate, creamware sibyl finials, traces of gilding, black basalt base, imp wafer Wedgwood & Bentley marks, gilt rim wear, covers with rim chips, nicks to bases, pr, c1770, 9-1/2" h **$7,500**

Artist designed

Bowl, Norman Wilson "Unique Ware" design, moonstone ground exterior, interior with translucent green glaze shading to blue center, impressed mark, England, 1930-60, 8-1/8" d **$400**

Inkstand, Keith Murray design, rect form pen tray with shallow wells and central cov box supporting two inkpots, matte green ground, imp and printed marks, slight chip under cover's rim, c1936, 10-1/8" l **$590**

Wedgwood kingfisher and low bowl, black basalt, bird on pierced rocky base, 7-1/2" h, low bowl has relief fruiting grapevine border, impressed marks, England, c1915, 14" d, **$585.**
Photo courtesy of Skinner, Inc.

Wedgwood tall jug, crimson Jasper dip, applied white classical subject, running grapevine border, impressed mark, c1920, 4-3/4" h, **$1,530.**
Photo courtesy of Skinner, Inc.

Wedgwood, tall jug, crimson Jasper dip, applied white fruiting grapevine border, classical figures, impressed mark, England, c1920, 7-3/4" h, **$530.**
Photo courtesy of Skinner, Inc.

Wedgwood Dragon Lustre vase, porcelain, magenta ground with gild dragon motif, 9" h, **$450.**
Photo courtesy of Sloans & Kenyon Auctioneers and Appraisers.

Jug, Keith Murray design, celadon slip, cream colored ground, imp and printed marks, c1940, 8" h..........**$210**

Vase, Keith Murray design
Globular, engine turned banding, imp and printed marks, c1935, 6" h
....**$650**
Straw glaze, horizontally turned body, printed mark, c1940, 7-1/4" h
....**$765**

Basalt

Bough pot, cov, scrolled handles terminating in ram's heads, pierced disc lid with removable candle nozzle, imp mark, restored nozzle and one handle, mid-19th C, 7" h **$1,265**

Bowl, engine turned dec, imp mark, early 20th C, 10-1/8" d **$230**

Bust, Horace, mounted on waisted circular socle, titled on reverse, impressed Wedgwood & Bentley marks to bust and base, c1775, 14" h
....**$3,100**

Candlestick, Ceres, modeled holding cornucopia form candle sconce and mounted to stepped circular base, imp title and mark, restored candle nozzle, rim nicks to base, 19th C, 11-1/2" h
....**$1,265**

Canopic jar, cov, bands of hieroglyphs and zodiac symbols in relief on jar, cover modeled as Egyptian head, impressed marks, price for pr, restored, c1867, 10" h...............**$3,820**

Cream jug, Encaustic dec, green, black and white enamels, leaf and

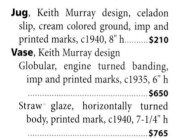

berry swags terminating at ribbon bows, below gilt trimmed band of foliage, impressed mark, early 19th C, 4-3/8" h......................................**$1,800**

Crocus pot and tray, hedgehog shape, imp marks, repaired chips, c1800, 9-3/4" l.............................**$920**

Cup and saucer, iron red and white banded palmette borders, Encaustic dec, imp lower case mark, slight enamel flake to saucer rim, late 18th C, 5" d saucer...................**$1,265**

Figure
Adonis, standing nude male modeled with cloth over his shoulder, impressed mark, 20th C, 12-1/4" h
....**$2,235**
Rousseau, standing figure modeled holding bunch of flowers in one hand and walking stick in other, impressed upper-lower case mark, chip to end of flower bunch, stick possibly replaced, late 18th C, 11-1/2" h **$4,000**
Venus, standing nude woman modeled by tree trunk on circular base, impressed title and mark, 19th C, 9-1/2" h **$950**

Hanging flower vase, bottle shape, overhead loop handle, impressed mark, early 19th C, 7-3/8" h **$1,765**

Inkstand, relief of classical figures bordered in oak leaves, gilted and bronzed, impressed marks, corner footrim nick, wear to gilt at top rim, c1875, 2-1/4" h sq shaped inkpot with insert **$5,875**

Jug, central putti-relief between bands of engine turning, mask head to handle terminal, metal mounts, imp lower case mark, late 19th C, 7-1/4" h
....**$2,875**

Lamp, vestal and reading, cov, female figure seated on oval lamps, applied acanthus leaves and bellflowers, imp marks, slight flake to book of reading lamp, ball finial reglued, finial and pitcher missing on vestal lamp, rim chip repair, price for pr, 19th C, 8-3/8" h..**$920**

Miniature, bust, Zeus, half-bust modeled wearing crown, impressed mark, mounted to silver collar with screw thread, 19th C, 1-3/4" h **$500**

Model
Bulldog, glass eyes, by Ernest Light, imp mark, imp nick to ear, c1915, 2-3/4" h **$345**
Sphinx, female figure, lion body, stepped rect base, imp mark, chips to footrim and headdress, early 19th C, 11-1/4" h **$865**

Plaque
Oval, classical figures in relief depicting seasons, impressed marks, price for pr, mounted to velvet lined wood frames, 19th C, 4-1/4" l............**$825**
Oval, relief depicting groups of three Graces, impressed marks, price for pr, 19th C, 6-1/2" x 8-1/2"........**$900**
Self-framed, oval, relief representing Day and Night, impressed marks, mounted in gilt wood frames, price for pr, 19th C, 5" x 6-1/4".........**$765**

Self-framed, oval, relief representing Day and Night, impressed marks, mounted in velvet lined painted wood frames, price for pr, early 19th C, 5" x 6-1/2" **$450**

Portrait medallion, oval

Captain Cook, black basalt, relief bust above impressed title, scooped back, self-framed, impressed Wedgwood & Bentley mark, shallow back edge chips, c1779, 3-1/8" x 4" **$4,410**

Martin Heinrich Klaproth, German chemist, black basalt, applied rosso antico bust above an impressed title, impressed mark, c1815, 2-1/2" x 3-1/4" **$650**

Oliver Cromwell, black basalt, relief bust above impressed title, scooped back, impressed mark, Wedgwood & Bentley mark, slight edge nick, c1779, 3" x 3-3/4" **$650**

Potpourri, cov, globular, upturned loop handles, enamel and gilt dec tropical bird and flowers in famille rose style, impressed mark, finial possibly re-cemented at join, inner disc lid missing, c1820, 13" h **$3,055**

Slave Medallion, oval, slave relief centering verse "Am I not a man and a brother?" imp mark and date, c1891, 1-1/8" x 1-1/4" **$635**

Rum kettle, body with bacchanalian boys in relief above engine turned band, shaped bale handle, Sybil finial, imp lower case mark, restored chip on cov rim and finial, late 18th C, 5-3/4" h **$600**

Tankard, cylindrical form, applied classical figures in relief, imp mark, restored rim chip, 19th C, 4-1/4" h **$360**

Tea cup and saucer, Iris Kenlock Ware, enamel dec floral design, imp mark, c1895 .... **$815**

Teapot, cov, oval, molded arabesque floral body, sunflower finial, imp mark, rim nick to cover, tip of spout slightly ground, early 19th C, 3-3/4" h **$290**

Carrara

Bust, Stephenson, mounted on waisted circular socle, impressed mark, title, publish date and sculptor, E.W. Wyon. F, c1858, 14-3/4" h **$900**

Figure, Venus Victrix, semi-nude figure modeled standing on freeform base, inscribed title, imp mark, shallow chip and nick to base, mid-19th C, 20-1/4" h.......................... **$1,450**

Vase, cov, trophy relief between floral festoons terminating at ram's heads, foliate borders, bronzed and gilt, imp and printed marks, cover restored, c1900, 7-1/2" h.............. **$1,495**

Creamware

Bowl

Reticulated, molded fiddleback ladle, imp "Wedgwood," stains, edge chip, 8-1/8" l...................... **$160**

Scalloped edge, cut-out design, imp "Wedgwood," 7-1/2" d **$600**

Plate, scenic, little girl and mother buying buns from the Bun Man, back titled "Buns!, Buns!, Buns!," 1863 mark and artist sgd "Lessore," 9-1/8" d **$335**

Vase, molded grape vines and foliage, painted band of strawberries, mid-19th C, 6" h **$250**

Drabware

Club jug, molded body, hunt subject, applied white fruiting grapevine border, imp mark, shallow rim chip, c1830, 7-3/8" h **$490**

Potpourri, cov, upturned loop handles, bulbous middle applied with band of blue foliage, pierced cover, acorn finial, solid insert disc lid, impressed mark, c1825, 10" h.................... **$1,650**

Tea set, 6-1/2" h cov teapot (slight chips to spout and sibyl finial), 4-1/4" h creamer (rim chip), 5" h cov sugar, imp marks, c1830 .... **$575**

Jasper

Barber bottle, three color, solid white body, applied bacchus heads at shoulder, classical relief, green foliate and lilac ground medallions, ram's heads and berries, impressed mark, cover married, mid 19th C, 10" h **$1,775**

Biscuit jar, cov

Three color dip, applied white classical figures in relief on black ground bordered with yellow ground bands, silver plated rim, handle and cover, impressed mark, needs replating, late 19th C, 5-1/4" h **$1,000**

Three color dip, applied white relief with classical figures and floral festoons terminating at ram's heads on green ground, bordered in lilac with foliate borders, silver plated rim, handle and cover, impressed mark, footrim nick, repaired chips to trim rings, needs replating, mid 19th C, 5-1/4" h **$600**

Bough pot, solid light blue, sq shape with arched recesses to paneled sides, applied white relief figures representing four seasons within palm framed corners, impressed mark, missing lid, restored foot, late 18th C, 6-3/8" h **$1,175**

Bowl

Black dip, applied white Dancing Hours figures in relief, running laurel and berry and acanthus leaf borders, impressed mark, c1959, 10" d **$720**

Dark blue dip, applied white Dancing Hours relief, imp mark, mid-19th C, 7-1/8" d **$920**

Solid blue, basketweave body, imp mark, early 19th C, 6-5/8" d... **$1,380**

Bowl, cov, crimson dip, applied white classical figures in relief within foliate framed panels, acanthus leaves on cover, impressed mark, c1920, 5-1/8" d.............................. **$1,880**

Brooch, octagonal, three-color, applied white classical relief on green ground, solid light blue medallion, gold mounted frame, imp mark, 19th C, 1" x 1-1/4" **$490**

Cache pot, undertray, dark blue dip, pot with applied white classical relief, band of flowers on tray, impressed marks, price for pr, 19th C, 5" h **$1,100**

Candlesticks, pr

Black dip, applied white classical relief within bands of foliage and arabesque floral design, impressed mark, one with edge nick, early 20th C, 4-1/4" h **$715**

Yellow dip, applied black classical relief and arabesque floral banded border, impressed marks, stain in drip dish, c1930, 7-3/4" h **$1,100**

Candy dish, cov

Lilac dip, applied white classical relief figures, silver plated rim, handle, and cov, imp mark, imp mark, light crazing, slight pitting to surface, c1877, 2-5/8" h......................... **$690**

Three-color dip, dark blue ground with applied yellow zigzags and white florets, foliage, and diamond border, silver plated rim, handle, and cov, imp mark, slight foot rim chip repaired, c1881, 2-1/4" h **$550**

Goblet, dark blue dip, applied white stiff leaves, impressed mark, 19th C, 5-7/8" h.......................... **$500**

Hair receiver, crimson dip, applied white classical relief and foliage designs, imp mark, slight loss to one figure, c1920, 4-3/8" d............. **$1,265**

Wedgwood vase and cover, light blue Jasper dip, white muses and upturned loop handles, floral garland, foliate borders, England, impressed mark, plinth staining, replacement cover, early 19th century, 11-1/4" h, **$880.**
Photo courtesy of Skinner, Inc.

Wedgwood Apollo vase and cover, light blue dip, white relief and finial, Jasper dip, England, 1930, "CC Postnatum Conditorem Anno Viget ARs Etruriae Redintegrata," commemorates 200th Anniversary of the birth of Josiah Wedgwood, no. 22 of 50 limited edition, ebonized wood base, impressed mark, 1930, 9-1/4" h, **$880.**
Photo courtesy of Skinner, Inc.

Wedgwood vase, dark blue Jasper dip, applied white relief of muses and laurel, acanthus leaves, arabesque floral, fruiting grapevine motifs, England, impressed mark, rim chip slight relief loss, early 19th century, 13-3/4" h, **$1,175.**
Photo courtesy of Skinner, Inc.

Humidor, cov, solid light blue, applied white relief with classical figures and urns framed within palm tree panels, banded arabesque floral dec, engine turned dome cover with Diana finial, limited edition in Masterpiece series, numbered 59 in edition of 200, printed and impressed marks, c1985, 9-3/8" h.................................**$720**

Inkstand, solid pale blue, sarcophagus form supporting two pots, applied white relief with central medallion of The Sacrifice to Hymen within drapery enclosure, impressed mark, missing covers, crazing throughout, old restorations to pots, backside of stand, and scrolled foliate relief, late 18th C, 6-7/8" h **$1,495**

Jam jar, cov, three-color dip, central light green ground band bordered in lilac, applied white classical figures below floral festoons and foliate border, silver plated rim, handle, and cov, imp mark, mid-19th C, 3-3/4" h **$650**

Jardinière
Black dip, applied white classical

relief, impressed mark, price for pr, one with rim repair, marks partially removed, early 20th C, 7-1/8" h **$825**

Olive green dip, applied white classical Muses in relief below fruiting grapevine festoon terminating at lion masks and rings, impressed mark, c1920, 8" h **$400**

Three-color, solid white ground, applied green floral festoons and foliate borders, lilac ram's heads and trophy drops, imp mark, 19th C, 5-1/4" h **$1,035**

Jewel box, cov, dark blue dip, oval, classical subject medallion mounted to three of paneled sides, larger medallion set on hinged lid, gilt brass mountings, 19th C, 4-1/2" h **$1,100**

Jug
Crimson dip, barrel shape with applied white classical Muses in relief within foliate framed panels, trophy below spout, impressed mark, c1920, 3-7/8" h...........**$1,530**

Crimson dip, applied white classical relief below border of floral

garlands, impressed mark, shallow chip to side of spout, c1920, 6-1/2" h **$940**

Three color, solid white body, applied pale lilac trophies terminating at ram's heads, green floral festoon, oak leaf bands and acanthus leaves, impressed mark, shallow foot-rim chips, some discoloration to white jasper, mid-19th C, 7-1/4" h **$1,650**

Mustard pot, cov, yellow dip, attached underplate, applied black fruiting grapevine relief, pot with lion masks and rings, silver plated cover, impressed mark, rim chip, stained interior, dish rim restored, c1930, 4" h **$325**

Necklace, lilac dip, 21 assorted beads, each with applied relief, 14 teardrop-shaped with classical subjects, seven oval with stars and stiff leaves, unmarked, 19th C, 21" l.............**$920**

Oenochoe jug, dark blue dip, applied white classical relief, scrolled handle terminating at female mask head, impressed mark, early 19th C, 11" h **$3,100**

Oil lamp, dark blue dip, applied white classical relief, Zodiac signs border, imp mark, early 19th C, 5-1/4" l **$1,265**

Perfume bottle, solid light blue, applied white relief portraits of George III on one side, reverse with Queen Charlotte, each bordered by floral festoons, unmarked, repair, chips to neck, late 18th/early 19th C, 1-7/8" d **$490**

Plaque

Black dip, rect, applied white relief depictions of Domestic Employment from design by Lady Templetown, impressed mark, England, painted wood frame, 19th C, 3" x 8-1/4" **$765**

Black dip, rect, applied white relief of children with fruit, reading and playing musical instruments, impressed mark, mid-19th C, 4" x 9" **$1,300**

Green dip, rect, applied white relief of children at play, impressed mark, England, gilded and ebonized wood frame, 19th C, 2-1/2" x 7-1/4" **$1,120**

Portrait plaque, green dip, Ariadne, oval, applied white relief, inscribed title and impressed mark, giltwood frame, 19th C, 8" d **$650**

Potpourri, cov, solid light blue, squat cylindrical shape, applied white stiff leaves below running laurel border, impressed mark, 19th C, 2-1/2" h ... **$825**

Salad bowl

Dark blue dip, applied white classical relief below floral festoons terminating in ram's heads, foliate borders, silver plated rim, imp mark, 19th C, 5-3/4" d **$375**

Three-color dip, dark blue ground with applied relief alternating as bands of yellow trellis and white scrolls, silver plated rim, imp mark, old repairs to rim and foot rim chip, c1882, 10-3/8" d **$460**

Salad set, 7-1/2" d bowl, dark blue dip, applied white classical relief, silver plated rim, 11" l silver plate fork and spoon servers with dark blue handles, applied foliate relief, late 19th C **$350**

Salt, open, solid light blue, applied white Dancing Hours in relief, imp marks, one with rim chip, other with relief loss to figure, price for pr, 19th C, 2-7/8" d **$750**

Slave medallion, solid white, raised verse surrounding applied black fig-

ure in relief, partial impressed mark, lacquered wood and brass frame, late 18th C, 1" x 1-1/4" **$1,765**

Spill vase, three-color dip, light blue ground, engine turned fluting below lilac ground medallions, applied white classical relief above floral festoons terminating at ram's heads, imp mark, mid-19th C, 3" h **$1,035**

Sugar bowl, cov, crimson dip, applied white classical relief, imp mark, restored chip on cover collar and two areas of relief, c1920 .... **$290**

Syrup jug

Dark blue dip, applied white birds in relief below oak leaf banded border, silver plated insert cov, imp mark, early 20th C, 6-1/4" h **$550**

Three-color dip, dark blue ground with applied vertical bands of yellow trellis and white scrolls, hinged pewter lid, imp mark, restored, late 19th C, 7-3/4" h **$350**

Tea bowl and saucer, solid pale blue, applied white relief, children playing above band of engine turning on cup, 5" d saucer with acanthus and stiff leaves bordering engine turned center, imp mark, late 18th C **$980**

Tea service, dark blue dip, 4-1/2" h cov teapot, 6" d waste bowl, twelve 6-1/8" d plates, seven 5-1/2" d tea cups, seven saucers, each with applied white grass and foliate border, impressed marks, few rim chips, 19th C **$1,765**

Vase, cov

Crimson dip, upturned loop handles, applied white classical relief and foliate borders, impressed mark, cover with hairlines, restored finial, c1920, 11" h **$3,525**

Dark blue dip, applied white bacchus head handles and Dancing Hours in relief, foliate framed borders, impressed marks, price for pr, one handle simply reglued, late 19th C, 6-1/2" h **$1,880**

Dark blue dip, bottle shape with applied white classical figures in relief within foliate frames, impressed marks, price for pr, early 19th C, 7-1/4" h **$1,765**

Dark blue dip, upturned loop handles, applied white classical relief, acanthus leaf borders, impressed marks, price for pr, mid-19th C, 9-1/2" h **$1,530**

Green dip, applied white relief with Dancing Hours, foliate borders,

bacchus head handles, impressed marks, price for pr, one finial reglued, one handle repaired, chip to socle rim, mid-19th C, 8-1/2" h **$2,115**

Vase

Black dip, applied white relief with classical muses below fruiting festoons terminating at lion masks and rings, trophies to shoulder, fruiting grapevine and acanthus leaf borders, impressed mark, late 19th C, 15" h **$2,585**

Light blue dip, bottle shape, applied white classical relief within foliate framed panels, neck with floral festoons terminating at ram's heads, impressed marks, price for pr, c1867, 8" h **$1,000**

Solid light blue, applied white relief with columnar framed panels of floral festoons and classical medallions below band of vine and scrolled ribbon, impressed mark, slight discoloration to foot, 19th C, 6-3/4" h **$825**

Three color dip, green ground, applied lilac medallions, white portraits in relief between drapery swags, imp mark, rim and foot rim chips, 19th C, 3" h **$435**

Yellow dip, applied blue relief with classical figures within foliate framed panels, fruiting grapevine and stiff leaf borders, impressed mark, missing disc lid, chips restored below base, 19th C, 5-1/2" h **$940**

Lusters

Bough pot, cov, Moonlight, wall pocket modeled as nautilus shell, pierced insert grid, impressed mark, cover repaired, slight chip to spine, c1815, 10" l **$940**

Box, cov, Dragon, pattern Z4829, mottled blue glaze, mother-of-pearl int., printed mark, c1920, 4" x 7" **$1,850**

Bowl

Dragon, octagonal, mottled blue ground ext., mother-of-pearl int., Z4829, printed mark, slight glaze scratches, c1920, 7-1/8" d **$470**

Fairyland Lustre, octagonal, exterior with "Castle on a Road" on deep blue shaded sky, interior with "Fairy in a Cage" with daylight sky, Z5125, printed mark, slight wear to center, c1920, 9" d **$3,820**

Wedgwood, Thomas Allen earthenware pedestal, hexagonal shape, blue transfer printed muses and floral borders, impressed mark, middle join and top rim restoration, staining, glaze wear, England, c1880, 35-1/4" h, **$1,000.**

Photo courtesy of Skinner, Inc.

Fairyland Lustre, octagonal, exterior with "Moorish" design on black ground, interior with "Smoke Ribbons" on daylight sky, Z5125, printed mark, c1920, 7-3/4" d **$5,875**

Fish dec, mottled blue ext., mother-of-pearl int., printed mark, c1920, 4" d...**$350**

Oriental motifs, mottled green/black ext. with dragon, mother-of-pearl int., printed mark, c1920, 3-1/8" d **$400**

Chalice bowl, Fairyland Lustre, exterior with "Twyford Garlands" on flame ground, interior with "Fairy Gondola" on flame sky, Z5360, printed mark, stem restored, hairlines to base, c1920, 10-5/8" d **$6,500**

Coffeepot, cov, Moonlight, imp mark, small chips to spout and cover, c1810, 5-1/2" h...**$690**

Cup, three handles, Dragon, blue ext., gilt reptiles, eggshell int. with central dragon, printed mark, c1920, 2" h **$275**

Dish, Dragon, Daisy Makeig Jones marks, Z4831, c1914-31, 4-3/4" d.............**$675**

Imperial bowl

Fairyland Lustre, exterior with firbolg design on red ground, mother-of-pearl interior with Thumbelina center, Z5275, printed mark, light glaze scratches to exterior, c1920, 10-1/2" d **$2,250**

Fairyland Lustre, exterior "Poplar Trees" on night sky, interior "Feather Hat" on daylight sky, Z4968, printed mark, center gilt wear, c1920, 10" d **$5,000**

Malfrey pot, cov, Fairyland Lustre, "Candlemas" pattern, Z5157, printed mark, vase rim regilded, c1920, 8-1/4" h......................................**$3,820**

Punch bowl, Butterfly, ruby lustre exterior with butterflies and insects, mother-of-pearl interior with butterflies, Z4827, printed mark, c1920, 11" d..**$2,820**

Teapot, cov, Moonlight, drum form, imp mark, rim chips restored, nicks to spout rim, c1810, 3" h.............**$575**

Vase

Dragon, pattern Z4829, mottled blue ext., mother-of-pearl int., Chinese pagoda panels, printed mark, c1920, 11" h **$1,150**

Fairyland, black, trumpet, shape 2810, Z4968, Butterfly Women, printed marks, pr, c1920, 9-3/4" h **$4,000**

Fairyland, exterior with "Firbolgs" on deep ruby ground, interior rim dec with fish from Thumbelina motifs on mother-of-pearl ground, printed mark, c1920, 8-3/4" h...........**$2,590**

Hummingbird, mottled blue exterior, orange/red mottled interior, Z5294, printed mark, c1920, 8-1/2" h **$1,175**

Paneled Daventry design, pale plum ground, Z5418, printed mark, c1920, 8-1/2" h......................**$3,300**

Wall pocket, Moonlight, nautilus shell, restorations, pr, c1810, 10" l **$575**

Majolica

Barber bottle, cov, cobalt blue ground, molded body with festooning fruiting grapevines between Bacchus mask heads applied to shoulder bordered in laurel and berries, imp mark, cover collar restored, c1869, 11" h..**$1,840**

Biscuit jar, cov, jar with molded dec of elephants within floral framed cartouches flanked by elephant masks, silver plated rim, bale handle and cover, imp mark, cover possibly married, c1867, 5-1/2" h **$1,250**

Bowl, cauliflower, multicolored, cobalt blue, rim nick on back, 11" d......**$495**

Compote, bowl molded as nautilus shell, base molded as two dolphins with entwined tails, impressed mark, possibly married, base chips, c1866, 16" h..**$1,100**

Crocus pot, hedgehog, oval shaped pierced body, green glaze, impressed mark, missing undertray, slight footrim chips, c1865, 6" h.................**$645**

Fish platter, Argenta, oval, scalloped rim, molded in relief with large fish atop vegetation, impressed mark, staining, c1878, 25-1/4" l **$825**

Floor urn, cobalt blue, ladies seated at top of bulbous vase, drapes of laurel wreaths and ladies head at base, turquoise, yellow, white, brown, green, and pink, repair to one base, minor nicks and repair to feet of ladies, pr, 26" h......................................**$5,500**

Jug, applied central fruiting grapevine band, imp marks, one with slight relief loss, price for pr, c1868, 8-3/4" h **$1,300**

Oyster plate, brown basketweave and shell **$1,210**

Pitcher, sunflower and urn, turquoise, 7" h...**$770**

Plate

Crane, 9" d..................................**$690**

Mottled, reticulated, 8-3/4" d **$165**

Salt, open, modeled as scantily clad boy holding basket, freeform base, imp mark, slight hairlines to rim, glaze flakes, restored base chips, c1889, 5-1/2" h...**$350**

Sugar, Argenta, bird and fan, repair to lid, hairline in base.....................**$125**

Umbrella stand, Argenta Fan, hairlines, 24" h...............................**$1,760**

Vase, bottle shape, raised bands of foliage, flowers and fruiting festoons surrounding oval medallions, impressed mark, c1870, 10" h......................**$900**

Pearlware

Candlesticks, pr, turquoise glaze, modeled as classical female holding cornucopia form base, supporting leafy sconce, imp mark, glaze wear, nicks to glaze surface, c1872 ....$1,380

Fruit basket, 10-5/8" on stand, oval, basketweave molded center, pierced gallery, green enamel trim, imp mark, early 19th C, some damage to strapping of basket, glaze wear on stand $320

Platter, well and tree, gaudy cobalt blue and rust Chrysanthemum pattern, repaired, c1800 ....$595

Potpourri vase, pierced cov, blue ground, white relief floral swags, band above engine-turned fluting, imp mark, body restoration, married cover, c1800 ....$230

Tea tray, rect, cut corners, red/pink transfer printed border, c1886, 18-1/8" l......................................$200

Vase, upturned loop handles, red ground with gilt trimmed blue transfer printed floral and bird design, impressed mark, cover missing, repaired handle, mid-19th C, 12-3/4" h......................................$500

Queen's Ware

Basket, oval, twisted overhead handles, molded basketweave body, pierced rim, enamel and gilt dec, impressed marks, price for pr, early 19th C, 9" l $1,175

Bidet, fitted mahogany stand with cov, imp mark, 21-1/2" l....................$425

Bough pot, cov, sq form, paneled sides, relief alternating with two figures representing Seasons and two urns, foliate molded sq disc lid and center insert, imp mark, old repair to hairline on disc lid, mid-19th C, 6" h $460

Box, cov, flat cylindrical form, gilt trim to green transfer printed foliate design, imp mark, light wear, c1882, 3-3/4" d $500

Dish, diamond shape, enamel painted Emile Lessore dec cherubs, artist sgd, impressed mark, c1860, 5-1/8" d $600

Flemish jug, molded body with majolica glazes, blue incised designs, relief portrait of Queen Victoria below spout, brown banded neck and foot, imp mark, 1877, 8-1/4" h $375

Orange bowl, cov, low pedestal foot, wide lobe-fluted flaring rim, high domed pieced cover with long tapering ovals framed

by molded scroll lattice and floral designs, imp mark, 20th C, 9-1/2" h $635

Plate, molded border, enamel dec center with Cupid and Psyche, artist sgd "E. Lossore," imp mark, c1870, 8-3/4" d......................................$635

Platter, oval, polychrome bird and floral dec in Chelsea style, imp mark, 1871, 15-3/4" x 20-3/8" $375

Sauceboat, molded trellis and scroll pattern after 19th C salt glaze stoneware model, imp mark, 19th C, 8" l..$460

Soup ladle, bowl with yellow ground banding, black enamel foliate vine dec, imp mark, early 19th C, 11-1/4" l $320

Rosso Antico

Bowl

Applied black basalt relief, fern dec, imp mark, early 19th C, 6-3/4" d $850

Egyptian, applied black basalt meander band above stylized foliate molded body, imp mark, early 19th C, 7-7/8" d $1,300

Box, cov, flat cylindrical form, enamel painted flowers, imp mark, base rim chip, c1860, 3-1/2" d..................$175

Bust, Matthew Prior, mounted on raised circular base, imp mark and title, restorations, 7-1/4" h..........$420

Candlesticks, pr, polychrome floral sprays, imp mark, each sconce restored, mid-19th C, 7" h..........$415

Club jug, polychrome floral sprays, imp mark, mid-19th C, 6-1/4" h..........$520

Cream jug, hexagonal form, banded Greek key relief, imp mark, early 19th C, 2-1/4" h..................................$450

Inkstand, applied black basalt leaf and

berry border on stand, supported by three dolphin feet, central pot insert, imp mark, foot rim restored, early 19th C, 4" h $550

Jug, oval, molded lobed body, foliage, stem, and flower relief, imp mark, restored spout rim chip, early 19th C, 5-1/8" l..................................$675

Tray, oval, Egyptian, applied black basalt hieroglyphs in relief, imp mark, early 19th C, 8-1/2" l $1,100

Vase, cov, tripod, applied black basalt Egyptian relief with central hieroglyph band, impressed mark, repair to one leg and finial, early 19th C, 8" h..................................$1,880

Stoneware

Bough pot, cov, D-shape, mottled green and white relief floral swags, acanthus, stiff leaves, England, impressed mark, chip to pot back corner and interior edge, cover as is, c1785, 4-3/4" h............................$775

Crocus basket, cov, pierced and engine turned body with overhead bow handle, dark blue dip dicing, impressed mark, early 19th C, 6-1/2" l.......$2,585

Dish, leaf form, white, enamel floral sprays, imp mark, very slight rim nick, early 19th C, 9-3/8" l..........$230

Mortar and pestle, 7-1/2" d mortar with spout, 10-1/4" l pestle with wood handle, vitrified, impressed marks, early 19th C, wear, chip on head $360

Vase, goblet shape, sponged brown and blue underglaze enamels, raised black basalt base, England, wafer Wedgwood & Bentley mark, slight flake to base, missing cover, c1775, 5-7/8" h..................................$600

Wedgwood Rosso Antico oil lamp and cover, applied black relief of dancing figures, scrolled foliate handle, England, early 19th century, handle restoration, chip to cover rim, impressed mark, 4-3/4" l, **$530.**
Photo courtesy of Skinner, Inc.

Weller basket, Ardsley, unmarked, 12-1/4", $750.
Photo courtesy of David Rago Auctions, Inc.

Weller vase, Coppertone, tall, curved handles, 1/4" base nick, marked in script, 10-3/4", $499.
Photo courtesy of David Rago Auctions, Inc.

Weller Hudson vase, floral decoration, artist signed "Pillsbury," half-kiln ink stamp, light crazing, first half 20th century, 6" h x 5-3/4" d, $300.
Photo courtesy of Green Valley Auctions.

WELLER POTTERY

History: In 1872, Samuel A. Weller opened a small factory in Fultonham, near Zanesville, Ohio. There he produced utilitarian stoneware, such as milk pans and sewer tile. In 1882, he moved his facilities to Zanesville. Then in 1890 Weller built a new plant in the Putnam section of Zanesville along the tracks of the Cincinnati and Muskingum Railway. Additions followed in 1892 and 1894.

In 1894, Weller entered into an agreement with William A. Long to purchase the Lonhuda Faience Company, which had developed an art pottery line under the guidance of Laura A. Fry, formerly of Rookwood. Long left in 1895, but Weller continued to produce Lonhuda under the new name "Louwelsa." Replacing Long as art director was Charles Babcock Upjohn. He, along with Jacques Sicard, Frederick Hurten Rhead, and Gazo Fudji, developed Weller's art pottery lines.

At the end of World War I, many prestige lines were discontinued and Weller concentrated on commercial wares. Rudolph Lorber joined the staff and designed lines such as Roma, Forest, and Knifewood. In 1920, Weller purchased the plant of the Zanesville Art Pottery and claimed to produce more pottery than anyone else in the country.

Art pottery enjoyed a revival when the Hudson Line was introduced in the early 1920s. The 1930s saw Coppertone and Graystone Garden ware added. However, the Depression forced the closing of the Putnam plant and one on Marietta Street in Zanesville. After World War II, inexpensive Japanese imports took over Weller's market. In 1947, Essex Wire Company of Detroit bought the controlling stock, but early in 1948, operations ceased.

Additional Listings: See *Warman's Americana & Collectibles* for more examples.

Bowl

Ardsley, flaring, stamped mark .. **$265**

Coppertone, perched frogs and lily-pads, stamped mark................. **$550**

Glendale, flaring, birds and waves crashing over rocks dec, stamped mark, few minor firing separations
....**$350**

Cabinet jug, Louwelsa, small yellow blossoms, silver overlay, imp mark, 3-3/4" x 2-3/4"........................**$1,000**

Candlestick

Round rim, sq pyramid form, reticulated arches near base, raised flowers and berries on vine, matted brown glaze, pink, blue, and highlights, one imp "Weller" on base, price for pr, late 1920s, 9-3/8" h....................**$150**

Glendale, owl dec, 13-1/2" h.......**$520**

Console set, pr candlesticks, green, Tutone, stamped marks, 7" d, 3-1/2" h three-sided bowl.........................**$250**

Ewer, Jap Birdimal, squeezebag trees and geisha dec by Rheadin, incised mark **$3,000**

Figure, turtle, Coppertown, unmarked, 2-1/2" x 6"....................................**$450**

Frog tray, oval, raised edge, frog and water lily on one side, lily pads on other, blotchy semi-gloss green glaze, "Weller Pottery" ink stamp, 15-1/2" l
....**$635**

Hanging basket

Forest, unmarked, 7-3/4" x 3-1/2"
....**$300**

Parian, conical, unmarked, 9-1/4" x 5-3/4"...**$125**

Garden ornament, swan, ivory glaze, minor flakes, 20" x 18".............**$6,500**

Jardinière

Aurelian, brown glaze, painted fruit, sgd "Frank Ferrell"................**$1,100**

Sicard, sunflowers, emerald green and gold on deep purple ground
....**$2,900**

Lamp base

Forest, unmarked, 2" chip next to hole at base, 5" d, 11-1/4" h **$460**

Louwelsa, by Hattie Mitchell, gourd shape, painted yellow cherry blos-

Weller Hudson vase, white and decorated, painted roses of deep pink and ivory, impressed mark, 13" x 6-1/2", **$780.**
Photo courtesy of David Rago Auctions, Inc.

Weller Hudson vase, floral decoration, artist signed "S.T.," impressed mark, early 20th century, 7-3/4" h x 3-1/2" d, **$165.**
Photo courtesy of Green Valley Auctions.

Weller Hudson vase, blue and yellow irises painted on both sides by Pillsbury, stamped mark, artist's signature, 1" blue glaze run next to iris on one side, 7" d, 15-1/2" h, **$1,700.**
Photo courtesy of David Rago Auctions, Inc.

soms, stamped "Weller Louwelsa," sgd "H. Mitchell" on body, 10" d, 13-1/4" h **$460**

Mug, Dickensware, dolphin handle and band, sgraffito ducks **$250**

Pitcher

Marvo, pink, unmarked, 8" h, 8" d
.... **$250**

Zona, kingfisher and cattails, imp mark, glaze nick at base, 9" h, 8-1/2" d.................................. **$250**

Planter

Rosemont, unmarked, several lines, 7-1/2" x 9-1/2" **$350**

Woodcraft, applied squirrel climbing up tree, 2" tight line **$375**

Vase

Aurelia, singing monk playing the mandolin in earthtone glazes, mkd "Aurelian" on base, numbered, decorator's signature for R. G. Turner on side, crazing, c1904, 19" h **$1,530**

Aurelia, tapering, berries and leaves, imp mark, 9-1/2" h, 4" d **$300**

Baldin, blue, imp mark, glaze nick at rim, 9" h, 9" d.......................... **$475**

Burntwood, bulbous, band of flowers, unmarked, 4-1/4" h, 3-3/4" d
.... **$100**

Eocean, short rim on cylindrical form, thistle plants in pink, maroon, and cream, green stems on brown to green to cream-colored ground, incised "Eocean Rose Weller," numbered "547," letter "Y" on base, artist's initials on side for Eugene Roberts, crazing and areas of glaze roughness, c1907, 21" h
.... **$1,880**

Fru Russet, emb flowers, pale bluegray and green glaze, imp mark, 14" h, 5-3/4".......................... **$2,600**

Greora, flaring, etched mark, 11-1/2" h, 7" d.......................... **$450**

Hudson, bulbous, painted band of white blossoms and leaves, Timberlake, stamped mark, artist's signature, 6-3/4" h, 6-1/2" h **$500**

Hudson, bulbous, painted pink tulips, imp mark, 10-1/2" h, 4-3/4" d................................ **$425**

Hudson, trumpet shape, painted berries and leaves, imp mark, 11" h, 4" d
.... **$400**

L'Art Nouveau, pillow, one side with maiden in profile, other with shell, stamped mark partially obscured, 9-1/2" h, 8-1/2" w **$450**

L'Art Nouveau, shell shape, painted maiden and flowers, imp mark, 1" line, two minor glaze flakes, 10" h, 8" d **$450**

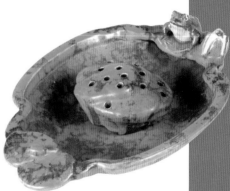

Weller bowl and flower frog set, Coppertone, frog perched on lilypad, small for head nick, stamped mark, 15-1/2" x 10", **$530.**
Photo courtesy of David Rago Auctions, Inc.

Weller bowl, Muskota turtle, built-in flower frog, unmarked, 9" l, 4" h, **$850.**
Photo courtesy of David Rago Auctions, Inc.

Weller umbrella stand, Flemish, decorated with maidens, chains of pink blossoms and ivy, stamped mark, few minor abrasions, 20", $1,190.
Photo courtesy of David Rago Auctions, Inc.

Weller ewer, Jap Birdimal, finely decorated by Rhead in squeezebag, trees and geisha, incised "Weller Faience Rhead G580," pinhead size fleck to spout, 10-3/4" x 7", $3,000.
Photo courtesy of David Rago Auctions, Inc.

Weller vase, L'Art Nouveau, embossed orange poppies, impressed "WELLER," 14" h, $475.
Photo courtesy of David Rago Auctions, Inc.

Weller jardinière, Burntwood, carved roosters, impressed mark, 2" line from rim, 9-1/2" d, 8-1/2" h, $225.
Photo courtesy of David Rago Auctions, Inc.

Weller vase, Coppertone, flaring, a frog on both sides, kiln stamp, 8-1/4" x 9-1/4", $1,140.
Photo courtesy of David Rago Auctions, Inc.

Weller hanging basket, Woodcraft, large, 4-3/4" x 10", $270.
Photo courtesy of David Rago Auctions, Inc.

Louwelsa, bulbous, orange and yellow carnations, imp mark, few short shallow scratches, 12" h, 3-1/4" h **$100**

Louwelsa, ovoid, gooseberries and leaves, imp mark, fleck to rim, few shallow scratches, 10-1/2" h, 5-1/2" d **$100**

Louwelsa, vasiform body, yellow rose stems on brown ground, decorator's signature on side for Hattie Mitchell, imp maker's mark on base, numbered "466" and "1,"

minor glaze loss, c1900, 20-3/4" h **$1,880**

Rosemont, bulbous, flaring rim, imp mark, 10" h, 4-1/2" d **$450**

Silverton, bulbous, pink chrysanthemums, ink stamp mark, 9" h, 5-1/2" h **$395**

Silverton, cylindrical, pink and white flowers, ink stamp mark, 8" h, 3-1/2" d **$300**

Silverton, flaring, calla lilies dec, ink stamp mark, 11-3/4" h, 5" d **$375**

Silverton, gourd shape, twisted

handles, yellow flowers, ink stamp mark, 6-1/2" h, 6" d.................**$275**

Silverton, two angular handles, pink and white flowers, Silverton and Weller paper labels, 10" h, 5-1/2" d **$300**

Warwick, unmarked, 10" h, 4-1/2" d **$200**

Wall pocket

Glendale, imp mark, restoration, 12" h **$250**

Suevo, conical, unmarked, minor wear to glaze, 12-1/4" h **$250**

WHITE-PATTERNED IRONSTONE

History: White-patterned ironstone is a heavy earthenware, first patented under the name "Patent Ironstone China" in 1813 by Charles Mason, Staffordshire, England. Other English potters soon began copying this opaque, feldspathic, white china.

All-white ironstone dishes first became available in the American market in the early 1840s. The first patterns had simple Gothic lines similar to the shapes used in transfer wares. Pattern shapes, such as New York, Union, and Atlantic, were designed to appeal to the American housewife. Motifs, such as wheat, corn, oats, and poppies, were embossed on the pieces as the American prairie influenced design. Eventually, more than 200 shapes and patterns, with variations on finials and handles, were made.

White-patterned ironstone is identified by shape names and pattern names. Many potters only identified the shape in their catalogs. Pattern names usually refer to the decorative motif.

Butter dish, cov, Athens, Podmore Walker, c1857.................................**$95**
Cake plate, Brocade, Mason, handled, 9" d...**$180**
Chamber pot, cov, emb Fleur-De-Lis & Daisy on handle, 1883-1913, marked "Johnson Bros.".............**$165**
Coffeepot, cov
  Laurel Wreath.................................**$275**
  Wheat and Blackberry, Clementson Bros...**$220**
Compote, ftd, Taylor & Davis, 10" d, 6" h...**$220**
Creamer
  Fig, Davenport.................................**$95**
  Wheat in the Meadow, Powell & Bishop, 1870.................................**$85**
Creamer and sugar, Scroll pattern, E. Walley, repaired finial, luster dec
....**$170**
Cup and saucer
  Acorn and Tiny Oak, Parkhurst...**$35**
  Grape and Medallion, Challinor...**$40**
  Wheat, Brockhurst, handleless, luster dec...**$25**
Ewer, Scalloped Decagon, Wedgwood
....**$150**
Gravy boat
  Bordered Fuchsia, Anthony Shaw..**$75**
  Wheat & Blackberry, Meakin.......**$65**
Milk pitcher, Leaf, marked "Royal Ironstone China, Alfred Meakin, England," 9" h.................................**$245**
Nappy, Prairie Flowers, Livesley & Powell...**$20**
Pitcher
  Berlin Swirl, Mayer & Elliot........**$120**
  Japan, Mason, c1915.................**$275**
  Syndenhaum, T. & R. Boote.......**$195**
  Thomas Furnival, 9" w, 9-1/2" h
....**$220**
Plate
  Ceres, Elsmore & Forster, 8-1/2" d.**$15**
  Corn, Davenport, 10-1/2" d..........**$20**
  Fluted Pearl, Wedgwood, 9-1/2" d**$15**
  Laurel Wreath, set of 13, 10".......**$325**

Prairie, Clementson, Hanley, 6-5/8" d
....**$15**
Scroll pattern, E. Walley, 8" d.......**$55**
Wheat and Clover, Turner & Tomkinson...**$24**
Platter
  Columbia, 20" x 15".....................**$125**
  Laurel Wreath, three graduated sizes
....**$325**
  Wheat, Meakin, 20-3/4" x 15-3/4"
....**$95**
Punch bowl
  Berry Cluster, J. Furnival...........**$175**
  Rosettes, handles, Thomas Furnival & Sons, c1851-90, 9-1/2", 6" h.....**$315**
Relish
  Laurel Wreath, diamond shape....**$25**
  Wheat, W. E. corn.......................**$30**
Sauce tureen, cov
  Columbia, underplate, Joseph Goodwin, 1855.................................**$315**
  Prize Bloom, T.J. & J. Mayer, Dale Hall Pottery.................................**$320**

Wheat & Blackberry, Clementson Bros...**$275**
Soap dish, Bordered Hyacinth, cov, insert, W. Baker & Co., 1860s.....**$150**
Sugar bowl, cov
  Hyacinth, Wedgwood.................**$145**
  Fuchsia, Meakin.........................**$140**
  Livesley Powell & Co., registry mark, 8" h...**$295**
Teapot, cov, T & R Boote, Burslem, registry mark for Nov. 26, 1879, 9-1/2" h.................................**$240**
Toothbrush holder
  Bell Flower, Burgess.....................**$50**
  Cable and Ring, Cockson & Seddon
....**$40**
Tureen, cov, underplate, Grape, matching ladle, chips.........................**$135**
Vegetable, cov
  Blackberry.................................**$95**
  Lily of the Valley, pear finial.......**$110**
Vegetable, open, Laurel Wreath, pr..**$200**
Waste bowl, Laurel Wreath..........**$45**

White-patterned ironstone tureen, covered, underplate, small, original ladle, **$125.**

WILLOW PATTERN CHINA

History: Josiah Spode developed the first "traditional" willow pattern in 1810. The components, all motifs taken from Chinese export china, are a willow tree, "apple" tree, two pagodas, fence, two birds, and three figures crossing a bridge. The legend, in its many versions, is an English invention based on this scenic design.

By 1830, there were more than 200 makers of willow pattern china in England. The pattern has remained in continuous production. Some of the English firms that still produce it are Burleigh, Johnson Bros. (Wedgwood Group), Royal Doulton (continuing production of the Booths' pattern), and Wedgwood.

By the end of the 19th century, production of this pattern spread to France, Germany, Holland, Ireland, Sweden, and the United States. Buffalo Pottery made the first willow pattern in the United States beginning in 1902. Many other companies followed, developing willow variants using rubber-stamp simplified patterns, as well as overglaze decals. The largest American manufacturers of the traditional willow pattern were Royal China and Homer Laughlin, usually preferred because it is dated. Shenango pieces are the most desirable among restaurant-quality wares.

Japan began producing large quantities of willow pattern china in the early 20th century. Noritake began about 1902. Most Japanese pieces are porous earthenware with a dark blue pattern using the traditional willow design, usually with no inner border. Noritake did put the pattern on china bodies. Unusual forms include salt and pepper shakers, one-quarter pound butter dishes, and canisters. The most desirable Japanese willow is the fine quality NKT Co. ironstone with a copy of the old Booths pattern. Recent Japanese willow is a paler shade of blue on a porcelain body.

The most common dinnerware color is blue. However, pieces can also be found in black (with clear glaze or mustard-colored glaze by Royal Doulton), brown, green, mulberry, pink (red), and polychrome.

Marks: Early pieces of Noritake have a Nippon "Royal Sometuke" mark. "Occupied Japan" may add a small percentage to the value of common tablewares. Pieces marked "Maruta" or "Moriyama" are especially valued.

Note: Although colors other than blue are hard to find, there is less demand; thus, pieces may not necessarily be higher priced.

Reproduction Alert. The Scio Pottery, Scio, Ohio, currently manufactures a willow pattern set sold in variety stores. The pieces have no marks or backstamps, and the transfer is of poor quality. The plates are flatter in shape than those of other manufacturers.

Willow Pattern grill plate, divided sections, marked "Made in Japan," **$24.**

Berry bowl, small
  Blue, Homer Laughlin Co. **$6.50**
  Pink, marked "Japan" **$5**
Bowl, Mason, 9" d **$45**
Cake plate, Newport Pottery Ltd., England, SP base, c1920 .... **$300**
Charger, 13" d **$55**
Coffeepot, cov, 10" h, 3" h warmer stand **$165**
Creamer, round handle, Royal China Co. **$12**
Cup and saucer
  Booths **$30**
  Buffalo Pottery **$25**
  Homer Laughlin **$10**
  Japanese, decal inside cup, pink ... **$25**
  Shenango **$15**
Dinner plate
  Allerton, 10" d **$25**
  Buffalo Pottery, 9" d **$20**
  Johnson Bros., 10" d **$15**
Egg, transfer printed pattern on ceramic body, early 20th C

Gray ground, 4-1/2" l **$95**
Light blue ground, 5-1/2" l **$85**
White ground, 5" l **$90**
Platter, marked "Copeland, Made in England," c1940, 19" x 14-1/2" ... **$195**
Sugar, cov, Allerton **$65**
Tea cup and saucer, scalloped, Allerton **$45**
Tea set, 5" h hexagonal teapot, creamer, cov sugar, tray, seven cups, six saucers, 20-3/4" d round tray with scalloped rim, gilt foo dog lid finials, gilt handles and rims, pattern registered January, 1879, printed at rim with quotation from Robert Burns' "Auld Lang Syne," Spode, retailed by Tiffany & Co., price for 17-pc set, late 19th C **$950**
Toby jug, overall crazing, 6" d **$930**
Wash bowl and pitcher, Adderlys Ltd., Staffordshire, age crack in pitcher, c1906, 7-1/2" h pitcher, 12" d bowl **$375**

YELLOWWARE

History: Yellowware is a heavy earthenware which varies in color from a rich pumpkin to lighter shades, which are more tan than yellow. The weight and strength varies from piece to piece. Although plates, nappies, and custard cups are found, kitchen bowls and other cooking utensils are most prevalent.

The first American yellowware was produced at Bennington, Vermont. English yellowware has additional ingredients that make its body much harder. Derbyshire and Sharp's were foremost among the English manufacturers.

Yellowware bowl, rolled rim, three brown stripes, 9" d, **$95.**

Yellowware mixing bowl, folded rim, green and white stripes, some wear from use, 10" d, **$85.**

Yellowware coffeepot, covered, top pot with pierced holes in base, covered, **$315.**

Bank, house shape, molded detail highlighted in black, roof marked "For My Dear Girl," firing crack at chimney, 3-5/8" h **$660**

Bean pot, cov, three white slip accent bands, bands repeated on orig matching lid, relief lines on both, Watt pottery logo on base, orig lid has been broken and reglued, bowl has some staining from use, 6-1/2" h **$165**

Bottle, slip dec attributed to Rudolph Christ, NC Moravian, early 19th C **$9,900**

Bowl, minor age crazing to glaze, 8-1/2" d, 4" h **$35**

Butter tub, twist handles, lead and manganese glaze, sgd "John Bell" **$6,050**

Candleholders, pr, Rockingham glaze, attributed to Bennington, replaced glass chimneys, c1850, 2-1/2" h **$615**

Canning jar, relief draped design, some crazing to glaze, rim surface chips, 6-1/2" h **$125**

Coffeepot, Rockingham glaze, relief of woman snorting snuff on one side,

man smoking pipe on other side, matching lid, c1850, 8-1/2" h **$50**

Creamer, brown stripes, white band, blue seaweed dec, shallow flake on inside edge of table ring, 4-3/4" h .. **$440**

Figure, recumbent lion, 8" l
Incised "Buck" on front **$4,000**
Plain front, chip **$2,600**

Flask, book shape, Rockingham glaze, two unglazed spots on one side, c1850, 7-3/4" h **$275**

Food mold
Miniature, Yellow Rock, Phila mark, 3-3/4" d, 1-1/4" h **$185**
Turk's head, 7-1/2" d, 2-3/4" h **$145**

Foot warmer, Rockingham glaze, relief scroll design at shoulder, c1850, 9" h **$440**

Lamp base, prominent rings, running brown and yellow/green glaze, partial lamp parts, 8-1/2" h **$115**

Measure, Spearpoint & Trellis, 5-3/4" h, 6-1/2" d **$300**

Miniature, chamber pot, cream and blue spongeware glaze, c1900, 1-1/2" h **$90**

Yellowware pitcher, white mid band, applied strap handle, **$225.**
Photo courtesy of Joseph P. Smalley, Jr., Auctioneer.

ZANE POTTERY

History: In 1921, Adam Reed and Harry McClelland bought the Peters and Reed Pottery in Zanesville, Ohio. The firm continued production of garden wares and introduced several new art lines: Sheen, Powder Blue, Crystalline, and Drip. The factory was sold in 1941 to Lawton Gonder.

Bowl
Blue, marked "Zanesware," 6-1/2" d **$35**
Brown and blue, 5" d **$45**

Figure, cat, black, green eyes, 10-1/8" h **$500**

Jardinière, green matte glaze, matching pedestal, artist sgd "Frank Ferreu," 34" h **$375**

Vase
Flowing medium green over dark forest green ground, 7" h **$85**

Green, cobalt blue drip glaze, 5" h **$30**
Ivory glaze, emb flowers and leaves, 8" h **$75**

Wall pocket, Moss Aztec, 8-1/4" l **$95**

ZANESVILLE POTTERY

History: Zanesville Art Pottery, one of several potteries located in Zanesville, Ohio, began production in 1900. At first, a line of utilitarian products was made; art pottery was introduced shortly thereafter. The major line was La Moro, which was hand painted and decorated under glaze. The firm was bought by S. A. Weller in 1920 and became known as Weller Plant No. 3.

LA MORO

Marks: The impressed block-print mark "La Moro" appears on the high-glazed and matte-glazed decorated ware.

Bowl, fluted edge, mottled blue glaze, 6-1/2" d..**$65**

Coffeepot, cov, stoneware, Bodine Pottery Co., sand colored, unglazed ext., Albany slip int., tin wire straps, handle, spout, lid, and wire bale handle, c1880, 8" h..........................**$1,020**

Jardinière

Ruffled rim, cream to light amber peony blossoms, shaded brown ground, 8-1/4" h..........................**$75**

Waisted cylindrical form, landscape scene, blue, green, and maroon matte glaze, c1908, 7-1/8" h, 8-1/2" d....**$175**

Vase

Cone-shaped top, bulbous base, La Moro, marked "2/802/4," 8-3/4" h **$350**

Light gray horse portrait, light olive green to blue-green ground, matte ext., glossy brown int., sgd "R. G. Turner," 10-1/4" h.....................**$825**

ZSOLNAY POTTERY

History: Vilmos Zsolnay (1828-1900) assumed control of his brother's factory in Pécs, Hungary, in the mid-19th century. In 1899, Miklos, Vilmos's son, became manager. The firm still produces ceramic ware.

The early wares are highly ornamental, glazed, and have a cream-colored ground. Eosin glaze, a deep rich play of colors reminiscent of Tiffany's iridescent wares, received a gold medal at the 1900 Paris exhibition. Zsolnay Art Nouveau pieces show great creativity.

Marks: Originally, no trademark was used; but in 1878 the company began to use a blue mark depicting the five towers of the cathedral at Pécs. The initials "TJM" represent the names of Miklos's three children.

Notes: Zsolnay's recent series of iridescent-glazed figurines, which initially were inexpensive, now are being sought by collectors and steadily increasing in value.

Zslonay vase, large, maiden embracing tree, green and purple lustered glaze, modeled by M.L., raised five-churches medallion/5955/ML., 17-1/2" x 9", **$3,600.**
Photo courtesy of David Rago Auctions, Inc.

Bowl, sea shell shape, hp florals, gold highlights and edging, blue mark "Zsolnay Pecs," castle mark, "Patent," imp factory mark and numbers, 6-1/2" l, 2-1/2" h..........................**$160**

Cache pot, young girls dance holding hands around stylized tree form, blue, pale silver, and pale lilac glazes, 13" d **$4,250**

Coffee set, cobalt blue and gold trim, white ground, creamer, sugar, cake plate, six cups, saucers, and dessert plates, 8-1/2" h cov coffeepot **$600**

Compote, ribbed, four caryatids molded as angels supports, blue-green irid glaze, 11" d..............**$1,100**

Creamer, fierce dragon handle, 6-1/2" l..**$250**

Figure

Bears, pair, emerald green glaze, 7-1/2" l, 5" h..............................**$695**

Spaniel, artist sgd, 5" h.................**$95**

Jardinière, ovoid, multicolored florals, protruding pierced roundels, cream ground, blue steep mark, 16" l ...**$450**

Pitcher, form #5064, red/maroon metallic Eosin ground, cream and pale brown flower dec, millennium factory mark, c1898, 7-1/2" h.....**$750**

Puzzle jug, pierced roundels, irid dec, cream ground, castle mark, imp "Zsolnay," 6-1/2" h.....................**$195**

Vase

Classic shape, flaring rim, nacreous chartreuse glaze, stylized suns and flowers, gold stamp mark, 11" h, 5" d.....................................**$495**

Furniture

STATE OF THE MARKET:
ARTS & CRAFTS FURNITURE

by Jerry Cohen partner in Craftsman Auctions
www.craftsman-auctions.com
Owner, The Mission Oak Shop
www.artsncrafts.com

Having specialized in Arts & Crafts furniture for the past twenty-eight years, I have seen how consistently the market value of furniture has mirrored the economic well-being of collectors. Because the supply of interesting material is limited, and because this style is popular, there are always more potential buyers than sellers; and prices tend to rise and fall based on the wealth of the buyers. In a typical year, we sell Stickley furniture ranging in individual values from around $500 to $150,000. This furniture goes to people with widely varying budgets, and prices of some items can be moving up while prices of other items are moving down. Overall, the past year has seen a small increase in the values of Arts & Crafts furniture across the entire price and style range.

Today, the vast majority of buyers' budgets fit into the $500 to $5,000 range, resulting in the strongest demand for furniture in this price range. Pieces in this price range are at their strongest levels since 2001, when the economy was in recession. This is not only a range attractive to the average collector, but also to non-collectors who are looking to furnish homes in the Arts & Crafts style. In many cases, vintage period pieces can be purchased for the same or less than the cost of reproductions. While pieces over $5,000 are usually worth far more in original condition versus refinished, lesser pieces are not highly affected by whether or not they are in original finish; what most buyers want are pieces that are ready to place in their homes without needing a lot of work. A typical Stickley sideboard that sells for $3,500 in good original finish will still bring $3,000 to $3,500 if nicely refinished; but a rare Stickley sideboard that brings $50,000 in pristine condition may only bring $10,000-15,000 once refinished. As price goes up, condition becomes of paramount importance; the wealthiest buyers will gladly pay a substantial premium to get pristine objects.

In the late 1990s, when the stock market seemed to be doubling almost every year, many pieces that had been selling for $5,000 to $8,000 saw their prices soar to the $10,000 to $20,000 range. The $5,000 to $20,000 price level is populated with serious buyers having a desire for higher quality pieces yet without either the ability or desire to buy the rarest and most expensive items. The years 2000 and 2001 saw a major change in the economy, and a drop in prices within this range. The end result has been a stron-

Gustav Stickley pair of V-back billiards chairs with five vertical back slats and tacked-on leather seats, both have orig finish, replaced burgundy leather, one has replaced foot support, red decal lower back stretchers, 45" x 26" x 20", **$19,200.**
Photo courtesy of David Rago Auctions, Inc.

ger market either below $5,000 or above $20,000 – with the market struggling in between. Bookcases and Morris Chairs were the hardest hit items in this segment, with pieces that sold for $8,000-14,000 in the late 1990s are often bringing only $5,000-7,000 today. Some settles that hit $18,000 or $20,000 in 1999 can be bought for $9,000 to $12,000 today. Depending on your point of view, this can be seen as a great opportunity to pick up hard-to-find and desirable pieces at prices that are a bargain compared to levels of seven or eight years ago.

The $20,000 and up market has seen volatility both up and down, as really rare pieces in great condition have brought tremendous prices, sometimes four to five times their previous values, while other items in this group have proved to be not as rare as once believed, and their prices have fallen. A Gustav Stickley work cabinet, a small piece that was bringing $15,000-20,000 in the mid-1990s, recently brought over $85,000—being the first example of this form to come to auction in the past ten years. The lucky consignor who brings a form to market that has not been offered in many years often reaps a windfall price that won't get repeated if another example surfaces soon after.

Whether Queen Anne, Empire, Art Deco, Modern, or any other furniture style, the most highly valued pieces are ones that can be attributed to the designers, makers, or communities that have been recognized as the best in their league. High values for various furniture styles can range from the tens of thousands up to the millions of dollars, depending upon the popularity of each style; and one thing every style has in common is a group of serious and deep-pocketed collectors willing and able to pay record prices for the best examples from each period.

Popularity of particular furniture styles tends to wax and wane in a cyclical manner. Centennial years, museum exhibitions, trendy interior designers, and home magazines have a tremendous impact on what people choose to collect and how they furnish their homes. When I started in this business 31 years ago in California, Victorian golden oak furniture was the rage out West, walnut Victorian furniture was what people wanted in the South, and New England loved its antiques pre-dating the Civil War. Today, the more common furniture from the 18th and 19th centuries brings less than it did 30 years ago, although the best pieces in original condition often bring a substantial premium, especially those that date to the 18th century.

Interest in twentieth century furniture has swelled over the past 35 years, partly for cultural reasons, but also for reasons of availability. About sixty years ago, today's senior citizens started buying mid-century modern furniture to furnish their homes; and about ten years ago, as people from that generation began to downsize and their estates started coming on the market, furniture by makers like George Nakashima, Charles Eames, and Vladimir Kagan came to market for the first time since being purchased new. Older furniture styles had already been absorbed by the market and were familiar to collectors, but these pieces were fresh and created a new wave of interest among dealers and the public alike.

One thing that creates a frenzy in the market, whether in 18th century furniture or late 20th century, is the appearance of a fine item that has never been on the resale market before. At the auctions we host, it is always that somewhat dirty and untouched item that was put away in a basement or attic 50 years ago, and is now seeing the light of day for the first time in decades, that steals the show and garners a record price.

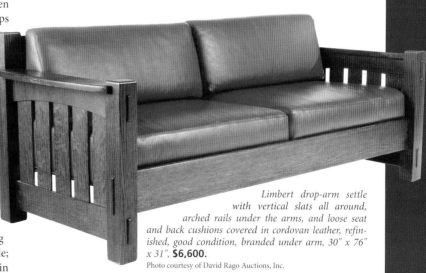

Limbert drop-arm settle with vertical slats all around, arched rails under the arms, and loose seat and back cushions covered in cordovan leather, refinished, good condition, branded under arm, 30" x 76" x 31", **$6,600.**
Photo courtesy of David Rago Auctions, Inc.

RESOURCES

Furniture Field Guide, Krause Publications, Iola, WI.

Antique Trunks Identification & Price Guide by Linda Edelstein and Paul Pat Morse, Krause Publications, Iola, WI.

Warman's American Furniture, Ellen T. Schroy ed., Krause Publications, Iola, WI.

Warman's Arts & Crafts Furniture Identification & Price Guide by Mark F. Moran, Krause Publications, Iola, WI.

Antique Trader Furniture Price Guide by Kyle Husfloen, Mark F. Moran contrib. ed., published by Krause Publications, Iola, WI.

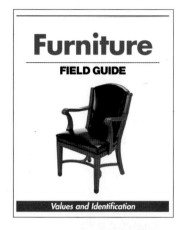

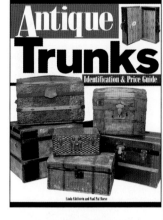

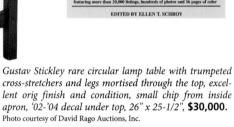

Gustav Stickley rare circular lamp table with trumpeted cross-stretchers and legs mortised through the top, excellent orig finish and condition, small chip from inside apron, '02-'04 decal under top, 26" x 25-1/2", **$30,000.**
Photo courtesy of David Rago Auctions, Inc.

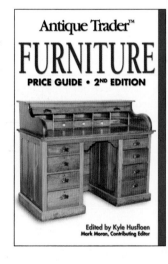

Gustav Stickley server (no. 818) with three drawers, oval pulls, overhanging top, and lower shelf, orig finish, stain and finish loss to top, minor separation to top, decal inside right drawer, 39" x 48" x 20", **$2,820.**
Photo courtesy of David Rago Auctions, Inc.

Roycroft sideboard with leaded-glass cabinet doors over a mirrored back, three small drawers flanked by cupboard doors over a linen drawer all having original copper hardware, beautiful orig finish and patina, top re-joined to lower portion with pegs, one side panel has a seam separation, carved orb and cross mark on center stile, 75-1/2" x 65-1/2" x 21", **$42,000.**

Photo courtesy of David Rago Auctions, Inc.

Gustav Stickley china cabinet designed by Harvey Ellis with overhanging top, three shelves, an arched apron and a hammered copper V-pull, excellent original finish and condition with original key, branded, paper label, 60" x 36" x 15", **$7,800.**

Photo courtesy of David Rago Auctions, Inc.

Sideboard, late Federal, tiger maple and cherry, arched pediment, three drawers, four cupboard doors, turned columns, turned feet, Pennsylvania, c1830, 55" h, 59-3/4" w, **$1,872.**

Photo courtesy of Pook & Pook, Inc.

Gustav Stickley Harvey Ellis-designed library table with single drawer, arched aprons and shoe feet, its sides having delicate inlay of pewter, brass and copper, and medallions inlaid with gallions in various fruitwood, orig finish with minor touch-ups to base, touch-ups and color added to top, red decal under bottom, 30" x 29-3/4" x 17-3/4", **$78,000.**

Photo courtesy of David Rago Auctions, Inc.

FURNITURE

History: Two major currents dominate the American furniture marketplace—furniture made in Great Britain and furniture made in the United States. American buyers continue to show a strong prejudice for objects manufactured in the United States. They will pay a premium for such pieces and accept them above technically superior and more aesthetically appealing English examples.

Until the last half of the 19th century, English examples and design books dictated formal American styles. Regional furniture, such as the Hudson River Valley (Dutch) and the Pennsylvania German styles, did develop. Less-formal furniture, often designated as "country" or vernacular style, developed throughout the 19th and early 20th centuries. These country pieces deviated from the accepted formal styles and have a charm that many collectors find irresistible.

America did contribute a number of unique decorative elements to English styles. The American Federal period is a reaction to the English Hepplewhite period. American designers created furniture that influenced, rather than reacted to, world taste in the Gothic-Revival style and Arts and Crafts, Art Deco, and Modern International movements.

Furniture styles

Furniture styles can be determined by careful study and remembering what design elements each one embraces. To help understand what defines each period, here are some of the major design elements for each period.

William and Mary, 1690-1730: The style is named for the English King William of Orange and his consort, Mary. New colonists in America brought their English furniture traditions with them and tried to translate these styles using native woods. Their furniture was practical and sturdy. Lines of this furniture style tend to be crisp, while facades might be decorated with bold grains of walnut or maple veneers, framed by inlaid bands. Moldings and turnings are exaggerated in size. Turnings are baluster-shaped and the use of C-scrolls was quite common, giving some look of movement to a piece of furniture. Feet found in this period generally are round or oval. One exception to this is known as the Spanish foot, which flares to a scroll. Woods tend to be maple, walnut, white pine, or Southern yellow pine. One type of decoration that begins in the William and Mary period and extends through to Queen Anne and Chippendale styles is known as japanning, referring to an imitation lacquering process.

Spice chest, Queen Anne, walnut and yellow poplar, molded edge, single long secret drawer, Quaker lock, double raised panel door, 12 interior drawers, molded base, bracket feet, c1760, 24-1/2" h, 17-1/2" w, 10-1/2" d, **$11,115.**
Photo courtesy of Pook & Pook, Inc.

Queen Anne, 1720-1760: Evolution of this design style is from Queen Anne's court, 1702 to 1714, and lasted until the Revolution. This style of furniture is much more delicate than its predecessor. It was one way for the young Colonists to show their own unique style, with each regional area initiating special design elements. Forms tend to be attenuated in New England. Chair rails were more often mortised through the back legs when made in Philadelphia. New England furniture makers preferred pad feet, while the makers in Philadelphia used triffid feet. Makers in Connecticut and New York often preferred slipper and claw and ball feet. The most popular woods were walnut, poplar, cherry, and maple. Japanned decoration tends to be in red, green and gilt, often on a blue-green field. A new furniture form of this period was the tilting tea table.

Chippendale, 1755-1790: This period is named for the famous English cabinetmaker, Thomas Chippendale, who wrote a book of furniture designs, *Gentlemen and Cabinet-Makers Director*, published in 1754, 1755, and 1762. This book gave cabinetmakers real direction and they soon eagerly copied the styles presented. Chippendale was influenced by ancient cultures, such as the Romans, and Gothic influences. Look for Gothic arches, Chinese fretwork, columns, capitals, C-scrolls, S-scrolls, ribbons, flowers, leaves, scallop shells, gadrooning, and acanthus. The most popular wood used in this period was mahogany, with walnut, maple, and cherry also present. Legs become straight and regional differences still exist in design elements, such as feet. Claw and ball feet become even larger and more decorative. Pennsylvania cabinetmakers used Marlborough feet, while other regions favored ogee bracket feet. The center of furniture manufacturing gradually shifts from New England and Mid-Atlantic city centers to Charleston. One of the most popular forms of this period was a card table that sported five legs instead of the four of Queen Anne designs.

Federal (Hepplewhite), 1790-1815: This period reflects the growing patriotism felt in the young American states. Their desire to develop their own distinctive furniture style was apparent. Stylistically it also reflects the architectural style known as Federal, where balance and symmetry were extremely important. Woods used during this period were first and foremost mahogany and mahogany veneer, but other native woods, such as maple, birch, or satinwood, were used. Reflecting the architectural ornamentation of the period, inlays were popular, as was carving, and even painted highlights. The motifs used for inlay included bellflowers, urns, festoons, acanthus leaves, and pilasters to name but a few. Inlaid bands and lines were also popular and often used in combination with other inlay. Legs of this period tend to be straight or tapered to the foot. The foot might be a simple extension of the leg or bulbous, or spade shaped. Two new furniture forms were created in this period. They are the sideboard and the worktable, reflecting forms that came into favor as they served a very functional use. Expect to find a little more comfort in chairs and sofas, but not very thick cushions or seats.

When a piece of furniture is made in England, or styled after an English example, it may be known as Hepplewhite. The time frame is the same. Robert Adam is credited with creating the style known as Hepplewhite during the 1760s and leading the form. Another English book heavily influenced the designers of the day. This one was by Alice Hepplewhite, and titled *The Cabinet Maker and Upholsterer's Guide,* with publisher dates of 1788, 1789, and 1794.

Sheraton, 1790-1810: The style known as Sheraton closely resembles Federal. The lines are somewhat straighter and the designs plainer than Federal. Sheraton pieces are more closely associated with rural cabinetmakers. Woods would include mahogany, mahogany veneer, maple, and pine, as well as other native woods. This period was heavily influenced by the work of Thomas Sheraton and his series of books, *The Cabinet Maker and Upholster's Drawing Book*, from 1791-1794, and his *The Cabinet Directory,* 1803, and *The Cabinet-Maker, Upholsterer, and General Artist's Encyclopedia* of 1804.

Empire (Classical), 1805-1830: By the beginning of the 19th Century, a new design style was emerging. Known as Empire, it had an emphasis on the classical world of Greece, Egypt, and other ancient European influences. The American craftsmen began to incorporate more flowing patriotic motifs, such as eagles with spread wings. The basic wood used in the Empire period was mahogany. However, during this period, dark woods were so favored that often mahogany was painted black. Inlays were popular when made of ebony or maple veneer. The dark woods offset gilt highlights, as were the brass ormolu mountings often found in this period. The legs of this period are substantial and more flowing than those found in the Federal or Sheraton periods. Feet can be highly ornamental as when they are carved to look like lion feet, or plain when they extend to the floor with a swept leg. Regional differences in this style are very apparent, with New York City being the center of the design style as it was also the center of fashion at the time.

New furniture forms of this period include a bed known as a sleigh bed, with the headboard and footboard forming a graceful arch, similar to that found on a sleigh, hence the name. Several new forms of tables also came into being, especially the sofa table. Because the architectural style of the Empire period used big open rooms, the sofa

Candlestand, Federal, mahogany, octagonal inlaid top, urn turned standard, downward sloping legs, spade feet, New England, c1810, 29″ h, 21-1/4″ x 14-1/4″, **$700.**
Photo courtesy of Pook & Pook, Inc.

Secretary bookcase, two parts, Sheraton, mahogany, c1810, 76″ h x 45-1/4″ w x 22″ d, **$1,100.**
Photo courtesy of Wiederseim Associates, Inc.

was now allowed to be in the center of the room, with a table behind it. Former architectural periods found most furniture placed against the outside perimeter of the walls and brought forward to be used.

Victorian, 1830-1890: The Victorian period as it relates to furniture styles can be divided into several distinct styles. However, not every piece of furniture can be dated or definitely identified, so the generic term "Victorian" will apply to those pieces. Queen Victoria's reign affected the design styles of furniture, clothing, and all sorts of items used in daily living. Her love of ornate styles is well known. When thinking of the general term, Victorian, it is best to think of a cluttered environment, full of heavy furniture, and surrounded by plants, heavy fabrics, and lots of china and glassware.

French Restauration, 1830-1850: This is the first sub-category of the Victoria era. This style is best simplified as the plainest of the Victorian styles. Lines tend to be sweeping, undulating curves. It is named for the style that was popular in France as the Bourbons tried to restore their claim to the French throne, from 1814 to 1848. The Empire (Classical) period influence is felt, but French Restauration lacks some of the ornamentation and fussiness of that period. Design motifs continue to reflect an interest in the classics of Greece and Egypt. Chair backs are styled with curved and concave crest rails, making them a little more comfortable than earlier straight back chairs. The use of bolster pillows and more upholstery is starting to emerge. The style was only popular in clusters, but did entice makers from larger metropolitan areas, such as Boston, and New Orleans, to embrace the style.

The Gothic Revival period, 1840-1860: This is one relatively easy to identify for collectors. It is one of the few styles that celebrates elements found in the corresponding architectural style: turrets, pointed arches, and quatrefoils—things found in 12th and 16th centuries that were adapted to this interesting mid-century furniture style. The furniture shelving form known as an étagère is born in this period, allowing Victorians to have more room to display their treasured collections. Furniture that had mechanical parts also was embraced by the Victorians of this era. The woods preferred by makers of this period were walnut and oak, with some use of mahogany and rosewood. The scale used ranged from large and grand to small and petite. Carved details gave dimension and interest.

Stool, Victorian giltwood, needlework upholstery, foliate carved apron, cabriole legs, 19th century, 11" h x 13-1/2" l, **$352.**
Photo courtesy of Skinner, Inc.

Rococo Revival, 1845-1870: This design style features the use of scrolls, either in a "C" shape or the more fluid "S" shape. Carved decoration in the form of scallop shells, leaves, and flowers, particularly roses, and acanthus further add to the ornamentation of this style of furniture. Legs and feet of this form are cabriole or scrolling. Other than what might be needed structurally, it is often difficult to find a straight element in Rococo Revival furniture. The use of marble for tabletops was quite popular, but expect to find the corners shaped to conform to the overall scrolling form. To accomplish all this carving, walnut, rosewood, and mahogany were common choices. When lesser woods were used, they were often painted to reflect these more expensive woods. Some cast iron elements can be found on furniture from this period, especially if it was cast as scrolls. The style began in France and England, but eventually migrated to America where it evolved into two other furniture styles, Naturalistic and Renaissance Revival.

Elizabethan, 1850-1915: This sub-category of the Victorian era is probably the most feminine-influenced style. It also makes use of the new machine turned spools and spiral turnings that were fast becoming popular with furniture makers. New technology advancements allowed more machined parts to be generated. By adding flowers, either carved, or painted, the furniture pieces of this era had a softness to them that made them highly suitable. Chair backs tend to be high and narrow, having a slight back tilt. Legs vary from straight to baluster turned types to spindle turned. This period of furniture design saw more usage of needlework upholstery and decoratively painted surfaces.

Sofa, Rococo Revival, medallion back, carved triple arching crest rail, padded back, cabriole legs and castors, 19th century, 38" x 64" x 30", **$472.**
Photo courtesy of Sloans & Kenyon Auctioneers and Appraisers.

Louis XVI, 1850-1914: One period of the Victorian era that flies away with straight lines is Louis XVI. However, this furniture style is not austere; it is adorned with ovals, arches, applied medallions, wreaths, garlands, urns, and other Victorian flourishes. As the period aged, more ornamentation became present on the finished furniture styles. Furniture of this time was made from more expensive woods, such as ebonized woods or rosewood. Walnut was popular around the 1890s. Other dark woods were featured, often to contrast the lighter ornaments. Expect to find straight legs or fluted and slightly tapered legs.

Naturalistic, 1850-1914: This furniture period takes the scrolling effects of the Rococo Revival designs and adds more flowers and fruits to the styles. More detail is spent on the leaves—so much that one can tell if they are to represent grape, rose, or oak leaves. Technology advances enhanced this design style as manufacturers developed a way of laminating woods together. This layered effect was achieved by gluing thin layers together, with the grains running at right angles on each new layer. The thick panels created were then steamed in molds to create the illusion of carving. The woods used as a basis for the heavy ornamentation were mahogany, walnut, and some rosewood. Upholstery of this period is often tufted, eliminating any large flat surface, as the tufting creates curved peaks and valleys. The name of John Henry Belter is often connected with this period, for it was when he did some of his best design work. John and Joseph W. Meeks also enjoyed success with laminated furniture. Original labels bearing these names are sometimes found on furniture pieces from this period, giving further provenance.

Renaissance Revival, 1850-1880: Furniture made in this style period reflects how cabinetmakers interpreted 16th and 17th century French designs. Their designs range from curvilinear and florid early in the period to angular and almost severe by the end of the period. Dark woods, such as mahogany and walnut, were primary with some use of rosewood and ebony. Walnut veneer panels were a real favorite in the 1870s designs. Upholstery, usually of a more generous nature, was also often incorporated into this design style. Ornamentation and high relief carving included flowers, fruits, game, classical busts, acanthus scrolls, strapwork, tassels, and masks. Architectural motifs, such as pilasters, columns, pediments, balusters, and brackets are another prominent design feature. Legs are usually cabriole or pretty substantial turned legs.

Néo-Greek, 1855-1885: This design style easily merges with both the Louis XVI and Renaissance Revival styles. It is characterized by elements reminiscent of Greek architecture, such as pilasters, flutes, column, acanthus, foliate scrolls, Greek key motifs, and anthemion high relief carving. This style originated with the French, but was embraced by American furniture manufacturers. Woods are dark and often ebonized. Ornamentation may be gilded or bronzed. Legs tend to be curved to scrolled or cloven hoof feet.

Eastlake, 1870-1890: This design style is named for Charles Locke Eastlake who wrote a very popular book in 1872 called *Hints on Household Taste*. It was originally published in London. One of his principles was the relationship between function, form, and craftsmanship. Shapes of furniture from this style tend to be more rectangular. Ornamentation was created through the use of brackets, grooves, chamfers, and geometric designs. American furniture manufacturers were enthusiastic about this style since it was so easy to adapt for mass production. Woods used were again dark, but more native woods, such as maple and pine were incorporated. Legs and chair backs are straighter, often with incised decoration.

Art Furniture, 1880-1914: This design period represents furniture designs gone mad, almost an "anything goes" school of thought. The style embraces both straight and angular with some pieces that are much more fluid, reflecting several earlier design periods. This period sees the wide usage of turned moldings and dark woods, but this time stained to imitate ebony and lacquer. The growing Oriental influence is seen in furniture from this period, including the use of bamboo, which was imported and included in the designs. Legs tend to be straight; feet tend to be small.

Arts & Crafts, 1895-1915: The Arts and Crafts period furniture represents one of the strongest periods for current collectors. Quality period Arts and Crafts furniture is available through most of the major auction houses. And, for those desiring the look, good quality modern furniture is also made in this style. The Arts and Crafts period furniture is generally rectilinear and a definite correlation is seen between form and function. The primary designers of this period were George Stickley, Leopold Stickley, J. George Stickley, George Niedeken, Elbert Hubbard, Frank Lloyd Wright, and the Englishman William Morris. Their furniture designs often overlapped into architectural and interior design including rugs, textiles, and other accessories. Woods used for Arts and Crafts furniture is primarily oak. Finishes

Cupboard, Court, Italian Renaissance Revival, upper section with molded cornice over series of small drawers, central prospect drawer resting on lower section, two arched panel cupboard doors, classical figures and lion details, 19th century, 82" h x 44" w, **$6,325.**
Photo courtesy of Pook & Pook, Inc.

Arts & Crafts china cabinet, trapezoidal, overhanging top supported by corbels, keyed through tenons, arched apron, orig finish, missing one tenon and one corbel, stenciled no. 6012, 61-1/4" x 42" x 14-1/4", **$3,600.**
Photo courtesy of David Rago Auctions, Inc.

Desk, Art Nouveau, made for Boys Lyman St. School, Westborough, MA, mahogany, cast iron mounts, drop front, fitted interior, open shelves, weighted pulleys working sliding panel which opens to reveal drawers and shelves, three drawers, open shelf, paw feet, 33-1/2" w, 17" d, 83-1/2" h, **$3,525.**
Photo courtesy of Skinner, Inc.

Bedside tables, Art Deco style, ebonized supports and plinth bases, pair, 14-1/2" w, 24" d, 24" h, **$750.**
Photo courtesy of Sloans & Kenyon Auctioneers and Appraisers.

Sideboard, International Movement, Heywood-Wakefield, champagne finish, drawers over three cabinet doors, two interior drawers and single shelf, branded mark, 59-3/4" l, 19" d, 32-1/2" h, **$500.**
Photo courtesy of David Rago Auctions, Inc.

were natural, fumed, or painted. Upholstery is leather or of a fabric design also created by the same hand. Hardware was often made in copper. Legs are straight and feet are small, if present at all, as they were often a simple extension of the leg. Some inlay of natural materials was used, such as silver, copper, and abalone shells.

Art Nouveau, 1896-1914: Just as the Art Nouveau period is known for women with long hair, flowers, and curves, so is Art Nouveau furniture. The Paris Exposition of 1900 introduced furniture styles reflecting what was happening in the rest of the design world, such as jewelry and silver. This style of furniture was not warmly embraced, as the sweeping lines were not very conducive to mass production. The few manufacturers that did interpret it for their factories found interest to be slight in America. The French held it in higher esteem. Woods used were dark, stylized lilies, poppies, and other more fluid designs were included. Legs tend to be sweeping or cabriole. Upholstery becomes slimmer.

Art Deco, 1920-1945: Furniture of the Art Deco period reflects the general feel of the period. The Paris *"l Exposition International des Arts Décorative et Industriels Modernes"* became the mantra for designs of everything in this period. Lines are crisp, with some use of controlled curves. The Chrysler Building in New York City remains the finest example of Art Deco architecture and those same straight lines and gentle curves are found in furniture. Furniture makers used expensive materials, such as veneers, lacquered woods, glass, and steel. The cocktail table first enters the furniture scene during this period. Upholstery can be vinyl or smooth fabrics. Legs are straight or slightly tapered; chair backs tend to be either low or extremely high.

International Movement, 1940-present: Furniture designed and produced during this period is distinctive as it represents the usage of some new materials, like plastic, aluminum, and molded laminates. The Bauhaus and also the Museum of Modern Art heavily influenced some designers. In 1940, the museum organized competitions for domestic furnishings. Designers Eero Saarien and Charles Eames won first prize for their designs. A new chair design combined the back, seat, and arms together as one unit. Tables were designed that incorporated the top, pedestal, and base as one. Shelf units were also designed in this manner. These styles could easily be mass-produced in plastic, plywood, or metal.

Additional Listings: Arts and Craft Movement, Art Deco, Art Nouveau, Children's Nursery Items, Orientalia, and Shaker Items.
Notes: Furniture is one of the types of antiques for which regional preferences are a factor in pricing. Victorian furniture is popular in New Orleans and unpopular in New England. Oak is in demand in the Northwest, but not as much so in the middle Atlantic states.

Prices vary considerably on furniture. Shop around. Furniture is plentiful unless you are after a truly rare example. Examine all pieces thoroughly—avoid buying on impulse. Turn items upside down; take them apart. Price is heavily influenced by the amount of repairs and restoration. Make certain you know if any such work has been done to a piece before buying it.

The prices listed here are "average" prices. They are only a guide. High and low prices are given to show market range.

Reproduction Alert. Beware of the large number of reproductions. During the 25 years following the American Centennial of 1876, there was a great revival in copying furniture styles and manufacturing techniques of earlier eras. These centennial pieces now are more than 100 years old. They confuse many dealers, as well as collectors.

Feet

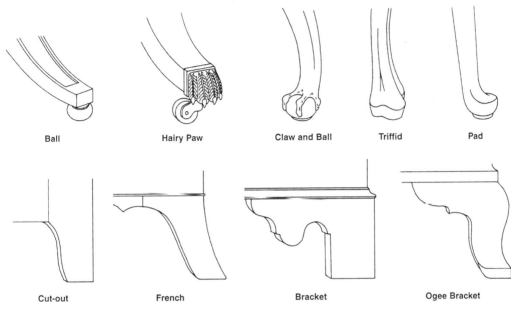

Ball

Hairy Paw

Claw and Ball

Triffid

Pad

Cut-out

French

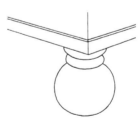

Bracket

Ogee Bracket

Marlborough

Spanish

Turmed Ball

Spider

Spade

Snake

Legs

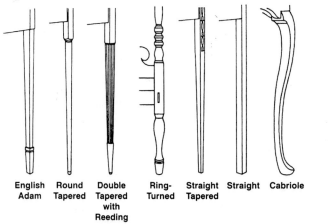

English Adam   Round Tapered   Double Tapered with Reeding   Ring-Turned   Straight Tapered   Straight   Cabriole

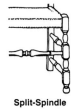

Split-Spindle

Ring-turned

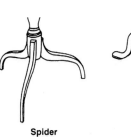

Spider

Snake

Hardware

Bail Handle

Teardrop Pull

Oval Brass

Brass

Pressed Glass

Eagle Brass

Construction Details

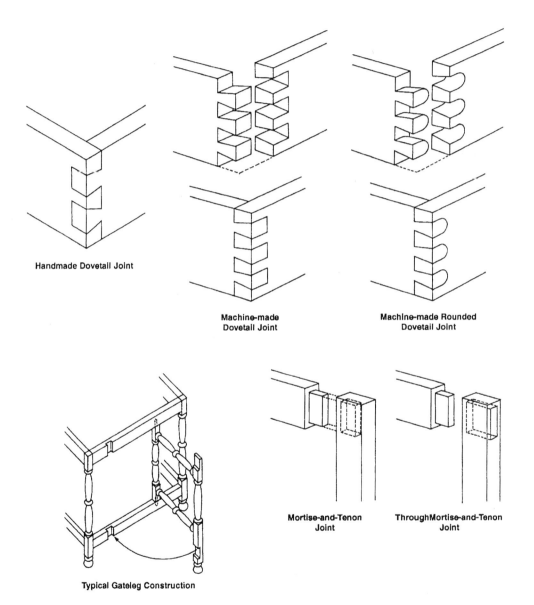

Handmade Dovetail Joint

Machine-made
Dovetail Joint

Machine-made Rounded
Dovetail Joint

Typical Gateleg Construction

Mortise-and-Tenon
Joint

ThroughMortise-and-Tenon
Joint

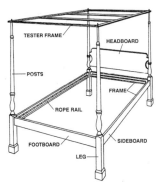

Typical Parts of a Bed

Cannonball bed, painted, Maine, red and black grain dec, early/mid-19th century, 49-1/2" h, 55" w, 79" d, **$645.**
Photo courtesy of Pook & Pook, Inc.

Beds

Art Deco, France, single curvilinear bed frame with hanging shelf compartments, price for pr, c1930, 82" l...................................**$1,410**

Art Nouveau, Emile Galle, French, satin wood and marquetry inlay, mirrored armoire, single size bed, bed stand, floral inlays of iris in walnut, kingwood, and tulipwood, mother-of-pearl accents, headboard sgd in marquetry "Galle," c1890
....**$3,800**

Arts and Crafts

Limbert, #651, daybed, angled headrest with spade cut-out, orig finish, recovered cushions, branded, numbered, 74" w, 25" d, 23" h........**$650**

Stickley Bros, attributed to, headboard with narrow vertical slats and panels, tapered feet, orig side rails, orig finish, minor scratches, stenciled "9001-1/2," 80-1/2" l, 56-1/2" w, 30" h.....................**$1,355**

Stickley, Gustav, single size, pyramidal posts, nine spindles to the head and footboard, complete with side rails, branded mark, 79-1/2" l, 43-3/4" w, 49-1/4" h................................**$8,575**

Baroque, Italian, simulated marble high scrolling headboard dec in patiglia with vacant cartouches and foliage, carved scrolling feet, painted, green and blue marbleized dec, losses to paint and gilt, pr, 45-3/4" w, 84" h.....................**$3,750**

Belle Epoque, French, walnut, each pc mounted with bronze floral wreaths, hardware, and claw feet, three-door armoire, two twin beds, four drawer

dresser, two dressing chairs, wall unit with chests, c1910, mounted with 20" x 12" bronze plaque of mother and child
....**$4,200**

Biedermeier, figured mahogany veneer, octagonal posts, turned feet and finials, paneled head and footboards, orig rails, some veneer damage, 38" w, 72" l, 45" h, pr...........**$750**

Chippendale, tall post, curly maple, turned posts, scrolled headboard with poplar panel, orig side rails, old mellow refinishing, minor repairs to posts, 60" w, 72" l, 80" h..........**$3,000**

Classical

Massachusetts, carved mahogany, tall post, scrolled mahogany headboard flanked by reeded, carved, and ring-turned posts, acanthus leaf, beading, gothic arches, and foliage carving, reeded and turned feet, orig rails later fitted for angle irons and bed bolts, orig surface, central finial missing, c1825-35, 59" w, 81" d, 98" h...........................**$6,900**

Middle Atlantic States, carved mahogany veneer, low post, scrolled and paneled headboard, leaf-carved finials flanked by posts with pineapple finials, acanthus leaves above spiral carved and ring-turned posts, orig rails, bed bolts, and covers, refinished, imperfections, 1835-45, 58-1/2" w, 78" d, 56-1/2" h....**$1,100**

New England, painted, turned tall post, turned and tapering head posts flanking shaped headboard, spiral-carved foot post joined by rails fitted for roping, accompanying tester, old red paint, restored, c1820, 54" w, 79" l, 60-1/2" h...........**$1,400**

Country, American, rope, high post, curly maple, areas of tight curl, evidence of old red wash, turned and tapered legs, boldly turned posts taper toward the top, paneled headboard with scrolled crest, turned top finial, pierced restorations, 53-1/2" w, 70" l rails with orig bolts..........**$1,890**

Country, American, day bed, birch, old red paint, tapered supports on head and footboards, tapered legs, raised turned feet, casters, contemporary blue and white upholstery, 74" l, 25-1/2" d, 27-1/4" h....................**$400**

Country, American, trundle, southwestern PA, walnut, mortised joints, turned posts, and finials, shaped corners along top edge of head, foot, and sideboards, refinished, 71-1/2" l, 44" d..**$125**

Daybed, Pennsylvania, William and Mary, cherry, scalloped crest rail over three vasiform splats, rush seat, turned baulester legs and stretchers, c1740, 15-1/4" h x 22-1/2" w x 67" l, **$2,290.**
Photo courtesy of Pook & Pook, Inc.

Edwardian, A. H. Davenport, painted maple, bed, two door side cabinet, two chairs, dressing table, early 20th C **$5,450**

Empire, American

Single, fitted as daybed or sofa, mahogany and mahogany figured veneer, turned and acanthus carved posts, upholstered cushion, 31-1/2" x 80" x 43-3/4" h **$825**

Tall post, curly maple posts, poplar scrolled headboard with old soft finish, turned detail, acorn finials, rails and headboard replaced, 57-1/4" w, 72-1/2" l rails, 89" h **$1,650**

Empire-style, sleigh, red painted, scrolled ends, bronze mounted foliate and mask mounts, price for pr, 20th C **$1,650**

Federal

American, cherry, tester, three-quarter, rect headboard with concave side edges, footboard lower, baluster-turned posts continuing to turned legs, rails with rope pegs, first half 19th C, 81-1/2" l, 53-1/2" w, 78-1/4" h **$500**

Massachusetts, attributed to Abner Toppan, Newburyport, canopy, cherry, vase and ring-turned, reeded, and swelled foot posts joined to chamfered tapering head posts and arched headboard by an arched canopy frame, old red stained surface, 72" l, 49" w, 83" h; accompanied by chamber stand with sq pierced top on beaded sq legs joined by cutout skirt and medial shelf with incised beaded drawer, refinished, remnants of red stain, also accompanied by orig receipt, 1810, 12" top, 31" h..............................**$9,400**

New England, maple, arched canopy above vase and ring-turned reeded and swelled foot posts, vase and ring-turned legs joined to ring-turned tapering head posts and arched headboard, old red-stained surface, minor imperfections, c1815, 51" w, 70" l, 80" h **$5,000**

New England, tester, maple, vase and ring-turned foot posts continuing to tapering sq legs and molded spade feet joined to sq tapering head posts continuing to sq legs, arched headboard, later arched canopy, refinished, c1810, 51" w, 83-3/4" h ...**$815**

New England, mahogany, turned and carved, tall post tester, arched canopy frame on vase and ring-turned spiral carved fluted taper-ing foot posts, joined to the turned tapering head posts with shaped headboard, ring-turned tapering feet, c1810-15, 45-1/2" w, 72" d, 61" h **$1,775**

Salem, Massachusetts, mahogany, tall post, vase and ring-turned swelled fluted foot post with leaf carving on fluted plinths continuing to vase and ring-turned legs joined to ring-turned tapering head posts, shaped headboard, old surface, c1810, 51" w, 71" d, 65" h.................**$3,175**

George III, four poster, carved walnut, brass mounted, circular tapered head posts, shaped mahogany headboard, reeded and acanthus-carved foot posts, ring-turned feet, casters, 9-1/2" h.................................**$10,000**

Gothic Revival, American, carved mahogany, tall headboard with three Gothic arch panels, leaf-carved crest rail, flanked by heavy round ribbed posts topped by ring-turned finials, arched and paneled footboard flanked by lower foot posts, heavy bun feet, c1850 ....**$4,750**

Hepplewhite-style, Philadelphia, mahogany, four tall posts each with reeded slender vasiform section over short vasiform turned carved with continuous swag designs, upholstered tester, c1943, 82" l, 62" w, 93" h.......**$1,550**

International Movement, George Nelson for Howard Miller, Thin Edge, caned headboard, 34" x 76" x 35" **$1,610**

International Movement, day bed Tugendhat-style, after design by Mies van der Rohe, rect black leather cushion with head rest, webbed wood frame, four cylindrical legs, 77" l, 38" w, 15-1/2" h **$2,350**

Hans Wegner, Denmark, retailed by Georg Jensen Inc., New York, natural woven backrest, lifts and folds to create upholstered day bed, retail label on base, c1965 teak, 78" l, 33-3/4" d, 28-3/4" h ...**$2,710**

Louis XV-style, carved walnut, upholstered, orig rails, pr **$600**

Queen Anne, Pennsylvania, low poster, turned and painted pine, head and footposts with flattened ball finials, shaped head and footboards, tapered feet, orig rope rails, orig green paint, early 19th C, 48-1/2" w, 74-3/4" h..................................**$3,600**

Renaissance Revival, walnut, double, high headboard topped by rounded pediment, pointed finial **$1,700**

Canopy bed, Federal, mahogany, reeded post, central foliate carving, Massachusetts, c1815, **$1,405.**
Photo courtesy of Pook & Pook, Inc.

Bed, attributed to Old Hickory, spindled and reed paneled head and foot boards, orig finish, unmarked, full size, 62" x 54" x 79", **$650.**
Photo courtesy of David Rago Auctions, Inc.

Poster bed, Empire, mahogany, acanthus-carved and spiral-turned posts, carved and cutout headboard, canopy top, custom bedding, second quarter 19th century, 79" h x 61" w x 72" l, **$1,210.**
Photo courtesy of Green Valley Auctions.

Rope

Country, curly maple and cherry, old mellow finish, urn shaped finials, scrolled headboard, large turned foot rail, 68-1/2" l orig rails, 51-1/2" w, 47" h **$200**

Country, pine and poplar, old dark red over orig lighter red paint, short turned finials and feet, 69" l orig rails, 51" w, 31" h headboard...**$250**

Pennsylvania, summer/winter, softwood, painted blue, removable turned posts, arched headboard, replacement canopy support, 50-1/2" w, 77" l, 80-1/2" h **$2,200**

Sheraton, canopy

Carved mahogany, headboard posts simple turned with ring and block turnings, simple headboard, heavily carved footboard posts with spiral turnings and acanthus leaf bell, sq tester with curtains, 58" w, 73-1/2" l, 88" without finials ..**$3,200**

Painted, headboard with D-type cut outs on side, footboard with reeded

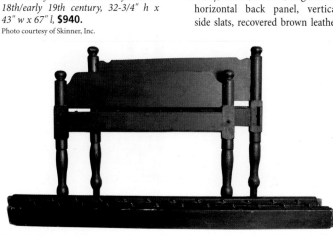

Bed, turned post, New England, painted blue, block-turned posts with knob finials, swelled ring-turned feet, peaked head and footboards, old surface, late 18th/early 19th century, 32-3/4" h x 43" w x 67" l, **$940.**
Photo courtesy of Skinner, Inc.

Rope bed, painted blue, turned posts, Pennsylvania, c1810, 35-3/4" h, 41-3/4" w, 75-1/2" l, **$450.**
Photo courtesy of Pook & Pook, Inc.

and turned posts, canopy frame, painted red, 52" w, 76" l, 68" h ..**$750**

Sheraton, country, day, pine, old brown finish, ring turned and tapered legs, ball feet, pegged construction, adjustable back, large dovetails at corners, contemporary cushions, 20" d, 70-1/2" l **$900**

Victorian, high headboard

Brass, four capped corner posts, fine applied brass scroll on headboard and footboard, c1900, 57" w, 78" l, 69" h **$1,850**

Brass, straight top rail, curved corners, ring-shaped capitals, cast iron side rails, c1900, 55" w, 61" h **$1,200**

Walnut, plain, 52" w, 50" h **$250**

Walnut and burlwood, ornately carved crest, 56" w, 90" h **$1,150**

Benches

Arts & Crafts, settle

Stickley Bros, cube, vertical slats, orig drop-in seat covered in new green leather, excellent orig finish, stenciled number, 50" l, 22-1/2" d, 33" h **$2,530**

Stickley, Gustav, No. 208, even arm, vertical slats all around, top rail mortised through legs, drop-in spring seat covered in new green leather, red Gustav decal, light sanding, some color added to orig finish, 76-1/2" l, 32" d, 29-1/4" h **$6,900**

Stickley, tapering posts, tightly spaced canted slats to back and sides, leather upholstered drop-in seat, fine orig finish, red decal, minor veneer chips, 36" x 80" x 32", Gustav, No. 222 ....**$11,500**

Stickley, Gustav, No. 225, single board horizontal back panel, vertical side slats, recovered brown leather

drop-in seat, over-coated orig finish, unmarked, 59-3/4" l, 31" d, 29-1/4" h **$7,475**

Stickley, L. & J. G., cube, border vertical panels on back and under each arm, brown leather cushion, orig condition and finish, orig upholstery, "The Work of L. and J. G. Stickley" label, 72" l, 27" w, 28" h **$3,450**

Stickley, L. & J. G., open arm, cloud lift top rail, horizontal backslat and corbels, new tan leather upholstered seat cushion, new finish, The Work of L & J. G. Stickley label, 53" l, 26" w, 36" h, some looseness ..**$1,650**

Young, J. M., cube, capped top rail, vertical slats all around, fabric cov drop-in spring seat, refinished, unmarked, 78" l, 29-1/2" h, 34" h **$2,870**

Art Deco, painted cast iron, re-upholstered top, small...........................**$95**

Bucket

Country, walnut, sq nail construction, shaped ends, four mortised shelves, old dry brown finish, age splits, one shelf notched out in back, 39-1/2" w, 12-1/2" d, 44" h **$1,700**

Pennsylvania, softwood, mortised construction, shaped cut-out legs, blue-green over earlier red surface, 80" l, 18" d, 29-1/2" h **$2,750**

Pennsylvania, softwood, beaded sides and shelves, stepped lower shelf with shaped cut-out feet, dovetailed, mortised, and nailed construction, old red painted surface, two shelves, 34-1/2" w, 14" d, 47-1/2" h....**$5,225**

Classical, window

Boston, carved mahogany veneer, upholstered seat, veneered rail, leaf-carved cyma curved ends, joined by ring-turned medial stretcher, 1835-45, 48" w, 16-1/4" d, 17-1/2" h........**$2,185**

New York, mahogany veneer, curving upholstered seat flanked by scrolled ends, scrolled base, old refinish, some veneer cracking and loss, 20th C olive green velvet upholstery, 1815-25, 39-1/2" w, 14" d, 23-5/8" h....**$3,500**

Classical Revival, mahogany, carved paw feet and lion's heads, maroon velvet cushion, old finish, 16-1/2" l, 29-1/4" w, 23" h...........................**$600**

Country

Pennsylvania, softwood, mortised leg, double skirt, shaped cut-out legs, old orange painted surface, 36" l, 13-1/2" d, 15-1/2" h **$3,520**

Pennsylvania, softwood, mortised leg, shaped cut-out legs, double molded skirt and towel bars, old blue-gray painted base, 38" l, 12" d, 20" h **$6,600**

Pennsylvania, softwood, mortised leg, shaped cut-out legs, reinforcing slats, old red painted surface, 53" l, 11-1/2" d, 17-3/4" h **$1,430**

Pine, old worn and weathered green repaint, one board top with rounded front corners, beaded edge apron, cut-out feet mortised through top, age crack in one end of top, 104" l, 13-1/2" w **$325**

Decorated, orig dark green with reddish brown paint, yellow line dec, mortised construction, some sq nails, arched end panels, replaced shoe feet, some later nails added, 33" w, 14" d, 23-1/4" h **$275**

Federal

New England, window, mahogany, upholstered seat and rolled arms, sq tapering legs, H-form stretchers, refinished, minor repair to one leg, c1810, 39-1/2" l, 16" d, 29" h ... **$900**

New York, window, figured mahogany, each end with rect crotch-figured crest centering removable slip seat, matching seat rail, saber legs, c1825, 40-1/2" l **$3,500**

George III, English, window, mahogany, rect seat, scrolling arms, later velvet cov, straight legs, blind fret carved, H-form stretcher, pr, mid-18th C, 38" l **$4,750**

Gothic Revival, American, carved mahogany, angled over-upholstered seat, carved seat rails centering quatrefoil, facet lancet-carved legs, mold-

ed faceted feet, c1820-40, 65" l, 20" d, 15-1/2" h **$1,750**

Kneeling, Pennsylvania, walnut, mortised, turned splayed legs, oval cut top, 36" l, 10" d, 9" h **$250**

Louis XVI-style, window, carved cherry, overstuffed seat, channeled rails, flanked by molded, overscroll arms carved with be-ribboned foliate sprays, turned, tapered, and leaf-capped legs **$200**

Meeting hall, pine and butternut, old sun bleached finish, tapered pencil post legs mortised through single board seat, narrow crest rail and supports, from Amana Colonies, 93" w, 19" d, 35" h **$600**

Piano, Arts & Crafts, Gustav Stickley, cut-out handles on plank sides, plank top, broad up-ended cross-stretcher, orig finish, red decal, 36" l, 12-3/4" w, 22" h **$4,600**

Victorian-style, chaise lounge, Chesterfield, tufted brown leather, adjustable backrest, casters, early 20th C, 62" l **$3,000**

Wagon seat, New England, painted, two pairs of arched slats joining three turned stiles, double rush seat flanked by turned arms ending in turned hand-holds, tapering legs, old brown paint over earlier gray, late 18th C, 15" h seat, 30" h **$1,200**

Wicker, painted white, hooped crest rail flanked by rows of dec curlicues, spiral wrapped posts and six spindles, pressed-in oval seat, dec curlicue apron, wrapped cabriole legs, X-form stretcher, 35" w, 31" h **$500**

Windsor, settle, 20th C green paint, yellow in turnings, 29 spindles with bamboo turnings across back with turned arms, well-shaped seat with incised rain gutter around back, eight splayed legs joined by cross stretchers, splits in seat, old iron braces added underneath for support, 77-1/2" w, 22" d, 36-3/4" h **$2,100**

Arts & Crafts, Roycroft Ali Baba bench with canted, A-shaped sides, lower stretcher mortised through the sides and half-log seat, excellent orig finish, carved orb and cross mark, 19-1/4" x 42" x 11", **$8,850.**
Photo courtesy of David Rago Auctions, Inc.

Trestle bench, Arts & Crafts, Rose Valley, carved oak, stretcher mortised through flaring plank legs, keyed through-tenons, orig finish, seam separation at top, branded, 18" x 60" x 15-1/2", sold at auction for **$10,000.**
Photo courtesy of David Rago Auctions, Inc.

Settle bench, Arts & Crafts, Gustav Stickley, No. 173, even-arms crib type, canted sides, loose seat cushion, fine orig finish, leather and cane decking, unmarked, tear to leather, small veneer repairs to top right post, 38-3/4" x 70" x 32", **$22,500.**
Photo courtesy of David Rago Auctions, Inc.

Bench, English, Cornwall, country, pine, high back, shaped sides, 19th century, 61" x 39" x 22", **$950.**
Photo courtesy of David Rago Auctions, Inc.

Lounge chair, Thonet, rocking, cane paneled back and seat, 40" x 26" x 38", **$175.**
Photo courtesy of David Rago Auctions, Inc.

Dower chest, painted pine, lift lid, three tombstone panels with pinwheels, tulips, etc., "Sara Farne 1808," Dauphin County Pennsylvania, dated 1808, 24-1/2" h, 50-1/2" w, **$4,915.**
Photo courtesy of Pook & Pook, Inc.

Bentwood

In 1856, Michael Thonet of Vienna perfected the process of bending wood using steam. Shortly afterward, Bentwood furniture became popular. Other manufacturers of Bentwood furniture were Jacob and Joseph Kohn, Philip Strobel and Son, Sheboygan Chair Co., and Tidoute Chair Co. Bentwood furniture is still being produced today by the Thonet firm and others.

Box
Circular, blue and white open and closed tulips dec on dry salmon ground, c1780, 5" d **$10,000**

Oval, laced seams on lid and base, old dark green paint on ext., dark red on int., dark red "AKHD Anno 1804" on lid, wear, splits, 12" l, 6" h **$300**

Continuous scene of man, woman, two dogs, tulips, rose trees, bulging crack, no lid, 13" d **$16,000**

Oval, dark green paint, laced seams, replaced lacing, glued edge splits, 17-3/4" w, 9-3/4" d, 7-3/8" h **$150**

Oval, laced seams, orig blue paint, black and red foliage around borders, initials "F.G.S.B. 1836," sq nails around base, edge damage, age splits, 22" l, 13" d, 8-1/4" h **$700**

Chair, Austrian, Vienna Secession-style, side, back splat with three circular perforations, three slender spindles, painted black, set of eight, c1910.........**$5,500**

Cradle, ivory fittings, 41" l, 39" h .. **$440**

Hall tree, Thonet, bentwood frame, contrasting striped wood inlay, coat hooks with central beveled mirror above one door, metal drip pan, orig label, c1910, 57" w, 13" d, 76" h **$2,750**

Plant stand, Thonet, Austria, round top with black printed classical urn and flower motif, bentwood tripod base, imp "Thonet," paper label, wear,

couple of breaks on feet, late 19th C, 18-5/8" d, 30-5/8" h **$210**

Rocker, Thonet, arched twined top rail, cut-velvet fabric fitted back, armrests, and seat, elaborate scrolling frame, curved runners, 53" l..................**$750**

Stool, Thonet, attributed to Marcel Kammerer, Austria, beech, sq seat, four legs, U-shaped braces forming spandrels, shaped bronze sabot feet, 1901, 14-1/4" sq, 18-1/2" h **$1,500**

Table, Josef Hoffman, c1905, circular top, wooden spheres dec below rim, 21-1/4" h **$500**

Blanket chests

Chippendale
Country, attributed to southwest PA, cherry, chestnut secondary wood, dovetailed case, cov interior till, dovetailed drawers, molded base, shaped bracket feet with scalloped returns, wrought iron strap hinges, old refinishing, replaced brass pulls, restorations and replacements to feet and lid, 22-3/4" d, 28-1/2" h....**$1,050**

Pennsylvania, figured walnut, molded rect hinged top opens to interior with lidded till, dovetailed case inlaid with "17 MM 85" with panel bordered by geometric banding, horizontal applied molding below, two thumb molded half drawers, bracket feet, two orig escutcheons, old surface, minor imperfections, 1785, 47" w, 22" d, 47" h **$14,100**

Decorated
American, poplar, orig black over red sponge dec, one board top, molded trim, arched cut-outs on end aprons, scalloped front apron, int. fitted with covered till, dovetailed drawer, cast iron hinges, minor touch-up, later coat of varnish,

43-1/4" w, 17" d, 21-1/4" h.......**$495**

New York, Schohaire County, 6 board, painted blue, molded top, dovetailed constructed base with painted diamond and draped frieze with Chinese export punchbowl and ladle, dotted, banded, vine, and diamond border flanked by enamel Stiegel flip glasses with circular borders, minor imperfections, early 19th C, 37" w, 17" d, 15" h.................**$6,900**

Ohio, pine and poplar, six-board construction, eagle dec, cover with considerable paint wear, restoration, c1820-40, 49-1/2" w, 21" d, 23-3/4" h **$2,300**

Ohio, attributed to Knox County, dovetailed poplar, orig sponged circles and meandering borders, two board top with molding, scalloped base painted black, beveled aprons, fitted int. with covered till, early iron casters, 39" w, 29-1/2" d...**$825**

Pennsylvania, Dauphin County, made for Madlen Nafrez, three blue panels on front, center one with name and date, other two panels with six pointed stars, 1808.............**$35,000**

Pennsylvania, softwood, front panel dec with six arched top panels, potted floral and foliate motif in style of Heinrich Otto, side panels dec with eight-point stars, molded lid and base, wrought iron strap hinges, interior till, 51" w, 23" d, 22-1/2" h.............**$11,000**

Pennsylvania, three tombstone shaped panels with stylized flowers, unicorns in center, reddish brown ground, loss to paint on lid, c1780...............**$9,500**

Dowry, Mahantango Valley, Pennsylvania, "Samuel Grebiel 1799," orig paint dec, red, blue, mustard, black, and white, two shaped polygons painted in blue grain painting, identical polygons

Blanket chest, painted pine, Pennsylvania, red and yellow striped dec, c1820, 21" h, 35" w, **$440.**
Photo courtesy of Pook & Pook, Inc.

Dower chest, painted, lift lid, panels with white and blue swirl dec on red ground, bracket feet, Pennsylvania, late 18th century, 21-3/4" h, 47-1/2" w, 20-3/4" d, **$1,170.**
Photo courtesy of Pook & Pook, Inc.

Mule chest, painted pine, old salmon surface, New England, c1760, 35" h, 42-1/2" w, **$1,220.**
Photo courtesy of Pook & Pook, Inc.

Blanket chest, late 18th century, 51-1/2" l x 23-1/2" d x 24-1/2" h, **$400.**
Photo courtesy of Wiederseim Associates, Inc.

Blanket chest, stencil and grain paint decorated, lid with applied edge moldings, dovetailed case, applied base moldings, turned feet, int. till with two concealed drawers, Western Pennsylvania, paint wear, loss to till's side, second half 19th century, 23" h x 44" w x 19-1/2" d, **$415.**
Photo courtesy of Green Valley Auctions.

Blanket chest, painted, rectangular, top, molded edge, dovetailed case, three arched panels, red and blue tulips in black urns, inscribed "Johanns Rank," dated 1798, molded base, cutout bracket feet, Pennsylvania, late 18th century, 22-1/2" h, 51-1/2" w, **$19,890.**
Photo courtesy of Pook & Pook, Inc.

on each side, two in front with banner above with name and date, int. lidded till, black painted dovetailed bracket base, off-set strap hinges, orig lock, 48-1/2" w, 21" d, 23-1/2" h **$3,000**

Federal, Pennsylvania, pine and cherry, molded lift top, well with till, case with two thumb-molded graduated drawers, dovetailed bracket feet, old refinish, minor imperfections, early 18th C, 40" w, 20-1/2" d, 43" h **$1,880**

Grain painted, New York state, molded hinged lift top, lidded till, molded bracket black painted base, orig fanciful ochre and raw umber graining, c1830, 48" w, 22" d, 29" h **$1,265**

Jacobean, oak, paneled construction with relief carving, drawer and feet replaced, repairs to lid and molding, old dark finish, 44-1/2" w, 19-1/2" d, 31-3/4" h **$825**

Miniature, England, mahogany, molded lift-top with wire hinges, dovetail constructed box base, mid molding trim, heavy molded bracket base, worm holes, wear, early 19th C, 14-1/4" l, 6-3/4" h **$1,035**

Mule, America, pine, thumb-molded top, two overlapping dovetailed drawers, bracket feet, old dark finishing, int. lined with 1875 Boston newspaper, pierced repairs to feet and drawer fronts, 40" w, 18" d, 34-3/4" h **$700**

Painted
Interior lid inscribed "Painted by D. Ellinger," also marked "D.Y. Ellinger 1957" on heart on front, pair of flower vases on front and each end, 31-3/4" w, 14-3/4" d, 19-1/2" h **$9,000**
Massachusetts, molded hinged top, case of two drawers, tall cut-out feet with valanced skirt, orig red-brown grain paint with contrasting beige grained drawers, orig pulls, first quarter 19th C, 36-3/4" w, 17-1/4" d, 37-3/4" h **$11,750**
New England, hinged top, well with

till, case with single drawer, cut-out base, orig mustard-brown graining resembling wood, minor imperfections, early 19th C, 39-1/4" w, 18-1/4" d, 40" h **$850**
New England, six-board, rect top, case with two drawer, cut-out feet joined by straight skirt, all-over orig reddish brown and yellow grain paint resembling exotic wood, old brass pulls, minor imperfections, minor paint wear, early 19th C, 41-1/4" w, 18-1/2" d, 32-1/4" h **$2,115**
Ohio, wide poplar boards, orig red paint, traces of silvery white star designs on lid and front, dovetailed case, molded top edge, bracket feet, small scalloped returns, molded base, int. till with lid, hinges and narrow hinge rail old replacements, minor edge wear, 49-1/4" w, 21" d, 26" h **$650**
Pennsylvania, Bucks County, red moldings and base, mottled reddish-brown ground, large triple banded hearts on front and sides, corners with half-hearts, over lozenges with names and date, two lower drawers, molded skirt with central drop, cut-out bracket feet, int. till, secret drawers, orig paint, minor losses, one side foot and back braces replaced, dated 1770, 49" l, 24" d, 29-1/2" h **$18,750**

Queen Anne, New England, marriage chest, pine, hinged rect lift lid, upper half faced with faux drawer fronts, brown paint, c1750, 35" **$4,000**

Sheraton, country, pine and poplar, orig red paint, molded edge top, paneled front and ends, sq corner posts, mortised and pinned frame, scalloped apron, turned feet, 44" w, 19-1/2" d, 25-1/2" h **$900**

William and Mary, New England, oak and yellow pine, joined, drawer base, old finish, minor imperfections, c1700, 48-1/2" w, 22" d, 32-3/4" h **$4,500**

Bookcase, two doors, Gustav Stickley, no. 717, gallery top, eight panes per door, hammered copper v-pulls, orig key, orig finish, sides and front color loss, top discoloration, red decal inside right, remnant of paper label on back, 56" x 47-1/2" x 13", $5,875.

Photo courtesy of David Rago Auctions, Inc.

Bookcase, L. & J.G. Stickley two-door with gallery top, twelve panes per door, keyed through-tenons, and hammered copper pulls, excellent original finish and condition, branded, 55" x 49" x 12", $7,200.

Photo courtesy of David Rago Auctions, Inc.

Bookcase, Gustav Stickley Harvey Ellis-designed two-door with leaded panes, refinished, good condition, seam separations on sides, paper label on back, 57" x 54" x 14", $8,400.

Photo courtesy of David Rago Auctions, Inc.

Bookcases
Arts & Crafts

English, double door, corbelled overhanging top, inlaid pewter, ebony, and fruitwood tulips, leaded glass panels with green tear-shaped inserts, curvilinear backsplash, emb strap handles, orig finish, unmarked, some corbels loose, 46" w, 12-1/2" d, 52-1/2" h....**$2,615**

Limbert, Grand Rapids, Michigan, oak, two elongated glass panels on each of two doors, three adjustable shelves on each side, round copper pulls, medium brown finish, branded mark on reverse, imperfections, early 20th C, 40-1/2" l, 14" d, 57-1/2" h **$2,775**

Stickley Bros, quarter-sawn oak, double door, slatted gallery top, single panes of glass, orig medium finish, brass tag, 35-1/2" w, 12" d, 50" h **$4,875**

Stickley, Gustav, quarter sawn oak, double door, eight glass panes to each door, gallery top, hammered copper V-pulls, three int. shelves, top and bottom mortised thru sides, red decal and paper Craftsman label, refinished, 42-3/4" w, 13" d, 56-1/4" h **$5,175**

Stickley, Gustav, quarter sawn oak, double door, 12 panes per door, gallery top, brass V-pulls, mortised top, paper label, refinished, warp in right door, stripped hardware, 54" w, 13" d, 55" h..................**$5,175**

Stickley, L. & J. G., Fayetteville, New York, oak, No. 641, gallery top with through tenons, Handcraft decal, some stains, door missing, c1912, 30" w, 55" h **$1,300**

Biedermeier-style, inlaid cherry, outset molded cornice with ebonized bead, front with two recessed glazed doors, four shelves, outset molded base raised on black feet, burr poplar panels, ebonized stringing, 53-1/2" w, 21" d, 72" h..................................**$700**

Chippendale

English, two pcs, mahogany, oak and pine secondary woods, top with two doors with geometric mullions and old glass, four adjustable shelves, two dovetailed drawers with beaded edges, short bracket feet, molded base, old replaced oval brasses, old refinishing, restorations to cornice and feet, later backboards, 32-3/8" w, 14" d, 83-1/4" h....**$2,300**

New England, southern, mahogany and maple, scroll top, top section with molded scrolled cresting, carved pinwheel terminals centering carved fan and bordered with punchwork flanked by flame urn-turned finials, two thumb-molded recessed panel doors opening to compartmented shelved int., lower section with fall front desk opening to stepped multi-drawer compartmented int. above case of four graduated scratchbeaded drawers, bracket feet, replaced brasses, refinished, imperfections, late 18th C, 39" w, 21" d, 84-3/4" h..........**$7,100**

Chippendale-style, New England, mahogany, broken arch pedestal over two arched-paneled doors, fitted secretary int. with pigeonholes, six small drawers, lower section with fall front, stepped fitted int., straight front, two small and two wide drawers, brass bail handle, escutcheons, lock plates, straight bracket feet, 42" w, 24" d, 93-3/4" h **$3,200**

Classical, Boston, carved mahogany veneer, cove molded cornice above two glazed doors flanked by columns with leaf carved tops and turned bases, fold-out felt lined writing surface, sectioned for writing implements, two small cock-beaded drawers over two long drawers, flanked by similar columns with carved tops, four reeded and carved bulbous feet, glazed doors open to bird's eye maple veneered int. with two adjustable shelves, valanced open compartments, five small drawers, brasses and wooden pulls appear to be orig, old refinish, imperfections, 1830s, 44-3/4" w, 22-1/4" d, 88" h..........................**$11,500**

Eastlake

America, ebonized, three glazed doors flanked by turned carved columns, incised and gilt dec, three drawer base, c1785, 58" w, 14" d, 74-1/2" h **$1,850**

America, cherry, rect top, flaring bead trimmed cornice, pair of single-pan glazed cupboard doors, carved oval paterae and scrolls across top, adjustable shelved int., stepped base with line-incised drawers, bail handles, c1880, 47-1/2" w, 15-1/4" d, 69-1/4" h...............**$1,200**

Empire, crotch mahogany veneers, top section: large architectural type cornice, two large glass doors with cathedral top muttons, three adjustable shelves; base: 11 drawers, oval brass knobs, applied base molding, two panes of glass cracked, 66" w, 83" h..**$5,500**

Empire style, French, ormolu mounted mahogany, fitted with four tall grill-inset and paneled doors, shelved interior, corners mounted with herm-form pilasters, wreath and paw feet, 19th C, 108" w, 12" d, 84-1/2" h....................................**$5,900**

Federal

Boston or Salem, Massachusetts, carved mahogany and mahogany veneer, top section with shaped gallery joining square plinths above flat cornice molding, two hinged glazed doors with beaded Gothic arches, four adjustable shelves, projecting base of four cockbeaded short drawers, corners carved with acanthus leaves and fluting, punchwork above vase and ring-turned reeded tapering legs, old refinish, imperfections, c1815-1820, 50" w, 18-1/2" d, 87-1/2" h..............**$9,900**

Southern States, attributed to, mahogany, veneered pediment embellished with inlaid floral vines and leaves above mullioned glazed doors, int. adjustable beaded shelves, lower case as hinged butler's desk with int. of valanced compartments and small drawers outlined with stringing, case of three graduated string inlaid drawers, skirt with inlaid vines and leaves, French feet, old refinish, replaced brasses, restored, 1790-1810, 40-1/2" w, 21-1/2" d, 93-1/2" h **$4,700**

George III, inlaid mahogany, dentil-molded cornice above two paneled doors, shelved interior, two candle slides, slant front enclosing fitted interior, two short and three graduated drawers, bracket feet, third quarter 18th C, 37" w, 22" d, 85-1/2" h...**$4,600**

George III-style, with 18th century elements, mahogany, later swan's neck cresting above pair of paneled doors opening to shelves, fitted with candle rests, lower section with slant lid enclosing a fitted int., all above three long drawers, ogee bracket feet, 35" w, 20" d, 95" h....................**$2,650**

George III style/Edwardian, painted satinwood, breakfront, upper section with four glazed doors; lower section fitted with five drawers on each end, projecting center section with secretaire drawer over pair of cabinet doors, polychrome dec, early 20th C, 75" w, 18" d, 88" h......**$11,750**

Georgian, early 18th C

Inlaid walnut, bureau bookcase, rect cornice, two paneled doors opening to shelves, fitted slant-lid desk, two short over two long drawers, bracket feet, inlaid all over with scrolling vines, 44" w, 22" d, 89" h...... **$10,575**

Mahogany, shaped octagonal cornice over glazed doors, above two cabinet doors, bracket feet **$2,900**

International Movement

Delineator Series, designed by Paul McCobb, manufactured by The Lane Co., retailed by Angelus Furniture Showroom, Los Angeles and San Francisco, walnut, upper cabinet fitted with open shelf over six cubby holes and two drawers, open shelf over pull-out writing surface, lower cabinet fitted with median shelves, one round pull missing, mid-20th C, 36-3/8" w, 15" d, 78" h **$600**

Unknown maker, teak, three fully finished modular sections in metal framework, with panel to create right angle, accompanied by magazine illus of unit, c1960, each 35-1/4" w, 17" d, 68-1/2" h....**$2,350**

Louis XV-style, block front, ormolu mounts, floral marquetry, banded inlay, top surface worn, scratches, 56" w, 16" d, 55" h.....................**$2,500**

Regency, late, mahogany, bookcase/breakfront, concave fronted cornice, frieze carved with anthemion, upper section fitted with four arched and glazed doors; lower section fitted with fall front writing surface and fitted int., all above two pedestals fitted with shelves and drawers, early 19th C, 84" w, 26" d, 93" h.....................**$7,475**

Renaissance Revival, American, late 19th C

Carved mahogany, two glass doors, shelved interior, case carved with central portrait bust and scrolling foliage, two columns, gadrooned ball feet, 61" w, 18" d, 64" h **$2,115**

Walnut, rect case carved with foliage and angular flowerheads, two doors, two base drawers, 54" w, 16" d, 57" h.............................**$1,550**

Walnut, rect top, three shaped, foliate, and corbel carved doors, shelved interior, plinth base, 73" w, 13" d, 49" h..................**$2,350**

Walnut, three tall glazed doors, shelved interior, projecting base with three drawers, 74" w, 20-1/2" d, 90" h.....................**$3,850**

Bookcase, Arts & Crafts, three door, each has four panes over two larger ones, three adjustable shelves per section, arched apron, orig finish, missing center mullion from middle door, unmarked, 56" x 63-1/2" x 14", **$2,880.**
Photo courtesy of David Rago Auctions, Inc.

Bookcase, Limbert single-door three adjustable shelves, corbels under a shaped top, and an arched apron, refinished, very good condition, branded on back, 57-1/4" x 29-1/2" x 14", **$5,400.**
Photo courtesy of David Rago Auctions, Inc.

Bookcase, Roycroft mahogany thirty-third degree single-door with sixteen panes, fixed shelves, shaped front and side posts, and a hammered copper escutcheon and knob-pull, orig finish, good condition, carved orb and cross on door, 56-1/2" x 40" x 15", **$9,000.**
Photo courtesy of David Rago Auctions, Inc.

Revolving, American, oak, molded rect top, five compartmentalized shelves with slatted ends, quadruped base with casters, stamped "Danners Revolving Book Case…Ohio," second half 19th C, 24" w, 24" d, 68-1/4" h **$1,200**

Rococo-style, Italian, serpentine front with three shelves, cabriole legs, dec with Chinoiserie scenes, green ground, late 19th C, 38" w, 14" d, 49" h **$690**

Victorian, Globe-Wernicke, barrister type, stacking, three sections, oak, glass fronted drawers, drawer in base, metal bands, orig finish **$900**

Boxes

Artist's, Pennsylvania, fancy inlay, tiger maple, bird's eye maple, and walnut, 1850-70 .... **$950**

Ballot, walnut, eight slide lid compartments, names of election officials and writing under lid, 19th C voting forms from East Berlin, Pennsylvania, last used in 1892, 32-1/2" l, 8-1/4" w, 4-1/4" h **$2,200**

Band, oval

Bucher-type paint dec, black ground, house and trees on center of lid, red/orange, white, and green floral tulip on top and sides, yellow highlights, provenance: Eugene and Dorothy Elgin collection, Conestoga Auction Co., April 3, 2004, 9-1/4" l, 6-1/8" w, 4-1/2" h **$15,950**

Unknown artist, nailed construction, painted light blue with patina turning blue to gray, pencil sgd "Elisha Whipple" under lid, 6-3/4" l, 5" w, 4" h **$2,530**

Box, Charles Rohlfs ornately carved, cedar-lined oak box with hinged lid and hammered copper escutcheon, cleaned original finish, small split to interior cedar, signed and dated 1901, 5-7/8" x 14-1/2" x 8-1/2", $14,400.
Photo courtesy of David Rago Auctions, Inc.

Candlebox, Pennsylvania, painted poplar slide lid, retaining yellow and ochre grain, plume decoration, mid-19th century, 8-1/4" h x 17-1/2" l, $4,600.
Photo courtesy of Pook & Pook, Inc.

Bible, chestnut, some curl in lid, molded edges, front panel with punched design, initials and date "L. T. 1705," int. with cov till and single drawer, wrought-iron lock, old dark patina, hasp missing, some edge damage, pulls added to drawer, 27" l **$650**

Book, Pennsylvania, ftd, drawer, top painted with arabesque design, spine with geometric devices in red and gilt, black ground, red borders, mottled mustard painted edges, minor paint war, c1860, 6-3/8" w, 5-1/8" d, 2-5/8" h **$250**

Bride's, oval, bentwood, overlapping laced scenes, orig painted dec, couple in colonial dress, white, red, brown, and black on brown stained ground, edge damage, German inscription and 1796 in white, 15-7/8" l, 10" w, 6-1/2" h .. **$495**

Candle, hanging

Poplar, orig dry red paint, peaked back two-board back, base board extends beyond lower front and includes six cut-outs for spoons, reeded sides, wire nail construction, small chip on front, 12" w, 7" d, 6" h **$285**

Walnut, poplar secondary wood, dovetailed case, hinged lid, good figure on front and lid, arched backboard, one drawer in lower front with orig turned walnut pull, mellow old finish, minor glued split, 14" w, 7-14" d, 8-3/4" h **$600**

Cheese, pine, circular, incised "E. Temple" on lid, painted blue, America, cracks, paint wear, minor losses, 19th C, 6-1/2" h, 12-1/8" d **$175**

Collar, wallpaper covering, oval, marked "E. Stone No. 116 1/2 William Street, New York," 13" l, 5" h **$575**

Cutlery, walnut, dovetailed, int. divided into two compartments, pierced handle, later tapered leg stretcher base, dark finish, 15-5/8" w, 10-1/2" d, 23" h **$300**

Storage box, dovetailed, inside lid "Presented to the Methodist Church at New Mills by John Wright A.D. 1824," Pennsylvania, 6-1/2" h x 13" w, $585.
Photo courtesy of Pook & Pook, Inc.

Decorated, dovetailed, pine, orig grain painting, rect, dovetailed, conforming hinged lid, ochre ground paint with red putty or vinegar painted seaweed-like designs, orig lock, wallpaper lined int., New England, missing top bail handle, later waxing of surface, 1820s, 14-5/8" w, 7-1/8" d, 6-3/4" h **$690**

Document

Grain painted and gilt stenciled, America, pine, rect, hinged lid, grain painted exterior simulating rosewood with gilt stenciled designs of fruit and foliage on top, gilt stenciled floral designs with green highlights on front and sides, leaf and pendant pinecone motifs on black borders with ovolo corners, minor paint losses, c1825, 18-5/8" w, 8-1/8" d, 6-3/4" h **$2,350**

Grain painted, pine, old brown wavy dec over mustard ground, dovetailed, orig internal lock, old padlock on outside, insect damage, 17-1/4" w, 11-3/4" d, 11-1/2" h... **$250**

Pine, gilt stenciled, New York State or New England, hinged dovetail constructed, rect, brass swing handle, top with gilt-stenciled flowers in footed bowl, sides with fruit and flowers, geometric borders, black ground, crack, minor paint wear, c1825, 14-3/4" w, 9-3/8" d, 5-1/4" h **$1,000**

Pine, painted, rect, hinged lid, carved and scribed compass stars and rosettes, incised checkerboard, foliate, and heart motifs, painted in shades of red, black, and mustard, wallpaper-lined interior with till, name "Peter Glawson, August 11th, 1863" inscribed on the back, small corner losses, minor paint wear, 13" w, 7-1/8" d, 5-3/4" h **$5,590**

Federal, America, inlaid mahogany, rect dovetail construction, hinged lid, bracket feet, inlaid oval paterae

Box, Bucher, lid with central building in a landscape, red, green and yellow tulip decoration, sides with similar decoration, 2-3/4" h x 9-1/2" w x 8-1/4" d, **$2,530.**
Photo courtesy of Pook & Pook, Inc.

Candlebox, painted pine, slide lid, heart and oak leaf dec, Pennsylvania, 19th century, 4-1/2" x 10-3/4" x 8", **$645.**
Photo courtesy of Pook & Pook, Inc.

Document box, hide covered, brass tacks and ring handle, paper covered int, lacking lock hasp, wear and cracking to covering, first half 19th century, 4" h, 5-1/8" x 8-1/8", **$90.**
Photo courtesy of Green Valley Auctions.

on top, circular paterae on front, top and sides bordered by string inlay, kite-shaped escutcheon, early 19th C, 11" w, 7-1/2" d, 7" h **$825**
Paint decorated, America, pine, rect, hinged lid, iron latch, vinegar painted graining with dark brown over pinkish-brown base color, c1830, 15" w, 8-1/2" d, 5-5/8" h **$600**

Dome-top, paint decorated
America, poplar, dovetailed, orig stenciled black and bittersweet colored vining on front, worn red and black on top, yellow brown ground on ends, some areas of green remain on side, orig iron lock and hasp, age splits, 24" l, 14" d, 12-3/4" h **$980**
Dec by Bucher, white ground, red houses and tulips on top and all sides, borders picked out in blue, early 19th C, 9" l **$13,500**
Schoharie, New York, pine, painted blue, hinged top with iron latch, decorated with letters "RM" in rectangle and linear borders in black, white, red, yellow, and green, front with flowers and floral border in similar colors, wear, cracks, early 19th C, 27" w, 12-1/4" d, 11" h **$1,880**
Worcester County, Massachusetts, paint dec, rect. wire hinged lid, painted black, foliate, swag, and linear embellishments in shades of yellow and red, iron latch and handles, paint wear, crack, early 19th C, 20-1/4" w, 10" d, 7-3/4" h **$2,235**

Dough, pine and poplar, rect removable top, tapering well, splayed ring-turned legs, ball feet, Pennsylvania, 19th C, 38" w, 19-3/4" w, 29-1/2" h **$500**

Grain painted, America, rect, carved from one piece of pine, sliding lid, incised compass, chip-carved dec on top and sides, brass escutcheon on side, old green surface, wear, age crack, early 19th C, 8-3/4" l, 5" w, 1-7/8" h **$2,000**

Knife
English, inlaid flame mahogany veneer over pine, bow front, scalloped corners with banded inlay, brass handles on both sides, star inlay on int. of lid, old refinish, contemporary, dovetailed int. lifts out, slotted for letters, hidden compartment below, some sections of inlay missing, age splits in veneer, 9" w, 10" d, 15-3/4" h **$550**
Federal, flamed grained mahogany, serpentine and block front, reeded front columns, fitted int., orig keys, pr, 16" h, 9-3/4" w, 14-1/2" d ... **$2,500**
Knife, Georgian, inlaid mahogany, sloping lid with patera, fitted int., 14-3/4" h, some lifting of patera inlay, pr **$6,900**
Mahogany veneer with inlay, edge veneer damage, int. incomplete, inlaid oval on inside of lid, 14-1/2" h **$225**

Letter box, Victorian, English, satinwood veneer, mahogany secondary wood, ebonized moldings, recesses for pens, drop front with divided letter compartments, old finish, two polished glass inkwells, 12-1/2" w, 8-1/2" d, 11-1/4" h **$920**

Pantry, America, pine top and bottom, oval, lapped maple sides fastened with copper tacks, painted blue, 19th C, 4-1/4" d, 1-1/2" h **$950**

Pencil box, child's, slide-lid, carved from single pc of cherry, carved heart shaped handle, compass wheel dec, 10" l, 2-1/2" h **$1,045**

Pipe box, hanging, New England, lollipop top, poplar and pine, c1800 .... **$6,250**

Presentation, walnut, simulated inlay, carved spread wing eagle on lid, presented to Gen George McClellan by Rauch Club, Milwaukee, Nov. 8, 1864 .... **$6,800**

Razor, sailor's, carved cherry, rect, heart-shaped handle, chip carved borders, incised sailing vessel on swivel top, 19th C, 10-3/4" l, 1-3/4" w, 1-1/2" h......... **$325**

Salt, hanging, walnut, sq nail construction, base molding, heart shaped wall mounted, hinged lid, paint dec, tan ground, brown highlighted graining, 8-1/2" l, 8-3/4" w, 13-1/8" h **$1,320**

Sewing
America, mahogany inlaid, hinged lid, center inlaid oval reserve with shell motif, ext. with inlaid borders and corners, int. lid centered with diamond motif, lift-out tray with several compartments, minor imperfections, 19th C, 12-1/4" w, 7-1/4" d, 5-5/8" h **$1,000**
Chinese Export, lacquered, Chinoiserie dec, scenic panels surrounded by mosaic patterns, Greek key border, brass bail handles on each end, int. with mirrored lid and fitted compartments, single fitted drawer, containing various sewing implements, minor wear and crackling, 19th C, 17-1/4" w, 11-1/2" d, 5-3/4" h **$475**

Slide lid
America, decorated, pine, bittersweet and white scrolling, initials "A.H.D. 1826" on blue ground, dovetailed corners, reeded lid, mix of orig rose head and later nails in bottom, age splits in base, some rim damage, replaced int. runner, 24-1/2" l, 15-1/2" d, 8-1/2" h **$420**
America, oak, lid with unusual reeded diamond design, dovetailed corners, old dark refinishing, pieced restorations to edges, 19-1/2" w, 12-1/4" d, 10-1/2" h **$250**
America, pine and poplar, orig reddish brown surface, sq cut nails on base, small lock with key inlet in one end, 16" l, 10" d, 10" h **$175**

Prison vanity box, mixed woods, parquetry, ebonized and satinwood inlay, interior lined tray over single compartment, later feet, late 19th century, 10" x 6-1/4" x 7", **$535.**
Photo courtesy of Sloans & Kenyon Auctioneers and Appraisers.

Box, lap desk, painted black exterior with polychrome floral decoration, gold trim, unfolds to writing surface, **$95.**
Photo courtesy of Dotta Auction Co., Inc.

Document box, walnut, straight bracket feet, Pennsylvania, c1800, 10-1/2" h x 22-1/2" w, 12-1/2" d, **$410.**
Photo courtesy of Pook & Pook, Inc.

Dome-top box, grain painted pine box with hinged lid, iron latch, black borders, ovolo corners, base crack, minor wear, American, early 19th century, 11-3/8" h x 24-5/8" w x 12-1/8" deep, **$820.**
Photo courtesy of Skinner, Inc.

America, walnut, dovetailed joints, pegged base, paneled lid with gouge carved finger pull, four interior compartments, orig finish, 10-1/4" l, 4-3/4" w, 3" h **$770**

European, pine, dovetailed, comb graining around sides, floral dec and molded edge on lid, European inscription on base with "1815," pieced restorations and touch up to ends, 10-3/4" w, 7-3/8" d, 5-5/8" h **$230**

Pennsylvania, John Drissel, Bucks County, attributed to, pine, pegged construction, gouge-carved edge and finger pull, painted red ground with red, blue, white, and green PA German compass, floral and tulip designs, name on lid "Peter Nehs," German text "I came to a country where I read on the wall be God fearing and don't break what doesn't belong to you," provenance: Eugene and Dorothy Elgin collection, Conestoga Auction Co., April 3, 2004, c1790, 11" l, 6-3/4" w, 4-1/4" h **$82,500**

Spice box

America, pine and poplar, eight drawer, dovetailed, molding at top and base, brass pulls, orig red-brown finish, pencil drawing of man and horse with illegible name on one drawer side, 13-1/4" l, 10-1/2" w, 12-1/8" h **$1,100**

Pennsylvania, attributed to Mahantongo Valley, slide lid, dovetailed, dusty blue ground, white, salmon, green and yellow tulip dec on four sides and top, c1780, 9" x 5" **$33,000**

Storage

America, pine, painted red, floral and linear dec, int. paper lined, late 19th C, 8-1/2" l, 6-1/2" w, 3-1/2" h...**$635**

Massachusetts, ochre-painted pine, six board, dovetailed, thumb molded lid dec with flags, shield, and banner inscribed "Mass. Militia 2nd Regt. 1st B. 2nd D," partial paper tag tacked to lid inscribed "...K Rogers Boston," minor imperfections, early 19th C, 18-7/8" l, 8-3/4" h.....**$1,150**

Sugar box

Amish, pyramid shaped lid, brass knob, black and salmon painted sides, five-point yellow and black star on front, 7" sq...............**$11,500**

Country, fruitwood, single base drawer with holes drilled in interior, wrought iron cane cutter mounted at middle, brass pull on lid, old mellow refinishing, 14" w, 9-3/4" d, 9" h **$250**

Tea bin, dec of gentleman toasting lady, dec by Ralph Cahoon, oil on wood, with certificate of authenticity from Cahoon Museum of American Art, 24-1/8" h, 17-1/2" w, 25" d.........**$2,530**

Utensil box, poplar, dovetailed, sq nail construction, scrolled sides and handle dividers, worn salmon painted finish, 11-1/2" l, 9" w, 5" h **$1,100**

Vegetable shredding, hanging, orig dry red paint, chestnut and pine, c1850 ....**$3,500**

Wall

America, pine, one drawer, dovetailed, sq nail construction drawer with four-part divider, brass pull, wood hinges, old leather repair, 10-3/4" l, 10" d, 17-3/4" h **$1,045**

America, poplar, early round head nail construction, paint dec, eight drawers, green ground, sponged and fanned graining, yellow and black highlights, green trim around drawers, red base, porcelain drawer pulls, 8-1/8" l, 4" w, 14" h....**$19,800**

Pennsylvania, attributed to Henry Lapp, Lancaster County, PA, sq and early round head nail construction, eight drawers, red ground with

Letter box, painted poplar, dome lid, orig red, green, yellow, and black checkerboard dec, Pennsylvania or New York, 19th century, 4-1/2" h, 12-1/2" w, **$820.**
Photo courtesy of Pook & Pook, Inc.

comb graining, yellow drawers, porcelain pulls, one drawer repaired, 8-1/2" l, 3-3/4" d, 14-1/2" h **$9,075**

Wallpaper covered, paper and wood construction

Eight-sides, blue, orange, and yellow foliage, 22-3/4" l, 18-1/2" w, 16-1/2" h **$4,675**

Oval, blue ground wallpaper with orange highlights, geometric and floral dec, int. lined with German and English text newspaper, paper label mkd "Laura May, Jack's Box, Dec 29, 1890," 8" l, 5-1/4" w, 3-3/4" h **$910**

Oval, eagle, yellow ground, green and pink highlights, int. lined with German text newspaper, 5-1/2" l, 3-3/4" h, 3" h **$580**

Oval, green ground, yellow and red highlights, lid lined with Lancaster German text newspaper, mkd "Dr. C. Weaver," 6-1/4" l, 4-1/2" w, 3-1/2" h **$1,540**

Oval, light green ground, maroon, green, and black highlights, bird and floral dec, int. lined with English text PA newspaper, 8-1/4" l, 5-1/8" w, 4-1/8" h.................**$420**

Rectangular, pink ground, red and white floral dec, int. lined with German text newspaper, 4-1/4" l, 3" w, 1-1/2" h **$715**

Round, pink ground, red and white floral highlights, int. lined with German and English text newspaper, 3" d, 1-7/8" h **$1,650**

Slide lid, pine, nailed construction, red base, green, white, and black wallpaper, minor usage wear, 7" l, 4-1/4" w, 3-1/4" h **$880**

Work, European, marquetry inlaid mahogany veneer, pine secondary wood, slant top lid with pincushion covered in old burgundy velvet, paper lined int., till with lid, engraved strap hinges, old finish, repairs, 12" w, 10-1/2" d, 7-1/4" h **$275**

Writing, English, 20th C

Mahogany, dovetailed case and two drawers, red velvet liners, compartment with lift lid on top, ivory pulls on top drawer, replaced wooden pulls on lower drawer **$230**

Mahogany, old ebonized finish, dovetailed drawer in base, divided int., open compartment behind roll top, two small int. drawers top, ivory pulls, sgd drawer "Sawlish, Sunday, 27th of February, 1820, J. H. Jacob," and religious verse, 14-1/2" w, 10-1/2" d, 6-1/2" h **$200**

Cabinets

Apothecary, pine, yellow grain dec, 29 drawers over two open shelves, cut-out base and sides, bracket feet, open back, 62" l, 12" d, 54" h ...**$1,550**

Bar, Art Deco, walnut, sarcophagus form, two doors, sq top with drop-front cabinet on left, mirrored bar, small drawer on right between two open bays, 48" w, 21" d, 54-1/2" d.................**$600**

Cellaret, George III, mahogany, serpentine, top enclosing a green baize interior, brass handles at sides, square-section tapering legs, 18" w, 18" d, 25" h.................**$1,675**

China

Art Moderne, mahogany, double doors, floral-carved relief panels, int. shelves, two drawers below, 45" w, 17" d, 62" h.................**$2,000**

Arts & Crafts, Limbert, #428, trapezoidal form, two doors, each with four windows at top over one large window, orig copper pulls, sides with two windows over one, refinished, branded, 40" w, 19" d, 63" h ...**$4,250**

Edwardian-style, curved glass sides, single flat glazed door, illuminated int., mirrored back, 42" w, 16" d, 64" h, pr.................**$1,675**

International Movement, Gilbert Rhode, manufactured by Herman Miller, glass-sided china cabinet top over two doors with burled fronts, brushed steel pulls, refinished, glass doors and shelves missing, 36" w, 17" d, 58" h.................**$800**

Victorian, American, oak, ornate, crest with carved wind god, leaves, and scrolls, curved glass door and side panels, four glass shelves, mirrored back, column supports, claw feet, c1900, 51" w, 19" d, 77" h.................**$2,650**

Chinoiserie, two drawers, double doors, two adjustable int. shelves, walnut veneer with inlay and black lacquer, gilded detail, attached base with turned legs, 20th C, 43" w, 15-1/2" d, 63" h.................**$625**

Corner

George III style, inlaid mahogany, molded swan's neck cresting, pair of mullioned glass doors, shelved interior, two lower paneled doors, bracket feet, inlaid with fans, 20th C, 45" w, 22" d, 91" h.................**$1,410**

Georgian, early, japanned, two part, molded cornice and outset corners above two pairs of doors flanked by solid pilasters, shaped plinth base,

decorated overall with Chinoiserie scenes on black ground, 18th C, 35" w, 19" d, 90" h.................**$7,650**

Renaissance Revival, American, walnut, hanging, spindle-inset cornice, two glazed doors and reeded pilasters **$400**

Curio, French

Bombé-shaped base, ornate, old gold repaint, carved rococo dec and gesso, beveled glass front, glass side panels, high scrolled feet, scalloped base aprons, 35" w, 15" d, 71-1/2" h....**$950**

Serpentine front, flowers around case, courting scene on lower case and door, metallic gold ground, ormolu dec around edges and arched crest, two removable glass shelves, worn red velvet covering bottom shelf, mirrored back, 33-1/2" w, 17" d, 74" h.................**$850**

Display

Biedermeier-style, poplar and burr-poplar, single door, outset molded cornice, three-pane glazed door flanked by similar stiles and sides, three mirror-backed shelves supporting shaped half shelves, block feet, 41" w, 16" d, 68" h **$800**

Edwardian, rosewood, dentil molded cornice, two glazed doors and projecting lower section fitted with three drawers, sq tapered legs joined by shelf stretcher, late 19th C, 25" w, 15" d, 56" h.................**$2,415**

Empire-style, gilt metal mounted mahogany, rect case fitted with arched glass door, stemmed bun feet, foliate cast mounts, 33" w, 16" d, 68" h.................**$1,975**

Queen Anne style, green japanned, pair of shaped and mullioned glass doors, shelved int., cabriole legs, Spanish feet, multicolored chinoiserie scenes, 38" w, 15-1/2" d, 80-1/2" h.................**$1,530**

Renaissance Revival, oak, foliate and fruit carved borders, shaped feet, glass front and sides, late 19th/early 20th C.................**$6,500**

Dressing, Art Deco, France, rect curvilinear top, centered mirror over four drawers flanked on each side by full-length curvilinear cabinets, shaped foot skirt, c1925, 68-1/2" w, 19-1/2" d, 66-7/8" h.................**$1,100**

Fall front, Renaissance Revival, American, ebonized and parcel gilt, angular cresting, fall front enclosing plain interior, trestle base, curved legs, 26" w, 45" h **$900**

China cabinet, Gustav Stickley, Harvey Ellis design, overhanging top, three shelves, arched apron, hammered copper V-pull, orig finish, orig key, branded, paper label, 60" x 36" x 15", **$7,800.**
Photo courtesy of David Rago Auctions, Inc.

Cabinet-on-chest, William and Mary, inlaid burl walnut, two parts, rect molded crown, top has two glazed panel doors, lower body has seven drawers, shaped apron, bun feet, early 18th century, 70-3/4" x 43-1/2" x 20", **$4,500.**
Photo courtesy of Sloans & Kenyon Auctioneers and Appraisers.

Filing, Arts & Crafts

American, golden oak, plain vertical stack, five drawers, orig brass nameplates and pulls, c1910 ... **$650**

Stickley, L. & J. G., Manlius, New York, reissue, two-drawer, rect, hammered copper hardware, branded "Stickley," round yellow and red decal in int. drawer, wear to top finish, 21-3/8" w, 28" l, 31" h **$360**

Hanging

Middle Eastern, inlaid mother-of-pearl, lancet molded cornice, turned shelf supports, spindle inset door above three small open shelves, 20" w, 7-1/2" d, 20" h **$425**

Renaissance Revival, American, walnut, spindle-inset gallery, floral incised door and shelved interior, shaped and angular pendant, 26" w, 8" d, 26" h **$765**

Ledger, American, walnut and mixed hardwoods, poplar secondary wood, dovetailed case, single paneled door, int. with divided compartments, later salmon paint, pr, 19th C, 15-1/2" w, 12" d, 24" h **$600**

Sheet music, first half 20th C

Mahogany, rect top over door, opening to 21 doors of graduated sizes, 20" w, 14-1/2" d, 34" h **$325**

Mahogany, one door, back rail with

beveled mirror, drawer, 18" w, 47" h **$225**

Side

Aesthetic Movement, American, ebonized and parcel gilt, upper section with spindle galleries and mirrored back, lower section with central door with angular foliate designs, flanked by open shelves, angular gilt foliage throughout, 43" w, 14" d, 66" h **$3,410**

Arts & Crafts, oak, single door, orig sq copper pull, notched toe-board, refinished, 22" w, 22" d, 38" h .. **$700**

Baroque, Dutch, oak, rect case fitted with three paneled doors, borders carved in shallow relief with scrolling tulip vines, stemmed bun feet, 82" w, 20" d, 53" h **$1,380**

Biedermeier, fruitwood parquetry, rect top, canted corners, pr of cabinet doors enclosing shelves, bracket feet, late 19th C, 55-1/4" w, 24-3/4" d, 40-1/2" h **$1,725**

Empire-style, gilt bronze mounted mahogany, rect marble top, conforming case fitted with cabinet door, pull-out shelves, plinth base, late 19th/early 20th C, 20-3/4" w, 16-1/4" d, 52-1/4" h **$750**

Gothic-style, oak, rect case fitted with two doors, upper door carved with gothic tracery, lower with linen-

fold paneling, sides with linenfold paneling, block feet, late 19th/early 20th C, 22" w, 19" d, 52" h **$450**

Louis XVI, Provincial, oak, paneled door carved with urns, late 18th/early 19th C, 41" w, 18-1/2" d, 73" h **$1,380**

Napoleon III, brass and mother-of-pearl inlaid, ormolu mounts, white serpentine marble top, conforming case, fitted with door, bracket feet, c1850-70, 35-1/2" w, 16" d, 41" h **$2,645**

Regency, rosewood, shelf with gallery above mirrored back over single drawer above grilled door flanked by columns with maiden terms on squared plinth base, price for pr, early 19th C, 24-1/2" w, 17-1/2" d, 45-1/2" h **$14,160**

Renaissance Revival, attributed to New York, ebonized, marquetry, and parcel-gilt, central elevated cupboard flanked by two similar cupboards, c1865-75, 75" w, 15" d, 64" h **$4,900**

Spice

Counter-type, poplar, old brown sponge dec, vertical stack with four sq nailed drawers with beveled edges, turned wooden pulls, chamfered side moldings, tongue and groove boards on sides of case, one drawer front split, 8-3/8" w, 17-1/2" d, 19-5/8" h **$495**

Hanging, rope twist top molding over geometric border flanking eight drawers, inlaid star and heart dec, porcelain knobs, inlaid with ivory and mixed woods, minor losses, second half 20th C, 15" w, 8" d, 18" h **$475**

Spool

J. & P. Coats, six drawers, each with original black stenciled dec, brass rosette pulls, flanking columns on each side, 26" w, 19-1/4" d, 22-1/4" h **$1,400**

Sloping lid, green leather top, low shelf at rear, six small drawers in two stacks, brass rosette pulls, 32-3/4" w, 23" d, 17-3/8" h, leather replaced **$400**

Vitrine

Biedermeier, part ebonized, triangular pediment and dentilled cornice above two mullioned glazed doors flanked by two columns, block feet, first half 19th C, 47" w, 21" d, 67" h **$4,600**

Biedermeier-style, peaked crest over two glazed doors flanked by ebonized columns, square block feet, price for pr, 45-1/4" w, 18-1/2" d, 73" h......................**$5,350**

George III-style, mahogany, open swan's neck cresting, glazed doors, lower section with glass top shelf, sq legs joined by stretchers, early 20th C, 22" w, 18-1/2" d, 68" h **$1,495**

Louis XVI-style, giltwood, outset molded rect top, frieze with beribboned floral garlands, front with glazed door with inset corners, flanked by fluted stiles, opening to two shelves, glazed sides, paneled skirt with swags, turned, tapered, and fluted legs with paterae, c1850, 27-1/4" w, 16" d, 61-1/2" h **$1,200**

Louis XV-style, Vernis Martin, bow front glazed door flanked by twin bow front glazed panels, glass shelves, painted scene including couple, music, and art trophies, 27" w, 17" d, 59" h..................**$1,500**

Candlestands
Adjustable

American, central cherry shaft, turned double adjustable candle arm, ring turned burl base, orig patination, c1780, 29" h........**$9,000**

American, maple, screw-post, traces of orig salmon paint, c1790.......**$4,500**

Chippendale

America, mahogany, round single board top, vase shaped column, cabriole legs, padded snake feet, old finish, well executed repair to one leg, reduced in size, 17-1/2" d, 28-1/4" h.............**$875**

Boston or Salem, Massachusetts, mahogany, carved oval tilt top, vase and ring-turned post, tripod cabriole leg base ending in arris pad feet on platforms, refinished, one leg repaired, late 18th C, 16-1/2" w, 22-3/4" d, 27-1/2" h.............**$1,535**

Massachusetts, mahogany, serpentine molded tilt top, vase and ring-turned post on tripod cabriole leg base, arris pad feet on platforms, old finish, very minor imperfections, late 18th C, 28" w, 27-3/4" d, 28-3/4" h **$4,200**

New England, tilt-top, walnut, circular molded top, vase and ring-turned post and tripod cabriole leg base, arris pad feet, old refinish, imperfections, minor repair, late 18th C, 17" d, 28" h **$2,500**

New Hampshire, attributed to Lt.

Candlestand, Federal, mahogany, rectangular line inlaid top, urn standard, downward-sloping inlaid legs, Maryland, c1805, 29-1/2" h, 19-1/2" w, **$2,224.**
Photo courtesy of Pook & Pook, Inc.

Candlestand, New England, maple, circular top on a vase and ring-turned post, tripod cabriole leg base, pad feet, old brown varnished surface, minor imperfections, late 18th century, 26" h x 16-1/2", **$820.**
Photo courtesy of Skinner, Inc.

Samuel Dunlap, old refinish, birch, painted red, imperfections, 16-1/2" w, 16-1/8" d, 26-1/2" h...**$2,950**

Pennsylvania, Chester County, Octorora, walnut, tilt top, molded edge burl top, bird cage support, ball turned pedestal, cabriole legs, well executed carved feet, 6" age crack in top, 24" d top, 29-1/2" h **$4,400**

Chippendale-style, America, inlaid mahogany, round tilt top with small raised edge, circular inlaid center fan, reeded urn shaped column, tripod base, well carved claw and ball feet, orig dark finish, early 20th C, 23-3/4" d top, 28-1/2" h..............**$225**

Country, cherry and maple, southeastern New England, circular top, vase and ring turned post and tripod base, three tapering legs, remnants of old dark green paint, imperfections, late 18th C, 12" d, 25" h.................**$1,150**

Federal

Connecticut, attributed to, cherry inlaid, rect top with string inlaid border, vase and ring-turned chip carved post, tripod base of arris cabriole legs, imperfections, c1790, 15" l, 13-3/4" w, 26-3/4" h.....**$1,120**

Connecticut River Valley, cherry, shaped top with serpentine sides and ovolo corners, vase and ring-turned post, tripod cabriole leg

base, arris pad feet, refinished, minor restoration, c1790, 17-3/4" l, 18" w, 26" h **$3,000**

Dunlap School, Antrim, New Hampshire area, painted, octagonal top with shaped underside, turned tapering pedestal ending in turned cap flanked by cabriole leg base ending in pad feet, Victorian polychrome dec with gilt highlight, minor imperfections, late 18th century, 13-5/8" x 13-1/2" top, 26-1/2" h..........**$25,850**

Massachusetts, inlaid birch and maple, scroll-shaped tilt top centering inlaid oval wavy birch panel, vase and ring-turned and reeded post, tripod shaped tapering legs, refinished, c1820, 15-1/8" w, 21-3/4" d, 29" h **$5,760**

Massachusetts, cherry, sq top with serpentine sides and rounded corners, vase and ring-turned post, tripod cabriole legs, arris feet, refinished, imperfections, note taped to underside of top reads "candlestand Starr-Allen family of Deerfield," late 18th C, 14-3/8" w, 15" d, 26-1/4" h....**$950**

Massachusetts, mahogany, oval tilt top, vase and ring-turned post, tripod base with cabriole legs, arris pointed pad feet on platforms, old surface, very minor imperfections, late 18th C, 23-1/4" w, 17-1/4" d, 27" h...**$8,850**

New England, cherry, serpentine

Candlestand, Federal, New York, rectangular top, ovolo corners, tilting, urnturned standard, downward curving legs, 28-1/4" h, 21-3/4" w, **$440.**
Photo courtesy of Pook & Pook, Inc.

Candlestand, Federal, New England, square top, ovolo corners, vase and ringturned post and tripod base, shaped tapering legs, old black paint over earlier red, c1800, 27-3/4" h x 17" w x 16-3/4" deep, **$880.**
Photo courtesy of Skinner, Inc.

Candlestand, George II, c1750, mahogany, circular tilt top, birdcage support, baluster standard, cabriole legs, pad feet, 26-1/2" d, 27-1/2" h, **$800.**
Photo courtesy of Pook & Pook, Inc.

top, vase and ring-turned post, tripod cabriole leg base, pad feet, old refinish, imperfections, c1790, 15-1/2" l, 16" w, 24-3/4" h **$775**

New England, painted, circular top, vase and ring-turned post and tripod cabriole leg base, old black paint over earlier red stain, polychrome floral cluster dec and pin striping, c1800, 16-1/4" d, 26" h **$2,115**

New England, cherry, rect octagonal top with applied cockbeaded edge, swelled ring-turned post, tripod base of arched, shaped, tapering legs ending in plain feet, refinished, imperfections, late 18th/early 19th C, 20-1/2" w, 16-3/4" d, 28-1/4" h **$825**

New Hampshire, birch, painted, sq top with rounded corners, urn shaped turned pedestal, high arched cabriole tripod base, pad feet, old red paint, imperfections, early 19th C, 13-3/4" w, 13-1/4" d, 26-1/4" h **$7,475**

Rhode Island, cherry, circular top with scratch-beaded edge, ring-turned tapering column, tripod cabriole leg base ending in arris pad feet, old finish, minor imperfections, late 18th century, 17-1/2" d, 27-3/4" h ..**$1,100**

Hepplewhite, country, birch and maple, old dark brown surface, round single board top, vase turned column, three serpentine tapered legs, old shims, 18" d, 27-1/2" h **$1,050**

Painted and decorated, Connecticut, cherry, octagonal top with molded edge, turned pedestal with urn shaping over high-arched cabriole leg base ending in pad feet, early black paint with 19th C yellow

Candlestand, Chippendale, attributed to England, walnut, circular molded top, vase and ring turned support, tripod cabriole leg base, arris pad feet on platforms, possible height loss, 18th century, 20-3/4" d, 22-1/2" h, **$450.**
Photo courtesy of Skinner, Inc.

striping on pedestal and legs, minor imperfections, late 19th C, 15-1/4" w, 15-3/4" d, 29-1/2" h **$4,025**

Primitive, wooden, adjustable candle arm, dark brown patina, early 19th C, 40" h **$715**

Queen Anne

New England, butternut and maple, octagonal, applied molded edge, baluster turned support, tripod cabriole leg base, old refinish, traces of red paint, imperfections, mid-18th C, 17-1/2" l, 17" w, 29" h **$1,530**

New England, cherry, round top, single double-sided candle drawer below, tapering and ring-turned post, tripod cabriole base, pad feet, old dark stain, alterations and repairs, late 18th C/early 19th C, 16-1/2" d, 26-1/4" h **$850**

Southern New England, cherry, tilt top with molded edge, swelled ring-turned pedestal, cabriole legs, pad feet, refinished, repairs, alterations, late 18th C, 18" w, 18-1/4" d, 27-1/4" h **$1,410**

Regency, English, mahogany, tilttop, scalloped one board top, boldly turned column, tripod base, saber legs with beaded edges, old refinish, repairs and restoration to top, label underneath "From the summer home (1890-1929) Goshen, NY of Charlotte Beardsley (1852-1914) and George Van Riper (1845-1925), 24" w, 17-1/2" d, 28" h **$595**

Windsor, walnut and curly maple, octagonal top, turned column, octagonal platform base, three turned legs, pegged and wedged construction, old brown finish, 12" w, 11-1/4" d, 24-3/4" h....................................... **$980**

Chairs

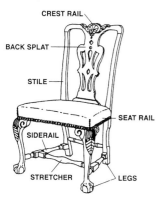

Typical Parts of a Chair

Slipper chair, Victorian, upholstered in brocade fabric, painted gold base, braided rope and tassels dec, 32" x 24" x 33", **$350.**
Photo courtesy of David Rago Auctions, Inc.

Side chairs, pair, English Yorkshire, carved walnut, arching crest, scrolling bracket finials, block-and ball legs, ring-and-ball front stretcher, 39" x 18-3/4" x 16-1/2", **$885.**
Photo courtesy of Sloans & Kenyon Auctioneers and Appraisers.

Armchair

Adirondack-style, rustic twig construction, including small arms, green paint, roped seat, c1910 .... **$2,300**

Aesthetic Movement, after Philip Webb's Sussex chair for Morris & Co., new natural rush seat, turned spindles, orig black paint, unmarked, c1885, 21-1/4" w, 19" d, 36-1/4" h **$1,045**

Art Deco, France, giltwood, sloping U-form back rail ending in gently swollen reeded arm supports, D-shaped seat upholstered seat cushion, pr, c1925 .... **$15,750**

Art Nouveau, L. Majorelle, France, carved mahogany, horseshoe-shaped back rail, upholstered back, front of arm supports carved with pine cones and needles, continuing to form molded front legs with similar carving, dark green leather upholstery, c1900 .... **$7,000**

Arts & Crafts

Indiana Hickory, twig construction, orig hickory splint seat, weathered finish, branded signature, 26" w, 17" d, 37" h................................ **$50**

Olbrich, Joseph Marie, Jugendstil, mahogany, small back panel inlaid with fruitwood floral pattern, inset upholstered seat, unmarked, good old refinish, 23-1/2" w, 19" d, 41-1/2" h **$1,840**

Stickley, Charles, four back slats, recovered spring cushion seat, orig finish, remnant of decal, 26" w, 22" d, 41" h **$230**

Stickley, Gustav, Model no. 2604, oak, arched crest rail over three horizontal back slats, shaped flat open arms, prominent front leg posts, offset front, back, and side stretchers, dark brown finish, red decal under arm, c1902, wear, 26-3/4" w, 26" d, 37" h **$1,840**

Stickley, Gustav, Thornden, two horizontal back slats, narrow arms, 1902-04 red decal, replaced seat, orig finish, minor edge wear, 37" x 21" x 21-1/2" **$3,105**

Stickley, Gustav, V-back, vertical back slats, replaced leather seat, orig faceted tacks, good orig finish, red decal, 27" w, 20-1/2" d, 37" h.............. **$1,045**

Stickley, L. & J. G., fixed back, drop arm, slats to seat, corbels, replaced drop-in green leather spring seat and back cushion, waxed finish, L & J. G. Stickley Handcraft label, 32-1/2" w, 33" d, 41" h.......... **$5,750**

Stickley, L. & J. G., spindled back, open arms, corbels, seat recovered in leather, refinished, unmarked, 24-1/2" w, 21" d, 38-1/2" h **$690**

Banister-back, New England, mid-18th C, turned maple, yoked crest rail above four molded banisters joining vase and ring-turned stiles, shaped scrolled arms on vase and ring-turned supports continuing to legs, turned feet joined by double sausage-turned stretchers, early splint seat, old refinish, imperfections, 14-1/2" h seat, 43" h.......... **$1,175**

Centennial, Colonial Revival, Queen-Anne style, wing back, hardwood cabriole legs, turned stretcher, upholstery removed, old dark finish, 46" h **$900**

Chippendale, English or Irish, walnut, pierced Gothic back splat, scrolled handholds, slip seat cov in cream colored silk upholstery, sq legs, small scalloped returns on front apron, refinished, one foot ended out, 19" h seat, 37" h back **$400**

Armchair, Chippendale, mahogany, serpentine carved crest, pierced and carved gothic splat, curved arms, slip seat, molded Marlborough legs, H-stretcher, Delaware Valley, c1790, **$2,575.**
Photo courtesy of Pook & Pook, Inc.

Armchair, George III, mahogany, arched crest, downward scrolled and stop fluted arms, square legs, c1790, **$1,990.**
Photo courtesy of Pook & Pook, Inc.

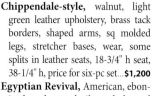

Armchair, rustic twig, pieced latticework back, spindled seat, simple legs, late 19th century, 45-1/2" x 23" x 19", **$940.**
Photo courtesy of David Rago Auctions, Inc.

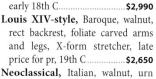

Armchair, Queen Anne, Delaware Valley, walnut, yoke crest, vasiform splat, serpentine arms, slip seat, carved skirt, cabriole legs, drake feet, c1745, **$8,775.**
Photo courtesy of Pook & Pook, Inc.

Armchair, French Louis XIV, carved oak, arching crest rail, vasi-form splat, plank seat, scrolled arms, block-and-ball turned stretchers and legs, 17th century, **$765.**
Photo courtesy of Sloans & Kenyon Auctioneers and Appraisers.

Chippendale-style, walnut, light green leather upholstery, brass tack borders, shaped arms, sq molded legs, stretcher bases, wear, some splits in leather seats, 18-3/4" h seat, 38-1/4" h, price for six-pc set... **$1,200**

Egyptian Revival, American, ebonized and parcel-gilt, upholstered scrolling back and seat, matching upholstered arm pads, sphinx head arm supports, claw feet, c1865, 39-1/2" h **$8,050**

Empire-style, mahogany, rect padded back, padded arms, ormolu-mounted classical busts, bowed padded seat, sq tapering legs with brass caps, white striped upholstery .. **$850**

George III, mahogany, shaped top rail, three pc vertical splat, upholstered seat, tapering sq section legs **$475**

Gothic Revival, America, walnut, old finish, reupholstered in damask, age cracks, 52-1/2" h **$200**

Hepplewhite, birch, pegged construction, eight vertical posts across back, slip seat, tapered legs with broadly shaped stretchers, relief arched fans on front and sides, old mellow refinishing, originally potty seat, base reworked, arms repegged, age splits, 18-1/2" h seat, 37" h back **$450**

Louis XIV, fauteuil, giltwood, serpentine cresting, scrolled and reeded arms, over upholstered seat, scrolled legs joined by stretchers, early 18th C **$2,990**

Louis XIV-style, Baroque, walnut, rect backrest, foliate carved arms and legs, X-form stretcher, late price for pr, 19th C **$2,650**

Neoclassical, Italian, walnut, urn and wheat carved splat, downswept arms, raised sq tapering legs, late 18th/ early 19th C, 34-1/4" h **$1,100**

Queen Anne
Middle Atlantic states, arched crest with square corners, raked stiles, scrolled arms on vasiform supports, trapezoidal seat, frontal cabriole legs ending in pad feet, raked rear legs, imperfections, last half 18th C, 16-1/2" h seat, 49" h **$21,150**

New Hampshire, hardwood with old black repaint, molded and curved back posts with vase splat and carved crest, turned posts support molded and scrolled arms, turned legs, Spanish feet, turned rungs with bulbous front stretcher, old rush seat, some loss to feet, 15-3/8" seat, 41" h **$4,125**

Regency
Mahogany, octagonal crest rail over shaped horizontal splat, open arms, shaped padded seat, sq tapering legs **$600**

Mahogany, rect top rail above horizontal spiral-turned splat and reeded scrolling arms, upholstered seat, ring turned front legs, rear saber legs **$600**

Regency-style, mahogany, bent reeded crest rail over shaped splat, upholstered seat, tapering turned legs **$200**

Renaissance Revival, attributed to Pottier & Stymus, New York, walnut, scrolled arms, upholstered back and seed, spherules on seat rail, 1865, 38" h **$1,100**

Rococo Revival, John H. Belter, rosewood, Rosalie pattern, laminated, solid back, crest carved with large rose, fruit, and grape clusters, yellow silk upholstery, tufted back, 42-1/2" h **$3,500**

Rococo-style, Italian, grotto, scallop shell seat, dolphin-shaped arms, rusticated legs, late 19th/early 20th C **$1,725**

Savonarola-style, mahogany, Old Man of the North carved in crest rail **$230**

Shaker, attributed to Canterbury, New Hampshire, birch and pine, concave rect back rail, turned stiles, four spindles, shaped seat, splayed turned tapering legs joined by stretchers, old refinish, traces of red stain, minor imperfections, c1835, 17" h seat, 24-1/2" h **$600**

Victorian, George Huntzinger, New York, patent March 30, 1869, walnut, pierce carved crest, rect upholstered back panel flanked by

Armchair, George II style, carved mahogany, foliate carved cresting with eagle heads above pierced baluster splat, carved arms, overupholstered leather seat, foliate carved cabriole legs, hairy paw feet, c1875-1880, 19" h to seat, **$1,880.**
Photo courtesy of Skinner, Inc.

Armchair, ladderback, Hudson River Valley, painted, ram's horn hand holds, sausage turned stretchers, 19th century black surface and gilt highlights, inscribed "Leah 1769," mid-18th century, **$2,340.**
Photo courtesy of Pook & Pook, Inc.

Armchair, mahogany, spoon-back, English William IV, arching down-swept crest rail, padded back, D-shaped cushion seat, turned front legs with castors, square tapering splayed rear legs, early 19th century, 39-3/4" x 23" x 34", **$825.**
Photo courtesy of Sloans & Kenyon Auctioneers and Appraisers.

turned and curved slats and stiles, low upholstered barrel-back, arm frame carved with classical heads, upholstered seat, pierced and scroll-carved front drop under seat connected to turned rung joining carved and turned front legs, ball feet, front leg stamped **$2,100**

Windsor

Bow-back, Pennsylvania, scrolled arms, bamboo turned spindles and legs, later tan and brown swirl paint dec seat, black frame, 16" h seat, 35" h **$470**

Brace-back, continuous arm, B. Green, Connecticut, bowed crest rail continuing to shaped arms above six spindles, vase and ring-turned arm supports, shaped saddle seat, splayed vase and ring-turned legs joined by swelled stretchers, repairs, late 18th C, 16" h seat, 37" h **$950**

Comb-back, attributed to Philadelphia, mixed woods, areas of old dark green paint, arched top with finely scrolled ears, nine back spindles, bentwood arm rain ending in shaped hand rests, D-shaped seat with incised line borders around edges, baluster and ring turned legs, blunt arrow feet, stretcher base, old pegged restoration on arm rail, 23-1/2" w, 17-1/2" h seat, 42" h **$11,275**

Comb-back, old worn red paint over yellow, evidence of earlier paint

history, seven spindle back with well shaped crest, bowed arm rain with turned supports, oval seat with incised detailing around spindles, splayed baluster and ring turned legs, "H" stretcher, 17-5/8" h seat, 41-1/4" h back **$20,700**

Continuous arm, New England, nine-spindle back, saddle seat, stamped "J Ash," c1815, 36" h **$1,100**

Continuous arm, Pennsylvania, nine-spindle back, bamboo turnings, early 19th C, 38" h **$275**

Double bow-back, New England, maple, ash, and pine, incised crest rail above seven spindles, applied scrolled arm, writing surface to right, both with bamboo-turned supports on shaped seat, centering drawer mounted on underside, splayed bamboo-turned feet joined by stretchers, orig red-brown stained surface, imperfections, c1800-15, 16" h seat, 45-1/2" h **$3,525**

Sack-back, Lancaster County, Pennsylvania, carved knuckles, D-shaped seat, bulbous "H" stretcher, turned splayed legs, blunt arrow feet, worn green-black paint, 16" h seat, 36" h **$3,025**

Sack-back, Rhode Island, painted maple and ash, arched crest above tapering spindles through crest which continues to shaped handholds above turned arm supports

on incised plank seat with pommel on swelled and ring-turned splayed legs joined by swelled stretchers, old black paint, worn surface, imperfections, 1790-1800, 16" h seat, 39-3/4" h **$2,250**

Slough-back, English, George III, yew and elm, back with turned spindles, center vasiform splat framed by pair of flattened stoles surmounting serpentine crest rail, shaped arm rail on plain spindles, saddle shaped seat, cabriole legs, pad feet, repairs, refinished, late 18th C, 29" w, 15-1/2" d, 46" h **$500**

Corner

Aesthetic Movement, American, possibly by Tisch, rosewood, cushioned and spindle-inset arms, lappet and scroll carved sq tapering legs
.... **$1,650**

Chippendale, walnut, rolled back rest with stepped detail, pierced harp shape splats, serpentine arm supports, scrolled handholds, molded seal frame, slip seat covered in worn upholstery, scalloped aprons, cabriole legs with relief carved shells on knees, claw and ball feet, old dark surface, restorations and replacements
.... **$1,870**

Chippendale-style, mahogany, shaped arms, openwork splats, rush slip seat raised on cabriole legs, claw and ball feet, 20th C **$575**

Country, New England, maple, arms with scrolled terminals, shaped crest, scrolled horizontal splats attached to swelled and turned baluster forms continuing to turned legs, joined to similar stretchers, old surface, replaced rush seat, minor imperfections, late 18th/early 19th C, 16-3/8" h seat, 30-1/2" h back **$1,610**

Queen Anne, country, old black and gold paint, shaped crest rail with medallion handholds, rose head nails, replaced paper rush seat, turned legs and supports, 16" h seat, 28-1/4" h back **$520**

William and Mary, New England, shaped backrest and chamfered crest, scrolled handholds, three vase and ring-turned stiles continuing to turned legs, joined to front leg by turned double stretchers, old dark brown paint, replaced wood seat, 18th C, 30" h **$1,380**

Dining

Arts & Crafts

Stickley, Gustav, ladder-back, four slats, cloud-lift aprons, drop-in seats recovered in leather, overcoat finish, roughness to edges, some with red Gustav decal, set of eight, 37" h **$6,300**

Stickley, L. & J.G., arched vertical back slats, drop-in spring seat, covered in new green leather, good new finish, orig labels, price for set of four, 37-1/2" h, 17" w **$3,335**

Assembled set, English, turned ash and alder, open spindle back with two or three tiers of short turnings between flattened stiles, rush seat, tapered round legs, pad feet, bulbous turned front stretcher, plain turned side and rear stretchers, two-arm chairs, 10-side chairs, some with feet ended out, price for set of 12, c1800-60, 19" w, 16" d, 38" h **$1,875**

Biedermeier, fruitwood and part ebonized, black faux-leather upholstery, restorations, set of four, 36" h **$2,500**

Centennial, Colonial Revival, Sheraton-style, mahogany, two arms, eight sides, shield back, reeded front legs, corner posts with carving of urns, needlepoint slip seats, 19-1/2" w, 17-1/4" d, 37-1/2" h................**$3,000**

Chippendale-style, Baker, Connecticut, black lacquer, saber-leg, set of eight, c1960.................**$2,100**

Classical, New England, figured maple, concave crests above vasiform splats and rails, scrolled and raked stiles, caned seats with serpentine fronts, saber legs joined by stretchers, old refinish, set of six, c1830-40, 17-1/4" h seat, 32" h...................**$950**

Eastlake, American, mahogany, one armchair, six side chairs, fan-carved crest rail, reeded stiles and stretchers, block-carved front legs, minor damage, set of seven, c1870, 35" h.....**$850**

Federal, Rhode Island or Salem, Massachusetts, mahogany carved, set of four side and matching arm chair, shield back with molded crest and stiles above carved kylix with festoons draped from flanking carved rosettes, pierced splat terminating in carved lunette at base above molded rear seat rail, seat with serpentine front rail, sq tapering legs joined by stretchers, over-upholstered seats covered in old black horsehair with scalloped trim, old surface, c1795, 16-1/2" h seat, 37-3/4" h......................**$23,000**

George III, mahogany, squared inlaid crest, reeded stiles, pierced and inlaid splat, upholstered seat,

Side chair, Windsor, fan back, red stain, New England, concave, serpentine crest rail, seven spindles, vase and ring-turned styles, carved saddle seat, ring-turned legs, swelled stretchers, c1780, 36" h, **$440.**
Photo courtesy of Skinner, Inc.

square tapering legs joined by an H-form stretcher, set of six....**$2,600**

George III-style

Mahogany, comprising two armchairs and 10 side chairs, serpentine cresting, pierced vasiform splat, and drop seat, sq legs, price for set of 10, 20th C...............................**$3,525**

Mahogany, foliate carved openwork baluster splat, trapezoidal slip-seat, sq legs joined by stretchers, price for set of 12, two armchairs and 10 side chairs **$9,400**

International Movement, manufactured by Oda, similar to design by Neils O. Moller, Denmark, two armchairs and four side chairs, teak, new upholstery over original, price for set of six, c1960, 31" h **$1,530**

Louis XVI-style beechwood, incorporating antique elements, comprising two armchairs and 10 side chairs, solid baluster splat, green leather drop-seat, circular fluted and tapered legs, price for set of 12 ....**$2,585**

Regency-style, mahogany and inlay, two armchairs, six side chairs, curved inlaid crest rail, dec horizontal splats, pale blue silk upholstery, Greek key design, late 19th/early 20th C, 33-3/4" h **$10,350**

Plantation chair, mahogany and canvas, 19th century, 32-1/2" h x 66" l x 27" w, **$550.**
Photo courtesy of Wiederseim Associates, Inc.

Side chair, Queen Anne, English, walnut and mahogany, shaped crest and splat, pad feet, H-stretcher, replaced seat frame, c1760, 18" h seat, 38-1/2" h back, **$425.**

Photo courtesy of Alderfer Auction Co.

Renaissance Revival, America, oak, two arm and eight side chairs, each with foliate and beast carved cresting, paneled seat rail and turned legs, set of 10, c1870 .... **$3,105**

Sheraton, one armchair, five side chairs, walnut and mahogany, mahogany flame veneer panels, rect crests with brass line inlay, rope twist carving on back crosspieces, reeded serpentine rear stiles, ring turned front legs, old refinishing, contemporary burgundy upholstered seats, restorations, 17" h seats, 31" h backs.................. **$1,150**

William IV, mahogany, shaped carved crest rail above horizontal splat, trapezoid slip seat, circular fluted tapering legs, set of six: one arm chair, five side chairs, second quarter 19th C **$3,600**

Easy (Wing, Great chair)

Boston, maple, crest continues to shaped wings above outwardly scrolling arms, serpentine shirt joins block and ring-turned front legs connected to sq raking rear legs by similar side stretchers, ring-turned swelled and blocked medial stretcher, old black paint, 20th C cotton show cover, restoration, 1710-1725, 19" h seat, 49" h **$15,275**

Connecticut, attributed to, turned and painted, yoked crest rail above vasiform splat joining turned stiles with canted vase and ring-turned arms ending in knob handholds on vase and ring-turned supports continuing to button feet joined by double bulbous front stretchers and planed side stretchers, painted red/brown over earlier paint, minor imperfections, mid-18th C, 16-1/2" h seat, 48" h **$6,500**

Federal, New England, birch, serpentine crest continues to shaped wings, out scrolled arms, tight seat over sq tapering front legs joined by sq stretchers to rear sq raking legs, floral upholstery, minor imperfections, early 19th C, 14-1/2" h seat, 47-1/4" h **$3,410**

Fauteuil

Louis XV-style, beechwood, frames carved with foliage, price for pr **$2,710**

Louis XV-style, painted, typical form with foliate carved frames, price for pr **$1,300**

Louis XVI-style, painted, floral and foliate carved top rail, upholstered back and seat, carved apron, cabriole legs, price for pr **$2,600**

Neoclassical, Continental, possibly Italian, painted green, carved floral crest and oval back, out scrolling arms, fluted tapering legs, painted throughout with flowers, price for pr, early 19th C and later **$4,780**

Neoclassical, Continental, possibly Italian, painted, chapeau de gendarme crest rail above out scrolling

arms, fluted tapering legs, blue and gray floral tapestry, price for pr, early 19th C and later **$4,100**

Sheraton-style, English, mahogany, green faux leather upholstery, scrolled and molded arms, balloon shaped seat, turned and reeded legs, matching arm supports, brass tack trim, early to mid-20th C, 17" h seat, 34" h back **$450**

Folding

Austrian, Thonet, bentwood, oval backrest and seat, scrolling arms and legs, late 19th C **$600**

Hall

William IV, octagonal scrolled backrest, center painted crest, shaped seat, turned tapering legs ending in peg feet **$475**

Highchair, child's

New England, attributed to, turned maple and birch, turned tapering stiles with finials joining three arched slats, shaped arms on vase and ring-turned supports, splayed legs joined by double stretchers, old refinish, late 18th C, 20" h seat, 40" h **$1,100**

Shaker-style, ladder back, woven splint seat, turned finials, foot rest, mustard paint, 24" h seat, 38" h back **$880**

Windsor, New England, rect crest above three spindles and outward flaring stiles, turned hand-holds on shaped seat, splayed turned tapering legs joined by stretchers, vestiges of stippled red and black paint, "M.H. Spencer, N.Y." in script on bottom of seat, 1825-40, 22-1/2" h seat, 31-1/2" h **$775**

Morris chair, Arts & Crafts, Gustav Stickley flat-arm (no. 332) with five vertical back slats under each arm, drop-in spring seat and loose back cushion newly recovered in dark brown leather, orig finish, color added to arms, red decal inside leg, 39" x 32" x 38", **$10,200.**

Photo courtesy of David Rago Auctions, Inc.

Armchairs, Louis XVI-style, new frame, price for pr, upholstered in 18th century tapestry, 40-1/2" x 24" x 24", **$2,600.**
Photo courtesy of David Rago Auctions, Inc.

Ladderback

Child's, woven splint seat, turned finials, red finish, 6-1/2" h seat, 3" h back **$250**

Connecticut, mixed hardwoods, old deep brown finish, bowed arms, turned supports continue down to medallions on top run of base, back with four arched slats, high finials, replaced woven splint seat, turned posts and stretchers, 14-1/2" h seat, 42" h back **$375**

Pennsylvania, woven splint seat, turned finials, painted red, 13" h seat, 42" h back **$150**

Library

George III, mahogany and caned, pink upholstered loose cushion, c1800, 33-1/2" h **$2,070**

Lolling, Federal

Massachusetts, mahogany, serpentine crest above half serpentine molded shaped arms, concave supports, over-upholstered serpentine seat on sq tapering frontal legs, raked rear legs, casters missing, minor imperfections, 1790-1800, 16-1/2" h seat, 42" h **$4,700**

New England, mahogany, reverse serpentine crest over upholstered back joining shaped arms and molded concave supports on four tapering sq legs, joined by sq stretchers, old refinish, imperfections, c1790, 17" h seat, 43-1/4" h **$6,900**

Lounge, International Movement

Charles and Ray Eames, MI, molded plywood mahogany seat and legs, purchased c1949, 22" w, 26" h **$1,880**

George Nakashima, New Hope, Pennsylvania, walnut conoid lounge chair, c1975, 31" w, 33-1/3" d, 30-1/2" h chair, 24" w, 24" d, 10-1/4" h ottoman **$4,700**

Hans Wegner, Denmark, teak, reclining upholstered cushion seat, c1960, 29-1/4" w, 48" d, 34-1/2" h chair, 29-1/2" w, 23-1/2" d, 13-1/2" h ottoman **$4,700**

Morris chair, Arts & Crafts

Stickley, Gustav, No. 332, slats to the floor under flat arms, orig brown leather cushions, orig finish, red decal, arms re-pegged and re-glued, 31-1/2" w, 36" d, 37" h **$6,275**

Stickley, L. & J. G., Fayetteville, New York, chair model No. 411, matching model No. 397 footstool, four carved slats on adjustable back, flat open arms with through tenon leg posts and four corbel supports with upholstered spring cushion seat and back, light brown finish, c1915, 29-1/4" w, 35" d, 40-1/4" h; footstool with spring cushion, 20" w, 14" d, 16-1/2" h, both with red and yellow decal "The Work of L. & J. G. Stickley" **$1,725**

Wainscot, Pennsylvania, walnut, pegged construction, shaped crest,

raised paneled back, shaped arms, turned legs, stretcher base, 18th C, 24-1/4" w, 19-1/2" d, 17-1/2" h seat, 42" h back **$7,150**

Side Chairs

Arrowback, tan, brown, red, and black dec of cornucopias on crest, leaves on back and front stretcher, incising around seat, brushed detain between, evidence of earlier green, bamboo turned base, 19th C mustard paint, 15-3/4" h seat, 32" h **$935**

Art Deco, Europe, wooden gondola backs, ivory sabots on front legs, cream striped fabric upholstery, pr, 25" h **$2,000**

Arts & Crafts

Stickley, Gustav, H-back, drop-in seat recovered in burgundy leather, red decal, over-coated orig dark finish, roughness to leg edges, 17" w, 16" d, 40" h **$690**

Stickley, L. & J.G., Fayetteville, New York, oak, model No. 940, three vertical slats below crest rail, slip seat, double side stretcher, branded mark, price for set of six, c1916, 35-3/4" h **$2,235**

Banister back

New England, paint dec, shaped crest above four split balusters joining vase and ring-turned stiles, trapezoidal rush seat, vase and ring-turned legs joined to rear legs by turned double stretchers, old surface painted dark brown with gilt stencil and polychrome floral designs, last half 18th C, 17-1/2" h seat, 44" h **$1,100**

New Hampshire, coastal, painted black, flaring fishtail carved crest over three split banisters flanked by vase and ring-turned stiles with ball finials, trapezoidal rush seat over ring-turned frontal legs joined by double turned stretchers, rear legs with old piecing, mid to late 18th C, 17" h seat, 43" h **$1,425**

Biedermeier, curved crest rail, central horizontal splat joined by three vertical splats, upholstered seat, squared tapering legs, set of four **$1,675**

Centennial, Queen Anne style, European, walnut, pierced and scrolled back splat, serpentine real stiles, balloon shaped slip seat, cabriole legs, scrolled knees, pad feet, old mellow finish, price for pr, 18-1/2" h seat, 41-1/2" h back **$600**

Chippendale

America, mahogany, arched crests,

interlaced double scroll back splat with piercing, old slip seat cov in black faux leather, sq legs with beaded edges, stretcher base, old dark finish, restorations, price for pr, 19-1/2" h seat, 38" h back **$1,785**

America, mahogany, serpentine crest with beaded edges, pierced vase shaped back splat, tapered rear stiles, replacement slip seat, sq legs with chamfered backs and beaded corners, stretcher base, old finish, rockers added at one time, now with pieced restorations as it was converted back to chair, 17" h seat, 35-3/4" h **$450**

Boston or Salem, Massachusetts area, carved mahogany, serpentine crests end in raked molded ears, center carved shells above owl-shaped splats with carved volutes above slip seats, Marlborough front legs with beaded outer edges, joined by similar sq stretchers to rear raking legs, old refinish, minor imperfections, price for pr, 1755-85, 16-5/8" h seat, 38" h **$4,200**

Connecticut River Valley, tiger maple, serpentine crest with raked molded terminals above pierced splat, old rush seat, block and vase turned front legs joined by turned stretcher, old refinish, 17-1/4" h seat, 39" h **$900**

Country, maple with some curl, pierced spat and shaped crest with carved ears, sq legs, mortised and pinned stretchers, old mellow refinishing, damage to paper rush seat because of breaks in front seal rail, 39" h **$110**

Massachusetts, cherry, shaped crest rail above pierced splat and raked stiles, upholstered slip seat, sq chamfered legs joined to raking rear legs by sq stretchers, refinished, repairs, late 18th C, 17-1/2" h, 38" h **$600**

Massachusetts, mahogany, shaped crest rail above pierced scroll and diamond splat flanked by raked stiles, trapezoidal upholstered slip seat, beaded straight legs joined to raking rear legs by sq stretchers, imperfections, late 18th C, 18" h seat, 37-1/2" h **$500**

New London, CT, carved cherry, serpentine crest rails, pierced splats with C-scrolls and beaded edges, molded shoes, flanked by stiles and rounded backs, molded seat frames

Chair, Modern, Eero Saarinen for Knoll, bent plywood legs, Knoll Assoc. label, price for set of four, 30-1/2" x 26" x 19", **$500.**
Photo courtesy of David Rago Auctions, Inc.

and straight legs with beaded edges, pierced brackets joined by sq stretchers, old refinish, set of five, 1760-95, 17" h seat, 39" h ...**$10,350**

New York, carved mahogany, carved crest ending in raked molded terminals above pierced splat with C-scrolls, slip seat, molded seat frame, front carved cabriole legs ending in ball and claw feet, rear raked legs, old surface, imperfections, 1755-65, 18" h seat, 39-1/2" h **$2,990**

Pennsylvania, attributed to, carved mahogany, serpentine crest rail with cockbeaded edge and scrolled terminals above pierced shaped splat, molded raking stiles, trapezoidal slip seat, beaded Marlborough front legs joined to raking rear legs by sq stretchers, restored, late 18th C, 17" h seat, 36-1/2" h **$1,775**

Rhode Island, mahogany, shaped and carved crest rail, pierced splat, raked stiles, trapezoidal slip seat, molded front legs joined to raked rear legs by sq stretchers, old finish, imperfections, c1765-95, 18" h seat, 38" h **$1,100**

Chippendale-style, country, mixed hardwoods, dark reddish-brown finish, pierced heart and scroll back splat, tapered real stiles, paper rush seat, turned legs and stretchers, Spanish feet, late 19th or early 20th C, 18-1/2" h seat, 40" h back....**$435**

Classical

Baltimore, painted and dec, scrolled crest above inverted vase-shaped splat, cane seat, dec front legs joined by medial stretcher, stencil dec, orig gilt classical motifs on black ground, 34-1/2" h **$750**

Boston, MA, attributed to, mahogany veneer, curving crest with the continuous stile and rail construction, shaped splats, bowed veneered front seat rails, frontal curving legs, rear raking legs, price for set of six, minor imperfections, c1835, 17" h seat, 31" h...............................**$4,350**

New England, carved and turned tiger maple, baluster turned cresting above acanthus carved, pierced splat joining raked stiles above trapezoidal rush seat, vase and ring-turned outward flaring frontal legs and turned stretchers, refinished, imperfections, price for set of six, c1825, 18" h seat, 34-1/2" h ..**$1,765**

New York, carved mahogany veneer, scroll back, beaded edges, horizontal splats carved with leafage and other classical motifs, slip seat, curving legs, old surface, set of six, 1810-20, 16-1/2" h seat, 32" h **$5,200**

Country, Ohio, painted mustard, black, and gold fruit and leaves, red painted surface in the manner of J. Huey, Zanesville, OH, c1840 ..**$7,500**

Armchair, Arts & Crafts, Limbert, Ebon-oak, geometric inlay, drop-in cushion seat newly decorated in wool Navajo print, branded under arm, refinished, some looseness, 38" x 27" x 23-1/2", $1,400.

Photo courtesy of David Rago Auctions, Inc.

Decorated, attributed to Carlisle, PA, plank seat, orig black over red dec, floral panels surrounded by gold stencils, bordered with salmon and yellow line border dec, carefully cleaned, applied coat of protective varnish, professionally executed slight touch-up, price for set of six, 17" h seat, 31" h **$3,650**

Federal

Boston, MA, or Portsmouth, New Hampshire, mahogany, square back with scratch beading enclose three pierced splats above trapezoidal shaped over upholstered seats, sq tapering front legs outlined in stringing and joined by sq stretchers to raked rear legs, refinished, one chair with a pierced rear stile, price for set of four, c1800, 18" h seat, 35-1/2" h.................. **$1,175**

Massachusetts or Rhode Island, mahogany inlaid, shield back, arched molded crest above five molded spindles and inlaid quarter fan, over-upholstered seats with serpentine fronts, molded tapering legs joined by stretchers, c1780, 17-1/2" h seat, 37" h, pr....................................**$5,475**

New England, attributed to, maple, rush seat, dec with polychrome flowers on yellow ground, price for pr, 18" w, 16" d, 35" h **$500**

New Hampshire, Portsmouth, attributed to Langley Boardman, mahogany, sq back, reeded on rest rail, stiles, and stay rail, over upholstered serpentine seat, molded sq tapering front

legs, sq stretchers and rakes rear legs, refinish, minor imperfections, 1774-1833, 18" h seat, 36" h **$1,035**

George III, mahogany, yoke shaped crest rail, pierced splat carved with wheat sheaves, slip-in padded seat, squared molded legs, price for pr, late 18th C................................ **$650**

Gothic Revival, New York City, mahogany veneer, trefoil pierced splats, curved stay rails, veneered seal rails, curving rococo legs, old refinish, 20th C upholstery, set of eight, 1850s, 16-1/2" h seat, 33-1/2" h **$6,900**

Hepplewhite

American, mahogany, shield back, rush seat.................................... **$325**

Shield back, mahogany, pierced scrolled splat with fluted urn, over-upholstered serpentine seat, tapered sq legs with inlaid pendants and cuffs, pr, black legs spliced, 38-1/2" h........ **$750**

Hitchcock, Hitchcocksville, Connecticut, rosewood grained surface, orig gilt dec, urn centering cornucopia splat, old rush seats, ring-turned legs, orig surface, price for set of four, 1825-32, 35-1/2" h.......... **$1,265**

International Movement

Designed by Mies van der Rohe, manufactured by Knoll Associates, New York, cantilevered tubular steel frame, green leather padded and upholstered seat, price for pr, 33-1/2" h **$6,450**

Mies van der Rohe Barcelona chairs, attributed to Knoll Associates, New York, black leather cushions on flat bar base, price for pr, 29-1/2" w, 29-1/2" d, 29-1/2" h................ **$5,590**

Warren McArthur Corporation, machined and tubular anodized aluminum with original upholstery, green decal labels. Height 32 inches .. **$2,150**

Ladderback

Pennsylvania, rush seat, ball turned finials, turned front stretcher, old mustard paint, wear to feet, 14-1/2" h seat, 41" h back........ **$385**

Pennsylvania, woven splint seat, turned finials, boldly turned front stretcher, turned legs, old brown paint, 14" h seat, 38-1/2" h back.................... **$525**

Pennsylvania, woven splint seat, turned finials, boldly turned front stretcher, reddish-brown finish, 16" h seat, 40" h back **$330**

Pennsylvania, woven splint seat, turned finials, boldly turned front stretcher, old green-black paint, 17" h seat, 40" h back **$385**

Pennsylvania, woven splint seat, turned finials and front stretcher, reddish-brown finish, 16-1/2" h seat, 39-1/2" h back................ **$360**

Neoclassical, Boston, 1815-20, mahogany, curving carved crests flanked by gadrooning above similarly curved horizontal splats enclosing carved elements flanked by reeded curving stiles that continue to half way on front legs and also elaborate front seat rails, curving rear legs and slip seats, upholstered in 20th C green watered moiré fabric, price for pair, 17-1/4" h seat, 33-1/2" h back.. **$1,175**

Plank seat, Pennsylvania, orig paint dec, fruit with green leaves on crest, yellow and white line borders on reddish brown ground, wear, old touch up, set of six, 18-1/2" h seat, 33-1/4" h back........................... **$700**

Queen Anne

American, burl walnut, shaped cresting, serpentine slat, slip-seat raised on shell carved cabriole legs, hoof feet, price for pr, early 18th C **$1,650**

Country, finely alligatored black paint, double arched crest, pierced vase shaped back splat, tapered rear stiles, replaced paper rush seat, pad feet, boldly turned front stretcher, small glued splits on crest, 17" h seat, 38-1/2" h back........................... **$375**

English, mahogany, scalloped and scrolled real splat, serpentine rear stiles, later red velvet covering on balloon seat, cabriole legs, relief carved shells on knees, pad feet, old refinishing, two returns replaced, 17" h seat, 39-1/2" back **$1,610**

New England, painted, carved and spooned crest rail above vasiform splat and raking stiles, trapezoidal slip seat, blocked vase and ring-turned legs, carved Spanish feet joined by bulbous turned front stretcher and straight side stretchers, old black paint over earlier paint, imperfections, mid-18th C, 16-1/2" h seat, 41" h back **$600**

Newport, Rhode Island, black walnut, curving crest above vase-shaped pierced splat, compass seat, front and side rail shaping, cabriole front legs joined to rear sq tapering legs by block and vase-swelled side stretchers, swelled and turned medial stretchers, rear feet without chamfering, old refinish, minor repairs, affixed brass plaque reads

"Ebenezer Storer 1730-1807," 1750-75, 17" h seat, 38-1/4" h **$2,990**

Regency-style, walnut, five brass rods as back splats, balloon seats with old replaced upholstery, applied ormolu mounts, tapered and fluted legs and rear stiles, old finish, set of four, 17-1/2" h seat, 32" h back **$450**

Rococo Revival, John H. Belter, rosewood, Rosalie without the Grapes pattern, laminated, solid back, crest carved with large rose and fruit, red silk upholstery, casters, pr, 37-1/2" h **$2,550**

Sheraton, walnut, raised medallion crest, rope twist detail on back slats, ring-turned and reeded front legs, rear saber legs, serpentine stiles, old finish, contemporary upholstered seats, restorations, one crest pieced, set of six, 19" h seat, 33" h back..**$750**

Slat back, Delaware River Valley, turned maple, five reverse graduated concave arched slats joining turned stiles with bulbous finials, rush seat, vase and ring-turned frontal legs joined by bulbous turned front stretcher and side stretchers, old surface, late 18th C, 17" h seat, 45-1/2" h **$4,120**

Victorian, ebonized, lacquered, Wedgwood mounts, openwork backrest, caned seat, turned legs, price for pr...........................**$1,410**

William IV, England, carved rosewood, foliate carved backrest with central diamond-shaped upholstered panel, slip seat, leaf carved circular legs, price for pr, c1835.............**$700**

Windsor
Bamboo turned, Pennsylvania, grain dec, red, green, and yellow floral, bud, and foliate dec crest rail, 18" h seat, 34" h back.....................**$935**

Birdcage, New England, two horizontal spindles and seven vertical spindles joining bamboo-turned slightly swelled stiles, shaped seats, splayed swelled bamboo-turned legs and stretchers, old worn black paint, price for set of five, 18" h seat, c1810, 35-1/2" h **$3,300**

Bow-back, New England, bowed crest rail above seven spindles and shaped saddle seat, splayed swelled bamboo-turned legs and stretchers, some paint loss to black paint, c1810, 17-1/2" h seat, 39" h **$650**

Bow-back, New England, black painted, molded bowed crest rails above

seven spindles and shaped saddle seat on splayed vase and ring-turned legs and swelled stretchers, price for pr, imperfections, late 18th C, 17-1/4" seat, 38-1/4" h **$2,820**

Brace-back, nine spindles bow back, well shaped seat with incised detail around spindles, vase and ring turned legs, turned "H" stretcher, old mellow refinish, restorations, 17-1/2" h, seat, 36-3/4" h **$385**

Butterfly, Pennsylvania, seven-spindle back, bamboo turnings, poplar seats, hickory legs and spindles, refinished, price for pr, one with crack in top rail **$285**

Clerk's, attributed to New England, ash, shaped concave crest above seven spindles, vase and ring-turned stiles, shaped saddle seat, splayed vase and ring-turned legs joined by turned, swelled stretchers, old refinish, imperfections, c1790, 26" h, 41-1/2" h......................**$1,430**

Comb-back, mixed woods, arched crest with flared ears, seven-spindle back, turned arms, bentwood arm rail, shield shaped seat, vase and ring turned legs, stretcher base, light refinish, 17" h seat, 38-1/4" h....**$800**

Fan-back, Massachusetts, attributed to, shaped crest rail with scroll carved terminals above seven spindles, vase and ring turned stiles and shaped saddle seat, splayed vase and ring turned legs joined by swelled stretchers, old black paint, late 18th C, 18" h seat, 36-1/2" h **$715**

Fan-back, New England, red stained, shaped crest rail above seven spindles, vase and ring-turned stiles, shaped saddle seat, splayed vase and ring-turned legs joined by swelled stretchers, imperfections, late 18th C, 17" h seat, 36" h....**$775**

Fan-back, New England, shaped crest rail above seven spindles and vase and ring-turned stiles, shaped saddle seat and splayed vase and ring-turned legs joined by swelled stretchers, old brown paint, late 18th C, 17" h seat, 37" h..........**$600**

Fan-back, New England, shaped crest rail with scroll-carved terminals above seven spindles and vase and ring-turned stiles, shaped saddle seat and splayed vase and ring-turned legs and swelled stretchers, old black/brown paint over earlier green and red paints, late 18th C, 17" h seat, 36" h....................**$7,675**

Armchair, Louis XVI provincial, fruitwood fauteuil, molded-edge medallion back, needlepoint panel, upholstered seat, ball feet, 18th century, 34" x 22-1/4" x 18-3/4", **$750.**
Photo courtesy of Sloans & Kenyon Auctioneers and Appraisers.

Slipper
Aesthetic Movement, American, walnut, V-shaped cresting, openwork floral and disc carved frieze, angular floral carved legs **$500**

Arts & Crafts, Gustav Stickley, spindled back, drop-in spring seat recovered in brown leather, orig finish, black decal, 17-3/4" w, 16" d, 37" h.............**$1,150**

Victorian, rosewood, angular foliate carved backrest with urn form splat, over upholstered seat and circular turned legs, c1875..........**$300**

Victorian, late, ebonized and bobbin turned needlepoint upholstery, foliate dec seat, c1880....................**$175**

Morris chair, Aesthetic Movement, in the style of William Morris, mahogany, spindled sides and back, loose tufted pillows, upholstered arms, casters, unmarked, orig finish, minor roughness to leg edges, 42-1/2" x 29" x 31", **$800.**
Photo courtesy of David Rago Auctions, Inc.

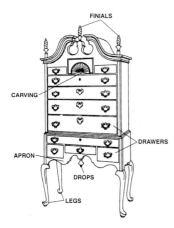

FINIALS

CARVING

DRAWERS

APRON

DROPS

LEGS

Typical Parts of a Highboy

Empire chest of drawers, American, mahogany, half-round upper drawer, three lower drawers, columnar front posts, turned feet, period pressed glass knobs, second quarter 19th century, 41" h x 44" w x 20" d, **$300.**
Photo courtesy of Green Valley Auctions.

Chest on chest, Georgian, possibly Scottish, rect. molded cornice, seven drawers top section, projecting lower section with four drawers, bracket feet, third quarter 18th century, **$2,940.**
Photo courtesy of Skinner, Inc.

Chests of drawers

Art Deco, Quigley, France, parchment covered, rect top, three tapering drawers, pyramid mirrored stiles, bracket feet, back branded, c1925, 44-1/2" x 35"...**$2,750**

Arts & Crafts, English, dresser, orig pivoting mirror with chamberstick shelves, glove boxes, copper repoussé panels, two drawers over one long drawer, orig medium-dark finish, unmarked, split to side, 42-3/4" w, 21-1/2" d, 64" h..........................**$1,725**

Biedermeier, maple, rect case fitted with two drawers, splayed sq legs, c1820, 36" w, 19" d, 31" h.........**$1,725**

Chippendale

Baltimore, Maryland, mahogany, line inlaid, two split upper drawers, three lower full width graduated cock beaded dovetailed drawers, molded base, ogee bracket feet, 35-1/4" w, 19-1/2" d, 33-1/2" h.................**$6,050**

Boston, Massachusetts area, carved mahogany, reverse serpentine, shaped mahogany top with veneered edge overhangs case of conforming veneered drawers, cockbeaded drawer separators, molded base, ball and claw feet, old refinish, veneer losses, 1770-80, 38-1/4" w, 20-3/4" d, 34-1/4" h...................................**$3,525**

Connecticut, carved cherry, rect top with molded edge, cockbeaded case of four graduated drawers, gadrooned carved ogee bracket base, replaced brasses, refinished, imperfections, late 18th C, 36-1/2" w, 17" d, 37-1/2" h....**$4,450**

English, mahogany, oak secondary wood, molded top with pull-out writing surface, four dovetailed graduated drawers with molded edges, old brass pulls, ogee feet, molded base, old refinishing, old restorations, backboards renailed, 34" w, 18" d, 33-1/4" h...........**$2,875**

Massachusetts, maple, rect overhanging top, four thumb-molded graduated drawers, ogee bracket feet, replaced brass pulls, old refinish, imperfections, losses, c1780, 32-1/2" w, 17" d, 33" h...........**$4,700**

Massachusetts, attributed to, maple, flat molded cornice, case of two thumb-molded short drawers and six graduated long drawers, bracket feet, brasses appear to be orig, old red stained surface, minor imperfections, last half 18th C, 36" w, 18-1/2" d, 57" h...........**$8,820**

New England, cherry, rect overhanging top, case of five graduated thumb-molded drawers, base with ogee feet, replaced brass, refinished, restored, late 18th C, 36-3/4" w, 17-3/4" d, 34-3/4" h..............**$2,350**

New England, maple, flat molded cornice, case of two thumb molded short drawers and four graduated long drawers, ogee bracket feet, brasses appear to be original, refinished, minor restoration, late 18th C, 36" w, 18" d, 42" h............**$4,200**

New England, maple, molded cornice overhangs case of five thumb-molded graduated drawers, molded bracket base, original brass, refinished, imperfections, late 18th C, 35-1/2" w, 18-1/8" d, 47" h......**$3,100**

Pennsylvania, walnut, five drawers, reeded quarter columns, ogee bracket feet, orig varnish, c1780 ....**$12,000**

Pennsylvania, high chest, walnut, cove-molded cornice, three small thumb-molded drawers over five graduated thumb-molded drawers, tall ogee bracket feet, two small locks removed, repairs, c1780, 41" w, 23" d, 62-1/2" h...........**$1,840**

Pennsylvania, walnut, three small thumb-molded drawers over two small thumb-molded drawers over three graduated thumb-molded drawers, twin fluted quarter-columns, ogee bracket feet, top not orig, two small locks removed, repairs, 40-1/4" w, 21-5/8" d, 46-3/4" h **$1,725**

Rhode Island, carved tiger maple, tall, cornice with dentil molding, case of seven graduated thumb-molded drawers, molded tall bracket base with central drop, top drawer with fan-carving, orig brasses, early surface, late 18th C, 38" w, 18-3/4" d, 63-3/4" h............**$27,600**

Southern, walnut, yellow pine secondary wood, orig two-board top with variegated fan inlays in corners, double star in middle, chamfered corners on case, with small urns and line inlay, five dovetailed drawers with banded inlay borders, ogee feet with scalloped returns, molded base, refinished, old replaced brasses, small areas of veneer damage, inlay restorations, minor insect damage, feet are old well-executed replacements, 39" w, 21-1/4" d, 38-1/8" h..............**$2,645**

Chippendale to Hepplewhite, transitional, cherry, pine secondary wood, dovetailed case with reeded quarter columns, cove molded cornice, eight dovetailed graduated drawers, French feet with scalloped returns, molding around base, orig oval brasses, old mellow refinishing, 42-1/2" w, 23" d, 63-3/4" h.................................**$5,300**

Chippendale-style, America, black walnut, mahogany, pine secondary wood, two board top, five finely dovetailed drawers with beaded edges, two drawers with divided interiors, bracket base with thin molded edge, brass bale pulls, wire nails, late 19th/early 20th C, 42" w, 20" d, 41-1/2" h.................**$900**

Classical

New England, bird's eye maple, rect top, case with projecting cockbeaded bird's-eye maple veneered drawers, above three graduated drawers with flanking engaged vase and ring-turned spiral carved columns continuing to turned feet, opalescent pattern glass pulls, refinished, 1825-30, 41" w, 20" d, 47-1/2" h ...**$1,530**

Ohio, attributed to, tiger and bird's-eye maple, backsplash above overhanging top, case with recessed panel sides, cockbeaded graduated drawers flanked by spiral carved columns and colonettes above dies, turned tapering legs and feet, shaped skirt, refinished, replaced glass pulls, imperfections, 1830s, 46" w, 19-3/4" d, 57-1/4" h....**$2,000**

Eastlake, American

Curly walnut, burl veneer, carved detail, scrolled crest, four dovetailed drawers, two handkerchief drawers, well detailed molded panel fronts, refinished, 39" w, 17-1/2" d, 46" h **$750**

Mahogany, five full drawers, two half drawers, carved leaf and branch dec, 38" w, 55" h **$300**

Empire

America, cherry, orig dark red flame graining over salmon ground on façade, worn orig red on sides, maple and poplar secondary woods, two-board top with old chip along back edge, serpentine pilasters on either side of four dovetailed drawers, old clear glass pulls, inset panels on ends, turned feet, age splits in top, c1830, 43" w, 22-5/8" d, 46-3/5" h **$500**

America, tiger maple, rect top, protruding frieze section fitted with single wide drawer over three drawers between applied half-round turnings, vase and ball turned feet, period round brass pulls, c1830, 42-1/2" w, 21-1/2" d, 44-1/2" h.................**$2,750**

Maine, attributed to, cherry, mahogany veneer, pine secondary wood, two-board top has shaped back splash, four dovetailed drawers with orig brass pulls and key escutcheons, high crisply turned feet, refinished, veneer repairs, pulls cleaned, minor dents, 41-1/4" w, 20" d, 41-1/2" h **$1,100**

Federal

America, bowfront, mahogany, flame mahogany veneer, pine secondary wood, old replaced top with biscuit corners, four dovetailed drawers with applied beading, replaced brass pulls, rope twist carvings on front pilasters, high boldly turned feet, refinished, pierced restorations, one rear foot replaced, 40-1/2" w, 19" d, 36-3/4" h.......**$770**

Baltimore, Maryland, mahogany veneered and inlaid, serpentine, top with veneered edge overhangs conforming case of four graduated drawers outlined in narrow banding and stringing with ovolo corners, shaped skirt, flaring French feet connected to shaped sides, replaced brasses, old refinish, imperfections, c1810, 45-3/4" w, 22-1/4" d, 38" h **$5,585**

Connecticut, attributed to, cherry, rect overhanging top with string inlaid edge, case with four scratch-beaded graduated drawers, bracket base, replaced brasses, refinished, minor imperfections, c1790-1810, 37-3/4" w, 19-1/2" d, 35" h....**$4,415**

Maryland, attributed to, cherry and poplar inlaid, rect top with string inlaid edge, case of four graduated drawers with cockbeaded surrounds flanked by quarter-engaged columns, base with scalloped front skirt and flaring feet, refinished, replaced brass, repairs, 1810-20, 40-1/4" w, 18-5/8" d, 35-1/2" h **$2,115**

Maryland, attributed to, mahogany inlaid, mahogany veneered top with inlaid edge, case of cockbeaded drawers with oval stringing, serpentine veneered skirt flanked by tapering French feet, refinished, old replaced brass, some restoration, early 19th C, 44-1/2" w, 20-1/8" d, 43" h **$1,880**

Chest of drawers, Hepplewhite, cherry, c1790, 39-1/2" x 42-3/4" w x 22" d, **$950.**
Photo courtesy of Wiederseim Associates, Inc.

Massachusetts, cherry, rect top with cross banded edge overhangs conforming case of four graduated scratch beaded drawers, cut-out bracket base, replaced brass, refinished, early 19th C, 40-1/4" w, 20-5/8" d, 35-1/2" h...............**$2,750**

Massachusetts, mahogany veneer, bowed top with cross-banded veneered overhanging edge, conforming case of cockbeaded veneered drawers, molded base with shaped feet, original brass, old refinish, early 19th C, 41-1/4" w, 23-1/2" d, 35" h.....................**$4,125**

Middle Atlantic states, mahogany, mahogany veneer, and cherry, rect, top above case of four graduated, cockbeaded drawers, upper drawer with cross banded mahogany inlay, shaped veneered skirt, slightly flaring French feet, refinished, replaced brasses, restored, 1815-25, 44-1/4" w, 19-7/8" d, 45-1/2" h **$2,115**

New England, inlaid cherry, bow front top with string-inlaid edge overhangs conforming case of inlaid drawers, stringing in outline, quarter fans, and central paterae above shaped skirt flanked by flaring French feet, replaced brass, old refinish, repairs, early 19th C, 42-3/4" w, 21" d, 36-3/4" h....**$3,100**

New Hampshire, possibly by the Dunlaps, carved and inlaid wavy birch, rect top with inlaid edge overhangs case of four drawers with stringing in ovolo outline; flanked by quarter-engaged columns wrapped with vine-like stringing, diminutive fan carving above and below columns, molded base with carved geometric shapes, sharply spurred bracket feet, mostly original brass, old refinish, imperfections, early 19th C, 38-1/2" w, 19-1/4" d, 38-1/2" h...............**$11,200**

Portsmouth or Greenland, New Hampshire, bow front, mahogany and flame birch veneer, bow front mahogany top with inlaid edge overhanging conforming case, four cockbeaded three-paneled drawers, divisions outlined with mahogany cross banded veneer and stringing above skirt, central veneered rect drop panel, high bracket feet joined by shaped side skirts, similar rear feet, turned pulls appear to be orig, old refinish, minor repairs, 1810-14, 40-1/4" w, 21-1/4" d, 39" h **$28,750**

Rhode Island, maple, rect top, molded edge, case of four thumb-molded graduated drawers, valanced skirt joining shaped French feet, orig oval brasses, old refinish, imperfections, c1800-10, 42" w, 18-1/4" d, 38-3/4" h **$1,765**

George III, bachelor's, mahogany, rect top over two short and three long drawers, bracket feet, 24-1/2" w, 18-1/2" d, 34" h **$2,600**

George III-style, mahogany, serpentine-front, thumb-molded top above four graduated and cockbeaded drawers, channel-carved bracket feet, 19th C, 43" w, 24" d, 43" h **$4,415**

Grain painted, attributed to Maine or New Hampshire, carved pine, central fan-carved drawer flanked by four small drawers above four long drawers, base with front and side shaping, restoration, late 18th C, 41-1/2" w, 18-3/4" d, 49-1/4" h **$4,410**

Hepplewhite

America, mahogany, straight front, four cockbeaded drawers, eagle-punched brasses, plain plant sides, bracket feet, shaped interiors, replaced top band, repairs to feet, lightly refinished, c1800, 42-1/2" w, 21" d, 37" h **$1,550**

America, mahogany, poplar secondary wood, two-board top, four dovetailed drawers with beaded edges, older replaced emb brasses, scalloped fan inlay on lower apron, banding around lower case, French feet, refinished, restorations, replacements, c1810, 39" w, 19-3/4" d, 42-5/8" h **$1,475**

American, bow front, cherry, shaped top, four graduated drawers, flared

---

Modern pieces with an antique look

Furniture makers have long copied each other's styles, and the 20th century furniture makers are continuing that practice. Collectors should be aware what some of today's well-made replica furniture may sell for. Here are some examples:

Breakfront secretary, Hendredon, Georgian-style, mahogany, shaped cornice over four glazed doors above secretary drawer, over two cabinet doors, flanked on each side by five graduated drawers, 26-1/2" w, 17-1/2" d, 87-1/2" h **$1,770**

Chest of drawers, Hendredon, dark brown, gold sponge dec finish simulating tortoise shell, four drawers, short block feet, flush mounted brass handles on drawers and sides of cases, branded signature inside drawers, price for pr, 28" w, 12-1/2" d, 28-1/4" h **$500**

Chest on chest, Virginia Crafters, walnut, oak and poplar secondary woods, urn and flame finials, broken arch top with carved rosettes, reeded columns, 11 drawers with carved shell on top drawer, ogee feet with scalloped returns, batwing brasses, branded signature on back, 40-1/4" w, 22-1/4" d, 90-1/2" h **$1,610**

Credenza, Chippendale-style, Kittinger, mahogany and mahogany veneer, oak secondary wood, four dovetailed drawers down left, smaller center drawer with cabinet below, longer drawer over open compartment flanking on right with adjustable shelf, molded edge

and base trip, branded label, emb metallic emblem in drawer, 81-1/2" l, 19-1/2" d, 30" h **$900**

Desk, Chippendale-style, Kittinger, mahogany and mahogany veneers, oak secondary wood, four dovetailed drawers on both sides, center drawer, thin applied moldings create decorative panels on sides and front, shaped bracket feet, molding around bases, emb metallic label, 72" w, 36-1/4" d, 30-1/2" h **$1,695**

Dining chairs, Baker, Regency-style, four side and two arm chairs ... **$4,250**

Dining table, Regency-style, Baker, 20th C, satinwood cross banded mahogany, rect top, three leaves, double reeded pedestals, downswept legs, casters, 132" l extended, 48" w, 30" h **$2,585**

Settee, Windsor, continuous arm, by Steve, painted by Peter Deen, cherry, scrolled arms, spindle back, turned legs, stretchers, distressed green paint, 56-1/2" l, 17-1/2" d, 17-1/2" h seat, 29" h back **$2,475**

Sugar chest, Sheraton-style, country, cherry, poplar secondary wood, hand made, two hinged lids, two dovetailed drawers, high turned feet, turned cherry pulls, interior divided into four compartments, small pieced repairs, 47-1/2" w, 20-1/4" d, 34-3/4" h **$900**

Table, lamp, Kittinger, mahogany, concave shaped top, one drawer, shelf in base, branded and metal labels inside dovetailed drawer, tapered legs, casters, 19" w, 18" d, 26" h **$250**

Windsor side chairs, set of six, painted red-brown, sgd "R. D. L." (Drew Lausch), painted by Peter Deen, 17-1/2" h seat, 37" h back **$4,675**

High chest, Chippendale, Pennsylvania, ogee cornice above Greek key molding, nine drawers flanked by fluted quarter columns, spurred ogee bracket feet, c1775, 39" w, 63-3/4" h, **$12,650.**
Photo courtesy of Pook & Pook, Inc.

feet, 19th C, 38-3/4" w, 22" d, 40" h **$3,600**

Country, refinished pine, red stain, solid bird's eye maple drawer fronts with natural finish, four dovetailed drawers, cut out feet and apron, old brass knobs, age cracks in front feet, 37-3/4" w, 35-3/4" h **$1,100**

Louis Philippe, walnut, later rect top, conforming case fitted with three drawers, shaped bracket feet, second quarter 19th C, 47" w, 20" d, 31" h **$425**

Queen Anne, Southeastern New England, painted oak, cedar, and yellow pine, rect top with applied edge, case of four drawers each with molded fronts, chamfered mitered borders, separated by applied horizontal moldings, sides with two recessed vertical molded panels above single horizontal panel, base with applied molding, four turned ball feet, old red paint, minor imperfections, c1700, 37-3/4" w, 20-1/2" w, 35" h **$26,450**

Renaissance, Italian, walnut, composed of antique elements, fitted with three long drawers, foliate and shield shaped carved drawer pulls, paw feet, 36" w, 17" d, 37" h **$2,450**

Sheraton

Cherry, two-board top with step down and molded edge, case with reeded pilasters and inset side panels, four dovetailed and beaded drawers, turned legs, ball feet, old refinishing, old replaced brass pulls, traces of red wash on front, 41-3/4" w, 21-3/4" d, 40-1/2" h .. **$990**

Cherry, walnut secondary wood, six dovetailed drawers, small variegated sq inlays at upper corners, turned legs with reeding on front two, similar reeding up front posts, paneled ends, refinished, replaced eagle brasses, top reset with small bow-tie shaped splice added below, minor edge restoration to drawers, 42-3/4" w, 18-3/4" w, 44-1/2" h **$1,500**

Transitional, New England, cherry, overhanging rect top, conforming case, four graduated drawers with cockbeaded surrounds, serpentine skirt flanked by flaring veneered French feet, period brasses, refinished, late 18th or early 19th C, 45-3/4" w, 20-3/4" d, 36-1/2" h **$1,410**

Victorian

American, oak, rect mirror, pair of handkerchief boxes, two small draw-

ers over three graduated long drawers, emb design creates circular decoration on top three drawers, orig brass hardware, 40" w, 68" h **$375**

American, poplar, mahogany veneer facade, serpentine top drawer, two serpentine stepback drawers, five dovetailed drawers, applied beading, worn finish, 40" w, 19-3/4" d, 47" h **$330**

American, walnut, white marble top, three drawers, one hidden drawer in base, carved fruit and nut pulls, 39" w, 32" h **$700**

William and Mary

American, burl veneer, bachelor's, five dovetailed drawers, pull-out shelf, worn finish, veneer damage, replaced base molding, turned feet, and backboards, orig brasses, 30" w, 19" d, 35" h **$1,980**

Southern Massachusetts or Rhode Island, tiger maple, graduated drawer construction, two over four drawers, applied moldings to top and bottom, turned turnip feet, old grunge finish, three escutcheon plates present, rest of hardware missing, some repair, 36-1/4" w, 18-1/4" d, 48" h **$2,950**

Chests of drawers, other

Apothecary, painted blue, two drawers, 96" l **$2,900**

Bureau a Cylindre, Louis XV-style, gilt-bronze mounted rosewood and marquetry, rect top with pierced gallery above roll-top enclosing fitted interior, above single drawer, cabriole legs, allover dec with flowers and scrolling foliage, 29-1/2" w, 21" d, 42" h **$1,420**

Campaign, mahogany, pine secondary wood, brass trim, dovetailed case, int. with lift-out tray, one dovetailed drawer, some shrinkage to lid, 30-3/4" w, 18-1/4" d, 19" h **$385**

Chamber, Federal, attributed to the Seymour Workshop, Boston, mahogany inlaid, rect top, inlaid edge overhangs case with single tripartite drawer above six smaller drawers flanking central cabinet on arched inlaid skirt, four turned reeded and tapering legs, similar arched side skirts, upper drawer with oval central stringing reserve, all drawers are outlined in ebonized inlay, missing dressing mirror from int. drawer, minor imperfections, c1915, 44-3/4" w, 19-1/2" d, 34-1/4" h .. **$42,550**

Chest on chest

Biedermeier, walnut and ebonized, molded plinth cornice, five upper drawers, lower section with two drawers, bun feet, 41" w, 22" d, 64" h **$2,300**

Chippendale, RI, carved tiger maple, scrolled molded top with flame carved side finials, raised paneled faux drawers and six thumb-molded working drawers, lower case of four similar graduated drawers on molded base with ogee feet, some dark mahogany stain, some original brass, central finial is later addition, feet repairs, other imperfections, 1750-1796, 38-1/2" w, 18-7/8" d, 87" h **$23,500**

George III

Mahogany, rect cornice with molding and dentil trim, three short drawers over three graduated drawers, lower section with three graduated drawers, bracket feet, 31-1/2" w, 17-1/2" d, 59-1/2" h **$4,720**

Mahogany, rect molded and dentillated cornice above three short drawers, over three graduated drawers, lower section with three graduated drawers supported by bracket feet, 31-1/2" w, 17-1/2" d, 59-1/2" h **$4,720**

Queen Anne

Salem, Massachusetts, attributed to, tiger maple, upper case with molded cornice, five graduated thumb-molded drawers, lower case with one long drawer with two drawer façade, and one long drawer with three short drawer façade, centrally carved fan, four arris cabriole legs with high pad feet on platforms, joined by cyma-curved skirt centering scrolled drops, possibly old brasses, old refinish, minor imperfections, c1740-60, 38-3/4" w, 19-1/2" d, 73-3/4" h **$16,450**

Southern New Hampshire, maple, upper case with cove molded cornice, five graduated thumb-molded drawers, lower case with three graduated drawers, valanced frame joining four short cabriole legs on high pad on platform feet, old refinish, replaced brasses, drawers with chalk and pencil inscriptions, vestiges of old red paint, minor imperfections, late 19th C, 40-1/2" w, 20" d, 80" h **$11,750**

Commode, Louis Phillipe, walnut, rectangular replaced top, three drawers, gilt metal mounted pilasters, carved paw feet, mid-19th century, 32-1/2" x 43-1/2" x 24", **$945.**

Photo courtesy of Sloans & Kenyon Auctioneers and Appraisers.

Commode, Louis Phillipe, slate top, rectangular, slab, frieze drawer, three long drawers, scalloped apron, block feet, mid-19th century, 36-1/4" x 43-1/8" x 21-1/2", **$1,180.**

Photo courtesy of Sloans & Kenyon Auctioneers and Appraisers.

Chest of drawers, other, lingerie chest, Louis XV-style, book-matched rosewood veneer with doré bronze mounts, bombe top with embossed leather drawer fronts, base with tambour doors, cabriole legs, 1890, 71" x 54" x 18", **$5,000.**

Photo courtesy of David Rago Auctions, Inc.

Chest on frame

Queen Anne, Connecticut, painted, flaring cornice with cove molding, case of thumb-molded drawers, arranged in two over four graduating pattern, frame with vigorously scrolling front and side skirts joined to cabriole legs with arris knees, arris disc feet, old red repaint, imperfections, 1740-70, 40" w, 23-1/4" d, 63-1/2" h.............**$9,200**

Queen Anne-style, English, walnut and burl veneer, mahogany secondary wood, case with four dovetailed drawers, brass teardrop pulls, cabriole legs, duck feet, 20th C, 19-1/4" x 33-1/2" base, 38-1/2" h **$825**

Chest over drawers

Chippendale, New England, painted, molded lift-top above double-arch molded case of two graduated false drawers and two working drawers, turned wooden pulls, high bracket feet centering cut-out pendant, orig red painted surface, 18th C, 37-3/4" w, 18" d, 45-1/2" h......**$8,900**

Grain painted, Northern New England, pine, hinged top opens to storage cavity above two thumb-molded drawers, vigorously shaped front and side skirts, faux bois done with ochre and burnt umber, old brasses, minor imperfections, early 19th C, 39-3/4" w, 18-7/8" d, 39-7/8" h **$2,350**

William and Mary, New Jersey, cherry, poplar secondary wood, molded lift-lid, cotter-pin hinges, two faux upper drawer fronts, two full width dovetailed lower drawers, molded base, cut-out feet, incised brass Chinese drop pulls, shaped key escutcheons, replaced hardware, 42-1/2" w, 17-1/4" d, 44-1/2" h.................**$2,750**

Commode

Baroque, North Italian, walnut, molded rect top above frieze drawer and three long drawers, sides with fielded panels, bracket feet, early 18th C and later, 48" w, 23" d, 35-1/2" h **$5,100**

Biedermeier, birch and ebonized wood, rect top above four drawers flanked by columns, shaped skirt, bracket feet, price for pr, 34-3/4" w, 16-1/2" d, 35-1/2" h...............**$2,950**

Louis XV, tulipwood and kingwood parquetry inlaid, serpentine front, two short over three long serpentine drawers, flared feet, foliate cast

mounts, mid-18th C, 50" w, 24" d, 32" h **$4,700**

Louis XV, Provincial, walnut, serpentine top, case fitted with two short and two long drawers, each carved with rocaille and channel dec, third quarter 18th C, 51" w, 24" d, 31" h............**$4,700**

Louis XV-style

Tulipwood and marquetry, gray shaped rect marble top over three graduated drawers, slightly splayed feet ending in gilt metal sabots, 44" d, 19-1/2" d, 34-1/4" h **$2,850**

Tulipwood and marquetry, tan and caramel rect mottled marble top above an apron of intertwined gilt-metal laurel garlands above two drawers, tapering legs ending in floral sabots, price for pr, 40-3/8" w, 18-7/8" d, 33-3/4" h............**$21,240**

Louis XV/XVI-style transitional

Ormolu mounted marquetry, inlaid tulipwood, serpentine marble top, conforming case, two drawers and angular legs, floral inlay, 20th C, 36" w, 20" d, 36" h.................**$1,410**

Parquetry inlaid, reverse breakfronted marble top, conforming case fitted with three drawers, short angular cabriole feet, checkered crossbanding throughout, c1770, 47" w, 20" d, 34" h **$2,530**

Neoclassical, petit, mahogany and marquetry, molded rect top above three drawers decorated with griffins, sphinxes, and rinceaux, tapering square-section feet, 29" w, 18-1/2" d, 33-1/2" h..............**$2,600**

Regency, French, 18th C

Bronze and brass mounted kingwood parquetry, marble top, three drawers flanked by brass inset and fluted stiles, shaped feet, 30" w, 18" d, 30-1/2" h......................**$4,600**

Serpentine marble top, conforming kingwood case, brass fluting, two drawers, cabriole legs, 29" w, 19" d, 30" h **$4,700**

Gentleman's dressing chest

Regency, English, mahogany, bow-fronted case fitted with hinged top enclosing mirror, lower case fitted with two long drawers, flared feet, c1820, 36" w, 24" d, 35" h......**$1,880**

Highboy

Chippendale, associated with John Goddard and Job Townsend, Newport, RI, carved mahogany, enclosed scrolled pediment centering fluted plinth surrounded by urns and flame finials above two applied plaques over two short and three long graduated thumb-molded drawers, set into lower case of one long and three short drawers above cyma- curved skirt, centered carved shell, frontal cabriole legs ending in ball and claw feet, similar rear legs ending in pad feet, old replaced brasses, refinished, repairs, 1760-80, 39" w, 20-1/2" d, 84" h...**$36,550**

Chippendale-style, America, mahogany, broken arch pediment, flame finials, reeded quarter columns at corners, inset panels on either end of top, eight dovetailed drawers with brass pulls, gadrooning around base and edges of base and lower section, cabriole legs with scrolled returns, raised acanthus leaf carvings, claw and ball feet, old reddish brown finish, late 19th/early 20th C, 48-1/2" w, 24-1/4" d, 81" h......**$1,200**

Queen Anne

America, cherry, poplar and pine secondary wood, top dovetailed case, circular fan at top, replaced molded cornice, seven graduated drawers on top, four drawers on base, base with pegged construction, molded trim on dovetailed drawers, carved fan at lower center, scalloped aprons, shaped returns, well shaped cabriole legs, pad feet, mellow refinish, replaced bat wing brasses, pierced restorations to some drawer fronts, replaced returns and waist molding, 35" w top, 40" w base, 22" d, 71-1/2" h......**$6,200**

Connecticut, attributed to, cherry and maple, broken arch pediment with three flame finials on fluted plinths, upper case with fan carved thumb-molded short drawer flanked by two shaped short drawers, four graduated long drawers, lower case with long drawer over two short drawers flanking fan carved drawer, carved scrolling skirt joining four cabriole legs, pad feet, replaced brasses and finials, old refinish, repairs and imperfections, c1760-80, 38-1/4" w, 19" d, 86" h......**$24,675**

Dunlap School, New Hampshire, carved maple, cove-molded cornice over upper case of five graduated long drawers, lower case of three graduated thumb-molded long drawers, upper and lowermost

drawers each fan carved, cyma-curved skirt centering scrolling drops, joining four cabriole legs with shaped returns, pad feet on platforms, dark stained surface, possibly orig brasses, minor imperfections, chalk inscriptions on drawer backs, c1770-80, 39-1/4" w, 21-1/2" d, 78-3/4" h......**$14,100**

Massachusetts or southern New Hampshire, tiger maple, flaring cornice above four thumb-molded drawers on lower case of one long drawer and three small drawers, the central one with fan carving above three flat-headed arches, cabriole legs, high pad feet, replaced brasses, refinished, minor imperfections, 1760-80, 37-3/4" w at mid molding, 19-5/8" d at mid molding, 72" h......**$16,450**

North Shore, Massachusetts, maple, flaring cove-molded cornice with concealed drawer above four thumb-molded graduated drawers in upper case over mid-molding, two long drawers, lower case visually divided into three drawers centering by carved fan over cyma-curved side skirts, cabriole legs and high pad feet, old surface, old brasses, imperfections, 18th C, 35-1/2" w, 17-5/8" d, 71" h...**$31,050**

Rhode Island, attributed to Abram Utter, tiger maple and cherry, top section with flat molded cornice, case of two thumb-molded short drawers, three long drawers, lower section with projecting molding above case of central thumb-molded short drawer flanked by deeper drawers, four arris cabriole legs, pad feet, all joined to deeply valanced skirt with applied cock beading and two turned drop pendants, replaced brasses, old refinish, minor imperfections, c1730-60, 37" w, 19-1/4" d, 63-3/4" h......**$29,375**

William and Mary-style, cross banded walnut, upper section with two short over three long drawers, base with three drawers on trumpet turned legs, 18th C, 40" w, 21" d, 69" h......**$1,850**

Linen chest

Georgian, shaped rect cornice over two doors opening to drawers above two short and two long drawers, splayed feet, 48" w, 21" d, 84" h......**$3,100**

Highboy, Queen Anne, mahogany, two sections, upper case with bonnet top, three over two over three lip-molded drawers, base has two lip-molded drawers, tall cabriole legs ending in pad feet, oak and pine secondary woods, replaced brasses, second half 18th century, VG condition, some repairs and alterations, 82-1/2" h, 38-1/2" w, 21" d, **$2,530.**
Photo courtesy of Green Valley Auctions.

Hepplewhite, English, two pcs, mahogany and mahogany flame veneer, oak secondary wood, two door with flame veneer panels, divided int. with five drawers on right side, brass bar and hooks on other, three dovetailed drawers in base with mahogany border inlay with beaded edges, shaped apron, French feet, refinished, old replaced brass pulls, fitted int. top drawer with four small drawers and eleven pigeon holes, pieced restorations, 49" w, 23" d, 83-1/2" h......**$1,200**

Liquor chest

Early 19th century, mahogany veneer, chest with brass swing handles opens to reveal compartmented int., 12 blown molded wine and spirit bottles, each with inscribed paper labels and dec with gilt flowers, bowknots, and borders about the neck and shoulders, lift out tray fitted with tumblers, funnel and stemware with similar gilt decoration, one tumbler cracked, some veneer loss, 17" w, 12-1/2" d, 11-1/2" h......**$1,410**

Lowboy

Queen Anne, mahogany, oblong molded top, three drawers with fan curved center drawer, drop brass handles, angular cabriole legs, pad feet with tongue, 38-3/4" w, 23-3/4" d, 31" h **$2,000**

Queen Anne, Rhode Island, maple, pine secondary wood, case dovetailed at rear, pegged at sides, old replaced two-board curly maple top, four dovetailed drawers with beaded edges, batwing brasses, scalloped aprons, cabriole legs, slipper feet, refinished, small insect holes, restorations with some alterations, 32-1/2" w, 22-1/2" d, 30-1/4" h **$1,760**

William and Mary style, red japanned, serpentine black marble top, conforming case fitted with five small drawers, shaped kneehole, cabriole legs, pad feet, price for pr, early 20th C, 28-1/2" w, 17" d, 29-1/2" h **$3,400**

Mule chest

New England, poplar, old dark red wash, rect lid, single board ends, two dovetailed drawers in base, well shaped serpentine bracket feet, orig wood pulls, glued split in lid, replaced hinges, added supports, 45-3/4" l, 20-3/4" d, 44" h **$850**

Spice

Ohio, attributed to, walnut, poplar secondary wood, mortised and paneled front door, small brass pull, three drawers with orig turned walnut pulls, turned feet, 14-1/2" w, 12-1/4" d, 18-3/4" h **$2,400**

Pennsylvania, walnut, dovetailed, cove-molded cornice, raised panel hinged door, opens to int. of 11 small drawers, brass pulls, molded base, old surface, 1780-1800, 15-1/2" w, 11" d, 18-1/4" h..**$14,950**

Sugar chest

Middle Atlantic states, attributed to, inlaid cherry, hinged lid with molded edge, interior cavity with single (missing) divider over facade with stringing in outline, oval inlaid central reserve and quarter corner inlays, restoration, early 19th C, 32-1/4" w, 16-1/2" d, 34-3/4" h **$12,925**

Tall

Federal, New England, tiger maple, cove molded top, case with six thumb-molded drawers, central fan carved drop pendant flanked by high bracket feet, orig brasses, old refinish, repairs, late 18th C, 41" w, 54-5/8" h **$8,625**

Cradle, dovetailed, scrolled rockers, **$350.**
Photo courtesy of Alderfer Auction Co.

Cradle, Victorian, stained pine, 30" x 41" x 20", **$175.**
Photo courtesy of David Rago Auctions, Inc.

Cradles

Chippendale-style, birch, canted sides, scalloped headboard, turned posts and rails, refinished, 37-1/2" l **$400**

Country

America, tiger maple, dovetailed, heart cut-outs, large rockers, 36" l, 26" w, 16" h **$675**

Eastlake, walnut, paneled headboard, footboard, and sides, scrolling crest above short turned spindles, platform support, orig finish, dated, 1875 .... **$495**

New England, painted pine, arched hood continuing to shaped and carved dovetailed sides, rockers, old light green paint, old repairs, 18th C, 40" l **$300**

Pennsylvania, dovetailed, refinished curly maple, cut-out hearts, age cracks and shrinkage, late 18th C, 41" l **$550**

Rustic, twig construction, rocker base, unsigned, 33" l, 22" d, 22" h **$120**

Windsor, New England, bamboo turned spindles, worn finish, c1800-20.................................... **$850**

Victorian, painted wrought wire and cast iron, scrolled trestle base, later int. inset rect marble plaque, 19th C, 40" l, 37" h **$940**

Cupboards

Armoire

Art Deco, France, sycamore and fruitwood, interior fitted with top shelf over divided compartment, hardware fitted for wardrobe, flanked by two shelves, lollipop-shaped key, c1928, 51-1/4" w, 19" d, 71" h **$1,650**

Arts & Crafts, English, single-door, overhanging top supported by corbels, mirror, emb copper pan-

els of stylized flowers, unmarked, refinished, new back and shelves, one corbel missing, 40" w, 18" d, 75" h **$1,050**

Classical, New York, mahogany, bold projecting molded Roman arch cornice, two paneled doors flanked by tapered veneered columns, ogee bracket feet, c1835, 74" w, 31" d, 94" h **$3,200**

Empire-style, Continental, mahogany, shaped cornice above two paneled doors opening to shelves, ribbed lunette-shaped feet, early 19th C, 42" w, 17" d, 74" h **$1,610**

Louis XV/XVI-style, transitional, kingwood and parquetry, molded marble top with serpentine sides, pair of doors, each with two shaped and quarter-veneered flush panels, serpentine sides, coated stiles with gilt-brass chutes, sq-section cabriole legs joined by shaped skirt, stamped "Dubreuil," 19th C, 44" w, 18-1/2" d, 59" h........................ **$950**

Restoration, New York, mahogany, flat top with cornice molding, two doors, birds' eye maple lined int., concealed drawer below, ribbed blocked feet, c1830, 56" w, 19-1/2" d, 90" h.................... **$2,800**

Victorian, American, walnut, bold double ogee molded cornice, two arched paneled doors, shelved int., plinth base, ogee bracket feet, c1840, 62" w, 24" d, 89" h......**$1,400**

Bee keeper's hutch, Canadian, pine, orig red and black painted top panel, paneled door on lower front, door on either end, drop front covers interior workshelf, hinged lid, pegged construction, lid marked "Patent Union, Bee Hive, W. Phelps Pat." 47" w, 19" d, 43-1/4" h................ **$750**

Chifforobe, Art Deco, herringbone

Cupboard, stepback, New England, pine, one piece, molded cornice, three shelves, case with two candle drawers, two raised panel doors, flat molded base, c1810, 75" h x 55-1/2" w, **$4,915.**
Photo courtesy of Pook & Pook, Inc.

Cupboard, two part, painted pine, upper section two raised panel doors, lower section two drawers, two panel doors, cut-out bracket feet, red painted surface, New England, c1800, 83" h, 54" w, **$1,585.**
Photo courtesy of Pook & Pook, Inc.

Cupboard, wall, pine, one piece, molded cornice, two raised panel doors, shelf, two raised cupboard doors, flat base, New England, early 19th century, 78-1/2" h, 49-1/2" w, 23" d, **$1,872.**
Photo courtesy of Pook & Pook, Inc.

design waterfall veneer, arched center mirror, dropped center section, four deep drawers flanked by tall cupboard doors, shaped apron, 1935............**$450**

Chimney, country, pine, old blue-gray paint, picture frame molding around front of case, single door, beaded panel, brass pull, four int. shelves, age splits, 29" w, 12-1/2" d, 55-1/4" h
....**$575**

Corner

Blind paneled doors, Kentucky, walnut, bracket feet..................**$3,000**

One piece, Chippendale, inlaid walnut, upper section with broken scroll pediment with twin rosettes, three finials, arched glazed door, white painted interior, lower section with single frieze drawer, twin paneled doors, turned bun feet, drawer bottom inscribed "Made by Wm Cassell 1840," 42-1/2" w, 93-1/2" h
....**$2,200**

One piece, Chippendale, Southern states, pine, heavy projecting cornice molding above arched molded surround, flanking similarly shaped raised panel doors opening to two shelves above two additional fielded panel doors, flanked by fluted pilasters, opening to single serpentine shelf, refinished, hardware replaced, repairs, 1760s, 64" w, 30" d, 93-3/4" h **$7,475**

One piece, paneled pine, New England, flat ogee molded cornice, arched opening flanks three painted

scalloped shelves, two fielded panel cupboard doors, single int. shelf, old refinish on ext., old red color on shelves, 19th C, 50" w, 20" d, 88" h
....**$4,255**

Two pieces, cherry, two doors, orig six wavy glass panes over two doors with four tin panels punch dec with cornflower motif, replacement wooden knobs, repairs, restoration, refinished **$1,425**

Two pieces, Pennsylvania, grain painted, eight light glazed doors, single drawer over two cabinet doors, shaped apron, bracket feet, orig paint dec, 45" w, 86-3/4" h **$2,500**

Two pieces, Pennsylvania, softwood, molded cornice, reeded stiles, arched top glazed door, serpentine shelves with spoon notches, two dovetailed drawers, two lower paneled doors, molded bracket base, dry blue painted surface, white door, black painted interior, 49" w, 30" d, 89-1/2" h, ex-Elgin
....**$29,700**

Court, European, oak, two-pc, mortised construction, top section with two doors and central panel

Incised diamonds and pinwheels, free standing turned pilasters on either side, scrollwork with date "16MIVI" below cornice, two doors with three inset panels each on lower case doors and ends separated by molded T-shaped cross pieces, well executed

replaced scrolled wrought iron butterfly hinges, old dark finish, restorations, old alterations, age splits, 63" w, 19-1/4" d, 62-1/2" h.....**$2,950**

Relief flowers, scrolled vining, matching vining below cornice, leaf and arch carvings across center, three inset panels each on lower case doors and ends separated by molded T-shaped cross pieces, well executed replaced scrolled wrought iron butterfly hinges, old dark finish, restorations, old alterations, 49-1/2" w, 20-1/8" d, 67" h.....**$1,200**

Desk top, New England, pine, old grain painted dec, two solid doors with relief carved vertical panels, brass hinges, moldings at top and bottom, shaped feet are extensions of case, 10 cubby holes in int., orig green paint on ext. and int., 29" w, 12" d, 27-1/4" h
....**$1,750**

Dresser, Provincial, English, oak, plate rack with four shelves flanked by architectural uprights, two paneled doors centered by three drawers, bracket feet, 18th C, 83" w, 19" d, 71" h
....**$4,720**

Hanging

Carlisle, Cumberland County, Pennsylvania, poplar, molded cornice, raised paneled door, int. shelf, lip molded dovetailed drawer, bold scalloped cut-outs, stained to resemble walnut, restoration to cornice, 27" w, 11-1/2" d, 35" h
....**$7,975**

Cupboard, corner, hanging, one door, wooden, stained, **$264.**
Photo courtesy of Skinner, Inc.

Cupboard, corner, cherry, two pieces, c1830, 82" x 34-3/4", **$2,200.**
Photo courtesy of Wiederseim Associates, Inc.

Breakfront wardrobe, Victorian three sections, center crest, two doors, four drawers, molded cornices, second half 19th century, 80" h x 22" d, **$1,045.**
Photo courtesy of Green Valley Auctions.

Country, decorated, dovetailed case, painted green, brick red, brown, and white dec on sponged ground, initialed and dated "F.P.S. 1855," molded cornice and base, two dovetailed drawers below two doors, two int. shelves, pierced restorations, areas of insect damage, 28-3/4" w, 10-3/4" d, 29-3/4" h **$750**

English, Chippendale, corner, oak, pine secondary wood, cove molded cornice, dovetailed case, single door with beaded edges, geometric mullions with old wavy glass, molded base, three int. shelves, old brown finish, old repairs, 30-1/4" w, 16-1/2" d, 43" h **$2,530**

Pennsylvania, softwood, painted red, molded cornice, raised carved circular trim, serpentine molded door, interior shelf, lip molded dovetailed drawer, molded base, restoration to door, 27-1/2" w, 14" d, 31-1/4" h
.... **$3,025**

Jelly, country, central Pennsylvania, poplar, old salmon paint, sq nail construction, gallery top, two paneled doors, well-shaped apron, bracket feet, three shelved int., wear, 43-3/4" w, 18-1/2" d, 54" h **$1,380**

Kas, Long Island, New York, cherry, pine, and polar, architectural cornice molding, two raised panel thumbmolded doors flanked by reeded pilasters, applied moldings, single drawer, painted detachable disc and stretcher feet, replaced hardware, refinished, restored, c1730-80, 65-1/2" w, 26-1/4" d, 77-1/4" h **$4,500**

Kitchen, orig blue paint, six center drawers with porcelain pulls, two side bins, one bin lid sgd "Ezra Woodside Montare, April 20, 1905," cutting board, continuous scalloped face board covering lower front and feet, back shaped like picket fence, 72" l, 21" d, 54" h **$7,200**

Linen press, Federal, Boston, mahogany veneer, three parts, veneered entablature with central rect outlined in stringing above veneered frieze, pair of recessed panel doors which open to five pull-out drawers with shaped sides, lower case with molding and three cockbeaded drawers, flaring high bracket feet, inlaid escutcheons, orig brasses, feet restored, surface imperfections, 1820-25, 48" w, 22-1/4" h, 83-1/2" h
.... **$6,900**

Milk, Pennsylvania, primitive, soft-

wood, molded edge, vertical beaded board door, wrought iron strap hinges with penny ends, cut-out block feet, three interior shelves, red painted surface, 38-1/2" w, 15" d, 58" h
.... **$4,400**

Pewter

Country, one pc, cherry and walnut, beveled cornice with flat top, four shelves flanked by tapered sideboards, notched aprons on ends, two doors in base, old refinishing, originally built-in, edge wear, repairs, 36" w, 16" d, 81-1/2" h **$920**

New England, two part, dark maple and cherry, cornice molding above molded sides and plate rails, stepped out surface, three drawers above recessed panel cupboard doors, single shelved interiors, sq feet, straight skirt, turned wooden pulls, restored, 58-3/4" w, 17-1/2" d, 79" h **$4,500**

Pennsylvania, walnut, scalloped cornice, three open shelves, lollipop one board side, two cupboard doors with batwing hinges, worn and scrubbed patina, c1780 .... **$40,000**

Pie safe

Georgia, pine and cherry, six tin panels, punched sunflower and heart motifs, double door cupboard base
.... **$4,800**

Kentucky, orig red grain paint, pegged construction, six punched tins, punched circular motif, as found condition **$1,200**

Southeastern United States, walnut, rect top above along drawer, two hinged cupboard doors each with two pierced tin panels with designs of hearts and initials "J.B." flanked by leafy branches, ends with three conforming decorated panels, sq tapering legs, refinished, minor imperfections, early 19th C, 39-1/2" w, 17" d, 49-1/2" h
.... **$5,300**

Tennessee, cherry, 12 tin panels, punched fylfots **$4,250**

Schrank, Pennsylvania, poplar, decorated, orig paint, sponged brown, salmon, green, and blue, two panels dec with maker's name and date, Philip-Man, 1796-28 Mey (sic), dentil cornice, reeded quarter columns, ogee feet, ex-Clark Garrett, 62" w, 70" h **$300,000**

Slant back, New England, pine, flat molded cornice above beaded canted front flanking shelves, projecting base with single raised panel door, old refinish, doors missing from top, imperfections, late 18th C, 37-1/2" w, 18" d, 73" h..............**$2,300**

Spice, northern Europe, wall-type, painted, flat molded cornice, hinged cupboard door, molded recessed panel opening, compartmentalized int., molded base, old dark green paint bordered by red, int. drawers missing, imperfections, last half 18th C, 16" w, 8" d, 17" h.................**$1,500**

Step-back, wall

America, Empire, mahogany and mahogany veneer, molded cornice top, three eight-light doors, adjustable shelves, cabinet base with three cupboard doors, sliding center doors in top and base, c1830, 73-1/2" w, 21" d, 93" h.........**$11,100**

Pennsylvania, attributed to, one piece, curly maple, mellow golden color, two mortised and paneled doors on top, one int. shelf, two board top with high pie shelf, five dovetailed drawers in base in three-over-two configuration, turned legs with excellent figure, replaced brass pulls, one glued break on the lower corner of door, 44-1/2" w, 19-1/2" d, 60-1/4" h **$8,525**

Pennsylvania or Ohio, attributed to, painted cherry, flaring cornice molding above fluted frieze, pair of glazed doors open to two-shelf int., flanked by fluting above stepped out surface, two drawers over two recessed panel doors opening to single shelf int., recessed panel sides, four short turned legs, all over red paint, brass pulls, imperfections, 1830-40, 50" w, 21-1/2" d, 88" h...................**$18,400**

Storage, Montgomery County, Pennsylvania, poplar, dovetailed case, molded top, two paneled doors, French bracket feet, int. shelves, scraped finish down to red, replaced back boards, moldings, 49" w, 18" d, 72" h...**$1,100**

Wall

America, two pieces, pine and walnut, old mustard paint and faint brown grain dec, traces of earlier red in some areas, brown sponging to three curved front drawers and on raised panels of lower doors, cove molded cornice, two-door top with six panes of glass in each door, vertical central panel with three panels, all top panes are tombstone

shaped, chamfered corners, turned feet with applied half turned pilasters, blue painted int. with cut-outs for spoons, 61" w, 21" d, 85-3/4" h **$5,500**

Canadian, Hepplewhite, two pieces, pine, beveled and cove molded cornice, two doors in top section with two panes of glass each, two int. shelves with red and white paint, molded waist, five drawers in base with incised beading, turned wooden pulls, well scalloped base, high bracket feet, refinished, evidence of earlier red paint, edge chips, couple of glued splits to feet, 48" w, 23-1/2" d, 78-1/2" h................**$935**

Federal, New England, second quarter painted, two parts, paneled, cornice molding, chamfered front corners, stepped-out surface with three scratch beaded drawers above two paneled doors, single shelved int., molded base, bracket feet, orig red surface, turned wood pulls probably original, repairs, 19th C, 57-1/2" w, 23-1/4" d, 85" h....................**$6,500**

Jacobean, oak and part painted, two parts, upper section with pegs and shelves, projecting lower section with two doors, each with geometric and floral carving, 64" w, 20" d, 80" h **$3,000**

New England, possibly Vermont, hooded, lollipop one board sides, three open shelves on top, single paneled cupboard door in base, dark green paint.................**$11,500**

New York, upstate, painted, flat cornice, case with two hinged doors each with two recessed vertical panels, shelved int., old gray paint, imperfections, early 19th C, 43" w, 18" d, 78" h............................**$1,000**

Wardrobe

Chippendale, English, mahogany, pine secondary wood, cove molded cornice, two-door front with three raised panels each, three inset panels on each side, scalloped bracket feet, molded base, brass lock escutcheons, refinished, formerly fitted with shelves and rod, restorations, replacements, 53-3/4" w, 24" d, 78" h...........**$1,500**

French, walnut, walnut veneer applied in herringbone pattern on ends, open pediment crest, double door mirrors with pillars on each side, late 19th C, 50" w, 98-1/2" h **$1,000**

Cupboard, English country Georgian style, scrubbed pine, molded-edge crown, glazed panel doors, long drawer, shelving, solid wood panel doors, additional shelving, plinth base, 19th century, 74" x 32-3/4" x 18-7/8", $710.
Photo courtesy of Sloans & Kenyon Auctioneers and Appraisers.

Cupboard, wall, pine, scalloped gallery, two short drawers, recessed panel door, bracket feet, 19th century, 45-1/4" h, 25" w, $500.
Photo courtesy of Pook & Pook, Inc.

Desk, schoolmaster's, Pennsylvania, slant lid, six drawer int., frame with single drawer, turned legs, orig red and green surface, early/mid-19th century, 44-3/4" h, 37" w, **$1,755.**
Photo courtesy of Pook & Pook, Inc.

Desk, Arts & Crafts, Gustav Stickley, postcard desk, letterholder backsplash, two drawers, paneled back and sides, recessed bookshelf below, original finish, early red decal, 39-1/2" l, 22" d, 36" h, **$1,610.**
Photo courtesy of David Rago Auctions, Inc.

Desk, child, Queen Anne, New England, slant front, slant lid, fitted interior, two long drawers, molded base, bun feet, c1730, 21-1/4", 18-1/4", 10-3/4" d, **$5,620.**
Photo courtesy of Pook & Pook, Inc.

Desks

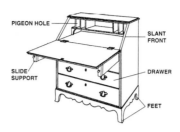

Typical Parts of a Desk

Aesthetic Movement, Herter Brothers, Washburn Commission, mahogany, fall front, top section: shelf with gallery top supported by turned and blocked posts, back panel with dec gold threaded material; middle section: slant lid, two supporting pull-out arms, central panel of marquetry inlaid with garland of flowers ending in bows, int. with two drawers, five cubbyholes, supported by two turned front legs, two bottom section with shelf and paneled back, missing orig writing surface, raised panel back, needs restoration, commissioned by Hon. William Drew Washburn for Minnesota Greek Revival house, copy of orig bill of sale, 30" w, 20" w, 53-1/2" h **$9,000**

Art Deco, Leopold Corp, Burlington, Iowa, walnut veneered, semi-oval top over center drawer flanked by pull-out writing surface and two drawers, bronze handles, light brown finish, "Charles S. Nathan Office Equipment New York" distributor's metal tag in drawer, veneer loss, wear, 66-1/8" l, 36-1/8" d, 29" h **$900**

Arts & Crafts, Stickley, Gustav, Syracuse, New York, lady's, model No. 720, cabinet with four vertical shelves, two small drawers, three horizontal shelves, rect top, two short drawers, paper Craftsman label, c1912, 38" w, 23" d, 37" h **$1,725**

Chippendale
Connecticut, mahogany, block front, slant front lid, fitted tiered int. with nine dovetailed drawers, pigeonholes, two pull-out letter drawers with fluted columns, flame-carved finials and door with blocking and fan carving, dovetailed case, four dovetailed drawers, conforming apron, bracket feet, replaced brasses, old refinishing, feet replaced, repairs to case, late 18th C, 41-3/4" w, 21-1/2" d, 42-3/4" h **$3,850**

Massachusetts, slant lid, mahogany, lid opens to int. of central fan, concave carved drawer, two conforming drawers flanked by document drawers with half-baluster fronts, four valanced compartments, two drawers, cockbeaded case of four graduated drawers, ogee bracket feet, center drop pendant, old brass bail pulls, refinished, imperfections, c1770-80, 40" w, 20" d, 43" h .. **$9,400**

New England, cherry, slant lid opens to an interior of open valanced compartments above small blocked drawers flanking central open compartment, thumb-molded graduated drawers, molded bracket base with central pendant, replaced brass, old refinish, repairs, late 18th C, 38" w, 19-3/4" d, 40-3/4" h **$2,500**

New England, maple, pine secondary wood, old dark brown surface, slant lid, interior with nine pigeonholes over five small drawers, dovetailed case, four dovetailed graduated drawers with beaded edges, molded base, bracket feet, old replaced batwing brasses, old repairs, late 18th C, 36" w, 17-1/2" d, 41-1/4" h **$4,900**

Rhode Island, cherry, slant front, stepped int. of small drawers, central one with shaping, case of beaded graduated drawers, ogee bracket feet, orig brasses, old refinish, restoration, late 18th C, 39" w, 20" d, 43" h **$3,800**

Virginia, attributed to, carved walnut, slant lid opens to stepped interior of six valanced small compartments flanked by pinwheel carved end-drawers above small drawers, case of graduated drawers with cockbeaded surrounds, molded bracket base, brasses appear early, refinished, repairs, late 18th C, 40" h, 19" d, 41-3/4" h **$3,820**

Drop-front, Philadelphia, tiger maple, mahoganized finish, 1830 .... **$6,000**

Eastlake, lady's, walnut, two parts, top section sits on pegs, top: mirror with two columns supported shelves, fancy carving, pressed dec; base section: double hinged writing surface with dec floral carving, writing surface with two panels of green felt, lifts to reveal compartment desk int. with two drawers, one side fitted with two long drawers, gallery shelf in base, dec applied pieces, shoe foot base, metal casters, 31-1/2" w, 19" d, 57" h **$1,150**

Edwardian, kneehole, mahogany, rect cross banded top with central oval medallion, front canted corners, long frieze drawer, two banks of three drawers, center cupboard door, foliate marquetry dec, c1900, 37-1/2" w, 31" h..................................**$600**

Edwardian-style, marquetry inlaid mahogany, U-shaped superstructure fitted with drawers and doors, serpentine case fitted with drawers, sq tapered legs, 20th C, 35" w, 24" d, 37" h..................................**$2,645**

Empire, butler's, cherry and curly maple, poplar secondary wood, scrolled crest with turned rosettes, pull-out desk drawer with arched pigeonholes and three dovetailed drawers, three dovetailed drawers with applied edge beading, turned and carved pilasters, paneled ends, paw feet, old finish, some edge damage, 44-1/2" w, 23" d, 57-3/4" h.................................**$1,925**

Federal

America, butler's, mahogany and mahogany veneer, rect top, case of three cockbeaded short drawers, pull-out desk with cockbeaded drawer facade flanked by wide drawers opening to prospect door over short drawer flanked by document drawer, two short drawers, two compartments, one long drawer, all-over pull-out shelf, three graduated cockbeaded long drawers, cut-out feet joined by shaped skirt, old refinish, 47" w, 19" d, 45-1/2" h..............................**$1,300**

American, mahogany and bird's eye maple, two cabinet doors, fitted interior with bird's eye maple drawer fronts, lower section with three cockbeaded drawers, fold-out writing surface, turned round legs with fluted bands, 43-1/4" w, 20" d, 52-5/8" h..............................**$2,400**

Massachusetts, eastern, tambour, mahogany and mahogany veneer inlaid, upper section with tambour doors flanked by pilasters with chevron inlay enclosing two short drawers over three valanced compartments centering prospect door with inlaid stringing enclosing two short drawers over double valanced compartments, lower section with folding lid over case of two cockbeaded string inlaid long drawers, legs inlaid with bellflowers and stringing tapering to inlaid cuffs, old replaced brasses, old

refinish, blue painted int., repairs and imperfections, c1800-10, 38" w, 19-1/4" d, 34-1/2" h.............**$11,750**

Massachusetts, possibly Worcester County, inlaid mahogany and cherry, slant thumb molded lid centering inlaid satinwood diamond panel bordered by rosewood crossbanding and stringing, fitted int. of eight drawers and seven valanced compartments, swelled case of four graduated cockbeaded drawers bordered by crossbanding on inlaid base, flaring French feet, replaced brasses, old refinish, minor imperfections, chalk inscriptions, c1800, 38-3/4" w, 21" d, 44" h...........**$4,450**

New England, mahogany and mahogany veneer inlaid, top section shaped gallery above flat molded cornice, two glazed doors enclosing compartments and drawer, flanking door and small drawer; projecting base with fold-out writing surface, two cockbeaded short drawers, two graduated long drawers, four sq tapering legs, inlaid cross-banding, old refinish, some restoration, inscribed "22 Geo. L. Deblois Sept. 12th 1810," early 19th C, 37-1/8" w, 20" d, 51-1/2".........................**$3,000**

New Hampshire, slant lid, wavy birch, lid opens to two-stepped int. case of drawers with four cockbeaded surrounds, serpentine skirt, tall arched feet, orig brasses, old refinish, repairs, early 19th C, 37-1/2" w, 18-1/4" d, 45" h....**$2,760**

New York State, mahogany veneer inlaid, slant lid and three graduated drawers outlined in stringing with ovolo corners, int. of veneer and outline stringing on drawers, valanced compartments, prospect door opening to inner compartments and drawers, flanking document drawers, orig brasses, old surface, veneer cracking loss and patching, other surface imperfections, early 19th C, 41-1/2" w, 21-1/2" d, 44" h..................**$2,550**

Pennsylvania, walnut inlaid, slant front, lid and cockbeaded drawers outlined in stringing, base with band of contrasting veneers, int. of small drawers above valanced compartments, scrolled dividers flanking prospect door which opens to two small drawers, three drawers, old refinish, repairs, early 19th C, 40" w, 20" d, 44-1/2" h...........**$3,550**

Desk, drop-front, German, walnut veneer, replaced pulls, rectangular top, slant front lid with molded edge, three drawers plus additional three hidden drawers behind flanking door, square tapering cabriole legs, 18th century, 41-3/4" x 47-3/4" x 25", **$7,690.**
Photo courtesy of Sloan's & Kenyon Auctioneers and Appraisers.

Desk, Flowertown, Pennsylvania, mahogany slant lid, Hepplewhite, William Sinclair label, fall front, fitted int, inlaid eagle on prospect drawer, case with four drawers, scalloped skirt, flaring French feet, c1810, 44" h, 40" w, **$4,915.**
Photo courtesy of Pook & Pook, Inc.

Desk, lady's writing, French inlaid, Kingwood, two sections, gilt-metal mounts, hand-painted porcelain inset panels, two upper doors above full-length lower drawer, 19th century, 52" h x 40" w x 20" d, **$1,760.**
Photo courtesy of Green Valley Auctions.

Desk, plantation, American, fold-down front, molded cornice, large ledger shelf, fitted interior with four pigeonholes over larger valanced section, four vertical dividers, single drawer, turned legs, 19th century, **$750.**
Photo courtesy of Dotta Auction Co., Inc.

Desk, slant front, New England tiger maple, c1780, 44" h x 37-1/2" w x 20". **$3,000.**
Photo courtesy of Wiederseim Associates, Inc.

Desk, slant front, Chippendale, Pennsylvania, walnut, fall front, fitted interior, serpentine front drawers, prospect door with shell carving, case has four graduated drawers, fluted quarter columns, ogee bracket feet, c1770, 44" h, 39" w, 22" d, **$5,850.**
Photo courtesy of Pook & Pook, Inc.

George III, English

Mahogany, oak secondary wood, kneehole, molded top, single cabinet door in center, single long drawer with divided interior over two banks of three dovetailed drawers with beaded edges and old brasses, bracket feet, molded base, old refinishing, some splits, restoration to veneer, 40-1/4" w, 20-1/2" d, 33" h **$2,650**

Mahogany, rect top with partial gallery above a long drawer, kneehole flanked by two short drawers, ring-turned legs, brass casters, 34" w, 20" d, 31" h **$700**

George III-style, pedestal, walnut, gilt-tooled brown leather top, central frieze drawer, two pedestals fitted on both sides with drawers and paneled doors, 65-1/2" w, 35" d, 30" h **$2,585**

Hepplewhite, oxbow slant front, maple and birch, pine secondary wood, int. with ten small drawers with brass knobs, seven pigeonholes, four graduated dovetailed drawers with beaded edges, old replaced oval brasses, high French feet, scalloped returns, band of inlay around base, refinished, restorations to scalloped valances and lid supports, 39-1/2" w, 18" d, 47" h **$2,100**

Louis XV, tulipwood and gilt bronze mounted, top having central writing stand, flanked by two hinged doors opening to storage, central frieze drawer; lower section: black lacquered shaped rect top with Chinoi-

Desk, lap, early 19th century on stand of later date, 24" x 15-3/4" x 9-1/2" d, **$200.**
Photo courtesy of Wiederseim Associates, Inc.

serie scene, central faux drawer, sides each having single drawer raised on cabriole legs with gilt bronze mounts ending in sabots, stamped "Durand," 25" w, 15-1/2" d, 31-3/8" h **$11,800**

Louis XV-style, parquetry, shaped rect top with inset red leather top, single drawer, cabriole legs, gilt bronze sabots, 23-1/2" w, 20" d, 27-5/8" h **$3,800**

Provincial, English, rect top, central drawer, shaped octagonal standards, H-form stretcher, octagonal block feet, early 19th C **$1,660**

Queen Anne

America, cross banded walnut, slant-lid, rect top, fitted interior of stepped pigeonholes and drawers, split lower case fitted with two short over three long graduated drawers, bracket feet, early 18th C, 35-3/4" w, 23" d, 39-1/2" h **$5,885**

Northern Maine, maple, slant front, int. with valanced compartments above small drawers, end drawers separated by scrolled dividers, case of three thumb-molded drawers, molded bracket base with central drop pendant, old darkened surface, 19th C, 35-1/2" w, 17-1/2" d, 40-1/4" h..**$5,175**

Vermont, tiger maple and cherry, slant front, int. with central fan-carved drawer, two valanced compartments flanked by molded document drawers, four valanced compartments, three drawers, case with four thumb-molded graduated drawers, bracket feet, replaced brasses, old refinish, imperfections, and repairs, c1750, 36" w, 18" d, 41-1/2" h............**$3,220**

Regency, English, lady's, cylinder, mahogany, tambour top, fitted int., slide-out writing surface, over two drawers, lyre base, 30" h writing surface, c1850, 35-1/2" w, 20" d, 38" h **$3,000**

Renaissance Revival, American, fall front, turned spindle cresting, paneled fall front and fitted interior, angular trestle base, 26-1/2" w, 16" d, 53" h **$850**

Rococo-style, Italian, painted, slant-lid, fitted interior, serpentine case fitted with three conforming drawers, flared bracket feet, 35" w, 17" d, 40-1/2" h............ **$4,465**

Schoolmaster's, Pennsylvania, walnut, interior drawers and compartments, molded lid, dovetailed skirt drawer, tapered legs, early 19th C, 34-1/2" w, 24" d, 37-1/2" h **$4,400**

Sheraton

American, stand-up, walnut, slant front, four graduated drawers, turned feet, ivory escutcheons, Sandwich glass pulls, flanked by paint dec columns, simply fitted int. with secret drawers, one pull replaced, repair to lid, hinges replaced, int. refitted, 35" h writing surface, 35" w, 43" h **$1,200**

Country, slant lid, cherry, pine and poplar secondary wood, two dovetailed drawers behind slant lid, two large compartments, three dovetailed drawers in base, turned feet, orig oval brasses with emb pineapple in basket design, refinished, alternations, restored break on one back leg, 37" w, 19-1/4" d, 38-1/2" h......... **$990**

Victorian

Bamboo, lacquered rect top with leather inset over long drawer and four vertical drawers, 35" w, 20" d, 29" h... **$720**

Walnut, hinged rect top, fitted int., single frieze drawer, turned legs, 28" w, 20-1/4" d, 33" h.............. **$400**

William and Mary, attributed to CT, tulipwood and oak, fall-front lid with raised panel, int. of four compartments, three drawers, well with sliding closure, double arched molded front, base with long drawer, four turned legs, joined by valanced skirt, shaped flat cross stretchers, turned feet, replaced brasses, old refinish, minor imperfections, early 18th C, 24-3/4" w, 15" d, 42-1/2" h **$17,250**

William and Mary-style, American, oak, seven dovetailed drawers, applied moldings, molded edge top, brass tear drop pulls, old finish, turned legs and stretchers, one piece of molding missing from drawer, 20th C, 27-3/4" x 59" x 31" h... **$500**

Dry sinks

Curly maple, rect well, work surface on right with small drawer, two poplar wood cupboard doors, short bracket feet, hardwood edge stripes, minor repairs, refinished, 55" w, 34-1/2" h.................................. **$2,400**

Grain painted, New England, rect well with tin lining, rounded splashboard, two small drawers, two cupboard doors, shelf int., bracket feet, brown and yellow pine graining, 49" w, 38" h.............. **$900**

Painted, attributed to Pennsylvania, rect overhanging top, well, cut-out ends with exposed tenons, joined by medial shield fitted with later copper insert, painted red, early 19th C, 44-3/4" w, 18-1/2" d, 32" h **$2,645**

Pine, three drawers on high back, sink with back-curved sides, paneled doors opening to self, stile feet, c1900, 43" w, 18-1/2" d, 33-1/2" h **$900**

Pine and poplar, galleried well, one small dovetailed drawer, two paneled doors, cut-out feet, 46" w, 18-1/4" d, 37-3/4" h...................................... **$600**

Poplar, painted, rect well above pair of paneled cupboard doors, scroll-cut apron continuing to low bracket feet, cast iron thumb latch replaced, layers of old worn green paint, 39-1/2" w, 16-1/4" d, 33" h **$650**

Hall trees and hat racks

Bench

Gothic Revival, oak, composed of some antique elements, tall backrest inset with foliate and figural panels, lift seat and foliate carved lower panels, 34" w, 73" h **$690**

Gothic-style, oak, tall backrest fitted with three figural, foliate, and seraph carved panels, lift seat, chip-carved sq legs, late 19th C, 60" w, 66-1/2" h **$1,855**

Chair

Arts & Crafts, Limbert, #79, hall chair, unique "bicycle" shape, orig leather back and shaped seat over slab leg with keyed construction, orig finish, branded and numbered, orig leather has been reinforced, 19" w, 20" d, 42" h................... **$1,100**

Cast iron, Union Army motif, patch boxes on base, belt with buckle carved for cane holder, swords and rifles forming back, topped with Union shield, piece found in Pennsylvania GAR hall **$10,500**

William IV, octagonal scroll worked backrest, center painted crest,

Dry sink, country, pine, dovetailed well top, two drawers over pair of cupboard doors, straight bracket feet, 19th century, **$775.**
Photo courtesy of Wiederseim Associates, Inc.

shaped seat, turned tapering legs, peg feet...................................... **$475**

Hall rack

Art Nouveau, France, mahogany, flaring mahogany panel, five brass curved coat hooks centered by mirror, umbrella stand below, early 20th C, 47" w, 85" h **$1,200**

Arts & Crafts, attributed to Charles Rohls, oak, tall sq shaft, two tiers of four wooden hooks, each near the top, half buttresses running up from the cross base on all four sides, sq wafer feet, early 20th C, 64" h **$1,100**

Bavarian, figural carved wood, mountain goat standing before tree branches, base carved with ferns and flowerheads, ovoid umbrella well, late 19th/early 20th C... **$2,250**

Colonial Revival, Baroque-style, American, cherry, shell carved crest over cartouche and griffin carved panel back, lift seat, high arms, mask carved base, paw feet, 1910, 39-1/2" w, 21-1/2" d, 51" h...... **$700**

Reformed Gothic, American, mahogany, angular superstructure with mirror and pegs, cane well, circular legs, 25" w, 13" d, 84" h **$750**

Renaissance Revival, American, walnut and part ebonized, upper section with arched cornice, rect mirror plate, turned hat pegs; lower section with marble top, curved cane supports, medial drawer, circular fluted legs, base fitted with shell-form cast iron pans, 51" w, 16" d, 89" h... **$3,200**

Victorian, American, burl walnut, ball finials above paneled and shaped cornice, rect mirror flanked by turned garment holders, marble top drawer supported by turned legs, shaped base, painted metal plant holders, 29" w, 14" d, 93" h.....**$1,400**

Hall tree (costumer), Arts & Crafts, Gustav Stickley, tapering post, four iron hooks, orig finish with overcoat, unmarked, 72" h, **$1,200.**
Photo courtesy of David Rago Auctions, Inc.

Hat rack

Arts & Crafts, wrought steel, hat and coat style, four sided, double hooks and spindles, unmarked, 21" w, 21" d, 75" h.................................**$865**

International Movement, Charles Eames, "Hang-It-All," manufactured by Tigrett Enterprises, white enameled metal frame, multicolored wooden balls, c1953, 20" w, 6" d, 16" h.................................**$800**

Windsor, American, pine, bamboo turned, six knob-like hooks, orig yellow varnish, black striping, 33-3/4" w.................................**$200**

Stand, Arts & Crafts, coat and umbrella type, wrought steel, cut-out apron, spindles, brass hooks, unmarked, 27" w, 10-1/2" d, 73" h.................**$850**

Umbrella stand, Black Forest, Germany, carved walnut, figural bear, fierce expression, loose chain around neck, holding tray in raised paw, porcelain base liner, early 20th C, 48" h
.................................**$5,750**

Mirrors

Adams-style, oval frame, relief molded gesso, urn and feather crest, scrolled foliage and swags, restored split on crest, few chips, 20th C, 23-1/2" w, 42" h.................................**$460**

Aesthetic Movement, America, overmantel, gilt, central cornice supported by two small columns over frieze dec with scene of snake attacking bird in tree, mirror plate highly dec with leaves, orig label of L. Utler, 47 Royal St., New Orleans, c1880, 64" w, 6" d, 84" h.................**$3,600**

Art Deco, France, octagonal mirror in wrought iron frame, rose and leaf dec, 1930, 36" w, 24" h.................**$250**

Arts & Crafts

Boston Society of Arts and Crafts, carved wood, rect, carved and gilded frame, ink mark, initials, orig paper label, 1910, 11-1/4" w, 18-1/2" h.................................**$700**

Limbert, oak, frame with geometric inlaid design over rect cane panel shoe-foot base, recoated orig frame, orig glass, 20" w, 8" d, 22" h.....**$600**

Baroque, Continental, second quarter giltwood, fruit-filled cartouche form resting, mirrored borders with grapevines and scrolls, foliate carved pendant, 18th C, 63" h.............**$5,750**

Baroque-style, gilt scrolling frames, price for pr 37-1/2" x 42-1/2" ..**$1,610**

Biedermeier, walnut, ogee molded cresting, paneled sides, c1830, 26" w, 37" h.................................**$350**

Centennial, Chippendale-style, mahogany and mahogany veneer, pine secondary wood, broken arch crest with gilt eagle, gesso liners with orig gilding and rosettes, leaf vining down each side, refinished, restoration and touchup to eagle and areas of gilding, 26-1/4" w, 56-1/2" h.................**$950**

Cheval, German, ebonized, swivel rect mirror, rounded ends, low sq mount, artist sgd, 70" h.................................**$425**

Chippendale

America, mahogany and gilt gesso, scrolled frame, molded gilt incised liner enclosing glass, old surface, late 18th C, 21-3/4" w, 44" h..**$3,100**

England or America, mahogany and parcel gilt, scrolled frame, molded and gilt incised liner, old refinish, replaced glass, late 18th C, 20-1/2" w, 36" h.........................**$500**

England, walnut and parcel-gilt, gilt-gessoed carved phoenix on leafy branch above scrolled frame with applied gilt leafy floral and fruit devices, gilt incised liner framing beveled glass, restoration, mid-18th C, 20-1/2" w, 44" h.................**$6,465**

New England, mahogany and gilt gesso, scrolled frame centering gilt gesso eagle in crest above gilt incised molded liner, imperfections, late 18th C, 18-1/2" w, 40" h....**$500**

Pennsylvania, mahogany and gilt gesso, labeled John Elliot & Son, Philadelphia, scrolled frame with pierced cresting centering phoenix above molded gilt incised liner, label affixed to backboard is last one used by the firm, imperfections, repairs, 1804-1810, 19-1/2" w, 34" h.................................**$950**

Chippendale-style

Cheval, carved mahogany, oval plate, four-legged base carved with foliage, claw and ball feet, late 19th C, 75" h
.................................**$635**

Table top, carved wood, black lacquer, and polychrome florals, central top figure of Oriental man with umbrella, hinged prop on verso, suspension loop, mid-18th C, 20" w, 29" h.................................**$1,150**

Classical

Dressing, America or England, carved mahogany and mahogany veneer, cylinder top opens to reveal four drawers, centering one door, ivory pulls, above single divided long drawer, restoration, 1810-20, 19" w, 10-5/8" d, 32" h......................**$1,610**

Girandole, America or England, crest with eagle flanked by acanthus leaves, convex glass, ebonized molded liner with affixed candle branches, foliate and floral pendant, imperfections, gilt gesso, 1810-20, 23" w, 35" h...........................**$5,175**

Overmantel, New England, painted and giltwood, rect mirror frame with sq corner blocks, applied floral bosses joined by vase and ring-turned split baluster columns, molded black liner, old gilt surface, replaced mirror glass, surface imperfections, c1820-40, 46" w, 23" h...**$920**

Wall, New York, carved and eglomise, entablature overhangs veneered frieze, reverse painted land and waterscape flanked by leaf carved split balusters, orig eglomise and mirror glass, old refinish, minor losses and crazing, 1830s, 38" h **$460**

Courting, wooden frame, reverse painted glass inserts and crest with bird and flowers, orig mirror glass with worn silvering, penciled inscription on back with "restored 1914," touch-up to reverse painting, brass back corner braces, 10-7/8" w, 16-1/2" h......................................**$935**

Eastlake, walnut, carved crest, 29" w, 63" h..**$575**

Edwardian, overmantel, boxwood marquetry inlaid, arched cresting inlaid with musical still life and scrolling vines, shaped mirror plate flanked by cross banded stiles, late 19th C, 60" w, 68" h **$900**

Empire, flame mahogany veneer over pine, scalloped crest with scrolled ends, inset oval panel at top, applied half turned pilasters, ogee base, worn silvering, glue repairs at ends of crest, old alligatored varnish finish, 21" w, 51" h..**$770**

Federal

America, two parts, orig gilding, black painted on applied half turnings, raised floral corner blocks, orig reverse painting with lady and child on recamier, repainted floral borders, touch up on panel, minor wear, 18-3/4" w, 39-3/4" h **$550**

Architectural, two parts, pine, old alligatored white paint over orig gilding, stepped cornice with applied ball dec, molded pilasters

on sides, applied corner blocks at bottom, reverse dec with ribbons, silver, and black leaves on white ground, edge damage, 15-1/4" w, 24-1/4" h **$450**

Convex, giltwood, spread wing eagle on rocky plinth, left claw on sphere, small ball on chain suspended from beak, oak leaf and acorn ornamentation, pair of coiled snakes at base, ebonized reeded bezel, c1820, 21-1/2" d, 43-1/2" h...............**$8,500**

Massachusetts, gilt gesso and wood, molded cornice with applied spheres above reverse painted tablet showing sea battle, glass below flanked by rope twist molded pilasters, imperfections, c1820, 19" w, 32-1/2" h **$1,300**

Massachusetts, gilt gesso and wood, molded cornice with applied spheres above reverse painted and stenciled tablet showing a cottage and bridge arching a brook, glass flanked by rope twist molded pilasters, minor imperfections, c1875-20, 17" w, 28-1/4" h **$600**

Massachusetts, giltwood and eglomise, turned engaged columns enclose reverse-painted tablet showing woman seated on red and gold neoclassical stool, holding parrot, flanked by red and gold drapery above a mirrored glass, old regilding, replaced mirror glass, early 19th C, 15-3/4" w, 32" h **$500**

New England, mahogany, scrolled frame, rect mitered liner with inlaid contrasting stringing, refinished, c1800, 20-3/4" w, 38" h **$1,000**

New England, mahogany and mahogany veneer, molded cornice above sq and reeded capitals, half engraved vase and ring-turned, acanthus leaf, diamond faceted columns on sq plinths, refinished, replaced glass, imperfections, c1820-25, 18-1/2" w, 40-1/2" h **$355**

New York City, mahogany, swan's neck crest, carved urn, bouquet-type finial with carved florets on wires, veneered frame flanked by wirebound wood vine work pendants, scrolled apron, heavily reworked, refinished, gold paint, c1780-1800, 21-1/2" w, 53" h **$675**

Reverse painted glass, gilt harbor scene with castle, figures, and sailing vessels, rope twist column sides, rosette motif, 34-5/8" w, 51-1/2" h, losses **$750**

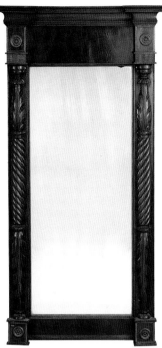

Mirror, late Federal, New York, mahogany, John Williams label, c1825, 51-1/2", **$820.**
Photo courtesy of Pook & Pook, Inc.

Mirror, wall, Italian Florentine painted and parcel-gilt, arching pediment, recessed panel, griffins, Medici family crest, arabesque decorated pilasters, mask-painted plinth base, molded edges, 24-3/4" x 16-3/4" x 1-1/2", **$1,120.**
Photo courtesy of Sloans & Kenyon Auctioneers and Appraisers.

Mirror, gesso-over-wood, pierced, scrolling foliate, rect, molded edge fillet, heavily patinated finish, late 19th century, 32" x 27-3/4", **$325.**
Photo courtesy of Sloans & Kenyon Auctioneers and Appraisers.

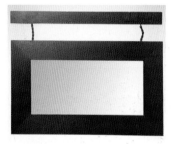

Mirror, Arts & Crafts, Roycroft, provenance: from family of Roycroft artisan, orig hanging chain and board, dark orig finish, broad 6-1/4" moldings, 50" x 30" mirror frame, 50" x 4" hanging board, 5-1/2" chain, **$4,000.**
Photo courtesy of David Rago Auctions, Inc.

Mirror, wall, American, giltwood, reverse painted, rectangular, projecting reverse breakfronted crest, painted spread wing eagle, 19th century, 24-1/2" x 13-1/2" x 2", **$560.**
Photo courtesy of Sloans & Kenyon Auctioneers and Appraisers.

Tabernacle, attributed to New York or Albany, gilt gesso, molded cornice with pendant spherules over frieze with applied sunflower and wheat sheaf device, flanked by checkered panels over two-part looking glass, flanked by applied double half columns, gilt surface, replaced glass tablet, 1795-1810, 14" w, 30-1/2" h **$865**

Wall, giltwood, labeled "Parker and Clover Looking Glass and Picture Frame Makers 180 Fulton St. New York," molded cornice with applied spherules above eglomise table of girl in pasture landscape holding dove, mirror flanked by spiral carved pilasters, 13-3/4" w, 29-1/8" h **$2,875**

Federal, late, attributed to New England, gilt gesso, molded cornice with acorn form drops over frieze centering carved leaf motif flanked by vine and leaf applied devices, two-part mirror glass with grape and leaf designs, flanked by vase, ring, and spiral turned split balusters, old gilt surface, minor imperfections, including replaced mirror glass, c1820-30, 19" w, 37" h **$700**

Federal-style, convex, eagle crest, worn gilding, ebonized liner, eagle with small chain, ball in beak, restorations to wings, late 19th or early 20th C, 16-1/2" w, 24-1/2" h **$700**

Folk Art, America, possibly prisoner made, pine, carved hearts, stars, and various numerals and patterns, year "1902," minor wear, 1902, 29-1/2" x 29-7/8" **$1,410**

George II-style, English, carved gesso and giltwood, C-scroll and shell carved arched crest, serpentine and rect mirror plate, scrolled foliate corner pendants, C-scroll, shell, and acanthus carved shaped apron, 19th C, 29" w, 65-1/2" h **$1,800**

George III, giltwood, crest centered by hoho bird over C-scrolls, flanked by swag-draped urns, frame sides with further C-scrolls, late 18th C, 26-1/2" w, 52" h........................ **$3,100**

Hepplewhite, shaving, mahogany, inlay, two dovetailed drawers, feet, posts, and mirror are old replacements, 17-3/4" h **$225**

Louis XV-style, pier, carved giltwood, large rect mirror topped by crest carved with leafy scrolls and rocaille, marble-topped ovolo 19-1/4" h shelf, flat leaf edge, gilt metal brackets,

reeded scrolls with anthemion and female mask terminals, 19th C, 33" w, 73" h...**$1,725**

Neoclassical, Trumeau, painted gray, parcel gilt, top with gilt molding over gilt gesso figure of reclining goddess flanked by urns, over rect two-part mirror plate in gilt floral and leaftip surround, continental 19th C, 40" x 98"...**$3,820**

Neoclassical-style, pier, gilt wood, crest with roundel with urn issuing foliage flanked by cornucopias, beveled rect plate within surround decorated with garlands of flowers, corners with Greek key motif, 20th C, 35" w, 68" h **$1,200**

Painted, attributed to the work of Nehemiah Partridge, eastern Massachusetts, rect molded frame painted red, intersecting linear designs in black, wear, first quarter 18th C, 7-7/8" w, 9-1/4" h.....................**$4,700**

Queen Anne

American, walnut and pine, old reddish brown paint, beveled glass, orig hand planed backboard, scrolled crest with replacements and veneer, 12-1/4" w, 23" h **$650**

Scroll, mahogany, old finish, molded frame, detailed scrolled crest, minor split in bottom edge of frame, 9" w, 16-1/4" h **$550**

Walnut, scrolled crest above molded rect frame enclosing beveled mirror glass, backboard inscribed "Capt S Cobb," refinished, glass resilvered, 10-1/2" w, 22-1/2" h **$1,175**

Renaissance Revival, American

Hall, parcel gilt walnut, openwork lappet and floral cresting, shaped plate, frame carved with leaftips, pegs and incised lines, 35" w, 75" h **$950**

Over mantel, parcel gilt walnut, arched mirror plate, carved in high relief with lappets, roundels and architectural motifs, 62" w, 60" h **$750**

Pier, walnut and parcel gilt, molded cornice carved with sawtooth and paterae, long mirror plate flanked by columns, low marble top, turned legs, 27" w, 12" d, 100" h **$500**

Wall, walnut and parcel gilt, sawtooth and spindle cresting, shaped plate, fluted pilasters, 45" w, 31" h **$425**

Rococo

Continental, giltwood, shaped mirror plate, arched top, frame carved with

Rocker, Victorian, carved face on curved back crest rail, shaped back splat, turned spindles, arms, and stretchers, **$135.**
Photo courtesy of Dotta Auction Co., Inc.

Rocker, Arts & Crafts, Gustav Stickley five vertical slats under each arm and a drop-in spring seat with loose back cushion covered in dark brown leather, old refinish, very good condition, unmarked, 38" x 29" x 30", **$2,760.**
Photo courtesy of David Rago Auctions, Inc.

Rocker, Arts & Crafts, L. & J. G. Stickley six slats under each arm and a drop-in spring seat and loose back cushion recovered in light brown leather, original finish, several chips, repair to right rocker, shadow of "The Work of..." decal, back stretcher, 36-1/2" x 31-1/2" x 35", **$3,360.**
Photo courtesy of David Rago Auctions, Inc.

foliage and C-scrolls, third quarter 18th C, 28" w, 54" h **$4,025**
Northern Europe, walnut and gilt gesso, shaped molded cresting with foliate devices enclosing reverse painted tablet showing man in powdered wig above rect molded walnut veneered gilt-lined frame on shaped pierced bracket, imperfections, late 18th C, 14" w, 31" h **$950**

Rococo-style, gilt wood, cartouche form, surround carved with scrolls hung with icicles, plate replaced, possibly re-gilt, c19th C, 47" h **$1,315**

Sheraton, mahogany, spiral turned split columns and bottom rail, inlaid panels of mahogany, rosewood, and cherry, architectural top cornice, split mirror, 24-1/2" w, 47" h **$300**

Victorian, Renaissance Revival, pier, walnut, molded cornice, molded leaf band, beveled oblong mirror, oblong white marble base shelf, fluted column sides, molded base, 32" w, 9" d, 94" h.. **$950**

Victorian, Rococo Revival, giltwood, shaped mirror plate, frame with foliate canopy cresting and mirrored borders, elaborately carved all over in high relief with birds, icicles, columns, and foliage, 19th C, 35" w, 64" h... **$1,900**

Rockers

Art Nouveau, American, oak, fumed finish, carved arms, saddle seat, three splats with floral-type capitals, c1900 .... **$400**

Arts & Crafts

American, oak, four vertical back slats, corbel supports under arms,

recovered orig spring cushion, orig finish, 29" w, 34" d, 36" h........ **$200**
Limbert, #580, oak, T-back design, orig recovered drop-in cushion, recent finish, branded, 24" w, 29" d, 34" h **$150**
Plail, oak, slatted barrel back, D-shaped recovered seat, refinished, unsigned, 26" w, 28" d, 31" h **$2,500**
Stickley Brothers, oak, six vertical back slats, recovered orig spring cushion, worn orig finish, branded, 25" w, 27" d, 35" h.................... **$220**

Bentwood, rustic, hickory and pine, old finish, repairs, 15-3/4" h seat, 37-1/2" h back.............................. **$225**

Boston, American, maple, spindle back, 19th C **$200**

Colonial Revival, Windsor-style, Colonial Furniture Co., Grand Rapids, MI, comb back, birch, mahogany finish, turned legs, 21" w, 17" d, 27-1/2" h.. **$200**

Decorated
America, orig black over red dec, gold stenciled urn of fruit and flowers on crest, shaped seat, scrolled arms, well turned legs, repaired damage to arms, 15" h seat, 40" h **$220**
Pennsylvania, dark green, gold foliate on crest, slats, and seat, red border with yellow line detail, turned legs, shaped medallion stretcher, scrolled arms, repaired break in one arm, 17" h seat, 42" h **$220**

International Movement, Charles Eames, manufactured by Herman Miller, salmon fiberglass Zenith shell, rope edge, black wire struts, birch runners, c1950, 25" w, 27" d, 27" h **$1,400**

Rocker, International Movement, Charles Eames for Zenith, yellow fiberglass, rope edge, black wire cat's cradle base, birch runners, Zenith label, one re-glued shock mount, some staining to seat, 27-1/4" x 25" x 27", **$865.**
Photo courtesy of David Rago Auctions, Inc.

Rocker, Eastlake style, platform type, reupholstered padded backrest, seat, and head rest, turned spindles, **$250.**
Photo courtesy of Joseph P. Smalley, Jr.

Ladderback, Pennsylvania, orig rush seat, turned finials, block and turned arm supports, painted green, 15" h seat, 39-1/2" h back **$315**

Wicker, painted white, sq back, basket weave pattern over openwork back, rect armrests with wrapped braces, openwork sides, braided edge on basketweave seat and skirt, X-form stretcher, 32" w, 33" h **$200**

Windsor

American, grain painted, stencil dec, scrolled crest, tail spindle back, shaped seat, bamboo turned legs, box stretcher, c1850 .... **$450**

New England, rect splat stencil dec with grapevines highlighted in freehand yellow fancy work above the raked spindles and stiles, scrolled arms, shaped seat, bamboo-turned legs on rockers, all-over burntsienna and black dec, early 19th C, 15" h seat, 43" h **$1,300**

Pennsylvania, bamboo turnings, cheese cutter rockers, yellow ground paint with smoke dec, red highlights, floral and strawberry dec crest, 17" h seat, 30-1/2" h **$3,300**

Secretaries

Biedermeier-style, inlaid walnut, molded rect top, four drawers, top drawer with fall front, fitted int. with ebonized writing-surface, molded block feet, 50-1/4" w, 23-3/4" d, 35-1/2" h **$1,000**

Centennial, inlay mahogany, two parts: top with four drawers over six cubbyholes center, line inlay door opening to reveal two cubbyholes and large drawer, sliding tambour flanked by inlay panels with simulated columns; lower: fold-over line inlay lid, two drawers with line inlay, diamond inlay on legs, some lifting to veneer, replaced cloth writing surface, 37-1/4" w, 19-3/4" d, 46" h **$800**

Chippendale

Connecticut, two pcs, maple and curly maple, pr of panel doors over fall front, fitted int., four drawers, orig pierced brass drop bail hardware **$45,000**

Maryland, attributed to, inlaid walnut, top with molded and pierced swan's-neck cresting with inlaid terminals centering a plinth with cross banded border and urn finial above cross banded frieze, two glazed doors enclosing adjustable shelves,

candle slides below on base with fall front opening, central prospect door flanked by string-inlaid document boxes, three drawers and four valanced compartments, case of four cockbeaded graduated drawers, ogee bracket feet, replaced brasses, refinished, restoration, late 18th C, 40" w, 22" d, 95" h **$7,700**

Massachusetts, carved mahogany, scrolled and molded pediment above tympanum with projecting shell and arched raised panel doors flanked by fluted pilasters, candle slides, raised panel slant lid with blocked facade, molded conforming base, bracket feet, int. of upper bookcase divided into open compartments above four small drawers, int. of lower case with two fan-carved blocked drawers, similar prospect door, small blocked and plain drawers, scrolled compartment dividers, replaced brasses, old finish, restored, c1770-90, 39" w, 22" d, 93-1/2" h **$19,550**

New England, block front, two pieces, upper section: flame finial, two blind doors, cyma-carved panels, various-sized open compartments on int., lower section with four front drawers, plain slant front, fitted int., some later replacements, late 18th C, 91" h **$38,180**

Rhode Island, Providence area, carved cherry, scrolled molded pediment flanks central plinth and finial above applied shell carving atop central fluted and stop-fluted column flanked by raised panel doors, shelved int. enclosed by quarter-engaged fluted and stop-fluted columns, lower case of two stepped int, serpentine end-blocked drawers with serpentine dividers, valanced compartments, central document drawers with applied columns, above four graduated thumb-molded drawers flanked by fluted and stop-fluted engaged quarter-columns, shaped bracket feet ending in platforms, old surface, some original brasses, presumed owners' names scratched on underside of case: "Abner Lampson, 1743-1797 and Ward Lampson, 1773-1850, Washington N.H." imperfections, 1765-85, 38-1/4" w, 21" d, 80" h **$55,815**

Classical, Boston, secretaire a'abattant, carved mahogany and mahogany veneer, marble top above cove

Secrétiare á abattant, Biedermeier birch and parcel-ebonized rectangular top, molded edge, fitted interior, leather top inset writing surface, three drawers, block feet, c1840, 46" x 43-3/4" x 16-1/2", **$1,652.**
Photo courtesy of Sloans & Kenyon Auctioneers and Appraisers.

molding, mahogany veneer facade flanked by veneered columns topped by Corinthian capitals, terminating in ebonized ball feet, recessed panel sides, fall front opens to desk int. over two cupboard doors, old refinish, 1820-25, 35" w, 17-1/2" d, 57-1/2" h **$16,100**

Colonial Revival, Colonial Desk Co., Rockford, IL, mahogany, broken arch pediment, center finial, two glazed mullioned doors, fluted columns, center prospect with acanthus carving flanked by columns, four graduated drawers, brass eagle, carved claw and ball feet, c1930, 41" w, 21" d, 87" h **$1,000**

Eastlake, American, burl walnut and mahogany, shaped cornice, pair of glazed cabinet doors, cylinder front, writing surface, two doors in base, shaped apron, 27" w, 22" d, 66" h **$1,500**

Empire, America, mahogany veneer, fall-front, dovetailed construction, two sections, top with two four-light cathedral glass doors, base with fall-front deck, five-drawer int., over three drawers flanked by curved columns, turned feet, c1840, 41-1/2" w, 20" d, 7' 4" h **$1,425**

Empire-style, gilt bronze mounted mahogany, rect top, fall front with fitted int., over pr of recessed cupboard doors, flanked by columns, paw feet, late 19th C, 44-1/4" w, 23-1/2" d, 49-1/4" h **$1,955**

Federal

Massachusetts, Boston or North Shore, mahogany inlaid, top section: central panel of bird's eye maple with cross banded mahogany veneer border and stringing joined to the plinths by a curving gallery above flat molded cornice, glazed beaded doors with Gothic arches and bird's eye maple panels and mahogany cross-banding and stringing enclosing shelves, compartments, and drawers; lower: projecting section with fold-out surface inlaid with oval bird's eye maple panel set in mitered rect with cross banded border and cockbeaded case, two drawers veneered with bird's eye maple panels bordered by mahogany cross-banding and stringing, flanked by inlaid panels continuing to sq double tapered legs, lower edge of case and leg cuffs with lunette inlaid banding, old finish, replaced brasses, imperfections, early 19th, 41" w, 21 3/4" d, 71 1/2" h **$9,775**

Massachusetts, coastal southern, inscribed "Wood" in chalk, mahogany, three pcs, molded cornice with inlaid dentiling above diamond inlaid frieze over two paneled cupboard doors with quarter-fan inlays opening to eight-compartment int., center case with tambour doors centering oval veneered prospect door, flanked by inlaid and reeded applied pilasters, valanced compartments, prospect door opens to single valanced compartment with drawer below, lower case with string inlaid fold-out writing surface, similarly inlaid drawers flanked by stiles, panel inlays, skirt, inlaid dentiling above legs with inlaid bellflowers, line inlay and inlaid cuffs, early surface, replaced pulls, minor veneer loss, c1816, 40" w, 20-1/2" d, 81-3/4" h **$34,500**

New Hampshire, paint decoration, two pieces, pine, old alligatored reddish-brown and yellow dec over earlier red, chamfered corners on dovetailed cases, molded cove cornice, tree dec on two paneled doors, slant front with tree dec, int. with 13 dovetailed drawers with central prospect door, four dovetailed drawers in base with applied beading, slightly shaped bracket feet with applied base molding, replaced wooden pulls, replaced H hinges, touch-up to top doors **$7,425**

George III, last quarter 18th C Mahogany, molded cornice, two

glazed doors, fitted interior with three shelves, rect molded base with pull out secretary drawer, two short and two long graduated drawers, 48" w, 18" d, 98" h **$9,440**

Mahogany, upper section with two mullioned and glazed doors; lower section fitted with secretary drawer over three long drawers, bracket feet **$1,645**

George III/Early Federal, America, mahogany, two sections, upper: shaped architectural pediment with gilt-metal ball and spike finials, cavetto cornice over cross banded frieze, chequer-banding, front with pair of 13-pane astragal doors, two adjustable shelves; base: outset fall-front opening, fitted int., four graduated cockbeaded oxbow-fronted drawers, conforming molded plinth base, molded and spurred bracket feet, third quarter 18th C, 44-1/4" w, 24-1/4" d, 93-1/2" h **$17,000**

Hepplewhite, North Shore, MA, mahogany, bookcase upper section, slant front desk **$6,250**

International Movement, Gilbert Rhode, manufactured by Herman Miller, upper bookcase with drop front desk over four doors, carved wooden pulls in burl and paldio veneers, refinished, c1940, 66" w, 15" d, 72" h **$2,600**

Louis XV-style, rosewood, bombe form, inset shaped white marble top, fall front, fitted interior, above four aligned drawers, cabriole legs with gilt metal paw feet, 37" w, 19" d, 66-3/4" h **$2,125**

Renaissance Revival, American, walnut, two sections, upper: bookcase section, S-curved pediment with center applied grapes and foliage carving, two arched and molded glazed doors, shelved int., three small drawers with applied grapes and foliage carved pulls; lower: fold-out writing surface, two short drawers over two long drawers with oval molding and applied grapes and foliage carved pulls, matching ornamentation on skirt, c1865, 48" w, 21" d, 95" h **$5,000**

Sheraton, New England, mahogany and mahogany flame veneer, cove molded cornice, three drawers across top with oval brasses, two paneled doors in top with fine flame veneer, three interior drawers, four pigeon holes with adjustable shelf, three dovetailed drawers with applied beading,

figured book page veneer, reeded legs with ring turnings and molded surround at base of case, refinished, few repaired veneer splits, pierced repairs, stains in bottom, replaced brasses, 42" w, 20" d, 50-1/2" h **$1,760**

Federal secretary, New England, cross-banded cherry, two sections, upper doors contain fitted interior, base has fold-down writing surface above three graduated drawers, turned feet, minor repairs, early 19th century, 55" h x 42" w x 21" d, **$605.**
Photo courtesy of Green Valley Auctions.

Secretary bookcase, Victorian, oak, cut-out and carved crest, two pane door, dropfront desk, beveled mirror, drawer, minor repairs, late 19th century, 68" h x 39" w x 13" d, **$550.**
Photo courtesy of Green Valley Auctions.

Settee, Louis XVI-style, newer frame, upholstered in 18th C tapestry, 44" x 76" x 31", **$1,200.**
Photo courtesy of David Rago Auctions, Inc.

Settee, Federal style, carved mahogany, downcurving reeded arms, reeded tapering legs ending in peg feet, 60-1/2" l, **$850+.**
Photo courtesy of Sloans & Kenyon Auctioneers and Appraisers.

Victorian, two pieces, walnut, top: crown molding cornice, two glazed doors with burl and walnut buttons; base: burl cylinder roll with two-drawer walnut int., pigeon-holes, slide-out writing surface, base: three long drawers with burl dec, tear drop pulls, refinished, 40" w, 23" d, 86" h............**$1,850**

William III, English, burl walnut veneer, two sections, recessed upper with double-domical crest, pair of domically crested doors mounted with beveled glass mirror panels of conforming upper outline, plain int. of three adjustable wood shelves above pr of candle slides; lower section with canted front, hinged fall-front writing board, shaped desk int. with valanced central cubbyhole between two pairs of valanced narrow cubby holes over two shaped drawers each, horizontal sliding door, flanked by two-tier side units with single-drawer bases, straight front of two graduated narrow drawers over two graduated wide drawers, highly figured burl on drawers matches writing board and doors, engraved period brasses, later short straight bracket feet, minor veneer damage, c1700-10, 40" w, 23-1/2" d, 84" h........................**$18,750**

Settees

Art Deco, attributed to Warren McArthur, tubular aluminum frame, sheet aluminum seat and back supports, removable vinyl cushions, c1930, 68" l
....**$5,750**

Arts & Crafts
  Limbert, #939, oak, 11 back slats, corbels under arm, recovered orig drop-in cushion, branded, refinished, 75" w, 27" d, 40" h.........**$800**

Stickley, Gustav, No. 222, tapering posts, tightly spaced canted slats to back and sides, leather upholstered drop-in seat, fine orig finish, red decal, minor veneer chips, 36" x 80" x 32"......................................**$11,500**
Stickley, L. & J.G., oak, drop-arm form, 12 vertical slats to back and drop-in orig spring cushion, recovered in brown leather, refinished, unsigned, 65" w, 25" d, 36" h..................**$1,800**
Unknown America maker, even arm, oak, crest rail over nine wide vertical slats, three on each side, joined by sq vertical posts, medium brown finish, replaced seat, joint separation, 20th C, 65" w, 25-3/4" d, 32" h........**$2,650**

Biedermeier-style, beechwood, curved open back, three vasiform splats, outcurved arms, caned seat raised on six sq-section sabre legs.......................**$650**

Classical, American, mahogany, serpentine front, carved crest, transitional rococo design elements, c1850, 82" l
....**$600**

Colonial Revival, William and Mary style, American, loose cushions, turned baluster legs and stretcher, c1930, 48" l.................................**$750**

Eastlake-style, Confidant, walnut, upholstered scrolling backs with horizontal pierced splats, upholstered seats, tapering square-section legs, 26" w, 26" d, 46" h........................**$600**

Empire-style, late 19th/early 20th C
Gilt bronze mounted mahogany, settee, pair of side chairs, each with foliate and figural mounts, 80" l settee, price for three pieces..**$1,725**
Mahogany, two seats, curved backs, each armrest ending on ram's head, hoof-foot feet.........................**$2,100**

French Restauration, New York City, rosewood, arched upholstered back, scrolled arms outlined in satinwood terminating in volutes, rect seat frame with similar inlay, bracket feet, c1840, 80" l, 27" d, 33-1/2" h ...**$1,200**

George II, mahogany, serpentine crest over upholstered back and seat, round reeded, tapering legs................**$1,500**

George III, black lacquer and faux bamboo, settee, pair of arm chairs, price for three pieces, early 19th C..........**$1,265**

Gothic Revival, American, carved walnut, shaped crest rail surmounted by center carved finial, stiles with arched recessed panel and similarly carved finials, upholstered back and seat, open arms with padded armrests and scrolled handholds, carved seat rail, ring turned legs, ball feet, c1850, 67-1/2" w, 23-1/2" d, 49-3/4" h ...**$800**

Louis XVI-style, gilt bronze mounted ebonized maple, Leon Marcotte, New York City, c1860, 55-1/2" l, 25" d, 41-1/2" h....................................**$2,185**

Queen Anne-style, inlaid back flanked by shepherd's crook arms, cabriole legs **$2,250**

Renaissance Revival, America, carved walnut, triple back, each having carved crest and ebonized plaque inlaid with musical instruments, red floral damask upholstery, c1875
....**$1,200**

Rococo Revival
  Attributed to John Henry Belter, 65" l settee, pair of lady's chairs, pair of side chairs, each with laminated rose and foliate carved cresting, grapevine openwork sides, cabriole legs, price for three pieces, c1885
....**$14,375**

Settee, Windsor, arrow back, bamboo turnings, red and black rosewood graining, Pennsylvania, 35" h, 79" w, 18-1/2" d, **$1,755.**
Photo courtesy of Pook & Pook, Inc.

Settee, Federal, Baltimore, attributed to Renshaw, triple chairback, downward sloping arms with urn-turned supports, bowfront seat supported by turned legs, original overall gilt decoration on black painted ground, c1800, 48" l, 18-1/2" w, 34" h, **$5,750.**
Photo courtesy of Pook & Pook, Inc.

Attributed to J. & J. Meeks, rosewood, laminated curved backs, Stanton Hall pattern, rose crest in scrolled foliage and vintage, tufted gold velvet brocade reupholstery, age cracks and some edge damage, 65-1/2" l.................... **$5,500**

Victorian, carved rosewood, shaped and padded back, two arched end sections joined by dipped section, each with pierced foliate crest, over upholstered serpentine front seat, flanked by scroll arms, conforming rail continue to cabriole legs, frame leaf carved, c1870 .... **$850**

Victorian, Renaissance Revival, carved walnut, upholstered, twin chair backs with arched crest rails, center oval, all surmounted by masks, heads and foliage, out-scrolled arms with rosettes, ring-turned tapering front legs, casters, 58" w **$700**

Wicker, tightly woven rect back, inverted triangle-dec, tightly woven arms, rect seat with woven diamond herringbone pattern, continuous braided edging from crest to front legs, turned spindle apron, 43" w, 36" h **$500**

Windsor, New England, birdcage, maple, ash, and hickory, bamboo turned birdcage crest over 27 turned spindles flanked by stiles joining bamboo-turned arms and supports over bench seat, eight bamboo-turned legs joined by stretchers, old refinish, imperfections, early 19th C, 72" l, 14-1/2" h seat, 31-1/2" h **$2,415**

Windsor, painted, half spindle-back, shaped crest rail, shaped plank seat, painted fruit dec on green ground, 79" l **$2,400**

Sideboards

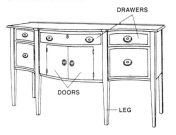

Typical Parts of a Sideboard

Aesthetic, inlaid and ebonized satinwood, raised centered pedestal fronted by demilune panel with inlaid bird motif, panel below with tied ribbon and trophy dec franked by two doors, burlwood reserves, brass borders, canted corners, label on back "J. Ziegler & Co., Furniture & Decorations Warehouse, No. 42 Bleeker Street, New York," 66-1/2" w, 18-1/4" d, 57-1/4" h **$6,325**

Art Deco, France, walnut and burl book-matched veneer, Bakelite cabinet doors and drawer pulls, c1928, 76" l, 19-1/2" d, 50-5/8" h........... **$900**

Art Nouveau, Louis Majorelle, oak and mahogany, rect, bowed front, inset marble top, two long drawers, undulating brass pulls cast with sheaves of wheat, two cupboard doors with large applied brass sheaves of wheat and undulating leaves, molded apron, four lug feet, 1900, 65" w, 39-1/8" h **$6,000**

Arts & Crafts

English, attributed to, with two "V" backsplashes, two drawers with ring pulls, bottom shelf, casters, orig finish, marked

"S79FUM90," 42" l, 20" d, 45-1/4" h **$1,150**

Limbert, Charles P., Grand Rapids, Michigan, oak, oblong top, mirrored back above case, three short drawers flanked by paneled cupboard doors over long drawer, copper pulls and strap hinges, sq legs, chamfered tenons, branded mark, c1910, 49-1/2" w, 53-1/2" h **$900**

Stickley Brothers, backsplash, single drawer with hammered brass hardware, lower shelf, good orig finish, branded "Stickley Brothers," stenciled "B735," light edge wear, 36" l, 19" d, 37" h **$2,185**

Stickley Brothers, paneled plate rack, four drawers, three panel doors with hammered brass hardware, good orig finish, branded "Stickley Brothers," stenciled "8833," wear to copper patina on iron hardware **$4,025**

Stickley, Gustav, model no. 967, gallery top over two short drawers and long drawer, two cupboard doors below, iron strap hinges and door pulls, red decal, imperfections, 1902, 59-3/4" w, 23-3/4" w, 43-3/4" h **$32,300**

Stickley, L. & J.G., Fayetteville, New York, oak, plate rail on rect top, three central drawers flanked by two cabinet doors, over single long drawer, branded mark, c1916, 47" w, 19-3/4" d, 44" h........... **$5,300**

Centennial, Chippendale-style, America, mahogany, block front with shell carving, four drawers, front cabinet doors, gadrooned apron, cabriole legs, claw and ball feet, late 19th C, 68" w, 24" d, 40" h **$950**

Sideboard, Arts & Crafts, Gustav Stickley, two small drawers over single long drawer, chamfered sides, wooden pyramidal knob-pulls, dark brown original finish, large red decal, c1902, 44-1/2" x 59" x 23-1/2", **$50,000.**
Photo courtesy of David Rago Auctions, Inc.

Sideboard, Arts & Crafts, Gustav Stickley with plate rack, linen drawer over two small drawers, an arched opening and two cupboard doors, fine orig dark finish with overcoat to top, red decal in top drawer, 45" x 48" x 18", **$4,113.**
Photo courtesy of David Rago Auctions, Inc.

Classical

Mid Atlantic States, carved mahogany and cherry veneer, rect top over mahogany veneered drawer, two recessed panel doors opening to one shelf int., flanked by veneered scrolled supports, veneered base, old refinish, hardware changes, splashboard missing, 1840-45, 40" w, 18-3/4" d, 40-1/8" h **$2,550**

New York, carved mahogany veneer, splashboard with molded edge and four spiral carved and turned columns, topped by urn-shaped finials, rect top overhands recessed paneled case, cockbeaded drawers and cupboards outlined with crass banded mahogany veneer, two top drawers with dividers above short drawers, bottle drawers flanked by end recessed panel doors, left one with single shelf int., right one with two-shelf int., flanked by columnar leaf carved supports over frontal carved paw feet, rear feet are heavily turned and tapering, old refinish, imperfections, 1830s, 60-1/4" w, 23-5/8" d, 56-3/4" h **$2,760**

Empire

American, carved mahogany and figured veneers, break front, three drawers, four doors across base with inset gothic panels of figured veneer, well carved paw feet, orig brass hardware, old dark finish, 73-1/2" l, 23" d, 42" h **$1,650**

French, gilt bronze mounted mahogany, shaped mottled green marble top above three frieze drawers decorated with palmettes, three cupboard doors decorated with mask in laurel surround and winged maidens, flanked by pilasters with sphinx head capitals, shaped base, gilt bronze feet; top bearing old paper label "BEDEL & CIE/ LE GARDE MEUBLE PUBLIC," late 19th C, 71" w, 23" d, 40" h **$8,400**

French, gilt bronze-mounted mahogany, shaped mottled green marble top above three frieze drawers decorated with scrollwork and palmettes, three cupboard doors decorated with portrait medallion, cornucopias, and torches, flanked by pilasters with sphinx head capitals, shaped base, late 19th/early 20th C, 78" w, 25" d, 40" h.................**$6,000**

Federal

Baltimore, Maryland, mahogany inlaid, veneered top with ovolo corners and string inlay in outline, case of central drawer and four cupboard doors all embellished with veneered ovals outlined in banding and interspersed with maple veneered rectangles, sq tapering legs with stringing in outline and forming five graduated loops above cuff inlays, case with old surface, replaced brass, imperfections, 1790-1810, 75-1/8" w, 25-1/2" d, 39-3/4" h **$14,100**

Massachusetts, Boston, mahogany, maple, and rosewood veneer, two-tiered case, demilune superstructure, maple inlaid panels surrounded by cross banded rosewood veneer above cockbeaded end drawers, small central drawer flanked by end cupboards, six ring turned tapering legs, case with concentric turnings, reeding, cock beading, and scenic landscape jointed on underside of arched opening, old surface, replaced pulls, replaced leg, veneer loss, later landscape painting, 1810-20, 74-1/2" l, 24-1/2" d, 44-3/4" h **$9,200**

Massachusetts or Rhode Island, mahogany, cross banded, rect top with ovolo corners and reeded edge overhangs case of cockbeaded drawers and central cupboards flanked by turned columns continuing to reeding above ring-turned swelled legs, turned feet, refinished, restored, replaced legs, early 19th C, 42-3/4" w, 21-1/2" d, 41-1/4" h **$8,820**

Middle Atlantic States, attributed to, mahogany and cherry inlaid, overhanging top with canted corners and serpentine front, central cockbeaded door inlaid with cherry panel with quarter fan inlays and mahogany mitered border, cockbeaded wine drawer with three-drawer facade at one end, three cockbeaded graduated drawers on other, ends with cherry veneered panels, four sq inlaid tapering legs ending in

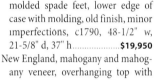

Sideboard, Empire, American, mahogany and burl veneer, four carved columns and capitals, turned feet, castors, 47-1/2" x 57" x 24", **$1,175.**
Photo courtesy of David Rago Auctions, Inc.

Sideboard, late Federal, Pennsylvania, tiger maple and cherry, arched pediment, three drawers, four cupboard doors, turned columns, turned feet, c1830, 55" h, 59-3/4" w, **$1,872.**
Photo courtesy of Pook & Pook, Inc.

Sideboard, Louis XV, provincial, elm, later paint, rectangular plank top, breadboard ends, carved molded edge, two drawers, two doors, serpentine apron, short curved legs, late 18th/early 19th century, 42" x 50-3/4" x 24", **$2,245.**
Photo courtesy of Sloans & Kenyon Auctioneers and Appraisers.

molded spade feet, lower edge of case with molding, old finish, minor imperfections, c1790, 48-1/2" w, 21-5/8" d, 37" h.................**$19,950**
New England, mahogany and mahogany veneer, overhanging top with shaped front, conforming case, central pullout surface, bowed cockbeaded drawers, two cupboard doors flanked by concave drawers and cupboard doors, six sq tapering legs, replaced brasses, old refinish, imperfections, c1790, 64" w, 20-1/8" d, 37-1/2" h.............**$5,500**
Southern States, attributed to Francis Marion Kay, cherry and other hardwoods, yellow pine secondary wood, replaced rest, three drawers over two doors, another drawer over prospect door at center, lower doors divided by half turned pilasters, six turned legs, one door is restored, hinges replaced, 1816-87, 60-1/4" w, 21-1/4" d, 49" h....**$3,410**
Virginia, walnut and yellow pine, molded rect top, cockbeaded case with end drawers, right drawer visually divided into two drawers, left with two working drawers, central cupboard cockbeaded door, four square tapering legs, old brass pulls, old refinish, repairs, inscription on drawer reads "Virginia Hunt Board, early 19th cent. from family of Admiral Todd, Naval Commander prior to and during the Civil War, Virginia," 1790-1810, 56" w, 22" d, 39" h **$5,520**
Federal-style, Southern States, huntboard, yellow pine, overhanging rect top, case with three drawers, skirt with central shaping, four sq tapering

legs, orig brasses, refinished, 21" w, 19-1/2" h..................................**$1,840**
George III, inlaid mahogany, cross banded and bowfronted top, case fitted with four drawers, sq tapered legs, inlaid throughout with stringing and quarter fans, c1790, 79" w, 24" d, 34-1/2" h...............................**$5,875**
George III-style
Mahogany, bow front, shaped top, single drawer flanked by doors, sq tapering legs, spade feet, late 19th C, 54" w, 26-1/2" d, 36" h......**$2,000**
Mahogany, inlaid, satinwood crossbanding, serpentine top, conforming case fitted with five drawers and two doors, sq tapered legs, late 19th C, 64" w, 22" d, 38-1/4" h......**$1,175**
George III/Hepplewhite, mahogany, flame grain mahogany, satinwood, and oak, paterae and shell inlay, 36" h...**$11,160**
Gothic, Kimbel & Cabus, New York, design no. 377, walnut, galleried top over two cupboard doors over open shelf over slant front over central drawer over open well flanked by two cupboard doors, galleried base shelf, bracket feet, c1875, 39-1/4" w, 17-3/4" d, 73" h **$9,775**
Hepplewhite, mahogany and mahogany veneer with inlay, bowed center section with conforming doors and dovetailed drawer, two flat side doors, sq tapered legs, banding and stringing with bellflowers on legs, corner fans on doors and drawers, reworked, repairs, replaced brasses, 58-1/4" w, 18-1/2" d, 37-3/4" h **$2,200**
Louis XV, Provincial, oak, rect top and case, fluted frieze, three paneled doors enclosing re-fitted interior of drawers,

short cabriole legs, 85" w, 19" d, 40" h **$3,525**
Neoclassical, Boston, mahogany veneer, corner style, paneled and scrolled splashboard over top with veneered molded edge, curving front which overhangs conforming case of three veneered drawers over two recessed paneled doors, single shelved int., similar recessed panel sides above flattened ball feet with brass banding, replaced brass pulls, old surface with some imperfections, 1820-25, 60" w, 35" d, 42" h...**$55,200**
Queen Anne, converted from highboy base, walnut, pine secondary wood, pegged construction, two dovetailed drawers, one with relief carved shell, scalloped aprons, cabriole legs, pad feet, old dark surface, age splits, replaced returns, 38-1/2" w, 20-1/2" d, 35" h..**$1,150**
Regency-style, inlaid mahogany, serpentine top, conforming case fitted with three central long drawers, drawer and door at each side, inlaid with quarter fans and checkering, 20th C, 65" w, 21-1/2" d, 40" h **$2,000**
Renaissance Revival, America, cherry, curled mahogany drawer fronts, burled arched panel doors...........**$900**
Second Empire, French, ebonized wood, scrolled crest with pierte dure florals within gilt metal cartouche, three section mirrored back divided by ebonized brackets, three drawers, center cupboard door flanked by two glazed cupboard doors, shelved int., figural gilt metal mounts, pietre dura floral and bird dec within gilt bronze cartouche, c1870, 67" w, 18" d, 77" h **$4,600**

Sheraton, country, walnut and curly maple, beaded edge top, four dovetailed drawers, scalloped aprons, turned legs, line inlay around apron and drawer fronts, old varnish finish, replaced glass pulls, wear and edge damage, one heart inlay missing, large water stain on top, 69-1/2" w, 21-1/2" d, 43-1/2" h.....**$5,500**

Southern, Kentucky, walnut and cherry, gallery on three sides of rect top, four drawers over four cupboard doors with punched tin panels dec with quarter fans and fylfots, c1850, 66" l.....**$17,500**

Victorian, American pine, serpentine crest, rect top, four small drawers over two banks of four drawers, center cupboard, late 19th C, 65" w, 19" d, 51-1/2" h.....**$750**

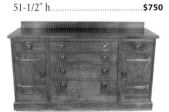

Sideboard, Arts & Crafts Gustav Stickley, #841, six drawers and two cabinets, hammered copper strap hardware with ring pulls, heavy construction, backsplash, orig finish and patina, top drawer orig leather lining, 41-1/2" x 72-1/4" x 22-1/4", $21,150.
Photo courtesy of David Rago Auctions, Inc.

Sideboard, Hepplewhite, Pennsylvania, cherry, bowfront top over frieze drawer flanked by two short drawers above two cupboard doors flanked by bottle drawers, all with line inlaid edges, square tapering legs with bellflower inlay and banded cuffs, c1810, 67" w, 41" h, $7,475.
Photo courtesy of Pook & Pook, Inc.

Sideboard, George III, mahogany, bowfront, long center drawer, two cellarettes concealed as two short drawers, square tapering legs, spade feet, early 19th century, 35-1/4" x 59-1/2" x 22", $825.
Photo courtesy of Sloans & Kenyon Auctioneers and Appraisers.

Sofa, Philadelphia or Baltimore Chippendale, arched back over scrolled arms, serpentine front seat, square legs with stretchers, c1780, 39-1/2" h x 92" w, **$4,370.**
Photo courtesy of Pook & Pook, Inc.

Sofas

Aesthetic Movement, American, walnut, shaped backrest, scrolled end above arcaded apron, circular turned legs, matching bolt of orig fabric, 70" l.....**$1,200**

Art Nouveau, Carlo Bugatti, ebonized wood, rect back, mechanical seat, slightly scrolling rect arms, parchment upholstery, painted swallows and leafy branches, hammered brass trim, four block form feet, 1900, 68-3/8" l.....**$1,900**

Centennial, Chippendale-style, American, mahogany, shaped back, rolled arms, yellow velvet upholstered seat, gadrooned apron, cabriole legs with carved knees, claw and ball feet, late 19th C, 62" l.....**$1,500**

Chippendale, country, step down back with step down arms, bowed front with large down filled cushions, eight molded carved legs, cup caster feet, reupholstered, 76" w, 32" d, 36" h.....**$3,000**

Classical

Mid-Atlantic States, carved mahogany and bird's eye-maple veneer, Grecian style, scrolled and reeded arm and foot, punctuated with brass rosettes, continuing to similar reeded seat rail with inlaid dies, reeded saber legs flanked by brass flowerettes, brass paw feet on casters, old surface, 1805-20, 75" l, 14-1/2" h seat, 35" h.....**$3,680**

New England, carved mahogany veneer, cylindrical crest ends, leaf carved volutes, upholstered seat and rolled veneer seat rail, leaf carved supports, carved paw feet, 1820-40, 92" w, 16-1/2" h seat, 34-3/4" h.....**$1,650**

Duncan Phyfe-style, recamier style, molded back with scrolled head and foot, roundel motif, molded apron, splayed saber legs, brass paw feet, casters, upholstery stained, price for pr, 35-3/4" h.....**$2,300**

Edwardian-style, Chesterfield, tufted brown leather, flattened bun feet, 81" l.....**$5,000**

Empire, mahogany and figured mahogany veneer frame, well-detailed carving with sea serpent front legs, turned back legs, lyre arms with relief carved flowers and cornucopia, rope-turned crest rail, refinished, reupholstered in floral tapestry on ivory ground, bolster pillows, 107" l.....**$3,850**

Federal

America, carved mahogany, mahogany veer paneled top crest with scrolled sides, front carved with rosette and leaf dec, carved paw feet with front stylized wings, red flower dec upholstery, 96" w, 19-1/2" d, 32" h.....**$1,000**

Massachusetts or New Hampshire, mahogany veneer paneled crest topped with reeding that continues on top of arms to reeded arm supports, bird's-eye maple inlaid dies on front swelled and reeded legs, turned feet with sq raked rear legs, old refinish, feet repairs, early 19th C, 32-1/4" h.....**$2,820**

New Hampshire, carved mahogany, upholstered, straight crest continuing to shaped sides with carved arms on vase and ring reeded and swelled posts and cockbeaded panels, bowed seat rail, vase and ring-turned legs with cockbeaded rect inlaid dies, old finish, minor imperfections, c1815, 78" w, 24" d, 17" h seat, 34" h back.....**$2,415**

Sofa, Biedermeier, mahogany, downswept inlaid crest rail, padded back, curving cornucopia arms with bolsters, padded tight seat, serpentine apron, reeded side scrolling legs, c1840, 37-3/4" x 74-3/4" x 25-5/8", **$3,660.**
Photo courtesy of Sloans & Kenyon Auctioneers and Appraisers.

Sofa, Chesterfield-style, tufted, taupe leather upholstery, turned feet, wear and tears to leather, 92" x 36" x 29", **$325.**
Photo courtesy of David Rago Auctions, Inc.

Sofa, International Movement, Charles Eames for Herman Miller, upholstered in original orange and red Alexander Girard fabric, chromed and black enameled flat steel frame, unmarked, 72-1/4" l, 28-1/2" d, 35-3/4" h, **$1,400.**
Photo courtesy of David Rago Auctions, Inc.

George III-style, English, carved oak, double arched upholstered high backrest, scrolled arms, loose cushion seat, acanthus carved legs, claw and ball feet, 58" l **$1,200**

Louis XV style, recamier
Mahogany, tied ribbon and wheat-sheaf carved backrest, scrolled end, foliate carved terminals on gadrooned feet, casters, 91" l **$1,410**
Walnut, high scrolled backrest, carved foliate on armrests and cabriole legs, 90" l **$650**

Neoclassical, Baltic, carved mahogany, paneled cresting, padded arms with lions heads and anthemia, upholstered seat and back, shaped feet, c1825, 68" l **$2,185**

Regency-style, heavily carved, acanthus leaves and claw feet, 89" l, 31-1/2" h **$260**

Renaissance Revival, American, carved walnut, five armchairs in two sizes, angular carved frames, 72" l settee... **$2,350**

Rococo Revival, John B. Belter, carved rosewood, triple back, carved central rose and fruit on sides, scroll band underneath, carved segmented scroll, tufted back red silk upholstery, brass caster feet, old restoration to central crest, worn seat fabric, 62" w, 42" h **$4,500**

Sheraton to Empire, transitional, carved mahogany, scrolled arms with molded detail, applied rosettes, relief carved leaf supports, brass caps on turned front legs, relief twist carvings, applied moldings on front panels, casters on base, dark refinish, glued break in one scroll, reupholstered, 70" w, 17-1/2" h seat, 34-1/2" h back **$550**

Victorian, late, American, camel back, reupholstered, turned legs, c1890, 60" l
.... **$750**

Stands

Baker, wrought iron, 48" h, 14-1/2" d, 84" h.. **$500**

Basin, Federal, New England, mahogany veneer, scalloped backsplash above basin cut outs, shaped skirt over medial shelf with one working and one faux cockbeaded drawer outlined in cross-banded veneer, four reeded legs, turned feet, old surface, replaced brass, minor imperfections, early 19th C, 24" w, 16-1/4" d, 43-1/2" h **$1,300**

Bird cage, wicker, painted white, tightly woven quarter moon-shaped cage holder, wrapped pole standard, tightly woven conical base, 74" h
.... **$225**

Book, Arts & Crafts, oak, four open shelves with cutout sides and through tenons, 45-3/4" h **$500**

Canterbury, Regency, mahogany, drawer with paper label for "G. Ibison Furniture Broker & Appraiser, Cumberland Place, Near the Elephant & Castle," restoration, early 19th C, 19-1/4" l, 14" d, 22-1/2" h **$1,380**

Card, Aesthetic Movement, American Marquetry inlaid and parcel gilt, circular top inlaid with floral marquetry, fluted and turned pedestal with turned rod decoration, splayed legs, 17-1/2" d, 33-1/2" h **$450**
Polychrome and part gilded walnut, circular top, turned and fluted stem, four turned and splayed legs, 12-1/2" d, 33" h **$530**

Cellarette

Arts & Crafts

Stickley, Gustav, flush top, pull-out copper shelf, single drawer, cabinet door, copper pulls, orig finish, large red decal, veneer lifting on sides and back, 22" w, 16" d, 39-1/2" h
.... **$4,315**

Stand, Sheraton, two drawers, c1820, 38" x 18-1/2", **$600.**
Photo courtesy of Wiederseim Associates, Inc.

Washstand, mixed woods, New England, scrolled sides, two small drawers, medial shelf, tapering legs, peg feet, early 19th century, 31" x 27-1/4" x 17-1/2", **$944.**
Photo courtesy of Sloans & Kenyon Auctioneers and Appraisers.

Music stand, Arts & Crafts, Gustav Stickley, four shelves, tapered posts, shaped apron, orig finish, decal on leg, paper label, missing small piece from side stretcher, stains, 39" x 22" x 15", **$2,600.**
Photo courtesy of David Rago Auctions, Inc.

Telephone stand, Arts & Crafts, L. & J. G. Stickley, no. 587, square overhanging top and apron, Handcraft decal inside leg, very good orig finish, minor separation to top, 27" x 16" x 16", **$1,400.**
Photo courtesy of David Rago Auctions, Inc.

Magazine stand, Harvey Ellis design, overhanging top, three shelves, arched side aprons, orig finish, wear and stains, branded under bottom shelf, 41-1/2" x 22" x 13", **$1,800.**
Photo courtesy of David Rago Auctions, Inc.

Stickley, L. & J.G., arched backsplash, pull-out copper shelf, two-door cabinet, hammered copper strap hinges, ring pulls, top refinished, orig finish on base, "The Work of ..." decal, 35-1/2" x 32" x 16"..**$13,800**

Federal, attributed to Middle Atlantic states, mahogany inlaid, octagonal top, conforming case, both inlaid with contrasting stringing, interior well with removable lead liner, four sq tapering legs inlaid with bellflowers and stringing, brasses appear to be orig, old refinish, sun faded top, imperfections, c1790-1800, 22-1/4" w, 17-1/4" w, 25-1/4" h **$28,200**

George III, English, mahogany, lozenge form, brass bands, twin loop carry handles, racked chamfered tapering legs, mid-19th C, 24" w, 17-1/2" d, 27-1/2" h **$7,500**

Chamber, Federal
New England, painted and dec, dec splashboard above washstand top with round cut-out for basin, medial shelf with drawer below, orig yellow paint with green and gold stenciling and striping, paint wear, imperfections, early 19th C, 18-1/4" h, 1" d, 39-1/4" h **$350**
North Shore, MA, carved mahogany, shaped splashboard, veneered cabinet door flanked by ovolu corners, carved columns of leaves and

grapes on punchwork ground, ring-turned tapering legs, brass casters, old replaced brasses, old refinish, minor restoration, c1815-25, 21-1/2" w, 16" d, 35-5/8" h....**$2,300**
Portsmouth, New Hampshire, mahogany inlaid, shaped splashboard with center quarter round shelf, pierced top with bow front, square string inlaid supports continue to outward flaring legs with patterned inlays, medial shelf, satinwood skirt, small center drawer with patterned inlaid lower edge, shaped stretchers with inlaid paterae, old finish, minor imperfections, c1800, 23" w, 16-1/2" d, 41" h **$5,750**

Demilune, Hepplewhite, country, pine, salmon paint, dark red fingerline dec, c1800 ....**$10,000**

Dumbwaiter
Georgian, three tiered, mahogany, each graduated dished tier raised on turned standard, three down swept legs, 22-1/2" d largest tier, 38-1/2" h **$600**
Queen-Anne style, walnut, three circular shelves, splayed legs, pad feet, 21" d, 39" h **$300**

Easel
Aesthetic Movement, ash, cresting with stylized scroll, rod and ball design, straight legs and spindle-inset supports, 19th C, 64" h ...**$275**
Louis XVI-style, mahogany and parcel-gilt, picture support hung

with berried laurel swags, trestle-end frame carved with acanthus, imbrications, and dolphins, 25" w, 23-1/2" d, 82" h.........................**$950**

Étagère
Classical, New England, mahogany and mahogany veneer, spool-turned gallery, ball finials, three shelves with similar supports, two recessed panel cupboard doors, single shelf int., ball-turned feet, old refinish, imperfections, 1860s, 35-1/4" w, 15-3/4" d, 66" h.........................**$990**
Regency, late, English, six tiers, corner, columnar supports, basal drawer, brass casters, early 19th C, 18" w, 14" d, 62" h...................**$3,000**
Victorian, three rect tiers raised by turned columns over two cabinet doors, ball feet, casters, 20-1/2" w, 16" d, 51-1/2" h......................**$1,180**
Victorian, Rococo Revival, carved rosewood, center upright mirrored section with asymmetrical leaf scroll cresting, conforming mirrored side panels with three shelves on each side, scrolled supports, serpentine variegated marble top on lower section, single drawer, scroll feet, minor damage to top, 51" w, 88-3/4" l................................**$4,025**

Folding, Chippendale
New York State or Pennsylvania, cherry, dished top rotates and tilts, birdcage support, swelled and

Plant stand, Old Hickory/Paine, spindled sides, orig finish, nails added, Paine furniture Co. label, stenciled no. 1207.152, 30" x 13" x 13", **$825.**
Photo courtesy of David Rago Auctions, Inc.

Magazine stand, Arts & Crafts, Gustav Stickley, No. 514, oak, tongue-and-groove paneled sides, square posts, leather strips tacked to shelf ends, original finish, early red decal under top shelf, wear to top, 35-1/2" x 14-1/4" x 14-1/2", **$8,100.**
Photo courtesy of David Rago Auctions, Inc.

Washstand, New England, paint decorated, scrolled splash back has freehand and stenciled floral dec, pierced top, medial shelf with drawer, vase and ring-turned legs, old surface, imperfections, c1830, 36" h x 16-1/2" w x 14-1/2" d, **$470.**
Photo courtesy of Skinner, Inc.

turned pedestal, cabriole tripod base, pad feet, old refinish, imperfections, 1755-1775, 17-1/2" d, 26" h **$3,220**
Pennsylvania, walnut, molded dish top, inscribed edge tilts, tapering pedestal with suppressed ball, cabriole legs ending in pad feet, imperfections, 1760-80, 22" d, 29" h
.... **$4,600**

Magazine
Arts & Crafts
Stickley, Gustav, Tree of Life, carved sides, four shelves, orig finish and tacks, unmarked, minor edge wear, 14" sq, 43-1/2" h **$1,610**
Stickley, L. & J.G., single broad slat on either side, arched toe board, new finish, "The Work of L. & J. G. Stickley" decal, 36" w, 12" d, 30" h
.... **$2,990**
Eastlake, carved maple, walnut, and bird's eye maple veneer, finely turned posts with ball finials on top corners, turned legs, dovetailed drawer, drop pulls, old finish, old gold paint in carving and turnings, one corner restored, 22" w, 14-1/2" d **$230**
Regency-style, mahogany, four divisions, dipped dividers, frieze drawer, turned legs on casters, late 19th C, 23" w, 16" d, 24" h **$1,775**
Renaissance Revival, mahogany, walnut, parcel-gilt, and ebonized

gilt-metal, hanging, back plate with acanthus crest flanked by fleur-de-lis and bellflowers, uprights mounted on top with gilt-metal bust roundels, central hinged magazine folio set with gilt composition oval bust of Mercury, gilt incised detailing, third quarter 19th C, 19-3/4" w, 21-1/2" h
.... **$300**
Victorian, mahogany, burled walnut veneer, turned corner posts and finials with scrolled and pierced panels, short boxed stops which conform to ends, dovetailed drawer with carved pull and applied fretwork, four trumpet turned legs, brass casters, late 19th or early 20th C, 28-1/2" w, 16" d, 21" h **$1,150**
Night, Art Deco, attributed to Maurice Defrene, France, amboyna wood inlaid with stylized flowers in various fruitwoods and mother-of-pearl, price for pr, c1925, 15" w, 18" d, 29-1/2" h
.... **$2,235**

Pedestal
Aesthetic Movement, American
Ebonized, rect top, turned stem, angular supports, four curved legs, 17" w, 14" d, 35-1/2" h **$500**
Gilded and velvet mounted walnut, sq top, gilded lappet corners, sq base, 12" sq, 37-1/2" h **$750**
Renaissance Revival, American, ebonized walnut, sawtooth frieze, turned

supports, four-footed circular base, 18" w, 12-1/2" d, 34" h **$450**
Pier, Empire-style, mahogany, gray marble top, part ebonized, gilded, mirrored back **$650**

Plant
Arts & Crafts
Limbert, ebon-oak line, overhanging top, four caned panels on each side, recent finish, branded signature, 14" w, 14" d, 34" h **$2,100**
Stickley, Gustav, sq top flush with cloud-lift apron, narrow board mortised through corseted stretchers with tenon and key, orig finish, crack in one stretcher, 1902-04 red decal, 14" sq, 27" h **$3,450**
French-style, black lacquered finish, turtle-shaped top with open well, ormolu wreath and quiver designs, acanthus leaves, hoof-shaped caps on feet, 20th C, 19-1/4" w, 14-1/2" d, 30" h **$275**
Folk Art, carved and painted root, America, polychrome painted animal heads radiating from entwined root base, inscribed "MAS 1897," 23" w, 38-1/2" h **$1,725**
Victorian, walnut and pine, three tiers, two top round, larger one octagonal, turned legs, scalloped aprons, old finish, 31" d, 37-1/2" h **$420**
Portfolio, William IV, English, carved rosewood, folding mechanism, c1830
.... **$3,500**

Tea stand, folding tray, later needlepoint with English storefronts, **$150.**
Photo courtesy of Dotta Auction Co., Inc.

Quilt rack, Renaissance Revival, American, walnut, faceted turned rods on trestle base, 27" w, 35" h **$200**

Reading, Federal, Albany, NY, mahogany, reading stand above ring-turned tapering post on rect shaped canterbury, turned tapering spindles, casters, early 19th C, 22-1/4" w, 14" d, 47-1/2" h **$3,200**

Sewing, Sheraton, country, black walnut, poplar secondary wood, lift top, fitted int. compartment with four int. dovetailed drawers and pigeon holes, single dovetailed drawer with figured front and incised beading, well-turned legs with ring turnings, replaced brass pull, pegged construction, lock missing, one leg with well-executed repair, 20" w, 19-1/2" d, 29" h **$1,155**

Sheet music stand, Aesthetic Movement, American, rosewood, hinged sides, pedestal, four downswept legs, 18" w, 5" d, 36" h **$500**

Side, Aesthetic, ebonized walnut, circular top, turned and fluted pedestal, circular base, three flaring feet with stylized carved leaves, presentation plaque "F. B. Parrish, April 1875," 34-1/2" h **$900**

Single drawer

Country, mahogany and fruitwood, incised monogram on left apron "SC" in script, two board top with gallery, small dovetailed drawer in apron, turned legs and supports, base shelf, old mellow refinishing, insect damage, 16-1/2" w, 16-1/4" d, 28" h **$450**

English, rosewood veneer, mahogany secondary wood, small urn-shaped finials on top, dovetailed center drawer, wooden pulls, three shelves, turned legs, old refinishing, minor edge chips, filled splits, 19th C, 19-1/4" w, 14-1/2" d, 39-1/2" h **$1,050**

Hepplewhite, cherry, pine and poplar secondary wood, two-board top, dovetailed drawer with brass pull, slender legs taper to feet, refinished, old tin patch over knot hole in drawer bottom, 17-3/4" w, 18" d, 27-1/2" h **$500**

Pennsylvania, early, softwood, one molded drawer, deeply beaded skirt, splayed tapered legs, scrubbed top, old tan over red painted base, 21-3/4" w, 21-1/2" d, 30" h **$1,650**

Sheraton, country, curly maple and walnut, poplar secondary wood, two board top, dovetailed drawer, turned legs, old replaced brass pull, old finish, chip on foot ring, 18" w, 17-1/4" d, 28-3/8" h **$700**

Sheraton, country, decorated, orig brown sponged dec over bittersweet colored ground, old dry varnish, pine, two board top, sq nail construction in drawer, splayed ring-turned legs, ball feet, minor wear, 21" w, 20-3/4" d, 31" h **$3,335**

Sheraton, country, walnut and cherry, poplar secondary wood, single board top, well turned legs with raised panels that flank dovetailed beveled edge drawer, orig glass pull, dark refinishing, old repairs, 20-1/2" w, 18" d, 28-3/4" h **$500**

Tabouret, Regency-style, carved oak, cushioned top above frame carved with elaborate floral sprays, raised and scrolled toes, 23" w, 19" h **$500**

Tavern, Federal, country, pine, breadboard top, single long drawer **$350**

Tier

Classical Revival, sq onyx top, two tiers, scrolled metal skirt, legs with central leaf tip band, second medial shelf, outward scrolled feet, late 19th C, 31-3/4" h **$360**

English, mahogany, small gallery on top, four shelves, ring-turned columns, half turned moldings resemble bamboo, brass casters, refinished, few trim pcs replaced, putty restorations under shelves, 16" sq, 44-3/4" h **$350**

Federal, New England, mahogany, three trays of diminishing size, molded edges, each rotates on turned urn-shaped shaft, cabriole leg tripod base, arris pad feet, old refinish, minor imperfections, late 18th/early 19th C, largest tier 23-1/4" d, 43-1/4" h **$7,650**

Two drawers, Hepplewhite, cherry, pine secondary wood, single board top, two dovetailed and beaded drawers with orig brass pulls, high tapered legs, old mellow finish, 14-3/8" w, 17" d, 28-7/8" h **$1,050**

Umbrella, Arts & Crafts, early 20th C, oak, sq form, four posts, top and bottom stretchers with mortise and tenon joinery, one dark brown finish, other medium brown finish, marked "Cedric S. Sweeter Jan 23, 1920," price for pr, 12" w, one 28-3/4" h, other 29" h . **$230**

Vitrine, Mahogany, line border inlay, satinwood panels, top with drop front, molded edges, tapered sq legs, brass casters, joined by stretcher base, 21-1/2" w, 16-1/2" d, 28" h **$600**

Wash

Eastlake, walnut and burlwood, three drawers, replaced white marble top, 29" w, 38" h **$265**

Empire, figured mahogany veneer, poplar secondary wood, dovetailed gallery fitted with narrow shelf, bowed top with cut-outs for wash bowl and two jars, serpentine front supports, turned rear posts, dovetailed drawer in base with brass pulls, high well turned legs, refinished, edge chips, 18" w, 16" d, 37-3/4" h **$385**

Federal

American, mahogany and figured mahogany veneer, bow front with two small drawers, cutout for bowl, cutout sides, single dovetailed drawer in base, turned legs, worn finish, some water damage, replaced top and two small drawers, 20-1/4" w, 17-1/4" d, 30-1/4" h **$275**

Rhode Island, mahogany veneer, top with four shaped corners, canted corners, engaged ring-turned columns ending in reeded legs flanking cock-beaded drawers outlined in cross-banded veneer, top two drawers with sections, replaced brasses, old refinish, imperfections, c1790, 20-3/4" w, 15-1/2" d, 28-1/2" h **$4,025**

Hepplewhite, bow front, mahogany and figured veneer, pine and poplar secondary woods, dovetailed gallery, top with cutout for bowl and two cup inserts, dovetailed beaded drawer below door with brass pull, tapered legs with beaded panels on front, restoration to center leg, 24" w, 17" d, 40" h **$600**

Victorian, walnut, white marble top, one drawer, pr lower cupboard doors, carved fruit and nut pulls, 30" w, 30" h **$300**

Whatnot, Corner, Victorian, Chinoiserie bamboo and lacquer, frame set with two diamond-shaped mirrors and shelves, late 19th C, 22" w, 13" d, 56" h **$250**

Work

Classical, carved maple and rosewood veneer, top outlined with rosewood veneer banding above sectional veneered drawer, lower drawer flanked by short columns, tapering pedestal joining four leaf carved legs ending in carved hairy paw feet on castors, old refinish, early 19th C, 20-3/4" w, 18-1/2" d, 28-3/4" h .. **$500**

Federal

Middle Atlantic region, bird's eye maple and oak veneer, top with hinged leaves, two working and two faux string inlaid drawers, top one fitted, ring-turned swelled legs joined by similar double stretchers, curving legs, scrolled feet, old refinish, imperfections, 1815-25, 17-1/4" w, 18" d, 28-1/4" h **$2,750**

New England, mahogany, rect top, single drawer, turned and reeded legs, old refinish, imperfections, early 19th C, 22" w, 16-3/4" d, 28-1/2" h **$750**

Hepplewhite, New England, cherry inlaid, sq top, outline stringing and quarter fan inlays on ovolo corners, line inlaid drawer and skirt, line inlaid sq tapering legs, crossbanded cuffs, brass drawer pull, refinished, c1810, 19" w, 19" d, 27" h **$2,650**

Renaissance Revival, American, lift top opening to real satinwood interior fitted with compartments, nar-

row drawer above semi-circular bag drawer, pair of stylized lyre form ends jointed by arched stretcher surmounted by turned finial, c1860 .... **$875**

Sheraton, New England, mahogany, veneered, outset rounded corners, shaped top, pull-out suspended fabric bag below single drawer, ring-turned and reeded round tapering legs ending in ring-turned tapering vasiform feet, old refinish, 1805-15, 16-1/2" w, 18-1/2" d, 28-1/4" h **$3,500**

Steps

Bed, New England, pine and tulipwood, two steps, thumb-molded drawer below bottom one, flanked by shaped sides, demilune base, old color, repaired, early 19th C, 15-1/2" w, 10" d, 17-1/2" h **$575**

Circus, America, painted white stringers, red, yellow, and blue treads, early 20th C, 25" w, 90" d, 27" h **$435**

Library

George III, English, mahogany, rect molded hinged top, eight steps, late 18th C, 49-1/2" w, 53-1/2" h ... **$2,500**

Regency, English, mahogany, three steps, inset green leather treads, scrolling banister, sq balusters, feet with brass casters, early 19th C, 46" w, 27" w, 56" h **$2,400**

Stools

Cricket, Arts & Crafts, Limbert, #205-1/2", rect top covered with new leather, splayed sides, inverted heart cut-out, single stretcher with through-tenon, replaced keys, orig finish, branded, 20" w, 15" d, 18" h **$950**

Foot

Arts & Crafts, oak

Barber Brothers, oak, nicely replaced leather seat, some color added to orig finish, paper label, 13" w, 13" d, 11" h **$110**

Limbert, cricket, #205-1/2, rect orig leather top and tacks, splayed sides with inverted heart cut-out having single stretcher with through-tenon construction, orig finish, branded and numbered, 20" w, 15" d, 19" h **$2,000**

Painted, attributed to York County, Pennsylvania, pine, paint dec, man eating oysters in center of top, red ground, scalloped border, inscription "By D. J. Rash for C. F. Rash," stylized leaves on sides and feet, 15-5/8" l, 9-3/4" w, 10-3/4" h **$18,700**

Stool, primitive pine, 19th century, **$225.**
Photo courtesy of Wiederseim Associates Inc.

Pair of stools, rectangular, pierced hand grip, block, ball and baluster legs, stretchers, 23-1/2" x 13-1/2" x 7-3/4", **$2,000.**
Photo courtesy of Sloans & Kenyon Auctioneers and Appraisers.

Queen Anne, walnut, rect frieze, 4 cabriole legs each with shell carving on knees, pad feet, slip seat, 18th C, 22-1/2" w, 17" d, 17" h **$1,950**

Sheraton, curly and bird's eye maple, old finish, cane top, minor damage to top, 7-3/4" w, 13" l, 6-1/2" h .. **$440**

Victorian, carved walnut, short cabriole legs carved at knees with shells, shaped skirting carved with acanthus, velveteen upholstery, late 19th C, 12-3/4" w, 16" l, 11" h **$175**

Windsor, attributed to Maine, early 19th C, rect top, four swelled legs joined by X-form stretchers, orig dark brown grain paint which resembles exotic wood, yellow line accents, paint imperfections, 12" w, 8" d, 7" h **$625**

Joint

Early, oak, old finish, wear and age cracks, 11" w, 16-1/2" l, 17-3/4" h. **$990**

Jacobean-style, oak, rect plank top, shaped skirt, block and ring-turned legs joined by box stretcher, 18" w, 11-1/4" d, 21" h **$700**

Footstools, pr, rectangular, upholstered, square molded legs, c1770, 11-1/2" h, **$2,225.**
Photo courtesy of Pook & Pook, Inc.

Footstool, Victorian, walnut, needle-point upholstery, fabric loss, leg wear, second half 19th century, 13" h x 16" w x 16" l, **$55.**
Photo courtesy of Green Valley Auctions.

Footstool, Early Victorian giltwood, bead and needlework top, four turned feet, third quarter 19th century, 4-3/4" h x 8-1/2" w x 20-1/2" l, **$140.**
Photo courtesy of Green Valley Auctions.

Footstool, attributed to Old Hickory, reed top over spindled sides, overcoated orig finish, unmarked, 13" x 17" x 11-1/2", **$500.**
Photo courtesy of David Rago Auctions, Inc.

Milking stool, well turned round wooden seat, splayed bamboo legs and stretchers, old red and yellow graining over cream ground, wear, 10" d, 6-1/4" h **$180**

Ottoman, Classical, attributed to Boston, Massachusetts, mahogany veneer, overstuffed cushions rest inside mitred frame atop molded base, ogee bracket feet, wooden casters, refinished, minor imperfections, price for pr, c1830, 20" w, 18" d, 17-1/2" h **$2,235**

Piano

Louis XVI-style, carved beech, circular, adjustable, close-nailed over stuffed top, petal-carved frieze, leaf-capped turned, tapered, and fluted legs, wavy cross-stretcher, late 19th C.......... **$850**

Renaissance Revival, American, telescopic, X-form, turned wooden screws adjust height, 20" h **$325**

Victorian, mahogany, upholstered, revolving, 20" h, early 19th...... **$200**

Seat-type

Country, folk art, attributed to Fredericksburg, PA, painted and dec, octagonal seat, chamfered edge, trimmed with border band of carved hearts, tall splayed and chamfered legs also trimmed with carved hearts and joined by slender rungs, overall polychrome, late 19th/early 20th C **$1,850**

George III, mahogany, gold floral satin upholstered rest seat, sq tapering supports, molded H-form stretchers, pr, late 19th C, 19-1/2" l, 17" h **$1,650**

International Movement

Eames, Charles, manufactured by Herman Miller, Time-Life, walnut, concave seat, 13" d, 15" h...... **$1,000**

Platner, Warren, manufactured by Knoll, bronze wire base, peach fabric upholstered seat, 17" d, 21" h **$325**

Renaissance Revival, American, walnut, cushioned and hinged seat opening to well, trestle base with angular supports, 23-1/2" w, 11" d, 19" h **$265**

Windsor, American, oblong plant seat raised on three tall, turned and slightly swelled legs joined by T-stretcher, traces of old green paint, 19th C, 15" w, 24-1/2" h **$200**

Tables

Typical Parts of a Table

Architect's, George III, English, mahogany, hinged tooled leather work surface above opposing hinged work surface, turned pedestal on three splayed legs, pad feet, some reconstruction, late 19th C, 29" w, 19-1/4" d, 29-1/2" h **$2,300**

Bank, Neoclassical-style, brass and metal, rect glass-inset top above frieze pierced with putti and scrolling foliage, trestle end supports cast as sphinxes, joined by stretcher, black marble block supports, removed from Hyde Park Bank of Chicago, 62" w, 39" d, 40" h **$800**

Banquet

Federal, mahogany and mahogany veneer, two-part, D-shaped drop leaf, two leaves..................... **$1,450**

Regency-style, mahogany, five leaves **$4,200**

Breakfast

Chippendale to Hepplewhite, transitional, walnut, one board top, beaded edge apron, sq legs with slight taper, molded corner, and inside chamfer, H stretcher, old finish, stains on top, 19" w, 29-1/4" l, 28-1/4" h **$8,250**

Tavern table, Pennsylvania, walnut, rectangular top, case with single drawer, baluster turned legs, stretchers, 18th century, 29-1/2" h, 36" w, 26-3/4" d, **$1,405.**
Photo courtesy of Pook & Pook, Inc.

Dining table, Queen Anne, Delaware Valley, walnut, rectangular top, frame with scalloped ends, cabriole legs, trifid feet, c1760, 28" h, 44" w, **$1,640.**
Photo courtesy of Pook & Pook, Inc.

Gateleg table, William & Mary, Pennsylvania, rectangular top, two D-shaped leaves, single long drawer, turned and blocked legs and stretchers, c1730, 29" h, 15" w, 34-3/4" d, **$3,045.**
Photo courtesy of Pook & Pook, Inc.

Classical, New York, carved mahogany inlaid, top with brass inlay in outline, stamped brass on edge of shaped leaves, one working and one faux drawers, flanked by drop pendants, four pillar curved platform support, leafage carved legs, carved paw feet, casters, replaced pulls, old finish, repairs, losses, 1820-30, 39" w, 24" d, 28" h.................**$2,450**

Federal
Massachusetts, central, inlaid cherry, rect hinged top with ovolo corners, base with straight skirt, edged with lunette inlay, flanked by sq tapering legs outlined in stringing, topped with icicle inlay, old refinish, c1810, 36" w, 17" d, 29" h.................**$1,150**

Massachusetts or New England, mahogany oval top, hinged leaves, flanking two drawers, one working, one faux, both outlined in stringing and have central panel of figured mahogany veneer above chevron-style inlaid banding, reeded, turned, tapering legs, turned feet, old refinish, surface imperfections, 1815, 35-3/8" w, 20-1/4" d, 29-3/4" h.................**$8,225**

New York City, carved mahogany veneer, rect top, shaped leaves, one working and one faux end drawers, cross banded mahogany veneer, turned acanthus leaf carved pedestal, four acanthus leaf carved legs, brass hairy paw feet, old refinish, repairs, c1815, 25" w closed, 38-1/2" l, 30-1/4" h.................**$1,725**

Bureau Plat, Louis XV-style, tulipwood, shaped top with leather insert, four ormolu-mounted shell ornaments at corners, frieze drawer flanked by two small drawers, angular cabriole legs with ormolu mounts, paw-form feet, minor veneer loss, 50-3/4" w, 30" h.................**$1,725**

Card
Classical
Attributed to firm of Isaac Vine and Isaac Vine Jr., Boston, carved mahogany and mahogany veneer, rect top with beaded edges, skirt with recessed panel, C-scrolls and carved volutes over tapering pedestal accented by carved leafage above serpentine veneered platform with carved and scrolled feet on casters, old refinish, imperfections, 1819-24, 37" w, 17-1/2" d, 28-1/2" h....**$1,840**

Attributed to Thomas Astens, New York City, carved mahogany and satinwood, rect swivel top with rounded ends, outlined in cross banded mahogany veneer, satinwood veneered skirt, faceted pineapple-like carving above acanthus leaf carving on pedestal, shaped legs, carved paw feet on casters, old refinish, imperfections, 1822, 36" w, 18-1/4" d, 28" h.................**$3,335**

New York, carved mahogany, mahogany veneer rect swivel top with rounded front carved corners, leaf carved and shaped shaft, curving platform which joins 4 scrolling leaf carved legs ending in carved paw feet, refinished, minor imperfections, 1820-30, 36" w, 17-1/2" d, 30" h.............**$1,495**

Federal
Boston or Charlestown, Massachusetts, mahogany inlaid, demilune top with inlaid top edge above undercut lower edge, three-paneled conforming skirt with outline stringing, interspersed with inlaid dies, string inlaid legs, refinished, top detached, other imperfections, c1800, 35-3/4" w, 17-1/2" d, 30" h......**$2,500**

Boston or Charlestown, Massachusetts, mahogany and figured maple inlaid, rect top with ovolo corners and inlaid top edge above undercut lower edge, skirt with figured maple rect panel and inlaid rect dies, sq double tapering legs ending in cuff inlays, old refinish, imperfections, early 19th C, 35-3/4" w, 17" d, 29-1/2" h.................**$2,235**

North Shore, Massachusetts, mahogany veneer carved, serpentine facade with ovolo front corners, ring-turned leaf and spiral carved legs, turned feet, old refinish, imperfections, c1815, 37-1/2" w, 17-5/8" d, 30-1/4" h.................**$900**

Philadelphia, mahogany and satinwood veneer, serpentine top, string inlaid skirt flanking rect satinwood center, sq tapering legs outlined in stringing with diamond-shaped die, terminating in cuff inlays, refinished, imperfections, c1800, 36" w, 18-3/8" d, 29-3/4" h.............**$5,600**

Sheraton
American, pine, old brown flame graining, top with later black paint, finely turned legs with raised acanthus leaf bands below serpentine apron, large raised relief leaf carvings at corners, ball feet, 34-1/2" w, 17-1/2" d, 30" h.................**$1,725**

English, mahogany, mahogany flame veneer, banded inlay around top, old red felt insert on interior surfaces, inlaid panels and diamonds on aprons, turned legs, relief ring detail, tapered to applied ormolu paw feet, old finish, pieced repair at one hinge, minor edge damage, 36" w, 16-7/8" d, 29-3/4" h....**$2,100**

Victorian, rosewood, rounded rect top with red baize surface, quadripartite base, scrolling feet, 36" w, 36" d, 29-1/2" h **$950**

Tea table, Arts & Crafts, Gustav Stickley, arched stretchers, splayed legs, mortised top inset with 12 Grueby tiles, old restored finish, unmarked, c1902, 26" x 24-1/2" x 20-1/8", **$27,500.**
Photo courtesy of David Rago Auctions, Inc.

Library table, Arts & Crafts, Limbert, No. 158, oval, plank legs, cut-out stretchers supporting oval-shaped lower shelf with brand underneath, fine original finish, 28-3/4" x 48" x 37", **$14,000.**
Photo courtesy of David Rago Auctions, Inc.

Trestle billiard table/settee, Arts & Crafts, Brunswick-Balke-Collenver Co., convertible, lower drawer with cues, rack, and balls, orig finish, new felt and pockets, metal tag, 31-1/4" x 70" x 39", **$15,000.**
Photo courtesy of David Rago Auctions, Inc.

Side table, Queen Ann, mahogany, single drawer, Queen Anne feet, seam separation on top, 18th century, 27" x 27" x 16", **$900.**
Photo courtesy of David Rago Auctions, Inc.

Tea table, George III, mahogany and burlwood, circular top, turned standard, cabriole legs, pad feet, c1750, 26" h, 25" d, **$880.**
Photo courtesy of Pook & Pook, Inc.

Center

Aesthetic Movement, American

John Jeliff, attributed to, inset white marble top and turret-form corners, paneled frieze with angular pendants, boldly scrolled and faceted trumpet legs joined by an H-form stretcher, delicately carved elongated leaftips, 46-1/2" w, 30-1/2" d, 30-1/2" h **$4,000**

Aesthetic, inlaid and ebonized, shield-form top with oval reserve of musical trophies, two roundels with birds, molded brass border, conforming apron, four gilt and inlaid medallions, tapered sq legs, curule stretcher with large centering urn, bun feet, 54-1/4" l, 32" w, 29-3/4" h **$4,025**

Walnut, white marble top, paneled frieze, four angular legs on scrolled base, 36" w, 24" d, 30" h **$1,650**

Baroque-style, painted, parcel gilt, octagonal marble veined rose colored top above plain frieze, acanthus carved, shaped and tapered legs, late 19th C, 44-1/2" w, 30" h **$2,820**

Biedermeier, inlaid walnut, shaped rect top, molded frieze with drawer, canted, sq-section cabriole legs, 25" w, 37" l, 27-3/4" h **$1,100**

Classical

Boston, attributed to, carved mahogany and mahogany veneer, circular top with inset leather surface, cross banded border, conforming base with four drawers, gilt brass lion's head ring pulls, vase and ring-turned spiral carved center support, gadrooned circular platform, four scrolled reeded and paneled legs,

gilt brass hairy paw feet and casters, refinished, minor imperfections, c1825, 27-3/4" d, 28" h **$12,925**

Philadelphia, carved mahogany veneer, rect top with molded edge, cockbeaded frieze with single central working drawer flanked by faux drawers, turned and carved pedestal ending in gadrooning above stepped, curved pedestal, 4 belted ball feet, old surface, minor imperfections, carving similar to work of Anthony G. Quervelle (1789-1856), Philadelphia, c1827, 45-1/4" w, 20" d, 34-3/4" h **$2,550**

Gothic Revival, attributed to New York State, mahogany veneer, hexagonal top with molded edge overhangs shaped frieze, three faceted columns atop flat base with concave sides on scrolled feet, old refinish, restored, 1935-45, 34-1/4" d, 31" h **$1,120**

International Movement, Wiener-werkstatte, mahogany and brass, circular top with cross banded edge, conforming frieze, sq-section support flanked by four further cylindrical supports, raised on truncated pyramidal base, c1930, 25-1/4" d, 30-1/2" h **$550**

Louis XV-style, mahogany inlaid, ormolu mounted walnut, shaped rect top, one short drawer, opposite faux drawer, cabriole legs, cast sabots, 19th C, 35" w, 22" d, 28" h .. **$600**

Napoleon III, top inset with porcelain plaque depicting Figuros Dining, surrounded by portrait plaques depicting interior scenes, circular carved base mounted with gilt bronze flowers and rams

Game table, Continental, mahogany, triangular top, marquetry floral inlay, fluted tapering legs, spade feet, early 19th century, 30" h, 39-1/2" w, 19-1/4" d, **$935.**
Photo courtesy of Pook & Pook, Inc.

Tavern table, rectangular top, splayed legs, box stretcher, c1735, 25" h, 32-1/2" w, 20-1/4" d, **$995.**
Photo courtesy of Pook & Pook, Inc.

Dressing table, painted pine, scrolled backsplash, case with single drawer, turned legs, orig yellow surface with green highlights, c1830, 34" h x 31-1/2" w, 15-1/2" d, **$2,225.**
Photo courtesy of Pook & Pook, Inc.

heads, three-sided concave plinth, 35-1/2" d, 34" h **$20,100**

Renaissance Revival, inlaid profile portrait of George Washington, eagle, American flags, images of farming, industry, sailing, and travel, c1876 .... **$20,900**

Victorian, bamboo, lacquer octagonal top, four legs joined by a stretcher with medial shelves, 28" w, 20" d, 28" h **$600**

Chair

American, cherry, three-board top, hinged seat lid, scalloped edge sides, apron, shoe feet, black paint on underside of top, old refinishing on base, minor repairs, late 18th C, 45-1/2" d top, 28-1/2" h **$9,350**

New England, pine and birch, top tilts above plant seat flanked by sq tapering arm supports which continue to chamfered legs, four sq stretchers, old refinish, late 18th C, 40-1/2" w, 42" d, 28-3/4" h **$1,100**

New England, pine, maple, and walnut, three-board top tilts above plank seat, walnut arms with turned tapering supports, similar legs terminate in ball and pad feet, old stained red brown surface, repairs, early 19th C, 48-1/4" w, 46-3/4" d, 27-3/4" h **$3,300**

Coach, Georgian, split leather writing surface closing to box form, S-curve legs joined by stretchers, 24-1/4" w, 24-1/4" d, 31-1/4" h **$1,180**

Console

Empire, American, rect white marble top over single drawer, down swept legs joined by medial shelf, mid-19th C, 28-3/4" w, 17" d, 28-1/2" h **$1,800**

George III, mahogany, rect banded top over two drawers, square tapering legs, 51-1/2" w, 23-1/2" d, 34" h **$1,400**

Neoclassical, attributed to Italy, parcel gilt and painted, inset marble top above frieze painted with rinceaux and scrolling foliage, centered by carved portrait medallion, stop-fluted tapering legs, first half 19th C and later, 38" w, 19-1/2" d, 33" h ...**$3,350**

Neoclassical-style, green painted, parcel gilt, brown marble top above frieze decorated with scrolling foliage, fluted tapering legs, price for pr, 20th C, 31" w, 14-1/2" d, 35" h **$2,400**

Rococo-style, polychrome painted and parcel gilt, veneered green marble top, heavily carved scrolling legs joined by stretcher surmounted by shell, 45" w, 23" d, 34" h **$4,600**

Dining

Arts & Crafts

Limbert, #403, cut-corner top over intricate base, slab supports with three spindles in an oval cut-out keyed stretchers connecting to a center leg, one leaf, orig finish, numbered, 50" w, 50" d, 30" h **$2,500**

Stickley, Gustav, variant of model 634, oak, oval top, six leaves, sq leg posts with mortise and tenon joinery, c1920, 46" w, 54-3/4" to 120-3/4" d, 30" h **$11,500**

Unknown maker, possibly California, oak, rect board on board top, lower median shelf with through tenons, cutout sides, shoe foot base, deep brown restored finish, c1912, 83-1/2" w, 35-1/4" d, 29" h **$3,200**

Gaming table, Hepplewhite, tiger maple, demilune form, c1790, 28-1/2" x 32" w x 16" d, **$900.**
Photo courtesy of Wiederseim Associates, Inc.

Dressing table, Queen Anne, Delaware Valley, walnut, rectangular molded top, one long and three short drawers, scalloped skirt, square cabriole legs, Spanish feet, c1750, 29-3/4" h, 30-1/4" w, 18" d, **$7,605.**
Photo courtesy of Pook & Pook, Inc.

Library table, Arts & Crafts, Gustav Stickley, spindled with rect top, broad lower stretcher, orig finish, minor warping to spindles, paper label under top, 29" x 36" x 24", **$3,000.**
Photo courtesy of David Rago Auctions, Inc.

Empire, carved figure mahogany, mahogany veneer, pine secondary wood, two board top, two 14-3/4" d scalloped leaves, pineapple carved column, short turned drops on corners, brass line inlay along aprons, finely carved paw feet and relief hair on legs, refinished, splits in column, repairs, 39" w, 23-1/4" d, 27-3/4" h **$1,560**

Federal
Massachusetts, mahogany, rect top with similar drop leaves, straight skirts, molded tapering legs ending in casters, refinished, repairs, provenance: according to family verbal history, this table belonged to General Benjamin Lincoln, who served in Washington's Army during the American Revolution, and accepted the sword of Cornwallis when the British surrendered, late 18th C, 46-3/4" w, 47-3/4" extended, 28-3/4" h **$1,550**

New England, cherry and bird's eye maple, two parts, two rect ends each with hinged drop-leaf, ring-turned tapering legs ending in ball feet, orig surface, minor surface mars, c1820-25, 82" w, 44-1/2" d, 28-3/4" h **$1,725**

Federal-style, mahogany, three part drop leaf sections, turned, octagonal legs with casters, 19th C, 162" l, 48" d, 29" h............................. **$6,375**

George III, late 19th C
Mahogany, drop leaf, gate leg, 55-1/4" w, 18-1/2" d, 29-1/4" h **$1,770**

Mahogany, rect top with rounded corners and reeded edge, double turned pedestals on paneled and reeded downswept legs, brass cap casters, two leaves, 48" w, 115" l with leaves, 28-3/4" h **$9,990**

George III-style
Cross banded mahogany, wide inlaid borders, three turned pedestals, downswept feet, brass cap casters, two leaves, 13' l extended, 53" w, 29" h **$5,875**

Mahogany, D-shaped top with rounded corners and reeded edge, twin pedestal bases of column raised on tripod base, downswept legs, brass toe caps and casters, 120" l, 44" w, 29-1/4" h.......... **$2,100**

Mahogany, rect top, rounded corners, reeded edge, triple turned pedestals, reeded downswept legs, brass cap casters, two additional leaves, 12' 6" l extended, 53-1/2" w, 29-1/2" h **$7,100**

Georgian-style, painted green, rect top, gadrooned edge, plain frieze, shell carved cabriole legs, claw and ball feet, 53" w, 39" d, 28" h **$900**

International Movement, Hans Wegner, c1960, teak, circular top fitted on cross stretcher frame with metal mounts set into four tapered circular legs, 61" d **$1,880**

Louis XVI-style, walnut, circular top splitting to accommodate eight leaves, plain frieze, circular tapered legs, 54-1/2" w, 30-1/2" h **$1,175**

Queen Anne
Boston area, c1740-50, inlaid figured walnut, top heavy thumb-molded edge outlined in stringing, hinged leaves flank serpentine shaped skirts above the cabriole legs, pad feet, old surface, imperfections, 42" w, 14-1/4" d, 40-3/4" d extended, 28" h **$11,200**

Virginia or North Carolina, walnut, top with molded edge, hinged demilune leaves flank straight skirts above block and swelled turned straight legs, pad feet, old refinish, imperfections, 1760-70, 50-1/2" w, 18-3/4" d, 57-3/4" extended, 29-1/2" h **$5,600**

Regency, late, inlaid mahogany, three parts, D-shaped ends, rect center section, all cross banded in satinwood, checker cross banded frieze and sq tapered legs ending in spade feet, four leaves, early 19th C, 155" l, 54" w, 29" h................. **$5,175**

Regency-style, mahogany, rect top, reeded edge, rounded corners, three ring-turned pedestals, molded cabriole legs, casters, two leaves, late 19th C, 48" w, 177" l, 29" h **$17,250**

Display, Edwardian, inlaid mahogany, shaped rect glazed top on sq tapering legs joined by X-form stretcher **$600**

Dressing
Chippendale, attributed to Pennsylvania, carved mahogany, rect molded top, case of two cockbeaded graduated drawers flanked by reeded stop-fluted lambrequin corners, cabriole legs, pad feet on platforms, all joined by shaped apron, old brasses, refinished, restored, c1760-80, 31" w, 18" d, 29-1/2" h **$5,875**

Classical, New England, grain painted and dec, scrolling crest over two short drawers, projecting top with rounded corners on conforming base, single drawer, ring-turned and incised tapering legs, allover grain paint resembling rosewood, highlighted by stencils of fruit bowls and scrolling leaves and flowers, gold, green, and black line dec, minor imperfections, c1820-40, 30" w, 15-1/4" d, 39" h............ **$1,550**

Empire, mahogany, small case top with drawer, dovetailed drawer in center, thin molding around lower apron, figured mahogany veneer over pine, high ring turned legs with relief rope twist carvings, small pieced restorations, 35-1/2" w, 17-3/4" d, 36-1/2" h................ **$1,650**

Federal, New York state, carved mahogany and mahogany veneer, brass inlaid, cockbeaded rect mirror, scrolled acanthus leaf carved supports with brass emb rosettes above three short drawers, projecting case of two short drawers, one long drawer joining four vase and ring-turned acanthus carved legs, casters, refinished, repaired, c1825, 36-1/4" w, 21-1/2" d, 55" h..................... **$1,725**

George I/II, English, walnut veneer, banded rect top with rounded front corners overhanging shallow straight front fitted with five shallow drawers of banded treatment, plain cabriole legs, pad feet, veneer losses, worm damage, c1725, 32" w, 17" d, 30" h............................ **$1,875**

Drop leaf
Chippendale
New England, southern, cherry, oval overhanging drop leaf top, cutout apron, scrolled returns, four cabriole legs ending in claw and ball feet, imperfections, c1760-80, 44-1/2" l open, 15-1/2" w, 27" h **$4,410**

Pennsylvania, walnut, shaped skirt, molded Marlborough legs, old surface, minor imperfections, late 18th C, 15-1/2" w, 46-3/4" l, 29" h ... **$550**

Rhode Island, carved mahogany, rect drop leaf top, four sq molded stop fluted legs joined by cut-out apron, repairs, c1780, 47-3/4" w, 38-1/4" d, 29" h **$2,100**

Classical, attributed to New York, carved mahogany and mahogany veneer, rect top, overhanging shaped leaves, conforming base with single drawer, beaded skirt, suspending four circular drops on leaf carved pedestal, four curved scrolling acanthus leaf carved and molded legs, brass paw feet on casters, possibly orig glass drawer pull, old refinish, very minor imperfections, c1820 .... **$1,650**

Federal, New England, mahogany, rect overhanging top, straight skirt, four sq tapering legs, old refinish, imperfections, 1795-1810, 14-1/2" w, 28" l extended, 26-1/2" h **$1,300**

Georgian, oak, shaped rect top opening to round surface, six round tapering legs ending in pad feet two legs swing out to support raised leaves, 42-1/2" w, 47" w open, 29" h **$900**

Hepplewhite, American

Birch, old reddish brown surface, two board top, single board leaves, tapered legs, old split in top, 48" w, 19" d, 29-1/2" h **$750**

Cherry, pegged joints, single board top, scalloped leaves, dovetailed corners on aprons, tapered legs, old mellow finish, old replaced hinges, iron braces added beneath top, 52" l, 19-1/2" d, 18-1/2" leaves, 29" h **$575**

Queen Anne, mahogany, D-shaped leaves, shaped apron, circular tapering legs, pad feet, early 18th C, 54" w, 49-1/2" h, 28" h **$1,765**

Regency, mahogany, oak secondary wood, figured veneer on top and D-shaped leaves with banding, single dovetailed drawer on one side with line inlay on front, false drawer on opposite end, urn shaped column with raised rings, tapered saber legs with inlaid ebony dec, brass caps and casters, old refinishing, old restorations, black staining on underside, 13-1/2" w, 18" d, 27" h **$1,035**

Sheraton, figured birch, single board top, warped single board leaves, one

dovetailed beaded edged drawer, well turned legs, band inlay below end aprons, old finish, replaced brass pull, wear, some replaced supports, 41-3/4" w, 18-1/4" d **$700**

Game

Arts & Crafts, Miller Furniture Co., removable circular top, four plank legs inlaid with stylized floral design, paper label, felted gaming surface missing, overcoated top, 36" d, 31" h **$1,150**

Empire, tilt-top, mahogany and mahogany flame veneer, top with ogee aprons on sides, turned drops, carved pineapple column, platform base with scrolled leaf returns to carved paw feet, one drawer on side, old dark finish, 40-1/2" w, 20" d, 30" h **$450**

George III, English, cross banded mahogany, D-shaped, plain frieze, sq tapered and molded legs, c1790, 35" w, 17" d, 28" h **$1,150**

Hepplewhite, American, inlaid cherry, hinged demilune to, conforming apron, sq tapering legs, 19th C **$400**

Phyfe, Duncan, mahogany, top with band of line inlay on edge, urn pedestal, saber legs, top loose, minor veneer loss, c1820, 39" w top open, 29" h **$1,875**

Queen Anne, English, mahogany, hinged two-board top with molded edge, dovetailed drawer, shaped returns, relief carved detail at knees, well shaped cabriole legs, pad feet, rear swing legs, old dark finish, old replaced brass pulls, minor restoration, side returns missing, old splits in top, 35-1/2" w, 16" d, 28-3/4" h **$1,550**

Renaissance Revival, A. Cutler & Son, Buffalo, NY, ebonized and parcel-gilt, drop leaf, orig paper label, wear to baise surface, c1874, 36" w, 13-3/4" d, 28-3/4" h **$700**

Sheraton, mahogany, shaped top, cookie corners, shaped frieze, turned reeded legs, replaced supports under top, 36" w, 30-1/2" h **$1,225**

Victorian, mahogany, rect top, felt playing surface, frieze drawer, Wedgwood mounts, sq tapered legs, late 19th C, 25" w, 15-3/4" d, 30" h **$5,000**

William and Mary-style, with antique elements, seaweed marquetry inlaid walnut, D-shaped top with concave front, frieze similar shaped, frieze drawer, turned legs joined by stretchers, 32" w, 14" d, 30" h **$2,875**

Lamp table, Arts & Crafts, Limbert, corbels oval top, canted, cut-out sides, rectangular lower shelf with brand mark underneath, cleaned orig finish, 29" x 45" x 29-1/2", **$4,000.**
Photo courtesy of David Rago Auctions, Inc.

Library

Arts & Crafts

English, overhanging top, arched apron, legs carved with stylized tulips, unmarked, refinished, seam separation to top, minor nicks and edge roughness at feet, 46" w, 27" d, 30" h **$1,955**

Robertson Co., H. P., Jamestown, New Jersey, early 20th C, oak, oval top over single drawer, flanked by side shelves, lower median shelf, imperfections, 48" w, 29-1/4" d, 29-1/4" h **$950**

Stickley, Gustav, three drawers, hammered copper pulls, sq posts, broad lower shelf, red decal, refinished, 66" l, 36" w, 30-1/2" h **$3,775**

Stickley, L. & J. G., Fayetteville, New York, similar to model no. 520, oak, rect top, single drawer, corbel supports, low median shelf with through tenons, red and yellow decal "The Work of L. & J. G. Stickley" on int. drawer, imperfections, 42" w, 28-1/8" d, 29-1/4" h **$1,265**

Classical, attributed to Boston, carved mahogany and mahogany veneer, rect top with rounded corners, conforming skirt with two working drawers and four faux drawers, carved shaped supports with scrolled brackets and applied bosses on platforms, scrolled feet joined by medial vase and ring-turned stretcher, old refinish, minor imperfections, c1825-35, 54-1/2" w, 26-1/2" d, 29-3/4" h **$4,410**

Georgian-style, Morris and Co., mahogany, tooled red leather top and gadrooned edge, two end drawers, boldly carved cabriole legs, claw and ball feet, late 19th/early 20th C, 90" l, 53" d, 30" h **$3,450**

Chair table, New England, pine, circular top, frame with square legs and box stretchers, early 19th century, 27-1/4" x 55-1/2" w, **$935.**

Photo courtesy of Pook & Pook, Inc.

Renaissance Revival, carved oak, rect top, two frieze drawers with mask form pulls, griffin form legs, shaped plinth, third quarter 19th C, 54" w, 28" d, 30" h..............................**$3,910**

Low table, International Movement, triangular glass top with rounded corners, conforming geometric base, mid-20th C, 26-3/4" w, 19-1/4" h **$360**

Night, Louis XV/XVI style, inlaid marquetry, oval, sliding cup rest at side, fitted with three drawers, cabriole legs joined by medial shelf, inlaid all-over with flower filled vases, pitchers and table articles, price for pr, 19th C, 12" w, 9-1/2" d, 26-1/2" h **$940**

Occasional

Aesthetic Movement, American, two circular mahogany veneer tiers on stylized tree branch-form legs, 12-1/2" w, 33" h **$500**

Arts & Crafts, Gustav Stickley, circular overhanging top, faceted finial over arched cross-stretchers, very good orig finish, red decal, 24" d, 29" h..............................**$2,185**

Biedermeier, birchwood, solid gallery top, inset petit point needlework panel, plain frieze, turned legs joined by stretchers, casters, inscription underneath reading "J. J. Werner, Paris," early 19th C, 21-1/2" w, 18-1/2" d, 29-3/4" h **$2,760**

International Movement, Mies van der Rohe design, Knoll Associates, NY, circular smoked glass top, tubular metal base, 27-3/8" d, 19-1/2" h **$765**

Refectory, oak, 1-1/2" thick three-board top, two large turned and carved supports, stretcher base, shoe feet, old dark finish, late 19th or early 20th C, 71-1/2" l, 27-1/2" d, 30-1/2" h **$1,550**

Sawbuck, primitive, pine, sq nail construction, two board top, sq legs

with chamfered outer corners, old refinishing, old repairs, 48-1/2" l, 34-3/4" w, 28" h............................**$900**

Serving

Federal, New England, inlaid mahogany, band inlay around top and leaves, large satinwood oval on top, single dovetailed drawer with satinwood band inlay, bow-front top with end-blocking and serpentine sides with string-inlaid edge above conforming base, single drawer outlined in veneer banding flanked by rect dies above similar banding and string inlaid legs, brasses appear original, old refinish, imperfections, c1800, 34-1/2" w, 17" d, 32" h.........................**$16,450**

George III, Mahogany, slightly bowed top, pair of drawers, sq tapering legs, c1800 ....**$1,725**

Satinwood and marquetry, demilune, later fitted with spring action drawers, restoration, 62-1/4" w, 23-1/2" d, 32-3/4" h............**$19,550**

Sewing

Federal

Boston, mahogany veneer, mahogany top with outset corners above two veneered cockbeaded drawers, sliding bag frame, flanked by legs with colonettes above reeding, ending in turned tapering feet, old brass, old finish, c1805, 20-3/4" w, 15-3/4" d, 28-1/4" h **$1,610**

New England, mahogany veneer, mahogany top with hinged drop leaves, reeded edge, flanking three veneered drawers, top fitted for writing, bottom with sliding sewing bag frame, ring-turned and spiral carved legs, casters, old refinish, replaced brasses, 18-1/2" w, 18-1/8" d, 29-1/4" h..............**$1,150**

French-style, inlaid mahogany, hinged scalloped top finely inlaid with flowers and scrolled leaves, scalloped aprons, delicate cabriole legs with beaded edging, applied ormolu on apron, knees, and feet, shallow int. compartment, old refinish, some alterations, early 20th C, 25" w, 18-1/2" d, 30-1/2" h.................**$600**

Sheraton, mahogany, drop leaf, two drawers over one drawer, ring and spiral turned legs, brass cup and caster feet, 20-1/2" closed, 27-3/4" open, 18" d, 28-1/2" h **$1,200**

Side

Baroque, Continental, walnut, rect top, tapered frieze, scalework and

scrolling vine carved legs joined by X-form stretcher, 17th C and later, 49-1/2" w, 23-1/2" d, 31" h.......**$600**

Classical, New York, mahogany, rect marble top with rounded corners, conforming ogee molded skirt, pierced and scrolled supports, pillar and scroll bases, applied ripple molding joining scrolled medial shelf, casters, old finish, minor imperfections, 1835-45, 31" w, 18-1/2" d, 31" h....................**$3,750**

Federal, attributed to southern New England, mahogany and tiger maple veneer inlay, serpentine top with elliptic ends, conforming base, frieze drawer, inlaid tiger maple veneer panels outlined with crossbanding and stringing, four sq tapering legs with conforming inlay continuing to inlaid cuffs, restored, c1800-10, 23-1/4" w, 17" d, 28-1/4" h **$10,575**

Louis XV, beechwood, demilune, gray and white marble top, plain frieze, sq cabriole legs, third quarter 18th C, 42-1/2" w, 22" d, 27" h.............**$1,530**

Louis XV-style

Marquetry inlaid mahogany, kidney-shaped top above lower shelf, cabriole legs..**$830**

Parquetry inlaid, kidney shaped marble top, three-quarter gallery, sq tapered legs, three drawers, 18" w, 11" d, 30-1/2" h **$950**

Tulipwood, parquetry inlaid, oval marble top, three drawers, sq tapered legs, 18-1/2" w, 12" d, 30-1/2" h **$1,100**

Neoclassical, Italian, fruitwood, inlaid walnut, rect case, two drawers, sq tapered legs, inlaid with leafy vines, price for pr, c1800, 20-1/2" w, 13" d, 29-1/2" h....................**$3,525**

Regency-style, shaped top inset with needlework, turned standard, tripartite base **$250**

Renaissance Revival, American, walnut, marble top, thumb molded edge, shaped corners, four angular legs with central turned post, mounted with roundels, casters, 28-1/2" w, 20" d, 29" h.............**$750**

Rococo, Italian, walnut, serpentine top and case, foliate carved apron, two drawers, cabriole legs, 19th C, 36" w, 18" d, 34" h.................**$1,765**

Rococo-style, cross banded fruitwood, serpentine top and case, three drawers, 19th C, 13" w, 10-1/2" d, 29" h........................**$450**

Victorian

Bamboo, octagonal lacquer top over four drop leaves, four legs joined by stretcher with medial shelf, 22" w, 22" d, 28" h **$600**

Mahogany, sq top, frieze with applied branch form carvings, branch form legs, 27" w, 25-3/4" d, 29-3/4" h **$250**

Silver, George III, carved mahogany, galleried tray top, low relief carved everted lip, repeating border of C-scrolls and foliage, swirling scroll bordered apron, molded sq cabriole supports with trailing acanthus carving at knees, Spanish feet, alternations to top, repairs, c1765, 31-3/4" l, 28-3/4" h **$2,000**

Sofa

Edwardian, painted satinwood, rounded drop leaves, two frieze drawers, trestle supports ending in brass paw casters, c1895, 36" w closed, 26-1/2" d, 28-1/2" h **$8,100**

Regency, cross banded mahogany, wide rect top, drop leaves with canted corners, frieze drawers to both sides, turned trestle bases, inlaid with boxwood and ebony, c1820, 52" w, 36" d, 28-1/2" h **$3,525**

Tavern

Country, Pennsylvania, softwood, circular top, stretcher base, beaded skirt, legs with old orange painted surface, most orig wrought brass and iron tacks, many with remnants of probably orig muslin-like fabric underneath tack head, 28" d, 25-1/2" h **$4,950**

Moravian, Pennsylvania, walnut, pegged construction, pin top, three board thumb molded top, dovetailed drawer, boldly turned legs, horizontal stretchers, turned feet, restoration to feet, 18th C, 61" w, 34" d, 30" h **$6,050**

Tea

Art Deco, France, walnut, rect top opens and swivels on U-shaped base, c1928, 44" l open, 22" closed, 35-1/4" w, 28-1/4" h **$1,880**

Chippendale

America, possibly Philadelphia, piecrust tilt top, figured mahogany one-piece circular top, ogee and crescent form carving, birdcage support, fluted column, compressed ball knop, three legs with plain knees, ball and claw feet, 28-1/2" h **$10,575**

Connecticut, cherry, round top tilts and revolves above birdcage mechanism, tapering shaft with suppressed ball and ring turnings, tripod cabriole leg base, pad feet, refinished, imperfections, late 18th C, 36-1/2" d, 28-3/4" h **$3,100**

Country, mahogany, two board dish top and key old replacements, urn shaped column with birdcage, cabriole legs, padded snake feet, old refinishing, shims added, 29-1/4" d, 26-3/4" h **$850**

Chippendale-style, America, mahogany, round tilt-top, well turned column, cabriole legs, snake feet, orig dark finish, minor edge wear, block needs stabilization, 32" d top, 27-1/2" h **$500**

George III, mahogany, circular tilt top, ring turned standard, tripod legs, pad feet, 32-1/4" d, 28-1/2" h **$1,100**

Hepplewhite, tilt top, poplar one board top with cut corners, birch tripod base with spider legs, turned column, old refinishing with painted foliage border designs in shades of gold and black, top replaced, repairs, 15-1/2" w, 23-1/2" l, 28-3/4" h **$440**

Queen Anne

Massachusetts, maple, oval overhanging drop-leaf top, cabriole legs, pad feet on platforms joined by cutout apron, old refinish, repairs, 1740-60, 31" w, 32-1/2" d, 27" h ... **$30,550**

New England, cherry, circular tilt top, vase and ring-turned post and tripod cabriole leg base, pad feet, refinished, minor imperfections, c1760-80, 34-1/4" d, 27-1/2" h **$1,175**

Victorian, papier-mâché, gilt and mother-of-pearl inlaid, shaped round tilt top, dec with urn of flowers, turned standard, tripartite base, 22" w, 22" d, 29" h **$885**

Tilt-Top

Federal, New England, mahogany inlaid, octagonal top with string inlay in outline, urn shaped pedestal, cabriole legs, arris pad feet on platforms, orig surface, very minor imperfections, 22" w, 14-3/4" d, 29-1/2" h **$3,750**

Georgian, mahogany, plain circular top over turned baluster standard, three cabriole legs ending in shaped pad feet, late 18th C, 32" d, 27-3/8" h **$1,100**

Tray, Edwardian, satinwood and inlay, two oval tiers, removable wood and

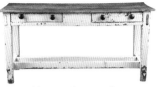

Farm table, French, painted pine, rectangular plank top, two frieze drawers, square tapering legs, double rail, early 19th century, 28-1/2" x 24" x 60-1/4", **$825.**
Photo courtesy of Sloan's & Kenyon Auctioneers and Appraisers.

glass tray, slightly splayed sq tapering legs joined by stretcher, c1900, 36" w, 20-1/4" d, 32" h **$1,150**

Trestle

Country, Pennsylvania, removable sliding scrubbed top, shaped cut-out legs, mortise and tenon stretcher, old green painted surface, 66" l, 16" d, 28-1/2" h **$3,575**

William IV, parquetry inlaid specimen wood, rect top, pendant applied frieze, trestle with turned ends and stretcher, cabriole legs, c1835, 33-1/4" w, 17-1/2" d, 29-1/2" h **$2,000**

Tripod

George III-style, mahogany, tilt-top, piecrust edge, acanthus carved stem and tripod base, slipper feet, 22-1/2" d, 28" h **$825**

Georgian-style, mahogany, silver plated mounts, serpentine reticulated gallery, turned stem, cabriole legs, price for pr, 20th C, 15" d, 22" h **$450**

Work

Biedermeier, walnut and mahogany, rect top with line inlay around center panel, dovetailed drawer with divided interior, beaded aprons, exaggerated serpentine legs, central stretcher, stamped signature "A. Gastaldi" on back of drawer, old refinishing, restorations, 24-1/2" w, 16-3/4" d, 31-1/4" h **$665**

Classical, Boston, mahogany veneer, solid top, hinged rounded drop leaves with beaded edges, flank two convex veneered drawers, top one fitted for writing, lower with replaced fabric sewing fabric bag, turned tapering legs which flank shaped veneered platform, ebonized bun feet, orig stamped brass pulls, imperfections, minor warp in leaf, 1830, 19" w, 19" d, 28-3/4" h **$980**

Federal

Massachusetts, early mahogany veneer, sq top with molded edge, hinged leaves flank two working drawers and bag frame, spiral carved legs, turned feet, casters, original brass, old refinish, 19th C, 18-1/4" w, 17-1/4" d, 29-7/8" h **$1,645**

New England, butternut, birch, and bird's eye maple, overhanging rect top, two drawers, straight skirt, vase and ring-turned legs, old brass pulls, refinished, minor imperfections, c1825, 20" w, 18-3/4" d, 29" h **$1,175**

Federal, late, New York State, tiger maple, shaped hinged top lifts above two drawer facade, upper faux one, lower working one with divided interior, turned pedestal, four incurvate legs ending in tiny ball feet, brasses replaced, refinished, c1820, 22-1/2" w, 15-7/8" d, 32" h **$2,820**

George III, mahogany, rect top, canted corners, fitted int., sq tapered and slightly splayed legs joined by stretchers, early 19th C **$2,380**

Oak trunk, English, rectangular top with three recessed panels, mortise and tenon joints, blind fretwork frieze, fluted pilasters, post feet, late 17th/early 18th century, 27-1/4" x 48-1/2" x 20-3/4", **$500.**
Photo courtesy of Sloan's & Kenyon Auctioneers and Appraisers.

Marriage trunk, Continental, walnut marquetry-inlaid, domed, inlaid oval medallion, butterflies and flowers, early 19th century, later bun feet, 28" x 52-1/2" x 26", **$2,950.**
Photo courtesy of Sloan's & Kenyon Auctioneers and Appraisers.

Trunk, flat top, French Provincial, walnut, rect plank top, pierced cartouche escutcheon plate with fitted hinged latch, 17th/18th century, 21-1/2" x 36-3/4" x 15-1/2", **$800.**
Photo courtesy of Sloans & Kenyon Auctioneers and Appraisers.

Trunks

History: Trunks are portable containers that clasp shut and are used for the storage or transportation of personal possessions. Normally "trunk" means the ribbed flat- or domed-top models of the second half of the 19th century.

Early trunks frequently were painted, stenciled, grained, or covered with wallpaper. These are collected for their folk-art qualities and, as such, demand high prices.

Dome top

Arched top with "L G" in scripted yellow paint, nail construction box, all grain painted to simulate mahogany, and outlined in yellow striping with yellow floral device centered under the lock, imperfections and repairs, New England, early 19th C, 28-1/4" l, 13-3/4" w, 13-1/2" h **$235**

Black japanned brass mounts, gilt Chinoisiere dec of figures in garden landscape, side handles, restoration, late 18th/early 19th C, 33-1/4" w, 16-1/4" d, 18-3/4" h **$750**

Fabric on wood, worn painted dec in ivory and green, red border designs and flowers, interior lined with green marbleized paper, worn, 19" l **$425**

Hinged top, dovetailed box, white painted vine, floral and leaf dec over black painted ground, int. papered with early 19th C Boston area broadsides, attributed to Massachusetts, some later paint, 19th C, 44-1/2" w, 22-3/4" d, 19-1/2" h **$1,035**

Paper-covered box green and red sponge dec, blue line and dot patterned paper-lined int., brass ring and iron latch, America, wear, 19th C, 6" l, 3-1/2" w, 2-5/8" h **$265**

Paint dec, black painted ground, central vined pinwheel bordered

Painted early wooden trunk with iron banding, decorated with flowers and scrolls, with painted names and dates "JTD – 1801" and "Johanes Larssen Roorvig 1853," 39" l, 18" d, 17" h, **$350.**
Photo courtesy of Joy Luke Auctions.

by meandering floral and arched vines, front with tassel and drape border, central MA, early 19th C, 11-1/2" h, 28" w, 14" d **$1,035**

Dovetailed, old dark brown finish, finely painted panels with Chinoiserie vases and planters of flowers in red, tan, and green on front and sides, wrought iron handles on ends, large brass hasp and moon escutcheon on front, 41-3/4" w, 24-3/4" h, 27-1/2" h **$320**

Flat top

Chinese, pigskin, red, painted Oriental maidens and landscapes within quatrefoils, brass loop handles and lock, 19th C, 14" x 8" **$125**

Copper and iron, Arts & Crafts strapwork and pyramidal tack mounts, black paint, hinged slant lid revealing rect box, 30-1/2" w, 16-1/2" d, 17-1/2" h **$200**

Poplar, old black paint, tacks border sides, top, lock, and handles, initials "P.L." on top, leather straps beneath tacks, worn cloth lining, age splits, 24" w, 14" d, 11" h **$150**

Tooled leather on pine, iron straps, brass buttons and lock, lined with worn newspaper dated 1871, hinged replaced, some edge damage, 15-1/4" l **$385**

Military, brass bound camphor wood, hinged rect top, storage well, brass bail handles, English, second half 19th C, 21-3/4" w, 17" d, 12-1/2" h **$200**

Vuitton, Louis

Fitted int., orig label, imp marks, early 20th C **$1,880**

Wardrobe, rect, wooden strapping, leather handles on ends, brass corners and clasps, int. with hanger bars, eight Vuitton hangers, early 20th C, 21-1/2" d, 15-1/2" d, 40-1/2" h **$1,100**

Glass

STATE OF THE EARLY AMERICAN GLASS MARKET

by Jeffrey S. Evans,
President of Green Valley Auctions, Inc.

The Early American glass market, which includes free-blown, molded, and pressed glass from the fourth quarter of the 18th century to the end of the 19th century, continues its slow but steady recovery from the doldrums of the 1990s. While it will probably never return to the pinnacle it achieved in the first half of the 20th century, select categories as well as top rarities in most categories have proven to be reasonable investments. If you are collecting with an eye towards investment it is essential that you learn what is truly rare and unquestionably American. Condition is also an extremely important factor in the glass world, probably more so than in any other category of collecting. Pieces in the best possible condition will always increase in value faster than pieces with damage. While it is perfectly accept-able to purchase great rarities with damage, make sure that you pay accordingly.

EARLY PRESSED GLASS

The market for early pressed glass from the 1828 to 1865 period has experienced new highs and lows over the past year. One contributing factor was the unusually large number of old collections that came to the market. In general, colored examples are bringing two to five times the prices that they achieved thirty years ago; while colorless examples (with the exception of the great rarities) are difficult to sell at half of their 1970s and 80s prices. The hottest categories continue to be colored vases and candlesticks. Lacy period (1828-1845) master salts are still in high demand with extremely rare specimens bringing record prices. An opaque violet blue Lyre salt retaining its original cover (one of only six recorded complete examples in this color) recently sold through our galleries for $34,000, tripling the previous record price for a lacy salt. The cup plate market seems to be maintaining its revival although most new collectors are entering at the lower strata; however, this should transfer to the middle and upper market in the future. Demand for children's toys from this period is closely following the trend of cup plates with colorless examples selling for a fraction of their 1980s prices while extremely rare colored examples would now be considered real bargains at their 1980s levels.

EARLY AMERICAN PATTERN GLASS

Demand for EAPG from the flint period (1850-1870) has remained steady with the most sought after patterns being Bellflower, Early Thumbprint, and Diamond Thumbprint. Goblets, tumblers, milk and water pitchers, and handled whisky tumblers or lemonades, are the most collected forms. Of course colored pieces from this period are rare and consistently bring premium prices.

EAPG from the non-flint or soda lime period (1870-1910) has been somewhat less predictable recently. Prices for rarities in most of the animal and historical patterns have remained steady and even climbed for extremely rare specimens. Patterns seeing the most demand include Three Face, U.S. Coin, Log Cabin, and Jumbo. There has been a notable resurgence in the popularity of glass produced at the Indiana Tumbler & Goblet Co. in Greentown, IN which can be attributed to the recent publication of several excellent Greentown specific reference volumes. A recent auction record was set when a possibly unique Greentown Rose Agate Holly spooner sold for $25,000. Non-souvenir ruby stained EAPG continues to be in high demand despite a fairly consistent supply that has been coming to the market.

Vaseline is still the most collected EAPG color followed by blue and then green; most anything in amber remains very hard to sell. Goblets are still the most widely collected form from this

Pressed salt, CD-4 covered Lyre, opaque soft violet blue, mottling, four scrolled feet, variant cover, pine cone finial, rim interior beads, shallow chip, minor flaking, Boston & Sandwich, 1835-1845, 3" h, sold at auction for **$34,000.**
Photo courtesy of Green Valley Auctions.

period with rare examples maintaining fairly steady prices. The past several years saw a surge of popularity and demand for cake stands or salvers, due largely to exposure from Martha Stewart. This demand has now begun to decrease and prices are seeing a slight decline, especially for rather generic patterns.

FREE-BLOWN AND BLOWN-MOLDED GLASS

The market for free-blown glass from the late 18th to the mid 19th centuries continues to evolve and attract many younger collectors. Due to the lack of glasshouse catalogs and original source reference material for this type of ware, many attributions have changed since the pioneering reference volumes were published in the 1930s and 1940s. The largest majority of the glass which was originally credited to the late 18th century American glasshouses of Amelung and Stiegel is now generally accepted as being produced in Central Europe. Because of this, specimens that can be firmly attributed to either house are now extremely rare and will bring exorbitant prices; the remaining loosely or reattributed examples remain at prices equal to or even below what they drew 50 years ago.

The market for New England and New York blown glass from the first half of the 19th century is extremely active with strongly attributed examples easily reaching into the five-figure price range. Mid-Western blown and pattern-molded glass also continues to draw tremendous interest, but here again it is very important to distinguish the American products from their similar European counterparts; price differences between the two can be ten fold.

Interest in New England blown-molded wares from the first half of the 19th century has remained steady; prices for rare colored examples remain on a constant upswing, while the more common colorless specimens haven't seen

any appreciable increase in the recent past.

Bottles, flasks, and fruit jars from the 19th century continue to attract serious interest from collectors and dealers, young and old alike. Historical and figured flasks in rare colors are in high demand, as are rare bitters bottles. Surprisingly, more common material has proven to be particularly sellable, at reasonable prices, primarily due to the entrance of Civil War reenactors into the market. Interest in 19th century fruit jars continues to escalate with rare colored examples and early jars complete with their original closures bringing record prices.

LIGHTING

The market for lighting from the whale oil, fluid, and kerosene periods has been somewhat soft except for very rare specimens. Colorless stand lamps from any period are slow to sell, but the demand for hand and finger lamps seems to be holding steady. Colored whale oil, fluid, and early kerosene lamps are bringing strong prices—examples complete with original burners will bring a premium. Cut overlay lamps are still drawing strong interest, especially the large banquet sizes and examples with strong gilt decoration. Prices for Victorian opalescent lamps have leveled off, and to some extent fallen off, from the highs of the past several years. Interest in Victorian miniature lamps remains strong with steady to slightly higher price levels. The recent interest in early burners and chimneys continues to increase and evolve—extremely rare burners have recently sold for over $2,000. This often overlooked category should provide many exciting discoveries in the years to come.

VICTORIAN OPALESCENT GLASS

While colored opalescent glass from the late 19th and early 20th centuries does not technically fall within the Early American Glass category, it does represent an ex-

*Tulip vase, deep violet blue, white striations, octagonal base, wafer construction, Boston & Sandwich Glass Co., 1845-1865, 10-1/4" h, 5-5/8" d rim, sold at auction for **$22,000**.*
Photo courtesy of Green Valley Auctions.

tremely hot market. Cranberry continues to be the king of all colors with some extremely rare water pitchers approaching $10,000. Other popular colors include vaseline and blue. The most widely collected Victorian forms continue to be sugar shakers, syrup jugs, and toothpick holders, but tumblers have seen a strong resurgence over the last two years.

In general Early American glass continues to be a specialized and fickle market. That said, it remains one of the last categories of antiques where great discoveries are still made on a regular basis. The past year has seen a deep violet blue with white striations Sandwich Tulip vase surface at a thrift store for $15 and sell for $22,000; an extremely rare cup plate, which was part of a $25 PA auction tray lot, fetch $6,600; and a Bank of Philadelphia cut tumbler, originally part of a $100 table lot at a big city auction house, nearly break the $10,000 mark. These examples, which may be viewed on our Web site at www.greenvalleyauctions.com, demonstrate that the high end of the market is healthy and thriving. However, the middle and lower stratas continue at the same or even lower levels than years past—a common trend in most all categories of antiques today.

RESOURCES
Magazines

Antique Trader®, published by Krause Publications, Iola, WI.

Books

Antique Trader® Bottles Identificaton & Price Guide, by Michael Polak, Krause Publications, Iola, WI.

Art Glass Identification & Price Guide, by John A. Shuman, III, Krause Publications, Iola, WI.

Carnival Glass A Warman´s® Companion, by Ellen T. Schroy, Krause Publications, Iola, WI.

Collecting Swarovski, by Dean A. Genth, Krause Publications, Iola, WI.

Early American Pattern Glass, 2nd Ed., by Darryl Reilly & Bill Jenks, Krause Publications, Iola, WI.

Fenton Glass A Warman´s® Companion, by Mark F. Moran, Krause Publications, Iola, WI.

Glass A to Z, by David J. Shotwell, Krause Publications, Iola, WI.

Heisey Glass The Early Years 1896-1924, by Shirley Dunbar, Krause Publications, Iola, WI.

Warman´s® Bottles Field Guide, by Michael Polak, Krause Publications, Iola, WI.

Warman´s® Carnival Glass, by Ellen T. Schroy, Krause Publications, Iola, WI.

Warman´s® Depression Glass, 4th Ed., by Ellen T. Schroy, Krause Publications, Iola, WI.

Warman´s® Depression Glass Field Guide, 2nd Ed., by Ellen T. Schroy, Krause Publications, Iola, WI.

Warman´s® Fenton Glass, by Mark F. Moran, Krause Publications, Iola, WI.

Warman´s® Glass, 4th Ed., by Ellen T. Schroy, Krause Publications, Iola, WI.

Warman´s® Lalique, by Mark F. Moran, Krause Publications, Iola, WI.

Warman´s® Pattern Glass, 2nd Ed., by Ellen T. Schroy, Krause Publications, Iola, WI.

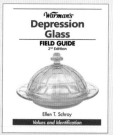
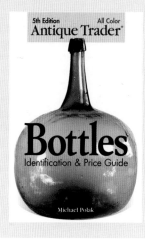

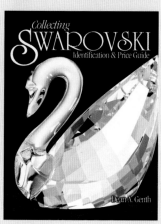

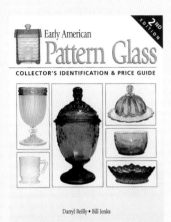

Early American Pattern Glass
COLLECTOR'S IDENTIFICATION & PRICE GUIDE
2ND EDITION
Darryl Reilly • Bill Jenks

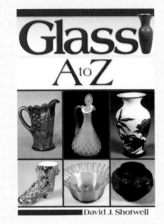

Glass A to Z
David J. Shotwell

Heisey Glass
The Early Years: 1896-1924
• Comprehensive price and identification guide
• Illustrations and descriptions of more than 50 patterns, marked and unmarked
• Color photos of more than 200 pieces
Shirley Dunbar

Warman's Carnival Glass
Ellen T. Schroy
Identification and Price Guide

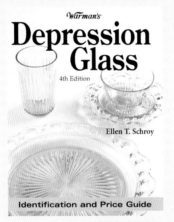

Warman's Depression Glass
4th Edition
Ellen T. Schroy
Identification and Price Guide

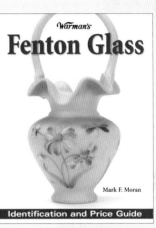

Warman's Fenton Glass
Mark F. Moran
Identification and Price Guide

Warman's GLASS
A Value & Identification Guide
4TH EDITION
A Fully Illustrated Price Guide to More Than 200 Types of American and European Glass, from ABC to Zanesville, with Histories, References, Clubs and Museums
Edited by Ellen T. Schroy

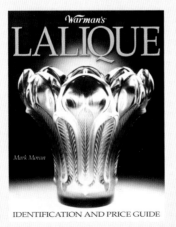

Warman's LALIQUE
Mark Moran
IDENTIFICATION AND PRICE GUIDE

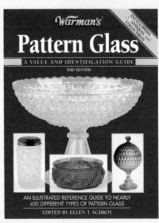

Warman's Pattern Glass
A VALUE AND IDENTIFICATION GUIDE
2ND EDITION
AN ILLUSTRATED REFERENCE GUIDE TO NEARLY 450 DIFFERENT TYPES OF PATTERN GLASS
EDITED BY ELLEN T. SCHROY

GALLERY

Window pane, Diamond Scrolls and Fans, colorless, band of prisms around outer edge, unpatterned side beveled at edges, minor edge flaking, Boston & Sandwich Glass Co., 1835-1850, 8" x 10", sold at auction for $4,180.
Photo courtesy of Green Valley Auctions.

Sugar bowl with cover, deep semi-translucent milky blue, bowl has eight vertical ribs, galleried rim, heavy domed foot, rough pontil mark, cover has ten ribs, folded rim, button finial, rough pontil mark, first half 19th century, 6-3/4" h, sold at auction for $6,050.
Photo courtesy of Green Valley Auctions.

Cologne, blown-molded heart, cobalt blue, from Heart kerosene lamp font mold, orig factory polished flat-top pressed stopper, polished pontil mark, Boston & Sandwich Glass Co., 1840-1886, 6-3/4" h overall, 5-5/8" h bottle, sold at auction for $3,850.
Photo courtesy of Green Valley Auctions.

Stand lamp, Circle and Ellipse, whale oil/fluid period, emerald green, pressed hexagonal base, wafer construction, period fine line collar, double tube fluid burner with caps and chain, New England, reworked collar, 1840-1860, 8-5/8" h, 45-5/8" d base, sold at auction for $4,290.
Photo courtesy of Green Valley Auctions.

Coinspot water pitcher, Ribbon-Tie mould, cranberry opalescent, crimped rim, eight panels below waist ring, applied colorless handle, V-shape exfoliation fracture to body at upper handle juncture, probably Dugan Glass Co., 12-1/4" h, sold at auction for $9,350.
Photo courtesy of Green Valley Auctions.

Covered nappie on standard, hexagonal, brilliant cobalt blue, eight scallop rim, standard with eight rib stem, three step base, extended round corners, rough pontil mark on stem int, wafer construction, several chips, probably Pittsburgh, 1840-1860, 7-1/2" overall, 5-1/2" h base, 3-1/2" h cover, sold at auction for $11,000.
Photo courtesy of Green Valley Auctions.

Plate, Lee/Rose No. 2287-B, deep green, nine pairs large scallops, four smaller between, some scallop loss, slight rim flaking, probably Union Glass Works, Philadelphia area, 3-7/16" d, sold at auction for **$6,600.**
Photo courtesy of Green Valley Auctions.

Tumbler/spill holder, pressed and cut, Philadelphia view, cylindrical form, colorless, "BANK OF PENNSYLVANIA/ PHILADELPHIA," plain panel, cross hatched frame, reverse three diamond point swags above nine wide pillar ribs, base has 24 cut rays, sold at auction for **$9,625.**
Photo courtesy of Green Valley Auctions.

Pair of Loop (Leaf) stand lamps, whale oil/fluid period, amber, pressed square base, wafer construction, period pewter collars, one period and one late whale oil burner, minor chips and flakes, collar dent, 1840-1860, 9-3/4" h, 3" sq base, sold at auction for **$15,950.**
Photo courtesy of Green Valley Auctions.

Portrait flask, GI-94 Franklin/Dyott, pint, black olive amber, embossed "BENJAMIN FRANKLIN" on obverse, "T.W. DYOTT, M.D." on reverse, "WHERE LIBERTY DWELLS THERE IS MY COUNTRY" and "KENSINGTON GLASS WORKS PHILADELPHIA" on edges, sheared lip, rough pontil mark, second to third quarter 19th century, 6-3/4" h, sold at auction for **$8,250.**
Photo courtesy of Green Valley Auctions.

Cruet, pattern molded, brilliant amethyst, globular body, long tapering neck, sixteen vertical ribs, applied hollow handle, hollow unpatterned stopper, kick-up base, rough pontil mark, Pittsburgh, possibly Bakewell, Page & Bakewells, 1830-1860, 8-1/4" h overall, 7-1/4" h to lip, proof **$9,900.**
Photo courtesy of Green Valley Auctions.

Blown ball font on pressed lion head and basket of flowers base, stand lamp, whale oil/fluid period, opaque to white opalescent, wafer construction, inverted conical stem, #1 fine line collar, double tube fluid burner with caps and chain, normal corner chipping, New England, 1830-1845, 13-7/8" h, 3-5/8" d base, sold at auction for **$6,600.**
Photo courtesy of Green Valley Auctions.

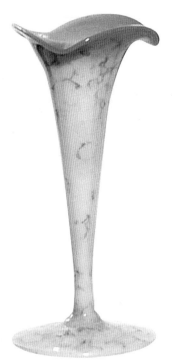

Agata vase, New England, footed lily form, tri-fold rim, 6" h, **$475.**
Photo courtesy of The Early Auction Company, LLC.

AGATA GLASS

History: Agata glass was invented in 1887 by Joseph Locke of the New England Glass Company, Cambridge, Massachusetts.

Agata glass was produced by coating a piece of peachblow glass with metallic stain, spattering the surface with alcohol, and firing. The resulting high-gloss, mottled finish looked like oil droplets floating on a watery surface. Shading usually ranged from opaque pink to dark rose, although pieces in a pastel opaque green also exist. A few pieces have been found in a satin finish.

Bowl

Crimped rim, Wild Rose shading, strong mineral staining, ex-Maude Feld, 8-1/4" d, 3-1/8" h **$2,250**

Waisted, crimped trefoil rim, overall mineral staining, ex-Maude Feld, 5-1/2" d, 3-1/2" h **$750**

Celery vase, satin, very heavy staining, 6-1/4" h **$8,960**

Cruet, flat bottom, 5-3/4" h **$5,320**

Tankard pitcher, tapering cylindrical body, Wild Rose with strong all over mineral staining, ex-Maude Feld, 8-1/2" h....................................**$5,000**

Toothpick holder, tricorn, gold metallic tracery and mottling **$645**

Tumbler, gold tracery, peachblow ground, black splotches, 3-3/4" h ..**$635**

Vase

Bowl shape, mottled blue mineral stain on matte ground, ex-Maude Feld, 5" h **$10,000**

Lily, Wild Rose shading, mineral staining, 7" h............................**$700**

Lily, shades from salmon pink to cream, ex-Maude Feld, 7-1/4" h..........**$1,200**

Morgan, Wild Rose color, overall mineral staining, orig amber griffin holder, orig Maude Feld label, ex-Maude Feld, 10-1/4" h **$5,250**

Water pitcher, amethyst staining framed with perfect gold, 5" crack to body, 7" h **$200**

AMBERINA GLASS

History: Joseph Locke developed Amberina glass in 1883 for the New England Glass Works. "Amberina," a trade name, describes a transparent glass that shades from deep ruby to amber. It was made by adding powdered gold to the ingredients for an amber-glass batch. A portion of the glass was reheated later to produce the shading effect. Usually it was the bottom that was reheated to form the deep red; however, reverse examples have been found.

Most early Amberina is flint-quality glass, blown or pattern molded. Patterns include Diamond Quilted, Daisy and Button, Venetian Diamond, Diamond and Star, and Thumbprint.

In addition to the New England Glass Works, the Mount Washington Glass Company of New Bedford, Massachusetts, copied the glass in the 1880s and sold it at first under the Amberina trade name and later as "Rose Amber." It is difficult to distinguish pieces from these two New England factories. Boston and Sandwich Glass Works never produced the glass.

Amberina glass also was made in the 1890s by several Midwest factories, among which was Hobbs, Brockunier & Co. Trade names included "Ruby Amber Ware" and "Watermelon." The Midwest glass shaded from cranberry to amber, and the color resulted from the application of a thin flashing of cranberry to the reheated portion. This created a sharp demarcation between the two colors. This less-expensive version was the death knell for the New England variety.

In 1884, Edward D. Libbey was given the use of the trade name "Amberina" by the New England Glass Works. Production took place during 1900, but ceased shortly thereafter. In the 1920s, Edward Libbey renewed production at his Toledo, Ohio, plant for a short period. The glass was of high quality.

Marks: Amberina made by Edward Libbey in the 1920s is marked "Libbey" in script on the pontil.

Additional Listings: Libbey, Mount Washington.

Reproduction Alert. Reproductions abound.

Basket, wide flared rim, enameled and gilt dec florals, polished pontil, mounted with finely sculpted gilt bronze dragon form handle, Victorian, 10-1/2" l **$690**

Biscuit jar, Diamond Quilted pattern, polished pontil, lid missing, 5" h **$50**

Bonbon, double reeded handles, 6-1/2" d..**$90**

Amberina toothpick, square mouth, diamond quilted pattern, 2-1/4" h, **$250.**
Photo courtesy of The Early Auction Company, LLC.

Amberina water pitcher, Reverse Dot Optic, lobed form, applied reed handle, polished pontil mark, late 19th/early 20th century, 8" h, **$165.**
Photo courtesy of Green Valley Auctions.

Amberina basket, New England Glass Works, shading with optical ribs and ornate fold rim, amber handle applied, 6-1/4" h, **$2,250.**
Photo courtesy of The Early Auction Company, LLC.

Bottle, Coin Spot pattern, attributed to Libbey, 8" h **$375**

Bowl
Crimson shading to amber, Diamond Quilted pattern, applied amber peaked overlay extends mid-length, orig Libbey paper label, ex-Maude, 5-1/8" h **$2,100**
Tricorn, amber base, Mt. Washington, 5" l sides, 2" h **$235**

Celery vase, cylindrical, tightly crimped thumbprint pattern, 6-1/2" h.. **$575**

Compote, catalog #3017, Libbey acid stamp mark, partial paper label, ex-Maud Feld, 7-1/4" d, 8-3/8" h ..**$4,000**

Creamer, Thumbprint pattern, polished pontil, Victorian, 4-1/2" h .. **$85**

Cruet
Inverted Thumbprint pattern, fuchsia trefoil spout, neck, and shoulder, Mt. Washington, 5-1/2" h **$435**
Inverted Thumbprint pattern, gilt dec, replaced stopper, wear to gilt, 6" h **$90**
Thumbprint pattern, replaced stopper, Victorian, 6" h **$95**

Decanter, Optic Diamond Quilted pattern, solid amber faceted stopper, 12" h.. **$475**

Demitasse cup, 16 optic panels, applied reeded handle, 2-1/8" h ..**$185**

Finger bowl, crimped ruffled rim, 5-1/2" d.. **$200**

Juice glass, Coin Spot pattern, 3-3/4" h **$75**

Lemonade, ribbed, applied amber ring handle, price for set of three, 5" h... **$425**

Miniature pitcher, crimson sq mouth extends to amber bulbous body, Inverted Coin Dot pattern, applied reeded handle, 3" h **$400**

Mug, 3-7/8" h.............................. **$1,000**

Nappy, handle, enameled dec, polished pontil, Victorian, 6" l........ **$140**

Punch cup
Coin Spot pattern, reverse Amberina, 2-3/4" h **$50**
Optic Diamond Quilted pattern, fuchsia to amber body with 20 panels, applied ribbed handle, New England, 2-1/2" d **$185**
Optic Ribbed pattern, applied reeded handle, 3-1/2" h **$100**

Shot glass, faint Diamond Quilted pattern, attributed to Brayden Pairpoint, 2-1/4" h............................. **$110**

Spooner, Diamond Quilted pattern, crimped scalloped rim, 4-3/4" h **$250**

Sugar, ovoid, Coin Spot pattern, two applied reeded handles, 4-1/4" h **$450**

Sweetmeat, Baby Thumbprint pattern, applied colorless florals, feet, and rim, polished pontil, 6" d.... **$320**

Syrup pitcher, Hobnail pattern, orig pewter top std "Pat. Jan 29 84," Hobbs, Brockunier & Co., three hobs chipped... **$300**

Tankard pitcher, New England, Optic Diamond Quilt pattern, 4-1/4" h..**$685**

Toothpick holder, sq mouth, 2-1/4" h.. **$250**

Tumbler
Coin Spot pattern, ground rim, 3-3/4" h **$125**
Coin Spot pattern, barrel shape, 4" h **$165**

Amberina glass and metal oil lamp, ovoid ruffled rim shade, two-handled pierced metal base stamped patent Aug 4, 1896, burner mkd Royal Pat. Apr 11, 93, 23" h, **$1,000.**
Photo courtesy of The Early Auction Company, LLC.

Vase

Swirled mold, enameled flowers, gilt scrolling, polished pontil, French, c1890, 8-1/4" h..........................**$150**

Swirl pattern, applied amber rigaree around crown-form top, applied amber petal feet, polished pontil, Victorian, 8" h **$150**

Tri-fold lily blossom, 6-3/4" h ...**$250**

Tri-fold lily blossom, 16 optic ribs, deep fuchsia and honey amber, attributed to Mt. Washington, 9-1/4" h, 4-1/4" w **$485**

Water pitcher

Bulbous, tricorn mouth shades to amber Coin Spot patterned body, applied reeded amber handle, 8-1/4" h **$295**

Coin Spot pattern, ftd, applied colorless reeded handle, 7" h **$225**

Optic Ribbed pattern, applied amber reeded handle, 8" h **$165**

Ovoid, sq mouth, Thumbprint pattern, faint optic ribbing at rim, applied reeded handle, 5-1/2" h **$175**

Wine, Optic Ribbed pattern, 4-3/4" h **$300**

AMBERINA GLASS, PLATED

History: The New England Glass Company, Cambridge, Massachusetts, first made plated Amberina in 1886; Edward Libbey patented the process for the company in 1889.

Plated Amberina was made by taking a gather of chartreuse or cream opalescent glass, dipping it in Amberina, and working the two, often utilizing a mold. The finished product had a deep amber to deep ruby red shading, a fiery opalescent lining, and often vertical ribbing for enhancement. Designs ranged from simple forms to complex pieces with collars, feet, gilding and etching.

A cased Wheeling glass of similar appearance had an opaque white lining, but is not opalescent and does not have a ribbed body.

Plated Amberina bowl, fuchsia shading to cream, amber ribbing, 5" d x 2-1/2" h, **$3,000.**
Photo courtesy of The Early Auction Company, LLC.

Cruet, high color, cut amber faceted stopper, applied amber handle, ex-Maud Feld, 7" h........................**$9,000**

Finger bowl, ruffled, tightly crimped rim with 12 distinct ribs, 5-1/2" d **$5,750**

Lemonade, applied amber handle, 5" h..**$3,500**

Pitcher, very rare, one of three known, ex-Maude Feld, 8" h **$37,520**

Toothpick holder, 2-1/4" h ...**$15,680**

Tumbler, thin layered bottom with rare citron hue, ex-Maude Feld, 3-3/4" h......................................**$1,600**

Vase

Lily, 8" h **$4,480**

Lily, deep crimson shading to custard yellow, clear amber raised disc base, orig Maude B. Feld label, 9-5/8" h **$6,000**

Water carafe, bulbous body, circular neck, 12 protruding amber ribs, orig New England Glass Works paper label, ex-Maude Feld, 8-1/2" h........**$42,000**

Water pitcher, bulbous, deep mahogany extending to cream on lower body, 12 well-defined protruding ribs, trefoil spout, applied amber handle, ex-Maude Feld, 7-1/2" h.........**$14,000**

Plated Amberina tankard pitcher, New England, cylindrical, glossy ribbed finish, amber to fuchsia, deep amber handle with rose hues, orig oval Amberina paper label, 8-1/2" h, **$28,000.**
Photo courtesy of The Early Auction Company, LLC.

Plated Amberina lemonade, cylindrical, glossy ribbed finish, amber to fuchsia, applied amber handle, 5" h, **$3,500.**
Photo courtesy of The Early Auction Company, LLC.

Plated Amberina celery vase, New England, cylindrical, glossy ribbed body, amber to fuchsia, 6-1/8" h , **$7,000.**
Photo courtesy of The Early Auction Company, LLC.

BACCARAT GLASS

History: The Sainte-Anne glassworks at Baccarat in Voges, France, was founded in 1764 and produced utilitarian soda glass. In 1816, Aime-Gabriel d'Artiques purchased the glassworks, and a Royal Warrant was issued in 1817 for the opening of Verrerie de Vonâoche éa Baccarat. The firm concentrated on lead-crystal glass products. In 1824, a limited company was created.

From 1823 to 1857, Baccarat and Saint-Louis glassworks had a commercial agreement and used the same outlets. No merger occurred. Baccarat began the production of paperweights in 1846. In the late 19th century the firm achieved an international reputation for cut glass table services, chandeliers, display vases, centerpieces, and sculptures. Products eventually included all forms of glassware.

Additional Listings: Paperweights.

Bonbon, amberina, swirled mold, pedestal foot, emb "Baccarat," 5-3/4" d **$150**

Candelabra, pr, crystal, four light, diamond-cut baluster standard, four scrolling candle arms terminating urn-form sockets, etched glass globes hung with prisms, 32" h **$2,000**

Cologne bottle, Rose Tiente, matching stopper, price for pr, 6" h **$100**

Decanter, flattened ovoid, scalloped edge, etched flat sides with hunter on horseback, forest animals, scrolling vine, neck with vine etching, similarly shaped and etched stopper, price for pr, 20th C, 11-5/8" h **$550**

Figure, porcupine, clear, trademark on base, 5" l, 3" h **$150**

Finger bowl, ruby ground, gold medallions and flowers dec, 4-3/4" d, 6-3/4" d underplate **$350**

Garniture, five-light candelabrum and four candlesticks, all hung with pendants, 22" h **$2,275**

Lamp, central cut glass urn on short brass stem, two horizontal reeded candle arms, fan cut drip pans suspending cut prisms, ovoid glass knop stem, paneled trumpet foot cut with roundels, brass flat leaf base, one with collar at urn for further prisms, other with collars for two etched-glass shades, electrified, price for pr, early 20th C, 19-1/2" l, 24-1/2" h **$2,875**

Liquor set, 10 matching cordials, gilt dec Neoclassical motif, 8-1/2" h decanter **$450**

Vase, colorless, tapered cylindrical, slightly everted rim, vertical tapered flutes on body, press-cut, 20th C, 9-3/4" h **$165**

Wash bowl and pitcher, colorless, swirled rib design, pitcher with applied handle and polished base, ground table ring on bowl, polished chip, 12-1/2" h pitcher, 16-1/2" d bowl **$250**

Baccarat, 21" x 12-1/4" three-light candelabra with drop prisms, matching candleholder, both red fading to yellow crystal, imprinted "Baccarat" on base, **$1,100.**
Photo courtesy of David Rago Auctions, Inc.

BARBER BOTTLES

History: Barber bottles, colorful glass bottles found on shelves and counters in barber shops, held the liquids barbers used daily. A specific liquid was kept in a specific bottle, which the barber knew by color, design, or lettering. The bulk liquids were kept in utilitarian containers under the counter or in a storage room.

Barber bottles are found in many types of glass—art glass with various decorations, pattern glass, and commercially prepared and labeled bottles.

Note: Prices are for bottles without original stoppers, unless otherwise noted.

Barber bottles, milk glass, opaque white body, green fern decoration, black lettering, one reads "Bay Rum," the other "Toilet Water," worn gold trim, pontil marks, no stoppers, price for pair, **$165.**

Advertising

Koken's Quinine Tonic for the Hair, clear, label under glass, 7-1/2" h **$195**

Lucky Tiger, red, green, yellow, black, and gilt label under glass, emb on reverse **$85**

Vegederma, cylindrical, bulbous, long neck, amethyst, white enamel dec of bust of woman with long flower hair, tooled mouth, pontil scar, 8" h.... **$130**

Amber, Hobb's Hobnail **$250**

Amethyst, Mary Gregory type dec, white enameled child and flowers, 8" h.... **$200**

Cobalt blue, cylindrical, bulbous body, long neck, white enamel, traces of gold dec, tooled mouth, pontil scar, 7-1/4" h **$100**

Emerald green, cylindrical bell form, long neck, orange and white enameled floral dec, sheared mouth, pontil scar, some int. haze, 8-1/2" h **$210**

Latticino, cylindrical, bulbous, long neck, clear frosted glass, white, red, and pale green vertical stripes, tooled mouth, pontil scar, 8-1/4" h **$200**

Milk glass, Witch Hazel, painted letters and flowers, 9" h **$115**

Opal glass, squatty, blue and purple pansies dec, Mt Washington, numbered 1039, 7" h **$100**

Opalescent

Coin Spot, blue **$300**

Seaweed, cranberry, bulbous **$465**

Sapphire blue, enameled white and yellow daisies, green leaves, 8-5/8" h ... **$125**

Mt. Washington, Crown Milano, biscuit jar, cream body with peach ribbing, dec with gold ivy, embossed lid, stamped "MW," 5" h, **$550.**
Photo courtesy of The Early Auction Company, LLC.

Webb Burmese biscuit jar, stemmed blossoming flowers and buds dec, 8-1/2" h to handle top, **$375.**
Photo courtesy of The Early Auction Company.

Crown Milano biscuit jar, powder blue fading to white, Art Nouveau polychrome design, lid stamped "P" in diamond trademark, 7" h, **$800.**
Photo courtesy of The Early Auction Company, LLC.

BISCUIT JARS

History: The biscuit or cracker jar was the forerunner of the cookie jar. Biscuit jars were made of various materials by leading glassworks and potteries of the late 19th and early 20th centuries.

Note: All items listed have silver-plated (SP) mountings unless otherwise noted.

Burmese glass, raised gold oak leaves and pastel flowers, Mt. Washington, possibly replaced lid, 9" h **$450**

Cranberry glass, two applied clear ring handles, applied clear feet and flower prunt pontil, ribbed finial knob, 9" h, 6-1/4" d **$195**

Glass
Blue, black scenic dec, pewter lid and handle, 9-1/2" h **$175**

Pale yellow ground, green, gold, and rose floral dec, tooled silver-plated cover, handle, and rim, unsigned, Mt. Washington, New Bedford, MA, 8-1/4" h **$150**

Opal glass, shading from white to blue, purple and crimson stemmed flowers, attributed to Wave Crest, 11" h **$325**

Satin glass, floral dec, pewter lid and handle, 11" h **$175**

BOHEMIAN GLASS

History: The once independent country of Bohemia, now a part of the Czech Republic, produced a variety of fine glassware: etched, cut, overlay, and colored. Its glassware, which first appeared in America in the early 1820s, continues to be exported to the U.S. today.

Bohemia is known for its "flashed" glass that was produced in the familiar ruby color, as well as in amber, green, blue, and black. Common patterns include Deer and Castle, Deer and Pine Tree, and Vintage.

Most of the Bohemian glass encountered in today's market is from 1875 to 1900. Bohemian-type glass also was made in England, Switzerland, and Germany.

Basket
Irid green, ruffled, applied reeded handle, gilt dragonfly and fern dec, 6-1/2" h **$175**
Irid green body dec with amethyst straw marks, metal rim and handle, Wilhelm Kralik, 8" d **$150**

Bowl, green ground, random ruby threading, c1910, 6" d **$175**

Candlesticks, set of four, cranberry flashed, cut to clear, wide drip pan cut with guilloche band accented with stars and roundels, similarly cut elongated egg-shaped stem, panel-cut domed foot, late 19th/early 20th C, 10-1/2" h....................................**$1,645**

Compote, irid green, threaded glass trim on bowl, pedestal, and foot, c1900, 9-1/4" h.............................**$175**

Dresser bottle, cut panel body, enameled dec, c1890, 8-1/4" h **$90**

Ewer, ftd, blue cut to clear, horizontal gray panels, dec with cameo carved white and blue grapes and leaves, price for pr, 14" h **$1,050**

Goblet, white and cranberry overlay, thistle form bowl, six teardrop panels alternately enameled with floral bouquets and cut with blocks of diamonds, faceted knob and spreading scalloped foot, gilt trim, 6-3/4" h **$600**

Low bowl, ftd, optic ribbed, blue, large enameled roses and foliage, three figural fish form feet, accented with jeweled eyes, and pointillism enamel, Harrach, 8-1/2" d........**$1,500**

Mantel lusters, pr, trumpet shaped body cased in white, enamel dec floral sprays and gilt moss, cut to ruby flashing, crenellated edge and trumpet foot, hung with long faceted colorless lusters, late 19th C, 12" h
....**$650**

Mantel urns, cov, pr, amber flashed, tapered octagonal bodies etched with continuous scene of deer in wooded landscape, domed lids with paneled baluster finials, faceted knop, trumpet foot with scalloped rim, star-cut base, late 19th C, 18-1/2" h **$2,500**

Portrait vase, slender baluster-form cranberry flashed body over-enameled with gilt vines, one side with white cased oval painted with portrait of young lady, late 19th C, 9-1/2" h .. **$250**

Ramekin, translucent yellow and clear, dec with red, green, yellow, and blue scrolling, white dotted and gold horizontal band, price for set of eight, 3" w **$100**

Rose bowl, optic ribbed body, applied ruffled rim, cobalt blue, Harrach, 5" h **$110**

Toothpick holder, tapering body, brass rim, threaded irid body, Pallme-Koening, 2-1/2" h **$115**

Urn, ftd, cranberry, medallion coat of arms, gold encrustations, polychrome floral scrolling, raised glass jewels, two jewels missing, 11" h **$175**

Vase

Baluster, clear, applied snake dec, 7-1/2" h **$75**

Bulbous stick, mottled red, colorful scrolling foliage, Graf Harrach propeller mark, 7-1/2" h **$350**

Bulbous stick, quadra-fold rim, deep amethyst, irid blue oil spot finish, 8-1/4" h **$120**

Bulbous stick, tri-fold rim, cranberry, overall gold oil spot finish, random threading at rim, 8-1/4" h **$150**

Cylindrical, shading from amber green to rose, Grenada Line, Rindskopf, 10" h **$175**

Cylindrical tapering body, irid citron, applied irid threading, Pallme-Koening, 12" h **$400**

Cylindrical, tri-fold inverted rim, irid blue, white draped loops, Rindskopf, 9" h **$150**

Paneled shouldered body, irid dark olive green/ brown, 3-1/4" h **$35**

Tapering ovoid body, blue cut to clear, notched rims, overlaid circular bases, clear floral pattern cutting, price for pr, 6" h **$200**

Tapered conical body with slightly flared rim, Azure blue, cut with daisy heads between navettes, cut and gilded chinoiserie hunting scenes and florals on smoked ground, paneled foot, early 20th C, 12-1/8" h **$250**

Wide cylindrical, irid green, shades of blue and purple in undulating design, 10-1/2" h **$600**

Water set, 11" h covered water jug, four matching 5" cups, cobalt blue ground, gilt bands, raised pink flowers, mkd "Made in Czecho-Slovakia" **$125**

Wine bottle, ruby flashed, engraved florals, matching stopper, c1890, 10" h **$90**

Bohemian cordial set, decanter with four matching wines, ruby flashed, grape and foliage etched decoration, matching tray, **$375.**

BOTTLES, GENERAL

History: Cosmetic bottles held special creams, oils, and cosmetics designed to enhance the beauty of the user. Some also claimed, especially on their colorful labels, to cure or provide relief from common ailments.

A number of household items, e.g., cleaning fluids and polishes, required glass storage containers. Many are collected for their fine lithographed labels.

Mineral water bottles contained water from a natural spring. Spring water was favored by health-conscious people between the 1850s and 1900s.

Nursing bottles, used to feed the young and sickly, were a great help to the housewife because of their graduated measure markings, replaceable nipples, and the ease with which they could be cleaned, sterilized, and reused.

A. M. Binninger & Co., 338 Broadway, NY, Distilled in 1848, Old Kentucky Bourbon, 1849 Reserve, true green, applied lip, iron pontil **$6,000**

Beehive, pattern molded, Midwestern 24 ribs swirled to right, open pontil, wear, light scratches, 9" h **$70**

24 vertical ribs, single roll collar, light green, unusual lip, 7-1/2" d **$180**

Empire Soda Works, San Francisco, aqua, 1861-71 ....**$400**

Excelsior Water, eight-sided, iron pontil, dug, uncleaned, some white paint on pontil **$450**

Miller's Extra Old Bourbon, E. Martin & Co., light amber, c1871-75, placed bubbles on front **$12,000**

Napa Soda Natural Mineral Water, sapphire blue, "W" on base, needs int. cleaning, few scratches, wear **$140**

Thos. Taylor & Co., Virginia, Nevada, medium to deep reddish-chocolate color, c1874-80, few scratches ...**$4,400**

Union Glass Works Phila Superior Mineral Water, deep cobalt blue, iron pontil, mug base, some int. stain, few scratches **$350**

Williams & Severance San Francisco Calsoda Mineral Waters, light green, orig graphite **$700**

Cosmetic

Kickapoo Sage Hair Tonic, cylindrical, cobalt blue, tooled mouth, matching stopper, smooth base, 5" h **$160**

Kranks Cold Cream, milk glass, 2-3/4" h................................**$6.50**

Pompeian Massage Cream, amethyst, 2-3/4" h **$9**

National Bitters, yellow green coloration, about mint, **$2,200.**
Photo courtesy of American Bottle Auctions.

Imperial Cabinet Whiskey, 5th sized back bar, tooled top, white enameled back bar on amber glass, near mint, **$700.**
Photo courtesy of American Bottle Auctions.

Ammonia MNFD by S.F. Gaslight Co., tooled top, light to medium citron, about mint, **$850.**
Photo courtesy of American Bottle Auctions.

Forest Lawn JVH, applied lip, iron pontil, about mint, 7" h, **$450.**
Photo courtesy of American Bottle Auctions.

Food and household

Ink, Waterman's, paper label with bottle of ink, wooden bullet-shaped case, orig paper label, 4-1/4" h **$10**

Pickle

Cathedral, pale aqua, sq applied top, sticky ball type pontil, 12" h **$190**

W. D. Smith, N.Y., deep aqua, pint, applied lip, graphite pontil, 8-1/2" h **$1,000**

Sewing Machine Oil, Sperm Brand, clear, 5-1/2" h **$5**

Shoe Polish, Everett & Barron Co., oval, clear, 4-3/4" **$5**

Nursing

Acme, clear, lay-down, emb **$65**

Cala Nurser, oval, clear, emb, ring on neck, 7-1/8" h **$12**

Empire Nursing Bottle, bent neck, 6-1/2" h **$50**

Mother's Comfort, clear, turtle type **$25**

Fell's Point with bust of George Washington and Valto monument on reverse, amethystine color, about mint, quart, **$1,600.**
Photo courtesy of American Bottle Auctions.

Buffalo Brewing Co. S.F. Agency beer bottle, applied top, green whittled, about mint, pint, **$240.**
Photo courtesy of American Bottle Auctions.

J & A Dearborn & Co. New York Soda Water D., applied top, blue coloration, near mint, **$200.**
Photo courtesy of American Bottle Auctions.

National Bottle Works San Francisco beer bottle, eagle, original stopper, about mint, quart, **$130.**
Photo courtesy of American Bottle Auctions.

Bride's basket, cased glass bowl with cherub transfers and polychrome dec, Holman silver-plate frame with handle, undetermined association, late 19th century, 12-1/2" h, bowl 11-3/8" d, **$330.**

Photo courtesy of Green Valley Auctions.

Bride's basket, cased mica fleck glass bowl, unmarked silver-plate stand, undetermined association, late 19th century, 8-1/2" h, 10" d, **$175.**

Photo courtesy of Green Valley Auctions.

BRIDE'S BASKETS

History: A ruffled-edge glass bowl in a metal holder was a popular wedding gift between 1880 and 1910, hence the name "bride's basket." These bowls can be found in most glass types of the period. The metal holder was generally silver-plated with a bail handle, thus enhancing the basket image.

Over the years, bowls and bases became separated and married pieces resulted. If the base has been lost, the bowl should be sold separately.

Reproduction Alert. The glass bowls have been reproduced.

Amber, enameled berries and buds, SP holder, 8-1/2" d, 12" h **$1,195**

Blue and white glass bowl, enameled floral dec, SP holder, 6" d, 5-1/2" h...**$250**

Bowl only, overlay, heavenly blue, enameled white flowers, green leaves, white underside, ruffled, 10-3/4" d, 3-1/2" h...**$215**

Crown Milano, ruffled edge bowl, heavy hand applied gold encrustation on mottled ground, pontil sgd with trademark, 13" l, 5" h **$2,000**

Custard, melon ribbed, enameled daisies, applied Rubena crystal rim, twisted and beaded handle, ftd, emb SP frame, marked "Wilcox," sq, 10" w **$450**

Opalescent Rubena Verde, applied lime stepped flower feet, thorny twist handle, Victorian, 11-1/4" h **$425**

Opaline cased in pink, ruffled amber rim, married plated holder, 9-3/4" h...**$150**

Peachblow, bowl only, glossy finish, deep pink shading to pale, 9-7/8" d, 3" h, 3-3/4" base.........................**$250**

Peachblow, cased rose shading to pink ground, applied amber stem, green leaves, amber handle, four applied feet, some losses, 10-1/2" h **$200**

Pink hobnail bowl, blue ruffled rim, SP holder dec with leaves, 10" d, 11" h...**$525**

Rubena Verde, sculptured, vaseline shading to pink, yellow and green enameled flowers, Benedict SP holder, 10-1/2" d, 12-1/2" h...............**$460**

Satin, deep pink ruffled bowl, white ext., marked "Nemasket Silver Co." SP holder, 9-1/2" d, 12" h.................**$275**

Satin, light beige shading to orange ruffled bowl, hp pink, purple and yellow flowers, green leaves, raised gold outlines, blue int., sgd "Simpson, Hall, Miller Co. Quad Plate" holder, 11" d, 7-1/2" h.......................................**$895**

Satin, bowl only, brown shaded to cream overlay, raised dots, dainty gold and silver flowers and leaves dec, ruffled, 11-1/8" d, 3-3/4" h **$250**

White opal basket, cranberry ruffled rim, applied vaseline rope handle, no holder, 9" h.....................................**$95**

White opaline, cased in pink, overall colorful enameled dec, emb Middletown plated holder, applied fruit handles, Victorian, minor losses, 12" d, 7-1/2" h..............................**$525**

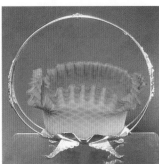

Bride's basket, diamond quilted Rubena, blue ruffled rim, silverplate frame with embossed floral sprays, 10" h overall, **$400.**

Photo courtesy of The Early Auction Company, LLC.

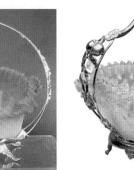

Bride's basket, cased mica fleck glass bowl, unmarked stand with handle, undetermined association, late 19th century, 10" h, 8-1/4" sq bowl , **$230.**

Photo courtesy of Green Valley Auctions.

Bride's basket, cased glass bowl, unmarked frame, undetermined association, late 19th century, 11-3/4" h, 12" d, **$230.**

Photo courtesy of Green Valley Auctions.

BRISTOL GLASS

History: Bristol glass is a designation given to a semi-opaque glass, usually decorated with enamel and cased with another color.

Initially, the term referred only to glass made in Bristol, England, in the 17th and 18th centuries. By the Victorian era, firms on the Continent and in America were copying the glass and its forms.

Bowl, light blue, Cupid playing mandolin, gold trim......................**$45**

Box, cov, oblong, blue, gilt-metal mounts and escutcheon, 4-1/8" l, 2-3/4" d, 3-1/2" h......................**$550**

Cake stand, celadon green, enameled herons in flight, gold trim.........**$135**

Candlesticks, pr, soft green, gold band, 7" h......................**$75**

Decanter, ruffled stopper, enameled flowers and butterfly, 11-1/2" h....**$75**

Dresser set, two cologne bottles, cov powder jar, white, gilt butterflies dec, clear stoppers......................**$75**

Ewer, pink ground, fancy gold designs, bands, and leaves, applied handle with gold trim, 6-3/8" h, 2-5/8" d......**$135**

Finger bowl, blue, faceted sides, early 20th C, eight-pc set, 4-3/8" d......**$500**

Hatpin holder, ftd, blue, enameled jewels, gold dec, 6-1/8" h...........**$100**

Perfume bottle, squatty, blue, gold band, white enameled flowers and leaves, matching stopper, 3-1/4" h **$100**

Puff box, cov, round, blue, gold dec **$35**

Sugar shaker, white, hp flowers, 4-3/4" h......................**$65**

Sweetmeat jar, deep pink, enameled flying duck, leaves, blue flower dec, white lining, SP rim, lid, and bail handle, 3" x 5-1/2"......................**$110**

Urn, cov, pink opaque, hp bird and branch dec, base mkd "251," 17" h..........**$150**

Vase, bulbous stick, Delft windmill dec, 11" h......................**$100**

Bristol vase, monumental, hp decoration, bird in flowering tree branches, polychrome on white ground, blue footed base, gilt leaf decoration, wooden reeded column base, 24-1/2" h vase, **$450.**
Photo courtesy of Alderfer Auction Co.

CAMBRIDGE GLASS

History: Cambridge Glass Company, Cambridge, Ohio, was incorporated in 1901. Initially, the company made clear tableware, later expanding into colored, etched, and engraved glass. More than 40 different hues were produced in blown and pressed glass.

The plant closed in 1954 and some of the molds were later sold to the Imperial Glass Company, Bellaire, Ohio.

Marks: Five different marks were employed during the production years, but not every piece was marked.

Basket, Apple Blossom, crystal, 7"...**$475**

Bonbon, Chantilly, crystal, Martha blank, two handles, 6"..................**$35**

Bowl, Wildflower, flared rim, three-ftd, 9-3/8" d......................**$85**

Butter dish, cov, Gadroon, crystal...**$45**

Candy jar, cov, Rose, green rose-shaped finial, 8" h......................**$250**

Candlestick
　Caprice, blue, Alpine, #70, prisms, 7" h......................**$195**
　Doric, black, pr, 9-1/2" h............**$160**
　Rose Point, crystal, two-lite, keyhole, pr......................**$95**

Celery, Gloria, five-part, 12-1/2" l..**$70**

Champagne
　Adonis, crystal, #3500..................**$35**
　Chantilly, crystal......................**$30**

　Roxbury, crystal......................**$30**

Cocktail
　Apple Blossom, Gold Krystal, #3130..**$48**
　Caprice, blue......................**$55**
　Chantilly, crystal......................**$42**

Cocktail icer and liner, Adonis, #968......................**$65**

Cocktail shaker, Chantilly, crystal, glass lid......................**$250**

Comport, Honeycomb, Rubena, ftd, 9" d, 4-3/4" h......................**$150**

Cordial
　Caprice, blue......................**$120**
　Chantilly, crystal......................**$75**
　Rose Point, #3121......................**$78**

Corn dish, Rose Point......................**$88**

Cornucopia vase, Chantilly, 9-1/8" h **$195**

Cambridge seashell, Crown Tuscan, #44, roses and butterflies, polychrome and gilt dec, Cambridge Glass Co., early/mid 20th century, light gilt wear, 8-3/4" h, base 5-1/4" d, **$120.**
Photo courtesy of Green Valley Auctions.

Creamer
Chantilly, crystal, individual size . $22
Tempo, #1029................................$15

Creamer and sugar, tray, Caprice,
crystal...$40

Cream soup, orig liner, Decagon,
green..$35

Cup and saucer
Caprice, crystal............................$14
Decagon, pink..............................$10
Martha Washington, amber..........$12

Decanter set, decanter, stopper, six-
handled 2-1/2 oz tumblers, Tally Ho,
amethyst.....................................$195

Flower frog
Draped Lady, dark pink, 8-1/2" h
....$185
Eagle, pink..................................$365
Jay, green....................................$365
Nude, clear, 6-1/2" h, 3-1/4" d $145
Rose Lady, amber, 8-1/2" h.........$350
Seagull...$85
Two Kids, clear.............................$155

Fruit bowl, Decagon, pink, 5-1/2".. $6

Goblet
Chantilly, crystal, #3600..............$45
Diane, crystal, #3122...................$45
Roxbury, crystal...........................$30
Tempo, #1029/3700.....................$15
Wildflower, gold trim, #3121.......$45

Ice bucket
Chrysanthemum, pink, silver handle
....$85
Wildflower, #3400/851...............$225

Iced tea tumbler, Chantilly.........$45

Ivy ball, Nude Stem, Statuesque
#3011/2, 9-1/2" h, 4-1/4" h d ruby ball,
4" d base.....................................$500

Jug
Gloria, ftd, 9-3/4" h....................$325
Rose Point, Doulton...................$595

Lemon plate, Caprice, blue, 5" d. $15

Marmalade, sterling silver cover, orig
spoon, Rose Point, #68...............$225

Mayonnaise set
Chantilly, divided bowl, underplate,
ladle, #3900/111.........................$95
Wildflower, bowl, underplate,
#3900/139...................................$55

Oyster cocktail, Portia, crystal....$40

Pitcher, cov, Forest Green, #3400/107,
1931..$500

Plate
Apple Blossom, pink, 8-1/2" d......$20
Chantilly, #3900/22, 8" d.............$18
Dianthus, pink, triangle C mark, 7" d
....$10
Diane, rolled edge, #3900/166, 14" d
....$75
Rose Point, crystal, ftd, 8" d.........$70

Relish
Apple Blossom, Gold Krystal, five-
part, #3400/67, 12" l..................$125
Caprice, club, #170, blue.............$115
Mt. Vernon, crystal, five-part........$35
Wildflower, three-part, three handles,
8"..$45

Salt and pepper shakers, pr, Wildflower, chrome tops, one slightly
cloudy...$40

Seafood cocktail, Seashell, #110,
Crown Tuscan, 4-1/2"..................$95

Server, center handle, Apple Blossom,
amber..$30

Sherbet
Diane, crystal, low.......................$20
Tempo, #1029..........................$12.50

Sherry, Portia, gold encrusted.......$60

Sugar
Rose Point, gold encrusted, #3900
....$75
Tempo, #1029..............................$15

Swan, 3-1/2" h
Crown Tuscan...............................$60
Crown Tuscan, gold encrusted....$125
Crystal...$40

Torte plate, Rose Point, crystal, three
ftd, 13" d......................................$95

Tray, Gloria, four part, center handle,
8-3/4" d..$70

Tumbler
Adam, yellow, ftd.........................$25
Carmine, crystal, 12 oz................$25
Chantilly......................................$42
Rose Point, #3500, 10 oz..............$35

Vase
Diane, crystal, keyhole, 12" h.....$110
Songbird and Butterfly, #402, blue,
12" h..$375
Wildflower, #3400, 10-3/4" h......$175

Whiskey, Caprice, blue, 2-1/2 oz
....$225

Wine
Caprice, crystal............................$24
Diane, crystal, 2-1/2 oz................$30

*Cameo glass vase, scenic, amber wood-
ed lakeland landscape, cameo signature,
Gallé, c1900, 7-3/4",* **$2,640.**
Photo courtesy of David Rago Auctions, Inc.

CAMEO GLASS

History: Cameo glass is a form of cased glass. A shell of glass was prepared, and then one or more layers of glass of a different color(s) was faced
to the first. A design was then cut through the outer layer(s), leaving the
inner layer(s) exposed.

This type of art glass originated in Alexandria, Egypt, between 100 and 200
A.D. The oldest and most famous example of cameo glass is the Barberini
or Portland vase found near Rome in 1582. It contained the ashes of Emperor Alexander Severus, who was assassinated in 235 A.D.

Emile Gallé is probably one of the best-known cameo-glass artists. He established a factory at Nancy, France, in 1884. Although much of the glass
bears his signature, he was primarily the designer. Assistants did the actual
work on many pieces, even signing Gallé's name. Other makers of French-
cameo glass include D'Argental, Daum Nancy, LeGras, and Delatte.

English-cameo pieces do not have as many layers of glass (colors) and cuttings as do French pieces. The outer layer is usually white, and cuttings are
very fine and delicate. Most pieces are not signed. The best-known makers
are Thomas Webb & Sons, and Stevens and Williams.

Marks: A star before the name Gallé on a piece by that company indicates
that it was made after Gallé's death in 1904.

Reproduction Alert.

Atomizer, amethyst floral cutting on pumpkin orange ground, sgd in cameo "Ciriama," French, 8" h....**$200**

Basket, textured ground, cameo carved gold highlighted green ferns, metal collar and handle, sgd with ship mark and initials "V.S.," French, 5" h....**$250**

Biscuit jar, cov, Webb, white cameo dec, single-petaled blossoms, leafed branch, ruby red ground, silver plate fittings, 6" d, 7-1/4" h.............**$2,950**

Bowl

Algues pattern, ovoid, three-pointed rim, underwater scene, sgd in cameo "Legras," slight chips to points, 4" d...............................**$225**

Ftd, four pulled points, pale pink ground, light yellow-green and amber overlay, etched clusters of blossoms on leafy branches, sgd "Galle" among leaves, several bubble bursts and int. wear, 7-3/4" d, 4-1/4" h **$690**

Mottled yellow and amethyst-gray ground, overlaid with vitrified green, red, and yellow powders, cameo cut with stemmed leafy red berries, sgd in cameo "Daum Nancy" with Croix de Lorraine, c1900, 8" d **$2,760**

Olive-green body, heavily etched and engraved Art-Deco swag and drapery design, fire polished, acid-etched "Legras" near base, 10" d, 3-3/4" h **$825**

Box, cov, Triangular form sloping from round opening, cameo cut and etched mountain landscape in blues and greens, sterling silver lid, cameo-etched "Lamartine" on side, int. rim nicks, 3" h................................**$360**

Cabinet vase, opal, internally dec with mottled green and amber glass, finely etched dandelion flower heads, fluffy windblown seed pods, gilt highlights, sgd in gilt "Daum Nancy Croix de Lorraine," 3-1/2" h **$2,415**

Cologne bottle

Frosted cylindrical body, cameo cranberry floral relief, cut faceted stopper, Val St. Lambert, 4-3/8" h ..**$175**

Lay down, teardrop shaped body, green ground, carved water lily, Webb, 3-3/4" l **$1,900**

Mottled gray to yellow ground, cameo and enameled branching acorns silhouetted against distant forested shoreline, sgd in cameo "Daum Nancy" with Cross of Lorraine, 7" h **$1,550**

Cruet, ruby-red body, textured white enamel meadowland scene, Meadowlark on tall plant stalk, smaller scene on reverse, white rim, trefoil spout, clear frosted handle, teardrop-shaped stopper, pontil mark sgd "59," Florentine Art, 6-1/2" h **$50**

Decanter, flattened oval body, upturned rim, conical stopper, frosted colorless and purple ground, overlaid in deep purple, etched iris, engraved "Cristallerie de Galle Nancy modele et decor deposes" on base, 10-1/4" h **$2,530**

Epergne, five 6" h etched cameo cylindrical flower holders, stylized naturalistic brass frame, Val St. Lambert, 10-1/2" h.................................**$1,800**

Ewer

Cranberry ground, highlighted in gold, overlaid in deep purple, cameo cut grapevine motif, metal mount flip lid and handle, emb with matching grape dec, sgd in gold "Daum Nancy," c1895, 7-1/2" h **$1,380**

Textured translucent glass, gold highlighted ruby cameo with random trailing flowers, silver-gilt emb collar, handle, and lid with raspberry finial, sgd in gold "Daum Nancy," c1895, 10-1/2".....................**$1,955**

Flask, tapered cylindrical bottle, translucent colorless body cameo cut with violet blossoms, enameled purple, yellow, orange and white, gilt highlights, inscribed "Daum (cross) Nancy," mounted with bulbed silver cap with emb flower blossoms, engraved "Lola," small cup with raised leaf blade design, emb "SH" in diamond, cap loose, 5-5/8" h **$375**

Floor vase, rose amber ground, overlaid in green, cameo cut towering trees above deep forested lake scene, sgd "Legras" in cameo, c1910, price for pr, 24" h **$4,025**

Incense burner, bell shaped vessel, shading from citron to frosted, wine-red and amethyst floral cameo cutting, lower body sgd in cameo relief "D'Argental," 7" h **$700**

Inkwell, mottled green and purple ground, cameo cut falling oak leaves, five jeweled carved insect and acorn cabochons, sgd "Daum Nancy," c1900, 4-1/4" d, 3-1/2" h **$1,265**

Lamp base

Blue-gray ground, overlaid with cinnamon and orange, cameo cut cascading leafy stemmed fruit, sgd "Galle" in cameo, lamp fittings, 16-3/4" h **$1,330**

Flattened circular body, Prussian blue, detailed white opaque floral cameo relief, butterfly, three frosted feet, English, 4" h, 4-1/2" w **$900**

Lamp, table

Mushroom shape, yellow overlaid in dark brown, cut frosted lake scene and oak leaves, French, c1920, 12-1/2" h **$600**

Textured frosted ground, cascading crimson leafy vines, sgd in cameo "Legras," 15" h **$250**

Daum Nancy pillow vase, amethyst to powder blue, stemmed iris dec, sgd in cameo Daum Nancy, 1-1/2" h, **$1,200.**
Photo courtesy of The Early Auction Company.

Cameo vase, Daum Nancy, shouldered, mottled amethyst graduating to yellow, long green-stemmed red flowers, signed in cameo Daum Nancy France, 5" h, **$1,150.**
Photo courtesy of The Early Auction Company, LLC.

Stevens and Williams cameo vase, gourd form, citron with branch and blooming flowers, 8-1/2" h, **$600.**
Photo courtesy of The Early Auction Company, LLC.

Cameo glass vase, French Gallé banjo form, green and white maple leaves and seed pods dec, frosted amethyst ground, sgd in cameo Gallé, 6-1/2" h, **$400.**
Photo courtesy of The Early Auction Company, LLC.

Cameo glass vase, cylindrical form, translucent green, amethyst wheel-carved stemmed flowers, c1900, 8" h, **$325.**
Photo courtesy of The Early Auction Company, LLC.

Pitcher, vitrified fall color leaves, mottled earth tone ground, applied gold enameled bug and handle, base engraved with block letters "Mueller Croismare," 7-1/2" h **$2,700**

Tray, triangular, inverted rim, frosted to orange, overlaid and cut large green-stemmed oak leaves and acorns, sgd in cameo "Galle," 9" w **$700**

Tumbler, gray ground mottled in yellow and amethyst, cameo cut purple and yellow enameled flowers, green leafy stems, sgd in cameo "Daum Nancy" with Croix de Lorraine, c1900, 3-1/4" h **$1,035**

Vase
Amber glass overlaid in orange and green, cut mountainous lake scene outlined with towering pine trees, sgd in cameo "Daum Nancy" with Croix de Lorraine, c1910, 13" h **$3,115**

Baluster, camellias in polished red and orange, pale ground, sgd "Galle" in cameo, 8" h **$1,300**

Bottle form, martele frosted ground, amethyst gold highlighted cameo stemmed flowers, icicle body, sgd with Burgun Schverer thistle and cross monogram, 9" h **$3,950**

Conical, green ground, bands of stylized flower blossoms on etched and polished surfaces, gilt highlights, inscribed "Daum (cross) Nancy" on base, gilt wear, 4-1/4" h **$325**

Cylindrical citron body, dark crim-son and rose colored maple leaves and seed pods, sgd in cameo "D'Argental," 10" h **$900**

Cylindrical, cameo cut trailing vines and flowers in green and brown over frosted ground, Foussin signature at side, 20th C, 14-3/8" h **$500**

Dark amber ground, overlaid in plum and burgundy, cut cascading branches of seed pods and leaves, sgd "D'Argental" in cameo, c1910, 11-3/4" h **$1,610**

Etched colorless body, white and pale yellow overlapping petals emerging from transparent green base, ftd, rolled base rim, rough pontil, sgd "L.C. Tiffany Favrile," numbered "4053D," 5-3/8" h **$11,200**

Ftd, cylindrical matte finish amber body, long-stemmed blue flowers and leaves, attributed to Mueller, engraved signature "Crois Mare," 12-1/2" h **$1,500**

Frosted gray ground overlaid in chartreuse and white, cut with trailing leaves and seed pods, sgd "Galle" with star in cameo, c1900, 7-1/2" h **$1,035**

Frosted ground with flecks of orange and green, orange and burgundy orchid, Daum Nancy, signature on side, c1905, 13-3/4" h **$3,525**

Gray and rose mottled ground, overlaid in amethyst, cameo cut shoreline castle between towering trees,

Cameo tumbler, Daum Nancy, mustard yellow mottled ground, sailing vessels against shoreline, sgd in enamel Daum Nancy, 5" h, **$1,700.**
Photo courtesy of The Early Auction Company, LLC.

Cameo glass vase, Muller Fres, French, bulbous, cylindrical, mottled yellow and blue to citron, crimson stemmed ruby flowers, sgd. Muller Fres Luneville, 14" h, **$4,250.**
Photo courtesy of The Early Auction Company, LLC.

Cameo glass vase, "Jeanne D'Arc," commemorative, panel with Joan of Arc on ground of arabesques, verso has panel with Cross of Lorraine, deep amethyst, shaded lemon yellow ground, cameo signature Galle, c1895, 11", **$16,800.**
Photo courtesy of David Rago Auctions, Inc.

distant mountains, sgd "Richard" in cameo, c1915, 22-1/2" h........**$1,495**

Gray ground, overlaid with amethyst, cameo cut mountainous lake scene and medieval castle, sgd "Richard" in cameo, drilled, c1915, 21-1/2"....**$650**

Gray ground internally dec with amber and frost mottling, cameo carved vitrified leaves, stemmed red bleeding hearts, sgd in cameo "Daum Nancy" with Croix de Lorraine, c1910, 4-1/2" h..........**$1,100**

Gray ground internally dec with mottled custard, overlaid in variegated orange and brown, cameo cut leafage and buds, inscribed "Degue," c1925, 10-3/4" h **$750**

Lemon yellow ground, cameo cut royal blue thistles, sgd "Richard" in cameo, c1915, 6" h **$320**

Olive green cased to salmon and translucent colorless glass, cameo cut and etched leaves and pendant seed pods, sgd "Galle" in cameo on side, polished pontil, rim possibly ground, base wear, 9-3/4" h.....**$460**

Ovoid cylindrical bulbous mottled green body, seven brown sailing ships, crimson and yellow sky, sgd in cameo "Daum Nancy" with Cross of Lorraine, 5-3/4" h..............**$1,200**

Ovoid, cameo carved red lily on gold Aventurine internally dec ruby and yellow body, sgd "Desiré Christian Meisenthal Loth," 7" h..........**$2,850**

Pale ground, red and orange polished trumpet vines, cameo signature "D'Argental," 12-3/4" h..........**$1,800**

Pillow shape, scenic, snow covered barren trees against distant gray forest, mottled yellow ground, sgd in cameo "Daum Nancy" with Cross of Lorraine, 4-3/4" h, 5-1/2" w ...**$2,450**

Shaded yellow ground, polished dark green blossoming branches, cameo sgd "Galle," 10-1/2" h **$1,500**

Squatty, Prussian blue, cameo carved tropical design, bamboo tree trunks and palms, double banded rim, top band carved with arrow dec, Webb, 5" h **$600**

Swollen elongated neck, flared base, opaque orange glass overlaid in black, cameo cut and etched tall leafy stems, scrolled lower border, cameo-etched "Richard," 11-1/2" h **$300**

Tapering ovoid body, frosted with swirled amethyst, overlaid with detailed summer forest scene, circular base sgd "Lamartine," numbered "327-604," 6-3/4" h **$1,000**

Triangular frosted blue body with blue mottling, cameo carved wisteria blossoms and vines, sgd in cameo "Legras," 8-1/4" h **$675**

Whiskey jug, textured translucent ground, cameo cut and enameled grapevine and leaves, metal lid and handle in form of knight's helmet, lion finial on flip lid, unsigned, c1895, 10-1/2" h **$815**

Cameo glass vase, cylindrical, amethyst and white flowering branches, frosted pink ground, sgd in cameo Gallé, 6-1/2" h, **$500.**
Photo courtesy of The Early Auction Company, LLC.

CARNIVAL GLASS

History: Carnival glass, an American invention, is colored-pressed glass with a fired-on iridescent finish. It was first manufactured about 1905 and was immensely popular both in America and abroad. More than 1,000 different patterns have been identified. Production of old carnival-glass patterns ended in 1930.

Most of the popular patterns of carnival glass were produced by five companies: Dugan, Fenton, Imperial, Millersburg, and Northwood.

Marks: Northwood patterns frequently are found with the "N" trademark. Dugan used a diamond trademark on several patterns.

Notes: Color is the most important factor in pricing carnival glass. The color of a piece is determined by holding it to the light and looking through it.

Butterfly & Berry

Made by Fenton.

Colors known: amethyst, blue, green, marigold, red, and white.

Forms: bowls, hatpin holders, table set, vases, water sets, and whimsies.

Identifying characteristics: This pattern is found in a paneled form with alternating butterflies and leaves in one panel, blackberries and leaves in other panels. This popular pattern was also used as an exterior pattern on Fenton bowls in the Hearts & Trees, Fantail, and Panther patterns. The pattern was produced from 1911 to 1926.

Also known as: Butterfly and Grape.

> **Reproduction Alert.** The large bowl has been reproduced in purple and white. Tumblers have been reproduced in amethyst.

Berry set, 7 pcs, blue .... $300-$325
Bowl, 5" d, ftd
   Amethyst .... $65-$85
   Blue .... $100-$125
   Green .... $90-$110

Butterfly & Berry, Fenton, water pitcher, amethyst, **$3,000.**

   Marigold .... $20-$25
   White .... $75-$95
Bowl, 9" d, scalloped, three claw feet, blue .... $425-$450
Bowl, 10" d, ftd
   Amethyst .... $175-$225
   Blue .... $85-$115
   Green .... $175-$200
   Marigold .... $65-$85
   White .... $600-$725
Butter dish, cov
   Amethyst .... $200-$240
   Blue .... $200-$225
   Green .... $250-$300
   Marigold .... $45-$80
Creamer
   Amethyst .... $100-$150
   Blue .... $85-$90
   Green .... $175-$200
   Marigold .... $30-$35
Hatpin holder
   Blue .... Rare-$1,200
   Marigold .... Rare-$1,300
Spooner
   Amethyst .... $100-$150
   Blue .... $85-$90
   Green .... $175-$200
   Marigold .... $30-$35
Sugar bowl, cov
   Amethyst .... $100-$150
   Blue .... $85-$90
   Green .... $175-$200
   Marigold .... $30-$35
Tumbler, 4-1/4" h, ftd
   Amethyst .... $45-$65
   Blue .... $65-$85
   Green .... $115-$125
   Marigold .... $10-$30
   Vaseline .... $350-$450
Vase, 6-1/2" h to 9" h
   Amethyst .... $65-$85
   Blue .... $45-$80
   Green .... $200-$300
   Horehound .... $100-$125
   Marigold .... $25-$35
   Red .... $600-$750
   White .... $100-$150

Water pitcher
   Amethyst .... $500-$3,000
   Blue .... $325-$500
   Green .... $600-$750
   Marigold .... $175-$300
   White .... Rare-$1,400

Cherry Chain

Made by Fenton.

Colors known: amethyst, blue, clambroth, electric blue, marigold, red, vaseline, and white.

Forms: bowls and plates.

Identifying characteristics: This cherry pattern features clusters of three plump cherries within a circle, surrounded by foliage and other elements. Another cluster of cherries is in the center. The Orange Tree pattern was used as the exterior design for this busy pattern. A pattern known as Cherry Chain Variant has clusters with five cherries each.

> **Reproduction Alert.** Fenton reissued this pattern in a number of shapes, such as the round bowl, ruffled bowl, chop plates, and rose bowls.

Bowl, IC shape, ruffled, or 3-in-1 edge, 9" d to 10" d
   Amethyst, IC shape .... $300-$325
   Blue .... $65-$100
   Clambroth .... $50-$95
   Marigold .... $40-$75
   Red .... Rare-$6,500
   Vaseline .... Rare-$200
   White .... Rare-$100
Chop plate, 11" d
   Marigold .... Rare-$2,000
   White .... $600-$900
Plate, 6" d to 6-1/2" d
   Amethyst .... Rare-$800
   Blue .... $85-$135
   Lavender .... Rare-$800
   Marigold .... $40-$105
   Marigold, dark .... $60-$65

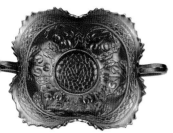

Cherry Chain, Fenton, bon bon, red, large, **$5,000.**

White	$200-$300

Sauce, IC shape or ruffled

Blue	$30-$50
Marigold	$20-$35
White	$20-$35

Diamond & Rib

Made by Fenton.

Colors known: amethyst, blue, green, marigold, and white.

Forms: jardinières and vases.

Identifying characteristics: This pattern features elongated ovals with ribbing in each one. Production began in 1911.

Also known as: Fenton's #504; Melon and Fan.

Reproduction Alert. Fenton has re-issued vases, but most are marked.

Jardinière, whimsy, flared and ruffled or straight-sided

Amethyst	Rare-$1,200
Blue	Rare-$1,300
Green	Rare-$1,400
Marigold	Rare-$1,400

Funeral vase, 17" h to 22" h

Amethyst	Rare-$1,600
Blue	Rare-$1,900
Green	Rare-$1,600
Marigold	Rare-$2,000
White	Rare-$850

Vase, whimsy, pinched in flared top, green, 5-1/2" h ... Rare-$1,000

Vase, squatty, amethyst, 7" h ... $25-$30

Vase, white, 10" h ... $80-$85

Vase, 11" h to 12" h

Amethyst	$40-$45
Blue	$80-$100
Green	$40-$45
Marigold	$35-$45
Smoke	$50-$75
White	$150-$155

Field Flower

Made by Imperial.

Colors known: amber, aqua, clambroth, cobalt blue, helios, marigold, olive, purple, red, smoke, and violet.

Forms: milk pitchers and water sets.

Identifying characteristics: The design is a flower framed by two strands of wheat, all on a stippled background, double arches border the stippling and serve as panels. Production began in 1912.

Also known as: Imperial's #494; Sunflower and Wheat.

Reproduction Alert. Water sets have been re-issued in contemporary colors.

Milk pitcher

Clambroth	$200-$250
Helios	$220-$320
Marigold	$95-$160
Purple	$200-$400

Tumbler

Amber	$50-$75
Cobalt blue	$275-$350
Helios	$40-$70
Marigold	$35-$45
Olive	$75-$100
Purple	$115-$145
Red	Rare-$1,500
Violet	$95-$200

Water pitcher

Amber	$285-$415
Aqua	$500-$550
Cobalt blue	Rare-$2,000
Helios	$300-$450
Marigold	$115-$175
Purple	$350-$550
Smoke	$600-$700

Gothic Arches

Made by Imperial.

Colors known: marigold and smoke.

Forms: vases.

Identifying Characteristics: This interesting pattern has large graceful arched loops that start at the flared top and gently flow to the round base.

Reproduction Alert. Reproduction vases have been made by Imperial in ice blue and pale yellow.

Vase, 10" h to 12" h

Marigold	$175-$1,200
Smoke	$410-$700

Vase, 14" h to 18" h, marigold ... $350-$500

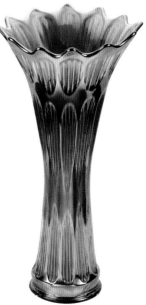

Diamond and Rib, Fenton, funeral vase, 19", 9" mouth, green, **$1,200.**

Field Flower, Imperial, tumbler, 4", purple, **$125.**

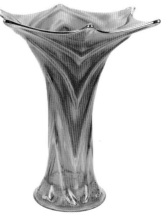

Gothic Arches, Imperial, vase, marigold, 11", mouth 8", **$1,200.**

Greek Key, Northwood, water pitcher, purple, 11-1/2", $900.

Hattie, Imperial, chop plate, purple, 10", $2,000.

Greek Key

Made by Northwood.

Colors known: amethyst/purple, blue, green, ice green, and marigold.

Forms: bowls, plates, and water sets.

Identifying characteristics: A band of a traditional Greek Key design flows through this pattern. This pattern began production in 1909 and found such favor with buyers that it was expanded to other forms in 1911 and production continued until 1913.

Bowl, dome base, 7" d to 8" d

Amethyst/purple	**$45-$85**
Green	**$50-$75**
Marigold	**$35-$50**

Bowl, flat, 8" d to 9-1/2" d

Amethyst/purple	**$150-$200**
Blue	**$300-$400**
Green	**$175-$225**
Ice green	**Rare-$2,000**
Marigold	**$150-$475**

Bowl, piecrust edge, basketweave back

Amethyst/purple	**$200-$250**
Blue	**Rare-$1,100**
Green	**$250-$850**
Marigold	**$200-$275**

Bowl, ruffled, basketweave back, 9" d

Amethyst/purple	**$60-$200**
Blue	**$450-$700**
Green	**$165-$215**
Marigold	**$475-$500**

Bowl, ruffled, plain back, amethyst/purple, 9" d .... **$85-$90**

Plate, basketweave back, 9" d

Amethyst/purple	**$400-$415**
Blue	**Rare-$2,000**
Green	**$625-$900**
Marigold	**$900-$1,250**

Plate, ribbed back, 9" d, marigold .... **$550-$3,000**

Tumbler, 4-1/4" h

Amethyst/purple	**$100-$200**
Green	**$45-$170**
Marigold	**$85-$125**

Water pitcher

Amethyst/purple	**$600-$900**
Green	**$900-$1,500**
Marigold	**$650-$1,150**

Hattie

Made by Imperial.

Colors known: amber, clambroth, helios, marigold, purple, and smoke.

Forms: bowls, chop plates, and rose bowls.

Identifying characteristics: This detailed pattern features arched lines and floral elements and is the only carnival glass pattern used on both the interior and exterior. Production began in 1911.

Also known as: Imperial's #496; Busy Lizzie.

> **Reproduction Alert.** Reproduction bowls are known in green, pink, smoke, and white. These bowls are all marked with the IG trademark.

Bowl, ruffled or round, 8" d to 9" d

Amber	**$155-$200**
Helios	**$55-$75**
Marigold	**$35-$70**
Purple	**$100-$250**
Smoke	**$50-$75**

Bowl, ruffled, 9-1/2" d

Marigold	**$35-$70**
Purple	**$245-$265**

Chop plate, 10" d to 10-1/4" d

Amber	**$2,000-$3,200**
Clambroth	**$600-$700**
Helios	**$250-$350**
Marigold	**$1,050-$2,400**
Purple	**$2,000-$3,500**

Rose bowl

Amber	**Rare-$1,600**
Marigold	**$95-$450**
Purple	**Rare-$2,500**

Holly

Made by Fenton.

Colors known: amethyst, aqua opalescent, blue, blue opalescent, celeste blue, green, lime green, lime green opalescent, marigold, marigold on milk glass, moonstone, powder blue, red, vaseline, and white.

Forms: bowls, compotes, goblets, hat, plates, rose bowls, and vases.

Identifying characteristics: Fenton's popular Holly pattern features sprigs of holly berries and leaves that converge in the center and radiate to the edges of the pattern. Production began in 1911.

Also known as: Carnival Holly.

> **Reproduction Alert.** Ruffled bowls have been reproduced in aqua opalescent and amethyst.

Bowl, CRE, 9" d

Amethyst	**$80-$90**
Marigold	**$135-$145**

Bowl, deep, round

Black amethyst	**$75-$95**
Blue	**$65-$85**
Lime green, marigold overlay	**$95-$100**

Marigold .... $40-$45

Bowl, IC shape, 9" d

Amber .... $100-$120
Amethyst .... $140-$150
Aqua opalescent .... $150-$350
Blue .... $65-$135
Celeste blue .... Rare-$5,250
Green .... $45-$160
Ice blue .... Rare-$2,700
Ice green .... Rare-$2,000
Lime green .... $145-$175
Marigold .... $30-$225
Powder blue, marigold overlay
.... $120-$135
Red .... Rare-$2,700
Vaseline .... $150-$275
White .... $160-$175

Bowl, ruffled, 9" d

Amber .... $105-$125
Amethyst .... $60-$80
Aqua .... $100-$115
Black amethyst .... $200-$300
Blue .... $70-$150
Blue opalescent .... $1,200-$1,300
Green .... $85-$130
Lavender .... $65-$95
Lime green .... $130-$150
Marigold .... $115-$125
Marigold on milk glass
.... Rare-$2,700
Powder blue .... $65-$150
Red .... $1,200-$1,800
Teal .... $115-$200
Vaseline .... $115-$200
White .... $85-$195

Bowl, 3-in-1 edge

Amethyst .... $115-$145
Aqua .... $135-$395
Aqua opalescent .... $375-$395
Blue .... $35-$135
Green .... $75-$125
Lime green, marigold overlay
.... $85-$140
Marigold .... $55-$250
Marigold on milk glass ... Rare-$1,900
Olive green .... $70-$75
Powder blue, marigold overlay
.... $100-$115
Red .... $1,200-$1,800
Teal .... $115-$200
Vaseline .... $115-$200
White .... $170-$190

Compote, CRE, ruffled

Lime green .... $100-$110
Marigold .... $25-$35

Compote, goblet shape

Aqua .... $120-$140
Blue .... $50-$75
Green .... $100-$120
Lime green, marigold overlay
.... $65-$90

Lime green opalescent ...... $400-$425
Marigold .... $25-$35
Powder blue .... $50-$75
Red .... $275-$875
Vaseline .... $55-$125

Compote, ruffled

Amber, light .... $65-$75
Amethyst .... $75-$175
Aqua, marigold overlay .... $90-$215
Aqua opalescent .... $75-$90
Black amethyst .... $150-$175
Blue .... $30-$55
Green .... $85-$135
Lime green .... $60-$110
Lime green, marigold overlay
.... $65-$175
Marigold .... $25-$35
Olive green .... $45-$85
Pink .... $50-$60
Powder blue .... $105-$125
Red .... $400-$450
Yellow-green .... $100-$115

Compote, two sides up

Marigold .... $150-$165
Violet blue .... $125-$150

Hat, CRE, flattened

Amber .... $60-$80
Amethyst opalescent .... $275-$300
Aqua .... $65-$90
Aqua opalescent .... Rare-$1,200
Blue .... $25-$45
Marigold .... $15-$35
Red .... $300-$450
Vaseline .... $50-$85

Hat, ruffled

Amber .... $60-$80
Amethyst opalescent .... $200-$235
Aqua .... $65-$90
Aqua opalescent .... $300-$700
Blue .... $35-$40
Green .... $40-$50
Lime green .... $35-$45
Marigold .... $15-$35
Marigold on milk glass ...... $115-$155
Purple, dark .... $60-$90
Red .... $200-$350

Hat, square

Amberina .... $100-$125
Aqua .... $35-$40
Blue .... $30-$50
Green .... $40-$60
Marigold .... $15-$35
Red .... $125-$165
Vaseline .... $115-$145

Hat, two sides up

Aqua .... $45-$70
Blue .... $30-$35
Lime green .... $65-$85
Marigold .... $95-$125
Red .... $500-$525
Vaseline .... $50-$85

Holly, Fenton, plate, blue, 9-1/2", **$400.**

Jack-in-the-pulpit, CRE, hat shape

Amber .... $80-$95
Amberina .... $200-$300
Aqua .... $100-$115
Blue .... $45-$115
Lime green .... $120-$135
Marigold .... $40-$50
Powder blue .... $40-$45
Red .... $200-$250
Vaseline .... $65-$125

Plate, 9" d to 10" d

Amethyst .... $250-$650
Aqua opalescent .... Rare-$2,400
Black amethyst .... $600-$1,000
Blue .... $300-$500
Celeste blue .... Rare-$1,750
Clambroth .... $135-$195
Green .... $125-$800
Marigold .... $185-$375
Pastel marigold .... $75-$110
Teal .... Rare-$1,000
White .... $135-$315

Rose bowl

Aqua opalescent .... $185-$195
Blue .... $175-$225
Marigold .... $120-$135
Vaseline .... Rare-$650

Lustre Rose

Made by Imperial.

Colors known: amber, amberina, aqua, clambroth, cobalt blue, emerald green, helios, lavender, light blue with marigold overlay, lime green, marigold, marigold on milk glass, purple, olive, red, smoke, teal, vaseline, and white.

Forms: berry sets, bowls, plates, table sets, vases, and water sets.

Identifying characteristics: Modern researchers have agreed that the patterns known as Lustre Rose and

Open Rose are actually the same pattern. The pattern can be identified by the three-dimensional open rose and foliage that dominates each form. The backgrounds have a pebbly or stippled effect. This pattern was made from 1911 until 1914.

Also known as: Imperial's #489; Imperial Rose; Open Rose.

Reproduction Alert. Bowls, plates, table sets, and water sets have been reproduced in amber, helios, meadow green, marigold, pink, purple, red, smoke, and white. These reproductions were made by Imperial and those who succeeded them. Imperial reproductions are marked with IG, LIG, or ALIG logos.

Berry bowl, master, ftd, 8" d to 10" d
Amber	**$80-$100**
Aqua	**$100-$150**
Clambroth	**$30-$50**
Cobalt blue	**$300-$400**
Helios	**$60-$70**
Marigold	**$30-$50**
Purple	**$85-$185**
Smoke	**$250-$300**
Vaseline	**$200-$275**

Berry bowl, small, ftd, 5" d
Amber	**$35-$40**
Aqua	**$40-$60**
Clambroth	**$15-$20**
Cobalt blue	**$100-$125**
Helios	**$60-$80**
Marigold	**$15-$20**
Marigold on milk glass	**$90-$110**
Purple	**$35-$40**

Lustre Rose, Imperial, bowl, red, footed, large, **$2,500.**

Bowl, ftd, 8" d to 9" d
Amber	**$90-$110**
Clambroth	**$40-$60**
Cobalt blue	**$245-$290**
Helios	**$50-$75**
Marigold	**$40-$60**
Olive	**$125-$145**
Purple	**$135-$170**
Red	**$2,000-$2,500**
Smoke	**$150-$200**
Vaseline	**$150-$225**

Bowl, IC shape, flared, 10" d
Marigold, ftd	**$200-$220**
Smoke, collared base	**$125-$150**

Bowl, ruffled, collar base, 8" d to 8-1/2" d
Amber	**$35-$45**
Electric purple	**$85-$100**
Purple	**$100-$115**

Butter dish, cov, 6" x 7-1/2"
Amber	**$185-$225**
Helios	**$70-$90**
Light blue with marigold overlay	**$125-$175**
Marigold	**$60-$100**
Purple	**$250-$275**
Teal	**$250-$300**

Centerpiece bowl, ftd
Amber	**$135-$200**
Clambroth	**$125-$145**
Helios	**$100-$200**
Marigold	**$100-$175**
Purple	**$350-$400**
Smoke	**$200-$250**

Creamer
Amber	**$60-$90**
Helios	**$35-$50**
Light blue with marigold overlay	**$80-$100**
Marigold	**$35-$50**
Purple	**$130-$150**
Teal	**$100-$120**

Fernery, three scrolled feet
Amberina	**$500-$750**
Aqua	**$85-$95**
Clambroth	**$40-$60**
Cobalt blue	**$150-$185**
Marigold	**$30-$45**
Olive	**$50-$90**
Purple	**$125-$250**
Smoke	**$75-$95**
White	**$300-$350**

Fruit bowl, deep, ftd, 11" d to 12" d
Amber	**$70-$90**
Aqua	**$185-$220**
Clambroth	**$45-$50**
Helios	**$100-$125**
Marigold	**$20-$40**
Purple	**$600-$700**
Red	**Rare-$2,000**
Smoke	**$55-$90**

Vaseline	**$250-$300**

Milk pitcher
Clambroth	**$100-$125**
Marigold	**$80-$100**

Plate, 8" d to 9" d
Amber	**$100-$120**
Aqua	**$110-$130**
Clambroth	**$185-$200**
Helios	**$160-$185**
Lime green	**$200-$225**
Marigold	**$200-$250**
Purple	**Rare-$2,000**

Rose bowl
Amber	**$40-$60**
Helios	**$40-$45**
Lime green	**$150-$200**
Marigold	**$30-$35**
Olive	**$115-$135**
Purple	**$600-$625**
Smoke	**$100-$185**

Spooner
Amber	**$60-$90**
Helios	**$35-$50**
Light blue with marigold overlay	**$80-$100**
Marigold	**$35-$50**
Purple	**$130-$150**
Teal	**$100-$120**

Sugar bowl, cov
Amber	**$80-$100**
Helios	**$50-$70**
Light blue with marigold overlay	**$80-$100**
Marigold	**$50-$70**
Purple	**$130-$150**
Teal	**$100-$120**

Tumbler
Amber	**$50-$85**
Aqua	**$45-$65**
Clambroth	**$95-$110**
Marigold	**$15-$20**
Olive	**$30-$50**
Purple	**$55-$90**
Teal	**$135-$160**
White	**$300-$325**

Water pitcher
Amber	**$300-$350**
Clambroth	**$95-$125**
Helios	**$300-$350**
Light blue with marigold overlay	**$200-$225**
Marigold	**$100-$125**
Purple	**$550-$600**

Nippon

Made by Northwood.

Colors known: amethyst, aqua, blue, green, ice blue, ice green, lime green, lime green opalescent, marigold, teal, and white.

Forms: bowls and plates.

Identifying characteristics: This design is based on graceful peacock feathers, each radiating from the center flower design. The pattern was first advertised in 1912.

Bowl, PCE, basketweave back

Green	**$300-$500**
Ice blue	**$250-$450**
Ice green	**$600-$800**
Marigold	**$200-$300**
Purple	**$375-$500**

Bowl, PCE, plain back

Aqua	**Rare-$3,300**
Ice blue	**$235-$375**
White	**$265-$285**

Bowl, PCE, ribbed back

Amethyst/purple	**$250-$450**
Aqua/teal	**Rare-$1,700**
Green	**$300-$500**
Ice blue	**$250-$450**
Ice green	**$600-$800**
Lime green	**$650-$850**
Marigold	**$200-$300**
White	**$175-$275**

Bowl, ruffled

Amethyst/purple	**$150-$200**
Green	**$200-$400**
Ice blue	**$300-$400**
Ice green	**$400-$500**
Marigold	**$100-$200**
White	**$150-$250**

Plate, 9" d

Amethyst/purple	**$800-$1,000**
Green	**Rare-$1,100**
Ice blue	**Rare-$8,500**
Marigold	**$550-$750**
White	**Rare-$1,200**

Ohio Star

Made by Millersburg.

Colors known: amethyst, clambroth, crystal, green, marigold, and white.

Forms: compotes, relishes, and vases.

Identifying characteristics: The design includes a circled six-pointed star over another, and another with graceful caned arches between each vertical row. This pattern was first made by Millersburg in crystal in 1909.

Compote, 4-1/2" d

Crystal	**$30-$35**
Marigold	**Rare-$1,300**
Relish, cloverleaf shape, marigold	**Rare-$3,000**

Vase, 10" h

Amethyst	**$2,000-$2,500**
Clambroth	**$1,500-$2,000**
Green, radium	**$1,750-$4,400**
Marigold	**$2,000-$3,000**

Peacock & Grape

Made by Fenton.

Colors known: amethyst, aqua, blue, green, lime green opalescent, marigold, peach opalescent, pumpkin marigold, and red.

Forms: bowls and plates.

Identifying characteristics: This pattern is similar to Peacock & Dahlia, but instead of a dahlia, there is a cluster of grapes and leaves. The top of the wedges have a flat border rather than a scallop. Production began in 1911.

Also known as: Fenton's #1646.

Bowl, ftd, 8" d to 9" d

Amethyst	**$125-$175**
Blue	**$80-$100**
Green	**$100-$150**
Lime green opalescent	**$500-$585**
Marigold	**$40-$60**
Red	**$700-$900**

Bowl, IC shape, spatula foot

Amethyst	**$90-$120**
Blue	**$50-$80**
Green	**$40-$60**
Marigold	**$20-$25**
Red	**$350-$400**

Bowl, ruffled

Amethyst	**$55-$80**
Blue	**$100-$175**
Green	**$30-$65**
Electric green	**$300-$400**
Marigold	**$20-$30**
Peach opalescent	**$300-$400**
Pumpkin marigold	**$250-$325**

Bowl, 3-in-1 edge

Amethyst	**$105-$165**
Green	**$45-$70**
Marigold	**$20-$25**

Nut bowl, ftd

Blue	**$100-$130**
Marigold	**$35-$55**

Plate, 9" d to 9-1/2" d

Blue	**Rare-$1,200**
Green	**Rare-$1,000**
Lavender	**$300-$500**
Marigold	**$450-$1,750**

Plate, collar base, 9" d

Electric blue	**Rare-$2,500**
Marigold	**$900-$1,100**

Plate, spatula ftd, 9" d

Blue	**$400-$500**
Green	**$300-$400**
Lavender	**$200-$300**
Marigold	**$85-$200**

Ribbon Tie

Made by Fenton.

Colors known: amethyst, black amethyst, blue, green, marigold, purple, and red.

Nippon, Northwood, PCE, ruffled bowl with basket-weave exterior, purple with near-electric iridescence, **$475.**

Ohio Star, Millersburg, vase, green, 10" **$4,400.**

Peacock and Grape, Fenton, bowl, 9", ruffle, marigold over moonstone, **$500.**

Ribbon Tie, Fenton, 3-in-1 bowl, electric amethyst, 8-1/2", $125.

Tornado, Northwood, vase, 6", ribbed flared top, amethyst, $1,800.

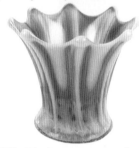

Wide Rib, Dugan, vase, peach opal, 5", $130.

Forms: bowls and plates.

Identifying characteristics: This pattern takes six ribbon segments and swirls them to the perimeter while other ribbons ring the bowl horizontally. Production began in 1911.

Also known as: Comet.

Bowl, candy ribbon edge

Amethyst/purple	**$40-$90**
Blue	**$95-$135**
Marigold	**$45-$65**

Bowl, ruffled or 3-in-1 edge, 8" d to 9" d

Amethyst/purple	**$125-$400**
Black amethyst	**$95-$115**
Blue	**$160-$250**
Green	**$45-$90**
Marigold	**$35-$65**
Powder blue	**$70-$90**
Red	**Rare-$10,500**

Plate, ruffled or 3-in-1 edge, 8" d to 9" d

Amethyst/purple	**$130-$400**
Blue	**$200-$300**

Tornado

Made by Northwood.

Colors known: amethyst, blue, green, ice blue, lavender, marigold, and white.

Forms: vases.

Identifying characteristics: This pattern has a swirling raised tornado-type eye that trails to the base of this vase. It is found with either a rib element on the sides or plain. Production was centered in the 1911 to 1912 period.

Also known as: Tadpole.

Vase, large, 6-1/2" h, 3" d base

Amethyst	**$400-$600**
Green	**$400-$800**
Marigold	**$300-$500**
Purple	**$450-$650**
White	**Rare-$6,750**

Vase, ribbed

Amethyst	**$1,500-$2,000**
Blue	**$3,100-$3,600**
Ice blue	**$3,600-$6,500**
Lavender	**$1,500-$2,000**
Marigold	**$1,000-$2,000**
Purple	**$800-$1,500**

Vase, small, 6" h, 2-5/8" d base

Amethyst	**$1,000-$1,800**
Green	**$400-$900**
Lavender	**$1,000-$1,300**
Marigold	**$225-$625**
Purple	**$215-$515**
White	**Rare-$5,500**

Vase, whimsy

Marigold, green tornado medallions	**$2,100-$4,750**
Marigold, pedestal base	**Rare-$1,900**

Wide Rib

Made by Dugan/Diamond.

Colors known: amethyst, blue, peach opalescent, white.

Forms: vases.

Identifying characteristics: This ribbed pattern is identified as Dugan/Diamond when the ends of each of the eight ribs have knob-like tips.

Also known as: Dugan's #1016.

Vase

Amethyst	**$75-$400**
Blue, 11" h	**$50-$100**
Peach opalescent	**$75-$135**
White	**$45-$80**

CONSOLIDATED GLASS COMPANY

History: The Consolidated Lamp and Glass Company was formed as a result of the 1893 merger of the Wallace and McAfee Company, glass and lamp jobbers of Pittsburgh, and the Fostoria Shade & Lamp Company of Fostoria, Ohio. When the Fostoria, Ohio, plant burned down in 1895, Corapolis, Pennsylvania, donated a seven-acre tract of land near the center of town for a new factory. In 1911, the company was the largest lamp, globe, and shade works in the United States, employing more than 400 workers.

In 1925, Reuben Haley, owner of an independent-design firm, convinced John Lewis, president of Consolidated, to enter the giftware field utilizing a series of designs inspired by the 1925 Paris Exposition (l'Exposition Internationale des Arts Décorative et Industriels Modernes) and the work of René Lalique. Initially, the glass was marketed by Howard Selden through his showroom at 225 Fifth Avenue in New York City. The first two lines were Catalonian and Martele.

Additional patterns were added in the late 1920s: Florentine (January 1927), Chintz (January 1927), Ruba Rombic (January 1928), and Line 700 (January 1929). On April 2, 1932, Consolidated closed it doors. Kenneth Harley moved about 40 molds to Phoenix. In March 1936, Consolidated reopened under new management, and the "Harley" molds were returned. During this period, the famous Dancing Nymph line, based on an eight-inch salad plate in the 1926 Martele series, was introduced.

In August 1962, Consolidated was sold to Dietz Brothers. A major fire damaged the plant during a 1963 labor dispute, and in 1964 the company permanently closed its doors.

Bonbon, cov, Ruba Rhombic, faceted, smoky topaz, catalog #832, c1931, 8" d **$325**

Bowl, Coronation, Martelé, flared, blue, 5-1/2" d................................ **$75**

Box, cov, Martelé line, Fruit and Leaf pattern, scalloped edge, 7" l, 5" w .. **$85**

Butter dish, cov, Cosmos, white custard glass, blue, pink, and yellow daisies, 6" h **$250**

Candlesticks, pr, Hummingbird, Martelé line, oval body, jade green, 6-3/4" h.. **$248**

Cocktail, Dancing Nymph, French Crystal **$90**

Cookie jar, Regent Line, #3758, Florette, rose pink over white opal casing, 6-1/2" h.. **$370**

Cup and saucer, Dancing Nymph, ruby flashed **$265**

Dinner service, Five Fruits, service for six, goblet, plate, sherbet, one large serving plate, purple wash, mold imperfections, wear...................... **$375**

Goblet, Dancing Nymph, French Crystal **$90**

Jar, cov, Con-Cora, #3758-9, pine cone dec, irid **$165**

Lamp
  Cockatoo, figural, orange and blue, black beak, brown stump, black base, 13" h................................. **$450**
  Flower basket, bouquet of roses and poppies, yellows, pinks, green leaves, brown basketweave, black glass base, 8" h.......................... **$300**

Mayonnaise comport, Martelé, Iris, green wash **$55**

Miniature lamp, opalescent blue, 10" h.. **$380**

Night light, Santa Maria, block base **$450**

Old-fashioned tumbler, Catalonian, yellow, 3-7/8" h **$20**

Perfume bottle, Ruba Rombic, gray frosted body, nick on stopper, 5-1/2" h **$1,420**

Plate
  Bird of Paradise, amber wash, 8-1/4" d **$40**
  Catalonian, yellow, 10-1/4" d **$45**
  Martelé, Orchid, pink, birds and flowers, 12" d **$115**

Puff box, cov, Lovebirds, blue **$95**

Salt and pepper shakers, pr
  Cone, pink.................................. **$75**
  Cosmos...................................... **$115**
  Guttate, green **$85**

Sauce dish, Criss-Cross, cranberry opalescent.................................. **$55**

Sherbet, ftd, Catalonian, green **$20**

Snack set, Martelé Fruits, pink..... **$45**

Sugar bowl, cov, Guttate, cased pink **$120**

Sugar shaker, puff quilted body, pink, brass lid, 3-1/2" d **$150**

Sundae, Martelé, Russet Yellow Fruits **$35**

Syrup, Cone, squatty, pink **$295**

Toothpick holder, Florette, cased pink.. **$75**

Tumbler
  Catalonian, ftd, green, 5-1/4" h **$30**
  Guttate, pink satin...................... **$65**
  Katydid, clambroth...................... **$165**
  Ruba Rhombic, faceted, ftd, silver gray, 6" h **$210**

Umbrella vase, Blackberry **$550**

Vase
  Katydid, blue wash, fan-shaped top, 8-1/2" h **$300**
  Regent Line, #3758, cased blue stretch over white opal, pinched, 6" h... **$175**
  Sea foam green, lavender, and tan, floral pattern, 6-1/2" h **$150**

Whiskey glass, Ruba Rhombic, faceted, transparent jungle green, catalog #823, 2-5/8" h....................... **$265**
  Duck **$60**

Consolidated sugar shaker, Cone pattern, tall, pink blushed milk glass, 2" d base, 5-1/4" h, **$150.**

Consolidated vase, Lovebirds, opaque white body, turquoise overlay, **$95.**

CRANBERRY GLASS

History: Cranberry glass is transparent and named for its color, achieved by adding powdered gold to a molten batch of amber glass and reheating at a low temperature to develop the cranberry or ruby color. The glass color first appeared in the last half of the 17th century, but was not made in American glass factories until the last half of the 19th century.

Cranberry glass was blown, mold blown, or pressed. Examples often are decorated with gold or enamel. Less-expensive cranberry glass, made by substituting copper for gold, can be identified by its bluish-purple tint.

Reproduction Alert. Reproductions abound. These pieces are heavier, off-color, and lack the quality of older examples.

Cranberry Nailsea sweetmeat, white drag loops, 5-1/4" w, **$300.**
Photo courtesy of The Early Auction Company, LLC.

Cranberry glass pitcher, tankard, gilt and enamel polychrome floral dec, applied colorless handle, Bastow Glass Co., Coudersport, Pa., 1900-1904, 11-3/4" h, 4" d, **$110.**
Photo courtesy of Green Valley Auctions.

Cranberry opalescent celery, fern pattern, open bubble to int., late 19th century, 6" h, **$140.**
Photo courtesy of Green Valley Auctions.

Cranberry crackle pitcher, Moser, pinch sided, medallions of floral sprays, applied, reeded gold highlighted handle, signed, 9" h, **$1,100.**
Photo courtesy of The Early Auction Company, LLC.

Cranberry glass, epergne, cased opalescent shading to clear, ruffled bowl, four lilies, with spiraling colorless rigaree, late 19th century, 19-1/2" h, 10" d bowl, **$935.**
Photo courtesy of Green Valley Auctions.

Basket, ruffled edge, petticoat shape, crystal loop handle, c1890, 7" h x 5" w **$250**

Bride's basket, German silver-filigree frame, plain cranberry bowl, 5" h, 3-1/2" d bowl **$115**

Centerpiece, central trumpet-form vase, shallow dish, pedestal foot, gilt Greek-key dec, Victorian, 19-1/2" h **$300**

Cologne bottle, faceted, finely cut faceted stopper, 7" h **$175**

Condiment dish, underplate, scrolling vines and grapes dec, Continental, 6-1/2" h..**$175**

Creamer, Optic pattern, fluted to applied clear handle, 5" h, 2-3/4" d **$95**

Cruet, Optic ribbed body, trifold rim, applied clear handled, 9" h **$100**

Decanter, craquelle, bulbous stick form, pinch-sided, crystal collar, oval stopper, 10-1/2" h **$150**

Dresser box, blown out melon ribs, enameled scrolling on bronze feet, French, late 19th C, 5" d..............**$175**

Epergne, five pcs, large ruffled bowl, tall center lily, three jack-in-the-pulpit vases, 19" h, 11" d **$1,200**

Finger bowl, Inverted Thumbprint pattern, deep color **$200**

Garniture, cranberry overlay cut to clear, faceted cut dec, Continental, 14" d bowl, pr 11" h candlesticks........................**$450**

Goblet, acanthus scrolling, clear banded cut stem with polychrome scrolling, foot dec with band of peacock eyes, mkd "Royal Baron," Meyrs Neff crown, Lobmeyer, 6" h **$550**

Lamp, fluid, deep cranberry font connected to sq black base, later electric socket base soldered over early brass collar, brass connector, 1860-75, 8" h **$880**

Nappy, heart shape, tooled crystal feet and handle, English, 5-1/2" d **$100**

Pipe, hand blown, tapering-bent neck, bulbous bowl, three bulbs at base, white-enamel dec at outer rim of bowl, 18" l....................................**$250**

Pitcher
  Bulbous, ice bladder int., applied clear handle, 10" h, 5" d **$250**
  Ripple and Thumbprint pattern, bulbous, round mouth, applied clear handle, 6-1/2" h, 4-1/8" d **$175**

Salt, master, ftd, enameled floral dec **$200**

Sherbet
  Ftd, polychrome and acanthus scrolling, various colored dotted peacock eyes, Lobmeyer, 4-1/4" h..........**$400**
  Translucent cranberry, dec with purple, red, yellow, green, and white scrolling flowers on horizontal gilt bands, beaded highlights, Moser, 4-1/2" h **$500**

Sugar shaker, molded fern pattern, 4-1/2" h..**$150**

Tankard water pitcher, acanthus scrollwork in shades of purple, red, green, and blue, gilt peacock eyes with various color dots, applied clear handle, Lobmeyer, 11" h **$1,100**

Tumble-up, Inverted Thumbprint pattern **$195**

Tumbler, Inverted Thumbprint pattern **$65**

Vase
  Bulbous, white-enameled lilies of the valley dec, cylindrical neck, 8-7/8" h **$150**
  Bulbous stick, flaring rim, cranberry, banded gold and silver collar, polychrome scrolling, dots, and florals, Moser, 9" h **$300**
  Ribbed body, heavy application of colorless leaves, collar, and scrolled feet, berry pontil, attributed to Harrach, c1890, 5-3/4" h..........**$100**

Watch stand, figural gilt bronze base with stork, hook for suspending pocket watch, cranberry glass posy vase set in reticulated scroll holder, Austrian or French, c1870, 7" h **$700**

CRUETS

History: Cruets are small glass bottles used on the table holding condiments such as oil, vinegar, and wine. The pinnacle of cruet use occurred during the Victorian era, when a myriad of glass manufacturers made cruets in a wide assortment of patterns, colors, and sizes. All cruets had stoppers; most had handles.

Aventurine, applied clear reeded handle, cut faceted stopper, 6-1/2" h **$375**

Bluerina, deep royal blue neck fades to clear at shoulder, optic inverted thumbprint design in body, applied clear glass handle, teardrop-shaped airtrap stopper, in-the-making thin elongated bubble in neck, 7-1/4" h **$500**

Bohemian, amber cut to clear, floral arrangement intaglio carved on ruby flashed ground of three oval panels with carved frames of floral swags, five cut-to-clear panels at neck, three embellished with gold scrolls, all edged in brilliant gold, 16 decorative panels edged in gold, base and stopper both sgd "4"...........................**$750**

Burmese, Mt. Washington, shiny finish, butter-yellow ribbed body, applied handle, and mushroom stopper, 7" h **$1,250**

Chocolate, opaque, Greentown Cactus, no stopper.....................**$125**

Leaf Bracket, orig stopper...........**$295**

Cranberry, optic ribbed body, trifold rim, applied clear handle, 9" h ...**$100**

Custard glass, Wild Bouquet pattern, fired-on dec...................................**$500**

Moser, eight raised cabochon-like ruby gems, deep cut edges of burnished gold, mounted on colorless body, eight alternating panels of brilliant gold squiggles and stylized leaves, handle cut in three sharp edges, six gold dec panels on stopper, each set with ruby cabochon, inside of mouth and base of stopper sgd "4," some loss to gold squiggles, 6" h **$585**

Pattern glass, orig stopper
  Amazon, bar-in-hand stopper, 8-1/2" h **$185**
  Beveled Star, green **$225**
  Croesus, large, green, gold trim ...**$395**
  Daisy and Button with Crossbars **$75**
  Delaware, cranberry, gold trim **$295**
  Esther, green, gold trim **$465**

Fluted Scrolls, blue dec **$265**
Millard, amber stain....................**$350**
Riverside's Ransom, Vaseline......**$225**
Tiny Optic, green, dec..................**$150**
Peachblow, New England, shiny finish, Wild Rose, pink-white handle, orig white stopper **$1,500**

Rubena Verde, Hobbs, Brockunier & Co., Polka Dot No. 308, flashed ruby red trefoil spout and upper half, intense Vaseline base, handle, and stopper, slight flake at tip of stopper, 7" h...**$585**

Sapphire blue
  Hobnail, faceted stopper, applied blue handle, damage to three hobs, 7-1/4" h **$385**
  Enameled pink, yellow, and blue flowers, green leaves, applied clear handle and foot, cut clear stopper, 7-1/2" h, 3-1/4" d **$165**

Satin, blue Raindrop MOP, clear frosted reeded handle, clear cut faceted stopper, flake, 7-1/2" h **$385**

Cruet, white spatter over amber ground, applied amber handle, matching amber ball stopper, **$65.**

Rubina Verde teepee cruet, coinspot pattern, faceted Vaseline stopper, applied handle, 6-3/4" h, **$400.**
Photo courtesy of The Early Auction Company, LLC.

Agata cruet, New England, bulbous body, tri-fold rim, light pink stopper, applied handle, 6" h, **$750.**
Photo courtesy of The Early Auction Company, LLC.

CUSTARD GLASS

Reproduction Alert. L. G. Wright Glass Co. has reproduced pieces in the Argonaut Shell and Grape and Cable patterns. It also introduced new patterns, such as Floral and Grape and Vintage Band. Mosser reproduced toothpicks in Argonaut Shell, Chrysanthemum Sprig, and Inverted Fan & Feather.

History: Custard glass was developed in England in the early 1880s. Harry Northwood made the first American custard glass at his Indiana, Pennsylvania, factory in 1898.

From 1898 until 1915, many manufacturers produced custard-glass patterns, e.g., Dugan Glass, Fenton, A. H. Heisey Glass Co., Jefferson Glass, Northwood, Tarentum Glass, and U.S. Glass. Cambridge and McKee continued the production of custard glass into the Depression.

The ivory or creamy yellow-custard color is achieved by adding uranium salts to the molten hot glass. The chemical content makes the glass glow when held under a black light. The more uranium, the more luminous the color. Northwood's custard glass has the smallest amount of uranium, creating an ivory color; Heisey used more, creating a deep yellow color.

Custard glass was made in patterned tableware pieces. It also was made as souvenir items and novelty pieces. Souvenir pieces include a place name or hand-painted decorations, e.g., flowers. Patterns of custard glass often were highlighted in gold, enameled colors, and stains.

Banana stand, Grape and Cable, Northwood, nutmeg stain...........**$315**

Berry bowl, individual size, Chrysanthemum Sprig, blue, slight loss to gold, sgd "Northwood," 5" l x 3-3/4" w, 2-5/8" h..............**$165**

Berry bowl, master
Beaded Circle, scalloped top, Northwood, 8-5/8" d, 5" h **$485**
Bonbon, Fruits and Flowers, Northwood, nutmeg stain **$225**
Chrysanthemum Sprig, blue, slight loss to gold, sgd "Northwood," 10-1/2" l x 8" w, 4-7/8" h..........**$385**

Bowl, Grape and Cable, Northwood, basketweave ext., nutmeg stain, 7-1/2" d **$70**

Butter dish, cov
Everglades **$375**
Grape & Cable, Northwood, nutmeg stain................................**$450**
Tiny Thumbprint, Tarentum, rose dec **$300**
Victoria..**$300**

Compote, Geneva............................**$65**

Creamer, Heart with Thumbprint .. **$85**

Cruet, Argonaut Shell, orig stopper, minimal loss to gold dec, 6-1/2" h **$985**

Goblet, Grape and Gothic Arches, nutmeg stain...**$80**

Hair receiver, Winged Scroll **$125**

Jelly compote, Argonaut Shell, gold edge, raised green leaves, gold seashells, 5" h **$235**

Nappy, Northwood Grape **$60**

Pitcher, Argonaut Shell **$325**

Plate, Grape and Cable, Northwood **$45**

Punch cup
Diamond with Peg.....................**$40**
Louis XV..................................**$35**

Salt and pepper shakers, pr, Chrysanthemum Sprig **$165**

Spooner
Beaded Circle, Northwood, wear to gold, 4-1/4" h **$195**
Wild Bouquet, Northwood, good floral dec, wear to gold, 4-1/2" h.........**$285**

Sugar, cov
Diamond with Peg.....................**$175**
Georgia Gem, pink floral dec **$185**

Tiny Thumbprint, rose dec.........**$185**

Table set, Inverted Fan and Feather, cov butter, creamer, spooner, cov sugar, Northwood, gold dec........**$500**

Tankard pitcher, Diamond with Peg **$275**

Toothpick holder
Chrysanthemum Sprig, blue, gold leaves and blossoms, sgd "Northwood," tiny inside edge base flake, 2-3/4" h **$545**
Chrysanthemum Sprig, custard, gold dec, script sgd "Northwood," 2-3/4" h **$100**
Louis XV **$200**

Tumbler
Beaded Circle, each circle with one blue blossom, and six pink blossoms and two green leaves, Northwood, worn gold rim trim, 4" h **$165**
Chrysanthemum Sprig, blue, slight loss to gold dec, 3-3/4" h..........**$185**
Wild Bouquet, Northwood, 3-3/4" h **$285**

Custard table set, left: sugar, covered; creamer; butter dish, covered; salt shaker; spooner, Chrysanthemum Sprig, blue custard, gold trim, **$800.**
Photo courtesy of Joy Luke.

CUT GLASS, AMERICAN

History: Glass is cut by grinding decorations into the glass by means of abrasive-carrying metal or stone wheels. A very ancient craft, it was revived in 1600 by Bohemians and spread through Europe to Great Britain and America.

American cut glass came of age at the Centennial Exposition in 1876 and the World Columbian Exposition in 1893. The American public recognized American cut glass to be exceptional in quality and workmanship. America's most significant output of this high-quality glass occurred from 1880 to 1917, a period now known as the Brilliant Period.

Marks: Around 1890, some companies began adding an acid-etched "signature" to their glass. This signature may be the actual company name, its logo, or a chosen symbol. Today, signed pieces command a premium over unsigned pieces since the signature clearly establishes the origin. However, signatures should be carefully verified for authenticity since objects with forged signatures have been in existence for some time. One way to check is to run a fingertip or fingernail lightly over the signature area. As a general rule, a genuine signature cannot be felt; a forged signature has a raised surface.

Many companies never used the acid-etched signature on their glass and may or may not have affixed paper labels to the items originally. Dorflinger Glass and the Meriden Glass Co. made cut glass of the highest quality, yet never used an acid-etched signature. Furthermore, cut glass made before the 1890s was not signed. Many of these wood-polished items, cut on blown blanks, were of excellent quality and often won awards at exhibitions.

Banana bowl, Harvard pattern, hobstar bottom, 11" l, 6-1/2" d **$220**

Basket

Five large hobstars, fancy emb floral silver handle and rim, 9-1/2" h, 11-1/2" d **$225**

Four large hobstars, two fans applied, crystal rope-twisted handle, 7-1/2" h, 8-1/2" d **$350**

Bonbon, Broadway pattern, Huntly, minor flakes, 8" d, 2" h **$135**

Bowl, cov, steeple form finial, flared scalloped rim, ftd, flute, oval, punty and vesica cuts, eastern United States, several edge nicks, repairs, c1840, 17-1/2" h **$215**

Bowl, open

Brilliant cut, cross bars and flowers, scalloped rim, sgd "Libbey" in circle, some grinding to edge, 8" d, 2" h **$175**

Deep-cut buttons, stars, and fans, 10" d **$220**

Hartford, stars with button border, scalloped edge, minor edge flakes, 9" d, 4" h **$125**

Rayed base, diamond point border, sgd "Libbey" in circle, 8" d, 1-1/2" h **$150**

Rolled-down edge, cut and engraved flowers, leaves, and center thistle, notched-serrated edge, 12" d, 4-1/2" h **$275**

Three brilliant cut thistles surround bowl, flower in center, scalloped edge, etched "Libbey" label, price for pr, 8" d, 4" h **$400**

Box, cov, cut-paneled base, cover cut with large eight-pointed star with hobstar center surrounded by fans, C. F. Monroe, 5" d, 2-3/4" h **$275**

Bread tray, Anita, Libbey in circle mark, 8" x 12" **$535**

Butter dish, cov, Hobstar **$250**

Candlesticks, pr

Adelaide pattern, amber, Pairpoint, 12" h **$250**

Faceted cut knobs, large teardrop stems, ray base, 10" h **$425**

Celery dish, sgd "J. Hoare" **$350**

Centerpiece, wheel cut and etched, molded, fruiting foliage, chips, 10-3/4" d **$490**

Champagne, Kalana Lily pattern, Dorflinger **$75**

Champagne bucket, sgd "Hoare," 7" h, 7" d **$400**

Champagne pitcher, Prism pattern, triple notch handle, monogram sterling silver top, 11" h **$425**

Cheese dish, cov, plate, cobalt blue cut to clear, bull's eye and panel, large miter splints on bottom of plate, 6" h dome, 9" d **$250**

Cider pitcher, hobstars, zippers, fine diamonds, honeycomb-cut handle, 7" h **$225**

Cologne bottle

Hob and Lace pattern, green cased to clear, pattern-cut stopper, Dorflinger, 6" h **$625**

Holland pattern, faceted-cut stopper, 7-1/2" h **$275**

Compote

Deep bowl with trefoil, curved edge, three hobstars, and panels with diamond point, fan, and zipper patterns, short pedestal, round base, etched maple leaf mark of T. B.

Cut Glass bowl, Pitney and Brooks, hobstars over a band of straight miters, marked bottom "P & B" in diamond, early 20th century, 4" h x 8" d, **$85.**
Photo courtesy of Green Valley Auctions.

Clark & Co., Honesdale, PA, minor grinding to sawtooth edge, 6-3/4" d, 5-1/2" h **$395**

Hobstars on scalloped edge bowl, straight paneled stem with zipper cut edges, minor flakes, 9-1/8" d, 6-1/4" h **$400**

Russian cut, scalloped rim and foot, zipper cut faceted stem teardrop center, minor pinpoints and grinding, 8-1/4" d, 8-3/4" h **$500**

Strawberry and chain pattern, serrated edge, low pedestal base, minor roughness and grinding, 7" d, 4-1/4" h..............................**$95**

Creamer and sugar, pr

Hobstar designs, handles with oval cutting, minor roughness on spout, 3-1/4" h, 3-3/4" h......................**$250**

Pedestal, geometric cuttings, zippered handles, teardrop full length of handle, sgd "Hawkes," 4-1/2" h
....**$750**

Pedestal, Carolyn variation, notched handles, 5-1/2" h **$895**

Cruet, round, stars on body, paneled neck with zipper cut edges, scallop cut handle, rayed base, faceted stopper, handle sgd "Tuthill," 6-7/8" h
....**$250**

Decanter, orig stopper

Pineapple and zipper cut designs, paneled neck with zipper cut designs, diamond pattern on base, faint label of "J. Hoare & Co. Corning 1853," 7-7/8" h **$350**

Quart, triple ring, strawberry diamonds and fans separated by rayed vesicas, flute-cut shoulder and base, polished pontil mark, non-matching cut hollow stopper, Pittsburgh, very minor rim flake, second quarter 19th C, 10-1/2" h
....**$220**

Russian pattern, pr, 11" h............**$600**

Stars, arches, fans, cut neck, star cut mushroom stopper, 11-1/2" h
....**$125**

Dish

Hobstar, pineapple, palm leaf, 5" d
....**$45**

Scalloped edge, allover hobstar medallions and hobs, 8" d **$175**

Dresser box, cov, Harvard pattern variation, three-ftd, silver-plated fittings, orig beveled mirror on swivel hinge under lid, cut by Bergen Glass Co., couple of minute flakes, 7" h, 7" w
....**$750**

Fern dish, round, silver-plate rim, C. F. Monroe, minor roughness to cut pattern, normal wear on base, no liner, 3-3/4" h, 8" w **$200**

Flower center

Etched and wheel cut motif, honeycomb flared neck, some wear, 7-3/4" h, 12" d.........................**$500**

Hobstars, flashed fans, hobstar chain and base, 5" h, 6" d.................**$325**

Goblet

Buzzstar, pineapple, marked "B & B," 7" h **$40**

Intaglio vintage cut, sgd "Sinclair," 8-1/2" h **$80**

Humidor, cov

Hobstars, beaded split vesicas, hobstar base, matching cut glass lid with hollow for sponge, 9" h....**$575**

Middlesex, hollow stopper, sponge holder in lid, Dorflinger, 7-1/2" d
....**$490**

Ice bucket

Colorless, body cut with vertical flutes, beaded silver-mounted rim with sterling silver swing handle marked for Wilcox Silver Plate Co., early 20th C, 6-5/8" h.............**$320**

Hobstars and notched prisms, 8" d underplate, double handles, 7" h
....**$940**

Ice cream tray, Empress pattern variation, sgd "Libbey," 10" x 17-1/2"
....**$1,000**

Jar, cov, diamond cut finial on stepped lid, ftd ovoid vessel, four Oriental influenced cut medallions, cane and star-cut ground, several nicks, 20th C, 10" h..**$260**

Knife rest, 4" l **$95**

Lamp

Cut glass rounded shade with pointed top, inverted trumpet form base, both with etched rose dec, wide borders of geometric design, ring of cut glass prisms, 24" h **$525**

Hobstars, cross-cut diamonds, flashed star cuttings, triangular shaped hanging prisms, 23" h **$1,300**

Loving cup, three handles, sterling top
....**$350**

Nappy, two handles

Deep-cut arches, pointed sunbursts and medallions, 9" d **$135**

Hobstar center, intaglio floral, strawberry diamond button border, 6" d
....**$45**

Orange bowl, hobstars and strawberry diamond, 9-3/4" x 6-3/4" x 3-3/4" h
....**$200**

Perfume bottle

Bulbous, allover cutting, orig stopper, 6-1/2" h **$220**

Cranberry overlay, shaped sides, notched cuts, S. Mordan & Co., silver-mounted cap, 3-1/2" l
....**$325**

Perfume flask, pistol-form, etched silver-gilt mounts, short chain, spring-action trigger opens lid set with maker's medallion, French, late 19th/ early 20th C, 4-3/4" l **$1,380**

Pickle tray, checkerboard, hobstar, 7" x 3"..**$45**

Pitcher

Baluster form body, upper section vertically ribbed and cut, lower section with stylized flowerheads, facet cut handle, silver-plated rim mount with beaded edging, monogrammed, marked "Wilcox Silver Plate Co.," 8-7/8" h **$750**

Baluster, vertical flutes with bead and lozenge cuts, crosshatched and diamond-cut diamonds at base, mounted with sterling bead-edged spout, monogrammed, 14-1/8" h
....**$250**

Tapered body with quatrefoil flowers, tiny diamond point surface, surrounded by fans and hobstars, paneled neck with zipper cuts, spout with diamonds, cut ridges on applied handle, spout has been reworked on underside, 12-1/2" h
....**$475**

Plate

Alternating hobstar and pinwheel, 12" d **$100**

Carolyn pattern, J. Hoare, 10" d
....**$525**

Potpourri jar, baluster shaped cut glass base, silver lid with portrait medallion and floral banding, 6" h
....**$200**

Punch bowl

Rajah pattern, sgd "Pitkin and Brooks," 13-3/4" d, 15-1/4" h
....**$2,750**

Round, set into base, cut rim, miter star cut pattern, acid-etched maker's mark for T. G. Hawkes & Co., Corning, NY, on base, 14-3/8" d, 13-1/4" h **$1,880**

Two pcs, Elgin pattern, Quaker City, 11" h, 10" w............................**$600**

Punch ladle, silver plated emb shell bowl, cut and notched prism handle, 11-1/2" l....................................**$165**

Relish

Leaf shape, Clear Button Russian pattern, 13" l **$375**

Two handles, divided, Jupiter pattern, Meriden, 8" l............................**$120**

Salad bowl, Russian pattern.........$90
Salt, open, Russian pattern, master size
....$45
Salt shaker, prism columns...........$30
Serving dish, two layers, apple and
pear branches, grape vine dec, Gravic,
11" d...$395
Tankard pitcher
  Harvard cut sides, pinwheel top, mini
  hobnails, thumbprint notched han-
  dle, 10-1/4" h...............................$200
  Hobstar, strawberry diamond,
  notched prism and fan, flared base
  with bull's eye, double thumbprint
  handle, 11" h................................$275
Tobacco humidor, Flute pattern,
ornate Whiting sterling lid with
sponge holder, 7" h.......................$650
Tray
  Hobstars, caning, and notched prisms
  inside vesicas arranged around center star, sgd "Libbey" twice, 12" d
  ....$2,000
  Round, Monarch, sgd "Hoare," 12" d
  ....$975
  Sillsbee pattern, Pairpoint, 14" x
  7-1/2"..$335
Tumbler
  Band of strawberry diamonds and
  fans, plain base edge, polished pon-
  til, Pittsburgh-type, first half 19th
  C, 3-1/4" h, 3-1/8" d..................$150
  Harvard, rayed base......................$45
  Hobstars..$40
Urn, cov, Russian pattern............$175
Vase
  Corset shape, well-cut hobstar, straw-
  berry diamond, prism, flashed star
  and fan, 16" h..............................$300
  Fan, amber, engraved grape leaves
  and vines, round disk base, acid-
  etched Hawkes mark, small chip on
  base, 11" h.....................................$300
  Floral and diamond point engraving,
  sgd "Hawkes," 12-1/2" h, 6-1/2" d
  ....$250
  Lobed rim, alternating vertical cut
  patterns, star-cut disk base, 20th C,
  19-1/2" h.......................................$750
  Monarch pattern, sgd "J. Hoare,"
  24-1/2" h....................................$3,750
  Ruffled edge, cut iris dec, Gravic,
  14" h..$295
  Squatty body, short flaring neck, scal-
  loped rim, 8" h, 11" d.................$550
  Two pcs, trumpet shape, hobstars
  and paneled ring design, base and
  top joined with metal post covered with diamond faceted ball,
  23-1/4" h....................................$1,350

Cut glass, decanters, iris design, sterling silver stoppers, Hawkes, price for pair, **$600.**
Photo courtesy of David Rago Auctions, Inc.

*Cut glass, water gob-
lets, iris design, square
base, Hawkes, price for
set of 12,* **$550.**
Photo courtesy of David Rago
Auctions, Inc.

DEPRESSION GLASS

History: Depression glass was made from 1920 to 1940. It was an inexpensive machine-made glass and produced by several companies in various patterns and colors. The number of forms made in different patterns also varied.

Depression glass was sold through variety stores, given away as premiums, or packaged with certain products. Movie houses gave it away from 1935 until well into the 1940s.

Like pattern glass, knowing the proper name of a pattern is the key to collecting. Collectors should be prepared to do research.

Reproduction Alert. The number of Depression glass patterns that have been reproduced continues to grow. Reproductions exist in many patterns, forms, and colors. Beware of colors and forms that were not made in the original production of the pattern. Carefully examine every piece that seems questionable and look for loss of details, poor impressions, and slight differences in sizes.

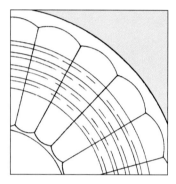

Circle

Manufactured by Hocking Glass Company, Lancaster, Ohio, in the 1930s.

Made in crystal, green, and pink. Crystal is listed in the original catalogs, but few pieces have surfaced to date. A 3-1/8" d sherbet is known and valued at $4.

Item	Green	Pink
Bowl, 4-1/2" d	$15	$15
Bowl, 5-1/2" d, flared	17.50	17.50
Bowl, 8" d	16	16
Bowl, 9-3/8" d	18.50	18.50
Creamer, ftd	9	16
Cup	6	7.50
Goblet, 8 oz, 5-3/4" h	16.50	15
Iced tea tumbler, 10 oz	17.50	17.50
Juice tumbler, 4 oz	9.50	9

Item	Green	Pink
Pitcher, 60 oz	35	35
Pitcher, 80 oz	30	32
Plate, 6" d, sherbet	3	3
Plate, 8-1/4" d, luncheon	11	11
Plate, 9-1/2" d, dinner	12	12
Sandwich plate, 10" d	15	17.50
Saucer, 6" d	2.50	2.50
Sherbet, 3-1/8"	5	5
Sherbet, 4-3/4"	12	12
Sugar, ftd	12	16
Tumbler, 8 oz	10	10
Tumbler, 15 oz, flat	17.50	17.50
Wine, 4-1/2" h	15	15

Circle, green pitcher, 80 oz, **$30.**

Circle, green cup, **$6.**

Colonial

Knife and Fork

Manufactured by Hocking Glass Company, Lancaster, Ohio, from 1934 to 1938.

Made in crystal, green, and pink.

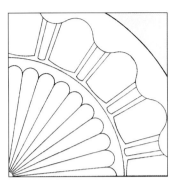

Item	Crystal	Green	Pink
Berry bowl, 3-3/4" d	$-	$-	$60
Berry bowl, 9" d	24	30	35
Butter dish, cov	40	60	700
Cereal bowl, 5-1/2" d	32	85	60
Cocktail, 3 oz, 4" h	15	25	-
Cordial, 1 oz, 3-3/4" h	20	30	-
Creamer, 8 oz, 5" h	25	25	65
Cup	8	15	12
Goblet, 8-1/2 oz, 5-3/4" h	25	35	40
Ice tea tumbler, 12 oz	28	55	45
Juice tumbler, 5 oz, 3" h	17.50	27.50	22
Lemonade tumbler, 15 oz	47.50	75	65
Milk pitcher, 8 oz, 5" h	25	25	65
Mug, 12 oz, 5-1/2" h	-	825	500
Pitcher, 54 oz, 7" h, ice lip	40	45	48
Pitcher, 68 oz, 7-3/4" h, no lip	45	72	65
Plate, 6" d, sherbet	4.50	8	7
Plate, 8-1/2" d, luncheon	6	8	10
Plate, 10" d, dinner	35	65	55
Plate, 12" d, oval	17.50	25	30
Platter, 12" l, oval	17.50	25	35
Salt and pepper shakers, pr	60	160	150
Saucer	4.50	7.50	6.50
Sherbet, 3-3/8" h	10	18	12
Soup bowl, 7" d	30	85	85
Spoon holder or celery vase	105	130	135
Sugar, cov	90	55	50
Sugar, 5", open	10	12	15
Tumbler, 3 oz, 3-1/4" h, ftd	18	20	16
Tumbler, 9 oz, 4" h	15	20	25
Tumbler, 10 oz, 5-1/4" h, ftd	30	48.50	50
Tumbler, 11 oz, 5-1/8" h	25	37.50	45
Vegetable bowl, 10" l, oval	18	25	30
Whiskey, 2-1/2" h, 1-1/2 oz	9	20	18
Wine, 4-1/2" h, 2-1/2 oz	18	30	15

Colonial, crystal wine, **$17.**

Colonial, green creamer, **$25;** *and sugar,* **$12.**

Colonial, green saucer, **$7.50.**

Laurel, Jade-ite dinner plate **$25.**

Laurel

Manufactured by McKee Glass Company, Pittsburgh, Pa., 1930s.

Made in French Ivory, Jade Green, Poudre Blue, and White Opal.

Item	French Ivory	Jade-ite	Poudre Blue	White Opal
Berry bowl, 4-3/4" d	$9	$15	$16	$14
Berry bowl, 9" d	28.50	40	55	30
Bowl, 6" d, three legs	15	25	-	15
Bowl, 10-1/2" d, three legs	37.50	50	68	45
Bowl, 11" d	40	55	85	37.50
Candlesticks, pr, 4" h	50	65	-	45
Cereal bowl, 6" d	12	25	28	20
Cheese dish, cov	60	95	-	75
Creamer, short	12	25	-	18
Creamer, tall	15	28	40	24
Cup	9.50	15	20	12
Plate, 6" d, sherbet	6	15	10	8
Plate, 7-1/2" d, salad	10	20	17.50	12
Plate, 9-1/8" d, dinner	15	25	30	18.50
Plate, 9-1/8" d, grill, round	15	25	-	18.50
Plate, 9-1/8" d, grill, scalloped	15	25	-	18.50
Platter, 10-3/4" l, oval	32	48	45	30
Salt and pepper shakers, pr	60	85	-	65
Saucer	3.25	4.50	7.50	3.50
Sherbet	12.50	20	-	18
Sherbet/champagne, 5"	50	72	-	60
Soup bowl, 7-7/8" d	35	40	-	40
Sugar, short	12	25	-	18
Sugar, tall	15	28	40	24
Tumbler, 9 oz, 4-1/2" h, flat	40	60	-	60
Tumbler, 12 oz, 5" h, flat	60	-	-	-
Vegetable bowl, 9-3/4" l, oval	18.50	480	45	20

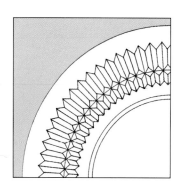

Lincoln Inn

Manufactured by Fenton Art Glass Company, Williamstown, W. Va., late 1920s.

Pieces are made in amber, amethyst, black, cobalt blue, crystal, green, green opalescent, light blue, opaque jade, pink, and red. Production in black was limited to salt and pepper shakers, valued at $325. Some rare pieces have been identified in several other colors.

Item	Cobalt Blue	Crystal	Other Colors	Red
Bonbon, oval, handle	$17.50	$12	$14	$18
Bonbon, sq, handle	15	12	14	15
Bowl, 6" d, crimped	14.50	7.50	10	14.50
Bowl, 9" d, shallow	—	9	—	—
Bowl, 9-1/4" d, ftd	42	18	20	45
Bowl, 10-1/2" d, ftd	50	28	30	50
Candy dish, ftd, oval	24	14.50	14.50	24
Cereal bowl, 6" d	12.50	7.50	9.50	12.50
Comport	25	14	15	25
Creamer	24	12	15	24
Cup	17.50	8.50	9.50	18
Finger bowl	20	14	14.50	20

Item	Cobalt Blue	Crystal	Other Colors	Red
Goblet, 6" h	30	12.50	16	30
Iced tea tumbler, 12 oz, ftd	50	24	28	40
Juice tumbler, 4 oz, flat	35	12	18	30
Nut dish, ftd	20	14.50	16	20
Olive bowl, handle	15	8.50	12	15
Pitcher, 46 oz, 7-1/4" h	820	700	715	820
Plate, 6" d	19.50	12	12.50	19.50
Plate, 8" d	27.50	15	14	27.50
Plate, 9-1/4" d	30	15	16.50	30
Plate, 12" d	35	16	18	35
Salt and pepper shakers, pr	265	175	175	265
Sandwich server, center handle	175	110	110	175
Saucer	5	4	4.50	5
Sherbet, 4-1/2" h, cone shape	18	12	14	18
Sherbet, 4-3/4" h	10	14	20	20
Sugar	18	12	15	24
Tumbler, 5 oz, ftd	24	14	14.50	24
Tumbler, 9 oz, ftd	28	32	35	30
Vase, 9-3/4" h	160	85	95	145
Vase, 12" h, ftd	225	115	125	175
Wine	35	20	24	40

Lincoln Inn, cobalt blue goblet, **$30.**

Newport
Hairpin

Manufactured by Hazel Atlas Glass Company, Clarksburg, W. Va., and Zanesville, Ohio, from 1936 to the early 1950s.

Made in amethyst, cobalt blue, pink (from 1936 to 1940), Platonite white, and fired-on colors (from the 1940s to early 1950s).

Item	Ameth.	Cobalt Blue	Fired-On	Pink	Platon.
Berry bowl, 8-1/4" d	$50	$50	$16	$25	$10
Cream soup, 4-3/4" d	25	25	10	17.50	8.50
Creamer	20	22	8.50	10	3
Cup	12	15	9	6	4.50
Plate, 6" d, sherbet	7.50	10	5	3.50	2
Plate, 8-1/2" d, luncheon	15	22	9	8	4.50
Plate, 8-13/16" d, dinner	32	35	15	15	12
Platter, 11-3/4" l, oval	42	48	18	20	12
Salt and pepper shakers, pr	60	65	32	30	18
Saucer	5.25	6	3	2.50	2
Sherbet	15	18.50	10	8	4
Sugar	20	22	9.50	10	5
Tumbler, 9 oz, 4-1/2" h	40	48	15	20	-

Newport, amethyst dinner plate, **$32;** *sugar,* **$20;** *creamer,* **$20;** *and cream soup bowl,* **$25.**

Ships
Sailboat
Sportsman Series

Manufactured by Hazel Atlas Glass Company, Clarksburg, W.V., and Zanesville, Ohio, late 1930s.

Made in cobalt blue with white, yellow, and red decoration. Pieces with yellow or red decoration are valued slightly higher than the traditional white decoration.

Ships, cobalt blue salad plate, **$27.50.**

Item	Cobalt Blue with White Decoration
Ashtray	$60
Ashtray, metal sailboat	120
Box, cov, three parts	250
Cocktail mixer, stirrer	45
Cocktail shaker	45
Cup	15
Ice bowl	45
Iced tea tumbler, 10-1/2 oz, 4-7/8" h	22
Iced tea tumbler, 12 oz	24
Old fashioned tumbler, 8 oz, 3-3/8" h	22

Item	Cobalt Blue with White Decoration
Pitcher, 82 oz, no ice lip	85
Pitcher, 86 oz, ice lip	75
Plate, 5-7/8" d, bread & butter	24
Plate, 8" d, salad	27.50
Plate, 9" d, dinner	32
Saucer	18
Tumbler, 4 oz, 3-1/4" h, heavy bottom	27.50
Tumbler, 9 oz, 3-3/4" h	18
Whiskey, 3-1/2" h	45

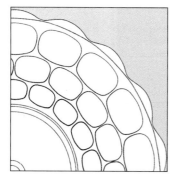

Yorktown

Manufactured by Federal Glass Company, in the mid-1950s.

Made in crystal, iridescent, smoke, white, and yellow. Values for all the colors are about the same.

Yorktown, yellow relish, **$3.**

Item	Crystal, etc.
Berry bowl, 5-1/2" d	$4.50
Berry bowl, 9-1/2" d	10
Celery tray, 10" l	10
Creamer	5
Cup	3.50
Fruit bowl, 10" d, ftd	18
Iced tea tumbler, 5-1/4" h, 13 oz	7.50
Juice tumbler, 3-7/8" h, 6 oz	4.50
Mug	15
Plate, 8-1/4" d	4.50

Item	Crystal, etc.
Plate, 11-1/2" d	8.50
Punch bowl set	40
Punch cup	2.50
Relish	3
Sandwich server	4.50
Saucer	1
Sherbet, 7 oz	3.50
Snack cup	2.50
Snack plate with indent	3.50
Sugar	5
Tumbler, 4-3/4" h, 10 oz	6
Vase, 8" h	15

DUNCAN AND MILLER

History: George Duncan, and Harry B. and James B., his sons, and Augustus Heisey, his son-in-law, formed George Duncan & Sons in Pittsburgh, Pennsylvania, in 1865. The factory was located just two blocks from the Monongahela River, providing easy and inexpensive access by barge for materials needed to produce glass. The men, from Pittsburgh's south side, were descendants of generations of skilled glassmakers.

The plant burned to the ground in 1892. James E. Duncan Sr. selected a site for a new factory in Washington, Pennsylvania, where operations began on February 9, 1893. The plant prospered, producing fine glassware and table services for many years.

John E. Miller, one of the stockholders, was responsible for designing many fine patterns, the most famous being Three Face. The firm incorporated and used the name The Duncan and Miller Glass Company until the plant closed in 1955. The company's slogan was, "The Loveliest Glassware in America." The U.S. Glass Co. purchased the molds, equipment, and machinery in 1956.

Additional Listing: Pattern Glass.

Animal
Heron, crystal $125
Swan, Sanibel, blue opalescent, 8" h
.... $165
Bowl, First Love, crystal, scalloped, 11" d $72
Bud vase, First Love, crystal, 9" h $75
Candlestick, Canterbury, orchid carving, 3" h $68
Candy box, cov, Canterbury, crystal, three parts, 6" d $70
Champagne
Cascade, crystal, #17365, 4-3/4" h .. $25
Lily of the Valley, crystal $35
Cocktail
Caribbean, blue, 3-3/4 oz $45
Cascade, crystal, #17365, 4-1/2" h .. $55
Lily of the Valley, crystal $32.50
Compote, Spiral Flutes, amber, 6" d
.... $20

Console bowl, Rose etch, crystal, 11" d $37.50
Cordial, Cascade, crystal, #17365 .... $55
Cornucopia, #121, Swirl, blue opalescent, shape #2, upswept tail $75
Creamer and sugar, Passion Flower, crystal $42
Cup, Sandwich, crystal $9
Finger bowl, Astaire, red $65
Fruit bowl, Sanibel, pink opalescent, 6-1/2" l $40
Goblet, water
Caribbean, crystal $37
Cascade, crystal, #17365, 6-1/4" h ... $25
First Love, crystal, 10 oz $35
Lily of the Valley, crystal $30
Plaza, cobalt blue $40
Sandwich, crystal $24
Iced tea tumbler, Cascade, crystal, #17365, 6" h $25

Juice tumbler
Lily of the Valley, crystal $28
Sandwich, crystal, ftd, 3-3/4" h $12
Sherbet
Canterbury, chartreuse $15
Sandwich, crystal $20
Sugar shaker, Duncan Block, crystal
.... $42
Tray, Sanibel, blue opalescent, 13" l
.... $125
Tumbler, Chanticleer, 3 oz, crystal satin $45
Vase, American Way, 9" h, flared, crystal, amber and cranberry vine dec...... $195
Whiskey, sea horse, etch #502, red and crystal $48
Wine
Cascade, crystal, 5-1/4" h, #17365
.... $25
Lily of the Valley, crystal $30
Sandwich, crystal $24

EARLY AMERICAN GLASS

History: The term "Early American glass" covers glass made in America from the colonial period through the mid-19th century. As such, it includes the early pressed glass and lacy glass made between 1827 and 1840.

Major glass-producing centers prior to 1850 were Massachusetts (New England Glass Company and the Boston and Sandwich Glass Company), South Jersey, Pennsylvania (Stiegel's Manheim factory and many Pittsburgh-area firms), and Ohio (several different companies in Kent, Mantua, and Zanesville).

Early American glass was popular with collectors from 1920 to 1950. It has now regained some of its earlier prominence. Leading auction sources for early American glass include American Bottle Auctions, Garth's, Green Valley Auctions, Heckler & Company, James D. Julia, and Skinner, Inc. A standard reference book used by early collectors as well as collectors today was written by George and Helen McKearin, *American Glass*, Crown Publishers in 1941. Many collectors and dealers refer to the "McKearin" plate numbers when describing early American glass.

Additional Listings: Cup Plates; Flasks; Sandwich Glass; Stiegel-Type Glass.

Bottle, blown, half post case, colorless, copper wheel engraved flowers on all sides, larger two resembling crosshatched tulips, chipped lip, 9-7/8" h $200
Bowl, free-blown, deep
Concave shoulder, folded rim, amber, slightly domed base, rough pontil mark, American, mid-19th C, 5-7/8" d, 1-3/8" h $1,100
Flaring folded rim, light amber, slightly domed base, rough pontil mark, American, first half 19th C, 5-1/4" d, 2" h $525

Flaring folded rim, amber, slightly domed base, rough pontil mark, American, first half 19th C, 8-1/2" d, 3-3/4" h $1,650
Slightly concave sides, delicate folded rim, deep muddy black amber, domed base, rough pontil mark,

American, first half 19th C, 7" d, 4-1/4" h **$1,980**

Slightly flaring folded rim, light ruby, domed base, rough pontil mark, American, second half 19th C, 6" d, 4" h **$440**

Slightly flaring folded rim, brilliant emerald green, slightly domed base, rough pontil mark, American, mid-19th C, 6-7/8" d, 3-5/8" h **$1,870**

Wide folded rim, aquamarine, slight kick-up, rough pontil mark, New York state, possibly Cleveland Glass Works, mid-19th C, 13" d, 5" h.................**$880**

Celery vase, Diamond Thumbprint, flint, scalloped rim, bulbous ribbed stem, round base, 9-1/4" h **$175**

Compote

Free-blown, colorless, applied blue threading around outside of bowl, applied hollow reverse baluster stem, high domed circular foot with folded rim, rough pontil mark, American or European, late 18th/ early 19th C, 4-1/8" h, 4-3/8" d rim, 3-3/8" d foot.........................**$1,155**

Pressed, Diamond Thumbprint, flint, scalloped rim, bulbous ribbed stem, round base, 9" h, 11-1/2" d **$230**

Cordial, blown, clear, red, dark green, and cotton twist stem, 4-1/2" h **$175**

Creamer, pressed, Gothic Arch, Palm, and Chain, colorless, lightly scalloped rim, molded handle, circular even scallop foot, Boston & Sandwich and others, chip under spout, 1835-45, 4-1/8" h...**$135**

Cream jug, free-blown, deep olive amber with white flecks, crude applied strap-type handle, circular foot, heavy rough pontil mark, possibly Saratoga Glass Works, first half 19th C, 5" h, 3" d rim, 2-5/8" d foot.....................**$1,100**

Decanter

Blown molded, pint, deep olive green, slightly flaring plain lip, rayed base, rough pontil mark, Keene, NH, McKearin GIII-16, 1820-40, 7" h, 3" d base....................................**$825**

Pressed, double Bellflower, ribbed, medium green to olive, second period, 9-5/8" h **$175**

Dish

Gothic Arch and Plume, oval, colorless, center with stippled background, plain table ring, even scallop rim, Midwestern, large shallow rim spall, 1835-45, 6-1/4" x 9-1/4" x 1-5/8" **$235**

Eagle, octagonal, colorless, central design of eagle with Ameri-

can shield surrounded by 13 stars, shoulder with three alternating designs of shields, acanthus leaves and five-point star medallions, plain even scallop rim, possibly Boston & Sandwich, loss of scallops, rim chipping, 1835-45, 7" d, 1-5/8" d **$100**

Flip, etched, blown, colorless copper wheel engraved borders of crosshatched ovals, wide fluting, 3-7/8" h...**$295**

Copper wheel engraved tulip in basket, 4-1/4" h **$350**

Copper wheel engraved border with crosshatched ovals, three-quarter ribbing, 6-1/4" h **$400**

Copper wheel engraved designs of four floral panels, 6-1/2" h **$500**

Hat, blown molded, colorless, inward folded rim, rayed base, rough pontil mark, possibly Boston & Sandwich Glass Co., 1825-35, McKearin GII-18, 2-1/8" h, 2-5/8" d rim, 1-3/4" d base..................**$145**

Hurricane shades, pr, blown, colorless, baluster form, medial frosted band with wheel-etched flowering vine, circular folded foot, America, 19th C, 21-3/4" h **$2,235**

Hyacinth vase

Amethyst, good color, minor wear, 8" h **$100**

Amethyst, medium color, added foot with folded rim, minor wear, 8-1/4" h **$575**

Inkwell, blown molded, dark olive amber, 14 diamond base, rough pontil mark, Keene, NH, 1820-1840, McKearin GII-18, top and side wear, 2" h, 2-5/8" d **$160**

Jar, blown molded, olive-green, wide rim, ten panels about shoulder, eastern United States, minor scratches, early 19th C, 8-1/2" h **$2,115**

Milk pan, free-blown, flaring folded rim, deep brilliant teal, slightly domed base, small rough pontil mark, second half 19th C, 7-1/2" d, 2-1/4" h **$470**

Nappy, Paneled Diamond, colorless, each panel topped by fan, point, and five scallop rim, possibly Boston & Sandwich, light flaking/mold roughness, 1828-1835, 6-5/8" d, 1-3/8" h......................**$70**

Pan

Free-blown, lily pad dec, flaring folded rim, brilliant light green, slightly domed base, rough pontil mark, New York, probably Redford or Redwood Glass Works, 19th C, 7-5/8" d, 1-3/4" h.................**$11,000**

Free-blown, slightly flaring folded rim, brilliant amethyst, nearly flat

base, polished pontil mark, second half 19th C, 8-7/8" d, 3" h **$330**

Pitcher, free-blown

Ftd, applied reeded handle, cobalt blue, eastern United States, early 19th C, 5" h **$1,200**

Threaded neck, applied strap-type handle, heavy medial rib, aquamarine, kick-up base, rough pontil mark, New York state, possibly Cleveland Glass Works, first half 19th C, 8" h, 6" d rim **$3,300**

Plate, Anchor and Shield, deep olive green, Midwestern, rim chip, 7" d, 1-1/8" d..**$315**

Storage jar, blown, olive green, flared rim, minor scratches, 11-3/4" h ...**$95**

Sugar bowl, cov

Pressed, Colonial variant, hexagonal, emerald green, polished finial, base with high scallop rim, rayed and polished underneath, under rim chip on cov, mid-19th C, 4-3/4" h, 4-3/8" d rim **$660**

Free-blown, cobalt blue, domed cov, galleried rim, ftd, eastern United States, early 19th C, 5-3/4" h **$1,500**

Translucent blood red bowl and stem, swirled grass green and red foot and cover, bowl slightly compressed bulbous form, galleried rim, wafer attached to hollow knop stem, lower wafer, circular foot with slight red swirls, strongly swirled boldly domed cover with applied mushroom type finial, rough pontil on both base and cov, possibly New England, mid-19th C, rim chip and flake on bowl, 8-1/4" h, 4-1/4" d, rim, 3-3/4" d foot.....................**$880**

Toddy plate, Lee-Rose No. 802, fiery opalescent alabaster, 76 even scallops, rim chip, 1830-45, 4-1/4" d.........**$110**

Tumbler

Blown molded, taper, colorless, rayed base, rough pontil mark, probably Boston & Sandwich Glass Co., McKearin GII-19, 1825-35, 2-1/2" h, 2-3/8" d rim, 1-3/4" d base **$165**

Blown molded, cylindrical, colorless, rayed base, rough pontil mark, probably Boston & Sandwich Glass Co., McKearin GV-4, 1825-35, 3-3/8" h, 2-7/8" d.....................**$275**

Nine-panel, brilliant teal, panels arched at top, American, probably New England, mid-19th C, 3-1/2" h, 3-3/8" d rim **$615**

Eight panel, ftd, translucent light starch blue, alabaster surface, third quarter 19th C, 4-1/2" h.............**$80**

Twine holder, Punty, deep red overlay cut to clear, orig metal reinforcement ring, probably New England, c1875, 4-1/4" h, 4" d **$150**

Vase, free-blown

Bright grass green, opal loopings, Marbrie, baluster, applied circular foot, rough pontil mark, South Jersey, second half 19th C, 7-1/2" h, 3-3/4" d rim, 2-3/4" foot **$550**

Colorless body, opal loopings, Marbrie, rolled over rim, applied triple shoulder ring, colorless applied solid stem, circular foot, rough pontil mark, Pittsburgh or New Jersey, mid-19th C, 11" h, 4" d rim, 4-1/4" d foot **$1,155**

Medium amethyst, trumpet, applied waist ring, solid plain stem, circular foot, faint pontil mark, second half 19th C, 11-1/2" h, 5" d rim, 3-3/4" d foot **$220**

Water jug, blown molded, colorless, applied hollow handle, light horizontal rings, rayed base, rough pontil mark, Boston & Sandwich Glass Co., McKearin GV-17, 1825-35, 8-1/4" h, 5" d rim, 4" d base **$3,100**

Window pane, Gothic Arch, colorless, six individual arches, scrolls, and rosettes above, faintly sgd "Bakewell" on reverse, Pittsburgh Flint Glass Manufactory of Benjamin Bakewell, broken into two pcs, several edge chips, 1830-45, 4-7/8" x 6-7/8" **$1,100**

Wine glass, blown molded, colorless, button stem, rough pontil mark, possibly Boston & Sandwich Glass Co., 1820-40, McKearin GII-19, small flake, 3-1/4" h, 2" d **$210**

Wine glass, free-blown

Colorless, blown ogee bowl with basal molding, fine enamel twist stem with single white opaque enamel ribbon central twist column, wide conical foot, rough pontil mark, third quarter 18th C, 5-3/4" h **$475**

Colorless, blown twisted bowl, multiple spiral air twist stem, wide conical foot, rough pontil mark, mid-18th C, 6-3/4" h **$500**

Colorless, plain pointed bowl with shoulder, angular knop stem, conical foot with faint pontil mark, mid-18th C, 6" h **$420**

Witch ball and stand, free-blown, aquamarine, trumpet vase form stand with applied threading, circular foot with four point rough pontil mark, ball with rough open pontil mark, mid-19th C, 4-3/4" d ball, 7-1/2" h, 4-7/8" d stand **$450**

FENTON GLASS

History: The Fenton Art Glass company was founded in 1905 and celebrated the centennial of its founding in 2005—a milestone for the American glass-making industry, as Fenton is the oldest continuously running American glass company.

The company produced its first piece of glass in 1907. Early production included carnival, chocolate, custard, and pressed glass, plus mold-blown opalescent glass.

In the 1920s, stretch glass and colors of jade green, ruby, and other art glass were added. In the 1930s, boudoir lamps and slag glass in various colors were produced. The 1940s saw crests of different colors being added to each piece by hand. Hobnail, opalescent, and two-color overlay pieces were popular items.

Handles were added to different shapes to make Fenton baskets, which are identified by the handler's mark at the point where the handle attaches to the basket. Each of these marks is unique to a given Fenton handler, adding to the hand-made charm of these items.

Through the years, Fenton has beautified its glass by decorating it with hand painting, acid etching, and copper-wheel cutting. Today, collectors are especially interested in cranberry opalescent glass, topaz (vaseline) opalescent, Burmese, and Rosalene (an opaque pink glass with colors shaded more deeply toward the edges). Hand-painting on these treatments is especially sought. Items decorated at the factory are usually signed by the painters who worked on them (one means of distinguishing Fenton-decorated pieces from those decorated later by someone outside the company).

Fenton has something for everyone and for every price point, which is one of the factors accounting for its customer loyalty over the last century. People whose purses or living spaces will not accommodate larger pieces have made Fenton's whimsical animal figurines very popular—so much so that these are seldom seen on the secondary market. High-end collectors are particularly interested in items made for the Connoisseur Series, which includes the best—and most expensive—art glass treatments in the Fenton line.

Historically, marks have consisted of various iterations of paper labels, many of which do not permanently adhere. Collectors rely on shapes, glass colors, and decorator signatures to identify older Fenton items. In 1970, the company began to mark its pieces with an embossed company name inside an oval. The numbers 8, 9, and 0 were added under the name for items produced in the decade of the 1980s, 1990s, and 2000s respectively. Burmese and other satin glass doesn't "take" the embossed logo very well and items made in the 70s and later often have the logo barely visible in the glass. Because of this problem, Fenton recently began adding a scripted green "F" stamp to the base of such treatments. The latest sticker mark includes the legend "100 years."

Fenton "seconds" are usually identified by an acid-etched stencil-style "F" on the bottom. This mark can be difficult to see without tilting the item to the proper light. As with many "seconds" produced by companies of quality, it will often be unclear why the piece was rejected as a first-quality item. Nevertheless, these items are considered, for collecting purposes, to be not as valuable as first-quality items.

Fenton, Hobnail, ruby basket, early 1970s, 7-3/4" h, **$35.**

Fenton, Vasa Murrhina melon vase, aventurine green, mid-1960s, 11-1/2" h, **$95.**

Fenton slag glass trumpet vase, mottled red body, c1932, 8-1/4" h, **$475.**
Photo courtesy of Sloans & Kenyon Auctioneers and Appraisers.

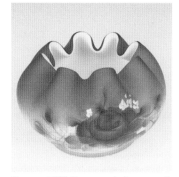

Fenton, Wild Rose cased-glass sample rose bowl, satin finish, unusual, hand painted, 1940s, 6-1/2" d, **$275.**

Basket

1925ic, Ivory Crest, 1940, 7" **$125**
3834rp, Rose Pastel Hobnail, 1954, 4-1/2"...**$55**
3837cr, Cranberry Opalescent Hobnail, 1940, 7"...............................**$110**
3837rp, Rose Pastel Hobnail, 1954 ....**$75**
3839po, Oval, Plum Opalescent, 1959, 12"...**$400**
7237bl, Blue Roses On Blue Satin, 1978, 7" **$65**
7237ec, Ebony Crest, 1968, 7" **$175**
7437bc, Bluebirds On Custard, 1977, 8"...**$75**
8435re, Threaded, Rosalene, 1976, 7" **$125**
9138ba, Poppy, Blue Satin, 1973, 7" **$65**
9138rs, Poppy, Rose Satin, 1974, 7" **$125**
9235mb, Roses In Blue Marble, 1970, 9"...**$75**

Bell, General Issue

1127se, Magnolia And Berry On Spruce, 1997, 6-1/2" **$40**
1145dx, Trellis On French Opalescent, 1999, 6-1/2"...............................**$45**
3645rn, Red Carnival, 1993, 5-1/2" **$30**
3645rv, Rose Magnolia Hobnail, 1993, 5-1/2"...**$25**
3645xc, Persian Blue Opalescent, 1989...**$25**
6761ru, Paisley, Ruby, 1997, 7".....**$35**
8267bc, Medallion, Bluebirds On Custard, 1977 ....**$45**
8267rc, Medallion, Roses On Custard, 1978...**$40**
8267ru, Medallion, White Roses On Ruby, 1979 ....**$40**
8465cb, Threaded Diamond-Optic With Diamond Handle, Colonial Blue, 1977 ....**$30**

Fenton, carnival glass, crimped bowl, Holly, cobalt blue, 1911, 9" d, **$275.**

8465wt, Threaded Diamond Optic with Diamond Handle, Wisteria, 1977...**$45**
8466re, Faberge, Rosalene, 1976 ....**$55**
8467ch, Patriots In Chocolate Glass (Bicentennial), 1974...................**$45**
8467ib, Patriots In Independence Blue (Bicentennial), 1974...................**$45**
8467pr, Patriots In Patriot Red (Bicentennial), 1974...............................**$45**
8467vw, Patriots In Valley Forge White, 1974...............................**$30**

Bowl

8520bb, Sculptured Ice Optic, Glacial Blue, 1982, 12"...........................**$50**
9425io, Tibbon Edge, Aqua Blue Carnival, (Made For Levay), 1980, 8" **$85**
K7722kn, Medium Flared, Banded Color (Katja), 1983...................**$65**
K7724ko, Flame Band (Katja), 1983, 9-3/4" **$75**
R9426ru, Faberge, Ribbed, Ruby (Made For A.L. Randall Co.), 1982 ....**$30**
R9430gs, Water Lily, Green (Made For A.L. Randall Co.), 1982, 6" **$35**
R9430ru, Faberge, Ribbed, Ruby, 1982, 6" **$35**

Box, Hen On Nest

5182cn, Large, Original (Amethyst) Carnival, 1970...........................**$95**
5182mb, Large, Blue Marble, 1971 ....**$125**
5186cn, Original (Amethyst) Carnival, 1970 ....**$65**
5186cu, Custard Satin, 1971 ....**$45**
5186ls, Lime Sherbet Satin, 1973 ....**$50**
5186mb, Blue Marble, 1971 ....**$75**

Candleholder

3870cr, Handled, Cranberry Opalescent Hobnail, 1953, pr **$80**

3874bo, Cornucopia, Blue Opalescent Hobnail, 1943, pr........................**$70**

3971bo, Mini Cornucopia, Blue Opalescent Hobnail, 1943, pr **$50**

Comport

3522dv, Footed, Spanish Lace, Violets In The Snow, 1971 ....**$65**

3522sc, Spanish Lace In Silver Crest, 1975 ....**$45**

3728po, Footed, Plum Opalescent, 1959 ....**$85**

3731go, Footed, Green Opalescent Hobnail, 1959 ....**$125**

3731mb, Footed, Blue Marble Hobnail, 1978 ....**$75**

3920gp, Footed, Green Pastel Hobnail, 1954 ....**$60**

3920mi, Footed, Milk Glass Hobnail, 1970 ....**$25**

628bo, Footed, Blue Opalescent Hobnail, 1941, 6" **$50**

7329ab, Low Footed, Apple Blossom On Silver Crest, 1969 ....**$50**

7429dc, Footed, Daisies On Custard, 1970 ....**$50**

7429eg, Rose Garden On Opal Satin, 1975 ....**$75**

7429sc, Silver Crest, 1961 ....**$40**

7429sf, Strawberries On French Opalescent, 1997 ....**$40**

Creamer

1461bo, Blue Opalescent Coin Dot, 1948, 5" **$55**

1461cr, Cranberry Coin Dot, 1948, 5" **$65**

1924ac, Aqua Crest, 1942, 5" **$50**

1924pc, Peach Crest, 1942, 5" **$50**

1924rc, Rose Crest, 1946, 5" **$50**

1924sc, Silver Crest, 1947, 5" **$35**

3901to, Topaz Opalescent Hobnail, 1941 ....**$50**

7261ec, Emerald Crest, 1949 ....**$50**

Cruet With Stopper

3863bo, Round, Blue Opalescent Hobnail, 1941 ....**$125**

3863cr, Round, Cranberry Opalescent Hobnail, 1941 ....**$145**

3869cr, Oil (Straight Sides), Cranberry Opalescent Hobnail, 1949 ....**$125**

3869fo, Oil (Straight Sides), French Opalescent Hobnail, 1942 ....**$40**

3869to, Oil (Straight Sides), Topaz Opalescent Hobnail, 1942 ....**$95**

Epergne

1522ic, 1-Horn, 4-Piece (includes base), Ivory Crest, 1940 ....**$175**

1948bo, 3-Horn, Blue Opalescent With Silver Crest, 1948, 12" bowl, ...**$225**

1948fo, 3-Horn, French Opalescent With Aqua Crest, 1948, 12" bowl **$200**

3800mi, 4-Horn, Milk Glass Hobnail, 1954 ....**$150**

3801bo, 3-Horn, Miniature, Blue Opalescent Hobnail, 1949 ....**$145**

3801fo, 3-Horn, Miniature, French Opalescent Hobnail, 1949 ....**$85**

3801go, 3-Horn, Miniature, Green Opalescent Hobnail, 1959 ....**$175**

3801gp, 3-Horn, Miniature, Green Pastel Hobnail, 1954 ....**$125**

3801mi, 3-Horn, Miniature, Milk Glass Hobnail, 1950 ....**$55**

Fairy Light

5108ba, Owl In Blue Satin, 1975 .. **$45**

5108cs, Owl In Custard Satin, 1975 ....**$35**

5108ls, Owl In Lime Sherbet Satin, 1975 ....**$40**

5108re, Owl In Rosalene, 1976.....**$55**

5406re, Heart In Rosalene, 1976 ..**$75**

7300by, Butterflies On White Milk Glass, 1977 ....**$45**

7300cv, Christmas Morn, 1978.....**$65**

7300cw, Cardinals In Winter, 1977 ....**$55**

7392db, One-Piece, Autumn Leaves Transfer On Burmese, 1970.....**$165**

7492db, Two-Piece, Autumn Leaves Transfer On Burmese, 1972.....**$150**

Figurine

Angel

Praying Boy, 5113rn, Berries & Blossoms, 1985 ....**$75**

Praying Girl, 5114ns, Natural Series, 1985 ....**$65**

Praying Girl, 5114rk, Berries & Blossoms, 1985 ....**$75**

Bird

5163bd, Blue Dogwood On Cameo Satin, 1980 ....**$45**

Happiness, 5197ba, Blue Satin, 1978 ....**$45**

Happiness, 5197bc, Bluebirds On Custard, 1977 ....**$50**

Bunny

5162bd, Blue Dogwood On Cameo Satin, 1980 ....**$55**

5162bj, Pekin Blue, 1980...............**$45**

5162cd, Daisies On Custard, 1978 ....**$45**

5162dv, Violets In The Snow, 1978 ....**$75**

5162ja, Jade Green, 1980...............**$50**

Butterfly On Stand, Wings Open 5171dk, Dusty Rose, 1986 ....**$45**

Cat

5165dv, Violets In The Snow, 1979 ....**$55**

5165ws, White Satin, 1971............**$55**

Happy 5277br, Burmese (Made In Both Satin And Gloss), 1966 .....**$95**

Doll, "Almost Heaven" Blue Slag (Sold Through Fenton Gift Shop), 1985..**$65**

Fawn

5160br, Burmese, 1986.................**$95**

5160ub, Blue Burmese, 1984 .....**$125**

Frog

5166dv, Violets In The Snow, 1979 ....**$175**

5166ls, Lime Sherbet, 1979...........**$65**

Kitten, 5119rk, Berries & Blossoms, 1984..**$75**

Mouse, 5148dc, Daisies On Custard, 1978..**$40**

Owl, 5158fn, Favrene, 6, 1993 .. **$125**

Pig, 5220ws, White Satin, 1972 .. **$65**

Puppies, 5159sp, Cocker Spaniels, Natural Series, 1985 ....**$65**

Rabbit, 5178cn, Original (Amethyst) Carnival, 1971...........................**$75**

Slipper, Cat, 3995bj, Pekin Blue Hobnail, 1968 ....**$25**

Snail, 5135re, Rosalene, 1993......**$65**

Swan

5161dc, Daisies On Cameo Satin, 1978..**$50**

5161ln, Lavender Satin, 1977 ....**$65**

5161py, Pink Blossom On Custard, 1978..**$50**

5161re, Rosalene, 1978 ....**$75**

Hat

1492bo, Coin Dot In Blue Opalescent, 1948..**$55**

1492cr, Coin Dot In Cranberry Opalescent, 1948 ....**$65**

1492fo, French Opalescent, 1948 ....**$45**

1492lo, Lime Opalescent, 1952.....**$75**

1492xc, Persian Blue Opalescent, 1989..**$35**

1920bo, Stiegel Blue Spiral Optic, 1939, 12" **$325**

1920cr, Cranberry Spiral Optic, 1938, 12" **$400**

1920fo, French Opalescent Spiral Optic, 1939, 12" **$150**

1920go, Green Opalescent Spiral Optic, 1939, 12" **$300**

1920to, Topaz Opalescent Spiral Optic, 1940, 12" **$325**

1921bi, Blue Ridge (Early), 1939, 10" **$250**

1921bo, Stiegel Blue Spiral Optic, 1939, 10" **$250**

1921cr, Cranberry Spiral Optic, 1938, 10" **$350**

1921go, Green Opalescent Spiral Optic, 1939, 10" **$265**

1921go, Green Opalescent Spiral Optic, (Made In Both Crimp And Straight Edge), 1939, 9" **$225**

1923bo, Stiegel Blue Spiral Optic, 1939, 6" **$60**

1923cr, Cranberry Spiral Optic, 1938, 6" **$95**

1923ic, Ivory Crest, 1940, 6" **$50**

1923pc, Peach Crest, 1940, 7" **$65**

Jar, Candy

Covered 6688uo, Peaches 'N Cream Opalescent, 1986 .... **$45**

Covered 7380wd, Footed, White Daisies On Ebony, 1973 .... **$75**

Covered 8489bx, Sapphire Blue Opalescent, 1990, 7" **$45**

Pitcher (aka "Jug")

2060cc, Feather In Country Cranberry, 1982, 70 oz. **$150**

2664bi, Blue Ridge, 9" 1985 .... **$145**

3664cr, With Ice Lip, Cranberry Opalescent Hobnail, 70 oz., 1965 .... **$275**

3664mi, Milk Glass Hobnail, 70 oz., 1987 .... **$55**

3664po, Plum Opalescent with Ice Lip (Made For Levay), 1984, 70 oz **$200**

3762go, Syrup, Green Opalescent Hobnail, 1959 .... **$85**

Fenton, Diamond Optic, tangerine stretch-glass tidbit tray, late 1920s, 10" d, **$125.**

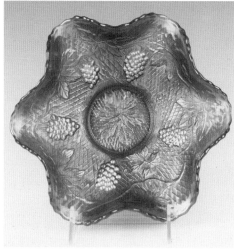

Fenton, carnival glass deep bowl with ruffled edge, paneled back, Lattice and Grape, green 9" d, **$400.**

3764rv, Rose Magnolia Hobnail, 1940, 54 oz. **$250**

3964bo, Blue Opalescent Hobnail, 1941, 4-1/2" **$45**

3965bo, Blue Opalescent Hobnail, 1940, 32 oz. **$85**

Plate, Designer Series

7418fv, Down Home On Custard, (Designer: Finn), 1983, 8" **$75**

7418hf, In Season (Hunter), (Designer: Dickinson), 1985, 8" **$95**

7418lt, Lighthouse Point On Custard Satin, (Designer: Dickinson), 1983, 8" **$75**

7618ee, Majestic Flight (Eagle) On White Satin (Designer: Cumberledge), 1984 .... **$85**

7618tl, Smoke And Cinders On White Satin (Designer: Dickinson), 1984 .... **$95**

8011le, Sandcarved Statue Of Liberty On Crystal, 1985, 9" **$60**

Punchbowl Set

3712go, 14-Piece, Green Opalescent Hobnail, 1985 .... **$475**

3712xc, 14-Piece, Persian Blue Opalescent Hobnail, 1989 .... **$400**

A3712uo, 14-Piece, Peaches 'N Cream Hobnail, 1988 .... **$325**

Vase

1353xc, Tulip, Fine Dot Optic In Persian Blue Opalescent, 1989, 10" **$75**

1354cr, Cranberry Dot Optic, 1982, 7" **$75**

1824cc, Fern In Country Cranberry, 1982, 4-1/2" **$50**

1850oh, Heritage Green Overlay, 1983, 7-1/2" **$45**

3551dv, Spanish Lace, Violets In The Snow, 1974, 8" **$65**

3752cr, Cranberry Opalescent Hobnail, 1941 .... **$225**

3759go, Swung, Green Opalescent Hobnail, 1959, 18" **$200**

3759mi, Swung, Milk Glass Hobnail, 1959, 18" **$50**

5750dk, Dusty Rose, 1982, 9" **$30**

6854iu, Aurora, Americana With Blue Crest, 7-1/2" (Family Signature, Mike Fenton), 1982 .... **$90**

7051wa, Spiral Ribbed, Rosebuds On Rosalene, 1982, 6" **$125**

7241ba, Blue Satin, 1982, 4-1/2" **$25**

7241vi, Vintage On Cameo Satin, 1980, 4-1/2" **$30**

7252bd, Blue Dogwood On Cameo Satin, 1976, 7" **$45**

7252qh, Raspberry Burmese, (Connoisseur), 1983, 7-1/2" **$175**

7252xa, Clydesdales, (Made For Budweiser), 1977, 7" **$300**

7257bc, Bluebirds On Custard, 1977, 10" **$75**

7554bq, Blue Roses On Custard Satin, 1981, 5" **$45**

7557in, Iris On Bone White, 1982, 9" **$65**

7557ja, Jade, 1980, 10" **$50**

7557pe, Silver Poppies On Ebony, 1981, 9-1/2" **$50**

8251hu, Mandarin, Blue On Cameo Satin, 1982, 9" **$150**

8251ja, Mandarin, Jade Green, 1980 .... **$75**

8252hu, Empress, Blue On Cameo Satin, 1982 .... **$85**

8452re, Fan, Rosalene, 1976 .... **$225**

8455vy, Diamond And Thread, Purple Stretch (Made For Levay), 1981 ... **$60**

8458bo, Bud, Blue Opalescent Hobnail, 1981, 11" **$35**

8956ci, Hanging Hearts In Custard, (Robert Barber Collection), 1976, 6" **$150**

8958ci, Pinch, Hanging Hearts In Custard, (Robert Barber Collection), 1976, 8" **$165**

8958th, Pinch, Hanging Hearts In Turquoise, (Robert Barber), 1975, 8" **$175**

9054ja, Bud, Jade Green, 1980 ...... **$25**

9054rd, Bud, Roses On Ruby, 1981 ..... **$30**

9055br, Ribbed Burmese, 1971, 5" . **$135**

9056bd, Bud, Blue Dogwood On Cameo Satin, 1980 .... **$25**

Water Set (Pitcher With Glasses)

3407io, 7-Piece, Cactus In Aqua Opal Carnival (Made For Levay), 1980 .... **$400**

3407rn, 7-Piece With Goblets, Red Sunset Carnival (Made For Levay), 1982 .... **$350**

FOSTORIA GLASS

History: Fostoria Glass Co. began operations at Fostoria, Ohio, in 1887, and moved to Moundsville, West Virginia, its present location, in 1891. By 1925, Fostoria had five furnaces and a variety of special shops. In 1924, a line of colored tableware was introduced. Fostoria was purchased by Lancaster Colony in 1983.

Fostoria, American pattern, 8" deep, **$50.**

Fostoria, Coin, red candy dish with cover, **$70.**

Ashtray
- American, 2-7/8" sq **$7.50**
- Coin, crystal **$30**
- June, blue **$75**

Baker, June, topaz, oval, 9" **$195**

Bell, Chintz, orig label **$130**

Berry bowl, June, blue, 5" d **$50**

Bonbon, Bridal Wreath, #2630 Century, cut 833, three toes **$75**

Bouillon, Versailles, topaz **$30**

Bowl
- American, oval, 10" l **$30**
- Baroque, blue, 4" sq, one handle .. **$22**
- Corsage, flared, 12" d **$110**
- Grape Leaf, green, 12" d **$175**
- June, 12" d, blue **$125**

Bread and butter plate, Trojan, topaz, 6" d **$10**

Cake salver
- Century, crystal **$60**
- Coin, crystal **$98**
- Corsage, 10-1/2" d **$32**
- Navarre, crystal, handles, 10" d ... **$60**

Candleholders, pr
- Baroque, one-lite, silver deposit Vintage dec on base, 4" h, #2496 .... **$75**
- Baroque, two-lite, removable bobeche and prisms, 8-1/2" h, 10" w, #2484 .... **$375**
- Buttercup, 5-1/2" h, #2594, etch 340 .... **$250**
- Coin, red, tall **$150**
- Meadow Rose **$185**
- Trojan, topaz, 2", #2394, etch 280 .. **$145**
- Trindle, #2594, three-lite, Buttercup etch, 8" h, 6-1/2" w **$250**

Candy dish, cov
- Baroque, crystal **$40**
- June, yellow **$370**
- Navarre, three parts **$175**
- Versailles, blue, three parts **$345**

Card tray, Brocaded Daffodil, two handles, pink, gold trim **$40**

Celery tray, Trojan, topaz **$100**

Cereal bowl, June, rose, 6" d **$85**

Champagne
- Bridal Wreath, #6051, cut 833 .... **$35**
- Buttercup, #6030, etch 340 .... **$32**
- Corsage, #6014, etch 325 .... **$32**
- Dolley Madison **$18**
- June, saucer, petal stem **$27**
- Versailles, pink **$40**

Cheese and cracker
- Chintz **$70**
- Colony **$55**

Cigarette box, cov
- Cigarette set, Baroque, azure, #2496, five pcs **$450**
- Morning Glory etching **$65**
- Oriental **$170**

Claret
- Bridal Wreath, #6051, cut 833 .... **$38**
- Camelia **$30**
- June, pink **$175**
- Navarre **$80**
- Trojan, yellow, 6" h **$100**

Cocktail
- Baroque, yellow **$15**
- Vesper, amber **$30**

Compote
- Baroque, crystal, 6" **$18**
- Corsage, #2496 Baroque, etch 325 .... **$75**
- Trojan, topaz, #2400, etch 280 ... **$85**

Condiment set, American, pr salt and pepper shakers, pr, cloverleaf tray, pr cruets **$200**

Console set, Baroque, azure, #2496, pr candlesticks, 10-1/2" d bowl **$300**

Cordial, Dolley Madison **$30**

Cosmetic box, cov, American, flake on bottom, 2-1/2" d **$900**

Courting lamp, Coin, amber **$150**

Creamer, individual size
- Bridal Wreath, #2630 Century, cut 833 .... **$30**
- Century **$9**
- Raleigh **$8**

Creamer, table size
- Baroque, azure, #2496 .... **$55**
- Chintz **$20**
- Raleigh **$10**
- Trojan, topaz **$22**

Creamer, sugar, tray, individual size
- Camelia **$45**
- Century **$30**

Cream soup
- Colony **$95**
- Versailles, pink **$65**
- Vesper, amber **$30**

Cruet, June, yellow **$700**

Crushed fruit jar, cov, America, c1915-25, 5-7/8" d, 6" h **$1,600**

Cup and saucer
- Baroque, blue **$35**

Buttercup **$34**
Camelia **$20**
June, azure **$45**
Minuet, green **$55**
Trojan, topaz, #2375 Fairfax, etch 280 .... **$40**

Decanter, orig stopper, Hermitage, amber, #2449 .... **$125**

Dinner plate
- Versailles, pink, slight use **$75**
- Vesper, amber **$30**

Figure
- Deer, standing, crystal, 4-1/2" h .. **$45**
- Lute and Lotus, ebony, gold highlights, price for pr, 12-1/2" h .. **$975**
- Mermaid, crystal, 10-3/8" h **$225**

Fruit cocktail, Hermitage, topaz, #2449 .... **$22**

Goblet, water
- Baroque, azure, #2496 .... **$45**
- Bouquet, crystal, #6033, etch 342 .. **$35**
- Buttercup, #6030, etch 340 .... **$40**
- Dolley Madison **$20**
- Golden Lace, gold trim **$24**
- Meadow Rose **$30**
- Navarre **$40**
- Trojan, topaz **$75**

Grapefruit, Coronet **$9**

Gravy boat, liner, Kasmir, blue .. **$180**

Ice bucket, Versailles, pink **$155**

Iced-tea tumbler
- Bouquet, crystal, #6033, etch 342 .. **$35**
- Navarre, pink **$75**

Jelly, cov

Coin, amber **$30**

Meadow Rose, 7-1/2" d **$90**

Jug

Hermitage, green, #2449, three pints

.... **$145**

Manor, #4020, wisteria foot ...**$1,500**

Trojan, topaz, #5000, etch 280 ....**$600**

Juice tumbler, June, topaz, ftd ...**$30**

Lily pond, Buttercup, 12" d **$55**

Marmalade, cov, American **$125**

Mayonnaise

Baroque, azure, #2496 ....**$95**

Bouquet, #2360 Century, etch 342

.... **$110**

Buttercup **$90**

Navarre **$90**

Milk pitcher, Century **$60**

Mint, Baroque, azure, #2496, handle,

4" d **$48**

Nappy, handle

Baroque, azure, #2496 ....**$48**

Coin, blue, 5-3/8" d **$30**

Nut cup, Fairfax, amber **$15**

Oil cruet, Versailles, yellow **$550**

Old-fashioned tumbler, Hermitage,

azure **$35**

Olive, Hermitage, amber, #2449 ....**$32**

Oyster cocktail, Hermitage, amber,

#2449 .... **$18**

Parfait, June, pink **$180**

Pickle castor, American, ornate silver

plated frame, 11" h **$900**

Pickle tray, Century, 8-3/4" **$15**

Pitcher, Lido, ftd **$225**

Plate

Baroque, green, 7-1/2" d **$28**

Century, 9-1/2" d **$30**

Corsage, etch 325, 8" d **$22**

Rose, 9" d **$15**

Platter

June, topaz, oval, 12" l **$145**

Trojan, topaz, oval, 12" l **$80**

Punch bowl, ftd, Baroque, crystal,

orig label **$425**

Relish dish, cov, Brocaded Summer

Gardens, three sections, white **$75**

Relish dish, open

Corsage, three parts, #2496, Baroque,

etch 325 ....**$75**

June, topaz, two parts, 8-1/4" l **$40**

Ring holder, American, 4-1/2" l, 3" h

.... **$800**

Rose bowl, American, small **$18**

Salad plate, Buttercup **$12**

Salt and pepper shakers, pr

Bridal Wreath, #2630 Century, cut

833, chrome tops **$95**

Coin, red **$60**

Coronet **$15**

Versailles, topaz, ftd **$200**

Sauce boat, Versailles, pink, match-

ing liner **$300**

Server, center handle, Trojan, topaz,

etch 280 .... **$135**

Sherbet

Baroque, azure, #2496 ....**$45**

Buttercup, #6030, etch 340 ....**$32**

Hermitage, green, #2449 ....**$22**

June, azure **$40**

Trojan, topaz, #5099, etch 280 ......**$48**

Snack plate, Century, 8" d **$25**

Sugar, individual size, Baroque, blue

.... **$4**

Sugar, cov, table size, Trojan, topaz ..**$22**

Syrup, American, Bakelite handle

.... **$200**

Sweetmeat, Baroque, azure, #2496

.... **$58**

Torte plate

Baroque, azure, #2496, 14" d **$125**

Colony, 15" d **$80**

Heather, 13" d **$45**

Tray, Navarre, 8" l **$100**

Tumbler, water

Hermitage, topaz, #2449 ....**$30**

June, ftd **$55**

Trojan, topaz, 5 oz, 4-1/2" h **$30**

Urn, cov, Coin, amber, 12-3/4" h **$68**

Vase

Baroque, azure, #2496, 8" h **$225**

Flying Fish, teal, 7" h **$65**

Hermitage, topaz, #2449, 6" h **$45**

Oak Leaf Brocade, c1929-31, 8" h

.... **$240**

Versailles, yellow, flip, 8" h **$395**

Whipped-cream pail, Versailles,

blue **$270**

Whiskey, Hermitage, topaz, #2449 ..**$20**

Wine

Buttercup, #6030, etch 340 ....**$45**

Chintz **$40**

Coin, red **$90**

Corsage, #6014, etch 325 ....**$45**

Hermitage, amber, #2449 ....**$20**

FRUIT JARS

History: Fruit jars are canning jars used to preserve food. Thomas W. Dyott, one of Philadelphia's earliest and most innovative glassmakers, was promoting his glass canning jars in 1829. John Landis Mason patented his screw-type canning jar on November 30, 1858. This date refers to the patent date, not the age of the jar. There are thousands of different jars and a variety of colors, types of closures, sizes, and embossings.

Collectors refer to fruit jars by the numbering system "RB," which was established by Douglas M. Leybourne Jr. in his book, *The Collector's Guide to Old Fruit Jars, Red Book 9.*

A. & D. H. Chambers Union, quart, yellow, olive green tint, applied groove ring wax sealer, tin lid mkd "A. & D. H. Chambers Pittsburgh, Pa (five-point star in center)," wire yoke, 7-5/8" h, 3-3/4" d base, RB 582 .... **$990**

A. Stone & Co. (arched), Philada Manufactured by Cunningham & Co. Pittsburgh PA" (on five lines), half gallon, aqua, high kick up, bare iron pontil mark, applied lip groove ring wax sealer, 9-3/4" h, 4-1/2" d base, RB 2752 .... **$1,320**

All Right

Half gallon, aqua, reverse mkd "Patd Jan. 28th 1868," base mkd "Pat Nov 26 1867," ground lip, unmarked metal dome shaped lid, wire clamp, two rim chips, 7-1/4" h, 4-1/2" d base, RB 61-3 .... **$90**

Quart, aqua, reverse mkd "Patd Jan 26th 1868," base mkd "PAT Nov 26 1867" and "12" in center, ground lip, unmarked metal dome shaped lid, wire clamp, 7-3/4" h, 3-3/4" d base, RB 59 .... **$110**

Almy (arched), quart, aqua, base mkd "Patented Dec 25, 1877 (star)" and "B," lid mkd "C," ground lip, Mason shoulder seal, glass screw-on lid, chips on lid, 7-1/8" h, 3-7/8" d base, RB 63 .... **$100**

Banner (encircled by), Patd Feby 9th 1864 Reisd Jan 22D 1867," quart, aqua, ground lip, press-down glass lid, neck indentation in rear, several rim flakes, 7-1/2" h, 3-3/4" d base, RB 403 .... **$135**

Beaver, facing right, chewing log, over

Fruit jar, Flaccus Bros., steer's head, amber, matching reproduction lid, RB 1014, **$220.**
Photo courtesy of American Bottle Auctions.

Fruit jar, Star and Crescent, self-sealing jar, embossed star and crescent moon, pint, ground lip, **$450.**
Photo courtesy of American Bottle Auctions.

Fruit jar, Mason's Patent Nov. 30th 1858, quart, teal, RB 1787, rough ground lip, **$275.**
Photo courtesy of American Bottle Auctions.

word "Beaver," midget pint, Ball blue, base mkd "3," unmarked glass insert and screw band, stippled tail, 5-5/8" h, 3-1/4" d base **$385**

Bloeser Jar, quart, aqua, ground rim, glass lid mkd "Pat Sept 27, 1887," orig wire and metal clamp with necktie wire, rim chip, 8" h, 3-3/4" d, RB 468 .... **$90**

Cohansey Glass Mf'g Co., Pat Mar 20. 77 (on base), half gallon, aqua, barrel shape, base also mkd "3," glass lid mkd "Cohansey Glass Mfg Co., Philada. PA," and "Y" in center, groove ring wax sealer, roughness, bruise on lid rim, 9-1/8" h, 4" d base, RB 633-1 .... **$70**

Cunningham & Co., Pittsburgh (on base), half gallon, deep aqua, bottom push up, bare iron pontil mark, applied lip to receive cork stopper, 9-3/4" h, 4-5/8" d base, RB 721 .. **$310**

Eagle
Half gallon, aqua, unmarked glass lid, iron yoke clamp with six-pointed star-shape thumbscrew, applied lip, 10" h, 4-1/2" d base, RB 872 .... **$110**
Quart, aqua, applied smooth lip, fabricated closure, 7-5/8" h, 3-7/8" d base, RB 871 .... **$90**

F & J Bodine Manufacturers, Philadelphia PA, quart, aqua, unmarked tin lid, soldered wire clamp, small open bubble under base edge, 7-1/8" h, 3-7/8" d base, RB 374 .... **$70**

Fahnestock Albree & Co., quart, dark aqua, pushed up bottom, pontil mark, Willoughby stopple mkd "J. O. Willoughby Patented, January 4, 1859," replaced wing nut, surface wear, 8-1/2" h, 3-3/4" d base, RB 970 .... **$360**

Gem, three gallon, aqua, reverse mkd

"Manufactured by The Hero Glass Works, Philadelphia PA," ground lip, glass insert mkd "Pat. Feb 12. 56. Dec 17.61. Nov 4.62. Dec 6.94, June 9.68. Sept 1.68. Sep 8.68. Dec.22.68. Jan 9 69," screw band, 17-5/8" h, 8-3/8" d base, RB 1058 .... **$3,575**

Glass Pail, one-half pint, teal, base mkd "Glass Pail Pat. Boston Mass June 24. 84," unmarked metal two pc lid with bail handle, 4-1/2" h overall, 3" d base, RB 20 .... **$525**

Globe, quart, red amber, base mkd "65," ground lip, red amber glass lid mkd "Patented May 15 1886," iron clamp and metal band around neck, 8-1/8" h, 3-3/4" d base, RB 1123 .... **$135**

Griffen's, Patent Oct 7 1862 (on lid), quart, amber, ground lip, glass lid with cage-like clamp, rim chip and flake, 7" h, 3-3/4" d base, RB 1154 .... **$70**

Hansee's, (PH monogram) Palace Home Jar, quart, clear, base mkd "Pat. Dec 19 1899," ground lip, monogrammed glass lid, wire clamp and neck tire wire, edge chips and flakes, 7-1/2" h, 3-3/4" d base, RB 1206 .. **$50**

Johnson & Johnson, New York (vertically), quart, cobalt blue, ground lip, cobalt lid, screw band, 7-1/8" h, 3-3/8" sq base, RB 1344 .... **$360**

Joshua Wright Philada, half gallon, aqua, barrel shape, applied lip, 10-1/2" h, 3-3/4" d base, RB 3036 variant **$180**

Lafayette, (in script, underlined), quart, aqua, base mkd "2," stopper neck finish three-pc glass and metal stopper, mkd "Patented Sept 2 1884 Aug 4 1885," 8-1/2" h, 3-5/8" d, RB 1452 .... **$110**

Mansfield
Pint, clear, base mkd "Mansfield Knowlton May '03 Pat. Glass W'K'S," and "2" in circle, glass lid, metal screw cap, light 1/4" crack, lid mkd "Mansfield Glass W'ks Knowlton Pat. May .03," 5-1/8" h, 3-1/8" d base, RB 1619 .... **$15**
Quart, clear with light aqua tint, base mkd "Mansfield Knowlton May '03 Pat. Glass W'K'S," glass lid, metal screw cap, lid mkd "Mansfield Glass W'ks Knowlton Pat. May .03," rim flake, 7" h, 3-5/8" d base, RB 1619 .... **$80**

Mansfield Improved Mason, quart, lavender tint, glass insert, screw band, rim flake, 7" h, B 1621 variant **$60**

Mason's (cross) Patent Nov. 30th 1858, (erased The Pearl), gallon, dark aqua, ground lip, Mason shoulder seal, plain zinc lid, rim flakes, 12" h, 5-7/8" d base, RB 1943 .. **$1,100**

Mason's CFJCO Improved, half gallon, amber, base mkd "H43," ground lip, amber insert mkd "P," screw band illegibly mkd, rim chip and flake, 9-1/8" h, 4-1/2" d base, RB 1711 **$190**

Mason's CFJCO Improved Patent Nov. 30th, 1858, gallon, aqua, base mkd "E122," ground lip, Mason's shoulder seal, metal lid mkd "Trademark Boyd's Porcelain Lined Patd Mar.30.58. June 9.63.Mar.30.69 Extd. Mar.30.72," partially open bubble, rim wear, lid cleaned, 12" h, 6" d, base, RB 1920 .... **$2,310**

Mason's Patent Nov. 30th, 1858, half gallon, green, amber swirls, smooth lip, metal "Ball" lid with milk glass insert mkd "Boyd's Genuine Porcelain Lined Cap 18V," 8-3/4" h, 4-3/8" d base, RB 1787 .... **$360**

Mason's Patent Nov. 30th, 1858, quart, Ball blue, reverse mkd with Tudor rose emblem, base mkd "A 83," ground lip, disk immerser lid, ext. mkd "TradeMark The Mason Disk Protector Cap Patd. Nov 30 1880," and Tudor rose emblem in center, bottom of disk mkd "Pat. Nov 23.75. Sept 12.76. Nov 30.80, July 20. 1886," 7-1/4" h, 3-3/4" d base, RB 1875 .... **$125**

Millville Atmospheric Fruit Jar, 56 oz, aqua, reverse mkd "Whitall's Patent June 18th 1861," glass lid, squared iron yoke clamp with thumbscrew, 9" h, 4-3/8" d base, RB 2181 .... **$45**

Moore's Patent Dec 3D 1861, quart, aqua, correct but slightly ill-fitting lid, rounded iron yoke clamp with thumbscrew, edge flakes on lid, flakes on interior jar flange, 8-1/8" h, 3-5/8" d base, RB 2204 .... **$55**

Owl, pint, milk glass, glass insert emb with daisy rosette, serrated screw band, 6-1/8" h, 2-1/2" d base, RB 3085 .... **$100**

Pansy (superimposed over erased Best), quart, amber, 20 vertical panels, ground lip, glass insert, screw band, rim flaking, 5-1/4" h, 4-1/2" d base, RB 2287 .... **$220**

Patented Oct. 19, 1858 (on lid), quart, aqua, ground lip, glass lid with internal lugs, lugs on neck of jar, 7" h, 3-7/8" d base, RB 1212 .... **$45**

PET, half gallon, aqua, correct glass lid, spring wire clamp, lid mkd "Patented Aug 21st 1869. T.G. Otterson," 9-7/8" h, 4-3/8" d base, RB 2359 .. **$200**

Potter & Bodine Airtight Fruit Jar Philada, half gallon, reverse mkd "Patented April 13th 1858," groove ring wax sealer, patched hole on edge of base, 2-1/4" h crack, 8-1/4" h, 4-1/4" d base, RB 2383 .... **$70**

Safety Valve Patd May 21, 1895 HC, over triangle on base, half gallon, dark aqua, Greek Key design around shoulder and base, glass lid mkd "1," ground lip, metal band clamp with bail handle, 8" h, 5-1/8" d base, RB 2539 .... **$55**

Safety Valve Patd May 21, 1895 HC, over triangle on base, pint, emerald green, partially ground lip, emerald green glass lid, metal band clamp, stamped "Safety Valve Patd May 21, 1895," 5-3/4" h, 3" d base, RB 2538 .... **$210**

Smalley Full Measure AGS (monogram), quart, amber, base mkd "Patented Dec 13 1892 April 7 1896, Dec 1, 1896," 7-1/4" h, 3-5/8" sq base, RB 2648 .... **$90**

Standard (arched), quart, light cobalt blue, reverse heel mkd "W. McC & Co," applied groove ring wax sealer, four-point star under base, tin lid mkd "W. McCully & Co. Glass Pittsburg," 1/2" wide chip on outer rim, 7-1/2" h, 3-3/4" d base, RB 2701-variant ... **$880**

Star, emblem encircled by fruit, quart, aqua, ground lip, neck slopes inward to opening, zinc insert and screw band, 7-3/4" h, 3-3/4" d base, RB 2724 .... **$150**

Sun (in circle with radiating lines) Trade Mark, quart, aqua, base mkd "J. P. Barstow," and "4," ground lip, unmarked glass lid, metal yoke clamp, mkd "Monier's Pat April 1 90 Mar 12 95," 7-3/4" h, 3-7/8" d base, RB 2761 .... **$100**

The Empire, quart, aqua, base mkd "Pat Feb 13 1866," ground rim, glass lid, chipping, bruise to ground rim, 8-1/2" h, 3-3/4" d base, RB 927 .... **$80**

The Gem, gallon, aqua, base mkd "H. Brooke Mould Maker NY Pat'd Nov 26th 1868. Patd Dec 17th 1861 Reis' Sept 1st 1868," ground lip, glass insert mkd "Mason's Improved May 10 1870," screw band, loss of lip flange, 12-3/8" h, 5-7/8" d base, RB 1071 .... **$880**

The Hero, half gallon, deep aqua, base mkd "Patd Nov 26 1867" and "5" in center, ground lip, glass insert with "WHA" monogram on interior center, series of patent dates on exterior, screw band, two rim chips, 9" h, 4-1/2" d base, RB 1242 .... **$15**

The Hero, quart, aqua, base mkd "Patd Nov 26 1867. Pat'd Dec 17 '61 Nov 4 '62 Dec 14 '69 Reis's Sept 1 '68 June 9' 69," and "87" in center, ground lip, glass insert with "WHA," monogram on interior center, series of patent dates on exterior, screw band, rim roughness, 7-1/8" h overall, 3-3/4" base, RB 1244 .... **$25**

The Hero, quart, honey amber, base mkd "Pat Nov 26 1867," and "6 (reversed) 7" in center, ground lip, metal lid with partially legible patent dates from 1862 through 1869 including Dec. 22, 1868 and Dec. 14, 1869," 7-1/2" h, 3-3/4" d base, RB 1242 .... **$6,600**

The Heroine, pint, aqua base mkd "22," ground lip, glass inset mkd "Pat. Feb 12.59 Dec. 17.61. Nov 4. 62.Dec 6.64. June 9.68. Jan 1.68. Sep 1.68. Sep 8.68 Dec 22.68," screw band, rim chip with flakes, 6-5/8" h, 3-1/4" d base, RB 1248 .... **$125**

The King, Pat Nov 2, 1869, quart, aqua, base mkd "3," ground lip, glass lid and iron yoke clamp, one half of rim broken out, 7-1/2" h, 3-3/4" d base, RB 1418 .... **$125**

The Valve Jar Co., Philadelphia, quart, aqua, base mkd "Patd Mar 1-th 1868," ground lip, glass lid, wire coil clamp, open bubble on edge of base, 7-1/2" h, 4" d base, RB 2873 .... **$385**

The Van Vliet Jar of 1881, half gallon, aqua, base mkd "6," ground lip, glass lid mkd "Pt May 3d 1881," metal yoke clamp with unmarked thumbscrew, attached wire extending vertically around entire jar, bruises, 9-1/4" h, 4-1/2" d base, RB 2878 ..... **$525**

Trade Marks Mason's CFJCO Improved, midget pint, aqua, base mkd "C178," ground lip, glass insert mkd "Trade Mark Mason's Improved Registered May 23d 1871" (CFJCo monogram in center) screw band stamped "Consolidated Fruit Jar Co. New York. Trade Mark Mason's Improved Registered May 23 1871," 6" h, 3-1/4" d base, RB 1722 .... **$25**

W. Chrysler, Pat. Nov. 21, 1865, quart, aqua, applied lip, three annealing lines, 7-3/4" h, 3-3/4" d base, RB 597-1 .... **$1,210**

GOOFUS GLASS

History: Goofus glass, also known as Mexican ware, hooligan glass, and pickle glass, is a pressed glass with relief designs that were painted either on the back or front. The designs are usually in red and green with a metallic gold ground. It was popular from 1890 to 1920 and was used as a premium at carnivals.

It was produced by several companies: Crescent Glass Company, Wellsburg, West Virginia; Imperial Glass Corporation, Bellaire, Ohio; LaBelle Glass Works, Bridgeport, Ohio; and Northwood Glass Co., Indiana, Pennsylvania, Wheeling, West Virginia, and Bridgeport, Ohio.

Goofus glass lost its popularity when people found that the paint tarnished or scaled off after repeated washings and wear. No record of its manufacture has been found after 1920.

Marks: Goofus glass made by Northwood includes one of the following marks: "N," "N" in one circle, "N" in two circles, or one or two circles without the "N."

Goofus bowl, Leaf and Beads, Northwood, c1906-08, opalescent ruffled ring around center design of leafs, center cold painted gold and red, N mark, 9" d, **$55.**

Ashtray, red rose dec, emb adv **$18**

Basket, strawberry dec, 5" h **$50**

Bonbon, Strawberry pattern, gold, red, and green dec, 4" d **$40**

Bowl
Cherries, gold leaves, red cherries, 10-1/2" d, 2-1/2" h **$35**
Grape and Lattice pattern, red grapes, gold ground, ruffled rim, 6-1/2" d **$45**

Bread plate, Last Supper pattern, red and gold, grapes and foliage border, 7" w, 11" l **$65**

Candy dish, figure-eight design, serrated rim, dome foot, 8-1/2" d **$60**

Charger, grape and leaves center **$125**

Coaster, red floral dec, gold ground, 3" d **$12**

Compote
Grape and Cable pattern, 4" d **$35**
Poppy pattern, red flowers, gold foliage, green ground, sgd "Northwood," 6-1/2" d **$40**
Strawberry pattern, red and green strawberries and foliage, ruffled, 6" d **$40**

Decanter, orig stopper, La Belle Rose **$50**

Dresser tray, Cabbage Rose pattern, red roses dec, gold foliage, clear ground, 6" l **$35**

Jewel box, basketweave, rose dec, 4" d, 2" h **$50**

Mug, Cabbage Rose pattern, gold ground **$35**

Nappy, Cherries pattern, red cherries, gold foliage, clear ground, 6-1/2" d . **$35**

Perfume bottle, pink tulips dec, 3-1/2" h **$20**

Pickle jar, aqua, molded, gold, blue, and red painted floral design **$50**

Pin dish, oval, red and black florals, 6-1/2" l **$20**

Plate
Carnations pattern, red carnations, gold ground, 7-3/4" d **$20**
Cherries, some paint worn off, 11" d **$35**
Sunflower pattern, red dec center, relief molded, 6" d **$20**

Platter, red rose dec, gold ground, 18" l **$65**

Powder jar, cov, puffy, rose dec, red and gold, 3" d **$40**

Salt and pepper shakers, pr, Grape and Leaf pattern **$45**

Syrup, relief molded, red roses dec, lattice work ground, orig top **$85**

Toothpick holder, red rose and foliage dec, gold ground **$40**

Tray, red chrysanthemum dec, gold ground, 8-1/4" d, 11" d **$45**

Tumbler, red rose dec, gold ground, 6" h **$35**

Vase
Cabbage Rose pattern, red dec, gold ground, 6" h **$45**
Poppies pattern, blue and red dec, gold ground, 9" h **$45**

Goofus plate, gold ground, two bright red roses in center, border with diamond quilting and acanthus scrolling, **$45.**

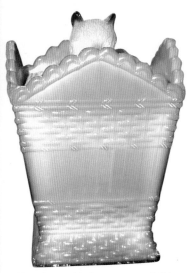

Greentown cat in hamper covered dish, chocolate glass, **$225.**

GREENTOWN GLASS

History: The Indiana Tumbler and Goblet Co., Greentown, Indiana, produced its first clear, pressed glass table and bar wares in late 1894. Initial success led to a doubling of the plant size in 1895 and other subsequent expansions, one in 1897 to allow for the manufacture of colored glass. In 1899, the firm joined the combine known as the National Glass Company.

In 1900, just before arriving in Greentown, Jacob Rosenthal developed an opaque brown glass, called "chocolate," which ranged in color from a dark, rich chocolate to a lighter coffee-with-cream hue. Production of chocolate glass saved the financially pressed Indiana Tumbler and Goblet Works. The Cactus and Leaf Bracket patterns were made almost exclusively in chocolate glass. Other popular chocolate patterns include Austrian, Dewey, Shuttle, and Teardrop and Tassel. In 1902, National Glass Company bought Rosenthal's chocolate glass formula so other plants in the combine could use the color.

In 1902, Rosenthal developed the Golden Agate and Rose Agate colors. All work ceased on June 13, 1903, when a fire of suspicious origin destroyed the Indiana Tumbler and Goblet Company Works.

After the fire, other companies, e.g., McKee and Brothers, produced chocolate glass in the same pattern designs used by Greentown. Later reproductions also have been made, with Cactus among the most heavily copied patterns.

Animal-covered dish
Dolphin, chocolate **$225**
Rabbit, dome top, amber **$250**
Bowl, Herringbone Buttress, green, 7-1/4" d...**$135**
Butter, cov, Cupid, chocolate **$575**
Celery vase, Beaded Panel, clear **$100**
Compote, Teardrop and Tassel, clear, 5-1/4" d, 5-1/8" h **$50**
Creamer
Cactus, chocolate...........................**$85**
Indian Head, opaque white.........**$450**

Goblet
Overall Lattice................................**$40**
Shuttle, chocolate **$500**
Mug, indoor drinking scene, chocolate, 6" w, 8" h..................................**$400**
Mustard, cov, Daisy, opaque white... **$75**
Paperweight, Buffalo, Nile green **$575**
Pitcher, cov, Dewey, chocolate, 5-1/4" h **$115**
Plate, Serenade, chocolate..............**$65**
Relish, Leaf Bracket, oval, chocolate, 8" l..**$75**

Salt and pepper shakers, pr, Cactus, chocolate **$130**
Sugar, cov, Dewey, cobalt blue.....**$125**
Syrup, Cord Drapery, chocolate, plated lid, 6-3/4" h **$295**
Toothpick holder, Hobnail and Shell, chocolate **$185**
Tumbler
Cactus, chocolate...........................**$60**
Dewey, canary................................**$65**
Vase, Austrian, 8" h........................**$55**

HEISEY GLASS

Heisey jug, Grecian border, colorless, three pint, applied handle, base marked, A. H. Heisey & Co., early 20th century, 6-1/4" h, **$155.**
Photo courtesy of Green Valley Auctions.

History: The A. H. Heisey Glass Co. began producing glasswares in April 1896, in Newark, Ohio. Heisey, the firm's founder, was not a newcomer to the field, having been associated with the craft since his youth.

Many blown and molded patterns were produced in crystal, colored, milk (opalescent), and Ivorina Verde (custard) glass. Decorative techniques of cutting, etching, and silver deposit were employed. Glass figurines were introduced in 1933 and continued in production until 1957 when the factory closed. All Heisey glass is notable for its clarity.

Marks: Not all pieces have the familiar H-within-a-diamond mark.

1900-58

Reproduction Alert. Some Heisey molds were sold to Imperial Glass of Bellaire, Ohio, and certain items were reissued. These pieces may be mistaken for the original Heisey. Some of the reproductions were produced in colors never made by Heisey and have become collectible in their own right. Examples include: the Colt family in Crystal, Caramel Slag, Ultra Blue, and Horizon Blue; the mallard with wings up in Caramel Slag; Whirlpool (Provincial) in crystal and colors; and Waverly, a seven-inch, oval, footed compote in Caramel Slag.

Animal

Gazelle **$1,450**

Plug horse, Oscar **$115**

Pony, kicking **$175**

Sealyham terrier **$145**

Sparrow **$150**

Ashtray

Old Sandwich, #1404, moongleam, individual size **$68**

Ridgeleigh, #1469, club shape **$10**

Bitters bottle, #5003, tube **$165**

Bowl

Plantation Ivy, crystal, 10" d **$65**

Queen Anne, light use, 8" d **$25**

Buffet plate, Lariat, #1540, 21" ... **$70**

Butter dish, cov, Rose **$200**

Cake plate, Rose, pedestal, 15" d
.... **$325**

Camellia bowl, Lariat, #1540, 9-1/2" d
.... **$40**

Candelabra, crystal, price for pr, 10" w, 16-1/2" h **$695**

Candlesticks, pr

Flamingo, #112 .... **$150**

Mercury, #122 .... **$70**

New Era, #3877 .... **$90**

Orchid, Trident, two-lite **$155**

Pinwheel, #121 .... **$90**

Regency, two-lite, #1504 .... **$98**

Thumbprint and Panel, #1433 ... **$140**

Trophy, #126, Flamingo **$275**

Windsor, #22, 7-1/2" h **$140**

Caramel, cov, Lariat, #1540, 7" **$75**

Celery, Empress, Sahara, 10" l **$45**

Centerpiece bowl, Ridgeleigh, #1469, 11" d **$225**

Champagne, Duquesne, tangerine, saucer **$235**

Cheese dish, cov, Lariat, #1540, ftd
.... **$40**

Cheese plate, Twist, #1252, Kraft, Moongleam **$63**

Cigarette holder, Crystolite **$25**

Claret

Carassone, Sahara, 4 oz **$68**

Orchid, Tyrolean line, 4-1/2 oz ... **$150**

Coaster

Colonial **$10**

Plantation **$50**

Cocktail

Lariat, #1540, Moonglo cut **$12**

Rose Etch **$33**

Seahorse, crystal **$145**

Cocktail shaker

Cobel, #4225, quart **$55**

Orchid Etch, sterling foot **$200**

Console set, Twist, Moongleam, Cattail cutting, 12" oval ftd bowl, pr 2" candles **$295**

Cordial

Carcassone, #390, Sahara **$115**

Minuet, crystal **$150**

Peerless, crystal **$28**

Creamer and sugar

Twist, #1252, oval, Sahara **$165**

Waverly, #1519, orchid etch **$75**

Cream soup, Queen Anne, etching
.... **$20**

Cruet, Greek Key, crystal **$145**

Cup and saucer

Empress, Sahara yellow, round **$40**

Twist, #1252, flamingo **$55**

Custard cup, Queen Anne **$15**

Floral bowl, Orchid, Waverly, crimped, some scratches, 12" d, 4" h **$55**

Gardenia bowl, Orchid, Waverly, 13" d **$90**

Goblet

Galaxy, #8005 .... **$25**

Moonglo, crystal **$35**

Narrow Flute, #393 .... **$29**

Plantation Ivy, crystal **$36**

Provincial, #1506 .... **$15**

Spanish, #3404, cobalt blue **$155**

Tudor **$12**

Honey, Plantation, #1567, ivy etch, 6-1/2" **$80**

Hurricane lamp base, Lariat, #1540, pr **$85**

Iced-tea tumbler, Moonglo, crystal
.... **$35**

Jug, Old Sandwich, #1404, Sahara, half gallon **$225**

Luster, Ipswich, crystal **$465**

Mayonnaise bowl, Orchid, two-part, Queen Anne **$65**

Mayonnaise ladle, #6, Alexandrite
.... **$245**

Muffin plate, Octagon #1229, Moongleam, 12" d **$48**

Nut dish

Empress, #1401, individual, Alexandrite **$175**

Narrow Flute, #393, Moongleam
.... **$15**

Oyster cocktail, Pied Piper **$15**

Paperweight, rabbit **$225**

Parfait glass, Orchid, price for set of eight, 5-1/2" h, 2-7/8" d, ... **$480**

Pitcher, Orchid, tankard **$625**

Plate

Colonial, 4-3/4" d **$5**

Empress, Moongleam, 7" d **$25**

Minuet, 8" d **$20**

Orchid, Waverly, 8" d **$40**

Ridgeleigh, #1469, 8" d **$10**

Punch bowl set, Crystolite, punch bowl, 12 cups, ladle **$400**

Relish

Normandie etch, star, #1466 .... **$95**

Orchid, three-part, three handles, 7-1/4" d **$55**

Heisey toothpick holder, Fancy Loop, green A. H. Heisey Glass Co., late 19th/ early 20th century, 2-1/4" h, **$70.**
Photo courtesy of Green Valley Auctions.

Provincial, #1506, 12" **$35**

Twist, #1252, flamingo, 13" l **$40**

Waverly, two-part **$25**

Rose bowl, Plateau, #3369, flamingo
.... **$65**

Salt shaker, Old Sandwich, #1404
.... **$30**

Sandwich plate, Rose **$220**

Serving tray, center handle, Orchid etch **$150**

Sherbet, Moonglo, crystal **$35**

Soda

Coronation, #4054, 10 oz **$10**

Duquesne, #3389, 12 oz, ftd, tangerine **$210**

Newton, #2351, 8 oz, Fronetnac etch
.... **$20**

Strawberry dip plate, Narrow Flute, #393, with rim **$195**

Sugar, Crystolite, individual **$18**

Tankard, Orchid, ice lip, 9-1/2" h, 7" w
.... **$480**

Toothpick holder, Fancy Loop, emerald **$70**

Tumbler, Carassone, Sahara, ftd, 2 oz
.... **$72**

Vase

Prison Stripe, #357, cupped, 5" **$55**

Ridgeleigh, #1469, Sahara, cylinder, 8" h **$245**

Water bottle, Banded Flute, #150
.... **$125**

Wine

Creole, Alexandrite, 5-1/2" h **$175**

Minuet, crystal, 6" h **$85**

Imperial vase, baluster, green heart-shaped leaves and stems, bright white lustered ground, unmarked, minute flecks around rim, 8" x 7-3/4", $700.
Photo courtesy of David Rago Auctions, Inc.

IMPERIAL GLASS

History: Imperial Glass Co., Bellaire, Ohio, was organized in 1901. Its primary product was pattern (pressed) glass. Soon other lines were added, including carnival glass, Nuart, Nucut, and Near Cut. In 1916, the company introduced Free-Hand, a lustered art glass line, and Imperial Jewels, an iridescent stretch glass that carried the Imperial cross trademark. In the 1930s, the company was reorganized into the Imperial Glass Corporation. The firm was sold to Lenox in 1976, and ceased all operations by 1984.

Imperial acquired the molds and equipment of several other glass companies—Central, Cambridge, and Heisey. Many of the retired molds of these companies were once again in use for a short period of time before Imperial closed.

Marks: The Imperial reissues are marked to distinguish them from the originals.

Engraved or hand cut

Bowl, flower and leaf, molded star base, 6-1/2" d **$25**
Candlesticks, pr, Amelia, 7" h **$35**
Celery vase, three-side stars, cut star base **$25**
Pitcher, tankard, Design No. 110, flowers, foliage, and butterfly cutting . **$60**
Plate, Design No. 12, 5-1/2" d **$15**

Jewels

Bowl, purple Pearl Green luster, marked, 6-1/2" d **$75**
Console set, Golden Green, 1920s, 10-1/2" d bowl, pr 9-1/2" h candlesticks **$350**
Rose bowl, amethyst, green irid ... **$75**
Vase
  Bulbous, mustard yellow, orange irid int., shape #1690, 6-1/2" h **$100**
  Cylindrical bud, emerald green, orange irid int., 8-1/2" h **$100**
  Cylindrical, irid marigold, wear at collar, 11" h **$75**

Lustered (freehand)

Candlestick, slender baluster, cushion foot, clear, white heart and vine dec, tall cylindrical irid dark blue socket, orig paper label, 10" h **$440**
Hat, ruffled rim, cobalt blue, embedded irid white vines and leaves, 9" w **$120**
Ivy ball, Spun, red, crystal foot, 4" h **$90**
Vase
  Bulbous shouldered, irid marigold, price for pr, 6-1/2" h **$300**
  Bulbous, strong marigold irid, random blue heart and vine dec, 10" h **$550**

Corset shape, irid green, white heart and vine dec, orange int., 10" h .. **$550**

Nuart
Ashtray **$20**
Lamp shade, marigold **$50**
Vase, bulbous, irid green, 7" h **$125**

Nucut
Berry bowl, handles, 4-1/2" d **$15**
Celery tray, 11" l **$18**
Creamer **$20**
Fern dish, brass lining, ftd, 8" l ... **$30**
Orange bowl, Rose Marie, 12" d .. **$48**

Pressed
Bar bottle, Cape Cod **$150**
Basket, Cape Cod, No. 160/73/0 .. **$350**
Birthday cake plate, Cape Cod **$325**
Bowl
  Cape Cod, 11" l, oval **$90**
Windmill, amethyst, fluted, 8" d, 3" h **$45**
Bread and butter plate, Cape Cod **$7**
Canapé plate, matching tumbler, #400/36 .... **$36**
Center bowl, Cape Cod, No. 160/751, ruffled edge **$65**
Champagne, Cape Cod, azalea **$22**
Coaster, Cape Cod, No. 160/76 ..... **$10**
Creamer, #400/30 .... **$9**
Cruet, orig stopper, Cape Cod, No. 160/119, amber **$28**
Decanter, orig stopper, Cape Cod, No. 160/163 .... **$75**
Dish, covered
  Dog, caramel slag, ALIG 1982 .... **$165**
  Dove, satin crystal, IG mark **$75**

Lion, amber, from Heisey mold mkd "CG" **$125**
Pie wagon, caramel slag, ALIG 1982 .... **$225**
Figure
  Chipmunk, Ultra Blue, ALIG mark **$195**
  Clydesdale, Ultra Blue, ALIG mark **$250**
  Wood Duck, Ultra Blue, IG mark .. **$225**
Goblet
  Cape Cod, No. 1602, Verde green .. **$20**
  Traditional **$15**
Jar, cov
  Cathay, Verde Green **$135**
  Owl, green and white slag, IG mark **$85**
Nappy, Quilted Diamond, marigold, ring handle **$35**
Pitcher, Cape Cod, No. 160/19, ice lip **$85**
Plate, Windmill, caramel slag, IG mark **$75**
Relish
  Candlewick, two-part, 6-1/2" **$25**
  Cape Cod, three-part **$35**
Rose bowl, Molly, black, silver deposit floral dec, 5" h **$45**
Salad plate, Cape Cod, use scratches, 8" d **$11**
Sherbet
  Cape Cod **$10**
  Traditional **$10**
Sugar, #400/30 .... **$9**
Tea cup, #400/35 .... **$8**
Toothpick holder, carnival or milk white, IG mark, 2-1/2" h **$30**
Tumbler, Georgian, red **$18**
Whiskey set, Cape Cod, No. 160/280, metal rack, clear bottles, raised letters Bourbon, Rye, and Scotch **$650**

LALIQUE

History: René Lalique (1860-1945) first gained prominence as a jewelry designer. Around 1900, he began experimenting with molded-glass brooches and pendants, often embellishing them with semiprecious stones. By 1905, he was devoting himself exclusively to the manufacture of glass articles.

LALIQUE

R.LALIQUE

In 1908, Lalique began designing packaging for the French cosmetic houses. He also produced many objects, especially vases, bowls, and figurines, in the Art Nouveau and Art Deco styles. The full scope of Lalique's genius was seen at the 1925 Paris l'Exposition Internationale des Arts Décorative et Industriels Modernes.

Marks: The mark "R. LALIQUE FRANCE" in block letters is found on pressed articles, tableware, vases, paperweights, and automobile mascots. The script signature, with or without "France," is found on hand-blown objects. Occasionally, a design number is included. The word "France" in any form indicates a piece made after 1926.

The post-1945 mark is generally "Lalique France" without the "R," but there are exceptions.

Reproduction Alert. The Lalique signature has often been forged; the most common fake includes an "R" with the post-1945 mark.

Ashtray

Irene, bright green, white patina, stenciled "R. Lalique France," Marcilhac pg 276, no. 304, c1931, 3-3/4" d **$1,100**

Jamaique, clear and frosted, sepia patina, engraved "R. Lalique France," Marcilhac pg 274, no. 296, 5-1/2" d **$225**

Simone, clear and frosted, sepia patina, stenciled "R. Lalique France," Marcilhac pg 275, no. 300, c1929, 4-1/2" d **$300**

Bookends, pr, Hirondelles, sgd "Lalique, France," 6-1/4" h **$500**

Bowl

Acacia No. 2, opalescent, stenciled "R. LALIQUE FRANCE," c1928, Marchilhac pg 755, no. 3249, 8-5/8" d **$300**

Cremieu, opalescent, molded "R. LALIQUE FRANCE," engraved No. 400, c1928, Marchilhac pg 297, no.x 400, 11-7/8" d **$550**

Doves, frosted doves with spread wings, oval, etched "Lalique (r in circle) France" in small script, 9" d, 6-1/4" h **$400**

Daisy, deep rim relief dec with band of overlapping daisies, colorless body fluted, brown patina accents, acid-etched mark "Lalique Cristal France," post WWII, 14-1/2" d, 2-3/4" h **$425**

Box, cov

Pommier du Japon, black, whitish patina, molded "R. LALIQUE,"

Marcilhac pg 227, no. 26, c1919, 3-1/4" d **$1,200**

Quatre Scarabees, black, whitish patina, molded "R. LALIQUE," Marcilhac pg 225, no. 15, c1911, 3-1/4" d **$1,600**

Veronique, black, whitish patina, molded "R. LALIQUE," Marcilhac pg 227, no. 25, c1919, 3-1/4" d **$1,700**

Cane handle, clear and frosted, sepia patina, Marcilhac pg 141, c1905, 3-3/8" l **$900**

Car mascot

No. 1124, Faucon, molded signature "R.Lalique" and etched "France," orig Breves Galleries metal mount, 6-1/4" h **$2,100**

No. 1138, Tete D'Aigle, later example, molded signature "R. LALIQUE" and engraved "Lalique France," 4-1/2" h **$300**

Coupe, Graines d'Asperges No. 2, opalescent, molded DVA mark, Marcilhac pg 751, no. 3221, 8-1/4" **$350**

Figure

Bamara, lion, designed by Marie Claude Lalique, MIB, introduced 1987, 8" h **$1,200**

Black panther, designed by Marie Claude Lalique, introduced 1989, MIB, 14-3/8" l, 4-3/8" h **$1,300**

Cat, crouching, frosted, designed by Rene Lalique, 1932, 4" h **$1,200**

Cheetah, designed by Marie Claude Lalique, MIB, 10" h, 8-1/4" l .. **$2,600**

Hat pin, clear and frosted, sepia patina over gilt metal foil, orig silvered metal mounting and shaft, c1912, 7-3/4" l shaft, 10" l overall

Feuilles, Marcilhac pg 566, no. 1558 .... **$2,800**

Scarabees, Marcilhac pg 566, no. 1559 .... **$1,800**

R. Lalique vase, "Acanthes," cased butterscotch yellow, orig bronze stand, molded R. LALIQUE, c1921, vase 10-7/8" x 12-1/2", **$28,800.**
Photo courtesy of David Rago Auctions, Inc.

R. Lalique vase, "Florence," clear and frosted, brown enamel and sepia patina, stenciled R. LALIQUE FRANCE, c1937, 7-5/8" h, **$6,000.**
Photo courtesy of David Rago Auctions, Inc.

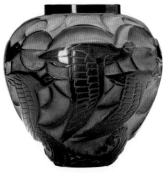

R. Lalique vase, "Courlis," deep green, whitish patina, stenciled R. LALIQUE FRANCE, c1931, 6-1/2", **$6,600.**
Photo courtesy of David Rago Auctions, Inc.

R. Lalique vase, "Bresse," amber, whitish patina, stenciled R. LALIQUE FRANCE, 6-1/2" h, **$3,000.**
Photo courtesy of David Rago Auctions, Inc.

R. Lalique vase, "Nivernais," bright green, engraved R. Lalique France, no. 1005, c1927, 6-5/8", **$3,360.**
Photo courtesy of David Rago Auctions, Inc.

R. Lalique vase, "Espalion," cased jade green, engraved R. Lalique France, no. 996, c1927, 7" h, **$5,700.**
Photo courtesy of David Rago Auctions, Inc.

R. Lalique vase, "Avallon," deep yellow amber, original wood stand, wheel cut R. LALIQUE FRANCE, engraved no. 986, c1927, vase 5-3/4" h, overall 6-3/8" h, **$6,000.**
Photo courtesy of David Rago Auctions, Inc.

Inkwell

Biches, clear and frosted, gray patina, engraved "R. Lalique," Marcilhac pg 315, no. 427, c1912, 6" sq base **$2,700**

Cernay, clear and frosted, green patina, molded "R. LALIQUE," Marcilhac pg 318, no. 437, c1924, 3-1/2" x 4"......................................**$5,000**

Mures, clear and frosted, blue patina, engraved "R. Lalique France, No. 431," Marcilhac pg 316, no. 421, c1920, 2" x 6-1/4" **$8,500**

Jewelry

Bracelet, Cerisier, peacock blue, engraved "Lalique," Marchilhac pg 532, no. 1329, small chips, one element reglued, c1928, 12 1-1/8" h elements **$2,000**

Brooch, Trois Anges, clear, sepia patina, gold reflecting foil, gilt metal backing, stamped "Lalique poincon," Marcilhac pg 545, no. 1373, c1912, 1-1/4" d..........................**$800**

Brooch, Chauve-Souris, electric blue, white patina, silver reflecting foil, gilt metal mount, stamped "Lalique poincon," Marcilhac pg 538, no. G.L., c1912, 2-1/8" d **$6,000**

Pendant, Cigognes, clear and frosted, gray patina, molded "LALIQUE," Marchilac pg 581, no. 1663, c1919, 2-1/8" d **$250**

Letter seal, R. Lalique
Rapace, blue, engraved "R. Lalique," Marcilhac pg 257, no. 234, c1931, 2" h **$1,700**

Sauterelle, electric blue, molded "LALIQUE," Marchilhac pg 249, no. 183, c1913, 1-5/8" h **$650**

Statuette Drapee, clear and frosted glass with green patina, early engraved signature, Marcilhac pg 249, no. 181, c1913, 2-1/2" h **$3,000**

Tete D'Aigle, dark amber, engraved "R. Lalique France," Marcilhac pg 248, no. 175, c1911, 3-1/8" h **$1,700**

Paperweight

Bird, Ailes Fermees, clear and frosted, engraved "R. Lalique France," Marcilhac pg 386, no. 1156, 4-1/2"..**$375**

Toby, clear and frosted, stenciled "R. Lalique France," Marcilhac pg 391, no. 1192, c1929, 3-1/2" **$1,200**

Perfume bottle

Bouquet de Faunes, for Guerlain, clear and frosted, gray patina, orig black leather presentation case, unmarked, orig retailer labels on base, c1925, Marchilhac pg 940, no. 1, 3-7/8" h **$1,300**

Camille, electric blue, white patina, molded "R. LALIQUE FRANCE," engraved "R. Lalique France," Marcilhac pg 335, no. 516, c1927, 2-3/8" h **$3,000**

Heart shape, Coeur-Joie, Nina Ricci, 5-7/8" h, 3-3/4" w **$825**

Narkiss, for Roger et Gallet, clear and frosted patina, black enamel, modeled "R.L. FRANCE," Marcilhac pg 947, no. 1, 3-7/8" h................**$2,700**

Vase

Amiens, topaz, whitish patina, stenciled "R. LALIQUE," Marcilhac pg 443, no. 1023, some int. staining, int. flaw in one handle, c1929, 7-1/4" h **$1,200**

Coquillles, clear and frosted, blue patina, molded "R. LALIQUE," Marcilhac pg 424, no. 932, c1920, 7-1/4" h **$1,100**

Dahlias, clear and frosted, sepia patina, black enamel, molded "R

R. Lalique lemonade set, "Hesperides," jug and eight tumblers on tray, clear and frosted, stenciled R. LALIQUE FRANCE, 1931, tray 16-1/2" d, **$2,160.**
Photo courtesy of David Rago Auctions, Inc.

R. Lalique ashtray, "Archer," opalescent, molded R. LALIQUE, c1922, 4-1/2" d, **$1,140.**
Photo courtesy of David Rago Auctions, Inc.

R. Lalique bowl, "Fleur," clear and frosted with gray patina, black enamel, molded R. LALIQUE, engraved France No. 3100, c1912, 4-1/2" d, **$900.**
Photo courtesy of David Rago Auctions, Inc.

LALIQUE," Marcilhac pg 425, no., 938, c1925, 4-7/8" h **$2,300**

Dauphins, opalescent, blue patina, stenciled "R. LALIQUE," engraved "France," Marcilhac pg 464, no. 10-900, 5-3/8" h **$2,200**

Douze Figurines Avec Bouchon, clear and frosted, engraved "R. Lalique France," Marcilhac pg 420, no. 914, small bruise to base of stopper barrel, c1920, 11-3/8" h **$7,000**

Espalion, electric blue, engraved "R. Lalique, France No. 996," Marcilhac pg 438, no. 996, c1927, 6-7/8" h **$1,300**

Frosted colorless bulbous body, repeating open-petal dahlias with black centers, etched mark "R.

Lalique France," Marcilhac no. 3938, model created in 1923, 5" h ...**$1,410**

Nivernais, bright green, engraved "R. Lalique France, No. 1005," Marcilhac pg 440, no. 1005, c1927, 6-5/8" h **$3,360**

Rampillon, opalescent, stenciled "R. LALIQUE FRANCE," two shallow chips, Marcilhac pg 437, no. 991, c1927, 5" h **$1,100**

Soudan Art, ovoid body, relief dec with three bands of running stags and flowers, sgd "R. Lalique France" on base, Marcilhac no. 1016, design created in 1928, 6-1/2" h.......**$1,120**

Tourterelles, opalescent, blue patina, engraved "R Lalique," Marcilhac pg 431, no. 963, c1925, 11-1/4" h....... **$14,000**

R. Lalique vase, "Malesherbes," clear and frosted, sepia patina, engraved R. Lalique France No. 1014, 1927, 9-1/8" h, **$3,000.**
Photo courtesy of David Rago Auctions, Inc.

R. Lalique shallow dish, "Gazelles," opalescent with blue patina, molded R. LALIQUE, wheel cut FRANCE, c1925, 11-5/8" d, **$1,800.**
Photo courtesy of David Rago Auctions, Inc.

R. Lalique vase, "Domremy," emerald green, whitish patina, engraved, R. Lalique France, No. 979, c1926, 8-1/4" h, **$4,800.**
Photo courtesy of David Rago Auctions, Inc.

Libbey rose bowl, Maize pattern, cased, yellow exterior, creamy white interior, **$195.**

Photo courtesy of Alderfer Auction Co.

LIBBEY GLASS

History: Edward Libbey established the Libbey Glass Company in Toledo, Ohio, in 1888 after the New England Glass Works of W. L. Libbey and Son closed in East Cambridge, Massachusetts. The new Libbey company produced quality cut glass, which today is considered to belong to the brilliant period.

In 1930, Libbey's interest in art-glass production was renewed, and A. Douglas Nash was employed as a designer in 1931.

Libbey Amberina vase, bud form, amber to rich fuchsia, optic ribbed, footed, sgd acid stamp Libbey, 9" h, **$500.**

Photo courtesy of The Early Auction Company, LLC.

Art glass

Bowl, amberina, crimson shading to amber, Diamond Quilted pattern, applied amber peaked overlay extends mid length, orig Libbey paper label, ex-Maude Feld, 5-1/8" h...........**$2,100**

Bud vase, shape #3008, amberina, slender neck, wafer base, c1917, 9" h **$500**

Center bowl, shape #3019, amberina, pedestal base, pontil sgd with trademark, ex-Maude Feld, c1917, 12" d, 5-3/4" h......................................**$6,250**

Cologne bottle, catalog #3041, amberina, ribbed elongated body shading from fuchsia to amber, raised disk base, blown stopper-dauber with fuchsia amber shading, pontil sgd with trademark, 8-3/4" h **$1,100**

Compote, catalog #3017, amberina, Libbey acid stamp mark, partial paper label, ex-Maude Feld, 7-1/4" d, 8-3/8" h......................................**$4,000**

Creamer and sugar, crystal, blue-green opaque dot trim, dark blue-green glass feet, polished pontil, 5-3/8" h creamer, 3-1/2" h, 4-3/4" d sugar **$475**

Miniature, vase, amberina, flattened oval neck extend to flaring circular body, fuchsia shading to amber, applied rigaree collar, raised dec, ex-Maude Feld, 3-1/4" h...................**$850**

Sugar bowl, open, opaque blue, satin finish, two handles, c1893, 4-1/2" w, 2-3/4" h...**$550**

Toothpick holder
Amberina, crimped bulbous body, deep red to amber, Inverted Baby Thumbprint pattern, ex-Maude Feld, 2-1/4" h **$600**
Amberina, Diamond Quilted pattern, barrel shape, 2-1/2" h...............**$250**

Underplate, amberina, Swirl pattern, scalloped rim, 6-1/4" d...............**$150**

Vase
Amberina, Optic Ribbed pattern, acid stamped "Libbey Amberina," ftd, 8" h **$500**
Mushroom shape, clear ribbed glass, allover yellow finish, 7-1/2" d..**$120**
Sq mouth, deep crimson extending to graduated double circular body, raised ovals, inverted circular dec, four applied amber shells, ex-Maude Feld, 4-3/4" h............**$2,100**
Tapering ovoid, circular neck, amberina, shades from very deep ruby to amber, raised and imp dec, orig "Libbey Amberina" label, ex-Maude Feld, 2-7/8" h **$750**

Cut glass

Banana boat, scalloped pedestal base, 24-point hobstar, hobstar, cane, vesica, and fan motifs, sgd, 13" x 7" x 7"..**$1,500**

Bowl, three brilliant cut thistles surround bowl, flower in center, scalloped edge, etched "Libbey" label, price for pr, 8" d, 4" h **$400**

Charger, hobstar, cane, and wreath motifs, sgd, 14" d........................**$300**

Miniature lamp, pinwheel design, sgd, 2" sq base, 10-3/8" h **$425**

Tumble-up, star burst, hobstar, fern, and fan motifs, minor handle check **$725**

Vase, No. 982, Senora pattern, cut glass, ftd, hexed vesicas, deep miter cuts, three 24-point hobstars at top between crossed miter cuts, small stars and trellises, clear knob and stem, scalloped foot cut with extended single star, Libbey over saber mark, some flaws, c1896-1906, 18" h **$2,500**

LOETZ

History: Loetz is a type of iridescent art glass that was made in Austria by J. Loetz Witwe in the late 1890s. The Loetz factory at Klostermule produced items with fine cameos on cased glass, good quality glassware for others to decorate, as well as the iridescent glasswares more commonly associated with the Loetz name.

Marks: Some pieces are signed "Loetz," "Loetz, Austria," or "Austria."

Atomizer, cameo, lemon yellow ground overlaid in blue, cameo cut leafy stemmed cockle shell flowers, sgd "Loetz" in cameo, no stopper, c1910, 7" h..............**$435**

Bowl

Opalescent, pinched rim, columnar support, triangular foot, engraved with artist cipher for Maria Kirschner, 7" d, 8-1/2" d.............**$3,585**

Ovoid body, quadrafold pinched rim, irid amber green, undulating irid blue horizontal dec, sgd "Loetz Austria," 5-1/2" h.............**$1,900**

Ruffled rim, wide body with dimpled shoulder, irid red, gold linear dec, polished pontil, unsigned, 13-1/2" d, 7-1/2" h.............**$825**

Squatty, everted quadrafold rim, irid green, three applied tadpoles, 5" h.............**$175**

Schaumglas, green and white mottled body, 13" d.............**$125**

Bud vase, figural flower form, irid, ruffled, crystallized leafy foot, irid gold entwining leafy branch, 8-1/2" h.............**$1,000**

Cabinet vase, bulbous, tricorn rim, green, overall blue finish, 3" h....**$130**

Candlestick, irid finish, base chip, 15-1/2" h.............**$115**

Cup, round bowl, gold and polychrome irid, applied handle, incised "Loetz Austria," 3-3/4" d.............**$290**

Decanter, Orpheus pattern, irid green, turquoise medallions, controlled threading, slight loss to threading at top, 11-1/4" h.............**$175**

Low bowl, fold down rim, int. with bluish-gold irid, ext with detailed irid oil spot dec, slight rim roughness, 8-1/2" d, 3" h.............**$250**

Mantel lamp, Federzeichnung, satin, cased in blue, airtrapped dec, overall gold tracery, enameled dec rim, 11" h.............**$1,100**

Rose bowl, ruffled purple irid raindrop dec, 6-1/2" d.............**$265**

Sweetmeat jar, cov, irid silver spider web dec, green ground, sgd, 5" h..**$450**

Urn, ovoid, irid, blue oil spot dec, inscribed "Loetz, Austria," 9-1/4" h............. **$1,600**

Vase

Bulbous stick, deep irid amber, irid blue pulled work dec, gold highlights, 8-1/2" h.............**$1,300**

Cylindrical, irid opal, applied branch dec, losses, 8" h.............**$110**

Corset shape, irid gold body cased in pink, sterling silver overlay, 4-1/4" h.............**$1,000**

Deep red, silver blue irid "Rubin Phanomen" finish, c1890, 12-3/4" h.............**$3,450**

Emerald green, diamond quilted mother of pearl pattern, overlaid sterling silver florals, trailing vines, inscribed "L" and "Sterling," c1890, 7-1/4" h.............**$1,850**

Feerzeichnung, flattened bulbous body extends to cylindrical neck, ruffled rim, shading from green to opal, gilt highlights, floral leaf and vine dec, 5-1/2" h.............**$900**

Figural, fish, gold body, irid Papillon finish, applied green fin feet, 7" h.............**$700**

Gold colored, irid finish, c1900, 7" h.............**$250**

Marmorierteglas, tapered polished marble ground, enameled dec at shoulder and fluted rim, pastel interior, c1890-1910, 7" h.............**$500**

Melon ribbed, everted rim, irid green, blue coin spots, vertical lines, 5" h.............**$500**

Olive green, wavy silver blue irid stripes, "Loetz Austria" inscribed on pontil, 5-1/4" h.............**$1,150**

Ovoid, quadrafold pinched rim, irid green graduating to cinnamon, blue oil spots and wavy lines dec, 8" h.............**$1,200**

Ovoid shouldered, bright lemon yellow, irid blue undulating lines, sgd "Loetz Austria," 6" h.............**$1,200**

Rusticana, waisted cylindrical, irid blue on green body, 9-1/2" h....**$250**

Schaumglas, green and white mottled body, orig paper label, 8" h.......**$250**

Schaumglas, red and white mottled bulbous body, 6-1/2" h.............**$315**

Loetz vase, heart-shaped leaves in yellow, gold luster finish, unmarked, two small abraded areas on body, 11-1/2" x 5", $1,600.
Photo courtesy of David Rago Auctions, Inc.

Loetz, iridescent green vase, internal trailing tendril, trefoil lip, engraved Loetz Austria, 9-1/2" d, $1,920.
Photo courtesy of David Rago Auctions, Inc.

Loetz, Art Nouveau vase, applied iridescent handles, blue oil-spot body, 7-1/2", $1,060.
Photo courtesy of David Rago Auctions, Inc.

Shouldered, irid green textured body, blue thumbprints, undulating lines, 4" h.............**$1,000**

Squatty stick, irid blue, 4-3/4" h....**$200**

Titania, shading from deep ruby to emerald, overall silver irid, 5" h....**$2,200**

MCKEE GLASS

History: The McKee Glass Co. was established in 1843 in Pittsburgh, Pennsylvania. In 1852, it opened a factory to produce pattern glass. In 1888, the factory was relocated to Jeannette, Pennsylvania, and began to produce many types of glass kitchenware, including several patterns of Depression glass. The factory continued until 1951, when it was sold to the Thatcher Manufacturing Co.

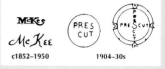

McKee named its colors Chalaine Blue, Custard, Seville Yellow, and Skokie Green. McKee glass may also be found with painted patterns, e.g., dots and ships. A few items were decaled. Many of the canisters and shakers were lettered in black to show the purpose for which they were intended.

Berry set, Hobnail with Fan pattern, blue, master berry and eight sauce dishes...**$170**

Candleholder, Rock Crystal, clear, double light, 6-3/4" w, 5-1/2" h.....**$65**

Candy dish, cov, Rock Crystal, red, 4-1/2" w, 10-1/2" h......................**$400**

Canister, cov, 10 oz, custard.........**$75**

Cereal canister, cov, custard, 48 oz **$145**

Child's, butter dish, opaque blue, 5" w base, 3-3/4" h **$55**

Creamer, Aztec, purple carnival **$125**

Egg beater bowl, spout, Ships, black dec on white...................................**$70**

Flour shaker, Seville Yellow **$65**

Grill plate, custard, marked "McK" **$25**

Kitchen bowl, spout, Skokie Green, 7" d...**$75**

Measuring cup, four-cup, Seville Yellow **$185**

Mixing bowls, nested set, Ships, red dec on white, 6", 7", 8", 9" **$185**

Pepper shaker, Roman Arch, black, "P"..**$40**

Pitcher, Wild Rose and Bowknot, frosted, gilt dec, 8" h **$65**

Reamer, pointed top, Skokie Green **$45**

Refrigerator dish, cov, Custard, 4" x 9"...**$35**

Ring box, cov, Seville Yellow **$20**

Server, center handle, Rock Crystal, red...**$140**

Sugar bowl, Aztec, purple carnival **$125**

Sugar shaker, Skokie Green, orig label and top, 2-3/8" sq, 5" h.....**$115**

Tea canister, custard, 48 oz **$145**

Tom and Jerry punch bowl set, 11-1/2" d, 5" h punch bowl, eight 3-1/2" h mugs, white, black lettering and trim **$95**

Tray, Rock Crystal, red, rolled rim, 13-1/2" l, 6-1/2" w, 2-1/2" h **$120**

Tumbler, Bottoms Up, caramel, 3-1/8" h, 2-3/4" d **$90**

Water cooler, spigot, Vaseline, two pcs, 21" h **$325**

MERCURY GLASS

History: Mercury glass is a light-bodied, double-walled glass that was "silvered" by applying a solution of silver nitrate to the inside of the object through a hole in its base.

F. Hale Thomas of London patented the method in 1849. In 1855, the New England Glass Co. filed a patent for the same type of process. Other American glassmakers soon followed. The glass reached the height of its popularity in the early 20th century.

Mercury compote, white enameled floral decoration, **$195.**
Photo courtesy of Dotta Auction Co., Inc.

Bowl, small plug in bottom, some wear, 8" d...**$120**

Cake stand, pedestal base, emb floral dec, 8" d..**$80**

Candlestick, 10-1/2" h................**$110**

Cologne bottle, bulbous, flashed amber panel, cut neck, etched grapes and leaves, corked metal stopper, c1840, 4-1/4" x 7-1/2"..................**$160**

Creamer, etched ferns, applied clear handle, attributed to Sandwich, 6-1/2" h......................................**$140**

Curtain tiebacks, etched grape design, price for pr, 3-1/8" d, 4-1/2" l **$140**

Door knob set, 2-1/4" d **$80**

Goblet, gold, white lily of the valley dec, 5" d...**$40**

Pitcher, bulbous, panel cut neck, engraved lacy florals and leaves, applied clear handle, c1840, 5-1/2" x 9-3/4" h...**$225**

Salt, master, circular, ftd, orig base cork, possibly Boston & Sandwich Glass Co., 1860-87, 2-1/4" h, 2-3/4" d.............**$50**

Sugar bowl, cov, low foot, enameled white foliage dec, knob finial, 4-1/4" x 6-1/4"...**$65**

Vase, cylindrical, raised circular foot, everted rim, bright enameled yellow, orange, and blue floral sprays and insects, pr, 9-3/4" h.....................**$225**

MILK GLASS

History: Opaque white glass attained its greatest popularity at the end of the 19th century. American glass manufacturers made opaque white tablewares as a substitute for costly European china and glass. Other opaque colors, e.g., blue and green, also were made. Production of milk-glass novelties came in with the Edwardian era.

The surge of popularity in milk glass subsided after World War I. However, milk glass continues to be made in the 20th century. Some modern products are reissues and reproductions of earlier forms. This presents a significant problem for collectors, although it is partially obviated by patent dates or company markings on the originals and by the telltale signs of age.

Collectors favor milk glass from the pre-World War I era, especially animal-covered dishes. The most prolific manufacturers of these animal covers were Atterbury, Challinor-Taylor, Flaccus, and McKee.

Notes: There are many so-called "McKee" animal-covered dishes. Caution must be exercised in evaluating pieces because some authentic covers were not signed. Furthermore, many factories have made split-rib bases with McKee-like animal covers or with different animal covers.

Milk glass, Victorian, painted lamp base, winter scene of farmer and cottage in woods, brass base, 10" h without chimney, **$90.** Photo courtesy of The Early Auction Company, LLC.

Animal dish, cov

Cat on drum...................................**$195**
Cat on hamper, green, V mark ...**$115**
Chick on sleigh, white.................**$115**
Dolphin **$145**
Kitten, ribbed base, Westmoreland, white..**$130**
Lion, reclining, white, criss-cross base **$135**
Robin on nest, med blue.............**$165**
Setter dog, blue............................**$265**
Swan, closed neck, white **$120**
Turkey, amethyst head, white body **$220**
Turkey, white head, dark amethyst body..**$170**

Bowl, Daisy, allover leaves and flower design, open scalloped edge, 8-1/4" d **$85**

Bust, Admiral Dewey, 5-1/2" h **$300**

Butter dish, cov, Roman Cross pattern, sq, ftd base curves outward toward top, cube-shape finial, 4-7/8" l...**$75**

Calling card receiver, bird, wings extended over fanned tail, head resting on leaf, detailed feather pattern **$150**

Compote, Atlas, lacy edge, blue **$185**

Creamer and sugar, Trumpet Vine, fire painted dec, sgd "SV" **$130**

Egg cup, cov, bird, round, fluted, Atterbury, 4-1/4" h **$135**

Hat, Stars and Stripes, black rim ..**$235**

Lamp, Goddess of Liberty, bust, three stepped hexagonal bases, clear and frosted font, brass screw connector, patent date, Atterbury, 11" h.......**$300**

Milk pitcher, Wild Iris, gilt trim, c1825, 8-3/4" h............................**$125**

Mug, Medallion, c1870, 3-1/4" **$50**

Plate

Donkey...**$50**
Easter, bunny, basket of eggs........**$35**
Fort Necessity, Indian chief, some orig paint, edge chip **$30**
Indian Chief, no paint...................**$70**
Rabbit center, horseshoe and clover border...**$145**
Three dogs and squirrel................**$65**

Spooner, monkey, scalloped top, 5-1/8" h..**$95**

Sugar shaker, Forget-me-not, green, orig top..**$50**

Syrup, plain, hp red flowers, damage to pewter top..................................**$65**

Tumbler, Royal Oak, orig fired paint, green band.....................................**$50**

Vanity box, cov, hand painted enamel floral dec, gold trim, imp "16" on both lid and base, 7" l, 2" w, 2" h **$250**

Milk Glass spooner/vase, Westmoreland, Charlton decoration, **$35.**

MILLEFIORI

Millefiori swan, 6" h, $50; rose bowl, 3" h, $65; and vase, 8" h, $45.
Photo courtesy of Joy Luke Auctions.

Reproduction Alert. Many modern companies are making Millefiori items, such as paperweights, cruets, and toothpicks.

Barber bottle, orig top, red, white dec $350

Beads, multicolored millefiori beads, blue glass bead spacers, 16" l $55

Bowl, tricorn, scalloped, folded sides, amethyst and silver deposit, 8" d ...$125

Candy dish, light blue, various sized multicolored millefiori flowers, swirled shape, Murano, c1950, 11-1/2" l, 9" w $85

History: Millefiori (thousand flowers) is an ornamental glass composed of bundles of colored glass rods fused together into canes. The canes were pulled to the desired length while still ductile, sliced, arranged in a pattern, and fused together again. The Egyptians developed this technique in the first century B.C. It was revived in the 1880s.

Creamer, white and cobalt blue canes, yellow centers, satin finish, 3" x 4-1/2" $110

Cruet, bulbous, multicolored canes, applied camphor handle, matching stopper..$120

Decanter, deep black ground, allover multicolored flux and canes, including peachblow, and opal, enamel dec, Gundersen, 12" h $1,450

Demittase cup and saucer, red and white millefiori, angular applied pink handle, broken pontil scars, Italian $275

Door knob, paperweight, New England Glass Co., center cane dated 1852, 2-1/2" d..............................$395

Goblet, multicolored canes, clear stem and base, 7-1/2" h.......................$150

Lamp, two-pcs, baluster stem, tall mushroom shape shade dec with large and small colorful canes, 16-1/2" h.......$850

Pitcher, multicolored canes, applied candy cane handle, 6-1/2" h $195

Slipper, camphor ruffle and heel, 5" l $125

Sugar bowl, cov, white canes, yellow centers, satin finish, 4" x 4-1/2" $125

Sugar shaker, bulbous, reds and yellows, orig top $275

Syrup, pewter top, dark green, browns, blues, applied colorless handle $295

Vase

Ftd baluster, large cane dec, 8" h ...$150

Ftd urn shape, small cane dec, 4-1/2" h $150

Ftd urn shape, small cane dec, 6" h $100

MORGANTOWN GLASS WORKS

History: The Morgantown Glass Works, Morgantown, West Virginia, was founded in 1899 and began production in 1901. Reorganized in 1903, it operated as the Economy Tumbler Company for 20 years until, in 1923, the word "Tumbler" was dropped from the corporate title. The firm was then known as The Economy Glass Company until reversion to its original name, Morgantown Glass Works, Inc., in 1929, the name it kept until its first closing in 1937. In 1939, the factory was reopened under the aegis of a guild of glassworkers and operated as the Morgantown Glassware Guild from that time until its final closing. Purchased by Fostoria in 1965, the factory operated as a subsidiary of the Moundsville-based parent company until 1971, when Fostoria opted to terminate production of glass at the Morgantown facility. Today, collectors use the generic term, "Morgantown Glass," to include all periods of production from 1901 to 1971.

Morgantown was a 1920s leader in the manufacture of colorful wares for table and ornamental use in American homes. The company pioneered the processes of iridization on glass, as well as gold and platinum encrustation of patterns. It enhanced Crystal offerings with contrasting handle and foot of India Black, Spanish Red (ruby), and Ritz Blue (cobalt blue), and other intense and pastel colors for which it is also famous. The company conceived the use of contrasting shades of fired enamel to add color to its etchings. It was the only American company to use a chromatic silk-screen printing process on glass, its two most famous and collectible designs being Queen Louise and Manchester Pheasant.

The company is also known for ornamental "open stems" produced during the late 1920s. Open stems separate to form an open design midway between the bowl and foot, e.g., an open square, a "Y," or two diamond-shaped designs. Many of these open stems were purchased and decorated by Dorothy C. Thorpe in her California studio, and her signed open stems command high prices from today's collectors. Morgantown also produced figural stems for commercial clients such as Koscherak Brothers and Marks & Rosenfeld. Chanticleer (rooster) and Mai Tai (Polynesian bis) cocktails are two of the most popular figurals collected today.

Morgantown is best known for the diversity of design in its stemware patterns, as well as for its four patented optics: Festoon, Palm, Peacock, and Pineapple. These optics were used to embellish stems, jugs, bowls, liquor sets, guest sets, salvers, ivy and witch balls, vases, and smoking items.

Most glass collectors recognize two well-known lines of Morgantown Glass today: #758 Sunrise Medallion and #7643 Golf Ball Stem Line. When Economy introduced #758 in 1928, it was originally identified as "Nymph." By 1931, the Morgantown front office had renamed it Sunrise Medallion. Recent publications erred in labeling it "dancing girl." Upon careful study of the medallion, you can see the figure is poised on one tiptoe, musically saluting the dawn with her horn. The second well-known line, #7643 Golf Ball, was patented in 1928; production commenced immediately and continued until the company closed in 1971. More Golf Ball than any other Morgantown product is found on the market today.

Basket

Patrick, #19-4358, Ritz Blue, applied crystal twisted handle, mint leaf prunts, 5" d, 9-3/4" h.............**$750**

Quilt, crystal, black/amethyst rope-twist handle, leaf form appliqués where handle joins basket, ground pontil...............**$1,100**

Trindle, #4357, amethyst, applied crystal twisted reed handle, c1930, 9".............**$725**

Berry jug, Palm Optic, #37, pink, 8-1/2" w, 9-1/8" h.............**$235**

Bowl

Fantassia, #67, Bristol Blue, 5-1/2" d.**$95**

Janice, Ritz Blue, #4355, 13" d....**$475**

Woodsfield, Genova Line, 12-1/2" d, #12-1/2.............**$565**

Brandy snifter, Golf Ball, #7643, red, crystal base, 4" w, 6-1/4" h.........**$130**

Candleholders, pr

Golf Ball, #7643, Torch Candle, single, Ritz Blue, 6" h.............**$300**

Hamilton, #87, Evergreen, 5" h......**$65**

Modern, #80, Moss Green, 7-1/2" h..**$90**

Candle vase, ruby, 5-1/2" h.........**$55**

Candy jar, cov

Mansfield, #200, burgundy matte, 12" h.............**$200**

Rachael, crystal, Pandora cutting, 6" h.............**$395**

Champagne

#7617, ruby bowl.............**$48**

#7643, Golf Ball, Ritz Blue, 5"......**$55**

#7860, Lawton, Azure, Festoon Optic, 5 oz.............**$50**

Cocktail

Chanticleer, crystal.............**$30**

Elizabeth, blue, twisted stem, 5-3/4" h.............**$75**

Filament stem, crystal, ruby filament, 4-1/2" h.............**$48**

Golf Ball, #7643, crystal, Chateau cutting.............**$25**

Ruby bowl, #7617.............**$45**

Venus, #7577, Anna Rose, Palm Optic, 3 oz.............**$40**

Cocktail set, Deco, black, 7-3/4" h pitcher with weighted base, five 3" w, 3" h cocktail glasses.............**$65**

Compote, Reverse Twist, #7654, aquamarine, 6-1/2" d, 6-3/4" h.........**$225**

Console bowl, El Mexicana, #12933, Seaweed, 10" d.............**$425**

Cordial, 1-1/2 oz

Brilliant, #7617, Spanish Red....**$140**

Golf Ball, #7643, Ritz Blue.........**$68**

Mikado, crystal.............**$30**

Finger bowl, Art Moderne, #7640, Faun etch, crystal and black, 4-1/2" d, ftd.............**$150**

Goblet

Art Moderne, #7640, Faun etch, crystal and black, 7-3/4" h.......**$125**

Golf Ball, #7643, Ritz Blue.........**$60**

Paragon, #7624, ebony open stem, 10 oz.............**$215**

Queen Louise, #7664, 3-1/2" d, 7-1/2" h.............**$400**

Guest set, Trudy, #23, Bristol Blue, 6-3/8" h.............**$145**

Iced tea tumbler, Vision, white on white.............**$45**

Ice tub, El Mexicana, #1933, Seaweed, 6" d.............**$225**

Jug

Kaufmann, #6, Doric star sand blast, 54 oz.............**$295**

Melon, #20069, Alabaster, Ritz Blue trim.............**$1,450**

Measuring cup, adv "Your Credit is Good Pickerings, Furnishings, 10th & Penn, Pittsburgh," clear, 3-1/8" d, 2-7/8" h.............**$315**

Oyster cup, Sunrise Medallion, blue, 2-3/8" d.............**$190**

Pilsner, Floret, etch #796, Lando, 12 oz.............**$65**

Morgantown champagne, Old English pattern, Spanish Red and crystal, **$70.**

Plate

Anna Rose, #734 American Beauty etch, 7" d.............**$65**

Carlton Madrid, topaz, 6" d.........**$35**

Sherbet

Crinkle, #1962, pink, 6 oz.............**$30**

Golf Ball, #7643, Ritz Blue.........**$50**

Sophisticate, #7646, Picardy etch, 5-1/2 oz.............**$55**

Sherry, Golf Ball, #7643, Spanish Red.............**$43**

Tumbler, water, Owl

Brown.............**$60**

Gold.............**$65**

Urn, #1160, Bristol Blue, ftd, 6-1/2" h.............**$650**

Vase

Catherine, #26, Azure, #758 Sunrise Medallion etch, bud, 10" h......**$265**

Gypsy Fire, orig sticker, 4".........**$68**

Raindrop pattern, red/orange, yellow base, hobnail design on inside graduating in size down to base, 4-1/2" d, 10" h.............**$35**

Wine

#7617, ruby bowl.............**$65**

Empress, #7680-1/2, Spanish Red, 3 oz.............**$90**

Filament stem, crystal, cobalt blue filament, 4-1/2" h.............**$65**

Golf Ball, Ritz Blue, 4-5/8" h.........**$58**

Vision, white on white.............**$45**

MOSER GLASS

History: Ludwig Moser (1833-1916) founded his polishing and engraving workshop in 1857 in Karlsbad (Karlovy Vary), Czechoslovakia. He employed many famous glass designers, e.g., Johann Hoffmann, Josef Urban, and Rudolf Miller. In 1900, Moser and his sons, Rudolf and Gustav, incorporated Ludwig Moser & Söhne.

Moser art glass included clear pieces with inserted blobs of colored glass, cut colored glass with classical scenes, cameo glass, and intaglio cut items. Many inexpensive enameled pieces also were made.

In 1922, Leo and Richard Moser bought Meyr's Neffe, their biggest Bohemian art glass rival. Moser executed many pieces for the Wiener Werkstätte in the 1920s.

Moser intaglio cut vase, triangular shape, translucent glass shading to purple, deep cut stem flowers, 4" h, **$425.**
Photo courtesy of The Early Auction Company, LLC.

Moser dresser jar, Alexandrite, two rows of eight ovals each, polished base, etched "Alexandrite" and "Moser/Karlsbad," early/mid-20th century, 5" h, base 3-3/4" d, **$80.**

Photo courtesy of Green Valley Auctions.

Moser vase, cylindrical optic ribbed, clear to amethyst glass, sculptured eagle in flight above pond scene, 1' 3-1/2" h, **$2,250.**

Photo courtesy of The Early Auction Company, LLC.

Basket, cranberry, gold encrusted handle, high relief enameled flowers, 7" h...**$450**

Box, cov, amethyst, base dec with band of Amazon warriors, lid with medallion of Spanish galleon, sgd "Moser," 5-1/4" w..**$350**

Bowl

Enameled scrolled foliate dec, cranberry shaded rim, matching underplate, c1900, 7" d...................**$1,035**

Horizontal band of cranberry cut to clear, gilt scrolling, pink roses, pr, 7-1/4" w and 9-1/4" w..............**$200**

Oblong paneled amber bowl, detailed engraving of bull elk in forest, sgd, signature on base, orig lined and fitted box, 9" l, 3-3/4" h.........**$1,000**

Candy dish, cov, green cut to clear, matching lid, acid stamped "Moser Karlsbad," 7-1/2" h.......................**$150**

Cologne bottle, amethyst shaded to clear, deep intaglio cut flowers and leaves, orig stopper, sgd, 7-1/2" h, 3-1/2" d...**$695**

Cordial, cranberry bowl, crystal stem, horizontal gilt bands dec with colorful enameled florals and scrolling, price for matched set of six, 4" h **$400**

Cream pitcher, translucent body shading to green, gilt medallions, raised green "jewels," 3-1/4" h....**$350**

Cup and saucer, clear graduating to translucent green, yellow and gold scrolling daffodils, script sgd "Moser" in body, price for matched sets, 4-1/2" w, 2-1/2" h........................**$275**

Decanter, flat sided, green translucent glass, gilt collar dec with overall gold floral scrolling, 8-3/4" h.............**$325**

Decanter set, 11" h faceted stopper bottle dec with green medallion and fine gold scrolling, six matching 3" h cordials, matching 9-1/2" d tray, chips to stopper finial and cordials......**$750**

Dresser box, cov, hinged

Rect, Prussian Blue, multicolored fans and foliage dec, small foot chips, 11" l, 4" h.................................**$375**

Round, translucent green, autumn oak leaves on brown branches, raised acorn jewels, 5" d.........**$475**

Egg cup, thumbprint patterned translucent colorless ground, red, blue, yellow, and green leaves on brown and yellow vines, chip on foot, 4-1/4" h..**$230**

Ewer, cranberry, gilt surface, applied acorns and clear jewels, 10-3/4" h **$2,000**

Finger bowl, underplate

Cranberry, overall gold scrolling and foliate, 6" w, 3" h......................**$250**

Green, overall gold florals and scrolling, 6" w, 3" h............................**$175**

Scalloped underplate, clear ground, red, blue, green, and pink acanthus scrollwork, accented with banded peacock eyes, attributed to Lobmeyer, 7" w, 3-1/2" h...............**$800**

Translucent amethyst, intaglio cut leafy stemmed flowers, 4-1/2" d bowl, 6" d underplate, price for set of four......................................**$850**

Translucent green, gold gilt horizontal bands, pastel scrolling and flowers, 7" w, 3-1/2" h...........................**$600**

Goblet

Enameled scrolled foliage, gilt ground, green tinted rim, price for pr, c1900, 6-3/4" h **$1,265**

Hand painted pastel scrolling flowers on body and foot, gilt bands, rim chip, 7" h............................**$475**

Shamrock shape, spreading foot, translucent blue body, overall gold flowers and scrolling, gold encrusted stalactite panels with silver scrolling, price for pr, 6-1/4" h **$675**

Juice glass, cranberry, blue and pink flowers, gold scrolling over horizontal gilt bands, set of six, 2-1/2" h **$200**

Pitcher, amberina, IVT, four yellow, red, blue, and green applied glass beaded bunches of grapes, pinched-in sides, three-dimensional bird beneath spout, allover enamel and gold leaves, vines, and tendrils, 6-3/4" h **$3,200**

Portrait vase, woman, gold leaves, light wear, 8-1/2" h **$450**

Rose bowl, cranberry ground, enameled florals and butterfly, applied acorns, c1900, 3-1/2" h................**$750**

Sherbet

Enameled scrolled foliage, cranberry shaded rim, price for pr, c1900, 4-1/2" h **$1,100**

Translucent cranberry, dec with purple, red, yellow, green, and white scrolling flowers on horizontal gilt bands, beaded highlights, 4-1/2" h **$500**

Tumbler, enameled dec, c1910, 3-3/4" h

Pale amber **$50**

Pale blue....................................**$50**

Urn, cranberry, two gilt handles, studded with green, blue, clear, and red stones, highly enameled surface, multicolored and gilt Moorish dec, 15-3/4" h..................................**$3,500**

Vase

Bulbous stick, flaring rim, cranberry, banded gold and silver collar, polychrome scrolling, dots, and florals, 9" h **$300**

Faceted cylindrical, clear graduating to translucent green, four gilt and engraved medallion cartouches, blue accents, script sgd "Moser Karlsbad," 5-3/4" h **$150**

Marquetry, ribbed, expanded bowl, tapering stem, intaglio cutting, cinnamon-colored marquetry flowers, pontil sgd "Moser Carlsbad," 13" h **$4,250**

Trumpet, ftd, optic ribbed, clear shading to pumpkin body, blue and yellow flowers, gray and orange scrolling, 16-1/4" h **$500**

Wall vase, conical, crackle body, enameled raised fish, colorful seaweed, 10" h **$900**

Water pitcher, alternating gilt and translucent vertical bands dec with white, blue, and amethyst flowers, 6-3/4" h **$700**

Wine

Elongated gold highlighted faceted stem, overall polychrome enameled scrolling on gold bands, 8" h **$600**

Shamrock shape, trumpet foot, translucent green body, gold scrolling dec, price for pr, 7" h **$125**

MOUNT WASHINGTON GLASS COMPANY

History: In 1837, Deming Jarves, founder of the Boston and Sandwich Glass Company, established for George D. Jarves, his son, the Mount Washington Glass Company in Boston, Massachusetts. In the following years, the leadership and the name of the company changed several times as George Jarves formed different associations

In the 1860s, the company was owned and operated by Timothy Howe and William L. Libbey. In 1869, Libbey bought a new factory in New Bedford, Massachusetts. The Mount Washington Glass Company began operating again there under its original name. Henry Libbey became associated with the company early in 1871. He resigned in 1874 during the Depression, and the glassworks was closed. William Libbey had resigned in 1872, when he went to work for the New England Glass Company.

The Mount Washington Glass Company opened again in the fall of 1874 under the presidency of A. H. Seabury and the management of Frederick S. Shirley. In 1894, the glassworks became a part of the Pairpoint Manufacturing Company.

Throughout its history, the Mount Washington Glass Company made different types of glass including pressed, blown, art, lava, Napoli, cameo, cut, Albertine, Peachblow, Burmese, Crown Milano, Royal Flemish and Verona.

Mt. Washington, Crown Milano, ewer, bulbous body in Nile green to opal, floral and gilt dec, twisted and curled handle, firm's trademark stamp, #559, 10-3/4" h, **$1,900.**
Photo courtesy of The Early Auction Company, LLC.

Banquet lamp, Colonial Ware (shiny Crown Milano), white ground, sprays of golden roses and single petaled blossoms on globe shaped shade and base, molded-in floral, swag, and geometric dec on base, possibly orig opaque white chimney, burner sgd "Made in United States of America," 23" h **$2,950**

Beverage set, satin, mother-of-pearl, yellow seaweed coralene dec, glossy finish, 9" h, bulbous water pitcher, three spout top, applied reeded shell handle, three matching 4" h tumblers, two blisters on pitcher, three-pc set **$750**

Bowl, Rose amber, fuchsia, blue swirl bands, bell tone flint, 4-1/2" d, 2-3/4" h **$295**

Collars and cuffs box, opalware, shaped as two collars with big bow in front, cov dec with orange and pink Oriental poppies, silver poppy-shaped finial with gold trim, base with poppies, white ground, gold trim, bright blue bow, white polka dots, buckle on back, sgd "Patent applied for April 10, 1894," #2390/128 .... **$950**

Compote, Napoli, crystal clear ground, ten hp pink full bloom tea roses, green foliage, 6" d bowl, 9-1/2" h **$875**

Condiment set, opaque white salt and pepper shakers, cov mustard, hp floral dec, 6-1/2" h silver plated holder sgd "Wilcox Silverplate Co." **$235**

Cracker jar, opal glass, Egyptian motif, several camels at oasis, distant pyramid and mosque, sgd in lid with Pairpoint Diamond P, #3910, corresponding #3910/530 on jar, 8" h **$2,760**

Mt. Washington, Crown Milano biscuit jar, ovoid, beige glass, gold mums and earth-tone leaves, sgd with CM crown mark, lid stamped MW, 10" h, **$700.**
Photo courtesy of The Early Auction Company, LLC.

Cruet, Burmese, shiny finish, butter-yellow body, applied handle, mushroom stopper, each of 30 ribs with hint of pink, color blush intensifies on neck and spout, Mt. Washington, 7" h............**$1,250**

Dresser box, portrait of young girl on cov, indigo blue ground, fancy embellishments at collar and other highlights, opaque white body, orig burgundy color satin lining, sgd "4622/206," 4-3/4" d, 3" h............**$750**

Flower holder, mushroom shape, white ground, blue dot and oak leaf dec, 5-1/4" d, 3-1/2" h **$425**

Fruit bowl, Napoli, solid dark green ground painted on clear glass, outside dec with pale pink and white pond lilies, green and pink leaves and blossoms, int. dec with gold highlight traceries, silver-plated base with pond lily design, two applied loop handles, four buds form fcct, base sgd "Pairpoint Mfg. Co. B4704," 10" d, 7-1/2" h............**$2,200**

Humidor, hinged silver-plated metalwork rim and edge, blown-out rococo scroll pattern, brilliant blue Delft windmills, ships, and landscape, Pairpoint, 5-1/2" h, 4-1/2" d top **$950**

Jar, cov, peachblow, rim of jar and rim of lid cased in gold metal with raised leaves, 6" w, 5-1/2" h............**$400**

Jewel box, opalware, Monk drinking glass of red wine on lid, solid shaded green background on cover and base, fancy gold-washed, silver-plated rim and hinge, orig satin lining, artist sgd "Schindler," 4-1/2" d top, 5-1/4" d base, 3-1/4" h **$550**

Mt. Washington, barrel-shaped toothpick holder, amethyst and blue stemmed flowers, 2-1/2" h, **$275.**
Photo courtesy of The Early Auction Company, LLC.

Jug, satin, Polka Dot, deep peachblow pink, white air traps, DQ, unlined, applied frosted loop handle, 6" h, 4" w **$475**

Lamp, parlor, four dec glass oval insert panels, orig dec white opalware ball shade with deep red carnations, sgd "Pairpoint" base, c1890............**$1,750**

Lamp shade, rose amber, ruffled, fuschia shading to deep blue, DQ, 4-1/4" h, 5" d across top, 2" d fitter **$575**

Miniature lamp, banquet style, milk glass, bright blue Delft dec of houses and trees, orig metal fittings, attributed to Frank Guba, 17" h, 4-1/2" d shade............**$795**

Mustard pot, ribbed, bright yellow and pink background, painted white and magenta wild roses, orig silver-plated hardware, 4-1/2" h **$185**

Perfume bottle, opalware, dark green and brown glossy ground, red and yellow nasturtiums, green leaves, sprinkler top, 5-1/4" h, 3" d **$375**

Pitcher, satin, DQ, MOP, large frosted camphor shell loop handle, 6" h, 3" w **$325**

Plate, Colonial Ware (shiny Crown Milano), white ground, pink cabbage rose, sprays of blue forget-me-nots, yellow daisies, purple chrysanthemums, dark red tulips, coral nasturtiums, white apple blossoms, white begonias, five raised gold rococo embellishments, sgd, 7" d **$550**

Rose bowl, satin, blue shading to white base, 5" d............**$45**

Salt and pepper shakers, pr, Four Lobe shape, white ground, colorful violet nosegays, salt top corroded **$235**

Sugar shaker (muffineer)

Egg shape, white shading to blue ground, pink and gold chrysanthemums, 4-1/4" h............**$385**

Egg shape, satin finish, overall green tint shading to pale green at base, vine laden with green leaves, naturalistically colored violet blossoms, 4-1/2" h **$385**

Fig shape, bridal white body, daffodil yellow and pink blossoms, 4" h **$1,950**

Melon ribbed, opaque white ground, daffodil yellow orchid blossoms, two-part metal collar with emb butterfly, dragonfly, and blossom, 3" h, 4" d............**$400**

Sweet meat, opaque ground, pseudo Burmese enameling, gilt flowers and leaves, accented with jeweled cabochons, emb bail handle, sgd, lid #P4408, one jewel missing, 5-1/2" h **$815**

Syrup pitcher, Colonial Ware (shiny Crown Milano), white melon ribbed body, 15 sprays of flowers, gold scrollwork, pewter-like collar and lid **$950**

Tumbler, Burmese, shiny finish, thin satin body, soft color blushes from rim to center then shading to pastel yellow base, Mt. Washington......**$375**

Vase

Burmese, satin finish, double gourd shape, finely drawn green and coral leafy tendrils, seven nosegays of blossoms, raised blue enamel forget-me-nots, each with pastel center with five coral dots, Mt. Washington, #147, c1885, 7-3/4" h **$985**

Gourd shape, 6" l flaring neck, satin, deep brown shading to gold, white lining, allover enameled seaweed design, 11 1/4" h **$550**

Lava, jet black ground, blue, jade green, gray, white, red, and black chips, small in-the-making blister on one color chip, 5-3/8" h, 4-1/8" d **$2,500**

Stick, Burmese, yellow shading to pink, multicolored flowers dec, remnants of orig paper label, 10-1/4" h **$1,035**

Verona, stylized florals outlined in gold and silver, pastel pink background wash, sgd "Verona 918," 9" h **$1,250**

NASH GLASS

History: Nash glass is a type of art glass attributed to Arthur John Nash and his sons, Leslie H. and A. Douglas. Arthur John Nash, originally employed by Webb in Stourbridge, England, came to America and was employed in 1889 by Tiffany Furnaces at its Corona, Long Island, plant.

While managing the plant for Tiffany, Nash designed and produced iridescent glass. In 1928, A. Douglas Nash purchased the facilities of Tiffany Furnaces. The A. Douglas Nash Corporation remained in operation until 1931.

Bowl, Jewel pattern, gold phantom luster, 7-3/4" x 2-1/2" **$285**

Candlesticks, pr, irid gold, large disc foot and top separated with baluster stem, sgd "650 Nash," 4" h **$350**

Compote, Chintz, transparent aquamarine, wide flat rim of red and gray-green controlled stripe dec, base inscribed "Nash RD89," 7-1/2" d, 4-1/2" h **$865**

Cordial, Chintz, green and blue, 5-1/2" h **$125**

Creamer and sugar, blue-green opaque dots, dark blue-green base, creamer with polished pontil, sugar with waffle pontil, 5-3/8" h creamer, 3-1/2" h sugar **$475**

Goblet, feathered leaf motif, gilt dec, sgd, 6-3/4" h **$295**

Sherbet, bluish-gold texture, ftd, sgd, #417 .... **$275**

Vase

Chintz, pastel, transparent oval, internally striped with pastel orange alternating with yellow chintz dec, 5-1/2" h **$275**

Polka Dot, deep opaque red oval, molded with prominent 16 ribs, dec by spaced white opal dots, base inscribed "Nash GD154," 9" h **$1,100**

OPALESCENT GLASS

History: Opalescent glass, a clear or colored glass with milky white decorations, looks fiery or opalescent when held to light. This effect was achieved by applying bone ash chemicals to designated areas while a piece was still hot and then refiring it at extremely high temperatures.

There are three basic categories of opalescent glass: (1) blown (or mold blown) patterns, e.g., Daisy & Fern and Spanish Lace; (2) novelties, pressed glass patterns made in limited quantity and often in unusual shapes such as corn or a trough; and (3) traditional pattern (pressed) glass forms.

Opalescent glass was produced in England in the 1870s. Northwood began the American production in 1897 at its Indiana, Pennsylvania, plant. Jefferson, National Glass, Hobbs, and Fenton soon followed.

Blown

Basket, cranberry, shading from translucent opalescent to deep rose, crystal handle, 6-3/4" h **$115**

Barber bottle, Raised Swirl, cranberry **$295**

Berry bowl, master, Chrysanthemum Base Swirl, blue, satin **$95**

Biscuit jar, cov, Spanish Lace, Vaseline **$275**

Bride's basket, Poinsettia, ruffled top **$275**

Butter dish, cov, Hobbs Hobnail, vaseline **$250**

Celery vase, Seaweed, cranberry .. **$250**

Creamer

Coin Dot, cranberry **$190**

Windows Swirl, cranberry **$500**

Cruet

Chrysanthemum Base Swirl, white, satin **$175**

Ribbed Opal Lattice, white **$135**

Finger bowl, Hobbs Hobnail, cranberry **$65**

Lamp, oil

Inverted Thumbprint, white, amber fan base **$145**

Snowflake, cranberry **$800**

Pickle castor, Daisy and Fern, blue, emb floral jar, DQ, resilvered frame **$650**

Pitcher

Arabian Nights, white **$450**

Hobbs Hobnail, cranberry **$315**

Seaweed, blue **$525**

Rose bowl, Double Diamond, pink opalescent, gold enameled flowers, 5" h **$90**

Salt shaker, orig top. Ribbed Opal Lattice, cranberry **$95**

Spooner, Reverse Swirl, cranberry **$175**

Sugar, cov, Reverse Swirl, cranberry **$350**

Sugar shaker

Daisy & Fern, cranberry, 4-1/2" h **$230**

Poinsettia, blue, roughness to fitter rim, 5" h **$375**

Opalescent vase, Corn pattern, blue, **$115.**

Opalescent basket, Vaseline, **$145.**

Spanish Lace, blue, roughness to fitter rim, 4-1/2" h **$200**

Windows, blue, roughness to fitter rim, 4-1/2" h **$250**

Syrup, Coin Spot, cranberry **$175**

Tumbler

Acanthus, blue **$90**

Christmas Snowflake, blue, ribbed... **$125**

Maze, swirling, green **$95**

Reverse Swirl, cranberry **$65**

Waste bowl, Hobbs Hobnail, Vaseline **$75**

Novelties

Back bar bottle, robin's egg blue ground, opalescent stripes swirled to the right, 12-1/4" h **$100**

Barber bottle, sq, diamond pattern molded form, light cranberry, white

vertical stripes, 8" h **$275**

Bowl, Winter Cabbage, white.......... **$45**

Bushel basket, blue **$75**

Chalice, Maple Leaf, Vaseline **$45**

Hat, Opal Swirl, white, blue edge **$95**

Jack-in-the-pulpit vase, green swirl, applied red flower, crystal stem, 6" h **$115**

Whimsy, 9" h trumpet vase with 7-1/2" d bowl in 13" h orig bronzed metal holder, aqua to clear, hp white enamel flowers, vase with ribbed clear stem, Victorian **$850**

Pressed

Berry bowl, master, Tokyo, green **$60**

Butter dish, cov, Water Lily and Cat-

tails, blue **$300**

Card receiver, Fluted Scrolls, white **$40**

Cracker jar, cov, Wreath and Shell, Vaseline **$750**

Creamer, Inverted Fan and Feather, blue **$125**

Cruet, Stars and Stripes, cranberry **$575**

Salt and pepper shakers, pr, Jewel and Flower, canary yellow, orig tops **$250**

Spooner, Swag with Brackets, blue **$70**

Toothpick holder, Ribbed Spiral, blue **$90**

Tumbler, Jeweled Heart, blue **$85**

Vase, Northwood Diamond Point, blue **$75**

OPALINE GLASS

History: Opaline glass was a popular mid-to late-19th century European glass. The glass has a certain amount of translucency and often is found decorated with enamel designs and trimmed in gold.

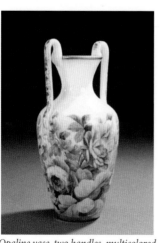

Opaline vase, two handles, multicolored floral decoration, 8-1/4" h, **$450.**

Photo courtesy of Sloans & Kenyon Auctions.

Basket, opaque white ground, applied amber stemmed pink flowers, amber twist handle, 7-1/4" h **$90**

Bouquet holder, blue opaline cornucopia-shaped gilt dec flower holders issuing from bronze stag heads, Belgian black marble base, English, Victorian, pr, early 19th C, 7" h **$725**

Box, cov, oblong, green, serpentine scrolled ends, gilt-metal mounts and escutcheon, Continental, mid-19th C, 6" l, 4-3/4" d, 5" h........................ **$920**

Bride's basket, white opaline, cased in pink, overall colorful enameled dec, emb Middletown plated holder, applied fruit handles, Victorian, minor losses, 12" d, 7-1/2" h **$525**

Candelabra, Louis XV style

Two light, gilt bronze and blue opaline, scrolled candle arms and base, late 19th C, 18-1/2" h **$175**

Five-light, gilt metal and blue opaline, 26-1/2" h **$400**

Chalice, white ground, Diamond Point pattern **$35**

Dresser jar, egg shape, blue ground, heavy gold dec, 5-1/2" d.............. **$200**

Ewer, white ground, Diamond Point pattern, 13-1/4" h **$135**

Jardinières, gilt bronze and blue opaline, sq, Empire style, tasseled chains, paw feet, pr, early 20th C, 5-1/4" h................................ **$1,610**

Mantel lusters, blue, gilt dec, slender faceted prisms, Victorian, damage, pr, c1880, 12-3/4" h.......................... **$250**

Oil lamp, dolphin-form stepped base, clear glass oil well, frosted glass shade, converted to electric, chips, late 19th C, 24" h **$460**

Oil lamp base, blue, baluster turned standard on circular foot, converted to electric, pr, 20th C, 22" h **$635**

Perfume bottle, baluster form, blue opaline bottle, gilt metal floral overlay, foot, and neck mounts, hinged lid set with shell cameo of young man in feathered cap, French, late 19th/ early 20th C, 4" h **$200**

Salt, boat shaped, blue dec, white enamel garland and scrolling **$75**

Vase

Cased pink ground, colorful enameled flower spray, 6-1/4" h **$225**

Fireglow, gilded banding, price for pr, 13-3/4" h **$115**

Homogenized gray ground, enameled perched birds, price for matched pr, 19th C, 10" h **$175**

Opaque white ground, applied amber stemmed acorn and red leaves, 4-1/2" h **$90**

Pink cased ground, enameled gold day lilies, three rolled over handled rim, Victorian, 9-1/2" h **$125**

Water pitcher, blue, high looped handle, bulbous, early 20th C, 12-1/4" h................................ **$240**

PADEN CITY GLASS

History: Paden City Glass Manufacturing Co. was founded in 1916 in Paden City, West Virginia. David Fisher, formerly of the New Martinsville Glass Manufacturing Co., operated the company until his death in 1933, at which time his son, Samuel, became president. A management decision in 1949 to expand Paden City's production by acquiring American Glass Company, an automated manufacturer of bottles, ashtrays, and novelties, strained the company's finances, forcing it to close permanently in 1951.

Contrary to popular belief and previously incorrect printed references, the Paden City Glass Manufacturing Company had absolutely no connection with the Paden City Pottery Company, other than its identical locale.

Although Paden City glass is often lumped with mass-produced, machine-made wares into the Depression Glass category, Paden City's wares were, until 1948, all handmade. Its products are better classified as "Elegant Glass" of the era, as it ranks in quality with the wares produced by contemporaries such as Fostoria, New Martinsville, and Morgantown.

Paden City kept a low profile, never advertising in consumer magazines of the day. It never marked its glass in any way because a large portion of its business consisted of sales to decorating companies, mounters, and fitters. The firm also supplied bars, restaurants, and soda fountains with glassware, as evidenced by the wide range of tumblers, ice cream dishes, and institutional products available in several Paden City patterns.

Paden City's decorating shop also etched, cut, hand painted, and applied silver overlay and gold encrustation. However, not every decoration found on Paden City shapes will necessarily have come from the factory. Cupid, Peacock and Rose, and several other etchings depicting birds are among the most sought-after decorations. Pieces with these etchings are commanding higher and higher prices even though they were apparently made in greater quantities than some of the etchings that are less known, but are just as beautiful.

Paden City is noted for its colors: opal (opaque white), ebony, mulberry (amethyst), Cheriglo (delicate pink), yellow, dark green (forest), crystal, amber, blue, and great quantities of ruby (red). The firm also produced transparent green in numerous shades, ranging from yellowish to a distinctive electric green that always alerts knowledgeable collectors to its Paden City origin.

Rising collector interest in Paden City glass has resulted in a sharp spike in prices on some patterns. Currently, pieces with Orchid or Cupid etch are bringing the highest prices. Several truly rare items in these etchings have recently topped the $1,000 mark. Advanced collectors seek out examples with unusual and/or undocumented etchings. Colored pieces, which sport an etching that is not usually found on that particular color, are especially sought after and bring strong prices. In contrast, prices for common items with Peacock and Rose etch remain static, and the prices for dinnerware in ruby Penny Line and pink or green Party Line have inched up only slightly, due to its greater availability.

Adviser: Michael Krumme.

Bowl, nappy
#215 Glades, ruby, 7" x 1-3/4" **$40**
#221 Maya, crimped, ruby, 7" **$50**
#412 Crow's Foot Square, Orchid etch, crystal, 7" **$55**

Bowl, two-handled serving type
#210 Regina, Black Forest etch, green **$125**
#215 Glades, Trumpet Flower etch, crystal...**$115**
#220 Largo, ruby.............................**$65**
#411 Mrs. B., Gothic Garden etch, crystal..**$45**
#412 Crow's Foot Square, cobalt **$95**
#412 Crow's Foot Square, green **$35**
#412 Crow's Foot Square, Ardith etch, yellow **$50**
#412 Crow's Foot Square, Delilah Bird etch, black................................**$130**
#412 Crow's Foot Square, Orchid etch, yellow **$150**

#412 Crow's Foot Square, Sasha Bird etch, yellow **$165**
#412 Crow's Foot Square, Trumpet Flower etch, ruby.....................**$165**
#412 Crow's Foot Square, Trumpet Flower etch, yellow..................**$225**
#881 Gadroon, Rose & Jasmine etch, crystal..**$50**

Cake salver, footed
#191 Party Line, high footed, Cheriglo **$65**
#191 Party Line, low, etched & gold encrusted border, crystal **$30**
#210 Regina, Black Forest etch, ebony or green......................................**$75**
#215 Glades, ruby...........................**$45**
#215 Glades, Spring Orchard etch, crystal..**$65**
#220 Largo, high footed, crystal **$50**
#220 Largo, low footed, ruby......**$140**
#300 Archaic, Cupid etch, Cheriglo **$125**

Paden City pitcher, #991 Penny Line, ruby, **$125.**

Paden City plate, #220 Largo, forest green, 9" d, **$25.**

Paden City cordial decanter on orig. matching tray, Ardith etch, Cheriglo, **$350.**
All Paden City photos courtesy of Ken Slater.

#330 Cavendish, gold encrusted border etch with roses, crystal........ **$50**

#411 Mrs. B, Ardith etch, green ... **$85**

#412 Crow's Foot Square, cobalt, 8-1/4" w, 4-1/2" h.................... **$125**

#411 Mrs. B, Gothic Garden etch, amber **$40**

#411 Mrs. B, Gothic Garden etch, Cheriglo **$50**

#412 Crow's Foot Square, Ardith etch, ruby **$190**

#412 Crow's Foot Square, Delilah Bird etch, yellow **$85**

Candleholders, pr

#210 Regina, Black Forest etch, ebony **$95**

#220 Largo, light blue................ **$130**

#220 Largo, Garden Magic etch, light blue **$90**

#300 Archaic, Cupid etch, Cheriglo **$115**

#411 Mrs. B, keyhole style, Ardith etch, ebony **$50**

#411 Mrs. B, keyhole style, Ardith etch, green **$80**

#411 Mrs. B., keyhole style, Gothic Garden etch, yellow.............. **$68.50**

#411 Mrs. B, keyhole style, no etching, ebony **$25**

#412 Crow's Foot Square, mushroom style, no etching, yellow............ **$30**

#412 Crow's Foot Square, keyhole style, Satin Rose etch, crystal **$45**

#412 Crow's Foot Square, keyhole style, mulberry **$50**

#412 Crow's Foot Square, keyhole style, ruby **$55**

#412 Crow's Foot Square, keyhole style, Orchid etch, crystal **$40**

#881 Gadroon, Irwin etch, crystal **$75**

#890 Crow's Foot Round triple, ruby **$125**

#895 Lucy double, crystal **$145**

Candy box, cov, flat

#215 Glades, ruby **$50**

#215 Glades, Spring Orchard etch, crystal, filigree base and finial .. **$60**

#300 Archaic, Cupid etch, Cheriglo **$145**

#411 Mrs. B, Ardith etch, yellow **$70**

#411 Mrs. B, Ardith etch, black .. **$125**

#411 Mrs. B, Delilah Bird etch, Cheriglo **$240**

#412 Crow's Foot Square, Satin Rose etch, crystal........................ **$35**

#412 Crow's Foot Square, Orchid etch, crystal.............................. **$60**

#412 Crow's Foot Square, Orchid etch, yellow **$155**

#412 Crow's Foot Square, Orchid etch, Cheriglo **$230**

#412 Crow's Foot Square, filigree holder, Orchid etch, ruby......... **$275**

#412 Crow's Foot Square, filigree holder, Delilah Bird etch, ruby. **$390**

#412-1/2, cloverleaf shape, Orchid etch, crystal, filigree holder, ruby...... **$425**

#555 heart shaped, Ardith etch, crystal................................... **$45**

Candy dish, cov, footed

#191 Party Line, green **$40**

#210/#503 Black Forest etch, ebony **$225**

#444 Bridal Wreath etch, ruby **$75**

#555 footed, light blue **$35**

#555 footed, ruby **$75**

#555 footed, wheel cut flowers, ruby **$65**

#701/#503 base, cutting, green..... **$30**

Cheese and cracker set

#210 Regina, Black Forest etch, green **$100**

#210 Regina, Black Forest etch, amber **$190**

#220 Largo, Garden Magic etch, crystal................................... **$30**

#221 Maya, dome lid style, light blue **$75**

#411 Mrs. B, Ardith etch, Cheriglo **$125**

#412 Crow's Foot Square, Orchid etch, Cheriglo **$200**

#777 Comet, domed lid style, cutting, light blue **$85**

Cigarette box, lid

#191 Party Line, footed jar, etched band of stylized roses, crystal ... **$50**

#215 Glades, ashtray lid, Spring Orchard etch, crystal.................. **$125**

Cocktail shaker

#156 cobalt................................. **$90**

#215 Glades, ruby, platinum band dec **$75**

#901 polished cutting, crystal **$40**

#901 Utopia etch, crystal **$130**

Cologne bottle

#191 Party Line, dauber stopper, green **$40**

#215 Glades, amber stopper **$20**

#215 Glades, black stopper **$30**

#502 dauber stopper, blue............ **$50**

Comport, footed, open

#210 Regina, Black Forest etch, green, 9-1/2" w **$100**

#211 Spire, Trumpet Flower etch, crystal................................... **$50**

#215 Glades, Forest Green, 6-1/2" w .. **$40**

#300 Archaic, turquoise blue........ **$45**

#300 Archaic, unusual flared shape, Peacock & Rose etch, green..... **$115**

#411 Mrs. B, Gothic Garden etch, Cheriglo, 4" h x 6" w.................. **$60**

#411 Mrs. B, Gothic Garden etch, yellow, 7" h x 7" w **$35**

#412 Crow's Foot Square, low footed, mulberry, 7" w **$45**

#412 Crow's Foot Square, low footed, Orchid etch, yellow, 7" w **$75**

#412 Crow's Foot Square, low footed, Ardith etch, ruby, 8" w............ **$175**

#412 Crow's Foot Square, low footed, Orchid etch, crystal, 10" w **$50**

#412 Crow's Foot Square, cupped sides, two flared sides, Delilah Bird etch, ruby, 5" w **$300**

#412 Crow's Foot Square, Orchid etch, crystal, 5" h x 9" w **$185**

#881 Gadroon, Irwin etch, ruby, 6-1/2" h x 7" w **$150**

#890 Crow's F Round, ruby, 6-1/2" h x 7" w **$40**

Nerva, Bridal Wreath, crystal, 9-1/2" w, 6" high **$45**

Compote, footed, covered, #211 Spire, Loopie etch, crystal, 8-1/2" h .. **$100**

Creamer and sugar

#210 Regina, Black Forest, ebony. **$75**

#220 Largo, light blue **$45**

#220 Largo, ruby **$62**

#300 Archaic, Cheriglo **$20**

#411 Mrs. B, amber or ebony **$20**

#411 Mrs. B, Ardith etch, green. **$165**

#411 Mrs. B, Gothic Garden etch, yellow **$90**

#412 Crow's Foot Square, cobalt .. **$35**

#412 Crow's Foot Square, mulberry **$100**

#412 Crow's Foot Square, opal **$85**

#412 Crow's Foot Square, Ardith etch, ruby **$180**

#412 Crow's Foot Square, Orchid etch, yellow **$135**

#701 Triumph, Nora Bird etch, crystal **$80**

#881 Gadroon, Irwin etch, crystal **$40**

#881 Gadroon, Irwin etch, ruby ... **$150**

#991 Penny Line, cobalt **$40**

Nerva, Rose Cascade etch **$65**

Cup and saucer

#210 Regina, Black Forest etch, Cheriglo **$180**

#210 Regina, Black Forest etch, ebony **$100**

#210 Regina, Black Forest etch, ebony, gold encrustation **$230**

#411 Mrs. B, Ardith etch, yellow .. **$35**

#881 Gadroon, ruby **$15**

#991 Penny Line, Black Forest etch **$100**

Decanter

#191 Party Line, cordial size, green **$35**

#210 Regina, Black Forest etch, green **$450**

#994 Popeye & Olive, ruby, orig ruby stopper **$130**

Decanter set

#191 Party Line, five blown whiskeys, Cheriglo **$75**

Oblong decanter, Ardith etch, six

shots, metal holder, Cheriglo .. **$275**

Egg cup

#210 Regina, Black Forest etch, green **$150**

#881 Gadroon, ruby **$75**

Ice bucket, metal bail

#191 Party Line, Peacock & Rose etch, amber **$120**

#902, Peacock & Rose etch, Cheriglo **$165**

#902, Eden Rose etch, green **$125**

#902, Cupid etch, Cheriglo **$195**

#902, Lela Bird etch, green **$225**

Ice tub, tab handles

#191 Party Line, Cheriglo **$30**

#300 Archaic, Cupid etch, green **$200**

#895 Lucy, Oriental Garden etch, crystal **$45**

#991 Penny Line, ruby **$125**

#411 Mrs. B, Ardith etch, yellow, liner and ladle **$60**

#412 Crow's Foot Square, Orchid etch, crystal **$48**

#412 Crow's Foot Square, Trumpet Flower etch, yellow **$125**

#881 Gadroon, Black Forest etch, crystal, liner and ladle **$115**

Napkin holder, #210 Regina, green **$100**

Night set, pitcher, inverted tumbler, #210 Regina, Black Forest etch, green **$450**

Pitcher, #191 Party Line 74 oz. pitcher, green **$75**

Plate

#210 Regina, 8", Black Forest etch, Cheriglo **$40**

#220 Largo, 9", amber **$10**

#220 Largo, 9", ruby **$25**

#300 Archaic, 8-1/4", Nora Bird etch, green **$35**

#411 8" plate, Ardith etch, yellow **$22**

#411 8" plate, Nora Bird etch, crystal **$50**

#412 8" plate, Orchid etch, green .. **$45**

#412 10" plate, Orchid etch, cobalt **$175**

#881 Gadroon, 8" plate, ruby **$15**

#890 Crow's Foot Round, 9" mulberry **$20**

#890 Crow's Foot Round, 10", Orchid etch, Cheriglo **$65**

Relish dish, #555 oblong, three parts, Gazebo etch, light blue **$40**

Sugar pourer

#94 Bullet, screw-on metal base, green **$145**

#191 Party Line, Cheriglo **$100**

Syrup pitcher

#185, amber **$22.50**

#185, gold encrusted band etch, amber **$40**

#185, cutting, green **$45**

#185, w/underplate, cutting, Cheriglo **$85**

#900 Emeraldglo, star cut, metal underplate **$45**

Tray, two handles

#220 Largo, ruby **$25**

#411 Mrs. B Ardith etch green ... **$100**

#412 Crow's Foot Square, hand painted tulips, opal **$195**

#412 Crow's Foot Square, Orchid etch, crystal **$40**

#412 Crow's Foot Square, Orchid etch, ruby **$200**

#412 Crow's Foot Square, Peacock & Rose etch, yellow **$100**

Tumblers and stemware

#191 Party Line, tumbler, Ardith etch, Cheriglo **$75**

#191 Party Line, banana split, flat, green **$25**

#215 Glades, whiskey, Ardith etch, crystal **$15**

#890 Crow's Foot Round, tumbler, amber **$40**

#890 Crow's Foot Round, tumbler, cobalt **$70**

#991 Penny Line, whiskey, mulberry **$5**

#991 Penny Line, tall stem goblet, ruby **$20**

#994 Popeye & Olive, goblet, Cheriglo **$20**

Vase

#61 hourglass shape, Zinnia & Butterfly etch, green, 8" **$125**

#61 hourglass shape, Zinnia & Butterfly etch, Cheriglo, 8" **$175**

#61 hourglass shape, Zinnia & Butterfly etch, amber, 8" **$325**

#61 hourglass shape, Zinnia & Butterfly etch, medium blue, 8" **$400**

#180 Butterfly & Zinnia etch, green, 12" **$200**

#180 Daisy etch, Cheriglo or green, 12" **$225**

#180 Daisy etch, gold encrusted Cosmos etch at top, Cheriglo, 12" **$225**

#180 Peacock & Rose etch, Cheriglo, 12" **$375**

#182 elliptical, ebony, silver overlay, 8" **$65**

#182 elliptical, gold encrusted Utopia etch, ebony, 8" **$250**

#182-1/2 elliptical, Ardith etch, crystal, 5" **$80**

#182-1/2 elliptical, Frost etch, crystal, 5" **$40**

#184, bulbous, Gothic Garden etch, green, 8" **$195**

#184, bulbous, Rose with Jasmine etch, crystal, 8" **$200**

#184, bulbous, Eden Rose etch, red and gold encrusted, 10" **$225**

#184, bulbous, Gothic Garden etch, black, 10" **$125**

#184, bulbous, Orchid etch, ruby, 10" **$365**

#191 Party Line, fan shape, Cheriglo or green **$35**

#191 Party Line, cuspidor shape, Ardith etch, black **$85**

#191 Party Line, blown, hourglass shape, crimped top, Cheriglo or green **$35**

#210 Regina, squatty, Harvesters etch, black, 7" **$195**

#210 Regina, cylinder shape, Harvesters etch, ebony, 9" **$225**

#210 Regina, Lela Bird etch, ebony, 10" bulbous bottom **$110**

#300 Archaic fan vase, Ardith etch, ebony **$400**

#411 Gothic Garden etch, black, 9" **$125**

#411 Gothic Garden etch, yellow, 9" **$165**

#411 Gothic Garden etch, green, 9" **$435**

#411 silver deposit dec, crystal, 9" **$50**

#411 Utopia etch, Cheriglo, 9" **$250**

#412 Crow's Foot Square, ruby, 8" cupped rim **$50**

#412 Crow's Foot Square, Irwin etch, 8" flared rim............................**$55**

#503 dome footed fan vase, ruby .**$95**

#994 Popeye & Olive, 7", ruby **$50**

Unknown #, Frost etch, 8" **$40**

Unknown #, paneled, floral silver overlay, cobalt, 10-1/2"..............**$90**

Unknown #, paneled, Gothic Garden etch, green, 10-1/2" **$300**

Unknown #, paneled, silver overlay, opal, 10-1/2" **$375**

PAIRPOINT

History: The Pairpoint Manufacturing Co. was organized in 1880 as a silver-plating firm in New Bedford, Massachusetts. The company merged with Mount Washington Glass Co. in 1894 and became the Pairpoint Corporation. The new company produced specialty glass items, often accented with metal frames.

Pairpoint Corp. was sold in 1938 and Robert Gunderson became manager. He operated it as the Gunderson Glass Works until his death in 1952. From 1952 until the plant closed in 1956, operations were maintained under the name Gunderson-Pairpoint. Robert Bryden reopened the glass manufacturing business in 1970, moving it back to the New Bedford area.

Pairpoint large cut chalice, bubble knopped baluster-shaped stem, blue cut to clear chalice, 11-1/2" h, **$300.**
Photo courtesy of The Early Auction Company, LLC.

Pairpoint table lamp, acid-etched shade, reverse painted with roses and poppies in pink and yellow on black ground, bronzed two-socket base, replaced cap and top screw, shade stamped "The Pairpoint Corp'n," base stamped 1915, 22" x 16", **$2,350.**
Photo courtesy of David Rago Auctions, Inc.

Box, cov, Russian pattern cut glass, silver mountings, sgd "Pairpoint," 7-1/4" d...**$410**

Candlesticks, pr, cobalt blue, controlled bubble sphere...................**$450**

Compote, glass bowl painted with yellow and blue poppies against a rose-colored ground, gilt accents, attributed to Mount Washington Glass Company, Pairpoint ribbed silver plated base with paw feet, sgd "Pairpoint" on base, dent, 7-1/4" d, 5-1/4" h **$470**

Console set, three-pc set, 12" d bowl, matching 3" h candlesticks, Tavern glass, bouquet of red, white, and green flowers................................**$575**

Dish, fish shape, teal blue, controlled bubbles dec, late **$275**

Ferner, elongated mold blown oval body, purple and crimson pansies dec, emb metal lid with two ring handles, numbered "5126-211," 8" w..........**$400**

Perfume bottle, amethyst, painted butterfly, teardrop stopper, "P" in diamond mark, 6-3/4" h...................**$375**

Pokal, cov, Chrysopras, dark yellow-green, wheelcut grapes and leaves, finial wheelcut with eight-petaled flower, 14" h **$625**

Vase

Flared colorless crystal trumpet form, bright-cut floral dec, gilt metal foliate molded weighted pedestal base, imp "Pairpoint C1509," 14-1/2" h **$490**

Tavern glass, bulbous, enameled floral dec of vase of flowers, base numbered, 5-1/2" h, 4-1/2" w..........**$225**

PATE-DE-VERRE

History: The term "pate-de-verre" can be translated simply as "glass paste." It is manufactured by grinding lead glass into a powder or crystal form, making it into a paste by adding a two percent or three percent solution of sodium silicate, molding, firing, and carving. The Egyptians discovered the process as early as 1500 B.C.

In the late 19th century, the process was rediscovered by a group of French glassmakers. Almaric Walter, Henri Cros, Georges Despret, and the Daum brothers were leading manufacturers.

Contemporary sculptors are creating a second renaissance, led by the technical research of Jacques Daum.

Bookends, pr, Buddha, yellow amber pressed molded design, seated in lotus position, inscribed "A Walter Nancy," 6-1/2" h.................................**$2,450**

Center bowl, blue, purple, and green press molded design, seven exotic long-legged birds, central multi-pearl blossom, repeating design on ext., raised pedestal foot, sgd "G. Argy-Rousseau," 10-3/8" d, 3-3/4" h.. **$6,750**

Clock, stars within pentagon and tapered sheaves motif, orange and black, molded sgd "G. Argy-Rousseau," clock by J. E. Caldwell, 4-1/2" sq......................**$2,750**

Dagger, frosted blade, relief design, green horse head handle, script sgd "Nancy France," 12" l................**$1,200**

Jewelry, pendant, round plaque, low relief molded rose blossom and branch, shaded rose, brown, and frosted glass, molded "G.A.R," (G. Argy-Rousseau), c1925, 2-1/4" d......... **$700**

Paperweight, large beetle, green leaves, mottled blue ground, intaglio "AW" mark, 3/4" w, 1-1/4" h.... **$6,800**

Sculpture, crab in sea grasses, lemon yellow, chocolate brown, pale mauve, and sea green, sgd "A. Walter/Nancy" and "Berge/ SC," 9-5/8" l........ **$8,500**

Tray

Molded as large moth, mottled blue, yellow, and emerald green, brown accents, emb "A. Walter," c1910, 5" d
.... **$1,150**

Green to yellow ground, molded school of swimming fish, sgd "A. Walter Nancy, Berge," 6" w ...**$1,450**

Vase, press molded and carved, mottled amethyst and frost ground, three black and green crabs, red eyes, naturalistic seaweed at rim, center imp "G. Argy-Rousseau," base imp "France," 5-1/2" h................................**$5,500**

Veilleuse, Gabriel Argy-Rousseau, press molded oval lamp shade, frosted mottled gray glass, elaborate purple arches with three teardrop-shaped windows of yellow, center teal-green stylized blossoms on black swirling stems, imp "G. Arty-Rousseau" at lower edge, wrought iron frame, three ball feet centering internal lamp socket, conforming iron cover, 8-1/2" h.............................**$6,900**

PAPERWEIGHTS

History: Although paperweights had their origin in ancient Egypt, it was in the mid-19th century that this art form reached its zenith. The finest paperweights were produced between 1834 and 1855 in France by the Clichy, Baccarat, and Saint Louis factories. Other weights made in England, Italy, and Bohemia during this period rarely match the quality of the French weights.

In the early 1850s, the New England Glass Co. in Cambridge, Massachusetts, and the Boston and Sandwich Glass Co. in Sandwich, Massachusetts, became the first American factories to make paperweights.

Popularity peaked during the classic period (1845-1855) and faded toward the end of the 19th century. Paperweight production was rediscovered nearly a century later in the mid-1900s. Baccarat, Saint Louis, Perthshire, and many studio craftsmen in the U.S. and Europe still make contemporary weights.

Antique

Baccarat, France, Double Garland, double trefoil garland of red and white canes centered by ring of blue canes; pink, white and green cane, minor wear, 19th C, 3" d, 2" h .. **$490**

Boston & Sandwich Glass Co., second half 19th C

Five large pears, four large leaves, four small vegetables, four small leaves, yellow, red, green, and rose, dew-like air traps, polished concave base, 1-1/2" h, 2-1/4" d **$315**

Flower, 10 bright blue petals with central cane, deep green stem, three leaves, dew-like air traps, polished concave base, 2" h, 2-3/4" d..... **$550**

Clichy, France, 19th C

Chequer, complex millefiori canes centered by pink and green Clichy rose, all divided by white latticinio twists, 2-3/4" d, 2" h..............**$1,265**

Millefiori, complex millefiori canes set in colorless crystal, 1-3/4" d, 1-3/8" h **$375**

Swirled, alternating purple and white pinwheels emanating from white, green, and pink pastry mold cane, minor bubbles, 2-5/8" d........**$2,200**

Degenhart, John, window, red crystal cube with yellow and orange upright center lily, one to window, four side windows, bubble in center of flower's stamens, 3-3/16" x 2-1/4" x 2-1/4" **$1,225**

Paperweight, R. Lalique, "Daim," clear and frosted, molded R. LALIQUE, c1929, 3-1/8", **$960.**

Photo courtesy of David Rago Auctions, Inc.

Aquamarine paperweight glass ornament, single fish swimming against aquatic foliage, aquamarine sea, engraved L.C. Tiffany Inc. Favrile 6508N, 6-1/4" x 5-3/4", **$20,400.**
Photo courtesy of David Rago Auctions, Inc.

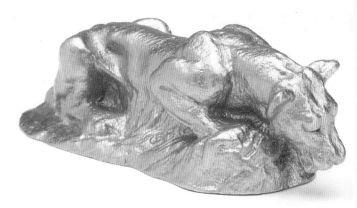

Paperweight, Tiffany Studios, gilt-parcel crouching panther, stamped "Tiffany Studios New York," 1-1/2" x 4", **$550.**
Photo courtesy of David Rago Auctions, Inc.

Gillinder, orange turtle with moving appendages in hollow center, pale orange ground, molded dome, 3-1/16" d ... **$500**

Millville, umbrella pedestal, red, white, green, blue, and yellow int., bubble in sphere center, 3-1/8" d, 3-3/8" h..**$800**

New England Glass Co.

Apple form, deep rose to bright yellow, clear circular base, engraved "K. A. Osgood," second half 19th C, 2-1/2" h, 3" d.......................**$990**

Pink flower, striated pink five-petal flowers, millefiori cane center, pink bud on deep green leafy stem, white latticino bed, minor wear, 2-1/4" d, 1-3/4" h **$690**

Pinchbeck, pastoral dancing scene, couple dancing before a group of onlookers, 3-3/16" d **$650**

Sandwich Glass Co.

Dahlia, red petaled flower, millefiori cane center, bright green leafy stem, highlighted by trapped bubble dec, white latticino ground, c1870, 2-1/2" d, 1-3/4" h **$650**

Poinsettia, double, red flower with double tier of petals, green and white Lutz rose, green stem and leaves, bubbles between petals, 3" d..**$1,200**

St. Louis, fruit basket, red and green ripening fruits, latticino base basket, central base cane, 3" d, 2-1/2" h..**$1,150**

Unknown maker, sulphide, silvery white figure of walking dog, polished base, light scratching and pitting, late 19th or early 20th C, 1-3/8" h, 2-1/8" d **$110**

Val St. Lambert, patterned millefiori, four red, white, blue, pistachio, and turquoise complex canes circlets spaced around central pink, turquoise and cadmium green canes circlet, canes set on stripes of lace encircled

by spiraling red and blue torsade, minor blocking crease, 3-1/2" d..**$950**

Modern

Ayotte, Rick, yellow finch, perched on branch, faceted, sgd and dated, limited edition, 1979 ....**$750**

Baccarat, Gridel pelican cane surrounded by five concentric rings of yellow, pink, green, and white complex canes, pink canes contain 18 Gridel silhouette canes, lace ground, signature cane, sgd and dated, limited ed. of 350, 1973 date cane, 3-1/16" d.............**$850**

Banford, Bob, cornflower, blue flower, yellow center, pink and white twisted torsade, "B" cane at stem, 3" d ...**$550**

Bryden Pairpoint Glass Co., red rose, green leaves, cut diamond-point panel base, second half 20th C, 2-1/4" h, 3-1/4" d **$210**

Kaziun, Charles, concentric millefiori, heart, turtle silhouette, shamrocks, six-pointed stars, and floret canes encircled by purple and white torsade, turquoise ground flecked with goldstone, K signature cane, 2-1/16" d................**$1,200**

Labino, free form, white, amber, and irid gold flower center, air bubbles, surrounded by green glass, sgd "Labino 1969," 2-1/2" d.........................**$210**

Orient and Flume, red butterfly with blue and white accents, brown and green vines, white millefiori blossoms over dark ground, orig sticker and box, 3-1/2" d, dated 1977............**$235**

Parabelle, tightly packed multicolored millefiori canes, dark blue ground, attributed to Gary and Doris Scrutton, signature and date cane, orig paper label, 2-3/4" d **$575**

Perthshire, miniature bouquet, yellow flowers, pink buds, basket of deep

blue canes, green and pink millefiori canes cut to form base, orig box and certificate, 2-1/2" d **$160**

Rosenfeld, Ken, Monarch butterfly, leafy stem, red blossom with three buds, R signature cane, inscribed "KR 2001," 1-7/8" h, 2-5/8" h.............**$350**

Salazar, David, compound floral, lavender six-petal poinsettia star blossom, three-leaf stem over green and red wreath, white ground, inscribed "David Salazar/111405/Lundberg Studios 1991," 3-1/4" d...............**$225**

Stankard, Paul, morning glory, bee on hive in center of two blue morning glories, three orange berries, two yellow flowers, sandy ground, root figure and word canes "Moist" and "Fertile" beneath, inscribed "Paul J. Stankard V32 '97," 2-3/8" h, 3-1/4" d **$2,875**

Tarsitano, Debbie, pansy, two central blue and yellow pansies flanked by three rose-pink blossoms, three yellow blossoms, green leafy stems, signature cane **$475**

Trabucco, Victor, Buffalo, NY, magnum pansy, purple pansy blossom and bud, leaf stem, white lace cushion, inscribed "Trabucco 1998," 2-1/2" h, 3-1/2" d **$635**

Whitefriars, Star of David, five rows of tightly packed blue and white millefiori canes, 3" d **$395**

Whittemore, Francis, two green and brown acorns on branch with three brown and yellow oak leaves, translucent cobalt blue ground, circular top facet five oval punties on sides, 20-3/8" d....................................**$300**

Ysart, Paul, green fish, yellow eye, yellow and white jasper ground encircled by pink, green, and white complex cane garland, PY signature cane **$550**

PATTERN GLASS

History: Pattern glass is clear or colored glass pressed into one of hundreds of patterns. Deming Jarves of the Boston and Sandwich Glass Co. invented one of the first successful pressing machines in 1828. By the 1860s, glass-pressing machinery had been improved, and mass production of good-quality matched tableware sets began. The idea of a matched glassware table service (including goblets, tumblers, creamers, sugars, compotes, cruets, etc.) quickly caught on in America. Many pattern glass table services had numerous accessory pieces such as banana stands, molasses cans, and water bottles.

Early pattern glass (flint) was made with a lead formula, giving many items a ringing sound when tapped. Lead became too valuable to be used in glass manufacturing during the Civil War, and in 1864, Hobbs, Brockunier & Co., West Virginia, developed a soda lime (non-flint) formula. Pattern glass also was produced in transparent colors, milk glass, opalescent glass, slag glass, and custard glass.

The hundreds of companies that produced pattern glass experienced periods of development, expansions, personnel problems, material and supply demands, fires, and mergers. In 1899, the National Glass Co. was formed as a combination of 19 glass companies in Pennsylvania, Ohio, Indiana, West Virginia, and Maryland. U.S. Glass, another consortium, was founded in 1891. These combines resulted from attempts to save small companies by pooling talents, resources, and patterns. Because of this pooling, the same pattern often can be attributed to several companies.

Additional Listings: Children's Toy Dishes, Cruets, Custard Glass, Milk Glass, Sugar Shakers, Toothpicks.

Reproduction Alert. Pattern glass has been widely reproduced.

Abbreviations

ah	applied handle
GUTDODB	Give Us This Day Our Daily Bread
hs	high standard
ind	individual
ls	low standard
os	original stopper

Arched Fleur-De-Lis

Late Fleur De-Lis

Manufactured by Bryce, Higbee and Company, c1897-88. Made in clear, clear with gilding, and ruby stained.

Items	Clear	Ruby Stained
Banana Stand	$42	$180
Bowl, oval, 9" l	110	—
Butter Dish, cov	48	142
Cake Stand	42	—
Creamer	36	72
Dish, shallow, 7" l	15	30
Jelly Compote	24	—
Mug, 3-1/4" h	24	48
Olive, handle	18	—
Pitcher, water	130	360
Plate, square, 7" w	15	410
Relish, 8" l	18	—
Salt Shaker	110	55
Sauce	10	24
Spooner, double handles	24	65
Sugar Bowl, cov, double handles	42	120
Toothpick Holder	36	120
Tumbler	18	55
Vase, 10" h	42	90
Wine	30	65

Aurora

Brilliant's Aurora, Diamond Horseshoe, Diamond Horse Shoe

Manufactured by the Brilliant Glass Works, 1888-1902. This company was acquired by the Greensburg Glass Company, which then continued the pattern. McKee & Brothers Glass Company, Pittsburgh, PA, c1902, made the pattern in chocolate glass only and in limited production. Pioneer Glass Company, Pittsburgh, PA, is credited with the ruby stain decoration. Made in clear and ruby stained. Also found with etching.

Items	Clear	Ruby Stained
Bowl, 5" or 6" d	$12	$24
Bread Plate, round, large star in center, 10" d	36	72
Bread Plate, round, plain center, 10" d	36	55
Butter Dish, cov	55	110
Cake Stand, hs	42	85
Celery Vase	42	72
Compote, cov, hs, 6" d	65	135
Compote, cov, hs, 7" d	65	115
Compote, cov, hs, 8" d	85	130
Compote, open, hs, 6", 7" or 8" d	24-30	36-55
Creamer	42	60
Decanter, os, 11-3/4" h	90	142
Goblet	60	65
Mug, handle	60	85
Olive, oval	24	42
Pickle Dish, fish shape	18	30
Pitcher, milk or water, quart or half gallon	48	120
Relish Scoop, handle	12	30
Salt and Pepper Shakers, pr	55	95
Sauce, flat or footed, sq, 4" w	10	18

Button Band

Umbilicated Hobnail, Wyandotte

Manufactured by Ripley and Company, in the late 1880s. Also reissued by United States Glass Company, after 1891, Factory "F." Made in non-flint, clear only. Some pieces are found with engraving. They are priced the same as plain clear pieces.

Items	Clear
Bowl, 10" d	$36
Butter Dish, cov	55
Cake Stand, hs, 10" d	85
Castor Set, 5 bottles, glass stand	142
Celery Vase	36
Compote, cov, hs, 6" d	124
Compote, open, ls	66
Cordial	42
Creamer, ftd or tankard	36

Items	Clear
Goblet	48
Jelly Compote, open, hs	36
Pitcher, milk, quart	48
Pitcher, water, tankard, half gallon	55
Plate, round	15
Spooner	30
Sugar Bowl, cov	42
Tumbler, flat	30
Water Tray	48
Wine	42

Daisy and Button with Crossbars

Daisy and Thumbprint Crossbar, Daisy and Button with Crossbar and Thumbprint Band, Daisy with Crossbar, Mikado

Manufactured by Richards & Hartley, Tarentum, PA, c1895. Reissued by United States Glass Company, Pittsburgh, PA, after 1891. Shards have been found at Burlington Glass Works, Hamilton, Ontario, Canada. Made in non-flint, amber, blue, clear, and vaseline.

Items	Amber	Blue	Clear	Vaseline
Bowl, oval, 6" l or 8" l	$24	$36	$18	$30
Bowl, oval, 9" l	48	48	30	42
Bread Plate	36	55	30	42
Butter Dish, cov, flat	55	55	55	55
Butter Dish, cov, footed	—	75	30	72
Celery Vase	42	48	36	60
Compote, cov, hs, 6" d	55	65	55	55
Compote, cov, hs, 8" d	65	75	55	65
Compote, cov, ls, 7" d	42	42	30	42
Compote, cov, ls, 8" d	48	48	36	48
Compote, open, hs, 7" d	48	55	30	48
Compote, open, hs, 8" d	55	60	36	55
Compote, open, ls, 7" or 8" d	36	42	24	55
Cordial	36	42	30	36
Creamer, individual	30	36	25	36
Creamer, regular	30	55	42	48
Cruet, os	75	85	42	120
Finger Bowl	55	48	36	42
Goblet	48	48	30	55
Ketchup Bottle	110	135	42	110
Lamp, oil, 4 sizes	130	155	110	130
Mug, large, 3" h; or small	18	35	15	24
Pickle Dish	24	24	12	24
Pickle Jar, cov	36	55	30	48
Pitcher, milk	65	72	55	110
Pitcher, water	115	85	65	130
Salt and Pepper Shakers, pr	48	5,000	36	55
Sauce, flat	18	25	12	18
Sauce, footed	25	30	18	30
Spooner, ftd	42	42	30	42
Sugar Bowl, cov, individual	30	42	12	30
Sugar Bowl, cov, regular	60	72	30	55
Syrup, orig top	120	130	65	130
Toothpick Holder	48	48	85	42
Tumbler, flat	24	30	25	30
Wine	36	42	30	36

Giant Bull's Eye

Bull's Eye and Spearhead, US Glass Pattern Line No. 157

Manufactured by Bellaire Glass Company, Findlay, OH, c1889, and Model Flint Glass Company, Findlay, OH, c1891, and continued by United States Glass Company, Pittsburgh, PA, after 1891. Made in non-flint, clear.

Items	Clear
Bowl, 8" d	$30
Brandy Bottle, os, tall, 12 oz, 16 oz, or 22 oz	55
Butter Dish, cov	55
Cake Stand, hs	36
Cheese Dish, cov	55
Claret Jug, tankard shape	72
Compote, cov	75
Compote, open, flared or scalloped rim	48
Condiment Set, cruet, salt and pepper shakers, mustard	85
Creamer	36
Cruet, os	72
Decanter, os	60

Items	Clear
Goblet	55
Lamp, handled	130
Perfume Bottle, os	36
Pitcher, water, half gallon	75
Relish Tray	18
Sauce, flat, 4" d	10
Spooner, scalloped	36
Sugar Bowl, cov	72
Syrup, orig nickel top, large or small	65
Tumbler	36
Vase, 7" h, 8" h, or 9" h	42
Water Tray	55
Wine	36
Wine Tray, 7-1/4" d	55

Hamilton

Cape Cod

Manufactured by Cape Cod Glass Company, Sandwich, MA, c1860. Shards have been found at the site of the Boston and Sandwich Glass Company, Sandwich, MA. Other companies also may have made this pattern. Made in flint, non-flint, and clear. Rare examples found in color.

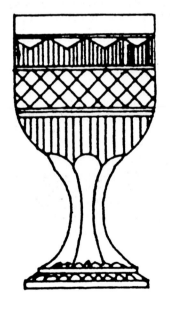

Items	Flint	Non-Flint
Butter Dish, cov	$90	$30
Castor Set, 4 bottles, pewter standard	190	130
Celery Vase, pedestal	72	24
Compote, cov, hs	115	42
Compote, open, ls, scalloped rim, 6" d	95	36
Creamer, ah	90	30
Creamer, ph	80	24
Decanter, os	160	60
Egg Cup	60	18
Goblet	55	15
Hat, made from tumbler mold	130	—

Items	Flint	Non-Flint
Honey Dish	18	12
Lamp, hand	105	42
Pitcher, water, ah, half gallon	290	130
Plate, 6" d	55	15
Salt, master, ftd	36	12
Sauce, 4-1/2" d	36	12
Spooner	42	15
Sugar Bowl, cov	90	30
Sweetmeat Dish, hs, cov	115	42
Syrup, ah, orig top	350	—
Tumbler, bar	105	42
Tumbler, water	95	36
Whiskey, ah	115	42
Wine	110	36

Paneled Daisy

Brazil, Daisy and Panel

Manufactured by Bryce Bros., Pittsburgh, PA, in the late 1880s. Reissued by United States Glass Company, Pittsburgh, PA, in 1891 at Factory "B." Made in non-flint, clear. Also found in amber (sugar shaker, $130) and blue (sugar shaker, $155). Milk glass pieces include 7" round plate ($48), 9" sq plate ($55), and sugar shaker ($95).

Items	Clear
Bowl, flared rim, 6" d or 7" d	$18
Bowl, shallow, 8" or 9" d; or square, 8" w	35
Bowl, square, 10-1/2" w	30
Butter Dish, cov, flat or footed	60
Cake Stand, hs, 8", 9", 10-1/4" or 11" d	36-60
Celery Vase	48
Compote, cov, hs, 5", 7", 8" d or 10" d	48-72
Compote, open, hs, 7", 9", 10" or 11" d	48
Creamer	42
Creamer, cov	75
Dish, oval, 9" l	35
Goblet	30
Jelly Compote, cov, hs, 6" d	55
Mug	36

Items	Clear
Pickle Jar	90
Pickle Scoop	18
Pitcher, water, half gallon	72
Plate, round, 7" or 9" d	36
Plate, square, 9-1/2" or 10" w	36-42
Relish, 5" x 7", wider at one end	25
Salt Shaker	30
Sauce, flat or footed, round, 4" d or 4-1/2" d	12
Spooner	30
Sugar Bowl, cov	48
Sugar Shaker	55
Syrup, orig top	85
Tumbler	30
Waste Bowl	18
Water Bottle	72
Water Tray	55

Reproduction Alert. Both the goblet and tumbler have been reproduced by L. G. Wright Glass Company, New Martinsville, WV, c1960, in amber, blue, clear, pink, and ruby. It also reproduced the relish scoop in amber, amethyst, blue, and green. Fenton Art Glass Company, Williamstown, WV, created a high standard covered compote in carnival, clear, and opalescent colors in 1970. A toothpick holder was added in 1973.

Pineapple and Fan #2

Cube with Fan, Holbrook

Manufactured by Adams & Company, Pittsburgh, PA. Reissued by United States Glass Company, Pittsburgh, PA, in 1891. Made in non-flint, clear. Also found in emerald green, ruby stained, and white milk glass trimmed in gold.

Items	Clear
Bowl, 8" d	$30
Butter Dish, cov	48
Cake Stand, hs, 9" d	42
Cologne Bottle	45
Creamer	30
Cruet, os	65
Decanter	48
Finger Bowl	30
Goblet	30
Ice Cream Tray	30
Pitcher, water, tankard	55

Items	Clear
Plate, 6-1/2" d	18
Punch Bowl, 12" d	72
Rose Bowl	35
Salt, individual	15
Spooner	30
Sugar Bowl, cov	36
Syrup, orig top	60
Tumbler	18
Waste Bowl	18
Whiskey	18
Wine	35

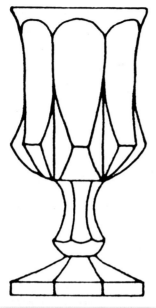

Reproduction Alert. Reproductions of this pattern have been made by Wheaton-Craft Giftware of Millville, NJ, c1976. It named the pattern Wheaton-Craft's Cape May. Its production was limited to clear, non-flint, creamer, nut dish, pickle tray, relish, and sugar bowl.

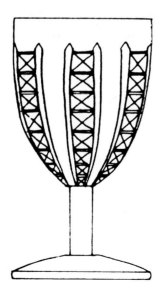

Portland

US Glass Pattern Line No. 15,121

Manufactured by Portland Glass Company, Portland, ME, late 1870s. Reissued by United States Glass Company, Pittsburgh, PA, c1910, at Factory "F" (Ripley & Co., Pittsburgh), Factory "O," (Central Glass Co., Wheeling, WV) and Factory "GP" (Glassport, PA). Made in non-flint, clear, and clear with gold trim. An oval pin tray in ruby souvenir ($35) is known and a flat sauce ($30).

Items	Clear w/Gold Trim
Basket, ah	$100
Biscuit Jar, cov	110
Berry Bowl, 6" or 7" d	35
Berry Bowl, 8" d	30
Bowl, cov, ftd	42
Butter Dish, cov	60
Cake Stand, hs, 10-1/2" d	55
Candlestick, 7" h, cupped or flared	100
Candlestick, 9" or 10-1/2" h	65-75
Celery Tray	30
Celery Vase	55
Compote, cov, hs, 6", 7" or 8"	72-85
Compote, open, hs, flared bowl, 7", 8-1/4" or 9-1/2" d	42-55
Compote, open, hs, straight sides, 6", 7" or 8" d	36-60
Compote, open, ls, 6", 7" or 8" d	48-60
Creamer, breakfast, table or tankard	35
Cruet, os	65
Custard Cup, handle	18
Decanter, qt, handled	60
Finger Bowl	30
Goblet	42
Jam Jar, silver plated cov	42

Items	Clear w/Gold Trim
Lamp, oil, orig burner and chimney, 9" h	110
Olive Dish, oval	35
Pickle Dish, boat shape	18
Pin Tray	35
Pitcher, water, bulbous; or straight sides, tankard	65
Pomade Jar, silver plated top	36
Puff Box, glass lid	42
Punch Bowl, ftd, 13-5/8" d	160
Punch Cup	18
Relish	18
Ring Tree	100
Salt Shaker	18
Sardine Box, 4-1/2" l	36
Sauce, flat, oval or square	10
Sauce, flat, round, flared or straight sides, 4" d	10
Spooner, large or small	36
Sugar Bowl, open, breakfast; or table	42-55
Sugar Shaker	48
Syrup, orig top	60
Toothpick Holder	30
Tumbler	30
Vase, 6" or 9" h	36-42
Water Bottle	48
Wine	36

Stars and Stripes

Brilliant, Federal Pattern Line No. 209 and 1903

Manufactured by Jenkins Glass Company, Kokomo, IN, in 1899. Also made by Federal Glass Company, Columbus, OH, c1914. Appeared in 1899 Montgomery Ward catalog as "Brilliant." Made in non-flint, clear.

Items	Clear
Berry Bowl, master	$18
Butter Dish, cov	36
Celery Vase	18
Cordial	18
Creamer	20
Cruet Set	45
Fruit Bowl, sq	18
Goblet	24
Pitcher, water	45

Items	Clear
Salt Shaker	18
Sauce, flat, round or square	10
Sherbet, handle	15
Spooner	18
Sugar Bowl, cov	24
Tumbler	18
Vase	12
Wine	18

PEACHBLOW

History: Peachblow, an art glass which derives its name from a fine Chinese glazed porcelain, resembles a peach or crushed strawberries in color. Three American glass manufacturers and two English firms produced peachblow glass in the late 1880s. A fourth American company resumed the process in the 1950s. The glass from each firm has its own identifying characteristics.

Hobbs, Brockunier & Co., Wheeling peachblow: Opalescent glass, plated or cased with a transparent amber glass; shading from yellow at the base to a deep red at top; glossy or satin finish.

Mt. Washington "Peach Blow": A homogeneous glass, shading from a pale gray-blue to a soft rose color; some pieces enhanced with glass appliqués, enameling, and gilding.

New England Glass Works, New England peachblow (advertised as Wild Rose, but called Peach Blow at the plant): Translucent, shading from rose to white; acid or glossy finish; some pieces enameled and gilded.

Thomas Webb & Sons and Stevens and Williams (English firms): Peachblow-style cased art glass, shading from yellow to red; some pieces with cameo-type relief designs.

Gunderson Glass Co.: Produced peachblow-type art glass to order during the 1950s; shades from an opaque faint tint of pink, which is almost white, to a deep rose.

Marks: Pieces made in England are marked "Peach Blow" or "Peach Bloom."

Peachblow water pitcher, square mouth, ovoid, deep amber handle, Hobbs Brockunier Wheeling, 8" h, **$1,100.**
Photo courtesy of The Early Auction Company, LLC.

Bowl

New England, Wild Rose, satin finish, smooth pontil mark, 3-3/4" d, 1-1/4" h **$495**

Acid finished, ftd, shaped trefoil fold down rim, soft pink shades to pale blue on bulbous rubbed body, three vertically ribbed feet, berry pontil, Mt. Washington, ex-Maude Feld, 7-1/2" d, 8" h **$12,000**

Bride's basket, Mount Washington, shades of pink, replated Meriden frame **$650**

Celery vase, New England, sq top, deep raspberry with purple highlights shading to white, 7" h, 4" w **$785**

Claret jug

Shape #322, Hobbs, Brockunier & Co., Wheeling, acid finish, applied reeded amber handle, ex-Maude Feld, 9-1/2" h **$5,500**

Shape #322, Hobbs, Brockunier & Co., Wheeling, shiny finish, applied reeded amber handle, ex-Maude Feld, 10" h **$6,500**

Cologne bottle, Webb, bulbous, raised gold floral branches, silver hallmarked dome top, 5" h **$900**

Cream pitcher

New England, satin finish, 2-3/4" h **$1,120**

Wheeling, applied amber handle, 3-1/4" h **$885**

Hobbs, Brockunier & Co., Wheeling, shiny, applied amber handle, 4-1/4" h, #319 .... **$650**

Cruet

Hobbs, Brockunier & Co., Wheeling, ruby reeded handle, amber faceted stopper, 7-1/4" h **$800**

Wheeling, ball shaped, mahogany colored trefoil spout and neck, paper label from Maude Feld, 6-1/2" h **$2,475**

Wheeling, glossy, petticoat, applied amber handle, cut and faceted stopper, orig Maude Feld label, ex-Maude Feld, 7" h **$850**

Wheeling, satin, teepee shape, applied amber handle, replacement faceted clear glass amber stopper, 7" h.. **$1,950**

Decanter, Gunderson, Pilgrim Canteen form, acid finish, deep raspberry to white, applied peachblow ribbed handle, deep raspberry stopper, 10" h, 5" w **$950**

Finger bowl, #93, Hobbs, Brockunier & Co., Wheeling, glossy, ovoid, 4-1/2" w, 2-3/4" h **$275**

Goblet, Gunderson, glossy finish, deep color, applied Burmese glass base, 7-1/4" h, 4" d top **$285**

Miniature, pitcher, #319, Hobbs, Brockunier & Co., Wheeling, glossy, sq mouth, orig Maude Feld paper label, ex-Maude Feld, 5" h **$700**

Peachblow tankard pitcher, cylindrical, amber to fuchsia, glossy applied amber handle, Hobbs Brockunier Wheeling, 9-1/2" h, **$4,000.**
Photo courtesy of The Early Auction Company, LLC.

Peachblow, Wheeling, square mouth vase, glossy finish, 4" h, **$500.**
Photo courtesy of The Early Auction Company, LLC.

Peachblow finger bow, pinched ruffled rim, acid finish, Mt. Washington, 5-1/2" d, **$1,800.**
Photo courtesy of The Early Auction Company, LLC.

Peachblow stick vase, bulbous, acid finish #12 in Hobbs Brockunier orig catalog, 10" h, **$850.**
Photo courtesy of The Early Auction Company, LLC.

Peachblow squatty vase, stick neck, glossy finish, Wheeling, 6" h, **$1,500.**
Photo courtesy of The Early Auction Company, LLC.

Mustard, cov, Wheeling, SP cov and handle.............................**$475**

Pitcher
Wheeling, Drape, squatty, mahogany shading to lemon yellow, sq mouth, applied clear reeded handle, 5-1/2" h **$350**
Wheeling, glossy finish, sq mouth, applied amber handle, orig Maude Feld label on int. of mouth, ex-Maude Feld, 5-1/2" h **$800**
Wheeling, acid finish, sq mouth, deep mahogany extends to lemon yellow, applied amber handle, orig Maude Feld label, ex-Maude Feld, 5-3/4" h **$1,200**
Wheeling, glossy, rect mouth, applied amber handle, 7" h................**$1,050**

Punch cup
Gundersen, acid finish...............**$275**

Hobbs, Brockunier, 2-1/2" h **$535**
Sugar shaker, Wheeling, 5-1/4" h" **$3,025**
Toothpick holder, Mt. Washington, dec, ex-Maude Feld, 2-1/2" h..**$15,680**
Tumbler
Gundersen, matte finish, 3-3/4" h **$275**
New England, satin finish, 3-3/4" h **$285**
New England, satin finish, deep raspberry red on upper third shading to creamy white, 3-3/4" h.............**$285**
New England, shiny finish, 3-3/4" h **$285**
Wheeling, matte finish, 3-1/2" h..**$200**
Wheeling, glossy finish, shading from fuchsia to yellow, 3-7/8" h **$200**
Vase
Mt. Washington, tapering ovoid,

raised enameled, Queens design dec, ex-Maude Feld, 9-1/4" h **$20,000**
New England, ovoid, peaked rim, shading from soft pink to cream, camphor tooled base, 7-1/4" h..**$250**
New England, satin finish, lily, fades to white stem and wafer base, 6-3/4" h **$635**
Wheeling glossy finish, sq mouth, 4" h **$500**
Wheeling, shiny finish, sq mouth, shouldered body, mahogany shading to custard yellow, white opaque liner, 4" h...............................**$550**
Wheeling, rare lavender casing, ex-Maude Feld, 4" h, 6" d....**$15,000**
Wheeling, Morgan, shiny finish, deep red shading to butterscotch, 8" h **$850**
Wheeling, Morgan, shiny finish, three minute-in-the-making rim flakes, 8" h **$1,750**
Webb, cased deep crimson to pink, cascading green leafy branch, gold highlights, 10" h **$1,265**
Wheeling, Morgan, acid finish, shades from mahogany to custard, orig acid finish holder, ex-Maude Feld, 10" h **$3,000**

PERFUME, COLOGNE, AND SCENT BOTTLES

Perfume, Steuben, gold, melon ribbed, missing stopper, 4" h, **$200.**
Photo courtesy of The Early Auction Company, LLC.

History: The second half of the 19th century was the golden age for decorative bottles made to hold scents. These bottles were made in a variety of shapes and sizes.

An atomizer is a perfume bottle with a spray mechanism. Cologne bottles usually are larger and have stoppers that also may be used as applicators. A perfume bottle has a stopper that often is elongated and designed to be an applicator.

Scent bottles are small bottles used to hold a scent or smelling salts. A vinaigrette is an ornamental box or bottle that has a perforated top and is used to hold aromatic vinegar or smelling salts. Fashionable women of the late 18th and 19th centuries carried them in purses or slipped them into gloves in case of a sudden fainting spell.

Perfume, Art Deco, emerald green, woman with arms outstretched embossed on base, original stopper, **$125.**

Perfume, Steuben, blue Aurene, bottle form, gold highlights, teardrop stopper, long dauber, sgd 3174 Steuben Aurene, 7-1/2" h, **$1,700.**
Photo courtesy of The Early Auction Company, LLC.

Cologne, Tiffany, gold Favrile, footed, frosted bulbous form, balled stopper, finial, iridescent gold band over pulled feathers dec, sgd D1407 L.C.T., c1895, 6-1/2" h, **$1,300.**
Photo courtesy of The Early Auction Company, LLC.

Atomizer

Cambridge, stippled gold, opaque jade, orig silk lined box, 6-1/4" h **$140**

Cameo, Gallé, lavender flowers and foliage, shaded yellow and frosted ground, 8" h **$1,250**

Moser, sapphire blue, gold florals, leaves, and swirls, melon ribbed body, orig gold top and bulb, 4-1/2" h ... **$275**

Cologne

Baccarat, colorless, panel cut, matching stopper, 5-7/8" h **$75**

Cameo glass
Bulbous, crimson satin, opaque white floral cutting, hallmarked British Sterling cap, 3-1/4" h **$1,400**
Citrine ground, white shaded star shaped blossoms, sterling mounts, English, very minor nick in foliage, c1900, 4" h **$1,495**
Finely etched ground, citron cameo stemmed flowers, French, attributed to St. Louis, faceted stopper, very minor chips on stopper and rim, 8" h **$300**

Cranberry glass, faceted, finely cut faceted stopper, 7" h **$175**

Cut glass, cranberry cut to colorless, cane cut, matching stopper, 7" h .. **$250**

Paperweight, double overlay, crimson red over white over colorless squatty bottle, five oval facet windows reveal concentric millefiore cane int., matching stopper, 7" h, 5" d **$460**

Vaseline, vaseline, attributed to New England Glass Co., flint, orig stopper, 4-1/2" h **$225**

Perfume
Glass
Continental, latticino, tapered ovoid, clear, white, and yellow strands, ext. of bottle with horizontal ribbing, silver gilt floral engraved hinged lid, enclosing glass stopper, early 19th C, 3-7/8" l **$425**
French, baluster form, blue opaline bottle, gilt metal floral overlay, foot, and neck mounts, hinged lid set with shell cameo of young man in feathered cap, late 19th/early 20th C, 4" h **$200**

Perfume, R. Lalique, D'Orsay "Ambre," black with whitish patina, molded LALIQUE, c1911, 5-1/4", **$1,800.**
Photo courtesy of David Rago Auctions, Inc.

Perfume, R. Lalique, Forvil, "La Perle Noire," clear and topaz, frozen stopper, molded R. LALIQUE PARIS FRANCE, c1922, 4-3/8", $2,880.
Photo courtesy of David Rago Auctions, Inc.

Cut glass, colorless, pistol-form, etched silver-gilt mounts, short chain, spring-action trigger opens lid set with maker's medallion, French, late 19th/early 20th C, 4-3/4" l......**$1,380**

Scent

Blown, colorless, cranberry and white stripes, white and gold metallic twist, 4-1/8" h............**$95**

Blown molded, sunburst, brilliant sapphire shading to cobalt blue, shield shaped body, plain lip, rough pontil break, early to mid-19th C, 2-3/4" h, 1-1/2" d............**$495**

Free-blown, dolphin or mermaid, colorless, opaque white stripes, applied cobalt blue rigaree, plain lip, possibly Boston & Sandwich Glass Co., some losses, 1825-50, 1-3/4" h............**$80**

Free-blown, dolphin or mermaid, colorless, applied rigaree, engraved "Eliz-h Richardson" on one side, sprig on other side, American or English, small rough spot on rigaree, mid-19th C, 3" h............**$50**

Pattern molded, flattened ovoid, brilliant peacock green, 20 ribs swirled to right, plain rim, rough pontil mark, American or English, early to mid-19th C, 2-1/4" h............**$265**

Pattern molded, flattened tapering ovoid, deep brilliant amethyst, 26 ribs swirled to right, plain rim, rough pontil mark, American or English, early to mid-19th C, 2-7/8" h............**$200**

Pattern molded, flattened tapering ovoid, teal blue, red swirl, 24 vertical ribs, plain rim, rough pontil mark, American or English, early to mid-19th C, 2-7/8" h............**$180**

Pattern molded, flattened tapering ovoid, deep cobalt blue, light iridescence, 24 ribs swirled to right, plain rim, rough pontil mark, American or English, rib flake, pinhead nicks, early to mid-19th C, 3" h............**$90**

Perfume, Moser cranberry, ovoid, gold medallions, polychrome acanthus scrolling, faceted stopper, 4-1/2" h, $575.
Photo courtesy of The Early Auction Company.

Pattern molded, flattened tapering ovoid form, pale yellow amber, 26 vertical ribs, plain rim, rough pontil mark, American or English, tiny flake on lip, early to mid-19th C, 3" h............**$165**

Vinaigrette

Cranberry glass, rect, allover cutting, enameled tiny pink roses, green leaves, gold dec, hinged lid, stopper, finger chain, 2-1/4" x 1"............**$185**

Cut glass, cobalt blue, yellow flashing, sterling silver overlay, emb sterling silver cap, 3-7/8" l............**$125**

Perfume, R. Lalique, "Aster," clear with blue patina, unsigned bottle, orig box engraved R. Lalique, c1913, bottle 4-1/4" h; box 3-1/2" d,
$5,400.
Photo courtesy of David Rago Auctions, Inc.

PHOENIX GLASS

History: Phoenix Glass Company, Beaver, Pennsylvania, was established in 1880. Known primarily for commercial glassware, the firm also produced a molded, sculptured, cameo-type line from the 1930s until the 1950s.

Ashtray, Phlox, large, white, frosted **$80**

Bowl, nude diving girl, white, 14" d ... **$495**

Creamer and sugar, Catalonia, light green **$45**

Lamp shade, ceiling type, pale pink, emb floral dec, 12" d **$115**

Umbrella stand, Thistle, pearlized blue ground, 18" h **$450**

Vase
Jewel, brown over milk glass,

4-3/4" d, 4-3/4" h **$200**
Daisy, pearlized daisies, light green ground, orig label, 8" h **$360**
Nude Scarf Dancers, light brown ground, cream figures, orig label, 8-1/8" d, 11-3/4" h **$650**
Dogwood, green and white, 10-3/4" h **$600**
Wild rose, blown out, pearlized dec, dark rose ground, orig label, 11" h **$275**

Phoenix vase, pink ground, raised white ferns and grasses, **$250.**

PICKLE CASTORS

History: A pickle castor is a table accessory used to serve pickles. It generally consists of a silver-plated frame fitted with a glass insert, matching silver-plated lid, and matching tongs. Pickle castors were very popular during the Victorian era. Inserts are found in pattern glass and colored art glass.

Amberina, melon ribbed IVT insert, SP lid, ftd frame, lid, tongs, c1875-95 .... **$700**

Colorless, diamond quilted pattern insert, silvered metal frame, 11-3/4" h **$200**

Cranberry, IVT insert, enameled blue and white florals, green leaves, shelf on frame dec with peacocks and other birds **$325**

Crown Milano, cylindrical hobnail insert shades from pink to opal, hand enameled dec, sgd "Pairpoint" silver

plate flower emb holder, orig tongs, 8-3/4" h **$2,150**
Double, vaseline, pickle leaves and pieces, resilvered frame **$800**
Mount Washington, opalescent stripes with light and dark pink, Pairpoint #604 frame, 11" h **$850**
Opalescent, cranberry, Daisy & Fern emb apple blossom mold, orig Empire frame, later tongs, Victorian, 11-1/2" h **$500**
Pink, shiny pink Florette pattern insert, white int., bowed out frame **$325**

Pickle castor, Westmoreland Block pattern jar, silver-plate stand with tongs, undetermined association, late 19th/early 20th century, **$120.**
Photo courtesy of Green Valley Auctions.

QUEZAL

History: The Quezal Art Glass Decorating Company, named for the quezal—a bird with brilliantly colored feathers—was organized in 1901 in Brooklyn, New York, by Martin Bach and Thomas Johnson, two disgruntled Tiffany workers. They soon hired Percy Britton and William Wiedebine, two more Tiffany employees.

The first products, which are unmarked, were exact Tiffany imitations. Quezal pieces differ from Tiffany pieces in that they are more defined and the decorations are more visible and brighter. No new techniques were developed by Quezal.

Johnson left in 1905. T. Conrad Vahlsing, Bach's son-in-law, joined the firm in 1918, but left with Paul Frank in 1920 to form Lustre Art Glass Company, which copied Quezal pieces. Martin Bach died in 1924, and by 1925, Quezal had ceased operations.

Marks: The "Quezal" trademark was first used in 1902 and placed on the base of vases and bowls and the rims of shades. The acid-etched or engraved letters vary in size and may be found in amber, black, or gold. A printed label that includes an illustration of a quetzal was used briefly in 1907.

Quezal lamp shade, feather-pull glass shade, signed, 5-1/4" h, **$175.**
Photo courtesy of David Rago Auctions, Inc.

Quezal vase, footed, ruffled opal rim, lamp shade shape, iridescent green and tan pulled feathers under feathered gold, sgd Quezal, 5" h, **$2,100.**
Photo courtesy of The Early Auction Company, LLC.

Quezal iridescent vase, shouldered form, everted opal rim, iridescent blue and yellow hooked feather, sgd Quezal 5-1/2" h, **$1,400.**
Photo courtesy of The Early Auction Company, LLC.

Quezal lamp shade, iridescent art glass, bell shape, gold zipper pattern, 5-1/2" h, **$145.**
Photo courtesy of The Early Auction Company, LLC.

Bowl, irid gold Calcite ground, stretch rim, pedestal foot, sgd "Quezal," 9-1/2" d..**$800**

Candlesticks, pr, irid blue, sgd, 7-3/4" h..**$575**

Ceiling lamp shade, drop, radiating irid gold and green leaf dec, domed irid ivory glass shade supported by brass ring suspended from three ball chains, two-socket fixture, shade inscribed "Quezal," Brooklyn, NY, early 20th C, 13-3/4" d, 21-1/2" l.....................**$6,325**

Chandelier, four elaborate gilt metal scroll arms, closed teardrop gold, green, and opal shades, inscribed "Quezal" at collet rim, very minor roughness at rim edge, 14" h ...**$2,000**

Cologne bottle, irid gold ground, Art Deco design, sgd "Q" and "Melba," 7-1/2" h..**$250**

Finger bowl and underplate, gold irid bowl, pontil sgd, ribbed underplate, sgd "Quezal," 4-1/2" d......................................**$300**

Jack-in-the-pulpit vase
Green pulled feather dec tipped in irid gold, alabaster body, shiny gold int., sgd "Quezal," 6-1/2" h....**$2,250**
Green pulled feather tipped in irid gold, sgd "Quezal," very minor wear to gold int., 6" h.....................**$2,000**

Lamp, desk, irid gold shade with green and white pulled feather dec, inscribed "Quezal" at rim, gilt metal adjustable crook-neck lamp, 14-1/2" h......................**$575**

Lamp shade
Aperture, irid gold, cylindrical, ruffled rims, signed, set of three, 4-3/4" h, 1-3/4" d....................**$235**
Aperture, ribbed bell form, calcite exterior, gold iridescent int., sgd on rim, 4-1/2" h, 2-3/16" d............**$180**

Low bowl, irid gold, ribbed shallow bowl, polished pontil, sgd, 4" d
....**$450**

Salt, open, shouldered, irid body, protruding ribs, pontil sgd "Quezal," 2-1/2" d, 1-1/4" h **$200**

Sherbet, irid gold body, blue coil dec, sgd "Quezal," 4" h **$700**

Toothpick holder, melon ribbed, pinched sides, irid blue, green, purple and gold, sgd, 2-1/4" h **$200**

Urn, cov, shouldered form, marigold body, overall green King Tut swirl pattern, matching lid, irid gold foot, sgd "Quezal" in silver, 13-1/2" h
....**$5,500**

Vase
Floriform, folded irid gold rim, green and gold leaf dec, sgd "Quezal S 651," 5-1/4" d **$2,350**
Floriform, wide mouth with stretched ruffled rim, irid gold interior, irid green, gold, and white ext., sgd "Quezal S 594," 6" h..............**$2,470**
Tri-fold flower form, random wintergreen loops over irid gold pulls, soft velvet gold irid int., sgd "Quezal," 5" h **$1,750**
Tulip-form body, pinched rim, green and gold irid pulled feather dec, circular foot with folded rim, base sgd "Quezal," 10-1/2" h **$18,800**

Whiskey taster, oval, irid gold, four pinched dimples, sgd "Quezal" on base, 2-3/4" h **$200**

Quezal Jack-in-Pulpit vase, flower form, iridescent gold, green pulled feathers, **$3,150.**
Photo courtesy of The Early Auction Company, LLC.

REVERSE PAINTING ON GLASS

History: The earliest examples of reverse painting on glass were produced in 13th-century Italy. By the 17th century, the technique had spread to central and eastern Europe. It spread westward as the center of the glassmaking industry moved to Germany in the late 17th century.

The Alsace and Black Forest regions developed a unique portraiture style. The half and three-quarter portraits often were titled below the portrait. Women tend to have generic names, while most males are likenesses of famous men.

The English used a mezzotint, rather than free-style, method to create their reverse paintings. Landscapes and allegorical figures were popular. The Chinese began working in the medium in the 17th century, eventually favoring marine and patriotic scenes.

Most American reverse painting was done by folk artists and is unsigned. Portraits, patriotic and mourning scenes, floral compositions, landscapes, and buildings are the favorite subjects. Known American artists include Benjamin Greenleaf, A. Cranfield, and Rowley Jacobs.

In the late 19th century, commercially produced reverse paintings, often decorated with mother-of-pearl, became popular. Themes included the Statue of Liberty, the capitol in Washington, D.C., and various world's fairs and expositions.

Today craftsmen are reviving this art, using some vintage-looking designs, but usually with brighter colors than their antique counterparts.

Mirrors

Reverse painted panel with fenced house, attributed to John Rupp, Hanover, York County, PA, Federal period, molding and columns, yellow and red grain paint dec frame, 12-1/4" w, 21" h.........................**$3,575**

Reverse painted white house, red and yellow roof, mahogany and mahogany veneer on pine, orig dark finish, reeded lower corner blocks and center divider, applied rope twist pilasters, scalloped cornice, turned acorn drops, orig backboards, some flaking to reverse panel, 13-1/4" w, 22-1/2" h.........................**$260**

Reverse painted panel with two men in boat on lake, cottage in background, attributed to John Rupp, Hanover, York County, PA, Federal period, molding and columns, yellow and red combed grain paint dec frame, 13-1/4" w, 25" h **$1,870**

Federal, primitive orig painting of houses with double chimneys near stream, mahogany frame with old reddish brown varnish, reeded pilasters, cove molded cornice and base, 18-1/4" w, 33-3/4" h.........................**$375**

Reverse painted panel with British naval battle scene, inner walnut veneered surround, giltwood and composition mirror with shaped crest centered by female mask and flanked by scrolls, mid-Georgian-style, 36-5/8" w, 38" h.........................**$4,700**

Portraits

Albert von England, military uniform with medal, sash, and epaulettes, titled in white bottom border, black painted frame, some flaking, damage to one corner, 9-1/4" w, 11-1/2" h.........................**$320**

George Washington, blue coat, ruffles, teal oval background, brown rect, white border, old burl walnut frame, 7-1/4" w, 9" h.........................**$690**

Lafayette, gray hair, blue and red military uniform, fur collared green coat, titled "Lafajetty" in bottom border, orig frame, some flaking, 9" w, 12" h.........................**$825**

Reverse painting sailing ship, windmill, original oval frame, **$95.**

Reverse painting portraits, left: gentleman in black suit, standing in room with dark green drape, patterned carpet, SRC, "B. F. Ferguson," shaped frame, slight losses, 16-1/4" w, 21-3/8" h, **$200;** *right: woman wearing royal blue gown, hook skirt, holding white fan and lace handkerchief, standing in room with pink drape, patterned carpet, S&DRC, "B. F. Ferguson 1867," shaped frame, stamp on reverse: "B. F. Ferguson Artist, S.W.Cor. 8th & Arch St., Philadelphia," 16-1/4" w, 21-3/8" h,* **$250.**
Photo courtesy of Alderfer Auction Co.

Reverse painting portrait of Martha Washington, c1830, 23-1/2" x 19-1/2", $250.

Photo courtesy of Pook & Pook, Inc.

Napoleon, military uniform, painted mat, cast plaster frame, 7-1/4" w, 8-1/4" h................................**$200**

Woman dressed in white, blue shawl, seated outdoors, holding basket of flowers on bounder in front, minor wear with flaking edges, possibly orig backboard, later gilt frame with black repaint, 11-1/2" w, 15-1/2" h **$920**

Young woman seated at tea table, holding white rose in hand, yellow skirt, blue jacket, white lace, white border mkd "Morgen," black painted frame, some flaking, corner cracked, 12" w, 15-3/8" h.............**$175**

Scenes

Perry's Lake Erie Victory, Sept. 10, 1813, naval battle scene, 7" x 9" ...**$250**

Mount Vernon, river, boat, and trees, old repainted frame, 8-1/4" w, 6-1/4" h **$550**

Country house in winter, gold painted frame, 10-1/2" h, 12-1/2" w........ **$75**

Ohio, side wheeler steamship, poplar frame, 10-1/2" h, 12-1/2" w **$175**

ROSE BOWLS

Reproduction Alert. Rose bowls have been widely reproduced. Be especially careful of Italian copies of satin, Mother of Pearl satin, peachblow, and Burmese, and recent Czechoslovakian ones with applied flowers.

History: A rose bowl is a decorative open bowl with a crimped, pinched, or petal top which turns in at the top, but does not then turn up or back out again. Rose bowls held fragrant rose petals or potpourri, which served as an air freshener in the late Victorian period. Practically every glass manufacturer made rose bowls in virtually every glass type, pattern, and style, including fine art glass.

Rose bowl, satin glass, herringbone pattern, dark pink shading to light pink, opal int., iron pontil mark, late 19th/early 20th century, 5-1/2" h, 5-1/2" d, $90.

Photo courtesy of Green Valley Auctions.

Amethyst and white leaf design, 5" d.......................................**$90**

Blue and white, shell design, floral dec, 6" d...................................**$120**

Blue and white, pleated, 5" d......**$95**

Bulbous ruffled top, pastel, frosted and opal vertical bands on body, English, Victorian, 4" h.....................**$125**

Cased, blue and white, flowers and leaf dec, 4" d..................................**$80**

Cased, orange and white satin, 5" d..**$100**

Cased, red and white satin, 5" d ...**$100**

Cased, yellow and white, 4" d **$75**

Diamond quilted, amethyst and white, 3" d **$100**

Green and white opalescent, ruffled rim, 5" d **$95**

Red and white shell design, 5-1/2" d.....................................**$110**

Satin, blue, 4" d **$90**

Satin, blue, ruffled, 5-1/2" h.........**$100**

Satin, crimped body, shading from medium to light blue, clear applied dec, 3" d, 1-3/4" d **$110**

Satin, diamond quilted mother of pearl, golden brown to golden cream, 3-1/2" d, 3-1/2" h **$495**

Satin, green, 4" d............................**$75**

Satin, green and white, leaf design, 4-1/2" d...**$115**

Satin, green and white, shell design, 5-1/2" d...**$125**

Satin, inverted crimped bulbous body shading from deep rose to pink, enamel floral dec, attributed to Thomas Webb & Sons, 3-3/4" h............**$100**

Spatter glass, orange and white, 5" d..**$90**

Rose bowl, Webb, Burmese, purple flower on green leaf Hawthorne branch, 2-1/2" h, $225.

Rose bowl, Harrach, blue, optic ribbed body, applied ruffled rim, 5" h, $75.

Photo courtesy of The Early Auction Company, LLC.

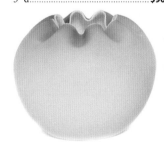

Rose bowl, satin, blue, large, ruffled rim, 5-1/2" h, $100.

Photo courtesy of The Early Auction Company, LLC.

SANDWICH GLASS

History: In 1818, Deming Jarves was listed in the Boston Directory as a glass maker. That same year, he was appointed general manager of the newly formed New England Glass Company. In 1824, Jarves toured the glassmaking factories in Pittsburgh, left New England Glass Company, and founded a glass factory in Sandwich.

Originally called the Sandwich Manufacturing Company, it was incorporated in April 1826 as the Boston & Sandwich Glass Company. From 1826 to 1858, Jarves served as general manager. The Boston & Sandwich Glass Company produced a wide variety of wares in differing levels of quality. The factory used the free-blown, blown three mold, and pressed glass manufacturing techniques. Both clear and colored glass were used.

Competition in the American glass industry in the mid-1850s resulted in lower-quality products. Jarves left the Boston & Sandwich company in 1858, founded the Cape Cod Glass Company, and tried to duplicate the high quality of the earlier glass. Meanwhile, at the Boston & Sandwich Glass Company, emphasis was placed on mass production. The development of a lime glass (non-flint) led to lower costs for pressed glass. Some free-blown and blown-and-molded pieces, mostly in color, were made. Most of this Victorian-era glass was enameled, painted, or acid etched.

By the 1880s, the Boston & Sandwich Glass Company was operating at a loss. Labor difficulties finally resulted in the closing of the factory on January 1, 1888.

Sandwich vase, trumpet, amethyst and colorless, gauffered rim, slightly twisted eight-panel vase, pestle stem fluted on inside, square base, 1840-60, McKearin plate 195, couple minor small base cracks, 10-1/8" h, **$5,000.**
Photo courtesy of Skinner, Inc.

Bowl, Gothic paneled arches, hexagonal, clambroth **$150**

Butter dish, cov, colorless, flint, Gothic pattern **$225**

Candlesticks, pr, pressed
Yellow, petal form candle cups, columnar shaft, sq stepped base, chips to petals on one, base edge and corner chips on both, c1850-65, 9-1/4" h **$600**
Translucent blue petal socket, clambroth dolphin standard, double-stepped sq base, few minor chips and cracks, c1845-70, 9-7/8" h **$1,530**
Translucent light lavender alabaster/clambroth, petal sockets, dolphins, wafer construction, double step base, 1845-70, 10" h **$3,300**

Champagne, Sandwich Star **$850**

Compote, cranberry overlay, oval cuts, enameled birds and flowers on inner surface, c1890, 10-1/2" w, 4-3/4" h **$495**

Creamer
Acanthus Leaf and Shield, colorless, plain rim, molded handle, octagonal even scallop foot, 1835-50, 4-1/4" h **$315**
Heart and Scale, colorless, molded handle, circular foot, 1838-45, 4-1/2" h **$220**

Decanter, blown-molded, quart, colorless, plain base, rough pontil mark, replacement pressed wheel stopper, McKearin GV-17, c1825-35, 11-1/2" h **$625**

Dish
Beaded Medallion and Urn, oval, colorless, shaped plain even scallop rim, chip under rim, 1835-45, 5-7/8" x 8" x 1-3/4" h **$90**
Double Peacock Eye, octagonal oblong, colorless, concave corners, variation with no background stippling on ends, plain cross bars in center, plain even scallop rim with interior beads, some loss to four corners, 1835-50, 9-1/8" x 12-1/4" x 2" h **$360**
Hairpin, colorless, scallop and point rim, near proof, shallow edge flake, 7-3/8" x 7-3/4" x 1-1/4" h, c1830-40 .... **$7,700**
Pipes of Pan, octagonal oblong, colorless, plain scallop and point rim, rope table ring, corner rim spall, 1930-40, 6-1/4" x 8-1/4" x 1-1/2" h **$310**

Fluid lamp
Bigler pattern, octagonal shaft, sq base, pewter collar, cobalt blue, 1840-65, 10-1/4" h **$1,120**
Circle and oval pressed fonts, pressed hexagonal baluster stem and base, clear, brass collars, base flakes, pr, 8-3/4" h **$250**
Colorless, conical font with button stem attached to pressed Lee/Rose No. 32 cup plate base, cork tube whale oil burner, rough pontil mark, minute base chips and flakes, 1828-35, 6-7/8" h **$1,980**
Cut overlay font of cobalt blue cut to clear, quatrefoil and punty cuts, brass columnar standard, sq marble base, minor base edge chips, 1840-65, 9-3/4" h **$950**
Sapphire blue, font wafer attached to pressed hexagonal base, early brass #1 collar, 1840-60, top of one loop chipped and later polished, 9-1/2" h **$1,045**

Fruit basket, on stand
Brilliant deep amethyst, basket with 32-point rim, 16 vertical openwork staves, 34-point star in sloping base, wafered to hexagonal knop and foot, possibly in-the-making shallow chip on knop, 1840-55, 8-1/4" d rim, 4-1/2" d foot, 8-1/4" h **$17,600**
Colorless, 32-point rim, 16 vertical openwork staves, 34-point star in sloping base, wafered to hexagonal knop and foot, 1840-55, 8-3/4" d rim, 4-1/2" d foot, 8-1/2" h **$615**
Cut overlay, triple dolphin base, font opaque white cut to colorless, connected to fiery opalescent base, heavily gilded dec on font, early #2 brass collar, brass connector, kerosene period, 1860-75, 11-3/4" h **$7,150**

Miscellaneous Sandwich glass: toothpick holder, footed compote, jar, lidded jar, four berry bowls, punch cup, rectangular tray, salt dip, miniature cup (damaged), saucer, creamer and three plates, **$380.**

Photo courtesy of Joy Luke Auctions.

Goblet, colorless, flint, Gothic pattern, 12-pc set **$650**

Inkwell, cylindrical-domed form, colorless, pink and white stripes, sheared mouth, applied pewter collar and cap, smooth base, 2-9/16" **$2,300**

Nappy

Crossed Peacock Eye, colorless, rayed center with alternating clear and stippled panels, shaped rim with plain even scallops, loss to several scallops, 1835-50, 9-1/4" d, 1-1/2" h **$150**

Plume and Acorn, medium amethyst, even scallop rim, small rim spall, 4-1/8" d, 1-1/8" h **$100**

Plume and Acorn, fiery opalescent, even scallop rim, minor flaking/ mold roughness, 5-1/8" d, 1-1/4" h **$55**

Paperweight, colorless and frosted, portraits of Queen Victoria and Prince Consort, 1851, 3-1/2" w, 1-1/4" h..**$220**

Pitcher

Amberina Verde, fluted top, 10" h..**$525**

Electric Blue, enameled floral dec, fluted top, threaded handle, 10" h.........**$425**

Plate, 6" d, lacy, Shell pattern.......**$175**

Pomade jar, cov

Bear, clambroth, emb "J Hauel & Co., Phila" under base, large chip to back of one ear, flange chips, 1850-87, 5" h **$490**

Bear, deep amethyst, polished around edge of cover and base, 1850-87, 3-3/4" h **$135**

Drum, slightly translucent jade green, plain shield, cover missing, minor rim flake, 3-1/2" h, 2-1/2" d **$360**

Salt, open, pressed, lacy

Shell pattern, red-amethyst, Neal SL 1, minor edge roughness, few base chips, c1825-50, 1-3/4" h **$650**

Beaded Scroll pattern, violet-blue, Neal Bs 3a, edge cracks and chips, c1825-50, 2" h **$360**

Sander, lacy, fiery opalescent, stippled rim with vertical chain of beads on body, rope-edge base, concentric circles under base, pewter cover missing, 2-3/4" x 2-3/4" d rim............**$470**

Spooner/spill, Sandwich Star, slightly translucent electric blue, hexagonal foot, polished pontil mark, 5" h, 3-3/4" d......................................**$1,265**

Sugar, cov, Star and Punty, colorless, octagonal, short paneled stem, circular foot, finial flake, roughness on rims, 1840-70, 8-3/4" h, 5-1/4" d base **$100**

Toddy, brilliant dark amethyst, lacy, Roman Rosette, edge chips, 5-3/8" d **$330**

Tray, oval, central butterfly and beaded bull's eyes, shoulder with fleur-de-lis, pinwheels, and fans, tiny even scallops on side rims, slight mold roughness, 1835-50, 6-1/8" x 9-1/8" x 1-3/8" h **$235**

Vase

Brilliant deep amethyst, panels continue to peg extension, wafered to octagonal base, 1845-65, 9-3/4" h, 5-1/2" d rim, 4-3/8" d foot **$4,950**

Elongated loop with bisecting lines, deep fiery opalescent/ opaque, hexagonal foot, polished table ring, 1835-50, 4-3/4" h, 3-1/2" d rim **$1,265**

Elongated loop with bisecting lines, medium brilliant amethyst, hexagonal foot, polished table ring, 1835-50, 4-3/4" h, 3-1/2" d rim.........**$990**

Pressed, tulip, amethyst, scalloped rim, paneled oval bowl, octagonal base, minor base chip, 10" h, c1840-60...................................**$2,115**

Pressed, tulip, dark amethyst, octagonal base, mid-19th C, price for pr, small chip on one petal, minor base chips, 10-1/4" h.....................**$9,400**

Pressed, tulip, dark amethyst, scalloped rim, octagonal base, very minor edge chips, c1845-65, 9-3/4" h **$4,600**

Ruby stained, acid etched leaves and polished grapes, notch-cut circular foot with polished center, tiny rim flake, 1880-87, 4" h, 3-3/4" d rim, 3-1/8" d foot............................**$145**

Whiskey taster, cobalt blue, nine panels **$175**

Satin glass pitcher, Diamond Quilted pattern, butterscotch shading to cream, ruffled and tooled rim, applied colorless handle, polished pontil mark, late 19th/ early 20th century, 8" h, 5" d, **$130.**

Photo courtesy of Green Valley Auctions.

SATIN GLASS

History: Satin glass, produced in the late 19th century, is an opaque art glass with a velvety matte (satin) finish achieved through treatment with hydrofluoric acid. A large majority of the pieces were cased or had a white lining.

While working at the Phoenix Glass Company, Beaver, Pennsylvania, Joseph Webb perfected mother-of-pearl (MOP) satin glass in 1885. Similar to plain satin glass in respect to casing, MOP satin glass has a distinctive surface finish and an integral or indented design, the most well known being diamond quilted (DQ).

The most common colors are yellow, rose, or blue. Rainbow coloring is considered choice.

Additional Listings: Cruets, Fairy Lamps, Miniature Lamps, and Rose Bowls.

Reproduction Alert. Satin glass, in both the plain and mother-of-pearl varieties, has been widely reproduced.

Bowl

DQ, MOP, rainbow, crimped, sgd "Patent," orig Maude B. Feld label, ex-Maude Feld, 4-1/2" d, 2-3/4" h **$1,100**

DQ, MOP, ruffled, shading from white to peach, 6" d, 1-1/2" h **$80**

DQ, MOP, rainbow, int. with fold down ruffled rim, four clear feet (slight roughness), berry pontil, mkd "Patent," ex-Maude Feld, 9-3/4" l, 6-1/4" h **$3,400**

Peacock Eye pattern, MOP, white, painted floral and ladybug dec, gilt highlights, scalloped, 10" d **$2,000**

Bride's basket
deep rose, enamel swan and floral dec, heavy bronze holder with birds perched at top, 15-1/2" h **$450**

Celery vase
MOP, cased blue, Herringbone pattern, waisted squared body, 5" h **$200**

Center bowl
DQ, MOP, rainbow, circular ovoid body, alternating bands of multicolored hues, heavily applied clear rigaree collar and thorn handles, clear stylized feet, ex-Maude Feld, 10" d, 9-1/2" h **$7,750**

Cologne bottle
Verre Moire, pulled three-color dec, coral and chartreuse on opaque white body, satin finish, crown-like cap attached to delicate chain to collar, anchor stamps and "cs fs" on collar, 3-1/2" d, 6-1/2" h **$750**

Cream pitcher

Blue, DQ, MOP, camphor reeded handle, 3-1/2" h **$200**

Blue, gold lettering "1893 World's Fair," made and dec by Mt. Washington, 2-1/2" h **$435**

Cruet
Rainbow, pastel blue, pink, and yellow swirls from base to trefoil spout, molded-in bulging ribs, polished pontil mark, ribbed applied handle, cut glass stopper, 7" h **$975**

Cup and saucer
Raindrop MOP, pink to white, 3" h cup, 5" d saucer **$385**

Epergne
pink and white, hobnail bowl, resilvered base and lily vase holder, 13-3/4" h, 10" d **$395**

Ewer

DQ, MOP, dusty pink shades to pale pink, air trays cross over 24 vertical ribs of melon shaped body, ruffled and crimped mouth, frosted clear handle with thorns, Victorian, 12" h **$350**

DQ, MOP, pink, fold over ruffled rim, applied rope handle, price for pr, 8-1/4" h **$100**

Glossy blue, tri-fold top, applied crystal twist handle, heat check in handles, price for pr, 9" h **$50**

Fairy lamp
blue shade and base, clear candle base insert, Victorian, 4-1/4" h **$225**

Lamp
white satin body, matching font with air-trapped Flower and Acorn design, enameled Japanese cherry blossoms, bronze ftd base with lions' heads, burner marked "Hinks & Sons Patent" and "Sherwoods Limited," retailer's soldered tag "T. R. Grimes, New Broad St., London," some flakes under font lip, 22" h **$1,260**

Mustard pot
bright yellow, gold prunus dec, SP top, Webb, 2-1/2" h **$450**

Rose bowl

Crimped body, shading from medium to light blue, clear applied dec, 3" h, 1-3/4" d **$110**

DQ, MOP, rainbow, trefoil shaped body, applied clear rigaree collar, berry pontil, three shaped clear feet, mkd "Patent," ex-Maude Feld, 4" h **$1,900**

Herringbone, blue MOP, crimped ruffled rim, 5" h **$50**

Inverted crimped bulbous body shading from deep rose to pink, enamel floral dec, attributed to Thomas Webb & Sons, 3-3/4" h **$100**

Salt shaker
rose shaded to white, MOP, DQ, tapered barrel, orig two-pc lid, 3-1/4" h **$550**

Spill vase
pale green body, hand enameled dec, Victorian, 10-1/8" h **$110**

Satin glass, gourd-shaped vase, pink shading to white, gilt and silver dec, opal int., late 19th/early 20th century, 8-3/4" h, 4-1/2" h, **$66.**
Photo courtesy of Green Valley Auctions.

Satin, pr. vases, Diamond Quilted pattern, 8" h, **$150.**
Photo courtesy of Joy Luke Auctions.

Satin glass basket, rainbow, Diamond Quilted, Mother-of-Pearl, ruffled rim, applied vaseline handle, sgd Patent, 8-1/2" h, **$1,150.**
Photo courtesy of The Early Auction Company, LLC.

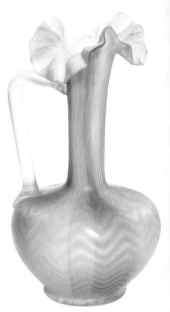

Satin glass ewer, rainbow, Diamond Quilted, Mother-of-Pearl, bulbous, footed, tri-fold rim, camphor handle, **$900.**

Photo courtesy of The Early Auction Company, LLC.

Satin glass, lace maker's lamp, pink mold blown shade, two-handled brass oil font holder, 17-1/2" h, **$825.**

Photo courtesy of The Early Auction Company, LLC.

Satin glass ewer, rainbow Mother-of-Pearl, alternating blue, red, and yellow panels, Herringbone pattern, ruffled rim, 9" h, **$800.**

Photo courtesy of The Early Auction Company, LLC.

Sugar shaker, Rainbow Mother-of-Pearl, ex-Maude Feld, 5-1/2" h **$4,760**

Tumbler, Rainbow, Diamond Quilted, enameled floral dec, pr, 3-1/2" h **$375**

Vase

Diamond Quilted, peach Mother-of-Pearl, bulbous, tight ruffled crimped rim, 7-1/2" h **$125**

Diamond Quilted, Mother-of-Pearl, flaring conical body, deep azure shading to pearl, gold prunus dec, applied thorn handles, attributed to Thomas Webb and Sons, 6-1/2" h.............**$800**

Diamond Quilted, Mother-of-Pearl, blue, shouldered, quadrafold rim, 7" h **$150**

Diamond Quilted, Mother-of-Pearl, butterscotch shading to pearl, 7" h **$85**

Diamond Quilted, Mother-of-Pearl, pink, bulbous, ruffled top, gilt design in center, 5-3/4" h.............**$150**

Diamond Quilted, Mother-of-Pearl, rainbow, bulbous, cylindrical neck, crimped fold down rim, 7" h **$800**

Diamond Quilted, yellow shading to white frost, gourd, 10-3/4" h **$170**

Herringbone, Mother-of-Pearl, top ground, 6" h **$50**

Pompeian Swirl, Mother-of-Pearl, blue shading to pale blue at base, pale blue cased int., two shiny upward spiraling ribbons, 5-1/2" h.........**$500**

Ribbed body, flaring ruffled to, shades from mahogany to lemon yellow, acid finish, 4-1/2" h.................**$325**

Stick, Mother-of-Pearl, blue, 5" h **$125**

Water pitcher, Mother-of-Pearl, cased, shading from rose to pink, Coinspot pattern, applied reeded handle, ground pontil, 8-1/2" h..**$425**

SCHNEIDER GLASS

History: Brothers Ernest and Charles Schneider founded a glassworks at Epiney-sur-Seine, France, in 1913. Charles, the artistic designer, previously had worked for Daum and Gallé. Robert, son of Charles, assumed art direction in 1948. Schneider moved to Loris in 1962.

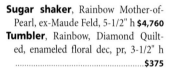

Although Schneider made tablewares, stained glass, and lighting fixtures, its best-known product is art glass that exhibits simplicity of design and often has bubbles and streaking in larger pieces. Other styles include cameo-cut and hydrofluoric-acid-etched designs.

Marks: Schneider glass was signed with a variety of script and block signatures, "Le Verre Francais," or "Charder."

Center bowl, rose and caramel-colored spattered glass, flared rim, wafer joined to ftd base with rolled lip, signed "Schneider" on side of base, 13-3/4" d, 7-3/4" h **$900**

Compote, shallow round bowl, pedestal base, mottled rose pink translucent glass with internal bubbles, shading to dark purple, polished pontil, acid etched "Schneider" on base, light edge wear, minor scratches, 8" d, 3-7/8" h **$300**

Ewer, elongated spout, mottled purples, pink, yellow, and orange splashes, applied purple handle, bulbed disk foot, acid stamp "France" on base, c1925, 10-3/4" h **$450**

Finger bowl and underplate, mottled red, burnt umber and clear, stamped mark, 4-1/2" d bowl, 7-1/4" d underplate **$350**

Tazza, shallow white bowl rising to mottled amethyst and blue inverted rim, amethyst double-bulbed stem, disk foot, sgd "Schneider," c1920, 7-5/8" h **$865**

Vase
Cameo dec, orange and mottled green against yellow body, base signature "Verre Francais," later marks "France Ovington New York," 12-1/2" h **$1,120**
Corset shape, internally dec, mottled amethyst and yellow, three amethyst Art Nouveau applied dec, sgd in hourglass in script, 8" h **$700**

Gold spattered body, coiled gold threading at shoulder, sgd with a vase and "Schneider," 3-1/8" h .. **$215**
Mottled orange ground, cameo cut with blue Art Deco design, candy-cane signature, c1920, 4-1/2" h . **$490**
Tapering cylindrical, baluster neck, orange overlay, five clusters of pendant grapes, geometric pattern cut foot over yellow mottled ground, inset cane at base, 14" h **$650**
Tapered form, incurvate rim, shaded orange overlaid in mottled brown, cameo-etched and cut cascading fruit and leaves, pedestal foot inscribed "Le Verre Francais," polished pontil, 17-3/4" h **$1,265**

SMITH BROS. GLASS

History: After establishing a decorating department at the Mount Washington Glass Works in 1871, Alfred and Harry Smith struck out on their own in 1875. Their New Bedford, Massachusetts, firm soon became known worldwide for its fine opalescent decorated wares, similar in style to those of Mount Washington.

Marks: Smith Bros. glass often is marked on the base with a red shield enclosing a rampant lion and the word "Trademark."

Reproduction Alert. Beware of examples marked "Smith Bros."

Atomizer, tan shading to cream opaque body, enameled amethyst and pink flowers, painted lion trademark, new hardware, 7" h **$260**

Biscuit jar
Green and pastel brown tendrils of ivy wind around melon ribbed body, gold plated fittings, sgd "405," 7" d, 8-1/2" h **$885**
Melon ribbed body shading from white to blue, polychrome enameled flowers, 6" d **$150**
Melon ribbed cream body, fall colored oak leaves, gold acorns, metal lid stamped "S.B.," 7" d, 7-1/4" h **$415**
Opaque cream ground, sculptured diagonal swirl pattern, polychrome

flower dec, red lion trademark, 7" h **$300**

Bowl
Lobed, pale pink ground, daisies dec, red rampant lion mark, 3" d **$150**
Melon ribbed, two shades of gold prunus dec, beaded white rim, 6" d, 2-3/4" h **$375**
Melon ribbed, beige ground, pink Moss Rose dec, blue flowers, green leaves, white beaded rim, 9" d, 4" h **$675**

Bride's bowl, opal glass bowl, painted ground, 2" band dec with cranes, fans, vases, and flowers, white and gray dec, fancy silver-plated holder sgd and numbered 2117, 9-1/2" d, 3" bowl, 16" h overall **$1,450**

Creamer and sugar, shaded blue

and beige ground, multicolored violet and leaves dec, fancy silverplated metalware, 4" d, 3-3/4" h **$750**

Humidor, cream ground, eight blue pansies, melon-ribbed cov, 6-1/2" h, 4" d **$850**

Mustard jar, cov, ribbed, gold prunus dec, white ground, 2" h **$300**

Plate, Santa Maria, beige, brown, and pale orange ship, 7-3/4" d **$635**

Ring vase, hand painted floral motif on vase, bamboo and butterfly motif silverplate stand, stamped "Tufts," 9" h **$75**

Salt and pepper shakers, silverplate napkin ring center on platform base, white shakers with blue floral trim, marked "Rockford #29" **$750**

SPANGLED GLASS

History: Spangled glass is a blown or blown-molded variegated art glass, similar to spatter glass, with the addition of flakes of mica or metallic aventurine. Many pieces are cased with a white or clear layer of glass. Spangled glass was developed in the late 19th century and still is being manufactured.

Originally, spangled glass was attributed only to the Vasa Murrhina Art Glass Company of Hartford, Connecticut, which distributed the glass for Dr. Flower of the Cape Cod Glassworks, Sandwich, Massachusetts. However, research has shown that many companies in Europe, England, and the United States made spangled glass, and attributing a piece to a specific source is very difficult.

Basket, ruffled edge, white int., deep apricot with spangled gold, applied crystal loop handle, slight flake, 7" h, 6" l **$225**

Bride's bowl, ruffled rim, yellow and white mottled ground, overall silver mica flakes, yellow stemmed blue daisies dec, 10-1/2" d **$90**

Candlesticks, pr, pink and white spatter, green aventurine flecks, cased white int., 8-1/8" h **$115**

Creamer, bulbous, molded swirled ribs, cylindrical neck, pinched spout, blue ground, swirled mica flecks, applied clear reeded handle, 3-1/4" d, 4-3/4" h **$225**

Cruet, Leaf Mold pattern, cranberry, mica flakes, white casing, Northwood **$450**

Ewer, raspberry pink ext., white int., mica flecks, twisted applied handle, rough pontil, 9-1/2" h **$250**

Jack-in-the-pulpit vase, oxblood, green, and white spatter, mica flakes, c1900, 6-1/4" h **$125**

Pitcher, white, and amber cased to clear, mica flakes, applied amber reeded handle, 8-1/2" h **$550**

Sugar shaker, cranberry, mica flakes, white casing, Northwood **$115**

Toothpick holder, alternating crimson and white mottled ground, gold mica, lattice stripes, 2-1/4" h **$65**

Tumbler, pink, gold, and brown spatter, mica flecks, white lining, 3-3/4" h **$90**

Vase
Glossy pink cased satin, silver mica, two applied crystal handles, 6-3/4" h **$75**
Stick, cased satin glass alternating pink and blue panels, overall silver mica, crystal rigaree around neck, 8-3/4" h **$75**

Water set, 9-1/2" h tankard pitcher, Aventurine, pink and white mottled ground, yellow and blue accents, metallic flecks, four matching 3-3/4" h tumblers **$350**

SPATTER GLASS

History: Spatter glass is a variegated blown or blown-molded art glass. It originally was called "end-of-day" glass, based on the assumption that it was made from batches of glass leftover at the end of the day. However, spatter glass was found to be a standard production item for many glass factories.

Spatter glass was developed at the end of the 19th century and is still being produced in the United States and Europe.

Spatter water pitcher, cranberry with opal spatter, triangular crimped top, polished pontil mark, colorless applied reeded handle, late 19th century, 8" h, $110.
Photo courtesy of Green Valley Auctions.

Reproduction Alert. Many modern examples come from the European area previously called Czechoslovakia.

Spatter bowl, tortoise shell pattern, amber ground, brown and black striations, $450.
Photo courtesy of Wiederseim Associates, Inc.

Basket, tortoiseshell, cream, tan, yellow, white, and brown spatter, white lining, rect, tightly crimped edge, colorless thorn handle **$120**

Berry set, master bowl and two sauces, Leaf Mold, cranberry vaseline **$300**

Bowl, amber and brown mottled tortoiseshell, 8-1/2" d **$90**

Box, cov, cranberry ground, white spatter, clear knob finial **$200**

Candlestick, yellow, red, and white streaks, clear overlay, vertical swirled molding, smooth base, flanged socket, 7-1/2" h **$60**

Cologne bottle, white spatter, enamel dec, orig stopper applicator, marked "Made in Czechoslovakia," price for pr, 5-1/2" h **$115**

Creamer, Leaf Mold, cranberry vaseline **$250**

Cruet, Aventurine, applied clear reeded handle, cut faceted stopper, 6-1/2" h **$375**

Darning egg, multicolored, attributed to Sandwich Glass **$125**

Ewer, yellow ground, white spatter, tri-fold spout, flared applied clear handle, sharp pontil, 8-3/4" h **$85**

Finger bowl and underplate, tortoiseshell, ruffled, 6" d, 3-1/4" d ... **$275**

Jack-in-the-pulpit, Vasa Murrhina, deep pink int., clear ruffled top, 5" h, 3-1/2" d **$115**

Pitcher, burgundy and white spatter, cased in clear, ground pontil, clear reeded handle, 6-1/2" d, 8" h **$395**

Rose bowl
Leaf Mold, cranberry ground, vaseline spatter **$250**
Mt. Washington, pink, blue, and white spatter on colorless ground, white opalescent scalloped top **$135**

Salt, maroon and pink, white spatter, applied clear feet and handle, 3" l **$125**

Sugar shaker, Leaf Umbrella pattern, cranberry **$495**

Toothpick holder, tubular design, crystal rigaree feet, 3" h **$60**

Tumbler, emb Swirl pattern, white, maroon, pink, yellow, and green, white int., 3-3/4" h **$65**

Vase
Aventurine, tapering global body, short cylindrical neck, white opaque lining, 4-3/4" h **$125**
Baluster shape, shades of blue, sgd "Czechoslovakia," 7" h **$50**

Watch holder, dish, ruffled rim, blue spatter, 7" h ormolu metal watch holder, 3-3/4" x 4-1/4" **$175**

STEUBEN GLASS

History: Frederick Carder, an Englishman, and Thomas G. Hawkes of Corning, New York, established the Steuben Glass Works in 1904. In 1918, the Corning Glass Company purchased the Steuben company. Carder remained with the firm and designed many of the pieces bearing the Steuben mark. Probably the most widely recognized wares are Aurene, Verre De Soie, and Rosaline, but many other types were produced.

1903–32

The firm is still operating, producing glass of exceptional quality.

Acid cut back

Lamp, table, ovoid shouldered form, blue Aurene cut to yellow jade, emb metal foot and collar, 22" h......**$2,000**

Vase
Catalog #7391, shouldered form, Green Jade, acid cut stemmed peony flowers and branches cut back to Alabaster, 10" h.......**$3,250**
Shape #5000, shouldered form, Green Jade over Alabaster, perched songbirds on leafy stems, sgd, 9-1/2" h.................**$2,000**

Animals

Colorless, NY, 20th C, inscribed "Steuben"

Donkey, standing, 10-1/2" h.......**$980**
Dove, on stand, abrasion to side of dove, 12-1/8" h..................**$635**
Eagle, imperfections, 4-3/4" h **$350**
Elephant, raised trunk, script sgd, 8" h
....**$100**
Frog, sitting, minor base wear, 4-1/4" l
....**$230**
Preening Goose, #8344, and Gander, #8355, clear, both sgd by artist Lloyd Atkins, orig box and pamphlet, price for pr, 5-1/4" h **$250**
Seal, resting on flippers, 8-1/2" l..**$375**
Shore Bird, light scratches to base, 8-3/8" l..............................**$115**
Snail, base scratch, 3-5/8" l..........**$115**
Squirrel, 4-1/8" h...................**$350**

Aurene

Atomizer, amber, gold irid finish, atomizer bulb missing, c1920, 6" h
....**$415**
Bowl, calcite int., remnants of orig paper label, 10" d........................**$450**
Bud vase, blue, gold highlights, sgd "Steuben Aurene 2556," 3" d base, 10" h..............................**$700**
Candlesticks, pr, catalog #686, amber, twist stems on applied disc foot,

strong gold luster, sgd "Aurene 686," c1920, 10-1/8" h................**$1,100**
Chandelier, five-light, gold Aurene ribbed bell-shaped shades, burnished bronze metal holder, five chain drop, dec griffin fleur-de-lis, refurbished and rewired, three shades sgd with fleur-de-lis mark, some damage to fitter ring of one, 40" h overall, 17" w........**$1,250**
Compote, shape #2604, gold, twist stem, applied cabochons, sgd "Aurene," 7" h **$1,600**
Darner, gold, some nicks and scratches from use, 5-1/2" l, 2-1/4" d.........**$850**
Goblet
Gold twist, stem, gold irid circular foot, sgd "Aurene 2361," 6" h ...**$250**
Gold, twist stem, sgd "Aurene 2861," 6" h **$250**
Grotesque bowl, 5" h, shape #7276, blue, strong coloring, sgd on bottom of one foot **$1,100**
Lamp base, 8-1/2" h shouldered form insert, pink, dec with gold Aurene random internal threading, acanthus leaf carving at stem, club shaped ftd base, dye stamped "Crest & Co.," 22" h overall **$3,000**
Lamp shade, irid green and gold drag loops, 5" h...........................**$225**
Low bowl, blue, three prunt feet, sgd "Aurene 2586," 12" d.................**$550**
Perfume, amber, irid gold finish, sgd "Aurene 1818," c1915, 6" h.........**$650**
Planter, blue, inverted rim, three applied prunt feet, engraved "Aurene 2586," 12" d **$775**
Sherbet, gold, stemmed, sgd "Aurene 2960," 3-1/4" h **$150**
Sherbet and underplate, gold, stemmed, sgd "Aurene 2680," 6" d, 4-1/2" h...............................**$250**
Vase
Shape #599, Style J, gold, leaf, vine, and millefiori dec, inscribed "Aurene" on bottom, 5-3/4" h **$3,750**

Steuben decanter, gold Aurene, footed bottle form, stopper, mkd in silver Aurene, c1910-1915, 10" h, **$1,200.**
Photo courtesy of The Early Auction Company, LLC.

Steuben trumpet vase, optic swirled, Green Jade body, applied disk foot, shape #6241, Steuben fleur-de-lis, 8" h, **$250.**
Photo courtesy of The Early Auction Company, LLC.

Steuben vase, iridescent blue Aurene, footed urn form, three attached ribbed handles, signed Steuben Aurene 6627, 6" h, **$900.**
Photo courtesy of The Early Auction Company, LLC.

Steuben, Aurene compote, blue twist stem, shape #686, signed Steuben Aurene 686, 6" h, **$1,100.**
Photo courtesy of The Early Auction Company, LLC.

Steuben bowl, gold Aurene, footed, flaring rim, signed Aurene 2851, 10" w, **$950.**
Photo courtesy of The Early Auction Company, LLC.

Steuben bowl, gold Aurene on Calcite, flaring form, large footed, #2851, 10" w, **$300.**
Photo courtesy of The Early Auction Company, LLC.

Shape #655, rich turquoise irid, dec with striated scrolling lappits, rich amber/pink irid, shouldered ovoid, inscribed "Aurene 655," 5-3/4" h **$17,000**

Shape #727, blue, flaring scalloped rim, sgd "Aurene 727," 6" h **$900**

Shape #2604, gold, corset shape, 7-1/4" h **$350**

Shape #2683, blue, sgd "Steuben Aurene," numbered, shouldered, 10" h **$1,600**

Shape #2683, gold, shouldered, sgd "Steuben," 6" h **$800**

Shape #2683, gold irid, brilliant pink and blue highlights, orig factory aperture filled, shouldered, 10-1/4" h **$950**

Shape #2909, flared rim, conical body, circular foot, rough pontil, gold, sgd "Steuben Aurene 2909," 5-7/8" h **$825**

Shade form, vertical ribbing, blue, sgd, 5" h **$900**

Squatty shouldered form, irid gold over calcite, sgd "Aurene F. Carder," 5-1/2" h **$475**

Calcite

Bowl
Ftd, opal, gold Aurene int., c1915, 8" d **$200**
Ftd, irid gold int., 10" d **$300**

Compote, amber bowl and foot, red and gold irid finish, irid blue rope twisted stem with gold finish, 8" h **$1,880**

Finger bowl and underplate, gold Aurene int., 6" w, 2-1/2" h **$200**

Lamp shade, dome, etched horizontal leaves, 5" h **$125**

Low bowl
Gold irid int., 10" d **$350**
Rolled rim, irid gold int., c1915, 12" d **$460**

Parfait and underplate, gold, partial paper label, 4-1/2" h, 5-1/4" d **$625**

Sherbet and underplate, stemmed, bright blue Aurene int., 6" d **$450**

Celeste Blue

Candlesticks, brilliant blue, applied foliate form bobeche and cups, bulbed shafts, c1920-33, set of four **$2,300**

Center bowl, catalog #112, swirled optic ribbed broad bowl, rolled rim, applied fluted foot, partially polished pontil, c1925, 16-1/4" d, 4-1/4" h **$400**

Finger bowl, underplate, catalog #2889, 5" d flared bowl, 6-1/2" underplate, swirled ribbed design, c1925, set of 12, some chips **$600**

Iced tea goblet, catalog #5192, blue, flared, light ribbon, set of eight, c1918-32, 6-1/2" h **$400**

Juice glass, catalog #5192, blue, flared, light ribbon, set of eight, c1918-32, 4-1/2" h **$375**

Luncheon plate, molded blue body, Kensington pattern variant, engraved border of leaves and dots, set of 12, c1918-32, 8-1/2" d **$550**

Sherbet, optic ribbed body, crystal stem, 4-1/2" h **$95**

Vase, clear glass handles, 10" d, 12-1/4" h **$1,700**

Wine glass, optic ribbed body, crystal stem, 4-3/4" h **$95**

Cluthra

Bowl, squatty shouldered form, pink shading to opal, 5-1/2" h **$600**

Lamp base, ovoid, creamy white cluthra acid-etched Art-Deco flowers, acid-etched fleur-de-lis mark near base, orig gilded foliate bronze lamp fittings, c1925, 12-1/2" **$2,070**

Vase, catalog #2683, rose, acid stamp script mark, 8" h **$2,600**

Wall pocket, half round flared bowl, black and white cluthra, cut and mounted to foliate gilt metal framework, polished pontil, slight corrosion to metal, c1930, 15-1/2" w, 8" h **$490**

Crystal

Bowl, basket shape, form #8079, inscribed "Steuben" on base, orig Steuben sock, 11-1/4" d **$150**

Calyx bowl, floriform oval, solid foot, inscribed "Steuben," 9-1/2" d, 3-3/8" h **$230**

Candlestick, shape #3178, green etched rim, 10" h **$150**

Center bowl, cov, dolphin and wave finial on cov, round bowl, applied wave motif on base, inscribed "Steuben," base scratches, 9" d, 12" h **$690**

Cocktail set, 15" h cocktail shaker, six matching 2-1/2" h glasses, two applied red cherries, wheel-cut leaves, and stems on shaker, ruby stopper, same dec on glasses, some with fleur-de-lis marks, slight damage to stopper **$3,700**

Goblet, flared cylindrical vessel,

knobbed stem, sq base, small "S" inscribed on base, designed by Arthur A. Houghton, Jr., Madigan catalog #7846, set of six, two with small chips, 1938, 7-1/16" h **$260**

Paperweight, sphere with randomly imp heart motifs, late 20th C, 2-1/2" d **$115**

Vase, catalog #SP919, flared wing form, pedestal base, inscribed "Steuben" on base, 7-3/8" h **$330**

Grotesque

Bowl, blue jade, Frederick Carder design, minor int. surface wear, fleur-de-lis mark, 11-1/2" l, 6-1/4" h **$3,850**

Vase

Amethyst, catalog #7090, pillar molded floriform body, ruffled rim shaded to colorless crystal at applied disk foot, acid script "Steuben" mark in polished pontil, c1930, 9-1/4" h **$525**

Ftd, cranberry at rim shades to clear, foot chipped, 11" h **$75**

Jade

Bowl, two-line pillar, ftd, alabaster int., fleur-de-lis acid stamp mark, 8" d, 6" h **$800**

Bud vase, green trumpet form vase with ruffled rim, supported on scrolled tripod hammered silver mount over round base, engraved "RAP" monogram, imp "Black Starr & Frost 7050 Sterling" on base, 7-3/4" h **$460**

Candlesticks, pr, No. 2956, jade candle cup and base, alabaster shaft, gold foil labels, 10" h **$550**

Compote, yellow, ftd, 10" h **$1,450**

Goblet, alabaster foot, 4-3/4" h **$95**

Lamp base, flared double gourd shaped dark amethyst body cased to alabaster int., overlaid with amethyst, cameo etched in Chinese pattern, double etched with scrolling design, gilt metal fittings with three scroll arms, shallow chip under fixture, 13" h **$1,850**

Parfait, applied alabaster foot, 6" h **$350**

Rose bowl, spherical, smooth jade crystal, 7" d, 7" h **$350**

Vase, catalog #1169, alabaster int., floral design, 3-1/2" d base, 8" h .. **$2,450**

Miscellaneous

Bowl, Old Ivory, catalog #7307, pillar ftd, applied raised foot, c1930, 6-1/2" h **$435**

Candlestick, shape #7564, Ivrene, ruffled collar, sgd "Steuben," 3-1/2" h **$200**

Center bowl, ftd, topaz body, celeste blue rims, eight swirl cabochons, 14" d, 8" h **$375**

Compote, stemmed, translucent body, translucent green rim, etched floral dec, 7" h **$175**

Cordial, optic ribbed body, gray blue, amber twisted stem, price of set of seven, 6" h **$450**

Finger bowl and underplate, optic ribbed amethyst body, turquoise lip wrap, bowls acid etched "Steuben" in block letters with fleur-de-lis mark, price for five matching sets, 7" w **$525**

Goblet

French blue, bubbles and reeding, corkscrewed stem, price for set of five, 8" h **$650**

Translucent, random bubbles, amber threading, 6-1/4" h **$115**

Lamp base, catalog #8023, urn form, swirled purple, blue, and red moss agate, gilt-metal lamp fittings, acanthus leaf dec, purple glass jewel at top, needs rewiring, 10-1/4" h **$2,415**

Paperweight, Excalibur, designed by James Houston, catalog #1000, faceted hand-polished solid crystal embedded with removable sterling silver sword, 18k gold scabbard, base inscribed "Steuben," 1963 .... **$1,955**

Serving plate, catalog #3579, Bristol Yellow, board convex and folded rim, slight optic ribbing, wear scratches, 14-1/4" d, 2" h **$200**

Sherbet and underplate, peach ground, intricately engraved, sgd in block letters, 5-1/2" h **$375**

Vase

Bristol Yellow, swirled, 10" h **$175**

Cintra, ftd ovoid, yellow, fleur-de-lis signature, 6-1/2" h **$850**

Green Silverina, ftd, translucent green, internal diamond quilted silver flecks, 7" h **$325**

Ivrene, flaring ruffled rim, 8" h **$425**

Wine glass, colorless, white air twist stems, script sgd, price for pr, 12" h **$300**

Oriental Poppy

Goblet, opalescent foot, 5-3/4" h ... **$325**

Wine glass, rose body, opalescent bands, vaseline tinted and opal rimmed foot, unmarked, 5-3/4" h **$320**

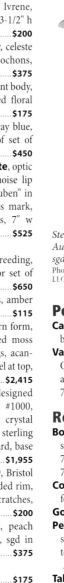

Steuben vase, trumpet flower form, gold Aurene, flaring ruffled rim, shape #346, sgd Aurene 346, 8" h, **$500**.
Photo courtesy of The Early Auction Company, LLC

Pomona Green

Candlestick, ornamental stem, acid block letters signature, 3-1/2" h ... **$200**

Vase, crystal, faint quilting, Pomona Green threading at top, shape #6980, acid stamped factory signature, 7-1/2" h **$325**

Rosaline

Bowl, one end folded in, other pinched spout, inscribed "F. Carder Steuben 723" on edge of polished pontil, 8" l, 7" w, 3-1/4" h **$350**

Compote, ruffled, alabaster stem and foot, 4" h **$275**

Goblet, crystal foot **$90**

Perfume, catalog #6412, teardrop shape, cloudy pink, applied alabaster glass foot, pr, c1925, 5-3/8" h **$435**

Table setting, four goblets with translucent rose bowl, clambroth foot, 7-1/2" h, four matching plates, 8-1/2" d **$1,260**

Selenium Red

Goblet, ftd, fleur-de-lis framing family crest, 4-1/2" h **$200**

Plate, acid etched factory mark and Carder post-production signature, 8-3/8" d **$200**

Spanish Green

Cordial, lead glass, applied ornamental stem, threading, random bubbles, acid stamped signature, set of six, one professionally repaired, 5-3/4" h **$475**

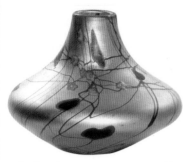

Steuben Aurene vase, squatty ovoid, gold Aurene dec with green leaf and vines, white millefiori highlights, shape #661, sgd Aurene 661, 3" h, **$3,250.**
Photo courtesy of The Early Auction Company, LLC.

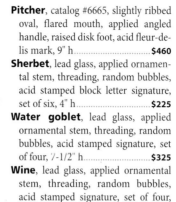

Pitcher, catalog #6665, slightly ribbed oval, flared mouth, applied angled handle, raised disk foot, acid fleur-de-lis mark, 9" h **$460**

Sherbet, lead glass, applied ornamental stem, threading, random bubbles, acid stamped block letter signature, set of six, 4" h **$225**

Water goblet, lead glass, applied ornamental stem, threading, random bubbles, acid stamped signature, set of four, 7-1/2" h **$325**

Wine, lead glass, applied ornamental stem, threading, random bubbles, acid stamped signature, set of four, 7-1/2" h **$325**

Verre De Soie

Bonbon, compote form, overall irid surface, swirled celeste blue finial, twisted stem, 6" h **$850**

Finger bowl and underplate, etched floral motif, 6" w, 2-1/2" h **$175**

Lamp shade, dome shape, price for pr, 3-1/2" d **$80**

Perfume, catalog #1455, ribbed body, celeste blue flame stopper, c1915, 4-1/2" h...............................**$400**

Vase

Classic form, notched rim, all over floral motif, 10" h **$450**

Ftd, lime green body, Verre de Soie irid finish, 6-3/4" h..................**$250**

STEVENS AND WILLIAMS

History: In 1824, Joseph Silvers and Joseph Stevens leased the Moor Lane Glass House at Briar Lea Hill (Brierley Hill), England, from the Honey-Borne family. In 1847, William Stevens and Samuel Cox Williams took over, giving the firm its present name. In 1870, the company moved to its Stourbridge plant. In the 1880s, the firm employed such renowned glass artisans as Frederick C. Carder, John Northwood, other Northwood family members, James Hill, and Joshua Hodgetts.

19th C

Stevens and Williams made cameo glass. Hodgetts developed a more commercial version using thinner-walled blanks, acid etching, and the engraving wheel. Hodgetts, an amateur botanist, was noted for his brilliant floral designs.

Other glass products and designs manufactured by Stevens and Williams include intaglio ware, Peach Bloom (a form of peachblow), moss agate, threaded ware, "jewell" ware, tapestry ware, and Silveria. Stevens and Williams made glass pieces covering the full range of late Victorian fashion.

After World War I, the firm concentrated on refining the production of lead crystal and achieving new glass colors. In 1932, Keith Murray came to Stevens and Williams as a designer. His work stressed the pure nature of the glass form. Murray stayed with Stevens and Williams until World War II and later followed a career in architecture.

Additional Listings: Cameo Glass.

Stevens and Williams vase, applied glass, optic ribbed corset body, clear glass to pink opalescent rim, four amber rigaree feet, two looped handles, central apple, four applied green leaves, 10" h, **$600.**
Photo courtesy of The Early Auction Company, LLC.

Stevens and Williams ewer, DQ, MOP, melon ribbed, pink, thorny camphor handle, **$700.**
Photo courtesy of The Early Auction Company, LLC.

Basket, tapering ivory body, inverted ruffled rim, appliqué of flowers and leaves, amber twist handle, Victorian, 8-1/2" h **$175**

Biscuit jar, cov, cream opaque, large amber and green applied ruffled leaves, rich pink int., SP rim, lid, and handle, 7-1/2" h, 5-1/2" d............**$300**

Bonbonniere, matching 4-3/4" d underplate, satin finish, swirling ribbon-like air traps on exterior of bowl and upper side of plate, crimson shading to golden pink at frilly edges, piecrust crimped edge underplate, bowl with robin's egg blue interior, under-plate with oyster white underside, 3-3/4" d, 2" h **$1,485**

Bowl, Osiris, mauve ground, swirling threaded dec, cased, 5" d **$1,430**

Box, cov, hinged, aventurine, green and red spatter, green metallic flakes, white lining, polished pontil, 4-1/2" d, 2-1/2" h..**$250**

Calling card receiver, applied amber handle, rolled edge, translucent opalescent ground, three applied berries, blossoms, and green leaves, three applied amber feet, 10" l **$750**

Ewer, Pompeiian Swirl, deep rose shading to yellow, off-white lining, frosted loop handle, all over gold enameled wild roses, ferns, and butterfly, 8-1/2" h, 5" w **$1,500**

Jardinière, pink opalescent, cut back, two spatter flowers and sunflowers, three applied opalescent thorn feet, leaves, and stems, minor damage, 6-1/2" d, 10" h **$350**

STIEGEL-TYPE GLASS

History: Baron Henry Stiegel founded America's first flint-glass factory at Manheim, Pennsylvania, in the 1760s. Although clear glass was the most common color made, amethyst, blue (cobalt), and fiery opalescent pieces also are found. Products included bottles, creamers, flasks, flips, perfumes, salts, tumblers, and whiskeys. Prosperity was short-lived; Stiegel's extravagant lifestyle forced the factory to close.

It is very difficult to identify a Stiegel-made item. As a result, the term "Stiegel-type" is used to identify glass made during the time period of Stiegel's firm and in the same shapes and colors as used by that company.

Enamel-decorated ware also is attributed to Stiegel. True Stiegel pieces are rare; an overwhelming majority is of European origin.

Reproduction Alert. Beware of modern reproductions, especially in enamel wares.

Bottle, blown

Brilliant deep peacock green, 15 diamonds, pot stone in neck, 5-3/8" h **$440**

Flattened octagonal, colorless, bright polychrome dec of deer on obverse, "1763" on reverse, floral dec on sides, flaring polished lip, kick up base, small flake, 6" h **$60**

Hexagonal, colorless, enameled white dove, red rose, scroll work, red, blue, yellow, and white floral designs, flared lip, 5-7/8" h **$175**

Bride's or cordial bottle

Blue, "VIVAT, es leben alle miller 1764," (long live all Miller's) central floral motifs surrounding folklore symbols, 6-1/8" h **$3,100**

Colorless, polychrome enamel floral dec, orig pewter collar with protruding threads, rough pontil mark, late 18th or 19th C, 4-3/4" h, 2-1/8" d x 2-1/2" **$315**

Flip glass, free-blown, polychrome enamel dec, colorless, rough pontil mark, late 18th or 19th C

Bird perched on heart and foliage, 3-1/8" h, 2-1/2" d rim, 1-5/8" d base **$440**

Bird perched on bright blue heart, above "3" and foliage, 3-1/2" h, 3-1/4" d rim, 2-1/8" d base **$385**

Bird perched on heart and foliage, 4-1/2" h, 3-3/4" d rim, 2-1/2" d base **$420**

Building, three tower wings, foliage, 3-1/4" h, 2-3/4" d rim, 1-7/8" d base **$425**

Front dec with bold tulip, back with stylized flower, 8" h, 6" d rim, 3-3/4" d base **$220**

Two double steepled buildings and foliage, 4-3/4" h, 3-3/4" d rim, 2-1/2" d base **$315**

Flask

Amethyst diamond and daisy, 4-3/4" h **$495**

Amethyst, globular, 20 molded ribs, minute rim chip, 5" h **$1,380**

Jar, cov, colorless, engraved sunflower and floral motifs, repeating dot and vine dec on cov, applied finial, sheared rim, pontil scar, form similar to McKearin plate 35, #2 and #3, 10-1/2" h **$750**

Tankard, handle, cylindrical, applied solid reeded handle, flared foot, sheared rim, pontil scar, form similar to McKearin plate 22, #4

Colorless, engraved with bird in elaborate sunburst motif, 5-3/4" h ... **$500**

Milk glass, red, yellow, blue, and green enameled dec of house on mountain with floral motif, old meandering fissure around body of vessel, 5-1/2" h **$150**

Tumbler, colorless, paneled, polychrome enameled flowers, 2-7/8" h **$220**

Steigel-type salt, master, cobalt blue, molded diamond quilted pattern, double ogee bowl, short stem, circular foot, tooled rim, pontil scars, 3-1/4" h, **$200.**

SUGAR SHAKERS

Amber, Paneled Daisy, Bryce Bros./US Glass Co., 4-1/4" h **$275**

Amethyst, nine panel, attributed to Northwood Glass Co., 4-1/2" h ...**$180**

Apple green, Inverted Thumbprint, tapered, 5-3/4" h **$160**

Blue, Inverted Fern, 5" h **$325**

Bristol, tall tapering cylinder, pink, blue flowers and green leaves dec, 6-1/4" h **$75**

Cobalt blue, Ridge Swirl, 4-3/4" h **$375**

Cranberry glass, molded fern pattern, 4-1/2" h **$150**

Custard, Paneled Teardrop, Tarentum Glass Co., 4-3/4" h **$110**

Cut glass, Russian pattern alternating with clear panels, orig SS top **$375**

Emerald green, Hobnail, US Glass Co., 4-1/4" h **$170**

Green, four blown molded panels, diamond and cross design, rib between each panel, lid mkd "E. P.," open bubble on surface, 5-3/4" h **$100**

Light blue, Paneled Daisy, Bryce Bros./US Glass Co., 4-1/4" h **$375**

Milk glass

Apple Blossom, Northwood Glass Co., 4-1/2" h **$160**

Quilted Phlox, white, hand painted blue flowers, Northwood Glass Co./ Dugan Glass Co. **$100**

Mt. Washington

Egg shape, yellow ground, blue, yellow, and amethyst mums, sgd, molded patent, 4-1/4" h **$200**

History: Sugar shakers, sugar castors, or muffineers all served the same purpose: to "sugar" muffins, scones, or toast. They are larger than salt and pepper shakers, were produced in a variety of materials, and were in vogue in the late Victorian era.

Fig shape, opalescent body, pansy dec, orig top, 4" h, 3-1/4" d ...**$1,200**

Light blue to white, enameled flowers, Pairpoint metal caddy, paper label from Mt. Washington Art Glass Society Annual Convention, 7" h ..**$950**

Melon ribbed, rose colored hues, raised blue and rust colored berries, emb metal lid, 4" h **$300**

Ribbed pillared body, enameled cascading Shasta daisies, emb metal lid, 5-1/2" h **$355**

Tomato shape, cream ground, raised white and blue flowers, 2-3/4" h **$230**

Opalescent glass

Beatty Honeycomb, white, Beatty & Sons, 3-1/2" h **$110**

Bubble Lattice, blue, 4-3/4" h **$325**

Chrysanthemum Base Swirl, blue, Buckeye Glass Co., 4-3/4" h **$275**

Coin Spot, bulbous base, blue, Hobbs, Brockunier & Co./Beaumont Glass Co., 4-3/4" h **$160**

Daisy & Fern, cranberry, 4-1/2" h **$230**

Poinsettia pattern, blue, roughness to fitter rim, 5" h **$375**

Reverse Swirl, white, Buckeye Glass Co./Model Flint Glass Co., 4-3/4" h **$120**

Spanish Lace, blue, roughness to fitter rim, 4-1/2" h **$200**

Swirl, cranberry, 5-1/4" h **$425**

Windows pattern, blue, roughness to fitter rim, 4-1/2" h **$250**

Opalware, Gillinder Melon, light blue shading to white, satin finish, hand painted multicolored floral dec, Gillinder & Sons, 4-1/2" h **$180**

Opaque

Acorn, blue, Beaumont Glass Co., 5" h **$230**

Alba, pink, Dithridge & Co., 4-1/2" h **$190**

Challinor's Forget-Me-Not, white, Challinor, Taylor & Co., 3-3/4" h **$90**

Cone, blue, Consolidated Lamp & Glass Co., 5-1/4" h **$140**

Little Shrimp, ivory, Dithridge & Co., 3" h **$100**

Parian Swirl, green, hand painted floral dec, Northwood Glass Co., 4-1/2" h **$175**

Quilted Phlox, light green, cased, Northwood Glass Co./Dugan Glass Co., 4-1/2" h **$210**

Rings & Ribs, white, hand painted floral dec, 4-1/2" h **$50**

Utopia Optic, green, hand painted floral dec, Buckeye Glass Co./ Northwood Glass Co., 4-1/2" h **$300**

Satin

Leaf Mold, light blue, Northwood Glass Co., 4" h **$325**

Leaf Umbrella, blue, Northwood Glass Co., 4-1/2" h **$425**

Slag, Creased Teardrop, brown shading to green, 4-3/4" h **$275**

Smith Bros

Blue body, polychrome flowers, 5" h **$125**

Melon ribbed, enameled flowers, 5" h **$250**

Spatter

Leaf Umbrella, cased cranberry, Northwood Glass Co., 4-1/2" h **$360**

Ring neck, cranberry and white, 4-3/4" h **$90**

Unidentified maker, opal glass body, blue stemmed flowers, Victorian, 4-3/4" h **$100**

Wave Crest, conical, polychrome fern dec, 5" h **$335**

Sugar shaker, ring neck, cranberry and white spatter, period lid split, late 19th century, 4-3/4" h, **$90.**
Photo courtesy of Green Valley Auctions.

Sugar shaker, Royal Ivy, cased spatter, period lid split and rusting, Northwood Glass Co., late 19th century, 4-1/2" h, **$360.**
Photo courtesy of Green Valley Auctions.

TIFFANY

History: Louis Comfort Tiffany (1849-1934) established a glass house in 1878 primarily to make stained glass windows. In 1890, in order to utilize surplus materials at the plant, Tiffany began to design and produce "small glass," such as iridescent glass lamp-shades, vases, stemware, and tableware in the Art Nouveau manner. Commercial production began in 1896.

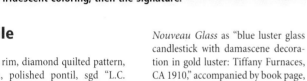

Tiffany developed a unique type of colored iridescent glass called Favrile, which differs from other art glass in that it was a composition of colored glass worked together while hot. The essential characteristic is that the ornamentation is found within the glass; Favrile was never further decorated. Different effects were achieved by varying the amount and position of colors.

Louis Tiffany and the artists in his studio also are well known for their fine work in other areas— bronzes, pottery, jewelry, silver, and enamels.

Marks: Most Tiffany wares are signed with the name "L. C. Tiffany" or the initials "L.C.T." Some pieces also are marked "Favrile," along with a number. A variety of other marks can be found, e.g., "Tiffany Studios" and "Louis C. Tiffany Furnaces."

Reproduction Alert. Tiffany glass can be found with a variety of marks, but the script signature is often faked or added later. When considering a purchase of Tiffany glass, look first to the shape, the depth of the iridescent coloring, then the signature.

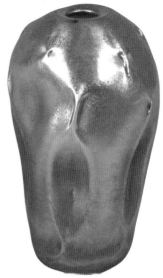

Tiffany Favrile vase, narrow mouth, swollen pinched shoulder tapers to base, indented sides, polished button pontil, paper label, c1902-1938, 5" h, **$1,175.**
Photo courtesy of Skinner, Inc.

Favrile

Bowl

Flared rim, diamond quilted pattern, aqua, polished pontil, sgd "L.C. Tiffany Favrile," numbered "1926," 8-1/8" d **$1,000**

Irid gold, sgd "L.C.T.," 6" d..........**$100**

Pastel, flattened flaring rim, yellow pastel body, opalescent feathering, stretch border, sgd around pontil "L.C.T. Favrile #1925," 5-3/4" d....................**$250**

Bowl and flower frog, irid gold, intaglio green lily pad and random green vines, double chain looped flower frog sgd "7127L L.C. Tiffany Favrile," 10" w **$3,900**

Bud vase

Flared rim, tapering cylindrical form, gold favrile, pulled blade dec, rough pontil, sgd "L. C. Tiffany-Favrile, Inc.," numbered "1504," 6" h ...**$825**

Ftd, irid gold, green pulled feather dec, sgd "1501 1980 LC Tiffany Favrile," 8" h...............................**$1,000**

Candle lamp shade, yellow pastel opal, pulled green and silvery irid feather dec, inscribed "L.C.T., N 841," c1900, 5-1/2" h..........................**$1,955**

Candlestick, baluster irid blue, King Tut pattern, gold int., attributed by Christian Revi in *American Art*

Nouveau Glass as "blue luster glass candlestick with damascene decoration in gold luster: Tiffany Furnaces, CA 1910," accompanied by book page, 10" h............................**$1,100**

Carafe, pinched ovoid body, elongated neck, topped with pinched and beaded stopper, ambergris, overall strong gold irid, polished pontil, base sgd "L. C. Tiffany Favrile 430," slight wear to rim, 11" h **$1,035**

Center bowl, deep blue irid swirling ribbed body, sgd "L.C.T. Favrile," orig paper label on pontil, 10" d, 3-3/4" h **$1,700**

Compote, floriform

Gold body, opal overlay, pulled green feathers, irid gold onion skin rim, inscribed "L.C. Tiffany Favrile 2648L," c1917, 4-1/2" h **$1,495**

Gold body, pinched ruffled rim, sgd "1504C L.C. Tiffany-Favrile," 4-3/4" h **$1,000**

Cordial, cylindrical flaring form, irid gold, sgd "L.C.T.," 3" h **$300**

Cup, gold, green arrowroot dec around the body, applied handle, sgd "L. C. Tiffany–Favrile," numbered "7246D," 2-1/4" h..**$650**

Decanter set, 11" h decanter with bulbous stopper, irid gold, fine hori-

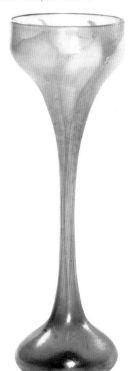

Tiffany flower form vase, bulbous stick form, iridescent green rim, white cala lily dec, signed T1179 L.C.T., c1903, 15-1/2" h, **$900.**
Photo courtesy of The Early Auction Company, LLC.

Tiffany candlestick lamp, gold Favrile, twisted base, ruffled shade, shade and base etched L.C.T., 13" x 7", **$1,800.**
Photo courtesy of David Rago Auctions, Inc.

Tiffany flower form vase, iridescent gold and amethyst optic ribbed foot, knopped amber standard, bulbous onion skin ruffled rim, gold Favrile, c1909, **$4,000.**
Photo courtesy of The Early Auction Company, LLC.

Tiffany blue Favrile vase, flower form, ribbed and footed, knopped stem, sgd. 1524-3372 M L. C. Tiffany Favrile Inc., c1900, **$1,600.**
Photo courtesy of The Early Auction Company, LLC.

zontal band of grapes dec, six matching sgd 4-1/4" h cordials **$5,500**

Dish

Extended ruffled rim, round form, blue, inscribed "L. C. Tiffany Favrile 1034-1595m," 5-1/4" d, 1-1/2" h.......... **$490**

Round rim, irid gold, inscribed "L.C.T.," paper label, polished pontil **$215**

Finger bowl, 4-1/4" d, pigtail prunts dec, sgd "L.C.T. T8919," 5-7/8" d ... **$475**

Finger bowl and undertray, gold favrile

Bowl with ruffled rim sgd "L. C. T.," 5-5/8" d undertray sgd "L. C. T." and numbered "R3491," 4-1/8" d ... **$500**

Bright blue hues, pigtail prunts, sgd "L.C.T. M9115," 6" w, 3" h **$450**

Flower frog, irid blue, two tiers of loops, sgd "L.C. Tiffany Inc. Favrile," numbered "488N," 1-1/2" d **$400**

Goblet, irid gold, sgd "LCT Favrile," 7" h **$550**

Lamp base, bulbous-shaped body, gold Cypriote finish, Doré foot, metal collar, foot die stamped "Cassidy Company Inc. New York," glass body sgd "Louis C. Tiffany Favrile," 25" h **$4,500**

Lamp shade, irid gold, inscribed "L.C.T. Favrile," c1900, 5" h **$575**

Low bowl, fold-over rim, optic ribbed body, irid gold, sgd "1883 L.C. Tiffany Favrile," paper label, 8" d **$550**

Nut dish

Gold swirled rib form, polished pontil, numbered "1401 L.C.T. Favrile," 3" d **$450**

Ruffled rim, irid gold, sgd "L.C.T. Favrile," 2-3/4" d **$175**

Punch cup, irid gold, dec with intaglio band of grapes and leaves, applied handle, sgd "L.C. Tiffany Favrile," 2-1/4" h.............................. **$400**

Rondel, circular disk, irid gold glass within metal rope-turned frame with loop handle, polished pontil, unsigned, minor wear, 17-3/8" d **$940**

Rose bowl, 10-ribbed form, ruffled rim, cobalt blue, overall blue irid luster, polished pontil sgd "L. C. Tiffany Favrile 1103-7725K," some scratches, 3-3/4" h.............................. **$865**

Salt, open

Gold, pinched inverted rim, polished pontil, paper label, 2-1/2" d **$300**

Gold, ruffled rim, polished pontil, sgd "L.C.T. Favrile," 2-1/2" d **$265**

Irid gold, four pronged feet, sgd "L.C.T.," 3-1/2" h **$450**

Tazza, pastel, aqua bowl, flattened stretch border, opalescent feathering, green tinted translucent stem, raised irid disc, sgd around pontil "L.C.T. Favrile 1702," 5-3/4" d, 6" h **$650**

Toothpick holder

Gold, trailing prunts, sgd "L. C. T.," numbered "D7626," 2-1/4" h ... **$250**

Tiffany decanter, gold Favrile, bulbous stick form, amethyst and red hues, matching stopper, sgd 595 L.C. Tiffany Favrile, 11-3/4" h, **$1,400.**
Photo courtesy of The Early Auction Company, LLC.

Tiffany Favrile vase, shouldered vessel, shading from opal to golden amber iridescence, random green decoration, signed "L.C.T. N 9919," c1900, 5-1/2" h, **$1,850.**
Photo courtesy of The Early Auction Company, LLC.

Tiffany lamp base, Favrile, iridescent, squatty stick form, opal glass, gren pulled feathers with blue iridescent Favrile, signed "56139H L.CV. Tiffany Favrile," 13" h, **$950.**
Photo courtesy of The Early Auction Company, LLC.

Gold, trailing prunts, sgd "L. C. T.," numbered "-3599," 2-3/8" h **$500**

Vase

10-ribbed gourd form, flared and ruffled rim above bulbed top, round disk foot, blue irid, inscribed "L. C. Tiffany Favrile 1089-68201," 10-1/4" h **$1,495**

Bulbous stick, flared rim, irid gold, sgd "2240J L.C. Tiffany Favrile," 4-1/4" h **$450**

Bulbous stick vase, flaring inverted rim, irid gold body dec with undulating white wave and gold zipper pattern, button pontil, sgd "A1493 L.C.T.," 10" h **$1,750**

Cameo, etched colorless body, white and pale yellow overlapping petals emerging from transparent green base, ftd, rolled base rim, rough pontil, sgd "L.C. Tiffany Favrile," numbered "4053D," 5-3/8" h
....**$11,200**

Colorless, alternating vertical bands of white opal, interior iridized in rich shaded azure blue, inscribed "L.C. Tiffany Favrile 1882," 8-7/8" h
....**$1,265**

Flared amber Favrile glass oval body, 25 tiny white cane blossoms among emerald green leaf leaves, amber stems, overall irid luster, inscribed "LCT Tiffany Favrile 2889C" around button pontil, 5" h **$2,415**

Flared rim, long cylindrical form, irid blue, sgd "L. C. T. Favrile," raised on pair of unsigned brass dolphin-form candlesticks, price for pr, 11-3/4" h **$2,235**

Floriform, blue, white and green hearts and vines dec, foot marked "5090 L. C. Tiffany Favrile," 6" h **$4,800**

Floriform, translucent green and variegated opal, pulled in feather design, slender stem, bell shape foot, inscribed "L.C.T. R 9927," 13" h **$7,130**

Floriform, wide circular opalescent glass cup with irid interior, ruffled edge, exterior dec with green striated leafage continuing to cylindrical stem, amber irid circular foot, unsgd, Corona period, 13-1/4" h **$3,000**

Floriform, gold int., green pulled feather on alabaster body, sgd "4749G L.C. Tiffany Favrile," 3" crack extends from rim into body, 4-1/2" h **$200**

Gold, high rounded shoulders with irid opal dec, marked "L. C. T. O1105," 7" h **$3,250**

Gourd form, random pulled designs in gold over yellow irid body, wafer pontil inscribed "LCT H1230," 9-1/2" h **$2,500**

Narrow mouth, bulbous body, blue, vertical tone on tone stripes, button pontil, sgd "L.C. Tiffany Favrile 7548H," 5-1/2" h **$1,880**

Tiffany vase, blue Favrile, flower form, tulip-form dec green hearts and vines, sgd 1220G L.C. Tiffany Favrile, c1912, 6-1/2" h, **$1,500.**
Photo courtesy of The Early Auction Company, LLC.

Tiffany bud vase, ribbed gold Favrile, flaring rim, etched 1730 L.C. Tiffany Favrile, 10" x 3-1/2", **$1,410.**

Photo courtesy of David Rago Auctions, Inc.

Tiffany Favrile vase, cylindrical, iridescent glass, internal tool design, sgd. 1168K L. C. Tiffany Favrile, c1916, 10-1/2", **$950.**

Photo courtesy of The Early Auction Company, LLC.

Tiffany Favrile glass vase, green leafage on gold, carved and internally decorated, engraved L.C.Tiffany Favrile 4252J, 6-1/4", **$6,000.**

Photo courtesy of David Rago Auctions, Inc.

Ovoid form, irid gold, covered in molded lily pad motif, conical pedestal, sgd "L.C. Tiffany-Favrile," 5-3/4" h **$950**

Ovoid tapering body, cylindrical neck, gold, covered in molded branch and leaf design, raised disc base, mkd "L.C. Tiffany Favrile 1559, 506P," 8-3/8" h **$1,500**

Protruding ribs, scalloped rim, irid gold, sgd "L.C. Tiffany Favrile #N5986," orig paper label on pontil, 8-1/2" h **$1,150**

Ribbed floriform body, ruffled rim, circular foot, irid gold, sgd "L. C. Tiffany Favrile," numbered "66D," 12-3/4" h **$2,710**

Swollen body tapering to bulbed stem, amber, dec with trailing vines and heart leaves, applied dark foot, sgd "L. C. Tiffany-Favrile 5603G," bubbles below surface, 9" h **$1,840**

Tapering, irid gold, intaglio butterfly and insect dec, sgd around pontil

Tiffany Favrile vase, ovoid form, iridescent gold with random brown vines w/iridescent green leaves, clusters of Millefiori, "4100H L. C. Tiffany Favrile," c1913, 4" h, **$2,750.**

Photo courtesy of The Early Auction Company, LLC.

"L.C. Tiffany Inc. Favrile 7924N," 4-3/4" h **$750**

Tapering ribbed body, irid waves, special order, sgd "L.C.T. 08136," 3-1/2" h **$1,200**

Translucent green, striking gold drips over rows of cascading irid drops, sgd "L.C.T. A214," 7-1/2" h **$2,500**

Trumpet, knopped stem, elongated irid gold body, flared rim, sgd "1509-9850L L.C. Tiffany-Favrile," 10" h **$1,300**

Wide mouth and shoulder, irid green, lower body shading to purple, polished pontil, sgd "L. C. Tiffany-Favrile," numbered "3525 L" on base, imperfections, 8-1/4" h **$1,880**

Vessel, gold, flared rim and shoulder on ribbed body, raised on circular foot, sgd "L. C. T. 63B," 3-5/8" h **$1,175**

Wine, irid gold, faceted stems, price for set of three, 3-3/4" h **$475**

Tiffany covered jar, Favrile, gold, two rows of lappets, jar etched "L.C.T. 1681," lid etched "M 7891," 9-1/2" x 6", **$18,000.**

Photo courtesy of David Rago Auctions, Inc.

Tiffany gold Favrile compote, flower form, scalloped rim, c1908 sgd 5934C L.C. Tiffany Favrile, 4-3/4" h, **$900.**

Photo courtesy of The Early Auction Company, LLC.

TIFFIN GLASS

History: A. J. Beatty & Sons built a glass manufacturing plant in Tiffin, Ohio, in 1888. On January 1, 1892, the firm joined the U. S. Glass Co. and was known as factory R. Fine-quality Depression-era items were made at this high-production factory.

From 1923 to 1936, Tiffin produced a line of black glassware called Black Satin. The company discontinued operation in 1980.

c1960

Marks: Beginning in 1916, wares were marked with a paper label.

Bell, June Night, crystal **$65**
Candlestick, June Night, duo, crystal
.... **$75**
Celery, Flanders, pink **$140**
Champagne
  Cherokee Rose, crystal **$20**
  June Night, #17358, crystal **$30**
  Palais Versailles, #17594, gold encrusted **$135**
  Plum, #17762 .... **$35**
Cocktail
  Byzantine, yellow **$15**
  Cerise, crystal **$28**
  Fuchsia, crystal **$20**
  June Night, #17538, crystal **$30**
Compote, cov, #17523, Wisteria, crystal Cellini foot, two minute rim nicks
.... **$395**
Console bowl, Fuchsia, crystal, flared, 12-5/8" d **$135**
Cordial
  Cordelia, crystal **$10**
  Flanders, pink **$150**
  Melrose Gold, #17356, crystal **$125**
  Persian Pheasant, crystal **$45**
  Westchester Gold, #17679, crystal ... **$95**
Cornucopia, Copen Blue, 8-1/4" ... **$90**
Creamer, Flanders, pink, flat **$230**
Cup and saucer, Flanders, yellow
.... **$100**
Decanter, Byzantine, crystal **$600**
Goblet
  Cherokee Rose, crystal **$28**

June Night, #17358, crystal **$35**
Palais Versailles, #17594, golden-crusted **$150**
Pink Rain, #17477, wisteria **$55**
Plum, #17662 .... **$35**
Iced tea tumbler
  Cerise, crystal **$28**
  June Night, #17358, crystal **$35**
  Pink Rain, #17477, wisteria **$55**
  Plum, #17662 .... **$35**
Juice tumbler
  Bouquet, gold encrusted, Killarney green **$75**
  June Night, #17358, crystal **$30**
  Palais Versailles, #17594, gold encrusted **$125**
Lamp, owl, rewired, 8-1/2" h, 5" d
.... **$500**
Martini glass, Shawl Dancer, set of four, 4-1/2" d, 3" h **$150**
Perfume bottle, parrot, slate gray painted finish, enamel dec, orig label, 4" h **$125**
Pickle, Flanders, yellow **$55**
Plate, Flanders, pink, 8" d **$35**
Rose bowl, Swedish Optic, citron green, mold #17430, c1960, 5-1/2" x 5" **$145**
Salad plate, June Night, crystal, 7-1/2" d **$22**
Seafood cocktail, liner, Palais Versailles, #17594, gold encrusted
.... **$175**

Tiffin lamp, figural, basket of fruit, **$250**.

Sherbet
  Cherokee Rose, crystal, tall **$24**
  Ramblin' Rose, crystal, low **$23**
Sherry
  June Night, crystal **$30**
  Shawl Dancer, crystal **$55**
Sugar
  Cerice, crystal **$25**
  La Fleure, yellow **$40**
Vase
  Crystal, artist sgd, 7-3/8" d, 14" h ... **$400**
  Dahlia, cupped, Reflex Green, allover silver overlay, 8" h **$225**
  Dark amethyst satin, poppy like flowers, 8-3/4" h **$200**
Wall pocket, ruby, 9" l, 3-1/4" w .. **$175**
Wine
  Byzantine, crystal **$18**
  Cherokee Rose, crystal **$40**
  Mirabelle, #17361, crystal, 6-1/4" h
.... **$48**
  Mystic, #17378, crystal, 5-5/8" h .. **$45**
  Palais Versailles, #17594, gold encrusted **$150**

TOOTHPICK HOLDERS

History: Toothpick holders, indispensable table accessories of the Victorian era, are small containers made specifically to hold toothpicks.

They were made in a wide range of materials: china (bisque and porcelain), glass (art, blown, cut, opalescent, pattern, etc.), and metals, especially silver plate. Makers include both American and European firms.

By applying a decal or transfer, a toothpick holder became a souvenir item; by changing the decal or transfer, the same blank could become a memento for any number of locations.

Toothpick holder, Diamond Spearhead, green opalescent, late 19th century, 2-1/4" h, **$44**.
Photo courtesy of Green Valley Auctions.

Toothpick holder, cranberry opalescent, Hobbs' no. 326 Windows Swirl, Hobbs, Brockunier & Co., late 19th century, 2-1/2" h, **$145.**
Photo courtesy of Green Valley Auctions.

Toothpick holder, Agata crimped top, 2-1/2" h, **$425.**
Photo courtesy of The Early Auction Company, LLC.

Toothpick holder, Hobbs' no. 101, Daisy and Button, Hobbs, Brockunier & Co., late 19th century, 2-3/4" h, **$145.**
Photo courtesy of Green Valley Auctions.

Bisque, skull, blue anchor-shape mark **$65**

China
Royal Bayreuth, elk **$120**
Royal Doulton, Santa scene, green handles **$75**
R. S. Germany, Schlegelmilch, MOP luster **$40**

Mt. Washington
10-lobe, crimson and blue floral dec, 2-1/4" h **$225**
Burmese, flared painted blue rim, mold-in ferns motif, scrolls at base, white blossoms with yellow dot centers, 2-1/2" h **$1,085**
Burmese, sq mouth, matte finish, diamond quilted, yellow rim,

2-3/4" h **$325**
Burmese, sq mouth toothpick holder, orig gilt, white, and yellow daisy dec, silvered plated Victorian frame mkd "James W. Tufts, Boston," 2-1/2" h **$1,000**
Burmese, tri-fold, ruffled rim, diamond quilted body, 1-3/4" h **$200**
Peachblow, sq mouth toothpick holder, shading from soft pink to soft blue, orig gilt dec and hp yellow daisies, silver plated Victorian holder mkd "James W. Tufts, Boston," 2-1/2" h **$9,500**
Ribbed pillar, blue flowers on leafy stem dec, 2" h **$175**

Pattern glass
Arched Fleur-De-Lis **$45**
Daisy and Button, blue **$75**
Fandango, Heisey **$55**
Hartford, Fostoria **$85**
Jewel with Dewdrop **$55**
Paneled 44, Reverse, platinum **$75**
Truncated Cube, ruby stained **$75**
US Coin, colorless, frosted Morgan one dollar coin, c1892 .... **$290**

Satin glass, 2-3/8" h, 3" d at top, 2" d base creamy white diamond quilted mother of pearl satin glass holder with tightly crimped top edge, polished pontil, hallmarked silver plated stand 7-3/4" l, 4" w, 3-1/8" h **$750**
Spatter glass, tubular design, crystal rigaree feet, 3" h **$60**

VAL ST.-LAMBERT

History: Val St.-Lambert, a 12th-century Cistercian abbey, was located during different historical periods in France, Netherlands, and Belgium (1930 to present). In 1822, Francois Kemlin and Auguste Lelievre, along with a group of financiers, bought the abbey and opened a glassworks. In 1846, Val St.-Lambert merged with the Socété Anonyme des Manufactures de Glaces, Verres à Vitre, Cristaux et Gobeletaries. The company bought many other glassworks.

Val St.-Lambert developed a reputation for technological progress in the glass industry. In 1879, Val St.-Lambert became an independent company employing 4,000 workers. The firm concentrated on the export market, making table glass, cut, engraved, etched, and molded pieces, and chandeliers. Some pieces were finished in other countries, e.g., silver mounts were added in the United States.

Val St.-Lambert executed many special commissions for the artists of the Art Nouveau and Art Deco periods. The tradition continues. The company also made cameo-etched vases, covered boxes, and bowls. The firm celebrated its 150th anniversary in 1975.

Ashtray, hexagon, colorless crystal, 6" w **$35**
Candlesticks, pr, colorless crystal, orig paper labels, 9-1/2" h **$250**
Cologne bottle, frosted cylindrical body, cameo cranberry floral relief, cut faceted stopper, 4-3/8" h **$175**
Cordial Glasses, set of six, bowls cased in cobalt blue, cut with band of circles over paneled flutes, single knopped

stem, spreading foot, 4-5/8" h **$250**
Epergne, five 6" h etched cameo cylindrical flower holders, stylized naturalistic brass frame, 10-1/2" h **$1,800**
Figure, parrot perched on bell, light cranberry, sgd "Val St Lambert, Belgique," 3-1/2" d base, 7-1/4" h **$275**
Paperweight, apple, colorless crystal, acid etched script signature, 4" h **$85**

Presentation vase, green ground, cameo cut chrysanthemums, maroon enameling, c1900, 14" h **$500**
Vase
Cobalt blue ground, overlaid in copper, all over emb rosettes, emb "Val St Lambert Belgique," c1910, 11-1/2" h **$575**
Emerald and colorless crystal, 8-3/4" d, 12" h **$550**

VALLERYSTHAL GLASS

History: Vallerysthal (Lorraine), France, has been a glass-producing center for centuries. In 1872, two major factories, Vallerysthal glassworks and Portieux glassworks, merged and produced art glass until 1898. Later, pressed glass animal-covered dishes were introduced. The factory continues to operate today.

Animal dish, cov
Hen on nest, opaque aqua, sgd..... **$95**
Rabbit, white, frosted **$85**
Swan, blue opaque glass **$110**

Butter dish, cov, turtle, opaque white, snail finial **$120**

Candlesticks, pr, Baroque pattern, amber **$75**

Compote, blue opaque glass, 6-1/4" sq **$75**

Mustard, cov, swirled ribs, scalloped blue opaque, matching cover with slot for spoon **$35**

Plate, Thistle pattern, green, 6" d
.... **$65**

Salt, cov, hen on nest, white opal
.... **$65**

Sugar, cov, Strawberry pattern, opaque white, gold trim, salamander finial, 5" h **$85**

Toothpick holder, hand holding ribbed vessel, opaque blue **$30**

Vase, flared folded burgundy red rim, oval pale green body, matching red enamel berry bush on front, inscribed "Vallerysthal" on base, 8" h **$490**

Two painted Vallerysthal milk glass strawberry-shaped sugar bowls, snail finials, 4-1/2" l, 5-1/2" h, each **$85**.
Photo courtesy of Joy Luke Auctions.

VENETIAN GLASS

History: Venetian glass has been made on the island of Murano, near Venice, since the 13th century. Most of the wares are thin walled. Many types of decoration have been used: embedded gold dust, lace work, and applied fruits or flowers.

Reproduction Alert. Venetian glass continues to be made today.

Bowl, deep quatraform bowl, applied quatraform rim, blue, clear internal dec, trapped air bubble square, circles, and gold inclusions, c1950, 7-1/2" w, 6-1/8" w **$360**

Candlesticks, pr, white and black glass, formed as coat on twisted stem coat rack on tripod base, black domed foot, 20th C **$275**

Centerpiece set, two 8-1/2" baluster ftd ewers, 8-1/2" ftd compote, red and white latticino stripes with gold flecks, applied clear handles and feet, three-pc set **$150**

Compote, cov, dusty amber body, blue lip wrap, floral finial, 7-1/2" d **$70**

Compote, open, pale green glass body, five gold metallic and colorless glass loop ornaments, price for pr, early 20th C, 7-7/8" h **$600**

Decanter, figural clown, bright red, yellow, black, and white, aventurine swirls, orig stopper, 13" h **$250**

Ewer, pinched sided, alternating green and opal panels, chain dec, 6" h ... **$65**

Goblet, shamrock shape, translucent, dec with pictorial medallions, intaglio cut gilt scrolling and flowers, Lobmeyer, price for pr, 6" h **$275**

Sherry, amber swirled bowls, blue beaded stems, eight-pc set **$495**

Table garniture, two 14-1/4" h clear glass dolphins on white diagonally fluted short pedestals, six 5-3/4" h to 7-3/4" h clear glass turtle, bird, seahorse, dolphin, two bunches of fruit in bowls, figures on similar white pedestals, including 20th C **$550**

Six Venetian birds on branch, 17" l, **$225**.
Photo courtesy of Joy Luke Auctions.

Vase, handkerchief shape, pale green and white pulled stripe, applied clear rope base, attributed to Barovier, 1930s, 8" h **$65**

Wine, alternating dec panels, 3-7/8" h
.... **$75**

Venetian glass, vases, swirled, price for pr, 20th C, 7" w, 9-1/2" h, **$300**.
Photo courtesy of David Rago Auctions, Inc.

WATERFORD

History: Waterford crystal is high-quality flint glass commonly decorated with cuttings. The original factory was established at Waterford, Ireland, in 1729. Glass made before 1830 is darker than the brilliantly clear glass of later production. The factory closed in 1852. One hundred years later it reopened and continues in production today.

Bowl, Kileen pattern, 9-3/4" d $260

Cake plate, sunburst center, geometric design, 10" d, 5-1/4" h $85

Cake server, cut-glass handle, orig box $80

Champagne flute, Coleen pattern, 12-pc set, 6" h $450

Christmas ornament, Twelve Days of Christmas Series, crystal, orig box, dated bag, orig sticker, brochure Partridge in Pear Tree, 1982 ....$450
Second, two turtle doves, 1985 ....$250
Four calling birds, 1987 ....$200

Compote, allover diamond cutting above double wafer stem, pr, 5-1/2" h $400

Creamer and sugar, Tralee pattern, 4" h creamer, 3-3/4" d sugar $85

Decanter, orig stopper, allover diamond cutting, monogram, pr, 12-3/4" h ... $300

Lamp, umbrella shade, blunt diamond cutting, Pattern L-1122, 23" h, 13" d $450

Napkin ring, 12-pc set, 2" h........$225

Tumbler, Colleen, set of six, orig box $400

Vase, diamond pattern, wreath around center, sgd, 6" h............................$225

Waterford, 5-1/2" d x 13" h vase with scalloped edge with mark; decanter and stopper with mark; open pitcher with mark; covered jar with mark; tall pitcher with long neck and stopper; two small pitchers; two small covered jars, one marked, price for grouping, **$700.**
Photo courtesy of David Rago Auctions, Inc.

WAVE CREST

History: The C. F. Monroe Company of Meriden, Connecticut, produced the opal glassware known as Wave Crest from 1898 until World War I. The company bought the opaque, blown-molded glass blanks from the Pairpoint Manufacturing Co. of New Bedford, Massachusetts, and other glassmakers, including European factories. The Monroe company then decorated the blanks, usually with floral patterns. Trade names used were "Wave Crest Ware," "Kelva," and "Nakara."

WAVE CREST WARE
c1892

Wave Crest biscuit jar, Helmschmeid Swirl, cylindrical form, mauve glass, cascading green stemmed white flowers, mkd in red Wave Crest C.F.M. Co., 10" h, **$350.**
Photo courtesy of The Early Auction Company, LLC.

Biscuit jar, cov, unmarked
Helmschmied swirl opaque white and tan body, red enameled flowers, 6-1/2" d **$460**
Pink and white background, melon ribbed, hp flowers, 5-1/2" d, 5-1/2" h **$250**
White ground, fern dec, 8" h **$200**

Bonbon, Venetian scene, multicolored landscape, dec rim, satin lining missing, 7" h, 6" w **$1,200**

Box, cov
Baroque Shell, Moorish Fantasy design, raised pink-gold rococo scrolls, fancy Arabic designs of pale turquoise and natural opaque white, lace-like network of raised white enamel beads, satin lining missing, 7-1/4" d, 3-3/4" h **$1,250**
Double Scroll, aqua blue tint, hp florals, sgd, no lining, 3" d **$275**
Heart-shape, opaque tan glass body, dec with red and yellow mums, Belle Ware, #4625/10, 6" d **$460**
Ormolu feet and handles, red banner back stamp, c1890, 5-3/4" l **$225**
Pink florals, fancy ormolu fittings, 7" w **$800**

Cigar humidor, blue body, single-petaled pink rose, pink "Cigar" signature, pewter collar, bail, and lid, flame-shaped finial, sgd "Kelva," 8-3/4" h **$685**

Cracker jar, blue and white hp florals, green and brown leaves, white Johnny jump-ups, puffy egg crate mold, 5-1/4" d, 10-1/2" h **$700**

Creamer and sugar, Helmschmeid pattern, pink stemmed flowers, 4-1/2" h **$350**

Dresser box, cov
Enameled violets, red banner back stamp, c1890, 4-1/4" d **$185**
Six-sided form, beaded enameling, unmarked, c1890, 4" d **$250**
Egg crate mold, enameled florals, un-marked, c1890, 5-3/4" l **$245**
Egg crate mold, hp florals, orig lining, red banner back stamp, 6-3/4" sq, 3-3/4" h **$320**
Egg crate mold, hp mums, shaded amber ground, ormolu mounted feet, reticulated shoulder, red banner back stamp, c1890, 6-3/4" w, 6-3/4" h **$2,425**
Florals, blue ground, mkd "Nakara C.F.M. Co.," c1890, 8" d **$900**

Wave Crest lamp base, opal vase, pink and white mums, amethyst scrolling, four-footed base, two-arm ormolu collar, 10" h vase, 24" overall, **$650.**
Photo courtesy of The Early Auction Company, LLC.

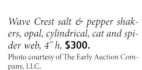

Wave Crest salt & pepper shakers, opal, cylindrical, cat and spider web, 4" h, **$300.**
Photo courtesy of The Early Auction Company, LLC.

Wave Crest powder box, blue floral dec, bronze mounts, complete with two ivory tipped feather powder puffs, 5-1/2" x 5", **$400.**
Photo courtesy of David Rago Auctions, Inc.

Wave Crest cracker jar, egg crate form, red and yellow roses, CF Monroe, 8" h, **$300.**
Photo courtesy of The Early Auction Company, LLC.

Wave Crest letter box, decorated with pink flowers, brass trim, 5-1/2" w, 4" h, **$350.**
Photo courtesy of Joy Luke Auctions.

Rococo mold, hp florals, orig interior, black block mark, c1890, 7-1/2" h **$525**

Swirl mold, enameled florals, red banner back stamp, hairline in lid, c1890, 7" h **$210**

Swirl mold, enameled florals, red banner back stamp, c1890, 5-3/4" d **$230**

Swirl mold, hp florals, unmarked, c1890, 7" h **$260**

Ewer, lavender, figural woman on handle, ornate base **$225**

Ferner, egg crate mold, enameled blue flowers, four lion emb feet, orig liner, 6-3/4" d **$520**

Mustard jar, cov, spoon, green ground, floral dec, unmarked **$140**

Pin dish, open

Pink and white, swirled, floral dec, unmarked, 3-1/2" d, 1-1/2" h **$35**

Pink and white, eggcrate mold, blue violets dec, marked, 4-1/4" d, 2" h **$80**

White, scrolls, pink floral dec, marked, 5" d, 1-1/2" h **$80**

Plate, reticulated border, pond lily dec, shaded pale blue ground, 7" d **$750**

Portrait box, cov, swirl mold, painted florals and cupid, block mark, c1890, 4-1/4" d **$250**

Salt and pepper shakers, pr

Swirled, light yellow ground, floral dec, unmarked **$75**

Tulip, brown and white ground, birds and floral dec **$70**

Sugar shaker, conical, polychrome fern dec, 5" h **$335**

Syrup pitcher, Helmschmied

Swirl, ivory-colored body, blue and white floral dec, smoky-gray leafy branches, SP lid and collar **$485**

Tray, flattened circular form, molded scrolled designs, hp floral dec in reserves, emb collar with openwork handles, sgd, discoloration to metal, 4-1/2" d, 1-3/4" h **$45**

Trinket dish, 1-1/2" x 5", blue and red flowers **$175**

Urn

Egg-shaped body, short pedestal, two ornate handles, centered raised gold, floral bouquet, pale green tinted ground, gold patina on metal fittings, 6-1/2" h **$445**

Horn shape over acorn-shaped body, short pedestal, two ornate handles, centered raised gold, floral bouquet, sea foam green tinted ground, gold patina on metal fittings, 6-1/2" h **$445**

Vase

Rococo mold, hp florals, ormolu ft base, red banner back stamp, c1890, 7-1/2" h **$275**

Swirl mold, ftd ormolu base, red banner back stamp, c1890, 7-1/2" h **$250**

White orchid blossoms with blue-gray shading, cobalt blue ground, gilt ormolu handles, 12-1/2" h **$2,450**

White wild rose blossoms, scattered sprays of gray rose buds, cobalt blue ground, gilt ormolu handles, 12-1/2" h **$2,450**

Vase ornament, light blue, detailed hand enameled dec, fine ormolu mounts, 6-1/4" h **$150**

WEBB, THOMAS & SONS

History: Thomas Webb & Sons was established in 1837 in Stourbridge, England. The company probably is best known for its very beautiful English cameo glass. However, many other types of colored art glass were produced, including enameled, iridescent, heavily ornamented, and cased.

Biscuit jar, cov, white cameo dec, single petaled blossoms, leafed branch, ruby red ground, silver plate fittings, 6" d, 7-1/4" h **$2,950**

Bowl

Alabaster, ruffled rim, hp silver and gold foliage and butterfly, turquoise int, 5" d **$250**

Burmese, lilac, prunus dec, 2" h **$6,000**

Burmese, silver rim, sgd "Thomas Webb & Sons," 4-1/2" d **$110**

Bride's bowl, hobnail, creamy opal body, rose int., ruffled rim, 10" d **$325**

Cabinet vase, rose ground, cameo carved white flower and butterfly, rim roughness, 2" h **$400**

Cane handle, globular form, cameo carved, intricate Moorish design, 3-1/2" h **$800**

Cologne bottle, Peachblow, bulbous, blue and white daisies, leafy green branches, two amethyst butterflies in flight, hallmarks on threaded ovoid cap, 5" h **$950**

Cream pitcher

Bulbous, round mouth, brown satin, cream lining, applied frosted handle, 3-3/4" h, 2-1/2" d **$210**

Sepia to pale tan ground, heavy gold burnished prunus blossoms, butterfly on back, gold rim and base, clear glass handle with brushed gold, 3-1/4" h **$385**

Epergne

Burmese, Hawthorne pattern, central post insert and three ruffled rim inserts, metal four-ftd base and holder, small chip, 11-1/2" h **$900**

Canary yellow center inverted pyriform vase with everted rim and rigaree collar, flanked by two peachblow apples, four downward curving vaseline leaves with amber stems, shaped mirrored plateau, ex-Maude Feld, 10-3/4" h **$18,000**

Ewer, satin, deep green shading to off-white, gold enameled leaves and branches, three naturalistic applies, applied ivory handle, long spout, numbered base, 9" h, 4" d **$425**

Figure, pig, solid Burmese body, pink tint to hind quarters, curly tail, four feet, ears, and snout, Webb, 3" l, 1-1/2" h **$750**

Flask, fish shape, lemon yellow glass overlaid in white, wheel carved features, sterling silver fish tail screw lid, cameo carved "Rd. 15711," lid imp "Sterling," hairline and cameo loss at mouth, 11-5/8" h **$9,500**

Lamp, kerosene, Burmese shade and base hand dec in Woodbine pattern, base with stamped trademark, 15" h **$4,250**

Perfume bottle, lay down style, circular, ivory, overall cameo flowers, emb flip lid, orig stopper, 2-3/4" h **$1,700**

Thomas Webb & Sons cameo decanter, three color, spherical body, white over crimson dogwoods, reverse with butterfly, embossed metal collar, flip lid with ornate chain, 9-1/2" h, **$3,250.**
Photo courtesy of The Early Auction Company, LLC.

Thomas Webb & Sons Diamond Quilted, Mother-Of-Pearl, rainbow epergne, three rose bowls, crystal stems, standard holds scalloped rim bowl, crystal acanthus leaf collar, mirror base, faceted undulating rim, all bowls sgd Patent 12" h, **$9,500.**
Photo courtesy of The Early Auction Company, LLC.

Thomas Webb & Sons double gourd vase, Peachblow, gold prunes dec, 7" h, **$500.**
Photo courtesy of The Early Auction Company, LLC.

Thomas Webb & Sons bride's bowl, pink satin, ruffled rim, glossy finish, stemmed gold branch dec, silver plate base, two lions, 11-1/2" h, **$2,450.**
Photo courtesy of The Early Auction Company, LLC.

Thomas Webb & Sons shouldered vase, opaque ivory, blue and pink stemmed flower dec, #16-27359, 10" h, **$100.**
Photo courtesy of The Early Auction Company, LLC.

Cameo carved leafy ferns and butterfly on reverse, monogrammed silver lid, 10" l **$1,650**

Rose bowl, Burmese, amethyst flowers, green and brown foliage, price for pr, 2-1/4" h, 2-1/2" h **$690**

Salad fork and spoon, ivory ground, cameo carved garden of stemmed flowers, hallmarked "F & Co." with crown and shield, 12" l **$700**

Scent bottle

Burmese, brilliant gold dec, restored gold cap, 3" d, 3-3/4" h
.... **$1,235**

Peacock Eye MOP, pearl white ground, sterling silver fittings, screw-on cap mkd "T. W. & S," hallmarks for 1902, "RD 58374" inscribed in base, minute dents in cap, 3" d, 4" h
.... **$950**

Sociable, Burmese, center crimped rim vase, three round covered dishes, delicate shading and dec, gilt metal ftd base, 8-3/4" h **$9,000**

Sugar shaker, herringbone MOP, tapering ovoid body shades from citron to pearl, British sterling silver cap with hallmark, acid stamped signature on base, 6-1/2" h **$500**

Vase

Alexandrite, honeycomb, 2-3/4" h
.... **$2,700**

Bulbous baluster, gold ground, carved white geraniums, carved white coral bells on reverse, sgd "Webb," 7-1/2" h **$1,750**

Bulbous stick, opal body, cinnamon iced crystal overlay, hand enameled gold flowering vine, numbered "1095-4P5aa," 6-1/4" h **$225**

Bulbous stick, tightly scalloped crimped rim, ivory ground, cascading honeysuckle dec, butterfly on reverse, sgd with half moon "Thos Webb and Sons," 7-3/4" h
.... **$1,000**

Burmese, trumpet, pink petaled rim shades to satin yellow, imp trademark, 8-1/4" h **$350**

Peachblow, tapering body, short everted neck, shades from deep cranberry to satin opal, allover applied coralene dec, 5-1/4" h **$200**

Peachblow, bulbous body extends to knopped conical neck, crimson to pink shading, enameled bird, butterfly, stylized flowers, gilt scrolls, 16" h **$1,200**

Shouldered, body shades from lime green rim to opal base, hp butterfly framed with leafy branch, mkd with registration number 676/5 R167, 7" h **$350**

Shouldered, deep crimson, enameled song birds perched on ginkgo flowering branches, numbered "893/7 P268," slight scratching on reverse, 7-1/2" h **$250**

Tapering ovoid, Prussian blue body, cameo carved opaque white floral cutting, cameo rings at top and base, butterfly on reverse, sgd, 7" h
.... **$1,700**

White blossoms and buds, carved pink folds and veins, frosted clear ground, butterfly on reverse, imp "Thomas Webb & Sons Cameo," 9" h **$3,450**

JEWELRY

STATE OF THE MARKET – COSTUME JEWELRY©

by Leigh Leshner

Collecting jewelry, just like collecting anything, can become an addiction. You find yourself looking for it everywhere. At garage sales, thrift stores, flea markets, auctions and the Internet. While the Internet has created a whole new market for collectibles by allowing anyone with a computer to sell their items worldwide, it has changed the field of collecting. Unfortunately, not necessarily for the better. Nationwide, well-established antique malls and stores have closed and attendance at antique shows is not what it used to be. People can now sit at home looking at a computer screen to find those rare one-of-a-kind items that they used to go out and hunt

for. The Internet has also opened up new sales arenas for dealers and individuals who want to sell their items. Now, instead of renting a mall space, they only need a computer and an Internet connection to reach a worldwide market. It's unfortunate to see this happening, because the fun of collecting is to go out and find that special item that you are looking for. It's the thrill of the hunt! Of finding that special item and holding it in your hands!

As with any collectible, when someone sees that money can be made, reproductions start to pop up. About ten years ago, there were some reproductions, but today the number of reproductions in the market have quadrupled. With the advent of technology, these reproductions often look very close to the originals. The pieces often have the company's signature and they have even perfected the pieces to show signs of age and wear. Some of the designers who are being reproduced are Weiss, Eisenberg, Staret, Trifari, Haskell and Coro. The best way to spot a reproduction is to be familiar with the way the originals look. Go out and look at the jewelry. Touch it, examine it, feel the weight of the piece. Look at the metal. Is it too bright? Does it seem new? By being exposed to a lot of jewelry, you become familiar with not only the pieces but familiar with the nuances which will be helpful in spotting reproductions.

Currently, there are reproductions and revivals of different styles and periods, especially Victorian and Edwardian pieces. Doing a search of the online auctions, approximately 50% of the Victorian and Edwardian pieces listed are reproductions. There are several things to look for to avoid buying a reproduction. One clue is the price. Most of these auctions start at 99 cents and have no reserve. That should be your first clue that they are not original pieces. Another basic hint to help you determine age is to look at the rhinestones in the piece. A lot of these reproductions use aurora borealis rhinestones. An aurora borealis rhinestone is a rhinestone that has an iridescent coating over it that gives it a rainbow effect. This type of rhinestone was not made until 1955 so it's not possible that these pieces were made prior to that date.

I always tell people don't be talked into buying a piece of jewelry simply because it is signed. Just because a piece of jewelry is signed, doesn't mean that it is more valuable. If it was ugly when it was made, it's still ugly now, no matter who made it. There are many pieces in the market that are unsigned and just as valuable as signed pieces. However, in today's marketplace, the pieces that are commanding the highest prices are signed costume jewelry. Among the designers that are bringing in top dollar are Miriam Haskell, Juliana, Kenneth Jay Lane, Schiaparelli, Eisenberg, Hollycraft and select pieces of Trifari and Coro. As a collector, you need to keep in mind hat a company made various lines of jewelry with varying quality. So while the piece may be signed, other factors such as the materials used, the design and the workmanship often determine the price that it will command. Looking online and in stores, flea markets and shows, this distinction is often not recognized and lower end, lesser quality jewelry is being priced disproportionately high.

For the past few years, Juliana jewelry has commanded high prices. This line of jewelry is unmarked but was originally sold with a hangtag indicating the maker. Very few of the Juliana pieces in today's marketplace still have their original hangtags, yet dealers and collectors continually attribute pieces to Juliana often citing the findings used on a piece of jewelry to "authenticate" that the piece is Juliana. What buyers and dealers alike should be aware of, is that the same findings were used by other makers as well. The findings were manufactured and then sold to many companies who used them in their designs. So unless the piece has a hangtag on it indicating the original maker, is signed or is authenticated by the company, it can't be definitively attributed to a specific maker.

Colorful, large rhinestone jewelry continues to be popular. Prices for the large ornate colorful rhinestone necklaces range between $250 - $1000 depending upon the size, maker and design. While the prices for clear rhinestone pieces have fallen, the clear rhinestone jewelry that still commands high prices are the ones that look like the "real thing." Art deco pieces reminiscent of precious gems such as diamonds, sapphires, rubies and emeralds continue to be sought after. Bakelite, a man-made plastic, is another type of costume jewelry that has retained its ability to demand high prices.

With the advent of the Internet, the market has been flooded with costume jewelry which, in turn, has brought the prices down for the average piece of jewelry. Pieces that had once been thought of as harder to find are now increasingly available on the Internet. The rare pieces, however, are still commanding high prices mostly due to the fact that they are becoming ever increasingly harder to find. Something that seems like an oxymoron, since there is a glut of jewelry available online.

With this overabundance of jewelry, comes a wide variety of condition levels. Unfortunately, many people who are selling the jewelry fail to distinguish the prices that should accompany the condition of the piece. As a buyer, you do need to focus on the condition and the quality. Is the piece well made? Is it missing any stones or pieces? Can the piece be repaired and how much will the repair cost? These are all questions that you need to ask yourself when you are purchasing a piece of jewelry. Be conscious of the condition of the piece, because it will effect the value. If the stones are yellowed, dark or missing, the value and the price should not be comparable to pieces that are in excellent to mint condition. Unless a piece is rare or one that you truly desire, think twice before purchasing it if it isn't in good condition. But if you can repair the piece yourself or have a jeweler do it and the price is reflective of the condition, low priced, then it might be worthwhile to purchase it. However, be advised that many jewelers will not work on costume jewelry.

Whatever you collect, just remember to collect what you like! Collecting, first and foremost, should be fun. Be conscious of the condition of the piece and don't be talked into buying a piece. Take your time to examine the piece. Use a loupe to look for signatures and other marks as well as damage. Learn as much as you can about the jewelry, so that you won't be fooled by reproductions or misinformation. By touching and seeking out the jewelry, you will become a wiser shopper.

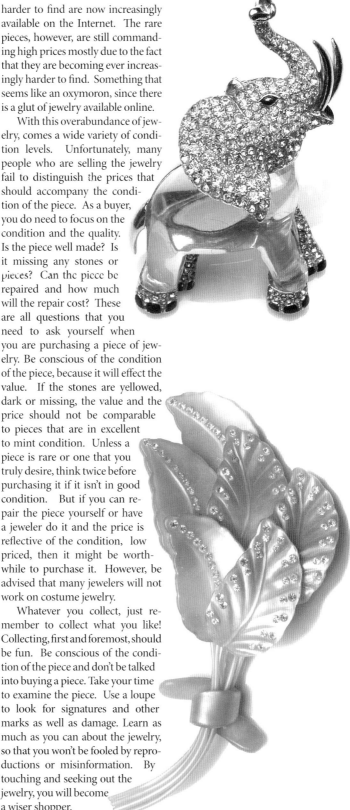

JEWELRY RESOURCES

100 Years of Vintage Watches, 2nd Ed., by Dean Judy, Krause Publications, Iola, WI.

Answers to Questions About Old Jewelry, 1840-1950, 6th Ed., by C. Jeanenne Bell, G.G., Krause Publications, Iola, WI.

Antique Trader Jewelry Price Guide, by Kyle Husfloen, ed., Marion Cohen contributing ed., Krause Publications, Iola, WI.

Collecting Art Plastic Jewelry, by Leigh Leshner, Krause Publications, Iola, WI.

Collecting Victorian Jewelry, by C. Jeanenne Bell, G.G., Krause Publications, Iola, WI.

Costume Jewelry, by Leigh Leshner, Krause Publications, Iola, WI.

Costume Jewelry Variations, by Marion Cohen, Krause Publications, Iola, WI.

Rhinestone Jewelry, by Leigh Leshner, Krause Publications, Iola, WI.

Secrets to Collecting Jewelry, by Leigh Leshner, Krause Publications, Iola, WI.

Vintage Jewelry, 1920-1940s, by Leigh Leshner, Krause Publications, Iola, WI.

Warman's© Jewelry, 3rd Ed., by Christie Romero, Krause Publications, Iola, WI.

Warman's© Jewelry Field Guide, by Leigh Leshner, Krause Publications, Iola, WI.

Warman's© Watches Field Guide, by Dean Judy, Krause Publications, Iola, WI.

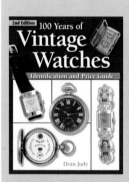

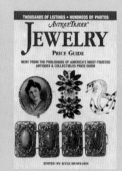
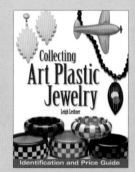

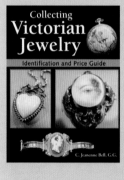

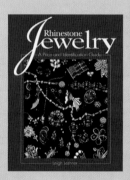

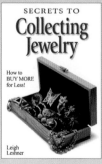

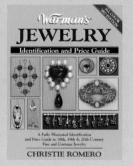

GALLERY

Brooch, Bakelite, horse head, seed pearl and gilt metal bridle, **$175.**
Photo courtesy of Skinner, Inc.

Egyptian Revival 14kt gold scarab brooch, ceramic scarab flanked by lotus flower, ankh and wing motifs, 1-7/8" w, **$705.**
Photo courtesy of Skinner, Inc.

Hatpin, Victorian, silver loops attached to brass, normal wear, early 20th century, 7" l, **$130.**
Photo courtesy of Green Valley Auctions.

R. Lalique brooch, "Meduse," profile version, clear and frosted, gray patina, orig gilt back, orig reflecting foil, stamped LALIQUE, c1912, 1-1/8" d, **$2,280.**
Photo courtesy of David Rago Auctions, Inc.

Haircomb, Georg Jensen, Skonvirke-aesthetic, symmetrical naturalistic flowers and leaves, scroll wire work, set with labradorites, marked G.J./830/S Denmark 43, 5" x 3-1/2", **$3,525.**
Photo courtesy of David Rago Auctions, Inc.

Shell cameo with sterling silver frame with marcasites, c. 1920, **$395.**

Necklace, Victorian, gold filled, wide mesh, cameo slide, 1873 patent date, 17-1/2" l, **$145.**
Photo courtesy of Green Valley Auctions.

Hinged bangle, Etruscan Revival, 18k yellow gold of Cerberus chained, naturalistic casting, minute granulations and beaded wire work, three rose-cut diamonds representing eyes, indistinct marks, 19th century, 29.5g gross weight, **$2,115.**
Photo courtesy of David Rago Auctions, Inc.

JEWELRY

History: Jewelry has been a part of every culture throughout time. It is often reflective of the times as well as social and aesthetic movements with each piece telling its own story through hidden clues that when interpreted will help solve the mysteries surrounding them. The jewelry is at times rich and elegant and at other times ornate yet simple. The pieces range in size and vary from delicate to bold made of both precious and non-precious materials.

Jewelry is generally divided into periods and styles. A circa date is only an approximation. It includes the period of ten years preceding and proceding the circa date. Each period may have several styles with some of the same styles and types of jewelry being made in both precious and non-precious materials. Additionally, there are recurring style revivals which are interpretations of styles from an earlier period. For example, the Egyptian revival that took place in the early and late 1800s, and then again in the 1920s.

Georgian, 1760-1837. Fine jewelry from this period is very desirable but few good quality pieces have found their way to auction in the last few years. Sadly, much jewelry from this period has been lost.

Victorian, 1837-1901. The Victorian period was named after Queen Victoria of England. She ascended the throne in 1837 and remained Queen until her death in 1901. The Victorian period is a long and prolific one; abundant with many styles of jewelry that it warrants being divided into three sub-periods: Early or Romantic period dating from 1837-1860; Mid or Grand period dating from 1860-1880; and Late or Aesthetic period dating from 1880-1901.

Sentiment and romance was a significant factor in Victorian jewelry. Often, symbols within jewelry and clothing represented love and affection with symbolic motifs such as hearts, crosses, hands, flowers, anchors, doves, crowns, knots, stars, thistles, wheat, garlands, horseshoes and moons. The materials of the times were also abundant and varied. They included silver, gold, diamonds, onyx, glass, cameos, paste, carnelian, agate, coral, amber, garnet, emeralds, opals, pearls, peridot, rubies, sapphires, marcasites, cut steel, enameling, tortoise shell, topaz, turquoise, bog oak, ivory, jet, hair, gutta percha and vulcanite.

Sentiments of love were often expressed in miniatures. Miniatures are portraits of a loved one. Sometimes they were representative of deceased persons, but often the miniatures were of the living. Occasionally, the miniatures depicted landscapes, cherubs or religious themes.

Hair jewelry was a popular form of jewelry that was an expression of love and sentiment. The jewelry was a way to keep the loved one near to you. The hair of a loved one was placed in a special compartment in a brooch or a locket or used to form a picture under the glass compartment. Later in the mid-nineteenth century pieces of jewelry were made completely of woven hair. Individual strands of hair would be woven together to create necklaces, watch chains, brooches, earrings and rings.

In 1861, Prince Albert died causing Victoria to go into mourning for the rest of her life. Victoria required that the royal court wear black. This atmosphere spread to the populace and created a demand for mourning jewelry. Mourning jewelry is another form of sentimentalism. It is a memento to remember a loved one. Mourning jewelry is typically black. When it first came into fashion, it was made from jet. Jet is a fossilized coal that was mined n Whitby, England. By 1850, there were fifty workshops that used jet o make brooches, lockets, bracelets nd necklaces. As the supply of jet dwindled, other materials were used such as vulcanite, gutta percha, bog oak and French jet.

By the 1880s, the dark, gloomy nd somber mourning jewelry was osing popularity. Mourning had beome relaxed. Fashions had changed. The clothing was simpler and had an air of delicacy. The Industrial Revolution which had begun in the early part of the century was now in full swing nd machine manufactured jewelry was affordable to the working class.

Edwardian, 1890-1920. The Edwardian period takes its name from n English Monarch, King Edward VII. Though Edward VII ascended the throne in 1901, he and his wife Alexandria of Denmark exerted influence over the style for the ten-year period before and after his ascension. The 1890s was known as La Belle Epoque. This was a time known for ostentation and extravagance. As the years moved on, the lines became simpler. The jewelry became smaller. Instead of wearing one large brooch, women were often found wearing several small lapel pins.

Into the 1900s, extravagance was again in vogue. Luxurious fabrics, sequins, beads and lace were used in clothing. Platinum, diamonds and pearls were prevalent in the jewelry of the wealthy, while paste was being used by the masses to imitate the real thing. The styles were reminiscent of the neo classical and rococo styles. The jewelry was lacy and ornate, feminine and delicate.

Arts and Crafts, 1890-1920. The Arts & Crafts movement was focused on the aesthetic appeal of a piece of jewelry. The heart of the movement was with artisans and handcraftsmanship. There was a simplification of form where the material was secondary to the design and craftsmanship. Guilds of artisans banded together. Some jewelry was mass-produced, but the most highly prized examples of this period are handmade and signed by their makers. The pieces were simple and at times abstract. They were handmade, hand hammered, patinated and acid etched. Common materials were brass, bronze, copper, silver, blister pearls, freshwater pearls, turquoise, agate, opals, moonstones, coral, horn, ivory, base metals, amber, cabachon cut garnets and amethysts.

Art Nouveau, 1895-1910. In 1895, Samuel Bing opened a shop called "L'Art Nouveau" at 22 Rue de Provence in Paris, France. He is credited with starting the Art Nouveau movement. Art Nouveau was influenced by the aestheticism of the late nineteenth century. The designs of the jewelry were characterized by a sensuality of the designs. Jewelry took on the forms of the female figure, butterflies, dragonflies, peacocks, snakes, wasps, swans, bats, orchids, irises and other exotic flowers. The lines were not angular. Instead, the designers used whiplash curves and exaggerated and stylized lines to create a feeling of lushness and opulence.

1920s-1930s. Costume jewelry was an outgrowth of the desire of the average person to have copies of the real jewelry that had previously been reserved to the wealthy. Costume jewelry began its steady ascent to popularity in the 1920s. Since it was relatively inexpensive to produce, there was mass production. The sizes and designs of the jewelry varied. Often, it was worn a few times, disposed of and then replaced with a new piece. It was thought of as expendable, a cheap throwaway to dress up an outfit. Costume jewelry became so popular that it was sold in both the upscale fine stores as well as the "five and dime."

During the 1920s, the fashion of the times was changing. These fashions were often accompanied by jewelry that drew on the Art Deco movement. The Art Deco movement, 1920—1935, got its beginning in Paris at the Exposition Internationale des Arts Decoratifs et Industriales Modernes. The idea behind this movement was that form follows function. The style was characterized by simple, straight clean lines, stylized motifs, geometric shapes and streamlined curves. Materials often used were chrome, rhodium, pot metal, glass, rhinestones, Bakelite and celluloid.

One designer who played an important role not only in clothing design but in costume jewelry design was Coco Chanel. She created costume jewelry to decorate her clothing. She knew the true meaning of the complete costume and she began wearing her costume jewelry; jewelry generally reserved for evening wear but Chanel wore it during the day, making it fashionable for millions of other women to do so too.

With the 1930s came the Depression and the advent of World War II. While life was often in turmoil, jewelry was one way to provide a respite. Women could purchase a relatively inexpensive piece of jewelry to spruce up an old outfit to make it look new. Designers began using enameling and brightly colored rhinestones to create wonderful whimsical designs of birds, flowers, circus animals, bows, dogs and just about every other figural you could imagine. Through the use of enameling and colored rhinestones, the jewelry was bright and festive.

Retro Modern, 1939-1950. World War II affected the world of fashion. The exportation of European clothing was down and domestic production was now at the forefront. The jewelry designs of the 1940s were big and bold. The jewelry had a more substantial feel to it and designers began using larger stones to enhance the dramatic pieces. The jewelry was stylized and exaggerated. The designers again indulged in their fantasies. Common motifs included flowing scrolls, bows, ribbons, birds, animals, snakes, flowers and knots.

Due to World War II, the use of pot metal (the tin and lead used in pot metal) was prohibited for use other than for the military. Sterling now became the metal of choice, often dipped in a gold wash known as vermeil. The vermeil was done in yellow, pink and rose gold.

Reflecting the world around them, the designers often created designs that had a militaristic feeling to it. The jewelry had themes of American flags, a v-sign for victory, Uncle Sam's hat, airplanes, anchors and eagles. These creations were made to be worn as a sign of support for the war effort and those involved in the fight for freedom.

Sterling pendant on black cord, designed by Björn Weckström, Finland, c1960s, **$900.**

Post-War Modern, 1945-1965. This was a movement similar to the arts & crafts movement that emphasized the artistic approach to jewelry making. It is also referred to as mid-century modern. This modernistic approach was occurring at a time when the beat generation was prevalent. These avant-garde designers created jewelry that was handcrafted to illustrate the artist's own concepts and ideas often manifesting itself in abstract and modern designs. The pieces were unusual and abstract. The emphasis was on the design. The materials often used in the jewelry were sterling, gold, copper, brass, enamel, cabochons, wood, quartz and amber.

1950s-1960s. The 1950s saw the rise of jewelry that was made purely of rhinestones. The stones had become the basis of necklaces, bracelets, earrings and pins.

The focus of the early 1960s was on the average woman. Functional clothing was back in style with Jackie Kennedy providing the role model. Clean lines, pill box hats and A-line dresses with short jackets were a mainstay for the conservative woman. The large bold rhinestone pieces were no longer the must have accessory. They were now replaced with smaller, more delicate gold-tone metal and faux pearls with only a hint of rhinestones.

At the other end of the spectrum was the beat collection which consisted of psychedelic colored clothing, Nehru jackets, thigh high mini skirts and go-go boots. These clothes were accessorized with beads, large metal pendants and occasionally big, bold rhinestones. However, times were changing and by the late 1960s, there was the movement back to mother nature and the "hippie" look was born. Ethnic clothing, tie dye, long skirts, fringe and jeans were the prevalent style and the rhinestone had, for the most part, been thrown to the wayside.

There are other areas of jewelry collecting that aren't defined by a period per se, but more by their styles and materials.

Novelty Jewelry is very popular. In the 1920s through the 1960s, new materials to jewelry making were used. Designers used celluloid, Bakelite, Lucite, wood, leather and ceramics to create whimsical figurals, flowers, vegetables, animals, people, western themes and geometric designs.

Mexican Silver: 1930-1970. Mexican silversmiths first made jewelry for tourists. The jewelry had pre-Hispanic and traditional Mexican motifs as well as some abstract modern designs. Artisans used silver, a combination of silver with brass or copper, alpaca, amethysts, malachite, obsidian, sodalite, tiger's eye, turquoise, abalone, ebony, rosewood and enameling to create their original designs. While hundreds of artists set up their shops in the town of Taxco, Mexico in the 30s and 40s creating a silversmith guild, there are only a relatively small number of well-known artisans who gained their reputation for their designs and craftsmanship.

Scandinavian Silver: 1900—1960. Scandinavian jewelry is another silver collectible that consists of jewelry manufactured in Denmark, Norway, Finland and Sweden. The jewelry has a distinct look and is often identified by its use of flowers, foliates, animal, modern, abstract and filigree designs. The material used included silver, bronze, gold, amber, amethyst, chrysoprase, citrine, crystal, lapis and enamel. The jewelry was generally produced in artist's studios and workshops where the focus was on design and craftsmanship. Import of the jewelry was relatively small with the large manufacturers being the exception.

Value: The value of a piece of jewelry is derived from several criteria, including condition, craftsmanship, scarcity and rarity, age and design. Condition is first and foremost. Don't overlook this. Be conscious of the condition of the piece because it will affect the value. The quality of the piece is also important. Look at the design of the piece. Is it intricate and ornate? Is it handmade or machine made? The more detail that is involved and the more handwork that is involved will generally make a piece more valuable.

While age does play a role in the value of a piece, don't be fooled into believing that antique jewelry has to be over 100 years old to have any value, and that the older the piece the more valuable it is- regardless of the condition.

Design: The factor of the design of the piece is a more subjective personal evaluation, more to do with your own personal taste. However, the design of the piece can help you determine the age of the piece and identify the period and style.

Scarcity and rarity play a role in the price of a piece. Obviously, if a piece is rare and hard to find, the price will reflect it.

The pieces listed here are antique or period and represent fine jewelry (i.e., made from gemstones and/or precious metals). The list contains no new reproduction pieces. Inexpensive and mass-produced costume jewelry is covered in *Warman's Americana & Collectibles.*

Adviser: Leigh Leshner

Note: The images used in this jewelry section are © Leigh Leshner, unless otherwise noted, and are used with permission. Leigh´s images were photographed by Maurice Childs.

FINE JEWELRY

Bar pin

Art Deco

Platinum and diamond, bezel and bead-set with old European and single-cut diamonds, approx. total wt. 2.74 cts.......................**$1,675**

Platinum and diamond, center old European-cut diamond weighing approx. 0.75 cts, further bead and bezel-set with fourteen old European-cut diamonds, millegrain accents, gold pin....................**$1,050**

Sapphires and pearls, A.J. Hedges & Co., alternately set with nine square sapphires and two rows of seed pearls, 14k yg mount, hallmark, 2-1/2" l.......................................**$300**

Edwardian, center line of bezel-set oval rubies, surrounded by 42 old European and full-cut diamonds, approx. total wt. 2.28 cts, platinum topped 14k gold mount, hallmark "AE K," Austrian guarantee mark...**$3,525**

Etruscan Revival, 14k gold, rose gold arched terminals, applied bead and wirework dec......................**$260**

Victorian, 14k yg, center carnelian intaglio of three cherubs within wirework frame, applied floral, bead, and ropetwist motifs..........................**$420**

Bracelet

Art Deco

Articulated geometric links bead and bezel-set throughout with 318 old European, square, and single-cut diamonds, approx. total wt. 11.79 cts, millegrain accents and open platinum gallery, French guarantee stamps, 7-3/8" l....................**$18,800**

Articulated links composed of 96 old European-cut and full-cut diamonds, approx. total wt 5.76 cts, channel-set onyx border, millegrain accents, platinum mount, sgd "Tiffany & Co.," one onyx missing, 7-1/8" l................................**$16,450**

Flexible links set with 191 full-and baguette-cut diamonds weighing approx. 5.53 cts, platinum mount, missing one small diamond, 7" l
....**$8,820**

Line of 40 prong-set old European-cut diamonds, framed by lines of channel-set square-cut emeralds, approx. total diamond wt. 3.98 cts,

platinum mount with 18k white gold clasp, engraved gallery, one emerald missing, 7-1/4" l......**$5,400**

Set throughout with old European, single, baguette, and marquise-cut diamonds, platinum mount, approx. total wt. 1.86 cts, 7" l.............**$3,000**

Seven center old mine and European-cut diamonds, approx. total wt. 1.75 cts, flanked by rect pierced links, 14k white gold, 7" l...............**$1,410**

Seven rect step-cut sapphires alternating with flexible honeycomb of bead-set old European and single-cut diamonds, approx. total wt. 4.64 cts, platinum mount, stamped "MD," French platinum guarantee stamps, 7-1/8" l....................**$16,500**

Art Nouveau, 14k yg, 10 openwork plaques in floral and scroll motif each centering collet-set sapphire, hallmark for Riker Bros., 7" l**$4,300**

Arts & Crafts, five bezel-set cushion-cut sapphires alternating with five old European-cut diamonds, approx. total diamond wt. 2.00 cts, joined by oval links, millegrain accents, c1915, 7-3/4" l...**$3,645**

Coin, 14k yg, heavy curb link chain suspending 1892 U.S. five-dollar coin in a wirework frame, 27.1 dwt., 6" l
....**$325**

Edwardian

Bangle, 14k yg, five bezel-set circular-cut sapphires within openwork design, 7" int. circumference...**$400**

Link, center old mine, European, and rose-cut diamonds in pierced and millegrain mount, flanked by knife-edge bar links, platinum-topped 18k gold, 6-1/2" l
....**$1,120**

Etruscan Revival, 18k yg, hinged bypass bangle terminating in two ram's heads, applied bead and wirework dec, 22.5 dwt, hallmark "P," evidence of solder, 6-1/2" int. circumference...**$2,585**

Post-War Modern, Van Gogh, hinged bangle, 14k yg, overlapping textured gold leaves highlighted by prong-set circular-cut ruby, emerald, and sapphire accents, 13.8 dwt, sgd "Van Gogh," c1950.............................**$530**

Retro Modern, double "tubogas"-style bracelet surmounted by bezel and bead-set old European-cut diamonds set in silver flowerheads,

Brooch, Czechoslovakian, garnet, mounted on brass, adapted for pendant, late 19th century, **$225.**
Photo courtesy of Sloans & Kenyon Auctioneers and Appraisers.

Victorian brooch, garnet carbuncle, bead-set pearls, coiled gold border, 14k yellow gold, c1880, 1-1/2", **$560.**
Photo courtesy of Sloans & Kenyon Auctioneers and Appraisers.

Ring, Georg Jensen, sterling Skonvirke, carnelian cabochon, no. 11A, c1933-1944, **$560.**
Photo courtesy of David Rago Auctions, Inc.

stems incorporating initials "H & L," 14k yg, French hallmarks **$420**

Victorian

Bangle, 14k yg, seed pearl buckle motif, black and brown enamel accents, small dents, 6-1/4" d interior circumference............**$550**

Slide, 18k yg, mesh design with adjustable oval slide engraved with scroll and fleur-de-lis motifs, edged

R. Lalique brooch, "Trois Anges," electric blue, orig gilt metal back, stamped LALIQUE FRANCE, c1912, 1-1/4" d, **$2,280.**

Photo courtesy of David Rago Auctions, Inc.

Late Georgian/early Victorian ring, silver and diamond, openwork navette form, river and single cut diamonds, 14k gold shank, size 5, **$500.**

Photo courtesy of Sloans & Kenyon Auctioneers and Appraisers.

Hair comb, micromosaic and silver filigree, curved panel, doves and foliage on blue field, minute shaded tesserrae, cannetille frame with trefoil, minor silver loss, 4" x 4", **$590.**

Photo courtesy of David Rago Auctions, Inc.

with palmettes dec with black tracery enamel, foxtail fringe terminals, 137.8 dwt **$1,200**

Brooch

Art Deco, diamond and platinum

Carved jade plaque depicting scrolling vines and gourds, corners accented by 22 single-cut diamonds, platinum frame, French guarantee stamps and hallmark **$2,585**

Center old European-cut diamond weighing approx. 1.29 cts, frame of 78 French, baguette, and circular-cut diamonds, millegrain accents, platinum frame, sgd "Raymond Yard"................................**$5,650**

Art Nouveau

Floral spray, white-cream translucent enamel lilies centered by cultured pearls, green enamel leaves, joined by gold coiled cord, 14k polished gold stems **$750**

Krementz & Co., light green enamel scrolling leaves centering heart-shape peridot, three old European-cut diamond accents, hallmark..........**$1,150**

Orchid, light greenish-yellow and purple openwork leaves, baroque pearl and old European-cut diamond highlights, retractable bail, 14k gold.................................**$1,275**

Pansy, yellow shading to purple enamel leaves edged by seed pearls, center old-European-cut diamond, retractable bail......................**$1,495**

Woman with flowing hair and dolphin with demantoid garnet eye amid waves within chased and engraved scallop shell, old mine-cut diamond moon, 14k yg mount...............**$400**

Arts & Crafts, Josephine Hartwell Shaw, 14k yg, center bezel-set oval amethyst surrounded by grapevine motif, sgd **$3,410**

Edwardian

Navette-form openwork brooch set with fancy-cut aquamarine and rose-cut diamonds **$600**

Sword and scabbard, 14k yg, connected by trace link chain, seed pearls, four prong-set old European-cut diamond accents **$235**

Post-War Modern

Robert Altman, 14k yg, seated poodle, prong-set with ruby, emerald, and sapphire highlights, 11.7 dwt, sgd **$470**

Richard Fishman, 24k yg, hand-formed openwork abstract circular brooch, sgd "Richard Fishman 1979" **$940**

Renaissance Revival, T.B. Starr, 18k yg, scrolling form, black and white enamel, seven cultured pearl accents, hair compartment on verso, sgd...**$1,645**

Retro Modern

Bow, pink and yellow gold, 14k, sgd "Tiffany & Co.," 5.4 dwt **$360**

Swirl, star and prong-set with full-cut diamond and ruby melee, flexible snake-chain terminals, 14k, 30.8 dwt..**$825**

Victorian

14k yg, boss framed by rope motifs terminating in double tassels star-set with rose-cut diamond melee **$300**

White gold, amethyst and cultured pearl, single oval amethyst with carved top of lady in profile, faceted bottom, white gold, 22 carats, surrounded by small pearls, 5.80 dwts **$800**

Buckle

Edwardian, rect openwork buckle edged with demantoid garnets spaced by old European-cut diamonds, silver-topped gold mount **$1,380**

Cuff links, pair

Platinum and diamond, geometric design, ten 0.10 carat round brilliant cut diamonds, 14.40 dwts **$490**

Platinum, ruby, and blue sapphire, two fine 0.40 carat rubies, two fine oval 0.40 carat blue sapphires, 12.40 dwts **$490**

Dress clips, pair

Art Deco

Platinum, two marquise shaped 1.20 carats diamonds, eighteen baguette cut 1.60 carats total diamonds, two 0.20 carat marquise shape diamonds, numerous small transitional round brilliant cut diamonds (2.50 carats total), 13.60 dwts **$5,260**

18k yg, WM Wise & Son, 18k yg, shield form, bead and bezel-set with old European-cut and single-cut diamonds, approx. total wt. 0.88 cts, millegrain accents, sgd **$1,880**

Earrings

Art Deco, pendant-type, each with jadeite cabochon and bead-set single-cut diamonds suspending jadeite drop, platinum mount, later silver screwback findings, missing one diamond **$1,765**

Etruscan Revival, 14k yg, pendant-type, coach cover, applied bead and wirework accents, later findings **$1,540**

Postwar Modern
Kanaris, 18k yg, dogwood blossoms, sgd "Kanaris," 14.3 dwt **$475**

Tiffany & Co., 18k yg, aventurine quartz, carved knot, sgd **$1,000**

Retro Modern, clips, 14k yg, abstracted floral form with circular-cut sapphires and cultured pearls, sgd "Tiffany & Co." **$450**

Victorian, pendant-type, gold, engraved foliate tops suspending two gold balls **$920**

Lavaliere
Edwardian
Amethyst, 14k gold, centered by oval amethyst within openwork scrolled frame surmounted by seed pearl trefoil, suspending similar drop, joined by trace link chain, 15" l **$450**

Platinum, heart-shape aquamarine suspends two collet-set old European-cut diamonds with pear-shape aquamarine terminal, three pearl accents, fine 14k white gold ropetwist chain **$1,410**

Egyptian Revival, 14k gold, centered by amethyst intaglio scarab within shaped lotus flower mount, baroque pearl drop terminal, stylized floral links, amethyst intaglio scarabs set at intervals, 16-1/2" l **$1,380**

Locket
Art Deco, 15k gold, sq black enamel locket unfolding to reveal six pages suspended from black enamel baton and fancy link chain, 28" l **$650**

Art Nouveau, 14k yg, helmeted Roman warrior in center, old European-cut diamond highlight, 4.4 dwt. **$150**

Edwardian
Carrington & Co., circular white enamel and green guilloche enamel locket accented by an old European-

cut diamond, platinum trace link chain alternating with green and white enamel baton links, hallmark, some enamel loss to locket, 20" l **$1,590**

French, 18k yg locket with pale blue guilloche enamel, rose and old European-cut diamond surmount, suspended from platinum chain with blue enamel baton links and seed pearls, French guarantee stamp on locket, 20" l **$2,700**

Victorian, 14k yg
Oval, turquoise enamel and five stars with old mine-cut diamond accents, reverse with hair compartment, pendant hook, later trace link chain, evidence of solder **$325**

Pale yellow gold engraved disc surrounded by deeper gold, heavily engraved frame, rose and white gold curb-link chain, 24.7 dwt **$365**

Necklace
Art Nouveau
Butterfly with bezel-set amethysts, seed pearl border, old European-cut diamond highlight, later amethyst drop, suspended later 14k gold and amethyst bead necklace, 16-1/2" l **$1,120**

Three center shaped cartouches designed with florettes and scrolls, joined by baton-shaped fancy links, 18k yg, French guarantee stamp, 6.5 dwt, 16" l **$1,000**

Arts and Crafts, elliptical-shaped jade within conforming enamel scrolled links joined by trace link chains, similarly set pendant suspending three jade drops, 18k gold, sgd "Tiffany & Co.," some enamel loss, 18" l .**$31,050**

Edwardian
Center articulated seed pearl and old European-cut diamond scrolling floral vine, joined by ropetwist chain, 15k gold, 15" l **$940**

Turquoise cabochons joined by delicate trace link chain, 10k gold mount, fringe loss to central tassel, 15" l **$450**

Etruscan Revival, Ivy leaf and berry motif, barrel clasp, 18kt yg, 15-3/8" l **$2,850**

Retro Modern, 14k yg, each link designed as leaf surmounting a ring, convertible to two bracelets, 72.8 dwt, 17" l **$1,120**

Victorian
14k gold and garnet, three floral engraved medallions surmounted by emerald-cut garnets set in ropetwist frames, reverse with plaited hair locket, suspended from snake chain, 16-1/2" l **$420**

18k yg, 18 concave disks centering coral bead within gold wirework frames, joined by oval-shaped links, some replaced beads and links **$1,650**

Negligee
Edwardian
Floral and foliate elements, old European and old mine-cut diamond, seed pearl accents, platinum mounts, one melee missing, later 19-1/2" l 14k white gold fancy link chain **$3,055**

Two rose-cut diamond flower terminals framed by calibre-cut rubies suspended from knife-edge bar links highlighted by bezel-set full and rose-cut diamonds, millegrain accents, platinum and 18k gold mount, orig fitted Parisian jeweler's box, 20" l fancy link chain **$4,935**

Pearls
Bracelet
Caged freshwater pearls interspersed with 18k gold beads with applied wirework, convertible to necklace with 14k gold rope chain, 8" l. **$425**

Seventy-two white cultured pearls with rose overtones, measuring approx. 5.90 to 6.0 mm, 14k white gold bar spacers and clasp with 11 full-cut diamond highlights, 7-1/4" l **$725**

Brooch, Mikimoto, 14k yg, designed as abstract leaf with clusters of cultured pearl flowers, sgd **$420**

Earclips, pr
Button pearl suspending chain link button pearl and diamond set cap terminating in teardrop shape pearl, set in 18k white gold, probably natural pearls **$3,300**

Elizabeth Locke, center gray pearl within 18k gold frame, hallmark **$1,880**

Necklace
Baroque, 31 South Sea Baroque pearls graduating in size from 10.70mm to 16.20mm, 14k white gold boule with diamond melee, 19-1/2" l **$4,700**

Ring, oval ring of diamonds, .33ct circular cut diamond, 14k white gold, central wire, c1935, .75ct total weight, size 5-1/2", **$558.**

Photo courtesy of David Rago Auctions, Inc.

Engagement ring, diamond, platinum box mount, flanked by channel-set rows of three single-cut diamonds, center European cut, 1.5 cts, size 7, **$2,938.**

Photo courtesy of David Rago Auctions, Inc.

Victorian carnelian cameo pin/pendant with earrings, c1870, profile of woman in relief, bezel set, 14k pink gold, pearl frame, 1-1/2" x 1-1/8"; earring converted to screw-back posts, 1" x 3/4", **$1,000.**

Photo courtesy of Sloan's & Kenyon Auctioneers and Appraisers.

Victorian pendant and earrings, yellow gold, enamel gentleman, freshwater pearl drop, 14k yellow gold, **$295.**

Photo courtesy of Sloans & Kenyon Auctioneers and Appraisers.

Cultured, David Webb, 31 graduated pearls measuring approx. 9.08 to 12.78 mm, invisible pearl and 14k white gold clasp, 16" l **$1,530**

Cultured, David Webb, 35 graduated pearls measuring approx. 11.02 to 13.12 mm, invisible pearl and 14k white gold clasp, 17" l, together with 3-3/4" l extension **$2,115**

Cultured, one hundred twenty-nine pearls ranging in size from 6.7 to 7.5 mm, 14k gold gem-set clasp, 14-1/2" l **$410**

Pendant

Art Deco

Platinum, numerous small old European cut diamonds (3.70 carats total), 18k white gold chain, 10.90 dwts **$4,185**

Sterling silver, coral and black enamel, Theodore Fahrner, offset by two rect faceted black stone panels (probably onyx), gilt chain mkd "935," pendant stamped "TF (linked) 935" **$1,880**

Art Nouveau

Collet-set sapphires and diamonds set within trefoil open wirework form, accented by rose-cut diamond points, joined by later festoons of fine trace link chain terminating in rose and circular-cut diamonds within triangular frames, later clasp, 18-1/2" l **$1,410**

Plique-a-jour enamel, lavender and green irid enamel flowers, green, pink, and white plique-a-jour enamel leaves, rose-cut diamonds and pearl accents, 18k gold mount with later faux pearl chain **$1,265**

Cartier, designed as cross composed of eleven rect-cut aquamarines, 18k yg, sgd, provenance: from estate of Reverend Thomas Mary O'Leary (1875-1949), Bishop of Springfield **$1,410**

Edwardian

Platinum top, 18k yg, four 3.00 mm pearls, one old European cut diamond, 24 rose-cut diamonds (0.34 carat total) 4.70 dwts **$1,100**

Platinum top, 18k yg, one old European 0.60 carat diamond, 59 rose-cut diamonds (0.70 carat total) suspended from 14k white gold chain, 3.40 dwts **$1,920**

Renaissance Revival, shield form with Renaissance motifs, rose-cut diamonds, rubies, pearls and emerald, cobalt blue enamel highlights, silver-topped 18k gold mount **$885**

Victorian

Circular pendant edged by gold beads and decorated with black tracery enamel, suspending gold bead pendants, fancy double trace link chain, 14k yg, 14.1 dwt., 23-1/2" l **$385**

Pietra dura, rose branch, one open flower, two buds, inlaid in shades of pink, varying shades of green as leaves, 14k rose gold bezel and bale **$400**

Pendant/brooch

Art Deco, platinum, navette set with five old mine and European-cut diamonds weighing approx. 5.33 cts, further surrounded by 142 bead-set old mine and European-cut diamonds weighing approx. 13.32 cts, approx. total wt. for all diamonds, 18.65 cts, provenance: accompanied by orig sketch by designer, Edmond Frisch, 336 Park Ave., New York.......... **$9,900**

Art Nouveau, 14k yg, circular-shaped, profile of classical woman accented by chased gold hair, enameled earring and face **$1,000**

Edwardian, 14k yg, scrolling form set throughout with rose-cut diamonds and pearls, three freshwater pearl and diamond drops **$715**

Victorian, 14k yg

Enameled inverted horseshoe framing three rounded forms, engraved accents, seed pearl highlights, 15.6 dwt, fitted box from Savage & Lyman Jewellers, Montreal **$600**

Openwork scrolling form bezel-set with three oval amethysts, suspending drop with pear-shape amethyst, chain festoons, 18.5 dwt, boxed **$1,000**

Pin

Art Nouveau

Dogwood blossom, center old European-cut diamond weighing approx. 0.50 cts, black enamel, 14k yg, American hallmark **$775**

Lady in profile, 18k yg, rose-cut diamond accent, French guarantee stamps, sgd "TW" **$325**

Edwardian, starburst, center 10.32 x 6.18 mm greenish-brown oval tourmaline, surrounded by sixteen old European-cut diamonds mounted on 14k gold rays, evidence of solder, possibly color change tourmaline, color changes to golden-olive color **$1,175**

Postwar Modern, duckling, 14k gold, freshwater pearl wings, red stone eye, sgd "Ruser" **$390**

Victorian, 18k, tapering silver-topped baton with graduated bead-set rose-cut diamonds, entwined with engraved yellow gold form completed by pearl, French guarantee stamp **$350**

Ring, Lady's

Art Deco, platinum and diamond

Center rect step-cut emerald framed by eight full-cut diamond melee, millegrain accents, open gallery and foliate engraved shoulders **$940**

Rounded form centering bezel-set old European-cut diamond flanked by lines of channel-set sapphires, set throughout with bead-set old European-cut diamonds, approx. total wt. 0.98 cts, millegrain accents **$1,175**

Art Deco, 14k white gold, center bead-set transitional-cut diamond within raised octagonal-shaped mount, openwork gallery with millegrain accents, approx. diamond wt. 0.87 cts **$2,350**

Art Nouveau, 18k yg, shaped rectangular plaque etched with initials "HP" flanked by stylized flowers within

open and ribbed shank, inscribed "Vitaline a Hubert, 2 Jan. 1910," size 7-1/2 .... **$355**

Arts & Crafts, 14k yg, three circular-cut pink sapphires, white pearl set among swirling leaves and vines continuing to shoulders, sized **$1,175**

Edwardian

Bezel-set fancy-cut aquamarine flanked by single rose-cut diamonds, silver-topped 18k gold mounts **$575**

Intaglio, orange and white carnelian, winged dragon with flower in mouth, 18k yg, 7.20 dwts **$160**

Retro Modern, Birks, platinum, pave-set single-cut diamond buckle motif, channel-set with graduating line of sq step-cut sapphires.................... **$2,000**

Victorian, snake, tri-color gold engraved body, (approx total 0.45 cts) old European-cut diamond, stones missing from eyes...................... **$410**

Stickpin

Art Deco, platinum

Cartier, Y-shaped form, two cultured pearls, bead-set diamond melee, no. 2608, French maker's mark, sgd **$765**

Channel set rubies with diamond melee **$475**

Sugarloaf sapphire cabochon with diamond melee and ruby accents **$425**

Art Nouveau

Crescent moon, 14k yg................. **$95**

Enameled woman, hallmark for Alling & Co., gold.................... **$400**

Edwardian, nine bead-set old European-cut diamonds, set in platinum, centered by cultured pearl in floret design, 14k gold shank................ **$775**

Egyptian Revival, enameled asps framing turquoise cabochon, 14k yg **$115**

Victorian, flowerhead design centering a round opal framed by 11 old mine-cut diamonds, 14k yg setting **$360**

Suite, Lady's

Brooch and ear pendants

Coral, agate chalcedony, brooch with center coral bead within engraved reserve framed by milky agate chalcedony, ear pendants ensuite .. **$625**

Victorian necklace and earrings, coral beads, three floral design cabochons, coral teardrops, four-strand necklace, orig box, c1850, **$765.**

Photo courtesy of Sloans & Kenyon Auctioneers and Appraisers.

Pendant, Edward Colonna for L'Art Nouveau Bing, Paris, light green enamel, triangular pearl and dentile pearl, mine-cut diamond, 28k yellow gold with platinum, each length of chain 9", c1900, 1-3/4" x 1-1/2", **$3,820.**

Photo courtesy of David Rago Auctions, Inc.

Early railroad pocket watch, English, signed Morton, **$649.**
Photo courtesy of Sloans & Kenyon Auctioneers and Appraisers.

Pocket watch, Waltham, hunter cased, 14k gold, 15 jewels, gold-filled chain, **$300.**
Photo courtesy of Wiederseim Associates, Inc.

Pocket watch, Tiffany & Co., 18kt gold, orig box, **$499.**
Photo courtesy of Skinner, Inc.

Coral, each with carved coral rose blossoms and foliage on 14k gold stems, boxed **$235**

Pendant/brooch and earclips, all with circular-cut amethysts and fox-tail fringe, 14k yg, brooch sgd "W. & S.B.," boxed, earrings with later screw-back findings, evidence of solder **$1,175**

Revival-style, bracelet and ring, 14k, hinged flexible braided bangle centering three contiguous balls with wirework and applied bead decoration, ring ensuite, 14.4 dwt, bangle slightly misshapen **$470**

Victorian, demi-parure

Bracelet and earrings, bracelet composed of 15k gold florets with turquoise cabochons; pr earrings each with two 14k gold circles with turquoise cabochons suspending three small drops, 7-3/4" l bracelet **$1,765**

Watches, Pocket

History: Pocket watches can be found in many places—from flea markets to the specialized jewelry auctions. Condition of movement is the first priority; design and detailing of the case is second.

Descriptions of pocket watches may include the size (16/0 to 20), number of jewels in the movement, whether the face is open or closed (hunter), and the composition (gold, gold filled, or some other metal). The movement is the critical element, since cases often were switched. However, an elaborate case, especially if gold, adds significantly to value.

Pocket watches designed to railroad specifications are desirable. They are between 16 and 18 in size, have a minimum of 17 jewels, adjust to at least five positions, and conform to many other specifications. All are open faced.

Study the field thoroughly before buying. There is a vast amount of literature, including books and newsletters from clubs and collectors.

Pocket, Gentleman's

Aurora, Size 18, Roman numeral dial, lever set 15 jewel gilt movement #38691, Grade 3 1/2 Guild, second model, yellow gold-filled hunting case #5161726 .... **$200**

Ball, Size 16, Arabic numeral dial, lever set 17 jewel nickel movement #134015, Official Standard, Waltham model, white gold-filled Illinois hunting case #51032 .... **$500**

Borel, Size 19, Roman numeral dial, lever set 20 jewel gilt movement #15110, Minute Repeater, chronograph, 14 karat yellow gold hunting case #6947 .... **$2,650**

Burlington, Size 16, open face Arabic numeral dial, lever set 17 jewel nickel movement #3447536, Illinois, yellow gold-filled case #5001237 .... **$110**

Elgin

Size 6, Roman numeral dial, pendant set 7 jewel nickel movement #10652232, first model, yellow gold-filled Wadsworth hunting case #316391 .... **$140**

Size 12, Arabic numeral dial, pendant set 17 jewel nickel movement #16472602, yellow gold-filled Dueber hunting case #9305829 ...... **$120**

Size 12, open face Arabic numeral dial, pendant set 19 jewel nickel movement #25254082, C.H. Hulburd 431, platinum case #103820 .... **$1,100**

Size 16, open face Arabic numeral dial, lever set 19 jewel nickel movement #21235315, B.W. Raymond, yellow gold-filled case #8048 .. **$215**

English, brass, key-wind, swing-out case, orig paper retailer's label "Thomas Harrison Silver-Smith Danville KY Clock and Watch Maker," iron forged chain and key, early 19th C **$1,700**

Hamilton

Size 16, Arabic numeral dial, lever set 21 jewel nickel movement #776560, Grade 993, yellow gold-filled Illinois engraved hunting case #2922269 .... **$330**

Size 16, open face Arabic numeral dial, lever set 21 jewel nickel movement #324343, Grade 960, model 960, 14k yellow gold-filled case # 5721 ... **$570**

Size 18, open face Arabic dial, lever set 17 jewel nickel movement #8023, Grade 936, silverode Keystone case #9158568, for American Jewelry Co., Leadville, CO. **$180**

Size 18, Roman numeral dial, lever set 17 jewel nickel movement #157179, Grade 925 The Union, yellow gold-filled hunting case **$175**

Hampden

Size 16, Arabic numeral dial, lever set 17 jewel nickel movement #1890116, William McKinley, BRDG, in a yellow gold-filled hunting case #6028660 .... **$165**

Size 16, open face Arabic numeral dial, lever set 23 jewel nickel movement #2801029, Grade 104, Bridge model, glass back nickel case .. **$350**

Size 18, Roman numeral dial, lever set 17 jewel nickel movement #1332191, Adjusted, silverine Dueber hunting case #2942431 .... **$90**

Howard

Size 12, open face Arabic numeral dial, pendant set 17 jewel nickel movement #1092624, Series 8, 14 karat yellow gold monogrammed case #121454 .... **$360**

Size 16, open face Arabic numeral dial, lever set 21 jewel nickel movement #1361149, RR Chronometer Ser, white gold-filled Keystone case #1554922 .... **$300**

Illinois

Size 16, open face Arabic numeral dial, pendant set 17 jewel nickel movement #3136048, Texas Special, yellow gold-filled case #6287230 ... **$120**

Size 18, Roman numeral dial, lever set 11 jewel nickel movement #231676, yellow gold-filled hunting case #143231 .... **$150**

Montgomery Ward

Size 18, open face Roman numeral dial, lever set 21 jewel nickel movement #1448074, Grade 61, sixth model, 10 karat yellow rolled gold plate Illinois case #7769495 .... **$175**

Size 18, open face Roman numeral dial, pendant set 11 jewel nickel movement #757650, 20th C, silverine Dueber case #4280 .... **$75**

Waltham

Size 14, Roman numeral dial, pendant set 13 jewel nickel movement #3127180, Chronograph, first model, coin silver American hunting case #21280 .... **$150**

Size 16, open face Arabic numeral dial, lever set 21 jewel nickel movement #20142536, Crescent St.U-D, model 1908, with wind indicator, yellow gold-filled case #9308103 .... **$900**

Size 18, open face Arabic numeral dial with 24 hour time, lever set 21 jewel nickel movement #10559638, Crescent St., first model, yellow gold-filled American case #405850 .... **$220**

Pocket, Lady's

Betsy Ross, Size 0, open face Arabic numeral dial, pendant set 7 jewel nickel movement #861180, yellow gold-filled Keystone case #8186017 .... **$100**

Elgin, Size 0, Roman numeral dial, pendant set 15 jewel nickel movement #8773791, first model, yellow gold-filled Wadsworth hunting case #667982 .... **$120**

Meylan, C. H., 18k gold and enamel, open-face, white enamel dial with black Arabic numerals, fancy scrolled hands, gray guilloche enamel bezel, cover enameled with gold flowers set with diamonds, suspended from platinum and purple guilloche enamel baton link chain, crystal replaced, minor enamel loss **$850**

Unknown maker, retro, pink gold, hinged rect cover surmounted by rubies and diamonds, similarly set scroll and geometric shoulders, snake link bracelet, 6-1/4" l **$750**

Vacheron & Constantin, 18k gold, hunting case, white enamel dial, Roman numerals, gilt bar movement, cylinder escapement, sgd on cuvette, engraved case, size 10 .... **$350**

Waltham, 14k yg, hunting case, white enamel dial, Arabic numeral indicators, subsidiary seconds dial, Lady Waltham jeweled nickel movement by A.W.W. Co., floral engraved case no. 224709, 0 size, gold ropetwist chain **$300**

Whipperman, A. J., Idaho Falls, Idaho, 14k yg, hunting case, white enamel dial, black Arabic numeral indicators, subsidiary seconds dial, 15 jewel nickel movement by Rode Watch Co., floral engraved case dec with pale pink guilloche enamel, old mine-cut diamond in center, signed Gruen, dust cover inscribed, "Father to Elsie 1914," 0 size, fancy 14k yg curb link and pink enamel baton link chain **$180**

Watches, Wrist

History: The definition of a wristwatch is simply "a small watch that is attached to a bracelet or strap and is worn around the wrist." However, a watch on a bracelet is not necessarily a wristwatch. The key is the ability to read the time. A true wristwatch allows you to read the time at a glance, without making any other motions. Early watches on an arm bracelet had the axis of their dials, from 6 to 12, perpendicular to the band. Reading them required some extensive arm movements.

The first true wristwatch appeared about 1850. However, the key date is 1880 when the stylish, decorative wristwatch appeared and almost universal acceptance occurred. The technology to create the wristwatch existed in the early 19th century with Brequet's shock-absorbing "Parachute System" for automatic watches and Ardien Philipe's winding stem.

Gentleman's

Boucheron, dress tank, A250565, white gold, reeded bezel and dial, invisible clasp, black leather Boucheron strap, French hallmarks, orig leather pouch **$2,150**

Bueche-Girod, 18k yg, gold curved dial, black Roman numerals, 17 jewel movement, integrated textural mesh bracelet; dial, movement, case back and clasp all signed "Bueche-Girod," 39.80 dwts **$360**

Cartier, 18k hg, rect convex white dial, black Roman numerals, round gold bezel, black leather strap **$1,380**

Concord, Delirium, 18k gold, round goldtone dial without indicators, flat rect bezel, quartz movement, Swiss hallmarks, orig crocodile band, 9" l .. **$1,265**

Garsons, 14k gold, sq goldtone dial with simulated jewel indicators, 17-jewel nickel movement, subsidiary seconds dial, integrated mesh band, 8-1/4" l **$345**

Hamilton, 14kt yg watch and band, needs repair **$575**

Lady's wristwatch, oval dial, Arabic numerals, platinum trim case with calibré-cut diamonds and sapphires, new leather strap, dial signed "Hamilton," c1930, 18k white gold and platinum, **$445.**

Photo courtesy of Sloans & Kenyon Auctioneers and Appraisers.

Hamilton, 18k yg, silverized rect dial, applied Arabic numerals, subsidiary seconds dial, 19 jewel movement, black leather strap **$180**

Jurgensen, Jules, dress, 14k white gold, Swiss movement, silvertone brushed dial, abstract indicators, diamond-set bevel, black faux alligator strap **$290**

Le Coultre, Futurematic, goldtone dial, subsidiary seconds dial, power reserve indicator, 10k yg-filled mount, lizard strap, 1950s **$425**

Longines, pale green rect dial, applied diamond set platinum Arabic numerals with small round and baguette cut diamonds, 15 jewel adjusted movement #3731402, case back engraved and dated 1935 ....**$2,035**

Mediator, 18kt yg band and watch, 17 jewel Swiss movement, sapphire crystal, 7" l **$350**

Nardin, Ulysse, 14k yg, chronometer, goldtone dial, luminescent quarter sections, applied abstract and Arabic numeral indicators, subsidiary seconds dial, lugs with scroll accents, leather strap, discoloration and scratches to dial **$270**

Omega, 18k yg, round cream dial, goldtone Arabic numeral and abstract indicators, heavy mesh bracelet, mild soil to dial, 44.80 dwt **$460**

Patek Philippe, 18k yg

Round ivory tone dial with stick indicators, later 18k gold band, c1960 ....**$2,700**

Silvertone metal dial with gold abstract numeral indicators joined by curved lugs to brown leather strap, replaced closure **$2,820**

Silvertone metal dial with raised indicators, subsidiary seconds dial, movement #977714, reference # 2470, triple sgd, leather strap, c1949 ....**$6,230**

Frattone, 14kt yg, 18 jewel Swiss movement, black leather band ...**$175**

Rolex, Oyster Perpetual

14k yg, goldtone dial, abstract indicators, sweep second hand, ostrich strap, slight spotting to dial **$850**

Datejust, two tone **$2,600**

Stainless steel, Air King, silvertone dial, applied abstract indicators, sweep second hand, oyster bracelet with deployant clasp, discoloration to crystal **$575**

Vacheron & Constantin, 18k gold, white round dial, abstract numeral indicators, 17-jewel nickel movements, associated 18k gold brickwork band, 7-1/4" l **$1,495**

Lady's

Bulova, small round dial with Arabic and baton numerals, 17 jewel movement, 14k white gold case and bracelet set with single cut and baguette cut diamonds weighing approx 1.50 carats total **$760**

Cartier, Tank Francaise, 18k yg, rect ivory tone dial with Roman numeral indicators, gold band with integral clasp **$5,875**

Chanel, 18k yg, black and white dial with Roman numeral indicators, onyx cabochon winding stem, enclosing Swiss quartz movement, adjustable black alligator band and 18k gold clasp, sgd **$1,300**

Elgin, platinum, rect ivory tone dial with Arabic numeral indicators, 17 jewel movement, bezel, lugs, and bracelet set with single-cut and baguette diamonds, 6-1/2" l **$1,410**

Grenchen, Nivada, Swiss, 14kt white gold, 17 jewels, six 2.2 mm round diamonds, 38 1.6 mm round diamonds on watch, band with 52 diamond accents, approx 1.50 ctw, 14.4 grams **$500**

Gruen, Art Deco, platinum, rect silvertone dial, black Arabic numerals, bezel enhanced with 32 circular-cut diamonds, mesh strap edged by box-set single-cut diamonds, highlighted by diamond-set floret shoulders, 6-1/4" l **$4,225**

Hamilton, platinum, rect ivory tone dial with Arabic numeral indicators, 17 jewel movement, bezel and lugs with single-cut and baguette diamonds, joining cord band. Missing winding stem **$300**

Helbros Watch Co., 17 jewels, Art Deco, combination of old European and single cut diamonds, approx 1 ct, case hinged to allow better contour when worn, calibre French cut sapphires, curved crystal, platinum setting **$995**

Movado

18k yg, rect gold tone dial with Arabic numeral and dot indicators, 15 jewel movement, 14k gold link band **$765**

Stainless steel, yg, mother-of-pearl dial, diamond set bezel containing thirty-six round brilliant cut diamonds weighing approx 0.72 carat total, quartz movement, deployment buckle **$525**

Pailet, Andrew, 14kt yg, diamonds around face, quartz movement, approx 1 ct TDW **$500**

Patek Philippe & Co., rect gold metallic enamel dial, Arabic and dot numerals, movement #940981, case # 509109; dial, movement, 18k yg, case and bracelet sgd "Patek-Philippe & Co Geneve," c1940, 46.60 dwt, 8-1/2" l **$3,350**

Rolex, 14kt yg, Spendel band, 17 jewels, face discolored **$60**

Rolex, Oyster Perpetual, stainless steel, round blue dial with stick indicators, date aperture, original band with integral clasp, boxed, crystal scratched **$1,530**

Rolex, platinum 3 extra diamond links, diamond bezel and diamond studded band, 2.38 ctw **$2,875**

Swiss, 18k yg, Swiss movement, manual wind, domed bezel, goldtone dial, black Roman numerals, hallmark, leather strap **$920**

Tiffany & Co., Art Deco, platinum and diamond, rect ivory-tone dial with Arabic numeral indicators, 17 jewel International Watch Company movement, bezel and lugs with bead-set diamond melee, engraved accents, black cord band, case with Krementz hallmark, 7" l **$940**

Watch fob
Art Nouveau

Carter Howe & Co., 14k yg, triple link chain composed of lotus buds and flowers joined by trace links suspending double griffin-head seal, hallmark **$940**

Whiteside & Blank, 14k yg, heart-shaped leaves and sinuous vine motifs joined by grosgrain strap, hallmark **$400**

Watch pin
Art Nouveau

Dragon clutching an arrow, 14k yg, partially obliterated American hallmark **$940**

Profile of young woman with flowing hair, encircled by enameled buds, foliage, and emerald-set blossom, 14k yg mount **$1,765**

Butterfly brooches with rhinestones and glass, c. 1925, **$285** each.

Coro owl Duette with enameling and rhinestones, c.1940s, **$345.**

From top: brooch with rhinestones, c. 1920, **$165.**

COSTUME JEWELRY

Bangle/Bracelet

Bakelite, Applejuice, carved, hinged bangle with rhinestones............ **$425**

Bakelite bangle, marbled green with rhinestones.................................. **$950**

Cameo bracelet, black Bakelite and celluloid....................................... **$350**

Jade, SS, four oval jade plaques pierced and carved with floral motifs, joined by woven foxtail chain bracelet, 7-1/4" l **$175**

Postwar Modern, Hermes, sterling silver, heavy flattened anchor links, sgd, 7-3/4" l **$1,100**

Rootbeer and tea, Bakelite bangle **$750**

Thermoplastic, yellow, five holes surrounded by aurora borealis rhinestones, hinged bangle **$225**

Victorian, French Jet snake wrap **$145**

Victorian, gold-filled wraparound bracelet **$185**

Brooch

Art Nouveau, Trout, basse-taille greenish-blue fading to pinkish-white iridescent translucent enamel **$850**

Cameo brooch, hardstone, gold-filled frame................................. **$195**

Edwardian, heart-shape form set throughout with seed pearls, highlighted by two bezel-set peridots,

English 9k stamp, 10k gold paper clip chain, 16-3/4" l............... **$500**

Jugendstil, SS, shaped pendant set with two oval green agate, reverse stamped "MiG, TF, 900, depose" for Max Joseph Gradl, Theodor Fahrner **$885**

Leaf brooch, cluster of stemmed leaves, moonglow with rhinestones on foliage.............................. **$110**

Nautical, intaglio of ship and water, Bakelite.................................. **$235**

Nautical, butterscotch Bakelite and wood.................................... **$350**

Turtle brooch, green Bakelite cabochon shell on wooden body **$225**

Buckle

Art Nouveau, sterling silver, two repoussé plaques of female faces with flowing hair and flower blossoms, hallmark for William B. Kerr & Co. **$300**

Cameo

Pendant/brooch, Victorian, 14k gold, shell cameo habille bead-set with an old European-cut diamond set within frame, retractable bail, solder to neck-chain on reverse......................... **$180**

Pendant necklace, Victorian, 14k gold, hardstone, carnelian agate cameo within oval frame with applied foliate motifs and flexible fringe, pendant bail missing suspended element, suspended from 18" l chain **$450**

Trifari elephant fur clip with Lucite body, enameling, and rhinestones, **$1,900-$2,300.**

Victorian micromosaic brooch, **$225.**

Celluloid and applejuice Bakelite necklace, **$325.**

Marbled green Bakelite stretch bracelet on elastic, **$225.**

Leaf brooch, moonglow with rhinestones, **$110.**

Locket on chain with seed pearls, gold filled, c. 1900, **$525.**

Earrings

Bow-shaped, brushed goldtone metal, 1960s...**$15**

Ear cover earrings, paisley shaped, covered with clear rhinestones...**$125**

Round-shaped, red enamel flower at center, surrounded by two rings of faux pearls, followed by a ring of red enamel fleurs-de-lis and a final row of faux pearls, Robert **$125**

Necklace

Art Deco, negligee, faux pearl drops, purple enameled links with faux pearl spacers, 1920s **$85**

Bakelite, butterscotch, beaded **$225**

Celluloid, with 21 assorted celluloid charms...**$325**

Handmade pendant, on goldtone chain, green glass, Denmark **$195**

Victorian, locket on chain, seed pearl cross motif, c.1880.....................**$225**

Opera glasses

Lefils, Paris, blue enamel dec with pink and gold floral sprays, mother-of-pearl eyepieces, engraved name, late 19th C, 4" w **$360**

Ring, gentleman's

Cameo

Black, white, and brown agate, carved Jesus profile, yellow gold setting, 4.80 dwts, late 19th C..............**$215**

Coral, red, Socrates portrait, 14k yg, 6.30 dwts, mid-19th C **$400**

Medium blue-green beryl, bearded soldier in high relief profile, vg, Victorian, 5.80 dwts................**$575**

Enamel, multicolored, black onyx, portrait of North African gentleman with red and green stripes, yg, Victorian, 5.00 dwts **$250**

Intaglio

Carnelian, Hermes with staff, 14k yg, 8.80 dwts....................................**$275**

Rhodolite garnet, Romulous and Remus in profile, yg, 5.10 dwts **$300**

Seal, black and white agate intaglio, coat of arms, 14k yg, 6.30 dwts **$120**

Watch fob chain

Victorian, gentleman's, yg, gold filled locket with black and white onyx cameo of soldier in neoclassical design, chain 12.90 dwts.............**$180**

Toys

TOYS–THE STATE OF THE HOBBY

by Karen O'Brien

COLLECTING TOYS

For more than a century, the materials and production techniques of the post-Industrial Revolution period have been put to good use creating toys. Indeed, the socio-political history of the 20th century can be extrapolated from the material, design, craftsmanship, and production methods employed in the creation of playthings.

Many toys owe their development to the need to make productive use of the scrap materials that were by-products of manufacturing processes. Not a new concept, the "never let anything go to waste" philosophy was put to use famously by the late Henry Ford, who contracted engines from the Dodge Brothers and requested that the wooden shipping crates be of a specific size—Ford then used the wood for the floorboards in early Model T production.

Early toy production enjoyed a similar "recycling" mindset. Cast-iron techniques employed to create salesman's samples of real stoves were used to make miniature replicas for children. Early pressed steel toys were produced from recycled sheet steel used in the fledgling automobile industry. Similar stories occur about the tangential creation of toys from companies utilizing tin, wood, rubber, and plastic.

What makes these toys collectible today? Nostalgia. Although experienced collectors appreciate the craftsmanship and mechanical engineering that qualifies many early toys as works of art, collectors are most often driven by the simple remembrances of childhood's carefree times. Nostalgia develops at its own pace for each generation, and while we gravitate towards the toys of our youths, we also appreciate the artistry of toys from eras other than our own. This appreciation ensures a long life for the toy collecting hobby, no matter what types of toys one prefers.

HOBBY PERSPECTIVE

I made my first trip to the Atlantique City show (held twice per year in Atlantic City, New Jersey) this fall and was amazed by the quality and quantity of vintage toys present. Toys that I've only seen in books were around each corner of the 10-acre facility. It is increasingly rare to see vintage tin wind-ups and cast-iron vehicles at local shows around the country, as these items become the stars of auction house catalogs. To see so many of the vintage favorites complete with their original boxes was a real privilege. Although many of the boxes were constructed of a simple cardboard, the box art was captivating.

Perhaps the real treat was discussing these beautiful toys with some of the most knowledgeable dealers in the world. It's worth the trip to Atlantique City to talk toys with dealers who can answer questions, discuss the operating features of their toys, and provide buyers with the story of a toy's history.

One of the prices paid as a result of the instant accessibility we enjoy from online auctions is that sellers are frequently unaware of the history, working features, and basic attributes of the toys that they sell. How many online auction listings have you read where the seller admits to having no knowledge regarding the item being sold? I'd guess it's quite a few, and because the seller has absolved himself of any responsibility regarding the toy, it is up to the buyer to become informed enough to know the simplest of facts. Do you know on sight whether or not the toy is complete? Does the toy work? Is there any damage that the photos aren't showing?

To be sure of your purchase, buyers need to see the toys they are considering in person or obtain them from a trustworthy source like an established auction house or a recommended dealer. Cast-iron and tin toys are hot this year, but because these toys also command premium prices, it's worth some effort to be sure of your source.

For additional perspectives on the hobby, I turned to Tom Bartsch, editor of *Toy Shop* magazine.

Toy Shop magazine is a monthly publication dedicated to toys old and new, and offers collectors a variety of perspectives on the hobby. "We're heading into some milestone anniversaries (40 years of Star Trek, 30 years of Star Wars), and as those properties get added publicity, the more product you will find on the secondary market," Bartsch said. "It's great for buyers because more product will be available, but sellers won't see the dividends with the glut of collectibles. Everything is about condition now. If you have a Mint toy complete with its box, you're going to find a buyer. It's as simple as that."

OTHER TRENDS

Space toys and western toys continue to do well at shows, and there is an increasing demand for these items when they are associated with early television shows. Items like Hopalong Cassidy cap pistols and outfits from the 1950s are in continual demand. Early space shows haven't appeared on DVD yet, and when they do, expect demand for the associated toys to increase. This has certainly happened with some of the 1970s television shows recently released on DVD like *Battlestar Galactica*, *The Dukes of Hazzard*, and *Wonder Woman*, as well as the 1960s classic *Lost in Space*. The collectibles associated with those shows are increasing in demand and value, and I expect this trend to be repeated when the 1950s shows are released to DVD. Now is the time to add Tom Corbett, Captain Video, Rex Mars, and similar space hero toys to your collection.

Grading Condition. The following numbers represent the standard grading system used by dealers, collectors, and auctioneers:

C.10	Mint
C.9	Near Mint
C.8.5	Outstanding
C.8	Excellent
C.7.5	Fine+
C.7	Fine
C.6.5	Fine - (good)
C.6	Poor

RESOURCES
Magazines

Antique Toy World
Classic Toy Trains
Old Toy Soldier
Toy Cars & Models
Toy Farmer
Toy Shop
Toy Trucker & Contractor
Toy Tractor Times (online-only)

Books

200 Years of Dolls, 3rd Ed., by Dawn Herlocher, Krause Publications, Iola, WI.

Hot Wheels™ Field Guide, by Michael Zarnock, Tracy Schmidt, ed., Krause Publications, Iola, WI.

Hot Wheels™ A Warman's Companion, by Michael Zarnock, Krause Publications, Iola, WI.

Hot Wheels™ Variations The Ultimate Guide, 2nd Ed., by Michael Zarnock, Krause Publications, Iola, WI.

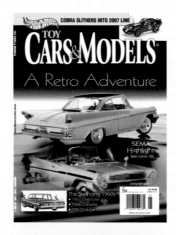

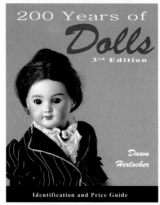

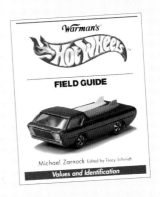

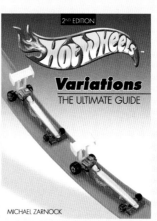

Fisher-Price: Historical, Rarity, and Value Guide 1931-Present, 3rd Ed., by Bruce R. Fox and John J. Murray, Krause Publications, Iola, WI.

O'Brien's Collecting Toys, 11th Ed., Karen O'Brien, ed., Krause Publications, Iola, WI.

O'Brien's Collecting Toy Cars & Trucks, 4th Ed., Karen O'Brien, ed., Krause Publications, Iola, WI.

Official Hake's Price Guide to Character Toys, 5th Ed., by Ted Hake, House of Collectibles.

Standard Catalog of Farm Toys, 2nd Ed., Karen O'Brien, ed., Krause Publications, Iola, WI.

Standard Catalog of Lionel Trains 1900-1942, by David Doyle, Krause Publications, Iola, WI.

Standard Catalog of Lionel Trains 1946-1969, by David Doyle, Krause Publications, Iola, WI.

The Ultimate Barbie® Doll Book, by Marcie Melillo, Krause Publications, Iola, WI.

Warman's Barbie® Doll Field Guide, by Paul Kennedy, ed., Krause Publications, Iola, WI.

Warman's® Dolls Antique to Modern, by Mark F. Moran, Krause Publications, Iola, WI.

Warman's Toys Field Guide, by Paul Kennedy, ed., Krause Publications, Iola, WI.

Toys & Prices 2007, 14th Ed., Karen O'Brien, ed., Krause Publications, Iola, WI.

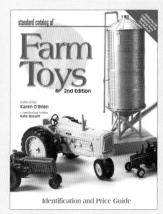

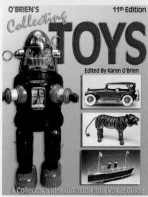

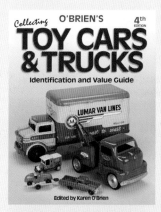

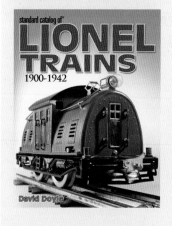

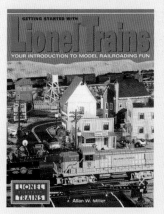

GALLERY

This Arcade Yellow Cab was released in 1932 and at auction, once brought **$62,000**.
Photo courtesy Bertoia Auctions.

Beat It! The Komical Kop, Marx, 1930s, **$650**.
Photo courtesy Scott Smiles.

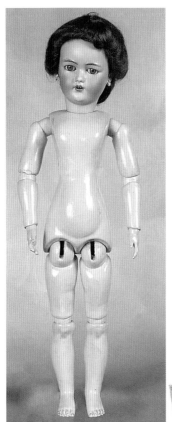

Enchanted Evening, #983, 1960-1963, pictured on a Bubblecut Barbie. This classic formal gown was offered on a collector doll in 1996, MIP, **$385**.

Simon & Halbig, 1159 Lady, bisque socket head, blue sleep eyes, real lash remnants, painted lower lashes, open mouth, original mohair wig, pierced ears, jointed wood and composition body, original clothing, marked: 1159//S &H//DEP//7 on head, Heinrich Handwerk//Germany//1 on body 1//H.H. (in heart) on shoes; minor wig pulls, 19", **$1,400**.
Photo courtesy of McMasters Harris Auction Co.

The Rebel, Ideal, 1961, **$100**.

BANKS, MECHANICAL

History: Banks which display some form of action while accepting a coin are considered mechanical banks. Mechanical banks date back to ancient Greece and Rome, but the majority of collectors are interested in those made between 1867 and 1928 in Germany, England, and the United States.

Initial research suggested that approximately 250 to 300 different or variant designs of banks were made in the early period. Today that number has been revised to 2,000-3,000 types and varieties. The field remains ripe for discovery and research.

More than 80 percent of all cast-iron mechanical banks produced between 1869 and 1928 were made by J. E. Stevens Co., Cromwell, Connecticut. Tin banks are usually of German origin.

Notes: While rarity is a factor in value, appeal of design, action, quality of manufacture, country of origin, and history of collector interest also are important. Radical price fluctuations may occur when there is an imbalance in these factors. Rare banks may sell for a few hundred dollars, while one of more common design with greater appeal will sell in the thousands.

Reproduction Alert. Reproductions, fakes, and forgeries exist for many banks. Forgeries of some mechanical banks were made as early as 1937, so age alone is not a guarantee of authenticity. In the following price listings, two asterisks indicate banks for which serious forgeries exist, and one asterisk indicates banks for which casual reproductions have been made.

The mechanical bank market has exploded upward in the last year. Vast sums of money are changing hands daily for high grade examples. Records are falling weekly as more and more new buyers enter the market and compete to previously unheard-of heights to secure superb examples. Both privately and at auction, astonishing amounts of money are being paid. Bargains, however, still remain available for banks with condition problems and those banks with less than 70 percent original paint. My projection for the next year is that superb condition bank prices will move to even more lofty heights, which will make the current numbers seem low. Also, I predict that few bargains in the lesser condition banks will remain available as the supply becomes exhausted by new buyers entering the market, who cannot afford the lofty numbers of the superb examples.

Additionally, there have been large sums of investment money coming onto the mechanical bank market, as of late, specifically directed at purchasing banks in the $20,000 to $100,000 and up levels per bank, causing an upward trend in these higher priced banks. It is my theory that much of this money has been moved into mechanical banks by non-collecting investors who have become fed up with the performance of the stock market and are searching for other directions of investment to protect their capital. I strongly suspect that this trend will continue.

The values listed here accurately represent the selling prices of mechanical banks in the specialized collectors' market. As some banks are hard to find, and the market is quite volatile both up and down in price structure, consultation of a competent specialist in mechanical banks, with up-to-the-moment information, is advised prior to selling any mechanical bank.

The prices listed are for original old mechanical banks with no repairs, in sound operating condition, and with at least 90 percent of the original paint intact. Banks that have touch-ups, flaws, repairs, or less than 90 percent of their original paint sell for much less than these prices. Banks with missing pieces often sell for as little as 10 percent to 20 percent of these prices.

Adviser: James S. Maxwell Jr.

Price note: Prices quoted are for 100 percent original examples with no repairs, no repaint, and which have at least 90 percent bright original paint. An asterisk * indicates casual reproductions; † denotes examples where casual reproductions and serious fakes exist.

Photo note: Photos in the mechanical and still banks sections courtesy Bertoia Auctions unless otherwise noted.

Upper left: Patronize the Blind Man and His Dog, J.&E. Stevens, 1878, **$8,500;** *lower left: Halls Liliput, J.&E. Stevens, 1877,* **$5,000;** *right: Uncle Sam, Shepard Hardware, 1886,* **$9,200.**

†**Acrobat** $3,700
†**Afghanistan** $1,800
African Bank, black bust, back emb
"African Bank" $1,500
American Bank, sewing machine
.... $9,500
***Artillery** $900
Atlas, iron, steel, wood, paper
.... $2,500
Automatic Chocolate Vending, tin
.... $450
Automatic Coin Savings, predicts
future, tin $150
Automatic Fortune Bank, tin
.... $4,200
Automatic Savings Bank, tin, soldier
.... $400
Automatic Savings Bank, tin, sailor
.... $450
Automatic Surprise Money Box,
wood $4,000
†**Baby Elephant X-O'clock**, lead
and wood $15,000
***Bad Accident** $2,800
Bambula, black bust, back emb "Bam-
bula" $3,700
Bank Teller, man behind three-sided
fancy grillwork $75,000
Bank of Education and Economy,
must have orig paper reel $1,200
Barking Dog, wood $2,000
Bear, tin $1,200
†**Bear and Tree Stump** $1,600
†**Bear**, slot in chest $320
†**Bill E. Grin** $900
†**Billy Goat Bank** $700
Bird in Cage, tin $3,200
Bird on Roof $1,200
Bismarck Bank $7,000
Bonzo, tin $2,500
Book-Keepers Magic Bank, tin
.... $7,500
Bowery Bank, iron, paper, wood
.... $42,000
Bowing Man in Cupola $4,500
†**Bowling Alley** $125,000
†**Boy Robbing Bird's Nest** ... $6,700
†**Boy and Bulldog** $2,800
†**Boy on Trapeze** $3,500
†**Boys Stealing Watermelons**
.... $3,200
Bread Winners $37,000
British Clown, tin $3,500
†**Bucking Mule** $1,500
***Bulldog**, place coin on nose
.... $1,800
†**Bull and Bear** $45,000
Bull Dog Savings, clockwork
.... $4,500
†**Bulldog**, standing $1,250
Bureau, wood, Serrill patent $3,200

Bank, mechanical, Magician, J. & E. Stevens Co., patented 9/17/1901, **$2,400.**
Photo courtesy of Pook & Pook, Inc.

Bank, mechanical, Bad Accident, J.& E. Stevens Co., patented 9/17/1901, **$1,020.**
Photo courtesy of Pook & Pook, Inc.

Bureau, Lewando's, wood $2,500
Bureau, wood, John R. Jennings Patent
.... $14,000
Burnett Postman, tin man with tray
.... $550
†**Butting Buffalo** $5,550
†**Butting Goat** $1,200
†**Butting Ram** $875
***Cabin**, black man flips $720
Caller Vending, tin $2,800
†**Calamity** $25,000
†**Called Out** $65,000
Calumet, tin and cardboard, with
Calumet Kid $200
Calumet, tin and cardboard, with sailor
.... $18,000
Calumet, tin and cardboard, with sol-
dier $20,000
†**Camera** $5,500
***Cat and Mouse** $3,200
†**Cat and Mouse**, giant cat standing
on top $22,000
Chandler's $550
Chandler's with clock $400
Child's Bank, wood $450
Chinaman in Boat, lead $37,000
Chinaman with queue, tin
.... $3,500
Chocolate Menier, tin $950
†**Chrysler Pig** $750
Cigarette Vending, tin $420
Cigarette Vending, lead $600
Circus, clown on cart in circular ring
.... $7,500
†**Circus**, ticket collector $950
Clever Dick, tin $400
Clown Bust, iron $4,500
Clown, Chein, tin $45
†**Clown on Bar**, tin and iron
.... $30,000
***Clown on Globe** $2,800
Clown and Dog, tin $950

Clown With Arched Top, tin
.... $150
Clown With Black Face, tin
.... $350
Clown With White Face, tin
.... $200
Clown With White Face, round, tin
.... $2,000
Cockatoo Pelican, tin $280
Coin Registering, many variants
.... $25-$1,000
Columbian Magic Savings, iron
.... $150
Columbian Magic Savings, wood
and paper $12,000
Coolie Bust, lead $2,000
Cowboy With Tray, Tin $1,600
†**Creedmoor** $950
Crescent Cash Register $2,000
Cross Legged Minstrel, tin ... $650
Crowing Rooster, circular base, tin
.... $2,000
Cupid at Piano, pot metal, musical
.... $26,000
Dapper Dan, tin $950
***Darktown Battery** $2,800
Darky Fisherman, lead $125,000
†**Darky Watermelon**, man kicks
football at watermelon $450,000
†**Dentist** $6,500
Dinah, iron $300
Dinah, aluminum $200
Ding Dong Bell, tin, windup
.... $65,000
Dog on Turntable $400
†**Dog With Tray** $2,000
Domed Vending, tin $1,600
Driver's Service Vending, tin
.... $1,500
Droste Chocolate $900
***Eagle and Eaglettes** $950
Electric Safe, steel $1,200

Left: Confectionary, Kyser & Rex, 1881, **$15,000;** *middle: Professor Pug Frog's Great Bicycle Feat, J.& E. Stevens, 1886,* **$10,000;** *right: Cupola Bank, J.&E. Stevens, 1874,* **$10,000.**

*Elephant and Three Clowns $2,800
*Elephant, locked howdah $260
Elephant, made in Canada ... $7,500
Elephant, man pops out, wood, cloth, iron $675
†Elephant, no stars $650
*Elephant, pull tail $70
Elephant, three stars $400
*Elephant, trunk swings, large ... $210
*Elephant, trunk swings, small $200
Elephant, trunk swings, raised coin slot $450
†Elephant with tusks, on wheels $300
Empire Cinema, tin $14,000
English Bulldog, tin $1,200
Feed the Goose, pot metal ... $480
5 Cents Adding $1,200
Flip the Frog, tin $2,700
Football, English football $2,800
Fortune Savings, tin, horse race $7,000
Fortune Teller, Savings, safe ... $1,320
†Fowler $45,000
†Freedman's Bank, wood, lead, brass, tin, paper, etc. $375,000
Frog on Arched Track, tin ... $26,000
Frog on Rock $575
Frog on Round Base $950
†Frogs, two frogs $2,200
Fun Producing Savings, tin ... $1,200
*Gem, dog with building $1,000
German Sportsman, lead and iron $17,000
German Vending, tin $1,200
†Germania Exchange, iron, lead, tin $32,000
†Giant in Tower $10,500
†Giant, standing by rock $30,000
Girl Feeding Geese, tin, paper, lead $9,500
†Girl Skipping Rope $32,000
†Girl in Victorian Chair $8,500
Give Me a Penny, wood $4,000

Grenadier $975
Guessing, man's figure, lead, steel, iron $8,200
Guessing, woman's figure, iron $55,000
Guessing, woman's figure, lead $22,000
Gwenda Money Box, tin $1,200
Hall's Excelsior, iron, wood $450
Hall's Liliput, no tray $500
Hall's Liliput, with tray $370
†Harlequin $85,000
Harold Lloyd, tin $3,200
Hartwig and Vogel, vending, tin $675
Hen and Chick $4,500
Highwayman, tin $12,000
Hillman Coin Target $18,000
*Hindu, bust $2,800
†Hold the Fort, two varieties, each $8,500
Home, iron $1,200
Home, tin building $570
Hoop-La $1,500
*Horse Race, two varieties, each $12,000
Humpty Dumpty, aluminum, English $210
†Humpty Dumpty, bust of clown with name on back, iron $1,680
Hunter and Palmers, tin, vending $550
*I Always Did 'spise a Mule, black man on bench $1,200
Ideal Bureau, tin $950
*Indian and Bear $4,000
†Indian Chief, black man bust with Indian feathered headdress, aluminum $28,000
Indiana Paddlewheel Boat ... $14,000
†Initiating Bank, first degree $9,500
Initiating Bank, second degree $16,000
Japanese Ball Tosser, tin, wood, paper $90,000
Joe Socko Novelty Bank, tin ... $400

John Bull's Money Box $20,000
John R. Jennings Trick Drawer Money Box, wood $10,500
Jolly Joe Clown, tin $1,200
*Jolly Nigger, American $390
*Jolly Nigger, English $210
Jolly Nigger, lettering in Greek $1,200
Jolly Nigger, lettering in Arabic $1,200
*Jolly Nigger, raises hat, lead $800
*Jolly Nigger, raises hat, iron . $1,320
*Jolly Nigger, stationary ears $150
*Jolly Nigger, stationary eyes $270
*Jolly Nigger, with fez, aluminum $1,200
Jolly Sambo Bank $1,680
†Jonah and The Whale Bank, stands on two ornate legs with rect coin box at center $125,000
†Jumbo, elephant on wheels $300
Kick Inn Bank, wood $1,500
Kiltie $390
Lawrence Steinberg's Bureau Bank, wood $15,000
†Leap Frog $3,200
Lehmann Berlin Tower, tin ... $1,500
Lehmann, London Tower, tin ... $1,500
†Light of Asia $1,600
Lighthouse Bank $2,800
Lion, tin $1,400
Lion Hunter $9,500
†Lion and Two Monkeys $1,800
*Little High Hat $900
Little Jocko, tin $390
*Little Joe Bank $570
Little Moe Bank $210
Lucky Wheel Money Box, tin $1,200
*Magic Bank, iron house $1,200
Magic Bank, tin $1,200
Magic, safe, tin $270
†Mama Katzenjammer $28,000
†Mammy and Child $5,700
*Mason $4,500
Memorial Money Box $240
*Merry-Go-Round, mechanical, coin activates $18,000
†Merry-Go-Round, semi-mechanical, spin by hand $280
Mickey Mouse, tin $30,000
Mikado Bank $60,000
†Milking Cow $6,500
Minstrel, tin $1,200
Model Railroad Drink Dispenser, tin $3,700
Model Savings Bank, tin, cash register $3,700
*Monkey and Coconut $3,200
Monkey and Parrot, tin $650
†Monkey Bank $650

Left: Jonah and the Whale, Shepard Hardware, 1890s, **$5,500;** *right: Chief Big Moon, J.&E. Stevens, 1899,* **$420.**

Bank, mechanical, Reclining Chinaman, J.&E.Stevens Co., c1885, **$2,880.**
Photo courtesy of Pook & Pook, Inc.

U.S. and Spain, J.&E. Stevens, 1898, **$NA.**

Monkey, chimpanzee in ornate circular bldg, iron $2,675
Monkey Face, tin with arched top $1,920
Monkey, pot metal, nods head.... $450
†Monkey, slot in stomach $2,200
Monkey, tin, tips hat $270
Monkey With Tray, tin $570
Mosque $1,450
Motor Bank, coin activates trolley $50,000
Mule Entering Barn $775
Music Bank, tin $225
Musical Church, wood............. $345
Musical Savings Bank, Regina $12,000
Musical Savings, tin $2,600
Musical Savings, velvet-covered easel $7,000
Musical Savings, velvet-covered frame $7,000
Musical Savings, wood house ... $570
National Bank $8,000
National, Your Savings, cash register $1,680
Nestle's Automatic Chocolate, cardboard, vending $1,200
*New Bank, lever at center $750
*New Bank, lever at left $750
†New Creedmoor Bank $675
Nodding Clown, pewter and brass $1,800
Nodding Dog, painted tin $7,500
†North Pole Bank $18,000
Novelty Bank $1,800
Octagonal Fort Bank............. $4,500
Old Mother Hubbard, tin $7,500
*Organ Bank, boy and girl $950
*Organ Bank, cat and dog........ $850
*Organ Bank, medium, only monkey figure $575
*Organ Bank, tiny, only monkey figure.................................. $650
Organ Grinder and Dancing Bear $4,500
Owl, slot in book................... $200
Owl, slot in head $280
*Owl, turns head $280
*Paddy and the Pig $4,200

Panorama Bank $22,000
Pascal Chocolate Cigarettes, vending, tin $1,080
Pay Phone Bank, iron $1,680
Pay Phone Bank, tin............... $450
†Peg-Leg Beggar $1,400
*Pelican, Arab head pops out... $1,200
*Pelican, Mammy head pops out $1,200
*Pelican, man thumbs nose ... $1,200
*Pelican, rabbit pops out $1,200
†Perfection Registering, girl and dog at blackboard $17,000
Piano, musical $1,600
*Picture Gallery $23,000
Pig in High Chair $950
Pinball Vending, tin $1,320
Pistol Bank, iron $1,400
Pistol Bank, iron, Uncle Sam figure pops out $22,000
Pistol Bank, litho, tin........... $3,700
Pistol Bank, sheet steel........... $1,120
Policeman, tin $300
Popeye Knockout, tin $750
Post Office Savings, steel $1,200
†Preacher in the Pulpit.... $150,000
†Presto, iron building $570
Presto, mouse on roof, wood and paper................................. $16,000
*Presto, penny changes optically to quarter $455
Pump and Bucket $2,000
*Punch and Judy, iron............ $2,400
Punch and Judy, iron front, tin back $4,200
Punch and Judy, litho tin, c1910 .... $1,400
Punch and Judy, litho tin, c1930 .... $400
†Queen Victoria, bust, brass .. $14,000
†Queen Victoria, bust, iron .. $32,000
Rabbit in Cabbage............... $575
†Rabbit Standing, large $1,600
†Rabbit Standing, small $950
Reclining Chinaman with Cards $7,500
Record Money Box, tin scales $6,700
†Red Riding Hood, iron $55,000

Red Riding Hood, tin, vending...$700
†Rival Bank..................... $65,000
Robot Bank, aluminum $1,500
Robot Bank, iron $3,500
Roller-Skating Bank............ $37,000
Rooster $1,200
Royal Trick Elephant, tin....... $5,500
Safe Deposit Bank, tin, elephant $45,000
Safety Locomotive, semi $950
Sailor Face, tin, pointed top ... $1,920
Sailor Money Box, wood $4,000
Saluting Sailor, tin $1,400
Sam Segal's Aim to Save, brass and wood $15,000
Sam Segal's Aim to Save, iron $22,000
*Santa Claus $2,800
Savo, circular, tin $200
Savo, rectangular, tin............... $200
†Schley Bottling Up Cevera $26,000
Schokolade Automat, tin, vending $1,200
School Teacher, tin and wood, American $15,000
School Teacher, tin, German .. $6,000
Scotchman, tin.................... $850
Seek Him Frisk $55,000
Sentry Bank, tin $375
Sentry Bugler, tin $165
†Shoot That Hat Bank......... $85,000
†Shoot the Chute Bank $60,000
Signal Cabin, tin $250
†Smith X-ray Bank $3,200
Snake and Frog in Pond, tin $4,200
*Snap-It Bank $840
Snow White, tin and lead........ $8,500
*Speaking Dog.................... $2,500
Spring Jawed Alligator, pot metal $2,000
Spring Jawed Bonzo, pot metal $2,000
Spring Jawed Bulldog, pot metal $2,000
Spring Jawed Cat, pot metal . $2,000
Spring Jawed Chinaman, pot metal $3,700

Left: Boy Robbing Bird's Nest, J.&E. Stevens, 1906, **$10,500;** *upper right: Boy Scout Camp, J.&E. Stevens, 1912,* **$6,000;** *lower right: Springing Cat, Charles A. Bailey, 1882,* **$15,000.**

Spring Jawed Donkey, pot metal $2,000
Spring Jawed Felix the Cat, pot metal...$3,700
Spring Jawed Mickey Mouse, pot metal...$22,000
Spring Jawed Monkey, pot metal $1,400
Spring Jawed Parrot, pot metal $1,400
Spring Jawed Penguin, pot metal $1,400
†**Squirrel and Tree Stump** $950
Starkies Aeroplane, aluminum, cardboard.................................$5,500
Starkies Aeroplane, aluminum, steel $8,500
Stollwerk Bros., large vending, tin $960
Stollwerk Bros., Progressive Sampler, tin.....................................$330
Stollwerk Bros., two penny, vending, tin $840
Stollwerk Bros., vending, tin $650
Stollwerk Bros., Victoria, sparautomat, tin.................................$570
*****Stump Speaker Bank** $1,200
Sweet Thrift, tin, vending..........$345
Symphonium Musical Savings, wood $1,200
†**Tabby**...$1,200
*****Tammany Bank**............................ $450
Tank and Cannon, aluminum ... $650
Tank and Cannon, iron...........$1,200

†**Target Bank**................................ $550
†**Target In Vestibule**..............$5,000
*****Teddy and The Bear** $2,600
Ten Cent Adding Bank...........$1,200
Thrifty Animal Bank, tin $300
Thrifty Scotchman, wood, paper $1,200
Thrifty Tom's Jigger, tin........$1,500
Tid-Bits Money Box, tin............$350
Tiger, tin.....................................$1,200
Time is Money...........................$750
Time Lock Savings.....................$950
Time Registering Bank..............$350
*****Toad on Stump**...........................$650
Toilet Bank, tin...........................$300
Tommy Bank...............................$500
Treasure Chest Music Bank $450
*****Trick Dog**, six-part base.............$875
*****Trick Dog**, solid base.................$400
*****Trick Pony Bank**.....................$1,200
Trick Savings, wood, end drawer ..$400
Trick Savings, wood, side drawer ..$350
Tropical Chocolate Vending, tin $1,800
Try Your Weight, tin, semi $400
Try Your Weight, tin, mechanical $950
†**Turtle Bank**............................$30,000
Twentieth Century Savings Bank $300
Two Ducks Bank, lead $2,000
U.S. Bank, building.....................$510
†**U.S. and Spain** $5,000
†**Uncle Remus Bank**................$4,000

†**Uncle Sam Bank**, standing figure with satchel $1,600
†**Uncle Sam**, bust....................$1,800
†**Uncle Tom**, no lapels, with star $850
†**Uncle Tom**, lapels, with star $850
†**Uncle Tom**, no star....................$800
United States Bank, safe........$4,000
Viennese soldier.........................$950
Volunteer Bank...........................$750
Watch Bank, blank face, tin........$120
Watch Bank, dime disappears, tin $165
Watch Bank, stamped face, tin.....$90
Watchdog Safe........................$2,200
Weeden's Plantation, tin, wood..$950
Weight Lifter, tin....................$3,000
Whale Bank, pot metal..............$300
*****William Tell**, iron.....................$775
William Tell, crossbow, Australian, sheet steel, aluminum $875
Wimbledon Bank.........................$750
Winner Savings Bank, tin ...$12,500
Wireless Bank, tin, wood, iron ..$300
Woodpecker Bank, large, tin, c1910 ....$2,800
Woodpecker Bank, small, tin, c1930-1960...$50
World's Banker, tin $5,500
*****World's Fair Bank** $2,300
Zentral Sparkasse, steel...........$750
Zig Zag Bank, iron, tin, papier-mâché $200,000
Zoo...$2,300

BANKS, STILL

History: Banks with no mechanical action are known as still banks. The first still banks were made of wood or pottery or from gourds. Redware and stoneware banks, made by America's early potters, are prized possessions of today's collectors.

Still banks reached a golden age with the arrival of the cast-iron bank. Leading manufacturing companies include Arcade Mfg. Co., J. Chein & Co., Hubley, J. & E. Stevens, and A. C. Williams. The banks often were ornately painted to enhance their appeal. During the cast-iron era, banks and other businesses used the still bank as a form of advertising.

The tin lithograph bank, again frequently a tool for advertising, reached its zenith from 1930 to 1955. The tin bank was an important premium, whether a Pabst Blue Ribbon beer can bank or a Gerber's Orange Juice bank. Most tin advertising banks resembled the packaging of the product.

Almost every substance has been used to make a still bank— die-cast white metal, aluminum, brass, plastic, glass, etc. Many of the early glass candy containers also converted to a bank after the candy was eaten. Thousands of varieties of still banks were made, and hundreds of new varieties appear on the market each year.

Brass, beehive, EOS, well detailed, base marked "A. B. Dalames Bank," 4" h, 4-1/2" d............................**$385**

Cast iron

Building, Kyser & Rex, Town Hall and Log Cabin, chimney on left side, "Town Hall Bank" painted yellow, c1882, 2-3/4" to 4-3/4" h.........**$260**

Bungalow, Grey Iron Ceiling Co., porch, painted, 3-3/4" h...........**$470**

Cab, Arcade, Yellow Cab, painted orange and black, stenciling on doors, seated driver, rubber tires, painted metal wheels, coin slot in roof, 7-3/4" l..............................**$935**

Cat With Ball, A. C. Williams, painted gray, gold ball, 2-1/2" x 5-11/16"............................**$190**

Circus Elephant, Hubley, colorfully painted, seated position, 3-7/8" h............................**$180**

Coronation, Syndeham & McOustra, England, ornately detailed, emb busts in center, England, c1911, 6-5/8" h...............................**$200**

Duck, Hubley, colorfully painted, outstretched wings, slot on back, 4-3/4" h............................**$165**

Dutch Boy and Girl, Hubley, colorfully painted, boy on barrel, girl holding flowers, price for pr, c1930, 5-1/4" and 5-1/8" h.................**$260**

Egyptian Tomb, green finish, pharaoh's tomb entrance, hieroglyphics on front panel, 6-1/4" x 5-1/4"............................**$275**

Elk, painted gold, full antlers, 9-1/2" h............................**$155**

Globe Safe, Kenton, round sphere, claw feet, nickeled combination lock on front hinged door, 5" h.........**$80**

Hall Clock, swinging pendulum visible through panel, 5-3/4" h **$110**

Horseshoe, Arcade, Buster Brown and Tige with horse, painted black and gold, 4-1/4" x 4-3/4"................**$125**

Husky, Grey Iron Casting Co., painted brown, black eyes, yellow box, repaired, 5" h **$365**

Jewel Chest, ornate casting, ftd bank, brass combination lock on front, top lifts for coin retrieval, crack at corner, 6-1/8" x 4-5/8"................**$90**

Kodak, J. & E. Stevens, nickeled, highly detailed casting, intricate pattern, emb "Kodak Bank" on front opening panel, c1905, 4-1/4" x 5" w .**$225**

North Pole, nickeled, Grey Iron Casting Co., depicts wooden pole with handle, emb lettering, 4-1/4" h............................**$415**

Mailbox, Hubley, painted green, emb "Air Mail," with eagle, standing type, 5-1/2" h **$220**

Maine, Grey Iron Casting Co., japanned, gold highlights, c1900, 4-5/8" l............................**$660**

Mammy, Hubley, hands on hips, colorfully painted, 5-1/4" h **$300**

Pagoda, England, gold trim, c1889, 5" x 3" x 3"............................**$240**

Pershing, General, Grey Iron Casting Co., full bust, detailed casting, 7-3/4" h **$65**

Pig, Hubley, laughing, painted brown, trap on bottom, 2-1/2" h, 5-1/4" l............................**$120**

Professor Pug Frog, A.C. Williams, painted gold, blue jacket, new twist pin, 3-1/4" h............................**$195**

Radio, Kenton, metal sides and back, painted green, nickeled front panel in Art-Deco style, 4-1/2" h **$445**

Reindeer, A. C. Williams, painted gold, full rack of antlers, replaced screw, 9-1/2" h, 5-1/4" l........................**$55**

Rumplestiltskin, painted gold, long red hat, base and feet, marked "Do You Know Me," c1910, 6" h......**$210**

Safe, Kyser & Rex, Young America, japanned, intricate casting, emb at top, c1882, 4-3/8" h............**$275**

Sharecropper, A. C. Williams, painted black, gold, and red, toes visible on one foot, 5-1/2" h.................**$240**

Spitz, Grey Iron Casting Co., painted gold, repaired, 4-1/4" x 4-1/2" h............................**$165**

Still bank, Independence Hall Tower centennial bank, cast iron, worn gilt surface, maker's marks on base "Made by Enterprise Mfg. Co. Phila. Pat. Sept 21, 75", 9-1/2" h, **$380.**
Photo courtesy of Skinner, Inc.

Steamboat, Arcade, painted gold, 7-1/2" l............................**$190**

Stove, Gem, Abendroth Bros., traces of bronzing, back marked "Gem Heaters Save Money," 4-3/4" h ..**$275**

Tank, Ferrosteel, side mounted guns, rear spoke wheels, emb on sides, c1919, 9-1/2" l, 4" w **$385**

U.S. Mail, Kenton, painted silver, gold painted emb eagle, red lettering large trap on back panel, 5-1/8" h **$180**

World Time, Arcade, paper time-tables of various cities around the world, 4-1/8" x 2-5/8"...............**$315**

Chalk

Cat, seated, stripes, red bow, 11" h **$200**

Winston Churchill, bust, painted green, back etched "Save for Victory," wood base, 5-1/4" h..........**$55**

Glass

Charles Chaplin, Geo Borgfeldt & Co., painted figure standing next to barrel slotted on lid, name emb on base, 3-3/4" h **$220**

Lead

Boxer, Germany, head, painted brown, black facial details, lock on collar, bent in back, 2-5/8" h...............**$130**

Burro, Japan, lock on saddle marked "Plymouth, VT," 3-1/2" x 3-1/2" .**$125**

Ocean liner, bronze electroplated, three smoking stacks, hinged trap on deck, small hole, 2-3/4" x 7-5/8" l......................................**$180**

Pug, Germany, painted, stenciled "Hershey Park" on side, lock on collar, 2-3/4" h **$300**

Pottery

Acorn, redware, paper label reads "Tithing Day/ At The/First Methodist Episcopal Church/Sunday January 2nd 1916/In the Interest of the Improvement Fund," 3-1/2" d, 4" h **$220**

Bulbous, redware, marked with initials "C.R.S.," flakes on base, 3-1/4" h **$220**

Dresser, redware, Empire chest of drawers shape, Philadelphia, PA, loss to feet, roughness on edges, 6-1/2" w, 4" d, 4-1/2" h.............**$220**

Hanging Persimmon, redware, yellow and red paint, 5" x 3" **$90**

House, redware, Georgian style house, brown glazed accents, good detail on windows and doorways, central chimney, Jim Seagreaves, sgd "JCS," 7-1/2" h **$425**

Jug, redware, bulbous, bird atop mouth, green and yellow graffito dev, Jim Seagreaves, sgd "JCS," 7-1/2" h **$515**

Steel

Lifeboat, pressed, painted yellow and blue, boat length decal marked "Contributions for Royal National Life Boat Institution," deck lifts for coin removal, over painted, 14" l **$360**

Postal Savings, copper finish, glass view front panel, paper registering strips, emb "U.S.Mail" on sides, top lifts to reveal four coin slots, patent 1902, 4-5/8" h, 5-3/8" w.............**$95**

Stoneware

Dog's Head, white clay, yellow glaze, two-tone brown sponging, shallow flakes, 4" h................................**$175**

Ovoid, brushed cobalt blue flowers, leaves, and finial, minor flakes at coin slot, 6" h **$6,875**

Pig, sitting, sgd in dark green "Delight M. Caskey Merry Christmas," 6-1/4" l **$3,000**

Tin litho, Keene Savings, Kingsbury, bank building shape, non-working tally wheels, 6-1/2" x 6" x 3" **$70**

White metal

Amish Boy, seated on bale of straw, U.S., painted in bright colors, key lock trap on bottom, 4-3/4" x 3-3/8"..**$55**

Cat With Bow, painted white, blue bow, 4-1/8" h............................**$155**

Gorilla, colorfully painted in brown hues, seated position, trap on bottom **$165**

Pig, painted white, decal marked "West Point, N.Y." on belly, 4-3/8" h **$30**

Rabbit, seated, painted brown, painted eyes, trap on bottom, crack in ear, 4-1/2" h **$30**

Spaniel, seated, painted white, black highlights, 4-1/2" h **$470**

Uncle Sam Hat, painted red, white, and blue, stars on brim, slot on top, trap on bottom, 3-1/2" h..........**$135**

Wood

Burlwood inlaid with exotic woods, top dec with geometric banding, front with sailing vessels, end panels with flags, Prisoner of War, late 19th C, imperfections, 5"x 8" x 5-1/4"...................................**$1,150**

Left: Bailey's Centennial Money Bank, 1875; right: City Bank with Chimney, 1870s, **$3,500.**

Bank, Mammy, cast iron, slot in back, painted red hat, dress, white kerchief and apron, some loss to paint, **$85.**

BARBIE®

History: In 1945, Harold Matson (MATT) and Ruth and Elliott (EL) Handler founded Mattel. Initially the company made picture frames but became involved in the toy market when Elliott Handler began to make doll furniture from scrap material. When Harold Matson left the firm, Elliott Handler became chief designer and Ruth Handler principal marketer. In 1955, Mattel advertised its products on "The Mickey Mouse Club," and the company prospered.

In 1958, Mattel patented a fashion doll. The doll was named "Barbie" and reached the toy shelves in 1959. By 1960, Barbie's popularity was assured.

Development of a boyfriend for Barbie, named Ken after the Handlers' son, began in 1960. Over the years, many other dolls were added. Clothing, vehicles, room settings, and other accessories became an integral part of the line.

From September 1961 through July 1972, Mattel published a Barbie magazine. At its peak, the Barbie Fan Club was second only to the Girl Scouts as the largest girls' organization in the United States.

Always remember that a large quantity of Barbie dolls and related material has been manufactured. Because of this easy availability, only objects in excellent to mint condition with original packaging (also in very good or better condition) have significant value. If items show signs of heavy use, their value is probably minimal.

Collectors prefer items from the first decade of production. Learn how to distinguish a Barbie #1 doll from its successors. The Barbie market is one of subtleties.

Recently, many collectors have shifted their focus from the dolls themselves to the accessories. There have been rapid price increases in early clothing and accessories.

Barbie is now a billion-dollar baby, the first toy in history to reach this prestigious mark—that's a billion dollars per year, just in case you're wondering.

Accessories

Alarm clock, beige plastic, gold clock numbers, gold metal knobs on back, 1964, VG, nonworking **$320**

Autographs book, black vinyl, graphics on cover, white and colored pages, age discolored rect sticker on upper left corner, 1961, NM/VG **$125**

Barbie Teen Dream Bedroom, MIB, discoloration to orig box, dated 1970 .... **$65**

Binder with pencil case, black vinyl covers, metal three-ring binder, Dennison Webster's Notebook Dictionary, Study-Aids in Arithmetic, English Grammar, American History, General Science, NJ, 1962 .... **$400**

Lunch kit, black vinyl, thermos, cardboard insert, plastic handle, metal closure, 1962 .... **$145**

Paper doll book, Whitman, uncut Barbie's Boutique, #1954, dated 1973, NM **$85**

Francie with Growing Pretty Hair, #1982, dated 1973, NM **$35**

Midge, #1962, dated 1963, NM **$150**

Play ring, adjustable, side view of Ponytail Barbie head surrounded by 10 clear rhinestones, clear plastic case with blue bottom, cardboard backing, pre-priced at .29, 1962, NRFC **$135**

Snaps n' Scraps, blue vinyl covers, graphics on front cover, nine construction paper-type pages, black plastic binder with cord ties, 1961, VG **$125**

Transistor radio, Vanity Fair, black vinyl case, Barbie graphics, metal closure, black velveteen liner, peach colored plastic radio, gold front, plastic dials, plastic and metal earphones, matching plastic case, 1962, VG **$700**

Wallet, red vinyl, graphic of Barbie wearing Enchanted Evening, zipper closure on coin compartment, attached metal bead chain, four clear plastic photo holders, black and white photo of Perry Como and Maureen O'Hara, cream colored plastic change holder, mirror, snap closure, 1962, VG **$145**

Barbie Dolls
American Girl Barbie

Brunette, tan lips, fingernails painted, bendable legs, knit Pak dress, fringe trim, cord belt, pale no box, VG **$300**

Golden blonde, beige lips, nostril paint, fingernails painted, orange one-pc swimsuit, no box, VG **$350**

Light blonde hair, peach lips, fingernails painted, bendable legs, Lunch

Commuter Set, #916, 1959-1960. This exciting fashion was reproduced in 1999 as part of Mattel's Collectors' Request series, MIP, orig, **$1,500.**

Date, Barbie Pak, sleeveless dress, olive green skirt, green and white bodice no box, VG.................**$450**

Titian hair, gold lips, fingernails painted, bendable legs, #1665 Here Comes the Bride outfit, white satin sleeveless gown, white tulle long veil, lace trim on gown and veil, ribbon bow accents, white nylon long gloves, blue nylon garter, white pointed toe shoes, box, VG......**$350**

Billions of Dreams Barbie, marked one billionth Barbie sold since 1959, #17641, serial #00305, orig shipping box, box dated 1997, NRFB, box slightly scuffed.............................**$275**

Bubblecut Barbie

Blonde, coral lips, nostril paint, fingernails and toenails painted, straight legs, #1610 Golden Evening outfit, gold knit shirt, matching long skirt with gold glitter, gold belt with buckle, mustard open toe shoes, three-charm bracelet, no box, VG, loss to glitter **$90**

Blonde, white lips with pink tint, white nostril paint, fingernails painted, toenails with faint paint, straight legs, one-pc red nylon swimsuit, red open toe shoes, orig box with gold wire stand, no box, VG **$250**

Brunette, red lips, fingernails and toenails painted lightly, straight legs, Pak outfit, red and white striped knit shirt, blue shorts, no box, VG/ G, frayed tag **$135**

Light blonde, pink lips, fingernails and toenails painted, straight legs, Best Bow Pak red dress, attached bow, floral print skirt, no box, VG **$125**

Titian hair, coral lips, nostril paint, fingernails and toenails painted, straight legs, black and white striped one-pc swimsuit, pearl earrings, black open toe shoes, white rimmed glasses with blue lenses, black white stand, booklet, orig box, VG **$200**

Color Magic Barbie

Lemon yellow hair, blue metal hair barrette, pink lips, cheek blush, fingernails painted, bendable legs, #1692 Patio Party, floral print nylon jumpsuit, blue and green satin overdress, blue pointed toe shoes, no box, NM **$550**

Red hair, green metal hair barrette, pink lips, fingernails painted, bendable legs, nude, no box, VG **$450**

Red hair, pink lips, cheek blush, fingernails painted, toenails with faint paint, bendable legs, nude, no box, NM/VG.....................................**$425**

Fashion Queen, painted brunette hair, blue vinyl headband, pink lips, fingernails and toenails painted, straight legs, gold and white striped swimsuit, matching turban cap, pearl earrings in box with white plastic wig stand with brunette pageboy, blonde bubblecut, and titian side-part wigs, black wire stand, orig box, MIB **$300**

Growin' Pretty Hair, blonde, peach lips, cheek blush, rooted eyelashes, bendable legs, pink satin dress, wrist tag, orig box with hair accessories, pink high tongue shoes, orig box, NRFB...**$475**

Hair Happenin's, titian hair, pink lips, cheek blush, rooted eyelashes, fingernails painted, bendable legs, nude, titan long hair piece braided with pink ribbon, no box, VG **$200**

Happy Holidays, orig box

1988, #1, NRFB...........................**$350**

1989, plastic window and box scuffed, NRFB....................................**$125**

1990, plastic window and box slightly scuffed, NRFB...........................**$70**

1991, box slightly scuffed and discolored, NRFB **$70**

Ponytail #1, model #850, brunette, striped white-striped swimsuit, white sunglasses, red lips and toenails, black shoes, MIB, $9,000.

1992, box slightly scuffed and worn, NRFB................................**$50**

Living Barbie, brunette, pink lips, cheek blush, rooted eyelashes, bendable arms, bendable legs, rotating wrists, orig silver and gold one-pc swimsuit, orange net cover-up with gold trim, booklet, no box, NM **$75**

Mackie, Bob

Gold Barbie, first in series, #5409, orig shipping box, 1990, NRFB........**$250**

Goddess of the Sun, eighth in series, #14056, certificate, stand, orig shipping box, 1995, NRFB..............**$65**

Madame Du Barbie, tenth in series, #17934, certificate, stand, 1997, MIB...**$145**

Queen of Hearts, seventh in series, #12056, certificate, stand, shipping box, 1994, NRFB **$150**

Ponytail

#1 ponytail

Blonde, red lips, fingernails and toenails painted, straight legs, black and white striped one-pc swimsuit, silver loop earrings, black #1 open-toe shoes with holes, white rimmed glasses with blue lenses, pink cover booklet, reproduction #1 stand, box with replaced insert, VG **$3,400**

Growing Up Skipper, Model #7259, blonde, red top, red and white hound's tooth skirt with blue band, red boots, MIB, $80.

Blonde, reset in ponytail, red lips, nostril paint, fingernails painted, TL, straight legs, black and white striped one-pc swimsuit, gold hoop earrings, one black #1 open toe shoe with hole (unmarked), white rimmed glasses with blue lenses, pink cov booklet, orig box with partial Marshall Field's sticker, VG **$3,200**

#3 ponytail, brunette, red lips, nostril paint, brown eyeliner, fingernails painted, straight legs, #976 Sweater Girl outfit, orange knit sweater, matching shell, gray skirt, black open toe shoes, pearl earrings, wooden bowl with orange, green and yellow yarn with two needles, metal scissors, *How to Knit* book, black pedestal with plastic base, pink cover booklet, white rimmed glasses with blue lenses, no box, hair and banks no box and fuzzy, VG/G **$475**

#5 ponytail, brunette, orig set, red lips, nostril paint, fingernails and toenails painted, straight legs, Pak outfit, black and white striped knit shirt, red shorts, no box, NM/VG **$300**

#6 ponytail

Brunette, orig ponytail top knot, coral lips, fingernails and toenails painted, straight legs, Japan market silver kimono, lavender lining, black and silver obi tied with silver and purple cord, attached bow, white nylon short gloves, black open toe shoes, silver and white purse with cord handle, VG **$375**

Titian hair, orig top knot, beige lips, fingernails and toenails painted, straight legs, blue two-pc pajamas with lace trim, button accents, no box, VG **$325**

Presidential Porcelain Collection, Royal Splendor, #01078, #10950, 1993, NRFB **$70**

Standard

Brunette, pink lips, cheek blush, fingernails painted, toenails with faint paint, straight legs, orig pink nylon swimsuit bottoms with plastic flower accent, #1804 Knit Hit blue and pink knit dress, pale blue high tongue shoes, no box, VG **$150**

Light brunette, pink lips, cheek blush, fingernails and toenails painted, straight legs, nude, no box, replaced rubber band, VG **$190**

Swirl ponytail

Brunette hair in orig set, coral lips, fingernails and toenails painted,

straight legs, #1638 Fraternity Dance gown, pink satin skirt, pink chiffon overskirt, white lacy bodice, blue and green nylon waist scarf, brooch accent, rose colored open toe shoes, single pearl necklace, white nylon long gloves, orig box, VG/G **$450**

Brunette hair in orig set, yellow ribbon, metal hair pin, coral lips, fingernails and toenails painted, straight legs, red nylon one-pc swimsuit, red open toe shoes, pearl earrings, wrist tag, box with gold metal stand, NM **$675**

Platinum hair in orig set, yellow ribbon, metal hair pin, white lips, fingernails painted, straight legs, nude, no box, NM-VG **$475**

Talking, brunette, ribbon bow ties, pink lips, cheek blush, rooted eyelashes, bendable legs, red nylon two pc swimsuit with metal accent on bottoms, white and silver net cover-up with red trim, no box, possible repairs to talker, working condition, VG **$275**

Twist 'n' Turn

Blonde, pink lips, cheek blush, fingernails and toenails painted, bendable legs, multicolored one-pc knit swimsuit, wrist tag, clear plastic stand, booklet, NRFB **$425**

Brunette, pink lips, cheek blush, fingernails painted, bendable legs, #1485 Gypsy Spirits outfit, pink nylon blouse, aqua suede skirt, matching vest, no box, VG **$125**

Pale blonde, pink lips, cheek blush, rooted eyelashes, fingernails painted, bendable legs, two-pc orange vinyl swimsuit, white net cover-up with orange trim, trade-in program doll, no box, VG **$475**

Friends and family dolls

Allan, painted red hair, pink lips, straight legs, #1409 Goin' Hunting, red plaid shirt, denim pants, red socks, black boots, red plastic cap, hunting rifle, frayed wrist tag, VG **$90**

Casey, blonde hair, clear plastic headband, peach lips, cheek blush, two-pc hot pink nylon swimsuit, orig clear plastic bag, cardboard hanger, orig price sticker, NRFP **$275**

Chris, Color Magic-type titian hair, green metal hair barrette, pink lips, cheek blush, bendable arms and legs,

Happy Holidays #1, 1988, Model #1703, blonde, MIB **$700.**

#3617 Birthday Beauties outfit, pink floral dress, white slip, white fishnet tights, white shoes with molded straps, gold wrapped present with white ribbon and pink flower accents, one pink crepe paper party favor with gold glitter, white paper invitation, orig box, VG **$125**

Christie

Talking, red hair, pink lips, cheek blush, rooted eyelashes, bendable legs, wrist tag, clear plastic stand, nonworking, box age discolored, scuffed, and worn, NRFM **$250**

Twist 'n' Turn, red hair, pink lips, cheek blush, rooted eyelashes, bendable legs, #1841 Night Clouds, yellow, orange and pink nylon ruffled nightgown with ribbon straps, matching yellow nylon robe with ribbon ties and flower accents, no box, VG **$125**

Francie

Brunette, clear plastic headband, peach lips, cheek blush, two-pc yellow nylon swimsuit, orig clear plastic bag, cardboard hanger, orig price sticker, NRFP **$250**

Brunette, pink lips, cheek blush, bent legs, ring earrings, Slightly Summery Pak dress, Barbie print top, green pleated skirt, VG **$100**

Malibu, The Sun Set, blonde, pink plastic sunglasses, plastic head cover, peach lips, painted teeth, bendable legs, pink and red nylon swimsuit, yellow vinyl waistband, orange terrycloth towel, box dated 1970, NRFB **$235**

Twist 'n' Turn, blonde, pink lips, cheek blush, rooted eyelashes, bendable legs, orig floral print outfit with lace trim, pink nylon bottoms, no box, VG **$300**

Ponytail #3, model #850, blonde, white-striped swimsuit, white sunglasses, red lips and toenails, black shoes, MIB, **$1,300.**

Roman Holiday (pictured on a Ponytail #4), Mattel, 1959, **$4,800.**

American Girl, first issue, 1965, model #1070, blonde, bendable legs, MIB, **$1,900.**

Jamie, walking, Furry Friends Gift Set, Sears Exclusive, titian hair, pink lips, cheek blush, rooted eyelashes, bendable legs, green, pink, and orange knit dress, orange belt with buckle, orange furry coat with pink vinyl trim, orange boots, gray dot with felt features, pink vinyl dog collar with silver accents, leash, no box, VG **$150**

Julia, talking, red hair, pink lips, cheek blush, rooted eyelashes, bendable legs, gold and silver jumpsuit with belt, wrist tag, clear plastic stand, NRFB, nonworking, box age discolored, scuffed, and worn **$225**

Ken

Brunette flocked hair, beige lips, straight legs, red swim trunks with white stripe, wrist tag, booklet, yellow terrycloth towel, cork sandals in cellophane bag, black white stand, orig box, oily face, worn wrist tag, VG **$155**

Brunette flocked hair, beige lips, straight legs, #790 Time for Tennis, white shirt and shorts, white sweater with navy and red trim, white socks and shoes, Tennis Rules book, tennis racquet and two balls, green plastic glasses, no box, NM **$115**

Brunette painted hair, beige lips, straight legs, #0782 Sleeper Set, blue and white striped pajamas, wax honey bun, metal alarm clock, glass of milk, no box, VG........... **$50**

Painted blond hair, peach lips, straight legs, #799 Touchdown red jersey with felt "7," red pants, white lacing closure, red socks with navy stripe, black cleats, red helmet, brown football, no box, VG **$50**

Painted brunette, peach lips, straight legs, #790 Time for Tennis outfit, white knit shirt, white sweater with blue and red trim, white shorts, socks, and shoes, tennis racquet and ball, no box, VG **$55**

Talking, painted brown hair, peach lips, painted teeth, bendable legs, #1435 Shore Lines outfit, blue nylon jacket with zipper closure, blue shorts, vinyl side stripes, multi-print pants with zipper closure, yellow plastic face mask with elastic head strap, swim fins, no box, non-working, stretched elastic on mask, NM **$100**

Midge

Blonde hair, pink lips, fingernails painted, white satin sleeveless shirt,

bolero jacket, wrap skirt, hat with bow accent, white open toe shoes, no box, VG **$85**

Titian hair, ribbon hair band, pink lips, fingernails painted, bendable legs, orig one-pc striped knit swimsuit, aqua open toe shoes, gold wire stand, orig box, VG **$425**

PJ, talking, blonde, beaded tie on left pigtail, replaced rubber-band on right pigtail, attached lavender plastic glasses, pink lips, cheek blush, rooted eyelashes, bendable legs, #1796 Fur Sighted outfit, orange jacket with fur trim, metallic gold tab and button closures, matching pants, zigzag print knit sweater, orange hat with fur trim, metallic gold chin strap, yellow high tongue shoes, no box, non-working, NM/VG **$155**

Ricky, painted red hair, peach lips, cheek blush, straight legs, striped jacket, blue shorts, cork sandals in bag, black wire stand, orig box with insert, wrist tag torn, NM **$140**

Skipper

Blonde, pink lips, straight legs, #1915 Outdoor Casuals, turquoise knit sweater, matching dickey with button closure, pants, white nylon

Bubblecut Barbie, second issue, 1962, model #850, blonde, wearing "Busy Morning" sundress, MIB, **$350.**

Hispanic Barbie, model #1292, black hair, 1980, MIB, **$75.**

Busy Barbie, model #3311, gripping hands, blonde, MIB, **$300.**

short gloves, white socks, white flat shoes, red wooden yo-yo, no box, VG... **$55**

Color Magic-type dark red hair, pink lips, straight legs, #1902 Silk 'n' Fancy dress, red velvet bodice, white skirt, red lace underskirt, gold braid waistband, white nylon socks, black flat shoes, NM **$90**

Color Magic-type titian hair, pink lips, straight legs, #1926 Chill Chasers, white fur coat, red cap with blue pompon, red flat shoes, no box, NM **$120**

Pose' n Play, blonde, blue ribbon ties, clear plastic headband, pink lips, cheek blush, bendable arms and legs, blue and white outfit with button accents, wrist tag, orig clear plastic bag, cardboard hanger, NRFP.. **$85**

Quick Curl, blonde hair, blue ribbon bow, pink lips, cheek blush, straight legs, blue and white long dress, orig clear plastic bag, NRFP **$150**

Skooter

Blonde, red ribbon bows, beige lips with tint of pink, cheek blush, straight legs, #1921 School Girl

outfit, red jacket with pocket insignia, red and white pleated skirt, white shirt, red felt hat with red and white band and feather accent, white nylon socks, red flat shoes, brown rimmed glasses, arithmetic, geography, and English books, black book strap, red and natural wooden pencils, orig box, VG **$90**

Brunette, hair in orig set with ribbons, pink lips, cheek blush, straight legs, #1901 Red Sensation dress, gold button accents, white nylon socks, red flat shoes, white nylon short gloves, straw hat with ribbon band and bow accent, NM **$70**

Brunette, retied with red cord, beige lips, cheek blush, straight legs, wearing Best Buy Fashions #9122, red plaid coat, black belt, matching cap with black ribbon accent, #9122 dress with red plaid skirt, black velveteen top, white nylon shirt, no box, VG **$70**

Tutti, Me and My Dog, brunette, red ribbon bow, pink lips, bendable arms and legs, red felt coat, fur trim, white fur hat with ribbon ties, red tights, white flat shoes, white dog with felt

features, attached red leash, no box, leash worn and knotted, VG **$70**

Outfits

Barbie

#934 black sleeveless dress, white collar, white hat with black ribbon accent, black open toe shoes, VG **$65**

#957 Knitting Pretty, pink sweater, matching sleeveless shell, pink flannel skirt, pink #1 open toe shoes, metal scissors, How to Knit book, wooden bowl with two needles, yellow, red, and pale pink yarn, VG/G **$160**

#958 Party Date, white satin dress, gold glitter accents, wide gold belt, gold clutch purse, clear open toe shoes, VG **$100**

#968 Roman Holiday, sheath, red and white striped bodice, navy blue skirt, matching red and white striped coat, black open toe #1 shoes, white nylon shirt gloves, red woven hat with bow accent, white vinyl clutch purse, black rimmed glasses, white hankie, pink plastic comb, brass compact, VG **$1,250**

Skipper, bendable leg, model #1030, brunette, MIB, **$250.**

Twist and Turn, model #1160, brunette, MIB, **$500.**

Busy Francie, model #3313, blonde MIB, **$425.**

#0873 Guinevere, royal blue velvet gown, embroidered and gold tri, attached chain belt, red and gold brocade slippers, red and gold brocade crown with navy blue and gold trim edging, attached gold nylon snood, red nylon armlets, NM/VG **$125**

#0874 Arabian Night, pink satin blouse, pink chiffon long skirt, matching pink sari with gold trim, gold foil slippers, gold plastic lamp, gold and turquoise beaded necklace, gold drop earrings, gold and turquoise plastic bracelets, paper theater program, VG **$95**

#1452 Now Knit, green, navy blue, and silver dress, matching green furry hat, blue nylon scarf with attached silver thread ring, NM/VG **$50**

#1489 Cloud 9, pale blue nylon short nightie with satin bodice, matching long robe, satin slippers, VG **$55**

#1593 Golden Groove, Sears Exclusive Gift Set, pink and gold lame jacket, matching short skirt, gold thigh-high boots, NM **$145**

#1612 Theatre Date, NRFB **$225**

#1615 Saturday Matinee, NM/VG

.... **$375**

#1617, Midnight Blue, NM/VG **$225**

#1620 Junior Designer, turquoise dress with green design, green pointed toe shoes, metal iron with black handle, *How to Design Your Own Fashion* book, VG **$80**

#1622 Student Teacher, red and white dress, white bodice inset with button accents, red vinyl belt, red pointed toe shoes, black rimmed glasses with clear lenses, plastic globe, wooden pointer stick, geography book, VG/G **$175**

#1629 Skater's Waltz, pink nylon skating suit, pink felt skirt, sheer nylon hose, white skates, pink fur muff, matching mittens, VG **$50**

#1635 Fashion Editor, sheath, turquoise skirt, floral print bodice, glitter accents, matching jacket, green ribbon trim, turquoise cap with flower bud accent and ribbon bow, turquoise pointed toe shoes, plastic camera, NM **$225**

#1637 Outdoor Life, blue and white checked coat, blue and white

houndstooth print pants, blue nylon shirt, white hat, tennis shoes, VG **$95**

#1644 On the Avenue, white and gold sheath with textured skirt, gold lame bodice, matching jacket, white nylon short gloves, cream-colored pointed toe shoes, gold clutch purse, jacket tag frayed, P condition belt, NM/VG **$150**

#1645 Golden Glory, gold floral lame long dress, green chiffon waist scarf, matching gold lame long coat with fur trim, white nylon short gloves, green satin clutch purse, VG ... **$120**

#1649 Lunch on the Terrace, green and white checkered dress with polka dot bodice, matching hat with white net cover, VG **$115**

#1650 Outdoor Art Show, VG **$145**

#1652, Pretty as a Picture, VG ... **$115**

#1656 Fashion Luncheon, VG/G .. **$225**

#1663, Music Center Matinee, NM/VG **$200**

#1678 Pan American Airways Stewardess, gray-blue jacket, attached metal wings, matching skirt, and cap, white shirt, white nylon short gloves, black pointed toe shoes, black vinyl shoulder bag, VG .. **$700**

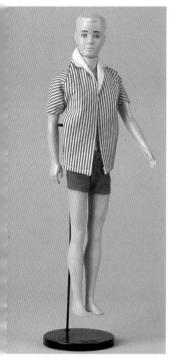

Ken, blond, painted hair, 1962 shorter doll, model #750, MIB, **$175.**

Talking P.J., model #1113, orange flowered dress, blonde, MIB, **$250.**

Skooter, first issue, straight leg, model #1040, blonde, MIB, **$180.**

#1687 Caribbean Cruise, yellow jumpsuit with halter top, yellow flat soft shoes, NM............................ **$50**

#1695 Evening Enchantment, red taffeta and chiffon long dress, marabou trim, matching chiffon cape, red pointed toe shoes, VG **$135**

#1792 Mood Matchers, paisley print nylon sleeveless blouse, matching pants, aqua nylon shirt, hot pink high tongue shoes, M **$65**

#1814 Sparkle Squares, checkerboard pattern coat with ruffle trim, rhinestone buttons, matching dress with pleated white nylon skirt, white sheet stockings, NM................ **$105**

#1848 All That Jazz, satin striped coat, matching dress with pleated skirt, beige sheer stockings, pink shoes with molded bows, VG .. **$140**

#1880 Winter Wedding, cream colored brocade gown with fur trim, brocade and fur trimmed cap with attached metal headband and tulle veil, white pointed-toe shoes, VG **$75**

#3428 The Zig Zag Bag, red and white zig zag pattern knit pants, orange terry cloth sleeveless shirt, zig-zag nylon shirt, red tennis shoes, M **$185**

#4041 Color Magic Fashion Fun, NM/VG... **$145**

Dressed Up, Barbie Pak, dress with pale blue satin skirt, gold and white striped bodice, attached belt and buckle accents, pale blue pointed toe shoes, NM/VG **$105**

Gala Abend, foreign market, white brocade gown, matching long coat with pale blue satin lining and fur collar, white nylon long gloves, white pointed toe shoes, VG **$700**

Francie

#1216 The Lace Pace, gold lame and pink coat cov with white lace, satin bow, matching dress with satin straps, pink shoes with molded bows, VG................................... **$105**

#1222 Gold Rush, orange satin dress, bright orange open toe shoes, VG **$40**

#1232 Two for the Ball, pink chiffon long coat, black velvet waistband, long dress with pink satin skirt, pink lace overskirt, black velvet bodice, pink soft pumps, coat tag frayed, VG/G **$45**

#3367 Right for Stripes, blue vest, blue and white striped pants, matching midriff top, floral print shoulder bag, aqua sneakers, VG............. **$65**

Pancho Bravo, Francie Pak, blue, pink, green, and white poncho, blue ankle boots, lavender plastic glasses, label, some age discoloration to cardboard backing, orig 99 cent price sticker, NRFP..................... **$40**

The Bridge Bit, white knit sweater, green and blue stitching, royal blue stretch pants with metal accent, pink pillow with flower design, NM **$65**

Ken

#788 Rally Day, NRFB.................. **$66**

#797 Army and Air Force, NRFB **$245**

#799 Touchdown, NRFB, box in F/P condition................................. **$125**

#0770 Campus Hero, NRFB......... **$95**

#0772 The Prince, green and gold lame coat, lace trim, rhinestone buttons, green velvet cape with gold lining, green nylon tights, green velvet shoes with gold trim, gold velvet hat with emerald, pearl, and feather accents, white collar with lace trim, velvet pillow with gold trim and tassels, paper program, VG **$150**

Supersize Barbie, model #9828, blonde, 18" h, MIB, **$200.**

Francie, straight leg, model #1140, brunette, MIB, **$400.**

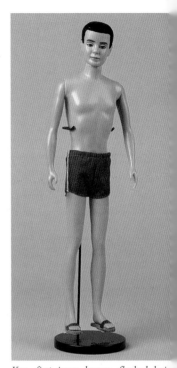

Ken, first issue, brown, flocked hair, model #750, red swimsuit, MIB, **$200.**

Earring Magic Ken, model #2290, painted hair with blond streaks, MIB, **$45.**

#0773 King Arthur, silver lame pants, shirt, and cap, red satin surcoat with gold griffin, gray plastic helmet and sword, brown scabbard, two red plastic spurs, cardboard shield, paper program, VG **$100**

#0779 American Airlines Captain, NRFB **$300**

#1404 Ken in Hawaii, VG **$40**

#1416 College Student, VG **$80**

#1417 Rovin' Reporter, red jacket, navy blue pants, white shirt, black socks and shoes, plastic camera, NM/VG
....**$75**

#1419 TV's Good Tonight, red robe, blue trim, pocket insignia, cork sandals with red straps, brown plastic TV with metal antenna, no tag on robe, VG **$60**

#1425 Best Man, VG-G **$150**

Ricky, #1502 Saturday Show, NRFB
....**$70**

Skipper

#1738 Fancy Pants, VG **$50**

#1901 Red Sensation, NRFB.......**$125**

#1912 Cookie Time, sleeveless dress, navy blue skirt, attached red belt, red flat shoes, miniature Barbie's Easy-As-Pie Cookbook, metal spoon with red plastic handle, gray bowl, Cookie Mix box, NM **$85**

#1913 Me n' My Doll, pink and white gingham checked dress, ribbon ties, flower embroidered accent, white nylon socks, white flat shoes, miniature plastic Barbie doll with painted features, pink and white checked skirt, VG **$80**

#1936 Sledding Fun, flower print jacket, fur collar, red sleeveless shirt, blue pans with sewn-on red socks, blue hat, one fur mitten, red boots, red and white plastic sled with cord handle, NM...............**$95**

#1972 Drizzle Sizzle, pink and Kelly green knit dress, orange vinyl appliqué flowers, clear plastic raincoat, cap, and boots, VG **$35**

DOLLS

History: Dolls have been children's play toys for centuries. Dolls also have served other functions. From the 14th through 18th centuries, doll making was centered in Europe, mainly in Germany and France. The French dolls produced in this era were representations of adults and dressed in the latest couturier designs. They were not children's toys.

During the mid-19th century, child and baby dolls, made in wax, cloth, bisque, and porcelain, were introduced. Facial features were hand painted, wigs were made of mohair and human hair, and the dolls were dressed in the current fashions for babies or children.

Doll making in the United States began to flourish in the 1900s with companies such as Effanbee, Madame Alexander, and Ideal.

Marks: Marks of the various manufacturers are found on the back of the head or neck or on the doll's back. These marks are very important in identifying a doll and its date of manufacture.

Additional Listings: See *Warman's Americana & Collectibles* for more examples.

Madame Alexander Susie-Q, all cloth, painted features, blue eyes, brown yarn wig, orig outfit, "Susie" Q//by Madame Alexander, N//ALL RIGHTS RESERVED on frayed clothing tag, light soil on costume, with orig label box, c1938, 15", **$575.**
Photo courtesy of McMasters Harris Auction Co.

Alt, Beck & Gottschalk, bisque shoulder head, blue paperweight eyes, multi-stroke brows, painted upper and lower lashes, closed mouth, molded blonde hair, kid body with pin joints at hips and knees, bisque lower arms, antique white dressing gown, blue coat, new underclothing, marked "998 No. 10" at back bottom of shoulder plate, 23" h
....**$950**

Amberg

Bottle Babe Twins, solid-dome bisque heads, light blue sleep eyes, softly blues brows, painted upper and lower lashes, open mouths, molded tongues, lightly molded and painted hair, cloth bodies with non-working criers, composition arms, right arms molded to hold celluloid bottles, orig white lace-trimmed baby dresses, slips, crocheted bonnets, diapers, and socks, hold orig celluloid baby bottle, blue and white celluloid rattle, marked "A.M./Germany/341/ 3" on back of heads, "Amberg's/Bottle Babe/Pat. Pending/Amberg Dolls/The World Standard" on dress, both dolls have light rubs on cheeks or hair, cloth bodies are aged, some flaking on arms, paint flaked off right arm of one, price for pr, 12-1/2" h................**$500**

New Born Babe, solid dome bisque head, blue sleep eyes, softly blushed brown, painted upper and lower lashes, closed mouth, lightly molded and painted hair, cloth body with composition hands, white lace-trimmed antique baby dress, slip and diaper, light dust in bisque, tiny run on upper lip, left side seam split near bottom of torso, 15" h
....**$315**

Armand Marseille

990 baby, bisque socket head, brown sleep eyes, feathered brows, painted upper and lower lashes, open mouth, well-accented lips, two upper teeth, antique human-hair wig, composition bent-limb baby body, antique baby dress, slip, diaper, new crocheted sweater, cap and booties, marked "Armand Marseille/ Germany/990/A 12 M" on back of head, heavy French-style body, arms repainted and have rough finish, right big toe missing, other toes repaired and repainted, normal wear at joints, 23" h....**$275**

Googly, bisque socket head, large slide glancing blue sleep eyes, single strike brows, closed smiling mouth, dark mohair wig, crude composition five-pc toddler body, lace-trimmed organdy baby dress, matching bonnet, slip, diaper, stockings, crocheted booties, marked "G. 253 B Germany A. 11/0 M" on back of head, repainted body, 6-1/2" h
....**$675**

Head circumference, Dream Baby, brown bisque socket head, brown sleep eyes, closed mouth, black painted hair, brown bent limb composition baby body, fine lawn christening gown with tucks, ruffles, and lace trim, c1920, 10" l, 9" d.....**$300**

Arranbee

Nancy Lee, composition head, brown sleep eyes with real lashes, painted lower lashes, single stroke brows, closed mouth, orig human-hair wig in orig set, five-pc composition body, orig brown flannel belted dress, white ruffle trim, orig underwear combination, orig socks and brown suede shoes with fringe tongue, marked "R & B" on back of head, unplayed with condition, 17" h
....**$300**

Nanette, hard plastic head, blue sleep eyes with real lashes, single-stroke brows, painted lower lashes, closed mouth, saran wig, five-pc hard-plastic walking body, orig red and white striped dress with red organdy sleeves and apron, blue vinyl wide belt with charms attached, wrist tag, curlers on card, comb, marked "R & B" on head, "Nanette/An R & B Quality Doll/R & B Dolly Company New York 3, NY" on label on end of box, "R & B/ Nanette/Walks/ Sits/Stands/ Turns Her Head/R & B Doll Company New York City" on wrist tag, near mint in aged box, lid damaged and repaired, 21" h...**$700**

Averill, Georgene

Bonnie Babe, solid dome bisque flange head, brown sleep eyes, softly brushed brows, painted upper and lower lashes, open mouth, two lower teeth, molded tongue, cloth mama doll body, composition lower arms and legs, antique long baby dress, marked "Copr by Georgene Averill 1005 3652 4 Germany" on back of head, body recovered, 20" h
....**$475**

Solid dome bisque flange head, blue sleep eyes, softly blushed brows, painted upper and lower lashes, open laughing mouth, two lower teeth, molded tongue, deeply molded dimples, lightly molded and painted curly hair, cloth mama-doll body, composition arms and lower legs, non-working crier, dressed in possibly orig white lace-trimmed baby dress, slip, underwear, socks, and knit booties, silk and lace bonnet, marked "Copr by Georgene Averill 1005 3652 3 Germany" on back of head, cloth body aged and lightly soiled, 17" h.................**$600**

Bahr & Proschild, 300, bisque socket head on bisque shoulder plate, blue set threaded paperweight eyes, feathered brows, painted upper and lower lashes, open mouth, four upper teeth, pierced tongue, orig human-hair wig, kid body with cloth torso, bisque lower arms, gussets at elbows, hips, and knees, antique white dress with lace trim, antique underclothing, orig blue velvet hat with flower trim, marked "300/10" on back of head, inherent red firing line at rim in back, minor wig pulls, tiny rub on right cheek, body aged and discolored, 19" h
....**$300**

Barrois, E., Poupee, pale bisque swivel head on shoulder plate, set blue eyes with threaded detail, fine multi-stroke brows, painted upper and lower lashes, closed mouth with accented lips, orig blonde mohair wig with orig tortoiseshell comb, kid body with kid-over-wood upper arms, mortise-and-tenon type knee joints, white dotted Swiss dress, possibly orig underclothing, socks, and shoes, marked "E 4 B," at rear edge of bisque shoulder plate, lower bisque arms replaced, 17-1/2" h.......................**$1,200**

Bisque

Oriental pair, olive-tone bisque socket heads, dark brown pupil-less set eyes, single stroke brows, painted upper and lower lashes, closed mouth, orig black mohair wigs, male with orig queue, five-pc olive-tone bisque bodies jointed at shoulders and hips, Oriental embroidered silk clothing, unmarked, price for pr, 4-1/2" h
....**$825**

Just Me, painted bisque socket head, blue side-glancing sleep eyes, single stroke brows, closed mouth, orig mohair wig, five-pc composition body jointed at shoulders and hips, orig white dress with orange and green felt trim, orig white cotton socks and white paper shoes with buckles, marked "Just Me/Registered/Germany/A 310/6/0 M" on back of head, needs to be restrung, 10" h
....**$900**

Miss Liberty, bisque shoulder head, painted blue eyes with molded lids, multi-stroke brows, tiny painted upper and lower lashes, closed mouth, molded earrings, molded and painted blonde hair with copper molded earrings, molded and painted blonde hair with copper tiara, two black ribbons across top of head and lay against left side of neck, molded bun with waterfall effect, cloth body, leather lower arms, red leather boots as part of lower leg, antique ecru wool dress with lace trim, antique underclothing, small holes in dress, 18" h
....**$1,650**

Bru Jne, bisque socket head, bulbous blue paperweight eyes, heavy feathered brows, painted upper and lower lashes, closed mouth, pierced ears, hand tied mohair wig, kid body with scalloped kid attaching body to shoulder plate, kid-over-wood upper arms, bisque lower arms, wooden lower legs, dressed in outfit made from antique ecru fabric and trims, beige and blue French style hat, French shoes marked "9," marked "Bru Jne/10" on back of head, "Bru" visible above kid on left rear shoulder, "No. 8" visible above kid on right rear shoulder, "Bebe Bru Bte S.G.D.G./Tout Contrefacteur sera saisi et poursuivi conformement a la Loi" on paper label on chest, 1" firing flaw on right forehead at crown, left little finger replaced, 22" h
....**$7,300**

Century Doll Co., bisque shoulder plate, blue sleep eyes, feathered brows, painted lashes, open mouth, four upper teeth, molded and painted hair, kid body pin jointed at hips and knees, jointed wood and composition arms, composition lower legs, redressed, marked "Made in Germany/Century Doll" on back of shoulder plate, 18" h
....**$325**

Chase, Martha, black cloth, dark brown painted on eyes, soft brick red painted mouth **$11,165**

China, unmarked

Frozen Charlie, pink tint, painted blue eyes, feathered brows, closed mouth, accent line between lips, painted blond hair with brush strokes around face, unjointed body with arms held in front, hands in fists, fingernails and toenails outlined, antique pink crocheted long dress and matching bonnet, 16" h
....**$675**

Open mouth, low brow, china shoulder head with turned head, painted blue eyes, red accent line, single stroke brows, open mouth, molded teeth, molded and painted wavy hair, cloth body, china lower arms and lower legs, painted garters, molded and painted brown shoes with heels, possibly orig beige print dress, underclothing, 18" h......**$850**

Cloth, Philadelphia Baby, painted head and shoulders, heavily lidded brown painted eyes, deeply modeled mouth, brown hair, cloth body, painted lower limbs, gray and white striped cotton shift, white undergarments, overall wear, paint rubs and loss, c1900, 21" h
....**$1,100**

Cochran, Dewees, Cindy, latex socket head, painted blue eyes, multi-stroke brows, painted upper lashes, closed mouth, human hair wig, five-pc latex body jointed at shoulders and hips, faded peach taffeta dress with tan collar and hem, purple velvet trim, marked "Dewees Cochran/Dolls" on torso under left arm, 15" h **$325**

Cuno & Otto Dressel

Bisque head, blue sleep eyes with lashes, open mouth, two upper teeth, replaced auburn mohair wig, fully articulated composition body, blue dress, imp "Cuno & Otto Dressel," some repair to body, early 20th C, 14" h **$200**

Girl, painted bisque socket head, blue sleep eyes with real lashes, feathered brows, shading around eyes, open mouth, four upper teeth, orig human-hair wig, jointed wood and composition teen-age body with high knee joints, orig clothing, short dress, slip, teddy, socks, and leather shoes, marked "Cuno & Otto Dressel/Germany" on back of head, 15-1/2" h **$450**

Demalcol, Googlie, bisque socket head, blue eyes set to side, single-stroke brows, painted upper and lower lashes, closed smiling mouth, human-hair wig, new jointed-composition body, blue and white flowered dress, matching bonnet, new underclothing, socks and shoes, marked "Demalcol/5/0/Germany" on back of head, 9-1/2" h **$525**

Eden Bebe, bisque socket head, blue paperweight eyes, feathered brows, painted upper and lower lashes, open mouth, six upper teeth, pierced ears, replaced mohair wig, jointed wood and composition French body, redressed, pale blue and ecru outfit, blue and beige jacket, antique underclothing, new stockings, and old shoes, marked "Eden Bebe/Paris/7/ Depose" on back of neck, "7" on front of neck, light kiln dust on left cheek, flaking at neck socket of body and on both lower legs, normal wear at joints and on hands, 16-1/2" h **$1,200**

Effanbee

American Child Boy, composition head, painted blue eyes, multi-stroke brows, tiny painted upper and lower lashes, closed smiling mouth, orig human-hair wig, five-pc composition child body, orig blue wool two-pc suit, jacket and shorts, white shirt, multicolored tie, orig socks and black leatherette shoes, unmarked, light facial crazing, few light lines of crazing on legs, 17" h **$1,050**

American Child, composition head, blue sleep eyes with real lashes, multi-stroke brows, painted lower lashes, closed mouth, orig human-hair wig with orig curlers, five-pc composition child body, orig blue and white striped zippered dress, nylon panties, orig white socks with blue trim, blue leatherette tie shoes, marked "Effanbee/American Children" on back of head, "Effanbee/Anne-Shirley" on back, unplayed with condition, 19-1/2" h **$1,500**

Grumpy Cowboy, composition shoulder head, painted blue eyes to side, single-stroke brows, closed pouty mouth, molded and painted hair, cloth body, composition arms and feet, cowboy outfit with plaid shirt, gold pants, green bandanna, imitation-leather chaps, holster with gun, replaced felt hat, marked "Effanbee/ Dolls/ Walk Talk Sleep" on back of shoulder plate, light crazing, light wear back of head, few flakes off shoulder plate, wear on edges of feet, 11" h **$475**

Gaultier, Francois

Bebe, bisque socket head, large blue paperweight eyes, feathered brows, painted upper and lower lashes, full-closed mouth, molded tongue, pierced ears, replaced mohair wig, jointed wood and composition body with straight wrists, new blue silk dress with matching bonnet, new underclothing, socks and lace-up boots, marked "F. G. (in scroll)/8" on back of head, fingers touched up, minor repairs, 21" h **$2,200**

Poupee, bisque socket head, bisque shoulder plate, light blue paperweight eyes, feathered brows, painted upper and lower lashes, closed mouth, pierced ears, orig mohair wig, cloth body with kid arms, individually stitched fingers, dressed in probably orig blue and white two-pc outfit with train, marked "2/0" on back of head, "F. G." on right shoulder, illegible mark on left shoulder, some age discoloration to body, one left finger missing, 10-1/2" h **$1,250**

Halbig, Simon

Bisque head, blue sleep eyes, open mouth, four molded teeth, pierced ears, blond mohair wig, chunky straight wrist articulated composition body, orig finish and stringing, new red faille dress, imp "1079 DEP," tiny chip to right ear hole, c1900, 8" h **$550**

C M Bergmann bisque head, brown sleep eyes with lashes, open mouth, synthetic auburn wig, jointed composition body, period white lawn dress with lace insertion, sprinkling of pepper spots primarily to the right cheek, early 20th C, 21" h **$260**

Oriental, bisque, medium skin tone, dark pupil-less stationary eyes, closed mouth orig black mohair Oriental-style wig, swivel neck, kid-lined neck socket and legs, long black stockings, brick red one-strap shoes, imp "852 3," some mottling/ soil to bisque, late 19th C, 7" h **$920**

Hamburger & Co., Viola, bisque socket head, blue sleep eyes, feathered brows, painted upper and lower lashes, open mouth, four upper teeth, synthetic wig, jointed wood and composition body, antique dress with lace trim, underclothing, new socks and leather shoes, marked "Made in/Germany/Viola/H & Co./ 7" on back of head, several wig pulls on right side of forehead, light rub on nose, small

Eden Bebe, bisque socket head, blue/ gray paperweight eyes, pierced ears, closed mouth, human hair wig, jointed French composition body, vintage clothing and shoes, new slip, Eden Bebe// Paris//M incised on head, with box, 23", $2,200.

Photo courtesy of McMasters Harris Auction Co.

inherent cut on H in back of head, repairs at neck socket of body, bottom of torso and left upper arm, normal wear at joints, finish of legs slightly different color than rest of body, 22-1/2" h **$300**

Hand sewn

Amish, OH, lavender dress, white apron, purple bonnet, arms and legs made from corn cobs, staining, 15" h **$345**

Amish, PA, green dress, black cape and bonnet, 16" h **$690**

Mennonite, PA, red and black checkered dress, black bonnet, fading, holes to cloth, 17-1/2" h **$965**

Handwerck, bisque head, blue sleep eyes, open mouth, pierced ears, orig blonde mohair wig, fully articulated composition body, Alice in Wonderland blue dress and white pinafore, dark brown shoes, imp "109-6 Germany Handwerck," 16" h **$460**

Handwerck, Heinrich

Bisque socket head, blue set eyes with real lashes, fur brows, painted lower lashes, open mouth, four upper teeth, pierced ears, antique human-hair wig, jointed wood and composition Handwerck body, new flowered dress, marked "Germany/Heinrich/ Handwerck/Simon & Halbig/ 5" on back of head, "Heinrich Handwerch/5" stamped in red, rub on right cheek, minor flake at earring hole, eyes, lashes, and brows replaced, 28" h **$300**

Kestner 172 "Gibson Girl," bisque shoulder head, blue sleep eyes with hair eyelashes, human hair wig, plaster pate, riveted jointed kid body, bisque lower arms, 172//3// Made in Germany on back of head, partial paper label on front, chipped fingertip, some body age, c1910, 17", $1,100.
Photo courtesy of McMasters Harris Auction Co.

Jumeau second series portrait Bebe, painted bisque socket head, brown paperweight eyes, mauve shadow, pierced ears, human hair wig, cork pate, incised 6 on head, Jumeau//Medaille D'Or//Paris stamped on body's lower back, antique clothing and hat, light wear, minor joint repair, lower arms repainted, replaced ball joint, c1880, 15", $4,800.
Photo courtesy of McMasters Harris Auction Co.

Bisque socket head, blue sleep eyes, molded and feathered brows, painted upper and lower lashes, open mouth, accented lips, four upper teeth, pierced ears, orig human-hair wig, jointed wood and composition Handwerck body with orig finish, antique white child's dress, antique underclothing, cotton socks, black patent leather shoes, marked "Germany/ Handwerck/Simon & Halbig/ 7" on back of head, "Heinrich Handwerck/Germany/7" stamped in red on lower back, finish flaking on lower left arm and knees, left knee ball replaced, 32-1/2" h **$1,025**

Handwerck, Max, bisque head, blue sleep eyes, open mouth, inset teeth, pierced ears, jointed-composition body, orig finish, newly made pink linen dress and hat, imp "421 10 Germany M HANDWERCK 2-1/2", bisque speckling, small chin pit, 21" h..**$320**

Harmann, Kurt, bisque head, brown sleep eyes, open mouth, replaced blonde mohair wig, fully articulated composition body, new blue satin and lace dress, worn period blue leather shoes, imp mark "30 5 K (over script H) 4," early 20th C, white scratch line each cheek, 26" h **$230**

Hertel, Schwab & Co.

140 character, bisque socket head, painted brown eyes, red accent line, feathered brows, closed mouth, accented lips, mohair wig, jointed wood and composition body, straight wrists, white factory chemise, dark green pants, matching cap, cotton socks, and new leather shoes, marked "140/4" on back of head, light rub on right cheek, minor repair at neck socket of body, light flaking on right upper leg, 15" h **$4,200**

Bisque socket head, blue paperweight eyes, feathered brows, painted upper and lower lashes, open mouth with accented lips and six upper teeth, pierced ears, replaced human-hair wig, jointed composition body with straight wrists, separate balls at shoulders, elbows, hips and knees, nicely redressed in pale pink French-style dress, new underclothing, socks and shoes, marks "8/0" on back of head and "Jumeau Medaille d'Or Paris" stamped in blue on lower back, replaced

antique paperweight eyes, tiny flake at each earring hole, tiny fleck on upper rim at inside corner of right eye, body has good orig finish with wear at all joints, on toes and heels, 20" h **$1,100**

Head circumference, twin character babies, blue sleep eyes, open mouths, two upper teeth, wispy blond tufts of hair, composition bent-limb bodies, matching period long white baby gown, one with pink, one blue ribbon trim, imp marks "152/2/0," price for pair, early 20th C, 9" l, 7" d **$635**

Heubach, Ernest

399 baby, solid dome painted bisque socket head, brown sleep eyes, single stroke brows, painted upper and lower lashes, closed mouth, lightly molded and painted hair, composition bent-limb baby body, orig multicolored "grass" skirt, marked "Heubach *Koppelsdorf/399*9/0, Germany" on back of head 12-1/2" h **$350**

300 baby, bisque socket head, set brown eyes, feathered brows, painted upper and lower lashes, open mouth, accented lips, four upper teeth, replaced wig, composition bent-limb baby body, antique white long baby dress, lace-trimmed antique baby bonnet, underclothing, diaper, and booties, marked "Heubach * Koppelsdorf/300 * 6/Germany" on back of head, arms and legs repainted, cracks in finish under repaint, neck socket touched up, repair on right arm joint and right wrist, 21" h **$275**

Heubach, Gebruder

Bisque shoulder head, blue intaglio eyes, two tone single stroke brows, closed mouth with shaded lips, molded and painted hair, tan oilcloth body with bisque lower arms, pin joints at hips and knees, cloth lower legs, new light blue velvet suit, white lace trimmed shirt, new socks and shoes, marked "8/Germany" on back of head, 22" h character **$350**

Heubach, Koppelsdorf

Screamer, bisque head, painted hair, painted blue intaglio eyes, open-closed screaming mouth, furrowed brow, straight-limb composition toddler body, maroon velvet short overalls, white shirt, imp "7684,"

sunburst mark, 10-1/2" h......... **$690**
Bisque head, blue sleep eyes with lashes, open mouth, brown human-hair wig, fully jointed wood and composition body, period underwear, new print cotton dress, imp mark "312," rub on cheek, early 20th C 24" h **$220**

Horsman, toddler, composition socket head, brown sleep eyes, single stroke brows, painted upper and lower lashes, mohair wig, jointed composition toddler body, straight wrists, diagonal hip joints, old white organdy dress with lace trim, underclothing, socks, high button boots, marked "E.I.H./ Co." on back, 15" h.................. **$650**

Ideal

Shirley Temple, composition head, hazel sleep eyes with real lashes, painted lower lashes, feathered brows, open mouth, six upper teeth, orig mohair wig in orig set, five-pc composition body, orig plaid "Bright Eyes" dress, underwear combination, replaced socks, orig shoes, marked "13/Shirley Temple" on head, "Shirley Temple/13" on back, 13" h .. **$700**

Shirley Temple, composition head, hazel sleep eyes, real lashes, painted lower lashes, feathered brows, open mouth, six upper teeth, molded tongue, orig mohair wig in orig set, five-pc composition child body, orig dotted organdy dress with pleats from "Curly Top" movie, orig underwear, combination socks and shoes, marks: "20/Shirley Temple/ Co. Ideal/N & T Co." on back of head, "Shirley Temple/20*" on back, and "Genuine/Shirley Temple/ registered U.S. Pat. Off/Ideal Nov & Toy Co./ Made in U.S.A." on dress tag, 20" h **$500**

Lori Martin, vinyl socket head, blue sleep eyes with real lashes, painted lower lashes, feathered brows, closed smiling mouth, rooted hair vinyl body jointed at waist, shoulders, hips, and ankles, orig tagged clothing, plaid shirt, jeans, vinyl boots with horses, marked "© Metro Goldwyn Mayer Inc./Mfg by/ Ideal Toy Corp/80" on back of head, "© Ideal Toy Corp./6-30-5" on back, "National Velvet's/Lori Martin/© Metro Goldwyn Mayer, Inc./All Rights Reserved" on shirt tag, 28" h **$550**

Jumeau

Bebe, bisque head, brown paper-

weight eyes, mauve eye shadow, closed mouth, pierced applied ears, orig red Jumeau earrings, imp DEPOSE E.9J, cork pate, orig blonde mohair wig, jointed straight wrist, eight-ball composition body marked "Jumeau Medaille d'Or," vintage commercial dress of aqua satin and ecru silk faille, brown leather shoes, marked "E.J., France," tiny red age line side of nose, c1885, 20" h **$5,475**

Bebe Soleil box, bisque socket head, blue paperweight eyes, feathered brows, painted upper and lower lashes, open mouth, accented lips, six upper teeth, human-hair wig, jointed wood and composition French body, dressed in factory chemise pants, "Tete Jumeau" stamped in red, "9" incised on back of head, "Bebe due Bon Marche" partial paper label on lower back, "10700" written upside down on upper back, "S.F.B. J. Paris Bebe Soleil Yeux Mobiles Formes Naturelles Entierement Articule" on label on end of box, 2" hairline on right side of forehead, body finish flaking or loose in places, wear on edges of feet, at joints and on hands, box bottom repaired, lid missing, 23" h Jumeau.................................. **$1,400**

Bisque socket head, brown paperweight eyes, heavy feathered brows, painted upper and lower lashes, open mouth, six upper teeth, pierced ears, human-hair wig over rock pate, jointed wood and composition French body with jointed wrists, working mama/papa pull strings, old white child's dress, underclothing, socks, black child's shoes, marked "14" on back of head, 35" h **$1,400**

Bisque socket head, paperweight eyes, multi-stroke brows, painted upper and lower lashes, open mouth, four upper teeth, pierced ears, orig mohair wig, orig pate, jointed wood and composition late French bodies, boy and girl doll dressed in orig ethnic costumes of Finistere Department of Brittany, France, marked "4" on back of heads, price for pr, 14" h **$2,000**

Great Ladies series, bisque socket head, blue paperweight eyes, single stroke brows, painted upper and lower lashes, closed mouth, orig mohair wig, five-pc composition

body, painted flat black shoes, orig white brocade gown with gold "diamond" jewelry, orig underclothing, marked "221/3/0" on back of head, "fabrication/Jumeau/Paris/ Made in France" on front of paper tag, "Marie-Louise/2, Femme de/ Napoleon Ier/ Epogue 1810" hand written on back of paper tag, 9" h **$475**

Jutta, bisque socket head, brown sleep eyes, feathered brows, painted upper and lower lashes, open mouth, two upper teeth, spring tongue, replaced human-hair wig, composition baby body, navy blue sailor top, hat, shorts, red and white striped socks, leather baby shoes, marked "Jutta/1914/14 1/2" on back of head, cracks on both hands, left little finger missing, 1914 baby, 26" h **$800**

Wooden doll, carved, gentleman with carved wooden head, hands and legs, original clothes include black wool frock coat, white linen shirt and stock, gold twill vest, brown trousers, New York state, wear, lacks feet, with stand, early to mid-19th century, 14-3/8" h, **$1,410.**

Photo courtesy of Skinner, Inc.

*K*R 128 Baby, bisque socket head, brown sleep eyes, open mouth, wobble tongue, composition body, original wig, antique clothing, marks: K*R//Simon & Halbig//128//56 on head; tiny wig pulls, 23", **$700.***
Photo courtesy of McMasters Harris Auction Co.

*Madame Alexander, "Margaret O'Brien" doll, composition, blue sleep eyes, painted features, jointed body, 21" h, **$175.***
Photo courtesy of Joy Luke Auctions.

Poupee Peau, bisque socket head on bisque shoulder plate, cobalt blue set eyes, multi-stroke brows, painted upper and lower lashes, closed mouth, pierced ears, orig mohair wig in orig curls, kid lady body with gussets at elbows, hips, and knees, individually stitched fingers, possibly orig clothing, factory chemise as blouse, ecru silk skirt with purple flowers, lavender and white striped under skirt, half slip, pants, socks, and boots with elastic inserts in sides, unmarked, one boot heel missing, 16" h **$3,750**

Kamkins, girl, cloth, molded face with painted features, blue eyes, orig brown mohair wig, cloth body and limbs, blue cotton dress, orig undergarments, purple Kamkins stamp mark on back of head, some soil and wear on face, early 20th C, 19" h **$1,150**

Kammer & Reinhardt (K*R)

100 baby, solid dome bisque socket head, painted blue eyes, single-stroke brows, open/closed mouth, molded and brush-stroked hair, bent limb composition baby body, possibly orig long baby dress, full slip half slip, diaper, undershirt, knit booties, long fleece coat, matching hat, marked "36/ K*R/100" on back of head, head perfect, orig body finish worn, 14" h.........................**$275**

115A baby, bisque socket head, blue sleep eyes, feathered brows, painted upper and lower lashes, closed mouth, orig mohair wig, five-pc composition baby body, antique-style white baby dress, slip, lace-trimmed panties, eyelet bonnet, marked "1/K*R/Simon & Halbig/115A/30" on back of head, wear to orig finish, arms mostly repainted, touch-up around neck socket, on toes, and feet, 10" h.............**$1,300**

115/A character toddler, bisque head, brown sleep eyes, closed pouty mouth, reddish-blond caracul wig, side-jointed composition toddler body, red and green plush jester's costume, also orig pink gingham outfit, imp "K*R Simon & Halbig 115/A, 48," c1910, 19" h **$4,320**

Kestner

161, bisque socket head, brown sleep eyes, feathered brows, painted upper and lower lashes, open mouth, four upper teeth, replaced human-hair wig, orig plaster pate, jointed wood and composition Kestner body, ecru dress with red cross stitch trim, marked "F 1/2 Made in Germany 10 1/2/161" on back of head, "Germany 3" stamped in red on right rear hip, 20-1/2" h......**$475**

164, bisque socket head, blue sleep eyes, molded and feathered brows, painted upper and lower lashes, open mouth, shapely accented lips, four upper teeth, skin wig, jointed wood and composition Kestner body, faded dark blue velvet sailor suit, white shirt, old socks and shoes, marked "M1/2 made in Germany 16 1/2/164" on back of head, "Excelsior/Germany/7" stamped in red on right lower back, body has orig finish with light wear, normal wear at joints, right finger repaired, 32" h **$1,200**

208, all bisque, stiff neck, brown sleep eyes, single-stroke brows, painted upper and lower lashes, open/closed mouth, orig mohair wig, all bisque body jointed at shoulders and hips, molded and painted white shirred socks and black one-strap shoes, marked "208/3" on back of head and on arms and legs at joints, "Made in Germany" round red stamp on back, "Baby Rose Germany" on round red label on tummy, orig box, 6" h **$300**

237, Hilda, bisque socket head, blue sleep eyes, feathered brows, painted upper and lower lashes, open mouth, two upper porcelain teeth, orig blond skin wig, composition Kestner baby body, white organdy baby dress, matching bonnet, marked "J Made in Germany 13/JD.K./237 ges gesch/N 1070" on back of head, 16" **$2,000**

257 baby, bisque socket head, brown sleep eyes, feathered brows, painted upper and lower lashes, open mouth, two upper teeth, antique mohair wig on old cardboard pate, composition baby body, new sailor romper, marked "Made in Germany/J.D.K/257/28" on back of head, 11" h
....**$350**

Kley & Hahn, 525Baby, solid dome bisque socket head, blue sleep eyes, feathered brows, painted upper and lower lashes, open-closed mouth, lightly molded and brush stroked hair, composition baby body, antique baby dress, marked "4/Germany/K&H (in banner)/525" on back of head, repainted, 11-1/2" h **$275**

Knickerbocker, Mickey Mouse, cloth swivel head, white facial, black oil-cloth pie eyes, large black nose, painted open/ closed smiling mouth with accent lines, black felt ears, unjointed black cloth body, orange hands with three fingers and a thumb, red over-sized composition feet, black rubber tail, orig shorts with two buttons on front and back, some fading, 11" h **$650**

Konig & Wernicke, Germany, early 20th C

Character baby, bisque head, early 20th century, blue sleep eyes, open mouth, two upper teeth, wobble tongue, orig brown mohair wig, bent limb composition baby body, red circle stamp "K & W," minor wear, 27" l, 16-1/2" d head circumference... **$815**

Character toddler, bisque head, brown sleep eyes, open mouth, two upper teeth, tongue, orig dark brown mohair wig, fully articulated side hip-joint composition toddler body marked "Made in Germany," period cotton sailor outfit, blue pants, white overblouse, white fabric shoes, imp "Made in Germany 99/7," some wear to finish of limbs, repaint to hands, 17" h............ **$750**

Kruse, Kathe

Kuhnlenz, Gebruder, 38 Girl, bisque shoulder head, blue threaded paperweight eyes, feathered brows, painted upper and lower lashes, closed mouth, human hair, cloth Goldsmith body, red corset, brown leather lower arms, red lower legs with red kid boots, silver two-pc outfit made from antique fabrics, marked "G.K." on back of head, "38-27.5" at bottom of shoulder plate, 22" h **$250**

Schlenkerchen, all-stockinette, pressed and oil-painted double-seam head, painted features, brown hair, shaded brown painted eyes with eyeliner, light upper lashes, closed mouth in smiling expression, cloth neck ring, stockinette covered, padded armature frame body, mitten hands, rounded feet, unlaundered off-white undergarments, soles stamped "Kathe Kruse, Germany," paint rub tip of nose, soil, c1922, 13" h **$5,475**

Sand Baby, hand painted head, painted blue eyes, single stroke brows, closed mouth, painted hair, stockinette covered body jointed at shoul-ders, loose joints at hips, formed navel, "Kathe Kruse" stamped on bottom of left foot, incomplete number stamped on bottom of right foot, 21" h **$550**

Lenci

Girl, pressed felt swivel head, painted brown side-glancing eyes, painted upper lashes, closed mouth with two-tone lips, orig mohair wig, cloth torso, felt limbs, orig pink felt dress with blue trim, blue felt coat with matching hat, orig underclothing, socks, blue felt shoes, marked "2" on bottom of right foot, "Lenci/ Made in Italy" on cloth label inside coat, 12" h **$400**

Lady, "Mary Pickford" felt face, light gray-blue painted eyes to right, long nose, closed mouth, long bare felt arms, classic Lenci fingers, white and green organdy summer frock, felt wide-brimmed bonnet, all trimmed with felt flowers and ruffles, silk stockings, pale green felt shoes with felt flowers, orig Lenci tag sewn to dress, small stain back of skirt, c1930, 28" h **$1,840**

Mascotte, pressed felt swivel head, painted brown "surprise" eyes to side, single-stroke brows, painted upper lashes, open-closed two-tone mouth, orig red mohair wig in braids, cloth body with felt arms and legs, orig blue and white polka dot nylon dress, white felt collar, red felt belt, orig one-pc underwear, red felt sandals, light display soil, front of dress faded, 8" h **$150**

Limbach, character, bisque socket head, blue sleep eyes with real lashes, painted upper and lower lashes, open mouth, accented lips, six upper teeth, human-hair wig, jointed wood and composition body, new white lacy dress, underclothing, new socks and shoes, marked "W/crown/17 72 in shamrock/Limbach" on back of head, two right fingers and three left fingers repaired, finish flaking around neck socket of body, cracks in finish on side seams of torso, wear at all sockets on torso, 23" h............................ **$625**

Madame Alexander

Marme from the Little Women Series, hard plastic head and body, gray sleep eyes, closed mouth, dark brown wig in snood, gray and pink print dress with orig tags, organdy shawl, shoes and socks, c1955, 14" h **$200**

K✱R 121 Baby, bisque socket head, blue sleep eyes, deep dimples, open mouth, original mohair wig, composition body, marks: K✱R//Simon & Halbig//121 on head; hands repainted, tiny rub on left side of head, 11", $360.
Photo courtesy of McMasters Harris Auction Co.

Gebruder Kuhnlenz 34, two dolls, dark brown bisque socket heads, set no pupil dark eyes, open mouths, original curly mohair wigs, crude five piece composition bodies, black molded and painted shoes, orange molded and painted stockings, marks: 34-13 and 34-16 on heads; small doll redressed in antique fabric clothing, large doll may have original dress, light touch up on small doll's legs, 6" (small) 8-1/2" (large), $950.
Photo courtesy of McMasters Harris Auction Co.

Special Girl, composition head, composition shoulder plate, blue sleep eyes with real lashes, painted lower lashes, feathered brows, closed mouth, orig human-hair wig in orig set, cloth torso with composition arms and legs, orig pale blue taffeta dress with lace and ribbon trim, attached blue panties, orig socks and center snap shoes, "Madame/Alexander/New York U.S.A." on dress tag, 23" h **$750**

Sweet Violet, hard plastic head, blue sleep eyes with real lashes, painted lower lashes, feathered brows, closed mouth, orig synthetic wig, hard plastic body jointed at shoulders, elbows, wrists, hips, and knees, walking mechanism, orig tagged blue cotton dress, underclothing, flowered bonnet, white gloves, black side-snap shoes, carrying orig pink Alexander hat box, marked "Alexander" on back of head, "Madame Alexander/All Rights Reserved/New York, U.S.A.," unplayed-with condition, comb and curlers missing, c1954, 18" h **$1,700**

Menjou, Adolph, composition shoulder head, painted brown eyes with accent line, molded monocle on right eye, feathered brows, molded and painted mustache, open-closed mouth, seven upper teeth, molded white shirt collar with hole, presumably for a tie, molded and painted hair, excelsior-stuffed cloth body with long limbs, composition white hands as gloves, composition lower legs as socks and shoes, orig black two-pc suit with satin lapels, 32" h **$725**

Motschmann-style, china, flange swivel head, painted blue eyes, single strike brows, closed mouth, molded and painted hair in "Alice" hairstyle, molded hair band, Taufling body, papier-mâché shoulder plate and hip section, china lower arms and legs, molded and painted boots, six painted side buttons, possibly orig homemade white dress, short chemise, leg covers, 14-1/2" h **$2,500**

Parian, untinted bisque shoulder head, painted blue eyes with red accent line, single stroke brows, closed mouth, pierced ears, molded and painted café au lait hair, molded blue tiara trimmed with gold, molded braid across top, on lower sides, and down middle of back of head, old cloth body with red leather boots as part of

leg, new arms by Emma Clear, white dotted Swiss and lace dress, antique underclothing, unmarked, old repair to tiara, body aged, 24" h **$1,900**

Petzold, Dora, composition head, painted blue eyes with eye shadow, single-stroke brows, accented nostrils, closed mouth, orig mohair wig, stockinette body stitch-jointed at shoulders and hips, mitten-type hands with stitched fingers, possibly orig white velvet dress with embroidery and lace trim, white teddy, orig socks and marked shoes, marked with girl in circle, "D P/7/7/0" on back of head, girl in circle with "D P" on bottom of shoes, 16-1/2" h **$275**

Poupee Bois, bisque socket head, bisque shoulder plate, pale blue threaded paperweight eyes, feathered brows, painted upper and lower lashes, closed mouth, pierced ears, orig human hair wig, wooden fashion body articulated at shoulders, elbows, wrists, hips, and knees, swivel joint on upper arms and upper legs, nicely redressed with antique fabric and lace, possibly orig stockings and high button boots, marked "4" on back of head, 17-1/2" h **$4,400**

Poupee Raynal, pressed felt swivel head, painted blue eyes, single-stroke brows, painted upper lashes, closed mouth with three-tone lips, orig mohair wig in orig set, five-pc cloth body with stitched fingers, orig light blue organdy dress with pink flower appliqués, matching hat, orig teddy, blue organdy slip, socks, white leather shoes, "Paris" typed on piece of paper pinned to back, unplayed-with condition, 19" h **$725**

Putnam, Grace

Bye-Lo Baby, solid dome bisque swivel head, tiny blue sleep eyes, softly blushed brows, painted upper and lower lashes, closed mouth, lightly molded and painted hair, all bisque baby body jointed at shoulders and hips, orig knit pink and white two-pc baby outfit with matching cap, marked "Bye-Lo Baby/©/Germany/G.S. Putnam" on label on chest, "6-20/Copr. By/Grace S. Putnam/ Germany" incised on back, "6-20" on hips and right arms, "20" on left arm, chip on right back of neck edge of head, minor firing line behind left ear, 8" h **$525**

Head circumference Bye-Lo Baby, solid dome bisque flange head, blue sleep eyes, softly blushed brows, painted upper and lower lashes, closed mouth, lightly molded and painted hair, cloth body with celluloid hands and "frog" legs, Bye-Lo baby gown, slip, orig flannel undershirt and diaper, cotton stockings, marked "Copr. by/Grace S. Putnam/Made in Germany" on back of head, "Bye-Lo Baby/ Pat Appl'd For/ Copy/by/Grace/ Storey/Putnman" stamped on front of body, 11" h, 10" d **$200**

Head circumference, Bye-Lo Baby, solid dome bisque flange head, blue sleep eyes, softly blushed brows, painted upper and lower lashes, closed mouth, lightly molded and painted hair, cloth body with "frog" legs, celluloid hands, antique baby christening dress, long slip, underskirt, socks and booties, marked "Copr. By/Grace S. Putnam/ Made in Germany" on back of head, partial Bye-Lo Baby stamp on front of torso, body aged and soiled, right hand missing two fingers, 20" h, 16-1/2" d **$250**

Recknagel, character, bisque socket head, tiny painted blue squinty eyes, single-stroke brows, open-closed mouth, five painted upper teeth, four lower teeth, molded tongue, molded and painted short hair with molded pink bow, five-pc chubby composition body, crude unpainted torso, molded and painted socks and shoes, redressed in pink lace-trimmed dress, matching hair ribbon, lace pants, marked "R 57 A/8/0" on back of head, light dust in bisque, light wear on orig body finish, 9" h **$675**

Redmond, Kathy

Eleanor Roosevelt, bisque shoulder head, well modeled painted features, molded and painted hair and necklace, cloth body, bisque arms and lower legs with molded black shoes, orig purple two-pc suit, marked "Eleanor Roosevelt R (in cat)" on back of shoulder plate, 13" h **$300**

Mary Todd Lincoln, bisque shoulder head, painted blue eyes, painted brows, closed mouth, molded brown hair, molded white roses and green leaves, molded white snood with gold highlights, molded necklace and earrings, molded white bisque ruffle with single rose on shoulder plate, cloth body, bisque lower arms and legs, black silk dress with blue accents, orig underclothing, marked "Mary Lincoln/R (in cat) 17" on back of shoulder plate, 14" h **$175**

S & Q, 201 baby, bisque socket head, set brown eyes, feathered brows, painted upper and lower lashes, open mouth, two upper teeth, molded tongue, mohair wig, composition baby body, navy blue velvet boy's shorts, jacket, and matching hat, white shirt, stockings, white baby shoes, marked "+ 201 SQ" (superimposed) "Germany 14" on back of head, 28" h **$700**

Schmidt, Bruno, 2042, solid dome bisque socket head, painted brown eyes, two-tone single-stroke brows, open-closed mouth, accented lips, brush-stroked hair, jointed composition body, redressed in maroon velour two-pc suit, ecru satin shirt with lace trim, black cotton socks, new black shoes, marked "5/B.S.W. in heart/2042" on back of head, "Handwerck" stamped in red in middle of lower back, 22" h **$1,500**

Schmidt, Franz, 1285 baby, solid dome bisque socket head, blue sleep eyes, softly blushed brows, painted upper and lower lashes, closed mouth, molded and painted hair, composition baby body, smocked baby dress, marked "1285/32/F S & C/Made in Germany" on back of head, 15" h **$575**

Schoenau & Hoffmeister, Masquerade set, bisque socket head, set brown eyes, single stroke brows, painted upper and lower lashes, open mouth, four upper teeth, antique mohair wig, five-pc composition body, walking mechanism, orig pastel dress with pale green ribbon trim, orig gauze-type underclothing, socks, leather shoes with black pompons, marked "4000 5/0/S PB (in star) H 10" on back of head, "F" on back of legs, "Germany" stamped on bottom of shoes, tied in red cardboard box with two lace-trimmed compartments, blue Pierrot costume brimmed with black, white, and ruffled collar, matching cone-shaped hat, black face mask with lace trim, light rub on nose, 13-1/2" h **$525**

Schoenhut

19/308 girl, wooden socket head,

Kestner Hilda Baby, bisque socket head, brown sleep eyes, two upper teeth in open mouth, 5 piece jointed composition body, mohair wig, antique clothing, marked J. made in 13.//Germany//237//JDK Jr.//1914//C in circle//Hilda//Ges. Gesch.//1070 incised on head, tight hairline front left rim to forehead, reset eyes, repainted lids, antique replacement arms, body wear, 17", **$1,500.**
Photo courtesy of McMasters Harris Auction Co.

brown intaglio eyes, feathered brow, closed mouth with excellent modeling, orig mohair wig, spring-jointed wooden body jointed at shoulders, elbows, wrists, hips, knees, and ankles, white dress with red dots in Schoenhut style, slip, knit union suit, replaced cotton socks and red flocked shoes, marked "Schoenhut Doll/Pat. Jan 17th 1911/ U.S.A." on oval label on back, very light touch up on left cheek, nose, edge of lips, craze lines on front of lower neck, light crazing on right cheek and outer corner of left eye, body has "suntan" color with normal wear at joints and light overall soil, few flakes off ankles, 19" h **$450**

Toddler, wood socket head, painted blue eyes, single-stroke brows, closed mouth, orig mohair wig, wooden body jointed at shoulders, elbows, wrists, hips, knees, and ankles, redressed, marked "Schoenhut/Doll/Pat Jan 17th 1911/USA" on oval label on back, "H. C. Schoenhut/©/ (illegible)" on round label on back of head, light wear on finish of face, rub on nose, wear on toes, 11" h **$425**

Schoenhut & Hoffmeister, character baby, bisque head, blue sleep eyes with lashes, hint of smile, open mouth, two upper teeth, pointy chin, orig dark brown mohair wig, bent-limb composition baby body, white cotton slip, imp "SHPB" in a star, "5,

Germany," white spot back of head at rim, early 20th C, 20" h, 13-1/2" d head circumference **$325**

S.F.B.J.

236 toddler, bisque socket head, blue sleep eyes, feathered brows, painted lower lashes, open/closed mouth, two upper teeth, orig mohair hair, jointed wood and composition toddler body, antique dark purple satin two pc outfit, matching cap, replaced socks and shoes, marked "S.F.B.J./236/Paris/8" on back of head, cracks in wood on lower half right arm, 18" h **$550**

301, bisque socket head, blue sleep eyes with real lashes, open mouth, four painted upper teeth, pierced ears, human-hair wig, jointed wood and composition body, jointed wrists, antique white lace dress and bonnet, marked "S.F.B.J./301/ Paris/1" on back of head, "2" incised between shoulders, "2" on bottom of feet, good original body finish, 11" h **$600**

Simon & Halbig

1428, bisque socket head, blue sleep eyes, single stroke brows, tiny painted upper lashes, open/closed mouth, replaced synthetic wig, jointed wood and composition body, new red velvet two pc boy's outfit, socks, new brown boots, marked "1428/4" on back of head, lower leg repainted, 12-1/2" h **$1,000**

1039, bisque socket head, bisque shoulder plate, blue flirty eyes, real lashes, feathered brow, painted lower lashes, open mouth with outlined lips, four upper teeth, pierced ears, orig mohair wig, orig white glass beads at neck joint, kid body, bisque lower arms, gussets at elbows, hips, and knees, cloth lower legs, pink silk two-pc outfit made from old fabric, antique underclothing, new socks and shoes, marked "S.H. 1038/DEP/6/Germany" on back of head, inherent firing line behind right ear, head loose on shoulder plate, normal aging and light soil to body, 18" h **$375**

1039, bisque socket heat, blue flirty eyes, real lashes, molded and feathered brows, painted upper and lower lashes, open mouth with accented lips, four upper teeth, pierced ears, human-hair wig, jointed wood and composition French type body, torso cut for working crier, both arms with kiss-throwing mechanism, knees jointed, both legs with walking mechanism, rose French-style new dress, antique underclothing, replaced socks and shoes, marked "1039/German/Simon & Halbig/S & H/10-1/2″ on back of head, 22" h **$500**

Terri Lee

Buddy Lee, hard plastic head with stiff neck, eyes painted to side, single-stroke brows, painted upper lashes, closed mouth, molded and painted hair, hard plastic body jointed at shoulders only, molded and painted black boots, orig Phillips 66 suit with labeled shirt and pants, black imitation-leather belt, marked "Buddy Lee" on back, "Union Made/Lee/Sanforized" on label on back of pants, "Phillips/66" on label on front of shirt, 12" h **$215**

Terri Lee, hard plastic head, oversized painted brown eyes, single-stroke brows, long painted upper and lower lashes, closed mouth, synthetic wig, five-pc hard plastic body jointed at shoulders and hips, orig yellow Evening Formal, #3570D orig socks and shoes, long white coat, #3690A, matching hat, marked "Terri Lee" on back, Terri Lee tag on coat, 1954, 16" h **$475**

Connie Lynn, hard plastic head, blue sleep eyes with real lashes, single-stroke brows, painted lower lashes at corners of eyes, closed mouth, orig skin wig, hard plastic baby body, orig two-pc pink baby outfit, plastic panties, orig socks and white baby shoes, Terri Lee Nursery Registration Form and three Admission Cards to Terri Lee Hospital, Connie Lynn tag on clothing, orig box, unplayed with condition, 18" .. **$625**

Unis France, 60, bisque socket head, light blue sleep eyes, single stroke brows, open mouth with 4 upper teeth, orig mohair wig, crude five-pc composition body, dressed in orig ethnic costume of Pont-l'Abbe in Brittany, France, marked "Unis/France/71 60 140/11/0" on back of head, 9-1/2" h **$175**

Vogue

Toddles, Hansel and Gretel, composition heads, painted blue eyes looking to the right, single stroke brows, painted upper lashes, closed mouths, orig mohair wigs, five-pc composition body, orig Tyrolean outfits, marked "Vogue" on back of head, orig clothing labels, orig boxes, price for pr, 7-1/2" h **$500**

Toddles, Nurse, composition, painted blue eyes looking to right, single stroke brows, painted upper lashes, closed mouth, orig mohair wig, body jointed at shoulders and hips, orig white nurse's outfit and hat, oilcloth snap shoes, marked "Vogue" on head, "Doll Co." on back, orig gold label on dress, 7-1/2" h **$475**

Wax, unmarked, reinforced poured-wax shoulder head, set blue glass eyes, multi-stroke brows, painted upper and lower lashes, closed smiling mouth, pierced ears, orig mohair wig, cloth body, wax-over composition lower arms and lower legs, antique red/white gingham dress, orig underclothing, socks and leather shoes, color worn on lips, eyelashes and brows, minor crack in wax on right front of shoulder plate, cracks on right leg, body is aged, soiled, and repaired, 18" h **$475**

Wislizenus, Adolph, girl, bisque socket head, brown sleep eyes, feathered brows, painted upper and lower lashes, open mouth, accented lips, pierced ears, replaced human-hair wig, jointed composition body with orig finish, possibly orig clothing, white low-waisted dress, antique underclothing, socks and shoes marked "8," blue velvet coat and matching hat with ribbon trim, marked "8/ A.W./Germany/6" on back of head, "46" stamped in red on bottom of feet, 18" h.. **$550**

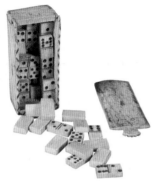

Miniature, rectangular whalebone box with 36 carved whalebone dominoes, sliding lid with worn, painted depiction of Neptune, 1" h x 1-1/4" w x 3" l, **$470.**
Photo courtesy of Skinner, Inc.

GAME BOARDS

History: Wooden game boards have a long history and were some of the first toys early Americans enjoyed. Games such as checkers, chess, and others were easy to play and required only simple markers or playing pieces. Most were handmade, but some machine-made examples exist.

Game boards can be found in interesting color combinations. Some include small drawers to hold the playing pieces. Others have an interesting molding or frame. Look for signs of use from long hours of enjoyment.

Today, game boards are popular with game collectors, folk art collectors, and decorators because of their interesting forms.

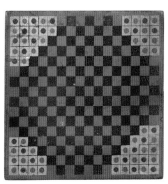

Checkered game board, painted wood, American, square with central field of painted green and salmon checks, corners have 13 white squares with alternating salmon and green dots, salmon painted ground, 19th century, 17" x 17-1/2", **$3,170.**

Photo courtesy of Skinner, Inc.

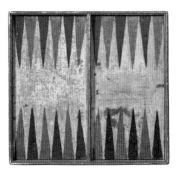

Backgammon/checkerboard double-sided game board, pine, painted, American, rectangular, red and black painted applied molding, red painted divider, backgammon in red, black and gray, checkerboard is black checks on natural ground, wear, 19th century, 17" x 19-3/4", **$1,525.**

Photo courtesy of Skinner, Inc.

Checkerboard/Nine Men's Morris double-sided game board, applied molding, inlaid diamond motifs, inlaid contrasting wood checkerboard, signed "SJH. 1876," in inlaid lettering and numerals, reverse centered with five-point star, crack, loss, 14-1/2" x 15", **$470.**

Photo courtesy of Skinner, Inc.

Checkerboard

Blue and white, yellowed varnish, New England, 19th C, 16" sq **$3,335**

Incised checkerboard under glass, red, lime green, yellow, and black, reverse painted in red, white, and blue, framed, America, minor paint wear, 20th C, 21-1/2" x 17-1/2" **$650**

Oak and mahogany squares, galleried edge with two reserves on sides with sliding lid compartments to hold checkers, two sets of checkers, one round, one square, minor wear, light alligatoring to old black paint on lids and gallery, 14" w, 20-1/4" h **$330**

Painted and gilt dec, molded edge, reverse marked "Saco Lodge No. 2," Saco, Maine, 19th C, 20" w, 18-3/4" h **$5,175**

Painted black and salmon, New England, 19th C, 15-1/4" sq **$2,300**

Painted black and white, tan colored ground, sgd "F. Smith," Pennsylvania, c1870, 12-1/2" w, 12-3/4" h **$1,955**

Painted green and white, unfinished, inscribed on reverse, late 19th/early 20th C, 17" w, 16" h **$460**

Painted green and yellow, paint imperfections, late 19th C, 10-1/2" w, 19-1/2" h **$1,955**

Painted hunter green and iron red, black frame, yellow grain paint on reverse, America, minor paint wear, 19th C, 13-7/8" w, 13-3/4" h **$1,380**

Painted red and black, yellow dec, Michigan, c1880, 18" w, 21" h **$2,415**

Painted red and white checkerboard, orig cherry frame, Newburyport, Massachusetts, c1850, 16" w, 17-1/2" h **$980**

Painted slate, incised geometric design, hand painted to resemble hardstones, shades of marbleized green and red, solid dark red checks, shaded yellow ground, mottled black border, New England, minor paint wear at margins, late 19th C, 19-1/2" sq **$1,645**

Painted yellow and black, green detailing, c1880, 18-1/2" sq **$5,465**

Pine, breadboard ends, additional strip on one side, old red and black checkerboard slightly off center, varnished, age split, minor edge wear, 17-1/2" x 24" **$200**

Poplar, old dry paint with gold and black blocks surrounded by red borders, black ground, red roundels with gold stars in each corner, reverse side painted red, breadboard ends with wire nails, 25" x 15" **$825**

Double-sided

Mustard and black, 14" sq **$975**

Obverse with Parcheesi, painted red, teal, orange, and green, checkerboard on reverse with orange, black, and yellow paint, paint wear to obverse at edges, c1900, 17" sq **$2,530**

Painted, applied molding, red and black checkerboard outlined in yellow on one side, Ouija board with black stenciled lettering and symbols on reverse, America, late 19th C, 21-1/4" x 21-1/2" **$470**

Painted, one side with Parcheesi game and primitive scene of hunter returning home in center, checkerboard on other side, small plated feet at corners, age split, 18-1/2" sq **$4,485**

Painted apple green, black, and red, checkerboard on obverse, backgammon on reverse, game piece compartments, America, c1870-80, 23" w, 17-1/4" h **$3,750**

Painted apple green, brown, and black, obverse with checkerboard, reverse with snake-motif game, America, mid-19th C, 12-1/4" w, 12" h **$36,800**

Painted black and red, obverse with checkerboard, reverse with Old Mill, applied molded edge, New England, c1850-70, 14-1/4" sq **$4,890**

Painted deep blue-green, red and black, checkerboard on obverse, backgammon on reverse, America, 19th C, 14-7/8" w, 15-7/8" h **$2,530**

Painted mustard, red, and green, checkerboard on obverse, backgammon on reverse, America, 19th C, 15" w, 16" h **$3,335**

Painted pine, brown and black checkerboard on one side, painted brown Old Mill game inscribed on reverse, two sliding panel compartments, New York State, early 19th C, 7-1/4" w, 7" h **$1,150**

Painted wood, sq board with applied frame, one side checkerboard painted yellow, black, green, and red, other side backgammon game in the same colors, America, wear, 19th C, 20-1/8" x 20-1/2" **$1,645**

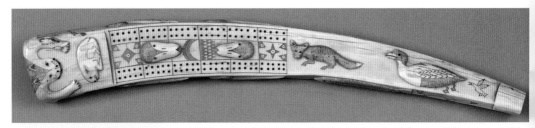

Cribbage board, Inuit, carved walrus tusk, animal figures, 19th century, 18" l,
$880.
Photo courtesy of Pook & Pook, Inc.

Parcheesi, painted pine board, American, wide panel with mitered molding, playing field painted in black, blue, green, red, yellow and white on iron red ground, green and black borders, 19th century, 23-3/4" x 28-3/4", **$5,875.**
Photo courtesy of Skinner, Inc.

Folding

Painted avocado green, colorful raised segmented tracks, opens for storage, wear, mid-20th C, 12-1/2" w, 31" h **$575**

Parcheesi

Folding, painted American flag and spade, heart, diamond, and club motifs, Massachusetts, minor paint imperfections, c1870, 18-1/2" sq **$46,000**

Folding, painted green, white, black, and yellow, varied geometric designs on game corners, America, 19th C, 19-1/2" sq **$2,875**

Folding, patriotic red, white, and blue stars and dec, New England, late 19th C, 18" w, 17-3/4" h **$4,350**

Painted, center rosette, bull's eye corners, attributed to Maine, wear, 19th C, 25" w, 24-1/2" h **$4,600**

Painted red, yellow, and green, New England, 1870-80, 27-1/2" w, 27" h **$5,750**

GAMES

History: Board games have been commercially produced in this country since at least 1822, and card games since the 1780s. However, it was not until the 1840s that large numbers of games were produced that survive to this day. The W. & S. B. Ives Company produced many board and card games in the 1840s and 1850s. Milton Bradley and McLoughlin Brothers became major producers of games starting in the 1860s, followed by Parker Brothers in the 1880s. Other major producers of games in this period were Bliss, Chaffee and Selchow, Selchow and Righter, and Singer.

Today, most games from the 19th century are rare and highly collectible, primarily because of their spectacular lithography. McLoughlin and Bliss command a premium because of the rarity, quality of materials, and the extraordinary art that was created to grace the covers and boards of their games.

In the 20th century, Milton Bradley, Selchow and Righter, and Parker Brothers became the primary manufacturers of boxed games. They have all now been absorbed by toy giant Hasbro Corporation. Other noteworthy producers were All-Fair, Pressman, and Transogram, all of which are no longer in business. Today, the hottest part of the game collecting market is in rare character games from the 1960s. Parker Brothers and All-Fair games from the 1920s to 1940s also have some excellent lithography and are highly collectible.

Additional Listings: See *Warman's Americana & Collectibles*.

Notes: While people collect games for many reasons, it is strong graphic images that bring the highest prices. Games collected because they are fun to play or for nostalgic reasons are still collectible, but will not bring high prices. Also, game collectors are not interested in common and "public domain" games such as checkers, tiddlywinks, Authors, Anagrams, Jackstraws, Rook, Pit, Flinch, and Peter Coodles. The game market today is characterized by fairly stable prices for ordinary items, increasing discrimination for grades of condition, and continually rising prices for rare material in excellent condition. Whether you are a dealer or collector, be careful to buy games in good condition. Avoid games with taped or split corners or other box damage. Games made after about 1950 are difficult to sell unless they are complete and in excellent condition. As games get older, there is a forgiveness factor for condition and completeness that increases with age.

These listings are for games that are complete and in excellent condition. Be sure the game you're looking to price is the same as the one described in the listing. The 19th century makers routinely published the same title on several different versions of the game, varying in size and graphics. Dimensions listed here are rounded to the nearest half inch.

Game of Dr. Busby, card game, Milton Bradley, 1910, **$45.**

Charlie McCarthy Game of Topper, Whitman, 1938, **$45.**

Reproduction Alert.

Across the Continent, Parker Bros, 1892 .... **$175**

A Knight's Journey **$125**

A New Game of History of England, published by J. Wallis, printed on linen, some wear, c1803, 6" x 8" **$190**

Bead-O-Rama **$50**

Bull in a China Shop, Milton Bradley, 1937 .... **$100**

Chiromagia Game, McLoughlin, three answer sheets, two question discs, lid missing **$125**

Clue, Parker Brothers, separate board and pieces box, c1949 .... **$35**

Des Mosaiques Humaines (Mosaic Faces), build-a-face, 30 top of head or shoulder pcs, profusion of noses, eyes, mouths, orig box, 6" x 9-1/2" **$2,000**

Dixie Pollyana, Parker Brothers, all wooden pcs, four orig dice and dice-cups, c1952, 8" x 18" **$100**

Elsie and Her Family, Selchow & Righter Co., 1941, 12-1/2" x 14-1/2" x 1-1/2" **$65**

Fish Pond, McLoughlin Bros., children on cover, c1898, 8" x 18" **$125**

Flying the United States Air Mail Game, Parker Bros, 17" x 27-1/2" playing board, orig playing pcs, deck of cards, 1929 copyright, 1-1/2" x 14-1/2" x 18" box **$100**

Game of Billy Possum, c1910, 8" x 15" **$600**

Game of Bo Peep, J.H. Singer, 8-1/2" x 14" **$250**

Game of Snow White and the Seven Dwarfs, The, Milton Bradley, Walt Disney Enterprises, 193? **$125**

Game of the Wizard of Oz, The, Whitman, c1939, 7" x 13-1/2" **$300**

Hi Ho Silhouette Game, 1932 ... **$30**

Limited Mail and Express Game, The, Parker Brothers, metal train playing pieces, c1894, 14" x 21" **$275**

Lone Ranger Hi Yo Silver Game, Parker Brothers, 1938 .... **$150**

Mansion of Happiness, The, W. & S. B. Ives, c1843 .... **$700**

Mickey Mantle's Big League Baseball Game, Gardner Games **$225**

Monopoly, Parker Brothers, white box edition #9, metal playing pieces and embossed hotels, c1935 .... **$150**

Monopoly, Parker Brothers, separate board and pieces box, 1946 Popular Edition **$50**

Motorcycle Game, Milton Bradley, c1905, 9" x 9" **$250**

New Board Game of the American Revolution, Lorenzo Borge, colored scenes and events, 1844, 18-1/2" w opened **$690**

New York Yacht Race, McLoughlin Bros, box bottom is playing board, two yacht tokens, teetotum, two markers, 19-3/4" w, 10-1/4" h, cover soiled, missing one short end **$390**

One Two, Button Your Shoe, Master Toy Company, 11" x 12" **$100**

Peter Coddles Trip to New York, Milton Bradley, orig instruction sheet, 6" x 8-1/2" **$65**

Pollyana **$75**

Radio Amateur Hour Game, 10" x 13" **$145**

Stick 'Em Pictures **$45**

Strange Game of Forbidden Fruit, Parker Brothers, c1900, 4" x 5-1/2" **$45**

Truth or Consequences, Gabriel, c1955, 14" x 19-1/2" **$40**

Uncle Sam's Mail, Milton Bradley, c1910, 16-1/4" x 15" x 1-1/4" **$225**

Uncle Wiggly **$75**

Young America Target, Parker Bros **$85**

Lindy The Flying Game, Parker Bros., "Improved Edition," original box, **$225.**

Action Figures, Star Trek, Cheron, 8″ figure, Mego, 1975, **$180.**

Space Patrol Rocket Lite, Rayovac, 1950s, **$350.**

Lost in Space 3-D Action Game, Remco, 1966, **$785.**

Battle of the Planets, Milton Bradley, 1970s, **$35.**

SPACE TOYS

One of the hottest trends in the toy-collecting hobby surrounds space toys. The children of the *Lost in Space* generation are today's avid collectors—and the demand for extra-terrestrial treasures is being felt at toy shows, flea markets, and even antique malls. The variety of space heroes extends from comic strip favorites Buck Rogers and Flash Gordon to the post-WWII emergence of television and the popularity of characters like Tom Corbett and Buzz Corey. By the 1960s, *Lost in Space* and *Star Trek* captivated youthful imaginations, and we all know what happened to the popularity of space toys with the 1977 release of *Star Wars*!

Toy spaceships, space guns, and space-themed characters are earning devoted followings among toy collectors and their popularity seems to be spreading at "warp speed."

Buck Rogers

25th Century Police Patrol Rocket, tin wind-up, Marx, 1939, 12″ l **$800**

Adventures of Buck Rogers Book, Whitman, 1934 ....**$100**

Battle Cruiser Rocket, two grooved wheels run along string, Tootsietoy, 1937 ....**$200**

Chemistry Set, beginners, Gropper, 1937 ....**$800**

Cut Out Adventure Book, Cocomalt premium, 1933 ....**$3,500**

Figure, cast metal, gray, Tootsietoy, 1937 ....**$150**

Helmet XC-34, leather, Daisy, 1935 ....**$500**

Interplanetary Space Fleet Model Kit, six different kits, 1935 ....**$200**

Punching Bag, balloon w/characters, Morton Salt, 1942 ....**$75**

Puzzle, space station scene, Milton Bradley, 1952 ....**$150**

Rubber Band Gun, advertising premium, 1930s **$75**

Satellite Pioneers Button, green or blue, 1958 ....**$50**

School Bag, suede cloth, 1935 ....**$150**

Sonic Ray Flashlight Gun, black, green, and yellow plastic wi/signal, Norton-Horner, 1955 ....**$150**

Super Scope Telescope, plastic telescope, Norton-Horner, 1955, 9″ l ..**$70**

Wristwatch, E. Ingraham, 1935..**$750**

XZ-35 Space Gun, blued metal ray gun, produces spark, Daisy, 1934, 7-1/2″ l **$275**

XZ-44 Liquid Helium Water Gun, red and yellow or copper finish, Daisy, 1936, 7-1/4″ l **$550**

Captain Video

Game, Milton Bradley, 1952.........**$150**

Galaxy Spaceship Riding Toy, 1950s...**$425**

Rite-O-Lite Flashlight Gun, Power House Candy premium, 1950s, 3″ l..**$95**

Rocket Tank, Lido, 1952...............**$95**

Space Port Play Set, tin, Superior, 1950s...**$430**

Flash Gordon

Air Ray Gun, pressed steel, air blaster, Budson, 1950s, 10″ l....................**$350**

Arresting Ray Gun, Marx, 1939, 12″ l..**$500**

Sci-Fi, Mystery Action Satellite, battery-powered, Cragstan, 1950s, **$1,350.**

Book Bag, 1950s, 12" w **$35**
Book, Flash Gordon and the Ape Men of Mor, Dell, 1942 .... **$150**
Hand Puppet, rubber head, 1950s **$145**
Paint Book, 1930s **$125**
Pencil Box, 1951 .... **$150**
Signal Pistol, tin/pressed steel, siren sounds when trigger is pulled, green w/red trim, Marx, 1930s, 7" l **$600**
View-Master Set, viewer, 3 reels "In the Planet Mongo," 1976 .... **$10**

Lost in Space
Costume, silver space suit w/logo, Ben Cooper, 1965 .... **$150**
Helmet and Gun Set, blue and red plastic gun, child-size helmet, Remco, 1967 .... **$530**
Jupiter-2 Model Kit, Marusan/ Japanese, molded in green plastic, 1966, 6" l **$650**
Puzzles, frame tray, Milton Bradley, 1966, 10"x14" **$65**
Robot, motorized w/blinking lights, Remco, 1966, 12" h **$365**
Trading Cards, 55 black and white cards, Topps, 1966 .... **$300**

Rocky Jones, Space Ranger
Coloring Book, Whitman, 1951 .... **$50**
Pin, Silvercup Bread premium, 1950s **$20**
Wristwatch, Ingraham, 1954 ..... **$150**

Space Patrol
Atomic Pistol Flashlight Gun, plastic, Marx, 1950s **$220**
Badge, metal oval on card, 1950s.. **$400**
Cosmic Glow Ring, red and blue, 1950s **$900**
Cosmic Ray Gun, tin body w/plastic barrel, Ranger Steel Products, 1954, 9" l **$90**
Drink Mixer, boxed, 1950s.......... **$100**
Interplanetary Space Patrol Credits Coins, different denominations **$16**
Non-Fall Space Patrol X-16, tin/ plastic, blinking lights, Masudaya, 1950s........................... **$150**
Periscope, paper w/mirrors, 1950s..**$200**
Rocket Lite Flashlight, Rayovac, 1950s........................... **$250**
Space Binoculars, green plastic, logo on sides, Ralston Purina, 1950s.. **$190**
Wristwatch, w/Terra compass, 1950s **$500**

Star Trek
Captain Kirk, plastic figure w/cloth costume, Mego, 1975, 8" h **$55**
Colorforms Set, 1975 .... **$20**
Communicators, blue plastic walkie talkies, Mego, 1976 .... **$150**
Controlled Space Flight, plastic Enterprise, battery-operated, Remco, 1976 .... **$125**
Enterprise Model Kit, from Star Trek: The Motion Picture, Mego/ Grand Toys, 1980 .... **$100**
Figurine Paint Set, Milton Bradley, 1979 .... **$25**
Flashlight, from Star Trek: The Motion Picture, Larami, 1979 .... **$10**
Helmet, plastic w/sound and lights, Remco, 1976 .... **$80**
Kirk Costume, Ben Cooper, 1975.. **$30**
Movie Viewer, red and black plastic, Chemtoy, 1967 .... **$16**
Needlepoint Kit, "Live Long and Prosper," Arista, 1980 .... **$23**
Paint-By-Numbers Set, Hasbro, 1972 .... **$35**
Phaser, black plastic, battery operated, Remco, 1975..................... **$100**
Puzzle, 150 pieces, Kirk, Spock, and McCoy, H.G. Toys, 1974 .... **$10**
Spock Bank, plastic, Play Pal, 1975, 12" h **$35**
Spock Wristwatch, from Star Trek: The Motion Picture, Bradley, 1979 .... **$30**
Telescreen, plastic, battery operated target game, Mego, 1976 .... **$100**
Tricorder, blue plastic tape recorder, Mego, 1976 .... **$135**
Vulcan Shuttle Model Kit, from Star Trek III, Ertl, 1984 .... **$20**
Water Pistol, white plastic shaped like the Enterprise, Azarak-Hamway, 1976 .... **$30**

Star Wars
3-3/4" Figures, 1977-78
Boba Fett **$19**
C-3PO **$20**
Chewbacca **$13**
Darth Vader **$15**
Death Squad Commander **$12**
Death Star Droid..................... **$30**
Greedo **$18**
Hammerhead **$15**
Han Solo **$22**
Jawa, cloth cape **$20**
Jawa, vinyl cape **$250**
Luke as X-Wing Pilot **$15**
Luke Skywalker....................... **$45**
Luke w/Telescoping Lightsaber .. **$185**
Obi-Wan Kenobi **$21**

Luke Skywalker as X Wing Pilot is one of the original 12 Star Wars figures released by Kenner in 1977-78, **$15.**

Power Droid **$11**
Princess Leia Organa **$28**
R2-D2 .... **$26**
R5-D4 .... **$17**
Sand People **$17**
Snaggletooth, red body **$10**
Stormtrooper **$30**
Walrus Man **$15**
12" Figures, 1978-79
Boba Fett **$175**
C-3PO **$35**
Chewbacca **$50**
Darth Vader **$75**
Han Solo **$110**
Jawa **$55**
Luke Skywalker....................... **$125**
Obi-Wan Kenobi **$125**
Princess Leia Organa **$85**
R2-D2 .... **$45**
Stormtrooper **$95**
Creatures/Play Sets, 1977-78
Creature Cantina **$25**
Death Star Station **$75**
Droid Factory......................... **$50**
Land of the Jawas **$45**
Patrol Dewback....................... **$20**
Vehicles
Darth Vader's TIE Fighter **$45**
Imperial TIE Fighter **$25**
Imperial Troop Transport **$35**
Jawa Sandcrawler..................... **$220**
Land Speeder **$13**
Millennium Falcon **$80**
X-Wing Fighter **$35**

Tom Corbett

Atomic Flashlight Pistol, "Tom Corbett Space Cadet" on handgrip, Marx, 1950s **$300**

Coloring Book, two versions, Saalfield, 1950s **$40**

Official Sparkling Space Gun, tin litho, Marx, 21" l **$150**

Polaris Wind-Up Spaceship, tin litho, blue and yellow, Marx, 1952, 12" l **$375**

Puzzle, frame tray, Saalfield, 1950s **$30**

School Bag, plastic/vinyl w/Tom's picture and rocketships on front, 1950s **$55**

Space Academy Play Set, large, plastic figures and vehicles, tin buildings, #7020, Marx, 1950s **$515**

Space Gun, light blue and black, sparks, 9-1/2" l **$130**

Guns, Cosmic Ray gun, Stevens, 1940s, **$175.**

The Arnold Mac 700 Motorcycle is propelled by a wind-up motor, **$650.**
Photo courtesy Kent M. Comstock.

Bing Yellow Taxi c1924, **$2,200.**
Photo courtesy Bob Smith.

The No. 201 "Ratchet" Dump Truck was produced from 1921-30, **$1,250.**
Photo courtesy Joe and Sharon Freed.

TOYS, GENERAL

History: The first cast-iron toys began to appear in America shortly after the Civil War. Leading 19th-century manufacturers include Hubley, Dent, Kenton, and Schoenhut. In the first decades of the 20th century, additional manufacturers joined these earlier firms; Arcade produced quality cast-iron toys, Buddy L and Marx used pressed steel and tin, and Tootsietoy explored die-casting. George Brown and other manufacturers who did not sign or label their work made wooden toys.

Nuremberg, Germany, was the European center for the toy industry from the late 18th through the mid-20th centuries. Companies such as Lehman and Märklin produced high-quality toys.

Today's toy collectors have a wonderful assortment to choose from. Many specialize in one company, time period, or type of toy, etc. Whatever their motivation, collections bring joy. Individual collectors must decide how they feel about the condition of their toys, whether they prefer mint-in-the-box or gently played with examples or perhaps even toys that have been played with extensively. Traditionally, the toys in better condition have retained their values more than those in played-with condition. Having the original box, instructions, and/or all the pieces, etc., adds greatly to the collectiblity, and therefore the value.

Toy collectors can find examples to add to their collections at most of the typical antique and collectibles marketplaces, from auctions to flea markets to great antique shows, like Atlantique City, and even shows and auctions that specialize only in toys. For a complete list of toy shows and auctions in your area, consult the Show Calendar section of *Toy Shop* magazine.

Additional Listings: Characters, Disneyana, and Dolls. Also see *Warman's Americana & Collectibles* and *Warman's Flea Market* for more examples. *Toys & Prices 2006* focuses on post-WWII toys, while *O'Brien's Collecting Toys 11th Edition* concentrates primarily on pre-WWII toys.

Notes: Every toy is collectible; the key is condition. Good working order is important when considering mechanical toys. Examples in this listing are considered to be at least in good condition, if not better, unless otherwise specified.

Adviser: Karen O'Brien

Mobilgas wind-up toy service station by Cragstan, very good condition, missing original key, **$40.**

On top is the Buddy "L" Baggage Truck No. 203B that was manufactured from 1929-31, **$3,500;** *the bottom truck is the Buddy "L" Auto Wrecker No. 209 released from 1928-31,* **$4,500.**
Photo courtesy Bertoia Auctions.

Arcade, USA

Auto, cast iron
Chevrolet, sedan, 1925, 7" l **$650**
DeSoto, sedan, painted gray, nickeled grill and bumper, decal on trunk reads "Sundial Shoes," rubber tires, 4" l **$325**
Ford coupe, Model A, No. 106, rumble seat, 1928, 6-3/4" l **$400**
Pontiac sedan, 1932, 6-1/2" l **$350**
Dump truck, cast iron, International Harvester, painted green, red chassis, yellow pressed steel dump body, 11-1/4" l.................................. **$600**
Fire trailer truck, red, blue fireman, detachable trailer, hose reel and ladder turntable, ladders missing, paint loss, 16" l.. **$450**
Ice truck, cast iron, Mack, railed open-bed body, rear platform, rubber tires, emb sides, painted blue, 6-7/8" l **$275**
Milk truck, cast iron, Borden's, painted green, classic milk bottle design, rubber tires **$1,200**
Pick-up truck, cast iron, "International" decals on door, painted bright yellow, black rubber tires, some rust on left side, 9-1/4" l **$500**
Racer, Bullet, cast iron, classic bullet-shaped body, painted red, nickeled driver and mechanic, side pipes, and disc wheels, emb "#9" on side **$500**
Stake truck
Chevrolet, 1925, 9" l **$950**
Ford Model T, 1927, 9" l............. **$700**
Mack, No. 246X, 1929, 12" l.....**$1,400**
Tank, cast iron, camouflage painting, large metal wheels, 7-1/4" l........ **$330**
Taxi, cast iron, painted blue, black trim, emb luggage rack, seated driver and passenger, rubber tires, 8-1/4" l ...**$660**

In 1941, Arcade released the No. 7100 International Dump Truck, **$1,250.**
Photo courtesy Tim Oei.

Thresher, McCormick-Deering, gray and cream wheels, red lining, chromed chute and stacker, 12" l **$320**
Tractor, cast iron
Farmall, "A", No. 7050, 1941, 7-1/2" l **$475**
Fordson, No. 273, 1928, 3-7/8" l **$125**
McCormick-Deering, No. 10-20, 1925, 6-3/4" l **$450**
Trolley, Greyhound, New York World's Fair, blue and orange, nickel driver, decals, three cars with tinplate canopies, black tires, some chipping and scratching, 16" l **$635**
Wrecker, cast iron
Ford Model T, 1927, 11" l...........**$750**
Mack, No. 255, 1930, 12-1/2" l...**$1,900**
Plymouth, No. 1830, 1933, 4-3/4" l **$450**

Arnold, USA

Motorcycle, civilian, litho tin wind-up, mkd "Made in US Zone Germany," tin wheels mkd "Union Cord," C.8+, 7-3/4" l... **$450**
Ocean liner, twin funnels, white superstructure, black and red hull, tinplate, clockwork motor, lg, 13" **$475**

Toy, delivery truck, Buddy L, pressed steel, yellow body, red, white, and black decals, no bottles, **$45.**
Photo courtesy of Dotta Auction Co., Inc.

Satellite, remote control, tin and plastic, orig box with graphics, C.9, 7" d **$180**

Bing, Gebruder, Germany

Auto, tin, clockwork, center door model, black, seated driver, radiator cap ornament, spare tire on rear, 6-1/4" l.................................. **$400**
Garage, litho tin, double doors, extensive graphics, houses sedan and roadster **$800**
Limousine, litho tin wind-up, red, maroon and orange striping, orig driver, c1910, 5-1/4" l................. **$750**
Open tourer, four seater, litho tinplate, gray-green, black and yellow lining, red button seats, black wings, front steering, orange and gray wheels, twin lamps, windscreen frame, hand-brake operated clockwork motor, chauffeur missing, lamps detached, c1915, 12-1/2" l **$2,400**
Union ferry boat, hand-painted tin, clockwork, red hull, brown open deck, white deck housing, railing on side, window cut-outs on both sides, stack on roof, 12" l.................... **$1,200**

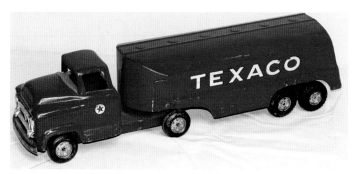

Tanker truck by Buddy L. Texaco tanker truck, **$100.**

This is the Chein Hercules Mack Motor Express Truck, **$1,450.**
Photo courtesy Bob Smith.

Buddy L, USA

Airmail truck, black front, hood fenders, enc cab, red body and chassis, 1930, 24" l...**$875**

Airplane, four-engine transport, monoplane, green wings, yellow fuselage and twin tails, 1949, 27" wingspan...**$405**

Auto
Flivver coupe, black, red spoke wheels, aluminum tires, 1924, 11" l......**$750**
Jr Camaro, metallic blue body, white racing stripes across hood, 1968, 9" l **$50**

Cement mixer truck, red body, white side ladder, water tank, mixing drum, 1965, 15-1/2" l....................**$80**

Dump truck
Husky, yellow hood, chrome one-pc wraparound bumper, 1969, 14-1/2" l **$100**
Hydraulic Construction, medium blue front, large green dumper, 1967, 15-1/4" l.................................**$150**
Jr Dumper, avocado cab, tiltback dump section, 1969, 7-1/2" l **$35**
Utility, duo-tone slant design, red front, gray chassis, royal blue dump body, yellow seat, 1940, 25-1/2" l........**$185**

Electric Emergency Unit wrecker, white pressed steel, rear hoist, paint wear and staining, 16-1/2" l........**$245**

Express Line delivery truck, black pressed-steel, front steering and rear doors, 24" l.................................**$750**

Fire truck
Aerial truck, red, nickel ladders, 1925, 39" l...**$850**
Extension ladder, rider, duo-tone slant design, white front, red hood top, cab, and frame, red semi-trailer, white ladders, 1949, 32-1/2" l....**$225**
Ladder truck, red, bright metal grille and headlights, two white ladders, 1939, 24" l..................................**$300**

Greyhound bus, pressed steel, clockwork, bright blue and white, "Greyhound Lines" on sides, rubber tires, 16"l **$325**

Outdoor railroad, No. 1000 4-6-2 locomotive and tender, No. 1001 caboose, No. 1003 tank, No. 1004 stock, No. 1005 coal cars (one with orig decal), 121-1/2" l, repainted **$2,750**

Steam shovel, No. 220, black, red corrugated roof and base, cast wheels, boiler, decal and winch, surface rust, paint crazing on roof, 14" h........**$125**

Telephone maintenance truck, No. 450, two-tone green, ladder, two poles, orig maker's box...............**$350**

Tractor
Husky, bright yellow body, large rear fenders, black engine block, 1966, 13" l **$80**
Ruff-n-Tuff, yellow grille, hood, and frame, black plastic engine block, 1971, 10-1/2" l **$50**

Wrecker, orig condition **$4,500**

Cast iron, unknown American makers

Dump truck, green Mack style front, C-cab, red bed with spring lever, spoked nickel wheels, 7-3/4" l....**$490**

Gasoline truck, blue, Mack-style front, C-cab, rubber tires, one tire missing. 7" l...**$225**

Milk wagon, black cast-iron horse, gilt harness, yellow wheels, blue steel wagon body, 6-3/4" l....................**$150**

Stake truck, Ford Model A, red, 7" l **$300**

Champion

Auto, cast iron, coupe, painted red, nickeled grille and headlights, rumble seat, rubber tires, spare mounted on trunk, 7" l, repainted..................**$250**

Gasoline truck, cast iron, painted red, Mack "C" cab, tanker body, emb on sides, rubber tires, 8-1/8" l....**$450**

Panel truck, cast iron, enclosed panel van, cast spare tires and headlights, traces of orig blue paint, spoked metal wheels, 7-1/2" l, poor condition **$400**

Racer, cast iron, painted red, silver trim, wind deflector on rear, separately cast driver painted blue, nickeled disc wheels, 8-1/2" l............**$650**

Stake truck, cast iron, painted red, Mack "C" cab, stake side body, nickeled spoke wheels, 7" l................**$660**

Truck, cast iron, "C" Mack cab, blue body, 7-3/4" l, replaced wheels...**$250**

Wrecker, cast iron, red C-cab with crane, nickel plated crank and barrel, rubber tires, 8-1/4" l....................**$600**

Chein

Barnacle Bill, litho tin wind-up, some loss of paint, C.7 ....**$325**

Bass drummer, litho tin wind-up, orig box missing end flap, C.9, 8-3/4" h, ...**$275**

Disneyland ferris wheel, clockwork motor, bell, six gondolas, litho Disney characters and fairgrounds scenes, distortion and paint loss, 16-3/4" h **$450**

Hercules ferris wheel, clockwork motor, bell, six gondolas, litho children and fairground scenes, 16-1/2" l **$375**

Popeye, in barrel, litho tin wind-up, C.8, 7" h **$650**

Roller coaster, litho tin wind-up, orig box, C.8-9, 19" l, 10" h.................**$525**

Wagon, horse-drawn, "Fine Groceries," tinplate, 12" l.......................**$290**

Converse, USA

Heffield Farms delivery wagon,

At left is Champion's Policeman on motorcycle #2, **$400;** *at right is #3,* **$425.**
Photo courtesy Kent M. Comstock.

This 1974 release from Corgi is a Citroen SM, #284, **$40.**
Photo courtesy Karen O'Brien.

Corgi's 1:43-scale Studebaker Golden Hawk, #211S, was produced from 1960-63, **$180.**
Photo courtesy Dr. Douglas Sadecky.

David P. Clark founded the Dayton Friction Toy Works after William Scheible purchased Clark's half of the David P. Clark Co. This is his 13-1/4"-long Seven Passenger Touring Car, c.1909, **$350.**
Photo courtesy Bob Smith.

articulated horse, considerable wear and paint loss, 21-1/2" l **$320**

Klondike Ice Co. delivery wagon, tinplate on wood, two litho horses, paint poor, 17" l **$175**

Trolley, open sides, pressed steel, blue and mustard, stenciled dec, marked "City Hall Park 175" on both ends, reversible benches, large clockwork motor, paint poor, destination boards missing, 16" l **$260**

Corgi

Ambulance, Chevrolet Superior, white body, orange roof, Red Cross decals, 4-3/4" l **$75**

Auto
Buick Riviera, #245, MIB **$85**
Chevrolet Caprice, #325, MIB **$60**
Circus, land rover and animal trailer, #30, MIB **$90**
Citreon DS 19, #210S, MIB **$84**
Ford Consol Saloon, #200M, MIB **$140**
Ford Zephyr Estate Car, light blue, 3-7/8" **$45**
Jeep CJ-5, dark metallic green body **$30**
Mercedes-Benz 220 SE coupe, #230 .... **$60**
Porsche Carrera 6, white body, red or blue trim **$60**
Volkswagen 1200 Driving School .. **$35**

Camera van, Commer Mobile, metallic blue body, black camera on gold tripod, cameraman, 3-1/2" **$120**

Car transporter, Bedford, black diecast cap, 10-1/4" l **$105**

Character cars
Batmobile, glossy black body, gold tow hook **$200**
Captain Marvel Porsche, white body, 4-3/4" l **$30**
Hardy Boys Rolls-Royce, red body, yellow hood **$70**

James Bond Aston Martin, metallic silver body, diecast base, red int., two figures, working roof hatch, ejector seat **$150**
Monkee Mobile, #277, MIB **$450**
Popeye's Paddy Wagon **$195**
Saint's Volvo P-1800, white body, silver trim **$55**

Tank truck, Mack Exxon, white cap and tank, red tank chassis, 10-3/4" l **$15**

Taxi
Austin, London, black, yellow plastic int. **$36**
Thunderbird Bermuda, white body, 4" l **$50**

Tractor, Ford 5000, blue body, yellow scoop arm and controls, chrome scoop, 3-1/8" l **$55**

Dayton Friction Co.

Patrol wagon, pressed metal and wood, friction driven, painted red, stenciled "Police Patrol" on front panel, seated driver on open bench seat, spoke wheels, 10" l **$350**

Touring car, pressed metal, painted red, gold spoke wheels, open sides, friction driver, 12" l **$500**

Dinky

Airplane
Autogyro, gold, blue rotor, 1934-41 .... **$125**
Bristol Beinhem, 1956-63 .... **$35**
Douglas DC3, silver, #60t, 1937-41 .... **$125**
Lockheed Constellation, #66b, 1940 .... **$90**
Percival Gull, camouflaged, #66c, 1940 .... **$100**
Twin Engine Fighter, silver, #70d/731, 1946-55 .... **$25**

Ambulance
Range Rover, #268, 1974-78 .... **$50**

This assortment of Dinky vehicles includes, Leyland Cement Wagon, **$250;** *Mighty Antar with Propeller,* **$400;** *Guy Slumberland Van, 1949-52,* **$575.**

Fisher-Price, Play Family Mini-Bus, Fisher-Price, early 1970s, **$50.**

The Fisher-Price Donald Duck Drum Major, #400-500, 1946, **$325.**

The Mickey Mouse Choo Choo from Fisher-Price, 1949, **$245.**

Fisher-Price's Quacky Family, with felt beaks and wooden dowels between the ducks, 1946, **$185.**

Superior Criterion, #263, 1962-68... **$50**

Auto

Austin Somerset Saloon, #161, MIB **$150**

Cadillac Eldorado, #131, 1956-62 .... **$60**

DeSoto, Diplomat, orange, F545, 1960-63 .... **$85**

Ford Fairlane, pale green, #148, 1962-66 .... **$60**

Jaguar XK 120, white, #157, 1954-62 .... **$125**

Mercury Cougar, #174, MIB **$95**

Plymouth Stockcar, #201, MIB..... **$40**

Studebaker Commander, F24Y, 1951-61 .... **$75**

Triumph TR-2, gray, #105, 1957-60 .... **$100**

Volkswagen 1300 sedan, #129, 1965-76 .... **$20**

Bulldozer, Blaw Knox, #561 .... **$45**

Bus

Routemaster, #289, 1964-80 .... **$75**

Silver Jubilee, #297, 1977 .... **$25**

Fire truck

Airport fire tender, #276, MIB ... **$125**

Fire chief's land rover, #195, MIB.. **$60**

Motorcycle

A. A. Motorcycle Patrol, #270/44B, 1946-44 .... **$30**

Police Motorcycle Patrol, #42B, 1946-53 .... **$45**

Police car

Citroen DS19, #F501, 1967-70 ..... **$95**

Plymouth, #244, 1977-80 .... **$35**

Taxi

Austin, #40H, 1951-52 .... **$70**

London, #284, MIB **$75**

Plymouth Plaza, #266, 1960-67 .... **$60**

Tractor

David Brown, #305 .... **$60**

Field Marshall, #37N/301 .... **$60**

Massey-Harris, #27A/300 .... **$60**

Truck

Austin Van, Nestle's, #471 .... **$65**

Brink's, #275, MIB **$65**

Coles Hydra, #980, MIB **$100**

Foden Mobilgas tanker, #941 ..... **$145**

Leland Tanker, Shell/BP, #944 ..... **$125**

Telephone service van, #261, MIB **$150**

Willeme log truck, #F36A/987 ..... **$75**

Fisher-Price, USA

American Airlines plane, paper litho over wood, bright orange and blue, extensive graphics, two propellers, 20" wingspan...................... **$500**

Chatter Telephone, 1962 .... **$30**

Donald Duck Xylphone, play wear, 1946 .... **$175**

Ducky Cart, 1950 .... **$45**

Easter Bunny, 1936...................... **$125**

Farmer in the Dell TV Radio, 1963 .... **$25**

Gabby Duck, 1952 .... **$55**

Jack n Jill TV Radio, #148, 1956 .... **$65**

Junior Circus, 1963 .... **$75**

Katy Kackler, #140, 1954............. **$80**

Lady Bug, 1961 .... **$35**

Merry Mousewife, #473, 1949 ... **$60**

Mickey Mouse Drummer **$250**

Mother Goose Music Cart, #784, 1955 .... **$35**

Nosey Pup, 1956 .... **$25**

Pinky Pig, 1958............................. **$35**

Pony Express, #733, 1941........... **$110**

Pushy Elephant, #525, 1934 ..... **$450**

Rock-A-Bye Baby Cart, #627, 1960 .... **$35**

Sleepy Sue, #632, 1960 .... **$55**

Streamline Express, #215, 1935 .... **$900**

Sunny Fish, #420, 1961 .... **$100**

Talky Parrot, 1963 .... **$145**

Teddy Drummer, #775, 1936..... **$300**

This Little Pig, #910, 1963............ **$30**

Uncle Timmy Turtle, #437, 1942 .... **$100**

Wiggily Woofer, #640, 1957........ **$85**

Ziggy Zilo, #737, 1958 .... **$50**

Hot Wheels, Mattel, MIP

American Hauler, redline, 1976 .. $70
American Tipper, redline, 1976 .. $65
Baja Bruiser, #8258, orange, 1974 .. $90
Beach Bomb, green .. $90
Boss Hoss, #6406, 1971 .. $250
Buzz Off, redline, 1973 .. $500
Captain America, #2879, white, 1979 .. $175
Cement Mixer, #6452, 1970 .. $125
Chevy, '57, Ultra Hots, #47 .. $100
Circus Cats, #3303, white, .. $75
Classic '36 Ford Coupe, redline, 1969 .. $125
Custom Police Cruiser, #6269, 2969 .. $200
Datsun 200XS, #3255, maroon, Canada, 1982 .. $125
Dune Daddy, #6967, light green, 1975 .. $75
Earthmover, #16 .. $85
El Rey Special, #8273, light blue, 1974 .. $1,100
Emergency Squad, #7650, red, 1975 .. $75
Fire Engine, redline, 1970 .. $165
Flat Out 442, green, Canada, 1984 .. $150
Fuel Tanker, #6018, 1971 .. $200
Heavy Chevy, #6408, 1970 .. $210
Hood, redline .. $150
Hot Heap, #6219, 1968 .. $110
Ice T, redline, 1971 .. $200
Jet Threat, #6179, 1976 .. $55
Light My Firebird, redline, 1970 .. $110
Lotus Turbine, #6262, 1969 .. $90
Mantis, #6423, 1970 .. $100
Maxi Taxi, #9184, yellow, blackwall, 1977 .. $50
Mongoose Funny Car, redline, 1970 .. $210
Moving van, redline, 1970 .. $150
Neet Streeter, #9510, chrome, 1976 .. $75
Olds 442, #6467, 1971 .. $800
Poison Pinto, #9240, green, blackwall, 1977 .. $30
Police Cruiser, #6963, white, 1973 .. $150
Porsche 911, #6972, orange, 1975 .. $65
Probe Funny Car, #84, Motorcraft .. $30
Race Ace, #2620, white, 1968 .. $75
Red Baron, #6963, red, blackwall, 1977 .. $25
Rig Wrecker, #45 .. $225
Road Roller, #55, yellow .. $25
Rock Buster, #9088, yellow, blackwall, 1977 .. $15
Sand Crab, #6403, 1970 .. $90

Scooper, redline, 1971 .. $220
Silhouette, #6209, 1979 .. $50
Sir Sidney Roadster, #8261, yellow, 1974 .. $90
Snake II, redline, 1971 .. $275
Super Van, #9205, chrome, 1976 .. $65
Sweet 16, #6422, 1970 .. $75
Tail Gunner, #29 .. $75
Team Trailer, redline, 1971 .. $225
Tow Truck, #6450, 1970 .. $120
T-Totaller, #9648, brown, blackwall, 1977 .. $40
Turbo Streak, #104 .. $75
Vega Bomb, #7654, green, 1975 .. $950
Volkswagen, #7620, orange, bug on roof, 1974 .. $75
Warpath, #7654, white, 1975 .. $115
Whip Creamer, redline, #1870 .. $60
Z Whiz, #9639, gray, redline, 1977 .. $70

Hubley, Lancaster, PA

Airplane, cast iron
American Eagle, WWII fighter 11" wingspan .. $200
Lindy Glider, painted red, yellow wings, driver seated on front, emb wings, 6-1/2" l .. $1,250
Navy fighter, DC, moving propeller, retractable landing gear, folding wings, orig box, C.9, 8-3/4" .. $225
Sea Plane, orange, and blue, two engines .. $75
Auto, cast iron
Chrysler Airflow, battery operated lights, 1934 .. $1,250
Coupe, 1928, 8-1/2" l .. $600
Lincoln Zephyr and trailer, painted green, nickeled grille and bumper, 13-1/2" l .. $825
Sedan and trailer, painted red sedan, trailer panted silver and red, rubber tires, factory sample tag, 9-1/2" l .. $725
Streamlined Racer, 5" l .. $375
Bell telephone, cast iron
Painted green, silver sides, emb company name, Mack "C" cab, nickeled ladders, long handled shovels, pole carrier, spoked wheels, repainted, 8-1/4" l .. $800
Painted green, winch, auger, nickel water barrel on side, ladders, and pole carrier, fatigued rubber tires, 9-1/4" l .. $1,300
Boat, cast iron, painted red, emb "Static" on sides, sleet form, seated driver, hand on throttle of attached motor, chromed air cleaner, painted orange, three tires, clicker, over painted, 9-1/2" l .. $1,650

Hubley Auto Transport with two Cadillacs, plastic, post-WWII, **$160.**
Photo courtesy Terry Sells.

This Hubley Motorcycle with two removable Policemen, cast iron, 9" l, **$1,200.**
Photo courtesy Kent M. Comstock.

This Hubley Packard from 1929 was cast in fifteen different parts and measures 11" l. One of the "Holy Grails" of Hubley collecting, this rarity, at auction, achieved **$16,000.**
Photo courtesy Bertoia Auctions.

Japanese Battery-Operated toys are popular with collectors, like this colorful Batmobile, **$400.**
Photo courtesy Heinz Mueller.

The Keystone Water Tower Pump truck is difficult to find with the water tank free from rust. This one has only minor rusting, **$1,500.**
Photo courtesy Karen O'Brien.

This is the plastic Kilgore Motorcycle, **$750.**

Photo courtesy Kent M. Comstock.

This is the Matchbox Regular Wheels Iron Fairy Crane from 1969-70, **$18.**

KP Photo courtesy George Cuhaj.

This 1969 Hot Wheels Redlines Custom Firebird was based on the Pontiac Firebird, **$250.**

KP Photo, Tom Michael collection.

The Hot Wheels Redlines Mantis was released in 1970, car out of pack, **$60.**

KP Photo, Tom Michael collection.

This is the Hot Wheels Paddy Wagon from 1970, **$75.**

KP Photo, Tom Michael collection.

Bus, cast iron, new tires, 5-3/4" l..**$125**

Cement mixer truck, cast iron, red and green, nickel tank, rubber wheels, Mack, restored, 8" l..................**$1,760**

Delivery truck, Merchants, 1925, 6-1/4" l..................................**$400**

Fire truck, cast iron
Fire Engine, 1930s, 5" l **$75**
Fire Patrol, 7-men, 1912, 5" l ...**$3,575**
Hook and ladder, 1912, 23" l ..**$1,850**
Ladder truck, 5-1/2" l....................**$70**

Gasoline truck, cast iron, painted silver, red spoked wheels, cast figure, round tank body, rear facets, c1920, 6" l...**$495**

Milk truck, cast iron, painted white, emb "Borden's" on side panel, rear opening door, nickeled grille, headlights, and spoke wheels, repaired headlights, 7-1/2" l
....**$1,980**

Motorcycle, cast iron
Harley-Davidson, 1932, 7-1/2" l.**$500**
Hill Climber, 1936, 6-1/2" l........**$450**
Indian Four Cylinder, 1929, 9" l
....**$1,800**
Motorcycle cop with sidecar.......**$700**
Patrol Motorcycle, green, 6-1/2" l
....**$275**
Parcel post, 90% orig paint, 10" l
....**$2,000**

Panama steam shovel, cast iron, painted red and green, large scale, nickeled shovel, cast people on trailer, dual rubbers on rear, 12" l **$935**

Pull toy, Old Dutch Girl, cast iron, white and blue dress, holding yellow can of cleanser, rubber tires, repaired stick, orig checker floor, c1932, 9" l
....**$4,100**

Racer, cast iron
Painted blue, painted red articulated pistons, seated driver, black tires, spoked wheels, 10-1/2" l.......**$1,760**
Painted green, red emb "5" on sides, hood opens on both sides to show extensively cast engine, disc wheels, seated driver, replaced hood doors, 9-1/2" l..............................**$1,500**
Painted red, seated driver, emb "#1" on sides, rubber tires, 7-3/4" l.......**$400**

Japanese

Haji, car with boat trailer, friction powered, blue Ford convertible, red and cream Speedo motor boat with friction-powered motor, red trailer, orig packing and maker's box, 8" l.....**$400**

Occupied Japan, Plymouth, litho tin wind-up, nickel trim, orig box, C.8+, 1942, 6" l....................................**$175**

SY, flying man robot, litho tin wind-up, orig box, C.9, 6" x 3" base, 11" h
....**$375**

T.N.

Dump Truck, friction powered tinplate, red and cream, automatic side dump action, orig maker's box, 11" l......................................**$150**

Great Swanee Paddle Wheeler, friction powered tinplate, whistle mechanism, orig maker's box, 10-1/4" l...............................**$175**

Koko the Sandwich Man, orig box, C.8, 1950s, 7" h.........................**$150**

TPS

Circus parade, tin litho wind-up, clowns and elephants, orig box, C.9, 11" l................**$275**

Moon patrol, tin, battery operated, tin astronaut driver, plastic dome, bump-and-go action, C.9, 8" l
....**$350**

Yone, swinging baby robot, litho tin wind-up, orig box, C.9, 4" x 4" base, 12" h..**$350**

Yonezawa

Missile launching tank, litho tin, battery operated, four targets, orig box, C.10, 6" l...............................**$155**

Happy n' sad magic face clown, battery operated, orig box, C.9, 10-1/2" h
....**$150**

Keystone Mfg. Co., Boston

Air mail plane, olive green, three propellers, 25".........................**$1,650**

Ambulance, canvas cover and stretcher, 27-1/2" l, C.8.................**$1,400**

Bus, Coast to Coast, blue, 31-1/4" l, C.8
....**$1,900**

Fighter plane, "Ride 'Em," silver pressed-steel, red wings, propeller and seat, 25" l.........................**$720**

Moving van, black cab, red body, rubber tires, 26-1/4"..................**$1,300**

Packard Ride 'Em water tower, tower, nozzle, tank, and seat, lg. 32" l
....**$850**

Police patrol truck, decals, 27-1/2" l
....**$700**

Steam shovel, 20-3/4" l.............**$250**

Kilgore, Canada

Airplane, cast iron, Seagull, painted red, nickeled wheels and wing mounted propeller, 7-3/4" l.........**$880**

Auto, open roadster, 1928, cast iron, painted blue, nickeled wheels and driver, decal reads "Kilgore, Made in Canada," 6-1/8" l.........................**$825**

The Lineol No. 1218 Bridge Truck is a rare vehicle, **$6,500.**
Photo courtesy Jack Matthews.

Delivery truck, cast iron, Toy Town, painted red, emb on side panels, gold highlights, silver disc wheels, repainted, 6-1/8" l **$360**

Dump truck, cast iron, painted blue enclosed cab, red dump body, lever to lift, nickeled disc wheels, 8-1/2" l **$450**

Ice cream truck, cast iron, enclosed cab painted blue, orange body, emb "Arctic Ice Cream" on sides, disc wheels, 8" l **$470**

Lehmann, Germany

Beetle, spring motor, crawling movement, flapping wings, maker's box, one leg detached, but present, early Adam trademark **$230**

Catalog, *Patent Lehmann Spielzug,* 1881, 21 pgs, orig order blank, 6" x 9", minor insect damage **$315**

Heinkel-Blitz He 70, tin, orig string, instructions, plane with Nazi swastika, orig box, C.10, 4-1/2" l **$575**

Na-Ob, red and yellow cart, blue eccentric wheels, gray donkey, marked "Lehmann Ehe & Co.," front wheel missing, 6" l **$145**

Oh-My Alabama coon jigger, lithograph tinplate, clockwork motor, 10" h **$480**

Sedan, EPL No. 765, litho tin wind-up, some edge and tire wear, C.7+, 5-1/2" l **$150**

Truck, tinplate, cream, red, and yellow, blue driver, fixed steering, clockwork motor, marked "Lehmann Ehe & Co.," 6-3/4" l **$435**

Tut Tut motor car, white suited driver, horn, front steering, bellows, coil springs, paint loss, rust spotting, 6-1/2" l **$650**

Linemar, Japan

Cabin cruiser, litho tin, battery operated, detailed interior, fabric covered seats, orig box, 12" l, C.9 .... **$250**

Clarabell Clown, tin mechanical action, 6-1/2" h, C.8 .... **$210**

Donald Duck, Walt Disney's mechanical tricycle, celluloid Donald Duck riding tin wind-up, box with illus of Mickey riding tricycle, 3-3/4" x 4" x 2-1/2" box **$325**

Feeding birdwatcher, litho tin and plush, battery operated, orig box, C.9, 7-1/2" h **$365**

Mickey Mouse

Moving van, litho tin friction, wear, 1950s, C.7, 13" l **$350**

Rocking on Pluto, litho tin wind-up, replaced ears and tail, C.7, 5-1/2" h **$850**

Music box, cowboy dancing to music, tin and plastic, battery operated, orig box, C.9, 5" h **$175**

Prehistoric animal, T-Rex, litho tin wind-up, orig box, 9" l, 6" h **$260**

Rocket express, litho tin wind-up, train and space ship, orig box, C.9, 5-1/2" sq **$575**

Smoking Popeye, tin, battery operated, orig box, C.7+ **$2,500**

Superman tank, tin, battery operated, orig box, © 1958, C.9, 5" h **$3,000**

Lineol, Germany

Armored car, litho tin clockwork, camouflage colors, revolving turret with gun, opening doors, spring lever for gun, wire guard covers vehicle, rubber tires, symbols repainted, minor paint loss, 10" l **$935**

Cannon, 88mm, litho tin, camouflage colors, stabilizer arms, elevation cranks, four-tire open frame, tow hook, 14-1/2" l **$935**

Pinocchio tin toy, Louis Marx & Co. for Walt Disney Productions, c1930, 15-1/2" x 11" x 2-1/4", **$355.**
Photo courtesy of David Rago Auctions, Inc.

This is the Marx Merchants Transfer truck from 1929, **$700.**
Photo courtesy Bob Smith.

This is the battery-operated Marx Combat Tank, "U.S. Tank Division," **$45.**
Photo courtesy Heinz Mueller.

Marx, Deluxe Delivery truck, 1948, **$200.**

This Matchbox Regular Wheels Road Roller was released in 1962, **$60.**

This is the Matchbox Models of Yesteryear Y-12 1909 Thomas Runabout that was issued in 1967, **$20.**

Photo courtesy Karen O'Brien.

Motorcycle with side car, composition figures, tin fenders, disc wheels, 4-1/2" l...........................**$500**

Marx, Louis & Co., NY

Airplane

American Airlines, flagship, pressed steel, wood wheels, 1940, 27" wingspan..........................**$170**

Bomber, metal, wind-up, four propellers, 14-1/2" wingspan.............**$100**

Floor Zeppelin, 1931, 9-1/2" l.....**$225**

Lucky Stunt Flyer, litho tin wind-up, 1928, 6" l...................................**$150**

Military litho tin wind-up, orig box, mounted to orig insert, 13" l, 18" wing span, C.9..........................**$260**

Pan American, pressed steel, four engines, 1940, 27" wingspan.....**$90**

Pursuit Plane, one propeller, 1930s, 8" wingspan...............................**$125**

Skybird flyer, litho tin wind-up, plane and zeppelin circling tower, orig box with wear, C.8, 26" w, 10" h........**$275**

Trans-Atlantic Zeppelin, litho tin wind-up, 1930, 10" l................**$225**

Auto

Army car, battery operated.........**$100**

Crazy Dan car, litho tin wind-up, 1930s, 6" l.............................**$395**

Dippy Dumper, celluloid Brutus, litho tin wind-up, 1930s, 9" l...........**$350**

Jalopy, tin driver, friction, 1950s..**$140**

Leaping Lizzie, litho tin wind-up, 1927, 7" l.............................**$250**

Queen of the Campus, four college students, 1950....................**$275**

Siren police car, 1930s, 15" l.........**$125**

Speed racer, 1937, 13" l.............**$250**

Streamline Speedway, two litho tin wind-up racing cars, 1936.......**$175**

Auto transport, plastic cab and cars, orig box, professional repairs, 23" l, C.9.......................................**$225**

Battleship, *U.S.S. Washington,* tin friction, orig box, 14" l, C.9.......**$275**

Bulldozer/tractor, gold body, rubber treads, plow and farmer driver, blue and red stake wagons, hitch, two discs, plow, corn planter, harvester.......**$275**

Drummer boy, litho tin wind-up, minor edge wear on drum, C.7+, 7-1/2" h.............................**$300**

Dumbo, the acrobatic elephant, litho tin wind-up, Disney, orig box, C.9, 1941, 4" h............................**$725**

Jazzbo Jim, litho tin wind-up, orig box, C.9, 9" h.......................**$575**

Lone Ranger, range rider, litho tin wind-up, C.9, 1938, 11" l, 9" h....**$350**

Merrymakers Band, tinplate, one dancer missing..........................**$850**

Pluto, litho tin wind-up, Walt Disney Productions, orig box, C.9, 6-1/2" h **$500**

Royal Bus Lines, litho tin wind-up, 1930s, 10-1/4" l...................**$135**

Set

Bulldog tractor, aluminum, litho wind-up, 1940, 9-1/2" l tractor...........**$250**

Sleeping Beauty, Prince Phillip, Samson the Horse, hard plastic, all accessories, orig box, 12" l, C.8+.......**$150**

Super Power Tractor and Trailer, litho tin wind-up, 1937, 8-1/2" l tractor **$125**

Truck

Dump truck, yellow cab, blue bum-per, red bed, 1950, 18" l...........**$10**

East-West Coast Van, tin litho, ten wheeler, tin balloon tires, ad graphics, orig box, C.9, 18" l.......**$32**

Gravel truck, pressed steel cab, red ti dumper, 1930, 10".................**$100**

Jalopy pickup, litho tin wind-up, 7" **$6**

Mack towing truck, dark green cab wind-up, 1926, 8" l.................**$175**

Pet shop truck, plastic, six compart ments with vinyl dogs, 11" l....**$125**

Royal Oil Co., Mack, dark red cab medium green tank, wind-up, 1927 8-1/4" l.................................**$200**

Searchlight, toolbox behind cab 1930s, 10" l.........................**$150**

Stake bed, pressed steel, wooder wheels, 1936, 7" l...................**$60**

TV and radio station, battery oper ated, orig box, C.8-9, 27" l, 10" w 8" h.......................................**$300**

Zippo the climbing monkey, mul ticolored litho tinplate, pull-string mechanism, 10" l.......................**$60**

Matchbox, England

Austin Taxi, #17, MIB, 1960.........**$75**

Atlantic Trailer, tan body, six meta wheels, MIB, 1956.....................**$70**

Atlas truck, metallic blue cab, orange dumper, labels on doors, 1975.......**$7**

Bedford Tipper, #3, gray cap, NM 1961.......................................**$25**

Blue Shark, #61, MIB, 1971.........**$15**

Caterpillar Tractor, #8, 1955......**$40**

Chevrolet Impala, taxi, orange, 1965 ....**$30**

Citreon DS19, #66, NM, 1959.....**$32**

Daimler ambulance, #14, NM, 1955 ....**$25**

Disney car, Donald Duck, 1989....**$40**

Ferrari Berlinetta, metallic green body, NM, 1965.......................**$25**

Fiat 1500, MIB, 1965.................**$15**

Foden Ready Mix concrete truck orange body, MIB, 1961.............**$45**

Ford Customline Station Wagon #31, yellow body, NM, 1957.........**$40**

Ford Zephyr 6, #33, MIB, 1963 ....**$33**

Fork Lift Truck, #15, red body, yellow hoist, MIP, 1973.....................**$95**

Harta Tractor Shovel, #69, orange MIB, 1965.................................**$30**

Honda Motorcycle with Trailer #38, MIB, 1968.........................**$40**

Horse Drawn Milk Float, #7, orange body, MIB, 1954.........................**$125**

Jaguar XK 140 coupe, #32, MIB 1957.......................................**$70**

Lambretta Motorscooter with Sidecar, #36, metallic green, MIP, 1961 .... **$95**

Land Rover Fire Truck, #57, NM, 1966 .... **$11**

Leyland Royal Tiger Coach, #40, silver-gray, NM, 1961 .... **$10**

London Bus, #5, MIB, 1954 .... **$80**

Mark Ten Jaguar, #28, NM, 1964. **$20**

Maserati 4CLT Racer, NM, 1958.. **$50**

Mercedes Benz Coach, white, 1965 .... **$30**

MGA sports car, #19, MIB, 1969 .. **$70**

Military scout car, #61, MIB, 1959 .... **$32**

Morris Minor 1000, dark green, 1958 .... **$20**

Pontiac convertible, #39, MIB, 1962 .... **$65**

Rolls-Royce Phantom V, 1964 ... **$15**

Scaffolding truck, silver body, green tinted windows, 1969 .... **$5**

Setra Coach, #12, 1970 .... **$5**

Snowtrac Tractor, red body, silver painted grille, 1964 .... **$10**

Swamp Rat, green deck, plastic hull, tan soldier, 1976 .... **$5**

Taxi Cab, Chevrolet Impala, #20, MIB, 1965 .... **$35**

Thames Wreck, red body, 1961, 2-1/2" **$15**

Volkswagon 1500 Saloon, #15, MIB, 1968 .... **$25**

Weatherhill Hydraulic Excavator, decal, 1956 .... **$20**

Pratt & Letchworth

Dray wagon, cast iron, open bed wagon, single slat slides, wooden floor, standing figure, red spoke wheels, one horse, 10-1/4" l **$275**

Hook and ladder truck, cast iron, horse drawn, one red and one white horse, black frame with red detailing, spoked wheels, seated front driver, seated rear driver, two wood ladders and bell, 23" l **$560**

Surrey, cast iron, open carriage, low splash board, two full width seams with arm and back rests, emb upholstering mounted on two prs of spoked wheels, pulled by one horse, c1900, 14" l **$990**

Schuco, trademark of Schreyer and Co., Germany

Acrobat bear, yellow mohair, glass eyes, embroidered nose and mouth, turns somersaults when wound, orig key, 1950s, 5" h **$575**

Ambulance, Mercedes 408 Servo, plastic, orig box, C.7+, 12-1/2" l **$125**

Mercedes Simplex, wind-up, 8-1/2" l **$125**

Monkey bellhops, Yes/No monkey with painted metal face, metal eyes, ginger mohair head and tail, red and black felt outfit and hands, Acrobatic monkey with painted metal face, metal eyes, ginger mohair head, red and black felt outfit and hands, winds by rotating arms, oak Mission style settee, moth damage on both, 1930s, 8-1/2" h **$435**

Monkey, tumbling **$110**

Porsche microracer, No. 1037, red, key missing **$100**

Racing kit, BMW Formula 2, tin and plastic, unassembled, orig box, C.10, 10" l **$165**

Set, Highway Patrol, squad car, 1958 .... **$140**

Tank, keywind **$50**

Teddy bear on roller skates, wind-up, beige mohair head, glass eyes, embroidered nose and mouth, cloth and metal body and legs, cotton shirt, felt overalls, hands, and boots, rubber wheels, marked "Schuco, U.S. Zone, Germany," clothes faded, key not orig **$490**

Teddy bear on scooter, friction auction, yellow mohair bear, black steel eyes, embroidered nose and mouth, black felt pants, blue litho scooter, 1920s, 5-3/4" h **$1,100**

Van, battery operated, 4" l **$75**

Smith-Miller

Chevy Ice Truck, c.1945 .... **$450**

GMC Dump Truck, 1950-53, six wheels **$350**

L Mack Aerial Ladder, SMFD, eight wheels **$550**

L Mack P.I.E. truck, fourteen wheels **$550**

MIC House Trailer **$450**

Structo

Bearcat Auto, 16" l, C.8, 1919 ... **$850**

Cement mixer truck, 1950s, 18-1/2" l, C.8, 9" h **$150**

Climbing military tank, green, 1929 .... **$500**

Contractor truck, orange dump truck, 1924 .... **$600**

Emergency van, blue and white, 1962 .... **$100**

Fire insurance patrol, 1928, 18" l **$200**

Here is the Schuco Old Timer 1913 Mercer windup, **$150.**
Photo courtesy Al Kasishke.

This Smith-Miller Dump has a working hand crank that operates the dump bed, **$500.**
KP Photo courtesy Larry Planer.

This is the Structo Weekender from the 1960s, **$180.**
KP Photo courtesy Ron O'Brien.

Fire truck, hydraulic hook and ladder, pressed steel, red, 3" l **$200**

Hydraulic dumper **$75**

Lone Eagle airplane, monoplane, spring drive motor, 1928 .... **$675**

Motor dispatch, blue, decals, 1929, 24" **$850**

Sky King airplane, blue, gray wings, 1929 .... **$900**

Tinplate, unknown makers

Clown violinist, stilt-legs, striped trousers, clockwork motor, poor condition, 9" h **$65**

Delivery carriage, litho, black, red, yellow, and pink, flywheel drive, 4-1/4" l **$150**

Horse-drawn omnibus, attributed to Francis, Field and Francis, Philadel-

This Tonka Suburban Pumper is from the early 1960s and its two-piece grille is indicative of trucks made before 1962, **$350.**
KP Photo courtesy Ron O'Brien.

A 1963 Tonka Wrecker, **$150.**
KP Photo courtesy Karen O'Brien.

The Buck Rogers No. 1033 Attack Ship from Tootsietoy, **$225.**

An art-deco influenced Wyandotte Boat-Tail Racer c1934, **$195.**
Photo courtesy Brian Seligman.

This 1950s Wyandotte Emergency Auto Service truck has a plastic cab and metal bed with litho graphics, **$145.**
Photo courtesy Brian Seligman.

Top row left to right: Gnom Series BV-Aral Tanker, 4-1/2", **$600;** *Gnom Series Ope Dump Truck, 4-1/2",* **$550;** *bottom row left to right: Gnom Series Racing Car, 4-1/2"* **$650;** *Gnom Series Sedan,* **$500.**
Photo courtesy Bob Smith.

phia, two white horses, black painted harnesses, wheel operated trotting, dark green roof with black fleur-de-lis and lining, emb gilt foliate surround, emb rear steps, door surround, driver's rear rest, emb window frames with painted curtains, front, rear upper section, lower half with hand-painted polychrome floral and foliate dec, over blue-gray, ochre int. with ochre vis-a-vis bench seating along sides, wheels, overall paint flaking, wheels detached, one window frame partially detached, 1850s, 23" l **$48,300**

Locomotive, attributed to Fallows, clockwork motor, cast wheels, high wings, cow catcher and bell, old repaint, 10" l **$460**

Locomotive, Victory, red boiler, bell, black and gilt stack, red and blue cab with green roof, silver stenciled windows, yellow chassis, spoked wheels, one wheel damaged, scratches and paint loss, 4-3/4" l **$990**

Porter and trolley, clockwork motor in hinged trunk, blue uniform, red and orange electric-type trolley, 4-1/2" l **$145**

Steamer, three funnels, hand painted, red, cream, and gray hull, cream superstructure, 10" l **$350**

Two-seater tourer, litho, red, yellow, and cream, driver, fly-wheel drive, 3" l **$425**

Tonka

Airlines tractor, set of two baggage carts, C.9, 1963 .... **$150**
Boat transport, 1960, 38" l **$250**
Construction
　Bulldozer, #300, 1962 .... **$35**
　Dump truck, #180, 1949 .... **$100**
　Dump truck and sand loader, #616,

　1963 .... **$100**
　Hydraulic Dump, #520, 1962 .... **$75**
　Road Grader, #12, 1958 .... **$75**
Fire truck
　Aerial ladder truck, 1957 .... **$250**
　Rescue Squad, 1960 .... **$100**
　Suburban Pumper, #46, 1960 ..... **$100**
Mini
　Camper, #0070, 1963 .... **$35**
　Jeep pickup, #50, 1963 .... **$35**
　Livestock Van, 1964, 16" l **$50**
　Stake truck, #56, 1963 .... **$40**
Truck
　Air Express, #16, 1959 .... **$350**
　Car Carrier, #40, 1960 .... **$100**
　Carnation Milk delivery van, #750,
　　1954 .... **$200**
　Deluxe Sportsman, #22, 1961 .... **$100**
　Farm state truck, 1957 .... **$190**
　Green Giant Transport semi, 1953 **$150**
　Minute Maid Orange Juice van, #725,
　　1955 .... **$275**
　Service truck, #01, 1960 .... **$100**
　Wrecker truck, #18, 1958 .... **$100**

Tootsietoy
Airplane
　Aero-Dawn, 1928 .... **$30**
　Beechcraft Bonanza, orange **$15**
　Curtis P-40, light green **$120**
　Navy Jet, red, 1970s **$5**
　P-38, WWII blue props **$225**
　Stratocruiser **$30**
　Transport plane, orange, 1941 ...... **$40**
Auto
　Andy Gump Car **$80**
　Bluebird Daytona Race Car **$20**
　Buick LaSabre, 1951 .... **$25**
　Buick Touring Car, HO series, 1960
　　.. **$30**
　Cadillac Coupe, blue and tan **$40**
　Chevrolet Roadster **$20**
　Corvette **$15**

Ford Fairlane Convertible, red **$6**

Ford V-8 Hotrod, 1940 .... **$15**

International Station Wagon, red and
yellow, 1939 .... **$15**

Lincoln Capri **$20**

Oldsmobile 98, red, 1955 .... **$20**

Packard, white, 1956 .... **$25**

Pontiac Fire Chief, red, 1959 .... **$20**

Boat

Battleship **$10**

Destroyer **$10**

Transport **$15**

Yacht **$10**

Doodlebug, die-cast, 4" l, orig paint

Green, C.8 .... **$65**

Red, C.9 .... **$75**

Set, fire department, 1947 Mack pumper, Mack fire trailer, Pontiac fire chief
sedan, 1950 Chevy panel truck ambulance, orig box, 1950s, C.9 .... **$265**

Unknown maker, American

Nine-pins, knockdown type, set of Indians, each with different polychrome
paint, 9" h to 10-1/2" h **$4,700**

Squeeze type, clown plays tambourine,
wood limbs, head loose, 7" l **$375**

Wooden crank, six soldiers on horses, move when handle is turned, orig

Vehicles, Structo, Moving Van, #710, 1956, **$210.**
Photo courtesy Randy Prasse.

polychrome paint, 19th C litho paper
base, 8-1/2" l **$3,700**

Wyandotte, USA

Airplane

Army bombing plane, 8-1/2" wingspan
.... **$85**

Defense bomber, 9-1/4" l **$75**

Stratoship mystery plane, 4-1/4" l ... **$50**

Ambulance, painted pressed steel,
nickeled grille, operating rear door,
minor scratches, 11" l **$170**

Car and trailer, painted pressed steel,
red, streamlined auto and travel trailer with operating rear door, replaced
white rubber tires, paint worn, chips,
and scratches, 25" l **$315**

Circus truck and wagon, red and
yellow, cardboard animals, 19" l
.... **$650**

Hoky & Poky, litho tin wind-up, play
wear, C.7, 6-3/4" l **$225**

Humphrey mobile, litho tinplate,
fixed steering, clockwork motor, rear
door, moving hat and arm, some
scratching, 9" l **$375**

Pan Am clipper, painted pressed
steel, red and white, brass engines,
nickeled propellers, 9" l **$275**

Streamlined Wagon, rubber wheels,
5-1/4" l **$45**

Zephyr roadster, rubber wheels,
13-3/8" l **$400**

TRAINS, TOY

History: Railroading remains an important collecting field to children of all ages, largely because of the "days-gone-by" romance associated with the rail travel and the prominence of toy trains.

The first toy trains were cast iron and tin; wind-up motors added movement. The golden age of toy trains was 1920 to 1955, when electric-powered units and high-quality rolling stock were available and names such as Ives, American Flyer, and Lionel were household words. The advent of plastic in the late 1950s resulted in considerably lower quality.

Toy trains are designated by a model scale or gauge. The most popular are HO, N, O and standard. Narrow gauge was a response to the modern capacity to miniaturize. Today train layouts in gardens are all the rage and those usually feature larger scale trains.

Additional Listings: See *The Standard Catalog of Lionel Trains 1945-69* for more examples.

Notes: Condition of trains is critical when establishing price. Items in fair condition and below (scratched, chipped, dented, rusted, or warped) generally have little value to a collector. Accurate restoration is accepted and may enhance the price by one or two grades. Prices listed are for trains in very good to excellent condition, unless otherwise noted.

Adviser: Karen O'Brien.

American Flyer

Boxcar, #33514, HO gauge, Silver
Meteor, brown **$50**

Caboose, #935, S gauge, bay window,
brown, 1957 .... **$60**

Circus Pullman, #649, S gauge, minor
wear to orig box, C.9 .... **$125**

Flat car, #24558, S gauge, Canadian
Pacific, Christmas tree load, 1959-60
.... **$145**

Gondola

#941, S gauge, Frisco, 1953-57 ..... **$15**

#33507, HO gauge, D&H, brown, can-
ister load **$60**

Handcar, #742, S gauge, some wear to
orig box and insert, C.8 .... **$75**

Locomotive

#354, S gauge, steam, Silver Bullet,
Pacific, 4-6-2, 1954 .... **$200**

#425, decals and paint chipped, 426
tender, decals chipped, C.5 .... **$75**

#435 locomotive, 433A tender,
unnatural wear to drivers, C.7-8
.... **$220**

#3020, O gauge, electric, 4-4-4,
c1922-25 .... **$375**

#3307 locomotive, 3189 tender, decals
chipped, C.5 .... **$100**

#3322 locomotive, 3199 tender, C.4-5
.... **$110**

Set, O gauge

Freight, #476 gondola, #478 boxcar,
#480 tank car, #484 caboose **$140**

Passenger, Railway Post Office car,
Paul Revere coach, Lexington
observation, orange **$125**

Lionel Trains, No. 385E locomotive and tender, 1933, **$500.**

Lionel Trains, No. 384 locomotive and tender, 1930, **$600.**

Set, standard gauge

#12 locomotive, painted cast iron, working clockwork, 120 tender, 1119 cattle car, 1109 gondola, 1111 IC caboose, tunnel, track, switches, C.4-5 ...... **$350**

#20 locomotive, 1131 tender, 1126 hopper, 1113 hopper, two 1223 coaches, C.4-5 .... **$130**

#423 locomotive, 426 tender, 415 searchlight car, 416 wrecker, 410 tank car, 408 box car, 407 gondola, C.5-7 .. **$240**

#434, 282 loco and tender, 500 combine, 501 coach, 502 vista dome, 503 observation, worn orig boxes, C.8-9 .... **$2,000**

#3315 locomotive, 3319 tender, 3380 combine, 3382 observation, C.5-6 **$280**

#3322 locomotive, 3189 tender, two 3208 box cars, 3206 lumber car, 3211 caboose, C.5-6 .... **$175**

#4644 locomotive, rewheeled, 4151 coach, 4152 observation, Eagle train, C.6 .... **$350**

#K5364W Silver Rocket, 474 and 475 Rocker AA, three 962 vista domes, 963 observation, orig boxes with some wear, C.6-8 .... **$1,550**

#20305, 21800-355 Baldwin diesel, 702 box of track, orig boxes, C.8-9 .. **$410**

#20740 Defender, 234 logo, 24557 Navy flat with Jeeps, 25056 USM box car and rocket launcher flat car, 24549 searchlight car, 24631 caboose, C.6-8 .... **$950**

Tank car, #24323, Baker's Chocolate, S gauge, gray tank ends, minor wear to orig box, C.8 .... **$350**

Bing, German

Locomotive, O gauge, pre-war

Clockwork, cast iron, no tender, headlight missing **$125**

Live steam, 0-4-0, minor fire damage, no tender **$800**

Set, O gauge, passenger, litho, #2395 combine, Winnebago coach, Lakewood observation, green with brown roofs **$350**

Set, #1 gauge, passenger, litho, dark maroon, lettered "Pennsylvania Lines," combine #1250, coach #1207 ...... **$525**

Ives

Baggage car

#50, O gauge, four wheels, red litho frame, striped steps, white/silver body, sides marked "Limited Vestibule Express, United States Mail Baggage Co." and "Express Service No. 50," three doors on both sides, one on each end, black roof with celestory, 1908-09 .... **$190**

#70, O gauge, eight wheels, red litho body, simulates steel, tin roof with celestory stripe, sliding center door, marked "The Ives Railway Lines, Express Baggage Service, 60, U. S. Mail," 1923-25 .... **$75**

Caboose, #67, O gauge, eight wheels, red litho body, sliding door on each side, gray painted tin roof with red cupola, "The Ives Railway Lines," 1918 .... **$85**

Gravel car, #63, O gauge, eight wheels, gray litho, rounded truss rods, marked "63" on sides, 1913-14 .... **$75**

Livestock car, #65, O gauge, eight wheels, orange-yellow litho body, type D trucks, gray painted roof with catwalk, sides marked "Livestock Transportation, Ives RR," c1918 ... **$95**

Locomotive

#19, O gauge, 0-4-0, black cast iron boiler and cab, two arched windows and "IVES No. 19" beneath, cast-iron wheels, NYC & HR No. 17 tender, 1917-25 .... **$225**

#25, O gauge, 4-4-2, black body, boiler tapers towards front, four separate boiler bands, three square windows on both sides of cab, gold frames and stripes, tin pony wheels, four-wheel L.V.E. No. 25 tender, 1906-07 .... **$310**

#3200, O gauge, 0-4-0, cast iron S-type electric center cab, green body, gold trim, cast iron six-spoke wheels, center door flanked by two windows, raised lettering "Ives" and "3200" below windows, 1911 .. **$285**

Lionel

Baggage car, #2602, O gauge, red body and roof, 1938 .... **$100**

Boxcar

#00-44, OO gauge, 1939 .... **$45**

#HO-874, HO gauge, NYC, 1964 .. **$25**

#6464-375 Central of Georgia, unrun, minor wear to orig box, C.7 .... **$120**

Caboose

#217, S gauge, 1926-40, orange and maroon **$250**

#HO-841, HO gauge, 1961, NYC .. **$20**

Cattle car, #213, S gauge, cream body, maroon roof, 1926-40 .... **$425**

Coal loader, #397, coal shield broken, minor wear and tape on orig box, 1948-57, C.6-7 .... **$100**

Derrick, #219, S gauge, C.7 .... **$270**

Dump, #218, S gauge Mojave end plates, minor wear to orig box, C.7 .... **$290**

Hopper, #516, S gauge, coal loads, minor chips, incomplete orig box, 1928-40, C.6-7 .... **$200**

Horse car, #3356, unrun, separate sale orig box, 1956-60 & 1964-66, C.9. **$125**

Locomotive

#8, S gauge, rewheeled, replaced headlights, minor touchup, C.6 .... **$190**

#156, O gauge, electric, 4-4-4, dark green, 1917-23 .... **$465**

#256 locomotive, RS, 1924-30, C.6 .... **$480**

#258 locomotive, 257T tender, wear to paint, 1930-35, C.5-6 .... **$120**

#265E, 265W tender, scratched, black, 1935-40, C.5 .... **$175**

Observation car

#322, S gauge, 1924-27 .... **$100**

#754, O gauge, streamliner, 1936 . **$95**

Pullman

#35, S gauge, orange, c1915 .... **$65**

#607, O gauge, 1926 .... **$60**

Refrigerator car, #214R, Standard gauge, ivory body, peacock roof, 1929-40 .... **$400**

Set, O gauge

Passenger, #252 electric locomotive, #529 coach, #530 observation, olive green, c1926 .... **$225**

Passenger, Union Pacific, #752E power unit, #753 coach, #754 observation, silver, c1934 .... **$375**

Set, S gauge

#8 loco, rewheeled, replaced headlamps, 337 coach, 338 observation, C.7 .... **$250**

#218 SF Alco AA, dummy with crack, 3428 milk car, 2414 coach, two 2412 vista domes, 2416 observation, C-6 .... **$360**

#225E locomotive, 265W tender, three restored 3659 dump cars, 2657 caboose, C.5-8 .... **$285**

#254E locomotive, replaced headlamps, restored frame, two 610 coaches, 612 observation, C.5 .... **$180**

#380 locomotive, 320 baggage, 319 coach, 322 observation, restored, C.8 .... **$525**

MISCELLANEOUS

Watercolor advertisement, Pennsylvania, Oak Hall Tailors, Harrisburg, 19th century, 11" x 13", **$585.**
Photo courtesy of Pook & Pook, Inc.

Child's rocking chair, oak, pressback design of advertising character, the Yellow Kid blowing horn, repair to back support, **$650.**
Photo courtesy of Dotta Auction Co., Inc.

Saddlery trade sign, molded zinc horse head encircled by a horseshoe, painted gray, vestiges of gilt, American, late 19th century, 21" h x 17" w, **$1,175.**
Photo courtesy of Skinner, Inc.

ADVERTISING

History: Before the days of mass media, advertisers relied on colorful product labels and advertising giveaways to promote their products. Containers were made to appeal to the buyer through the use of stylish lithographs and bright colors. Many of the illustrations used the product in the advertisement so that even an illiterate buyer could identify a product.

Advertisements were put on almost every household object imaginable and became constant reminders to use the product or visit a certain establishment.

Additional Resources:

Antique Trader® Advertising Price Guide, by Kyle Husfloen, ed., and Rich Penn, contr. ed., Krause Publications, Iola, WI.

Warman's® Americana & Collectibles, 11th Ed., by Ellen T. Schroy, ed., Krause Publications, Iola, WI.

Ashtray, Buster Brown, glazed china, figural hat, Buster gesturing towards Tige balancing steaming teapot on nose, 4-7/8" l, 1" h **$135**

Bank, figural
Magic Chef, painted vinyl, 7" h
.... **$25**
RCA Nipper, light fuzzy flocked surface over metal, 6-1/4" h, C.8++
.... **$230**

Blotter, unused
Cotton Overshirts, ivory white and black celluloid cover, bound at each corner by metal mount, two remov-

able cardboard ink blotter ships image of "Oppenheim, Oberndor & Co.," 3" x 6" **$2**
Eppens, Smith Co., NY, Coffee and Tea Importer, full-color celluloid slight use, 1900 seasonal greeting
.... **$1**
Fairbanks Portable Pumping Out fit, graphics of metal vehicle, road paving machinery, 7-1/4" x 9-1/2"
.... **$1**

Booklet, Dutch Boy Paint, 20 pgs, 5" 6"................................ **$1.**

Bookmark, Rally Day, diecut celluloid Spirit of '76 fife and drummers, large American flag, string tassel, early 1900s................................ **$2**

Box
Proctor & Gamble, 1873, wood..**$20**
Weideman Oak Flakes, 14 oz, card board, 6-1/4" x 4-1/4" **$12**
Yanks Chewing Gum, counter display box, 20 orig packs of Yanks brand 5¢ Spearmint Chewing Gum, Gum Products Inc., Boston, MA 1" x 3-1/4" x 6-1/2" **$19**

Broom holder, DeLaval Cream Separators, tin litho, black and white, orig adv envelope, 3-1/2" d, C.8 .... **$45**

Calendar
Blue Ribbon Canned Foods, desk ivory-colored celluloid over tin 1916, 3-1/5" x 4-1/2" **$2**
Nevin's Candy, wall type, two-ply cardboard, 1917, 3-1/4" x 6-1/4"
.... **$1**
Red Goose Shoes, wall type, colorful print of mountain goat hunter titled "Getting His Goat," H. C. Edwards artist, ads for Red Goose Shoes Friedman-Shelby Shoe Col, Atlantic Shoes, Pacific Shoes, 1924, 8" x 19"
.... **$2**

Candy pail
Novia Kiddie Pops, pail shape, image of pops and children and dog on both sides, 3-3/4" d, 3-1/4" h, C.7.5+.................................. **$675**
Three Pigs, Mayfair Candy Co., NY, tin litho, 3-1/8" x 3-3/8", C.8-.........**$170**

Cigar box, Pittsburgh's Finest, wood, colorful paper labels with uniformed police officer, 10-7/8" x 7-5/8" x 7-1/2", C.8+.............................. **$275**

Cigar tin, tin litho
Izaak Walton, image of Walton, hunting and fishing scenes in background, 5-3/8" x 5-3/8", C.8.....**$190**
King Midas, image of king on both sides, 5-1/8" x 6-1/8" x 4-1/8", C.8+ tin, lid fair **$120**

Old Seneca Stogies, W. C. Kildow, colorful graphic Indian image, 5-3/4" x 4-3/8", C.8 .... **$425**

Orcico Cigars, 2 for 5¢, colorful graphic Indian image, 5-1/2" x 6-1/8" x 4-1/8", C.8.5 .... **$550**

Tobacco Girl, detailed image of trademark girl on both sides, 5-1/2" x 6-1/4" x 4-1/4", C.8.5 .... **$3,300**

White Owl Brand, General Cigar Co., blue ground, white owl perched on smoking cigar, 5-3/4" x 5-1/2", C.8+ **$675**

Clicker

Motorcycle Boy, litho tin, boy in yellow motorcycling outfit with goggles and neckerchief, riding red cycle, holding ice-cream cone in one hand, 1930s **$25**

Poll-Parrot Shoes, litho tin, red, yellow, blue parrot, yellow background, red lettering, 1930s **$25**

Twinkie Shoes, litho tin, full-color art of elf character standing on mushroom, dark green background, tiny inscription for "Hamilton-Brown Shoes Co.," 1930s **$30**

Clock

Calumet Baking Powder, Sessions clock, oak, wall-type, gold lettering, 39" x 18" x 5-1/2" **$2,600**

Iroquois Beverages, Buffalo, NY, light-up, double bubble, 16" d **$525**

None Such Mince Meat, Pumpkin-Squash, Like Mother Used to Make, ribbed cardboard, clock face shaped like pumpkin, tin back shaped like pie plate, easel, hanging hook, clock mechanism not working, 9-1/2" d **$1,150**

Coffee tin

Daisy Fresh Coffee, Euclid Coffee Co., Cleveland, l lb, key wind, 3-5/8" x 5", C.8 .... **$150**

Epicure Coffee, John Sills and Sons, 1 lb, image of butler serving cup of coffee, 6" x 4", C.8+ **$725**

Fairway Coffee, 1 lb, key wind, colorful image of children in field, steaming cup of coffee in background, 4" x 5", C.8.5 .... **$250**

First Pick Coffee, l lb, key wind, 4" x 5", C.8 .... **$350**

Jipco Coffee, Beckers-Prentiss Co., Buffalo, NY, 1 lb, key wind, blue and white, buffalo on front, steaming cup of coffee and blossoms on back, 4" x 5-1/8", C.7 .... **$250**

Loyl Coffee, Rochester Seed & Supply Co., 1 lb, 6-1/4" x 4", C.8.5+

.... **$120**

Publix Markets Coffee, Lakeland, FL, 1 lb, key wind, grocery store image, 3-5/8" x 5", C.8 .... **$200**

Red Turkey Coffee, Mailby's, Corning, NY, 1 lb, 5-3/4" x 4-1/4", C.8 .... **$375**

Ten Eyck Coffee, Bacon, Stickney & Co., Albany, NY, 1 lb, pry lid, detailed image of Ten Eyck Hotel, 5-1/2" x 4-1/ 4", C.8 .... **$375**

Turkey Coffee, Kasper Co., 1 lb, image of wild turkey on both sides, 5-3/4" x 4-1/4", C.8 .... **$375**

Wake-Em Up Coffee, Anderson-Ryan Coffee Co., Duluth, MN, 10 lb, wooden handle, green and gold, trademark Indian on both sides, 13-1/2" x 9", C.8+ **$475**

Yellow Bonnet Coffee, Springfield Grocer, 1 lb, key wind, white background, 4" x 5", C.7.5+/8- **$325**

Crock, stoneware

Bowers Three Thistles Snuff, cobalt blue lettering, 14" x 9-1/2", few chips **$450**

Heinz, detailed multicolored stone litho label, orig lid and closure, 8" x 4", C.8.5+ **$675**

Diecut, litho cardboard

Colgate Talcum Powder, two-sided, seated baby in cap and romper, holding product, price for pr, 1913, 14" x 8-1/2", C.8 .... **$675**

Johnson & Johnson Talcum Powder, baby on back playing with talc container, string hanger, 8-1/8" x 14-1/8", C-7.5 .... **$575**

Larkin Boraxine Laundry Soap, cream-colored cat, red bow at neck, easel back, 12" x 9", C.8.5 .... **$220**

Williard's Candy, 5¢ Nutritious, Wolf Co., Philadelphia Lithographers, blond boy in red sweater, blue shorts, easel back, 17" x 8-3/8" **$550**

Williard's Candy, 5¢ Nutritious, Wolf Co., Philadelphia Lithographers, blonde girl in blue blouse, red romper, easel back, 17" x 8-3/8" **$675**

Display cabinet, countertop

Blue Bird, A Man's Handkerchief, tin litho, hinged top with glass insert, holds four early product boxes, 1920s, 6-3/4" x 11-1/2" x 8", C.8 .... **$450**

Farnam's Famous Kalamazoo Celery and Pepsin Chewing Gum, wood, curved glass, gold lettering, 7-1/2" x 17" x 10" **$5,600**

Roseville pottery dealer's sign, ivory scrolled letters, blue ground, 4-1/2" x 8", **$2,585.**
Photo courtesy of David Rago Auctions, Inc.

Advertising clock, Erie Griswold, cast-iron skillet form, embossed around clock "WE SELL/ERIE/UP TO TIME/HOLLOW WARE," windup clock with second hand, dial lettered "TRADE (Spider) MARK/GRISWOLD MF'G. CO.,/ERIE PENN.," black painted surface, dial discoloration, late 19th century, 14-1/2" h, 9-3/4" d, **$2,530.**
Photo courtesy of Green Valley Auctions.

Display, tin litho, For Real Satisfaction Smoke a Pipe With This Trademark, WDC, gent smoking pipe and pointing to red triangular trademark, four pipes, easel back, c1918, **$145.**
Photo courtesy of Dotta Auction Co., Inc.

Lard pail, Swift's Silver-Leaf Pure Lard Kettle, red, black, and gold label, original handle and lid, some rust, **$25.**

Trade card, Metropolitan Life Insurance Co., "The Leading Industrial Insurance Company of America," little girl standing next to chair, branch addresses on other side, scrolling borders, oversized, copyright 1902, **$45.**

Chair, folding, blue and white enamel plaque on back, "Smoke Piedmont, The Cigarette of Quality," **$300.**
Photo courtesy of Alderfer Auction Co.

J & P Coats, thread spools **$1,800**
Nestles, Hazelnut Chocolate Bars, adv labels inside glass lift top, 4-3/4" x 10-1/8" x 7-1/2", C.8 ....**$500**
Tootsie Roll Candies, tin litho, 13" x 8-3/4" x 8-1/4", C.8...................**$700**
Van Haagen's Fine Toilet Soaps, German silver, curved corners, front glass etched with name, some denting to moldings **$525**
Zeno Gum, wood, emb Zeno marquee with fancy filigree, 18" h, 10-1/2" w, 8" d **$575**

Display
Red Goose Shoes, figural, papier-mâché, glass eyes, 10-1/2" x 9" x 4-1/2", C.7.5 ....**$250**
Tennyson 5¢ Cigars Always Fresh, Mazer Cressman, tin litho, 8" x 5-3/4" x 5-3/4", C.8+ **$400**

Display rack, Chesterfield/L & M/Oasis Cigarettes, painted wood **$120**

Door push
Canada Dry, multicolored bottle and slogan, emb tin litho, 9" x 3" **$210**
Crescent Flour, Voight Milling Co., Grand Rapids, MI, emb tin litho, 9-5/8" x 3-3/4", C.8.5................**$300**
Domino Cigarettes, emb tin litho, 14" x 4", C.8.5 ....**$100**
Edgeworth Tobacco, red, white, and blue, emb tin litho, 14" x 4" **$170**
Ex-Lax, multicolored porcelain, 8" x 4" **$375**

Fan, hand held
Alka-Seltzer, cartoon illus, cardboard mounted on wooden rod, late 1930s-40s, 8-1/2" x 9-1/2" **$25**
Planters Peanuts, Mr. Peanut driving peanut shaped car, adv on back, 1940s, 5-1/4" x 8", C.8..............**$250**

Gauge, Standard Roller Bearing Co., 3" x 3" celluloid covers, diecut openings, inner disk wheels to use in determining precise measurements, requirements, etc. for ball bearings, c1920 ....**$20**

Lapel stud
Alaska Stove Trimmings, brown and white celluloid, metal lapel stud fastener, stove lid lifter illus, plus inscription "Mama! Do You Use Alaska Stove Trimmings-Always Cold" **$20**
Widow Jones Suits Me, multicolored celluloid on metal, young lady in stylish gray outfit and hat, pale blue to white background, blue lettering, New England clothing store sponsor, 1-1/4".....................................**$40**

Lunch box
Dan Patch Cut Plug, Scotten Dillion Co., tin litho, bale handle, yellow, red, and black, 4-3/8" x 6-7/8" x 4-5/8", tin C.8+, lid C.7+ **$325**
Green Turtle Cigars, Gordon Cigar Co., tin litho, turtle on rock smoking cigar, 5-1/4" x 7-1/2" x 4-1/2", front C.8-, back C.7 ....**$350**

Match safe, Advance Farm Equipment, silvered brass, hinged, celluloid wrapper print in color, one side with medieval figure raising Advance banner on rocky height, opposite side with "Simple Traction Engine," two smaller panels each with lists of offices by city, early 1900s **$115**

Mirror, pocket
Berry Bros Varnishes, celluloid, multicolored, little boy pulling dog in Berry Co. adv wagon, 1-3/4" x 2-3/4"..**$200**
I Wear Kleinert's Dress Shields, brown on cream, 2" d............................**$45**
The Lincoln Savings Bank, blue on white, bright red center stripe surrounding profile of Lincoln above text "Vote for Lincoln As Your Bank," c1940, 2-1/8" d................**$30**

Oyster pail, Fresh Oysters, Schneier's Co., Akron, OH, 1 gal, orig lid, 7-3/8" x 6-5/8", C.8+............................**$250**

Paperweight, Southern Fruit Julep Co., glass, reverse adv on all four sides, five-year monthly scrolling calendar inside, 1-3/8" x 4" x 2-7/8" **$325**

Peanut butter pail, tin litho
Armour's Veribest Peanut Butter, 2 lb, nursery rhyme characters, yellow ground, 4-5/8" x 4-3/8", C.7.5 ....**$190**
Clark's Peanut Butter, Canadian, 1 lb, sporting images, 3-3/8" x 3-3/4", C.8++ **$875**
Monarch Peanut Butter, Teenie Weenie, 1 lb, colorful image of children and giant peanuts, c1920, 3-3/4" x 3-3/8", C.8++ **$300**

O! Boy Peanut Butter, Stone Ordean Wells Co., Duluth, 1 lb, children eating sandwiches on front, seashore scene on back, 3-3/8" x 3-3/4", C.8+ **$650**

Planters High Grade Peanut Butter, 25 lbs, 9-1/4" x 10-1/4", C.7.5 .. **$575**

Squirrel, Canadian, 3 lb, pry lid, squirrel eating peanut, 4-3/4" x 5-1/8", C.8.5 .... **$425**

Pencil clip

Ardee Flour, red, yellow, blue logo, celluloid on brass wire clip, Hubbard Milling Co., Mankato, Minn, sponsor, early 1900s **$25**

Red Man Cigar Leaf, multicolored, tobacco pack mounted on brass wire spring clip, early 1900s **$55**

The Metropolitan, black, white, and red celluloid, mounted on brass wire spring clip, sponsor store designates "Hats" and "Furnishings" **$20**

Pinback button

Cherry-Ripe Ice Cream, two dark red cherries on green, c1940, 3-1/2" d **$20**

Davis OK Baking Powder, multicolored, bottle flanked by slogans, black lettering, back paper, c1896 .... **$20**

Empire Cream Separator, black and white image, blue letters, rim inscription "I Chirp for the Empire because it makes the most dollars

for me," clicker hanging from bottom rim **$50**

Farm Boy Bread, red, white, and blue, center bluetone photo of young farm lad posed next to cow and rooster, blue and red lettering, 1930s **$15**

Hessler Rural Mailbox, illus of sample mailbox, "Approved By Postmaster General" **$75**

Kar-A-Van Coffee, multicolored, loaded camel, early 1900s **$20**

Lekko Scouring Powder, multicolored, image of product canister, and housewife on knees scrubbing floor, 1920s **$35**

Mephisto Auger Bits, black and red lettering, white ground **$15**

Metzer's Milk Infant Keeps Them Smiling, tinted flesh-tone face, white background, blue and red lettering, c1930, 1" d **$12**

O.I.C. Hogs, black and white art and inscription, patriotic red, white, blue, and silver outer rim, back paper with lengthy text for "Famous O.I.C. Hogs," c1900 .... **$50**

RCA Micro Mike, ivory white celluloid, red image and title, 3" d **$18**

Stetson Hats Best in the World, multicolored logo, celluloid, oval **$12**

Vote Betty Crocker, red, white, and blue litho, c1960 .... **$12**

Widow Hoffman System-Boys Clothing-Harris Clothing Co., Baltimore,

black and white celluloid, young lad in cap and jacket **$15**

Wilbur's Cocoa, multicolored, cherub trademark stirring Wilbur mug, orig back paper, c1896 .... **$20**

Plate, Old Barbee Whiskey, Vienna Art, center with peasants and cabin, tin litho, 10" d, C.8 .... **$400**

Pot scraper, tin litho

MB Flavoring Extracts, Day-Bergwall Co., Milwaukee, Shonk Litho, slight wear, 2-7/8" x 3", C.7+ **$375**

Nesco Royal Graniteware, 3-1/2" x 3", C.8 .... **$500**

Print, Falls City Clothing Co., Imperial Clothes, Louisville, Ky, titled Elsie, sgd B. Tichman, woman in red duster and bonnet, printed by Meek Co., Coshocton, OH, framed, copyright 1908, 30" x 15" **$235**

Rolling pin, Royal Household Flour, Canadian, china body, wooden handles, blue and red printing, mkd "Hand-painted Nippon" on side, 19-1/4" x 3" **$230**

Salesman's sample

Dilworth's Golden Urn Brand Coffee, Pittsburgh, tin litho, 2-1/2" x 2", C.8+ **$150**

Goldsmith & Sons boxing gloves, leather, lace-up, two 4-1/4" x 2-1/2" gloves stamped "GoldSmith 01" in silver, 2-1/2" x 5-1/4" x 5-3/4" orig box **$350**

South Bend store display, die cut countertop display, shows Bass Oreno, Improved Surf Oreno, Tarp Oreno, and Trout Oreno, "Fish and feel fit," tape repair on back, orig cardboard shipping box, 1927, **$2,750.**
Photo courtesy of Lang's Sporting Collectables.

Wall pocket, embossed multicolored stiff paper, woodland scene, text on pocket "Compliments of L. F. Harpel, General Merchandise, Richlandtown, Pa," **$35.**

Sign, Columbia Records, litho tin, yellow, red, white, and black, Accredited Dealer, **$125.**

Display, Brown's Jumbo Bread, elephant shape, framed, 19" w, 17" h, **$300.**
Photo courtesy of Joy Luke Auctions.

Home plate, rubber, emb lettering, 4" x 4-1/8" **$180**

Lawnmower, mkd "H. A. Daum, Locksmith" **$3,950**

Toilet, Ariston Silent, Made of Durock, heavy ceramic bowl, orig hardware and seat, spider line to glaze on int., 7-3/4" x 14" x 7" **$825**

Sharpening stone, Pike Mfg. Co., Pike, NH, gold luster finish metal case, pike fish passing through letter "P," rect whetstone, some wear to stone and luster **$45**

Sign

Algo Spearmint Chewing Gum, cardboard, 4-1/2" x 7-3/4", C.8 .... **$160**

Collins Honey Scotch Candy, Minneapolis, emb tin, 7" x 19-1/2" **$210**

Continental Insurance, framed paper in three sections, left panel with Victorian Brooklyn, Continental Insurance Building with signage on front, right panel with New York Continental Insurance Building with multiple horse-drawn carriages in front, center with Indian tribe watching as wild animals run out of burning forest, J. Ottoman litho, some minor staining to orig matting, ©1895, 34-1/2" h, 68-1/2" w **$1,450**

Cracker Jack The More You Eat, The More You Want, F.W. Rueckheim & Bros., Chicago, mother holding child reaching for box, 1900, 14-1/2" x 10-3/4", C.8.5 .... **$5,000**

Dakota Maid Flour, emb tin litho, yellow and blue, 9" x 19-1/2", C.8+ **$120**

De Laval Cream Separators, tin, emb frame **$2,800**

Drink Palmer's Root Beer, It's Better, Palmer Candy Co., Kaufman, TX, heavy porcelain, slightly curved, 14" x 21", C.8+ **$300**

Drink Moxie, emb tin litho, 6-1/4" x 19", C.9 .... **$250**

Elgin Watch, reverse painting on glass, trademark Father Time, gold on black, framed, 23-1/2" h, 17-1/2" w **$500**

Enjoy Hires, it's always pure, emb tin litho, girl in red hat, 9-3/4" x 27-3/4", C.8+ **$475**

Enjoy Hires Healthful Delicious, 9-1/2" x 27-1/2", emb tin litho, C.7.5 .... **$250**

Everybody Likes Popsicle Refreshing Easy to Eat, emb tin litho, red, black, yellow, 9-7/8" x 27-3/4", C.8+ **$325**

Foster Hose Supporters, celluloid, 17" x 9" **$425**

Gail Borden Eagle Brand Condensed Milk, cardboard litho, puppy drinking from sleeping baby's glass nursing bottle, 15" x 10-1/2", C.8- **$450**

Georgia Stages, Inc. Ticket Office, Bus Station, porcelain, double-sided, graphics of bus, 1930s **$10,500**

Good Humor Ice Cream, six-color porcelain, 1930s, 18" x 26", C.8+ **$1,200**

John P. Squire & Co., self framed emb tin, pig in center, titled "Squires Arlington, Hams-Bacon-Sausage," ©1906, 24" h, 20" w **$800**

Jersey Crème The Perfect Drink At Fountains, 5¢ Also in Bottles, two-sided tin litho flange, yellow and black, 6" d, C.9 .... **$725**

Kis-Me-Gum, emb cardboard diecut, lady in diaphanous top, framed, ©1905, 8" h, 13" w **$500**

Korbel California Champagne, tin litho over cardboard, 13" x 19", C.8 .... **$250**

Lee Union-Alls, porcelain **$2,800**

McCormick, The King of the Harvest, stone litho, image of well dressed farmer harvesting in field with team of horses, 15-1/2" x 21-1/2", C.8 .... **$475**

Merry Widow Gum, cardboard, hanging type, 8" x 3", C.8 .... **$375**

Pearl Oil, flanged tin, diecut kerosene can shape **$3,100**

Star Brand Shoes, self framed tin, bust of young lady with flowing hair, advertising "Women's Mayflower Shoe, $2.50," some overall spotting, 26" h, 19" w **$300**

Sterling Super-Bru, Sterling Brewers, Evansville, IN, emb tin, trapezoid, 17-5/8" x 9-3/8", C.8.5+ **$450**

Sunkist Grower, porcelain, black, white, and red, green border, 11-1/2" x 19-1/2" **$375**

Tom Keene Cigar, curved corner type, heavy porcelain, orig Ingram-Richardson paper manufacturer's label on back, 15" x 14-3/4", C.8.5 .... **$575**

United Motor Service, porcelain, double sided **$3,000**

Valentine's Valspar Varnish, It's The Coat That Makes The Boat, hanging, tin litho over cardboard, man varnishing 1920s wooden racing boat, 13" x 19", C.8+ **$3,400**

Wonder Bread, porcelain, dark blue, red, and white, 8-5/8" x 20, C.8 .... **$375**

Woolworth's, fiberboard, diamond-shape, "Woolworth's, Satisfaction Guaranteed, Replacement Or Money Refunded," white and black letters, red and white ground, some paint chipping and flaking **$35**

W W W Rings, tin over cardboard, lady in vintage clothing at college football game, some damage, 9-1/4" h, 6-1/4" l **$100**

Y & S Licorice, figural, pc of black licorice, orig paper label, hanging, 18" x 3-1/2", C.8- **$275**

Zenith Radios, enamel, bright blue and white letters on red field, yellow background, "Long Distance Radio," 60" l, 18" w **$200**

Spinner top

Hurd Shoes, black and white celluloid, wooden red spinner dowel, Parisian Novelty Co., maker name on rim curl, 1930s **$20**

Poll-Parrot Shoes, litho tin, wooden spinner dowel, red and yellow parrot striding between black shoes, yellow background, red rim, red star logo, 1930s **$25**

Woodmen of the World, blue lettering on white celluloid, wooden red spinner dowel, Parisian Novelty Co., maker name on rim curl, 1930s **$18**

Store bin, tin litho

Beech Nut Chewing Tobacco, slant front, green ground, white lettering, 6" w, 10" l, 8" h **$400**

Light Sweet Burley Tobacco, Spaulding Merrick, 10-3/4" x 8-1/4", C.8 .... **$210**

Sure Shot Chewing Tobacco, graphic of Indian brave taking aim with bow and arrow, 6-1/2" x 15-1/4" x 10-1/4", C.8++ **$950**

Sweet Cuba Tobacco, slant front, 10" l, 8" w **$365**

Sweet Mist Chewing Tobacco, children in fountain, 11-1/2" x 8-1/4", C.8 .... **$300**

Tiger Chewing Tobacco, Lorrilard Co., round, blue, 11-3/4" h, 8-3/4" d **$850**

Tape measure

Fox's Guernsey Dairy, black lettering on yellow ground, red rim, four red carnations on black ground on reverse **$25**

Sears, Roebuck & Co., white lettering, black ground, lightning bolt-style lettering for "WLS" (World's Largest Store), red, white, blue, and green stylized floral design on back **$15**

Thermometer

Calumet Baking Powder, wood, black,

red, and white, yellow ground, 27" x 7-1/4", C.8+ **$1,100**

Hills Bros. Coffee, porcelain, 1915, 8-3/4" w, 21" h **$825**

Kentucky Club Pure Tobacco, painted metal, 38-1/2" x 8", C.8++ **$200**

Wool Soap, black and white, metal case, glass front, 1895 copyright, 6" d **$600**

Tin, miscellaneous

Busy Biddy Spice, Davies Strass Stauffer Co., red, white, and black, 3-1/8" x 1-3/4" x 1-1/4", C.7.5+ **$120**

Cadette Tooth Powder, figural tin litho soldier, red cap and coat, full, 7-3/8" x 2-1/4" x 1-1/4", C.8 .... **$625**

F. W. Cough Drops, Geo Miller & Co., Phila, "Cured My Cough," detailed graphics, 8" x 5-1/8" x 5-1/8", C.9 .... **$1,400**

Planters Nuts & Chocolate Co., Egyptian design on lid and sides, c1919, 6-1/4" d, 4" h, C.8 .... **$1,050**

Popeye Pop Corn, Purity Mills, Dixon, IL, pry lid, 4-3/4" x 3-1/4" x 2-1/8", C.8++ **$160**

W. Phillips Ltd., London, biscuits, Egyptian images on shaped hinged lid, 6" x 6-3/4" x 3-1/8", C.8- **$90**

Tip tray, Cunard Lines, Aquitania ocean liner, tin litho, 4-5/8" x 6-5/8", C.8+ **$350**

Tobacco tin, tin litho

Bulldog Smoking Tobacco, Lowville Buffington Co., vertical pocket, 4-1/2" x 3" x 7/8", C.8 .... **$675**

C.H.Y.P. Inter-Collegiate Mixture, 2-1/4" x 4-1/2" x 3-3/8", C.8- **$160**

Checkers, Weisert Bros, St. Louis, vertical pocket, white, black, and red, 4-1/2" x 3" x 7/8", C.8.5 .... **$525**

Crane's Private Mixture, House of Crane, Indianapolis, vertical pocket, 4-1/4" x 3-3/8" x 1-1/4", C.8 .... **$425**

Dixie Queen, canister, trademark girl in large hat on both sides, 6-1/2" x 4-1/4", C.8.5 .... **$600**

Forest & Stream, Imperial Tobacco Co., Canada, vertical pocket, fisherman in canoe, 4-1/8" x 3" x 7/8", C.8 .... **$475**

Guide Pipe & Cigarette Tobacco, Larus & Bros., vertical pocket, 4-1/4" x 3" x 7/8", C.8+ **$230**

Long Distance, Scotten Dillon Co., pail, multicolored graphics with battleship, 6-1/2" x 5-1/2", C.8+ **$190**

North Pole Tobacco, United States Tobacco Co., hinged box, 3-1/8" x 6-1/8" x 3-7/8", C.8+ **$220**

Pat Hand, Globe Tobacco Co., vertical pocket, full, 2-3/4" x 2-1/2" x 1-3/8", C.8.5 .... **$130**

Trade sign, wooden, two crossed over, carved handled blades, painted green with polychrome floral embellishments, inscribed "PPD 1860" on one blade, American, c1860, 18" x 17", $350.
Photo courtesy of Skinner, Inc.

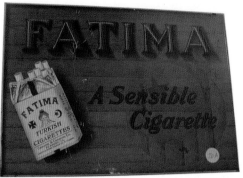

Sign, Fatima, A Sensible Cigarette, tin litho, multi-colored pack of cigarettes, green background, 12" x 8-1/2", $165.
Photo courtesy of Dotta Auction Co., Inc.

Plate, advertising, "Chocolate Drops" in gold, center design of black child, white dress, yellow ribbons, gold rim, $80.

Lunch pail, Just Suits Tobacco, P. Lorillard Co., tin, red, gold text accented in black, lid hinged, clasp on left, wire handle, designed to be reused as lunch pail, bright glossy finish, gold luster, c1900, 7-3/4" l, 5-1/4" w, 4" h, $150.
Photo courtesy of Hake's Americana & Collectibles.

Paul Jones, shield with Paul Jones on front, image of battleship on back, vertical pocket, 4-1/2" x 3" x 7/8", C.8+ **$1,750**

Pipe Major, Brown & Williamson, vertical pocket, 4-1/2" x 3" x 7/8", C.8+ **$325**

Princeton Mixture, Marburg Bros., paper label, 4-1/2" x 3" x 1-7/8", C.8+ **$400**

Puritan, Phillip Morris, vertical pocket, 4-3/8" x 3" x 7/8", C.8.5 .... **$300**

Seal of North Carolina, Marburg Bros., canister, multicolored graphic trademark on both sides, 6-1/2" x 4-7/8", C.8+ **$375**

Trout-Line, vertical pocket, fly fisherman in stream, 3-3/4" x 3-1/2" x 1-1/8", C.8++ **$675**

Weyman's Cutty Pipe, canister, green ground, red and yellow lettering, 13-1/2" x 10-1/4" x 9-3/8", C.8.5 .... **$1,400**

Whip, Patterson Bros., vertical pocket, rider in red coat, white pants, black boots, brown horse's head, 4-1/2" x 3" x 7/8", C.8- **$850**

White Manor, Penn Tobacco, vertical pocket, 3" x 3-1/2" x 1", C.8++ **$210**

Token, Sambo's Coffee, wooden, printed in red on both sides, one side with patriotic design featuring coffee mug, inscription "What This Country Needs Is A Good 10 Cent Cup of Coffee-Sambo's Has It," reverse inscribed "Sambo's Restaurants Anywhere," late 1970s, 1-1/2" d **$10**

Trade card

Ayer's Sarsaparilla, "Ayer's Sarsaparilla Makes the Weak Strong," two gentlemen **$18**

Child's & Staples, Gilbertsville, Maine,

young girl chasing butterfly, 2-3/4 x 4-1/2" **$1**

Czar Baking Powder, black woman and boy with giant biscuit **$2**

Granite Iron Ware, three ladies gossiping over tea **$2**

Hadfield's Premium Fireworks, G Parsons agent, 24 John Street, New York, c1860, 2" x 3" **$30**

Heinz Apple Butter, diecut, pickle shape **$60**

Hoyt's German Cologne, E.M. Hoyt & Co., mother cat and kittens **$25**

J. & P. Coats, Best Silk Thread, "We Never Fade," black youngster and spool of thread **$18**

New Essay Lawn Mower, scene of Statue of Liberty, New York harbor **$35**

Norton Bros., sign and tin manufacturers, c1870, 2-3/4" x 4" **$575**

Perry Davis, Pain Killer for Wounds armored man of war ships battle scene **$25**

Reid's Flower Seeds, two high wheeled bicyclers admiring flowers held by three ladies **$25**

Scott's Emulsion of Cod Liver Oil, man with large fish over back, vertical format **$20**

Thompson's Glove Fitting Corsets, lady and cupids **$35**

White Sewing Machine Co., elves working at sewing machine **$15**

Tray, tin litho

J. Leisy Brewing, Cleveland, OH, multicolored graphic of factory, horse-drawn delivery wagons, oval, 13-5/8" x 16-5/8", C.8+ **$775**

Nova Kola, American Art Works, center graphic of well dressed couple clinging to world while raising glasses together, 13-1/4" x 13-1/4", C.8 .... **$375**

Pabst Brewerys, black ground, gold dec, multicolored graphic of factory, rect, 12-1/4" x 17-1/4", C.8++ **$550**

Stroh's Lager Beer, Detroit, heavy porcelain enamel center insert, 12" d, C.8+ **$1,050**

Watch fob, Corby's Canadian Whiskey, silvered white metal frame, four large flower blossoms surround color insert of pretty woman reclining against stone wall, robe falling open, Whitehead & Hoag **$175**

ANIMAL COLLECTIBLES

History: The representation of animals in fine arts, decorative arts, and on utilitarian products dates back to antiquity. Some religions endowed certain animals with mystical properties. Authors throughout written history used human characteristics when portraying animals.

The formation of collectors' clubs and marketing crazes, e.g., flamingo, pig, and penguin, during the 1970s increased the popularity of this collecting field.

Additional Resources:

Warman's® Americana & Collectibles, 11th Ed., by Ellen T. Schroy, ed., Krause Publications, Iola, WI.

Barnyard

Carving, folk art, wood

Peep, painted, with stand, c1900, 7" l **$9,545**

Rooster, polychrome red, mustard yellow, and brown, base with indistinct pencil inscription, Pennsylvania, c1840, 9-1/2" l, 2-1/2" w, 8" h **$4,320**

Rooster, old cream-colored paint, 3/4 flat body, stand, 17" l, 15" h **$460**

Chopper, rooster, iron, fanciful silhouette, incised feather detail, mounted on wooden fragment, with stand, lacks wooden handle, late 18th/early 19th C, 12" l, 7-1/2" d, 7-1/4" h **$1,035**

Doorstop, lamb, polychrome glazed molded earthenware, attributed to J Eberly & Co., Strasburg, Virginia **$34,100**

Figure, sewer tile

Frog on log, hand modeled, tooled bark, inscribed initials "H.S." on base, dark brown, slightly metallic glaze, traces of gold on one end of log, 5-1/4" l, 5" h **$425**

Pig, standing, wearing pants, vest, and bow tie, reddish-brown glaze, few spots of wear, 7-7/8" h **$320**

Hooked rug, owl in front of a full moon, oval, late 19th C **$950**

Jar, cov, stoneware, figure of pig eating from trough on lid, German, some damage to base, 6" d, 6-1/2" h **$115**

Lithograph, Prize Poultry, from Cassell's Poultry Book, printed by Vincent, Brooks, Day & Son, each specimen titled including "Mr. Henry Belden's Pair of Golden Spangled Polish," etc., French matted, 21-1/8" x 18-1/2" ebonized and parcel gilt frames, England, price for set of eight, late 19th C, 10" x 7-1/2" **$1,530**

Painting, gouache, 12-1/4" h, 20" w, sheep grazing in hilly pasture, sgd "H. I. Marlatt," (H. Irving Marlatt, Mt. Vernon, New York, 1867-1929, gouache sketch on heavy paper, matted, 22-1/4" h, 29-3/4" w frame, some edge wear **$250**

Painting, oil on canvas, sheep and lambs in stable, nearby chickens, ornate frame with copper and gold repaint, rebacked on board, revarnished, minor touch up, 29-1/8" h, 36-1/2" w **$920**

Pull toy, billy goat, gray fur, papier-mâché horns, leather harness, orig cream painted cart with gold and blue stripes, goat moves with rocking motion, one wheel knob replaced, wear, 23" l **$815**

Tin, Dr. Daniels' Cow Invigorator, 18 oz pry lid tin litho, image of cow on each side, C-8+ **$275**

Birds

Architectural element, owl, pottery, unglazed, traces of old silver paint, base imp "Owens and Howard, St. Louis, MO," minor hairlines, 18-1/2" h **$550**

Eagle, cast iron, painted, black with white spots, America, late 19th C, 11" l, 5-1/2" d, 3-1/2" h **$250**

Figure, sewer tile, horned owl, perched on round pedestal base, orange glaze, 10-1/2" h **$450**

Plaque, ebonized frame, pietra dura, colorful parrot on perch, Italian, early 20th C, 7" x 4" sight, 11-1/2" x 8-1/2" **$250**

Sculpture, eagle, carved wood, standing, spread wings, 15-1/2" wingspan, 20" h **$395**

Terriers, bronze, designed by M. Kirmse, one seated, one crouched, both signed by artist, Gorham, tallest 1-1/2" x 3/4", **$1,600.**
Photo courtesy of David Rago Auctions, Inc.

"Nipper," papier-mâché, RCA Victor trademark, early 20th century, 35" h, **$525.**
Photo courtesy of Pook & Pook, Inc.

Bear figurine, bisque, sitting up, unmarked, late 19th/early 20th century, 11" h, **$145.**
Photo courtesy of Green Valley Auctions.

Dog, boot scraper, bronze, dachshund shape, detailed, **$115.**

Photo courtesy of Dotta Auction Co., Inc.

Hippos, paperweight, crystal, etched marked "Mats Jonasson, Sweden" on original label, **$125.**

Horse, award, crystal Tiffany vase, engraved "Pennsylvania Horse Breeders Association 1993 Iroquois Award, Pennfield Farms, Inc., breeder of Fleeced," **$125.**

Trivet, parrot, pastel central figure with intricate flower and vine pattern, eight triangular feet, Rookwood marks, 1929, 5-3/4" sq **$325**

Wall shelf, eagle, carved wood, shaped shelf supported by eagle with spread wings, loss to gilt, 16-1/2" w **$475**

Cats

Bank, chalkware, seated, wearing red bow, minor loss, 11" h **$200**

Cane

Carved ivory ball handle with cat face emerging from one side, 1/3" sterling collar with Chester hallmarks for 1903, dark Malacca shaft, 3/4" brass ferrule, 34-1/2" l, 1-3/4" d x 1-3/4" h **$450**

Carved wood head, nicely detailed features, when button on back is pressed, red eyes change to blue, long red tongue shoots out, 1-1/4" dec silver collar, Malacca shaft, 7/8" replaced brass ferrule, German, c1880, 36" l, 2" w x 3-1/2" **$2,020**

Figure

Carved pine, fat cat, incised "E. Sweet," cracks, 20th C, 9-1/2" w, 7" d, 17-1/4" h **$435**

Glass, cast, blue, sgd "Daum France," 20th C, 3-1/4" h **$185**

Glass, cast, colorless, sgd "Baccarat," orig box, 3-7/8" h **$175**

Sewer tile, elongated form, head cocked to one side, curious look, hand tooled eyelashes, metallic glaze, Ohio, 13-1/4" h.............**$660**

White cotton batting clad, green glass eyes.............**$110**

Sewer tile, reclining, hand-tooled eyelashes, white glazed eyes, 9" l **$360**

Paperweight, hunchback cat, cast iron, adv "Walter A. Zelnicker Supply Co. in St. Louis, U.S.A." on base, rare, excellent, 3-7/8" x 2-1/2".............**$515**

Painting

Brown Tabby Kitten with a Rose Bow, John Henry Dolph, sgd "JHDolph" lower left, oil on board, framed, scattered retouch, 12" x 9" **$4,700**

Gray Tiger Cat with a Blue Bow, sgd "MABrown" lower right, American School, oil on canvas, framed, minor scattered retouch, varnish inconsistencies, 19th C, 17" x 21" **$2,000**

Sleepy Tabby, Franklin W. Rogers, sgd "F.W. Roger" lower right, label on reverse, oil on canvas, framed, scattered retouch, varnish inconsistencies, craquelure, 21" x 17" **$1,175**

The Sleeping Tabby, monogrammed and dated "JLC 1881" lower left, American School, oil on canvas, framed, scattered retouch, craquelure, 19th C, 9" x 12" **$3,300**

Stamp box, carved fruitwood, figural cat lying inside shoe, glass eyes, hinged lid, early 20th C, 4-3/4" l **$225**

Tip tray, cast iron, figural black kitten's face, "Baker," excellent, 4" x 4"....**$150**

Dogs

Ashtray, Scottish Terrier, sq, porcelain, center black terrier, images of hounds and rabbits, green and white ground, Hermes.............**$50**

Cane

Carved elephant ivory handle, 3-1/2" l x 1-1/2" h, pug family consisting of father, mother, three pups in line, 1" gold filled collar dec in "C" scrolls, orig owner's elaborate initials, ebony shaft carved with simulated thorns, 1-1/8" burnished brass and iron ferrule, English, c1890, 35" l **$1,570**

Carved ivory handle, 1-3/4" d x 4-3/4" h, performing poodle, wearing toy soldier's cap, holding toy gun, 3/4" silver collar, tan Malacca shaft, 1" replaced brass ferrule, England, c1890, 35-1/4" l **$1,120**

Elephant ivory handle carved as mastiff emerging from seashell, 2" w x 2-3/4" h brown glass eyes, maccassar ebony shaft, 1-1/2" white metal and iron ferrule, Continental, c1890, 36-7/8" l.............**$1,680**

Purple quartz handle carved as French bulldog, 2-1/2" w x 2" h, upright ears, dec gold plated collar, ebony shaft, 1" brass and iron ferrule, Continental, c1890, 36-1/2" l **$950**

Cigarette case, enameled portrait of hunting dogs, French, mkd ".900 fine" **$1,175**

Figure, bronze, terrier with bone, bronze dog standing possessively over carved ivory bone on ground before him, oblong base, mold incised signature for Friedrich Gornik, founder's monogram AR, 5" l, 3-1/2" h **$900**

Figure, clay

Newcomerstown, Ohio, pottery, seated, unglazed clay, good detail, shallow front chip, 10" h.............**$3,750**

Ohio white clay, seated, short ears and tail, long jowls, grown glaze, chip on back of base, small flake on ear, 8-1/8" h **$110**

Seated, freestanding front legs, yellow Ohio clay, mottled green glaze on base, brown dec on dog, black eyes, blue ink stamp label "E. Houghton & Co. Dalton, Ohio, 1928," hairline in base, 7" w, 3-1/2" d, 9-1/2" h **$1,450**

Seated, freestanding front legs, gray clay, cream-colored glaze, brown and blue polka dots, long tail with brown, one ear brown, other blue, chips on base, 7-1/4" l, 9-1/4" h **$6,270**

Figure, pearlware, long hair seated dog, white, brown and gold spots, minor flakes on base, short hairline, 2-7/8" l, 3-1/4" h **$520**

Figure, sewer tile

Collie, standing, reddish brown glaze, rect molded base, firing separations, small chips on ears, 10-1/2" l, 5-1/2" w, 11-1/2" h **$935**

Seated, hand modeled, tooled fur and facial features, mat glaze with metallic speckles, traces of white paint, 7-1/2" h........................... **$110**

Seated, molded with hand tooled details on ears and face, long eyelashes, glaze varies from light tan to dark reddish brown, Ohio, minor flakes on base, 11" h................ **$660**

Figure, stoneware, Spaniels, tan and brown speckled matte glaze, glass eyes, oval bases, England, repair to base of one, glaze flakes, price for pr, c1875, 13-1/2" h **$6,465**

Folk art painting, King Charles spaniel and her two pups, 8-7/8" x 11" **$2,800**

Jewelry, brooch

Micromosaic, recumbent King Charles spaniel, gold ropetwist frame, minor lead solder on verso **$900**

Platinum and diamond, terrier, pave setting, green stone eyes....... **$1,725**

Reverse painted crystal, standing boxer, oval 14k gold frame, sgd "W. F. Marcus" **$920**

Painting, pastel on paper

Naughty puppy worrying a piece of lace, unsigned, American School, molded gilt frame, rippling, 19th C, 13-1/4" x 17-1/4" **$1,295**

Puppy sleeping on green cushion, unsigned, American School, gilt

frame, small ear at center right edge, 19th C, 12-1/2" x 17-1/4" **$1,175**

Shaving mug, hp, two hunting dogs, brown background, mkd "St. Louis Electronic Grinding Co., Barber Supplies," some wear to gold trim, crack in ring handle, 4-1/8" x 3-3/4" **$120**

Vase, Lenox, marked "Hunter Arms Co., First Prize, Class A," image of pointer in clearing, sgd "Delan," stamped Lenox logo, 10" h **$3,665**

Watch fob, four graduated round 14k gold plaques depicting dog's heads in repoussé, suspended by trace link chains, monogrammed, swivel clasp, 15.0 dwt.................................... **$575**

Horses

Blanket, needlework design of horse, red ground, diamond design in field, black border with cross-stitched multicolored floral design, red yarn fringe, wool backing, reverse stitched with owner's name "Jacob Weber 1871," minor restoration, moth damage in backing, 68" sq **$175**

Book, Rodeo, *A Collection of Tales & Sketches* by R.B. Cunningham Graham, selected by A.F. Tschiffeley, Literary Guild, 1936 .... **$10**

Cane, 4" l x 2-1/4" h elephant ivory handle carved as two riding horse heads, carved simulated leather tack, 1/2" sterling collar marked "Brigg," London hallmarks for 1897, ebony shaft, 7/8" brass and iron ferrule, 35-3/4" l.................................... **$1,350**

Condiment set, electroplate, base formed as horseshoe, spur-form handle, toothpick holder flanked by boot form castor, mustard pot with whip-form spoon, central jockey cap open salt, Elkington & Co., England, late 19th C, 5" l, 3-5/8" h **$175**

Figure, carved and painted wood

Articulated circus figure with red textile shoulder girth, riding horse with glass bead eyes, attributed to Connecticut, stand, minor wear, paint imperfections, c1900-10, 10-1/2" l, 14-1/2" h **$2,530**

Laminated, stylized form, grommet eyes, orig glossy black paint, America, losses to tail, late 19th C, 7-1/2" h **$1,610**

Plaque, Black Forest carved leaping stag, late 19th century, 27" l, **$490.**
Photo courtesy of Pook & Pook, Inc.

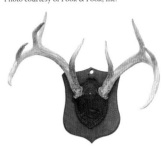

Early deer rack, 10 points, iron skull plate, pat. date May 26, 1891, plate depicts rifle, powder horn, hunting bag, etc., **$225.**
Photo courtesy of Lang's Sporting Collectables.

Hunting dog, painting, oil on canvas, retouch, surface grime, losses, framed, signed and dated "Henry Stull, 1980," 12" x 12", **$5,875.**
Photo courtesy of Skinner, Inc.

Puzzle, Joseph Strauss, Happy Hunter, plywood, 500 pcs, orig box, 1940/50, 15-3/4" x 20", **$100.**
Photo courtesy of Bob Armstrong.

Lithograph, equine, trotters, Gen. Butler, Silus Rich & Bashaw, Jr., 1869, 17-1/2" x 25", **$1,000.**

Photo courtesy of Wiederseim Associates, Inc.

Bull, cast bronze, wooden base, unmarked, break to horns, 20th century, 10", **$475.**

Photo courtesy of David Rago Auctions, Inc.

Musical picture, tin figures of adult cat playing fiddle, kittens dancing, tin figures move in conjunction with music box attached to back, German, missing key, losses to frame, 8-3/4" x 12", **$10,450.**

Photo courtesy of Alderfer Auction Co.

Figure, porcelain
Man in colonial dress riding white horse, 18" l, 20" h **$290**
Woman in colonial dress riding dappled brown horse, 18" l, 20" h **$660**

Painting, oil on canvas, portrait of horse standing in barnyard, sgd and dated "E. Corbet 1881" lower right, identified as Irish race horse by note on reverse, framed, small areas of paint loss, craquelure, varnish inconsistencies, 18-1/4" x 24-1/4" **$2,000**

Pull toy, painted and laminated carved pine, full stride, horsehair tail, wheeled platform base, America, early 20th C, 11-1/4" l **$635**

Sign, The Stewart Clipping Machine, colorful image of horses in court room jury box, machine in center, cardboard litho, 14" x 20", C.8.5 .... **$475**

Toy, Arabian Trotter, tin and composition wind-up, orig key, orig box **$130**

Watch holder, figural, silver plated metal, detailed jockey and race horse figure, mkd "Reed & Barton," loss to orig silver plate, 10" h, 5-3/8" d **$525**

Weathervane, full-bodied trotting horse, copper, verdigris surface, black metal stand, America, minor dents, late 19th C, 26-1/2" l, 16-1/2" h **$4,325**

Wild animals
Bookends, pr, rabbits, modeled poised on back legs, painted copper over plaster, red square bases, Aesthetic Movement, late 19th/early 20th C, 5" h **$300**

Cane
Elephant ivory handle carved as

American bison, amber glass eyes, finely fashioned features, 1/2" sterling collar with London hallmarks for 1920, heavy ebony shaft, 7/8" brass and iron ferrule, 36" l, 2-1/3" w x 3-1/4" h **$1,120**
Elephant ivory handle carved as six male lions, amber eyes, alternate with mouths open and closed, 1/3" ringed silver collar, thick Malacca shaft, 1-1/2" horn ferrule, English, c1890, 36-1/4" l, 2" d x 3" h **$1,460**

Figure
Carved alabaster, reclining rabbit, full relief, rect base, 9" l, 5" d, 6" h **$2,185**
Carved bone, elephant, carved bone, carved wooden armature overlaid with bone tiles in contrasting patterns, India, c1900, 24" l **$1,610**
Ceramic, white elephant figures, gray and pink enamel detailing, sq bronze bases with gilt rocaille scrollwork to sides, price for pr, early 20th C, 10" w, 5-3/4" d, 10-1/2" h **$2,760**
Kangaroo, Fred Alten (1872-1945, Wyandotte, Michigan), body with traces of brown stain, red glass eyes, shaped base, with stand, 3-1/4" w, 7-1/4" h **$575**
Polychromed carved wood deer, worn brown paint, white accents on nose and underbelly, green ground stand, America, missing one antler and part of right foreleg, 19th C, 18" l, 3-1/4" d, 17-3/4" h **$3,450**

Shooting gallery target, rabbit, Massachusetts, some paint remaining, with stand, c1940, 21" w, 7" d, 31-1/2" h **$815**

Tin, litho
Jumbo Peanut Butter, Frank Tea & Spice Co., one-lb size, 3-3/8" x 3-7/8" **$775**
Red Wolf Coffee, Ridenour-Baker Co., Kansas City, one-lb size, vacuum pack, trademark wolf, 5" d, 4" h **$575**
Tiger Bright Sweet Chewing Tobacco, P. Lorillard Co., vertical pocket size, 3" w, 7/8" d, 2-7/8" h **$275**

ARCHITECTURAL ELEMENTS

History: Architectural elements, many of which are handcrafted, are those items which have been removed or salvaged from buildings, ships, or gardens. Part of their desirability is due to the fact that it would be extremely costly to duplicate the items today.

Beginning about 1840, decorative building styles began to feature carved wood and stone, stained glass, and ornate ironwork. At the same time, builders and manufacturers also began to use fancy doorknobs, doorplates, hinges, bells, window locks, shutter pulls, and other decorative hardware as finishing touches to elaborate new homes and commercial buildings.

Hardware was primarily produced from bronze, brass, and iron, and doorknobs also were made from clear, colored, and cut glass. Highly ornate hardware began appearing in the late 1860s and remained popular through the early 1900s. Figural pieces that featured animals, birds, and heroic and mythological images were very popular, as were ornate and very graphic designs that complimented the many architectural styles that emerged in the late 19th century.

Fraternal groups, government and educational institutions, and individual businesses all ordered special hardware for their buildings. Catalogs from the era show hundreds of patterns, often with a dozen different pieces available in each design.

The current trends of preservation and recycling of architectural elements has led to the establishment and growth of organized salvage operations that specialize in removal and resale of elements. Special auctions are now held to sell architectural elements from churches, mansions, office buildings, etc. Today's decorators often design an entire room around one architectural element, such as a Victorian marble bar or mural, or use several as key accent pieces.

Arch, fragmentary, sandstone, carved figures, including Buddha seated on dais, central India, c15th/16th C, 36" l **$1,495**

Bird bath, cast iron, shallow basin, gadrooned rim mounted by two doves, fluted baluster form standard on circular base cast with pierced rose design, 19" d, 33-1/2" h **$300**

Bird cage, house form, grand entrance, front porch, bay windows, dormers, cupola, painted green, trimmed with red painted wooden buttons, knobs, and perches, some paint loss, 21" x 19-1/2" x 18" **$230**

Bracket

Carved wood, mermaids, gilded, bifurcated scrolled tails, America, some loss, pr, 19th C, 19-3/4" h, 10-1/2" d, ...**$4,230**

Galvanized tin, arched bracket, center keystone, pilaster base, Renaissance Revival, price for pr.................**$900**

Capitals, galvanized tin, flat tops, raised star and rope twist details, one stripped, other old gray and white paint, wear and split seams, price for pr, 16" w, 10" d, 21" h **$250**

Catalog

Hudson Equipment Co., Chicago, IL, 256 pgs, Hudson Barn Equipment Catalog No. B-31, stalls, stan-

chions, bull stall, etc., 1940, 6-1/2" x 9-3/4" **$30**

Morgan Sash & Door Co., Chicago, IL, 180 pgs, Catalog & Price List No. 553, Morgan-Anderson Woodwork, c1953, 8-1/2" x 11" **$35**

Chimneypiece, carved pine, molded shelf above dentilled frieze with central roundel decorated with putto flanked by swags of flowers, jambs decorated with urns above scrolled brackets, acanthus leaves at feet, late Victorian or Edwardian, c1900, 96" w, 7" d, 72" h **$1,800**

Curtain tiebacks, mercury glass, grape dec, pewter collars, price for set of six, some chips, minor wear **$175**

Door

Raised panel, pegged construction, orig red paint, wrought iron thumb latch, old corner chip, 27-1/4" w, 69-1/2" h **$580**

Architectural, wooden element, painted green, American, large semi-wheel shaped, seven spokes, late 19th century, 33-1/4" h x 35" w, **$880.**
Photo courtesy of Skinner, Inc.

Architectural, wrought iron hinged door or screen, rings joined by barbed knots, black enamel wear, Samuel Yellin, stamped 33, 25-1/2" x 20-1/2", **$1,295.**
Photo courtesy of David Rago Auctions, Inc.

Architectural, eagle, Bellamy-style, gilt carved, inscribed blue banner: "Live and Let Live," 72" wingspan, **$5,500.**
Photo courtesy of David Rago Auctions, Inc.

Architectural, tile frieze, Arts & Crafts, 12 Grueby Pottery tiles modeled with red blossoms and green foliage, banded ochre and red ground, unmarked, few minor nicks, 6" x 6" corners, 5" x 9" rectangles, **$2,600.**
Photo courtesy of David Rago Auctions, Inc.

Architectural, fountain, carved alabaster and marble, base with female figure in draped cloth, incised floral decoration, fitted as lamp, chips to base, repairs, turn of the century, 18-1/2" d, 43-1/2" h, **$2,500.**
Photo courtesy of David Rago Auctions, Inc.

Architectural, lantern brackets, wrought iron, spiral support and scrolled back-plate, set of four, 32" x 42" x 5", **$475.**
Photo courtesy of David Rago Auctions, Inc.

Architectural, fountain, bronze, mermaid and dolphin, wave-form base encrusted with turtle, crab, and shells, 38" d, 85" h, **$3,315.**
Photo courtesy of Sloans & Kenyon Auctioneers and Appraisers.

Architectural, vault door, center plaque reads "Herring Hall Marvin Safe Co., Hamilton, OH," **$195.**
Photo courtesy of Alderfer Auction Co.

Two molded recessed panels, grain painted to resemble exotic wood, attributed to Maine, very minor surface imperfections, early 19th C, 31-1/2" w, 78-1/2" h **$920**

Doorknob, brown pottery agateware, 2-1/8" d, price for pr **$90**

Door knocker, wrought and hammered copper, tulip shape, monogrammed "IGW," orig dark patina, 4" w, 11-1/4" h **$175**

Door pull, brass, Arts & Crafts, round, grimacing figure wearing head covering, holding ring in its mouth, 8" d **$270**

Eagle
Carved mahogany, bas-relief carving, perched on arrow, gilt highlights, America, 12-3/4" w, 5" h **$530**
Carved giltwood, perched on carved rockery, Pilot House type, America, old regilding, minor wear, c1875, 26" w, 31" l, 25" h **$2,415**
Gilded tin, outstretched wings, perched on rockery weighted base, holds scales in beak, metal manufacturer M.F. Frand Co., Camden, New Jersey, tag on lower base, imperfections, late 19th C, 32-3/4" w, 19-1/4" h **$1,880**

Finials, pr
Cast stone, cov urn draped with floral swags, fluted socle, sq base, pr, 19th C, 25" h **$1,800**
Molded copper, star and crescent on ball above ring and baluster-form base, all-over verdigris surface, America, purportedly from an Odd Fellows Lodge, minor dents, late 19th/early 20th C, 31" h **$3,525**

Floor vase, alabaster, urn form, scalloped rim, leaftip neck band, vertically fluted body with double leaftip stem, trumpet foot, plinth base, Classical Revival, late 19th C, 28-1/4" h **$325**

Garden bench, cast iron
Openwork vintage design, scrolled seat, worn white paint, price for pr, 36" w, 13-1/2" d, 28" h **$350**
Openwork fern design on back and legs, geometric cast designs on seat, old white repaint, two hairlines, chip near front corner, 43-1/2" w, 15" d, 31" h **$325**

Garden furniture, cast iron, scrolled medallions on backs, scrolled arms, cast geometric stars on seats, Gothic style aprons, old white paint, price for two-pc set, 36" h chair, 45" l x 18" d x 37" h settee **$1,495**

Garden ornament
Rabbit, cast iron, seated figure, traces of white, green, and red paint wear, late 19th C, 10" l, 11-5/8" h **$345**
Urn with flame, carved and painted wood and gesso, painted tan, putty, and white, traces of gilt, 19th C, 16-1/2" l, 29-1/2" h **$2,185**

Garden seat, porcelain, detailed white relief floral and bird dec, dark blue ground, paneled sides with pierced dec on two sides and top, Oriental 14-1/4" d, 19-1/4" h **$425**

Garden table, cast iron, painted white, ornate detail, openwork inserts on top, high cabriole legs, scrolled feet, foliage returns, one insert missing, 44" w, 26-3/4" d, 30-1/4" h **$520**

Griffins, winged, stone-cut, English, pr **$4,200**

Hitching post, cast iron, jockey, yellow, red, green, black, and white painted detail, wired for lantern, 31" h **$275**

Joint cap, composition, gilt, shell form, bases with tapering acanthus, Georgian, set of four, 10-1/4" w, 12" l, ... **$900**

Library steps, metamorphic, mahogany, leather top, open position as rect low table, hinged to form four-tread library step, Regency style, 28" w, 17-1/2" d, 17-1/2" h **$900**

Lock, iron, rect plate with male and female silhouettes, key with quatrefoil terminal, stand, minor surface corrosion, 19th C, 8-1/2" w, 11" h **$650**

Obelisks, pr, black slate, parcel gilt, tapered form, front incised with pseudo hieroglyphics on gilt ground, stepped base, gilt metal feet, Egyptian Revival, late 19th C, 13-3/4" h **$940**

Pedestal
Antico-verde marble, round and octagonal tapered revolving top, columnar pedestal carved with band of anthemion between beading, base with further beaded band, sq plinth base, Classical Revival, Italian, late 19th C, 40" h **$2,750**
Burled veneer, applied moldings on columns, stepped molded bases, paper label "Made in Italy," price for pr, 27-1/2" h, 9-1/4" d **$250**

Carved walnut, turned top raised on figure of classical man, turned and bead-carved base, early 20th C, 27-1/2" h **$360**

Copper and brass, twist-turned legs, paw feet, urn finial on base, Renaissance Revival, 31-1/2" h, 14" w sq top **$425**

Mahogany, circular top, turned standard, three paw feet, Victorian, 31" h **$220**

White marble, dark gray striations, circular top, turned rings on column, octagonal base, small edge chips, 40" h, 9-1/4" d top **$450**

Planter, zinc, nautilus shell form, pr, 22" l, 20" h **$2,160**

Staircase and railing, oak, designed for the offices of Charles P. Limbert Co., Holland, Michigan, salvaged from building prior to demolition in 1990 .... **$3,350**

Sundial, lead, circular, alpha numerics, terra cotta base shaped like three gargoyles, shaped plinth, 17" d, 34" h **$850**

Terrarium, walnut and glass, rect body with four chamfered round uprights topped by turned finials, colorless glass sides, base with lead-lined interior, raised on bun feet, Victorian, late 19th C, 17" w, 21-3/8" h **$600**

Topiary form, lyre-shape, wire, conical base, painted green, America, late 19th/early 20th C, 13-1/2" w, 24" h **$150**

Urn, cast iron

Flared rim, shell design on lower reservoir, round stems, painted black, double handles, repairs, price for pr, 14-3/4" h **$200**

Flared rim, sq to round base, double handles, white paint, minor rim chip, 19-1/2" h **$420**

Fluting, relief acanthus leaves, raised cast scroll panels, pedestal base, removable handles, painted white, 37-3/4" h, 30" w **$575**

Ribbed tops and columns, sq base, painted white, price for pr, 20-1/2" h **$120**

Wall plaque, pine, eagle and shield, carved in the manner of John Haley Bellamy, America, painted white, early 20th C, 48-1/4" w, 10-1/2" h **$1,645**

Window frame, arched, mullions in gothic pattern, five small panes remaining, green paint, 20th C, 35-1/2" w, 35" h, ... **$55**

ART DECO

History: The Art-Deco period was named after an exhibition, "l'Exposition Internationale des Arts Décorative et Industriels Modernes," held in Paris in 1927. Its beginnings succeed those of the Art-Nouveau period, but the two overlap in time, as well as in style.

Art-Deco designs are angular with simple lines. This was the period of skyscrapers, movie idols, and the Cubist works of Picasso and Legras. Art Deco motifs were used for every conceivable object being produced in the 1920s and 1930s (ceramics, furniture, glass, and metals) not only in Europe but in America as well.

Additional Listings: Furniture and Jewelry. Also check glass, pottery, and metal categories.

Aquarium, stepped and paneled molded translucent yellow glass bowl, dec with six panels of stylized flowers, set in bronzed metal tripod stand, three enameled green handles, legs terminating in stylized dolphins, central light fixture, tri-part base, dark patina, chips, wear, c1925, 41-1/2" h **$2,415**

Armoire, sycamore and fruitwood, interior fitted with top shelf over divided compartment, hardware fitted for wardrobe, flanked by two shelves, lollipop-shaped key, France, c1928, 51-1/4" w, 19" d, 71" h **$1,650**

Ashtray, Frankart, America, second quarter 20th C, white metal striding nude female figure, painted light green, green glazed square pottery ash receptacle on base, raised marks on base "FRANKART. INC. PAT. APPLD FOR," lacking ceramic cigarette box, 12-7/8" h **$450**

Bed, single curvilinear bed frame with hanging shelf compartments, France, price for pr, c1930, 82" l **$1,410**

Bonbon dish, cov, colorless glass, relief etched dec of three nude mermaids on interior of cover, raised signature, Sabino Glass, Paris, France, wear, 20th C, 6-1/2" d, 1-1/4" h **$235**

Bookends, pr, bronze, cast as bust of woman, patinated, unmarked, 8" h **$360**

Art Deco, washbowl and pitcher, graniteware, white ground, light brown and blue decoration, chips, **$150.**

Art Deco, lamp, bronzed metal base with two figures, bright orange, white, and blue spatter globe shade, original wiring, **$250.**

Art Deco, vase, Rookwood Pottery, squeeze bag decorated by William Hentschel, nude, antelopes, and geese, matte brown and white glaze, flame mark/XXIX/6080/WEH, neatly drilled hole in bottom, 1929, 13-1/2" x 11", **$4,750.**

Photo courtesy of David Rago Auctions, Inc.

Cabinet, dressing, rect curvilinear top, centered mirror over four drawers flanked on each side by full-length curvilinear cabinets, shaped foot skirt, France, c1925, 68-1/2" w, 19-1/2" d, 66-7/8" h **$1,100**

Cabinet, gentleman's, burled veneer cabinet, Bakelite and chrome hardware, England, c1930, 28-1/2" l, 16-1/2" d, 40" h **$940**

Center bowl, by Grace Helen Talbot, Roman Bronze Works, fluted bowl, four bronze nude female figures with arms outstretched, dark green-brown patina, signed and dated on base, 1922, 16" d, 3-3/4" h **$5,875**

Chair, tub, mahogany frame, upholstered seat, price for pr, 20th C, 27" h **$600**

Chandelier, colorless mold-blown and etched glass shade with stylized flowers and leaves, wrought iron frame with vine ornamentation, sgd "Degue 534," France, c1930, 30" h, 19" d.. **$600**

Cigarette case, silver, interior with vermeil wash, engraved "Fran," leather case, 5-3/8" l, 3-1/8" w **$100**

Clock, table, Telechron, model 4F65, Ashland, Massachusetts, circular blue glass with Roman numeral dial raised on flat chromed metal bar with curvilinear foot, electric movement, c1935, 7-1/4" w, 6-1/4" h **$750**

Coffee set, silver plated, Wilcox, design attributed to Gene Theobald, faceted 10-1/2" h coffeepot, and sugar container with Bakelite finials, matching creamer, 20" l oblong tray, all marked "Wilcox S.P. Co/E.P.N.S./ International S.Co./W. M. Wounts/ 1981N." **$1,150**

Credenza, beveled glass cabinet over rect marble top, two drawers over two cabinet doors in burlwood with metal mounts, wear, escutcheon missing, c1930, 61" l, 20-1/2" w, 82" h **$600**

Desk

Leopold Corp, Burlington, IA, walnut veneered, semi-oval top over center drawer flanked by pull-out writing surface and two drawers, bronze handles, light brown finish, "Charles S. Nathan Office Equipment New York" distributor's metal tag in drawer, veneer loss, wear, 66-1/8" l, 36-1/8" d, 29" h **$900**

Plycraft, double pedestal, four drawers on each side, single center drawer, stenciled #331, 30" x 44" x 22-1/2" **$350**

Drawings, by Alexander Bronson, pencil drawings of two beds by Paul Frankl, other with pedestal table, sgd, mounted in natural wood frames, price for three-pc set, 13-1/2" x 17" **$750**

Dresser box, Egyptian Revival, bentwood Egyptian sarcophagus form, overlaid in emb copper with Egyptian motifs, blue opaque glass scarabs, sides trimmed in tooled leather, silk lining, dark rich patina with verdigris oxidation, c1925, 12" l **$460**

End table, mahogany and burlwood, orig marble tops over single drawers, one with two lower shelves, other with shelf and cabinet, raised rosettes on metal hardware, France, price for pr, c1930, 16-1/2" w, 14" d, 29" h **$1,400**

Figure, molded opalescent glass, nude female figure, triangular base with raised and etched marks, paper label, Sabino Glass, Paris, France, 20th C, 9-1/2" h **$390**

Fireplace screen, wrought iron, diagonal grid with spade elements at intersections, dark patina, attributed to Raymond Subes, France, c1925, 25-1/4" w, 35" h **$4,200**

Lamp base, etched brass, silver wash on ovoid brass form, etched nude female figures picking grape clusters from cascading grape vines, weighted round stepped base, France, wear, scattered corrosion, c1925, 21" h.................. **$520**

Lamp, boudoir, Danse De Lumiere, molded glass figure of woman with outstretched arms, bearing stylized feather drapery, oval platform base with internal light fixture, molded title and patent mark, mold imperfections, c1930, 11" h **$400**

Lamp, floor, domical orange and blue mold-blown shade, wrought iron framework, conforming metal base, France, c1930, 68" h **$3,290**

Lamp, hanging, silvered metal, three arms with white etched glass shades attributed to Schneider, France, c1925, 29" l **$800**

Lamp, table

Concentric ribbed pink satin shade with stylized rosebud center, shade emb "Vleighe France 1137," nickel-plated brass base with emb geometric designs, minor flakes on shade, 19" h, 11" d **$520**

Trefoil etched colorless glass shade, rosette and geometric designs, supported by wrought iron tripod with applied rosette accents and leaf motif, shade sgd "Degue," nicks and chips to shade, 19" h, 13" d shade **$920**

Mirror

Cast metal, circular plate supported by two figures with composition faces, stamped "Collection Francaise, made in USA," 10-1/4" h **$360**

Full-length mirror with arched top, asymmetrical rosewood base with geometric ivory inlay, France, c1925, 29" w, 15" d, 70-3/4" h............. **$1,530**

Octagonal mirror in wrought iron frame, rose and leaf dec, France, 1930, 36" w, 24" h **$250**

Oval beveled glass, wrought metal surround, France, c1928, 36-3/4" h **$1,645**

Nightstand, bird's-eye maple veneer, marble top, France, c1930, 15-1/2" w, 15-1/2" d, 31" h **$300**

Plaque, cast aluminum, Love Birds, sgd "Rene P. Chambllen" lower right, dedicatory inscription verso, c1930, 12" x 9" **$920**

Poufee, floral upholstered round seat in gold, blue-gray, melon, and brown, four reeded legs that taper at base, France, c1925, 23" d, 13-1/2" h **$300**

Punch bowl and cordial set, eight-sided finial on paneled cov, 7-1/2" h, 8-1/2" d bowl dec with silver and red geometric design, six 2-1/2" d paneled cordials with similar dec, 14" d round glass tray with multiple star cuts on base, chrome sides, chrome ladle, imperfections **$290**

Ring, lady's, rounded form bezel and bead-set with old European-cut diamonds, approx. total wt. 1.56 cts, millegrain accents, 18k white gold mount **$2,000**

Room divider, four panels, black lacquered arched frames inset with canvas, painted abstract gold and black pattern, slight damage to hinges, each panel 24" w, 71-1/2" h **$1,725**

Salon chair, U-shaped low chair, beige velvet and burlwood, metal tag on bases, "Hotel Le Malandre Modele Depose," price for pr, c1945, 28-1/2" w, 26-1/2" d, 24-1/2" h **$2,185**

Server, stepped rect top, curvilinear ends over fitted cabinet doors, English, c1930, 55" w, 20" d, 36" h.......... **$1,880**

Sideboard, walnut and burl book-matched veneer, Bakelite cabinet doors and drawer pulls, France, c1928, 76" l, 19-1/2" d, 50-5/8" h **$900**

Stand, amboyna wood inlaid with stylized flowers in various fruitwoods and mother-of-pearl, attributed to Maurice Defrene, France, price for pr, c1925, 15" w, 18" d, 29-1/2" h **$2,235**

Table, dining

Oval top, Burlwood, fine ebony and ash inlay dec, four canted legs, accompanied by two conforming 16" leaves, France, c1930, 79" l, 40" w, 29" h **$1,175**

Oval top with geometric inlay border with central medallion, angular center support, shaped platform base, US, c1930, 72" l, 43-1/2" w, 29-3/4" h **$1,410**

Table, tea, walnut, rect top opens and swivels on U-shaped base, France, c1928, 44" l open, 22" closed, 35-1/4" w, 28-1/4" h **$1,880**

Tea and coffee set, silver, oval tray, coffeepot, teapot, creamer and cov sugar accented by ebonized handles and finials, mkd "835," hallmarked, Germany, creamer handle restored, tray scratches, early 20th C, 18-3/4" d **$1,175**

Torchieres, gilt bronze, skyscraper design raised on four stepped feet, US, price for pr, c1930, 69" h **$2,750**

Tray, rect, two handles, hammered brass, stamped "M. Willig Freising Bavaria," 24" l **$110**

Vase

Cameo glass, black ground, stylized scene of three repeated terriers against bronzed and silvered ground, unsigned, French, c1925, 8-1/2" h **$300**

Ceramic, Boch Frères, extended rim, oval form, stylized light green blossoms, stems, and foliage, gold accents, turquoise ground, glossy glaze, painted "BFK/340," imp "708," minor crazing, minor light scratches, price for pr, 11-3/8" h **$920**

Citrine ground, stylized enameled flowers, sgd "Legras," minor heat check, 8-1/2" h **$200**

Frosted colorless glass angular bulbous body, octagonal rim, ftd, base, incised Sabino signature, France, edge nicks, c1930, 9-1/2" h **$275**

Mold blown art glass, relief vine and

leaf dec, remnants of silvered metal on interior, etched mark on base, France, interior rim ground, c1930, 10-1/4" h **$240**

Molded opalescent glass, Art Deco stylized scene of centaur and panther hunting gazelles, foliage background with blue patina, unmarked, attributed to Sabino, 12-1/2" h **$635**

Wiener Werkstatte, bulbous, flaring neck, painted white and black geometric pattern, brown ground, stamped "WWW/ Made in Austria/ HB," 12-1/4" h, 5-1/2" d **$175**

Wall hanging, cotton velvet rose-colored curtain with multicolored crewel work design of stylized lanterns and trailing decoration, France, c1925, 63" w, 100" l **$1,470**

Wall sconces, pr, colorless etched shades with vertical bands of flowers supported on bronze Dore mounts, shades signed, by Heiter Vincent, France, c1925, 20" l **$750**

Wrist watch

Concord Watch Co., platinum, ivory tone dial with Arabic numeral indicators, 17 jewel Concord Watch Co. movement, bezel with bead-set single-cut diamond melee, 14k gold band with bead-set diamond accents, 6-1/4" l **$530**

D & L Co., rect ivory tone dial with Arabic numeral indicators, 17 jewel movement, bezel with bead-set single-cut diamonds and channel-set French-cut sapphires,

18k white gold case, adjustable platinum mesh band, case sgd **$1,410**

Lady's Baume & Mercier, center platinum rect dial framed by alternating rows of bead-set single-cut diamonds and channel-set rect sapphires, millegrain accents, 18k mesh band, 14k closure **$1,410**

ART NOUVEAU

History: Art Nouveau is the French term for the "new art," which had its beginning in the early 1890s and continued for the next 40 years. The flowing and sensuous female forms used in this period were popular in Europe and America. Among the most recognized artists of this period were Gallé, Lalique, and Tiffany.

The Art-Nouveau style can be identified by flowing, sensuous lines, florals, insects, and the feminine form. These designs were incorporated into almost everything produced during the period, from art glass to furniture, silver, and personal objects. Later wares demonstrate some of the characteristics of the evolving Art-Deco style.

Additional Listings: Furniture and jewelry. Also check glass, pottery, and metal categories.

Bud vase, glass, deep crimson, cut back to citron, 8-3/4" h **$100**

Art Nouveau Pate-de-verre tabletop light, fan shaped, incised with red and black flowers on purple ground, mounted on later wood-grain iron stand, stamped FRANCE/G. ARGY-ROUSSEAU, 7-3/4" x 7-1/2", **$9,988.**
Photo courtesy of David Rago Auctions, Inc.

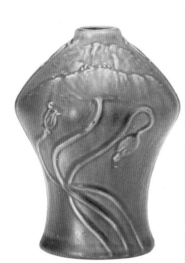

Art Nouveau vase, embossed with poppies under matte green vellum glaze, rim fleck, stamped mark and DENAURA 162 in ink, 6-1/2" x 5", $2,280.

Photo courtesy of David Rago Auctions, Inc.

Art Nouveau Amphora vase, floriform, polychrome and gilt water lily motif, four openwork handles, iridized finish, impressed under base crown, "AUSTRIA," "AMPHORA" and "8650/45," early 20th century, 19-1/2" h x 7" d, $550.

Photo courtesy of Green Valley Auctions.

Candlestick, patinated metal, figural, nymph standing on butterfly, holding flower form candle sconce, flower-form base, early 20th C, 11-3/8" h **$115**

Case, sterling silver, Tiffany & Co., rect, engraved on both sides, monogram "AJC," suspended from silver chain, brown leather interior with two pockets, orig silver retractable pencil, sgd **$215**

Center bowl, purple iridescent threaded glass within green oil spot ground, tooled copper rim, Art Nouveau shaped metalwork sides framing faces, unsgd, Austria, possibly Loetz, early 20th C, 12" d, 9" h **$650**

Clock

Desk, bronze, Chelsea Clock movement, gilt-metal and glass mount, red enamel dec devices, ftd base, circular face with Arabic chapters, imp "Chelsea Clock Co., Boston, USA, 155252" on inside clock works, worn patina, 3-3/4" w, 4-3/8" h **$460**

Figural, enameled cast white metal, relief of woman's head, flowing hair, leaves, thistles, Seth Thomas movement, circular dial with Roman numerals, minor wear, c1900, 12-1/2" h **$300**

Wall, carved walnut, two train movement, floral etched gilt metal dial sgd "Trilla, Barcelona," case topped by bust of young beauty on rocaille shell above iris flower, flanked by poppy roundels, case further carved with stylized florets, writing flower buds at corners, Spanish, early 20th C, 24-1/2" w, 10" d, 38" h **$490**

Desk lamp, two-light bypass fixture, base of colorless glass molded as ocean wave, top with gilt bronze figure of nubile mermaid, flanked by two lidded inkwells formed as fishing trap and whelk shell, flattened feet, early 20th C, 14-1/2" w base **$4,350**

Door pulls, bronze, whiplash handles, orig patina, Belgian, price for pr, 3" w, 15" h **$1,150**

Floor vase, glass, gray ground internally dec with streaked orange and mottled blue, blown-out into wrought iron armature with scrolled designs, stylized florals, Muller and Chapelle, glass damaged at base, c1910, 21" h **$1,100**

Garniture, centerpiece with bronze patina, female spelter figure of "L. Historie," flanked by spelter plinth with clock, enameled dial with painted Arabic numbers, sgd "L. Satre-A Pont. Aven," rect molded marble base with center bronze gilt neoclassical mounting, bronze gilded bun feet, pr of bronze patina spelter Louis XVI style urns, ribbons and swags centering figural medallion, sq marble base, bronze gilded feet **$950**

Inkwell, bronze, double inkwells flanking shaped pen tray, raised leaf and berry motif, sgd "C.H. Louchet," 7" x 13" **$460**

Lamp, table, opalescent shell held by arched foliage, supported by female figure in white metal, bronze patina, ruffled water-like base, early 20th C, imperfections, 18-1/4" h **$320**

Notebook, hammered sterling silver, Tiffany & Co., flying bird and branch dec, entwined starfish on reverse, contains celluloid cards with days of week, sgd, additional hallmark for Shiebler **$360**

Perfume bottle, paneled slender baluster form bottle painted with blue and gold flowers, gilt-metal hinged lid enclosing glass stopper, lid with short chain, 4-1/4" h **$520**

Picture frame

Sterling silver, oval, emb flowers and maiden, Unger Bros., Newark, 4-7/8" h **$175**

Wood, penwork and colored stained dec of stylized fruiting flowers, easel back, 8-1/2" w, 11-3/8" h **$100**

Pitcher, relief wheat dec, mottled blue, brown, and green, imp "Gres Mougin Nancy," by Joseph Victor Xavier, Nancy, France, c1900, 11-3/4" h **$865**

Plaque, 12-3/8" x 9-5/9", Summer Maiden, possibly Limoges, late 19th C, enameled rect plaque depicting profile bust of brunette among sunflowers, bordered by poppy stems, sgd "Dorval," gilt metal frame mounted with flowering branches, maroon velvet surround, 18-3/4" x 15-3/4" **$4,410**

Stove, coal, bronze and iron, shaped structure, pierced bronze plaque with "S"-scroll motifs centering pineapple, applied bronze medallions with female profiles, stamped "Deville Pailliette Forest, No. 17, Charlesville, Ardennes," c1900, 28-1/2" w, 22" d, 36" h **$375**

Art Nouveau, candelabra, bronze, four-branch, trumpet flowers on swirling stems attached to free-form organic Art Nouveau base, fine original patina, Jesse Preston, Chicago, 18" x 13", **$9,000.**
Photo courtesy of David Rago Auctions, Inc.

Art Nouveau, slipper chair, mother-of-pearl inlay, 32" x 28" x 20", **$300**.
Photo courtesy of David Rago Auctions, Inc.

Art Nouveau, vase, emerald glass, silver overlay with wild roses and vines, unmarked, 7-3/4" x 5-1/4", **$700.**
Photo courtesy of David Rago Auctions, Inc.

Art Nouveau vase, threaded, gold iridescence, green lappets, Victor Durand, minor losses to threading, polished pontil, 12", **$960.**
Photo courtesy of David Rago Auctions, Inc.

Art Nouveau, collector's cabinet, carved bellflower crown, carved figural panel, etched glass cabinets, mirrored backsplash and inlaid apron, some losses, 90" x 77" x 21-1/2", **$1,400.**
Photo courtesy of David Rago Auctions, Inc.

Arts & Crafts, lantern, hanging, Gustav Stickley, four sided, overhanging vented cap, pierced sides, hammered amber glass, die stamp compass mark, few scratches to original patina, 9" d x 4" h lantern, 21" l chain, **$3,400.**

Photo courtesy of David Rago Auctions, Inc.

Arts & Crafts, window, leaded polychrome slag glass, arched top, windmill on hill in front of large puffy clouds, unmarked, wooden frame, from a Michigan home, few minor breaks, 41" w, 78-1/2" h, **$4,025.**

Photo courtesy of David Rago Auctions, Inc.

Arts & Crafts, mantel, custom-designed, oak, carved tree of life flanked by stylized floral stained glass cupboard doors, original finish, unmarked, 59" w, 14" d, 82-1/2" h, **$4,100.**

Photo courtesy of David Rago Auctions, Inc.

Table, side, scallop-edge rect top inlaid with poppies in exotic woods, fluted legs, cabriole feet, lower shelf with variation of poppy motif, orig finish, inlaid "Galle" signature, 24" w, 17" d, 30" h, ... **$2,100**

Tea kettle, sterling silver, floral repoussé dec, curved handle, marked "J. E. Caldwell & Co., 925, Sterling, 1000, Philadelphia," 47 troy oz, 11" h **$550**

Tumbler, crystal tumbler, acid stamped "WMF," hallmarked silver handled holders, set of four, 4" h **$175**

Urn, conical pottery body, large white and red spring garden flowers, painted blue shiny glazed body, artist sgd, Continental, triple griffin bronze holder base, 17-1/2" h **$475**

Vase

Glass, Bohemian, irid, stylized floral metal frame, 7-1/2" h **$125**

Glass, Bohemian, gray ground internally dec with mottled light and dark blue, blown-out into wrought iron reeded armature, base inscribed "Daum Nancy" and "L Majorelle," c1920, 8 3/4" h **$1,610**

Glass, attributed to Pallme-Koenig, suppressed circular body, extended tapering neck, everted rim, pink, blue, green irid finish, embedded threaded dec, minute rim nicks, 17-1/2" h **$700**

Wine cabinet, carved walnut, panels elaborately carved with nymphs and grapevines, fitted with two pairs of doors and drawer, early 20th C, 46" w, 18" d, 68-1/2" h **$5,550**

ARTS & CRAFTS MOVEMENT

History: The Arts & Crafts Movement in American decorative arts took place between 1895 and 1920. Leading proponents of the movement were Elbert Hubbard and his Roycrofters, the brothers Stickley, Frank Lloyd Wright, Charles and Henry Greene, George Niedecken, and Lucia and Arthur Mathews.

The movement was marked by individualistic design (although the movement was national in scope) and re-emphasis on handcraftsmanship and appearance. A reform of industrial Society was part of the long-range goal. Most pieces of furniture favored a rectilinear approach and were made of oak.

The Arts & Crafts Movement embraced all aspects of the decorative arts, including metalwork, ceramics, embroidery, woodblock printing, and the crafting of jewelry.

Adviser: David Rago.

Additional Listings: Roycroft, Stickley, and art pottery categories.

Blanket chest, Greene & Greene, oak and yellow pine, unusually mortised corners fastened with sq dowel pegs, two lift-top doors, good orig finish, from Pratt residence, Ojai, California, 65" l, 23-3/4" w, 18-1/2" h **$22,500**

Bookcase, gallery top, adjustable shelves, small cabinet with leaded glass door, orig finish, Liberty & Co. tag, c1900, 37" w, 10-1/4" d, 47" h **$3,115**

Bookstand, oak, four open shelves with cutout sides and through tenons, 45-3/4" h **$500**

Box

Copper, hammered, riveted handles and strap hinges, Van Erp Workshop, orig patina, open box stamp, few scratches, 2-1/2" x 7" x 3-3/4" **$2,300**

Rect, hinged, enameled plaque of sailboat with marsh grasses and waterscape, Liberty Tudric, imp "Tudric," numbered "083," 6-1/8" l, 4-3/4" w **$940**

Silver and enamel rect, hinged lid cov with stylized enamel flowers and leaves in green, rose, blue, and white with applied wire and silver balls, raised artist's initials "EC," for Elizabeth Copeland, Boston, 1915-37, 3-7/8" w, 2-3/4" d, 2" h .. **$14,100**

Candlesticks, pr

Brass, two-branch, conical holders set in spirals, bright finish, orig bobeches, Omicron, incised "Jarvie," small scratches and dents, 10-3/4" h, 8" d **$6,500**

Cast copper, imp "1797" with double cross, no patina, unmarked, 11-3/4" h, 3-3/4" d **$195**

Chair, dining room, Limbert, side, single broad vertical back slat, tacked-on brown leather, orig finish with heavy overcoat, branded mark, 17" w, 37" h, price for set of four **$1,610**

Chair, side, L. & J. G. Stickley, Fayetteville, New York, oak, model no.

Arts & Crafts, coal bucket, Dirk Van Erp, hammered copper, riveted brass bands, flame shaped brass finial, original dark patina, stamped open box mark, normal wear around rim, 10" d, 17" h, **$4,600.**
Photo courtesy of David Rago Auctions, Inc.

Arts & Crafts, lamp, ceramic, bulbous base, four arms, turtle shade inset with several green slag glass panes, matte green glaze, unmarked, Chicago, restored cracks to arms, 16-1/2" x 11", **$3,335.**
Photo courtesy of David Rago Auctions, Inc.

Arts & Crafts, charger, Onodaga Metal Shops, hammered copper, embossed with leaves and pods, stamped "OMS 100," cleaned patina, 20" d, **$1,400.**
Photo courtesy of David Rago Auctions, Inc.

940, three vertical slats below crest rail, slip seat, double side stretcher, branded mark, price for set of six, c1916, 35-3/4" h **$2,235**

Chamberstick, hammered copper, cup-shaped bobeche, riveted angular handle, flaring base, stamped "OMS" for Onondaga Metal Shops, old cleaning and verdigris to patina, 6-1/4" h **$175**

Cigarette box, hammered copper, riveted trim, emb circular medallions, cedar lining, natural patina, unmarked, attributed to England, 2-1/4" x 5" x 4" **$260**

Clock, New Haven, Japanese-style, brass hands, keyed through-tenon sides, amber ripple glass, orig ebonized finish, paper label, 14" w, 4-3/4" d, 21-3/4" h **$490**

Coal scuttle, hammered copper, repoussé floral motif, riveted seams, rolled rim, new patina, some dents to body, some replaced rivets, 15" x 22" **$575**

Coffee and tea service, coffeepot, teapot, creamer, sugar, and tray, pewter, wicker handles, by Archibald Knox, stamped "Liberty/Tudric," price for five-pc set **$3,115**

Compote, pewter, cluthra green glass liner with opalescent and gold swirls, Liberty Tudric, Archibald Knox, 8" d, 6-3/4" h **$3,115**

Inkwell, faceted copper, curled, riveted feet, enameled green, red, and black, spade pattern, orig patina, unmarked Arts & Crafts Shop, couple of nicks to dec, 5-1/4" sq, 3-1/2" h **$250**

Lamp, ceiling, polished hammered brass, four arms, flame-shaped opalescent glass shade with green pulled feather pattern, English, 8-1/2" d, 11" h **$1,355**

Lamp, table, shade, eight panels of textured white glass with exterior green paint within bronzed metal strapwork frame, three sockets with acorn pulls on bulbous verdigris base, unsigned, paint wear, 21-1/2" h, 16-1/2" d **$1,060**

Lamp, student, Roycroft brass washed hammered copper base, Stickley Bros. copper and mica shades with silhouetted trees, orig finish, replaced mica, orb and cross mark, 16" h, 13" d **$1,840**

Library table
Double oval, flaring legs, cut-out stretchers, orig finish, branded Limbert mark, 1" cut off legs, 47-1/2" l, 36-1/4" w, 28-1/2" h **$7,475**
Two arched drawers, corbels, one shelf, orig finish, Lifetime Paine Furniture Co. metal tag, 52" l, 24" w, 29-1/2" h **$2,300**

Magazine stand
Gallery top, vertical slats all around, five tiers, fine orig dark finish, branded "CPM," 18-1/4" w, 14" d, 50-1/2" h **$2,415**
Three shelf, two short drawers, arched side rails over slatted sides, light finish, loose joints, 24" w, 12" d, 41-1/2" h **$630**

Music cabinet, attributed to G.M. Ellwood for J.S. Henry, English, mahogany, beveled top, paneled door inlaid with fruitwoods and mother-of-pearl, two drawers, brass hardware, good new finish, c1900, 21-1/2" w, 17" d, 42" h **$2,870**

Arts & Crafts, bookends, pr, embossed tall ships on waves, covered in fine curdled matte blue-green glaze, unmarked, glaze chip to one corner, 6" x 5-3/4" x 3-1/4", **$325.**
Photo courtesy of David Rago Auctions, Inc.

Arts & Crafts, candlestick, copper, tulip-shaped, enameled decorated in stylized floral pattern, The Arts Crafts Shop, Buffalo, New York, 8-1/3" x 5-1/4", **$1,000.**
Photo courtesy of David Rago Auctions, Inc.

Nut set, hammered copper, 8-1/2" d master bowl, six 3" d serving bowls, Benedict, some wear to patina, unmarked.....................**$290**

Occasional table, circular top over flaring legs joined by cut-out stretchers, orig finish, branded Limbert mark, wear and stains to top, 30" d, 29-1/2" h **$2,070**

Pagoda table, Limbert, corbels under sq top, flaring sides, arched apron, lower shelf, cut-out base, orig finish, heavy overcoat, paper label under top, 34" sq, 30-1/2" h **$13,800**

Picture frame, hammered sterling silver, emb daisies, English hallmarks, 6" w, 9" h.....................**$750**

Pillow, embroidered stylized orange and green poppies, beige linen ground, 16" x 25".....................**$400**

Plant stand, Limbert, quarter-round corbels under sq top, flaring sides, ovoid cut-outs, lower shelf, plank base, fine orig factory finish, factory edge repair to top, no visible mark, 20" sq, 29-1/2" h **$6,900**

Room divider, oak, grid-like top, three-panel, each panel cut-out with fern design, replaced linen panels, orig finish, unmarked, some minor chipping to edges, 68" h **$1,200**

Server, L. & J.G. Stickley, Fayetteville, New York, oak, rect top over single drawer, lower median shelf, branded mark, c1916, 32" w, 16" d, 33" h **$1,410**

Sideboard, L. & J.G. Stickley, Fayetteville, New York, oak, plate rail on rect top, three central drawers flanked by two cabinet doors, over single long drawer, branded mark, c1916, 47" w, 19-3/4" d, 44" h **$5,300**

String holder, sterling on bronze, bell shape, applied silver leaves and vines, orig patina, stamped "HAMS," Heintz, 3-3/4" d, 3-1/2" h **$535**

Tablecloth, circular, linen, embroidered red poppies, green leaves, 39" d.....................**$860**

Table, dining

Limbert, circular, extension, four-sided pedestal base, orig finish with heavy overcoat, 54" d, 27-1/4" h **$2,300**

Unknown maker, California, oak, rect board on board top, lower median shelf with through tenons, cutout

sides, shoe foot base, deep brown restored finish, c1912, 83-1/2" w, 35-1/4" d, 29" h.....................**$3,200**

Tabouret, Limbert, sq top, box construction, sq cut-outs, top refinished, orig finish on base, branded mark, 16-1/2" sq, 18" h **$2,615**

Trunk, copper and iron, strapwork and pyramidal tack mounts, black paint, hinged slant lid revealing rect box, 30-1/2" l, 16-1/2" d, 17-1/2" h.....**$200**

Vase, bulbous, curtained copper, dimpled and folded sides covered in rare orig red finish, Dirk Van Erp, windmill/ San Francisco mark with partial D'Arcy Gaw visible, 5" h, 6" d **$2,760**

Wall sconces, pr, 6" d shade, brass, emb stylized poppies, leaded glass period shades, English, 14-1/2" h **$2,530**

AUTOGRAPHS

History: Autographs appear on a wide variety of formats—letters, documents, photographs, books, cards, etc. Most collectors focus on a particular person, country, or category, e.g., signers of the Declaration of Independence.

Abbreviations: The following are used to describe autograph materials.

ADS	Autograph Document Signed
ALS	Autograph Letter Signed
AQS	Autograph Quotation Signed
CS	Card Signed
DS	Document Signed
FDC	First Day Cover
LS	Letter Signed
PS	Photograph Signed
TLS	Typed Letter Signed

Colonial America

Hancock, John, endorsement sgd, as Governor, approving sentences levied by garrison court martial against several convicts held on Castle Island, Boston, three pgs, folds, minor browning, Aug. 3, 1790

.....................**$3,910**

Jefferson, Thomas, partially printed vellum DS, sgd as president, granting 327 acres on Northwest Territory to Martha Walker, countersigned by Secretary of State James Madison, small hand colored manuscript map on verso, showing location of plot near junction of Scioto and Whetstone rivers, Washington, minor fading, Feb. 15, 1802, 10" x 12" **$4,370**

Nicolls, Richard, DS, as British colonial governor, confirming Peter Stuyvesant's land grant to Egbert van Borsum, for first Brooklyn ferry house, New York, March 12, 1666, 1-1/2 pgs, separated at folds, some loss, wax seal intact.....................**$2,990**

Foreign

Bonaparte, Napoleon, LS, sgd "Buonparte," to President of Military Council, in French, half pg, small 8vo sheet, General in Chief of the Army of the Interior stationery, c1794 ....**$1,610**

Disraeli, Benjamin, envelope, sgd "Disraeli," addressed to Lady Corneila Guest, matted and framed, 3" x 4" **$80**

Eiffel, Gustave, TLS, Paris, April 19, 1889, sgd "G. Eissel" to E. Hippeau, in French, business stationery, folds, one page, single 8" x 10" sheet.....................**$375**

Peron, Eva, PS, Buenos Aires, Oct. 10, 1950, bust portrait, sgd on mount beneath calligraphic inscription, signature light, framed, 9" x 6-1/2" photo on 13-1/2" x 9-1/2" mount.....................**$620**

General

Einstein, Albert, ALS, to his first wife Mileva, in German, regarding increase in monthly payments for son Tetel, praising his son Albert, acknowledging death of Dr. Zuercher, one page, Dec. 21, 1937 ....**$5,060**

Ford, Henry and Edsel, TLS, congratulating Albert W. Howard as a new dealer, Dearborn, Ford Motor Co. stationery, morocco folder with photograph, Aug. 1, 1939 ....**$1,725**

Freud, Sigmund, newspaper photo sgd, "Sigm. Freud," framed, certificate of authenticity by Charles Hamilton, wax seal on verso of frame, yellowed, 1932, 5-1/2" x 4" **$1,955**

Joffre, Joseph, general, framed page, program for Washington Birth-

day Dinner, American Club, Paris, Feb 22, 1926, 5" x 3-1/4", framed with colored print of Joffre, 14" x 8"
.... **$50**

Lindbergh, Charles A., PS, inscribed, large close-up portrait in aviator's cap, Acme Newspictures, 13-1/2" x 19-1/2"
.... **$1,840**

Ruth, Babe
Baseball, graded C.9-9.5 .... **$17,270**
Photo of Babe Ruth with golfer Rudy Jugan, sgd by Ruth **$1,430**

Tiffany, Charles Louis, ALS, sgd "C. L. Tiffany" to George Wilson, NY Chamber of Commerce, sending check for dinner honoring Seth Low, one pg, New York, Oct. 5, 1867
.... **$415**

Vanderbilt, William H., LS, to members of Special Committee of NY Chamber of Commerce, regarding railroad rate legislation, six pgs, New York Central & Hudson River Railroad Co. stationery, New York, Sept. 18, 1879, pin holes, inked stamp on first page **$2,760**

Wright, Orville and Wilbur, check sgd by both, payable to B.F. Goodrich Co., Winters National Bank, endorsement stamps on verso, cancellation perforation just above Orville's signature, Dayton, Jan. 26, 1911, 3" x 8-1/4"
.... **$4,830**

Literature

Aldrich, Thomas Bailey, poem sgd, titled "Three Flowers," inscribed to Bayard Taylor, 14 lines, one pg, 1876
.... **$260**

Browning Robert, ALS, granting permission to reprint two poems in volume edited by H.W. Dulcken, London, April 8, 1867 .... **$865**

Dickens, Charles, ALS, to J.P. Harley, inviting him for a visit, Twickenham Park, Thursday night, two pgs, toned, soiled, tape repairs, c1838
.... **$1,035**

Frost, Robert, book, *The Best Poems of 1922,* sgd and inscribed by Frost to Carl Bernheimer above poem, The Witch of Coos, page 16, also sgd by Gwendolen Haste on page 57, and Leonora Speyer, page 58, custom slipcase, London, 1923
.... **$690**

Hawthorne, Nathaniel, clipped signature, mounted to another sheet, 1" x 3-3/4" **$290**

Hemingway, Ernest, ALS, sgd "Papa," to Leonard Lyons, graphic

letter describing injuries from plane crash and brush fire while on safari in Africa, Venice, two pgs, April 8, 1954
.... **$4,370**

Shaw, George Bernard, ALS, to Bruno E Kohn, declining request, The Hydro Hotel stationery, Torquay, one pg, Oct. 10, 1915 .... **$230**

Stowe, Harriet Beecher, quotation sgd "I know that my redeemer liveth," March 13, 1889, trimmed, 4" x 5"
.... **$230**

Military

Beauregard, Pierre G. T., postcard sgd, thanking General for copies of order, congratulating him, New Orleans, repaired tear, staining on verso from prior mounting, Oct. 27, 1882 .... **$375**

Custer, George Armstrong, ALS, sgd "Armstrong," to his friend John Bulkley, regretting he declined position on Custer's staff, three pgs, orig envelope, Headquarters, 2nd Brigade, 3rd Div Cap Corp A.P., Summer, two minor tape repairs at folds, 1863
.... **$7,475**

Mussolini, Benito, PS, close-up bust portrait, looking downwards, sgd on sheet below image, red wax seal affixed to lower left corner, minor creases in image, emb stamp on lower right corner of image, framed, 11" x 7-1/2" **$520**

Pershing, John J., books, *My Experiences in the World War,* two volumes, publisher's cloth, author's autograph edition, one of 2,100 numbered copies, New York, 1931 .... **$290**

Sherman, William T, PS, sgd "W. T. Sherman, General, New York, Feb. 8, 1889," standing 3/4 portrait, in uniform, image size, matted, framed, 11-1/2" x 7" **$2,300**

Thomas, Lorenzo, PS, "Brig Genl I. Thomas, Adj. Genl U.S.A.," bust portrait carte-de-visite by Frederick Gutekunst, orig photographer's mount, sgd on recto at bottom of image, bit yellowed and soiled, revenue stamp affixed on verso **$260**

Music

Bernstein, Leonard, manuscript sgd, high school exam essay on religion and society, 3-1/2 pgs, April, 1935 .... **$520**

Puccini, Giacomo, clipped signature, framed, March 1916, 1-1/2" x 6-1/2" **$230**

Posters, framed under glass: The Monkees, autographed by Davie Jones, Mickey Dolenz, Peter Tork and Michael Nesmith, 14-1/2" x 18-1/2", **$125***; Batman movie poster, autographed by Adam West, Burt Ward, Lee Merriweather and Frank Gorshin, 20" x 24",* **$125.**
Photo courtesy of Joy Luke Auctions.

Lincoln, Abraham, sgd document, August 10, 1861, Corps of Engineers commission for William C. Paine, countersigned Simon Cameron, framed, minor smudging, 13-1/2" x 17", **$4,405.**
Photo courtesy of Skinner, Inc.

Hawthorne, Nathaniel, sgd document, December 12, 1853, declaration of material from vessel Arctic, as Customs Inspector, Port of Liverpool, folds, minor tearing, **$705.**
Photo courtesy of Skinner, Inc.

Washington, George, sgd, Philadelphia, May 30th, 1775, letter of recommendation for young man, to Burwek Basset, as Delegate to Continental Congress, holograph address leaf, wax seal, tears to address leaf, overlaid with japan, former fold separations, **$10,575.**
Photo courtesy of Skinner, Inc.

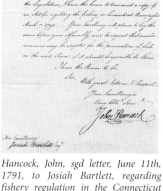

Hancock, John, sgd letter, June 11th, 1791, to Josiah Bartlett, regarding fishery regulation in the Connecticut River, as Governor of Massachusetts, very good, light lower edge toning, **$10,575.**
Photo courtesy of Skinner, Inc.

Hamilton, Alexander, sgd letter, Philadelphia, July 27, 1791, to Benjamin Lincoln regarding excursion, as Secretary of the Treasury, folds browning, minor losses, **$4,995.**
Photo courtesy of Skinner, Inc.

Stravinsky, Igor, musical quotation, sgd and inscribed, 20 note tone row from The Flood, Hotel Pierre stationery, New York, framed, May 4, 1962, 7-1/4" x 10-1/4" **$1,035**

Presidents

Cleveland, Grover, ALS, to William Steinway, thanking him for grand piano given as a wedding present, three pgs, Executive Mansion stationery, orig envelope, Washington, Aug. 14, 1886 ....**$490**

Eisenhower, Dwight D., typed quotation sgd, Presidential oath of office, Washington, framed, Jan. 20, 1953, 7" x 5-1/4"...**$815**

Grant, Ulysses, partly printed document, four language ship's papers to Captain West Mitchell for whaling voyage of the bark Mount Wollaston, countersigned by Secretary of State Hamilton Fish, Washington, one pg, folio, July 8, 1872 ....**$1,495**

Hayes, Rutherford B., Remarks of President Hayes, at Celebration of General Garfield's Election, inscribed and sgd "With compliments R. B. Hayes," orig Executive Mansion envelope addressed in Hayes' hand to Hon. George K. Forster, postmarked Washington, 2-1/2 pgs, Nov. 17, 1880 ...**$750**

Lincoln, Abraham, partially printed vellum DS, appointing Rowland C. Kellogg a Commissary with rank of Captain, countersigned by Edwin Stanton, Washington, faded, creased, June 8, 1864, 17" x 14-1/2"........**$4,140**

Nixon, Ford, Carter, Reagan, and Bush, PS, group portrait standing outside behind podium at dedication of Reagan Library, sgd in varying inks below image, Simi Valley, 1991, 7-3/4" x 10-3/4" **$3,450**

Roosevelt, Theodore, TLS, to Sereno E. Pratt, editor of Wall Street Journal, White House stationery, Washington, thanking him for article, 2-1/4 pgs, March 3, 1906 ....**$21,850**

Wilson, Woodrow, ALS, to W.A. Stein, request for autograph, Princeton, one pg, Feb. 4, 1901 ....**$320**

Show business

Barrymore, John, scrapbook assembled by Barrymore for his daughter, sgd and inscribed to her on front pastedown, hundreds of newspaper and magazine clippings relating to his performance in Hamlet at the Haymarket Theatre, other material, oblong folio, orig morocco, London, some clippings loose, 1925 .....**$1,035**

Holiday, Billie, PS, inscribed "To Norman Stay Happy," souvenir group photo taken in Chicago, showing "Lady Day" with five other people, sgd on mat above image, presentation folder of Garrick Stage Bar, also inscribed by another, inscriptions in pencil, 5" x 7" **$980**

Pavlova, Anna, PS, sgd and inscribed, silver print image by C Mishkin, en pointe, inscribed in blue ink on image, mounted in paper folder, Jan 1907, 7-1/2" x 5-1/2" **$635**

Statesmen

Churchill, Winston, TLS, discussing upcoming General Election, one pg, 28 Hyde Park Gate stationery, London, hole punched in upper left margin, minor toning, Jan. 22, 1950, ...**$2,760**

Mifflin, Thomas, ADS, March 8, 1756, land grant to James Strawbridge for 1098 acre parcel of land in Lycoming County, PA, sgd as Governor of PA, 11-1/2" x 20-1/2"....................**$60**

Roosevelt, Franklin D., TLS, sgd as Acting Secretary of the Navy, on Dept. of Navy letterhead, concerning investigation into collision between *USS Lake Tahoe* and scow *W.T.C. #35,* March 27, 1919, 10-1/2" x 8" **$500**

AUTOMOBILIA

History: Automobilia is a wide-ranging category. It includes just about anything that represents a vehicle, from cookie jars to toys. Car parts are not usually considered automobilia, although there are a few exceptions, like the Lalique radiator ornaments. Most sought after are automobile advertising, especially signs and dealer promotional models. The number of items related to the automobile is endless. Even collectors who do not own an antique car are interested in automobile, bus, truck, and motorcycle advertising memorabilia. Many people collect only items from a certain marque, like Hupmobiles or Mustangs, while others may collect all advertising, like matchbooks or color brochures showing the new models for a certain year. Most material changes hands at automobile swap meets, and specialty auctions held throughout the year. Notably "hot" items on the market are service station and trucking company hat badges.

Additional Resources:

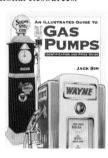

An Illustrated Guide to Gas Pumps, by Jack Sim, Krause Publications, Iola, WI.

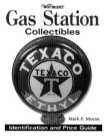

Warman's Gas Station Collectibles Identification and Price Guide, by Mark F. Moran, Krause Publications, Iola, WI.

Advertising button

Auto dealership, Butzer Bros, purple on white, early touring car, early 1900s **$25**

Buick Fireball 8, graphic red, white, and blue design, for introduction of high-power engine, 1940s **$45**

Fisk Tires, black, white, and yellow, symbolic youngster ready for bed holding candle and automobile tire, slogan "Time to Re-tire, Get a Fisk," 1930s **$20**

Hyvis Motor Oil, black on white, center red figure for "Automobile Con-

test" sponsored by Kapisco Oil Co., Shakopee, Minn., 1930s **$12**

Pyro-Action Spark Plugs, multicolored image of warrior in armor, orange rim inscribed "Crusade Against Spark Plug Paralysis-Sponsored by Robert Bosch," 1930s .. **$10**

Advertising tab, Ford Motors Merry Christmas, diecut thin metal tab, two gold lusters, red and green image of Santa in sleigh, red lettering, 1950s, 1-1/4" x 2-1/2" **$50**

Air station, Gilbarco, hose and "Air" sign **$1,100**

Badge, attendant's uniform type

Texaco, inlaid cloisonné enamel, 1-3/4" x 2-1/4" **$425**

Tydol Veedol Gasoline Motor Oil Serviceman, inlaid cloisonné enamel, orange and black on silver, 2-7/8" x 2-1/4" **$675**

Calendar, Harley-Davidson, South Dakota dealer, tin litho, detailed image of 1930s biker on Harley, full 1940 calendar pad, 3" x 5-3/4", C.8 ...... **$525**

Catalog

Buick Motor Co., Flint, Michigan, 16 pgs, illus of models, 1916, 5-3/4" x 7-1/2" **$100**

Curtis Aerocar Co., Inc., Coral Gables, Florida, 8 pgs, 1938, 7-1/4" x 11-3/4" **$40**

Compression tester, Hasting's Piston Ring advertising on dial, orig metal storage box **$45**

Dealership sign, Dodge Plymouth, enameled porcelain, neon **$4,000**

Display cabinet

Auto Lite Spark Plug, painted metal cabinet, glass front, 18-1/2" h, 13" w **$125**

Schrader tire gauge cabinet, figural tire gauge, opens to reveal parts **$350**

Gas pump globe

Atlantic, milk glass **$1,045**

Boron Supreme, plastic **$660**

British Shell, cased glass **$3,410**

White Eagle, eagle-shaped milk glass **$2,750**

Gas pump nozzle, brass **$110**

Island cabinet, Mobil, gargoyle type, orig porcelain signs, replaced globe, restored, 1920s **$1,045**

Key chain fob

Ford Tractors, dark gold plastic, showing key mechanism for "New Ford Select-O-Speed Tractors," reverse with "Greatest tractor advantage since hydraulics" and Ford logo, late 1940s **$12**

Crown Gasoline (Kentucky) globe, good condition, paint loss at edges of lenses, 16-1/2" lenses, **$700.**

Mobilgas (East Coast) pledge shield, excellent condition, 7-1/2" by 8", **$650.**

Bisonoil Motor Oil, quart tin can, near mint, **$300.**

R. Lalique hood ornament, "Perche," clear and frosted, gray patina, molded and stenciled R. LALIQUE, **$1,500.**
Photo courtesy of David Rago Auctions, Inc.

R. Lalique hood ornament, "Pintade," clear and frosted, wheel cut R. LALIQUE FRANCE, c1929, 5-7/8", **$6,600.**
Photo courtesy of David Rago Auctions, Inc.

R. Lalique hood ornament, "Tete de Coq," clear and frosted, Lucite stand, molded LALIQUE FRANCE, c1928, 7", **$2,400.**
Photo courtesy of David Rago Auctions, Inc.

R. Lalique hood ornament, "Tete D'Epervier," opalescent, molded LALIQUE FRANCE, c1928, 2 1/2", **$3,600.**
Photo courtesy of David Rago Auctions, Inc.

Shell Oil, silvered metal emblem, painted on reverse with instructions for return if lost, c1930 ..... **$10**

Key ring holder, silvered metal, double ring holder, centered by applied miniature metal 7/8" h figure of smiling and saluting Esso Happy Oil Drop figure finished in porcelain white enamel, copper luster face, Esso logo on chest in red on silver, blue oval logo, 1960s, 3-1/2" h **$25**

Lapel stud, brass, spoked automobile wheel, center engraved "327," tiny inscription on tire wall "Albany Automobile Show, Feb. 15-22," c1922 .. **$15**

Lube tank, double pump, oval, Texaco decals, mounted on wheels, restored, 43" x 17" x 29" h **$4,510**

Oil can

Hudson Motor Oil, Kansas City, quart, crimped seal, images of oil tanker, airplanes, and race cars, unopened, 5-1/2" x 4", C.8.5 ..... **$275**

Sohio Hand Separator Oil, quart, full **$220**

Oil carrier, wire

Esso, eight orig tall quart bottles with labels **$2,100**

Texaco, eight matching quart bottles, labels, restored spouts, restored carrier **$965**

Oil carrier, wood, Casto Penn Motor Oil, 12 matching tall quart bottles, 16" x 12" x 16" **$3,740**

Paperweight, Atlantic Richfield, trapezoid, clear Lucite, small dark amber vial holding liquid "Crude Oil Prudhoe Bay-North Slope, Alaska," and "Atlantic Richfield Co." with logo in internal blue lettering, 3" x 3" **$15**

Pencil clip, Studebaker, diecut and rolled dark thin brass with name diagonally across image of spoked automobile wheel, early 1900s **$35**

Pocket mirror

Celluloid, Oak Motoring Suits, man wearing suit standing in front of early car, 2-3/4" x 1-3/4" **$240**

Shaded black and white photo, standing man, trees and railing in background, hand on hood of his Ford, license plate "NY 31," 2-1/4" d **$35**

Pump

American Pump Co., octagon body, restored 10-gallon visible pump **$2,640**

Fry Mae West, 10-gallon visible pump, Shell decals, replaced globe, restored **$3,500**

Service Station Equipment Corp., Atlantic Richfield decals, twin 10 gallon visible tubes, restored, reproduced globes **$10,100**

R. Lalique hood ornament, frog, "Grenouille," clear and frosted, molded LALIQUE, engraved R. Lalique France, c1928, 2-1/2", **$13,200.**
Photo courtesy of David Rago Auctions, Inc.

Banjo barometer, Regency, mahogany, early 19th century, 39" h, **$645.**
Photo courtesy of Pook & Pook, Inc.

Banjo barometer, line inlaid mahogany, English, 19th century, 36-3/4" h x 10" w, **$450.**
Photo courtesy of Wiederseim Associates, Inc.

BAROMETERS

History: A barometer is an instrument that measures atmospheric pressure, which, in turn, aids weather forecasting. Low pressure indicates the coming of rain, snow, or storm; high pressure signifies fair weather.

Most barometers use an evacuated and graduated glass tube that contains a column of mercury. These are classified by the shape of the case. An aneroid barometer has no liquid and works by a needle connected to the top of a metal box in which a partial vacuum is maintained. The movement of the top moves the needle.

Reproduction Alert. Modern reproductions abound, made by diverse groups ranging from craft revivalists to foreign manufacturers.

Banjo, mahogany, dial engraved "P. Nossi & Co. Boston," broken pediment cresting above shaped case with thermometer, circular barometer dial, inlaid patera, 38-3/4" h **$690**

Banjo, shell inlaid, painted black, Kirner Bros., Oxford, Victorian, mid-19th C, 39-3/4" h **$460**

Barometer and wall clock, G. V. Mooney, NY, walnut, shaped backboard, molded wood and brass bezel framing paper dial and brass lever movement, printed paper dial "G.V. Mooney's Barometer Patented May 30th 1865— Sold by Arnaboldi & Co. 53 Fulton St. New York," mercury tube extending to the base with molded wooden boss, 50" h **$1,880**

Louis XV-style, gray painted, parcel gilt, case topped by urn flanked by husk swag, floral painted thermometer, barometer dial mkd "Bourgeois, Paris," late 19th C, 42-1/2" h.................. **$940**

Stick, sgd E. Kendall, N. Lebanon, mahogany, etched steel face, mirrored well cov, 34" l **$550**

Wheel, Aneroid, Swedish, part ebonized, arch top with acorn finials, painted milk glass thermometer between turned uprights, open dial with printed enamel bezel signed "C.L. Malmsjo, Guteborg," within turned frame, acorn pendant finial, late 19th C, 21-1/2" l **$300**

Wheel, carved oak, foliage and C-scrolls, English, late 19th C, 33" d **$230**

Wheel, English, Georgian, mahogany, dial signed "Dolland, London," rounded pediment over thermometer, urn inlaid central roundel, line inlay throughout, early 19th C, 36-1/2" l **$1,840**

Wheel, English, mahogany, broken pediment centered by finial, round hygrometer dial over vertical thermometer, convex mirror over barometer dial, ending in dial for level, early 20th C, 39" l **$815**

Wheel, Georgian, mahogany, dial sgd "Dolland, London," rounded pediment over thermometer, urn inlaid central roundel line inlay throughout, early 19th C, 26-1/2" h **$1,840**

Wheel, rosewood veneer, onion top cornice with hygrometer dial over thermometer over convex mirror, large barometric dial, small level at base, English, mid-19th C, 40" l........... **$350**

Wheel, rosewood case with thermometer over silvered barometer dial marked for J. Kienzly, Exeter, inlaid throughout with mother-of-pearl, abalone, and brass flowering vines, butterflies, and birds, Victorian, Anglo-Indian, late 19th C, 42-3/8" l **$1,410**

Wheel, Scottish, mahogany, swan's neck cresting over later German hygrometer, vertical thermometer, over painted roundel, signature roundel centered by level and sgd "F. Uago, Glasgow," mid-19th C, 38" l **$865**

BASKETS

History: Baskets were invented when man first required containers to gather, store, and transport goods. Today's collectors, influenced by the country look, focus on baskets made of splint, rye straw, or willow. Emphasis is placed on handmade examples. Nails or staples, wide splints that are thin and evenly cut, or a wire bail handle denote factory construction, which can date back to the mid-19th century. Decorated painted or woven baskets rarely are handmade, unless they are American Indian in origin.

Baskets are collected by (a) type— berry, egg, or field; (b) region—Nantucket or Shaker; and (c) composition—splint, rye, or willow.

Half buttocks, woven splint, thick brown paint, bentwood handle, 8" w, 5" h...**$200**

Miniature

Bushel, painted cream-white over red, America, 19th C, 5-3/4" d, 3-1/4" h **$760**

Woven splint, single handle, painted blue, 1-3/4" d, 2" h.....................**$550**

Nantucket Light Ship, America

Round, carved wooden bail handle, turned wood bottom with incised line dec, America, late 19th/early 20th C, 8-1/8" h **$650**

Round, carved wooden bail handle, turned wood bottom with incised line dec, inscribed "Eldridge" on base, America, losses, late 19th/early 20th C, 6-5/8" h **$700**

Round, carved wooden swing handle, turned wooden bottom with incised lines, America, minor wear, 20th C, 5-1/4" h **$675**

Round, carved wooden swing handle, turned wooden bottom with incised lines, stamped "Nantucket Mass.," paper label "Boyer 4 Federal Street Nantucket MA," minor wear, America, 20th C, 3-5/8" h **$900**

Native American

Covered, woven splint, attributed to New England Algonkian or Iroquois, round domed lid, round to square form, red and green flowering vine motif, side handles, minor wear, fading, early 19th C, 15-1/2" h **$2,000**

Splint, Schaticoke Tribe, CT, rect, two carved handles, decorative bands, polychrome blue, orange, green, and brown splints, 19th C, 13" l, 10-1/4" w, 7" h **$1,725**

Oak

Peach basket shape, initials "CMT," 11-1/2" h, 14" d top **$235**

Sewing, rect, compartments woven into one end, minor cracking, 21" l, 12" d, 6" h.................................**$250**

Rye straw

Bee skep, ovoid, wood base, 15" h, 15" d **$3,960**

Bulbous, flared rim, 11-1/2" h, 11-1/2" d **$990**

Child's, sewing, attached pin cushion, 1-1/2" h, 4-1/4" d.....................**$250**

Cov, bread rising, round, tapered sides, domed lid, wooden finial, two woven handles, attributed to Pennsylvania maker, 8-1/2" h, 17" d **$3,410**

Cov, hamper style, bulbous, 22" h, 16" d **$1,760**

Cov, hamper style, bulbous, 20" h, 22" d **$2,750**

Cov, hamper, bulbous, fitted lid and base, 12" h, 16-1/2" d **$1,155**

Cov, hamper style, oval, 15-1/2" h, 22" l, 17" w **$1,265**

Cov, oval, carved bentwood handles, attributed to Ephrata, PA, maker, 14-1/4" h, 32-1/2" l, 25" w **$3,850**

Cov, painted salmon dec, wooden knob finial, attributed to unknown maker, Hanover, York County, PA, 12" h, 18" d.......................**$2,970**

Cov, round, bread-rising, tapered sides, wooden finial, 5-1/4" h, 13" d **$3,850**

Hamper style, oval, hidden loss to inner rim, cov, 20" h, 17" d **$770**

Market, oval, pinned bentwood handle, 11-1/4" h, 17" l, 10-1/2" w **$1,980**

Miniature, cov, openwork, woven hinges and latch, 3" h, 4-1/2" d **$1,700**

Miniature, oval, bend handle, wooden base, straw openwork weave, Easter egg dated 1925, 3-1/2" h, 3-5/8" l, 2-1/2" w **$385**

Oval, cov, straight sides, 7" h, 12" l, 10-1/2" w **$1,320**

Oval, fruit, two woven handles, looped openwork splint trim, 4-1/2" h, 10" l, 8-3/4" w **$500**

Oval, market, attached bentwood handle, 9" h, 12" l, 8-1/2" w ..**$2,750**

Oval, openwork, attributed to unknown maker, Hanover, York County, PA, 4" h, 12-1/2" l, 7-5/8" w **$1,155**

Oval, openwork, two woven handles, attributed to unknown maker, Hanover, York County, PA, 6" h, 13" l, 8" w **$1,045**

Oval, table, painted green, woven handle, 4-5/8" h, 11-1/2" l, 7-3/4" w **$1,320**

Oval, table, tapered sides, two handles, 4" h, 17-1/2" l, 13-1/4" w **$330**

Round, drying, 3" h, 19-1/2" d **$95**

Round, field, bentwood handles, cross supports in base, 10-1/2" h, 23" d **$825**

Round, field, tapered sides, attached bentwood handle, 13-1/2" h, 16-1/2" d **$500**

Round, field, tapered sides, two woven handles, 8-1/2" h, 18" d **$880**

Round, openwork rim, color banding, attributed to Andrew Sheely, Hanover, York County, PA, 4" h, 9-1/4" d **$990**

Round, openwork, Pennsylvania maker, 4-1/2" h, 11" d **$770**

Round, openwork, table, 3-1/4" h, 11-1/4" d **$125**

Round, tapered sides, openwork rim, 2" h, 6-1/4" d.........................**$550**

Round, tapered sides, two attached bentwood handles, 8" h, 14-1/2" d **$1,760**

Round triangular openwork rim, single coil base, attributed to Cumberland County, PA, 3" h, 10-1/2" d **$660**

Serving tray, round, two woven handles, 19-1/2" d....................**$880**

Sewing, applied section for pin cushion, flared base rim, attributed to Hanover, York County, Pennsylvania maker, 7" h, 13" l, 7-3/4" w................................**$10,725**

Tapered, triple coil base, 10" h, 16" d **$880**

Splint

Oak, D-shape, hanger, rounded head nails, wooden base, 8" h, 5" l, 3-5/8" w.....................................**$470**

Oak, rect, market, tapered sides, bentwood handle, pinewood base, round head nails, attributed to Grantville, Dauphin County, PA, maker, 13" h, 16-1/4" l, 10-1/4" h **$990**

Oak, round, tapered sides, pine base, red stained rim and side banding, attributed to maker in Grantville, Dauphin County, PA, 4" h, 8" d **$180**

Oval, market, bentwood handle, pine wood base, attributed to Grantville, Dauphin County, PA, maker, 13-1/2" h, 14" l, 11-1/2" w **$1,210**

Wall pocket, bentwood handle, painted brown, 9-1/2" h, 6-3/4" l, 4" h **$250**

Wooden

Oval, painted green, wood slat and band construction, round head nails, metal support to bentwood handle, 15" h, 15" l, 11-1/2" w **$1,320**

Stave construction, vertical wood staves taper down at base, fixed with wire, dark orig finish over varnish, 13" d, 17" h **$250**

Round basket, cane and oak splint, raised interior, banded top and base, bentwood handle, 10" d, 12" h, **$220.**
Photo courtesy of Alderfer Auction Co.

Kettle basket, splint oak, fixed handle, 12" d, 12" h, **$150.**
Photo courtesy of Alderfer Auction Co.

Elliptical basket, two rows of rose-colored weave, flat wooden base, two small handles, 1950s, **$15.**

Round basket, white oak splints, carved notched handle, slight kick-up base, dry natural surface, found in Pendleton County West Virginia, minor breaks, late 19th/early 20th century, 11-1/2" h, 11" d, **$110.**
Photo courtesy of Green Valley Auctions.

Round basket, high handle, brown stained finish, damage to rim, dry condition, **$20.**

Round basket, white oak splints, dry worn red paint, mid-Atlantic, carved notched handle, slight kick-up base, some breaks and losses, late 19th/early 20th century, 11-1/2" h, 12-1/2" d, **$220.**
Photo courtesy of Green Valley Auctions.

Kidney basket, white oak splints, double rim, excellent dry natural surface, Shenandoah Co., VA, early 20th century, 9-1/2" h, 9" x 9-1/2" rim, **$195.**
Photo courtesy of Green Valley Auctions.

Key basket, leather, oval, tooled ext dec, shaped rim, orig rounded handle, with finger-like terminals overlayed and stitched to side exteriors, leather bottom, handle reattached, mid-19th century, 7" h x 8-1/4" l, **$4,125.**
Photo courtesy of Green Valley Auctions.

Kidney basket, white oak splints, mid-Atlantic, double rim, orig dry natural surface, early 20th century, 12" h, 12-3/4" x 13- 1/2", **$138.**
Photo courtesy of Green Valley Auctions.

BEATRIX POTTER COLLECTIBLES

History: Helen Beatrix Potter was born in 1864 in London. Her favorite pets were a mouse, rabbit, and a hedgehog. As a child, she loved to sketch these creatures and by 1893, she had created the characters of Flopsy, Mopsy, Cottontail, and Peter Rabbit. By December of 1901, Beatrix published 250 copies of her first book, *The Tale of Peter Rabbit*, which included 41 black and white illustrations. She gave many of these books to friends and family as gifts, but did sell some for a halfpenny each. In 1902, Frederick Warne & Co. published the first trade edition of this book and it became an instant bestseller. Beatrix went on to write 23 more tales and each is still in print today and they have been translated into more than 35 languages.

Clearly a clever businesswoman, Beatrix designed and licensed her Peter Rabbit doll in 1903, making him one of the first licensed literary characters. Steiff produced its own version of Peter Rabbit in 1903. Grimwades Pottery, Stoke-on-Trent, England, was granted permission in 1922 to use Potter's illustrations on children's dishes. John Beswick obtained copyrights in 1947 to use Potter's storybook characters as figurines. The first set of nine figures, including Jemima Puddle-Duck, were an instant hit. In 1969, the Royal Doulton Group acquired Beswick and continued to produce the charming characters. Josiah Wedgwood and Sons began to use Peter Rabbit in its designs in the late 1950s.

Backstamps are useful in determining the date of Beatrix Potter figures. A gold circular backstamp is the earliest, dating to the 1940s-50s. Royal Albert backstamps were used only from 1989 to 1998. Some characters, Susan and Old Mr. Pricklepin, and Thomasina Tittlemouse, were produced by Royal Albert for a short six-week period and are much more sought after by collectors.

In 2002, an exhibition to celebrate the 100th anniversary of the first

Egg-shaped covered jar, Benjamin Bunny on top, Mother Bunny attending at bed on base, **$65.**

Cup, Bunnykins figures, Royal Doulton, **$18.**

commercial publication was created by the Royal Ontario Museum and it has since traveled to other museums, like the Children's Museum in Indianapolis, delighting children of all ages.

Baby bowl, Peter Rabbit, Grimwades, 1920s 30s **$590**

Barbie, 2002 Peter Rabbit Centenary **$29.95**

Book

The Roly-Poly Pudding, Frederick Warne, NY, 1908......................**$80**

The Tailor of Gloucester, Frederick Warne & Co., first US printing, 1903 ....**$130**

The Tale of Peter Rabbit, orig privately printed version, 1901 ....**$110,000**

The Tale of Peter Rabbit, Frederick Warne, first edition, second or third printing, 1902-3..................**$18,500**

The Tale of Peter Rabbit, American printing, 1904 ....**$450**

Chamber pot, Peter Rabbit, Wedgwood..**$200**

Cup and saucer, Peter Rabbit, Wedgwood, 1958..................................**$140**

Dish, Peter Rabbit, jasperware, blue, Wedgwood, 1980s **$200**

Eggcup, Peter Rabbit, Grimwades, 1920s-30s **$400**

Figure

Duchess with Flowers, earthenware 1955-1967................................**$2,800**

Duchess with Pie, earthenware 1979-1982................................**$4,255**

Hunca Munca, Beswick, 2-5/8" h, 2-3/4" w......................................**$115**

Jeremy Fisher, Royal Albert, 1st version, 2nd variation, modeled by Arthur Gredington, 3-1/2" h ...**$135**

Mr. Benjamin Bunny, Beswick, brown mark, 4" h, 3-7/8" l.....................**$75**

Mrs. Rabbit with basket, F Warne Co., Beswick, England, 4" h **$35**

Mrs. Rabbit and bunnies, Beswick, brown mark, 3-5/8" h.................**$75**

Mrs. Ribby and the Patty Pan, Royal Albert, modeled by Martyn Alcock, 3-1/2" h **$50**

Peter Rabbit, Beswick, sky blue jacket, brown shoes, hp "77" on base in brown and "31" in black, 1948, 4-1/4" h **$120**

Pickles, earthenware 1971-1982 ....**$485**

Tailor of Groucester, Royal Albert, 3-1/2" h **$35**

Game, Peter Rabbit's Race Game....**$45**

Handkerchiefs, Peter Rabbit, orig package................................**$385**

Pendant, F. Warne, made in Italy

Knitting bunny in rocking chair, 3-1/4" h **$30**

Moma mouse, babe in her arms, 3-3/4" h **$30**

Mr Pig, cane in hand, 3" h **$32**

Mrs Pig at the market, 3" h **$30**

Print, Squirrel Nutkin from *Tale of Squirrel Nutkin*, published by F. Warne, 1950s **$25**

Tea set, Peter Rabbit, 17 pcs, Grimwades..............................**$5,100**

Watercolor, unpublished, Building a Snowman, 1893 ....**$75,000**

Aunt Jemima, cookie jar, salt and pepper shakers, range shakers, measuring cup, spice shakers, all plastic, **$250.**

BLACK MEMORABILIA

History: The term "Black memorabilia" refers to a broad range of collectibles that often overlap other collecting fields, e.g., toys and postcards. It also encompasses African artifacts, items created by slaves or related to the slavery era, modern Black cultural contributions to literature, art, etc., and material associated with the Civil Rights Movement and the Black experience throughout history.

The earliest known examples of Black memorabilia include primitive African designs and tribal artifacts. Black Americana dates back to the arrival of African natives upon American shores.

The advent of the 1900s saw an incredible amount and variety of material depicting Blacks, most often in a derogatory and dehumanizing manner that clearly reflected the stereotypical attitude held toward the Black race during this period. The popularity of Black portrayals in this unflattering fashion flourished as the century wore on.

As the growth of the Civil Rights Movement escalated and aroused public awareness to the Black plight, attitudes changed. Public outrage and pressure during the early 1950s eventually put a halt to these offensive stereotypes.

Black representations are still being produced in many forms, but no longer in the demoralizing designs of the past. These modern objects, while not as historically significant as earlier examples, will become the Black memorabilia of tomorrow.

Additional Resources:

Antique Trader® Black Americana Price Guide, 2nd Ed., by Kyle Husfloen, ed., Krause Publications, Iola, WI.

Autograph, Martin Luther King, Jr., photograph, sgd "with best wishes Martin Luther King," 11" x 14" **$3,220**

Baseball cap, Kansas City Black Royals Negro League, white, gray pinstripes, worn black visor, large black "KC" stitched on front, c1920 .... **$930**

Book

George Washington Carver, An American Biography, Rackham Colt, ex-library copy, 1943 .... **$5**

Who's Who in Colored America, Volume I, J. Joseph Boris, ed., New York, first edition, portrait plates, small 4to, orig cloth, 1927 .... **$375**

Women of Achievement, Benjamin Brawley, Woman's American Baptist Home Mission Society, portrait plates, small 8vo, orig cloth, 1919 .... **$375**

Bottle opener, cast iron

Alligator and boy with hands up, mkd "John Wright, Inc.," front of base mkd "Souvenir of Tyban Dam, Grafton, W.V.," 3" x 4-1/2" **$400**

Man's face, indented eyes, Wilton Products, damaged orig box, 4-1/8" x 3-1/2" **$150**

Nickel plated, painted, black caddy, mkd "Pat. #86,603," near mint, 1932, 5-13/16" x 1-7/8" **$1,460**

Cartes-de-visite

Colored Baptist Church, Petersburg, VA, Lazell & McMillin, Petersburg, photographers, ext. view, men and women sitting on front fence, pencil inscription "Church of Petersburg Negroes burned by rebels, given by Lottie, Feb. 9th, 1868," soil, wear, slight crimp, 1966 .... **$345**

Frederick Douglas, full-length portrait, erased pencil marks on top border, c1860 .... **$550**

Sojourner Truth, 3/4 view, seated at table, knitting, "I Sell the Shadow to Support the Substance," corners

Wool embroidery, young girl and attendant, 19th century, 7-1/2" x 9-1/4", $890.
Photo courtesy of Pook & Pook, Inc.

Egg rattle, bisque, child emerging from egg, unmarked, early 20th century, 2" h, $55.
Photo courtesy of Green Valley Auctions.

Advertising figure, life-size, polychrome papier-mâché, figure posed in seated position, hands poised as if holding newspaper, white hat with red band, dark blue jacket, white shirt, vest, pants, and shoes, red necktie, America, minor paint wear, separations, late 19th/early 20th century, 20" w, 33" d, 48-1/2" h, $5,900.
Photo courtesy of Skinner, Inc.

Sign, tin litho, tan ground, black lettering, red trim, child eating slice of bread with honey, honey pail to right, "Honey, dat's all! Rocky Mountain Honey Co., Producers of Choice Honey, Silver City, New Mexico," red border, some wear, $195.
Photo courtesy of Alderfer Auction Co.

clipped, toning, light browning, 1864 .... **$660**

Cigar box label, glossy paper label, Booker T., Perfecto Cigars, black and white portrait of Booker T. Washington, red, pale blue, and dark blue border, white stars, unused, c1930s, 6-1/4" x 10" **$20**

Circular, "The New York Association of the Friends for the Relief of those held in Slavery and Improvement of the free People of Color," Westbury, July 24, 1840, republished by the Philadelphia Assoc of Friends for Promoting the Abolition of Slavery, 10" x 7-3/4" **$50**

Doll

Golliwog, velveteen face, hands, and feet, applied felt eyes and mouth, inked nose, yellow checked shirt, golden crepe pants, red braid trim, removable gray and white checked wool jacket, some wear and soil, c1930, 20" h **$460**

Mammy, nut head, painted features, looped plush hair, whisk broom body, orig commercial assemblage, pink print dress, twin black babies in green print organdy outfits, early 20th C, 12" h **$635**

Mammy, stuffed cloth, hand-embroidered features, red trimmed dress, blue and white cap, wear, damage, 18" h **$220**

Door latch, carved wood, female with incised dec torso, Bamana, Africa, 18" h **$415**

Ephemera

Certificate of Freedom, for Thomas Chambers, resident of New York City, partly printed document, sgd, small folio, docketed on verso, September 1814 .... **$950**

Deposition of Thomas Cook, Shrewsbury, NJ, concerning slave trade and events on the sloop *Fanny*, Jan. 10, 1801, 12-1/2" x 8" **$175**

Depositions concerning slave trade by sloop *Fanny* between Africa and North America, 17 pgs, Oct 8, 1801, 9-1/2" x 7-1/2" **$550**

Notice, *The Charleston Daily Courier*, regarding issuing of slave badges, giving prices for various trades, Jan. 5, 1858 .... **$1,380**

Receipt, "Negro Apprenticeship 2/6," printed, "Bought of the Anti-Slavery Society, Office, No. 18, Aldermanbury," (England) signed and dated by Francis Wedgwood, Society seal, dated 1838 .... **$490**

Figure, carved wood, Dogon, curved form with arms to sides, oversized stylized head, wearing skull cap, African, wood loss, 23" h **$900**

Figure, cast iron, painted

Family, 2-1/2" h man, 3-1/4" h woman, two 2-3/8" boys, 2" h girl, Wilton, excellent **$620**

Sitting black boy and girl, Hubley, very good, 1-1/4", price for pr **$225**

Swing band, group of six musicians, Hubley, catalog #34, near mint, 2-1/2" x 1-7/8" **$1,680**

Game, Jolly Darkie Ten Pens, McLoughlin Bros, two wooden balls, ten 8" x 2-1/2" diecut cardboard black men figures on wooden bases, orig box, C.8, 14-7/8" x 9-1/2" x 1-1/2" **$1,000**

Headrest, carved wood, Senufo, elongated form on four round feet, female head with stylized coiffure on one end, dark patina, African, 30" l, 2-3/4" h, one foot broken off.............. **$1,530**

Heddle pulley, carved wood, Janushead form, dark patina, Africa, crack, 10" h.. **$1,410**

Nodder, black boy, clockwork, head nods up and down, eyes roll, one arm extended upward, other extended forward in greeting manner, papier-mâché, 30" h **$1,500**

Perfume bottle, Golliwog, stylized faces, black and brown hair covering stoppers, bulbous frosted glass body, painted white collar, black round feet, raised maker's mark for DeVigny, one with partial paper label, price for three-pc set, c1919, 4-3/4" to 6" h **$575**

Pinback button

Baltimore Elite Giants, Negro Leagues, red and white, glossy cello, c1940 .... **$45**

Gold Dust Washing Powder, multicolored trademark of Black twins seated in wash tub, white background, black letters **$60**

Pocket tin, tin litho, vertical pocket type, image of black man smoking pipe on front, mkd "Record Pipe Tobacco" on back, 4-1/4" x 3-3/4" x 7/8" **$625**

Puzzle, Darktown Fire Brigade, Parker Bros, heavy cardboard pcs, wear to orig box, c1890s, 7-1/2" x 9-1/2" x 1-1/8" **$425**

Receipt, to Mr. Stanley from H. Seymour, dated Nov 22, 1788, reading "Deliver Bob Negro the pair of small shoes you have made for him and send me the cost," 3" x 7-3/4" **$30**

Roly poly, Mayo's Roly Poly Tobacco, Mammy, litho tin, two pcs, C-8+, 7" x 5-1/4" **$825**

Slave tag, copper, Charlestown, 1834, 2" sq
Porter, No. 171 .... **$3,065**
Servant No. 205, wear, minor dents **$1,175**

Target game, McLoughlin Bros, image of black man holding musical instruments, C.8.5, 15-1/2" x 8" x 1-5/8" **$500**

Textile, printed, showing Little Black Sambo and tiger, earth tones of red, green, and dark brown, tan linen ground, folded, sewn seam with red ink label "WPA Handicraft Project #10235, Milwaukee, Wisconsin, Sponsored by Milwaukee County and Milwaukee State Teachers College," c1935-43, 32-1/2" x 42" **$1,350**

BOOKS, EARLY

History: Collecting early books is a popular segment of the antiques marketplace. Collectors of early books are rewarded with interesting titles, exquisite illustrations, as well as fascinating information and stories. The author, printer, and publisher, as well as the date of the printing, can increase the value of an early book. Watch for interesting paintings on the fore-edge of early books. These miniature works of art can greatly add to the value.

Scott, Sir Walter, The Waverly Novels, Boston: Estes and Lauriat, Edition de Luxe, edition of 1,000, 54 volumes, half crushed black morocco, 8vo, bumped, toned, chipped, 1893, **$1,350.**
Photo courtesy of Skinner, Inc.

Additional Resources:

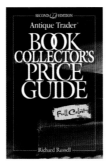

Antique Trader® Book Collector's Price Guide, 2nd Ed., by Richard Russell, Krause Publications, Iola, WI.

Aelianus, Claudis, Claudis Aelianus His Various History, translated by Thomas Stanley, London, Thomas Dring, first Stanley edition, small 8vo, modern 1/2 sheep gilt, first blank leaf missing, rubbed, some dampstaining in outer corners, 1665 .... **$130**

Armstrong, John, The Art of Preserving Health: A Poem, London, A. Millar, first edition, 134 pgs, 4to, modern 1/4 calf, title browned, 1774 .... **$70**

Bentley, Richard, The Folly and Unreasonableness of Atheism…In Eight Sermons Preached at the Lecture Founded by the Honourable Robert Boyle, Esquire, London, J. H. for H. Mortlock, eight parts in one volume, 4to, contemporary mottled sheep, rebacked, 1693 .... **$410**

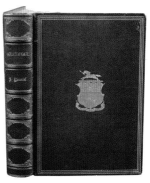

Colt, Samuel, Armsmear, The Home, the Arm, and the Armory of Samuel Colt, New York, first edition, orig gilt on binding by Mathews, scattered foxing, 1866, **$1,530.**
Photo courtesy of Skinner, Inc.

Bohn, Henry C, A Catalogue of Books, London, engraved frontispiece and title page, thick 8vo, contemporary 1/4 road, front cover detached, frontispiece adhere, heavy foxing, 1841 .... **$150**

Burke, Edmund, Reflections on the Revolution in France, London, J. Dodsley, second edition, second impression, 356 pgs, 8vo, contemporary calf, rebacked, hinges reinforced, cloth slipcase, 1790 .... **$165**

Burney, Frances, Evelina or A Young Lady's Entrance into the World, London, T. Lowndes, second edition, three volumes, 12mo, contemporary sheep, rebacked, 1779 .... **$130**

Dart, John, Westmonasterium; or, The History and Antiquities of the Abbey Church of St. Peters Westminster, London, John Coles, engraved titles, 148 of 149 plates, two volumes, folio, contemporary calf gilt, red and green morocco lettering pieces, joints cracked, foxing, 19th C armorial bookplate, c1723 .... **$350**

Dickinson, Emily, Poems, FE, 1890 .... **$6,500**

Fairbairn, James, Fairbairn's Crests of the Families of Great Britain and Ireland, Revised by Laurence Butters, Edinburgh and London, engraved titles, 148 plates, two volumes, 8vo, contemporary 1/2 levant gilt, rebacked retaining faded orig backstrips, later 19th C **$70**

Fielding, Henry, Amelia, London, A. Millar, first edition, integral ad leaf at end of Volume 2, four vol-

Hawthorne, Nathaniel, and Lowell, James Russell, Association Copy, The House of Seven Gables, A Romance, *Boston: Ticknor, Reed and Fields, first edition, brown cloth, from the library of James Russell Lowell, "From the Author" written by the publisher, 8vo, 1851,* **$2,470.**
Photo courtesy of Skinner, Inc.

Sinking of the Titanic, The World's Greatest Sea Disaster, *Official Edition, red cover,* **$75.**
Photo courtesy of Alderfer Auction Co.

Dreiser, Theodore, An American Tragedy, *New York, first edition, two volumes, Boni and Liveright imprint, cloth, slipcase, front edge chips, spine fading, 1925,* **$470.**
Photo courtesy of Skinner, Inc.

The Illustrated Historical Register of the Centennial Exposition, *1876, gold trim on black leather cover, illustrated,* **$250.**

Frost, Robert, A Masque of Mercy, *New York: Henry Holt and Company, numbered 699 of 751 signed copies, slipcase with minor wear, boards, 1947,* **$325.**
Photo courtesy of Skinner, Inc.

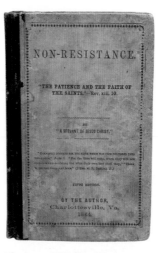

Thurman, W.C. "Non-Resistance, or the spirit of Christianity Restored," *Fifth Edition, Published by the author, Charlottesville, VA, hardcover, VG condition, silverfish damage to front cover, bumped corners, light spine wear, foxing inside covers, half of rear fly leaf lost, 1864 (on cover), 1862 (title page),* **$440.**
Photo courtesy of Green Valley Auctions.

Byrd, Richard Evelyn, Little America: Aerial Exploration in the Antarctic, *New York: G.P. Putnam's Sons, original half vellum, one of 1,000 sgd by author and publisher, slipcase, very good, 1930,* **$295.**
Photo courtesy of Skinner, Inc.

umes, 12 mo, modern beige calf gilt with morocco lettering pieces, 1752 .... **$490**

Gay, John, *The Shepherd's Week, In Six Pastorals,* London, Ferd. Burleigh, first edition, seven full-page etched illus by Louis Du Guernier, 8vo, modern 1/2 calf, 1714 .... **$865**

Gibson, Edward, *The History of the Decline and Fall of the Roman Empire,* London, A. Strahan and T. Cadell, six volumes, three engraved portrait, contemporary calf, map of Constantinople missing, 1782-88 .... **$320**

Godwin, William, *Things as They Are; or The Adventures of Caleb Williams,* London, B. Crosby, first edition, three volumes, 12mo, contemporary marbled boards with red morocco lettering, spines darkened, occasional light browning, armorial bookplates and signatures of SC rice planter Charles Izard Manigault (1795-1874), 1794 .... **$1,840**

Howell, William, *An Institution of General History; or The History of the World,* second edition with large additions, London, Thomas Bassett, four volumes in three, folio, modern 1/4 Morocco, 1680 .... **$435**

Hume, David, *The History of England,* London, A. Millar, six volumes, 4to, contemporary calf gilt with morocco lettering pieces, few joints cracked, 1754-59 .... **$980**

Johnson, Samuel, *Irene, A Tragedy,* London, R. Dodsley and M. Cooper, first edition, 8vo, joints rubbed, 1749 .... **$865**

Knight, Henrietta, Lady Luxborough, *Letters Written by the Late Right Honourable Lady Luxborough to William Shenstone, Esq.,* London, J. Dodsley, first edition, 416 pgs, 8vo, contemporary calf, rebacked, 1775 .... **$375**

Lackington, James, *Memoirs of the First Forty-Five Years of the Life of James Lackington, the Present Bookseller in Chiswell-street, Moorfields, London, Written by Himself,* printed for and sold by the author, first edition, engraved frontispiece portrait, 344 pages, 8vo, modern tree calf gilt, 1791 .... **$215**

Milton, John, *Paradise Lost, Paradise Regain'd,* Birmingham, John Baskerville for J. and R. Tonson, London, together, two volumes, large 8vo,

contemporary mottled calf, rebacked, 1760 .... **$575**

Nicolay, John G. and John Hay, *Abraham Lincoln, A History,* two-volume set, 1909 .... **$460**

Priestley, Joseph, *Lectures on History, and General Policy,* London, J. Johnson, 1793, two folding engraved tables, two volumes, 8vo, contemporary calf gilt, joints cracked **$200**

Shakespeare, William, *The Famous History of the Life of King Henry the Eight(h),* extracted from the second folio, London, modern cloth, calf lettering piece, some foxing and minor stains, 18th C owner's signature on last page, 1632 .... **$460**

Thomas, Gabriel, *An Historical Account of the Province and County of Pensilvania and of West-New Jersey in America,* 1698 .... **$27,000**

Unknown author

Confessions of a Medium, FE, London, 1882 .... **$250**

The Great Chinese Wizard's Handbook of Magic, Hurst & Co, NY, 1872 .... **$275**

BRASS

History: Brass is a durable, malleable, and ductile metal alloy consisting mainly of copper and zinc. The height of its popularity for utilitarian and decorative art items occurred in the 18th and 19th centuries.

Reproduction Alert. Many modern reproductions are being made of earlier brass forms, especially such items as buckets, fireplace equipment, and kettles.

Brass, box, Arts & Crafts, Carence Crafters, pagoda-shape, acid-etched wild roses, pristine copper patina, imp. "CC," 7" x 6" x 6", **$1,400.**
Photo courtesy of David Rago Auctions, Inc.

Brass, pipe mold, American, 18th century, 10" l, **$575.**
Photo courtesy of Pook & Pook.

Brass, snuff box, oval, three dials having Roman numerals and arrows for combination, hinged lid, 3-1/2" x 2-1/2", denting, brass button for opening detached, **$175.**
Photo courtesy of Alderfer Auction Co.

Brass, bowl, reticulated, incised center crest, price for pr, 20th century, 9" d, 6-1/2" h, **$425.**
Photo courtesy of David Rago Auctions, Inc.

Brass, foot warmer, hexagonal, wedding presentation type, pierced and embossed body, hearts, flowers, and busts of man and woman, Dutch, 18th century, 8-1/2" d, 7" h, **$2,530.**
Photo courtesy of Pook & Pook.

Additional Listings: Candlesticks, Fireplace Equipment, and Scientific Instruments.

Additional Resources:

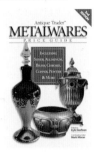

Antique Trader® Metalwares Price Guide, 2nd Ed., by Kyle Husfloen, ed., and Mark Moran, contr. ed., Krause Publications, Iola, WI.

Andirons, pr

Acorn tops, seamed columns, cabriole legs, ball feet, 17-1/2" h **$220**

Ring-turned columns, scalloped cabriole legs, ball feet, 18" h **$360**

Bed warmer

Engraved lid with large central flower surrounded by scrolls, maker's touchmark "ST," turned maple handle with old refinishing, minor damage near hinges, 42-1/2" l **$215**

Engraved lid with central flower surrounded by scrolls, turned wood handle with daubs of brown paint, wear, minor split in ferule, 43-3/4" l **$185**

Candlesticks, pr, pricket, ovoid drip pan on double baluster stem, domed cast foot, Continental, 18th C, 10-1/8" h..**$650**

Chandelier, cast, eight scrolled arms with torch shaped ends, each with small electric socket, simulated candle coverings, 20th C, 25" d, 20" h **$250**

Chestnut roaster, oval, pierced hinged lid, long handle, 18-3/4" l **$120**

Chimes, mahogany and rosewood frame, eight brass chimes, turned pilasters on either side, striker missing, 20th C, 18-1/2" w, 27-1/2" h **$220**

Coal bin, brass gallery, applied Wedgwood dec, paterae carved rosewood frieze, tilting bin, splayed legs, Aesthetic Movement, price for pr, c1875, 16-1/2" w, 15-1/2" d, 26" h **$4,410**

Coal grate, Neoclassical-style, back plate cast with scene of figures in revelry, grate with central horizontal bar over guillouche band, uprights with brass urn finials, rear plinth base, front tapered legs, late 19th C, 19-1/2" l, 10-1/4" d, 27" h............**$175**

Dresser mirror, French, gilt brass, mirrored glass, scrolls, floral pots, and garlands dec, cracks, loss to silvering 11" w, 18" h **$525**

Easel, A-frame topped by girdled round finial, late 19th/early 20th C, 61-5/8" h **$500**

Figure, Bodhisattva, dark patina, 10 arms, eight faces, single body, walnut block base, 31-1/2" h **$450**

Fireplace fender, pierced grapevines, applied bunches of grapes, rope twist detail, three cast brass paw feet, 47" w, 13" d, 9" h **$350**

Gong, dragons and tokugawa mons designs, Japan, early 20th C, 18" d **$325**

Ladle, brass bowl attached with copper rivets to wrought iron flattened handle, rattail hanging hook, 11-1/4" l **$300**

Letter sealer, 2" l brass tube, 23 double-sided brass discs with various sentimental seals for wax, 19th C **$100**

Oil lamp, Bouillote, three-light, squat ovoid font with short arms, suspending three tools from chains, spreading foot with ogee shaped rim, black tin frame, 19th C, 19-1/2" h **$420**

Palace jar, chased designs of various deities within scrolled field, India, 20th C, 17" d, 16" h....................**$420**

Plant stand, old gilding, round top with leaf drops and three scrolls, scrolled supports, leaves, and large flowers, eagle talon feet, lacquered, 14-1/2" d, 35-1/2" h **$450**

Samovar, worn partial marks, illegible from polishing, heavy cast base, replaced burner cover, damage to spout, repair, 19-1/2" h **$150**

Sconces, pr, hammered, gilt carved wooden foo dogs accents, 21" d **$360**

Steam whistle, single chime, lever control, 2-1/2" d, 12" h.................**$150**

Sundial, engraved markings, scrolls, and lettering "Merton Londini Anno Dom 1675" and "I stand amid ye Summere flowers To tell ye passinge of ye houres," imp "Made in England," early 20th C, 12-1/2" l, 12" w, 8-3/4" h **$265**

Trump indicator, circular flat brass disk, green enamel top, celluloid rotating suit and no trumps indicator **$130**

BRONZE

History: Bronze is an alloy of copper, tin, and traces of other metals. It has been used since Biblical times not only for art objects, but also for utilitarian wares. After a slump in the Middle Ages, the use of bronze was revived in the 17th century and continued to be popular until the early 20th century.

Notes: Do not confuse a "bronzed" object with a true bronze. A bronzed item usually is made of white metal and then coated with a reddish-brown material to give it a bronze appearance. A magnet will stick to it but not to anything made of true bronze.

A signed bronze commands a higher market price than an unsigned one. There also are "signed" reproductions on the market. It is very important to know the history of the mold and the background of the foundry.

Additional Resources:

Antique Trader® Metalwares Price Guide, 2nd Ed., by Kyle Husfloen, ed., and Mark Moran, contr. ed., Krause Publications, Iola, WI.

Basket, trompe l'oeil, folded linen form, woven handle, applied florals and insects, Japanese, 19th C, 10-1/4" **$350**

Box, chaise lounge form, topped with monkey on pillows, lid lifts to reveal erotic scene of man and woman with carved ivory features, gilt and polychrome dec, marble base, 20th C.....................**$1,495**

Bust, Napoleon, Sienna marble column with leaftip surround, plinth base, late 19th/early 20th C, 11-3/8" h **$1,410**

Candlesticks, pr, figural

Don Quixote standing and holding a lance, 11" h Pancho Sanchez, riding a donkey and holding a staff, each with inverted helmet-formed sconce, both on tripod base, early 20th C, 10" h **$300**

Owl, granite base, 6" h **$225**

Cauldron, four flanges with geometric decoration, two with handles, tripod base, Central Asia, Seljuk period, 15th C, 19" d **$1,100**

Clock, Chelsea Clock Co., Boston, silvered dial, round case, shaped rect base, ball feet, retailed by Tiffany & Co., 8" w, 3" d, 6-1/4" h **$650**

Clock garniture, parcel gilt bronze and slate, 20" h clock with two-train Hersant Freres chiming movement, case topped by griffin-handled urn, front set with female mask, raised front paw feet, pair of three-light candelabra, fruiting vine scrolled candle arms, similarly styled base, French, Renaissance Revival, late 19th C, 18" h **$1,175**

Figure and sculpture

Allegorial Autumn, standing figure holding sheaf of wheat and flowers, holding staff, fluted black slate base, grand tour, late 19th/early 20th C, 15" h **$600**

Cast from model by Vanetti, modeled as warrior in chariot drawn by three horses, rounded rect base, cast signature, 28" l, 13" h **$3,150**

Gentleman reading newspaper, oblong base, indistinct mold incised signature, Continental School, dated 1903, 13-1/2" d **$1,300**

Hockey player, cast, green patina, base sgd "Joe Brown 1956," 11-1/2" h, 12-1/2" w **$1,150**

Little girl covering giggle with her hand as she hides nosegay behind her back, medium brown patina, mold incised signature "Gaudez," (Adrien-Etienne Gaudez, 1845-1902), 23-1/2" h **$3,525**

Mythical beast, tail raised, supporting figure sitting on its back, table form base, Southeast Asia, 18th or 19th C, one leg loose, 3-1/4" w, 2-1/2" d, 5-7/8" h **$175**

Napoleon, standing by column, sq base with leaf-tip rim set with gilt eagle, late 19th C, 14" h **$940**

Seated woman with lyre resting on her lap, rect base with mold incised signature, for Georges Van der Straeten, Parisian foundry seal, late 19th C, 20-1/2" h **$1,650**

Shepherdess and her flock, woman in cape, standing with group of sheep by a stream, mold incised signature of Charles (Karl) Korschann, 15" w hexagonal green marble base, 12-1/2" h **$1,410**

Two Arabs, one man drawing water from well, other cooking, under grass roof, cold painted, Viennese, mounted with small electric bulb, early 20th C, 7-3/4" h **$2,350**

Nature Revealing Herself, standing woman in Doré and pewter patinated robe, carved malachite scarab set at bodice, carved ivory bust, arms, and feet, mold incised signature "E. Barrias," Susse Freres foundry seal, slate and onyx base, 2-3/4" h stone base, 22-1/4" h **$11,200**

Young Dionysus, standing, empty wine skin, after the antique, verdigris patination, early 20th C, 14" h **$500**

Garden lantern, jewel finials and eaves decorated with fish finials, pierced fire boxes, bases with cast foo dogs, Japan, price for pr, 19th C, 4" h **$2,115**

Jose stick holder, attendant holding cloth with censer on top, opening in censer to hold joss stick, dark brown patina, China, Ming Dynasty, several holes, 4-3/4" h **$200**

Incense burner, Oriental, circular base with relief birds and foliage, center medallions, applied handles, old clock set into one side which has a loose hand, some damage, soldered restorations, 22" h **$525**

Lamp, designs of birds and flowers in high relief, Japan, Meiji period (1868-1911), 68" h **$1,765**

Lamp base, gilt bronze, candelabra, five flower-form serpentine candle arms, raised on fluted rouge marble stem set with figure of cherub, ovoid base, black painted wood plinth, Louis XVI-style, price for pr, late 19th/early 20th C, electrified, 22" h **$2,235**

Letter holder, Doré, Silvercrest, double tiered, overlay of sailing ship in waves accented by linear decoration, imp mark, numbered "2222," 8-1/2" l, 2" d, 5" h **$300**

Parade helmet, cast

Depicting Hercules battling the hydra with cityscape in background, borders of military motifs and emperors, 19th C, 15-3/8" l, 11-1/4" h **$460**

Bronze, dogs, signed on base "P.J. Mene," Pierre Jules Mene, French, c1810-1879, 4-1/2" h x 5-1/2" w, **$980.**
Photo courtesy of Pook & Pook, Inc.

Bronze beaker vase, Chinese, everted mouth, scalloped rim, cast, high relief dragon, Ming Dynasty, 4-1/2" h, **$413.**
Photo courtesy of Sloans & Kenyon Auctioneers and Appraisers.

Bronze figure, dragon holding pearl, stamped on base, "H.A.M.," gilt-bronzed pearl, c1900, 12" h, **$265.**
Photo courtesy of Sloans & Kenyon Auctioneers and Appraisers.

Bronze, flower vessel, tightly curled lotus leaf resembling small boat, attached lotus blossoms, seed pods, crabs crawling to top, signed on rectangular reserve, Japanese, carved wooden stand, 19th century, 9-1/2" l, 3-1/4" h, **$2,450.**

Bronze, figure, standing peacock with long tail, cold painted, Bergmann, Austrian, loss to comb, 12" l, **$150.**
Photo courtesy of Alderfer Auction Co.

Bronze, stags feeding, signed on base "P.J. Mene," Pierre Jules Mene, French, c1810-1879, 7-1/4" h x 9" w, **$1,150**
Photo courtesy of Pook & Pook, Inc.

Bronze, Chinese tripod censer, ovoid, azurite encrusted, Eastern Zhou dynasty, 5" d, 4" h, **$530.**
Photo courtesy of Sloans & Kenyon Auctioneers and Appraisers.

Bronze, cast tobacco jar, wagon, foxes blacksmithing, late 19th century, 8-1/2" h, 12-1/2" d, **$995.**
Photo courtesy of Pook & Pook, Inc.

Bronze, stag, signed on base "P.J. Mene," Pierre Jules Mene, French, c1810-1879, 11-1/4" h x 11" w, **$575.**
Photo courtesy of Pook & Pook, Inc.

Bronze, figure, nomad riding camel, cold-painted, Vienna, mkd "2607" with other indiscernible marks, losses to camel leg, restorations, early 20th century, 8-1/4" x 6-3/4", **$1,100.**
Photo courtesy of David Rago Auctions, Inc.

Bronze, censor, foo dog, standing, three-dimensional features, open mouth, removable section in back, 20" l, 21" h, loss to tip of mane, **$715.**
Photo courtesy of Alderfer Auction Co.

Bronze, garden statue, figural, young boy holding lamp, verdigris patina, 20th century, 34" x 24" x 6", **$550.**
Photo courtesy of Sloans & Kenyon Auctioneers and Appraisers.

Gladiator's, Continental-style, China, four-part hinged visor comprising two-piece pierced eye guard, over two-piece face guard cast as figures before prison gates, helmet with high relief battle scene, further Roman-style figures, early 20th C, 18" l **$690**

Pen vase, gilt, cylindrical vessel, flared base, ribbed swirled design, unsigned, attributed to Tiffany Studios, New York, 3-1/2" h **$175**

Plaque

Circular, high relief design of lion's head, early 20th C, 14" d **$1,300**

Flower Maidens, profile busts of long-haired beauties, incised titles "Marguerite" and "Mignon," set in 11-3/4" sq maroon velvet frames, Aesthetic Movement, price for plate 19th/early 20th C, 5-5/8" sq **$715**

Scepter, three cast faces, paneled rod, engraved swirled designs, crown finials, Oriental, possible brazed repair on rod, 20-1/2" l **$175**

Smoking tray, Doré finish, applied scrolling on ash bowl, cigar rests, matchbox holder, unmarked, c1910, 6-1/4" d...............................**$70**

Tray, band of hammered designs, marked "Apollo Studios, New York" c1910, 9" d **$45**

Urn, cast, black patinated, everted reeded rim, central band of classical figures, two short handles with male masks, fluted foot, sq black marble base, Classical-style, price for pr, late 19th/early 20th C, 11-3/8" h **$2,530**

Vase, enameled dec of figures in ancient Roman garb, dragons on shoulder, butterflies on rim, mark on underside, possibly Japanese, slight loss to enamel, early 20th C, 13" h.........**$175**

Wall sconces

Pr, cast, Louis XV-style, two-light, rocaille-shaped candle arms and backplate, floriform drip pans hung with faceted colorless glass lusters, 11-7/8" h **$150**

Set of four, each with two candle sockets on cornucopia-shaped stems bound by ribbons, drapery-like wall plates with rosettes at top, gilded, 21" h **$700**

BUSTS

History: The portrait bust has its origins in pagan and Christian traditions. Greek and Roman heroes dominate the earliest examples. Later, images of Christian saints were used. Busts of the "ordinary man" first appeared during the Renaissance.

During the 18th and 19th centuries, nobility, poets, and other notable people were the most frequent subjects, especially on those busts designed for use in a home library. Because of the large number of these library busts, excellent examples can be found at reasonable prices, depending on artist, subject, and material.

Alabaster, woman in lace headdress and bodice, tapered alabaster socle, early 20th C, 17-1/4" h **$450**

Black basalt, Cicero, waisted circular socle, imp title and Wedgwood & Bentley mark, chips to socle rim, c1775, 10" h...........................**$2,300**

Bronze

Ajax, after the antique, helmet, beard, parcel gilt toga, sq base, dark green patination, 20th C, 16-1/4" h **$865**

Child, modeled as the head of a young child with curly hair, on cylindrical stone base, 20th C, 12-1/2" h **$635**

Cold painted, Bianca Capello, woman wearing classical clothing, Renaissance Revival motifs, sgd "C. Ceribelli," marble plinth, 24" h **$2,100**

Gentleman, Leo F. Nock, brown-green patina, sgd on base "Leo Nock Sc," stamped "Roman Bronze Works, NY," dated 1919, 22" h **$320**

Homer, dark brown patina, French, possibly Barbediene, 19th C, 8-1/2" h **$750**

Mercury, chocolate brown and parcel-gilt patina, short socle, sq base, after the antique, 20th C, 11-1/2" h **$410**

Nubian Princess, Edrmann Encke, Gladenbeck foundry mark, short socle, marble base, 7-1/2" h.....**$415**

Rembrandt, Albert-Ernest Carrier-Belleuse, silvered patination, bronze socle, marble plinth, 20-1/2" h **$2,300**

Virgin, dark brown patina, Leon Pilet, French, sgd, 1836-1916, 9-3/4" h **$575**

Watteau-style woman, tricorn hat, low décolletage, George (Joris) Van Der Straeten, Paris Bronze Society foundry mark, fluted marble socle, reddish brown and black patination, 10-7/8" h.........................**$460**

Winged cherub, seated on broken column, playing hornpipe, pair of doves perched opposite, after Mathurin Moreau, dark brown patination, green marble socle, 9" h **$250**

Bronze and marble, medieval woman, after Patricia by Roger Hart, young woman, sheer headdress, marked "Mino di Tiesole" on ovoid white marble base, 20th C, 11-1/4" h **$575**

Carved marble, Pharaoh's Daughter, John Adams-Acton, snake headdress, beaded necklace, tapered sq section base, carved on front with scene of the discovery of Moses and title, 13-3/8" w, 10-3/4" d, 39" h breche d'alep marble tapered sq section pedestal, England, late 19th C, 13-3/4" w, 9-3/4" d, 26" h **$16,100**

Carved marble, Jeanne D'Arc, white marble face and base, pink marble bodice, incised title on front, early 20th C, 15-1/4" w, 6-3/4" d, 15" h **$700**

Gamin, polychromed plaster, Augusta Christine Fells Savage, (American 1892-1962), imp on verse, c1930, 9-1/4" l.....................................**$33,350**

Lady, carved facial features, ears, and hair style, stepped base with dentil carving, stamped dec, old surface, America, early 20th C, 8-1/4" h **$650**

Majolica, young boy, French colonial dress, marked "BU 677," 19" h **$900**

Marble, lady with rose, incised "A. Testi," associated partial alabaster pedestal with spiral fluted stem, 20" h **$2,645**

Marble, young pious woman, lace and flower bodice, hair in long braid, matching 6" h marble socle, Italian, late 19th C, 26" h **$7,475**

Bust, Enid the Fair, George Frampton, 1907, signed, titled and dated in the mold, original dark patina, abrasion to nose, 20-1/2" x 9", **$7,500.**
Photo courtesy of David Rago Auctions, Inc.

Bust, giltwood and polychrome paint-ed, Roman soldier plumed helmet, cloak and shield, later paint restora-tions, late 18th/early 19th century, 37" x 25" x 15", **$3,070.**
Photo courtesy of Sloans & Kenyon Auctioneers and Appraisers.

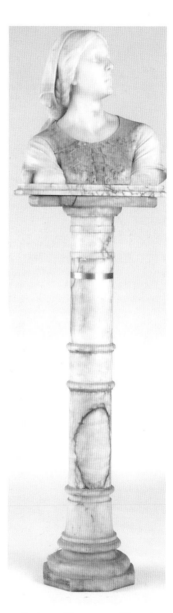

Bust, parian, child, by Isaac Broome stamped OTT & BREWER, incisec TRENTON N.J., 6-3/4" x 5", **$1,560**
Photo courtesy of David Rago Auctions, Inc.

Bust, marble, classical male, plinth base with natural weathering and wear, late 19th century, 32" x 21" x 10", **$2,700.**
Photo courtesy of David Rago Auctions, Inc.

Bust, marble, woman, Florentine-style, associated marble pedestal, 61" x 17" x 9", **$600.**
Photo courtesy of David Rago Auctions, Inc.

Bust, marble, classical woman, plinth base with natural weathering and wear, late 19th century, 32" x 21" x 10", **$2,700.**
Photo courtesy of David Rago Auctions, Inc.

BUTTER PRINTS

History: There are two types of butter prints: butter molds and butter stamps. Butter molds are generally of three-piece construction—the design, the screw-in handle, and the case. Molds both shape and stamp the butter at the same time. Butter stamps are generally of one-piece construction, but can be of two-piece construction if the handle is from a separate piece of wood. Stamps decorate the top of butter after it is molded.

The earliest prints are one piece and were hand carved, often heavily and deeply. Later prints were factory made with the design forced into the wood by a metal die.

Some of the most common designs are sheaves of wheat, leaves, flowers, and pineapples. Animal designs and Germanic tulips are difficult to find. Prints with designs on both sides are rare, as are those in unusual shapes, such as half-rounded or lollipop.

Reproduction Alert.
Reproductions of butter prints were made as early as the 1940s.

Butter mold

Pineapple, carved wood, 4-3/8" d **$325**

Roses, carved maple, serrated edges, 5" x 8" **$165**

Sunflower, carved wood, 3-1/2" d **$125**

Butter stamp

Carved fruitwood, strawberry, 2-7/8" d, 4-1/2" l **$50**

Double sided, oval, peony on one side, tulip on other, carved print on handle, age crack, 3-3/4" d **$295**

Eagle on laurel branch, star over its head, wavy feathers, one-pc handle, scrubbed surface, 4-1/2" d **$395**

Hexagonal, pineapple print, tall case, pewter straps, orig plunger, 4-1/2" l, 4-3/4" d **$100**

Lollipop style, carved pinwheel on one side, tulip with leaves on other, 6" l **$3,900**

Nesting swan, threaded handle, old refinishing, some worm holes, minor edge damage, 4" d **$500**

Pomegranate, concentric circle rim, one-pc handle, dark patina, 4-1/4" d **$100**

Rectangular, backward looking crested peafowl-type bird, sitting on flowering branch, turned inset handle, dark stains, 2-3/8" x 1-3/4" **$250**

Round, carved primitive eagle, rayed sunbursts, dark patina, worn finish, large one-piece handle, 4-3/8" d **$330**

Round, carved flower, one piece handle, 1-7/8" d **$175**

Round, carved wide-eyed cow and fence, threaded insert handle with chip on end, 3-1/4" d **$200**

Round, carved tulip, good patina, PA, age cracks, 5" d **$665**

Speckled rooster, leafy foliage, one-piece handle, small chip, 3" d **$275**

Stylized eagle with shield, natural finish, blue ink stain, 3-3/4" d **$110**

Stylized eagle with shield, concentric circle rim, dry surface, 3-7/8" d **$110**

Walnut, foliage and flowers, 4-3/4" d, 5-1/2" l **$115**

Butter print, leaf and vine design, round, single handle, **$65**.

Butter print, oval, wooden, hand-carved tulip and star design, some cracking and wear, VG condition, mid 19th century, 4" x 6-5/8", **$99**.
Photo courtesy of Green Valley Auctions.

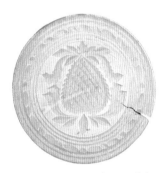

Butter print, pineapple carved butter print, round, single handle, age crack, **$85**.
Photo courtesy of Wiederseim Associates, Inc.

Butter print, lollipop style, wooden, hand-carved feather star design, VG condition, first half 19th century, 6-3/8" l, 3-5/8" d, **$120**.
Photo courtesy of Green Valley Auctions.

Butter print, flowers with center fern leaves, coggled edge, one-piece wooden handle, **$90**.

1908, pretty girl, calendar pages in center, gold lettering "Compliments of A. A. Eckert, General Merchandise, Packerton, PA," **$55.**
Photo courtesy of Dotta Auction Co., Inc.

1906, seasonal floral sprigs, scattered calendar pages, gold lettering "Prince Furniture Co., Complete Home Furnishers, No. 502 Hamilton St, Allentown, Pa," beaded edges, **$90.**
Photo courtesy of Dotta Auction Co., Inc.

1917, pair of grazing deer, calendar pages on border and flags, gold lettering "Compliments of E. D. Reitter, Hoppenville, PA," **$65.**
Photo courtesy of Dotta Auction Co., Inc.

Calling card stand, cased glass, ruffled and curled rim, polychrome floral dec, brass wire stand, late 19th/early 20th century, 4-3/4" h, 8-1/2" d, **$55.**
Photo courtesy of Green Valley Auctions.

CALENDAR PLATES

History: Calendar plates were first made in England in the late 1880s. They became popular in the United States after 1900, the peak years being 1909 to 1915. The majority of the advertising plates were made of porcelain or pottery and the design included a calendar, the name of a store or business, and either a scene, portrait, animal, or flowers. Some also were made of glass or tin.

Additional Resources:

Warman's® Americana & Collectibles, 11th Ed., by Ellen T. Schroy, ed., Krause Publications, Iola, WI.

1906, Compliments of A. K. Clemmer, Kulpsville, Pennsylvania, scattered florals and calendar pages **$60**

1908, hunting dog, Pittstown, Pennsylvania **$40**

1909, Compliments of John U. Francis, Jr., Fancy and Staple Groceries, Oaks, Pennsylvania, multicolored transfer of roses and grapes, calendar pages around rim with holly leaves and berries, worn gold trim, mkd "Iron Stone China, Extra Quality" with lion and shield mark **$35**

1911, Souvenir of Detroit, Michigan, months in center, hen and yellow chicks, gold edge............................ **$30**

1912, Winchester, rifle with grouse, autumn scene................................ **$75**

1913, boy in overalls, mkd "Our Art Dept, 1913" **$65**

1915, black boy eating watermelon, 9" d.. **$60**

1916, eagle with shield, American flag, 8-1/4" d.. **$40**

1917, cat center.............................. **$35**

1919, ship center **$30**

1920, The Great War, MO.............. **$30**

1921, bluebirds and fruit, 9" d........ **$35**

1922, dog watching rabbit **$35**

1969, Royal China, Currier & Ives green, 10" d **$40**

CALLING CARD CASES AND RECEIVERS

History: Calling cards, usually carried in specially designed cases, played an important social role in the United States from the Civil War until the end of World War I. When making formal visits, callers left their card in a receiver (card dish) in the front hall. Strict rules of etiquette developed. For example, the lady in a family was expected to make calls of congratulations and condolence and visits to the ill.

The cards themselves were small, embossed or engraved with the caller's name, and often decorated with a floral design. Many handmade examples, especially in Spencerian script, can be found. The cards themselves are considered collectible.

Note: Don't confuse a calling card case with a match safe.

Cases

Ivory, rect, wood inlay, block rows, center framed with diamond design rim band, 4" l............................. **$175**

Leather, sterling silver plaque depicting young woman in Renaissance costume, seed pearl accents, Art Nouveau, French hallmarks.............. **$300**

Silver, American, mid to late 19th C

Coin silver, Albert Coles, engraved dec, monogram **$350**

Coin silver, pointed arched base, engraved dec, monogram........ **$325**

Sterling silver, goldwashed, fitted leather case, engine turned dec, monogram **$250**

Sterling silver, Gorham, engraved dec, monogram **$325**

Silver, Chinese Export, rect, all-over hammered appearance, central monogrammed roundel, attributed to Tuck Chang & Co., late 19th/early 20th C, approx four troy oz, 2-7/8" x 3-7/8"... **$200**

Silver and ivory, silver filigree work over ivory panels, filigree depicts wild boar hunt on one side, cartouche with

Kodak, No. 14, Antographic Kodak Junior, original box, **$45.**

Eastman Kodak, field type camera, large, front view, **$125.**
Photo courtesy of Dotta Auction Co., Inc.

Camera, Reflex Obscura, tapering stained wood body, hinged pasteboard flap, removable 5" x 6" ground glass screen, card barrel with simple focusing lens, American, mid-19th century, 16-1/2" l, **$700.**
Photo courtesy of Skinner, Inc.

monogram framed by filigree border on reverse, engraved brass frame, lid needs regluing, loss to int, 5-1/2" x 3"..**$220**

Silver plate, quadruple silver plate, orig chain, Victorian, 3-1/2" x 3-3/4" **$125**

Tortoiseshell with stylized floral plique, hinged metal lid, 19th C, 4" x 3"..**$110**

Wood, burl, Victorian, 3" l............**$95**

Receivers

Bronze

Figural, bronze, monkey, Victorian, 7" l...**$135**

Hammered, ovoid, emb comedy and tragedy masks, orig dark patina, crisp details, Gorham stamp mark, 9-1/2" l, 6" w **$650**

Porcelain, hand painted, roses, foliage, gold handles, 10" l..............**$45**

Silver plate, marked "Meriden," wear to plating, 7-1/4" l, 5-1/2" h **$60**

Tile, emb monks, gun-metal glaze, raised AETCo medallion for American Encaustic Tiling Co., few edge nicks, 5-1/4" x 6-1/2"...........................**$95**

CAMERAS

History: Photography became a viable enterprise in the 1840s, but few early cameras have survived. Cameras made before the 1880s are seldom available on the market, and when found, their prices are prohibitive for most collectors.

George Eastman's introduction of the Kodak camera in 1888, the first commercially marketed roll-film camera,

put photography in the hands of the public.

Most collectors start with a general interest that becomes more defined. After collecting a broad range of Kodak cameras, a collector may decide to specialize in Retina models. Camera collectors tend to prefer unusual and scarce cameras to the most common models, which were mass-produced by the millions.

Because a surplus exists for many common cameras, such as most Kodak box and folding models, collectors are wise to acquire only examples in excellent condition. Shutters should function properly. Minimal wear is generally acceptable. Avoid cameras that have missing parts, damaged bellows, and major cosmetic problems.

Agfa, Germany, Billy O, vertical folding camera, uses 127 roll film, Solinar f3.9/75mm lens, Compur shutter, c1932-37...................................**$50**

American Optical Co., New York, Flammang's Patent Revolving Back View Camera, tan and red bellows, mahogany body with brass fittings, Prosh Triplex lens and external shutter, c1886, 5" x 7".......................**$625**

E. & H.T. Anthony & Co., NY, Anthony view camera, mahogany with nickel and brass fittings, folding bed, original "EA" stamped landscape lens, c1880, 5" x 8".............................**$350**

Bell & Howell, Chicago, Dial 35, unusually configured half frame camera, spring-powered motor drive, f2.8/28mm Canon lens, molded plastic case, c1968.............................**$35**

Foton, high quality 35mm rangefinder camera with spring-powered motor drive, Cooke Amotal f2/50mm lens, c1948 ....**$850**

Conley Camera Co., Rochester, Minnesota, Conley Folding 3A Kewpie, vertical folding camera with square corners and red bellows, 1916 ....**$40**

Eastman Kodak, Rochester, New York

Kodak Petite, Vest Pocket Kodak Model B, light green, orig faded green bellows (also available in blue, gray, lavender and rose), matching hard case, c1929 ....**$150**

Kodak Cirkut Camera No. 10, Folmer & Schwing Division, large format camera for photographing panoramic pictures on film up to 10" w, outfit includes Turner Reich lens, tripod and gearbox, c1917 ....**$2,700**

No. 4 Folding Pocket Kodak camera, vertical folding camera, 4" x 5" exposures on roll film, red bellows, polished wood insets on bed, c1907-15...................................**$80**

Ordinary Kodak Camera, c1891-95, wooden box camera, loaded with 24, 4" x 5" exposures on roll film, string set shutter **$900**

Franke & Heidecke, Germany, Rolleiflex 3.5F, twin lens reflex camera, Planar f3.5/75mm lens, light meter, excellent condition, c1961 ....**$900**

Heiland Photo Products, Premiere, 35mm non-range-finder camera, made in Germany, Steinheil Cassar f2.8/ 45mm lens, Pronto shutter, c1957 ....**$15**

Candelabra, Baccarat, matching candleholder, three lights, drop prism crystals, red fading to yellow crystal, imprinted Baccarat on base, 21" x 12-1/4", **$1,300.**

Photo courtesy of David Rago Auctions, Inc.

Ica, Germany, Polyscop, stereo camera with rigid nonfolding body, Tessar f4.5 or 6.3 lenses, c1911-25 .... **$200**

Lionel Manufacturing Co., NY, Linex, cast metal subminiature stereo camera, f8/30mm lenses, for taking pairs of 16mm by 20mm exposures on roll film, c1954 .... **$90**

Minolta, Japan, Autocord, twin lens reflex camera, Rokkor f3.5/75mm lens, Seikosha MX 1-500 shutter, non-metered, c1955 .... **$70**

Nippon Kogaku, Japan, Nikon S2, rangefinder camera, Nippon Nikkor f1.4/5cm lens, non-metered, chrome top, excellent condition, c1952 .... **$1,100**

Seneca Camera Co., Rochester, New York, Seneca No. 1, 4" x 5" folding camera, polished wood interior, red bellows, Wollensak Junior brass cased lens, carrying case containing two plate holders **$95**

Spencer Co., Chicago, Falcon Flash Camera, inexpensive plastic miniature camera using 127 roll film, flash attachment, orig box **$15**

Voigtlander, Germany, Vitomatic IIa, 35mm viewfinder camera, outfitted with superior Ultron f2/50mm lens, Prontor 500 SLK-shutter, c1959 .... **$185**

Yamato Koki, Japan, Pax, small 35mm rangefinder camera styled after Leica, Luminor f3.5/45mm lens, YKK shutter, c1952-55 .... **$40**

Yashica, Japan

Electro 35, 35mm rangefinder, Yashinon f1.7/45mm lens, screw-on telephoto and wide-angle adaptor lenses, c1974 .... **$50**

Yashica Flash-O-Set, 35mm camera, f4/4cm lens, single-speed leaf shutter, built-in light meter, AG-1 flash unit, c1961 .... **$24**

Zeiss, Germany

Contarex "Bull's-eye," 35mm camera, large round exposure meter window over lens, Tessar f2.8/50mm lens, c1959-66 .... **$425**

Super Ikonta III, folding rangefinder camera, Tessar f3.5/75mm coated lens, Synchro-Compur shutter to 1/500, c1954-1958 .... **$350**

CANDLESTICKS

History: The domestic use of candlesticks is traced to the 14th century. The earliest was a picket type, named for the sharp point used to hold the candle. The socket type was established by the mid-1660s.

From 1700 to the present, candlestick design mirrored furniture design. By the late 17th century, a baluster stem was introduced, replacing the earlier Doric or clustered column stem. After 1730, candlesticks reflected rococo ornateness. Neoclassic styles followed in the 1760s. Each new era produced a new style of candlesticks; however, some styles became universal and remained in production for centuries. Therefore, when attempting to date a candlestick, it is important to try to determine the techniques used to manufacture the piece.

Candelabras are included in this edition to show examples of the many interesting candelabras available in today's antiques marketplace. Check for completeness when purchasing candelabras; most are sold in pairs.

Candelabra

Brass

Baluster stems, scrolled tripod bases, cov with highly detailed cast grape vines, center and two branching arms with cast vines with leaves and bunches of grapes, leaves cover sockets, small dents on one, price for pr, 22-1/4" h **$1,155**

Three scrolled arms, center fruit finial, two Sevres-type blue porcelain pieces with white reserves filled with hand painted polychrome flowers, cast brass base with grape leaves and cherub faces, 14-1/2" h **$300**

Bronze

Bronze and gilt bronze, Victory, winged figure in flowing gown, rising from caramel colored marble plinth, four scrolled arms with candle sockets, later conversion to electric lamp, French Empire, 19th C, 33" h **$980**

Gilt bronze, shafts modeled as quivers rising from acanthus scrolled brackets, rouge marble plinths, columned feet, quiver tops emanating from

Pair of tall candlesticks, Fulper, covered in Mirror Black flambé glaze, base scratches on one, vertical marks, 11-1/2", **$558.**

Photo courtesy of David Rago Auctions, Inc.

Brass candlesticks, pr, bell base, 17th century, 7-1/4" h, **$995.**
Photo courtesy of Pook & Pook, Inc.

Candlesticks, pr, Tiffany blue pastel, opalescent baluster stems, onion skin borders, sgd 1927 L.C.T. Favrile, **$1,200.**
Photo courtesy of The Early Auction Company, LLC.

Steuben candlestick, blue, twist stem, shape #686, signed, 8" h, **$500.**
Photo courtesy of The Early Auction Company, LLC.

Turned wooden candlesticks, tin candlecups, early 19th c, 15-1/2" h, **$380.**
Photo courtesy of Pook & Pook, Inc.

scrolled arms, fluted candle socket, Napoleon III, French, c1855-70, pr, 27" h **$1,380**

Gilt bronze, ftd base supporting altar from which a column of clouds mounted with winged angels looking up toward five-arm candelabra, French, 19th C, 41" h **$865**

Gilt metal

Five-light candelabra centerpiece with scrolled foliate arms, colorless prisms supported on patinated baluster form shaft with gilt floral and foliate designs on black ground, two matching 16-5/8" h three-light candelabra, all on sq white marble bases, seam separation on shafts, lacking some prisms, 19-3/4" h **$360**

Victorian, Egyptian Revival style, scrolling candle arms supporting five candles, urn-shaped support, black marble plinth, 23" h **$360**

Glass

Deep amethyst base and column with cut panels, cut stars around center, detailed brass castings include four branches, all with scrolled acanthus leaves and sockets, emb "Made in France," wear to silver plating, center finial missing, 11-1/4" h **$550**

Pressed colorless glass, two-light, center faceted prism above drip pan hung with faceted prisms, suspending two chains of prisms to a pair of spiral twisted scrolled arms, flanked by two scrolled candlearms, drip pans hung with further prisms, single knob stem, stepped sq base, late 19th C, bases drilled, 20" h, 14-1/2" w, price for pr **$350**

Candlesticks

Art glass, iridescent gold, large disc foot and top separated with baluster stem, sgd "650 Nash," 4" h **$350**

Brass

Capstan base, damage, soldered repair, 6" h **$215**

Heavy stem threaded into saucer base, dings and scratches, 5-1/4" h **$320**

Mid-drip pans, baluster stems, round spun base, finely detailed turnings with extractor holes in sockets, Dutch, 19th C copies of earlier style, 9-1/8" h **$230**

Push-rod, round base, 8-3/8" h **$90**

Push-ups, saucer bases, tooled rings around columns, 4-1/2" h, pr **$175**

Removable candlecup, beaded on rim, octagonal, baluster shaft, domed base with ruffled edges, remnants of silver plating, France, early to mid-18th C, 9-3/4" h **$150**

Removable candlecup, octagonal, baluster shaft, domed base with ruffled edges, remnants of silver plating, France, early to mid-18th C, 10" h **$150**

Side push-up, threaded into domed base with scalloped edge, 8-3/4" h **$275**

Bronze, patinated bronze, silvered and gilt sconces over rouge marble drip pans, classical male bust, tapered stem, round base, Italian, late 19th C, 10" h **$600**

Cast brass and wrought iron, Gothic Revival, late 19th C, pricket, trefoil-edged drip pan, girdled multi-knopped cast brass standard, wrought-iron trefoil base with serpentine legs, acanthus knees and

Candlestick, Rockingham flint glaze, ring on upper and lower stem, second half 19th century, 8" h, **$770.**
Photo courtesy of Green Valley Auctions.

Steuben candlesticks, pr, gold Aurene, bluish highlights, shape #686, sgd Aurene, 8" h, **$850.**
Photo courtesy of The Early Auction Company, LLC.

Brass candlestick, circular base, trumpet-shaped shaft, medium patina, Jessie Preston, triangular stamp, 14" x 7-1/4", **$940.**
Photo courtesy of David Rago Auctions, Inc.

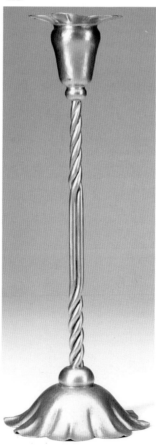

Candlestick, Arts & Crafts, gold-plated hammered copper, fluted candle-holder at top, twisted stem, fluted flower-form base, made by Marie Zimmerman, artist's cipher, 14" x 5-1/4", **$2,000.**
Photo courtesy of David Rago Auctions, Inc.

flowerhead scrolls, price for pr, 61" h **$1,610**

Glass, pressed, early

Alabaster/ clambroth, petal socket, dolphin, single-step base, orig gilt dec shells on base, wafer construction, Boston & Sandwich Glass Co., Sandwich, MA, 1845-70, 10-1/2" h **$1,155**

Canary, hexagonal, large base, wafer construction, Boston & Sandwich Glass Co., Sandwich, MA, socket flake, minor base flakes, 1840-60, 7-1/2" h **$190**

Dark blue-violet, faint white swirls within base, hexagonal socket, circular base, wafer construction, Boston & Sandwich Glass Co., Sandwich, MA, 1835-50, 6-3/4" h **$1,155**

Vaseline, hexagonal sockets, patterned hexagonal base, one pc construction, possibly European, minute socket rim flake, minor base nicks, second half 19th C, price for pr, 8" h **$125**

Gilt bronze

Base of sconce with acanthus, tapered stem with central guilloche band on fish scale ground, ovoid base with leaftip and patera roundels, Empire, French, early 19th C, 10" h **$900**

Gilt metal, Gothic Revival, hexagonal sconce, drip pan with pierced trefoil rim, hexagonal stem with bulbous shaped knop, loaded floriform base enameled with lion shields and griffins on trefoils, ropetwist foot trim, late 19th C, 11-3/4" h **$1,000**

Marble, Empire-style, late 19th C, engine turned and beaded ormolu nozzles, gray marble columns hung with gilt-metal chains suspending acorns, stepped white marble base with flat leaf and beaded mounts, flattened ball feet, price for pr, 8" h **$350**

Pewter, pricket, wide drip pan, double-baluster stem, shaped-tripartite base, three ball feet, Continental, 18th C, 22-3/4" h **$700**

Porcelain, figural, male and female flower gatherers, against brocage, rocaille base, attributed to Samson, France, late 19th C, price for pr, 10-5/8" h **$450**

Sterling silver, Neoclassical, England, emb gadrooned nozzle, campana-shape stems, foliate festoons and acanthus dec, waisted pedestal base, emb arms and beaded rims, price for pr, first half 19th C, 5-1/2" h.......**$280**

Tin

Adjustable push-up rod, pie plate base, ring handle, 5-1/2" h, 6" d **$550**

Hog scraper, adjustable push-rod, decorative brass ring, illegible name stamped on push-rod handle, 7-1/4" h, 3-3/4" d....................**$660**

Pie plate base, ring handle, 4-1/2" h, 7-1/2" d **$1,100**

Wrought iron

Scrolled handle and feet, lip handle, notched push-up, price for pr, 11-1/2" h **$550**

Spiral, scrolled push-up, turned wood base, 6-7/8" h............................**$300**

CANDY CONTAINERS

History: In 1876, Croft, Wilbur, and Co. filled small glass Liberty Bells with candy and sold them at the Centennial Exposition in Philadelphia. From that date until the 1960s, glass candy containers remained popular. They reflect historical changes, particularly in transportation.

Jeannette, Pennsylvania, a center for the packaging of candy in containers, was home for J. C. Crosetti, J. H. Millstein, T. H. Stough, and Victory Glass. Other early manufacturers included: George Borgfeldt, New York, New York; Cambridge Glass, Cambridge, Ohio; Eagle Glass, Wheeling, West Virginia; L. E. Smith, Mt. Pleasant, Pennsylvania; and West Brothers, Grapeville, Pennsylvania.

Notes: Candy containers with original paint, candy, and closures command a high premium, but beware of reproduced parts and repainting. The closure is a critical part of each container; if it is missing, the value of the container drops considerably. Small figural perfumes and other miniatures often are sold as candy containers.

Additional Resources:

Warman's® Americana & Collectibles, 11th Ed., by Ellen T. Schroy, ed., Krause Publications, Iola, WI.

Airplane, P-38 Lightning, orig wire clip, motors, and ground, no closure **$200**

Auto, coupe, long hood, orig tan snap-on strip, orig gold stamped tin wheels, orig closure **$120**

Barney Google, bank

Orig paint, orig closure **$650**

Repainted, orig closure **$450**

Baseball player, with bat, 50 percent orig paint, orig closure **$500**

Bear, on circus tub, orig tin, orig closure **$500**

Boat, USN Dreadnaught, orig closure **$350**

Bulldog, screw closure, 4-1/4" h....**$60**

Bus

Chicago, replaced closure **$275**

Heavy composition black cat candy container (bottom plug), Germany, repainted eyes, nose, and mouth, 1920s, 6" h, **$300.**
Photo courtesy of Mark B. Ledenbach.

Composition Veggie figural with original tag, Germany, 1920s, 4" h, **$185.**
Photo courtesy of Mark B. Ledenbach.

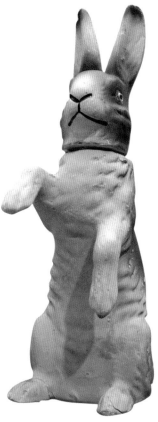

Candy container, rabbit, papier-mâché, original closure, **$550.**

New York-San Francisco, orig closure **$375**

Victory Glass Co., replaced closure **$300**

Camera, tripod base, 80 percent paint **$200**

Cannon

Cannon #1, orig carriage, orig closure **$375**

Two-Wheel Mount #1, orig carriage, orig closure **$220**

U. S. Defense Field Gun #17, orig closure **$380**

Cat, papier-mâché, seated, gray and white paint, pink ribbon, glass eyes, touch up and repairs, 3-3/4" h **$375**

Chick, composition, cardboard, base, Germany, 5" h **$20**

Dog, by barrel, 90 percent paint, chip on base, orig closure **$220**

Dog, papier-mâché, gray, painted and molded feathers, stamped "Made in Germany," repair at neck opening ... **$50**

Gadget cane, violin, large 3" h x 6-1/2" l mahogany tau handle, handle unscrews to reveal chamber holding a mahogany horsehair bow with ebony and MOP decoration. Instrument opens by removing a 21-1/2" panel held in place by nickel ring, maple sounding board and bridge, ebony seats, four pins and a key for tuning the strings, 1-3/4" brass ferrule, good condition, probably Austrian, c1860, 34-1/3" h x 6-1/2" l, **$6,700.**

Photo courtesy of Tradewinds Antiques, H.A. Taron.

Elf on rocking horse, pressed glass, no closure, 3-1/2" h **$160**

Felix the Cat, repainted, replaced closure **$550**

Fire truck, with ladders **$45**

George Washington, papier-mâché, with tricorn hat, white ponytail and blue coat, standing beside cardboard cabin with deep roof and chimney, unmarked, 3" h **$195**

Ghost head, papier-mâché, flannel shroud, 3-1/2" h **$150**

Gun, West Specialty Co., 5-3/4" l **$20**

Horse and wagon, pressed glass **$35**

Indian, pressed glass, riding motorcycle with sidecar, no closure, 5" l **$350**

Kettle, pressed glass, clear, T. H. Stough, cardboard closure, 2" h, 2-1/4" d **$50**

Limousine, orig wheels, orig closure, small chip **$600**

Little boy, papier-mâché head and hollow body, large pink nose, closed smiling mouth, painted brown eyes, molded and painted red vest, green jacket, yellow short pants, purple socks, black shoes, brown tie, 6" h **$210**

Locomotive, Mapother's 1892, orig closure **$125**

Man on motorcycle, side car, repainted, replaced closure **$525**

Mule, pulling two-wheeled barrel with driver, 95 percent paint, orig closure **$85**

Nursing bottle, pressed glass, clear, natural wood nipple closure, T. H. Stough, 1940-50 .... **$20**

Puppy, papier-mâché, painted, white, black muzzle, glass eyes, 2-1/2" h **$35**

Rabbit, glass

Rabbit pushing chick in shell cart, orig closure **$500**

Rabbit with basket on arm, no paint, orig closure **$120**

Rocking horse, small chips on rockers, no closure **$180**

Rooster, papier-mâché, pewter feet, orig polychrome paint, marked "Germany," 6-1/2" h **$225**

Sailor, papier-mâché head and hollow body, large pink nose, closed smiling mouth, protruding lower lip, molded and painted sideburns and hair, molded gray fez, painted blue eyes, molded and painted blue sailor uniform, black belt with knife case and sword, black shoes, unmarked, 6" h **$275**

Santa Claus, by sq chimney, 60 percent paint, replaced closure **$180**

Stop and Go, replaced switch handle, orig closure **$440**

Submarine F6, no periscope or flat, orig super structure, orig closure **$250**

Tank, World War I, traces of orig paint, no closure **$90**

Telephone, small glass receiver **$55**

Turkey, gobbler, small chip under orig closure **$100**

Village bank, with insert, log-cabin roof **$110**

Wagon, orig closure **$90**

Wheelbarrow, orig wheel, no closure **$35**

Windmill, five windows, ruby-flashed orig blades, orig closure **$495**

CANES

History: Canes or walking sticks have existed through the ages, first as staffs or symbols of authority, and then items like religious ceremonial pieces. They eventually evolved to the fashion accessory that is the highly desirable antique prized by today's collector for its beauty and lasting qualities. The best were created with rare materials such as carved ivory, precious metals, jewels, porcelain, and enamel, with many being very high-quality works of art. They were also fashioned of more mundane materials, with some displaying the skill of individual folk artists. Another category of interest to collectors is the gadget canes that contained a myriad of hidden utilitarian objects, from weapons to drinking flasks, telescopes, compasses, and even musical instruments, to cite just a few.

Adviser: Henry A. Taron.

Automata

English, 4-1/3" h x 2-1/4" handle, carved wood full-bodied pug, brown glass eyes, sitting on top of stump, short curly tail swings upward, long red tongue protrudes when button activated, 2/3" smooth gold collar mkd "Brigg, London," mahogany shaft, 7/8" brass ferrule, 36-1/4" l **$3,640**

English, 3-1/2" h x 3-1/2" w carved elephant ivory handle, fierce lion with flowing mane, button at back of neck causes tongue to protrude and eyes change from brown to red, 1/3" silver collar, brown hardwood shaft, 2/3" bone ferrule, c1900, 34-3/4" l **$2,200**

Bamboo, carved, Japanese, 1-1/2" h x 1-1/8" natural root handle, low relief carved shaft with leaves, insects, and moths, dark stained and chip carved background, 1" burnished brass ferrule, c1900, 36" l **$400**

Cameo glass, English, 3-2/3" h x 1-1/3" w pistol handle, cameo carved white palm trees on pale blue blown glass, 3/4" silver collar, rosewood shaft, 1-1/4" dark horn ferrule, c1895, 35-3/4" l **$2,920**

Campaign, American, McKinley, 4-1/4" l x 1-2/3" w tau horn handle, hollow tin, top engraved "Patriotism, Protection, Prosperity," shaft engraved "Pat. Apl'd For, The Winfield Mf'g, Warren, O," oval-shaped tin shaft with multiple small dents, capped end, 1896, 36" l **$450**

Cigarette holder with matchsafe, English, 2" h x 1-1/8" d sterling knob, dec with basketweave pattern, owner's initials on top, hinged lid opens to reveal compartment with central tube for cigarettes, hinged lid scored as striker, matches in crescent box with swing-open lid, London hallmarks, 7/8" horn ferrule, 1884, 37" l **$1,120**

Damascene, English, handle imported from Toledo, Spain, 6-1/2" l steel crook handle with gold damascene of dragons, flowers, geometric designs, ebony shaft, 1" burnished brass ferrule, c1890, 35-3/4" l **$4,370**

Ebony, carved, English, 5-1/4" h x 2" handle, grinning black man, wearing linked silver collar necklace, 1/4" elephant ivory ring collar, ebony shaft, 1-1/4" ivory ferrule, c1890, 35-1/2" l **$785**

Enamel, Continental, 1-1/2" h x 2-1/2" l duck handle, teal green enamel head, yellow glass eyes, painted yellow beak, 1/3" silver collar, black shaft, 1" horn ferrule, c1890, 36" l **$1,010**

Folk art, American, single piece of hickory, 2-1/3" cylindrical handle, high relief carving of religious and fraternal symbols including bible, all-seeing eyes, IOOF linked chain, bow and arrows, scales of justice, sheaf of wheat, skull and crossbones, caduceus staff, hourglass, heart-in-hand, beehive, coffin, peace dove, urn, crossed writing quills, crossed keys, crossed swords, crossed mallets, three baby bottles, c1895, 36" l **$2,600**

Gadget, English, tape measure, 1-1/2" h x 1-3/4" celluloid handle as Arab with turban, cigarette dangling from mouth, acts as handle for 3 foot cloth tape measure that pulls out of mouth, ringed brass collar, brown hardwood shaft, 1" horn ferrule, c1910, 36" l **$750**

Gold, American, 4-1/2" l x 2-1/4" gold filled handle shaped as finely detailed duck, yellow glass eyes, stepped partridgewood shaft, 7/8" brass ferrule, c1890, 33" l **$425**

Gold, Anglo/Indian, 1-7/8" h x 7/8" d knob, chased and raised owner's ini-

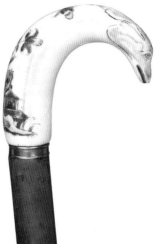

Cane, French, porcelain, bec-de-corbin handle, 4-3/4" along arc and 1" thick, painted bird face at pointed end, handle is painted in kakiemon style, 1/4" silver collar on Malacca shaft, 4-1/2" brass ferrule, Saint Cloud, very good, c1760, 33-3/4" l, **$3,920.**
Photo courtesy of Tradewinds Antiques, H.A. Taron.

Cane, lapis, gold and ebony, 2" h and 3/4" d lapis lazuli handle, 1/2" double-lined gold collar, ebony shaft, 2/3" horn ferrule, c1890, 35-3/4" l, **$1,344.**
Photo courtesy of Tradewinds Antiques, H.A. Taron.

Cane, folk art, by "Bally Carver," dog's head grip, shaft includes plumed heart, tulip, running horse, stars, buck, birds cows, etc., original varnished surface, 36" h, $4,830.
Photo courtesy of Pook & Pook, Inc.

Cane, elephant ivory pique, silver decoration, 3-3/4" h x 1-1/3" d handle, silver string inlay, silver overlay of bird, cat, flowers, leaves and butterflies, 4-1/8" brass ferrule, c1675, 36-1/4" l, value estimated at $12,000-$18,000; this cane sold at auction for $45,920.
Photo courtesy of Tradewinds Antiques, H.A. Taron.

tials on top, four standing Hindu gods in relief on side, single pc elephant ivory carved to simulate thorns, 1-1/4" brass ferrule, c1890, 33-1/2" l **$3,360**

Gun

Belgian, 6" l x 1" d black horn crook handle, 1-1/8" slotted nickel collar hides drop-down trigger, breech opened with quarter turn, 14mm breech with Belgian marks, rosewood veneer shaft, 1" removable ferrule/tampion, very minor crack in horn handle, c1895, 35-3/4" l **$1,200**

Continental, 2-1/2" l "L" handle, black painted metal, opens 4-1/2" down shaft, bayonet type socket for loading pin fire 12 mm cartridge, hammer on top of barrel pulls back with thong, 3/4" removable ferrule/tampion, c1885, 33-1/2" l **$1,100**

Historical, coaching, elephant ivory flat mushroom knob, 3/4" h, 1-2/3" d, scrimmed on top with detailed two-masted privateer, Prince George, inscribed "Prince George, 1762", owner's initials "I.D.," 3/4" scalloped silver collar with punch dec in diamond patterns, dark tropical wood shaft, 3-1/3" brass ferrule with circular mud flange, 1762, 56-1/4" l **$8,000**

Ivory, carved

Continental, 2-3/4" h x 1-7/8" d, high relief carved forest scene with dinosaurs, thick honey-toned Malacca shaft, 1" burnished brass ferrule, c1870, 36" l............................**$3,810**

Continental, 1-3/4" h x 4-1/3" l handle, semi-nude Cleopatra reclining on fancy divan, scratching dog's back while cat licking her foot, 3/4" silver collar, heavy ebony shaft, 1-1/2" replaced white metal and iron antique ferrule, small chip on divan, c1880, 36" l **$10,640**

English, automaton, wolf dressed as Red Riding Hood's Grandma,

2" l x 3-3/4" to side x 2-1/4" at thickest point elephant ivory "L" handle, detailed wolf with pale yellow eyes wearing Grandma's bonnet with round metal spectacles, when spring engaged, mouth swings open revealing large mouth with long fangs, 1-1/4" dec silver collar, Malacca shaft, 1" burnished brass and iron ferrule, c1885, 36" l **$3,600**

English, elephant ivory, 2-2/3" h x 4-1/2" l handle, detailed full-bodied leopard with yellow glass eyes, inlaid ebony spots, running pose, front paws on curved pedestal, 1" d sterling collar with worn owner's initials and London hallmarks, ebony shaft, 1" white metal and iron ferrule, c1900, 35-1/3" l **$8,000**

English, elephant ivory, 4" h x 1-1/4" w handle, carved rabbit with flute, yellow glass eyes, Alpine coat, 1/4" sterling collar, worn London hallmarks, rosewood shaft, 1" black horn ferrule, late 1890s, 36" l **$4,500**

English, elephant ivory "T" handle, 1-3/4" h x 4-1/4" l, detailed carved carp, yellow glass eyes, carp barbels, 1/3" dec silver collar, ebony shaft, 1" brass and iron ferrule, c1890, 35" l............................**$1,400**

English, piqué tau, 4" l elephant ivory handle, 1-1/4" w, classical shell carving on each end, circle and central cross piqué on top, circles and "C" scrolls on sides, 1/3" lined silver collar with "1691" above scrolling, stepped Malacca shaft, oval silver eyelets, 3-2/3" brass and iron ferrule, 34" l............................**$9,000**

German, William Tell, 5-1/3" h elephant ivory handle, 2" w, William standing on scrolled plinth, resting elbow while holding crossbow, fancy "T" carved in ivory below plinth, Malacca shaft, 1" silver band, 1-1/4" bone ferrule, c1860, 32-3/4" l **$2,000**

French, 2" h x 1" d Napoleon profile shadow handle, 2/3" silver collar, heavy ebony shaft, 1" horn ferrule, c1825, 36-1/4" l **$2,020**

French, 3-1/4" h x 1-1/4" d elephant ivory handle, carved panel on one side with silver lily overlay, 1-1/3" silver collar with French hallmarks, heavy rosewood shaft, 1" black horn ferrule, c1900, 36-1/3" l **$450**

German, 4" h x 2-1/2" handle, bearded troll kneeling on branch of oak tree, hand resting on rock hammer, 3/4" textured silver collar rimmed with two gold rings with gold tree trunk on side, worn Continental hallmark, ebony shaft, 1" replaced ferrule, c1800, 37-1/3" l **$1,800**

German, 7-1/2" h x 2-1/8" w pistol grip handle, carved coat of arms with plumed knight's helmet, detailed shield, inscribed Latin mottos "honestas, equitas, virtus," 1/3" carved ivory ring collar, dark rosewood shaft, 3/4" ivory ferrule, student type, c1885, 36" l **$2,690**

Ivory, hippo, carved, Continental, 4-1/8" h x 1-1/4" d fluted mushroom shaped top, graceful hand with fringed cuff holding ivory top, 3/4" rope turned ivory collar, finely figured thin snakewood shaft, 1-3/4" horn ferrule, c1895, 38" l **$1,010**

Ivory, walrus, carved

Continental, 2-3/4" h x 1-3/4" w, skeleton wearing ruffled collar, holding up bony hands and mask of human face, 1" textured silver collar with two simulated bucks and smooth cartouche, heavy ebony shaft, 1" brass and iron ferrule, c1880, 35-3/4" l **$4,250**

English, 5-1/4" h x 1-3/4" w handle with hunter leaning against tree with propped rifle, dog on hind legs sniffing game bag, hunter lighting pipe, 1" dec sterling collar with 1896 London hallmarks, tightly stepped partridgewood shaft, 7/8" replaced brass ferrule, made in England, imported German handle, 1896, 36-3/4" l **$1,460**

French, 4-1/2" h x 1-7/8" handle carved as young woman wearing fancy hat, blouse revealing breasts, opposite side inscribed "Madamd

Plaisir, Orleans," 3/4" rope turned silver collar, smooth partridgewood shaft, 1-1/2" white metal and iron ferrule, c1880, 36" l **$4,480**

Map, American Legion Convention, 6-1/2" wooden crook handle, 3/4" white metal collar with slot, spring-loaded cloth street map of Boston with metal edge and grip, paper label "American Legion Convention 1940," picture of Paul Revere, text "Paul Revere rides again," 2/3" white metal ferrule, 1940, 34-1/2" l **$535**

Marble, English, 4-1/2" h x 3-1/4" l gray opaque L handle, base with diamond overlay fashioned from four graduated pieces of different colored marble, shaft comprised of multicolored marble segments, 3" horn ferrule, c1900, 35-7/8" l **$2,650**

Merchant's measure, English, 2-1/2" h x 1-1/4" d ivory knob handle, rich yellow patina, unscrews to reveal long thin flexible Malacca rod with small round rosewood handle, 1-1/2" brass and iron tip, rod has line of dots to measure in one inch increments, 1" scalloped and punch dec silver collar, worn Malacca shaft, 3" brass ferrule, c1695, 36-1/2" l **$4,700**

Mixed metals

Japanese, 3-3/4" h x 1-1/4" d handle, silver, gold, and copper leaves and vines, silver praying mantis on brass background, artist sgd in small cartouche, dark bamboo shaft, 1-1/2" white metal and iron ferrule, c1890, 34-3/4" l **$2,000**

Japanese, fashioned in America, 2-1/2" h x 1" w brass knob with finely detailed standing crane holding plum branch in beak, silver body, copper crest, bamboo shaft with pyrography, sgd in Japanese characters by maker, 1-1/4" white metal and iron ferrule, c1895, 35" l **$1,500**

Mother of pearl, French, 2-2/3" h cylindrical knob handle, 7/8" d top made from eight diamond shaped pieces that come together at center point, sides with mother-of-pearl bars and vermeil silver overlay with festoons of roses and ribbons at top, center silver ring, chain of laurel leaves at base, French hallmarks and "935," ebony shaft, 1-1/3" white metal and iron ferrule, 36-1/4" l **$1,600**

Cane, Venetian millifiori, Pate de Verre glass paste 2" h handle, 1/3" gold gilt collar, honey-toned hardwood shaft, 1" replaced white metal ferrule, found in France, very good, c1915, 38-1/4", **$1,344.**
Photo courtesy of Tradewinds Antiques, H.A. Taron.

Cane, English, carved wood and gilt metal, 6" l slightly curved handle, 1-3/4" at widest point, jester has carved wood body and gilt metal boots, arms and head, holds a jester's rattle depicting Punch, 1/2" gilt collar marked "Brigg," very good, c1890, 34-3/4" l, **$1,230.**
Photo courtesy of Tradewinds Antiques, H.A. Taron.

Music box, Swiss, carved from single pc of hardwood, possibly birch, 3" l, 2" h smooth "L" handle, carved pug dog sitting upright on top of music box on top of shaft, separate winding key, carved shaft with simulated thorns, c1900, 34-3/4" l........... **$6,440**

Nautical

America, carved whale ivory and whalebone, 2-1/4" h x 1-1/8" d whale ivory mushroom handle, inlaid on top with 1/3" sq piece of baleen with round mother-of-pearl spherule in center, thin baleen separator, fully carved whalebone shaft with section of sawtooth pattern, section of convex fluting, then concave fluting raised stringing turns to left followed by raised piece, uniform yellow patina, c1840, 32-1/4" l................................. **$2,800**

Cane, American, Remington dog head gun cane curio, 2-1/3" h, 3-1/4" "L" handle, classic gutta-percha hound head, 1/3" nickel collar, shaft unscrews to receive 32 cal. rimfire cartridge, straight pull cocks gun and raises sight, round trigger under handle, shaft covered in gutta-percha, worn Remington marks, "PatFeb.9th 1872" and model number "890," 1-2/3" hollow nickel ferrule, matching model number "890," very good, c1875, 34" l, **$10,080.**
Photo courtesy of Tradewinds Antiques, H.A. Taron.

America, whale ivory and carved whalebone, 3" h x 1-1/2" d whale ivory handle, 1/3" round baleen spherule inlaid in flat top, three tin baleen spacers around two 1/4" whale ivory spacers, while whalebone shaft with angled twist carving, some age cracking, spacers cosmetically in-filled, c1850, 35" l
.... **$2,240**

Ophthalmologist, America, 1-1/2" elephant ivory ball handle, 1" brown glass eyes, 7/8" dec collar mkd "sterling," figured rosewood shaft, 1" black horn ferrule, c1890, 36" l **$840**

Pewter, 1-2/3" h x 1-1/4" d pewter knob handle, domed top inscribed "I.G.R., 1795," malacca one-step shaft with swing clevis for cord below handle, 1-3/4" lined pewter mount with scalloped edges pointed at top and bottom, 9-1/4" pewter ferrule, 3/4" dull-pointed iron tip, Continental, 49" l................................. **$3,000**

Phrenology, America, 36-1/3" l, 2-2/3" h x 1-1/4" w handle with markings and clear decoder, yellow patina, 2/3" beaded and lined silver collar, stepped partridgewood shaft, 1" burnished brass and iron ferrule, c1850, 36-1/3" l **$3,360**

Porcelain

English, 1-1/2" d pale blue porcelain ball, painted jockey and horse jumping over water hazard, green wreath of foliage frames scene, 1/4" gold ring collar, heavy ebony shaft, 1" replaced brass ferrule, c1900, 36-3/4" l..................................... **$500**

Royal Copenhagen, 2-1/4" h x 7/8" cylindrical handle, hand painted scene with sailboat, pale blue, green, gray, and pink, 1/2" gold wash collar, black enameled shaft, 7/8" horn ferrule, England, 1900
.... **$1,345**

Presentation, America, 18kt gold, double gold quartz inlays, 4" h, 4" l, 1" thick tau handle, inlaid on each end is 1" x 3/4" polished oval gold quartz stone, each matrix with gold flecking in gray/white background, inscribed fancy cartouches on handles, presenter's initials on side, receiver's name on shaft portion, dark tropical wood shaft, 1" white metal and iron ferrule, c1870, 36-1/4" l **$6,160**

Quartz, French, vermeil silver overlay, 2-3/4" h x 7/8" d pale pink rose quartz handle, internal crystalline fissures, two vermeil silver floral rings at top and bottom, three long classical columns topped with ferns, one column with French Minerva hallmark for 950 silver, ebony shaft, 1" burnished brass ferrule, c1900, 37" l................................. **$1,795**

Rock crystal

Bavaria, 3" h x 1" d rock crystal handle, top faceted like jewel, fourteen long smooth panels on sides, 2/3" silver collar with blue guilloche enamel, custom 4-1/4" l red leather case mkd "Berthold Fuchs," jewelry from Bad Kissingen, Bavaria, lined with satin and velvet, ebonized hardwood shaft, 1" horn ferrule, c1900, 36" l.......................... **$1,345**

French, 36" l, 2-3/4" h x 1" d rock crystal handle, reticulated overlay vermeil silver in diamond and swirled patterns, tiny French hallmarks, brown hardwood shaft, 7/8" horn ferrule, c1900, 36" l.............. **$1,345**

Shooting stick seat, French, birch and bamboo, iron slide fittings, two 6" x 4" folding seat, 3-1/2" pointed ferrule can be inserted into ground for stability, c1900, 34" l
.... **$500**

Silver

2-1/4" l x 1-1/4" d spherical handle of Chinese man with knotted pigtail queue, handle unscrews to reveal water receptacle and long metal siphon, when queue is lifted, man emits strong stream of water from mouth, maccassar ebony, Art Nouveau, Viennese, 1-1/3" horn ferrule, 37-1/8" l................................. **$2,000**

3" l silver dog head with amber glass eyes, mkd "800," partridgewood, 7" crook handle, 1-1/4" brass and iron ferrule, c1895, 36" l................. **$280**

3" h x 4-1/2" "T" handle, full-bodied mermaid reclining on floral bed with sinuous Art Nouveau flowers, swirling long hair, Continental hallmarks, snakewood shaft, 1-1/3" horn ferrule, c1900, 38" l...... **$3,000**

3-1/4" h x 3-3/4" l "L" handle shaped like golf putter, oval cartouche with owner's initials, dec with fancy scrolls and flowers, mkd "Sterling," opens to gold washed cigarette case, figured snakewood shaft, 1-1/2" burnished brass ferrule, American, c1895, 36" l **$1,120**

Snuff, Austro-Hungarian, 7" h x 1-1/2" d oval vermeil silver handle, engraved C-scrolls, raised spiral chain encrusted with rubies, emeralds, sapphires, garnets, pearls, and shell in raised mounts, shallow gold lined box with curved bottom for snuff under hinged top, ebony shaft, 1-3/4" white metal and iron ferrule, two stones missing, 40-1/2" l **$2,000**

Staghorn, English, 2" h x 4" l polished staghorn handle carved as African elephant, amber glass eyes, 1" gold collar initialed "C.J.W.," dated 1906, hallmarked 12K gold, mkd "Brigg," honey toned bamboo shaft, 3/4" burnished brass ferrule, 1906, 36" l **$840**

Sunday stick, English, tortoiseshell, 1-1/2" h x 3" l handle fashioned like golf driver, faux gold weight on side, inscribed "Good Luck," London hallmarks for 18k and 1905, mkd "Brigg," 7/8" gold collar, inscribed "Sir Louis Nuthsen," stepped partridgewood shelf, 1" burnished brass ferrule, storage bag, 1905, 37-1/4" l **$1,800**

Sword, English, 2-1/2" h x 1-1/4" gold knob handle, ducal stallion engraved on top, engraved with scrolls and flowers, two swimming swans, orig owner's name "E. Barnard" engraved on lower edge, thick Malacca shaft with gold mounts and swing clevis 2-1/2" d down 30" l triangular sword, tight tongue, groove metal fitting, twin blood grooves, minor age pitting, 5-7/8" brass ferrule, c1760, 44-1/4" l
.... **$3,810**

Wood

American, 3-1/2" l x 2-1/2" w carved half crook handle, single pc of ash, carved face of John Brown, revarnished, 2" l iron ferrule, c1860, 36" l **$1,120**

America, 5-1/2" l x 3" d "L" handle, high relief carving of rifle and game shoulder bag with roping, shield with roping at bottom of handle, 2/3" coin silver collar inscribed "F.K. Murray, Captain US Navy, 1868," knobby hickory shaft, 1" brass and iron ferrule, 1868, 34-1/2" l **$360**

Anglo-Indian, carved rosewood, 4-1/4" h x 1-1/3" w stylized bird handle, ivory and ebony eyes, ivory tail, two 1/2" ivory separators

Seven-bottle, George III, c1800, Anglo-Irish cut glass shakers, ewers, etc. with silver mounts, fitted oval tray with four feet, 11" h, 8-1/2" l, **$1,675.**
Photo courtesy of Pook & Pook, Inc.

and one horn separator, 2-3/4" of reticulated silver at top of rosewood shaft, three more separators, thin ivory ferrule, first half 20th C, 37-1/4" l **$400**

English, 2-2/3" h x 2" d dark wood handle carved as detailed monkey wearing collar and tie, when ivory button at back of head engaged, glass eyes roll and change color from blue to yellow, long red tongue shoots out, thin horn collar, dark rosewood shaft, 1" white metal and iron ferrule, c1890, 37-1/3" l **$1,900**

English, made from single piece of hardwood, perhaps birch, 4-3/4" l pistol grip handle carved as brown and white fox, stained dark brown shaft stepped to simulate bamboo, 1" white metal and iron ferrule, c1900, 39-1/2" l **$1,010**

CASTOR SETS

History: A castor set consists of matched condiment bottles held within a frame or holder. The bottles are for condiments such as salt, pepper, oil, vinegar, and mustard. The most commonly found castor sets consist of three, four, or five glass bottles in a silver-plated frame.

Although castor sets were made as early as the 1700s, most of the sets encountered today date from 1870 to 1915, the period when they enjoyed their greatest popularity.

2-bottle, Reed and Barton, Egyptian-style frame, two cranberry glass cruets and matching open salt elevated in center, 18" h **$600**

Eight-piece cruet set, George III, ovoid monogrammed stand, ogee-shaped gadrooned rim, wood base, tapered legs, ball feet, loop handled upright, holds colorless cut glass two casters, three cruets, and lidded jar all with silver mountings, maker's mark "CC," London, 1810, 10-1/4" h, **$410.**
Photo courtesy of Skinner, Inc.

3-bottle, Bohemian, three shouldered 14" h decanters, flashed blue, green, and cranberry, cut with circles, etched Greek key band, silver-plated stand with tall central handle above three cylindrical wells, with geometric engine turning, borders with fruiting grapevine, three grapevine feet, late 19th C, 10-1/4" w, 20-1/2" h **$865**

3-bottle, clear, Daisy-and-Button pattern, toothpick holder center, matching glass holder **$125**

4-bottle, cranberry bottles and jars, clear pressed-glass frame, silver-plated look handle, two brass caps, one pewter, 9-1/2" h **$275**

4-bottle, ruby stained, Ruby-Thumbprint pattern, glass frame **$360**

5-bottle, clear, New England Pineapple, two cruets with orig numbered cut and pressed panel hollow stoppers, two shakers with cut panel necks, period lids, mustard pot with period hinged lid, unmarked Brittania frame, 14-1/4" h, 7" d frame
.... **$330**

6-bottle, cut, diamond-point panels, rotating sterling-silver frame, all-over flowers, paw feet, loop handle, Gorham Mfg. Co., c1880, 11-1/2" h
.... **$2,500**

6-bottle, etched designs, revolving silvered metal stand, Victorian
.... **$175**

CATALOGS

History: The first American mail-order catalog was issued by Benjamin Franklin in 1744. This popular advertising tool helped to spread inventions, innovations, fashions, and necessities of life to rural America. Catalogs were profusely illustrated and are studied today to date an object, identify its manufacturer, study its distribution, and determine its historical importance.

Additional Resources:

Warman's® Americana & Collectibles, 11th Ed., by Ellen T. Schroy, ed., Krause Publications, Iola, WI.

A. B. See Electric Elev., New York, New York, 24 pgs, stiff wraps, 1908, 8-3/4" x 10" **$24**

A. Cutler & Son, Buffalo, New York, 86 pgs, Catalog No. 12, early 1900s, 6" x 8" **$75**

Baraca & Philathea Supply Co., Syracuse, New York, 32 pgs, 1923, 3-1/2" x 6" **$21**

Bullock & Crenshaw, Philadelphia, Pennsylvania, 60 pgs, 1857, 5-3/4" x 9" **$325**

Burstein-Applebee Co., Kansas City, Missouri, 114 pgs, wraps, 1948, 8" x 10-1/2" **$40**

Century Furniture Co., Grand Rapids, Michigan, 145 pgs, hardcover, 1927, 5-1/2" x 8-1/4" **$24**

Champion Corp, Hammond, Indiana, 39 pgs, vertical fold in center, c1929, 7" x 9-1/2" **$35**

Crane Co., Chicago, Illinois, 28 pgs, 1927, 3-1/2" x 6-1/4" **$15**

Crofts & Reed Co., Chicago, Illinois, 148 pgs, Spring & Summer catalog, 1916, 7-3/4" x 10-1/2" **$37**

Detroit Dental Mfg Co., Detroit, Michigan, 11 pgs, Gilmore Adjustable Attachments, c1924, 5-1/4" x 8-1/4" **$15**

Distinctive Weathervane, York, Pennsylvania, 15 pgs, 1930s, 6" x 9-1/4" **$80**

Eli Lilly & Co, Indianapolis, Indiana, 295 pgs, hardcover, Handbook of Pharmacy & Therapeutics, illus, 1925, 7" x 9-1/4" **$48**

Erie Engine Works, Erie, Pennsylvania, 48 pgs, 1901, 7-1/2" x 9-3/4" **$190**

Ernst Heinrich Roth, US, 40 pgs, photos of violins, 1924, 6-1/2" x 9-1/2" **$50**

Fairbanks, Morse & Co., Chicago, Illinois, 24 pgs, pictorial wraps, 1926, 8-1/2" x 11" **$20**

Flaig Bros, Pittsburgh, Pennsylvania, 24 pgs, c1930, 6-1/2" x 9" **$22**

Fuller Brush Co., Hartford, Connecticut, 12 pgs, full color, c1975, 8-1/4" x 11" **$10**

Geo. Delawrence, Berlin, Wisconsin, 25 pgs, c1929, 4-3/4" x 7" **$12**

George C. Frys Co., Portland, Maine, 78 pgs, Cat. No. 162, c1928, 8" x 10" **$48**

Horace Partridge Co., Boston, Massachusetts, 92 pgs, Catalog No. 139, 1932, 6-1/2" x 9-1/2" **$85**

Howard Tresses, New York, New York, 30 pgs, c1935, 5-3/4" x 9" **$16**

James B. Clow & Sons, Chicago, Illinois, 52 pgs, c1911, 9-1/4" x 12" **$45**

James Manufacturing Co., Ft. Atkinson, Wisconsin, 255 pgs, hardcover, 1914, 6-3/4" x 9-3/4" **$55**

King & Eisele Co., Buffalo, New York, 12 pgs, two pgs illus, order form laid-in, c1928, 9-1/2" x 12-1/4" **$55**

Krafft & Phillips Fashion, Philadelphia, Pennsylvania, 20 pgs, color, 1935, 10-3/4" x 15" **$45**

Liquid Carbonic Co., Chicago, Illinois, 72 pgs, 1914, 6" x 9" **$85**

Louden Machinery Co., Fairfield, Iowa, 50 pgs, illus, 1912, 7-3/4" x 10-3/4" **$42**

Luger Industries Inc., Burnsville, Minnesota, 80 pgs, in mail-out envelope, 1971, 8-1/4" x 11" **$30**

Lyons Band Instrument Co., Chicago, Illinois, 256 pgs, spiral bound, 1956, 9" x 11" **$40**

Marshall Field & Co., Chicago, Illinois, eight pgs, pocket folder of floor coverings, 1932, 6-1/4" x 8-1/4" **$20**

Norlin Music Inc., Lincolnwood, Illinois, 12 pgs, c1975, 7-1/2" x 11" **$15**

Northfolk Paint & Varnish, Norfolk Downs, Massachusetts, 26 pgs, 1930, 8-1/2" x 11" **$10**

Oakwood Manufacturing Co., Springfield, Ohio, 32 pgs, c1910, 8" x 7-1/2" **$18**

Ohio State Stove & Mfg Co., Columbus, Ohio, 12 pgs, six illus, pages laid-in, c1925, 7-3/4" x 10-1/2" **$26**

Old Town Canoe Co., Old Town, Maine, 48 pgs, 1956, 6" x 8" **$75**

Oskamp, Nolting & Co., Cincinnati, Ohio, 40 pgs, wraps, 8-3/4" x 11-3/4" **$65**

Pan-American Band Instruments, Elkhart, Indiana, 1930s, 3-1/4" x 6-1/4" **$30**

Pass & Seymour Inc., Syracuse, New York, 137 pgs, Catalog No. 25, 1919, 7-1/2" x 10-3/4" **$26**

Richmond Stove Co., Richmond, Virginia, 96 pgs, c1920, 3-1/2" x 6" **$40**

Rock Island Stove Co., Rock Island, Illinois, 63 pgs, Catalog No. 38, 1929, 7-3/4" x 10-1/2" **$32**

Sayre & Fisher Co., New York, New York, c1895, 122 pgs, hardcover, 6-3/4" x 10-1/2" **$32**

Sealed Power Corp, Muskegon, Michigan, 1943, 32 pgs, 8" x 10-1/2" **$14**

Sears, Roebuck & Co., Chicago, Illinois, 34 pgs, automobiles, 1911, 7" x 9-1/2" **$100**

Sears, Roebuck & Co., Chicago, Illinois, 19 pgs, rugs and carpets, 1936, 8-3/4" x 12-3/4" **$20**

Shakespeare Co., Kalamazoo, Michigan, 32 pgs, Angler's Catalog, 1959, 7" x 10" **$24**

Stewart & McGuire, New York, New York, eight pgs, silver gilt highlights, 8-1/4" x 11" **$45**

At left, teddy bear, Japanese, moveable arms and legs, bright pink, made in Occupied Japan, c1945, 4-1/4", $30; at right, bright red teddy bear, made in Occupied Japan, 6" h, $35.

St. Bernard, tan, black highlights, intertwined VCO/USA, c1925, 3-1/4", $18.

Societe Industrielle de Celluloid, fully jointed baby doll, dressed in vibrant fancy regional costume from Britany region, costume adds height to the doll. Trademarked with SIC in lozenge shape, c1920, 6", $65.

Stover Mfg & Engine Co., Freeport, Illinois, 24 pgs, folded vertical as issued, c1939, 8" x 9" **$35**

Targ & Dinner, Chicago, Illinois, 472 pgs, bound volume of catalogs, 1967, 9" x 12" **$55**

The Cloak-Drummer Co., Chicago, Illinois, 86 pgs, fall and winter, 1912, 7" x 9-1/2" **$30**

United States Rubber Co., New Orleans, Louisiana, 12 pgs, 1940, 9" x 12" **$32**

Victor Safe & Lock Co., Cincinnati, Ohio, 200 pgs, wear at binding, 1910, 6-1/2" x 9-3/4" **$110**

Weber Lifelike Fly Co., Stevens Point, Wisconsin, 96 pgs, No. 19, 1938, 6-1/4" x 9" **$60**

Westinghouse Machine Co., Pittsburgh, Pennsylvania, three pgs, c1895, 6" x 9" **$140**

Whitemore Associates Inc., Boston, Massachusetts, 160 pgs, 1950, 6" x 9" **$30**

Wright & Ditson, Boston, Massachusetts, 112 pgs, Spring & Summer Sports Equipment, 1928, 5-1/2" x 8" **$100**

Wright Co., Inc., Atlanta, Georgia, 212 pgs, kitchen equipment, 1928, 8-1/2" x 11-1/4" **$125**

Yale & Towne Mfg Co., Stamford, Connecticut, 450 pgs, hardcover, Catalog No. 25, 1921, 7-3/4" x 10-3/4" **$110**

CELLULOID ITEMS

History: In 1869, an Albany, New York, printer named John W. Hyatt developed and patented the world's first commercially successful semi-synthetic thermoplastic. The moldable material was made from a combination of camphor, the crystalline resin from the heart of a particular evergreen tree, and collodion, a type of nitrated-cellulose substance (also called Pyroxylin), which was extremely flammable. Hyatt and his brother, Isaiah, called their invention Celluloid, a name they made up by combining the words cellulose and colloid.

By 1873, the Hyatts were successfully producing raw pyroxylin plastic material at the Celluloid Manufacturing Company of Newark, NJ. In the early days of its commercial development, Celluloid was produced exclusively in two colors: flesh tone, for the manufacture of denture-base material, and off white, which was primarily used for utilitarian applications like harness trimmings and knife handles.

However, during the late 1870s, advances in plastics technology brought about a shift in the ways Celluloid could be used. Beautiful imitations of amber, ivory, tortoiseshell, jet, and coral were being produced and used in the fabrication of jewelry, fashion accessories, and hair ornaments. Because the faux-luxury materials were so realistic and affordable, Celluloid quickly advanced to the forefront of working and middle class consumerism.

Throughout the 1880s and 1890s, the Celluloid Manufacturing Company experienced stiff competition from a number of newly organized companies that began to aggressively produce their brands of pyroxylin plastic into a variety of products. By the early 20th century, there were four major American manufacturers firmly established as producers of quality pyroxylin plastics. In addition to the Celluloid Company of Newark, New Jersey, there was the Arlington Manufacturing Company of Arlington, New Jersey, which produced Pyralin; Fiberloid Corporation of Indian Orchard, Massachusetts, makers of Fiberloid; and the Viscoloid Company of Leominster, Massachusetts. Even though these companies branded their plastic products with registered trade names, today the word "celluloid" is used in a general sense for all forms of this type of early plastic.

Celluloid was imported into France during the mid 1870s for use in the fabrication of ornamental hair combs and its success was quickly recognized throughout Europe. By the 1880s it was being manufactured in factories throughout France and Germany. It was the German doll industry that made initial strides in utilizing the material for toys during the late 1890s. The first manufacturing plant for celluloid in Japan was built in 1908 and by the 1920s that country was the world's most prolific manufacturer and fabricator of pyroxylin plastic—due in most part to the island of Formosa's vast natural resources of camphor forests—an essential ingredient in the celluloid recipe.

Celluloid-type plastics were popular alternatives for costly and elusive natural substances. Within the fashion industry alone, it gained acceptance as a beautiful and affordable substitute for increasingly dwindling supplies of ivory and tortoiseshell. However, it should be noted that celluloid's most successful application during the late 19th century was realized in the clothing industry as an imitation of fine-grade linen that was fashioned into stylish waterproof cuffs and collars.

In sheet form, celluloid found many successful applications. Printed political and advertising premiums, pinback buttons, pocket mirrors, and keepsake items from 1890-1920 were turned out by the thousands. In addition, transparent-sheet celluloid was ornately decorated by embossing, reverse painting, and lamination, and then used in the production of decorative boxes, booklets, and albums. The toy industry also capitalized on the use of thin-celluloid sheet for the production of blow-molded dolls, animal toys, and figural novelties.

The development of the motion-picture industry helped celluloid fulfill a unique identity all its own; it was used for reels of camera film, as well as in sheet form by animation artists who drew cartoons. Known as animation cels, these are still readily available to the collector for a costly sum, but because of the degradation of old celluloid, many early movies and cels have been lost forever.

By 1930, and the advent of the modern-plastics age, the use of celluloid began to decline dramatically. The introduction of cellulose-acetate plastic replaced the flammable pyroxylin plastic in jewelry and toys, and the development of non-flammable safety film eventually put an end to its use in movies. By 1947, the major manufacturers of celluloid in the United States had ceased production; however, many foreign companies in Germany, France, Denmark, Italy and Japan continued manufacture and produced dolls and toys throughout the post World War II period. Today Japan, Italy and Korea continue to manufacture cellulose-nitrate plastics in small amounts for specialty items such as musical-instrument inlay, knife handles, ping-pong balls, and designer fountain pens.

Beware of celluloid items that show signs of deterioration: oily residue, cracking, discoloration, and crystallization. Take care when cleaning celluloid items; it is best to use mild soap and water, avoiding alcohol- or acetone-based cleansers. Keep celluloid from excessive heat or flame and avoid direct sunlight.

Marks: Viscoloid Co. of Leominster, Massachusetts manufactured a large variety of small hollow animals between 1914-1930, that ranged in size from two to eight inches. Most of these toys are embossed with one of three trademarks: "Made in USA," an intertwined "VCO," or an eagle with a shield. German and Japanese manufacturers of collectible figural toys numbered in the hundreds. All toys imported into the United States were either embossed with a trademark, and or stamped with country of origin, or carried an export inspection sticker. Many American and German toy designs were copied by the Japanese, particularly the Ando Togoro company, whose trademark resembles a crossed circle.

Adviser: Julie P. Robards.

Advertising and souvenir-keepsake items

Badge, 2-7/8" l shield shaped, on a lanyard, printed with two intertwined American flags, Chaplain Ladies Auxiliary, FOE, thick multiple layered celluloid, fraternal organization for Fraternal Order of Elks, made by Whitehead & Hoag Co., early 1900s, 5-3/4" l, 1-1/4" w **$20**

Bookmark, embossed with roses and embroidered, "Greetings" on the long flat surface, pink tassel, c1920 ...... **$25**

Card, delicate lacy embossed celluloid printed with floral motif in yellow and pink and the words "Fond Greetings," c1910, 3" x 2" **$30**

Clothing brush, celluloid-laminated photograph showing Pennsylvania State Memorial, Gettysburg, Pennsylvania, sepia, black and cream, c1920, 3-1/2" d **$75**

Compact, imitation ivory-grained celluloid with gold Elk motif and "Third Annual Ball, BPOE, Leominster Lodge No. 1237, Jan.

26, 1917," produced by the Viscoloid Co. of Leominster, MA, c1917, 1-3/4" d **$65**

Fan, when closed, cream colored celluloid Brise fan, peach colored ribbon, shows the Washington Monument and "Washington D.C." in goldtone paint. Celluloid loop, c1920, 4" h **$40**

Ink blotter, Christmas theme advertising premium. Printed celluloid cover with religious imagery of Shepherds and Sheep with Star of Bethlehem. "To our faithful old friends and cherished new friends we render this greeting. E. Keller & Sons," c1915, 7-3/4" x 3" **$65**

Match safe, souvenir metal safety-match holder, celluloid on cover showing colorized photo of Atlantic City, New Jersey boardwalk, c1920, 2-1/2" x 1" **$45**

Pinback button, printed cream colored celluloid with crossed American and Irish flags with shamrock and lyre motif in the center. "Erin Go Bragh," c1920, 3/4" d **$30**

Pin holder, celluloid disc, metal framework, "F Krupps Steel Works, Thomas Prosser & Son, NY," front shows advertising, back shows small child, engraved ivory-grained celluloid, c1890, 1-3/4" d **$40**

Pocket mirror, topsy-turvy image of a smiling man, "This man trades at Hager's Store, Frostburg, MD," turned upside down, the man is frowning and caption reads, "This man does not. For a satisfied customer see other side.," c1900, 1-3/4" d **$110**

Postcard, emb-fan motif with applied fabric and metal-script words, "Many Happy Returns," applied over fabric, c1908, 5-1/2" x 3-1/2" **$35**

Tape measure, pull-out tape, colorful pretty girl with flowers, adv for "The First National Bank of Boswell, The Same Old Bank in its New Home," printed by P.N. Co. (Parisian Novelty Co. of Chicago), Patent 7-10-17, emb in the side, c1920, 1-1/4" d **$65**

Animals, Toy

Among the most prolific manufacturer of American made celluloid toys was the Viscoloid Co. of Leominster, Massachusetts. This company manufactured a variety of small hollow toy animals, birds, and marine creatures, most of which are embossed with one of these three trademarks: "Made In USA," an intertwined "VCO," or an eagle with shield. A host of foreign countries also mass-produced celluloid toys for export into the United States. Among the most prolific manufacturers were Ando Togoro of Japan, whose toys bear the crossed-circle trademark, and Sekiguchi Co., which used a three-petal flower motif as its logo. Paul Haneaus of Germany used an intertwined PH trademark, and Petticolin of France branded its toys with an eagle head. Japanese-and American-made toys are plentiful, while those manufactured in Germany, England, and France, are more difficult to find.

Alligator, green, white-tail tip, VCO/USA, c1925, 3" **$18**

Animal set, Japanese, six circus animals, garish bright colors, marked "Made In Occupied Japan," elephant, gorilla, giraffe, tiger, lion, and hippo, set, c1945 .... **$85**

Bear, American, cream bear, pink and gray highlights, VCO/USA, c1920, 5" w **$20**

Bison, dark brown, eagle-and-shield trademark, c1920, 3-1/4" l **$18**

Boar, brown, Paul Haneaus of Germany/PH trademark, c1920, 3-1/4" l **$75**

Camel, peach celluloid, pink and black highlights, marked with crossed circle and "Made in Japan," c1930, 3-1/2" x 2-1/2" **$20**

Cat, Japanese, peach, flower trademark, c1935, 3-1/2" l **$30**

Chick, yellow, black eyes and beak, no trademark, c1925, 7/8" **$8**

Chicken, Japanese, metal feet, club trademark w/N, c1935, 1-1/2" **$30**

Cow

Cream-and-orange cow, intertwined VCO/USA, c1925, 4-1/2" **$25**

Nodder, French, realistic design w/ lozenge trademark w/SNF, c1930, rare **$175**

Dog

English Bulldog, spiked neck collar, translucent-green color, rhinestone eyes, intertwined VCO/USA, c1920, 4-3/4" l, 2-1/2" h **$35**

Hound, Japanese. Long tail, peach celluloid, gray highlights, crossed-circle Japan trademark, c1930, 5" **$25**

Scottie, plaster-filled cream-colored celluloid, no detailing, marked JAPAN, c1945, 3-1/4" l **$25**

Donkey, peach celluloid, nodder head, made in Occupied Japan, c1945, 4" l **$55**

Duck, standing, cream-colored celluloid, hand-painted eyes and bill, original paper label, Japan, c1935, 2-1/4" **$20**

Elephant

American Viscoloid gray elephant, tusks, USA, c1920, 6-3/4" x 4-3/4" **$45**

Nodder, trunk down, wide open ears, white, gray highlights, Bird trademark Japan, c1945, 3-3/4" **$45**

Fish

Bright red, USA, c1925, 2-1/4" l **$8**

Yellow with brown highlights, molded scales, intertwined VCO, circle, c1925, 2-7/8" l **$12**

Frog, green or yellow, stripe on back, intertwined VCO/USA, c1920, 1-1/4" **$25**

Giraffe, cream, painted yellow and brown spots, eagle trademark, French, c1940, 7" tall **$85**

Goat, white, curled horns, flower, "N" in circle represents Navy Goat, Japan, c1935, 3" **$35**

Hippopotamus, Japanese, pink, closed mouth, MIOJ, c1945, 3-3/4" **$18**

Horse

Bending to eat grass on base, Occupied Japan, c1945, 5" l **$30**

Cream, purple and pink highlights, USA, 7" l **$18**

Leopard, white, orange highlights, black spots, Occupied Japan, c1945, 4-1/2" **$30**

Lion

Japanese, tan, brown highlights, marked TS & Made in Japan, c1930, 3-3/4" **$20**

Japanese nodder, pink highlights on white celluloid, fierce open mouth, full mane, Japan, c1945, 5-1/4" l **$65**

Lobster, American Viscoloid,bright red, detailed shell, c1925, 1-3/4" .. **$65**

Penguin, Japanese, Diahachi Kobyashi trademark, nodder, black with red bill and feet, blue eyes, Japan, 4-1/2" **$65**

Pig, pull toy, pink pig on rectangular platform, four celluloid wheels, USA, 4-1/2" animal on 6" base **$65**

Polar Bear, white, USA, c1925, 2-1/4" l **$15**

Ram, cream, gray highlights, USA, c1925, 4-1/2" **$20**

Rhino, German, gray, fine detail, PH trademark, Paul Haneaus, c1920, 5" l **$65**

Seal, gray, balancing red ball, VCO/USA, c1925, 4-1/2" l **$70**

Squirrel, rare, brown, holding nut, USA, c1925, 2-7/8" h **$65**

Stork, Japanese, standing, white, pink legs, flower mark, Japan, c1950, 6-3/4" **$25**

Swan, Japanese, multicolored purple, pink, yellow, crossed circle trademark, c1935, 3-3/8" **$20**

Tiger, "P" painted on side for Princeton Mascot; Japanese, c1940, 6 1/2" l **$35**

Turtle, brown top, yellow bottom, USA on foot, c1925, 1-3/8" **$18**

Dolls

American

Marks Brothers, boy doll, molded hair, blue eyes, shoulder plate marked Marks Bros. Co., Boston, Mass, USA, celluloid arms and hands, cloth body and legs, rare, c1920, 18" **$200**

Jackson, Parsons, baby doll with jointed arms and legs, realistic detailing, bald headed, open mouth, trademark of stork on back w/ Parsons Jackson Co. Cleveland, Ohio, USA, c1914 .... **$200**

Sametz, Louis, Dutch girl, thin cream colored hollow celluloid, side glancing eyes, hands in pocket of long dress, ring attached to top, rattles, trademarked w/Indian profile on back, c1920 .... **$35**

Viscoloid, figural girl with short dress, hat and side glancing eyes, very well molded hair, socks and shoes, rattles, image of child star Baby Peggy, trademarked w/intertwined VCO/USA, c1925 .... **$45**

Viscoloid, jointed girl doll, naked with well molded shoes and socks, bobbed hair with bow. Marked USA, c1925, 7" tall....................**$55**

Denmark

Jeris Kofoed, Girl doll with short curly molded hair, naked except for shoes and socks, jointed arms and legs, hair painted blond pearlescent, pink cheeks. Trademarked with scalloped shell trademark, c1940, 4-1/2" tall **$55**

France

Petitcollin Co., Boy doll with jointed arms and legs, dressed as a shepherd. Trademarked with profile of eagle head, c1930, 8" **$55**

Society Nobel Francaise, realistic toddler doll with brown real hair wig, glass eyes that shift back and forth, flirty smile, fully jointed with socket head, trademarked SNF in lozenge, c1935, 18" tall, rare **$300**

Germany

Buschow & Beck, shoulder plate doll with real wig and blue glass eyes, beautifully molded facial features, slightly parted lips, helmet insignia on front of shoulder plate, kid body, composition arms and legs, c1910, 14" tall **$150**

Cellba, chubby girl with curly hair, pink cheeks and pursed lips, jointed arms, fixed legs, dressed in regional costume, trademark with crowned mermaid in shield, c1936, 4-1/2" tall **$45**

Schildkrott fashion doll, young girl with shoulder plate head, real hair wig, glass eyes, fully jointed arms and legs, dressed in blue satin and lace dress, original white leather shoes with fancy buckles, trademarked with turtle. c1920, 14" tall.........**$250**

Japan

Karl Standfuss Co. Kewpie with topknot, blue wings, fixed body with moving jointed arms, naked, Grace O'Neill copyright, trademarked JUNO in oval, c1920, 4" rare **$125**

Kewpie knock-off, top knot-no wings, naked with side glancing eyes, jointed legs and arms. Trademark Japan w/ top logo, c1925, 4" **$45**

Roly Poly, Easter related, duckling, peach hat trimmed in flowers, jacket,

necktie, green trim, cream celluloid, VCO trademark, 2-1/2" **$155**

Toy Boat, German ocean liner, gray and red, flag, intertwined PH, 4-1/2" **$50**

Fashion accessories

Bar pin, rect shape, translucent amber bar pin with applied center blue flower, c-clasp, c1920, 2-1/2" l **$30**

Belt, 3/4" x 1-1/2" rect mottled green celluloid slabs linked by chain, applied silver-tone filigree dec, 22" l **$35**

Comb and case, c1925

Cream-colored celluloid comb, 3-1/4" x 1" pearlized amber and gray rhinestone-studded case, 3" l **$25**

Folding molded case, emb rose motif, imitation ivory with brown highlights, 2-1/4" l **$30**

Eyeglasses, Harold Lloyd type, black frames...**$20**

Hair ornament, ornamental, imitation tortoiseshell, double prong, oblong shaped filigree hair ornament for securing upswept hairdo, c1900, 6"..**$65**

Hair comb, ornamental, imitation tortoiseshell, 24 teeth, applied-metal trim studded with rhinestones and brad fastened Egyptian Revival pink and gold metal floral and beetle dec., 1890, 4" x 5-1/4" **$145**

Hat pin, c1910

Elephant head, tusks, black glass eyes, imitation ivory, 4" head on 6" shank **$100**

Filigree-hollow egg, pale-green paint applied over grained celluloid, 10" l **$85**

Hat ornament, c1930

Art Deco, pearlized red and cream half circles, rhinestone trim, 3-1/2" h **$65**

Calla lily, cream-pearlized celluloid, white rhinestones, 1-1/2" l threaded pin with screw-on celluloid point, 4-1/2" h **$35**

Purse frame

Black pointed horseshoe shape, rhinestones, white molded cameo clasp, 4" l..**$95**

Imitation tortoiseshell, crescent shape, molded filigree and center

cameo, celluloid push-button latch and linked chain, 6" l **$110**

Purse, basketweave, link celluloid chain, mottled grain ivory and green 4-1/2" x 4-1/2"...............................**$200**

Holiday items

Angels, set of three, one holding cross star, or lantern, Japan, Mt. Fuji trademark, 1-1/2" h................................**$35**

Christmas decoration, roly poly-type house, opening in back for a small bulb, shows Santa approaching door, red and white, intertwined VCO/USA trademark **$125**

Christmas ornament

Little boy on swing, all celluloid, dark green highlights, holding onto string "ropes" for hanging on tree, 3-3/4"..**$95**

Santa, Horn and sack, hole in back for light bulb, trademarked "S" in circle, Japan, 3-3/4" **$65**

Striped green and white Christmas stocking filled with gifts including duck and kitten, crossed-circle trademark, Ando Togoro, 4" **$125**

Halloween favor, orange horn, black witch and trim, intertwined VCO/USA, 4" l....................................**$150**

Rattle, standing black cat, orange bow, intertwined VCO/USA, 3-3/4" l **$185**

Reindeer, white deer, gold glitter, red eyes and mouth, molded ears and antlers, USA, 3-1/2".......................**$20**

Roly poly, black cat on orange pumpkin, intertwined VCO/USA, 3-1/2" **$235**

Santa

Basket of flowers, fur-trimmed suit, nice detail, VCO/USA trademark, 5" h **$75**

Yellow or mint green translucent celluloid, holding lantern and sack, Japanese, Mt. in circle trademark, 4" **$55**

Novelty items

Letter opener

Bulldog on long pointed hollow blade, Made in Germany, 7-1/4" l **$75**

Ivory grained, magnifying glass in top, coiled-metal snake, red-glass eyes around the handle, 7-3/8" l **$85**

Pin cushion

Figural hen on weighted base, straight pins stick into holes in base, American VCO/USA, 2-1/4" h **$75**

Figural novelty rabbit with pin cushion baskets, marked "Germany" 2" h **$130**

Tape measure

Billiken, cream celluloid, applied-brown highlights, marked "Japan", 2-1/2" h **$185**

Utilitarian and household items

Bookends, pr, mottled-pink celluloid, emb ornamental gold neoclassic drape, plaster weighted, no trademark, c1930, 4-1/4" h, 3-1/4" w, 2-1/4" d............. **$45**

Clock

German Gothic cathedral design, round face, dark yellow ivory grained celluloid, 5-1/2" x 3" **$45**

New Haven Clock Co., alarm, folding travel case, pearlescent pink laminated over amber celluloid, 3" sq **$30**

Crumb tray set, two dustpan-shaped trays, ivory celluloid, dark blue dec border, monogrammed "T" in center of each tray, c1910 .... **$50**

CFrame

Pearlized-amber celluloid, diecut floral motif, attached over wood frame, celluloid butterflies in each corner, 5-1/2" x 7" **$35**

Round, ivory grained, easel back, 4" d **$25**

String holder, round sphere on a weighted base, twist apart, center hole in top for string, imitation-ivory grain, no trademark, c1910 .... **$65**

Watch holder, pearlescent blue, green, and amber, wall-hanging banjo-clock style, Wilcox trademark, late 1920s, 6-1/2" l... **$25**

Vanity items

Dresser boxes, oval-shaped pearlized peach boxes, dec-shaped lids, marked "Amerith," Lotus Pattern, c1929 pr **$35**

Dresser set

Eight-piece, pearlized yellow-laminated amber celluloid, black trim, mirror, brush, shoe horn, button hook, soap box, nail buffer, tooth-brush holder, hair-pin holder, marked "Arch Amereth, Windsor," orig box, c1928 .... **$75**

Seventeen-piece, Fairfax pattern, Fiberloid Company, mottled brown and gold, carved floral trim, comb, brush, mirror, powder box, hair receiver, nail file, scissors, button hook, and clothing brush, c1924................. **$125**

Dresser tray, pearlized cream color and amber framework, Normandy lace inserted between double-glass bottom, c1925 oval, 7-1/2" l, 5" w................. **$30**

CHARACTER AND PERSONALITY ITEMS

History: In many cases, toys and other products using the images of fictional comic, movie, and radio characters occur simultaneously with the origin of the character. The first Dick Tracy toy was manufactured within less than a year after the strip first appeared.

The golden age of character material is the TV era of the mid-1950s through the late 1960s; however, some radio-premium collectors might argue this point. Today, television and movie producers often have their product licensing arranged well in advance of the initial release.

Do not overlook characters created by advertising agencies, e.g., Tony the Tiger. They represent a major collecting sub-category.

Additional Resources:

Warman's® Americana & Collectibles, 11th Ed., by Ellen T. Schroy, ed., Krause Publications, Iola, WI.

Character

Andy Gump, pinback button, "Andy Gump For President/I Endorse The Atwater Kent Receiving Set," red,

Andy, litho tin wind up, yellow derby, light blue jacket, red and tan striped trousers, Louis Marx & Co., **$320.**
Photo courtesy of Pook & Pook, Inc.

Dionne Quintuplets, booklet, All Aboard for Shut-Eye Time, Dr. Dufoe and Quints on cover, **$25.**
Photo courtesy of Sky Hawk Auctions.

Katzenjammer Kids, original illustration, drawn by Harold H. Knerr, 11" x 8-1/2", **$475.**
Photo courtesy of David Rago Auctions, Inc.

white, blue, and fleshtone, 1-1/4" d
.... **$40**

Betty Boop

Book, Betty Boop Cartoon Lessons, Fleischer Studios, 1935, 12" x 9"
.... **$500**

Marble, Peltier Glass Co., black and white swirl, black transfer of Betty, c1932, 11/16" **$175**

String holder, chalk, head and shoulders, orig paint, 6-1/2" w, 7-1/2" h
.... **$625**

Brownies, Palmer Cox

Book, *The Brownies, Their Book*, Palmer Cox, NY, 1887, first edition, second issue, illus by Cox, 4to, pictorial glazed boards **$230**

Child's fork and spoon, emb Brownies on handles **$18**

Dolls, stuffed cloth, Uncle Sam, Indian, Highlander, Chinaman, German, Sailor, Soldier, Canadian, Irishman, Policeman, John-Bull, and Dude, each has name stitched on back, colorful-printed outfits, marked "Copyright 1892 by Palmer Cox" on back of each, "Brownie's" on right foot of each, set of 12, 8" dolls **$775**

Buster Brown

Bench, child size bench, four seats divided by diecut animal shapes, one black and white lion, black and white zebra, and orange tiger, red background, detailed illus of Buster and Tige on ends
.... **$6,000**

Children's feeding dish, Buster and Tige, wear to gold trim **$115**

Figure, bisque, red hat and suit, blue bowtie, black shoes, c1920, 2" h
.... **$100**

Sunday comics, St. Paul Daily News, full section, 1914 .... **$20**

Tray, Buster Brown Shoe's, brown grain painting, gold lettering, some wear, 13-3/8" d **$65**

Campbell's Kids

Child's feeding plate, two Campbell kids, one holding doll behind back, Buffalo Pottery **$45**

Doll, boy, orig clothing, 1970, 16" h
.... **$35**

String holder, chalk, incised "Copyright Campbell," 6-3/4" h **$395**

Charlie the Tuna

Animation cel, 10-1/2" x 12" clear acetate sheet, centered smiling full-figured 4" image of Charlie gesturing toward 4" image of goldfish holding scissors, 10-1/2" x 12-1/2" white paper sheet with matching blue/lead pencil, 4" tall image of Charlie, c1960 .... **$150**

Wristwatch, bright gold luster bezel, full-color image of Charlie on silver background, ©1971 Star-Kist Foods, grained purple leather band, 1-1/2" d bezel **$60**

Dutch Boy, string holder, diecut tin, Dutch Boy sitting on swing painting the sign for this product, White Lead Paint Bucket houses ball of string, 14-1/2" x 30" **$300**

Elsie the Cow, Borden

Display, mechanical milk carton, cardboard and papier-mâché, figural milk carton rocks back and forth, eyes and mouth move from side to side, made for MN state-fair circuit, 1940s **$500**

Lamp, Elsie and Baby, hollow ceramic figure base, Elsie reading to baby nestled on her lap, brass socket, c1950, 4" x 4" x 10" **$125**

Felix the Cat

Figure, dark copper-colored plastic, loop at top, 1950s, 1" h **$10**

Pinback button, Herald and Examiner, c1930s, 1" d **$45**

Valentine, diecut, jointed cardboard, full color, "Purr Around If You Want To Be My Valentine" inscription, ©Pat Sullivan, c1920 .... **$20**

Happy Hooligan

Figure, 8-1/4" h, bisque, worried expression, tin-can hat, orange, black, blue, and yellow **$75**

Stickpin, 2-1/4" l, brass **$25**

Howdy Doody

Belt, suede, emb face **$35**

Cake-decorating set, unused **$40**

Pencil case, vinyl, red **$25**

Jiggs and Maggie

Pinback button, The Knoxville Sentinel, black and white image of Jiggs, red bowtie, c1920, 3/4" d
.... **$15**

Salt and pepper shakers, pr, ceramic
.... **$48**

Katzenjammer Kids

Christmas card, copyright King Features Syndicate, 1951, 4-1/4" x 4-1/2" **$18**

Comic strip, Ovaltine ad on back **$15**

Li'l Abner

Bank, Schmoo, blue plastic............ **$50**

Pinback button, Li'l Abner, Saturday Daily News, black litho, cream ground, newspaper name in red, 13/16" **$20**

Little Annie Rooney, pinback button, comic-strip contest button serial-number type, c1930, 1-1/4" d
.... **$25**

Little Orphan Annie

Big Little Book, *Little Orphan Annie Secret of the Well*, No. 1417
.... **$85**

Book, *Little Orphan Annie and the Gila Monster Gang,* Harold Gray, Whitman Publishing, © 1944 licensed by Famous Artists Syndicate, 248 pgs, 5" x 8" **$12**

Toothbrush holder, bisque, back inscribed "Orphan Annie & Sandy, ©F.A.S., #1565," bottom stamped "Japan," some wear to paint, 4" h
.... **$165**

Mr. Peanut

Ashtray, Golden Jubilee, 50th Anniversary, gold-plated metal, figural, orig attached booklet, orig box, 5" h, 5-3/4" h **$130**

Bank, green, 8-1/4" h **$20**

Booklet, *Mr. Peanuts Guide to Tennis,* 24 illus pgs, ©1960, 6" x 9"
.... **$20**

Mug, green, c1960, 3-3/4" h **$18**

Paint book, Planter's Paint Book No. 2, 32 pgs, ©1929, 7-1/4" x 10-1/2" .. **$35**

Toy, trailer truck, red cab, yellow and blue plastic trailer, 5-1/2" l **$275**

Mutt & Jeff

Bank, cast iron, orig paint, 4-7/8" h
.... **$125**

Book, *The Mutt & Jeff Cartoon Book,* Bud Fisher, black and white illus by author, Ball Pub. Co., 1911
.... **$100**

Dolls, composition character heads, molded and painted features, molded mustaches, metal ball jointed body, composition hands, orig felt jackets, vests, ties, and pants, molded hat, Bucherer, 6-1/2" h and 8" h, price for pr ...**$500**

Popeye

Cereal bowl, plastic, white ground, red, blue, and black illus of Popeye and Olive Oyl **$5**

Charm, bright copper-luster plastic figure of Olive Oyl, 1930s, 1" h.. **$10**

Figure, chalkware, 14" h.............. **$150**

Mug, Olive Oyl, figural, 4" h **$20**

Reddy Kilowatt

Hot pad, laminated heat-resistant cardboard, textured top surface with art and verse inscription, "My name is Reddy Kilowatt-I keep things cold. I make things hot. I'm your cheap electric servant. Always ready on the spot," c1940, 6" d **$40**

Pinback button, "Please Don't Litter," blue and white, 1950s **$15**

Stickpin, red enamel and silvered-metal miniature diecut figure, c1950 .... **$30**

Speedy Alka Seltzer, patch, colorful stitched image of smiling Speedy waving his wand, pixie dust accent, 1960s **$35**

Yellow Kid

Cap bomb, cast iron, c1898, 1-1/2" h **$185**

Pinback button, #2, orig paper label, 1894.. **$60**

Personality

Amos and Andy

Photograph, framed black and white facsimile signed photograph and brochure.................................... **$95**

Toy, Andy, litho tin wind-up, yellow derby, light blue jacket, red and tan striped trousers, Louis Marx & Co. **$320**

Autry, Gene

Badge, Gene Autry Official Club Badge, black and white, bright orange top rim, c1940, 1-1/4" d **$50**

Child's book, *Gene Autry Makes a New Friend*, Elizabeth Beecher, color illus by Richard Case, Whitman Tell-A-Tale, 1952................. **$12**

Watch, orig band **$145**

Ball, Lucille

Magazine, Life, April 6, 1953, five-pg article, full-color cover of Lucy, Desi Arnaz, Desi IV, and Lucy Desiree **$30**

Movie-lobby card, full color, 1949 Columbia Picture "Miss Grant Takes Richmond," 11" x 14" **$40**

Cassidy, Hopalong

Coloring book, large size, 1950 .... **$30**

Tablet, color-photo cov, facsimile signature, unused, 8" x 10"............ **$24**

Wallet, leather, metal fringe, multicolored cover, made by Top Secret **$35**

Chaplin, Charlie

Candy container, glass, Charlie and barrel, small chip, 3-3/4" h **$100**

Magazine, *Life*, April 1, 1966, Chaplin and Sophia Loren **$10**

Dionne Quintuplets

Advertisement, Quintuplet Bread, Schultz Baking Co., diecut cardboard, loaf of bread, brown crust, bright red and blue letters, named silhouette portraits, text on reverse, 5" x 7" **$70**

Booklet, *All Aboard for Shut-Eye Time*, Dr. Dufoe and Quints on cover **$25**

Doll, Dr. Dufoe, composition, painted blue eyes, single stroke brows, closed smiling mouth, gray mohair wig, jointed at shoulders and hips, orig two-pc doctor's uniform, hat, socks, and shoes, marked "Madame Alexander New York" on clothing tag, doll unmarked, 14" h **$525**

Fan, diecut cardboard, titled, "Sweethearts of the World," full-color tinted portraits, light-blue ground, funeral director name on reverse, ©1936, 8-1/4" x 8-3/4" **$35**

Garland, Judy

Pinback button, "Judy Garland Doll," black and white photo, used on c1930 Ideal doll, name appears on curl, also "Metro-Goldwyn-Mayer Star" in tiny letters, 1" h **$125**

Sheet music, "On the Atchison, Topeka, and the Sante Fe," 1945 MGM movie, "The Harvey Girls," sepia photo, purple, light pink, and brown cov **$35**

Gleason, Jackie

Magazine, *TV Guide*, May 21, 1955, Philadelphia edition, three-pg article on the Honeymooners.......... **$18**

Pinback button, "Jackie Gleason Fan Club/ And Awa-a-ay We Go!," blue

on cream litho, checkered suit, 1950s, 1-5/8" d...................... **$65**

Laurel & Hardy

Movie poster, When Comedy Was King, 20th C Fox, Laurel and Hardy in center **$25**

Salt and pepper shakers, pr **$175**

Lone Ranger

Coloring book, unused.................. **$50**

Game board, target bull's eye **$185**

Ring, Cheerios premium, saddle type, filmstrip missing **$225**

Marx, Groucho, book, *Groucho and Me*, Groucho Marx, Bernard Geis, 1959, 22 photos **$10**

Mix, Tom

Big Little Book, Whitman, *Tom Mix and The Stranger from the Sea*, Pete Daryll, 1936, #1183 ...... **$75**

Premium, Tom Mix Ralston Telegraph Set, 1940...................... **$95**

Ring, magnet, 1946 .... **$145**

Scarf, Tom Mix Ralston Straight Shooters **$195**

Our Gang, Little Rascals, display sign, 23-1/4" x 32", heavy diecut cardboard, Felin's Meat Products, c1920, sign and individual 1-1/4" x 3" named figures **$4,700**

Rogers, Roy

Bank, Roy on Trigger, porcelain, sgd "Roy Rogers" and "Trigger".... **$200**

Charm, blue plastic frame, black and white glossy paper photo, 1" h . **$35**

Ring, litho tin, Post's Raisin Bran premium, Dale Evans, ©1942........ **$45**

Watch, Roy and Dale **$120**

Temple, Shirley

Child's book, *The Shirley Temple Edition of Susannah of the Mounties*, by Muriel Denison, Random House, New York, 1936, reprint orange cover with red and black lettering on front and end cover, orig dust jacket **$20**

Doll, composition, hazel sleep eyes, open mouth, orig mohair wig in orig set, jointed at shoulders and hips, dressed in tagged pajamas from Poor Little Rich Girl, orig shoes, mkd "Shirley Temple, Ideal, N & T Co.," 18" h **$575**

Figure, salt-glazed, 6-1/2" h.......... **$85**

Handkerchief, Little Colonel, boxed set of three **$200**

Magazine tear sheet, Lane Hope Chests adv, 1945 .... **$8**

Pinback button, brown-tone photo, light-pink rim, Ideal Dolls, 1930s, 1-1/4" d **$75**

Three Stooges

Autograph, letter, 4-1/2" x 5-1/2" mailing envelope, two folded 6" x 8" sheets of "Three Stooges" letterhead, personally inked response to fan, sgd "Moe Howard," March 10, 1964 Los Angeles postmark **$200**

Badge, cello, black and white upper face image of Curly-Joe on purple background, Clark Oil employee type, 4" d **$20**

Photo, glossy black and white, facsimile signatures of Curly-Joe, Larry, and Moe, plus personal inscription in blue ink by Moe, 4" x 5" **$95**

Wayne, John

Magazine, *Life*, Jan. 29, 1972........**$25**

Magazine tear sheet, "Back to Bataan," black and white, 1945, 10" x 13". **$15**

Movie poster, "McLintock," 1963 . **$250**

CHILDREN'S BOOKS

History: Because there is a bit of the child in all of us, collectors always have been attracted to children's books. In the 19th century, books were popular gifts for children, with many of the children's classics written and published during this time. These books were treasured and often kept throughout a lifetime.

Developments in printing made it possible to include more attractive black and white illustrations and color plates. The work of artists and illustrators has added value beyond the text itself.

Additional Resources:

Collecting Little Golden Books®, by Steve Santi, Krause Publications, Iola, WI.

Warman's® Americana & Collectibles, 11th Ed., by Ellen T. Schroy, ed., Krause Publications, Iola, WI.

Warman's® Little Golden Books®, by Steve Santi, Krause Publications, Iola, WI.

Warman's® Little Golden Books Field Guide, by Steve Santi, Krause Publications, Iola, WI.

A Child's Garden of Verses, illus by Myrtle Sheldon, Donahue Pub, 1st ed, 1916 .... **$25**

A Christmas Carol, Charles Dickens, Garden City Pub, color and black and white illus by Everett Shinn, red cover, fancy gold trim, ©1938 .... **$28**

Adventures of Tom Sawyer, Mark Twain, American Pub. Co., Hartford, Connecticut, blue and gold cover, 1899 .... **$45**

Alice's Adventures in Wonderland in Words of One Syllable, Saalfield, illus by John Tenniel, dj, ©1908 .... **$18**

American Girl Beauty Book, Bobbs-Merrill, New York, illus, 1945................ **$9**

And To Think That I Saw It On Mulberry Street, Dr. Seuss, Vanguard Pub., 3rd printing, ©1937 .... **$15**

An Old Fashioned Girl, Louisa M. Alcott, Robert Bros. Pub, 1870, 1st ed **$35**

Bobbsey Twins At The County Fair, The, Grossett & Dunlap, 1st ed., dj, 1922 .... **$28**

Book of the Camp Fire Girls, Rev. Ed., paperback, 1954.............................. **$6**

Boys Story of Lindbergh, The Lone Eagle, Richard Beamish, John C. Winston Co., dj, 1928 .... **$20**

Bunny Rabbit Concert, Lawrence Welk, illus Carol Bryan, Youth Pub. Sat Evening Post, 2nd printing, 1978......... **$8**

By the Shores of Silver Lake, Laura Ingalls Wilder, illus Garth Williams, Harper Collins, dj, 1953 .... **$10**

Christmas Eve on Lonesome and Other Stories, John Fox, Jr., Grossett & Dunlap, 1904 .... **$15**

Eric & Sally and Other Stories, Johanna Spyrl, Grossett & Dunlap, 342 pgs, 1932 .... **$7**

Freckles, Grossett & Dunlap, illus by E. Stetson Crawford, 1904 .... **$8**

Girl Scout Handbook, Rev. Ed., 1930 .... **$7**

Hardy Boys, Missing Chums, Franklin Dixon, illus by Walter Rogers, Grossett & Dunlap, 1st ed, 1928.......... **$25**

Helen's Babies, John Habberton, J. H. Sears & Co., colorful illus by Christopher Rule **$10**

How the Grinch Stole Christmas, Dr. Seuss, Random House, Grinch on red and green cover, ©1957 .... **$25**

Little Britches, Father and I Were Ranchers, Ralph Moody, illus Edward Shenton, Peoples Book Club, Chicago, 1950 .... **$8**

Lullaby Land, Eugene Field, Scribner, 1st ed, 1897 .... **$35**

Marcella Stories, Johnny Gruelle, M. A. Donohue Co., color and black and white illus, dj, 1930s...................... **$95**

Metropolitan Mother Goose, Elizabeth Watson, Metropolitan Insurance Co. promo, 1930s, 20 pgs **$18**

Mother Goose and Nursery Rhymes, Anthemum Pub., colored wood engravings by Philip Reed, 1st ed,

Mother Goose and gander on orange cover, 1963 .... **$35**

Mother Goose or The Old Nursery Rhymes, Warne, Kate Greenaway illus, pictures on both front and back cov, c1900, 44 rhymes **$45**

Moving Picture Boys and the Flood, The, Victor Appleton, Grossett & Dunlap, pictorial cover, 1914 .... **$15**

Mr. Winkle Goes to War, Theodore Pratt, Duell, Sloan & Pearce, 1st ed, dj, 1943 .... **$8**

Mrs. Appleyard's Year, Louise Andrews Kent, Hough. Mifflin, 195 pgs, rooster on cover, 1941 .... **$9.50**

Mrs. Wiggs of the Cabbage Patch, Alice Hegan Rice, Appleton-Century Co., hardbound, lady in red dress on cover, 1941 .... **$10**

My Very Own Fairy Stories, Johnny Grulle, P. F. Volland Co., 30th ed, color illus, 1917 .... **$65**

Nancy Drew, The Password to Larkspur Lane, illus by Russell Tandy, Grossett & Dunlap, some fading to blue cover, 1933 .... **$65**

Nelly's Silver Mine, Helen Hunt Jackson, Little Brown & Co., illus by Harriet Richards and Henry Pitz, dj, 1924 .... **$20**

Peter Rabbit and the Little Boy, Linda Almond, Platt & Munk, 1935 .... **$15**

Raggedy Ann's Wishing Pebble, Johnny Gruelle, M. A. Donohue Co., color and black and white illus, dj, 1930s **$85**

Riley's Songs O'Cheer, James Whitcomb, Bobbs Merrill Pub, six color illus, black and white illus by Will Vawter, 1905 .... **$35**

Six White Horses, Candy Geer, illus Leslie Bennet, M & W Quill Pub, 2nd printing, 1964 .... **$6**

Smoky The Cow Horse, Will James, Aladdin Books **$8**

Swiss Family Robinson, The, Johann Wyss, illus by Lynd Ward, Grosset & Dunlap, Junior Library edition, 1949 .... **$8**

Tarzan and City of the Gold, Edgar Rice Burroughs, Whitman, dj, 1952 .... **$15**

The Cat In The Hat Comes Back, Dr. Seuss, Random House, dj, 1958 .... **$185**

The New Our Friends, Dick and Jane, Scott Foresman, 1951 .... **$38**

The Night Before Christmas, A Little Golden Book, Simon Schuster, illus Cornelius DeWitt, 1946 .... **$45**

Tom Sawyer Detective, Mark Twain, Grossett & Dunlap, 1924 .... **$15**

Uncle Remus His Songs and Sayings, Joel Chandler Harris, 112 illus by A. B. Frost, D. Appleton & Co., 1916 .... **$75**

Uncle Wiggily and the Runaway Cheese, Howard R. Garis, color illus by A. Watson, Platt & Munk, oversize, 1977 .... **$13**

When We Were Very Young, A. A. Milne, Dutton, 3rd printing, 1924 .... **$17.50**

CHILDREN'S FEEDING DISHES

History: Unlike toy dishes meant for play, children's feeding dishes are the items actually used in the feeding of a child. Their colorful designs of animals, nursery rhymes, and children's activities are meant to appeal to the child and make meal times fun. Many plates have a unit to hold hot water, thus keeping the food warm.

Although glass and porcelain examples from the late 19th and early 20th centuries are most popular, collectors are beginning to seek some of the plastic examples from the 1920s to 1940s, especially those with Disney designs on them.

ABC plate

Aesop's Fables the Leopard and the Fox, black transfer print, pearlware, England, 19th C **$175**

Crusoe Finding the Foot Prints, color enhanced brown transfer, pearlware, England, minor discoloration, 19th C **$125**

Eye of the master will do no more than his hands, multicolored transfer **$145**

Franklin's Provbs, (sic) black transfer print, pearlware, England, 19th C **$175**

Old Mother Hubbard, brown transfer, polychrome enamel trim, alphabet border, marked "Tunstall," 7-1/2" d **$200**

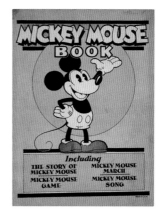

Mickey Mouse Book, second to fourth printing, Wynn Smith daily strips on page 8 and back cover, "Printed in USA" on front, complete copy, Bibo and Lang ©, light age, VG/Fine, 9" x 12", **$925.**
Photo courtesy of Hake's Auctions www.hakes.com.

Baby plate, rolled rim, decal decoration, verse "Baby Bunting Runs Away, And joins the little pigs at play," wear to gold trim on border, marked "D. E. McNichol, East Liverpool, O, 1218," **$95.**

Rocking horse, carved and painted, horsehair mane and tail, orig smoke surface and blue rockers, late 19th century, 28" h, 46-1/2" w, **$915.**
Photo courtesy of Pook & Pook, Inc.

Highchair, Windsor, bow-back, bamboo turned, painted, Pennsylvania, bowed crest rail on seven spindles, scrolled arms, shaped seat, splayed legs, footrest and stretchers, imperfections, c1810, overall 39" h, 24" h seat, **$880.**
Photo courtesy of Skinner, Inc.

Buffalo Pottery, Grace Drayton children, worn image, chip on inner rim, **$20.**

Take Your Time Miss Lucy, black transfer of money and cat, polychrome enamel, titled, molded hops rim, red trim, ironstone, imp "Meakin," 6" d **$125**

Bowl, Sunbonnet girls dec, pale orange band, cream colored ground, marked "Roseville," slight wear, inner rim chip **$200**

Butter pat, "A Present For Ann," blue transfer medallion, 3-1/4" d **$125**

Cereal set, Nursery Rhyme, amber, divided plate, Humpty Dumpty on mug and bowl, Tiara **$125**

Creamer, three yellow ducks, yellow band with black outline, cream-colored ground, marked "R12" **$125**

Cup, Raggedy Ann, Johnny Gruelle, Crooksville China, 1941 .... **$65**

Cup plate, "Constant dropping wears away stones and little strokes fell great oaks," green transfer, polychrome enamel dec, 4-5/8" d **$90**

Feeding dish

Kiddieware, pink, Stangl **$125**

Little Bo Peep, glass, divided, white, red trim **$65**

Nursery Rhyme, green enamelware, marked "Made in Germany" **$40**

Raggedy Ann, Johnny Gruelle, Crooksville China, 1941, 8-3/4" d **$85**

Mug

Pearlware, black transfer, girl jumping rope, England, early 19th C, 1-7/8" h **$275**

Pearlware, black transfer dec, Dr. Franklin's Maxim's on Industry, England, early 19th C, 2-1/2" h........ **$345**

Pearlware, blue transfer dec, "A Present for Charles," vine borders, England, early 19th C, 2-1/2" h **$325**

Pearlware, blue transfer dec, "A Present for Samuel," recumbent cow, England, early 19th C, 2-1/2" h........ **$275**

Pearlware, blue transfer dec of couple in boat in scene with deer, England, minor rim chip, early 19th C, 2-5/8" h **$195**

Pearlware, brown transfer motto "Better be alone than in bad Company," England, early 19th C, 2-5/8" h **$265**

Pearlware, dark red dec, poem for December, child with dog and cat pulling cart full of toys, England, early 19th C, 2-5/8" h............. **$295**

Pearlware, green and black transfer dec, "Dr. Franklin's Poor Richard Illustrated," on industry, England, early 19th C, 2-5/8" h............. **$285**

Pearlware, green transfer dec, "The Orchard," England, early 19th C, 2-5/8" h **$235**

Pearlware, maroon transfer, "Mr. Winkle's Horsemanship," England, early 19th C, 2-7/8" h............. **$295**

Pearlware, reddish-brown dec, "For loving a book," England, early 19th C, 2-1/2" h **$300**

Plate

Buster Brown, mint center image, 1910, 6" d **$135**

"Where Are You Going My Pretty Maid, See Saw Margery Daw," three parts, transparent-green Depression-era glass, 8" d **$45**

CHILDREN'S NURSERY ITEMS

History: The nursery is a place where children live in a miniature world. Things come in two sizes: Child scale designates items actually used for the care, housing, and feeding of the child; toy or doll scale denotes items used by the child in play and for creating a fantasy environment copying that of an adult or his own.

Cheap labor and building costs during the Victorian era encouraged the popularity of the nursery. Most collectors focus on items from 1880 to 1930.

Additional Listings: Children's Books, Children's Feeding Dishes, Children's Toy Dishes, Dolls, Games, Miniatures, and Toys.

Paint set, Alice in Wonderland, tin litho box, some original paints, marked "Made in England," **$25.**

Rocking horse, carved, orig painted surface, late 19th century, 20-1/2" h, 40-1/2" l, **$700.**
Photo courtesy of Pook & Pook, Inc.

Doll Bed, Mickey and Minnie Mouse, wood with fabric covering, English, Mickey on foot, Mickey and Minnie on headboard, moderate wear, Fine, 1930s, 10-1/2" x 20" x 12" h, **$280.**
Photo courtesy of Hake's Auctions www.hakes.com.

Papier-mache child's chair, ebonized, gilt decoration, MOP inlaid, arching crest rail, vasi-form splat, needlework stuff-over seat, ring-and ball turned legs, peg feet, mid-19th century, 28-1/4" x 13-3/4" x 14-1/2", **$445.**
Photo courtesy of Sloans & Kenyon Auctioneers and Appraisers.

Doll bed, red painted pine, four poster bed, arched head and foot boards, American, 19th century, 17-5/8" h x 9-7/8" w x 14" l, **$440.**
Photo courtesy of Skinner, Inc.

Child's table, Gustav Stickley, overhanging top, lower stretcher mortised through sides, orig finish on base, refinished top, loose, branded and paper label under top, 18-1/2" x 28" x 19-3/4", **$765.**
Photo courtesy of David Rago Auctions, Inc.

Crib, Sheraton, bird's-eye maple, headboard with cutout crest above fielded panel, turned posts and spindles, hinged side, custom mattress, second quarter 19th century, 42" h x 28" w x 51" d, **$275.**
Photo courtesy of Green Valley Auctions.

Child's rod back Windsor side chair, orig green painted surface, 19th century, 18" h, **$295.**
Photo courtesy of Pook & Pook, Inc.

Blocks, boxed set, ABCs, animals, litho of Noah and ark on cov, Victorian **$185**

Boat, play, ice, wood with iron runners, c1900, 24" l **$460**

Bucket, wooden-stave construction, orig yellow paint, blue-painted tin bands, stenciled stars, chick, and eagle, wood and wire bale handle, int. has some crayon marks, bottom band replaced, 5-1/2" d, 4-1/4" h **$660**

Carriage, wicker, brown and white hide-covered horse with glass eyes, leather tack, hair mane, horsehair tail, two-wheeled vehicle pushed by handle, horse sets between shafts on three-wheeled frame, wire wheels with rubber tread, some damage to hide, wear to paint, late 19th/early 20th C, 53" l, 37" h **$1,380**

Chair

America, pine, shaped crest rail over back splat with keyhole cut-out, shaped seat, splayed ring-turned legs, painted brown with polychrome floral dec on crest and splat, red and black striping, gilt accents, minor paint wear and cracks, 19th C, 9-5/8" h seat, 20-1/8" h back **$265**

Attributed to New England, turned ash, two turned stiles flanking two horizontal and two vertical spindles with turned arms, projecting hand-holds continuing to slightly tapering legs with stretchers, old refinish, imperfections, late 17th C, 8-1/2" h seat, 21-1/2" h back **$2,820**

Ladder-back, arms, leather seat, turned finials and legs, old blue-green paint, 6" h, 24" h back **$415**

Chest of drawers, child-size, Hepplewhite-style, curly maple, pine secondary wood, banded inlay around two-board top and base, four graduated dovetailed drawers with dark line inlay, and fans at corners, well-scalloped base, French feet, diamond-shaped escutcheons, emb brasses with cornucopia designs, 27" w, 17" d, 28" h **$1,320**

Crib, refinished birch, tapered high posts with incised line beading along edges, urn-shaped supports on all sides, narrow vertical slats added for stability, 38-3/4" d, 69-1/2" h, orig 48" l rails **$220**

Crib quilt, central diamond, needlework heart and foliate black bound edges, Amish, Lancaster County, Pennsylvania, 40" x 41" **$4,675**

Desk, Queen Anne, southeastern New England, cherry and poplar, slant lid, int. with four compartments over drawers, sliding panel revealing well, case with single thumb molded drawers, bracket feet, replaced brasses, old refinish, restorations, 18th C, 22-3/4" w, 14-1/4" d, 27" h **$4,120**

Doll bed, Arts & Crafts, oak, rect headboard with two cartoon-like images of baby dolls, footboard with two sq form cut-outs, imperfections, 28-5/8" l, 16" w, 15-3/4" h **$230**

Doll carriage

American, fringed top surrey, original dark green paint, gold stenciling, wooden wheels, platform top, fringe replaced, c1870, 32" l, 28" h **$350**

Heywood Wakefield, woven wicker, natural finish, diamond pattern weave, steel wheels, rubber tires, clamshell hood, maker's label on underside, early 20th C, 30" l, 28" h **$150**

Natural wicker wooden spoked wheels, original button-upholstered back, red cotton parasol on wire hook, late 19th C, 30" l, 28" h .. **$230**

Doll cradle, pine, sq and "T" head nails, footboard and part of hood are dovetailed, scrolled end rockers, layers of red paint, age cracks, wear, one rocker glued, 15" l, 8-1/4" w, 13" h **$150**

Doll crib, poplar, orig reddish-brown painted dec, shaped head and foot-boards, rockers, turned posts with ball finials, edge wear, finial chips, 16-1/2" l, 11-1/2" d, 11" h **$320**

Game, ring toss, green painted wood backplate set with small hooks, each with gold transfer printed number, four leather tossing rings, England, first quarter 20th C, 16" d **$175**

Highchair, pillow-back crest rail, rect splat flanked by raked stiles, scrolled arms, turned supports, rush seat, turned legs joined by stretchers, old beige paint, floral polychrome dec, 22" h seat, 33" h back **$1,000**

Horse, pull toy, carved wood, painted white ground, black sponge high-lights, horsehair mane and tail, applied saddle, bridle, and ears, metal wheel base, mid-1800s, 16-1/2" l, 6" w, 16" h **$2,860**

Needlework picture, silk thread and watercolor on silk, titled "The Mother's Hope," young girl in land-scape setting, Massachusetts, framed in oval format, minor scattered staining, small areas of fabric loss, replaced tablet, early 19th C .... **$1,72.**

Noah's Ark, painted red, blue, orange, white, and green wood, roof and one side of base open to inner compartments, six carved and painted animals, Noah, two ladies, one glued leg, some edge wear, 18-1/2" l, 5" d, 11-1/2" h..................................... **$750**

Potty chair, Windsor, attributed to New England, orig yellow paint, green and black striping, stenciled front on crest, potty chair hole in seat covered in old brown, green, and white chintz with large bird and foliage design, bamboo turnings, 10" h seat, 22" h back **$250**

Push cart, red and blue, gold stenciled dec, sgd "Wm F. Goodwin's Patents Jan. 22, 1867 & Aug. 25, 1868," black painted wheels, handles and under-carriage, corner joints need resoldering, 12" l, 5-1/4" h...................... **$250**

Rattle, sterling silver, pink coral handle below knopped body with emb dec, five silver bells, whistle, maker's mark "E.S.B.," Birmingham, England, 19th C, 4" l.............................. **$475**

Rocking chair

Plank seat, spindle back, salmon and brown paint, cheese-cutter rockers, 8" h seat, 19" h back **$200**

Shaker, production, Mt. Lebanon, New York, 1880-1930, incised "O" with decal on rocker, old varnished surface, replaced tape seat, minor imperfections, 7-3/4" h seat, 24" h back **$3,300**

Rocking horse, wooden, mortised and dovetailed, tacked leather seat, mustard paint, arched, gouged-carved tail, Adams County, Pennsylvania, use wear, 45" l, 12" w, 26" h **$6,380**

Schoolboy sketchbook, Thomas Stapler, attributed to New England, booklet with pen and ink inscription on cover reading "Thomas Stapler's Book 1803," six pages with pen and ink and watercolor pictures of birds, one titled "The Gull," one page with perspective drawing of a Federal-style building, one page depicting a mathematical problem, toning, light stains, 1803, 6-1/4" x 7-3/4" **$600**

Tea set, partial, porcelain, Buster Brown and girl having tea decoration, mug and two plates shown from 16-piece set, wear, some damage, $395.
Photo courtesy of Joy Luke Auctions.

Tea set, pink Sunderland luster, teapot, lidded sugar, creamer, three cups, three saucers, handle-less cup and saucer, $350.
Photo courtesy of Joy Luke Auctions.

Tea set, original box, white ground, multicolored floral decoration, service for six, Japan, $90.

Sled, carved oak and wrought iron, carved horse head, traces of polychrome dec, Pennsylvania, 19th C, 37" l, 12-1/4" w, 20" h **$3,110**

Sleigh, high sides, wooden runners, old repaint with scrollwork and foliage, red ground, yellow line borders, blue int., edge wear, 19" l, 13-1/2" w, 18" h............................ **$385**

Tricycle horse, painted wood horse model, glass eyes, suede saddle, velvet saddle blanket, single front wheel, two rear wheels, chain-driven mechanism, by Jugnet, Lyon, repainted, 39" l, 22-1/2" w, 33" h............................ **$850**

Wheelbarrow, painted red, hand painted scenes with American eagle and flags **$2,700**

CHILDREN'S TOY DISHES

History: Dishes made for children often served a dual purpose— playthings and a means of learning social graces. Dish sets came in two sizes. The first was for actual use by the child when entertaining friends. The second, a smaller size, was for use with dolls.

Children's dish sets often were made as a sideline to a major manufacturing line, either as a complement to the family service or as a way to use up the last of the day's batch of materials. The artwork of famous illustrators, such as Palmer Cox, Kate Greenaway, and Rose O'Neill, can be found on porcelain children's sets.

Akro Agate

Tea set, octagonal, large, green and white, Little American Maid, orig box, 17 pcs **$225**

Water set, Play Time, pink and blue, orig box, seven pcs **$125**

Bohemian glass, decanter set, ruby flashed, vintage dec, five pcs **$135**

Candlesticks, pr, hexagonal, colorless, tiny socket hole, rough pontil mark, 1850-70, 2" h, 1-3/8" d base **$50**

China

Cheese dish, cov, hunting scene, Royal Bayreuth................................... **$85**

Chocolate pot, Model-T car with passengers **$90**

Cup and saucer, Phoenix Bird **$15**

Dinner set, Willow Ware, blue and white, Japanese **$200**

Tea set, children playing, cov teapot, creamer, cov sugar, six cups, saucers, and tea plates, German, Victorian **$285**

Tureen, cov, Blue Willow, marked "Made in China," 3-1/2" w **$60**

Decanter, blown molded glass

Colorless, ringed type III base, rough pontil mark, no stopper, Boston & Sandwich Glass Co., 1825-35, 2-3/4" h **$220**

Colorless, rayed and ringed type I base, rough pontil mark, pressed sunburst stopper, Boston & Sandwich Glass Co., 1825-40, quarter pint, 5" h.................................. **$450**

Depression glass, 14-pc set

Cherry Blossom, pink **$390**

Laurel, McKee, red trim............. **$355**

Moderntone, turquoise, gold...... **$210**

Flat iron, light amethyst, Boston & Sandwich Glass Co., tip polished, 1850-70, 7/8" h, 1-5/8" l............. **$150**

Plate

Lacy Diamond and Scroll with Concentric Rings, amethyst, 49 even scallop rim, rope table ring, Boston & Sandwich Glass Co., loss to one scallop, 1835-50, 2-1/4" d **$440**

Lacy Scroll and Diamond Point, colorless, plain rim, American or possibly Continental, rim spall, minor roughness, 2-5/8" d **$25**

Tumbler

Lacy Pointed Oval, brilliant teal, ten scallop base rayed underneath, faint pontil mark, Boston & Sandwich Glass Co., 1835-50, 1-7/8" h, 1-5/8" d **$525**

Nine-Panel, canary, slightly rough pontil mark, Boston & Sandwich Glass Co., 1845-70, 1-5/8" h, 1-1/2" d **$100**

Nine-Panel, deep translucent starch blue, slightly rough pontil mark, Boston & Sandwich Glass Co., 1845-70, 1-5/8" h, 1-1/2" d **$110**

CHRISTMAS ITEMS

History: The celebration of Christmas dates back to Roman times. Several customs associated with modern Christmas celebrations are traced back to early pagan rituals.

Father Christmas, believed to have evolved in Europe in the 7th century, was a combination of the pagan god Thor, who judged and punished the good and bad, and St. Nicholas, the generous Bishop of Myra. Kris Kringle originated in Germany and was brought to America by the Germans and Swiss who settled in Pennsylvania in the late 18th century.

In 1822, Clement C. Moore wrote "A Visit From St. Nicholas" and developed the character of Santa

Reproduction Alert. Almost all holiday decorations, including Christmas, are now being skillfully reproduced. Only by knowing the source of a possible purchase, trusting the dealer, and careful observation can you be sure you are obtaining an antique.

Ornament set, 10 wood jointed Jaymar figures, goose, sailor, Betty Boop, Popeye, clown, bear, pig, Ed Wynn, Humpty Dumpty, Little Red Riding Hood, each with hook on top of head, text on lid "Hook These Ornaments Onto Your Christmas Tree. After Christmas, Detach Hook And You Have An Ornamental Gift Or Toy," some wear and loss to original 10-1/2" x 12-1/2" x 1-3/8" deep box, 1935, **$575.**

Photo courtesy of Hake's Americana & Collectibles.

Christmas Card, slightly textured white paper, full-color Christmas caroling scene of Mickey, Minnie, and Donald standing in front of The Little House, two of Donald's nephews watching them while holding snowballs behind their backs, card opens to reveal two-panel scene of Susie the Little Blue Coupe pulling wheeled wagons containing many Disney characters such as Seven Dwarfs, Gus and Jaq, Bambi, Pinocchio, etc.; each wagon has monthly calendar for 1952, back cover with illustrations of Robin Hood and Peter Pan, title "Coming Soon," 1951, 7" x 8", **$75.**

Photo courtesy of Hake's Americana & Collectibles.

Claus into the one we know today. Thomas Nast did a series of drawings for *Harper's Weekly* from 1863 until 1886 and further solidified the character and appearance of Santa Claus.

Additional Resources:

Warman's® Americana & Collectibles, 11th Ed., by Ellen T. Schroy, ed., Krause Publications, Iola, WI.

Advertising

Bank, molded rubber, Santa Claus holding a coin, toys in pack, marked "Christmas Club A. Corp, N.Y. 1972" **$6**

Booklet, *"When All The World Is Kin,"* collection of Christmas stories, Christmas giveaway, Fowler, Dick, and Walker, The Boston Store, Wilkes-Barre, Pennsylvania, 5" x 4" **$7**

Catalog, Boston Store, Milwaukee, WI, 1945, 48 pgs, "For An American Christmas," 8-1/2" x 11" **$20**

Display, Santa in sleigh with two reindeer, Snow King Baking Powder, diecut cardboard, 16-3/4" x 32" **$675**

Pinback button

American Red Cross, red, green, and white celluloid, Santa carrying toy sack with Red Cross symbol, 1916 .... **$60**

Eagle Tribune, 1991 Santa Fund, red, white, and blue portrait, two green holly sprigs **$25**

Esso, red, white, and blue, centered Santa, 1940 .... **$45**

Gilmore Brothers Santa, black and white portrait, fleshtone tinted face, red cap, black "Christmas Greetings-Gilmore Brothers," 1940s **$60**

Joske Bros Santason is Here, litho, color design on yellow ground, Santa and child **$60**

Macy's Santa Knows, red and white 1950s **$35**

National Tuberculosis Assn, Health for All, multicolored litho, Santa 1936 .... **$15**

Santa Claus at Schipper & Blocks multicolored, Santa wearing holly leaf and berry crown, nestled by blond child, pale blue blending to white background, early 1900s **$85**

Santa's Headquarters Namm's New Fulton Street Addition, Whitehead and Hag back paper, c1920, 1-1/4" d **$125**

Spiegel Toyland Santa, multicolored litho, black lettering, 1930s **$50**

Stickpin, diecut thin cello multicolored portrait of Santa on short hanger stickpin, back inscribed, "Meet Me At Bowman's," c1920 .... **$48**

The May Co. Santa, multicolored Santa surrounded by children in winter outfits, holly leaves and berries in background, red lettering "I Am At The May Co." **$95**

Trade card, child holding snowballs, "The White is King of all Sewing Machines, 80,000 now in use," reverse reads "J. Saltzer, Pianos, Organs, and Sewing Machines, Bloomsburg, Pa." **$10**

Candy box

Cardboard, four-sided cornucopia, Merry Christmas, Santa, sleigh, and reindeer over village rooftops, string bail, USA, 8" h **$35**

Cardboard, pocketbook style, tuck-in flap, Merry Christmas, Santa in store window with children outside, marked "USA," 6" x 5" **$15**

Candy pail, tin litho, holiday greetings and adv on front, color graphics of children sledding and skating on back, 2-7/8" x 2-7/8" **$525**

Children's books

A Certain Star, Pearl Buck, Herschel Levit illus, *American Weekly,* 1957 .... **$10**

How Santa Filled the Christmas Stockings, Carolyn Hodman, color illus by F. W. Stecher, Stecher Litho Co., 1916, 13" x 71" **$85**

Rudolph the Red-Nosed Reindeer, Robert I. May, Maxton Publishers, Inc., 1939 .... **$12**

The Bird's Christmas Carol, Kate Douglas Wiggin, Hough Miffin, dj, 1912 .... **$7.50**

The Littlest Snowman, Charles Tazewell, Grossett & Dunlap, New York, 1958 .... **$18**

Christmas-tree fence

Cast iron, silver, ornate gold trim, Germany, fifteen 10" l segments with posts **$600**

Wood, folding red and green sections, USA, 48" l **$35**

Feather tree

Green wooden base, 12" h **$95**

Green goose feather-wrapped branches with metal candleholders, painted white with green trim round wooden base, marked "Germany," 4' h **$420**

Red and green wooden base, 26" h **$225**

Figures

Belsnickle

Chalk, green-hooded coat with clear mica flecks, painted black base, feather tree missing, minor damage to base, 5-1/8" h **$275**

Composition, orig red, white, and black paint, gold mica flecks, green feather tree, blue pipe cleaner trim, minor wear on hood, 8-3/4" h **$980**

Father Christmas

Composition, pink face, red-cloth coat, painted blue pants, black boots, mounted on mica-covered cardboard base, marked "Japan," 7" h **$90**

Papier-mâché, hollow molded, plaster covered, white coat, black boots, sprinkled with mica, 8" h **$300**

Reindeer, pot metal, marked "Germany," 1" h **$20**

Santa Claus

Cotton batting, red, attached to cardboard house, marked "Japan," 3" h **$48**

Celluloid, molded, one-piece Santa, sleigh, and reindeer, 3" l **$35**

Hard plastic, Santa on green plastic skis, USA, 5" h **$120**

Pressed cardboard, red hat and jacket, black boots, 10" h **$90**

Sheep, composition body, carved wooden legs, covered with cloth or wool, glass eyes, 3" h **$40**

Greeting cards

"Sincere Good Wishes," purple pansy with green leaves, greeting inside, Raphael Tuck & Sons, 1892 ...... **$12**

"Loving Greetings," flat card, two girls pictured hanging garland, marked "Germany," 1910 .... **$10**

"Merry Christmas," series of six envelopes, decreasing in size, small card in last envelope, American Greeting Publishers, Cleveland, USA, 1933 .... **$12**

House, cardboard

Mica covered, wire loop on top, marked "Czechoslovakia," 2" x 2" **$10**

House and fence, sponge trees, marked "USA," 4" x 5" **$12**

Lantern, four sided, peaked top, wire bail, metal candleholder in base, black cardboard, colored tissue paper scenes, 1940s, 8" h **$25**

Magazine, St. Nicholas, color covers, ads, illus, story, bound edition of 1915 and 1916 .... **$15**

Ornaments

Angel, wax over composition, human-hair wig, spun-glass wings, cloth dress, Germany, 4" h **$60**

Ball, silvered glass, any color, 2" d **$4**

Beads, glass, half-inch multicolored beads, paper label marked "Japan," 72" l **$8**

Bulldog, Dresden, three-dimensional, marked "Germany," 3" h **$250**

Camel, cotton batting, Germany, 4" h **$160**

Cross, beaded, two-sided, silvered, wire hanger, paper label marked "Czechoslovakia," 4" h **$20**

Father Christmas on Donkey, chromolithograph, blue robe, tinsel trim, 10" h **$25**

Kugel, round, deep sapphire blue, brass hanger, 4-1/2" d **$120**

Mandolin, unsilvered glass, wrapped in lametta and tinsel, 5" h **$45**

Parakeet, multicolored glass, spun glass tail, mounted on metal clip, 5" h **$20**

Pear, cotton batting, mica highlights, paper leaf, wire hanger, Japan, 3" h **$15**

Santa Claus in Chimney, glass, Germany, 4" h **$75**

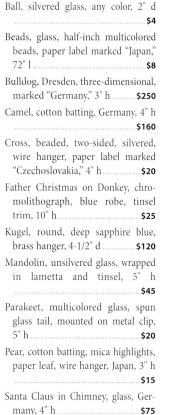

Harper's Christmas 1894 lithograph, signed "Edward Penfield," framed, 22-1/4" x 16-1/4", **$765.**
Photo courtesy of Skinner, Inc.

Tall case clock, pine, red paint, Silas Hoadley, Plymouth, Connecticut, flat-molded cresting on hood, glazed tombstone opening with cockbeaded surround, polychrome and gilt dial depicting Masonic symbols in arch, seconds and calendar indicators, mkd "S. Hoadley Plymouth," wooden weight-driven movement, molded cutout base, orig surface, early 19th century, 88-1/4" h, **$5,875.**

Photo courtesy of Skinner, Inc.

Swan, Dresden, flat, gold with silver, green, and red highlights, 5" x 6" **$150**

Tree top, three spheres stacked with small clear glass balls, silvered, lametta and tinsel trim, attached to blown glass hooks, 11" h **$90**

Postcards, Germany

Christmas bells and snow scene, marked "Made in Germany," used, one-cent stamp, 1911 .... **$20**

"Happy Christmas Wishes," Santa steering ship **$15**

"May Your Christmas Be Merry and Gay," photo card, sepia tones, Father Christmas peeking between two large wooden doors, wearing fur cap **$20**

Toys

Horse and wagon, composition, hand-painted workhorse, gray dappling, remnants of leather harness with brass rosettes, partial paper label, red and yellow painted wagon with sign "St. Claus Dealer in Good Things," wear, wagon fork replaced, 21" l, 9" h................................... **$575**

Jack-in-the-box, "Santa Pops," hard plastic, red-felt hat, orig box, Tigrette Industries, 1956, 9-1/2" h **$30**

Merry-go-round, wind-up, celluloid, green and red base, four white reindeer heads, Santa sitting under umbrella, Santa spins around, stars hanging from umbrella bounce off

Mantel clock, French, gilt bronze and porcelain, 20" x 9" x 4", **$375.**

Photo courtesy of Wiederseim Associates, Inc.

bobbing deer heads, orig box, Japan **$65**

Santa, battery operated, metal covered with red and white plush suit and hat, soft-plastic face, holding metal wand with white star light, wand moves up and down and lights up while Santa turns head, 10" h **$90**

Tree, brush style, green, mica-covered branches, wooden base, 6" h **$8**

Tree stand, cast iron, old worn green, gold, white, and red paint, relief tree trunk, foliage, and stairway design, 9-3/4" sq, 4" h............................. **$110**

CLOCKS

History: The sundial was the first man-made device for measuring time. Its basic disadvantage is well expressed by the saying: "Do like the sundial, count only the sunny days."

Needing greater dependability, man developed the water clock, oil clock, and sand clock, respectively. All these clocks worked on the same principle— time was measured by the amount of material passing from one container to another.

The wheel clock was the next major step. These clocks can be traced back to the 13th century. Many improvements on the basic wheel clock were made and continue to be made. In 1934, the quartz-crystal movement was introduced.

The first carriage clock was made about 1800 by Abraham Louis Breguet as he tried to develop a clock that would keep accurate time for Napoleon's officers. One special feature of a carriage clock was a device that allowed it to withstand the bumpy ride of a stagecoach. These small clocks usually are easy to carry with their own handle built into a rectangular case.

The recently invented atomic clock, which measures time by radiation frequency, only varies one second in a thousand years.

Notes: Identifying the proper model name for a clock is critical in establishing price. Condition of the works also is a critical factor. Examine the works to see how many original parts remain. If repairs are needed, try to include this in your estimate of purchase price. Few clocks are purchased purely for decorative value.

Additional Resources:

Antique Trader® Clocks Price Guide, by Kyle Husfloen, ed., and Mark F. Moran, contr. ed., Krause Publications, Iola, WI.

Encyclopedia of Antique American Clocks, 2nd Ed., by Robert W. and Harriet Swedberg, Krause Publications, Iola, WI.

Warman's® American Clocks Field Guide, by Robert W. and Harriet Swedberg, Krause Publications, Iola, WI.

Advertising

Chew Friendship Cub Plug, face of man with moving mouth 'chewing Friendship Tobacco to the tic of the clock, pat'd March 2, 1886, 4" h **$900**

Gruen Watch, Williams Jewelry Co. on marquee at bottom, blue neon around perimeter, 15" x 15" **$600**

Hire's Root Beer, "Drink Hires Root Beer with Root Barks, Herbs," 15" d **$250**

International Tailoring, Chicago, cast iron, emb design, bronzed, orig working clock, 12" w, 2-1/2" d, 16" h, C.8+ **$1,000**

Longine's Watches, "The World's Most Honored Watch," brass, 18-1/2" d **$300**

None Such Mincemeat, pumpkin face, some wear, 8-1/2" w **$300**

Victrola Records, orig pendulum **$2,100**

Alarm

Attleboro, 36 hours, nickel-plated case, owl dec, 9" h **$75**

Bradley, brass, double bells, Germany **$40**

Champion, 30 hours, American movement, metal frame, ornamental feet, 9" h **$75**

New Haven, 30 hours, SP case, perfume-bottle shape, beveled-glass mirror, removable cut-glass scent bottle, beaded handle, c1900 .... **$185**

Bracket

Louis XV, Corne Verte, gilt bronze mounts, bracket stamped "GOTER" and "JME," porcelain dial and backplate signed "F. cois Gilbert A. Paris," five turned pillar movement with silk suspension, recoil escapement with silk suspension, converted from verge escapement, eight-day time and strike movement with vertical striking, count wheel mounted on the back plate, 25-pc porcelain dial mounted on brass dial plate, Roman numeral hours and Arabic five-minute gradations, c1735, 11" w, 6" d, 26" h case, 12" w, 6-3/4" d, 12" h base **$5,500**

Regency, Bennett & Co., Norwich, brass inlaid and gilt bronze mounted mahogany, dial and back plate sgd, oak leaf spandrels, case inlaid with scrolls, gadrooned bun feet, chips, c1810, 17" h **$4,325**

Tiffany & Co., bronze, stepped rect-shaped top, four acorn finials, cast foliate frieze, four capitals with reeded columns, shaped and foliate cast base, beveled glass door and panels, circular face dial with Roman numerals, marked "Famiel Marti Medaille...Paris 1900, Tiffany & Co.", 13" h **$600**

Carriage

French, oval, brass, four beveled glass panels, fine cut flowers in border to sides, top oval glass panels initialed "M.E.H.," dial painted with woman

Mantel clock, R. Lalique, "Deaux Figurines," clear and frosted, orig decorated metal illuminating base, polished lower edge of clock, mostly inside base, one corner internal fracture, c1926, 15-1/4", $3,480.

Bracket clock, Philadelphia, Federal, mahogany, dial inscribed "John J. Parry Philad.," molded arch top over pierced and scrolled sound grills, matchstick molded base, brass ball feet, c1810, $4,140.

Mantle clock, French, gild metal and marble, two figures, plinth base, floral and c-scroll motif, late 19th century, 17" h, 18" w, **$645.**
Photo courtesy of Pook & Pook, Inc.

Mantel clock, fake graining, yellow ground, black "smoke" type graining, circular dial flanked by two columns on each side, marble base, applied ormolu on sides, no markings, **$200.**

Mantle clock, L and J.G. Stickley, Peter Hanson design, etched copper face, wooden square details, small glass window, beveled top and base, overcoated finish, replaced glass, unmarked, 22" x 16" x 8", **$7,638.**
Photo courtesy of David Rago Auctions, Inc.

and cupid, decorative D-shaped handle on top, 5-1/2" h **$1,150**

Grande Sonnerie, brass, dial marked for "Muiron & Cia., Mexico," phases of the moon, subsidiary day, date, and seconds dial, all enamel, set into brass plate engraved with leafy scrolls and dragons' heads, repeater button, strike/silent quarter strike lever, title on movement engraved in Spanish, made for Mexican market, early 20th C, 7-1/2" h **$7,475**

Japan, 19th C
Brass works and case, floral engraving on rect case, surmounted by bell, stand missing, 6-1/2" h
.... **$3,000**
Brass works, rosewood case, 7" h
.... **$7,100**

New Haven Clock Co., gilded brass case, beveled glass, gold repaint to case, orig pendulum and key, 11-1/2" h **$315**

Tiffany & Co., brass and glass, French half strike repeater movement marked for Souaillet Freres, enamel dial with Arabic numerals and subsidiary seconds dial, early 20th C, 3-3/8" w, 3" d, 7" h **$950**

Desk

American, shaped rect, brass case, white enamel bordering cobalt blue, stylized applied monogram, decorative brass corners, central dial with Arabic numerals, 4-3/4" h
.... **$150**

British United Clock Co., Ltd., Birmingham, England, brass, bracket cut-out edges on diamond-shaped brass clock frame, four pierced diamond patterns, floral, bowknot, and fleur-de-lis punch dec, wire easel stand, printed and imp maker's marks, spotty corrosion, 20th C, 6" w, 4-1/2" h **$260**

Enameled, gilt bronze, tombstone shape, front enameled in translucent emerald green enamel on wavy engine turned ground, c1910, 4-1/4" h **$350**

Mantel

Ansonia, French-style, rococo scroll dec, enameled face sgd "Ansonia," bronze-colored patina on spelter, orig pendulum, missing finial and key, 14-1/2" h **$275**

Birge, Mallory, and Co., Bristol, CT, Classical, mahogany and gilt gesso scrolled cornice with fruit-filled baske flanked by square plinths, glazed doo enclosing white painted and gilt dial seven-day brass strap weight-driver movement, mirror below, reverse painted tablet below that, all flanked by gilded engaged and free-standing columns on ball feet, refinished restoration, imperfections, c1830 17" w, 5" d, 38" h **$650**

Classical Revival, French, retailed by Theodore B. Starr, New York, two-train half-striking Japy Freres movement, ovoid case with beveled glass sides, dial with colorless paste-set bezel, pendulum centered by portrait miniature on ivory of lady in 18th C dress, double bezel of colorless pastes early 20th C, 12-1/4" h **$725**

French, Louis XVI-style, patinated metal, figural cherub painter with palette and wreath-draped easel, two-train half-striking movement with Japy Fils Medaille D'Argent seal, enamel dial with worn retailer's mark, set into beaded gilt-meta bezel, waisted black marble socle, late 19th C, 17-3/4" w, 7-1/2" d, 22" h
.... **$2,990**

George III, William Stephenson, London, maker, mahogany case, arch top with lifting handle, glass front and rear doors, side frets, brass bracket feet, two-train fusee striking movement, painted dial, c1800, 16-1/2" h **$1,650**

Gothic Revival, French, gilt bronze, two-train half-striking Japy Freres movement with pull repeater, retailed by Bourdin, Paris, case formed as pointed arch Gothic cathedral, central round dial, pierced curved arch revealing red glass panel at back, pair of columns, stacked plinth base, further ebonized wood platform, late 19th C, 20-3/8" h **$2,350**

Jugendstil, oak, retailed by Liberty & Co., exposed bell on top, open sides, copper face emb with violets, purple and yellow slag glass window, orig finish, working condition, unmarked, 9-3/4" w, 14-1/4" h **$1,840**

Leavenworth, Mark, Waterbury, CT, Federal, pillar and scroll, mahogany, scrolled cresting, three brass urn finials on sq plinths above glazed door, eglomise tablet showing house by lake flanked by freestanding columns, wooden dial with gilt dec housing thirty-hour wooden striking movement, cut-out valanced base, refinished, restoration to tablet, c1825, 16-1/2" w, 31-1/4" h..................**$3,820**

Louis Philippe style, retailed by Hollin, ormolu, figural, Vincenti two-train chiming movement set in bale, topped by hat and bag of coins, figure of boy holding anchor, rect plinth base set with scene of cherub loading ship, another bookkeeping, trumpet feet, late 19th C, 11-3/8" h
....**$1,880**

Louis XV, gilt bronze mounted, waisted ovoid tulipwood veneered case topped by rocaille urn and trimmed in rocaille C-scrolls, two-train half-striking movement, enamel dial with outer ring of seconds markers, 19" h
....**$1,175**

Louis XVI style, French, figural, bronze painted white metal figure of classical woman, holding gilt metal and engine-turned orb movement on white metal rod from her upraised hand, onyx plinth base, late 19th C, 26" h..................................**$7,050**

Shreve, Crump & Low, Gothic Revival, carved mahogany, French two-train half-strike movement, engraved silver dial, case formed as Gothic pointed and trefoil arch, paneled turrets, blocked base, late 19th C, 19-1/2" h................................**$850**

Terry, Samuel, Federal, pillar and scroll, mahogany, scrolled cresting, three brass urn finials on sq plinths above glazed door, eglomise tablet showing building in landscape, flanked by freestanding columns, wooden painted and gilt dial, thirty-day wooden movement, valanced cut-out base, refinished, tablet replaced, c1825, 17" w, 4-1/2" d, 31-1/2" h
....**$1,530**

Thomas, Seth, Plymouth Hollow, CT, Classical, carved mahogany and mahogany veneer, eagle and shield-carved scroll flanked by square plinths above glazed door with eglomise tablet showing public building with floral stenciled border, opening to wooden painted dial, 36 weight-driven movement, flanked by stencil decorated engaged columns on carved acanthus leaf and hairy paw feet, minor imperfections, c1825, 17" w, 4-3/4" d, 30" h..................**$775**

Tiffany & Co., marble and patinated metal, two-train half-striking movement sgd by Tiffany & Co., pink marble temple form case, pediment set with patinated metal plaque of putti with goat, round bezel set to center of case flanked by patinated pilasters, plinth base mounted with central cartouche and laurel branches, late 19th C, 12-1/4" w, 5-7/8" d, 13-1/8" h................................**$300**

Victorian, black, rect, two-train strike and bell movement, front with breche d'alep marble pilasters flanking round dial, plinth base with breche d'alep band and diamond inlay, gilt incised line dec, late 19th C, 9-3/4" w, 5-3/4" d, 10-3/4" h................**$425**

Waterbury, black lacquer, patinated metal scrolled feet, faceplate flanked by marbleized columns with patinated metal mounts, hourly chime, c1900, 15" l, 12" h......................**$300**

Porcelain

Ansonia, Royal Bonn, shelf, blue and white case dec with flowers, open escapement, time and strike, 9-1/2" w, 15" h..**$920**

French, possibly Sevres, architectural stepped-down form, roof with ormolu shell finial, ormolu mounted columns flanking central dial, figural garden scene over scrolled ormolu mounted base, chips, crazing, c1880, 10-1/2" h
....**$700**

Shelf

Atkins Clock Mfg., Bristol, CT, rosewood, 30-day wagon spring movement (invented by Joseph Ives), case with hinged door, zinc painted dial framed by eglomise tablet above lower mirrored door, iron and brass "patent equalizing lever spring" movement, flanked by canted recessed paneled corners, backboard with maker's label, c1855-58, 13-1/2" w, 4" d, 17-3/4" h

Original, untouched condition
....**$3,525**

Refinished, dial repaired..........**$2,235**

Birge and Fuller, Bristol, Connecticut, c1845-50

Gothic, candlestick, double steeple, mahogany, wagon spring, orig painted tablets, painted zinc dial,

Shelf clock, Ansonia, walnut, silver dec on tablet, star at top, pendulum and key, late 19th century, minor silver wear and dial discoloration, 22" h x 14-1/2" w, **$88.**
Photo courtesy of Green Valley Auctions.

Shelf clock, Ithaca, painted dial, paneled door, single glass pane, stamped on face, orig finish, veneer lifting on one side, 69" x 18" x 12", **$600.**
Photo courtesy of David Rago Auctions, Inc.

eight-day time and strike, "J. Ives Patent Accelerating Lever Spring" movement, 13-3/4" w, 4" d, 26" h **$8,225**

Gothic, double steeple, wagon spring, case with orig painted tablets, painted zinc dial, 30 hour "J. Ives Patent Accelerating Lever Spring Movement," 11-1/2" w, 4-1/4" d, 24-1/4" h **$3,300**

Brewster and Ingrahams, Bristol, Connecticut, Gothic twin steeple, mahogany, peaked cornice, glazed door, stenciled gilt-green on white table showing love birds, enclosing painted zinc dial, double fusee brass movement, flanked by two turned finials and columns, flat base, dial replaced, minor veneer loss, c1845, 19" h **$1,100**

Forestville Manufacturing Co., J.C. Brown, Bristol, Connecticut, Gothic, acorn, rosewood, shaped laminated case with orig reverse painted tablet, painted zinc dial and eight-day fusee movement, dial attributed to repainted, c1849, 10-1/8" w, 4" d, 20-1/4" h **$6,500**

New Haven, glass door, mirrored side panels, spelter standing cupids, walnut case with drawer at base, 24" h **$490**

North, Norris, Torrington, Connecticut, Classical, mahogany, flat cornice above glazed door, eglomise tablet of young woman flanked by engaged black paint stenciled columns, polychrome and gilt white painted dial, 30-hour wooden weight-driven movement, c1825, 23-3/4" h, 13-1/2" w, 5-1/4" d **$4,900**

Pomeroy, Noah, Bristol, Connecticut, mahogany veneer, movement marked "N. Pomeroy, Bristol, Conn," steeple frame encloses glass tablets, lower one with polychrome beehive imagery, imperfections, 1860s, 14-3/4" h **$1,150**

Terry, Eli and Sons, Plymouth, Connecticut, Federal, paper label "Eli Terry and Sons," mahogany, scrolled pediment, wooden painted dial with gilt spandrels, wooden 30-hour movement, eglomise glass, curving case skirt, French feet, restoration, c1810-15, 31-1/4" h **$1,955**

Thomas, Seth, Plymouth, Connecticut, calendar, double dial, time, and strike, glass door, c1820, 14" w, 27" h **$1,150**

Unidentified, Massachusetts maker, Federal, mahogany, pierced fret over unsigned painted dial, rocking ship and gilt spandrels, red, white, and blue shields, box base on feet, restorations, c1805, 38-1/2" h **$12,650**

Table

French, gilt bronze and enamel, case finely molded gilt bronze with hooved feet, translucent maroon panel enameled with cherubs and floral sprays, maroon enameled dial with circular florals, gilt numerals, surmounted by matching enameled dome, gilt acorn finial, works stamped "Etienne Maxant, Brevete, Paris made in France," c1900, 14" h **$2,590**

French, gilt bronze and guilloche enamel, round clock, Swiss movement, enameled in translucent azure blue on engraved radiating ground, enameled and gilt chapter ring, gilt bronze case surmounted by petal forms, 19th C, 4" d **$600**

Wendell, "Mr. Clock," sq ribbon-mahogany box, tall verdigris-patinated copper legs, sgd and dated 1988, 24" x 6" **$1,380**

Tall case, dwarf

Gilmanton, Noah Ranlet, New Hampshire, dial sgd "Noah Ranlet Gilmanton 1796," time and strike movement, pine, scrolled solid crest above bonnet that encloses sgd, painted dial, includes side lights, waist door, flanked by quarter-engaged columns above base box, later stenciled eagle dec, pine case with old refinish, replaced crest, other imperfections, 49-1/4" h **$18,400**

French, marble and agate, Egyptian revival style, ormolu anthemion corner pendants, female busts, swans, laurel wreaths, paw feet, 19th C, 52" h **$3,800**

Hingham, J. Wilder, dial face indistinctly sgd, reverse dial reads "J. Wilder Hingham" in period script, painted bowl of fruit in arch, gilt spandrels, eight-day timepiece with drop-off strike, mahogany and mahogany

veneer, bonnet flanked by free-standing tapering columns above waist door with applied molding, crossbanded veneer box base, curving skirt and feet, replaced crest, other minor imperfections, c1810-15, 47-1/2" h **$28,750**

Tower, Reuben, Plymouth, Massachusetts, alarm dial sgd "Reuben Tower Kingston," pine, pierced fret above bonnet flanked by free-standing mahogany columns, painted iron dial with spandrels and polychrome painted basket of flowers, fruit, and foliage above waist, box base over curving skirt, ogee feet, refinished case, replaced crest and columns, some height loss, c1820-30, 40-3/4" h **$12,650**

Tall case

Brokaw, Isaac, Federal, mahogany inlaid, dial marked "Isaac Brokaw Bridge Town" (New Jersey), shaped hood with inlaid patera and bookend inlays above glazed door, painted dial, eight-day weight-driven movement, seconds hand, calendar aperture, waist door with serpentine top and elliptical inlay, oval and quarter-fan inlays on lower case, similar embellishments above the bracket feet, refinished, restored, 1800-10, 94-1/2" h **$10,575**

Caldwell, J. E., Georgian-Revival, mahogany, dial sgd "Caldwell," subsidiary seconds dial, cast scroll and cherub detailing, phases of the moon, two train chiming movement, hood with swan's neck cresting centered by urn, carved scroll detailing, glass front door flanked by tapering and partially reeded circular section columns, case with beveled glass front door flanked by engaged partially reeded columns, paneled plinth base centered by carved shell, front paw feet, rear ogee feet, late 19th/early 20th C, 24" w, 15" d, 95" h **$2,895**

English

English, George III, oak case, broken scroll pediment with center brass finial, arched glazed door, white painted dial with small second hand, multicolored moon dial, works by William Bellmann/Broughton, shaped pendulum door with veneered border, fluted quarter columns, molded base, c1790-1812......................................**$2,000**

George III style, works attributed to Elliott of London, retailed by Bigelow, Kennard, three-train movement, quarter striking and chiming, nine tubes, pierced brass spandrels, inlaid mahogany case with swan's neck cresting, three ball and spire finials, mid-case with glass door and engaged columns, inlaid with fan and urn, 91" h **$5,600**

Victorian, dial painted with landscape scenes, sgd "Thompson of Huddersfield," two-train movement, oak case carved all over with flat foliage and lappets, swan's neck cresting, engaged columns, 95" h **$2,350**

Farquharson, Alexander, George III, mahogany, gilt bronze mounts, dial signed "Alexander Farquharson, Edinburgh," etched steel face with date aperture and seconds dial, case with broken pediment cresting, dentil molding, two columnar supports with gilt capitals, shaped long door and bracket feet, 89" h.................**$2,760**

Federal, inlaid mahogany, broken scroll pediment with twin inlaid stars, urn, and steeple finial, arched glazed door, white painted dial with floral spandrels, small second dial, four flanking colonettes, 8-day works, thumb-molded pendulum door with ovolo cut-outs above, trunk and line-inlaid chamfered corners, bracket feet, 92-3/4" h **$2,600**

French, Provincial Renaissance style, quarter strike mobilier, serpentine cresting above glass door, brass face depicting courting couple, single train movement with quarter chiming on two bells, hour strike on one bell, case carved with strap work and mask, 19th C, 94" h **$1,400**

Gothic-style, mahogany, cresting with 3 floral dec spires, glazed door with side panels, pointed arch mullins, steel dial, gilt metal Arabic numerals, center ornament and spandrels, multicolored moon dial, Canterbury, Westinster, and Whittington chimes, twin caved corner columns, low octagonal feet, 98" h, 24" w **$5,000**

Mulliken, Nathaniel, Lexington, Massachusetts, walnut, hood with molded flat cornice above arched molding, glazed tombstone door with flanking engraved columns, engraved brass dial with brass spandrel, boss in arch engraved "Nath Mulliken LEXINGTON" above chapter ring, seconds indicator, and calendar aperture, waist with thumb-molded door, base with applied thumb-molded panel, bracket feet, refinished, restored, c1760, 87" h **$7,650**

Mulliken, Joseph, Concord, Massachusetts, Federal, cherry, hood with pierced fretwork joining sq plinths and brass ball finials above arched cornice molding, iron painted tombstone dial with bird and floral designs inscribed "J. Mulliken Concord," eight-day weight-driven movement, flanked by free-standing reeded columns, waist with molded rect door flanked by reeded quarter columns on base with inlaid stringing joining corner quarter fans on flat molding, imperfections, lacks hood door and feet, c1800-10, 88-3/4" h..................**$4,700**

Mulliken II, Nathaniel, Lexington, Massachusetts, attributed to, mahogany and cherry, hood with broken arched cornice molding, three sq plinths, tombstone glazed door with flanking engaged columns, brass dial with cast spandrels, silvered banner in arch engraved "Nath. Mulliken + Lexington," above the boss with engraved eagle on branch, silvered chapter ring, seconds indicator, calendar aperture, eight-day weight-driven movement, waist with thumb-molded door, molded base, refinished, loss of height, restored, c1770-75, 88" h..................**$7,650**

Munroe, Daniel, Concord, Massachusetts, Federal, mahogany, hood with pierced fretwork joining three reeded brass stop fluted plinths above arched cornice molding, glazed inlaid tombstone door enclosing polychrome iron moon phase dial with floral spandrels, polychrome indicator, calendar aperture inscribed "Daniel Munroe," eight-day weight-driven movement, flanked by reeded brass stop-fluted columns, rect inlaid waist door flanked by reeded brass stop-fluted quarter columns on inlaid base ending in molding, feet missing, restored fretwork, c1810, 85-1/2" h......................**$17,625**

Nash, William, Bridge, England, George III, works signed, brass and steel face with date aperture and seconds dial, inlaid mahogany case with swan's neck cresting, colum-

Tall case, Pennsylvania Chippendale, cherry, carved bonnet, pineapple finial, dentil moldings, painted dial, bracket feet, inscribed "Solomon Parke, Philadelphia," ogee bracket feet, c1795, 92-1/2", **$17,250.**
Photo courtesy of Pook & Pook, Inc.

nar supports, cross-banded door inlaid with shell, bracket feet, 85" h **$6,900**

Smith, Benjamin, Provincial, works signed by Benjamin Smith, Leeds, brass face, steel chapter ring, two-train movement, lunar arch, date dial and subsidiary seconds hand, pierced spandrels, inlaid oak case with broken arch cresting, checkered banding, inlaid with shell and fans, bracket feet, 96" h **$7,495**

Solliday, Peter, Bedminster, Bucks County, PA, cherry, 30 hour works, broken scroll pediment with twin rosettes, two turned upper finials, space for three turned lower finials (one missing), painted dial with painted flower in arch with four floral spandrels, calendar dial, glazed door, four colonettes, arched truck door blanked by twin columns, base with twin columnal pilasters, short turned feet, c1795-1807, 93-1/2" h, 19-3/4" w, 10" d, chipped pigment on dial **$4,500**

Taber, Elnathan, Roxbury, Massachusetts , Federal, dial sgd "E. Taber, Roxbury," painted iron dial with calendar aperture, seconds hand, gilt spandrels, two ships, one flying American flag in the arch of dial, eight-day movement, mahogany veneer inlaid case with pierced fretwork, fluted plinths, brass stop fluted free-standing columns flanking bonnet above waist door with applied moldings, flanked by engaged brass stop fluted quarter columns with brass capitals and bases, waist door opens to reveal early 19th C label "Directions for Setting Up a Clock" above box base with inlay in outline, curving skirt, French feet, refinished, imperfections, c1815, 92" h **$48,875**

Unidentified American maker

Federal, Massachusetts, inlaid mahogany, upper case with three spire and ball finials, open fretwork cornice, arched door and painted metal face with flowerhead spandrels and portrait of Washington and flags in the arch, two-train movement and subsidiary seconds dial, mid case with rect door and brass stop-fluted quarter columns, plinth with flared French feet, inlaid checked banding throughout, restorations, c1810-20, 95" h **$9,990**

Hepplewhite, cherry, inlaid, swan neck pediment with carved rosettes, vase finial, barber pole and vine and

berry inlay on hood, barber pole, vine inlay, and inlaid oval at waist, 97" h **$15,275**

Weiser, Martin, Northampton, Pennsylvania, Chippendale, softwood, painted red, brown arch pediment, spiral carved finials, carved rosettes, arched side lights, turned and reeded column supports, shaped pendulum door with wrought iron rattail hinges, reeded quarter columns, molded base with raised panel with carved oblong rosette and ogee bracket feet, 30 hour movement, illuminated dial with bird and floral motif, dated register, some minor in-painting on dial, minor repair to bonnet, 92" h **$13,750**

Willard, Benjamin, Lexington, Massachusetts, cherry, brass dial inscribed "Benjamin Willard Lexington," boss inscribed "Tempus fugit," cast brass spandrels, silvered chapter ring, second hand, calendar aperture, eight-day time and strike movement, pagoda style bonnet, fluted plinths above scalloped waist door, molded box base, refinished case, restoration to bonnet, c1771, 82" h **$12,650**

Willard, Simon, Roxbury, Massachusetts, Federal, dial indistinctly sgd, eight-day time and strike movement, mahogany inlaid case with pierced fret on bonnet, American dial with "S+N" on reverse, rocking ship flying two American flags in arch of dial, painted rose spandrels and gilt outline, flanked by brass stop-fluted free-standing columns above waist door with applied molding, cross-banded veneer, boxed inlaid base, sq feet, refinished, height loss, replaced feet, c1800, 93-1/2" h **$37,375**

Wismer, Henry, Plumstead, Bucks County, Pennsylvania, cherry, hood with molded broken-arch resting, carved floral rosettes, three plinths with turned finials, glazed tombstone door, polychrome iron dial, basket of fruit in arch, seashell spandrels, calendar aperture signed "Henry Wismer B.C.," brass weight-driven striking pull-up movement, flanked by turned columns, waist with door flanked by four ring-turned columns, base with canted corners, flaring French feet, old surface, c1820, 95-1/2" h **$5,875**

Wood, David, Newburyport, Massachusetts, Federal, cherry and maple, hood with three reeded plinths above arched molding, glazed tombstone door, polychrome and gilt dial with

fruit designs, seconds indicator, calendar aperture inscribed "D. Wood," brass weight-driven movement, flanked by reeded columns, cockbeaded waist door flanked by reeded quarter columns, cove molding, base with reeded band and cut-out feet, engraved label affixed to back of door "David Wood, watch and clockmaker," refinished, imperfections, c1800-15, 89" h **$8,820**

Wall

Automaton movement, Friesland, arched hood, face painted with central landscape scene within chapter ring with hours and seconds, allegorical women in corners, arch with automaton figures of jumping dog, peddler, child on hobby horse, painted bracket case, 39" l **$765**

Banjo

Abbott, Samuel, Boston, Massachusetts, attributed to, Federal, mahogany, painted dial, "A"-shaped brass weight-driven eight-day movement, reverse painted throat glass flanked by gilded rope twist and brass side arms, lower eglomise glass depicting in polychrome "Lafayette the Friend of Liberty," restoration, c1815-25, 33-1/2" h **$1,955**

Cummens, William, Boston, Massachusetts, Federal, dial sgd "warranted by Wm. Cummens," convex painted iron dial enclosed by convex glass and bezel topped by acorn finial, molded mahogany veneer case, T-bridge eight-day weight-driven movement, reverse painted throat glass, flanked by side arms, eglomise tablet marked "Patent" in box base, restoration, c1820, 34" h **$6,325**

Currier, Edmund, Salem, Massachusetts, Federal, dial sgd "E. Currier Salem," eight-day weight-driven movement, throat glass panel reads "Patent," lower reverse painted glass reads "E. Currier Salem" above gilt bracket, restoration, c1820, 41-3/4" h **$3,335**

Curtis and Dunning, Concord, Massachusetts, Federal, dial sgd "warranted by Curtis and Dunning," eight-day weight-driven movement, mahogany case with brass bezel and convex glass, tapering throat with reverse painted glass flanked by brass side arms, box base with eglomise panel, rope twist giltwood in outline, period throat glass broken, c1815, 33-1/2" h **$5,175**

Curtis, Lemuel, Concord, Massachusetts, Federal, brass eagle finials, mahogany and gilt gesso case, brass bezel, painted and gilt iron dial inscribed "warranted by L. Curtis," eight-day weight-driven movement, throat glass enclosing thermometer, inscribed "L. Curtis Patent," lower tablet showing figures in farm landscape, both framed by gilt spiral moldings, flanked by brass side arms, restoration, imperfections, c1815, 33-1/4" h **$7,650**

Dyar, J., Concord, Massachusetts, Federal, mahogany, brass eagle finial above brass bezel, painted metal dial, reading "Warranted by J. Dyar," eight-day eight-drive movement, foliate throat glass reading "Patent," flanked by rope twist dec, brass side arms, lower tablet with eglomise naval battle framed by applied rope twist moldings, lower tablet replaced, other imperfections, c1815, 32-3/4" h **$2,820**

Munroe and Whiting, Concord, Massachusetts, Federal, gilt mahogany, acorn-form finial, iron painted dial enclosing eight-day weight-driven movement, foliate throat glass flanked by side arms, lower panel depicting ship battle, both within rope twist dec frames, lower tablet replaced, other imperfections, c1808-17, 33" h **$1,880**

Sawin, John and John W. Dyer, Boston, Massachusetts, Federal, giltwood and mahogany, dial sgd "Sawin and Dyer, Boston," acorn finial above convex glass and brass bezel, brass eight-day weight-driven movement, glass throat panel reads "Patent" flanked by brass side arms over lower glass eglomise tablet which depicts seaside hotel, reads "Nahant," minor restoration, c1825, 33" h **$4,025**

Unidentified maker

Concord, Massachusetts, Federal, gilt and mahogany brass ball finial above brass bezel and dial, eight-day weight-driven movement, foliate throat glass reading "PATENT"

flanked by brass side arms, lower tablet depicting battle between the Constitution and the Guerriere, both framed by applied rope twist dec, imperfections, c1815, 35" h **$2,475**

Unidentified Massachusetts maker, Classical, mahogany and mahogany veneer, acorn finial, molded bezel, painted metal dial, brass eight-day weight-driven movement, lyreform throat, rect pendulum box, both with eglomise tablets, molded bracket with acorn pendant, restored, c1825, 38-3/4" h **$1,300**

Willard, Aaron, Jr., Boston, Massachusetts

Classical, carved mahogany, lyre, urnturned finial above molded wooden bezel, painted metal dial inscribed "A Willard, Jr., Boston," eight-day weight-driven movement above acanthus leaf scroll-carved throat and pendulum box, both with eglomise tablets, molded bracket, old refinish, old replaced tablets, accompanied by bill of sale dated 1946 for $200, c1825, 40-1/2" h **$10,575**

Federal, mahogany case, molded brass bezel, painted zinc dial, brass eight-day weight-driven movement stamped "A Willard Jr Boston," above half-round molded throat and pendulum and eglomise tablets, imperfections, c1820, 28-1/2" h **$1,645**

Willard, Simon, Roxbury, Massachusetts, Federal, mahogany, unmarked dial, eight-day weight driven T-bridge movement with stepped train, escapement in case with cross-banded veneer, brass side arms, reverse painted throat glass above lower eglomise tablet which reads "S. Willard's Patent," restoration, c1805, 33-1/2" h **$10,350**

Girandole, J. L. Dunning, attributed to, Burlington, Vermont, Classical, carved mahogany, molded wooden bezel, painted iron dial inscribed "Dunning," brass weight-driven movement above tapering molded throat with mahogany panel flanked by carved scroll side pieces, circular molded door with pierced mahogany panel, scroll carved acanthus leaf bracket,

Wall clock, unidentified mark Regulator, walnut veneer, calendar movement, pendulum and key, marked "Regulator," minor separation, small veneer loss, replaced pendulum, second half 19th century, 32" h x 17-1/2" w, **$220.**
Photo courtesy of Green Valley Auctions.

imperfections, c1818-20, 39" h **$62,275**

Lyre, Chandler, Abiel, Concord, New Hampshire, Classical, dial sgd "A. Chandler," striking brass eight-day weight-driven movement, leaf carved mahogany veneer case with bracket, refinished, imperfections, c1825, 43" h **$17,250**

Mirror

Chandler, Abiel, Concord, New Hampshire, gilt gesso and wood, gilt and black painted split baluster door with stencil and painted tablet, mirror below, painted iron dial inscribed "A. Chandler," brass eight-day weight-driven movement, maker's label affixed to backboard, minor imperfections, c1825, 13-3/4" w, 4" d, 29" h **$8,225**

Morrill, Benjamin, Boscawen, New Hampshire, late Federal, dial sgd "B. Morrill Boscawen, N.H.," c1825,

Vase, Imperial Dragon, 18-1/4" h, **$265.**

Photo courtesy of Pook & Pook, Inc.

eight-day wheelbarrow movement surrounded by gilded spandrels above mirror glass, flanked by gilded and painted split baluster columns, restoration, c1825, 31-3/4" h **$3,740**

Unidentified, attributed to New Hampshire, giltwood and gesso, gilt split baluster framed door with eglomise tablet and mirror below, painted tin dial set into wooden frame enclosing a brass eight-day rack and snail movement, imperfections including replaced tablet, c1825, 13" w, 4-1/4" d, 29-1/2" h **$1,800**

Spiderweb, Nelson, George, for Howard Miller, wood center, white enameled metal rays, black string, black Howard Miller decal, No. 2214, 18-1/2" h **$1,150**

Watchman, Morrill, Benjamin, Boscawen, New Hampshire, 1860s, rect birch box case, painted iron dial marked "B. Morrill Boscawen," eight-day weight-driven brass movement, imperfections, 54-1/2" h **$2,875**

CLOISONNÉ

History: Cloisonné is the art of enameling on metal. The design is drawn on the metal body, then wires, which follow the design, are glued or soldered on. The cells thus created are packed with enamel and fired; this step is repeated several times until the level of enamel is higher than the wires. A buffing and polishing process brings the level of enamels flush to the surface of the wires.

This art form has been practiced in various countries since 1300 B.C. and in the Orient since the early 15th century. Most cloisonné found today is from the late Victorian era, 1870-1900, and was made in China or Japan.

Box, cov, rounded form, butterflies among flowering branches, turquoise ground, Chinese, 19th C, 4-3/4" d, 2-3/4" h **$345**

Candlesticks, pr, figural, brass, blue mythical animals seated on round dark red base with openwork sides, three feet, each animal holds flower

in mouth, red candle socket on back 7-1/8" h **$200**

Cane, Japanese cloisonné handle 1-1/3" d x 9-1/2" l, dark blue ground long scaly three-toed Japanese dragon in shades of white, pale blue, black, and brown, 1/3" gold gilt collar, black hardwood shaft, 7/8" horn ferrule fashioned in England, c1890, 36" l **$1,460**

Cup, ftd, butterflies and flowers, lappet borders, Chinese, 19th C, 4" h **$100**

Desk set, brush pot, pen, pen tray, blotter, and paper holder, Japanese, price for set **$130**

Figure, Killin, riders atop their backs, one saddle blanket dec with house floating on clouds above waves, other with crane flying above mountainous landscape, Chinese, losses to enamel, pr, late 19th or early 20th C, 11-3/4" h **$800**

Incense burner, globular, three dragon-head feet, high curving handles, scrolling lotus and ancient bronzes motif, openwork lid, dragon finial, raised Quinlong six-character mark, damage, 19-3/4" h **$815**

Jar, cov, ovoid, even green over central band of scrolling flowers, dome lid, ovoid finial, marked "Ando Jubei," 20th C, 6" h **$230**

Jardinière, bronze, bands of cloisonné designs, golden yellow and blue triangles, polychrome geometric designs on dark blue, chrysanthemums on light blue, cast relief scene of water lily, turtle, and flowering branches on int., soldered repair at foot, 13" d, 10" h **$220**

Planter, quatralobe, classical symbol and scroll dec, blue ground, Chinese, 11" l, pr **$200**

Scepter, three cloisonné plaques inset with wooden cloud-carved frame, China, early 20th C, 22" l **$125**

Tea kettle, multicolored scrolling lotus, medium-blue ground, lappets border, waisted neck with band of raised auspicious symbols between key-fret borders, floral form finial, double handles, Chinese, 19th C, 10-1/2" h **$690**

Teapot, central band of flowering chrysanthemums on pink ground, shoulder with shaped cartouches of phoenix and dragon on floral and patterned ground, lower border with chrysanthemum blossom on swirling ground, flat base with three small raised feet, single chrysanthemum design, spout and handle with floral design, lid with two writhing dragons on peach-colored ground, Japanese, late 19th/early 20th C, 4-3/4" d, 3-1/4" h...................................**$4,025**

Urn, ovoid, slightly waisted neck, peony dec, black ground, base plaque marked "Takeuchi Chubei," Japanese, Shichi Ho Company, Owari, late 19th C, 23-3/4" h
...................................**$690**

Vase

Animal head handles, gilt rims and bases, China, 19th C, pr, 3" h ..**$375**

Lobed form, blue ground, design of phoenix, dragons, and flowers, China, late 18th/early 19th C, 16-1/2" h **$1,530**

Surface of minuscule scrolling with scattered chrysanthemums, possibly by Namikawa, unsigned, Japan, Meiji period (1868-1911), 6" h **$725**

Two birds taking flight from flowering tree, cluster of plants on back side, gold wire cloisons on dark blue ground, band of shippo designs on mouth rim and base, silver rims, bottom rim mkd "silver," base with Hayashi Kondenji inlaid mark, Japan, Meiji period, 3-3/4" h...............**$3,750**

CLOTHING AND CLOTHING ACCESSORIES

History: While museums and a few private individuals have collected clothing for decades, it is only recently that collecting clothing has achieved a widespread popularity. Clothing reflects the social attitudes of a historical period.

Christening and wedding gowns abound and, hence, are not in large demand. Among the hardest items to find is men's clothing from the 19th and early 20th centuries. The most sought after clothing is by designers, such as Fortuny, Poirret, and Vionnet.

Note: Condition, size, age, and completeness are critical factors in purchasing clothing. Collectors divide into two groups: those collecting for aesthetic and historic value and those desiring to wear the garment. Prices are higher on the West Coast; major auction houses focus on designer clothes and high-fashion items.

Antique Trader® Vintage Clothing Price Guide, by Kyle Husfloen, ed., and Madeleine Kirsh and Nancy Wolfe, contr. eds., Krause Publications, Iola, WI.

Afternoon dress

Dark gray silk, pleated skirt, black lace trim on bodice, c1880 ....**$60**

Pale blue lawn, two-pc, white crocheted buttons, white dotted Swiss detailing on bodice, c1900.........**$95**

Rust silk, two-pc, train, fitted bodice trimmed with tan silk knotted fringe, silk covered buttons, c1880
...................................**$450**

White dotted tulle, two-pc, lace yoke, pin tucks, ruffles, lace cuffs, c1890
...................................**$75**

White lawn, white cotton embroidery, filet lace insertion, rows of mother-of-pearl buttons on front, c1910
...................................**$225**

White linen, elbow-length sleeves, fitted waistline, crocheted buttons up back of bodice, cotton floral embroidery and trim, c1900
...................................**$250**

Beaded dress, black silk crepe and silk chiffon over black taffeta, embroidered all over with black glass beads, black silk chiffon drape from waistline, labeled "Best & Co.," c1940
...................................**$200**

Bed jacket, pale blue quilted satin, c1950 ....**$40**

Belt, Hermes, wide beige leather belt, gold tone pyramidal hardware, 31" l
...................................**$200**

Bonnet, child's, brown crochet work, silk ribbon ties, mid-1800s, **$65.**

Shawl, all over paisley design in greens, roses, reds, blues, etc., black center, three sides with short fringe, late 1800s, 70" x 72", **$225.**
Photo courtesy of Alderfer Auction Co.

These ornate buckskin trousers were worn by Lt. Charles King while serving with the 5th US Cavalry. The trousers, decorated with white, red, pink, blue and yellow glass beads, were given to King by "Buffalo Bill" Cody probably after the war, although there are documented instances of some officers wearing flamboyant trousers ranging from buckskin to leopard skin, **$18,000.**
KP photo/Wisconsin Veterans Museum collection

Chatelaine hook and change purse, American silver, hook monogrammed "H.H.L.," purse inscribed "H.H. Lloyd 1852," velvet bag, $245.
Photo courtesy of Pook & Pook, Inc.

Flapper dress, beaded black velvet, 1920s, $200; yellow beaded velvet gown, 1930s, $125.
Photo courtesy of Skinner, Inc.

Blouse

Black dotted net, long sleeves, pin tucks, lace insertion at neckline, c1910 .... **$45**

Cream bobbin lace over net, Battenberg lace yoke, stand-up collar, elbow-length sleeves, c1900 .... **$90**

White lawn, embroidery and lace insertion, minor edge damage to collar, c1890 .... **$30**

Camisole, No. 5, black and white, cotton and Spandex, Chanel **$325**

Cardigan, gray, cotton, Chanel **$300**

Cape

Black, painted velvet, fur trim, early 20th C **$120**

Brown, feathers and appliqué, cat's eye patterned velvet, silk floral brocade lining, Edwardian **$775**

Capelet, black, glass beaded trim, openwork, fringe, c1890 .... **$40**

Chemise, linen, ruffles and lace at cuffs, late 18th/early 19th C **$25**

Collar

Black net, attached yoke, elaborately embroidered with black glass beads, c1890 .... **$30**

Black silk and velvet, steel beading, c1890 .... **$25**

Coat, woman's

Black silk velvet, black silk appliqués, cream silk satin lining, black soutache on lapels, red wool appliqué and gold embroidery, labeled "Lazarus Bros, Wilksbarre, PA," c1910 .... **$250**

Black wool cashmere, long sleeves, black satin lining, deep cape of black fur, labeled "Kraeler, Jeannette, Reading, Harrisburg," c1940 .... **$900**

Coat, man's

Cotton, red, black shawl collar and lining, black frog closures, full length, late Victorian **$125**

Pigskin, light brown, fur trimmed, matching hat, Hermes **$300**

Costume, clown, glazed cotton, blue and white, oversized buttons, ruffled cuffs, late 19th/early 20th C **$50**

Dress

Black silk crepe, scallops at sleeves, cream embroidered silk cuffs and collar, wrap style, labeled "Lucille Ltd., New York," c1915 .... **$195**

Burgundy satin brocade, wrap style bodice with frogs, mandarin collar, "Hand Made in Hong Kong, 100% Rayon Brocade," c1955 .... **$90**

Bustle, two-pc, brown silk damask and brown silk, ruching and ruffles on bustle skirt, tan shell buttons on front, later added collar, c1870 .... **$275**

Dressing gown, white voile, lace trim, blue and white flowers, c1950 .... **$65**

Evening coat, black, velvet, National Recovery Act label, lady's, 1930s **$100**

Evening dress

Beaded and sequined, silk, Bob Mackie Boutique, 1980s, size 10 .... **$150**

Beaded, black, silk, full length, sleeveless, 1920s **$500**

Beaded, black velvet, flapper style, 1920s **$200**

Beaded, mesh, black, feathered embellishments, matching hat, 1920s **$500**

Beaded, mesh, three-tier, pink, yellow, and blue, beaded floral design, sleeveless, 1920s **$940**

Beaded, yellow velvet, 1930s **$150**

Brocade, metallic, green and orange, belted, Galanos, 1980s **$360**

Satin, brown, sash bow, sleeveless, Christian Dior Boutique **$200**

Sequins, black and white, Chanel Boutique, c1980, size 6 .... **$335**

Evening jacket, black, acetate and rayon, Chanel, size 42 .... **$200**

Evening suit, sequin, silver, Eavis & Brown, 2 pc, v-neck, button down front, long sleeves with fringed cuffs to match hem of jacket, skirt, full length **$360**

Gown

Black velvet, full skirt, silk rose detailing, cream organdy collar, labeled "Trains-Norell," c1950 .... **$75**

Charcoal gray and green silk velvet, pin tucks and smocking on sleeves, deep V-neckline, c1930 .... **$95**

Deep aqua silk chiffon, elaborately embroidered with freeform shapes of clear glass beads, blue, rose, and white glass beaded Art Deco motifs, c1920 .... **$550**

Gold and rust floral printed silk chiffon, cape collar, underpinnings of tan silk crepe, c1930 .... **$85**

Gray and blue woven silk with cream stripe, pagoda sleeves, ruching on bodice, cream braid on sleeves and bodice, bodice lined with cream linen, c1865 .... **$95**

Mauve silk chiffon, sleeveless, elaborately embroidered with lilac satin threads, silver glass beads in Art Deco motif, lilac feather trim at hem, underpinnings of ivory silk chiffon, c1920 .... **$275**

Pale green silk chiffon, trimmed with pale green silk satin, embroidered at scalloped hem with silver and white glass beads, prong-set rhinestones, c1925 .... **$175**

Pale lilac silk, sq cut steel buttons, cream lace collar, bubble-effect skirt, draped back, wear, c1900 .... **$60**

Pumpkin and lilac silk etched velvet, sleeveless, floral design, fur at hem, c1920 .... **$275**

Sheer cream silk in windowpane weave, overprinted with sepia, rose, and blue floral pattern, silk trim at cuffs, bodice lined with cream muslin, c1820 .... **$500**

Tan silk, long sleeves, dropped waistline, button detailing, embroidery, c1920 .... **$75**

Handbag

Alligator, brown, brass clasp, brown leather lining, c1945 .... **$45**

Black silk faille, embroidered with black glass beads, matching fringe, c1900 .... **$95**

Floral tapestry, rose, green, and blue on cream ground, black border, brass frame with chain handle, c1940, 8 1/2" x 5 1/2" **$30**

Hermes, Cabana, large blue leather form, silver tone hardware, two shoulder straps, leather interior with four pockets, 37 cm **$1,765**

Hermes, Kelly, supple black calfskin form, gold tone hardware, detachable shoulder strap, leather interior with three pockets, 30 cm **$2,350**

Hermes, Kelly, rigid blue alligator form, gold tone hardware, detachable shoulder strap, leather interior with three pockets, boxed, orig felt protection insert, 33 cm **$10,340**

Hermes, Kelly, rigid pebbled brown leather form, gold tone hardware, detachable shoulder strap, leather interior with three pockets, boxed, orig felt protection insert, 32 cm **$4,820**

Mesh, 10k yg, pierced and scalloped top set with four old mine-cut diamonds, approx 1.12 cts., three oval cabochon turquoise, suspended by trace link chain and gold safety pin, stamped No. "6," European hallmark, c1915, 67.0 dwt. **$1,120**

Mesh, 14k yg, Edwardian, designed with a floral and scroll frame, the bypass-style thumb piece set with two sugarloaf sapphires joined by a trace link chain, 132.5 dwt. **$1,118**

Mesh, 14k yg, Edwardian, pierced, chased, and engraved floral and foliate closure, suspended from a curb link chain, 96.7 dwt. **$835**

Silver and enamel, Birmingham, England, 1938, maker's mark "EJH," oval, lid with lavender basse taille enamel, leather lined interior, silver link chain, monogrammed, 6-1/4" l, 3-7/8" d **$250**

Hat, lady's fashion type

Aqua silk pillbox, aqua veil, colorful beads, embroidery, c1960 .... **$50**

Black velour, wide brim, black feathers, black and white ostrich plumes, c1910 .... **$95**

Wide-brimmed black velvet, under brim of blue velvet, blue ostrich plume, silver stamped on the black silk lining "Dives Pomeroy & Stewart," c1910 .... **$150**

Wide-brimmed natural straw, gold grosgrain ribbon, white cotton daisies, labeled "Jean Allen," c1945 .... **$35**

Hat, man's, top hat, orig box **$85**

Jacket

Battenburg cream lace, long sleeves, gathering at shoulders, c1890 .... **$350**

Lace, cream Irish crochet, borders of elaborate Irish crochet with shamrock motif, V-neckline, four tan crocheted buttons, c1910 .... **$325**

Silk velvet, purple, lined with purple silk, fabric covered buttons, patch pockets, c1890 .... **$120**

Suede and cloth, olive green, Hermes, men's size large **$250**

Wool flannel, black, bolero, black taffeta lining, black fur trim, c1955 .... **$65**

Lingerie dress

White eyelet lace, white lawn, detailed bodice with pin tucks, lace yoke and collar, scalloped hem, c1900 ...... **$65**

White lawn, eyelet lace, lace insertion, ruffles at hem, c1790 .... **$375**

Nightgown

Pajamas, leopard print flannel, Dora Lee, unworn, c1950 .... **$35**

Pale pink satin, diminutive roses pattern, cut on bias, c1940 .... **$35**

White cotton, embroidered yoke, buttons up front, c1910 .... **$35**

White cotton, lace cutwork yoke, embroidered, matching lace cuffs, c1910 .... **$55**

Pants suit

Black and white, silk, Emilio Pucci, lady's size 14 .... **$470**

Charcoal gray wool flannel, long sleeved tunic top, high collar, straight legged pants, entirely set with prong-set rhinestones, fully lined, labeled "Made In The British Crown Colony of Hong Kong, Best & Co., Fifth Ave, New York," several rhinestones loose, c1960 .... **$70**

Petticoat

Cream organdy, pin tucks, lace, ruffles at hem, train, c1890 .... **$35**

White cotton, scalloped eyelet lace hem, front tucked panel, c1880 .... **$40**

Purse

Beaded, Art Deco, silver, red flowers, green leaves and vines, beaded fringe **$120**

Beaded, paisley pattern, sterling silver frame, reds, oranges, and cobalt blue, red and blue beaded fringe **$335**

Egg-shape, jeweled, gold toned chain handle, cream ground, purple, pink, and green floral dec, mirrored int., Judith Leiber **$200**

Lucite, butterscotch, unknown maker **$120**

Lucite, Feiner **$150**

Lucite, jeweled, Rialto **$250**

Robe, man's, orange and tan paisley print, orange lining, full length, late Victorian **$125**

Scarf, Hermes, silk

Cosmos, blue and white horse-drawn chariots riding upon clouds on light blue and purple background **$250**

Fetes Venitiennes, harlequins and guests at masquerade ball on background of brown, orange and purple **$200**

Shawl

Cream silk, floral cream satin embroidery, knotted fringe, braided dec, back tassel, c1890 .... **$150**

Ivory silk, floral ivory satin embroidery, knotted satin fringe, Spanish, c1900, 44" sq **$75**

Paisley, machine-woven, wool, dark int., orange patterned border .. **$150**

Red silk, embroidered, long fringe, Chinese **$470**

Slip

Ivory silk, net darning trim in floral design, camisole top lace straps, ivory satin embroidery, c1910 .... **$65**

Woven silk taffeta, light gray plaid, rose and green satin flowers, long knotted silk fringe, c1900, 70" sq **$125**

Skirt, lace alternating with voile, black, train, underpinnings of cream silk taffeta, pinking and ruffles, c1870, some minor damage on tulle and lining **$150**

Smoking jacket, man's, mauve and gray, early 20th C **$125**

Suit, gray wool tweed, fabric cov buttons, button detailing on jacket pockets, lined with pale gray crepe, flared skirt with gores, "Freiss Orig" label, c1945 .... **$110**

Sweater

Beige cashmere, double lining of beige lace and nylon, long sleeves, rhinestone buttons, rhinestone clasp at waistline, tan mink snap-on collar, some rhinestones missing from clasp, c1955 .... **$40**

Black cashmere, labeled "Made in Scotland for Liberty of London" **$35**

Vest, white cotton, mother-of-pearl buttons, c1910 .... **$65**

Visiting dress

Pale pink silk, two-pc, pintucks, lace appliqué, lace cuffs, c1890 .... **$65**

Purple linen, elaborate fabric-covered button detailing, purple silk net trim at neckline and cuffs, minor damage to net, c1910 .... **$40**

Waistcoat, gentleman's, silk, embroidered with floral vines and sprigs, two covered pockets, applied cherub-printed roundels below, England or France, restorations, late 18th C **$250**

Walking suit, wool, silk faille, chestnut brown, brown silk velvet trim, pleats at hem, fabric-covered buttons, lace collar **$325**

COCA-COLA ITEMS

History: The originator of Coca-Cola was John Pemberton, a pharmacist from Atlanta, Georgia. In 1886, Dr. Pemberton introduced a patent medicine to relieve headaches, stomach disorders, and other minor maladies. Unfortunately, his failing health and meager finances forced him to sell his interest.

In 1888, Asa G. Candler became the sole owner of Coca-Cola. Candler improved the formula, increased the advertising budget, and widened the distribution. A "patient" was accidentally given a dose of the syrup mixed with carbonated water instead of still water. The result was a tastier, more refreshing drink.

As sales increased in the 1890s, Candler recognized that the product was more suitable for the soft-drink market and began advertising it as such. From these beginnings, a myriad of advertising items have been issued to invite all to "Drink Coca-Cola."

Notes: "Coke" was first used in advertising in 1941. The distinctively shaped bottle was registered as a trademark on April 12, 1960.

Petretti's Coca-Cola® Collectibles Price Guide, 11th Ed., by Allan Petretti, Krause Publications, Iola, WI.

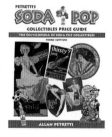

Petretti's Soda Pop Collectibles Price Guide, 3rd Ed., by Allan Petretti, Krause Publications, Iola, WI.

Warman's® Coca-Cola® Collectibles Identification and Price Guide, by Allan Petretti, Krause Publications, Iola, WI.

Warman's® Coca-Cola® Field Guide, by Allan Petretti, Krause Publications, Iola, WI.

Binder, rigid cardboard, red oilcloth cover, four-ring metal binder to hold advertising sales sheets, no contents, c1950, 13" x 15-1/2" **$48**

Bookmark, Romance of Coca-Cola, 1916 .... **$30**

Bottle

Amber, marked "Lewisburg" **$30**

Christmas, Williamstown, West Virginia **$15**

Commemorative, NASCAR Series, Bill Elliott, Dale Earnhardt, or Bobby Labonte **$5**

Bowl, Vernon Ware, green, artificial ice, C-9.8, 1930s, 10" w **$600**

Calendar, Hamilton King illus, 1913, 13-1/2" x 22-1/2" **$900**

Ceiling globe, milk glass, four logos, C-9.5, 1930s, 14" d **$990**

Clock, octagonal, neon, silhouette girl, C-8.5, 1939, 18" **$1,800**

Cooler, Victor, triple-door, attached counter, mounted jukebox, brass foot rail, three floor-mounted barstools, restored **$5,775**

Cut-out, 1926, girl under umbrella **$3,995**

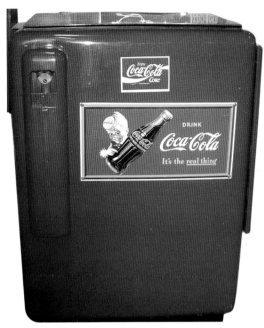

Cooler, red, "Drink Coca-Cola, It's The Real Thing," **$1,295.**

Tray, Springboard Girl, American Art Works, Coshocton, OH, 1939, 13-1/2" x 10-1/2", **$425.**
Photo courtesy of Joy Luke Auctions.

Bingo cards, diecut, lot of three, each 8-1/2" x 9" cardboard card printed on front in red and black, each has 25 diecut windows which reveal different numbers for use in calling Bingo game, text across bottom "Compliments Coca-Cola Bottling Co," issued by Kemper-Thomas, Cincinnati, OH. Some surface dust soil, bit of light wear around edges, right side of bottom of each has original owner's initials in blue ballpoint pen, 1940s, **$25.**
Photo courtesy of Hake's Americana & Collectibles.

Vending machine, red and white, working condition, **$950.**

Door kick plate, litho tin, scrolling Drink Coca-Cola logo, 11-1/2" x 35"

1923 bottle on left, C-9.9 .... **$1,765**

1942, couple on right, C-9.9 .... **$2,600**

Door pull, plastic and metal, bottle shape, orig instructions and screws, C-9.3-9.5, 8" h **$275**

Game board, Steps to Health, prepared and distributed by Coca-Cola Co. of Canada, Ltd., orig unmarked brown paper envelope, copyright 1938, 11-1/4" x 26-1/2" **$60**

Mileage meter, originating in Statesville, NC, C-8.4, 10" x 7" **$1,675**

Pin, Hi-Fi Club, gold luster finish, detailed plastic, short metal stickpin, miniature Coke bottle about name in red lettering, phonograph record background inscribed "Sponsored By Your Coca-Cola Bottler," Australian issue, c1950 .... **$40**

Plate, Vienna Art, topless woman **$1,610**

Pocket mirror, oval, celluloid, pretty girl, dark green ground, white and red lettering, 1914, 1-3/4" w, 2-3/4" h **$400**

Poster, two farm girls taking a break, caption "Work Refreshed," 1943 .... **$2,750**

Prize chance card, printed in red and black on white, unused, c1940, 4-1/4" x 5-1/4" **$12**

Radio

Bottle shape, 1930s, C-8.2, 24" h **$8,500**

Cooler shape, red, 1950s **$2,250**

Sandwich plate, white ground, script slogan, bottle and glass in center, Knowles, C-9.8, 7-1/4" d **$750**

Sign, porcelain

Diecut, two-color, script, orig box, attaching instructions, screws, C-10, 6" x 18" **$1,100**

Porcelain, diagonal slash, fountain service, C-9.7, 1934, 23" x 26" **$4,700**

Porcelain, single bottle in center, no slogan, C-9.2, 1950, 24" d **$1,800**

Porcelain, curb-side service, two-sided, green, red, and white, C-9.6, 1933, 60" x 42" **$3,000**

Sign, tin

Drink Coca-Cola, emb tin litho, vertical, C.8.5, c1931, 12-1/4" x 4-1/2" **$625**

Wood coffee mill, cast iron grinder and handle, Golden Rule, Columbus, Ohio, **$185.**
Photo courtesy of Dotta Auction Co., Inc.

Drink Coca-Cola, Ice Cold, Gas Today, tin, 1936 .... **$2,700**

Sign, wood, Drink Coca-Cola, fancy metal filigree at top, orig Kay Display label on back, C.8+, c1930, 11-3/8" x 9" **$775**

String holder, two-sided, showing six-lace and logo "Take Home in Cartons," C-9.5, 1940s **$4,000**

Thermometer, round, red and white, c1950, 12" d **$180**

Toy, van, Corgi, 5" l diecast metal and plastic replica, copyright 1978, 2-3/4" x 6" x 3-1/2" color box with display window **$35**

Tray

Bathing beauty, C-8, 1930 .... **$195**

Girl in convertible being waited on by another girl, C-9.5, 1942 .... **$450**

Madge Evans, C-7.5, 1935 .... **$165**

Oval, girl handing Coke to viewer, C-10, 1926, 13" x 19" **$15,250**

Vending machine, Select-O-Matic, Westinghouse, six dial selector, bottle opener set into front, c1960, 23-5/8" x 21-5/8" x 64" h **$3,200**

COFFEE MILLS

History: Coffee mills or grinders are utilitarian objects designed to grind fresh coffee beans. Before the advent of stay-fresh packaging, coffee mills were a necessity.

The first home-size coffee grinders were introduced about 1890. The large commercial grinders designed for use in stores, restaurants, and hotels often bear an earlier patent date.

Cast iron coffee mill, remnants of decorative decals at top, base embossed "Enterprise Mfg Co., Philadelphia, PA," **$500.**

Arcade, wall type, crystal jar, emb design, marked "Crystal" and "Arcade" orig lid rusted, 17" h **$185**

Crown Coffee Mill, cast iron, mounted on wood base, decal "Crown Coffee Mill Made By Landers, Frary, & Clark, New Britain, Conn, U.S.A.," number 11 emb on top lid **$525**

Enterprise

#00, two wheels, store type, orig paint, orig decals, C8+, 12-1/2" x 7-1/2" x 8-3/4" **$1,450**

#9, orig dec and decals, bright orange/ red paint, blue on top of base and edges of wheels, gold detailed lettering, drawer in base stenciled "No. 9," eagle finial, white porcelain knob, minor wear, restored break on lid, 28-1/2" h **$1,200**

Pine, fingered joints, one drawer, iron pull, iron top cup and handle, wooden knob, c1880, 5-3/4" sq, 6" h **$95**

Woodruff Edwards, Elgin, IL, store type, 28" d wheels, eagle finial, repainted, 66" h **$1,800**

COIN-OPERATED ITEMS

History: Coin-operated items include amusement games, pinball machines, jukeboxes, slot machines, vending machines, cash registers, and other items operated by coins.

The first jukebox was developed about 1934 and played 78-RPM records. Jukeboxes were important to teen-agers before the advent of portable radios and television.

The first pinball machine was introduced in 1931 by Gottlieb. Pinball machines continued to be popular until the advent of solid-state games in 1977 and advanced electronic video games after that.

The first three-reel slot machine, the Liberty Bell, was invented in 1905 by Charles Fey in San Francisco. In 1910, Mills Novelty Company copyrighted the classic fruit symbols. Improvements and advancements have led to the sophisticated machines of today.

Vending machines for candy, gum, and peanuts were popular from 1910 until 1940 and can be found in a wide range of sizes and shapes.

Adviser: Robert Levy.

Notes: Because of the heavy usage these coin-operated items received, many are restored or, at the very least, have been repainted by either the operator or manufacturer. Using reproduced mechanisms to restore pieces is acceptable in many cases, especially when the restored piece will then perform as originally intended.

Additional Resources:

Warman's® Americana & Collectibles, 11th Ed., by Ellen T. Schroy, ed., Krause Publications, Iola, WI.

Arcade

Bag Puncher, Mills Novelty, 1926 .... **$4,500**

Big Bronco, Exhibit Supply, 1951 .... **$1,300**

Bowling League, Genco, 1949 .. **$800**

Hunter, Silver King, 1949 .... **$500**

Mutascope, American, 1901 ..... **$3000**

Slugger, Marvel, 1948 .... **$550**

Gum

Big Top, Advance, capsule, 1969 .. **$300**

Slot machine, Mills, 5 cents, Castle, Gold Award, 1938, **$3,000.**

Cebco Hot Nut, two globes, 1930 .... **$600**

E-Z, Ad-Lee Novelty, gumballs, 1908 .... **$1,500**

Empire Vender, Lawrence, 1935 . **$600**

Master Novelty, Atlas, 1951 ...... **$150**

Jukeboxes

AMI, G200, 1950 .... **$700**

Rockola, Deluxe 20, 1939 .... **$1,700**

Seeburg, HF 100R **$3,000**

Seeburg, M100B, 1955 .... **$2,000**

Wurlitzer, 700, 1940 .... **$4,500**

Wurlitzer, 1015, 1946 .... **$6,000**

Slot machines

Caille, Cadet, 1934 .... **$900**

Caille, Superior, 1928 .... **$1,800**

Groetchen, Deluxe Columbia, 1938 .... **$900**

Jennings

Bronze Chief, 1940 .... **$1,600**

Dutchboys, 1928 .... **$1,700**

Sun Chief, 1948 .... **$3,100**

Today Vender, 1928 .... **$2,000**

Victoria Peacock, 1932 .... **$3,000**

Mills

Black Cherry, 1946 .... **$1,800**

Diamond Front, 1939 .... **$1,600**

Poinsettia, 1930 .... **$1,700**

Token Bell Hightop, 1948 .... **$1,800**

Torch Front, 1928 .... **$1,400**

War Eagle, 1931 .... **$2,200**

Slot machine, Mills, 1934, 5 cents, Chevron QT, **$2,200.**

Slot machine, Art Deco, standing club console, orig paint and gold token award, initially used in speakeasy, 1937, 60" x 19-1/2" x 13", **$3,820.**
Photo courtesy of David Rago Auctions, Inc.

Slot machine, Mills, 1938, 25 cents, Bursting Cherry, **$2,300.**

Slot machine, Roll-a-Top Bandit, Watling, three reels, 5c operation, twin jackpot, carousel, case with cast eagle and cascading coins, "Watling Scale Co. Inc.," transfers, 27" h, **$2,230.**
Photo courtesy of Skinner, Inc.

Slot machine, "Little Duke" fortune teller, sideways mechanism, minor wear, O.D. Jennings & Co., 1932, 20-1/2" x 8-3/4" x 13", **$1,410.**
Photo courtesy of David Rago Auctions, Inc.

Watermelon Hightop, 1948......**$2,200**

Pace

All Star Comet, 1936 ....**$1,800**

Bantam, 1930 ....**$1,800**

Deluxe Comet, 1939 ....**$1,400**

Whatling

Bird of Paradise, Rolatop, 1935...**$6,000**

Blue Seal, 1929 ....**$1,500**

Treasury, 1939 ....**$3,000**

Miscellaneous

American Scale, 1937 ....**$200**

Cigarette Machine, Stoner, 1950
....**$600**

Condom Machine, Advance, 1940 ...**$150**

Gillette Razor Blades, 1940 .....**$250**

Jergens Lotion, lotion dispenser, 1937 ....**$350**

Keen Kut Razor Blades, 1940 ..**$200**

Kitco Towels, Kirch, 1936 ....**$125**

National Postage, Northwestern, 1950 ....**$125**

Watling Horoscope Scale, 1957 ... **$350**

COINS

History: Coin collecting has long been one of the most respected and honored aspects of the collecting world. Today it still holds its fascination as new collectors come onto the scene every day.

And just like the old-time collectors, they should be ready to spend time reading and learning more about this fascinating hobby. The States Quarter Series has spurred many of us to save quarters again and that has encouraged all types of coin collecting.

After the Declaration of Independence, America realized it needed its own coinage. Before that time, foreign coins were used in addition to paper currency. The first coins issued by a young America were known as "Fugio" cents, struck on copper in 1787. Many of the early states created their own coins until the Federal Mint was constructed in Philadelphia after 1792. By 1837, the purity of silver was increased from 89.24 to 90 percent with minor adjustments to this weight occurring until 1873. Early dominations included a silver 3-cent piece, a gold $3 piece (1854), $1 and $20 (1849). The coinage law of 1857 eliminated the half-cent, changed the size of some coins, and forbid the use of foreign coins as legal tender. By the time of the Civil War, the bronze two-cent and nickel three-cent pieces and the five-cent nickel were created. The motto "In God We Trust" was added at this time. From the late 1870s, coins were plentiful. From 1873 to 1918, several laws were passed requiring the government to buy silver and strike an abundance of silver dollars. President Theodore Roosevelt is credited with

having encouraged Congress to pass legislation for providing dramatically new coin designs. As a result of his efforts, the Walking Liberty half-dollar, Mercury dime, Buffalo nickel, and the Saint-Gaudens $20 gold were created. Commemorative coins were also becoming very popular at this time. Designs on coins continue to change to reflect events, such as the Bicentennial.

It would be impossible to list values for all types of coins in a general price guide such as *Warman's*, so the following is included to give a general idea of coins. More information about specific coins is available in various publications, including the *2007 Standard Catalog of World Coins* and *2007 North American Coins & Prices: A guide to U.S., Canada and Mexican Coins,* published by Krause Publications.

Grading: The value placed on a coin is highly dependent on its "grade" or condition. The general accepted grades are as follows:

Brilliant Uncirculated (BU): No visible signs of wear or handling even under a 30-power microscope, full mint luster.

Uncirculated (Unc.): No visible signs of wear, even under a 30-power microscope, bag marks may be present.

Almost Uncirculated (AU): All detail will be visible, wear only exists to the highest point of the coin, half or more of the original mint luster must be present.

Extremely Fine (EF or XF): 95% of original detail visible, or, on a coin without an inner detail to wear, there will be light wear over nearly all the coin.

Very Fine (VF): 75% of the original detail visible, or, on a coin with no inner detail. There will be moderate wear over the entire coin. Letter and date number corners may be weak.

Fine (F): 50% of original detail is visible, or, on a coin with no inner detail, there will be heavy wear over all of the coin.

Very Good (VG): 25% of the original detail is visible, heavy wear on all of the coin.

Good (G): Coin's design clearly outlined but with substantial wear, larger detail may still be visible, rim may have a few weak spots of wear.

About Good (AG): Typically only a silhouette of a large design exists. The rim will be worn down into the letters if any.

Proof (PF): Refers to not a grade, but rather a special way of minting coins, usually as presentation pieces. Unlike coins produced for circulation, proof coins are double struck between highly polished dies on specially polished blanks. Today's modern proofs are mirror-like in appearance, often with frosty devices.

Advisor: James Bixler.

Reproduction Alert. Counterfeit coins of all denominations exist.

Additional Resources:

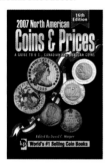

2007 North American Coins & Prices, 15th Ed., by David C. Harper, Krause Publications, Iola, WI.

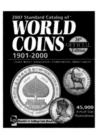

2007 Standard Catalog of World *Coins,* 34th Ed., Colin R. Bruce, II, senior ed, Thomas Michael, market analyst, Krause Publications, Iola, WI.

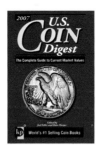

2007 U.S. Coin Digest, 5th Ed., by Joel T. Edler and Dave C. Harper, ed., Krause Publications, Iola, WI.

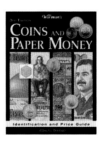

Warman's Coins & Paper Money, Identification and Price Guide, 3rd Ed., by Allen G. Berman, Krause Publications, Iola, WI.

Warman's U.S. Coins & Currency Field Guide, by Allen G. Berman, Krause Publications, Iola, WI.

Barber or Liberty Head Half Dollar (1892-1915), designed by Charles E. Barber.

1892, VG.............................**$42**

1913, VG.............................**$90**

1915, VF.............................**$380**

Indian Head or Buffalo Nickel (1913 to 1938), designed by James Earle Fraser.

1913 FIVE CENTS on raised ground, Unc.............................**$33**

1936D, 3-legged buffalo, VG.......**$600**

Eisenhower Dollar (1971-1978), designers Frank Gasparro and Dennis R. Williams.

1971D, copper-nickel clad, MS-63 .**$2**

1973S, silver clad, PF-65..............**$25**

1978D, EF.............................**$2**

Franklin Half Dollar (1948 to 1963), designed by John R. Sinnock.

1948, MS.............................**$15**

1950, XF.............................**$6**

1961, MS-65.............................**$145**

Half Cent (1793-1857).

1793 Liberty Cap type, VG......**$2,750**

1804 Draped Bust type, "Spiked Chin" variety, VG.............................**$90**

1810 Classic Head type, F..........**$120**

1849 Braided Hair type, original, small date, PF-60.................**$6,000**

Large Cents (1793-1857), various designers

1793, Flowing Hair type, chain reverse, AMERICA in legend, G **$7,750**

1794, Head of 1793, VG.........**$2,600**

1809, Classic Head type, Fine....**$600**

1813, Classic Head type, VG......**$175**

1847, Braided Hair, EF...............**$75**

Indian Head Cent (1859-1909), designed by James B. Longacre.

1860, variety 2, copper-nickel, oak wreath with shield, pointed bust, VF.............................**$34**

1867, variety 3, bronze, XF........**$175**

1900, variety 3, bronze, Proof-63 ....**$285**

1909S, variety 3, bronze, F.........**$480**

Lincoln Cent (1909 to date), designed by Victor D. Brenner.

1911D, VF.............................**$15**

1950, Proof-65.............................**$40**

2007, copper-plated zinc, Proof-65 ....**$4**

1925D Mercury Dime, MS-60, **$350.**
Photo courtesy of Heritage Numismatics Auctions, Inc.

1881CC Morgan Dollar, MS68, **$25,000.**
Photo courtesy of Heritage Numismatics Auctions, Inc.

1936D Washington Quarter, VF, **$15.**
Photo courtesy of Heritage Numismatics Auctions, Inc.

Silver Three-Cent Piece (1851-1873), designed by James B. Longacre.

1851-1853, G $27

1854, MS-60 .... $350

1859-1861, G $30

Liberty Head Five-Cent Piece (1883 to 1913), designed by Charles E. Barber.

1883, no CENTS variety 1, G $6

1901-1908, MS-60 .... $72

Indian Head or Buffalo Nickel (1913 to 1938), designed by James Earle Fraser.

1918S FIVE CENTS in recess, VG
.... $28

1936D, 3-legged buffalo, VG $600

Jefferson Five-Cent Piece (1938 to date), designed by Felix Schlag.

1938, MS-60 .... $4

1939D, VF $5

1942P-1945S, Wartime silver alloy, VF $1

1971S, Proof-65 .... $2

Liberty Seated Dime (1837-1891), designed by Christian Gobrecht.

1837-1838, no stars on obverse, G . $40

1838, large stars on obverse, MS-60
.... $280

1846, MS-60 .... $5,500

1860, variety 4, legend on obverse, G
.... $15

Winged Liberty Head or "Mercury" Dime (1916-1945), designed by Adolph Weinman.

1916, VF $7

1929S, MS-60 .... $33

1940, XF $3

1944D, MS-63 .... $12

Roosevelt Dime (1946 to date), designed by John R. Sinnock.

1946, BU $3

1949S, XF $3

Liberty Seated Quarter (1838-1891), designed by Christian Gobrecht, variations.

1840O, no drapery obverse, VG ... $29

1852, drapery added to Liberty's left elbow VF $185

1853, arrows at date, VG $15

1873, arrows at date, VG $23

1876, arrows removed, VG $17

Standing Liberty Quarter, (1916-1930), designed by Hermon A. MacNeil.

1930, type 2 obverse, AU $75

1930S, type 2 obverse, F $10

Washington Quarter (1932-1998), designed by John Flanagan.

1932, XF $10

1941D, VF $3

1972, copper-nickel clad, MS-65 ... $4

Liberty Seated Half Dollar (1839-1891), designed by Christian Gobrecht, variations.

1839, no drapery from elbow, G . $38

1857, arrows removed, VF $55

1866, "In God We Trust" above eagle reverse, VF $70

Barber or Liberty Head Half Dollar (1892-1915), designed by Charles E. Barber.

1892, VG $42

1913, VG $90

Walking Liberty Half Dollar (1916-1947), designed by Adolph A. Weinman.

1918, F $16

1933S, XF $60

1947, MS-65 .... $230

Franklin Half Dollar (1948 to 1963), designed by John R. Sinnock.

1948, MS-60 .... $15

1952, AU $7

1961, MS-65 .... $145

Kennedy Half Dollar (1964 to date). Obverse by Gilroy Roberts, reverse by Frank Gasparro.

1964, silver coinage, MS-60 .... **$3**

1970S, silver clad, Proof-65 .... **$15**

1979, filled "S," Proof-65 .... **$5**

1981S, Proof-65 .... **$15**

1989D, MS-65 .... **$3**

1995S, silver, Proof-65 .... **$100**

Liberty Seated Dollar (1840-1873)

1840, no motto above eagle reverse, G **$225**

1866, "In God We Trust" surmounting eagle reverse, G **$250**

Morgan Dollar (1878-1921), designed by George T. Morgan.

1878, 8 tail feathers, VF **$38**

1881S, VF **$19**

1921S, MS 60 .... **$31**

Eisenhower Dollar (1971-1978), designed by Frank Gasparro and Dennis R. Williams.

1971D, copper-nickel clad, MS-63 . **$2**

1973S, silver clad, PF-65 .... **$25**

COMIC BOOKS

History: Shortly after comics first appeared in newspapers of the 1890s, they were reprinted in book format and often used as promotional giveaways by manufacturers, movie theaters, and candy and stationery stores. The first modern-format comic was issued in 1933.

The magic date in comic collecting is June 1938, when DC issued Action Comics No. 1, marking the first ap-

Reproduction Alert. Publishers frequently reprint popular stories, even complete books, so the buyer must pay strict attention to the title, not just the portion printed in oversized letters on the front cover. If there is any doubt, look inside at the fine print on the bottom of the inside cover or first page. The correct title will be printed there in capital letters.

Also pay attention to the dimensions of the comic book. Reprints often differ in size from the original.

pearance of Superman. Thus began the Golden Age of comics, which lasted until the mid-1950s and witnessed the birth of the major comic-book publishers, titles, and characters.

In 1954, Fredric Wertham authored *Seduction of the Innocent*, a book that pointed a guilt-laden finger at the comics industry for corrupting youth, causing juvenile delinquency, and undermining American values. Many publishers were forced out of business, while others established a "comics code" to assure parents that their comics were compliant with morality and decency standards upheld by the code authority.

The silver age of comics, mid-1950s through the end of the 1960s, witnessed the revival of many of the characters from the Golden Age in new comic formats. The era began with Showcase No. 4 in October 1956, which marked the origin and first appearance of the Silver-Age Flash.

While comics survived into the 1970s, it was a low point for the genre; but in the early 1980s, a revival occurred. In 1983, comic-book publishers, other than Marvel and DC, issued more titles than had existed in total during the previous 40 years. The mid-and late-1980s were a boom time, a trend that appears to be continuing.

Note: The comics listed here are in near-mint condition, meaning they have a flat, clean, shiny cover that has no wear other than tiny corner creases; no subscription creases, writing, yellowing at margins, or tape repairs; staples are straight and rust free; pages are supple and like new; generally just-off-the-shelf quality.

Additional Resources:

2007 Comic Book Checklist and Price Guide, 13th Ed., by Maggie Thompson, Brent Frankenhoff, Peter Bickford, and John Jackson Miller, Krause Publications, Iola, WI.

Standard Catalog of® Comic Books, 4th Ed., by John Jackson Miller, Maggie Thompson, Peter Bickford, and Brent Frankenhoff, Krause Publications, Iola, WI.

Standard Guide to Golden Age Comics, by Alex G. Malloy and Stuart W. Wells, III, Krause Publications, Iola, WI.

Warman's® Comic Book Field Guide, by John Jackson Miller and Maggie Thompson, Krause Publications, Iola, WI.

Captain Marvel Adventures, Fawcett

1	$30,000
2	$3,650
3	$2,100
4	$1,500
5	$1,150
6	$1,000
7	$850
8	$800
9	$775
10	$750
11	$725
12	$700
13-15	$675
16-17	$650

Captain Marvel Adventures, #15, Sep 42, © 1942 Fawcett, **$675.**

Detective Comics, #40, Jun 40, © 1940 DC, **$5,850.**

Hopalong Cassidy, #16, Feb 48, cover photo of William Boyd (aka Bill Boyd), © 1966 Bill Boyd, **$180.**

18	**$1,450**
19	**$600**
20	**$550**
21	**$500**
22	**$475**
23	**$685**
24	**$450**
25	**$435**
26	**$425**
27	**$400**
28	**$425**
29	**$400**
30	**$375**
31-35	**$350**
36	**$360**
37	**$340**
38	**$300**
39	**$330**
40	**$325**
41-44	**$285**
45-47	**$250**
48	**$400**
49-50	**$250**
51	**$240**
52-55	**$220**
56-60	**$235**
61-65	**$230**
66-70	**$225**
71-75	**$200**
76-80	**$190**
81-85	**$175**
86-90	**$165**
91-120	**$150**

121	**$240**
122-130	**$140**
131-140	**$130**
141-150	**$125**

Detective Comics, DC

1	**$78,000**
2	**$16,500**
3	**$10,200**
4-5	**$6,450**
6-7	**$4,200**
8	**$5,800**
9-17	**$4,100**
18	**$4,850**
19	**$4,000**
20	**$5,900**
21	**$3,100**
22	**$3,900**
23-26	**$3,100**
27	**$206,000**
28	**$21,400**
29	**$29,800**
30	**$6,600**
31	**$26,000**
32	**$5,800**
33	**$42,000**
34	**$5,600**
35	**$8,200**
36	**$6,000**
37	**$5,650**
38	**$44,000**
39	**$5,400**
40	**$5,850**
41	**$3,200**

42-44	**$2,075**
45	**$3,000**
46-50	**$1,700**
51-57	**$1,285**
58	**$3,850**
59	**$1,750**
60	**$1,400**
61	**$1,150**
62	**$1,850**
63	**$1,150**
64	**$3,200**
65	**$2,000**
66	**$2,950**
67	**$1,625**
68-69	**$1,400**
70	**$985**
71	**$1,100**
72-75	**$850**
76	**$1,250**
77-79	**$850**
80	**$950**
81-82	**$760**
83	**$800**
84	**$760**
85	**$950**
86-90	**$760**
91	**$850**
92-98	**$625**
99	**$850**
100	**$900**
101	**$575**
102	**$800**
103-108	**$585**

Superman Vol. 1, #14 Jan 42, © 1942 DC, **$2,675.**

Uncle Scrooge, #5 May 54, © 1954 Walt Disney Productions, writer, artist, cover Carl Barks, **$220.**

Valor, #1 Apr 55, artist Al Williamson, Wally Wood, Angelo Torres, Bernie Krigstein, Graham Ingels,© 1955 E.C. , **$190.**

109	$775	180	$410	274-297	$100
110-113	$565	181-186	$360	298	$175
114	$750	187	$400	299-300	$70
115-117	$565	188-189	$360	301-326	$50
118	$750	190	$550	327	$175
119	$565	191-192	$360	328	$85
120	$800	193	$410	329-331	$40
121	$565	194-199	$360	332	$100
122	$975	200	$525	333-358	$30
123	$565	201-204	$360	359	$75
124	$710	205	$525	360-371	$30
125-127	$565	206-213	$450	372-386	$25
128	$710	214-224	$330	387-388	$45
129-130	$565	225	$4,400	389-390	$16
131-136	$465	226	$1,400	391-394	$13
137	$600	227-229	$460	395	$20
138	$850	230	$500	396	$13
139	$460	231	$340	397	$20
140	$3,750	232	$275	398-399	$13
141	$500	233	$1,100	400	$45
142	$950	234	$300	401-425	$20
143-148	$500	235	$565	426-445	$15
149	$625	236	$325	446-479	$10
150-151	$550	237-240	$275	480-500	$8
152-155	$485	241-260	$210	501-531	$3
156	$575	261-264	$165	532	$5
157-167	$485	265	$275	533-534	$3
168	$3,100	266	$165	535	$5
169-170	$475	267	$210	536-up	$3
171	$650	268-271	$65		
172-176	$475	272	$125		
177-179	$365	273	$160		

Superman Vol. 1, DC

1	$149,000

2	$12,500
3	$8,250
4	$5,500
5	$3,750
6-10	$2,700
11-13	$1,700
14	$2,675
15	$1,625
16-20	$1,390
21	$1,125
22-23	$960
24	$1,125
25	$935
26-29	$835
30	$1,525
31-40	$730
41-50	$580
51-52	$475
53	$2,200
54-60	$475
61	$1,000
62-70	$450
71-75	$425
76	$1,300
77-80	$375
81-95	$350
96-99	$300
100	$1,600
101-110	$260
111-115	$240
116-123	$225
124-126	$195
127-130	$185
131-135	$160
136-139	$145
140	$170
141-145	$110
146	$150
147	$135
148	$110
149	$125
150-161	$65
162-170	$55
171-180	$50
181-190	$35
191-198	$30
199	$200
200-239	$25
240-244	$8
245	$12
246-251	$6

252	$12
253	$6
254	$12
255-271	$3
272	$7
273-277	$3
278	$6
279-283	$3
284	$6
285-291	$2
292	$4
293-299	$2
300	$6
301-350	$2
351-399	$2
400	$5
401-422	$2
423	$8

Uncle Scrooge, Dell

4	$310
5	$220
6	$200
7	$185
8	$140
9	$130
10	$125
11	$120
12	$115
13	$120
14	$110
15	$100
16	$90
17	$100
18	$90
19	$85
20	$80
21-22	$75
23	$70
24	$80
25	$75
26	$70
27	$75
28-29	$70
30	$65
31-33	$55
34-35	$60
36	$55
37	$50
38	$60
39	$50
40	$55

86-87	$35
88	$30
89	$35
90	$32
91-92	$35
93-94	$30
95	$35
96-98	$30
99	$35
100	$32
101-120	$20
121-140	$18
141-160	$12
161-180	$8
181-200	$7
201-219	$6
220-240	$5
241-260	$4
261-299	$2
300	$3
301-308	$2
309-319	$6
320-up	$5

Valor, E.C.

1	$190
2	$140
3-4	$115
5	$105

COPPER

History: Copper objects, such as kettles, teakettles, warming pans, and measures, played an important part in the 19th-century household. Outdoors, the apple-butter kettle and still were the two principal copper items. Copper culinary objects were lined with a thin protective coating of tin to prevent poisoning. They were relined as needed.

Reproduction Alert. Many modern reproductions exist.

Additional Listings: Arts and Crafts Movement and Roycroft.

Notes: Collectors place great emphasis on signed pieces, especially those by American craftsmen. Since copper objects were made abroad as well, it is hard to identify unsigned examples.

Additional Resources:

Antique Trader® Metalwares Price Guide, 2nd Ed., by Kyle Husfloen, ed., and Mark Moran, contr. ed., Krause Publications, Iola, WI.

Breadbox, chamfered oblong rect form, hinged cov, paneled domical form, brass finial raising from lozenge-shaped plaque over brass ring handles, brass bottom, Neoclassical, possibly Dutch, c1800, 12" l x 7-1/2" w x 11" h **$165**

Carpenter's pot, globular, dovetailed body, raised on three plain strap work iron legs, conforming handle, 11" l x 8" h **$70**

Censer, lobed, carved and pierced lid set with white jade, China, 19th C, 13" d **$1,300**

Charger, hand hammered, emb high relief of owl on branch, naturally forming patina, Liberty paper label, 29-1/2" d **$3,110**

Desk set, hammered blotter, letter holder, bookends, stamp box, each with bone carved cabochon, branch and berry motif, Potter Studio, fine orig patina, die-stamp mark **$750**

Fish poacher, cov, oval, rolled rim, iron swing ball handle, 19th C, 20-1/2" l **$350**

Inglenook hood, hammered, emb Glasgow roses, English, small tear at bottom, 30" w, 8" d, 34-1/2" h **$1,610**

Panel, repoussè of Bodhisattva seated on lotus seat, high relief figure, chased detail, traces of red pigment and gilding, Southeast Asia, slight bends, 18th C, 6-3/8" h x 2-7/8" w **$500**

Pot, cov, twin handles, oval, raised on four strap work legs, fitted with tubu-

Copper bookends, pr, hammered copper, possibly by Potters Studio, inset large Grueby scarab paperweights, matte brown glaze, orig dark patina, scarabs marked, 5-1/2" x 6", **$2,500.**
Photo courtesy of David Rago Auctions, Inc.

lar end handles, shallow domed cov stamped with shield design, center stationary handle, English, 19th C, 19-1/2" l, 12" w, 16" h **$215**

Screen, Arts & Crafts, ruffled edges, repousse design of oak tree, acorns, sun behind it, iron supports with copper coils wrapped around on front, 24" w x 38-1/4" h **$495**

Teakettle, gooseneck, dovetailed construction, swivel handle, brass finial, stamped "W. Wolfe," 12" h **$3,520**

Tray, Stickley Brothers, hammered copper, loped rim emb with dots, stamped "36" no patina, 13-1/2" d **$800**

Umbrella stand, hand hammered, flared rim, cylindrical body, two-strap work-loop handles, repoussé medallion, riveted flared foot, c1910, 25" h **$650**

Vase, hammered, ovoid, Dirk Van Erp, fine orig mottled patina, D'Arcy Gaw box mark, small shallow dent on rim, 5-1/2" d x 7" h **$8,100**

Vessel, hammered, ovoid, closed-in rim, orig dark patina, Dirk Van Erp closed box mark, 4" d, 3-1/4" h **$2,300**

Wall sconce, hammered, flame head, riveted Arts & Crafts details, attributed to Dirk Van Erp, cleaned patina, 4-1/2" w x 11" h **$425**

Water urn, copper body, int. with capped warming tube, applied brass ram's head handles, urn finial, brass spout, sq base with four ball feet, unmarked, repairs to lid, 14" h **$125**

Copper candy kettle, iron handles, interior worn, 18-1/2" d, **$150.**
Photo courtesy of Joy Luke Auctions.

Copper gilded griffin staff ornament, late 19th century, 12" h, 14" w, **$1,170.**
Photo courtesy of Pook & Pook, Inc.

Copper, vase, Roycroft, hammered, four sided, two rows of pierced squares below rim, minor cleaning, orb and cross mark, **$7,200.**
Photo courtesy of David Rago Auctions, Inc.

Black duck decoy, early 20th century, carved with tack eyes, weathered paint, 6-1/8" h x 16-1/4" l, **$585.**
Photo courtesy of Skinner, Inc.

Canada goose decoy, worn orig paint, glass eyes of unknown assoc, crudely repaired neck break, beak loss, cracking/separations, late 19th/early 20th century, 12" h x 23" l, **$110.**
Photo courtesy of Green Valley Auctions.

Wooden duck decoy, old repaint, old nailed neck repair, bill chip, early 20th century, 8" h x 17-1/2" l, **$90.**
Photo courtesy of Green Valley Auctions.

DECOYS

History: During the past several years, carved wooden decoys, used to lure ducks and geese to the hunter, have become widely recognized as an indigenous American folk-art form. Many decoys are from 1880 to 1930, when commercial gunners commonly hunted and used rigs of several hundred decoys. Many fine carvers also worked through the 1930s and 1940s. Individuals and commercial decoy makers also carved fish decoys.

Because decoys were both hand-made and machine made, and many examples exist, firm pricing is difficult to establish. The skill of the carver, rarity, type of bird, and age all affect the value.

Reproduction Alert.

Notes: A decoy's value is based on several factors: (1) fame of the carver, (2) quality of the carving, (3) species of wild fowl—the most desirable are herons, swans, mergansers, and shorebirds—and (4) condition of the original paint.

The inexperienced collector should be aware of several facts. The age of a decoy, per se, is usually of no importance in determining value. However, age does have some influence when it comes to a rare or important example. Since very few decoys were ever signed, it is quite difficult to attribute most decoys to known carvers. Anyone who has not examined a known carver's work will be hard pressed to determine if the paint on one of his decoys is indeed original. Repainting severely decreases a decoy's value. In addition, there are many fakes and re-productions on the market and even experienced collectors are occasionally fooled. Decoys represent a subject where dealing with a reputable dealer or auction house is important, especially those who offer a guarantee as to authenticity.

Decoys listed here are of average wear, unless otherwise noted.

Additional Resources:

Collecting Antique Bird Decoys and Duck Calls, An Identification and Price Guide, 3rd Ed., by Carl F. Luckey and Russell E. Lewis, Krause Publications, Iola, WI.

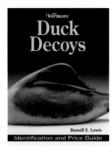

Warman's Duck Decoys, by Russell E. Lewis, Krause Publications, Iola, WI.

Atlantic Brant, Mason, Challenge grade, from the famous Barron rig (Virginia), nearly mint condition, age shrinkage neck crack repair, tight filled factory back crack, c1910 ....**$4,500**

Baldgate Wigeon Drake, miniature, A. Elmer, Crowell, East Harwich, MA identified in ink, rect stamp on base, 2-1/2" x 4" **$635**

Black Bellied Bustard, miniature, H Gills, initialed "H. G. 1957," identified in pencil, natural wood base, 3-1/2" x 4" **$230**

Black Bellied Plover, unknown American 20th C maker, orig paint, glass eyes, mounted on stick on lead base.
Minor paint loss, small chips to beak, 12-1/2" h **$2,530**
Minor paint loss, beak repair, 13-1/2" h **$1,725**

Black Breasted Plover, Harry C. Shourds, orig paint **$2,650**

Black Duck
A. Elmer Crowell, East Harwich, MA, orig paint, glass eyes, stamped mark in oval on base, sleeping, wear, crack, 5-1/4" h **$525**
Ira Hudson, preening, raised wings, outstretched neck, scratch feather paint **$8,500**
Mason, Premier, Atlantic Coast, oversized, solid-bodied special order, most desirable snaky head, excellent orig condition, some professional restoration, filled in-the-making back crack, tail chip on one side of crack, neck filler replacement, c1905 ....**$4,500**
Mason, Standard, painted eye, dry original paint, all of its original neck filler, invisible professional dry rot repair in the base, c1910 ....**$750**

Unknown maker, carved balsa body, wood head, glass eyes, orig paint, 15-1/2" l **$150**

Wildfowler, CT, inlet head, glass eyes, worn orig paint, green overpaint on bottom on sides, c1900, 13" l **$220**

Black Drake, miniature

A. Elmer Crowell, East Harwich, MA, identified in ink, rect stamp on base, break at neck, reglued, minor paint loss, 3-1/2" x 4-3/4" **$635**

James Lapham, Dennisport, MA, identified in black ink, oval stamp, minor imperfections, 2-1/2" x 4" **$290**

Bluebill Drake, carved by Robert Elliston, painted by wife Catherine Elliston, Illinois River, 19th C **$6,700**

Bluebill Hen, Mason Challenge, hollow, orig paint, c1910 ..... **$3,450**

Blue-Winged Teal Drake and Hen Pair, Davey W. Nichol, Smiths Falls, Ontario, Canada, matched pair, raised wings, scratch feather patterns, sgd on bottom, 1960 .... **$1,650**

Brant, old black, white and gray paint, glass eyes, age splits on base, minor chips to gesso on back, 14-1/2" l **$115**

Broadbill Drake and Hen Pair, Mason, painted eyes, rare gunning rigmates, untouched original condition, neck filler missing, some shot evidence, hen has small, superficial chip on one side, c1910 .... **$1,450**

Bufflehead Drake

Bob Kerr, carved detail, glass eyes, orig paint, scratch carved signature, c1980, 10-1/2" l **$250**

Harry M. Shrouds, carved, hollow body, painted eyes............. **$1,800**

James Lagham, Dennisport, MA, identified in ink, oval stamp on base, 3" x 4-1/2" **$345**

Canada Goose

Hurley Conklin, carved, hollow body, swimming position, branded "H. Conklin" on bottom **$600**

Unsigned, carved wood, shaped tin, canvas covering on body, later gray, brown, white, and black paint, glass eyes, restored splits in neck, 22-1/2" l........ **$100**

Unsigned, gray, black, and white paint, incised carved initials "P.C." on base, carved open

bill, relief detail on wings and tail feathers, glass eyes, iron legs, glued break at neck, 27" l, 26-5/8" h **$300**

Canvasback

Chesapeake Bay, carved and painted, glass eyes, metal ring, 12" l, 7-1/2" w, 10-3/4" h **$1,650**

Unknown carver, pine, paint dec, lead weight, metal ring, 8-3/4" l, 6" w, 5" h **$1,210**

Curlew

Dan Leeds, Pleasantville, NJ, carved and painted brown, stand, 1880-1900, 13" l **$2,415**

Harry V. Shrouds, orig paint **$2,000**

Curlew Oyster Eater, Samuel Jester, Tennessee, carved and painted, slight paint wear, age crack in body, stand, c1920, 16" l, 9" h **$1,035**

Elder Duck, old black and white paint, green stripe around head, yellow bill, Maine, unsigned, 17-3/4" l................................... **$250**

Flying Duck, glass-bead eyes, old natural surface, carved pine, attributed to Maine, c1930, 16" l, 11" h......................... **$2,300**

Goldeneye, drake, unknown Maine carver, oversized, classic Maine inletted neck and raised shoulders, worn orig paint with clear patterns, branded "Gigerrish" or "G.I. Gerrish," c1900, 13" l.................**$1,850**

Great Northern Pike, attributed to Menominee Indian, WI, painted green, glass eyes, ribbed sheet metal fin, tall stand, c1900, 36" l, 9" h......................... **$3,450**

Green Wing Teal Duck, miniature, A. Elmer Crowell, East Harwich, MA, identified in ink, rect stamp on base, 2-1/2" x 4" **$865**

Heron, unknown maker, carved wig and tail, wrought iron legs..... **$900**

Herring Gull, attributed to Gus Wilson, used as weathervane, traces of old paint, metal feet, weathered and worn, c1910-20, 18-3/4" l................................ **$3,110**

Hooded Merganser Drake, William Clarke, Oakville, Ontario, Canada, transitional plumage, excellent orig condition, minor in-use wear, c1900 .... **$2,450**

Loon, carved and painted, wooden rudder, America, stand, paint wear, 19th C, 27" l................ **$9,200**

Perch fish decoy, Andy Trombley, 1950s, 9", **$2,596.**
Photo courtesy of Lang's Sporting Collectables.

Pheasant decoy, wooden, carved and painted, painted brass tack eyes, no stand, old tail repair, late 19th/early 20th century, 10-3/4" x 33-1/2", **$1,650.**
Photo courtesy of Skinner, Inc.

Turtle fish decoy, Bud Stewart, signed, minor paint loss around weights, Near Mint, 6-1/2", **$305.**
Photo courtesy of Lang's Sporting Collectables.

Carved and painted duck decoy attributed to Bill Shaw, Lacon, Illinois, **$850.**
Photo courtesy of Joy Luke Auctions.

Canada goose decoy, carved and painted, mid-20th C, 15" h x 22" w, **$345.**
Photo courtesy of Pook & Pook, Inc.

Mallard Drake

Ben Schmidt, Detroit, relief carved, feather stamping, glass eyes, orig paint, orig keep, marked "Mallard drake Benj Schmidt, Detroit 1960," 15-1/4" l **$450**

Bert Graves, carved, hollow body, orig weighted bottom, branded "E. I. Rogers" and "Cleary" **$900**

James Lapham, Dennisport, MA, sgd and identified in ink on bottom, 4" x 5" **$435**

Mason, Challenge, rare hollow model with elaborate Mason Premier style paint patterns, no tail chip, professional repair to some splintering on end of bill, tight neck crack on left side, some shot evidence on right side, c1910 .... **$3,500**

Mason, Premier, hollow snakey head, orig condition, c1900 .... **$6,500**

Robert Elliston, carver, painted by wife Catherine Elliston, Illinois River, 19th C..................... **$6,200**

Mallard Drake and Hen Pair, Mason, glass eyes, gunning rigmates, excellent orig condition, some neck filler replaced, drake has filled factory crack on side, c1905 .... **$1,750**

Mallard Hen

Robert Elliston, carved, hollow body, orig paint **$1,800**

Mason Premier, hollow, excellent orig paint, rich red breast, professional tail chip repair and neck putty restoration, c1905 .... **$3,900**

Merganser Drake, Mason Challenge, Detroit, MI, strong orig paint with no cracks, some shot holes have been filled on one side, branded "C. Simpson," c1910..................... **$7,500**

Owl, carved wood, glass eyes, orig polychrome paint, 20" h...... **$1,700**

Perch, Heddon, ice-type **$800**

Pintail Duck

Drake, Paw Paw Bait Co., stenciled company name on bottom, c1932-36................................. **$800**

Drake and hen, John H. Baker, Bristol, PA, painted in naturalistic tones, glass eyes, sgd, imp maker's signature, lead ingot affixed to bases stamped "John Baker Bristol, PA," paint flakes on hen, 20th C.................. **$1,100**

Plover, Joe Lincoln, winter plumage, feather painting, orig paint **$800**

Red Breasted Merganser Drake

Amos Wallace, ME, inlet neck, carved crest, detailed feathered paint **$2,000**

George Boyd, NH, carved, orig paint **$8,000**

Redhead Drake, Dan Bartlett, Prince Edward County, Ontario, Canada, hollow, fine orig paint, c1920 .... **$950**

Robin Snipe, Obediah Verity, carved wings and eyes, orig paint **$4,400**

Ruddy Duck, miniature, maker unknown, identified in ink on base, paint loss to bill, 2" x 2-3/4" **$690**

Ruddy Duck Drake, Len Carmeghi, Mt. Clemens, MI, hollow body, glass eyes, orig paint, sgd and dated, 10-3/4" l..................... **$250**

Ruffled Grouse, miniature, A. Elmer Crowell, East Harwich, MA, rect stamp, mounted on natural wood base, 3-1/2" x 4-1/2"..... **$865**

Sea Gull, weathered surface, used as weathervane, attributed to WI, late 19th/early 20th C, 14" l **$1,840**

Shorebird, carved and painted, mounted on wooden stand, minor wear, America, early 20th C, 6-3/4" l, 9-1/2" h..................... **$775**

Swan, unknown Chesapeake Bay, MD, maker, carved wood, braced neck, white paint, 30" l........... **$900**

Widgeon, matted pair, Charlie Joiner, MD, sgd on bottom **$800**

Wood Duck Drake, D. W. Nichol, Smiths Falls, Ontario, slightly turned head, 1950s **$2,450**

Yellowlegs, carved and painted, New Jersey, stand, c1890, 11" l **$2,185**

DISNEYANA

History: Walt Disney and the creations of the famous Disney Studios hold a place of fondness and enchantment in the hearts of people throughout the world. The 1928 release of "Steamboat Willie," featuring Mickey Mouse, heralded an entertainment empire.

Walt and his brother, Roy, were shrewd businessmen. From the beginning, they licensed the reproduction of Disney characters on products ranging from wristwatches to clothing.

In 1984, Donald Duck celebrated his 50th birthday, and collectors took a renewed interest in material related to him.

Additional Resources:

Warman's® Americana & Collectibles, 11th Ed., by Ellen T. Schroy, ed., Krause Publications, Iola, WI.

O'Brien's Collecting Toys, 11th Edition, Karen O'Brien, ed., Krause Publications, Iola, WI.

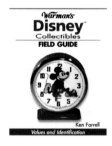

Warman's® Disney Collectibles Field Guide, by Ken Farrell, Krause Publications, Iola, WI.

Adviser: Theodore L. Hake. Author of the *Official Guide to Disneyana,* House of Collectibles, 2006, over 9,000 Disney items in color with values. Hake's auction site is: www. hakes.com.

Bambi

Book, *Bambi*, hardcover, Grossett & Dunlap, copyright 1942, 7" x 8-1/4" **$40**

Charm bracelet, gold luster metal link bracelet, five figural gold luster charms of red/brown Bambi and Faline, blue Thumper, black and white Flower, yellow/green Friend Owl, 1950s, 6" l **$20**

Figure, Goebel, full bee mark, incised "DIS 111," 1950s, orig string tag, 2-1/2" x 6-1/2" x 7" **$75**

Pencil sharpener, figural, "Walt Disney's Bambi," green catalin, color decal, early 1940s, 1-3/4" **$124**

Planter, glazed ceramic, Modern Ceramic Pottery, Australian, 1950s, 5" x 7" x 6" **$125**

Studio fan card, stiff buff paper, brown design, Walt Disney facsimile signature, small copyright, 1940s, 7" x 9" **$35**

Cinderella

Costume, two pcs, Ben Copper, copyright Walt Disney Productions, late 1960s, box illus include Spider-Man, Hulk, Thor, and Wonder Woman, wear to box, costume bright, 8-1/4" x 11" x 2-3/4" orig box **$30**

Planter, ceramic, Shaw Cinderella in serving clothes, 7-1/4" h **$425**

Prince Charming leaning against banister **$300**

Soaky, soft plastic body, hard plastic head, blue dress, movable arms, 10-1/2" h **$20**

Davy Crockett

Pencil case, "Official Davy Crockett Frontierland Pencil Case," vinyl, attached shoulder strap, snap closure with paper insert depicting Fess Parker as Davy, unused contents inc., composition book and sealed pencil/ruler assortment, one pencil mkd "Davy Crockett - King Of The Frontierland," 6-1/2" x 8-1/2" **$140**

Disney Family

Autograph, Walt Disney, 7" x 8-1/2" glossy photo of Walt standing next to bookcases, wearing tie with symbol for Smoke Tree Ranch, accompanied by letter of authenticity from Hake's Americana & Collectible Auction, 2-3/4" l signature, 11" x 14" cardboard mat **$750**

Autographed photo, Roy E. Disney, glossy photo boldly signed at

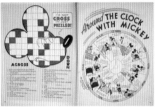

Mickey Mouse, magazine, first issue, 10-1/4" x 13-1/4", vol. 1, no. 1, 2" spine edge splits repaired, tape strip on cover, strong color, intact, Good, 44 pgs, by Hal Horne © 1935, **$900.**
Photo courtesy of Hake's Auctions www.hakes.com.

Pinocchio Coachman, cookie jar, whip and sword at left, pipe in right hand, minor flaws, Brayton/Laguna, Exc, 1939, 6" x 8" x 8-3/4", **$4,000.**
Photo courtesy of Hake's Auctions www.hakes.com.

Mickey's Nephew, celluloid figure with movable head, yellow nightshirt, red shoes, several shallow indents, Disney copyright, "Made in Japan," VF, 1930s, 5-1/4", $615.
Photo courtesy of Hake's Auctions www.hakes.com.

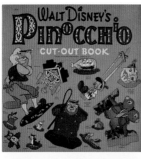

Pinocchio, cut-out book, card stock cover, Whitman No. 974, unused, 4 pgs, © 1939, 1" x 13", $500.
Photo courtesy of Hake's Auctions www.hakes.com.

right corner in black felt tip pen, reverse with sticker, "Roy Disney Vice Chairman The Walt Disney Company," accompanied by letter of authenticity from Hake's Americana & Collectibles Auction **$75**

Disneyland

Book, *A Visit to Disneyland,* Whitman Big Tell-A-Tale, 28 pgs, color photos, copyright 1965, 6" x 8-1/2" **$20**

Game, Disneyland Riverboat Game, Parker Bros, four different colored metal boat playing pcs, copyright 1960, 14-3/4" sq board, 8" x 16" x 1-3/4" deep box **$50**

Key chain, Mickey head and black text, brass chain, c1960, 1-1/4" d, 3/8" thick transparent plastic disc **$22**

Snow dome, hard plastic, 3-D castle, Tinkerbelle dangling from top, 1960s, 2-1/4" h **$50**

Disney World

Convention badge, black printing, gold background, "110 Club '79/ Disney World," 4" d **$10**

Flicker, I Like Walt Disney World, red metal case, text on reverse including "Vari-Vue" and Walt Disney World logo, black, white, and red image of Mickey wearing blue bowtie, changes to slogan in white on red background **$20**

Donald Duck

Book, *Donald's Penguin,* hardcover, Garden City Publishing, 24 pgs, copyright, 1940, 8-1/2" x 9-1/2" **$80**

Book, *The Wise Little Hen,* Donald Duck debut, Whitman, 40 pgs, © 1935. Fine condition. **$250**

Button, Birthday Club, black & white, inscribed "Member," issued by "Astor Theater, Burwood," (Australia), late 1930s or early 1940s, 13/16" **$135**

Button, club, Donald eating frozen treat reading "Icy-Frost Twins Club Of America Member," no backpaper as issued, tiny crack below bowtie, several small bumps/indents, c1950, 1-1/4" **$247**

Calendar, full color center scene titled "Bedtime," Donald making sure nephews are getting ready for bed, blue and white border with Mickey, Minnie, Pluto, Dumbo, Timothy, Bambi, and Thumper with stars, American Bedding Co., Portland OR, only December calendar

remains, 8" x 11" thin cardboar● **$145**

Christmas card, image of Donald as Santa, standing on rooftop giving victory symbol, next to sack of war-themed toys, bottom margin reads "Proceeds To The American Woman's Voluntary Services," card stock, orig plain envelope, World War II era, 6-1/4" x 9" **$80**

Doll, Knickerbocker, stuffed, movable head, oilcloth eyes, hat, collar and jacket buttons held on with safety pins, felt tail, 1930s, 7" x 10" x 17-1/2" h **$475**

Egg cup, color image of Donald pushing wheelbarrow, brown/iridescent tan, unmarked, 1950s 2-1/4" x 4" x 3-1/2" **$145**

Fan card, image of angry Donald clenched fists, card stock, facsimile Walt Disney signature, c1937, 7" x 9" **$200**

Figure, celluloid, plaster filled, metallic blue paint, 1930s, 3" h **$100**

Fun-E-Flex figure, wood body, fabric-covered arms, movable head, near complete decal on front of body, 1930s, 5" h **$1,150**

Juice glass, wrap-around images of Huey, Dewey, and Louie, names 1940s, 3-3/8" h **$125**

Little Golden Book, *Donald Duck in Disneyland,* Golden Press, copyright 1960, 4th printing, 24 pgs .... **$18●**

Pencil drawing, lead and blue pencil 4" x 4-1/2" image of Donald with green pencil underline, from "Honey Harvester," 1949, 10" x 12" sheet of animation paper **$200**

Pencil holder, celluloid, designed as lamp, 1" h, 3-D Donald figure on base with long bill, shade with images of Mickey and Donald, Disney copyright, mkd "Japan," 1930s, 3-1/4" h **$700**

Pencil sharpener, figural, dark red catalin, full color decal on front, 1-11/16" **$60**

Toy, Schuco, tin litho and hard plastic, felt hat and collar, wind-up, orig box, 1960s, 6" h **$300**

Dumbo

Bank, cast metal, copyright on back of base, mkd c1941, key missing, 4" h **$250**

Figurine, painted and glazed ceramic of newborn Dumbo, red, blue, and silver foil stick-on back, Disney copyright and "Modern Ceramic

Products PTY Ltd., Sydney," 1940s, 2" x 2-1/2" x 3-1/2" h.............. **$185**

Figurine, Dumbo with recessed ears for holding jewelry, Goebel, full bee mk and others, 1950s, 3-1/2" t **$252**

Premium button, black, white, red, and gray, "D-X" printed on platform, reverse Kay Kamen back paper includes small image of running Mickey, 1942, 1-1/4" d...... **$30**

Toothbrush holder, painted ceramic, matte finish, three openings for toothbrushes, incised 1942 copyright, 3-1/2" x 5-1/2" x 3-3/4"............. **$150**

Fantasia

Concept art, watercolor, Dance of the Hours, ominous-looking alligator backing hippopotamus against stone column, reverse with studio backstamp noting artist James Bodrero, sequence #10, sketch #374, July 11, 1939, 10" x 12" sheet of animation paper.............. **$2,000**

Figure, painted and glazed ceramic, Vernon Kilns, 1940 Disney copyright

Centaur, incised "31," 10" h **$1,000**

Centaurette, incised "24," 7-1/2" h **$750**

Plate, Flower Ballet, Vernon Kilns, dark maroon, yellow, green, and blue, copyright 1940, 9-1/2" d............... **$75**

Souvenir movie program, softcover, Western Printing Co., black and white photos of Walt Disney and other contributors, full color plates of scenes from film, from orig 1940 release, 9-1/2" x 12-1/2".. **$50**

Goofy

Animation cel, 4" x 5-1/2" image of Sport Goofy, color laser background of stadium, #A-76 from numbered sequence, from 1980s Disney TV show, 10-1/2" x 12-1/2" acetate sheet **$150**

Bank, molded hard vinyl head, Play Pal Plastics, Inc., copyright 1971, red shirt collar, bright yellow hat, trap missing, 5" x 9" 10-1/2" **$25**

Blotter, Sunoco Oil, Goofy and angry polar bear, broken-down car, unused, copyright 1939, 4" x 7"................. **$40**

Book, *Goofy Best Comics,* Abbeville Press, 184 pgs, title page boldly signed in black felt tip pen, "Very Best to Al, Floyd Gottfredson,"

hardcover, copyright 1979, 9-3/4" x 13-1/4"... **$75**

Figure, Hagen-Renaker, painted and glazed ceramic, green shirt and hat, tan vest, blue pants, brown shoes, foil sticker missing, 1950s, 2-1/2" h **$150**

Pencil drawing, lead and blue pencil, 4" x 5-1/2" image of Goofy from waist up as porter, #17.5 from "Baggage Buster," 1941, 10" x 12" sheet of animation paper **$250**

Toy, Goofy's Disneyland Stock Car, Linemar, Goofy as Driver, other characters riding, late 1950s, 6" l **$275**

Mickey Mouse

Bank, metal, chest with lightly emb oilcloth fabric, brass plated side panels, text, "Mickey and Minnie At The World's Fair, 1933 Chicago 1934," raised images of Hall of Science, Travel, and Transportation, Federal on front, Zell Products, scattered loss to brass luster, key missing, 2-1/4" x 4-1/4" x 2" h **$200**

Books

Big Little Book, *Mickey Mouse Sails for Treasure Island,* softcover premium for Kolynos Dental Cream Whitman, 1935........................... **$60**

Mickey Mouse Presents Santa's Workshop, hardcover 80 pgs, Collins, c1938, 7-1/4" x 10" **$250**

Mickey Mouse Waddle, Blue Ribbon Books, copyright 1934, orig dust jacket, perforated Waddle pages removed, 7-3/4" x 10-1/4"........ **$200**

The Adventures of Mickey Mouse, hardcover, 32 pgs, David McKay Co., copyright 1931, 5-1/2" x 7-3/4" **$150**

The Adventures of Mickey Mouse, softcover, Canadian version, Musson Book Co. Ltd., copyright 1934, 6-1/4" x 8-1/2" **$275**

Candle nightlight holder, ceramic, figural Mickey asleep in chair, 1-1/2" recessed area on front to hold candle, unmarked Crown Devon, 1930s, 2-1/2" x 5-1/2" x 4-1/2" **$235**

Card album, Mickey Mouse Picture, Vol. 2, issued by Gum Inc., for cards #49-96, front cover with Mickey holding open picture card album, mounted cards #77, 87, 90, and 95, 16pgs, 1930s, 6" x 10" **$250**

Mickey Mouse Club movie button, likely produced by local theater owner, VF, c1932, 1/2", **$645.**
Photo courtesy of Hake's Auctions www.hakes.com.

Donald Duck, bisque figure with red mandolin, "S1158," minor defects, 1930s, 4" h, **$745.**
Photo courtesy of Hake's Auctions www.hakes.com.

Pinocchio, composition bank, Pinocchio riding on turtle, metal trap beneath, small rubs, flakes and dust soiling, missing key, crown, fine, 6-1/2" h, **$420.**
Photo courtesy of Hake's Auctions www.hakes.com.

Mickey Mouse vase, Goebel, hunter pose with rifle, squirrel climbing up back of tree, complete foil sticker and markings on base, full bee, "Dis-75," 1950s, 5-1/2" h, **$220.**
Photo courtesy of Hake's Auctions www.hakes.com.

Mickey Mouse, tin-litho "Mickey The Driver" car, hard plastic Mickey with spring-mounted head, built in key, depicts Mickey, Minnie, Goofy, Pluto and Donald on car, box has light aging, Marx, F/VF, 1950s, 6.5" l, **$500.**
Photo courtesy of Hake's Auctions www.hakes.com.

Lunchbox with thermos, "Mickey Mouse Club," metal lunchbox with "Mickey Mouse Club Official Identification Card" printed on side, Alladin Industries, Inc., © Walt Disney Productions, VF, 1963, 6-1/2" thermos, **$200.**
Photo courtesy of Hake's Auctions www.hakes.com.

Car radiator ornament, stamped brass, relief design, dark patina, 1930s, 3" x 5-3/4" **$300**

Clock, metal, enameled front with two Mickeys, mkd "Made in Germany," 1930s, 2" x 3"x 3/4" **$800**

Comic book, Ghost of the Grotto, four color, Carl Barks art, Dell Publishing, CGC 6.5, #159, Aug. 1947 ....**$275**

Composition book, *Mickey Mouse Composition Book,* by Powers Paper Co., brown, black, and red illus of Mickey and Minnie walking, carrying school books, multiplication tables on back, some penciled school work on pages, dated 1934, 6-3/4" x 8-1/4" **$75**

Demitasse cup, china, highly-stylized image of Mickey on both sides, 1930s, 2-1/4" h..................**$90**

Dime register bank, tin litho, dark yellow border, top and sides with Mickey, Minnie, and nephews, copyright 1939, 2-1/2" x 2-1/2" x 3/4" **$250**

Doll, Knickerbocker, stuffed cloth, polished cotton face with printed details, separate fabric pants, felt ears, hands, and shoes, 10-1/2" h **$500**

Figure
Bisque, playing accordion, Disney copyright, mkd "Made in Japan," 1930s, 5-1/4" h..................**$225**
Celluloid, squatty body, oversized head, one arm reaching to back, c1930, 4-3/4" h..................**$225**
Glass, from 1937 sports set, Mickey as baseball player, 5-1/2" h **$350**

Gum card wrapper, Gum inc., waxed paper, illus of Mickey, Minnie, Pluto, Horace, and Clarabelle, text "Save the Wrappers," 1930s, 5" x 7-1/4"..................**$100**

Magazine, *Mickey Mouse Magazine,* Vol. 1, #7, 36 pgs, newsprint, Mickey and W.C. Fields dot-to-dot puzzle neatly done in pencil, near mint, April 1937 ....**$475**

Marionette, painted composition head, wood pegs hands and feet, 3-1/2" x 5" x 7" animal fur-covered body, 1930s, 7-1/2" l tail **$165**

Napkin ring, black enamel and silvered, diecut Mickey, on reverse stamped "E.P.N.S. R.R." early 1930s, 1-5/8" d **$135**

Pencil box
Cardboard, double snap closure front panel, Dixon, #2666, 1934, 5-3/4" x 10-3/4" x 2" **$250**
Mickey Mouse/Donald Duck, Dixon, front depicts Mickey and Donald, back shows Horace and Goofy behind house windows, textured paper-covered cardboard, snap closure, repeated Disney characters on interior, mkd "No. 3103," 1930s, 4-1/2" x 8-1/2" x 3/4" d **$225**

Pencil drawing, 3" x 4" lead pencil image of seated Mickey wearing policeman's hat, from "Dognapper," 1934, 9-1/2" x 12" sheet of animation paper..................**$300**

Pen clip, silvered metal, 9/16" domed metal attachment with colorful Mickey, tiny copyright initials below WDP, Bastian, early 1950s, 1-1/4" h **$35**

Pin, diecut brass, enamel, in boxing gloves, 1940s, 1" **$85**

Plate, china, images of Mickey playing musical instruments, dancing, Minnie wearing hat, mkd "Imperial Ironstoneware N.K.T. Made in Japan," 1930s, 8" d..................**$100**

Sand pail, tin litho, attached carrying handle, Ohio Art, golf theme, wrap-around illus with Mickey, Donald, Goofy, and black cat, play wear, copyright 1938, 5-3/4" h, 5-3/4" d at top **$300**

Sheet music, *The Wedding Party of Mickey Mouse,* Stasny Music Corp, orig copyright, 1931, 1936 issue, 8 pgs, 9" x 12"..................**$125**

Space heater, cast-iron front, steel heating element compartment on back, high-relief Mickey on front, hands on either side of center opening, Art Deco-style grills, text "Tabard Mickey Mouse Fire/By Permission of Walt Disney-Mickey Mouse Ltd.," English, 12" x 12" x 5" deep **$2,500**

Tea set, boxed, China, 11pcs, Mickey Mouse teapot, creamer and sugar, four cup and saucer sets, mkd "S.A." with crescent moon and star on teapot, slight crazing, 1930s **$560**

Toy
Celluloid, Mickey and Donald in rowboat, Disney copyright, mkd "Made in Japan," old repairs, 1930s, 2" x 6" x 2-1/4" h **$350**
Pressed steel, telephone, N. N. Hill Brass Co., rotary dial turns and rings, pop-up cardboard Mickey figure, c1934, 5" x 8" x 4-1/2" h **$300**

Mickey Mouse English Ingersoll pocket watch, first issue, celluloid dial, revolving second wheel, silvered brass case, NM, 1933, 2" d, **$1,650.**
Photo courtesy of Hake's Auctions www.hakes.com.

Alice In Wonderland figurine, Shaw, foil sticker on underside, c1951, 5-1/2" h, **$195.**
Photo courtesy of Hake's Auctions www.hakes.com.

Pinocchio "Good Teeth" premium, ADA Giveaway, ©WDP on bottom edge, NM, 1-1/4", **$240.**
Photo courtesy of Hake's Auctions www.hakes.com.

Pull, Fisher Price "Mickey Mouse Choo-Choo," Mickey rings bell as toy is pulled, bright paper labels, no. 485, 1949 update, 8-1/2" l **$210**

Watch fob, silvered brass, loop at top, black accents, reverse "Ingersoll Mickey Mouse Watches & Clocks Copyright Walt Disney," English, 1930s, 1-1/8" **$265**

Wristwatch, Ingersoll, dial with large black, white, and yellow Mickey, hands point to numerals, second wheel with three tiny Mickey images, vintage replacement strap, working order and clean dial, 1933, 1-1/4" d chromed metal case **$325**

Mickey Mouse Club

Australian, dark blue lettering, "New Lyric Theater Mickey Mouse Club," 1" d scrapbook, Whitman, 64 unused pgs, full color cover of Mouseketeers with art supplies, copyright 1957, but actually 1970s printing, 10-3/4" x 14-3/4" **$20**

Minnie Mouse

Bracelet, enameled and incised Mickey and Minnie standing back to back, 1930s, stamped "Sterling" **$200**

Child's feeding dish, divided, color images of Minnie, Mickey, and Salem China Co., 1930s, 8" d, 1-3/4" h **$150**

Cigarette holder, china, Minnie playing piano, mkd "Germany," incised "2885, " 1930s, 3-1/5" x 2-1/4" x 3" h **$200**

Figure

American Pottery, leaning against broom, 6" h **$250**

Shaw, pink outfit, orig label, mkd "Mexico," 4-1/2" h **$275**

Pencil drawing, lead pencil drawing of 2-1/2" x 3" Mickey and 1-1/2" x 2" Minnie, #73 from "Camping Out," 1934, 9-1/2" x 12" sheet of animation paper **$250**

Pencil sharpener, catalin, octagon, depicts full Minnie figure, minor oxidation on metal blade, 1-1/8" **$112**

Pin, Minnie and Mickey full figure, silvered brass, Mickey standing to right of Minnie, yellow enamel background, mkd "Sterling," missing bar pin and hinge, c1932, 1" t **$280**

Pull toy, celluloid figure attached to 4" long freewheeling wood scooter, 19" l string, wood knob on end, mkd "Made in Japan," small copyright symbol, 1930s, 3-1/4" h ..**$320**

Salt and pepper shakers, painted and glazed ceramic, Dan Brechner Exclusive foil sticker, ink stamp copyright, WD-52, standing on top of wood crates which house noisemakers, names on front of base, orig stoppers, 2" x 2" x 5-1/4" **$75**

Sign, Congoleum Gold Seal Rug, die-cut cardboard, text "3 Special Prizes Offered By This Store/Ask For A Free Entry Blank," image of Minnie mopping linoleum rug, 1930s, 19-1/2" d **$750**

Teapot, glazed yellow ceramic, full color image of Mickey, Minnie, and Donald, hand-in-hand, text "Ring-A-Ring of Roses," names in blue, roses, unmarked, possibly Wade, 1930s, 3-1/2" x 6" x 3-1/2" h **$90**

Pinocchio

Book, *Pinocchio Linen-Like, #1061*, Whitman, 12 pgs, full color art on each page, copyright 1940, 7" x 7-3/4" **$50**

Candy bar wrapper, Schutter Candy Co., black, white, yellow, and red image of Jiminy and premium "Official Conscience Medal," copyright 1940, 3-1/4" x 8-1/4" **$60**

Figure

Ceramic, Figaro, Goebel, foil sticker, 1950s, 4" h **$125**

Ceramic, Pinocchio and Figaro, Brayton Laguna, company name and "Gepetto Pottery" on underside, 1940s, 4-1/4" h **$950**

Wood, black, white, red, blue, and yellow, separate light blue wood ball hands attached by elastic string, paper label, "Pinocchio," copyright, Geo Borgfeldt Corp., 1940, 4-3/4" h **$125**

Game, Pinocchio Race Game, Chad Valley, scene of Pinocchio and Jiminy Cricket encountering Foulfellow and Gideon leaving Geppetto's workshop on box lid, some fading to box, 14-1/2" sq board, game pcs, c1940, 10" x 15" x 1-3/4" h **$140**

Lamp base, painted and glazed ceramic, donkey and high-relief flowers, Zaccagnini, W72, Disney

Children's premium book, Merry Christmas From Mickey Mouse, © 1939 K.K. Publications, Inc., Joslin's Department Store, Malden, Mass., intact, spine split but still intact, Fine, 16 pgs, 7" x 10", **$925.**

Photo courtesy of Hake's Auctions www.hakes.com.

copyright sticker, wiring missing, 5-1/2" x 4-1/2" **$150**

Planter, painted and glazed ceramic, Figaro dipping paw into aquarium planter, raised image of fish on front, c1940, 3" x 5-1/2" x 4-1/2" **$35**

Soaky, soft plastic body, hard plastic head, Pinocchio sitting on top of tree stump, holding school slate, 1960s, 9-3/4" h **$20**

Toy, walking Pinocchio, litho tin wind-up, Linemar, orig box, 1950s, 5-3/4" h **$750**

Pluto

Drinking glass, small W.D. Ent. Copyright, Pluto with eyes closed, mouth wide open belting out song, music stand in front of him, music notes scattered around front and back, 4-3/4" h **$320**

Novelty, Pluto pulling Donald in sleigh, Donald holds string reigns, celluloid, platform base, mkd "Made In Japan," 1930s, 1" x 4" base... **$647**

Pencil drawing, from flip book designed by Art Corner at Disneyland, Ralph Kent artist, 1955, 3-1/2" x 5" image in lead pencil and black crayon on 7-1/4" x 10-1/4" sheet **$100**

Pin, brass, rich yellow enamel, black, white, and red accents, WD copyright, 1930s, 1-1/4" **$85**

Push puppet, hard plastic, Kohner, c1960, green base, foil sticker with orange text, 2-1/2" h **$25**

Toy drum major windup, Linemar, orig rubber ears, tail missing, 1950s, 6-1/4" h **$175**

Roger Rabbit

Animation cel, pair, one with Jessica Rabbit, other with Weasel, background film scene on high quality Kodak paper, 1988, 7-1/2" x 16-1/2" acetate sheet, 4-1/2" x 7-1/2" certificate of authenticity issued by Walt Disney Co. **$200**

Production test cel, set of three, consecutively numbered, each with full figure image in slightly different pose of Roger as gray rabbit, three 11-1/2" x 16-1/2" acetate sheets **$100**

Sleeping Beauty

Book, *Sleeping Beauty,* Whitman, Story Hour series, 32 pgs, copyright 1959, 7-1/2" x 8-1/4" **$18**

Box proof, "Sleeping Beauty Colorforms Dress Designer Kit," full

color glossy paper, copyright 1959, 11-1/4" x 16-1/4" **$65**

Figure, Queen, Hagen-Renaker, painted and glazed ceramic, foil sticker, 1950s, 2-3/8" h............ **$600**

Snow White

Birthday card, White & Wyckoff, black, white, red, blue, and green design, front with Doc and Sleepy in front of doorway, opens to Snow White dancing with Doc as others play instruments, copyright 1938, 4-1/4" x 5-1/2" **$30**

Book, *Edgar Bergen's Charlie McCarthy Meets Walt Disney's Snow White,* Whitman Publishing, softcover, 24 pgs, copyright 1938, 9-1/2" x 11-1/2" **$110**

Comic book, full color, 16pgs, copyright 1958 by Western Printing Co., issued as premium by Reynolds Wrap, 5" x 7" **$22**

Figure, celluloid with plaster filling, marked "Foreign" on back, "Celluloid" on underside, some pulling at seams, c1938, 1-1/2" x 2-1/4" x 4-1/2" **$75**

Mechanical Valentine set, diecut, poems relating to each character, 8pcs, Snow White 6" t, dwarfs 5" t **$135**

Paper doll, Snow White Magic Doll, mkd "Made in Canada by Somerville Paper Boxes," copyright 1937, storage inside cover for 11" diecut cardboard doll and six different felt outfits, 9" x 13-1/2" cardboard folder **$200**

Pencil sharpener, figural, dark red catalin, full-color decal on front, 1-11/16".................................... **$75**

Pitcher, Sneezy, painted and glazed, relief and dimensional shape, marked "Wadeheath by Permission Walt Disney England," c1938, 3-3/4" h **$175**

Song folio, *Snow White and the Seven Dwarfs,* 9" x 12", 52 pgs, Bourne Inc. Music Publishers, copyright 1938, 1950s printing............................. **$25**

Song folio, *Snow White and the Seven Dwarfs,* 52 pgs, Bourne Inc. Music Publishers, copyright 1938, 1950s printing, 9" x 12".............. **$25**

Tea set, partial, cake plate with Snow White and Doc, six 4-1/4" d plates for Dopey, Grumpy, Bashful, Sleepy, Doc, and Sneezy; four 1-1/4" h tea cups for Dopey, Sneezy, Grumpy, and Sleepy; three 3-1/4" d saucers for Dopey, Sleepy, and Sneezy;

2-1/4" h creamer with Dopey; and 3" h cov sugar with Happy, mkd "Made in Japan," copyright 1937 ....**$200**

Umbrella, red, white, and blue wood handle and shaft, metal frame, white silk like synthetic fabric cover, full color images of Snow White and the Seven Dwarfs, names in black letters, copyright, c1938, 19" l, 24" d open..**$100**

Three Pigs

Game board, Marks Brothers Co., ominous image of Wolf towering over dancing Fiddler and Fifer Pigs, Practical Pig putting finishing touches on brick house, c1934, 16-3/4" sq board **$50**

Plate, white china, full-color center scene of Three Pigs, Little Red Riding Hood, and Grandmother knitting in rocking chair, blue rim trim, marked "Salem China Co./Patriot China," 1930s, 7-1/2" d **$75**

Postcard set, marked "Paris," French text, backs also marked "Disney," each with full color art telling story, sent by soldier to daughter in US, each with typed or handwritten note, sent on consecutive days in April, 1945, set of 12 numbered 3-1/2" x 5-1/5" cards **$150**

Radio, wood, front with 4" opening with pressed wood attachment with three pigs, fabric speaker cover, two pigs play fife and fiddle, while third dances, 5" x 7" x 9-1/4" **$1,000**

Sand pail, tin litho, Ohio Art, Wrap-around scene, Spanish version, 1934, 5" h **$300**

Toy, Big Bad Wolf and Three Little Pigs, litho tin wind-up, Linemar, key-wind, 1960s, each 4-1/2" h..............**$200 ea.**

Zorro

Costume, unused, attached to orig diecut cardboard hanger display, Lindsay, black diecut leatherette mask, black fabric cloak/sash, silver image of Zorro on rearing Tornado, 3-1/4" d Member Lindsay Ranch Club badge, late 1950s, 16" x 37" **$50**

Countertop standee, cardboard, easel on back, printed text on back, "New on TV From Disney Studios Zorro/ABC-TV/Brought To You By Seven-Up, imprint of Channel 6, Thursday 8 P.M.," copyright 1957, 12" x 16" **$50**

Figure, painted and glazed ceramic, Enesco, orig foil sticker, copyright, "WDE.140," attached foil-covered

cardboard string tag, replaced metal sword, 3" x 4" x 7" h **$125**

Game, Whitman, 15-1/2" sq board, complete set of picture letter cards, one generic plastic marker missing, copyright 1965, 8" x 15-1/2" x 1-1/2" deep box **$75**

Puzzle, frame tray, , Whitman, full-color Zorro and Captain Ramone sword fighting, copyright 1957, 11-1/2" x 14-1/2" **$25**

School bag, vinyl covered canvas, plastic carrying handle, vinyl carrying strap, unused store stock, c1958, 3-1/2" x 13" x 10" h....................**$90**

DOLLHOUSES

History: Dollhouses date from the 18th century to modern times. Early dollhouses often were handmade, sometimes with only one room. The most common type was made for a young girl to fill with replicas of furniture scaled especially to fit into a dollhouse. Specially sized dolls also were made for dollhouses. All types of accessories in all types of styles were available, and dollhouses could portray any historical period.

American

Gambrel roof, painted off-white, red pasteboard scalloped shingles, front opening half doors, six rooms, original paper wall and floor coverings, hinged door in rear roof,

front steps, orig furniture, bisque dolls, accessories, and rugs, some paint and paper wear, 28-1/4" w, 17-1/4" d, 32-1/2" h..................**$920**

Ivory-painted gable and center hallway, five large rooms and attic bedroom, attached garage, separate blue shutters and window boxes, most furnishings from same period as house, approx. 40 items, made by John Leonard Plock, NY architect, c1932, 21" w, 43" h **$250**

Victorian, two-story house, modified Federal style, mansard roof with widow's walk, fenced-in front garden, simulated grass and fountains, polychrome details, last quarter 19th C, 21-1/4" l, 28-3/4" h......**$400**

Bliss, chromolithograph paper on wood

Two-story, blue litho paper on roof, blue wood on back, red wood chimney and base, two open lower windows and two upper windows, house opens in front, litho wall and floor coverings inside, marked "R. Bliss" on door, some wear, one wall slightly warped, 14" h **$575**

Two-story, front porch with turned columns, working front door, overhanging roof with lattice-work balcony, blue-gray roof with dormer windows, hinged front, int. with two rooms, printed carpeting and wallpaper, celluloid windows with later lace curtains, electric lights,

Dollhouse, Ginny lithographed cardboard, Cape Cod style with tabs, one room, terrace and green grass, dormer window and chimney both marked "Ginny," c1940s, 24-3/4" h x 31" w x 22" d, **$645.**

Photo courtesy of Skinner, Inc.

two scratch-built chairs, 16-1/2" h **$1,725**

Two-story, two single windows down, one double window up, remnants of windows and curtains, small porch and balcony on front, marked "R. Bliss" on front door, soiling to paper, cardboard front warped, 12-1/2" h **$525**

Elastolin, Germany, farmyard, house, barn, fencing, trees, and various figures, 29" w................................**$1,150**

German, Nuremberg Kitchen, dark yellow walls with deep red trim, red and black checkerboard floor, cream stove hood, green furniture, tin stove, tin and copper pots, set of scales, wash boiler, baking pans, utensils, pottery, porcelain, and pewter tableware, some paint wear and imperfections, late 19th C, 35" w, 11-1/4" d, 17" h **$2,300**

McLoughlin, folding house, two rooms, dec int., orig box, 12" x 17" x 16".....................................**$950**

Schoenhut, mansion, two-story, eight rooms, attic, tan brick design, red roof, large dormer, 20 glass windows, orig decal, 1923, 20" x 26" x 30" **$1,750**

Tootsietoy, house, furniture, and accessories, printed Masonite, half-timbered style, two rooms down, two up, removable roof, open back, orchid and pink bedroom sets, orchid bathroom, brown dining room set, flocked sofa and chairs, green and white kitchen pcs, piano, bench, lamps, telephone, cane-back sofa, rocker, some damage and wear to 3/4 scale furniture, 21" w, 10-1/8" d, 16" h **$525**

DOORSTOPS

History: Doorstops became popular in the late 19th century. They are either flat or three-dimensional and were made out of a variety of different materials, such as cast iron, bronze, or wood. Hubley, a leading toy manufacturer, made many examples.

All prices listed are for excellent original paint unless otherwise noted. Original paint and condition greatly influence the price of a doorstop. To get top money, the original paint on a piece must be close to mint condition. Chipping of paint, paint loss, and wear reduce the value. Repaint-

Doorstop, cast iron, large footmen, Hubley, mkd "© FISH," orig paint, first half 20th century, 12" h x 8-1/4" l, $385.
Photo courtesy of Green Valley Auctions.

Doorstop, cast iron, Little Colonial Lady, orig paint, crazing, wear and paint flaking, first half 20th century, 4-1/2" h, $55.
Photo courtesy of Green Valley Auctions.

ing severely reduces value and eliminates a good deal of the piece's market value. A broken piece has little value to none.

Reproduction Alert. Reproductions are proliferating as prices on genuine doorstops continue to rise. A reproduced piece generally is slightly smaller than the original unless an original mold is used. The overall casting of reproductions is not as smooth as on the originals. Reproductions also lack the detail apparent in originals, including the appearance of the painted areas. Any bright orange rusting is strongly indicative of a new piece. Beware. If it looks too good to be true, it usually is.

Notes: Pieces described contain at least 80 percent or more of the original paint and are in very good condition. Repainting drastically reduces price and desirability. Poor original paint is preferred over repaint.

All listings are cast-iron and flat-back castings unless otherwise noted.

Art Deco woman, wedge sgd "Joe Wagner Realty Co." on front base, very good, 5-1/8" x 4-3/4" **$225**

Bathing beauties, Hubley, sgd "Fish, 240," two Art Deco bathers under bright umbrella, excellent, 10-7/8" x 5-1/4"...........................**$450**

Blue jay, standing in grass with flowers, good, 4-7/8" x 3-3/4" **$500**

Caddy golfer, white caddy, brown plaid knickers, turquoise necktie, excellent, 8" x 5-3/4"................**$1,910**

Cape cod, thatched roof, yellow hollyhocks, pink flowering vines, picket fence on side, near mint, 4-3/4" x 7-1/4" **$560**

Cat, sleeping
Hubley, repaint, 8-1/2" x 5-1/4" ..**$150**
Unknown maker, full figure, painted black, excellent, 5-1/4" x 12-1/4" x 10-1/4" dia **$1,460**

Clipper ship, *Charles W. Morgan*, back sgd "P. F. Gay, Dartmouth, Mass. Copyright 1932," ship at dock, flying American flag, near mint, 10-5/8" x 14-7/8" **$1,120**

Cottage, snow capped roofs, yellow clapboards, green trees, excellent, 7-3/4" x 7-1/8"........................**$4,480**

Elk, attributed to Albany Foundry, standing on rocks, excellent, 9-7/8" x 8-5/8" **$840**

Fawn, sgd "Taylor Cook C 1930, No. 6," Art Deco style, excellent, 9-7/8" x 5-3/4" **$560**

Flower basket, pansies and morning glories, angel-embossed basket, excellent, 11-1/2" x 7"................**$280**

Flying ducks, Spencer, realistic paint, near mint, 7-1/2" x 5-1/4".......**$1,000**

Fox terrier, Hubley, full standing figure, facing right, near mint, 8-3/4" x 8-1/4".......................**$450**

Fruit basket, mkd "16," fruit overflowing woven basket, two pcs of fruit lying at base, excellent, 5-1/8" x 5-3/8".......................**$225**

Heron, Albany Foundry, near mint, 7-1/2" x 5"................**$450**

Highland lighthouse, sgd "Highland Light Cape Cod," two pc casting, excellent, 9" x 7-3/4"................**$3,360**

Indian maiden, bright colors, excellent, 8-5/8" x 2-7/8"................**$340**

John Humphrey house, 3-story saltbox with dormer windows, gray clapboards, green base sgd "The John Humphrey House, Swampscott," excellent, 5-1/8" x 7-1/4"................**$1,100**

Medieval Knight in Armor, sgd "I.V.I. Pat Pend.," very good, 13-1/4" x 5-7/8"................**$120**

Narcissus, Hubley, flowers in ftd urn, mkd "266," near mint, 7-1/4" x 6-3/4"................**$310**

Old mill, Greenblatt Studios, old mill and stone bridge by stream and winding lane, near mint, 9-3/4" x 7-1/4"................**$8,400**

Palomino horse, Hubley, near mint, 7-3/4" x 10-3/4"................**$260**

Peter Rabbit, Albany or National Foundry, excellent, 8-1/4" x 4-7/8"................**$1,120**

Poppies, yellow flowers, slant handled basket, back sgd "C.H.F. CO. E110," excellent, 10-1/2" x 8"................**$840**

Puss in Boots, white kitten playing in black boot, sgd "Copyright 1930, Creations Co.," excellent, 8-3/8" x 5-3/4"................**$1,910**

Putting golfer, Hubley #34, red coat, gray pinstriped knickers, excellent, 8-3/8" x 7-1/8"................**$510**

Rabbit in top hat, blue jacket, red bowtie, plaid vest, National Foundry, #89, near mint, 9-7/8" x 4-5/8"................**$1,800**

Roses in planter, pastel roses, ribbed planter, near mint, 7" x 4-3/4"................**$400**

Saltbox house, stone fence, attributed to Sarah Symonds, mkd "Apple-

tree, Mass," red clapboard house, stone wall, excellent, 5-7/8" x 9-1/8"................**$4,200**

Spanish dancer, Hubley 193, ruffled flowered dress and shawl, holding fan, 8-7/8" x 5"................**$200**

Sulgrave manor house

A. M. Greenblatt, sgd "1 Copyright 1925 by A. M. Greenblatt Studios" on back, "Ancestral Home of George Washington" on front base, near mint, 9-1/8" x 10-7/8"................**$1,350**

National Foundry, excellent, 5-1/2" x 5-1/16"................**$115**

Three kittens, Bradley and Hubbard, sgd "B & H," three kittens seated in open book, orig rubber bumpers, excellent, 5-1/4" x 6-3/8"................**$1,100**

Tulips

Albany or National Foundry, mkd "41," multicolored tulips, ridged vase, green 2-tiered base, near mint, 8-1/4" h................**$340**

Connecticut Foundry, sgd "Conn Fdry Corp 1929," colored tulips in vase, excellent, 10-5/8" x 6-3/4"................**$225**

West Wind, CJO, Judd Co., 1253, sgd "The West Wind" on front of base, young girl walking in field of flowers, hair blowing, skirt billowing, rare, near mint, 18" x 8"................**$23,250**

Windmill with cottages, post and rail fence, excellent, 9-7/8" x 11-1/2"................**$1,100**

Doorstop, cast iron, bronze colored urn with flowers, orig paint with moderate loss, light base rust, first half 20th century, 7-1/4" h, 6" l, **$88.**
Photo courtesy of Green Valley Auctions.

Doorstop, cast iron, Little Southern Belle, orig paint, normal wear, first half 20th century, 6-1/2" h, 2-3/4" x 3-1/4", **$55.**
Photo courtesy of Green Valley Auctions.

Doorstop, mansion on bronzed top of hill, stamped "B&H" (Bradley & Hubbard), 9-1/2" x 8-1/2", **$2,900.**
Photo courtesy of David Rago Auctions, Inc.

FAIRY LAMPS

History: Fairy lamps, which originated in England in the 1840s, are candle-burning night lamps. They were used in nurseries, hallways, and dim corners of the home.

Two leading candle manufacturers, the Price Candle Company and the Samuel Clarke Company, promoted fairy lamps as a means to sell candles. Both contracted with glass, porcelain, and metal manufacturers to produce the needed shades and cups. For example, Clarke used Worcester Royal Porcelain Company, Stuart & Sons, and Red House Glass Works in England, plus firms in France and Germany.

Fittings were produced in a wide variety of styles. Shades ranged from pressed to cut glass, from Burmese to Nailsea. Cups are found in glass, porcelain, brass, nickel, and silver plate.

American firms selling fairy lamps included Diamond Candle Company of Brooklyn, Blue Cross Safety Candle Co., and Hobbs-Brockunier of Wheeling, West Virginia.

Two-piece (cup and shade) and three-piece (cup with matching shade and saucer) fairy lamps can be found. Married pieces are common.

Marks: Clarke's trademark was a small fairy with a wand surrounded by the words "Clarke Fairy Pyramid, Trade Mark."

Fairy lamp, Webb, Burmese, four parts, shaded shade and ruffled base, crystal candleholder, underplate marked with Clark's "Cricklite," base has Webb trademark, 6-1/2" d base, 5-1/2" h overall, **$750.**

Photo courtesy of The Early Auction Company, LLC.

Reproduction Alert. Reproductions abound.

Bisque, tri-face baby girl, 3-1/2" **$70**

Blue and white frosted ribbon glass dome top shade, ruffled base, clear marked "S. Clarke" insert, flakes on shade, 6" **$490**

Blue satin mother-of-pearl shade, clear Clarke Fairy pyramid insert, 3-3/4" **$225**

Blue satin swirl shade, matching base, ruffled top and edge, 5" **$325**

Burmese
Dec shade, clear Clark's Cricklite base, 4" **$900**
Egg-shaped shade, crystal insert, colorful porcelain bowl, stamped S. Clark's patent trademark, English trademark backstamp, 8" **$1,380**

Burmese Cricklite, dome shaped shade, pleated bowl shaped base, clear glass candle cup sgd "Clarke's Cricklite Trade Mark," 7-1/2" d, 5-1/2" h **$1,350**

Clarke Pyramid, light, holder, and white porcelain mug, frosted shade set on finger loop base, sgd "Clarke Food Warmer," adv slogans on mug, 8-1/2" **$125**

Clear molded flame shade, controlled bubbles, clear S. Clarke's Fairy Pyramid base, 4-1/2" **$60**

Figural green glass shade in shape of monk, set on frosted shoulders base, 4-1/2" **$110**

Green Nailsea shade, porcelain Doulton Lamplih dec base, sgd "S. Clarke's Fairy" in center, 5-1/2" **$1,300**

Green opaque shade, gold and blue enamel dec, clear pressed glass pedestal base, 8-3/4" **$275**

Lavender and frosted white shade, matching ruffled base, zigzag design, 5-1/2" **$150**

Metal, colored inset jewels, reticulated shade with bird designs, 4-1/2" **$185**

Ruby red, profuse white loopings, bowl shaped base with eight turned up scallops, clear glass candle cup holder marked "S. Clarke Patent Trade Mark Fairy," 5-3/4" **$1,250**

Ruby red, white loopings, matching piecrust crimped base, inclusion on shade, 4" d, 4-1/2" h **$585**

Ruby red Cricklite, white loopings dome shaped shade, bowl shaped base with 26 pleats, clear glass candle cup sgd "S. Clarke Patent Trade Mark Fairy," 7" d, 6" h **$975**

Ruby red Cricklite, white loopings satin dome shaped shade, clear cup mkd "S. Clarkes Patent Trade Mark," 4" h.. **$335**

Yellow satin shade, matching ftd base, clear sgd "S. Clarke Fairy" insert, 6-1/4" **$650**

Yellow satin swirl shade, clear S. Clarke's Fairy pyramid base, 4" **$150**

Webb, blue shade dec with bird and branch, clear Clarke's Cricklite insert, sq blue satin base, 6-1/2" **$1,500**

White and yellow striped shade, clear S. Clarke Fairy insert, nestled on matching white and yellow ruffled base, 6" h **$500**

FIREARM ACCESSORIES

History: Muzzle-loading weapons of the 18th and early 19th centuries varied in caliber and required the owner to carry a variety of equipment, including a powder horn or flask, patches, flints or percussion caps, bullets, and bullet molds. In addition, military personnel were responsible for bayonets, slings, and miscellaneous cleaning equipment and spare parts.

During the French and Indian War, soldiers began to personalize their powder horns with intricate engraving, in addition to the usual name or initial used for identification. Sometimes professional horn smiths were employed to customize these objects, which have been elevated to a form of folk art by some collectors.

In the mid-19th century, cartridge weapons replaced their black-powder ancestors. Collectors seek anything associated with early ammunition—from the cartridges themselves to advertising material. Handling old ammunition can be extremely dangerous because of decomposition of compounds. Seek advice from an experienced collector before becoming involved in this area.

Reproduction Alert. There are a large number of reproduction and fake powder horns. Be very cautious!

Notes: Military-related firearm accessories generally are worth more than their civilian counterparts.

Calendar, Marble Arms & Mfg Co., artwork by Philip R. Goodwin, top image of two hunters, one with gun raised at animal across river, bottom image with man by campfire, docked canoe, 1918 .... **$5,230**

Canteen, painted, cheese-box style, dark red paint overall, one side painted gold with a large primitive eagle with shield breast, the top of the shield red with cream lettering "No. 37," other side painted in gold letters, "Lt. Rufus Cook," pewter nozzle, sq nail construction, strap loops missing, 7" d, 2-5/8" deep **$1,650**

Cartridge board, 22" x 25", Winchester, New Haven, CT, 1874, showing range of rimfire cartridges, wood frame, some shelf spoiling, corner repair to frame **$12,915**

Cartridge box

Hall and Hubbard, .22 caliber, green and black label "100 No. 1/22-100/ Pistol Cartridges," cov with molded cream and black paper, empty, missing about half green side label, 3-7/8" x 2" x 1" **$300**

Union Metallic Cartridge Co., .32 caliber, cream and black label "Fifth .32 caliber/No. 2/Pistol Cartridges," engraving of Smith & Wesson 1st Model 3rd Issue, checked covering, orange and black side labels, unopened, 4" x 2-1/8" x 1-1/4" **$210**

Catalog

Colt's-The Arm of Law and Order, 42 pgs, black and white illus and specifications of 16 models of Colt revolvers and automatic pistols, 5-3/4" x 7-3/4" **$25**

Savage Arms Corp., Chicopee Falls, MA, 1951, 52 pgs, No. 51, *Component Parts Price List for Savage, Stevens, Fox Shotguns & Rifles,* 8-1/2" x 11" **$35**

Winchester Repeating Arms, New Haven, CT, 215 pgs, Cat No. 81, illus of repeating and single-shot rifles, repeating shotguns, cartridges, shells, primers, percussions caps, shot, 5-1/2" x 8-1/2" **$250**

Flask, brass, dead game, emb, stamped "Am. Flask & Cap Co.," 8" l **$200**

Knapsack, painted canvas, flap having American eagle with shield among stars and surrounded by oval cloud border, scrolled banner inscribed "RIFLE CADET," painted in red, white, blue, and gold on black ground, two leather strap and iron buckles, reverse with ink inscription, "Benjamin Pope Bridgewater July 4th 1820," minor paint losses, wooden hanger and twine attached to the back, 13-5/8" x 13-1/4" **$31,725**

Poster, store type, Winchester Rifles, Shotguns and Ammunition For Sale Here, two bear dogs in foreground, bloodhounds in back, 41-1/2" x 32" **$6,300**

Powder horn, engraved

America, incised animal figures, scallop, and linear borders on butt end, inscribed "M RIFLE COMP'Y 1823/ horne" next to the initials "AM," wood plug with applied wire staple for carrying strap, carved wooden stopper, c1823, 10-1/2" h **$450**

"JOB WATERMAN HIS HORN/ CALEB HARRIS/FEB,y THE 10 AD 1758/ PROVIDENCE," Providence, RI, in four circular or lobed reserves, applied silver plated brass mouthpiece, copper band around butt rim, leather band with woven twill strap sewn to neck, c1858, 14-1/8" l **$900**

John Goddard, incised dec, borders of wave-like and compass motifs, scene with figure driving horse and carriage with sun overhead and dog, sgd "JOHN GODDARD," indistinct date 1747 or 1777, butt end with extension lobe pierced for carrying strap, pine plug, late 18th C, 16" l **$1,175**

"Robert Guy's Horn" down side, smaller engraving near spout, dated "1840," domed pine plug, flared end for carrying strap, hole 1" above name, 16-1/2" l **$250**

"Stil not this horn for fear of shame for hear doth stand the oner name jacob lewis 1785, (sic) two rows of geometric devices round bottom, carved and incised lines at spout, dome-shaped wooden plug, America, small age crack, wear, late 18th C, 18" l **$1,610**

"Wm M. 1799," also "J. M. 1814," surrounded by series of inscribed

circles, flat pine plug, 18" l **$1,200**

Primer, engraved, New York scene, primitively engraved men and animals, date "1852" added later, c1800, 7" l **$1,155**

Product leaflet

Western Silvertip Ammunition, glossy paper, color printing, diecut upper corner, one side shows 18 variations of brass cartridges in differing gauges for large game hunting, one panel devoted to three Winchester hunting rifles, 1956, 3-1/2" x 6" closed **$25**

Western-Winchester, full color printing, illus and describes western Super-X and Xpert shotgun shells and cartridges, 1957, 3-1/4" x 6-1/2" closed **$15**

Shotgun box, empty

Austin Cartridge Co., Crack-Shot, 16 gauge, full-color scene of three hunting dogs on front **$2,310**

Chamberlin Cartridge Co., 12 gauge, Blue Rocks **$1,100**

Clinton Cartridge Co., Pointer Brand, 12 ga, smokeless powder, pointer in center with bird in mouth, light blue top and lettering, gold border, red ground, 4-1/8" x 4-1/8" x 2-1/2" **$350**

J. F. Schmelzer & Sons Arms Co., 12 gauge carver cartridges, illus of hunter and pointed on front **$1,750**

Peters Quick Shot, 12 gauge shotgun shells **$5,835**

Firearm accessory, gun cabinet, Arts & Crafts, three doors, mirrored pane over two drawers, 69-1/2" x 44-1/2" x 19", **$2,500.**

Photo courtesy of David Rago Auctions, Inc.

Hand-fabricated Confederate musket, **$2,500-$2,850.**

The .54 caliber, Richmond Sharps carbine (Confederate), is recognized by its brass furniture, **$13,500-$15,500.**

Robin Hood Eclipse Cartridge, 12 gauge, near smokeless powder shells **$2,550**

Sign, Winchester Guns and Ammo, guns and dead game image by Alexander Pope, tin litho, wood structural backing, dark green background, 36" x 30"..**$1,300**

Tin, Oriental Smokeless Gunpowder, half pound, four litho labels with full-color ducks **$1,810**

Tinder box, tin, candle socket, inside damper, flint, and steel, 4-3/8" d **$330**

Tinder lighter, flintlock
Rosewood pistol grip, tooled brass fittings, 5-1/2" l **$750**
Compartment for extra flint, taper holder, 6-1/2" l **$550**

Water keg, wooden, American, oval, flattened bottom, two Shaker-style wide-tongued wooden straps, large hand-forged nail on each end for carrying cord, orig wood stopper, late 18th/early 19th C, 9" x 7-1/2" x 9" **$400**

FIREARMS

History: The 15th-century Matchlock Arquebus was the forerunner of the modern firearm. The Germans refined the wheelock firing mechanism during the 16th and 17th centuries. English settlers arrived in America with the smoothbore musket; German settlers had rifled arms. Both used the new flintlock firing mechanism.

A major advance was achieved when Whitney introduced interchangeable parts into the manufacturing of rifles. Refinements in firearms continued in the 19th century. The percussion ignition system was developed by the 1840s. Minie, a French military officer, produced a viable projectile. By the end of the 19th century, cartridge weapons dominated the field.

Notes: Two factors control the pricing of firearms—condition and rarity. Variations in these factors can cause a wide range in the value of antique firearms. For instance, a Colt 1849 pocket-model revolver with a five-inch barrel can be priced from $100 to $700, depending on whether all the component parts are original, some are missing, how much of the original finish (bluing) remains on the barrel and frame, how much silver plating remains on the brass trigger guard and back strap, and the condition and finish of the walnut grips.

Be careful to note a weapon's negative qualities. A Colt Peterson belt revolver in fair condition will command a much higher price than the Colt pocket model in very fine condition. Know the production run of a firearm before buying it.

Laws regarding the sale of firearms have gotten stricter. Be sure to sell and buy firearms through auction houses and dealers properly licensed to transact business in this highly regulated area.

Additional Resources:

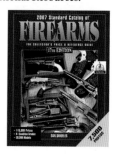

2007 Standard Catalog of® Firearms, 17th Ed., by Dan Shideler, ed., Krause Publications, Iola, WI.

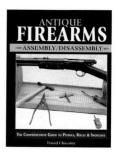

Antique Firearms Assembly/Disassembly, by David Chicoine, Krause Publications, Iola, WI.

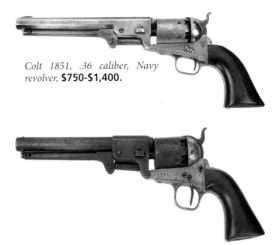

Colt 1851, .36 caliber, Navy revolver, **$750-$1,400.**

Cased set, Belgian dueling pistols, **$1,300-$1,700.**

Confederate, Griswold, .36 caliber, brass-frame revolver, **$22,000-$30,000.**

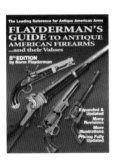

Flayderman's Guide to Antique American Firearms and Their Values, 8th Ed., by Norm Flayderman, Krause Publications, Iola, WI.

Standard Catalog of® Military Firearms, 3rd Ed., by Ned Schwing, Krause Publications, Iola, WI.

Warman's® Civil War Collectibles Field Guide, by John F. Graf, Krause Publications, Iola, WI.

Carbine

Hall-North, Model 1843, percussion, .52 caliber, rifled 21" barrel, bold metal stampings, signature and 1849 on receiver, traces of old brown finish, walnut stock with old split between trigger guard and barrel, small repairs near breech, 40" l **$935**

Joslyn Model 1862, .52 caliber, 22" round barrel, walnut stock, clear inspector's markings, brass buttplate, trigger guard and barrel band, stamped signatures on lock and breech block, 38-5/8" l **$650**

C. S. Richmond, .58 caliber, 25" barrel, all-steel hardware, brass nose cap, buttplate stamped "U.S.," Type 3, humpback lock, "C. S. Richmond, 1864" mark, no sling swivels, 43" l
....**$3,300**

Sharp's New Model 1863, breech loading, walnut stock and forearm, double inspectors markings, 22" blued barrel, areas of very light case coloring on lock, buttplate, hammer, barrel

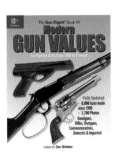

The Gun Digest Book of Modern Gun Values, 13th Ed., by Dan Shideler, ed., Krause Publications, Iola, WI.

Warman's® Civil War Collectibles, 2nd Ed., by John F. Graf, Krause Publications, Iola, WI.

band, and receiver, clear stampings on lock, 34" l **$1,980**

Spencer, Civil War Model, .52 caliber rimfire, 22" round barrel, overall brown finish on all metal surfaces, worn walnut stock, faint inspector's mark, forearm with additional coat of varnish, 39" l **$2,100**

Springfield, Model 1884 Trapdoor, saddle ring, mint bore, Buffington sight, stamped "C. Proper," range with inspector's cartouche.................**$825**

Wesson, Frank, 28" octagonal barrel, folding rear peep sight, walnut stock with orig dark finish, rear open sight missing, 43" l overall **$275**

Dueling pistols, percussion lock

English, London, dolphin hammer, belt clip, engraved scrollwork on frame, checkered burl-wood grip, barrel engraved "London," second quarter 19th C, 8-1/2" l, price for pr **$650**

English, Queen-Anne style, London, for J. Wilson, scrolled mask butt, grip set with small monogrammed cartouche, plain stylized dolphin hammer, cannon barrel engraved with cartouches, and maker's mark on underside, late 18th C, 8" l, price for pr...**$500**

Flintlock long arms

Buchele, W., Bicentennial, curly maple stock, relief carved bust of George Washington with flag behind cheekpiece along with acanthus leaves on either side of comb, brass hardware including engraved patch box with eagle finial, applied Liberty Bell, twelve inlays along with brass and nickel silver floral wire inlay, 58-1/2" l **$3,500**

Cooper, J, lock sgd "J. Cooper," engraved detail, brass hardware including patch box, curly maple stock with nickel silver escutcheons, thumb piece with faint checkering, 38-1/2" l octagonal barrel turned found for bayonet on last 3" with lug, conversion to flint with pieced repair to forend and other replacements, 54-1/2" l....................................**$950**

French, Model 1766 Charlesville Musket, lock plate only partially legible, matching ramrod, top jaw and top screw period replacements, 44-3/4" l orig barrel length **$1,250**

Golcher, Joseph, Philadelphia, PA, .54 caliber, octagonal barrel, brass patch box, buttplate, trigger guard, carved and brass-fitted pick compartment, brass and silver inlays along tiger maple stock, lock plate marked, barrel initialed, c1800, 54" l, 38-1/2" l **$4,750**

Kentucky, R. E. Leman, .38 caliber, small brass front sight and fixed rear sight, top flat in front of chamber area is marked "R.E. LEMAN/ LANCASTER PA/WARRANTED," unmarked flat lock plate, applied grain tiger striped stock, simple brass trigger guard, two-pc patch box with crescent buttplate and dbl. set triggers, ovoid forestock with integral ramrod groove and two small brass guides, dark heavy patina on iron and wood, 37-3/8" oct. bbl **$920**

Pennsylvania, attributed to W. Haga, Reading School, maple stock, relief carving, incised details, brass hardware with flintlock, some age cracks, glued repair, good patina, replaced patch box lid, 50-1/2" l octagon to round barrel **$1,760**

U. S. Model 1819, Hall, breech loading, second-production type, Harpers Ferry Armory, John Hall's patents, .52 caliber, single shot, three barrel bands, breechblock deeply stamped, 32-5/8" round barrel **$1,200**

Virginia, curly-maple stock with good figure, relief carving, old mellow varnished finish, brass hardware, engraved and pierced patch box, Ketland lock reconverted back to flint, silver thumb piece inlay, barrel and forend shortened slightly, small pierced repair at breech area, top flat engraved "H. B.," 41-1/2" l **$3,300**

Flintlock pistols-single shot
English

Blunderbuss, 14" round iron barrel with Birmingham proofs, fitted with 12-1/2" triangular snap bayonet, walnut full stock with lightly engraved brass furniture, two ramrod pipes, buttplate, trigger guard, small shield-shaped wrist plate, two lock-plate screw escutcheons, attributed to John Whitehouse, metal parts complete and orig throughout, missing sliver of wood along right side at muzzle, early 19th C, 29-1/2" overall **$1,500**

Tower, .60 caliber, 12" round barrel full-length military stock, brass trigger guard, butt cap and sidelined lock plate marked "Tower" behind hammer and crown over "GR" forward of hammer, proofed on left side of barrel at breech, crown on tang behind tang screw, good condition, re-browned and cleaned replaced front sight, working order **$700**

French, military, 9" round iron barrel flat beveled lock plate with faceted pan fitted with flat beveled reinforced hammer, brass furniture, unmarked 16" overall length........................**$800**

Halsbach & Sons, Baltimore, MD holster pistol, 9" brass part round part octagon barrel, .65 caliber, lock marked "Halsbach & Sons," large brass butt cap with massive spread wing eagle (primitive) in high relief surrounded by cluster of 13 stars large relief shell carving around tang of barrel, full walnut stock pin-fastened, c1785 to early 1800s **$1,750**

U. S. Model 1805, iron rib underneath holding ramrod pipe, lockplate marked with spread eagle and shield over "US" and vertically at rear "Harper's Ferry" over "1808", .54 caliber, walnut half stock with brass buttplate and trigger guard, Flayderman 6A-008, 10" round iron barrel **$3,000**

Musket

Colt, Model 1861, .58 caliber, "17th N.Y.V." beneath stock, good signature, date, and stampings on metal, inspector's cartouche on stock, bright gray metal, areas of pitting around bolster and lock, 39" barrel......**$1,375**

Enfield, .58 caliber, unmarked, percussion, square base front sight/bayonet lug with 800 meter military sight, lock plate has markings of a crown over "VR" and date "1856," right side of butt stock carries cartouche of circle with broad arrow and date "1856," three bbl bands with sling swivels and slotted head ramrod, upper bbl band and sling loop, as well as sling loop on trigger and ramrod, appear to be recent replacements, bbl retains smooth gray-brown patina with heavy pitting over breech end, light refinish to wood, worn and damaged nipple, dated 1856, 39" bbl.....................**$815**

.52 caliber, Spencer 7-shot repeater carbine, **$11,000-$20,000.**

Pistol, English boot of screw barrel, mkd "Freeman, London," Tower of London proof marks, late 18th century, 8" l, **$380.**
Photo courtesy of Pook & Pook, Inc.

Harpers Ferry, Model 1816 Conversion Musket, .69 caliber, standard 1816 Model, makers' name and date 1837 vertically behind hammer, small eagle over "US" in front of hammer on lock plate, top bayonet lug and front sight on rear strap of split front band, iron mounted with three bands and tulip head ramrod, left flat has inspector's initials "JAS," conversion accomplished by mounting nipple at breech end of bbl and filling flash pan cut-out with brass, fine condition, iron retains dark smoky patina with light pitting around nipple area, fine hand-rubbed patina, broken away nipple, 42" bbl **$690**

Parker Snow & Co., Miller conversion, 40" round barrel, bold stampings include signature, eagle, and 1864 on lock, 56" overall **$1,375**

Springfield, rifled musket
.58 caliber, dark bore, 1862-dated lock and breech, gray patina on all metal, extensive fine pitting, good lock markings, faint breech markings, slight handling marks on stock, two very good cartouches, good-plus with incorrect reproduction ramrod and a very good original bayonet, 40" barrel............ **$850**
.58 caliber, Model 1863, Type II, very good bore, lockplate marked, 1864-dated "US-Springfield," breech with 1864 date and "V/P (eagle head)" proof mks, light gray patina, sharp markings, muzzle with faint nipple pitting, old refinish on stock, two legible inspector cartouches, correct ramrod, very good, 40" barrel **$1,500**

Percussion pistol

American, engraved, sgd on lock "P. D. Gwaltney & Co., Norfolk, Va," conversion from flintlock, checkered walnut stock with steel hardware, pineapple finial on trigger guard, swamped octagonal barrel with thin gold band of inlay at breech, small chip, hairline at lock mortise, end cap missing, 15-3/4" l **$850**

English
Folding bayonet, simple engraving on frame, stands of flags and "Lenning," old hairlines in grip, 4" l barrel, 8-1/2" l **$250**
Single shot, sgd "W. Parker" on lock, "Maker to His Majesty, London" on barrel, finely checkered bag grip, narrow pierced repair just below lock, 8-1/4" l.............................. **$715**

Gibbs, Tiffany & Co., Sturbridge, MA, underhammer percussion pistol, 6" cast steel barrel with engraved flower and vine motifs and imp marks: "202," "E HUTCHINGS & CO AGENTS BALTO," "GIBBS TIFFANY & CO. STURBRIDGE MASS.," eagle motif; rosewood grips with geometric mother-of-pearl inlay, silver back strap engraved "Dr. C.A. Cheever;" mahogany hinged case with engraved silver plaque on top "From Eusebius Hutchings of Baltimore, Md. to Charles A. Cheever Portsmouth, New Hampshire," interior contour lined with black velvet, fitted with accessories including copper powder flask, brass bullet mold with mahogany handles marked "202," cleaning rod, ramrod, five small leather ammunition pouches, loss on underhammer, descended from Cheever family, early 19th C, 9-7/8" l pistol, 12-5/8" x 5-5/8" x 2-1/4" case.............................. **$3,200**

Remington, New Model, bold inspector's stamp on grips, sub inspector's initials on various other parts, old brown finish with some bluing remaining on cylinder, elevated front sight appears to be early addition, 1858 .... **$980**

Target, figured walnut buttstock, brass buttplate, steel trigger guard, 22-3/4" octagonal barrel stamped 340L at muzzle, single hammer mounted on breech/frame, ramrod missing, narrow pieced repair to stock, 38-1/2" l....................................... **$300**

Waters, 8-1/2" round barrel, bright metal, stamped address and "1838" on lock, double inspector markings on stock, 14" l.............................. **$660**

Pistol

Colt Model 1911 Army, .45 caliber auto, orig blued finish, checkered walnut grips, good signature and other stampings, 8-1/2" l....................... **$825**

Sharp's Pepperbox, four shot, .22 caliber, 3" barrels, traces of orig bluing, stamped signature, patent information around hammer screw, gutta percha grips with checkered design, 5-1/2" l.............................. **$220**

Volcanic Lever Action, Navy, .38 caliber, 8" barrel, signature "The Volcanic Repeating Arms Co." on top, walnut grips, brass frame with old patina, minor pitting on one side, tab for magazine tube broken, spring missing, 14-1/2" l **$9,900**

Revolver

Baby Dragoon, .31 caliber, standard 5" oct. bbl without rammer, cylinder has round stop holes, brass grip frame with one-pc wood grips, top flat of bbl is devoid of orig Colt markings, very faintly visible word "Orleans," presumably stamp of New Orleans retailer, medium gray-brown patina on iron, repaired and refinished grip, shoulder repairs on back strap, accompanied by handwritten letter stating that this revolver was owned and used by Confederate Col. Henry C. Kellogg **$4,025**

Colt

Model 1849 Pocket, 4" barrel, .31 caliber, faint New York address, all serial numbers matching, replaced catch **$495**

Model 1860 Army, matching serial numbers, butt signature, New York address, overall light brown to gray surface on metal, brass trigger guard, iron grip straps, 8" barrel, 14" overall, old corner chips on grips, period black leather holster with raised "U. S." design and eight or three over stamped "G" on front flap, worn to grain, 13" l **$675**

Model 1861 Navy, .36 caliber, 7-1/2" round bbl, case color frame with silver-plated trigger guard and back strap, Naval battle cylinder scene with one-pc fine old ivory grips, very deep relief Mexican eagle on left side, accompanied by orig Colt casing containing Colt's patent short angle spout flask and iron bullet mold, packet of Johnston & Dow's skin cartridges, Eley cap tin **$9,500**

Lefaucheux Pin Rimfire, old bright surface on barrel, frame, and cylinder, bold signature and proofmarks, walnut grips finely alligatored varnish, 6-3/8" octagon to round barrel, one Lefaucheux cartridge on mount, 12-1/2" l **$450**

Remington

Beals, 7-3/4" barrel, old dark finish, 13-1/2" l **$825**

Model 1858, .44 caliber, 8" octagonal barrel, good signature with faint inspector's stamp on grips, 14" l **$880**

Model 1861 Navy, 7-3/8" octagon barrel, all-over matte gray finish, signature stamp **$990**

Warner, pocket, .28 caliber, 3-3/4" round bbl, cased with small flask and incorrect accessories, gray-brown patina overall, faint Warner markings on top of frame, light surface rust overall, grips badly chipped at base, gun does not fit partitions in case very well **$920**

Rifle

Allin Conversion Model 1866, 40" round barrel, worn browned finish, three bands, "U. S. Springfield" lock with eagle and 1865 date, walnut stock, in-the-making file marks, 56" l **$250**

Conestoga Rifle Works, half-stock Kentucky, cal. 36, fixed sights, tiger striped stock, pewter nose cap, dbl. set triggers, two-pc patch box, brass furniture, dark brown iron, polished brass, fine dark wood, set trigger won't hold, hammer won't cock, bbl cut to 34-1/4" **$410**

Percussion, half stock

Fordney, Melchoir, Lancaster County, (died 1846), 39-1/4" octagon barrel, sgd "M. Fordney," curly maple stock, old mellow refinishing, checkered wrist, fine engraving on brass hardware, fair border engraving on barrel, chips around lock mortise, some age splits beneath forearm, small putty repair on one side of tang, front portion of triggerguard replaced, 55" l **$1,150**

McComas, Alexander, 1843-75, stamped "A. McComas, Baltimore" on top of barrel, checkered walnut stock with steel hardware, small cap box, beavertail cheekpiece, 34" l octagon barrel, restored stock split behind lock, chip off cap box, 49-1/2" l **$420**

Partial stamped signatures on lock and barrel for J. Henry & Son, 36-3/8" octagon barrel w/browned surface, walnut stock, stepped beaver tail, steel buttplate, brass trigger guard, nickel silver inlays, small "U. S." stamp below trigger guard, 52-1/2" l, orig powder horn **$950**

Remington, rolling block

Military, approx .45 caliber, full stock, three barrel bands, 35" tapered round barrel with adjustable rear sight, clear signature on tag, ramrod missing, 50-1/2" l **$220**

Remington signature and address on tang, crown proofs, "G" stamp on buttstock, old dark finish, brass handle bayonet, dents, one band spring mission, 50" l **$330**

Springfield, Model 1873 Trapdoor, 45-70 caliber, cadet model, 29-1/2" round blued barrel, three click tumbler, eagle mark and signature on lock with eagle's head and "V. P." on breech area, minor dents on stock, ramrod, 48-3/4" l **$450**

Winchester, Model 1873 Special Order, cal. 44 WCF, standard grade, 24" oct. bbl, half-nickel front sight, slot blank in rear dovetail, early Lyman tang sight, button magazine with uncheckered wood, straight stock and crescent steel buttplate with trap **$1,610**

Shotgun

European, double barrel, 12 gauge 30-1/2" damascus barrels, silver band overlay, sgd "R. Baumgarter in Bernburg" on barrel, engraved stag on tang, "Hubertus Geweher," figured walnut stock, horn trigger guard, 47" l **$275**

Fox Sterlingworth, 16 gauge, double barrel, 26" barrel, top lever break-open, hammerless, double trigger, blued, checkered walnut pistol grip stock and forearm **$400**

Parker Brothers, double barrel, "D" grade, Damascus steel barrels, figured walnut stock with checkering, finely engraved #2 frame with skeleton butt plate, 14" pull, extra barrel with own forearm, same serial number on both **$1,495**

Stevens, Model 970, 12 gauge, single shot, octagonal breech, top lever break-open, hammerless, automatic shell ejector, automatic safety, blued, case hardened frame, checkered walnut pistol grip stock and forearm, 32" l round barrel **$95**

FIREHOUSE COLLECTIBLES

History: The volunteer fire company has played a vital role in the protection and social growth of many towns and rural areas. Paid professional firemen usually are found only in large metropolitan areas. Each fire company prided itself on equipment and uniforms. Conventions and parades gave the fire companies a chance to show off their equipment. These events produced a wealth of firehouse-related memorabilia.

Additional Resources:

Warman's® Americana & Collectibles, 11th Ed., by Ellen T. Schroy, ed., Krause Publications, Iola, WI.

Advertising button

Baldwin II NO 22 May 26, '97, Williamsport, elderly gentleman, Whitehead & Hoag back paper, 1-1/4" d **$15**

Central NY Volunteer Fireman's Convention, Auspices Seward Tribe Alaska Esquimaus, June 26-28, 1910, Auburn, NY, 1-1/2" d **$20**

Keystone Fire Co. No. 1 Shillington, PA, Dedication May 31, 1924, real photo, man standing by doorway of two-story building, Keystone Badge paper, 1-1/4" d **$15**

Marion Fire Co. Stouchsburg, Pa, real photo, truck with ladders and hose reel parked on street in front of house and tree, men standing at left, 1-1/4" d................................. **$15**

Pennsylvania State Firemen's Convention, Allentown, multicolored, fireman in helmet, 1930, 1-1/4" d **$18**

Woodbury Fire Dept., black on gold, center pumper wagon, Friendship No. 1, 1930 event, attached to small red, white, and blue fabric ribbon **$20**

Badge

Columbia PA, arch reads "Centennial of Columbia Fire Co.," pumper, 1896 .... **$40**

Compliments of, diecut fire trumpets and hydrants on hanger, asst chief name, c1890, 2-1/2" h **$35**

15th Annual Convention National Ass'n Fire Engineers, 1887........ **$45**

Mapleton, Iowa, June 7, '06, multicolored scene of two firemen holding hose at left, larger scene of two firemen using tools against fire bursting thru doorway, Whitehead & Hoag back paper, 1-3/4" h **$40**

Wilmington, DE, 1907, fabric with celluloid pin **$15**

Bell, brass, iron back, 11"............. **$125**

Belt, red, black, and white, marked "Hampden," 43" l **$85**

Box, cov, oval, wallpaper covering with fire engine scene, blue ground, white and green highlights, inside lined with Der York Democrat 1834 newspaper, 17" l, 13-3/4" w, 14" h **$13,750**

Fire bucket

Leather, stitched seams, nailed strap handle, old black paint, brown painted int., wear, 12-1/2" h **$175**

Leather, leather handle attached with iron rings, old dark green paint over dark red with black painted

Helmet, leather, white, silvered front plate embossed "Rescue, AFD," crossed ladders motif, brass eagle, original liner, long back, **$225.**

handle and collar, black lettering "L.TOWER.-3.," in yellow outlined banner, America, alligatored paint surface, early 19th C, 19-1/4" h **$715**

Leather, painted red, black collar, leather handle, gilt lettering "1801. FOUNTAIN NO.2," with black shading, America, losses, handle wear, c1801, 21-1/2" h **$2,280**

Miniature, tin, bail handle, orange paint dec, "Fire Bucket" printed on side, 3" h, 1-7/8" d **$615**

Fire extinguisher

Babcock, American La France Fire Engine Co., Elmire, NY, grenade, amber glass................................. **$500**

Hayward's Hand Fire Grenade, yellow, ground mouth, smooth base, c1870, 6-1/4" h **$85**

Red Comet, red metal canister, red glass bulb **$50**

Fire mark, cast iron, oval

Black, gold eagle and banner dec, marked "Eagle Ins. Co. Cin O," 8" x 12"... **$950**

Polychrome paint, relief molded design, pumper framed by "Fire Department Insurance," 8" x 11-1/2" **$495**

Helmet

Leather, Anderson + Jones, Broad St., NY, emb and ribbed leather, brass trumpetered holder, painted tin front piece lettered "cataract hose 2 j.g.," manufacturer's stamp on underside of brim, repaint, leather losses, 9" x 14-1/4" x 11".......... **$635**

Stamped aluminum, black enameling, leather front panel marked "Chopmist, F.D.," interior makers

Fire mark, painted cast iron, William Penn in oval center, marked "Leader," **$225.**

Fireman Doll, commemorative, Philadelphia, composition head, painted features, stuffed body, kidskin hands, green painted cardboard hat, gilt lettered "INDEPENDENT," hand sewn green wool jacket with brass buttons, green wool trousers, white cotton shirt, black silk sash with gilt lettered "Committee of Arrangement Philadelphia Fire Dept. May 3, 1852.," brown leather shoes, with stand, wear and losses, 25" h, c1852, **$4,110.**
Photo courtesy of Skinner, Inc.

Andirons, turned brass finial, scrolling iron side mounts and raised down-swept legs, 11-3/4" x 9" x 15-1/2", **$825.**

Photo courtesy of Sloans & Kenyon Auctioneers and Appraisers.

Hearth trivet, forged iron, four penny feet, good condition, expected rust and pitting, 19th century, 3-1/2" h, 7-3/4" d, 19" l, **$110.**

Photo courtesy of Green Valley Auctions.

Fireplace fender, brass and iron, English, solid front, applied buttons, two rail top with central kettle trivet, early 19th century, 6" h, 47" w, 13" d, **$220.**

Photo courtesy of Green Valley Auctions.

Fender, gilt bronze, urn and garland motif, French, 20" x 12" x 6-1/2", **$600.**

Photo courtesy of David Rago Auctions, Inc.

Andirons, pr, bellmetal, urn finials, Philadelphia, c1810, 22-1/2" h, **$555.**

Photo courtesy of Pook & Pook, Inc.

label for Cairns & Brothers, Clifton, N.J." **$200**

Ink blotter, Fireman's Fund 75th Year, Allendale, CA, fireman with little child, 1938, 4" x 9" **$7.50**

Ledger marker, Caisse General Fire Insurance, Statue of Liberty illus, multicolored, tin litho, 12-1/4" l, 3" w **$275**

Medal, Jacksonville Fire Co., silvered brass, firefighting symbols circled by "I.A.F.E.-1917-Jacksonville, Fla.," reverse "Compliments of N. Snellenburg & Co. Uniforms, Philadelphia, Pa," looped ring **$15**

Nozzle, hose, brass, double handle, marked "Akron Brass Mfg. Co., Inc.," 16" l **$165**

Parade hat, painted leather, polychrome dec, green ground, front with eagle and harp, banner above "Hibernia," back inscribed "1752" in gilt, "1" on top, red brim underside, some age cracks, small losses to brim edge, 6-1/2" h **$3,335**

Print, color lithograph, *Engine of the Red Jacket Veteran Fireman's Association...Champion of the New England League, 1894,* printed for the Brooks Bank Note Company, Boston, folio, 22-1/2" x 17-1/4" **$1,410**

Sales sheet, glossy paper, Iron Horse Metal Ware Products, Rochester Can Co., NY, pictures five galvanized red fire pails, 8-1/2" x 11" **$20**

Sign, Philadelphia Underwriters, heavy porcelain, detailed graphic image in center with fire mark in upper right corner, made in England, 14" x 20" **$600**

Stickpin, Honor To Our Brave, fireman portrait, red shirt, blue helmet, 1900s, 7/8" celluloid button on 1-3/4" stickpin **$15**

Toy

Arcade, fire pumper, 1941 Ford, cast iron, painted red, emb sides, cast fireman, hose reel on bed, rubber tires, repaired fender, 13" l **$440**

Arcade, ladder truck, cast iron, painted red, two cast firemen, rubber tires, bed contains ladder supports, open frame design, 9-1/4" l **$440**

Hubley, Ahrens Fox fire engine, cast iron, rubber tires, 7-1/2" l **$475**

Kenton, fire pumper, cast iron, painted red, gold highlights on boiler, and ball, emb sides, disc wheels with spoke centers **$615**

Kingsbury, horse-drawn ladder wagon, sheet metal, painted red, wire supports, holding yellow wooden ladders, two seated drivers, pulled by two black horses, yellow spoke wheels, bell on frame rings as toy is pulled, 26" l **$2,150**

Williams, A. C., fire pumper, cast iron, painted red, gold highlights, cast driver, bell, and boiler, rear platform with railing, rubber tires, 7-1/2" l **$315**

Watch fob, presentation, two sided, embossed silver medal with crystal bezels, one side with raised female allegorical figure surrounded by 13 stars, other side with inscriptions "NORTHERN LIBERY FIRE CO. No 1./INSTITUTED MAY 1, 1756./ INCORPORATED MAR 18th 1833.," oval frame with scrolled crest engraved "Retired FROM Service SAM'L ALEXANDER Mar, 15, 1871," America, 19th C, solder repair to crest **$450**

FIREPLACE EQUIPMENT

History: In the colonial home, the fireplace was the gathering point for heat, meals, and social interaction. It maintained its dominant position until the introduction of central heating in the mid-19th century.

Because of the continued popularity of the fireplace, accessories still are manufactured, usually in an early-American motif.

Reproduction Alert. Modern blacksmiths are reproducing many old iron implements.

Andirons, pr, brass, round ball finials, scrolled spur legs, ball feet, 8-3/4" w, 16" d, 12" h **$385**

Andirons, pr, brass and iron

America, brass urn-tops over iron knife-blade shaft, lower brass shield, arched legs over penny feet, last quarter 18th C, 9-1/2" w, 16-1/2" d, 21-1/2" h **$650**

Ball top with concentric ring turnings, shaped columns, cabriole legs, spurred knees, slipper feet, conforming log stops, one imp "BOSTON," losses and cracks near log stops, c1800, 11-1/4" w, 25" d, 16-5/8" h **$600**

Belted ball tops, baluster ring-turned shaft, sq stepped base, conforming log stops on curved log supports, America, dents, mid-19th C, 8" w, 27" d, 14-3/4" h **$500**

Faceted steeples over belted balls, columnar shafts, spurred cabriole legs with slipper feet, conforming steeple-top log stops, signed "J DAVIS BOSTON" on billet bars, 10-5/8" w, 17-3/4" d, 18-1/2" h **$950**

New York, beaded belts on double lemon finials, round plinths supported on spurred cabriole legs with ball feet, minor wear, first quarter 19th C, 19" d, 9" h **$775**

Andirons, pr, bronze, ribbon-wrapped torches tapering to leaftip, reeded stem with husk-accented bifurcate base, Louis XVI-style, 19th C, 31" h **$2,400**

Andirons and matching tools, Federal, 24" h brass ring-turned shaft andirons with spurred legs, ball feet, similarly turned fireplace 32" h tongs and 33" h shovel **$1,100**

Bellows, wood and leather, brass tacks, brass wind spout, white ground paint with some dec on back, floral dec on front and handle, good condition leather, 17-3/4" l, 8" w **$550**

Coal grate, George II, brass-mounted iron, bowed central section of four rails over grate, ash drawer between bow front side panels, applied brass starbursts, surmounted with brass urn finials, English, last quarter 19th C, 26" w, 9-1/2" d, 16" h **$200**

Fireboard, wide central raised panel, paint dec to depict seaside village, ships, and houses, surround painted to depict tiles with numerous ships, houses, and trees, America, wear, fading, early 19th C, 36" x 44-3/8" **$7,650**

Fire dogs, pr
Brass, central horizontal reeded orb raised on three reeded legs, reeded horizontal bar on top, Aesthetic Movement, English, third quarter 19th C, 7-1/2" w, 6-1/2" h **$150**

Cast iron, rampant lion bearing twisted horizontal bars, seated on rope twist rounded and octagonal base, late 19th/early 20th C, 15" h **$700**

Gilt bronze, squat urns draped in husks on top, short fluted column with central leaf-scrolled band, large urn opposing berry finial

across horizontal cross bar, Louis XVI-style, 19th C, 16-1/4" w, 14" h **$1,300**

Fire fender
Brass rail on serpentine fender, vertical wirework with swag dec, England or America, minor wear to brass rail, loss of one wire, late 18th/early 19th C, 51-1/4" w, 18-1/2" d, 12-1/4" h **$5,600**

Wire and brass, serpentine, brass ball finials, 52" l, 18" d, 12-1/2" h **$1,155**

Fire screen
Bamboo, brass mounted, foliate painted panel, turned supports and trestle base, Victorian, 31" w, 40" h **$150**

Gilt bronze, cartouche-shaped wire firescreen with central floral stem within rocaille borders, Louis XV-style, together with set of brush, shovel, and tongs in 24" h beaded stand; pair of small 10-3/8" h firedogs formed as rocaille acanthus scrolls, 28-3/4" h **$600**

Leaded glass, tripartite, central square panel and two narrow side panels set with multicolored textured and bull's eye glass pieces, brass surround, griffin-form trestle feet, Renaissance Revival, late 19th/early 20th C, 32-3/4" h **$1,100**

Tubular frame, ormolu scrolling at top, scrolled feet, center oil on canvas with courting scene, French, sgd "G. Jones" on lower right, early 20th C, 33" w, 41-1/4" h **$700**

Walnut, openwork cresting, revolving screen painted with dec scenes, trestle base, Renaissance Revival, American, 26-1/2" w, 44" h **$300**

Wire and brass rail, 30-1/4" h, 36-3/8" l **$770**

Fire tools, brass and iron, ball finial on belted ball top, shovel and tongs, minor dents, scattered pitting, 30-7/8" and 31-3/8" l **$420**

Footman, brass, Georgian-style, rect top, turned side handles, pierced apron, cabriole front legs, straight round rear legs, English, 18" w, 15" d, 12" h **$365**

Hearth broom, hardwood handle, bristle holder, carved and painted face of black man, handle end stamped with rocket, inscribed "Forward Biltmore, NC," wear, 8-1/4" w, 22" l **$445**

Fire screen, brass, scene of farmer and horses plowing field, **$450.**
Photo courtesy of Joy Luke Auctions.

Bellows, painted gold fruit, green leaves, red and black decoration, front panel detached at nozzle, wear, 19th century, **$90.**
Photo courtesy of Pook & Pook, Inc.

Log holder, vertical slats and cut-out pulls, metal Stickley Brothers tag, new finish, some chips, loss of part of one copper strap, 19-1/2" x 20" x 18-1/2", **$1,000.**
Photo courtesy of David Rago Auctions, Inc.

Mantle, Federal, carved pine and plaster, molded and blocked cornice, swag applique and floral drop sides, late 18th century, **$2,500.**
Photo courtesy of Pook & Pook, Inc.

Iron fishing spear, painted wood, four-tined cast-iron spearhead, barbed terminals, octagonal pole with red and white painted stripes, American, 19th century, 9' 4-3/4" l, $560.
Photo courtesy of Skinner, Inc.

Hearth stand, Baroque-style, cast brass, sailing ship, five tools **$450**

Hearth toaster, America, wrought iron, toast support embellished with scrolled heart motifs, turned wooden handle with remains of green and red paint, late 18th C, 16-3/8" w, 23" l
....**$825**

Hearth trivet, wrought iron
Round, flattened handle, hanger hook, three-legged base, rust, 15-1/2" l, 6-1/4" d **$220**
Square grilling surface, flattened handle, circular end, four sun-like stamps, 23-1/2" l, 11-1/2" w
....**$250**

Kettle shelf, brass and wrought iron, "D" shape with cast top with pierced scrolling, floral medallions around skirt, iron cabriole legs ending in large penny feet, one decorative rosette missing from front, 13" w, 10-1/2" d, 13-1/2" h **$460**

Kettle stand, brass and wrought iron, tripod base, round column, painted black, circular brass top with pierced designs, scalloped edges, 10-3/4" h
....**$100**

Mantelpiece, faux marble painted, attributed to Vermont, early 19th C
Projecting shelf above molding, rect capitals on pilasters and plinths, orig gray-green paint with white veining, paint wear, 61" w, 6-1/2" d, 49-1/4" h **$1,000**
Rect shelf above cove molding, flanking rect capitals on pilasters and plinths, orig white paint with gray veining, surface wear, 60" w, 6-3/4" d, 48-1/4" h **$715**

Mantle urns, pr, gray marble with white striations, applied ormolu and gilded spelter dec, stamped "P.H. Mourey" around base, minor wear to gilding, 17-1/2" h **$500**

Pole screen
English, candle shield, orig green and mustard paint, table-top
....**$11,500**
English, mahogany, pole with shaped top, turned tapering urn-shaped pillar, cabriole leg base ending in arris pad feet on platforms, orig needlework panel, gold and blue floral pattern, brown ground, outlined with applied wood moldings, old surface, imperfections, 1760-80
....**$5,175**
Irish, Chippendale, inlaid walnut and fruitwood veneers, oblong panel with scalloped edges, orig silk needlework of a dragon, saber

legs with line border inlay graduate into triangular block with three turned supports, tripod base, short turned feet below applied blocks, some stains on fabric, few veneer chips missing, 53-1/2" h **$470**

Tinder lighter, pistol shape, flintlock striker
Mahogany, brass tinderbox, lyre-shaped front support, small candle socket with drop pan, etched scrollwork on the side, 5-1/8" l
....**$1,430**
Walnut, steel tinderbox, candle socket, simple curved support, front end with compartment for tinder/candles, inscribed "Laurent Gille," 8" l **$935**

FISHING COLLECTIBLES

History: Early man caught fish with crude spears and hooks made of bone, horn, or flint. By the mid-1800s, metal lures with attached hooks were produced in New York State. Later, the metal was curved and glass beads added to make them more attractive. Spinners with painted-wood bodies and glass eyes appeared around 1890. Soon after, many different makers were producing wood plugs with glass eyes. Patents, which were issued in large numbers around this time, covered the development of hook hangers, body styles, and devices to add movement to the plug as it was drawn through the water. The wood plug era lasted up to the mid-1930s when plugs constructed of plastic were introduced.

With the development of casting plugs, it became necessary to produce fishing reels capable of accomplishing the task with ease. Reels first appeared as a simple device to hold a fishing line. Improvements included multiplying gears, retrieving line levelers, drags, clicks, and a variety of construction materials. The range of quality in reel manufacture varied considerably. Collectors are mainly interested in reels made with high-quality materials and workmanship, or those exhibiting unusual features.

Early fishing rods, which were made of solid wood, were heavy and prone to breakage. By gluing together tapered strips of split bamboo, a rod was fashioned which was light in

South Bend Midget Underwater Minnow in Frog Spot, GE with marked blunt prop, small tail chip, slight varnish flaking on belly, EX-, **$236.**
Photo courtesy of Lang's Sporting Collectables.

Fish decoy, Bud Stewart, glass eyes, open mouth, signed "BS," 4-1/2", **$255.**
Photo courtesy of Lang's Sporting Collectables.

Pepper Roman Spider, notched head, solid yellow, blended green back, painted eyes, VG condition, wood chipping, **$275.**
Photo courtesy of Lang's Sporting Collectables.

weight and had greatly improved strength. The early split-bamboo rods were round and wrapped with silk to hold them together. As glue improved, fewer wrappings were needed, and rods became slim and lightweight. Rods were built in various lengths and thicknesses, depending upon the type of fishing and bait used. Rod makers' names and models can usually be found on the metal parts of the handle or on the rod near the handle.

Reproduction Alert. Lures and fish decoys.

Additional Resources:

Classic Fishing Lures, by Russell E. Lewis, Krause Publications, Iola, WI.

Fishing Collectibles Identification and Price Guide, by Russell E. Lewis, Krause Publications, Iola, WI.

Heddon Catalogs Over 50 Years of Great Fishing, 1902-1953, by Clyde A. Harbin, Sr. and Russell E. Lewis, Krause Publications, Iola, WI.

Heddon Plastic Lures, by Russell E. Lewis, Krause Publications, Iola, WI.

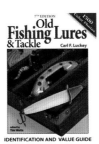

Old Fishing Lures, Identification and Value Guide, 7th Ed., by Carl F. Luckey, contributing editor Tim Watts, Krause Publications, Iola, WI.

Warman's® Fishing Lures, by Carl F. Luckey and Clyde A. Harbin, Sr., Krause Publications, Iola, WI.

Bait bucket, painted blue, stenciled "Falls City-Magic-Minnow Bucket" **$1,980**

Bait trap, Katch-N-Karry, Glassman Mfg. Co., Jackson, TN, patented 1941, wood, 4" d wire mesh circle, litho of bluegill and roach **$375**

Bank, painted composition, bobbing head, round fisherman in hat and sunglasses, mermaid by side, coin slot in back, felt covering over base, 1960s, 3-1/2" x 4" x 7" h **$30**

Bobber, hand painted
Panfish float, black, red, and white stripes, 5" l **$12**
Pike float, yellow, green, and red stripes, 12" l **$24**

Calendar print, Bristol, young couple and their guide getting ready for fishing excursion, cut down and laid down on old style mat board, old frame with wood backing, 1905, 12" x 13" **$330**

Canoe, Old Town Sponson, 16' **$1,430**

Catalog
Creek Chub Bait Co., Garrett, IN, 1934 ....**$330**
Evinrude Motors, Milwaukee, WI, 1961, Catalog of Outboard Motors **$32**

Trout rod, Goodwin Granger Victory 9', 3/2 rod, 2" repair wrap to tip, added stap-and-ring hookkeeper, orange and black jasper wraps, double black tipping, screwlocking type reel seat, orig bag and fiber tube with label, **$330.**
Photo courtesy of Lang's Sporting Collectables.

Garcia Fishing Equipment & Supplies, Garcia Corp., Teaneck, NY, c1955, accordion fold large 11-1/4" x 30" sheet **$20**

Hardy Brothers, 1910 .... **$495**

Montague Rod & Reel Co., Montague City, MA, c1949, Catalog No. 49-M **$55**

Orvis, c1900 .... **$330**

Penn Fishing Tackle Mfg., Philadelphia, PA, Catalog No. 17 of Penn Reels, 1952 .... **$32**

Shakespeare Co., Kalamazoo, Catalog No. 27, some pages uncut, 1927 .... **$175**

Wallsten Tackle Co., Chicago, IL, Fishing Tips, Courtesy of Cisco Kid Lures, 1940s **$21**

Weber Lifelike Fly Co., Stevens Point, WI, Catalog No. 22, Flies & Fly Tackle, 1941 .... **$70**

White, E. M. & Co., Old Town, ME, E. M. White Builders of White Canoes, c1922 .... **$40**

Child's kit, Mickey Mouse Fishing Kit, copyrighted "Walt Disney Enterprises," tin litho, C.8+, 1920s, 4-1/2" x 1-1/2" x 7-1/2" **$500**

Cigarette card, King of England deep-sea fishing, New Zealand, 1937 .... **$12**

Clock, mechanical, fish punching hole in side of boat with moving hammer, Hero Clock Co., wind-up, marked "Made in China" **$40**

Creel

Split, reinforced rim on lid, off center hole, orig split splint hinges, wire and loop lid latch, heavy fabric support attached to shoulder strap, 5" x 9" x 9" h **$2,200**

Turtle, bulbous shape, tight rattan weave, full length leather hinge, emb 98" rule, leather worker's stamp "ILHAN New Boulder Colo," leather harness, small mahogany priest attached with leather thong, 7" x 17" **$5,500**

Turtle, leather trimmed, bulbous shape, split reed and cord reinforcing on bottom, orig twisted reed hinges and harness loops, sliding figural turtle lid latch, wood rule on lid, dec cross hatch weaving on front, old leather harness, 5-1/2" x 13" x 7" h **$1,210**

Turtle, tight rattan weave, bulbous shape, orig twisted reed hinges and harness loops, split reed and cord reinforcing on bottom, figural turtle latch, wood rule on lid, dec cross hatch weaving on front, leather and web harness, 6" x 15" x 7" h **$1,650**

Decoy, fish, wood

Leroy Howell, gray body, black metal fins, 6-1/2" l **$115**

Ice King, perch, painted, Bear Creek Co., 7" l **$75**

Wood, paint dec, America, minor paint wear and losses, early 20th C, 31-1/2" l **$1,495**

Display, salesman's sample, Pequea, Strasburg, PA

Oilcloth cov box, two panels, lures, 9" x 13" **$1,870**

Oilcloth cov box, 19 round bodied cork floats, 9" x 15" **$1,100**

Oilcloth cov box, eight lures, 18 assorted feathered trebles, large weedless example, 9-1/2" x 13" **$330**

Two-sided, lures and pearl spoons, 9-1/2" x 13" **$1,650**

Two panels, assortment of 58 floats, 18" x 29-1/2" d **$18,700**

Display case, 33 different colorful winders with bobbers, 21" x 21" **$3,410**

Fishing license, for resident use
Connecticut, yellow, black, and white, 1935 .... **$65**

Pennsylvania, blue and white, black serial number, 1945 .... **$18**

Flask, pewter, emb on both sides, one side with fisherman landing trout, other side with fisherman netting catch, marked "Alchemy Pewter, Sheffield, England" **$175**

Float, Ideal **$200**

Fly, Carrie Stevens **$440**

Fly fishing display

C. J. Frost, Stevens Point, WI, c1910, 9' l **$3,080**

Painted wood trout replica, fly fishing reel, flies, net, wood case, c1911, 39-3/4" l, 3-3/4" d, 13-1/4" h ... **$195**

License holder, paper envelope, Florida Game and Fresh Water Commission, stamped with County Judge's name **$22**

Lure

Al Foss Dixie Wiggler, #13, 1928, metal box, extra hook, pocket catalog, 3-1/2" l **$100**

Allen, Vamp, stripy finish **$550**

Blee, Charles, submarine bait, all metal **$2,000**

Case Bait Co., rotary marvel, c1910 .... **$360**

Creek Chubb Bait Co.

Giant Pike, orig box, 12-1/2" x 2-3/4" **$195**

Glitter beetle, red and white **$615**

Jigger 4100, red side **$140**

Mouse **$470**

Pikie minnow, early orig box **$440**

Plunking dinger, all black **$100**

Red beetle **$315**

Sarasota, #3317, luminous yellow head, c1927-31 .... **$800**

Detroit Glass, minnow tube, fish form, four treble hooks, orig box, c1914 .... **$3,500**

DeWitt, minnow, orig box with papers **$90**

Dunk's Double Header, black plug, c1931 .... **$125**

Four Brothers, Neverfail Minnow, orig box **$615**

Garland Bros., Plant City, FL, cork head minnow **$315**

Hanson

GE pull-me-slow, two hooks **$90**

Muskegon spoon jack minnow, green back, five-hook **$275**

H. Comstock, 1883, Flying Helgramite **$4,400**

Heddon

#175, heavy casting minnow, worn leaping bass box **$420**

#300, Dowagiac surface minnow **$275**

#300, husky minnow, orig box ... **$660**

#400, bucktail surface minnow ... **$615**

#450, killer **$175**

#1500, dummy double, unmarked box, orig paper **$360**

Henning, glass minnow tube **$440**

J. A. Holzapfe, Jackson, MI, mushroom, bass, orig box **$660**

Jamison, wig-wag **$95**

K & K, animated minnow **$160**

Like Live Bait Co., Jacksonville, FL, mechanical, patent no. 1,7658,160, orig box **$13,200**

Manhattan Casting Bait, No. 2, White, orig box **$495**

Moonlight Bay #1, c1904, 4" shallow cup **$400**

Musky

Crazy crawler 2510 mouse **$250**

Giant vamp 7350, jointed, natural scales, c1930 ...... **$130**

Surfasser 300, two hooks, rainbow **$150**

Paw-Paw, sucker, perch finish, tack eyes **$30**

Pflueger

All-in-One **$470**

Floating monarch minnow, c1906 ...... **$90**

Never Fail Minnow, three hooks **$300**

Surprise minnow **$185**

Sam-Bo, bass, pike, pickerel, orig box, 4" l **$215**

Shakespeare

Mouse white and red, thin body, glass eyes, 3-5/8" l **$30**

Underwater minnow, five-hook, c1907 ...... **$150**

South Bend Tackle Co.

Panatellia, green crackle-back finish, glass eyes, boxed **$50**

Truck-Oreno, red and white wood **$2,970**

Vacuum Bait, red and white dec **$100**

Souvenir, Lucky Lure, Souv of Indian Lake, OH, nude black female, 3-1/2" l, MOC **$130**

Strike-It-Lure, green, yellow, and red spots, glass eyes **$40**

W. D. Chapman, Theresa, NY, metal minnow and propeller **$2,200**

Winchester

9011, three-hook **$500**

Green plug, repainted by Dale Roberts **$130**

Minnow bucket, green collapsible canvas, wire bail, orig black painted wooden handle, stamped "No. 08 Mfg for the Planet Co. Patent" **$155**

Net, boat, wooden 32" handle **$90**

Net, trout

Brodin, name branded on wood handle, unused **$50**

English, folding, triangular, alloy and brass construction, rubber grip, belt clip, mkd "Made in Great Britain," unused, 30" handle **$85**

Hardy, collapsible, alloy construction, belt clip, 24" handle **$27.50**

Patch, Atlantic City Surf Fishing Tournament, 3-3/4" x 5" **$12**

Pinback button, Johnsburg Fish & Game Club, red and white, forest safety theme, 1930s **$10**

Poacher's gig, hand forged five pronged rake-type device, long worn wooden handle, from Eastern Shore, MD or VA, 63" l **$145**

Pond boat, sailer, rudder, 30" h, 28" l, 10" w **$200**

Poster

Bristol Fishing Rod Co., colorful scene of young Victorian couple enjoying picnic while lad lifts edge of her dress with rod and line, gold frame, cloth liner, 13-1/2" x 18" **$4,400**

Kingfisher, They Can't Get Away From Kingfisher Lines, E. J. Martin's Sons Kingfisher Brand, Braided Silk Lines, Rockville, Conn, girl ice fishing, matted, 24" x 32" frame, 17" x 24" ... **$8,360**

Reel

ABU Ambassador 5000, bait casting, red finish, leather case with spare parts **$125**

A.L. Walker, Y, German silver

Model 100, 4/0, salmon **$1,650**

Model 200, 4/0, salmon **$1,870**

Anson Hatch, side mount C-1866, mkd "Hatch's Patent June 19, 1866" **$5,500**

Army and Navy, English alloy, trout, 2-1/8" d **$220**

Arthur Kovalovsky, No. 64, made for Zane Grey, patented 2,022,204, front plate mkd "Arthur Kovalovsky Hand Made Patented 1,958,919-Hollywood Cal," big game, 8-1/2" d, 6-1/2" w spool, 17 lbs **$20,900**

B. C. Milam, Frankford, KY, #2, casting **$1,760**

B. F. Meek & Sons

#2, casting **$935**

#8, mkd "Hand Made," German silver, bait casting **$6,160**

#33 Bluegrass **$85**

#44, trout, German silver **$5,280**

Bogdan, Model 200, salmon, right hand wind **$825**

Charles M. Clinton, Ithaca, NY, German Silver, c1900 ...... **$6,820**

DAM, quick casting, black finish, red agate line guide, orig box **$85**

Dr. Allonzo H. Fowler, Ithaca, NY, hard rubber, Fowler's Improved Gem Fly Reel **$6,600**

Edward R. Hewitt, custom made, initials "M.S.I.," aluminum, raised pillars, trout fly, orig leather case **$13,750**

Edw. Vom Hofe

German silver, tiny upright trout, c1870 ...... **$7,810**

Model 621, size 4/0 ...... **$250**

Perfection, Model 360, size 2, German silver and hard rubber, trout ... **$8,820**

Peerless, Model 355, size 3, German silver and hard rubber, trout **$5,280**

Salmon, Cascapedia **$4,290**

Hardy

Cascapedia, salmon, 2/0 size **$12,375**

Princess, trout, German silver reversible line guide **$200**

Uniqua, trout, 3-1/8", flat telephone latch **$275**

Hendryx Safety Reel, trout **$995**

H. L. Leonard

Model 50B, wide spool, fly **$1,760**

Patent 1877, upright trout **$3,080**

Horton Mfg.

#3, suede bag **$425**

#7 Bluegrass **$880**

#33 Bluegrass Simplex, suede bag **$425**

Julius Vom Hofe

Fly, plain, early size 3 ...... **$880**

Freshwater, casting, Pat. Nov. 17, 85, Oct. 8, 1887, torn bag **$165**

Meisselbach, #260, featherlight, skeleton, fly, vertical box **$330**

Morgan James, side mount, pillbox style, brass, c1860 ...... **$9,350**

Niangua, casting **$660**

Ocean, 3/0B **$300**

Orvis, presentation

EXR1, trout, right hand wind **$110**

EXR111, trout, spare spool, right hand wind **$110**

Otto Zwarg, Model 400, multiplying, salmon, 2/0 size **$1,710**

Pflueger

Atlapac, 9/0 size, 5" d **$330**

Hawkeye, bulldog logo, trout, German silver and hard rubber **$350**

Philbrook & Paine, handmade, raised pillar, trout, mkd "Pat Apld For" **$9,625**

Restigouche
1896 patent **$1,540**
1897 patent **$1,320**
1902 patent **$1,540**

Seamaster
Duel mode, anti-reverse, saltwater fly, all black.................................**$990**
Mark III, duel mode, anti-reverse, saltwater fly, gold and black **$880**

Shakespeare
Standard.................................**$150**
Standard, professional.................**$150**
Tournament **$110**

South Bend, #1131A, casting, shiny finish, orig box **$18**

Stan Bogdan, handmade, baby trout
Left hand wind, orig pouch, unused, 2-3/4" d, 3/4" w.....................**$1,732**
Spool, hard leather case, 2-3/4" d, 3/4" w **$1,485**
Talbot Star **$385**

Thos. J. Conroy, NY, Wells model, trout, c1889.........................**$3,300**

Union Hardware Co., raised pillar type, nickel and brass **$25**

Unmarked, wood, brass fittings, c1880-1920, 6" d......................**$85**

Walker, TR-4, fly....................**$1,210**

Waltonian, Square Stamping Co., Barneveld, NY, casting............**$660**

Winchester
Model #2844, raised pillar bay, 3" d, 1-7/8" w spool rest, nickel plated **$275**
Model #2944, raised pillar light saltwater, 3-1/4" d, 1-7/8" w spool, nickel plated **$250**

Wm. H. Talbot Eli, casting **$880**

Rod

C. W. Jenkins, CO, Model GA 70-39, trout, two-pc, two tips, for 4 wt line, orig bag and tube, 7'................**$935**

Dickerson, trout, Model 861711, Special 1937, three-pc, two tips, orig bag and tube, 8-1/2'......**$2,100**

E. C. Powell
Heavy trout or light salmon, Marysville, two-pc, two tips, patent numbers denoting hollow built configuration, orig bag, later tube, 8-1/2' **$910**
Trout, "A" taper, two-pc, two tips, (one replaced), hollow built, orig bag and tube, 8-1/2' **$770**
Trout, B-9, two-pcs, two tips, for 6 wt line, hollow built, profession-

ally restored, orig bag and tube, 9' **$825**
Trout, "C" taper, two-pc, two tips, hollow built, orig bag and tube, 8-1/2' **$990**

F. E. Thomas, Bangor, ME
Salmon, two handed, three-pc, two tips, canvas sack, tip tube, several wraps need replacing, 12' **$220**
Trout, Dirigo, three-pc, two tips, orig bag, later tube, 8' **$580**
Trout, Dirigo, three-pc, two tips, orig bag, later tube, varnish roughness, 9' **$165**
Trout, Special, three-pc, two tips, orig bag and tube, restored, 8-1/2' **$385**
Trout, Special, three-pc, two tips, cork spacer on reel seat, orig bag, hanging tag, and tube, 9'................**$440**

Gary Howells, trout, two-pc, two tips, for 5 wt line, possibly unused, orig bag and tube, 7-1/2'......**$2,750**

George Halstead, Danbury, CT, split bamboo, trout, 7-1/2' **$3,410**

Gillum, trout, two-pc, two-tip, light line, orig bag and tube, missing four guides, needs refinishing, 7-1/2' **$3,850**

Goodwin Granger, split bamboo, 7' **$1,100**

Hardy
Centenary set, commemorative, reproduction of 1890s 8' Gold Medal split bamboo rod, blued Houghton Perfect 2-5/8" reel, both numbered "64," of 100 sets made in 1992, rosewood chest with brass plaque **$2,915**
Salmon Deluxe Rod, extra tip, aluminum case, 9' **$175**

Harold Gillum, Ridgefield, CT, split bamboo, 6-1/2' and 7-1/2' sold as pr **$7,700**

H. L. Leonard
Fly, 6-1/2" **$1,450**
Fly, Leonard Tournament, extra tip, metal case, 9'.........................**$300**
Red wrap, 7-1/2'....................**$1,925**
Split bamboo, model 50DF, 8' **$880**
#37ACM-6' **$3,025**
#37-6' **$1,925**

Horrocks & Illotson, 9' 3", two tips, split-bamboo fly, maroon wraps **$50**

Montaque, bamboo, two tips, orig case **$135**

Omar Needham, Rangeley, ME, Needham's Special, light salmon,

two-pc, two tips, impregnated screw down-locking reel seat, orig condition, orig bag and tube, 9' **$220**

Orvis
Battenkill, two-pc, two tips, orig bag and tube, 8-1/2' **$425**
Light Spinning, two-pc, one tip, orig bag and tube, 7' **$220**
Model 1882, trout, three-pc, two tip, modern guide replacements, orig bag, 9-1/2' **$110**
Salmon, two-pc, two tips, orig bag and tube, 9-1/2' **$360**
Spinning, two-pc, one tip, superlight, orig bag and tube, 6-1/2'........**$250**

Paul H. Young, Perfectionist, trout, two-pc, two tips, orig bag and tube, 1978, 7-1/2' **$2,570**

Payne
Light trout, two-pc, three tips, 1-5/8 oz, orig bag, hanging tag, and tube, 4'4" **$7,975**
Salmon, three-pc, two tips, removable 6" butt extension, orig canvas sack, tip tube, and ferrule plugs, 10-1/2' **$450**
Salmon, dry fly, Model 430, two-pc, two tips, removable 6-3/4" butt extension, 6-1/8 oz, unused, orig bag, tube, and tube cover, 9' **$2,100**
Trolling, three-pc, two tips, restored butt and tip section, orig bag and tube, 9'................................**$410**
Trout, Model 96, two-pc, two tips, orig bag and tube, 6-1/2'......**$3,300**
Trout, Model 98, two-pc, two tips, extra tip, orig bag and tube, 7' **$3,850**
Trout, Model 200, three-pc, two tips, spare unfinished tip, five guides, orig bag and tube, 8'............**$3,080**
Trout, Model 204, three-pcs, two tips, screw-up locking over walnut reel seat, poor varnish, Abercrombie & Fitch & Fitch Co. stamp, orig bag and tube, 8-1/2' **$1,870**
Trout, three pcs, two tips, screw up-locking reel seat, orig bag and tube, 9' **$1,760**

R. L. Winston, San Francisco, trout, two-pc, one tip, for 7 wt line, hollow built, orig bag and tube, 8-1/2' **$525**

Sam Carlson
Light salmon, Four Quad, two-pc, two tips, 3" removable butt extension, orig bag and tube, 8-1/2' **$1,870**

Lure, Moonlight Pikaroon, pike size, black back, red sides, white belly, VG+, 5-1/4" l, **$235.**
Photo courtesy of Lang's Sporting Collectables.

Lure, Heddon no. 701 Musky Minnow, marked props, cup rigging rainbow finish, red handpainted gill marks, 1 belly weight paint chipped, flaking varnish, finish has heavy alligatoring, VG+ condition, **$1,180.**
Photo courtesy of Lang's Sporting Collectables.

Lure, Heddon 300 Surface Minnow, early, brass hardware, unmarked props, green crackleback, handpainted gill marks, wood chipping, varnish loss, **$385.**
Photo courtesy of Lang's Sporting Collectables.

Casting reel, MOP, hard rubber, German silver, "E. Holzmann – Pat. Oct 31, '05 – April 16, '07, Bklyn," two patent markings 850,580 and 803,165, oversized counter balance handle, freespool model, rim control lever disengages gear train, full size offset foot, unaltered and unpolished, spool reel 3-1/4" d, 1-3/8" w, **$6,490.**
Photo courtesy of Lang's Sporting Collectables.

Lure, Heddon Wilder-Dilg Flyrod lure, rare, EX condition, age lines where thread tied around body, **$360.**
Photo courtesy of Lang's Sporting Collectables.

Lure, South Bend Plug Oreno, butterfly finish, glass eyes, full weed guards rigged to top of head, slight varnish flaking, EX-, **$635.**
Photo courtesy of Lang's Sporting Collectables.

Lure, Heddon, Jeanette Hawley Mohawk, yellow body, green scale finish, **$15,000-$17,500.**

Lure, Heddon 700 Musky Minnow, rare, green crackleback finish, red handpainted gill marks, five trebles, unmarked spinners, light varnish flaking, 1911, 5" l, **$9,020.**
Photo courtesy of Lang's Sporting Collectables.

Lure, Heddon, Triple Teaser, Series No. 1000, white and red buck tail, minnow blades stamped, "Heddon Triple Teaser," **$30-$50.**

Creek Chub Ice Decoy, Fin Tail Shiner body, tiny paint flaking on metal tail, includes #2110 cardboard box, EX+ condition, **$3,630.**
Photo courtesy of Lang's Sporting Collectables.

Floating minnow bucket, Ideal #435, orig green finish, lift out int, stenciled stringer of three fish, Cream City, scratches, rust, bent lid, Good condition, 10-1/2" x 8-3/4" x 7", **$470.**
Photo courtesy of Lang's Sporting Collectables.

Flask, horse pulling cart/eagle, olive green, pint, pontil, McKearin GV-7a, **$700.**
Photo courtesy of American Bottle Auctions.

Flask, cornucopia/urn, emerald green, pint, pontil, McKearin GIII-17, **$450.**
Photo courtesy of American Bottle Auctions.

Flask, Redware pig, molded and incised anatomically correct, rear hole, incised with "Railroad & River Guide with a little Good Old Rye in," several landmarks noted include "Miss. River, St. Louis," ear chip, c1880, 7-1/2" l, **$7,635.**
Photo courtesy of Skinner, Inc.

Trout, Four, two-pc, two tips, orig bag and tube, 7-1/2' **$2,530**

Trout, Thomas Special, two-pc, two tips, orig bag and tube, 7' **$1,540**

Shakespeare, Premier Model, three-pc, two tips, split-bamboo fly, red silk wrappings, cloth bag, metal tube, 9' **$75**

Shakespeare Springbrook, fly fishing, orig bag **$100**

S. J. Small, split bamboo, three-rod set **$2,640**

Superlight, spinning rod, 5' **$660**

Thomas & Thomas, Caenis, light trout, blued hardware and ferrules, two-pc, two tips, orig bag and tube, 7-1/2' **$1,760**

Union Hardware Co., Kingfisher, saltwater boat rod, split-bamboo fly, dark brown wraps, 7-1/2' **$35**

Walt Carpenter

Trout, Browntone, Model No. 91276, two-pc, two tips, for 4-wt line, unused, orig bag, tube, and tube bag, 7-1/2' **$2,750**

Trout, Browntone Special, three-pc, two tips, dark flamed cane, cap, and ring reel seat, mahogany spacer, blue hardware, wrapper on handle, orig bag and tube, 8'3" **$3,300**

Trout, two-pc, two tips, for 5-wt line, blued hardware and ferrules, orig bag and tube, 7'9" **$2,530**

Trout, three-pc, two tips, for 5-wt line, light cane, screw up-locking reel seat, unused, orig bag and tube, 8' **$2,200**

Walton Powell, trout, two-pc, two tips, extra mid section, professionally restored, 9' **$220**

Scale, brass, "Chamllons Improved, New York, Pat. Dec 10 1967" **$30**

Tackle box, leather **$450**

Vise, fly tying

Steel and brass, bolts to table, 7" l, 2-1/2" w **$210**

Cast iron and steel, can be used free standing or bolted down, 7-1/2" l, 6" h **$240**

Wallet, H.L. Leonard, 30 plastic pockets displaying 30 different kinds of poly blend, orig contents, 5-1/2" x 12", opens to 12" x 19" **$40**

FLASKS

History: A flask, which usually has a narrow neck, is a container for liquids. Early American glass companies frequently formed them in molds that left a relief design on the front and/or back. Historical flasks with a portrait, building, scene, or name are the most desirable.

A chestnut is hand-blown, small, and has a flattened bulbous body. The pitkin has a blown globular body with a spiral rib overlay on vertical ribs. Teardrop flasks are generally fiddle shaped and have a scroll or geometric design.

Notes: Dimensions can differ for the same flask because of variations in the molding process. Color is important in determining value—aqua and amber are the most common colors; scarcer colors demand more money. Bottles with "sickness," an opalescent scaling that eliminates clarity, are

worth much less.

Historical

Baltimore monument/sailing boat, half pint, very pale green, open pontil, 5-3/4" h **$250**

Columbia, Liberty cap, eagle, Kensington and Union on reverse, pale aqua, bubbles **$800**

Eagle-Cornucopia, early Pittsburgh district, 1820-40, light greenish-aquamarine, sheared mouth, pontil scar, pint, McKearin GII-6 .... **$475**

Eagle-Willington/Glass Co., Willington glass Works, West Willington, CT, 1860-72, bright medium yellowish-olive, applied double-collared mouth, smooth base, half pint, McKearin GII-63 .... **$210**

For Pike's Peak, Prospector-Hunter Shooting Deer, attributed to Ravenna Glass Works, Ravenna, OH, 1860-80, aquamarine, applied mouth with ring, smooth base, quart, McKearin GXI-47, 1/4" shallow flake **$325**

Frigate Franklin/Masonic Arch, frigate sailing ship Franklin and "Free Trade and Sailors Rights" on front, reverse with Masonic Arch, green sheaf, "Kensington Glass Works Philadelphia," pint, pale aqua, open pontil, 6-7/8" h **$350**

Masonic Arch/eagle

Pint, olive green, Keene on back, open pontil, 7-1/2" h **$320**

"HP" below eagle, pint, light emerald green, open pontil, 7-1/4" h **$300**

"HP" below eagle, pint, medium emerald green, open pontil, 7-1/2" h **$1,100**

Railroad and eagle
Olive green, no inscriptions, pint, 6-5/8" h, McKearin GV-9 .... **$450**
Olive green, open pontil, pint, McKearin GV-9 .... **$375**
Railroad, medium blue green, emb "Success to the Railroad" on both sides, plain lip, rough pontil mark with straight seam, Lancaster Glass Works, pint, 1825-75, 6-3/4" h, McKearin GV-1 .... **$90**
Union and Wm Frank & Sons, Pitts on one side, cannon on other, aqua, pint, interior blisters, minor residue, flake on base, 7-1/2" h, McKearin GXII-39 .... **$100**

Pattern molded
Emil Larson, NJ, swirled to the right, amethyst, sheared mouth, pontil scar, some exterior high point wear, c1930, 7-3/8" l.. **$250**
Midwest, 24 ribs swirled to the right, golden amber, sheared mouth, pontil scar, 1800-30, 4-5/8" l........ **$190**
Pattern molded, Mid-western, blue aqua, handle, open pontil, 6-1/4" h **$2,300**

Pictorial
Cornucopia and urn of fruit
Aqua green, pint, McKearin GIII-4, minor int. residue, small pot stone, 7-1/4" h **$250**
Dark olive, pint, McKearin GIII-4, 6-1/2" h **$125**
Golden amber, half pint, minor surface wear, McKearin GIII-10, 5-1/2" h **$220**

Eagle
Coffin & Hay, Hammonton, NJ, spread-wing American eagle on reverse, blown, 8-3/4" h **$210**
Columbia/Eagle, bust of Columbia on front with "Kensington," eagle with "Union Co." on reverse, pint, pale aqua, open pontil, 7-1/8" h **$635**
Double eagle, pint size, olive green, 6-5/8" h **$320**
Eagle and cornucopia, pint, yellow olive green, open pontil, 6-3/4" h **$100**
Horseman and hound, mounted calvary officer on front, hound on reverse, quart, yellow olive, open pontil, 8-3/4" h **$1,610**
Horse pulling cart/eagle, pint, dark olive green, open pontil, 6-3/4" h **$200**
Hunter and fisherman, man shooting rifle, man fishing, cala-

bash style, teal green, open pontil, 9-1/8" h **$520**
Summer/Winter Tree, quart, aqua, open pontil, 8" h **$100**

Pitkin type
Midwest, ribbed and swirled to the right, 16 ribs, olive green with yellow tone, sheared mouth, pontil scar, some int. stain, 1800-30, 6-1/4" l **$300**
New England, sheared mouth, pontil scar, ribbed and swirled to the left, 36 ribs, light olive yellow, 1783-30, 5-1/4" l................................ **$375**
Pattern molded, flattened ovoid, medium olive amber, 36 rib broken swirl to right, short neck, plain lip, kick-up base, rough pontil mark, probably New England, pint, early 19th C, 6-3/4" h **$360**

Portrait
Adams-Jefferson, New England, yellow amber, sheared mouth, pontil scar, half pint, 1830-50, McKearin GI-114 .... **$325**
Byron/Scott, busts, half pint, yellow olive amber, open pontil, 5-3/4" h **$320**
General Jackson, Pittsburgh district, bluish-aquamarine, sheared mouth, pontil scar, pint, 1820-40, McKearin GI-68 .... **$1,500**
General Taylor, pale greenish aquamarine, emb "Genl Taylor Never Surrenders" and "A Little More Grape Capt Bragg," plain lip, rough pontil mark, probably Baltimore Glass Works, pint, 1825-75, 7-1/8" h, McKearin GS-4 .... **$160**
Jennings, bust of Wm Jennings Bryan with "In Silver We Trust" and "Bryan-1896-Sewall," reverse with American eagle "United Democratic Ticket, We Shall Vote, 16 to 1," coin shape, amber, lighter yellow amber edges, 5-1/4" h, small fracture visible on base and base edge **$920**
Jenny Lind, Fislerville Glass Works, aqua, calabash, several int. blisters, 9-1/4" h, McKearin GI-107 ...... **$115**
Lafayette-DeWitt Clinton, Coventry Glass Works, Coventry, CT, yellowish-olive, sheared mouth, pontil scar, half pint, 1/2" vertical crack, weakened impression, 1824-25, McKearin GI-82 .... **$2,100**
Pewter Pilgrim, shaped figural handles, moon-shaped body, molded foliage, pierced base, losses, 14" h, 16th C **$345**

Rough and Ready Taylor-Eagle, Midwest, aquamarine, sheared mouth, pontil scar, pint, 1830-40, McKearin GI-77.................... **$1,200**
Washington
Washington/eagle, bust of Washington on front with "Adams and Jefferson, July 4th A.D. 1776," eagle with motto, T.W.D. and Kensington Glass Works, pint, pale green, open pontil, 6-7/8" h **$290**
Washington/Bridgeton NJ, bust of Washington "Bridgeton New Jersey" on both sides, quart, aqua, open pontil, 8" h, some residue at base.. **$200**
Washington and Taylor
Ice blue, quart, bust of Washington "The father of his country," and bust of General Taylor "General Taylor NEVER SURRENDERS," open pontil, 8-1/4" h.................... **$1,000**
Olive green, pint, some surface wear and minor int. blisters, 6-1/2" h, McKearin GI-31...................... **$260**
Sapphire blue, soda style applied top, open pontil, quart, McKearin GI-54 .... **$2,600**

Pottery
Bennington, brown flint glaze, book form, 5-3/4" h **$460**
Majolica, polychrome dec bulldog, landscape, and crest design, Italy, 19th C, 4-1/2" h **$200**
Pig shape, brown Albany glaze, incised "Brachmann & Moosard, Importers and Dealers in Wines & Liquors, 81 West Third Street, Cincinnati," Anna Pottery, 7" l **$13,500**
Nailsea, pint, amber and white swirls, faint pontil mark, 7-5/8" h......... **$435**
Nailsea, pint, pink and white, faint pontil mark, 8-5/8" h.................. **$200**
Scroll
Aquamarine, flat ring below plain lip, faint large iron pontil mark, quart, 8-1/2" h, McKearin GIX-4, 1825-50 .... **$110**
Dark olive green, pint, open pontil, 6-7/8" h **$1,150**
Dark olive green, pint size, open pontil mark, 7-1/8" h **$1,100**
Greenish aquamarine, plain lip, rough pontil mark, quart, 8-7/8" h, McKearin GIX-2, 1825-50 .... **$90**
Honey amber, pint, minor surface wear, 7" h **$350**
Medium blue green, plain lip, rough pontil mark, quart, 8-3/4" h, McKearin GIX-1, 1825-50 .... **$190**

Folk art, carved and painted yoked oxen pr, wooden, American, oxen are painted red and white, iron tack eyes, blue yoke, string tail tufts, losses, 5-1/8" h, **$410.**
Photo courtesy of Skinner, Inc.

Folk art checker set, orig fitted hinged case, signed "David Wall" on int, carved and painted, reset brass hinges and hook/eye clasp, VG condition late 19th century, 2-1/2" h, 9-3/4" x 10-1/4", **$175.**
Photo courtesy of Green Valley Auctions.

Folk art, birth record, watercolor and ink on paper, two birds perched on fruiting branches, period molded wood frame, "Anna B. Cochran Born July 6, 1804," attributed to Moses Connor, Jr., sight size 8-1/2" x 6-1/4", **$4,700.**
Photo courtesy of Skinner, Inc.

Folk art, swan, painted wooden head, canvas-covered wire framed body, **$700.**
Photo courtesy of David Rago Auctions, Inc.

Sunburst

Deep blue green, tooled lip, rough pontil mark, three-quarter pint, 1825-75, 7" h, McKearin GVIII-29 .... **$220**

Medium green, plain lip, rough pontil mark, New England, pint, early to mid-19th C, 8" h, McKearin GVIII-2 .... **$440**

Medium yellow olive, plain lip, rough pontil mark, Coventry, CT, pint, early to mid-19th C, 7-1/2" h, McKearin GVIII-3 .... **$615**

FOLK ART

History: Exactly what constitutes folk art is a question still being vigorously debated among collectors, dealers, museum curators, and scholars. Some want to confine folk art to non-academic, handmade objects. Others are willing to include manufactured material. The term is used to cover objects ranging from crude drawings by children to academically trained artists' paintings of "common" people and scenery. Some record setting prices for folk art were achieved during the auction of the collection of Eugene and Dorothy Elgin, at Conestoga Auction Company, Inc., in April of 2004 (marked ex-Elgin).

Bald eagle, carved and painted wood, stylized, glass eyes, stippled surface, Ohio, mounted on carved pine base, minor age cracks, attributed to early 20th C, 26-3/8" h **$5,000**

Billfold, beadwork eagle with shield, two stars, crossed American flags, old label: "This pocketbook was made by a Mrs. Davis in the Virginia Colony AD 1758, was found in her son's HB Davis's pocket at the surrender of Lord Cornwallis from George Davis," some deterioration to fabric, some losses, 7-1/2" l **$950**

Bird tree, carved and polychromed, seven stylized birds on wire legs, base made from surface root, PA, c1890-1910, 20" h, 21" w **$17,050**

Birth record, watercolor and ink on paper, Mary Hoyt, born May 6, 1807, two cream, beige, and light brown birds in ovals, flanked by patterned outline and column-like lines, reverse sgd "Henniker May 7, 1829 by Moses Connor," unframed, minor staining, 9" x 7" **$8,225**

Box, cov, carved oak, America, figure of man wearing cap with visor, sitting cross-legged on large dog, both have tails, border of turned finials joined by spiral rails, dovetailed box, leaf-carved drawer, paneled sides, old variegated varnish finish, late 19th/early 20th C, 6" w, 3-1/2" d, 4-1/2" h **$1,265**

Bust, attributed to Albert Abelt, Cumberland County, PA, titled "My Favorite Teacher," carved and painted wood, fabric flowers on hat, soulful eyes, blue dress, ex-Elgin, 6" h **$24,200**

Candle stand, laminated hardwoods, sq top with egg and dart molding, four ladies legs shaped supports with turned drop, old mellow finish, repairs, 16" w, 15-1/2" d, 30-1/4" h **$375**

Carving angel

Bulls' heads, life-size, real horns, glass eyes, old weathered paint, carved by Noah Weiss (1842-1907, Northampton County, PA), dated 1870, price for pr **$38,500**

Pine plank naively carved with face of angel, outstretched wings, radiating layered feathers, remnants of orig polychrome dec, light weathering to gray patina, possibly PA, 19th C, 41" l, 9" h................................. **$900**

Relief carved angel holding star of Bethlehem and scroll, faded inscription begins "Glory to God in the...," right arm with old iron work repair, American, 19th C, 28" l, 17" h.............................. **$1,100**

Drawing, pencil, 13-7/8" x 17-1/4", farm scene, detailed two-story house, smaller barns, picket fence, hills and trees in background, stains and foxing, 16-1/2" x 20-3/4" gilt frame **$980**

Drawing, watercolor

American School, two girls standing, each holding red book, wearing applied gold foil brooch, lace collars accented with pinprick designs, framed, tear lower left, repaired tears on edges, 19th C, 9" x 7" **$1,410**

Girl in red dressed flanked by stylized tulip columns, inscribed "Ann Potter's profile drawn by Ruby Devol," verse "Can love for me inspire your tender heart. Dare I to hope and with that hope be blessed. Pursed we shall to us will him virtuous paths and find for time prove more," orig red painted frame, c1840 .... **$20,000**

Man and woman on either side of two handled urn of flowering roses, tulips, and other flowers, inscribed "A Walk in the Garden," Constructed by Michael Palmer, June 14, AD 1838-This is to certify that wife, Sarah B. Abrise, is superior in reciting first class this evening. May 21, 1841," 1841, 14" x 17" **$28,000**

Family record, Elijah and Mary Ann (Blew) Smalley, "Executed by E.S. Van Gleve," attributed to Indiana, pen and ink on paper, recording vital statistics of them and their 11 children, decorated with four columns and foliage, imperfections, c1866, 16-3/4" x 20-7/8" **$300**

Figure, carved and painted wood

Airplane, four engines, tin tail, 44" w wooden wings, propellers, orig red and white paint, some flaking and touch up, 30" l **$250**

Bird on pedestal, pegged articulated head, wings, and body, paper label on base "Done by Stanley Nick Gustwick, Coudersport, Pa," 7-1/2" h, 6-1/2" l, 4-1/2" h **$880**

Crane, carved wood body, neck, and legs, tin tail and wings, tack eyes, painted gray, green and red, aged patina, legs made from turned spindles of old chair, made by Emanuel Myers, York County, PA, broom maker, 20" h, 22" l, 7-1/2" w **$9,350**

Man with drum, Alabama, stand, late 19th/early 20th C, 5" h **$360**

Snake, old dark red paint, yellow polka dots, black, white, and blue eyes, old chip on tail, early 20th C, 25-1/2" l **$575**

Woman, standing, applied extended arms, metal tack eyes and buttons, alligatored surface, America, stand, late 19th C, 6-1/2" h **$600**

Grotesque face jug, stoneware, brown-speckled glaze, found in Ohio, imperfections, 19th C, 5-1/2" h **$14,950**

Hammer, oak and iron, figural, handle surmounted by carved man's head and upper torso, found in PA, 19th C, 13" l **$1,955**

Memorial, incised gilt and ebonized deep recessed shadow box frame, white painted cast iron profile of Lincoln surrounded by wreath of wire stemmed wax silk flowers, grouped with ribbon tied and waxed silk roses and calla lilies, surmounted by white dove with wings spread in flight, c1875, 31" x 23" x 6-1/2" **$700**

Model, Chinese-style side-wheel paddle boat, small horse-drawn cart, two horses powering wheels, carved man, minor breaks, 29" l, 11-1/4" d, 8" h **$115**

Picture frame, painted and incised wood, meandering vine and dot border, corner bosses, one corner boss missing, 12-5/8" w, 15-3/4" h **$920**

Plaque, sun face, carved polychrome, molded edge, America, minor imperfections, stand, early 19th C, 14" d **$16,100**

Schnerenschnitte, hearts, tulips, and paired birds cut in 12-1/4" d circle, reverse backing with drawing of tulip and "Love, D.Y. Ellinger/1960," smoke-dec 17-1/4" sq frame **$950**

Scherenschnitte, birth certificate, dated Sept. 5, 1780, for Anna Elizabeth Lauerin, Berks County, PA, Tolpehaden Township, cut-work and painted dec border of flowers, tulips, and hearts attached with vine-work, black ink text, glued down, staining, loss, 11-1/2" x 14-1/2" **$925**

Sculpture, seagull, wood and tin, orig paint, wooden ice fishing decoy in beak, standing on pylon surrounded by fishing related items including netting, lures, eel spear, bobbers, lead sinkers, wear, 34-1/2" h **$450**

Still life, watercolor on paper, American School, 19th C, framed

Fruit and foliage in gray bowl, shades of red, green, and blue, pinprick dec, general toning, tiny scattered stains, 10-3/4" x 9-1/2" **$1,150**

Bouquet of Spring Flowers in a Vase, sgd "Frances Thompson, 1841," tulips, narcissus, and other spring flowers, white handled urn-form vase dec with sea shells, very minor toning, 15" x 13" **$2,715**

Theorem

Basket of flowers, oil and watercolor, sgd "Julia P. Paine," c1840, 12-3/8" x 15" **$12,000**

Basket of fruit still life, watercolor on velvet, unsigned, American School, molded giltwood frame, toning, 19th C, 16-1/2" w, 13-1/2" h **$4,150**

Canton porcelain bowl of fruit, strawberries, pear, blueberries, bird nested in center, sgd "D. Ellinger," orig grain painted frame, 22-1/4" l, 17" h **$4,950**

Fruit compote, sgd "D.Y. Ellinger/1960" lower right, framed, 23-1/2" x 28-1/2" .... **6,325.**

Lady Liberty feeding eagle, basket of flowers, trees, and flag, on velvet, gilt frame, fading, discoloration to textile, c1790, 12-1/4" w, 15-1/2" h **$3,190**

Tinsel picture, flower arrangement, reverse-painted glass backed with foil and paper, American School, Victorian frame, repaired, late 19th C, 22" x 17" **$180**

Trivet, heart form, single pc carved chestnut, serrated edges, applied legs, wrought iron tacks on top, 11-1/2" l, 4" w, 1-3/4" h **$2,100**

Valentine, pinprick and watercolor on paper, woven, pink paper ribbon border, German verse, woman in pink carrying bottle, soldier in blue uniform on horseback, separated by medallion "Treue Liebe," (True Love) glued down to another pc of paper, some damage, translation included, 12-1/2" h, 8-1/4" w **$500**

Wall hanging, attributed to Noah Weiss, Northampton, Lehigh County, PA, relief carved pine, two hunting dogs and two quail, painted white, black, and brown dogs, green grass, mottled white sky, painted black frame, aged patina, ex-Elgin, 19-1/2" w, 19" h **$8,250**

FRAKTUR

History: Fraktur, the calligraphy associated with the Pennsylvania Germans, is named for the elaborate first letter found in many of the hand-drawn examples. Throughout its history, printed, partially printed/partially hand-drawn, and fully hand-drawn works existed side by side. Schoolteachers or ministers living in rural areas of Pennsylvania, Maryland, and Virginia often made frakturs. Many artists are unknown.

Fraktur, Pennsylvania, watercolor on paper, potted tulip, 19th century, 9-1/2" x 6-3/4", **$1,725.**
Photo courtesy of Pook & Pook, Inc.

Fraktur, watercolor and ink on paper, red, black, green and yellow tulips and birds, diamond border, Bucks County Pennsylvania, 8" x 6-1/4", **$1,112.**
Photo courtesy of Pook & Pook, Inc.

Fraktur, Sarah Kriebel (Montgomery County, PA, 1828-1908) Schwenkfelder watercolor, two birds perched on tulip vine, heart, 9-1/2" x 7-1/2", **$1,170.**
Photo courtesy of Pook & Pook, Inc.

Fraktur exists in several forms— geburts and taufschein (birth and baptismal certificates), vorschrift (writing examples, often with alphabet), haus segen (house blessings), bookplates and bookmarks, rewards of merit, illuminated religious texts, valentines, and drawings. Although collected for decoration, the key element in fraktur is the text.

Notes: Fraktur prices rise and fall along with the American folk-art market. The key marketplaces are Pennsylvania and the Middle Atlantic states.

Alphabet, upper and lower case written in fraktur schrift, orange and black ink, old inlaid frame, minor discoloration and tears, 9-3/4" w, 12" h...**$250**

Birth certificate, Geburts and Taufschein
Hand drawn, attributed to Samuel Bentz, Lancaster County, PA, for Susanna Hacker, born 1828, spherical, geometric, and stylized floral and finial dec, old frame, some staining, 6-7/8" w, 9" h.........**$4,950**
Hand drawn, attributed to Ehre Vater artist, for Margaretha Mayerin, Sept. 28, 1800, Cumberland County, PA, two columns, centralized heart and two birds, tulip and floral dec, illuminated in red, yellow, green, and blue, painted frame, minor folds, tears, small restoration to corner, 10-3/8" w, 17-3/4" h **$8,250**
Hand drawn, attributed to Joseph Lochbaum, for Johannes Schlichter, 1792, ink, illuminated in red, yellow, and green, floral motifs and hearts, two flying eagles, religious text in hearts, black painted frame, 15" w, 12-3/4" h **$4,675**
Hand drawn, Henry Young, watercolor, man in blue frock coat holding glass of wine, inscribed between two red, yellow, and blue eight-point stars, for "Mr. Michael Snyder-A Son of Andrew Snyder and his wife Catherine, born Seysel May 25 AD 1820 in Derry Township Columbia County State of Pennsylvania," 8" w, 11" h **$19,000**
Printed, Daniel May, York, PA, for William Brennemann, 1847, Codorus Township, York County, PA, hand illuminated in blue, green, pink, and yellow, filled by decorator, contemporary marbleized paint dec

frame, tears, minor discoloration, 9-1/2" w, 15" h **$180**
Printed and hand drawn, printed text for Johann Valentine Schuller, hand drawn potted flowers and text attributed to J. Schuller, for Marigreth Schneider, 1789, Pinecreek, Berks County, PA, illuminated in red, yellow, and green, black painted frame, 12-1/2" w, 7-1/2" h **$3,025**
Printed by J. Hartman, 1818, Lebanon County, PA, for Joseph Rudy, 1818, Dauphin County, PA, illuminated in brown and yellows, filled in and signed by Charles Overfield, Hannover, Germany, 1847, framed, 14-1/2" w, 12-1/2" h **$600**

Bookplate
Handwritten, "Jacob Witmeyer's Book, born in 1835," York County, PA, illuminated in yellow, red, green, and blue ink, red ochre painted frame, 6-3/4" l, 4" h **$385**
Watercolor on laid paper, tulips and other flowers, bright red, yellow, and green, yellow and black birds, worn gilt frame, PA origin, 6-1/2" w, 8-1/4" h **$2,990**

Child's Book of Moral Instruction (Metamorphis), watercolor, pen and ink on paper
Dec on both sides of four leaves, when folded reveals different versus and full-page color illus, executed by Sarah Ann Siger, Nazareth, PA, orig string hinges, 6-1/4" x 7" **$575**
Dec on both sides of four leaves, each with upper and lower flaps showing different versus and color illus, unknown illustrator, 5-3/4" x 7-1/2"...**$345**
Printed form on paper, hand colored elements, The Great American Metamorphosis, Philadelphia, printed by Benjamin Sands, 1805-06, printed on both sides of four leaves, each with upper and lower flaps, engraved collar illus by Poupard, 6" x 7"................................**$420**

Christmas card, German text, greeting inside stylized oval, circular border, framed, 6-1/2" w, 4" h **$825**

Confirmation certificate, watercolor, pen and ink on paper, David Schumacher, paired tulips and hearts, for Maria Magdalena Spengler, dated 1780, 6" x 7-3/4" **$4,600**

Copybook, Vorschrift, pen and ink, red watercolor, laid paper, German text with ornate Gothic letters in heading, blocked cut area in lower left unfin-

Fraktur, ink and watercolor, Southeastern Pennsylvania, central heart, birds and flowers, dated 1788, 12-1/2" x 15", $2,530.
Photo courtesy of Pook & Pook, Inc.

Fraktur, Pennsylvania, watercolor on paper, flowers and angel, dated 1795, 12-3/4" x 15-3/4", $2,760.
Photo courtesy of Pook & Pook, Inc.

Print, Grant Wood, "Shriners' Quartet," lithograph, pencil signed lower right, framed, 8" x 12" sight, $1,800.
Photo courtesy of David Rago Auctions, Inc.

ished, minor edge damage, 11-3/8" w, 9-1/2" h yellow and red leather covered frame, 8" w, 5-5/8" h **$250**

Drawing

Blue bird within two black snakes climbing poles to arch, decorative name "S. A. Kline," handwritten "A. C. Martin, April 22, 1823," orig frame, 4-1/4" w, 5-3/4" h.......**$1,980**

House and barn, farm life, cows, horses, rabbit, and snake, buggy and Conestoga wagon, sun with face, pen and green, orange, yellow and brown, dated 1856 in lower right corner, framed, 9-7/8" l, 5-1/8" h **$7,975**

Snow Hill Cloister, Franklin County, PA, potted flowers with compass wheels, tulips, and parrots, decorative border, drawn in red ink, colored in yellow, blue, and green, old painted frame, 8-1/4" w, 10-3/8" h **$6,600**

Ein brief, printed and hand illuminated, printed by King und Baird, Philadelphia, purple, orange, and yellow, ein brief to guard against fired, old frame, 11-1/2" w, 15" h **$315**

Family register, hand drawn, blue-green and red border with stars and flowers in corners, hearts, cherubs, and cross hatch work at center, German names, written in old brown ink, heart and hand medallion with inscription "Orphans Home and Ft. Wayne Hospital, Allen Co., Ind," sgd "John Cornelius Martin," old taped tear near top margin, small piece of corner missing, dates from 1814 to 1870, 19-3/4" w, 16" h **$1,100**

Himmelsbrief, printed, attributed to Stettinius and Leper, text, Hanover, York County, PA, wood blocks of

vases and flowers, hand illuminated in red, yellow, and green, old tiger maple frame, water stained, 9-3/4" w, 7-1/2" h..................................**$100**

House blessing (Haus Segen)

Block printed and hand drawn, printed text, dated 1787, hand dec attributed to Arnold Hovelmann, tulip and flowers, border dec, illuminated in red, yellow, green, and brown, old painted frame, 7-1/2" h, 12" w **$10,450**

Printed by Johann Ritter, Reading, hand colored, orange, green, blue, yellow, brown, and black, professionally repaired and rebacked on cloth, 18-1/4" h, 14-3/8" w old stenciled dec frame, 15-1/2" h, 11-3/4" w...........................**$500**

Marriage certificate, watercolor, pen and ink on paper, Daniel Schumacher, paired red, yellow and green birds flanking an arch with crown, for Johannes Haber and Elisabeth Stimmess, Windsor Township, Berks County, PA, dated 1777, 8" x 12-1/2" **$1,035**

Reward of merit, hand drawn, cut-work, attributed to Jacob Botz, Lancaster, PA, floral motif, two birds perched on tulips, cut-work to floral motif, name Salome Schmidin below, red, blue, and green, 3-1/4" w, 4-7/8" h **$3,740**

FRATERNAL ORGANIZATIONS

History: Benevolent and secret societies played an important part in America from the late 18th to the mid-20th centuries. Initially, the societies were organized to aid members and their families in times of

distress. They evolved from this purpose into important social clubs by the late 19th century.

In the 1950s, with the arrival of the civil rights movement, an attack occurred on the secretiveness and often-discriminatory practices of these societies. Membership in fraternal organizations, with the exception of the Masonic group, dropped significantly. Many local chapters closed and sold their lodge halls. This resulted in the appearance of many fraternal items in the antiques market.

Benevolent & Protective Order of the Elks, (BPOE)

Book, *National Memorial*, color illus, 1931 ....**$35**

Bookends, pr, bronzed cast iron, elk in high relief..................................**$75**

Pinback button, orange, lavender, and green, white accents, gold rim, brown elk symbol, tiny inscription "Souvenir Elks Convention Los Angeles 1909"....................................**$25**

Shaving mug, pink and white, gold elk head, crossed American flags and floral dec, marked "Germany" on bottom **$90**

Tip tray, Philadelphia, 21st Annual Reunion, July 1907, rect, 4-7/8" x 3-1/4"..**$135**

Eastern Star

Demitasse cup and saucer, porcelain...**$25**

Pendant, SP, rhinestones and rubies **$45**

Ring, gold, Past Matron, star-shape stone with diamond in center **$150**

Eastern Star, dresser tray, glass top, metal fittings, enameled emblem with gold trim in center, dried flowers under glass top, two handles, **$25.**

Knights Templar, plate, 51st Annual Conclave, Knights Templar, Penna, Gethsemane Commandry, No. 75, York, PA, 1904, blue transfer print, **$65.**

Cane, English, silver, 3" h x 1-2/3" unfolding Masonic ball handle, dec with C-scrolls, initialed, June 15th, 1891 on top, sides done in arched panels, four side latches, spreads to six linked pyramids, all engraved with secret symbols, ebony shaft, 2-3/4" horn ferrule, 1891, 35-3/4" l, **$1,900.**

Photo courtesy of Henry A. Taron.

Independent Order of Odd Fellows (I.O.O.F)

Ceremonial staff, polychrome carved wood, reverse tapering staff surmounted by carved open hand in cuffed sleeve holding heart in palm, old red, gold, and black painted surface, mounted on iron base, minor surface imperfections, 3" w, 1-1/2" d, 64" h **$2,300**

Gameboard, reverse painted black and gold metallic squares bordered by "I.O.O.F" chain links and other symbols, areas of flaking, black oak frame, 20-1/2" x 20-1/2" **$350**

Vignette, oil on board, hand beneath three links holding heart and card bearing archery scene, molded gilt gesso frame, flaking, subtle surface grime, 7-3/4" x 14-1/2" **$920**

Wall hanging, painted canvas, from Odd Fellows Lodge #4 in Whitehall, NY, several symbols reflecting high ideals, imperfections, 19th C, 75" l, 47-1/2" h **$2,990**

Watch fob, 94th Anniversary, April 12, 1913 ....**$30**

Knights Templar

Business card, Reynolds, J. P., Columbia Commandery No. 18 (K of P) Sturgis, MI, color logo, c1890 ....**$6**

Loving cup, china, three handles, green and white, gold tracery, Knights Templer insignia and Pittsburgh, 1907, marked "American China Co." **$75**

Shot glass, bowl supported by three golden swords, dated 1903, Pittsburgh **$25**

Tumbler, emb Indian head, dated 1903, Pittsburgh **$45**

Masonic

Advertising button, Illinois Masonic Hospital, black and white litho, c1920 ....**$10**

Apron, 14" x 12", leather, white, blue silk trim, white embroidery, silver fringe **$35**

Book, *An Inquiry In The Nature & Tendency of Speculative Freemasonry*, John Stearns, 210 pgs, 1829 ....**$65**

Bookends, pr, patinated metal, "appl'd for" on back **$200**

Box, cov, Chinese Export black lacquer, molded top with mother-of-pearl and lacquer Masonic devices, sides with floral dec, top loose, lock mecha-

nism missing, minor lacquer loss, 5" x 16-1/4" x 12-1/2" **$920**

Ceremonial cane, carved lizards, rounded top knop with emblem and eagle, metal top, several age cracks, 33-1/2" l **$350**

Fob, silvered brass, June 14-15, inscription for "Grand Lodge, F & A.M. Wisconson," blank reverse, 1927 event **$18**

Goblet, St. Paul, 1908 ....**$70**

Jug, lusterware, transfer printed and painted polychrome enamels, horseman, inscribed "James Hardman 1823," Masonic dec, royal coat of arms, minor wear, 5-5/8" h **$410**

Match holder, wall type, walnut, pierce carved symbols, 11" h **$75**

Painting, oil on canvas, "Our Motto," framed, retouched, craquelure, 23-1/4" h, 20" w **$2,645**

Pendant, 10k yg, designed as double-headed eagle, set with old European and single-cut diamonds, approx. total wt. 0.78 cts, opening to reveal various enameled emblems, 13.3 dwt, missing two stones **$500**

Pocket watch, Hiram Watch Inc., 14k yg, open face, blue dial with raised gold tone Masonic symbol indicators, case with engraved Masonic scenes and symbols, Hallmark 15 jewel movement, winding stem topped with blue stone cabochon **$2,115**

Ring, 14k rose gold, enameled cross on one side, enameled 32 degrees on other, double eagle head set with 10-point diamond, hand engraved, 1900-20 ....**$175**

Sign, shield shape, polychrome wood, several applied wood Masonic symbols, including All-Seeing Eye, sun, moon, stars, large central "G," pillars, etc., gilt highlights, blue field, red and white stripes below, molded gilt frame, wear and losses, 28-3/4" w, 34" h **$3,055**

Shriner

Cup and saucer, Los Angeles, 1906 ....**$70**

Dinnerware, Rajah, partial set, various marks, 52 pcs **$150**

Ice-cream mold, pewter, crescent with Egyptian head, marked "E & Co., NY," 4-1/4" d **$60**

Mug, Syria Temple, Pittsburgh, gold figures, 1895 ....**$125**

Shot glass, cranberry and clear, symbols and officers' names, St. Louis, 1909 ....**$300**

GAME PLATES

History: Game plates, popular between 1870 and 1915, are specially decorated plates used to serve fish and game. Sets originally included a platter, serving plates, and a sauce or gravy boat. Many sets have been divided. Today, individual plates are often used as wall hangings.

Birds

Plate

Each hand painted with gold trim, light and dark gray corners, center with game birds, gold outlines, mauve circular mark "Carlsbad Mark & Gutherz," price for 11-pc set, 8" sq **$700**

Hp, set of 12 with different center scene of shore birds in natural setting, apple green edge, printed gold scrolled rim dec, artist sgd "B. Albert," Theodore Haviland & Co., France, early 20th C, 9-1/4" d **$865**

Duck, pastel pink, blue, and cream ground, duck flying up from water, yellow flowers and grasses, sgd "Laury," marked "Limoges," not pierced for hanging, 9-1/2" d **$120**

Game bird and pheasant, heavy gold, scalloped emb rococo border, marked "Coronet Limoges, Bussilion," 13-1/4" d **$250**

Platter

Two handles, quail, hp gold trim, Limoges, 16" l **$150**

Flying grouse, scrolled gilt rim, hp, artist sgd "A. Brousselton," mkd "Limoges/Crown/Coronet/France," 18" d **$615**

Set

Fourteen pcs, 20-3/4" platter with strutting tom turkey, 9" gravy boat, twelve 10" d plates with different turkey designs, hp, artist sgd "Gasri," green "LDBC Hambeau Limoges" mark **$700**

Seven pcs, wild game birds, pastoral scene, molded edges, shell dec, Fazent Meheim, Bonn, Germany **$250**

Twelve pcs, 10-1/2" d plates, game birds in natural habitat, sgd "I. Bubedi" **$3,500**

Deer

Plate, buck and doe, forest scene, 9" d **$60**

Set, 13 pcs, platter, 12 plates, deer, bear, and game birds, yellow ground, scal-

Pair of blue glass mantel lusters decorated with white flowers, cut glass prisms, 10" h, **$225.**
Photo courtesy of Joy Luke Auctions.

loped border, "Haviland China," sgd "MC Haywood" **$3,200**

Fish

Plate

Bass, scalloped edge, gray-green trim, fern on side of fish, Limoges, 8" d **$65**

Colorful fish swimming on green shaded ground, scalloped border, gold trim, sgd "Lancy," "Bairritz, W. S. or S. W. Co. Limoges, France," pierced for hanging, 8-1/2" d **$50**

Platter

Bass on lure, sgd "RK Beck," 14" l **$125**

Hp, Charoone, Haviland, 23" l **$200**

Set

Seven pcs, platter, six serving plates, each with different fish dec, white ground, gold trim, Italian **$125**

Eight pcs, four plates, platter, sauce boat with attached plate, cov tureen, Rosenthal, 24" l **$425**

Eleven pcs, 10 plates, serving platter, sgd "Limoges" **$360**

Fifteen pcs, 12 9" plates, 24" platter, sauce boat with attached plate, cov tureen, hp, raised gold design edge, artist sgd, Limoges **$800**

GIRANDOLE AND MANTEL LUSTRES

History: A girandole is a very elaborate branched candleholder, often featuring cut glass prisms surrounding the mountings. A mantel lustre is a glass vase with attached cut glass prisms.

Girandoles and mantel lustres usually are found in pairs. It is not uncommon for girandoles to be part

Mantel lusters, pink cased glass, handpainted floral panel, gilt accents, large hanging prisms, gilt wear, flakes on rim, 14-1/4" h, **$650.**
Photo courtesy of Alderfer Auction Co.

of a large garniture set. Girandoles and mantel lustres achieved their greatest popularity in the last half of the 19th century both in the United States and Europe.

Girandoles

Brass, three songbirds on flowering vine, three socket top, cut glass prisms, white alabaster base, worn gilding, old patina, few flakes, 17-1/4" w, 16-1/2" w **$115**

Cast brass, East Indian man dressed in feathered turban, fancy robes, scimitar hanging from chain, white marble base, faceted prisms with cut stars and flowers, minor edge flakes, roughness to prisms, price for pr, 15" h **$115**

Cast brass, high relief rococo scrolling and vintage detail, applied flowers on base, columns shaped like large leaves about to burst into blossom, three sockets each with clear cut glass prisms, orig gilding and bobeches, soldered restorations on branches, price for pr, 18" h, 15" w **$990**

Longwy, Aesthetic Movement, two-light, rect, central beveled mirror plate, surrounded by Islamic-inspired tiles in brass frame, scrolled candle arm with two acorn-shaped nozzles, removable bobeches, third quarter 19th C, 9-7/8" w, 17" h **$750**

Pr candlesticks, center 15-1/4" h three-light candelabra, emerald green cut glass prisms, turned and tapered brass columns, white marble bases, worn gilding, 12" h **$575**

Mantel garnitures

Bronze and crystal, three-light candelabra, stylized lyre form garniture hung with cut and pressed glass prisms, above three scrolled

Teapot, sloping sides, gooseneck spout, original hinged lid and interior pouring strainer, gray and white, $125.

Wash basin, aqua and white speckle, stamp mark "Elite Austria Reg. No. (illegible) 26," chip, $45.

Dish pan, round, deep sides, two handles, green and white spatter, $40.

candle arms, trefoil base, price for pr, 20-5/8" h................................**$980**

Three cov baluster jars and two vases, Hundred Antiques dec, in famille rosé enamels, China, price for five-pc set, 19th C, 14" h, 12" h........................**$2,185**

Urn form, two short scroll handles, incised on side with Japonesque florals in silver and gold coloration, trumpet foot further dec with Japonesque patterning and insects, sq section marble base, inset to front with mixed metal-style patinated plaque depicting drummer and dancer, Aesthetic Movement, price for pr, third quarter 19th C, 10-1/4" h............**$690**

Mantel lustres

Blown translucent clambroth glass, gauffered rim, rough pontil, seven prisms, price for pr, late 19th C, 10-3/4" h, 5-3/8" d rim................**$150**

Cranberry glass, white enamel foliage dec rims, gilt trim, vining floral dec, cut faceted prisms, flakes and roughness to prisms, price for pr, 10" h................................**$615**

Overlay glass, white cut to pink, enamel flowers, gilt accents, cut glass prisms, Bohemian, price for pr, 9" h
................................**$425**

Ruby glass, overlay and enameled plaques, fluted, heavy gilt, cut glass prisms, France, price for pr, 19th C, 12" h................................**$2,645**

GRANITEWARE

History: Graniteware is the name commonly given to enamel-coated iron or steel kitchenware.

The first graniteware was made in Germany in the 1830s. Graniteware

was not produced in the United States until the 1860s. At the start of World War I, when European companies turned to manufacturing war weapons, American producers took over the market.

Gray and white were the most common graniteware colors, although each company made its own special color in shades of blue, green, brown, violet, cream, or red.

Older graniteware is heavier than the new. Pieces with cast-iron handles date between 1870 to 1890; wood handles between 1900 to 1910. Other dating clues are seams, wooden knobs, and tin lids.

Reproduction Alert. Graniteware still is manufactured in many of the traditional forms and colors.

Additional Resources:

Warman's® Americana & Collectibles, 11th Ed., by Ellen T. Schroy, ed., Krause Publications, Iola, WI.

Berry pail, cov, cobalt blue and white mottled, 7" d, 4-3/4" h................**$65**

Bowl, green and white, 11-3/4" d, 3-3/4" h................................**$50**

Cake pan, robin's egg blue and white marbleized, 7-1/2" d................**$45**

Coffeepot, gray, tin handle, spout and lid, 10" h................................**$525**

Colander, light blue, pedestal base, 12" d................................**$45**

Cookie sheet, mottled blue and white
................................**$225**

Cup, blue and white medium swirl, black trim and handle, 2-3/4" h
................................**$50**

Frying pan, blue and white mottled, white int., 10-1/4" d................**$135**

Funnel, cobalt blue and white marbleized, large................................**$50**

Grater, medium blue................**$115**

Kettle, cov, gray mottled, 9" h, 11-1/2" d................................**$50**

Measure, one cup, gray................**$45**

Mixing bowls, red and white, nested set of four, 1930s................**$155**

Muffin pan, blue and white mottled, eight cups................................**$250**

Pie pan, cobalt blue and white marbleized, 6" d................................**$25**

Pitcher, gray, ice lip, 11" h............**$110**

Roaster, emerald green swirl, large
................................**$250**

Skimmer, gray mottled, 10" l........**$25**

Teapot, enameled dec, small chips, 9-1/2" w, 5" h................................**$525**

Tube pan, octagonal, gray mottled
................................**$45**

Utensil rack, shaded orange, gray bowls, matching ladle, skimmer, and tasting spoon, 14-1/2" w, 22" h
................................**$400**

Wash basin, blue and white swirl, Blue Diamond Ware, 11-3/4" d............**$150**

Wash basin, brown and white speckle, pierced for hanging, chips, **$55.**

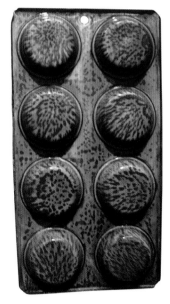

Muffin pan, eight muffins, gray and white, pierced to hang, **$85.**

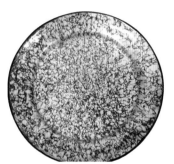

Dinner plate, dark blue and white spatter, **$30.**

Cup, gray, some rust, **$8.**

Roaster, three pieces, oval, green and white spatter, **$45.**

Roaster, covered, long, oval, gray speckled, **$90.**
Photo courtesy of Dotta Auction Co., Inc.

Shovel, solid white, some usage wear, wooden handle missing, **$35.**

Assorted blue spatter pieces, ranging from light blue to cobalt blue, from left: lid, two serving spoons, **$15 each;** *small open berry pail, white interior, wooden bail handle,* **$75;** *small mixing bowl,* **$20;** *coffee boiler,* **$85;** *inverted dish pan,* **$35;** *medium size colander,* **$65;** *inverted rectangular roaster with self handle,* **$30;** *inverted medium size dish pan,* **$25;** *inverted shallow pan,* **$25.**

Young broomed witch slot and tab dual-sided cardboard candy container, USA, 1950s, 5-1/2" h x 2-1/2" w x 5" l, **$95.**

HALLOWEEN

History: There are differing schools of thought as to how the origin of our Halloween celebrations came to be. There are those who believe that it got its beginning thousands of years ago from the beliefs of the Celts as well as those of their religious leaders, the Druids. Whatever the actual antecedents were are relatively unimportant. What is important is that Halloween became a key stop on the USA holiday circuit beginning in the first decade of the 1900s. From that time through the present day Halloween has been celebrated as a simple holiday free from any religious connotation. The Halloween parties held through the early 1930s were almost always for adults. The almost exclusively child-centric Halloween party familiar to us today really didn't get going until the middle 1930s. Trick-or-Treating, as we know it, did not come to the fore across wide swaths of the United States until the 1930s so until then, house parties were the norm. To help the party-giver, publications like the Halloween Bogie Books from the Dennison Company of Framingham, MA, were superb decorating guides containing tips on themes, games, menus and costumes easily fashioned from the firm's many crepe pa-

per creations. The Beistle Company of Shippensburg, PA was also a key contributor to the look of those early Halloween parties with an abundant array of diecuts, lanterns, table-top decorations, hats and fortune telling/stunt games just to name a few genres. The Gibson Art Company of Cincinnati, OH was also an important player in the Halloween decorations business with items more typically humorous in design than its two main competitors.

As the years passed, Halloween's popularity grew and with it came an artistic outpouring of seasonal items from the hands of some very talented artists, both domestically and from Germany. (Fewer items, typically of lesser quality, came from Japan.) Tin noisemakers like horns, clickers, shakers and tambourines, invitations, tally and place cards, seals, as well as other paper goods like tablecloths, napkins, doilies, etc. were just some of the wondrous bounty of items available to the determined party-giver.

The current market for items made pre-1940 is very strong, something that has been true since the early 1990s. Some genres wax and wane but the overall trend line for values has consistently pointed north since that time. Reproductions of certain

genres like composition candy containers and pressed paper or pulp lanterns have caused concerns in the hobby leading to suppression in the rate of growth in terms of value, although this has lessened somewhat since 2004. Hard plastic items from the 1950s, tin noisemakers, except for tambourines and output from the Bugle Toy Company, and common German diecuts have been market laggards. Early Beistle party sets, table-top decorations and diecuts as well as early Dennison boxed goods have been market leaders.

Many collectors of vintage Halloween pieces wax nostalgic about the 1980s and early 1990s when it was possible to buy vintage Halloween memorabilia at prices quite low compared to today's market. With the advent of the on-line auction venues, collectors now have the opportunity to peruse hundreds of items at a single sitting. Now you can bid on items of interest offered by a seller in a remote location while you're sitting at your home computer. There is a downside: where once you had the chance of acquiring a choice item and just had the locals to contend with, you now have collectors from all over the globe able to get in on the action.

Adviser: Mark B. Ledenbach

Additional Resources:

Vintage Halloween Collectibles, 2nd Ed., by Mark B. Ledenbach, Krause Publications, Iola, WI.

Bogie book, Dennison
    1912 .... **$850**
    1914 .... **$650**
    1922 .... **$125**
Candy container, champagne bucket shape, bottom slides out to place

candy inside bucket, German, some wear, 3-1/4" h..........................**$1,100**

Jol man, sack candy container, Fibro Toy, cardboard, c1950s, 6-1/2" h, 6" w...**$200**

Celluloid black cat rattle holding sack and bird cage, Japan, 1920s, 7" h **$800**

Jack-o-lantern Man, rattle Viscoloid, excellent condition, 4" h **$700**

Ceramic, Dept. 56 Snow Village, Halloween Haunted Mansion, 1998, green roof, MIB **$325**

Cymbals, tin litho, price for 2-piece set, 1920s, 5-1/2" d **$600**

Diecut (paper)

Cat in candle, Dennison, near mint, c1920, 6" h **$125**

Figurines, German, boxed set of eight, orig box, 3-1/4" h **$1,530**

Flying witch, Dennison, few creases, minor surface wear **$65**

Halloween Wumpus, devil lightning monster, Beistle, ...**$600**

Lightning Wampus, aka The Halloween Devil, Beistle, c1931, 30" h **$575**

Puss in Boots, German, early 1930s, 8-3/4" h **$1,000**

Tiara with devil face, 1920s, Germany, 5" h, 9-1/2" w **$600**

Witch, bat-winged, Beistle, c1925, 18" x 18-1/2" open **$245**

Game

"I'm a Dumbskull" game w/envelope, Beistle, 1920s **$225**

"Ring the Belle," ring toss game, Gibson Art Company, 16" h...........**$600**

"Wheel Witch Fortune," w/fortune card, Beistle, 9" h.....................**$215**

"Pick A Pumpkin" fortune game, litho paper, witch, brownie & black cat in center, 12 Pumpkin ring perimeter, Germany made for Beistle, c1920s **$2,000**

Katzy Party, Selchow, 1920s........**$105**

Halloween apron, crepe paper, decorated with witches, bats, jack-o-lanterns, and black cats, c1925, 22" h **$120**

Halloween party book, orange pages, Beistle, c1923..................**$375**

Jack-O-Lantern, pulp, F. N. Burt, 1940s...**$195**

Jack-O-Lantern, tin, horn nose with original wire bale..........................**$75**

Lantern, printed on cardboard, transparent eye, nose and mouth with honeycomb tissue folding sides, Beistle,

fitted for electric or candle light, some wear, c1931, 12" d **$800**

Lantern, Tommy Whiskers cat face Art Deco lantern, Beistle, c1938, 11" x 11-1/4"....................................**$200**

Nodder, composition, German, c1920, 8-1/2" h.....................................**$1,500**

Paper lantern, black cat head, accordion paper, heavy composition, orig wire handle, metal candleholder, German, early 1900s....................**$1,175**

Parade jack-o-lantern, tin, c1908, 7" d...**$1,500**

Pennant shaped devil face on top diecut, German, c1920s, 15-1/2" **$650**

Plastic candy container, witch rocket, pumpkin-shaped wheels, 1950s, 5-1/2" l, 4" h **$375**

Plastic pirate drummer, wheels, 1950s, 7-1/2" h............................**$500**

Plastic pirate auto with witch, Rosen/Tico...................................**$300**

Roly poly, witch and broom, celluloid, c1930, 3-1/2" h.........................**$775**

Teapot with lid, porcelain, Germany, c1915, 4" h **$650**

Sugar bowl with lid, porcelain, Germany, c1915, 2-1/2" h.............. **$300**

Tambourine, witch on goose flying over city, Chein, c1920s, 7" d......**$250**

HATPINS AND HATPIN HOLDERS

History: When oversized hats were in vogue, around 1850, hatpins became popular. Designers used a variety of materials to decorate the pin ends, including china, crystal, enamel, gem stones, precious metals, and shells. Decorative subjects ranged from commemorative designs to insects.

Hatpin holders, generally placed on a dresser, are porcelain containers that were designed specifically to hold these pins. The holders were produced by major manufacturers, among which were Meissen, Nippon, R. S. Germany, R. S. Prussia, and Wedgwood.

Hatpin
Brass

Child with flowing hair, flanked by sunflowers, Victorian, orig finish, 1-1/2" x 1-3/4", 9" l pin **$125**

Dual-sided cardboard black cat face lantern with slot and tab construction and original inserts, other side shows an angry cat face, USA, 1950s, 7-1/2" h x 3-1/4" w x 6-1/2" l, **$65.**

Composition jack-o-lantern headed man candy container (opens at neck) Germany late 1920s, 4-3/4" h, **$375.**
From the collection of Theresa Roberts.

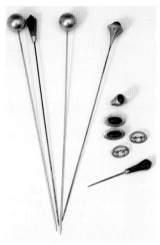

Hatpins, five gold 20mm hat pins; pair of gold ball topped pins by Carter & Gough; citrine cabochon, two jade topped pins by Sloan with two pairs of handy pins, and gypsy mount carnelian ring in celluloid box, price for lot as shown, **$275.**

Photo courtesy of David Rago Auctions, Inc.

Horn, snuff box, rectangular, hinged lid and oval sides, held together with white metal straps and brass nails, marked "L'Auvergnate; Marque Deposee, R.L.," French, late 19th century, 3-1/2" x 1-7/8" x 7/8", **$175.**

Photo courtesy of Gamal Amer.

Military button, 2" d, 9-1/2" l pin **$125**

Oxidized, four citrine-colored stones in each of four panels, citrine-colored stones on 1/2" bezel, 2-1/4" l **$315**

Enamel, 14k yg, hinged American flag, 5-1/2" l **$275**

Hand-painted china, violets, gold trim **$35**

Glass, 2" l faceted amber glass bead, 13-1/4" l japanned shaft **$125**

Ivory, ball shape, carved design **$65**

Jet, 1-1/4" elongated oval knobby bead, 8" l pin **$200**

Metal, round disk, Art-Nouveau style lady with flowing hair, 9-1/4" l ... **$125**

Satsuma, Geisha Girl dec **$245**

Sterling silver

Arts & Crafts motif of ivy leaf in circle, Charles Horner, hallmarks for Chester, England, 1911, 1-1/4" d, 11" l pin **$195**

Elongated tear shape, marked "Horner," 6-1/2" l **$95**

Hatpin holder

Belleek, relief pink and maroon floral dec, green leaves, gold top, marked "Willets Belleek," dated 1911, 5-1/4" h **$125**

Limoges, grapes, pink roses, matte finish, artist sgd **$60**

Nippon, hp blue daisy flowers, marked "E. O. China," 4-7/8" d **$185**

Royal Bayreuth, tapestry, portrait of lady wearing hat, blue mark **$575**

R. S. Germany, pink roses, green foliage, pink luster trim, 4-1/2" d ... **$315**

R. S. Prussia, peach flowers, green foliage, 7" h, 3" d **$180**

HORN

History: For centuries, horns from animals have been used for various items, e.g., drinking cups, spoons, powder horns, and small dishes. Some pieces of horn have designs scratched in them. Around 1880, furniture made from the horns of Texas longhorn steers was popular in Texas and the southwestern United States.

Ale set, silver plate-mounted cov 9-3/4" h jug, two 5-1/2" h beakers, fitted 17-3/4" l x 15" h plated frame with twisted gallery and upright handle, tripartite circular base with Greek Key border, raised on stepped block feet, English, early 20th C **$850**

Arm chair, steer horn, leather upholstered seat, four pairs of matched horns form base, American, 20th C **$575**

Cane

Dark horn handle, carved as perched eagle, clear and black glass eyes, lighter horn beak, 2/3" woven silver thread collar, blond Malacca shaft, 1-1/2" horn ferrule, Continental, c1895, 35" l, 1-3/4" w, 4" h **$490**

Staghorn "L"-shaped handle, high relief carved hunting scene, detailed family crest on top round portion, scene spirals around han-

dle starting at bottom continuing to top, medieval hunt with dogs, men with spears and lances pursing two bears, thin coin silver spacer, Malacca shaft with round silver eyelets, 2-1/4" polished staghorn ferrule, attributed to Germany, c1880, 33-3/4" l, 4" w x 5-1/4" h **$2,800**

Wild boar's tusk handle, pointed silver cap with leaf dec, marked "sterling" on one end, other end with sq cap inscribed "Judge Henry Bank Jr. from KeoKuK Bar Feb. 15, 1919," 1-1/8" dec silver collar, dark briarwood shaft, 1-1/4" white metal and iron ferrule, 34-1/8" l, 7-1/2" l **$1,100**

Case, two part, both sides with tiger underneath pine tree, top with ideogram within circle, written characters on inside flange, cord attached to lower part passes through hole in cover, Korea, cracking, some lifting of horn, 19th C, 6-1/8" l, 2-3/4" h **$150**

Cup, rhinoceros, carved as magnolia flower, base of branch and leaves, carved wood stand, losses, 18th C or earlier, 5" h **$1,100**

Furniture suite, American, 48" w x 25" d x 44" h loveseat, one 38" w x 24" d x 44" h chair, one 32" w x 28" d x 35" h chair, each upholstered, mounted with animal horns, wooden legs, brass casters, from William Wrigley residence, Chicago, IL, late 19th C **$6,375**

Snuff box, rect, carved PA motifs, floral dec, red paint on hinged lid, birds carved on sides, star on bottom, 2" l, 2-3/4" w, 3/4" h **$450**

Polychrome pot, Acoma, red, black and orange on cream ground with crosshatching, diamond, floral, and checkerboard decoration, red internal rim, c1890-1900, **$9,775.**
Photo courtesy of Pook & Pook, Inc.

San Ildefonso vase, black, matte glaze, dec geometric band, very good condition, signed "Desideria San Ildefonso," 6-1/2", **$705.**
Photo courtesy of David Rago Auctions, Inc.

Moccasins, fully beaded, Central Plains, Lakota, beaded bifurcated tongues, multicolored geometric devices using glass and faceted brass seed beads on light blue background, minor bead loss, circa late 19th century, 9-1/2" l, **$2,937.**
Photo courtesy of Skinner, Inc.

INDIAN ARTIFACTS, AMERICAN

History: During the historic period, there were approximately 350 Indian tribes grouped into the following regions: Eskimo, Northeast and Woodland, Northwest Coast, Plains, and West and Southwest.

American Indian artifacts are quite popular. Currently, the market is stable following a rapid increase in prices during the 1970s.

Additional Resources:

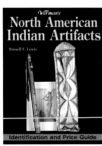

Warman's® North American Indian Artifacts, by Russell E. Lewis, Krause Publications, Iola, WI.

Bag

Northern Plains, Cree, buffalo hide, red cloth and remnant pony beaded edging, linear multicolored beaded pattern on front, 1870s, 6" l, damage **$530**

Plateau, pictorial, beaded cloth, flat, multicolored American eagle with flags, two arrow-pierced hearts, five-point start, bottle green ground, first quarter 20th C, 14" x 13", insect damage to cloth **$1,880**

Bandolier bag, Great Lakes, Ojibwa, beaded cloth, multicolored floral devices, white ground, loom-woven geometric tabs with red wool hang from bottom, c1900, 18" w, 20" l **$1,100**

Belt, Plains, buffalo rawhide, one side covered with flat brass Ute buttons, secured with long hide laces, insect damage to underside, late 19th C, 3-3/4" w, 31" l **$530**

Bird, Southwest, painted pottery, figural, stylized black on cream dec, red base, c1900, 8-1/4" l, crack **$590**

Blanket strip, beaded hide

Central Plains, dark blue Maltese cross and geometric devices on white ground, last quarter 19th C, 61-1/2" l **$3,300**

Plains, three large roundels, abstract bear paw devices, yellow, white center red, and dark translucent blue on medium blue ground, thread and sinew sewn, 1870s, 7-3/4" w, 54" l, bead loss **$15,275**

Bow, wood

Northern California, gracefully shaped, back painted with red and black geometric devices, late 19th C, 47" l **$1,175**

Southern Plains, Comanche, carved, long curved form, use patina, old tag reads "Comanche Indian Div. Picked up on battlefield 1845," first half 19th C, 58" l **$2,000**

Bow case and quiver

Southern Plains, Apache, hide quiver with wood support, remnant red trade cloth, both with fringe and

Totem, Haida, carved argillite, fish, man with wide and dentated mouth surmounting raven base, some restoration, 20th century, 9" h, **$1,500.**
Photo courtesy of David Rago Auctions, Inc.

perforated dec, sinew-backed bow with orig sinew string, last quarter 19th C, 41" l case, 42" l bow **$3,525**

Southern Plains, probably Comanche, horse hide, fringed at strap ends and ends of both cases, harness leather awl case dec with white seed beads, bone-handled awl, unique wood and buffalo hide arrow extractor, orig Osage orange wood bow with sinew string, inside of strap end written "Paint Creek Texas, March 7, 1868," mid 19th C, dark use patina, 52" l, 47" l bow, old repairs **$9,990**

Bow guard, Southwest, Navajo, silver, turquoise, unusual shape, stamp and repousse work, nine variously shaped turquoise stones, two with serrated bezels, commercial leather wrist strap, first quarter 20th C, 5" l **$3,175**

Bowl, carved wood, Northwest Coast, carved wood, abstract seal form, mother-of-pearl eyes, white glass

bead inlays, early 20th C, 8-1/2" l **$560**

Bowl, painted pottery

Mimbres, int. with red-brown zigzag, hatching, and geometric devices, cream-colored slip, hole, cracks, c950-1150 A.D., 12" d, 4-1/2" h **$1,300**

Southwest, Hopi, Fannie Nampeyo, seed jar form, black and red geometric devices, cream-orange slip ground, 9" d, 5-1/2" h **$2,585**

Southwest, Hopi, int. with abstract katchina, first half 20th C, 7-1/2" d, 2-1/4" h **$1,175**

Southwest, Zuni, flared form, black prehistoric-looking patterns on white slip, possibly made as a flower pot, hole in bottom, early 20th C, 5-3/4" d, 5" h **$250**

Bowl, redware, Southwest, Carmelita Dunlap, bulbous, feather design, sgd "Carmelita Dunlap," San Ildefonso Pueblo, surface marks, third quarter 20th C **$470**

Bracelet, Southwest, Zuni, silver and turquoise, cluster form, nineteen oval

stone settings, orig Pohndorf, Denver Colorado, box, 20th C, 3" l.........**$825**

Candleholder, Plains, Dakota, red pipestone, human head and quadruped, made in two pcs three lead inlays, c1900, 9" h **$825**

Canteen, Southwest, Cochiti, painted pottery, two lugs, black rain clouds, cream colore slip, late 19th C, 5-1/2" d **$560**

Courting flute, Plains, two pcs of cedar hollowed out and lashed together with buffalo hide wrappings, elk form flute block, incised detail, six finger holes, late 19th C, 25" l **$2,880**

Cradle board

Central Plains, Cheyenne, buffalo hide, painted parfleche liner, canvas backing, sack beaded with multicolored geometric devices on white ground, large trade bead and hawk bell drops, red pigment and brass tack dec on boards, last quarter 19th c, 44-1/2" h **$88,125**

Western, Ute, Comanche-style boards stained yellow on front, red on back, unusual beaded and stained hide attachments at tips, yellow stained cloth sac with beaded and fringed detail, metal concha, remnant Ute-style wicker hood, damage, last quarter 19th C, 29" h **$4,410**

Crook knife, Northeast, carved wood handle, incised grid and three-leaf clovers, finial with whimsical carved face, diamond-shaped brass pc attached, 9" l **$1,175**

Cuffs, pr, Plateau, cloth lined, beaded on one side with multicolored floral devices on light blue ground, long fringe, early 20th C, 9-1/2" l **$530**

Dagger, Northwest Coast, Tlingit, double tapered metal blades, central flute, copper cov grip with braided fiber wrapping, long hide wrist strap, includes stand, mid 19th C, 24" l **9,990**

Dance board, Southwest, Katcina, rect cottonwood form, painted on one side with box and border devices, six circular forms lashed with hide and projecting from sides, painted cross and four-color wedge shapes, cloth waist ties, late 19th/early 20th C, 15-1/2" w, 19" h.....................**$15,275**

Dance shield, Central Plains, Lakota, painted muslin, stretched over wood hoop, painted hawk framed by crescent moons and dash marks, late 19th C, 17" d, provenance: collect-

Women's dress, beaded hide, Southern Plains, Cheyenne, yellow stained yoke with red pigment details, multicolored geometric beaded detail, bottom tabs with three rows of beaded and tin cone decoration, circa third quarter 19th century, 56" l, **$47,000.**
Photo courtesy of Skinner, Inc.

ed by Henry W. Fischer, Presbyterian minister in South Dakota circuit, 1906-12, descended in family..**$7,650**

Doll

Southwest, Apache, hide, stylized form, hide ears, harness leather moccasin shoes, blue and black beaded detail, white cross on chest, large green bead for nose, minor bead loss, last quarter 19th C, 12-1/2" l **$2,585**

Southwest, Apache, female, rect wood form, thread-wrapped head, commercial leather hair bow at back of head, brass pinheads dec, elaborate two pc dress with long fringe, tin cone, traces of yellow, green, and red pigment, multicolored pony beads at yoke, "cactus kicker" high-top tin cone and moccasins with commercial leather soles, single brass tack on toe, beaded eardrops and necklace, last third 19th C, 14" h **$14,100**

Dough bowl, Southwest, San Ildefonso, polychrome pottery, inside and outside painted with red and black foliate devices, cream colored slip, first half 20th C, 15" d, 7" h **$800**

Drawing, Inuit, George Ahgupuk, hide, hunting and village scenes, sgd lower right corner, 20th C, framed, 31" x 13-1/2" image size **$9,400**

Dress, girl's

Central Plains, thick elk hide, yoke with beaded strips, multicolored cross and eight-point star devices of glass and metallic seed beads, c1900, 33" l, bottom cut off and then reattached, hide loss **$1,880**

Northern Plains, hide, open at sides, multiple rows of carved bone simulated elk teeth on both sides, three lanes of multicolored geometric beadwork, first quarter 20th C, 28" l **$3,525**

Dress, woman's, Southern Plains, Cheyenne, hide, yoke stained yellow with red pigment details, multicolored geometric beaded detail, bottom tabs with three rows of beaded and tin cone dec, profusely fringed in various lengths, third quarter 19th C, 56" l..**$47,000**

Dress yoke, girl's, Northern Plains, Yankton Sioux, beaded buffalo hide, fringed at arm openings, beaded on both sides, yellow, white center red, and dark blue geometric devices on medium blue ground, custom stand, 1870s, 17" l...............................**$9,400**

Drum, Plains, commercial wood drum body, two drum heads, painted image of bird and four dots framed by concentric circles, damage to hide, late 19th C, 24" d, 12" w **$2,350**

Drum beater, Plains, hide-covered handle and head, polychrome plaited quill work, long drop with multicolored geometric quill work, bottom fringe, quill loss, c1900, 20" l **$765**

Hair ornament, Central Plains, rawhide cross, multicolored geometric beadwork, rect red trade cloth panel with four brass conchas, ribbons, and hair attachments, late 19th C, 19" l ....**$715.**

Halibut hook, Northwest Coast, carved cedar, composite avian and octopus form, cedar bark wrappings, 19th C, 11" l **$1,100**

Holster, Southern Plains, Kiowa, commercial leather form, two beaded hide tabs with tin cones from bottom, front beaded with multicolored geometric and single thunderbird device on medium blue ground, minor bead loss, early 20th C, 14-1/2" l including tabs **$9,990**

Jar, Southwest, Santa Clara, Blackware, concave bottom, bulging mid-section, long flaring neck, slightly scalloped rim, crack, surface wear, chips, early 20th C, 12" d, 11" h..................**$1,410**

Katchina, polychrome carved wood

Southwest, Hopi, cottonwood form, large case mask, painted clothing, wood loss, early 20th C, 11-1/2" h **$3,100**

Southwest, Hopi, flat cottonwood form of butterfly maiden, Palhik Mana, missing part of tablita, late 19th C, 6-3/4" h **$3,410**

Knife case, Northern Plains, Cree, beaded hide, cloth lined soft form, beaded on front with striped and cross devices, tin cone danglers and bottom fringe, late 19th C, 9" l excluding fringe......................................**$950**

Knife sheath, Northern Plains, Crow, buffalo hide panel at top, cutout belt slot at side, top panel and single row down side with multicolored geometric device on pink ground, seed, real, and pony beads, fifteen remaining brass tacks, traces of red pigment, third quarter 19th C, 10-3/4" l **$14,100**

Leggings, boy's, Southern Plains, Kiowa, beaded hide, stained yellow, edge beading on side tabs and along cuffs, fringed at bottom halves and

Pipe bowl, inlaid stone, Eastern Plains, gray-brown, short prow, locomotive-style bowl, central silver band, geometric devises, two buffalo tracks on bowl, circa second quarter 19th century, 5-1/4", **$1,175.**
Photo courtesy of Skinner, Inc.

Pipe, wood and stone, Plains, long wooden stem, twisted and grooved, red pigment traces, red pipestone T-bowl, circa late 19th century, 31" l, **$499.**
Photo courtesy of Skinner, Inc.

Vision quest amulet, painted rawhide, Southern Plains or Ute, circular form, sun, moon, and human face likeness, multicolored elk on rev, yellow twisted fringe, brass beads, and two shells hang from bottom, includes stand, collected in 1895, disc is 3-3/4" d, **$4,700.**
Photo courtesy of Skinner, Inc.

Moccasins, beaded, Southern Plains, Cheyenne-Arapaho, hard sole forms partially beaded with multicolored checkered pattern, blue pigment down vamp, tag "Cheyenne-Arapaho near North Canadian River OKLA," late 19th century, 10-1/2", $528.
Photo courtesy of Skinner, Inc.

Pipe bag, beaded, Northern Plains, Cree, four edge-beaded tabs, beaded panel with floral devices, bottom fringe, circa late 19th century, 17" l, $530.
Photo courtesy of Skinner, Inc.

bottoms, multicolored brick-stitch tubes with hawk bell attachment hung from tab ends, c1900, 26" l **$1,830**

Leggings, man's, Southern Plains, Cheyenne, beaded hide, stained yellow and green, short fringe along side flaps and bottoms, partially beaded on both sides of flaps and edges, concentric circles, dragonflies, and lightning border, navy blue, white center red, and white seed beads, last quarter 19th C, 32" l **$3,525**

Leggings, woman's, Plains, Cheyenne, beaded hide, yellow stained uppers, panels with multicolored geometrid devices on white ground, some cut beads, last quarter 19th C, 22-1/2" l **$1,650**

Log caddy, Northeast, Penobscot, rect birch bark side panels dec with foliate and animal images, handle broken, damage, early 20th C, 14-1/2" w, 22" l, 20" h **$7,650**

Martingale, Northern Plains, Crow, beaded hide, red cloth insets, beaded Crow multicolored geometric devices, partially edged with large milky white beads, large bells, bugle beads on bottom, c1900, 33" l, cloth loss **$5,300**

Mask

Northwest Coast, forehead, carved polychrome wood, bird with articulated lower beak, remnant cedar bark head covering, second quarter 20th C, 18" l **$3,100**

Northwest Coast, Kwakiutl, painted hollow cedar form, pierced at mouth and eyes, deep stylized carving, human and avian features, commercial pigments, early 20th C, 10-1/2" h **$17,625**

Maul, Central Plains, Lakota, stone and wood, buffalo rawhide wrapped handle with traces of pigment, 19th C, 11" l **$590**

Mirror bag

Northern Plains, Crow, beaded hide, rect, Crow geometric designs on both sides and strap, bottom fringe, last quarter 19th C, 14" l with fringe, bead loss..................................**$3,100**

Southern Plains, Kiowa, beaded commercial leather, curved sides, beaded on both sides in dark blue, Kiowa blue, white, and Kiowa wine red geometric devices, flap with hide-fringe, commercial leather fringe on bottom, third quarter 19th C, 15-1/2" l

including fringe, some bead loss **$9,400**

Moccasins, child's, beaded hide

Central Plains, Cheyenne, hard soles, minimal multicolored geometric devices, single thunderbird on white ground, c1900, 7" l **$1,300**

Central Plains, Lakota, hard soles, multicolored geometric devices, cloth ankle wraps, c1900, 5-3/4" l **$1,650**

Central Plains, Lakota, hard soles, multicolored geometric devices on medium blue ground, c1900, 6" l **$350**

Moccasins, infant's, Southern Plains, Comanche, beaded hide, hard soles, partially beaded multicolored geometric devices, beaded tabs and cuff edges, minor bead loss, last quarter 19th C, 4-1/8" l **$765**

Moccasins, men's, beaded hide

Central plans, beaded and quilled, dark blue crosses on white border lane, vamp partially quilled, red trade cloth inset at tongues, quill loss, last quarter 19th C, 11" l **$1,175**

Central Plains, Lakota, hard sole, wine red and yellow geometric devices on light blue ground, c1900, 10" l **$450**

Northeast, Iroquois, beaded and quilled hide, soft sole forms, polychrome geometric quillwork on vamps, geometric beadwork on cloth edging on cuffs, second quarter 19th C, 8-1/2" l, quill loss **$11,750**

Plateau, soft soles, partially beaded with multicolored floral designs on vamps, muslin ankle coverings, late 19th C, 10" l **$950**

Southern Plains, Arapaho, hard soles, multicolored geometric, thunderbird, and dragonfly devices on white ground, some stiffness to hide, bead loss, provenance: descended in family of Capt Samuel S. Mathers, Special Land Agent for Dept of Interior, 1895, last quarter 19th C, 9-1/2" l **$1,530**

Southern Plains, Comanche, hard sole stained yellow, long heel fringe, partially beaded multicolored devices, row of tin cone danglers along vamps, c1900, 9-1/2" l **$3,175**

Southwest, Apache, painted high-top, soft forms, rawhide soles, red dots at top, red and blue details on foot, insect damage to soles, last quarter 19th C, 41" h **$2,000**

Southwest, probably Mescalero Apache, hard sole forms with red stained fringe from vamps and heels, bifurcated tongues and vamps with multicolored geometric beaded trim, traces of red and yellow pigments, c1870, 10-1/2" l **$7,050**

Necklace

Central Plains, woman's, bone hairpipes, rawhide spacers, gold painted and wood beads at neck, brass and glass beads at bottom, c1900, 33" l **$2,000**

Southwest, Zuni, squash blossom, silver and turquoise, twelve blossoms, one naja, all multiple stone settings, mid 20th C, 16" l **$470**

Olla

Santa Clara, Black Pottery, pumpkin shaped, polished, 20th C, 13" d, 14-1/2" h **$2,715**

Southwest, Acoma, bulbous, abstract black and cream devices, red ground, remnant green pigment, small hole, c1900, 10-1/2" d, 9" h **$1,410**

Southwest, Acoma, painted pottery, high shouldered, Zuni-like dec, large medallions with small birds, cross-hatched detail, early 20th C, 11" d, 10" h **$2,000**

Southwest Acoma, painted pottery, high shouldered, red-orange concave bottom and inner rim, black Zuni-like geometric and curvilinear devices, cream colored ground, 1920s, 11" d, 9" h **$2,585**

Southwest, Acoma, polychrome pottery, high shouldered, crimped rim, orange and black abstract curvilinear devices, cream colored slip, 1920s, 10-1/2" d, 8-1/2" h, rim crack **$2,115**

Southwest, Zia, polychrome pottery, red underbody, black and red-brown abstract foliate devices, four large birds, cream-colored slip, late 19th C, 12-1/2" d, 12" h, rim chip **$15,275**

Parfleche envelopes, pr, Plateau, polychrome, bold geometric red, green, blue, and orange

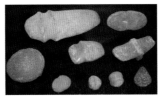

Stone implements: back, left to right: celt (axe head without grooves), attributed to eastern US, post 1500 A.D., 3-1/2" l, **$320;** *axe head, full groove, attributed to Ohio or Mid-West, believed to be pre-1500, 7" l, incomplete,* **$175;** *center row: mortar, volcanic stone, three feet, Columbia River region, 1,500 to 2,500 years old, 4" d, 2-1/2" h,* **$100;** *axe head, archaic, full groove, pecked hard stone, New England, pre-Columbian, 5" l,* **$100;** *axe head, probably ceremonial, eastern US, pre-Columbian, 5-3/4" l,* **$100;** *front row: axe head, full groove, Mid-West, 2000 to 2500 B.C.,* **$250;** *pestle or seed grinder, Mid-West, 2-7/8" h,* **$90;** *miniature mortar, 2-1/4" d,* **$65;** *full groove axe head, eastern US, probably New York, pre-historic, 1-3/4" l,* **$125.**
Photo courtesy of Alderfer Auction Co.

Saddlebags, double, beaded hide, Plains-style, Ute, fringed with two beaded panels, multicolored hourglass devices, white background, elk hide, c1870s, 90" l with fringe, **$8,225.**
Photo courtesy of Skinner, Inc.

Cradle, wood, hide and cloth, western, Ute(?), Comanche-style boards yellow on front, red on back, unusual beaded and stained hide attachments at tips, beaded and fringed cloth sack yellow stained, metal concha, remnant Ute-style wicker hood, circa last quarter 19th century, damage, 29" h, **$4,406.**
Photo courtesy of Skinner, Inc.

Pot, Santa Clara, gourd-shaped, signed by Marie Julian, small chip on top, 7-1/2" x 10", **$3,500.**
Photo courtesy of David Rago Auctions, Inc.

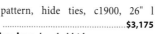

Bowl, Pueblo, San Ildefonso, shallow, black, attributed to Maria, c1920, 13-1/8" d, **$600.**
Photo courtesy of Pook & Pook, Inc.

Bowl, Navajo, geometric pattern, 13" d, 3" h, **$1,000.**
Photo courtesy of David Rago Auctions, Inc.

Hide Pipe Bag, beaded and quilled, Central Plains, Lakota, oversized bead panels, multicolored geometric and American flag designs, glass and metallic seed beads, multicolored quille rawhide slates and fringe, quill loss, circa late 19th century, 31" l (with fringe), **$4,000.**
Photo courtesy of Skinner, Inc.

pattern, hide ties, c1900, 26" l
....$3,175

Pipe bag, beaded hide
Central Plains, Lakota, beaded panels with multicolored glass and metallic seed beads in geometric designs on white ground, multicolored quill-wrapped rawhide slats, bottom fringe, tin cone and red horsehair danglers, late 19th C, 39" h
....$2,115

Central Plains, Lakota, both sides beaded with different multicolored geometric patterns on medium blue ground, polychrome quill-wrapped rawhide slats, bottom fringe, red ribbons on sides, first quarter 20th C, 25" l $450

Central Plains, Lakota, oversized beaded panels with multicolored geometric and American flag designs of glass and metallic seed beads, multicolored quill rawhide slats, bottom fringe, quill loss, late 19th C, 31" l
....$4,000

Northern Plains, Cree, four edge-beaded tabs at opening, beaded panel with floral devices, fringed bottom, late 19th C, 17" l
....$530

Pipe bowl
Eastern Plains, inlaid stone, gray-brown form, short prow, locomotive-style bowl, central silver band, inlaid lead geometric devices, two buffalo tracks on bowl, second quarter 19th C, 5-1/4" l
....$1,175

Great Lakes, Ojibwa, carved stone, probably carved on Manitoulin Island, sq shank with six small holes, tapering to horse head shaped prow, human head form bowl, white seed

bead eyes, one bead eye missing, mid-19th C, 6" l $17,625

Pipe stem, Great Lakes, wood, file branded, cutouts with remnant multicolored bird quill wrappings, damage, mid 19th C, 26-1/2" l $1,530

Pipe, wood and stone
Plains, red pipestone bowl in form of canoe prow, ash stem with spaced barrel-shaped forms, use patina, 26" l
....$2,235

Plains, red pipestone head, locomotive bowl, six lead ring inlays, slightly tapered ash stem, single carved round form, dark use patina, 28" l $2,200

Plate, Southwest, Blue Corn, San Ildefonso, painted pottery, cross device at center framed by feather pattern, sgd "Blue Corn San Ildefonso Pueblo," rim crack, 20th C, 14-3/4" d $2,115

Pouch, beaded hide
Apache, Mescalero, yellow stained hide front with multicolored geometric devices on a "pony trader" blue ground, commercial hide back, tin cone danglers from strap and bottom, late 19th C, 10-1/2" l including fringe
....$1,300

Plateau, pictorial, cloth backing, beaded on one side with standing man with bonnet waving at man and woman on horseback, multicolored figures on salt and pepper ground, second quarter 19th C, 19" l including fringe
....$950

Southern Plains, Comanche, brick-stitched U-shaped form, beaded on both sides with multicolored geometric devices on pink ground, late 19th C, 3-1/4" l $450

Southern Plains, tapered form, multicolored geometric devices on dark blue ground on flap and front, beaded border on back, tin cone danglers on bottom, last quarter 19th C, 7" l **$2,115**

Possible bags, pr

Central Plains, Lakota, buffalo hide, rect, beaded fronts, sides, and flap with multicolored geometric devices on white ground, red dyed tin cone danglers on sides and flap, minor bead loss, late 19th C, 21" l **$10,575**

Central Plains, Lakota, hide, rect, beaded front and sides with multicolored geometric devices on white ground, hide ties, late 19th C, 17" l **$2,820**

Northern Plains, Crow, buffalo hide, thick carrying strap, partially beaded front in classic Crow design, one bottom tab missing, split in side, last quarter 19th C, 16" l **$12,925**

Quirt, Northern Plains, Cree, brass tacks on carved rings, braided commercial leather strap, cloth wrist strap with multicolored floral devices, wool danglers, 1870s, use patina, 15" l wooden handle, bead loss **$5,875**

Rattle

Northern Plains, Crow, wood handle wrapped with red cloth and hide, hide head with red and yellow pigments, hide fringe, three hawk bell attachments, use patina, last quarter 19th C, 10-1/2" l **$1,000**

Northwest Coast, carved wood, raven, painted red and black, first half 20th C, 12-1/2" l, crack **$2,115**

Roach spreader, Plains, Pawnee, German silver, two feather sockets, crescent moon cutouts, stamped lightning devices, bottom engraved "Made by Caesar," signed "Chief Wolf Robe," 20th C, 7" l **$530**

Saddle and stirrups, woman's, Plateau, Flathead, rawhide covered wood frame with hide covering, large horns each with differing beaded drop, wooden stirrups with elaborate beaded cloth dec, old tag "Indian Woman's saddle made and ridden by Annie Martin Ronan Flathead Res. Mont.," bead loss, damage, late 19th C, 16" h, 26" l **$5,590**

Saddlebags, double

Plains-style, Ute, heavily fringed elk hide, two beaded panels, bold multicolored hourglass devices on white

ground, 1870s, 90" l including fringe **$8,225**

Southern Plains, Cheyenne, beaded buffalo hide, both ends with multicolored geometric details, red trade cloth inserts, long bottom fringe, beaded and cloth loss, minor stiffness to hide third quarter 19th C, 34" l folded **$5,875**

Southwest, Apache, buffalo hide, cutout designs backed with red commercial cloth, cutout tabs, tin cones, bottom fringe, black and white pony beaded detail, third quarter 19th C, 32" l folded, cloth loss **$14,100**

Shirt, man's, Southern Plains, probably Comanche, green dyed cloth, yellow stained hide fringe at collar, shoulders, elbows, cuffs, and bottom, hide strips beaded in simple barred pattern with white, white red, and medium blue pony beads, damage to cloth, second quarter 19th C, 30" l **$7,050**

Skull cracker club

Plains, Lakota, carved stone, oversized head carved as stylized animal head, short wood handle wrapped in green stained rawhide, late 19th C, 18" l **$590**

Plains, Sioux, round stone head with central ridge and knob at top to secure rawhide strap, trades of red pigment, rawhide wrapped wood handle with horsehair drop, old tag reads "Sioux, near White River S. Dak," last half 19th C, 27" l **$470**

Storage box, lidded, Northeast, Eastern Algonquin, birch bark, rect tapered form, avian and foliate devices dec, last quarter 19th C, 10" w, 13-1/2" l, 9-1/2" h, minor damage **$360**

Tomahawk, Plains, forged head with spike and three circular perforations, secured to handle with metal tack with human-like face, handle appears to be salvaged from early tribal artifact, cloth and bead drop, late 19th C, 17-1/4" l **$590**

Vest

Central Plains, Lakota, fully beaded on front and back, multicolored geometric and American flag devices on white ground, initials "S.S." beaded on upper back, red cloth trim, bead loss, old repairs, late 19th C, 20" l **$4,120**

Northern Plains, European-style, partially quilled on front with multicolored foliate devices, c1900, 22-1/2" l, quill loss **$1,200**

Vest and leggings, Central Plains, commercial cloth vest, front dec with cowrie shells, glass buttons, brass conchas, orange cloth back, blue wool leggings with beaded hide strips, multicolored geometric devices on white ground, first quarter 20th C, 25" l vest, 29" l leggings **$400**

Wedding jar, Southwest, Santa Clara, redware, double spout handled form, lobed mid-body, pedestal base, wear, early 20th C, 10" d, 12" h **$1,100**

INKWELLS

History: Most of the commonly found inkwells were produced in the United States or Europe between the early 1800s and the 1930s. The most popular materials were glass and pottery because these substances resisted the corrosive effects of ink.

Inkwells were a sign of the office or wealth of an individual. The common man tended to dip his ink directly from the bottle. The years between 1870 and 1920 represent the golden age of inkwells when elaborate designs were produced.

Brass, engraved peaked cornice-form backplate cut with central trefoil and flowers, cabochon bloodstone surrounded by four cabochon red stones, rect base with engraved border, central cut glass well flanked by turned pen supports, Gothic Revival style, England, third quarter 19th C, 9-1/4" l, 5-7/8" h **$250**

Bronze

Cast, Victorian, figural, greyhound dog chained to fencepost, two orig glass wells with covers, 12" l **$815**

Central lidded baluster form inkwell, round dish raised on quadripartite leaf-form bronze base, dark green enamel ground, stylized foliate bands with gilt accents, faux jewelling, French, late 19th C, 8" d, 5-1/2" h **$435**

Oval bronze tray, enameled in ivory and jewel dec, pen rest with urn-shaped inkwell, Viennese-style, mid-19th C, 7-1/4" l **$700**

Cast metal, figural, young girl and large dog, bronzed finish, Victorian, c1906, 12" l, 8-1/2" h **$750**

Copper, repoussé, inlays of men, woman, and monkeys, further

Inkwell, hinged bronze, embossed geometric swag pattern, complete with Davis glass liner, orig dark patina, Jessie Preston, stamped J.PRESTON CHICAGO, c1910, 3-1/4" x 5-1/2" x 5-1/2", **$2,115.**

Photo courtesy of David Rago Auctions, Inc.

Inkwell, George Ohr pottery, cottage shape, tile roof, two arches, swinging picket fence, green and amber speckled glaze, mkd "G. E. OHR BILOXI," short firing line to base, 3-1/2" x 6" x 4-1/4", **$5,500.**

Photo courtesy of David Rago Auctions, Inc.

Inkwell, bronze mounted "Sevres" porcelain, cylindrical, body enamel dec floral sprays, cobalt blue borders, gilt bronze reticulated neck, ram's head handles, leaf base, removable ink pot, lid has flat leaf finial, late 19th century, 4-3/4" h, **$470.**

Photo courtesy of Skinner, Inc.

Inkwell, bronze and glass, Tiffany Studios, 3-3/4" h, 6-1/2" w, **$430.**

Photo courtesy of Pook & Pook, Inc.

engraving and gilt, Japan, Meiji period (1868-1911), 3" d........ **$420**

Glass, crystal, square, four molded rococo feet, 3-1/4" w, 3-1/2" h **$175**

Gilt metal, bronze, French, rococo style, lion's head supporting pen rest above tray with two cov wells, dolphin feet, 14" l **$460**

Paperweight, multicolored concentric millefiori, base with 1848 date canes, Whitefriars, 6-1/4" h, 4-1/2" d.................................... **$175**

Pearlware, gilt highlights, imp "By F. Bridges, Phrenologist," and "EM" on base, England, very minor chips, gilt wear, 19th C, 5-1/2" h **$520**

Porcelain, formed as three crested birds, magenta, gilding, white band painted with polychrome flowers, insert and lid, underglaze blue crossed arrows, French, 5" h **$200**

Sterling silver, two bottles, matching pen tray, center sander, Victorian, hallmarked................... **$1,800**

Stoneware
Brushed cobalt blue on top, imp "C. Crolius. Manhattan-Wells, New York," few chips on base, 3-1/8" d, 1-5/8" h............... **$3,200**
Incised oval stamp "C. Crolius Stone Ware Manufacturer Manhatten Wells, New York," flat cylindrical form, incised edges, upper one enhanced with cobalt blue slip, center well surrounded by three pen holders, three lower edge chips, 3-1/2" d, 1-1/4" h **$2,990**

Wood, Matthew Bolton, Birmingham, rect, emb silver mounts,

Inkwell, bronze, wolf and bird dec, "Fables de La Fontaine," sgd "J. Moigniez," Jules Moigniez (French, 1835-1894), 5" h, 8" w, **$935.**

Photo courtesy of Pook & Pook, Inc.

gadroon and shell edge, two silver mounted cut glass inkwells in gadrooned holders, four scroll legs, paw feet, c1795, 14" l, 10" w **$1,725**

IRONS

History: Ironing devices have been used for many centuries, with the earliest references dating from 1100. Irons from the medieval, Renaissance, and early industrial eras can be found in Europe, but are rare. Fine engraved brass irons and hand-wrought irons predominated prior to 1850. After 1850, the iron underwent a series of rapid evolutionary changes.

Between 1850 and 1910, irons were heated in four ways: 1) a hot metal slug was inserted into the body, 2) a burning solid, e.g., coal or charcoal, was placed in the body, 3) a liquid or gas, e.g., alcohol, gasoline, or natural gas, was fed from an external tank and burned in the body, or 4) conduction heat, usually drawing heat from a stove top.

Electric irons are just beginning to find favor among iron collectors.

Additional Resources:

Warman's® Americana & Collectibles,

11th Ed., by Ellen T. Schroy, ed., Krause Publications, Iola, WI.

Advisers: David and Sue Irons.

Reproduction Alert. The highly detailed German charcoal iron known as "dragon chimney" is currently being reproduced in Europe.

There are more reproduction slug irons being hand crafted in Europe. They are well made, so look carefully for wear on handles, and inside parts.

Charcoal

Acme Carbon Iron, 1910 .... $125
Cummings & Bless, tall chimney, 1852 .... $110
Cutwork sides, wrought, French $350
Dragon chimney, highly detailed, German $450
Dutch Brass, cutwork sides $300
Eclipse, lift off top, 1903 .... $110
Improved Progress Iron, 1913 .... $250
Junior Carbon Iron, 1911 .... $200

Children's

Brass, ox tongue slug, 4" $180
Cap, oval, French, "WP," 3-1/2" $60
Charcoal, tall chimney, 3-1/2" $250
Cross Rib Handle, cast, 2-3/4" $30
Dover Sad Iron, No. 812, 4" $45
European Ox Tongue, all iron, 3" $110
Sensible No. 0, detachable handle, 4" $120
Sleeve, with rope handle, cast, 4-1/2" $50
Swan, all cast, 2" $125
Swan, all cast, 5" $450
Swan, original yellow paint with pin striping, 2-1/2" $300
The Gem No. 2, wood handle, 4-5/8" $200
The Pearl, 3-3/4" $75
Tri-bump handle, all cast, 2-3/8" $40
Wapak 2, cast, 4" $50

Electric

Knapp Monarch, round iron $200

Iron, polisher, MAB COOKS, patented Dec. 5, 1848, IBI 271(M), 5" l, **$135.**

Pacific Electric, 1905 .... $110
Petipoint Model 410, Art Deco-style fins on sides $200

Flat Iron

Best On Earth, Potts Iron, detachable $60
Czechoslovakia, green, detachable handle $125
Double Pointed, cast, 9" $160
Dover Sad Iron, detachable $40
Enterprise, boxed set of three, detachable handles, wooden box $350
Enterprise, boxed set, five irons, three handles, two trivets $500
Enterprise, "Star Iron," holes in handle $70
Eurpoean, wrought, bell in handle $80
French, Le Caiffa, cast, 2-3/4" .. $45
Hoods 1867, soapstone body $150
IXL, cast $20
LeGaulois, cast, French $50
Ober, #6, patent 1912 .... $50
Round back, "L" handle, Belgium $90
Sensible, detachable handle, No. 3 .... $75
Weida's Patent 1870, fold-back cold handle $350

Fluter, combination type

Eclipse, charcoal with side fluter plate $200
Hewitt, revolving, clamp-on side fluter plate $350
Knapp, cast, front latch and hinge, Aug. 2, '70 .... $150
Ladies Friend, revolving with slug, 1899 .... $600
Little Giant, fluter at angle $350

Iron, charcoal, Dutch brass, mid-1800, IBI 65, 8" l, **$425.**

Street's Magic, three pcs, 1876 .... $450

Fluter, machine type

Eagle, Nov. 2, 1875, American Machine Co. $100
English, fine flutes, cast frame $200
H. B. Adams, clamp-on $325
Manville, cone shape $400
Osborne, hand wheel for tension $450
The Knox Imperial, good paint $350

Fluter, rocker type

Geneva Hand Fluter, 1866 .... $80
Geneva Improved, brass plates $300
Howell's Wav Fluter, 1866 ...... $450
The Boss $300
The Erie Fluter, detachable handle $250
The Ladies Friend, 1875 .... $160

Fluter, roller type

American Machine $90
American Machine Co., Phila, PA $125
Clarks, holes in handle $180
Shepard Hardware, 1879 .... $130
Sundry Mfg. Co. $250

Goffering Irons

Clamp-on, single barrel, all wrought $350
Double barrel, cast base $500
Single, brass, ornate "S," oval base $250
"S" wire, single barrel, oval base $75

Liquid Fuel, gasoline, or kerosene

Coleman 4A, blue $125

Ironware, doorknocker, wrought iron serpent form, 19th century, 11" l, $460.
Photo courtesy of Pook & Pook, Inc.

Ironware, horse and buggy, cast iron, some original paint, 11" l, $250.
Photo courtesy of Joy Luke Auctions.

Ironware, sugar nippers, engraved and punched dec, mkd "A. Timmin & Sons," VG condition, late 18th/early 19th century, 9" l, $154.
Photo courtesy of Green Valley Auctions.

Ironware, cast iron doorknocker, figural, lady in bathing suit, orig paint, cheek touchups, normal paint, light rust, first half 20th century, 2-1/2" x 5-1/4", $88.
Photo courtesy of Green Valley Auctions.

Coleman 609, black $120
Diamond Akron Lamp Co. $70
Diamond, Self Heating Iron $80
Ellison Bros., revolving, tank in handle $900
Montgomery Ward, gasoline iron $75
Perfection $200
The Improved Easy Iron $110

Liquid Fuel, natural gas
Clarks, Fairy Prince, blue, English $150
English, Salter Gas Iron $160
European Ox Tongue, gas let "L" handle $100
Humphrey $125
Nu-Styl, La Rue Gas Iron, removable 2# weight $500
Uneedit Gas Iron, 1913 .... $100
Vulcan Gas Iron $75

Mangle Board
Horse handle, geometric design, with paint, 1790 .... $2,000
Turned handle, no carving, 1910 .... $100

Miscellaneous
Give-away, Lent Tailor Supplies $600
Iron sole plate to attach bottom of iron $30
Laundry stove, Prize No. 15, holds nine irons $450
Suitcase Iron, Iro-Case, iron is suitcase handle $350

Slug Irons
Austrian, brass box, turned posts $140
Austrian, ox tongue, brass, L handle $250
Bless-Drake, salamander box iron, top lifts off $250
Belgium, round back with trivet $250
Butters, lift off top, 1866 .... $650
Danish Brass Box, engraving, 1810 .... $450
Denmark, brass, vine engraving, dated 1810 .... $450
French, hand made, decorative posts, lift gate, c1800 .... $700
Majestic, combination, revolving $750
Scottish Box, turned brass posts $1,200

Special Purpose
Asbestos, sleeve $50
Billiard table iron, London $300
Egg iron, hand held $80
English
  Hot Water iron $350
  Round bottom polisher, Carron $75
Glove form, steam heated, brass $200
Hat
  Shackle, adjustable edge $135
  Tolliker, wood, curved shape $140
  Tolliker, wood, brass base $150
Polisher
  French, CF, raised pattern on bottom $200
  Hood's, patent 1867, soapstone body $400
  Star polisher $150
Sleeve iron
  Grand Union Tea Co. $60
  Hub $50
  Pluto, electric $200

IRONWARE

History: Iron, a metallic element that occurs abundantly in combined forms, has been known for centuries. Items made from iron range from the utilitarian to the decorative. Early hand-forged ironwares are of considerable interest to Americana collectors.

Additional Listings: Banks, Doorstops, Fireplace Equipment, Irons, Kitchen Collectibles, Lamps, and Tools.

Additional Resources:

Antique Trader® Metalwares Price Guide, 2nd Ed., by Kyle Husfloen, ed., and Mark Moran, contr. ed., Krause Publications, Iola WI.

Andirons, pr, cast, faceted ball finials, knife blade, arched bases, penny feet, rusted surface, 20" h **$325**

Apple roaster, wrought, hinged apple support, pierced heat end on slightly twisted projecting handle, late 18th C, 34-1/4" l **$1,650**

Baker's lamp, cast iron, attached pan, hinged lid, bottom marked "No. 2 B. L.," pitted, 4-1/4" h, 8-1/2" l **$250**

Bill holder, Atlantic Coast Line, cast, c1915, 4" h **$50**

Book press, cast iron, painted, dolphin-form **$420**

Boot scraper, cast, Scottie Dog, figural side profile, America, minor surface rust, early 20th C, 11-1/2" l, 18-1/2" h **$590**

Book press, cast iron, painted, dolphin-form **$420**

Bottle openers

Alligator, head up, John Wright Co., near mint, 2-1/2" x 5-1/8" **$200**

Alligator with boy, Wilton Products, excellent, 2-3/4" x 3-7/8" **$450**

Bear head, John Wright Co., wall mount, excellent, 3-3/4" x 3-1/8" **$115**

Beanie Bert, sgd "1988" on front of base, mint, 4" x 2" **$225**

Canada goose, Wilton Products, good, 1-11/16" x 3-5/8" **$85**

Canvasback duck, Wilton Products, near mint, 1-13/16" x 2-7/8" **$225**

Cathy Coed, L & L Favors, repainted, 4-1/2" **$340**

Cocker spaniel, brown, mkd "John Wright Inc., 1947," 2-3/4" x 3-3/4" **$85**

Cowboy holding onto signpost, John Wright, good, some paint loss, 4-1/8" x 2-3/4" **$70**

Cowboy in chaps, Wilton Products, near mint, 4-1/2" x 2-3/4" **$675**

Cowboy with guitar, John Wright Co., near mint, 4-3/4" x 3-1/8" **$115**

Dinky Dan, Gadzik Sales, sgd "Gadzik, Phil, Ivy Weekend 52," excellent, 3-7/8" x 2-1/8" **$310**

English setter, brown and white, mkd "John Wright Inc., 1947," 2-1/4" x 4-1/2" **$85**

Fish, tail up, mkd "John Wright, Inc., 1947," very good, 2-5/16" x 4-5/8" **$200**

Freddie Frosh, L & L Favors, front base sgd "Big Game '55," 4" x 2" **$340**

Grass skirt, Greek, Gadzik Sales, sgd "Gadzik Phil." 5" x 1-15/16" **$400**

Mr. Dry, Wilton Products, excellent, 5-1/2" x 3-1/2" **$115**

Monkey, brown paint, mkd "John Wright Inc.," near mint, 2-5/8" x 2-11/16" **$280**

Paddy the Pledgemaster, Gadzik Sales, sgd "Gadzik Phil, Dinner Dance '57" on front, near mint, 3-7/8" x 2-1/4" **$400**

Patty Pep, L & L Favors, Pittston, Pennsylvania, sgd "Women's Weekend '55" on front, excellent, 4" **$675**

Parrot, John Wright Co., near mint, 4-3/4" h **$310**

Parrot on perch, near mint, 4-5/8" x 3-1/4" **$620**

Toucan, John Wright Co., near mint, 3-3/8" x 2-7/8" **$450**

Calipers, pr, wrought

Double, two arms meeting at "Y"-shaped central piece, ring handle with old split, 18-1/2" l **$125**

Ending in delicate ladies legs, stamped "WTI 1863," 18-1/2" l **$115**

Candlestick, wrought, spiral iron stem, curled finger loop and tab, wooden push up, old, cone shaped wooden base with dark patina, 9-3/4" h **$160**

Carriage fenders, cast, shaped like horse leg, sgd "Fiske, New York," price for pr, c1880 .... **$4,800**

Cleaver, figural-shaped blade with eagle's head, handle terminating in brass boot, stand, minor surface corrosion, 20th C, 11-1/2" l, 4-1/2" h **$490**

Compote, cast, flower form bowl, shaped and molded star base, America, old rust surface, late 19th C, 10" w, 7" h **$200**

Cookie mold, oval, bird on branch, cast iron, 5-1/4" l **$335**

Door knocker, cast, fox head, ring hangs from mouth, 5-1/2" l **$85**

Embossing wheel, cast iron and bronze, scrolled foliate motif on wheel edge, imp maker's marks for M. W. Baldwin, Philadelphia, handle missing, 4" l, 1-3/4" w, 9-1/4" h **$460**

Figure, cast, Lady Liberty, Mott Foundry, New York, holding goblet and torch with octagonal marble base, later white wood plinth, c1850, 24-1/4" w, 39" h **$7,425**

Fireback, cast, late Regency-style, arch top flanked by dolphins, central polychrome scene of shepherd with his flock by fountain, beaded surround, scrolling leaf border, 21-1/2" w, 33" h **$300**

Herb grinder, cast, footed trough form, 6" d round disk-shaped crusher with wooden handle through center, late 18th/early

Reproduction Alert. Use the following checklist to determine if a metal object is a period piece or modern reproduction. This checklist applies to all cast-metal items, from mechanical banks to trivets.

Period cast-iron pieces feature well-defined details carefully fitted pieces, and carefully finished and smooth castings. Reproductions, especially those produced by making a new mold from a period piece, often lack detail in the casting (lines not well defined, surface details blurred) and parts have gaps at the seams and a rough surface. Reproductions from period pieces tend to be slightly smaller in size than the period piece from which they were copied.

Period paint mellows, i.e., softens in tone. Colors look aged. Beware of any cast-iron object whose paint is bright and fresh. Painted period pieces should show wear. Make sure the wear is in the places it is supposed to be.

Period cast-iron pieces develop a surface rust patina that prevents rust. When rust is encountered on a period piece, it generally has a greasy feel and is dark in color. The rust on the artificially aged reproductions is flaky and orange.

Ivory, ball, high relief carved flowers, stained details, carved wood stand, Japan, 19th century, 2-1/2" d ball, 4-1/2" h with stand, **$375.**

Ivory, plaque, carved warrior on horse back and pine tree in relief, reverse with calligraphy, Chinese, Qing Dynasty, 7" x 3", **$530.**
Photo courtesy of Sloans & Kenyon Auctioneers and Appraisers.

19th C, 16-1/2" l, 4-1/2" w, 4" h $980

Hitching post, cast, jockey, yellow, red, green, black, and white painted detail, wired for lantern, 31" h $275

Jousting helmet, wrought, cylindrical, tapering vertically at front, narrow eye slits, pierced circular and cruciform breaths, 12th C style, 19th C, 18" h $1,495

Kitchen utensils, 9" h hanging rack, wrought, step down crest with scrolled heart, cut out cross bar, three spatulas, two dippers, with tooling and initials, 16" l $675

Knife, folding, hand-forged blade with a trigger locking mechanism pivots into iron sheath bound with carved wood handle, held with two iron bands and six pins, blade illegibly marked, wear, late 18th/early 19th C, 8-1/4" l closed, 15-1/2" l open $150

Lamp, floor, arrow-shaped finial on shaft, two sockets, scrolled wrought iron tripod feet, woven striped paneled shades, scattered corrosion, price for pr $815

Letter sealer, coat of arms, European, late 18th/early 19th C, 1" d $40

Mirror, cast, gilt, rococo scrolled acanthus frame, oval beveled mirror, Victorian, 22" h $75

Mold, figural pumpkin, smiling man face, invented by John Czeszczicki, Ohio, used to grow pumpkins in human forms, surface corrosion, later stand, 1930, 7-1/4" w, 8" d, 8" h $635

Mortar and pestle, urn shape, cast iron, pitted, 10-1/2" d, 8-1/4" h $50

Pipe tongs, wrought iron, 18th C, 17-1/4" l $1,150

Rush light holder, wrought, twisted detail on stem and arm of counterweight, high tripod feet riveted to disk, traces of black paint, 15-3/4" h $330

Shelf brackets, pr, swivel, 5-1/2" h $20

Spittoon, cast iron, top hat, Standard Manuf Co., Pittsburgh, Pennsylvania, painted black, glazed porcelain int. $415

Sugar nippers, tooled flower at pivot points, 10" l $600

Trivet, round, marked "The Griswold Mfg. Co., Eire, PA, USA/8/ Trivet/206," 7-3/4" d $35

Umbrella stand, cast, backplate formed as figure of Admiral Nelson, titled at base, stepped base with double shell-form removable drip pan, 30-3/4" h $750

Utensil rack, wrought iron, scrolled crest, five hooks with acorn terminals, minor brazed repair, 10-3/4" l $770

Wafer iron, imp with seal of U.S., minor imperfections, c1800, 5-1/4" d, 24" l $550

Wall frame, cast iron, gilt eagle crest, elaborately dec frame, C-scrolls and foliate devices, 19th C, 8-1/2" h, 6" d $575

IVORY

History: Ivory, a yellowish white organic material, comes from the teeth or tusks of animals and lends itself to carving. Many cultures have used it for centuries to make artistic and utilitarian items.

A cross section of elephant ivory will have a reticulated crisscross pattern. Hippopotamus teeth, walrus tusks, whale teeth, narwhal tusks, and boar tusks also are forms of ivory. Vegetable ivory, bone, stag horn, and plastic are ivory substitutes, which often confuse collectors. Vegetable ivory is a term used to describe the nut of a South American palm, which is often carved. Look for a grain that is circular and dull in this softer-than-bone material.

Note: Dealers and collectors should be familiar with The Endangered Species Act of 1973, amended in 1978, which limits the importation and sale of antique ivory and tortoiseshell items.

Ball, carved, three boys forming circle, clothes with traces of paint, China, age cracks, 19th C, 2" d, 3-3/4" with base $115

Box, cov, cylindrical, carved scene of figures in landscape, screw-on lid, China, 19th C, 4-1/2" h $220

Bridge, carved from hippopotamus tusk, various figures in palace setting, 12" l $175

Brush pot

Incised and stained dec, mountainous landscape with people in foreground, ivory base, inscriptions around foot, China, age cracks, 19th C, 3-5/16" h, 1-7/8" d **$495**

Incised and stained dec, mountainous landscape with people in foreground, wooden base, China, age cracks, 19th C, 3-1/8" h, 2" d **$450**

Relief carving of figures and landscapes, China, 6" h **$500**

Shaped panels carved with people in landscape, base with openwork dec, China, crack on side of base, 19th C, 3-7/8" h, 1-7/8" d **$320**

Chess set

Chinese figures, detailed, 16 crimson stained pieces, 15 natural pieces, lacquered case, gilt dec scenes and mother-of-pearl inlay, Oriental, 20th C, 2-1/2" to 5" h **$1,100**

Chinese figures, 16 natural color, 16 tea stained, fitted wood case with playing field, Oriental, 20th C, 3-1/2" to 7" h **$920**

Chinese figures, natural and tea-stained pieces, each carved with figures standing on mystery ball bases, inlaid box with brass clasp, 3" to 7" h **$700**

Cup, cov, foliate finial, oval body, carved frieze of putti with hound, mask and acanthus baluster stem, round foot, Continental, early 18th C **$1,200**

Doctor model, carved, Chinese, 20th C

Embellish with coral and turquoise necklace and bracelets, holding fan, wooden stand, age crack, 13" l **$850**

Wooden stand, age crack, 10-3/4" l **$650**

Fan, carved, painted figures amidst courtyard setting, inlaid with painted ivory faces, black lacquer and parcel gilt can, base inscribed in gilt "E. Cardinal's Canton," Chinese export, 19th C, 11" l **$1,195**

Figure, carved

Ascetic in kneeling position, arms raised, body leaning forward in bowing motion, inlaid eyes, traces of red pigment on skirt, mounted on wooden base, China, right foot replaced, 18th or 19th C, 3-1/8" h **$260**

Bodhistiva, standing, elaborate dress, two lotus pods flanking head, sinuous tendrils held in each hand, mounted on carved wooden stand, China, 19th C, 13" h **$1,265**

Gentleman and woman, both carrying peony blossom spray and basket, following natural curve of tusk, painted details, China, pr, 20th C, 20" h **$1,675**

God of longevity, China, 11-3/4" h **$600**

Guardian, right hand resting on sword with dragon entwined around it, two curved ribbons framing head, wooden stand with cloud designs, well carved and stained detail, China, slight age cracks, missing right dragon whisker, 19th C, 12-3/16" h **$1,150**

Immortal, frog on left shoulder, black colored hair and shoes, China, 19th C, 5-3/4" h **$850**

Lady, body leaning to right, double gourd bottle on ribbon dangling from her waist, string of beads in her right hand, branch in her left, branch curving and resting behind head, stained details, carved wooden stand, China, age cracks in hand and left arm, 19th C, 5-1/2" h **$1,035**

Lady, holding wine pot, side with sages under pine trees, cov with foo dog, left hand holding handle, long flowing scarf with several joints, elaborate hair contained in phoenix headdress, China, wear to painted surface, age cracks and filled in areas, 18th or 19th C, 12-3/8" h **$1,265**

Ox, recumbent, head turned to right, halter attached to ring through nose, crossing over and resting on blanketed back, inlaid eyes, himotoshi and sgd "Gyokuzan" on base, lightly stained details, Japan, 19th C, 1" h, 1-7/8" l **$300**

Quanyin holding scroll in her left hand, standing on lotus pedestal, stained details, China, age cracks, ivory separated at mouth and reglued,

Ivory, figure of a Meiren, standing, loose robes and high chignon, Chinese early 20th century, 11-1/2" h, **$500.**

Ivory, vases, floral motifs, pr, Chinese, early Republic period, 7-3/4", **$550.** Photo courtesy of Sloans & Kenyon Auctioneers and Appraisers.

Ivory, musicians, each on a wooden barrel form stand, highly detailed, set of seven, 19th century, 6-3/4" x 2", **$1,500.** Photo courtesy of David Rago Auctions, Inc.

age cracks, 18th C, 7-1/4" h **$460**

Vishnu and his consort, Indian, 7-1/2" h **$300**

Woman in western attire, carrying purse and umbrella, China, 8-3/8" h **$300**

Woman holding a basket and flowers, China, 12-1/2" h **$600**

Jagging wheel, 19th C

Figural, unicorn, inlaid eyes and nostrils, minor losses, 7-1/8" l **$4,600**

Pierced carved, whalebone, minute losses, 5-3/4" l **$2,875**

Letter opener, oblong blade carved to end with writhing dragon, Chinese, early 20th C, 9-3/4" l **$115**

Mask, Jomen carved from one piece of ivory, old man, wrinkled face, deep sinuous curves, raised furrowed brow, locks of hair brought up from side and tied in bow, long beard, back side carved in narrow grooves, ears pierced with hole for hanging wire, unsigned, Japan, Meiji period, minor nick at tip of beard, 8-3/4" l, 4-3/8" w, 2" d **$2,875**

Okimono

Figure of young boy and dog, sgd on bottom, Japan, Meiji period, crack on boy's face, 2-1/8" h **$200**

Man sitting with his left arm resting on small chest, wood grain finely carved and stained, handles of dark horn, sake cup resting on top, holding pipe case in right hand, robes with geometric designs and medallions, part of robe overlapping underside of chest, sgd on base in sq seal, Japan, 19th C, 3" l **$1,000**

Man spilling from his hat cucumbers attached to vine, frog resting on top, details slightly stained, red signature tablet on base, Japan, 19th C, 5-1/2" h **$700**

Samuari holding double gourd sake bottle in his left hand, open fan in right, garment draped over large sword attached to cord over his right shoulder, man keeling beside him holding sake cap in his left hand, gift box wrapped by cord and a bucket lie on foreground, signature on underside of box, Japan, Meiji period, damage to sticks of fan, 6" h **$1,035**

Sectional, marine ivory, man and young boy standing on tree stumps, man playing samisen, small chest with fan on top hangs from his shoulder, child holding fan in left hand, right hand with upside down book with written pages, sgd on bases, Japan, missing pc from fan, traces of glue, c1900, 9-1/4" h **$250**

Seven gods of good fortune, faces emerging from basket, well carved details, lightly stained, sgd on base, Japan, Meiji period, age cracks, 2" d, 2" h **$300**

Takarabune, seven gods of good future, stained detail, sgd on base, Japan, Meiji period, 4-1/2" l **$375**

Young boy playing with toy model of horse, right hand gripping ribbon attached to horse's mouth, left hand passing under horse, holding drum, sgd on rect reserve, Japan, Meiji period,

crack on base, 3-1/8" l, 1-5/8" h **$250**

Page turner, Shibiyama, thin blade dec sparrows in flowering tree, gold and pewter colored paint, inlaid with nacre and coral, carved handle with sparrows being chased by rodent, Japanese, one inlay missing, 17" l **$520**

Parasol handle, carved

Monkeys and butterflies feasting on fruit, details partially colored and stained, Japan, crack on side, c1900, 8-3/8" l **$165**

Tapering form with dragons, phoenix, and other birds, blank cartouche with metal divider and tip, stained horn finial on end, China, 19th C, 13" l **$200**

Pickwick, carved, minor losses, repair, 19th C, 3-1/4" h **$210**

Plaque, carved

General (Mad Anthony) Wayne, America, round, relief carved three-quarter view bust length portrait, banner below inscribed with name, houses and foliage in background, age crack, conforming molded wood frame, late 18th/early 19th C, 3-7/8" d **$500**

Low relief carving of figures in garden landscape, letters ARDS on bottom, Chinese, slight staining and age cracks, 18th or 19th C, 4-7/8" l, 3" w **$575**

One side with plants emerging from rock, other side with figures in interior and pine trees in background, stylized wave border, Chinese, slightly curved, age cracks, 18th C, 7-5/8" l, 4-1/8" w **$650**

Jade spinach archaistic censer and cover, Fangding, Chinese, Qing dynasty, 9-1/2" h x 6-3/4" d, **$6,490.**
Photo courtesy of Sloans & Kenyon Auctioneers and Appraisers.

JADE

History: Jade is the generic name for two distinct minerals: nephrite and jadeite. Nephrite, an amphibole mineral from Central Asia that was used in pre-18th-century pieces, has a waxy surface and hues that range from white to an almost-black green. Jadeite, a pyroxene mineral found in Burma and used from 1700 to the present, has a glassy appearance and comes in various shades of white, green, yellow-brown, and violet.

Jade cannot be carved because of its hardness. Sawing and grinding with wet abrasives such as quartz, crushed garnets, and carborundum achieve shapes.

Prior to 1800, few items were signed or dated. Stylistic considerations are used to date pieces. The Ch'ien Lung period (1736-1795) is considered the golden age of jade.

Boulder, finely carved interior of Guanyin figure, light green tones, polished amber colored ext., Oriental, 20th C, 13" h **$815**

Box, rect, silver mounted, early 20th C, 3-3/8" l..**$320**

Bowl, carved

Two angular handles, carved studs and designs, China, 18th C or earlier, 2-11/16" d, 2-1/4" h...........**$290**

Russet inclusions, China, internal fissures on base, rim fissure, 19th C, 3-1/4" d, 2" h..............................**$435**

Bracelet, archaic carved black jade, white inclusions, outside carved with Zhuanshu script, mounted with silver colored metal, internal band with eight straps of different designs, four ending with ruyi heads, China, four old breaks and regluing, 3-3/8" d **$200**

Brush washer, carved

Gray color with russet inclusions on base, carved bat and leafy branch,

China, 18th C, 2-1/2" l, 1-3/8" h **$350**

Hollowed out peach form, animal head handle, apple green inclusions, China, filled-in fissure, minor fritting, 18th C or earlier, 3-5/8" l, 2-1/4" w, 1-1/8" h......................**$200**

Candlesticks, pr, dark green, carved low relief goose with outspread wings, stands on tortoise, head supports three-tiered pricket, tripod bowl with int. carving, reticulated wood base with carved key scroll motifs and floral scrolls, 12-7/8" h **$550**

Carving

Double gourd and foliage, pale green color stone, China, fitted stand, 18th/19th C, 4" x 2-1/2" **$2,250**

Figural woman, pale lavender stone with green and tan accents, China, 6-1/4" h **$360**

Horse, nephrite of celadon color with brown striations, China, 19th/20th C, 7" l...**$450**

Pair of birds on nests, long tails, forest green color stone, China, early 20th C, 7" l...**$710**

Pair of phoenixes, pale lavender stone with areas of apple green and russet, fitted, carved hardwood stands, repair to one crest, 13" h.......**$1,000**

Reclining hound, highly translucent green stone, 5" l.......................**$710**

Ceremonial knife, carved, archaic style designs, traces of red pigment, China, 18th C or earlier, 9-3/8" l **$90**

Dish, brownish-celadon, carved in Mughal style, open chrysanthemum flower, China, 19th C, 5-3/4" d...**$475**

Figure, carved

Carved yellow-green, dark gray inclusions, four birds perched on tree trunk, carved fitted wood stand, China, one foot missing from stand, 20th C, 7-1/4" to 9-1/4" h **$375**

Celadon, woman, whisk in her right hand, leafy branch in left, branch curving behind her neck and resting on left shoulder, hair styled with large chignon on top of head, russet inclusions on flower and part of garment, China, small fissure at back of head, 19th or 20th C, 10-1/2" h **$200**

Green, dark gray inclusion running vertically, maiden holding flowering branch in right hand and resting on her left shoulder, China, glued

Jade, bowl, lobed form, sides carved with lotus, two raised handles with carved rings, four scrolled feet, wooden base carved with openwork cash design, China, 19th or 20th century, 11-1/2" l x 7-1/4" w x 4-1/2" h bowl, **$650.**

to wooden stand, 20th C, 5-3/4" h **$135**

Lotus leaf forming elongated oval bowl with lobed edges, raised from bunch of branches, duck resting on lotus pod, carved and fitted wood stand with lotus design, China, small loss to stand, natural fissure conforming to design, small chips, 18th or 19th C, 4-3/4" h, 10-1/2" l **$650**

Mottled gray and black, Guandi in sitting position, long hair cascading down lower back, hole carved thru right clenched hand, carved wooden base, China, chips to right foot, glued to stand, 19th C, 7-1/8" h, 4-1/2" w **$1,035**

Mottled gray and black, lady holding teapot flanked by phoenix and attendant with fan, carved wood base, China, small chips, base glued on, 20th C, 9-5/8" h **$435**

Mottled, maiden with crane and sacred fungus, China, stand partially rebuilt with plaster, 19th C, 5-5/8" h **$625**

Off-white, mottled celadon, and gray-green color stone, mythical fierce beast with vase on its back, carved fitted wood stand with wire inlay, China, teeth broken, 19th or 20th C, 4-1/8" h, 6" l **$100**

Pale green jade with gray and russet inclusions, two ducks facing opposite directions, each holding lotus sprig in beak, carved fitted wood stand, China, small chip to edge of one leaf, 19th or 20th C, 3-1/4" h, 4-1/4" l **$325**

Turtle, celadon colored flat carapace and head, russet colored lower body and four feet, China, 18th C, 2-1/8" l, 2" w, 3/4" h **$175**

White, apple green inclusions, dark green underfoot, carved duck with fish in its beak, wings carved with tips pointed outwards, China, neck restored, over-painted, 19th C, 4-3/8" h, 4-1/2" l **$260**

White, apple green, russet, and gray inclusions, maiden holding vase, hair combed with large chignon, standing, glued to carved quartz base with flowers on side, hole pierced in base, China, base chipped, 19th or 20th C, 6" h **$135**

White, man with frog resting on his head, Chinese, 19th C, 2-5/8" h **$750**

Flute, light and dark colored cylinders of celadon green tone, wooden frame, India, early 20th C, 22" l **$75**

Inkstone, oval, depression to one side, black and white mottling, incised rim band, 3-5/8" l **$200**

Letter opener, carved interlocking C scrolls between keyfret bands handle, SS knife, 10-3/4" l **$250**

Libation cup, celadon jade, incised dec, dragon head handles, Chinese, Qing dynasty, price for pr, 5" l **$425**

Palace figure, carved herons, more than 200 pieces of dark green mottled jadeite feathers applied over wooden form, mahogany stained wooden plinth, minor losses, price for pr, 20th C, 76" h **$1,150**

Pendant, carved

Axe shape, white stone, China, 18th C **$215**

Chi dragon, pale mottled green, dark inclusions at base, openwork chi dragon on crescent, China, small rim chips, 18th or 19th C, 1-3/4" l, 2-1/4" d, 1-1/4" h **$200**

Duck and lotus plants, highly translucent brown color stone, China, 18th C **$300**

Ducks and lotuses, white stone, China, 18th C **$1,000**

Gourd shape, leafy branch, Chinese, 19th C, 1-3/4" l **$200**

Plaque, pale lavender, bright green spots, China, 18th C **$200**

Pi disk, carved

Thick, brown and russet inclusions, deep groove carved on one side near edge, China, 18th C, 2-1/2" d, 3/4" **$100**

Thick, pale green with russet inclusions, coiled fish nose to nose with chi dragon, stylized waves, ruyi designs, fitted stand carved with bats among clouds, areas of pitting, China, small crack on inner circle, old break to stand, small chips, 18th C or earlier, 8-3/8" d, 5/16" **$3,600**

Plaque, carved

Complex design of cranes with entwined lotus plants and tendrils, raised curved shape, back edge with carved holes for attachment, mounted with three silver colored metals on wood base, China, small fissure, 18th C, 3-3/8" w, 3-7/8" l, 5-3/8" h **$435**

Thick, oval, openwork dec, central figure holding flag surrounded by

flowers, center with carved quartz cabochon secured with metal pin, China, 20th C, 4-3/4" h, 3-1/2" w, 1/8" **$150**

Saucer, low relief carving of five bats around central longevity emblem, pale green color stone, price for pr, late 19th/early 20th C, 6" d **$650**

Seal, carved

Crouching boy, Chinese, 19th C, 1-1/8" h **$265**

Foo dog, Chinese, 19th C, 1-1/2" h **$245**

Recumbent foo dog, dark green spinach jade, Chinese, 19th or early 20th C, 1-1/8" h **$275**

Snuff bottle, grayish-white, mottled russet skin on one side, rose quartz stopper **$550**

Tablet, spinach, plain rect shape, carved and recessed wood stand, China, 19th C, 3-3/4" l, 1" h **$520**

Urn, cov, Buddhist figure, open work foliage, lavender and green jadeite, polished finish, Oriental, 20th C, 11" h **$1,100**

Vase, carved

Celadon, well carved figure riding dragon and chasing flaming pearl, phoenix with figure on back carved on shoulder, rocks emerging around base, well hollowed interior, China, natural fissure, 18th or 19th C, 6-5/8" h **$2,875**

Hu form, stone of celadon color with white striations and brown markings, China, 19th C, 7" h **$1,300**

Vase, cov, carved, spinach, flattened oval form, body carved with archaistic designs, stepped shoulder and plain neck, cov with large oval finial terminating with raised nipple, China, 18th or 19th C, 9-3/4" h **$220**

Water coupe, Mughal-style carving of peach and foliage, pale green color stone, 5" x 4" **$3,000**

Water dropper, celadon, carved wine pot, rat forming handle, leaf and tendril on side, lid and spout of silver metal with pearl and traces of enamel on carved round foot, China, small chip to foot, 18th or 19th C, 2-1/2" h **$290**

JUDAICA

History: Throughout history, Jews have expressed themselves artistically in both the religious and secular spheres. Most Jewish art objects were created as part of the concept

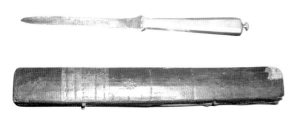

Judaica, circumcision knife, silver, original case, **$300.**

of Hiddur Mitzva, i.e., adornment of implements used in performing rituals both in the synagogue and home.

For almost 2,000 years, since the destruction of the Jerusalem Temple in 70 a.d., Jews have lived in many lands. The widely differing environments gave traditional Jewish life and art a multifaceted character. Unlike Greek, Byzantine, or Roman art, which has definite territorial and historical boundaries, Jewish art is found throughout Europe, the Middle East, North Africa, and other areas.

Ceremonial objects incorporated not only liturgical appurtenances, but also ethnographic artifacts such as amulets and ritual costumes. The style of each ceremonial object responded to the artistic and cultural milieu in which it was created. Although diverse stylistically, ceremonial objects, whether for Sabbath, holidays, or the life cycle, still possess a unity of purpose.

Notes: Judaica has been crafted in all media, though silver is the most collectible.

Astrolabe, bronze, finely chased lettering, symbols and foliage, 19th C, 5-1/4" h..**$200**

Award of merit badge, silver, Temple Ahawath Chesed Religious School, awarded to Walter R. Herschman, 1892, 2-1/2" h..............**$265**

Bible, Leviticus, Paris, Robert Estienne, 16 mo, vellum boards, printed in square Hebrew type with vowel points, surrounding Latin commentary in small and neat hand, fifty bound-in pages of theological treatise, 1544-1546......................**$900**

Box, cov, silver, dec with the Binding of Isaac, hinged lid, Dutch, 18th/19th C, 4" l...**$1,650**

Bridal necklace, silver, rows of rect plaques applied with granulation and

hung with filigree pendants, Yeminite **$470**

Carpet, Bezalel wool, design of Rachel's Tomb, flanked by seven-branch menorahs, stylized Zion lettering, cranberry, gray, green, and blue, sgd "Marvadia, Jerusalem," early 20th C, 19-3/4" x 43"..........................**$3,820**

Charger, majolica, depicting Joseph and his brothers, Italian, 19th C imperfections, 12-1/4" d............**$890**

Figure, old Jewish man, Gardiner, Russia, late 19th C, 9" h....................**$940**

Flagon, stoneware, with incised and blue glazed "Star of David," pewter lid, German, late 19th C, 8" h **$150**

Floor screen, three-panel, sgd G.D. Felice, polychrome dec, ceremonial scenes and fruit and foliage, 1940, 72" h..................................**$1,530**

Folk art, Wedding Feast, carved and painted wood and plaster, sgd J.J. Stark, 11-1/2" x 17-1/4"............**$275**

Haftorah scroll, square hand-lettered ink on vellum, cherry wood rollers, probably Germany, late 18th C, 22-1/2" h scroll..................**$4,120**

Hanukah lamp

Brass, backplate with lions, menorah, and "these lights are holy" in Hebrew, over candleholders, servant lamp to side, Bezalel, Jerusalem, early 20th C, 5-1/2" h **$715**

Havdalah compendium, candleholder with egg and dart and foliate designs, drawer for spices, base formed as full-figured bird, circular base, Czechoslovakian, mark for Prague, c1814-1866, 7" h **$3,055**

Havdalah plate, porcelain, hand painted and transfer dec, M.L. Schwab, Frankfurt a Main, Germany, late 19th C, 8-1/2" d **$235**

Kiddush cup

German silver, neoclassical motif, hand-hammered leaf and berry band at rim, reeded stem, circular

Judaica, Shiviti, ink and gouache, Star of David within architectural surround, 19th/20th century, framed, 15-1/2" x 10-1/2", **$1,175.**
Photo courtesy of Skinner, Inc.

Judaica, merit badge, American Silver Award, Temple Ahawath Chesed religious School, awarded to Walter R. Herschman, 1892, 2-1/2" h, **$265.**
Photo courtesy of Skinner, Inc.

Judaica, broadside, warning to the inhabitants of the city of Jerusalem, Palestine, signed R.N. O'Connor, text in English, Arabic and Hebrew, 19 October 1938, **$205.**
Photo courtesy of Skinner, Inc.

foot, German presentation inscription from "Israelitischen kultus-Gemeinde," mkd "800," German, early 20th C, 9-1/2" h **$1,530**

Silver and parcel gilt, beaker form with finely chased scrollwork and cartouche, mkd "800M," Continental, late 19th C, 2-3/4" h **$590**

Silver and silver filigree, applied filigree decoration and three medallions, Bezalel, Jerusalem, early 20th C, 4-3/4" h **$890**

Silver, beaker-form, rim with Hebrew inscription, wide band of foliage and scroll-work, mkd "12," Polish, 19th C, 2" h **$325**

Silver, flared rim over plain tapered body, Hebrew inscription pertaining to circumcision, Dutch, 833 fine, date letter for 1927, 3-1/2" h **$775**

Silver, tapered form, slightly flared foot, intricate acid etched vintage design, palm trees, appropriate Hebrew text, Bezalel, Jerusalem, second quarter 20th C, 3-3/4" h **$940**

Judaica, Lulav holder, enameled brass, Near Eastern, prob. Egyptian, cylindrical form, Hebrew text, 19th century, 28-1/4", **$1,525.**
Photo courtesy of Skinner, Inc.

Sterling silver, engraved "presented by Cong. Ahavath Achim, Revere, E. Kassoy," Russian-style, 2-1/2" h **$250**

Silver, flared cup with engine-turned detail, slender stem, square foot, Germany or Poland, first half 19th C, 5-1/2" h **$600**

Laver, copper, heavily cast foliate motifs, appropriate Hebrew inscription, Continental, 7" h **$1,120**

Lulav (palm branch) holder, enameled brass, cylindrical form, Hebrew text "Joseph is a fruitful bough...," probably Egyptian, 19th C, 28-1/4" h **$1,530**

Marriage box, pewter, circular, scene of couple, inscribed "Mazel Tov," 19th C, 4-1/4" d **$250**

Matzoh bag, embroidered silk, cream ground, colorful lion, crown, and foliage, Europe, early 20th C **$200**

Matzoh plate, Tepper blue transfer dec, vignettes of the Seder, identified in Hebrew and English, Ridgways, early 20th C, 10" d **$180**

Menorah/Candelabra, brass, Modernist design, movable candle arms, domed circular base with Hebrew inscription, 1920s, 19" h **$470**

Mezuzzah

Carved ivory front with lions, crown, and columns, silver rect backplate with scroll-work and cabochon coral, Polish style, 6-1/2" h **$325**

Silver gilt and enamel, foliate motifs, mounted on wooden backing, Russian-style, 6-3/8" h **$325**

New Year's card, lithographed diecut pop-up, Sukkot, Germany, c1890-1910, 6-3/4" h....................**$150**

Paper cut, rect format, delicate cut work deer and birds amidst foliage, text pertaining to protecting against evil eye, matted, late 19th/early 20th C, 9" x 7-1/2" **$1,000**

Painting, framed

Pondering Rabbi, Josef Johann Suss, sgd lower right, oil on canvas, 11-3/4" x 9" **$1,100**

Rabbi in His Study, Hans Winter, sgd lower right, identified on reverse, oil on board, 5-3/4" x 7-3/4" **$2,350**

Rabbi with Torah, Maria Szanthos, sgd lower right, oil on canvas, 23-1/4" x 19" **$1,000**

Still Life with Pomegranates, Reuven Rubin, sgd "Rubin" in Hebrew and

English lower left, oil on canvas board, 7-1/2" x 9-1/2" **$9,990**

Plaque, bronze, mother and child placing money in Tzdaka box, Boris Schatz insignia upper right, Bezalel, Jerusalem, early 20th C, 6-3/8" h **$825**

Plate, white molded ground with brown transfer depicting "Sacred History of Joseph and his Bretheren...," English, chips, early 19th C, 6-1/2" d **$130**

Pocket watch, Waltham, gilt, Hebrew numerals, subsidiary seconds dial, removable nickel silver case **$600**

Postcard album

113 cards, various Jewish personalities, late 19th/early 20th C.......**$825**

124 cards, New Year and holiday cards **$1,650**

Presentation bowl, sterling silver, shaped rim and foliate motifs, inscribed "presented by the Petoefi Sick & Benevolent Society," Theodore B. Starr, NY, c1910, 9" d **$360**

Purim noisemaker, silver and silver-gilt, applied turquoise, carnelian and paste stones, filigree work, appropriate Hebrew text, Turkmenistan, 11-3/4" h **$1,530**

Sabbath candlestick

Bronze, cast with fox hunt motifs, base with menorah's, Star of David and blessing for candles, France or America, c1875, 10-3/4" h **$235**

Repoussè silver, tulip-form candleholder over foliate cast baluster stem, plain square foot, Abraham Reiner, Warsaw, bobeches replaced, price for pr, c1862-68, 12" h **$1,300**

Silver plated, cast neoclassical motifs, leaf and scroll form feet, removable bobeches, Warsaw, price for pr, late 19th C, 12-3/4" h **$650**

Seder dish, bone china, plate and small dishes for implements of the Seder, illustrations by Eric Tunstall, RI, Royal Cauldon, England, 20th C, 16" d...**$300**

Seder plate, porcelain, transfer dec, center with order of the Seder in tones of rose, yellow and brown, shaped aqua rim with floral sprays, German, late 19th/early 20th C, 9-1/2" d **$590**

Shabbat knife, metal and mother-of-pearl, inscribed in Hebrew "Shabbat Kadosh," Czechoslovakian, early 20th C, 5-1/2" l............................**$180**

KITCHEN COLLECTIBLES

History: The kitchen was the focal point in a family's environment until the 1960s. Many early kitchen utensils were handmade and prized by their owners. Next came a period of utilitarian products made of tin and other metals. When the housewife no longer wished to work in a sterile environment, enamel and plastic products added color, and their unique design served both aesthetic and functional purposes.

The advent of home electricity changed the type and style of kitchen products. Fads affected many items. High technology already has made inroads into the kitchen, and another revolution seems at hand.

Additional Listings: Baskets, Brass, Butter Prints, Copper, Fruit Jars, Graniteware, Ironware, Tinware, and Woodenware. See *Warman's Americana & Collectibles* for more examples, including electrical appliances.

Additional Resources:

300 Years of Kitchen Collectibles, by Linda Campbell Franklin, Krause Publications, Iola, WI.

Spiffy Kitchen Collectibles, by Brian S. Alexander, Krause Publications, Iola, WI.

Warman's® Americana & Collectibles, 11th Ed., by Ellen T. Schroy, Krause Publications, Iola, WI.

Warman's® Flea Market Price Guide, 4th Ed., by Ellen T. Schroy, Krause Publications, Iola, WI.

Bean pot, cov, Bristol glaze, handle, c1900, 6-1/2" h **$25**

Broom holder, Little Polly Brooms, tin litho, image of little girl sweeping floor, 2-1/2" w, 6-1/4" h **$425**

Butter churn, old blue paint, America, minor imperfections, 19th C, 49" h **$345**

Butter paddle
Burl, dark patina, simple hooked handle, 9-3/4" l **$165**
Maple, unusual carved handle resembling bird with open beak, small rim chip, 6-1/4" l **$125**

Cheese sieve, plus handle, hand-molded yellow clay, Albany glaze, 10" d, 7" h **$320**

Colander, stoneware, brown Albany glaze, handled, attributed to Midwest, c1870, 13" h **$75**

Cookbook
Mastering the Art of French Cooking, Julia Child, volumes one and two, Knopf, 1971-76, dj **$27.50**
The Good Housekeeping Illustrated Book of Desserts, Step-by-Step Photographs, Hearst Books, 1991, 5th printing, dj **$12**

Cookie mold
Carved woman at well, man and woman near potted plant, few worm holes, 28" l, 3-3/8" w **$250**

*Fiesta Ware, cobalt blue, No. 4 mixing bowl, 5" x 7-3/4", **$200-$225.***

Covered dish, green and brown spongeware, cov with two open handles, dish two tab handles, light crazing and discoloration, early 20th century, 4-1/2" h, 8" d rim, **$110.**
Photo courtesy of Green Valley Auctions.

Pie crimper, carved bone, scrimshaw floral dec handle, 19th century, 6-1/2" l, **$878.**
Photo courtesy of Pook & Pook, Inc.

People and rooster on one side, four animals and two birds on other, minor edge wear, 23-1/2" l, 5-1/4" w **$125**

Cutting board, rect, hardwood, scrolled top edge and handle, minor splits, 13-3/4" w, 27-1/4" l **$615**

Dough box, pine and turned poplar, PA, rect removable top, tapering well, splayed ring-turned legs, ball feet, 19th C, 38" w, 19-1/4" d, 29-1/2" h **$425**

Egg beater, Jacquette Scissor, marked "Jacquette, Phila, PA, Patented No. 3," 10-1/2" l **$550**

Firkin, cov, wood, painted green, bentwood handle, wooden banding, splits on top, 15" d, 14-1/2" h **$990**

Flour sifter, Tilden's Universal, wood, partial intact paper label, 14" h, 12" w **$335**

Food chopper, wrought iron, scalloped edge blade, turned wood handle, 7" w **$270**

Fork

Two prongs, bone handle, 6-1/2" l **$65**

Two prongs, wrought iron, flattened handle, heart shaped hanger, 21" l **$550**

Grater

Pierced tin, hanging ring, 4-3/4" h, 2-1/2" w **$50**

Wooden, metal blade, hanger hole, 10-1/4" l, 4" w **$85**

Griddle, cast iron, Griswold, No. 10 ....**$70**

Ice bucket, Frigidaire, frosted green glass **$35**

Kettle, cast iron, Griswold No. 4 ....**$85**

Ladle, brass bowl, wrought iron handle with decorative heart hanger, 20" l, 5-3/8" d **$880**

Lemon squeezer, iron, glass insert, marked "Williams" **$50**

Meat tenderizer, stoneware, orig wood handle, marked "Pat'd Dec. 25, 1877" in relief on bottom, diamond point extensions with some use wear, 9-1/2" h **$90**

Nutmeg grater, Champion, brass and wood, 7" l **$635**

Pantry box, cov, oak, bail handle, 11-1/2" d, 6-1/2" h **$175**

Pastry board, wood, three sided **$32**

Pie crimper, carved bone, unicorn with carved fish tail, ball-shaped hooves, front leg glued, late replacement crimper, medium brown stain, 7" l **$220**

Pie lifter, wrought iron, turned wood handle, 18" l **$95**

Pie safe, hanging, mortised pine case, old thin red wash, door, sides, and back with punched tins with geometric circles and stars, white porcelain door pull, two int. shelves, edge damage, 31" w, 19" d, 31" h **$990**

Potato masher, turned maple, 9" l **$40**

Pot scraper, Sharples Tubular Separator, tin litho, graphic advertising on both sides, 3-1/8" x 2-1/4" **$275**

Rack, rect backplate with arched top, red and white enameled checkerboard pattern, narrow well, single rod suspending two strainer spoons, 20" l **$250**

Reamer

Grapefruit, green, US Glass, cone chips **$575**

Orange, pink, Hazel Atlas **$195**

Orange, Sunkist, blocked pattern, white milk glass, Walker #331b **$125**

Rolling pin

Curly maple, dark color, good patina, 16-1/2" l **$275**

Milk glass, cylindrical, turned wood handles, marked "Imperial Mfg., Co. July 25, 1921," 22" l **$95**

Wooden, turned handle, peg mortised joint, 23-1/2" l, 4-1/2" w **$1,320**

Sausage stuffer, turned wood plunger, 17-1/2" l **$30**

Scoop, rect, carved poplar, round handle, 5-1/2" w, 12-3/4" l **$55**

Sieve, brass, wrought iron scrolled handle with rattail hanging hook, 18-1/2" l, 5-1/2" d **$330**

Skillet, cast iron, Griswold, No. 14 ....**$165**

Slaw board

Tombstone shape, 6" w, 11" l **$220**

Two-tier, hickory or ash, old brown surface, pierced detail on either side, steel blade, brass fittings, age splits, one scallop missing, 13" l, 7" d, 7-1/4" h **$100**

Walnut, cut-out heart design, shaped neck on back, semi-circular base, 5-3/4" w, 21-1/4" h **$500**

Walnut, top with stylized heart cut-out, outlined by field of small carved dots, crowned by three six-pointed Germanic carved stars in field of impressed snowflakes, lower edge gouge carved, molded and dated siderails, hand wrought nut, bottom edge sgd "S.O.A.

Carved oak server, Renaissance Revival, rect top, two drawers, two tiers, carved block, baluster, ring-and ball turned supports, 19th century, 43" x 41-3/4" x 19-1/8", **$500.**
Photo courtesy of Sloans & Kenyon Auctioneers and Appraisers.

Kitchen, hanging salt box, painted pine, 19th century, arched back slant lid, single drawer, red stained surface, green and yellow swag, floral motif, 12" h, 12-1/2" w, **$1,055.**
Photo courtesy of Pook & Pook, Inc.

Buttermilk pitcher, blue and white salt glaze, Indian in war bonnet, light inner rim flake, early 20th century, 8-1/2" h, **$110.**
Photo courtesy of Green Valley Auctions.

Coffeepot, copper, conical form, hinged lid, applied handle, side spout, American, mid-19th century, 10" h, 4-1/4" d rim, **$88.**
Photo courtesy of Green Valley Auctions.

Bean pot, blue and white salt glaze, embossed "Boston Baked Beans," orig lid, acorn-style finial, minor rim flake, early 20th century, 7-1/2" h, **$230.**
Photo courtesy of Green Valley Auctions.

Flour bin, pine, lift top, two divided upper drawers, applied lower moldings, cutout feet, some repairs and wear, second half 19th century, 51" h x 51-1/2" w x 21-1/2" d, **$192.**
Photo courtesy of Green Valley Auctions.

Butter churn, painted, red and black dec, Pennsylvania, 19th century, **$525.**
Photo courtesy of Pook & Pook, Inc.

1887," York County, PA, 7" w, 16-1/2" h **$2,100**

Walnut, two metal blades, carved star dec, scalloped edges and borders, initialed "F.N.," 7" w, 19" h.......**$220**

Redware colander, with handle, 19th century, 15" h, **$470.**
Photo courtesy of Pook & Pook, Inc.

Soap cutting board, wooden, molded sections, use wear, 9" l, 6-1/2" w, 1-1/8" h.........................**$55**

Spatula, iron, D-shape, baluster like turnings on handle, 10" l **$200**

Spice set, Griffiths, set of 16 glass jars with yellow tops, each with spice name, orig rack...................**$160**

Stove, cast iron, chrome, nickel, colorful ceramic tile back.................**$6,000**

Sugar shaker, Dutch boy and girl, Tipp City **$22**

Syrup jug, adv, clay inscribed "W. D. Streeter, Richland, NY," Albany glaze, tight hairline on side, c1890, 8" h **$35**

Taster, brass and wrought iron, polished, 7" l......................................**$150**

Tin

Donovan's Baking Powder, Mt. Morris, NY, 1 lb, paper label, 5-1/4" h, 3" d............................**$475**

Egg-O Brand Baking Powder, paper label, 2-3/4" h, 1-1/4" d............**$110**

Kavanaugh's Tea, 1 lb, little girl on porch in dress, talking to doll, mother sipping tea in window, card-

board sides, tin top and bottom, 6" h, 4-1/2" w, 4-1/2" d.............**$500**

Miller's Gold Medal Breakfast Cocoa, red and black, c1890, 2" h, 1-5/8" w, 1-1/8" d **$250**

Opal Powdered Sugar, Hewitt & Sons, Des Moines, 8" h, 4-1/2" w, 3-1/4" d **$180**

Parrot and Monkey Baking Powder, 4 oz, full, 3-1/4" h, 2-1/8" d **$375**

Sunshine-Oxford Fruit Cake, sq corners, early 1900s......................**$20**

Towle's Log Cabin Brand Maple Syrup, cabin shaped, woman and girl in doorway, 4" h, 3-3/4" l, 2-1/2" d **$110**

Trivet, lyre form, wrought iron frame and turned handle, brass top, replaced foot, stamped maker's mark, 12" l **$45**

Wafer iron, cast iron, octagonal, church with steeple and trees dec on one side, pinwheel with plants and star flowers on reverse, wrought iron handles **$400**

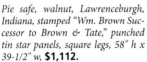

Pie safe, walnut, Lawrenceburgh, Indiana, stamped "Wm. Brown Successor to Brown & Tate," punched tin star panels, square legs, 58" h x 39-1/2" w, **$1,112.**
Photo courtesy of Pook & Pook, Inc.

Lamp shade, Quezal, green and gold pulled feather pattern, egg shape, 4-1/2" h, **$200.**
Photo courtesy of The Early Auction Company, LLC.

Lamp shades, cameo, satin, gold to clear, oak leaves and acorn dec, pr, 6-1/2" h, **$225.**
Photo courtesy of The Early Auction Company, LLC.

Lamp shade, Steuben, green and gold drag loop, ruffled rim, shape #819S, 5" h, **$225.**
Photo courtesy of The Early Auction Company, LLC.

LAMP SHADES

History: Lamp shades were made to diffuse the harsh light produced by early gas lighting fixtures. These early shades were made by popular Art Nouveau manufacturers including Durand, Quezal, Steuben, and Tiffany. Many shades are not marked.

Aladdin
Cased, green **$870**
Satin, white, dogwood dec **$65**
Cameo, gold satin glass cut to clear in acorn and leaves pattern, price for pr, 6-1/2" h **$225**

Fostoria
Gold, 24 ribs, 4-1/2" h **$85**
Iridescent gold, 24 ribs, 4-3/4" h
.... **$90**
Opal, ribbed, gold interior, 4-3/4" h
.... **$100**

Lustre Art, opal, gold ribbon dec, 5" h
.... **$100**

Palme-Koenig, opaline, pink drag loops, 6-3/4" h **$110**

Quezal
Chartreuse gold and dark green reverse drape pattern, ribbed, 5" h
.... **$575**
Cylindrical, vertical ribbing, irid calcite, inscribed "Quezal," 6" h ... **$150**
Egg shape, green and gold pulled feather design, 4-1/2" h **$200**
Gold snakeskin design, 4-3/4" h
.... **$170**
Green and gold leaf design, gold threading, 4-3/4" h **$150**
Irid, bell shaped, gold zipper pattern, 5-1/2" h **$145**

Irid gold, pulled feathers, 5-1/2" h
.... **$270**
Irid gold, white scaled pattern graduating to irid green rim, sgd "Quezal," 5-1/4" h **$225**
Irid opal, gold pulled feather design, fitter rim chips, 5" h **$75**
Opal, green and gold pulled feather design, 4" h **$375**
Opal ground, irid blue pulled feather dec, tipped in gold, 5" h **$300**
Trumpet shape, dark gold, ribbed, 6-1/2" h **$115**

Slag glass dome, caramel slag, curved, 24" d **$200**

Steuben
Acid etched calcite, scrolling pattern, fleur-de-lis mark, price for set of three, 5" h **$300**
Aurene, gold, ribbed, fleur-de-lis mark, 4-1/4" h **$125**
Bell shape, alabaster body, irid green and gold hooked feather, fleur-de-lis mark, price for pr, 4-1/2" h
.... **$1,200**
Mushroom shape, gold Aurene hooked pulled feather on opal ground, additional zipper dec, 5" w
.... **$350**
Shape #64, gold Aurene, scalloped rim, fleur-de-lis mark, price for matched set of four, 4" h
.... **$525**
Shape #672, verre-de-soie, trumpet shape, ribbed, price for pr, 5" h
.... **$125**
Shape #799, tulip shape, green and gold pulled feathers, 1" re-glued chip, 5" h **$65**
Shape #819S, green and gold drag loop design, ruffled rim, 5" h **$225**

Shape #823-1/2, verre-de-soie, engraved hanging flower pattern, 4-3/4" h **$175**
Shape #853, verre-de-soie, engraved festoon pattern, ruffled rim, 4-1/8" h **$200**
Shape #938A, gold, inverted urn form, ribbed, 4-1/4" h **$160**
Shape #985, opal, green and gold drag loops, straight rim, 3-1/2" h
.... **$250**
Shape #2268, verre-de-soie, ribbed, 4-1/4" h **$75**
Shape #2327, calcite, acid etched ivy pattern, price for three, 5-1/2" h
.... **$500**
Shape #2354, calcite, acid etched Lumene pattern, 5-1/2" h **$70**
Shape #2533, calcite, acid etched Warwick pattern, 4-1/2" h **$95**
Shape #2533, calcite, acid etched oak leaf and acorn pattern, 4-3/4" h **$90**
Shape #7198, opal, Marbellite, 4-3/4" h **$50**
Tulip shape, gold Aurene, fleur-de-lis mark, price for matched pr, 5" h
.... **$225**
Tulip shape, gold Aurene, unmarked, price for matched pr, 5-1/4" h
.... **$175**

Tiffany
Irid gold, internally dec in coin spot pattern, scalloped rim, price for matched set of four, one with minute fitter rim chip, 3" h **$500**
Ribbed, conical, Favrile, irid, price for matched set of five, two with very minor fitter rim chips, 5-1/4" h
.... **$1,200**

Lamp, metal newel post base, figural, woman, holding bird, Steuben pulled feather shade with silver fleur-de-lis mark, 21" h, **$450.**
Photo courtesy of The Early Auction Company, LLC.

Table lamp, Neoclassical, bronze and ormolu base, each with campana shaped urn with Bacchanalian group at the handles, standing on a plinth dec with alternating bountiful urn and musical instrument medallions, urn 19-3/4" h, 35" h with finial, **$6,000.**
Photo courtesy of David Rago Auctions, Inc.

Table lamp, Tiffany Studios, four opalescent and amber glass shades in four sockets pendant from curved tendrils, domed leaf decorated foot, bronze base, marked Tiffany Studios New York, no. 25861, 16-1/2", **$9,987.**
Photo courtesy of Skinner, Inc.

Table lamp, Daum Nancy cameo, French, shade depicts trees, lake and boats, pinecone design base, metal mounts, shade signed "DAUM/ NANCY" above Cross of Loraine, early 20th century, 14" h, 7" d shade, **$2,750.**
Photo courtesy of Green Valley Auctions.

Table lamp, Gone With the Wind style, hand painted red, white, and pink morning glories, red beaded fringe trim, electrified, **$350.**
Photo courtesy of Dotta Auction Co., Inc.

Newell post lamp pair, Gustav Stickley, hammered copper four-sided lanterns lined in period mica, possible not original, stained cedar posts, normal patina wear, original finish, missing several ball screws, unmarked, 29-1/2" x 9-1/2" x 11", **$5,875.**
Photo courtesy of David Rago Auctions, Inc.

Unidentified American maker

Bulbous, Calcite, price for pr, 5" h $100

Irid gold, bell shaped, 4" h............$80

Irid gold, bell shaped, 4-1/4" h.....$90

Irid gold, ribbed body, 4-1/4" h $85

Irid, gold and white pulled feather, 5-1/2" h $125

Irid, opal green pulled feather, 5-1/2" h $100

LAMPS AND LIGHTING

History: Lighting devices have evolved from simple stone-age oil lamps to the popular electrified models of today. Aimé Argand patented the first oil lamp in 1784. Around 1850, kerosene became a popular lamp-burning fluid, replacing whale oil and other fluids. In 1879, Thomas A. Edison invented the electric light, causing fluid lamps to lose favor and creating a new field for lamp manufacturers. Companies like Tiffany and Handel became skillful at manufacturing electric lamps, and their decorators produced beautiful bases and shades.

Reproduction Alert.

Additional Resources:

Antique Trader® Lamps & Lighting Price Guide, by Kyle Husfloen, ed., Krause Publications, Iola WI.

Astral

Cornelius & Co., gilt brass weighted base with Gothic detailing, applied prism ring with ovoid frosted etched glass globe with Greek key and floral designs, electrified, flakes on rim, patent 1897, 11" h globe, 26" h overall $775

Sq white marble base, ribbed then turned brass column, cut glass prisms, frosted shade with etched flowers and

vintage dec, electrified, 22-1/2" h $250

Grapevine etched colorless glass shade, gilt metal font, glass prisms, standard with Rococo bronze fittings, flared, ribbed, blue glass shaft with gilt highlights, white marble base, electrified, imperfections, America, 19th C, 24-5/8" h $920

Banquet

Classical Revival, Goldsmiths Co., English, silver plate and cut glass, bowl form cut glass oil font, fluted Corinthian column, tapered sq section loaded base with flower filled urns connected by swags, electrified, early 20th C, 21-3/8" h $800

Victorian, cranberry shading to pink satin glass shade, set with amber, red, and green jewels, pink-shaded cased glass font, column fitted on enameled iron base, burner mkd "Kosmos Brenner," c1880, 30-1/2" h $980

Boudoir

Aladdin, reverse painted bell shade, pine border, floral molded polychromed metal base, 14-1/2" h, 8" d..$225

Handel, gilt-finished spelter base, reverse painted etched glass shade with umber harbor scene, orange sky, shade stamped "Handel 6450," Handel Lamps cloth tag on base, chips to patina, 14" h, 7" d $1,150

Heintz Art Metal Shop, Buffalo, NY, bronze shade with cut-out Art Nouveau style flowers and foliage, in three sections, similar dec in silver overlay on round bronze base, paper label, two dents, 9-1/4" h, 8-1/2" d $1,265

Obverse painted scenic, closed top mushroom-cap glass shade with textured surface mounted on gilt metal handled lamp base, weighted foot, hand-painted silhouetted forested landscape scenes, rim marked "Patented April 29th, 1913," 13-1/2" h $1,150

Pittsburgh Lamp, Brass & Co., reverse painted ribbed shade, winter landscape of black barren trees on snowy ground, blue shading to yellow and orange ground, metal base with raised foliage dec, raised "P.I.B. & Co. 2080" on base, 14" h, 7" d shade $635

Van Erp, Dirk, hammered copper and mica, four panel shade, single socket, small beanpot base, orig patina, open box mark, 12" x 10-1/2" $9,000

Chandelier

Arts & Crafts

Hammered bronze frame with pierced designs, suspending hammered bronze socket holders with four gold Aurene glass shades, c1910, 18" h, 14-1/2" d....................$1,380

Six panels, red brass, replaced mica panels, three-light cluster, orig dark patina, period chain and ceiling cap, 27" h, 32" d....................$2,300

AVEM, mold blown art glass, six arms terminating in candle lights, alternating with scrolls, silvered metal mounts, wiring restored, c1935, 27-1/2" d................................$600

Degue, colorless mold-blown and etched glass shade with stylized flowers and leaves, wrought iron frame with vine ornamentation, sgd "Degue 534," France, c1930, 30" h, 19" d................................$600

Empire-style, gilt metal and cut glass, six light, top with six outscrolled flat leaves hung with crystals, slender reeded standard with central cut glass orb, flat leaf ring supporting six short serpentine scrolled candle arms offset by pierced ribbon-tied laurel wreaths, strung throughout with crystal strands, end of standard with further crystals, 20th C, 31" l $1,100

Morreau, gilt and emb iron frame suspending four leaded-glass domed shades, central matching spherical shade, frame emb "The Morreau Co.," 20" h, 20" d....................$1,100

Muller Freres, France, five triangular-etched glass shades with geometric designs, wrought iron frame, signed "Muller Freres Luneville," c1930, 31" h, 17-1/2" d........................$1,060

Desk

Handel, lobed harp base, swiveling single socket, leaded green slag glass geometric shade, orig dark bronzed patina, base and shade stamped "Handel," 18-1/2" h, 10-1/2" d............$2,200

Steuben, bronze, adjustable, irid hammered glass shade, orig patina, shade sgd "Steuben," 20" h, 7" d............$860

Student, brass frame and adjustable arm, white glass shade, early 20th C, 23-1/2" h....................$260

Tiffany, 13-1/2" h, 7" d swirl dec irid green ribbed dome Damascene shade cased to white, marked "L.C.T" on rim, swivel-socket bronze harp frame, rubbed cushion platform, five ball

Student lamp, Steuben, double scrolling adjustable arm base, two 10" Aurene shades, iridescent gold and white zigzag border, shades signed with fleur-de-lis, 24" h, **$5,500.**
Photo courtesy of The Early Auction Company, LLC.

Table lamp, brass, three light, three signed 4-3/4" h Quezal shades, 21" h, **$950.**
Photo courtesy of The Early Auction Company, LLC.

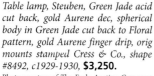

Table lamp, Steuben, Green Jade acid cut back, gold Aurene dec, spherical body in Green Jade cut back to Floral pattern, gold Aurene finger drip, orig mounts stamped Cress & Co., shape #8492, c1929-1930, **$3,250.**
Photo courtesy of The Early Auction Company, LLC.

Banquet lamp, Mt. Washington Crown Milano lamp, standard, font and shade, embossed gilt metal fitting separate glass components, opal glass with crimson, orange and yellow mums, green leafy stems over gray design, shade 12" w, 43" h overall, **$10,000.**
Photo courtesy of The Early Auction Company, LLC.

Parlor lamp, kerosene, hanging urn form, ?B & H, dec opal shade, patinated brass base with drop in font, undetermined association, electrified, late 19th century, 21" h, **$175.**
Photo courtesy of Green Valley Auctions.

Student lamp, Miller, brass, burner thumbnails mkd "E. MILLER & CO, DUPLEX," cased green ribbed shade, late 19th century, 22" h, 6-1/2" d base, **$412.**
Photo courtesy of Green Valley Auctions.

Table lamp, slag-glass shade, patinated white metal, 16 inset glass panels, early 20th century, electric, 26" h, 20" d shade, **$255.**
Photo courtesy of Green Valley Auctions.

Chandelier, hammered copper, conical shape, hangs from three long chains, cast hooks, ceiling plate, orig patina, Roycroft, orb and cross mark, 36" x 17", **$8,225.**
Photo courtesy of David Rago Auctions, Inc.

Table lamp, eight-light lily, gold iridescent shades, patinated unmarked metal base, shades engraved Quezal, c1920, 18", **$3,120.**
Photo courtesy of David Rago Auctions, Inc

Table lamp, Jefferson, reverse-painted hammered glass shade, branches of red and white flowers, ribbed two-socket patinated base, shade sgd "2369-R," base and shade stamped "Jefferson," 21-1/2" x 16", **$2,300.**

Photo courtesy of David Rago Auctions, Inc.

Hanging lamp, tin conical shade, embossed brass base, electrified, **$250.**

Boudoir lamp, reverse painted glass ovoid shade, green trees against blue sky, 13-1/2" h, **$200.**

Photo courtesy of The Early Auction Company, LLC.

Table lamp, Arts & Crafts, Heintz, sterling on bronze, helmet shade inset with "jewels," single-socket trumpet base, both with overlay of silver branches with leaves and berries, stamped "Pat. APD 4 1035," some cleaning to patina, 14" x 9", **$1,600.**

Photo courtesy of David Rago Auctions, Inc.

Banquet lamp, cast brass and silvered metal fittings, font, and base, marble pedestal, **$200.**

Photo courtesy of Dotta Auction Co., Inc.

Chandelier, Neoclassical-style, doré bronze, suspended by six rods terminating in figural mounts which support a bowl-shaped slag work glass shade screened by elaborate scroll work and swans, exterior with six electrified candles supported by acanthus leaf and column detail, all terminating in an acorn-shaped finial, **$6,500.**

Photo courtesy of David Rago Auctions, Inc.

feet, imp "Tiffany Studios New York 419" **$3,740**

Unknown maker

Brass, ribbed gold irid bell-form shade, unsgd, 20-1/4" h **$300**

Frosted blue satin shade with tadpole dec, adjustable brass arm and dome base, 25" h, 4" d **$200**

Early American

Betty lamp, tin, saucer base, weighted column, attached handle, some damage to wick support, 10" h **$150**

Cage lamp, wrought iron, spherical, self righting gyroscope font, two repaired spout burners, 6" d **$500**

Candle holder, wrought iron, hanging type, primitive twisted arms and conical socket, 19" h **$385**

Candle stand, wrought iron, double arms, brass candleholders and drip pans, attributed to PA, pitting, losses to drip pans, 18th C, 57-1/4" h, 24-1/2" w **$8,100**

Fluid

Blanc de chine, figural, small boy with heart-shaped medallions around necks, each holds small bowl on his head for lamp oil and small wick, minor rim flakes, price for pr, 5" h **$250**

Blown glass, colorless, ball font, wafer attached to pressed base with extended round corners, possibly Boston & Sandwich Glass Co., Sandwich, MA, minor base chips at low points, 1840-60, 5-1/4" h **$90**

Blown glass, colorless, blown font attached with wafers to pressed lacy base, drop burner, some roughness, edge flakes, 6-1/2" h **$265**

Blown glass, colorless, blown font with etched swag and tassel design, pressed stepped base, fluid burner, edge flakes, 6-3/4" h **$150**

Blown glass, colorless, bulbous font, bladed wafer, pressed paw-foot base, early pewter collar, possibly Boston & Sandwich Glass Co., Sandwich, MA, 1830-45, 10-1/2" h **$880**

Blown glass, colorless, bulbous font, ringed wafer attached to pressed base, early pewter collar with correct whale oil burner, possibly Boston & Sandwich Glass Co., Sandwich, MA, minor base chips, slight lean to font, 1830-45, 9-3/4" h **$200**

Blown glass, colorless, conical font, applied foot, applied angular handle with thumb rest and medial channel, rough pontil mark, 1820-40, 3-1/2" h **$250**

Blown glass, colorless, conical font, ringed wafer attached to pressed stepped base, possibly Boston & Sandwich Glass Co., Sandwich, MA, base chips, 1840-60, 6-3/4" h **$90**

Blown glass, colorless, flattened font, solid stem, round base, pewter collar, 6" h **$150**

Blown glass, colorless, urn shaped font, disk wafers, pressed sq stepped base with vertical ribbing between extended round corners, pewter collar, correct pewter and tin whale burner, rough pontil mark, possibly Boston & Sandwich Glass Co., Sandwich, MA, chips and flakes to base, 1830-45, 7-1/2" h **$115**

Blown glass, colorless, urn shaped font, ringed and disk wafer construction, large blown and hollow ball shaped knop, pressed stepped base, early brass collar, double tube fluid burner with caps and chain, possibly Boston & Sandwich Glass Co., Sandwich, MA, normal flakes under base, 1830-45, 10-1/2" h **$660**

Blown threaded glass, light cranberry with opposing white spiraling threads, font attached to reeded brass stem, single marble base, early #2 brass collar, probably Joseph Walter & Co. Flint Glass Works or Boston & Sandwich Glass Co., some manuf bubbles at base of font interior causing minor thread distortion, 1860-75, 7-1/2" h **$1,980**

Cut overlay, star and quatrefoil, opaque white cut to colorless font, connected to white alabaster/clambroth Baroque base, early #2 brass collar and connector, probably Boston & Sandwich Glass Co., overlay abrasions, 1860-80, 14-1/2" h **$990**

Pressed glass, colorless, loop font, paneled hexagonal base, pewter collar and cap, minor roughness, price for pr, 11-1/4" h **$200**

White cut to cranberry glass font, brass collar, marble and brass base with lime green glass stem insert, 13-3/4" h **$650**

Table lamp, four sided metal shade with pink slag glass inserts and pierced work gallery, wick adjuster marked "Made in US of America," square font with pierced floral decoration, waisted pedestal with square base supported on four paw feet, electrified, 22-1/2" h, **$300.**

Photo courtesy of Alderfer Auction Co.

Parlor lamp, pink D.Q.M.O.P., bulbous body, ruffled rim, metal collar and porcelain knobs, four applied rigaree feet, signed "Hinks Duplex Patent," 14" h, **$1,725.**

Photo courtesy of The Early Auction Company, LLC.

Table lamp, geometric shade, band of turtle-back tiles against yellow ground, Four Virtues gilt base, four sockets, a couple of short breaks, stamped TIFFANY STUDIOS NEW YORK, shade 1482, base 557, 25-1/2" x 18", $28,800.
Photo courtesy of David Rago Auctions, Inc.

Table lamp, Handel, reverse painted textured shade with wooded landscape, shade marked "Handel 6159, JB" with three slash marks below, bronze base stamped "Handel," cloth tag sewn to felt on underside, 23" h, $7,000.
Photo courtesy of Alderfer Auction Co.

Table lamp, dragonfly, cone-shade unsigned, orig Tiffany footed library base, mkd Tiffany Studios D794, Bakelite sockets, on/off switches, three-arm shade holder, 18" h, $27,500.
Photo courtesy of The Early Auction Company.

Grease, tin, brass labels "S.N. & H.C. Ufford, Boston," saucer base with concentric rings, one missing shade brackets and ring carrier, soldered repairs, price for pr, 6-1/2" h **$1,250**

Hanging, wrought iron, "U"-shaped swing hanger with long hook, wick holder with chicken finial, 22-1/2" l, 4-3/4" d **$175**

Lace maker's, colorless, round blown font attached to blown base, hollow stem, 7-3/4" h **$375**

Loom light, wrought iron, candle socket, trammel, 14-3/4" h **$500**

Miner's lamp, cast and wrought iron, chicken finial, replaced hanger, 7-3/8" h **$110**

Peg, overlay glass, pink cut to white cut to clear, frosted peg attached to clear wafer, brass collar, 2" d, 4-1/2" l **$450**

Petticoat, tin, round pan base, large ring handle applied to one side of column, small pick and chain attached to handle, 9" h **$260**

Rush light holder, wrought iron, candle socket counter weight, tripod base, penny feet, tooled brass disk at base of stem, simple tooling, 9-1/2" h **$470**

Skater's lamp, brass, clear glass globe marked "Perko Wonder Junior," polished, small splint in top of brass cap, 6-3/4" h **$160**

Student, brass, embossed "MILES PATENT" on whale oil font, adjustable candle holder and pierced shade, removable tin snuffer, brass ring finial, weighted dish base, traces of black paint, England, candle holder loose from drip pan, late 18th/early 19th C, 19" w, 7-1/4" h **$1,650**

Taper jack, Sheffield silver on copper, old repairs, 5" h **$195**

Floor

Bradley and Hubbard, small domed leaded glass shade, green slag glass, gold key border, open framework adjustable standard, domed circular foot, 56" h, 7" d **$400**

Faries Mfg. Co., Decatur, IL, bright chrome torchere, flaring trumpet shade, diecast mark, 65-1/4" h, 12" d **$150**

Handel
Chipped glass hemispherical reverse painted shade, moonlit tropical scene with tall ship, orig bronze patina, single socket harp, shade

mkd "Handel 65-749," cloth label on base, 56-1/2" h, 14" d **$7,000**
Yellow and amber opalescent bent glass paneled shade with faux lead came, green diamond details, five-light, patinated copper columnar base, scrolling feet, marked "HANDEL" on base, 64" h, 24" d **$9,780**

Sarfatti, Gino, manufactured by Arteluce, Italy, three arm, adjustable, steel, wood, and leather, c1950, 74-1/4" h **$3,750**

Tiffany/Aladdin, reflective white int., marked "Tiffany Studios New York," adjustable bridge lamp base with Arabian Nights motif, orig dark bronze patina, elaborate platform base, stamped "Tiffany Studios New York 576," 50" h, 10" d spun bronze shade **$2,990**

Unknown maker, black and gold painted metal, topped by three acanthus scrolls, tripartite base with pad feet, Baroque style, electrified, 57-1/4" h **$765**

Yellin, Samuel, wrought iron, twisted tripod base, conical finial, two socket frame, mkd "Samuel Yellin Phila PA," 61-1/2" h, 17-1/2" d **$4,000**

Hanging

American, patinated metal and cut glass, hall type, candle socket, Gothic arches, diamonds and flowerheads dec, 19th C, 18" h **$1,380**

Arts and Crafts

Brass and slag glass shade, linked metal chain suspending shade composed of eight panels of green, caramel, and white bent slag glass panels, dropped apron with emb and cut-out brass border overlay with Dutch windmills, trees, and cottages over band of multicolored slag glass, prisms below, 30" drop, 20-1/2" d **$920**

Four massive iron cross bars, hand hammered and bronzed surface, support chocolate slag glass shades with brass fleur-de-lis guards, electrified, 17" drop, 22-1/2" d **$950**

Handel, Meriden, CT, reverse painted, model number 6997, mushroom-shaped glass shade decorated on exterior and interior with exotic blue and gold birds, burgundy and green floral branches and leaves, bronzed metal fittings, stamped "Handel," shade sgd

and numbered, early 20th C, 11" d **$3,290**

Morgan, John, and Sons, NY, attributed to, verdigris bronze leaves surrounding ceiling hook suspending four chains supporting six-socket domed shade, similar bronze leaf dec, dropped apron, shade with striated green, amber, and white slag glass segments, round transparent purple "jewels" form grape-type clusters, few cracked segments, 39-1/2" h drop, 25-1/4" d, 11-1/2" h leaded shade **$6,325**

Perzel, chrome, metal, and glass, 40-1/4" d **$1,225**

Tiffany, attributed to Tiffany Glass and Decorating Co., square green and opalescent diamond-shaped glass jewels arranged as central pendant chandelier drop, twisted wire frame, late 19th C, 18" l, 15" d **$2,990**

Unknown maker, brass, slender hanging stem, repaired wiring, 32" h, two 6-1/2" h amber etched shades **$375**

Piano

Handel, gilt leaded lavender and opalescent yellow leaded shade suspended from bronze base, scrolled arm, unmarked, attributed to, c1915, 17" l **$750**

Tiffany, tripartite gold amber glass turtleback shade, framed in bronze, three center gold irid turtleback tiles, single-socket swiveling "dog leg" shaft, shade and weighted base imp "Tiffany Studios New York," 6-3/4" h, 19" l shade **$4,025**

Table

American, early 20th C

20 radiating caramel and white slag glass panels on domed shade, medial geometric green glass border, alternating green and caramel slag glass border, undulating dropped apron, two-socket fixture, ribbed trefoil base with brown/green patina, minor corrosion, some cracked segments, 19-1/4" h, 15-1/2" d **$920**

Reverse painted shade, hemispherical frosted glass shade, int. painted with trees and foliage silhouetted against yellow-orange shaded sky and water, two-socket bronze patinated cast metal base, raised scroll, foliate, and flower motif, base

Desk lamp, orange and white marbleized turtle shaped top panel, blue and white marbleized slag side panels, trophies on sides, acorn on pull chain, **$295.**

Photo courtesy of Dotta Auction Co., Inc.

Floor lamp, Roycroft, designed and executed by Dard Hunter and Victor Toothaker, gently sloping circular leaded glass shade, stylized pattern of fruit and foliage in yellow and green slag glass, three-socket wrought iron base with twist, in foliate and wood grain patterns, unmarked, few short breaks to glass, 61" x 20", from estate of Miriam Hubbard Roelofs, Elbert and Alice Hubbard's daughter, **$22,000.**

Photo courtesy of David Rago Auctions, Inc.

Table lamp, incense lamps, orig Durand glass shades, Egyptian figural bases, pr, **$1,300.**

Photo courtesy of David Rago Auctions, Inc.

Desk lamp, faceted slag glass shade, band of green maple leaves, single socket bronzed base, orig patina, orig on/off key, shade stamped HANDEL, base unmarked, shade 5" x 5-1/4", **$2,400.**

Photo courtesy of David Rago Auctions, Inc.

Table lamp, Woodbine shade, three-footed bronze lamp base, adapted oil-font, minor breaks, stamped TIFFANY STUDIOS NEW YORK, 17" x 14", **$24,000.**

Photo courtesy of David Rago Auctions, Inc.

marked "A & R Co.," minor wear, 24-3/4" h, 18" d........................**$920**

Baccarat, attributed to, blown molded glass, deep emerald green columns and fonts with relief twist designs, black marble bases, brass and brass plated fittings, harp and finial, fittings replaced, pr, 36" h......................**$1,380**

Bigelow Kennard, Boston, domed leaded shade, opalescent white segments in geometric progression border, brilliant green leaf forms repeating motif, edge imp "Bigelow Kennard Boston/Bigelow Studios," three socket over Oriental-style bronze base cast with foo dog handles, Japonesque devices, 26" h, 18" d shade.......**$2,875**

Boston Glass Works, floral and foliate overlay, bronze patina over six radiating striated caramel and white bent slag glass panels, two-socket fixture with similar illuminated base, minor patina wear, few dents, early 20th C, 22" h, 18-1/2" d bent panel slag glass shade..........................**$750**

Bradley and Hubbard, Meriden, CT, early 20th C

Frosted domed shade with stylized floral dec in burgundy, brown, and green, sgd urn form base, 18" h..............**$750**

Reverse-painted shade with eight lilies in gold and earthtones, shade decorated on exterior with textured brown blades, patinated brown metal strapwork base, maker's stamp on standard, one socket needs repair, 22" h, 15-3/4" d......................**$2,710**

Duffner and Kimberly, New York, dome leaded glass shade with tuckunder irregular rim, multicolored blossoms with yellow centers, green leaves, long stemmed flowers extending to top on segmented white background, three socket bronze lobed shaft with quatraform shaped base, 26" h, 24-1/2" d shade.............**$7,435**

Handel, Meriden, CT

Chipped glass reverse painted shade, moonlight forest scene with brook, three socket, four footed Arts & Crafts base with some verdigris to bronze patina, orig cap, Handel 6324, 25" h, 18" d.................**$6,000**

Chipped glass reverse painted shade, moonlit tropical scene with tall ship painted by John Bailey, three socket bronze base with clefs, orig cap, shade mkd "Handel 6391 John Bailey," base unmarked, 24" h, 18" d.............**$8,000**

Chipped reverse painted shade, pink and green bouquets of wild roses and butterflies, two socket base, orig pierced cap, some verdigris to bronze patina, shade mkd "Handel 6688," base unsigned, 23" h, 18" d **$9,000**

Conical shade with light green ground and blue gray lower border, segmented by band of pink apple blossoms on branches, stamped "Handel Lamps Pat'd No. 979664," sgd "Handel 6742," three sockets on bronze metal standard, some spotting, 23-1/2" h, 18" d **$3,820**

Reverse painted domical glass shade, band of black-eyed Susans with orange petals, brown centers, and green leaves against yellow ground, outlined on textured exterior in black, sgd "Handel 6956 BD," three sockets with acorn pulls, bronzed metal vasiform base, 22-1/2" h, 17-1/2" d **$3,290**

Ribbed glass reverse painted shade, tall ships on sea, classical acanthus leaf three-socket base, some verdigris to bronze patina, orig cap, Handel 5887R, base unsigned, small chips to edge of shade, 23-1/4" h, 15" d **$5,500**

Heintz, sterling on bronze, single socket, mushroom shaped shade and flaring base overlaid with delicate sprig pattern, bronze patina, few short scratches, 15" h, 13" d **$1,600**

Jefferson, reverse painted scenic shade with winter scene on textured satin shade, brass candlestick base, unsigned, c1915, 17" h, 12" d **$460**

La Verre Francais, cased glass, frosted ext. over swirled orange, yellow, and cobalt blue, sgd on both shade and base, electrified, replaced shade holder, 19" h **$1,350**

MB Co., paneled shade, conical base, openwork silver-plate grape vine designs, five panels of green and white slag glass, cast leaf finial, engraved leaves on base, base marked "Made and Guaranteed by the MB Co. USA," electrified, five sockets, 20-1/2" h **$1,200**

Muller Fres, frosted domed shade with mottled dec, inscribed "Mueller Fres Luneville," brass tri-support stylized fleur-de-lis base, 20" h **$1,000**

Pairpoint, domed closed top mushroom-cap glass shade, Vienna, coralene yellow int., painted stylized olive green leaves and red berries, gold outline on ext., ball-decorated ring supported by four arms, quatraform base molded with foliate devices, imp "Pairpoint Mfg Co., 3052," 20-1/2" h, 11-1/2" d shade.............**$2,070**

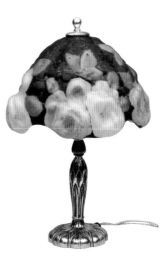

Table lamp, hammered copper metal overlay, caramel textured glass shade, tulip design riveted strapwork, signed Handel, no. 979664, three sockets, shaft on domed base, bronze patinated finish, wear, impressed Handel on base shade, 25" h, 17-3/4" d, **$3,055.**
Photo courtesy of Skinner, Inc.

Boudoir lamp, Pairpoint, roses and butterflies, black background, silvered base, signed and numbered "C 3064," early 20th century, 14-1/4" h, shade 9-1/2" d, **$2,420.**
Photo courtesy of Green Valley Auctions.

Table lamp, seven light lily, gold Favrile shades, bronze base, fine orig dark patina, TIFFANY STUDIOS NEW YORK/29788, impressed fleur-de-lys, shades marked LCT, 20" x 10", **$26,400.**
Photo courtesy of David Rago Auctions, Inc.

Hall lamp, hanging, rib optic, rubina opalescent, colorless glass font, brass mounts, chain and ceiling plate, late 19th century, 8" h x 8" d shade, overall 45-1/2" h, **$155.**
Photo courtesy of Green Valley Auctions.

Table lamp, Bigelow and Kennard, leaded glass shade, gothic geometric pattern in white and light green slag glass, three-socket bronze-patinated base, unmarked, 21-1/2" h, 16" d, **$4,025.**
Photo courtesy of David Rago Auctions, Inc.

Table lamp, Gorham, asymmetrically bordered leaded glass shade of white and pink cyclamen blossoms, green leaves, four-socket bronzed foliate base, unmarked, finial appears to be soldered to shade causing separation around top, few short lines to glass, 22-1/2" x 20", **$12,000.**
Photo courtesy of David Rago Auctions, Inc.

Floor lamp, iridescent pulled feather shade, single socket, Art Deco base, four lion feet, unsigned, American, 20th century, 66-3/4", **$825.**
Photo courtesy of Skinner, Inc.

Pittsburgh Lamp, Brass and Glass Co., Pittsburgh, model no. 1595, domed frosted and textured glass shade, interior painted with mountainous landscape, exterior painted with pine trees, paper manufacturer's label affixed to interior, three-socket patinated metal ribbed standard set into weighted metal base, scroll, shield, floral, and foliate motifs in relief, wear to patina, c1920, 27" h, 17-3/4" d shade **$1,955**

Steuben, attributed to, jade green long neck vasiform glass standard with white threading spiraling on neck, double socket, leaf-form bronzed metal mounts, 23" h **$420**

Suess Ornamental Glass Co., Chicago, leaded glass shade with stylized yellow, orange, green, and white slag flowers and leaves, brass-washed base, unmarked, 23" h, 22" d shade **$5,350**

Tiffany Studios, dome shade, layered and striated leaded glass segments designed as tulip blossoms and leaves, red, orange, amber, blue, and green, metal rim tag imp "Tiffany Studios New York 1456," three-socket bronze base with three pronged crutch supporting oval shaft, sq base with mottled brown and green patina, round disk on base imp "Tiffany Studios New York 444," 22-1/2" h, 16" d **$32,220**

Unidentified maker, alabaster, fluted gourd-shaped body with flared top, black marble base, brass paw feet and fittings, tall brass stem, double electric sockets, 52-1/2" h **$300**

Van Erp, Dirk, hammered copper classical base, four paneled mica shade with vented cap, single socket, fine orig patina and mica, open box mark/San Francisco, 17-1/2" h, 13" d **$9,200**

Williamson, Richard, & Co., Chicago, amber slag bordered by red tulips, pink and lavender-blue spring blossoms, green leaf stems, carved glass, mounted on four-socket integrated shaft with stylized tulip blossoms above leafy platform, imp "R. Williamson & Co./Washington & Jefferson Sts./Chicago, Ill," restored cap at top rim, 25" h, 20" d peaked leaded glass dome **$3,220**

LANTERNS

History: A lantern is an enclosed, portable light source, hand carried or attached to a bracket or pole to illuminate an area. Many lanterns have a protected flame and can be used both indoors and outdoors. Light-producing materials used in early lanterns included candles, kerosene, whale oil, and coal oil, and, later, gasoline, natural gas, and batteries.

Barn, mortised wood frame, four panes of glass, bentwood handle, tin cover over top vent, twisted wire latch, old patina, discolored glass in door, minor damage, make-do repaired split on top, 5-1/4" w, 5-3/4" d, 8-3/4" h..........................**$825**

Candle

Tin, double folding door covering orig glass panel, folding handle in back, brass candle socket with spring loaded push-up in base, traces of black paint, door hinges glued, lid possible replacement, 9-3/8" h **$230**

Tin, octagonal paneled glass globe, punched tin top, ring handle, and font, globe surrounded by wire guards, replaced tin font with candle socket, war, minor damage, traces of japanning on top, 11-1/4" h **$300**

Wood frame, beveled base and top, pegged construction, arched tin deflector on top, wire bale carrier, old refinishing, old pieced restoration on top, one pane cracked, minor insect damage, 12" h **$250**

Folding, tin, glass sides, emb "Stonebridge 1908," 10" h **$75**

Globe, fixed pear-shaped globe, pierced tin frame, ring handle, traces of black paint, America, mid-19th C, 17-1/2" h.......................................**$215**

Hall, glass and polychrome, gold painted flat leaf top suspending cut glass drops, joined by curved scrolls, suspending ovoid shade formed by five curved colorless glass panels in metal framework topped by ribbon tied laurel branches, accented with faceted bead trim, bead and glass prism trefoils, Italian, late 19th C, 26" h..**$2,100**

Japanese, Patterson Bros., Lansing, MI, adv, panes with General U. S. Grant, puppies, young girl, and wilderness scene **$195**

Jeweled, sheet brass, punched designs radiating out from faceted blue, red, green, and pale gold glass jewels, bottom marked "NH Car Trimming Co. New Haven, Conn," ring hanger, 11-1/2" h...................................**$250**

Painted tin, triangular black painted tin frame with glass panels, int. mirror paneled reflector, small tin kerosene lamp, glass chimney, America, seam separations, late 19th C, 15-3/4" l, 12" d, 19-3/4" h...........**$175**

Paul Revere Type, punched tin, circular punching on door and body, cone top, round handle, light overall pitting, 16" h **$275**

Railroad, Pennsylvania Railroad, marked "Keystone Lantern Co., Philadelphia," wire ring base, 5" h red globe...**$445**

Skater

Brass, grass green globe, 7" h **$550**

Tin, amethyst globe, top mkd "Jewel," rust, 7" h...................................**$835**

Tin, deep amethyst globe, top and globe both mkd "Jewel," rust, 7" h **$1,100**

Tin

Brass base and top with hinged, fluted peak, onion-shaped blown glass globe, wire guards, two wire bale handles, removable tin font held by two wires, burner missing, minor dents, 15" h **$230**

Pear-shaped mold blown glass globe, pierced tin top and base, ring handle, tin oil font with two spring clips, burner missing, soldered repairs, black repaint, 12-1/2" h **$300**

Tin, four panes of glass, hinged door, wire guards, wire bale handle, old worn gold paint, wear, 12" h **$115**

Tin, tin base and top with pierced stars and diamonds, molded glass globe with wire guards, ring handle, removable tin font, brass burner, traces of black paint, 12" h **$200**

Tin, old black paint, clear brown glass insert, applied rings top and bottom, pierced diamonds and stars, make-do candle socket is old glass inkwell, New England, edge dents on base, 16-1/2" h....................**$250**

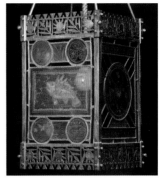

Lantern, hall, Aesthetic Movement, American, pierced bronze banding at top and bottom, four polychrome stained glass panels, each painted with flower, fish, duck, or dove, 19th century, **$2,400.**
Photo courtesy of David Rago Auctions, Inc.

Lantern, Dietz, Acme Inspector Lamp, embossed handle, L.V.R.R., **$395.**
Photo courtesy of Dotta Auction Co., Inc.

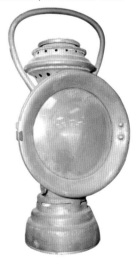

Lantern, Dietz, loop handle, large round clear lens, **$225.**
Photo courtesy of Dotta Auction Co., Inc.

Map, sampler, American silk on silk, depicting world map by Skinner, early 19th century, 9-5/8" x 17-1/2", **$3,910.**

Photo courtesy of Pook & Pook, Inc.

Two maps of America, A New and Accurate Map Of America by Thomas Bowen, c1800; "Carte de la Partie Sud des États-Unis," by M. Bonne, c1790, the larger 11" x 17-1/4", **$300.**

Photo courtesy of Sloans & Kenyon Auctioneers and Appraisers.

Map, New Jersey, geological survey, George Cook cartographer, 1889, sold as suite of 36" x 48" wall charts, index sheet, with original field box, **$300.**

Photo courtesy of David Rago Auctions, Inc.

Map, state off Rhode Island, engraving on paper from Cary's American Atlas 1796, "compiled from the Surveys and Observations of Caleb Harris by Harding Harris," toning, scattered light stains, contemporary molded wood frame, 14" x 9-7/8", **$700.**

Photo courtesy of Skinner, Inc.

MAPS

History: Maps provide one of the best ways to study the growth of a country or region. From the 16th to the early 20th century, maps were both informative and decorative. Engravers provided ornamental detailing, such as ornate calligraphy and scrolling, especially on bird's-eye views and city maps.

Maps generally were published as plates in books. Many of the maps available today are simply single sheets from cut-apart books.

In the last quarter of the 19th century, representatives from firms in Philadelphia, Chicago, and elsewhere traveled the United States preparing county atlases, often with a sheet for each township and each major city or town.

A Map of North America, Edward Wells, London, 1700, double page, engraved, wide margins, 355 x 480 mm **$635**

A Map of the British Empire in America, from the Head of Hudson's Bay to the Southern bounds of Georgia, London, engraved, folding, hand colored and in outline, wide margins, c1750, 265 x 325 mm **$260**

Americae Nova Tabula, Willem Blaeu, Amsterdam, double page engraved, wide margins, 1633, 365 x 465 mm **$2,990**

A New and Accurate Map of the World, John Overton, London, engraved, folding, double-hemispheric, margins trimmed, 1670, 390 x 515 mm **$8,625**

A New Map of Nova Scotia, Thomas Jeffreys, London, double page, engraved, very wide margins, all edges tissue-backed on verso, 1750, 325 x 415 mm **$220**

A Plan of the Town and Chart of the Harbour of Boston, London, February 1775, engraved, folding, extracted from 1775 issue of *Gentleman's Magazine,* 290 x 350 mm **$220**

Atlas, "New Historical Atlas of Montgomery County Pennsylvania" by J. D. Scott, Philadelphia, binding weak, insect damage to back flyleaf, 1877, 17-1/2" x 14" **$650**

British Dominions in America agreeable to the Treaty of 1763, Thomas Kitchin, Dury, London, double page, engraved, hand colored in outline, wide margins, 1777, 445 x 540 mm **$6,440**

Canada et Louisiane, George Louis Le Rouge, Paris, double page, engraved, wide margins, hand colored in outlined, 1755, 625 x 510 mm **$375**

Capt. James Lane Property, Bedford, Massachusetts, watercolor and ink on paper, shows distances, boundaries, and 223 acres, divided between sons James and Samuel in accordance with last will and testament, "Surveyed and divided by Stephen Davis, Surveyor of Lands," laid down on muslin, creases and separations, tears, fading, staining, 1773, 12-3/4" x 30-1/2" **$150**

Cruchley's New Plan of London, George Frederick Cruchley, London, engraved, 30-section map, hand colored, linen backed, orig board cover with publisher's label, 1836, 460 x 855 mm overall **$175**

Dutch, 7-3/8" x 12-1/4", black on white engraving by O. Lindeman, red, green, brown, and yellow hand coloring showing hemispheres, 2" tear repaired from back, contemporary

13-1/2" x 17-1/2" frame and matting **$250**

Haemisphaerium Stellatum Astrale Antiquum, Andres Cellarius, Amsterdam, double page, engraved celestial map, hand colored, wide margins, clear tear at vertical fold at lower margin just extending into image, 1660, 440 x 515 mm **$2,530**

Jamaica, John Thomson, Edinburgh, double page, engraved, two insets showing harbors of Bluefields and Kingston, wide margins, hand colored in outline, 1817, 440 x 630 mm **$320**

Land Survey Map of Boston Cabinet Maker Stephen Badlam, by Matthew Withington, pen and ink on paper showing parcel of land in Dorchester, Massachusetts, written description and compass star directional highlighted with watercolor, creases, small edge losses, repaired tears, stains, 1786, 20" x 11-1/2" **$650**

Map of Oregon and Upper California, John Charles Fremont, Washington, folding, lithographed, hand colored in outline, overall browning, 1848, 905 x 755 mm **$2,185**

Maryland, copper plate engraving, titled "Noua Terrae-Mariae tabula," by cartographer John Ogilby, London, 15-1/2" x 16-1/2", light foxing and toning **$3,500**

Northern America, including Russian Alaska, entire British Possessions & Danish Iceland, Colton, hand colored, 1857, 17" x 14" **$95**

Ohio, A J. Johnson, New York, with view of capitol building in corner, from *"New Illustrated Family Atlas of the World 1864,"* printed, hand colored, matted, unframed, 23" h, 29" w **$75**

Philadelphia, and Liberties section, set of three, published by John Reed, engraved by James Smithers, vignettes of Pennsylvania Hospital, House of Employment, State house, provenance descended from Gen George Meade family, each with some chipping, tears, foxing, late 18th C, each 31-1/2" x 24" **$9,750**

Sicily, copper plate engraving, titled "Europae Tabula VII" by Ptolmey,

some foxing, toning, text bleed through, 9" x 12" **$150**

United States of America, W. and D. Lizars, London, engraved, folding, hand colored, margins trimmed, several folds closed at lower edge with archival tape, c1810, 395 x 460 mm **$260**

MATCH HOLDERS

History: The friction match achieved popularity after 1850. The early matches were packaged and sold in sliding cardboard boxes. To facilitate storage and to eliminate the clumsiness of using the box, match holders were developed.

The first match holders were cast iron or tin, the latter often displaying advertisements. A patent for a wall-hanging match holder was issued in 1849. By 1880, match holders also

Match holder, Wedgwood, Jasper, blue, bottom marked only "Wedgwood," late 19th/early 20th century, 1-1/4" h x 2" x 3-3/4", $55.
Photo courtesy of Green Valley Auctions.

Match holder, figural, brass, Punch, second half 19th century, 2" h, $99.
Photo courtesy of Green Valley Auctions.

Match holder, bronze, pheasants, sgd "Cain," Auguste Nicolas Cain (French, 1821-1894), 4-1/4" h, 6-1/2" w, $350.
Photo courtesy of Pook & Pook, Inc.

Cigar and match holder, German bisque, fisherman smoking pipe, gilt dec, impressed mark, late 19th century, 8" h x 4-1/4" x 6-3/4", $65.
Photo courtesy of Green Valley Auctions.

Match holder, figural, brass, boy with drum on back, second half 19th century, 4-3/4" h x 2" x 2-3/4", $110.
Photo courtesy of Green Valley Auctions.

Match holder, hanging type, cream painted metal, black silhouette of girl with parasol in garden, **$35.**

Match safe, Stagecoach motif, enamel on sterling, English hallmarks, made by Sampson Mordan, London, 1899, 2-1/4" x 1-1/2", **$1,500-$2,000.**

Match safe, Cobra motif, sterling silver, Gorham Mfg Co., cat. #605, 2-1/2" x 1-3/8", **$2,000.**

were being made from glass and china. Match holders began to lose their popularity in the late 1930s, with the advent of gas and electric heat and ranges.

Advertising

Ballard Flour, tin litho, figural obelisk shape, Egyptian hieroglyphics, C.8-, 6-5/8" x 1-7/8" **$925**

Buster Brown Bread, tin litho, baker serving bread to Buster Brown and friends, wear to match basket, C.8-, 6-7/8" x 2-1/8" **$475**

Ceresota Prize Bread Flour, figural, diecut, tin litho, boy slicing bread, C.8+, 5-3/8" x 2-1/2" **$300**

Vulcan Plow Co., diecut, C.8+, 7-7/8" x 2-3/4" **$825**

Wrigley's Juicy Fruit Gum, tin litho, red, white, and black, C.8, 4-7/8" x 3-3/8" **$400**

Bisque, natural-colored rooster with beige basket, two compartments, round base with pink band, 4" h, 3-5/8" d **$135**

Brass, bear chained to post, cast, orig gilt trim, 3" h **$225**

Bronze, shoe, mouse in toe, 3" h . **$125**

Cast iron, figural, high-button shoe, black paint, c1890, 5-1/2" h **$50**

Glass, shaded rose to pink overlay satin, ball-shape, glossy off-white lining, ground pontil, 3" h, 3-1/4" d **$155**

Majolica

Happy Hooligan with suitcase, striker, rim nick to hat **$110**

Monk, striker, hairline in base ... **$140**

Papier-mâché, black lacquer, Oriental dec, 2-3/4" h **$25**

Grading Condition. The following numbers represent the standard grading system used by dealers, collectors, and auctioneers:

C.10 = Mint

C. 9 = Near mint

C.8.5 = Outstanding

C.8 = Excellent

C.7.5 = Fine +

C.7 = Fine

C.6.5 = Fine – (good)

C.6 = Poor

Porcelain, seated girl, feeding dog on table, sgd "Elbogen" **$125**

Sterling silver, hinged lid, diecut striking area, cigar cutter on one corner, lid inscription "H. R." and diamond, inside lid inscribed "Made for Tiffany & Co./Pat 12, 09/Sterling," 1-3/4" x 2-1/2" **$95**

Tin, top hat, hinged lid, orig green paint, black band, 2-3/8" h **$65**

Torquay pottery, ship scene, reads "A match for any Man, Shankin," 2" h, 3-1/8" d **$85**

MATCH SAFES

History: Pocket match safes are small containers used to safely carry matches in one's pocket. They were first used around the 1840s. Match safes can be found in various sizes and shapes, and were made from numerous materials such as sterling, brass, gold, nickel-plated brass, ivory and vulcanite. Some of the most interesting and sought after ones are figurals in the shapes of people, animals, and anything else imaginable. Match safes were also a very popular advertising means during the 1895-1910 period, and were used by both large and small businesses. Match safes are known as vesta cases in England.

Resources: Deborah Shinn, *Matchsafes,* Scala Publishers in association with the Cooper-Hewitt Museum, 2001; W. Eugene Sanders, Jr., and Christine C. Sanders, *Pocket Matchsafes, Reflections of Life & Art, 1840-1920,* Schiffer Publishing, 1997; Denis Alsford, *Match Holders, 100 Years of Ingenuity,* Schiffer Publishing, 1994; Audrey G. Sullivan, *History of Match Safes in the United States,* published by author, 1978; Roger Fresco-Corbu, *Vesta Boxes,* Lutterworth Press, 1983.

Collector Clubs: International Match Safe Association, PO Box 791, Malaga, NJ 08328-0791, www.matchsafe.org or IMSAoc@aol.com.

Note: While not all match safes have a striking surface, this is one test, besides size, to distinguish a match safe from a calling card case or other small period boxes. Values are based on match safes being in excellent condition.

Adviser: George Sparacio

Reproduction Alert. Copycat, reproduction, and fantasy match safes abound. Reproductions include Art Nouveau styles, figural/novelty shapes, nudes, and many others. Fantasy and fakes include Jack Daniel's and Coca-Cola.

A number of sterling reproduction match safes are marked "925" or "Sterling 925." Any match safe so marked requires careful inspection. Many period, American match safes have maker's marks, catalog numbers, 925/1000, or other markings. Period English safes have hallmarks. Beware of English reproduction match safes bearing the "DAB" marking. Always verify the date mark on English safes.

Check enameled safes closely. Today's technology allows for the economic faking of enamel motifs on old match safes. Carefully check condition of enameling for telltale clues.

Numerous reproduction brass match safes are appearing on the market. They are made to resemble original pieces, and do not have any maker marks or numbers to assist in their identification. Some plated brass match safes are also appearing.

1893 World's Fair/Columbus' egg, figural, sterling, 2-5/8" x 1-3/4", EX **$450**

Agate, black/brown/white banded agate, brass trim with engine turned design, push button lid release, abrasive striker inside lid, 2-3/4" x 1", EX **$75**

Agate sides, enameled floral decoration on brass edges, 2-5/8" x 1-1/8", EX **$125**

Aluminum, brite cut design, double lid, stamp combo, by August Goertz Co., patent #484,092, 2-5/8" x 1-3/8", EX **$45**

Anheuser Busch/Knights of Templar Conclave, Oct. 18, 1889, Wash-ington, DC, nickel plated, by Edward Hauck & Sons, patent Aug. 14, 1883, 3" x 1-1/2", EX............................**$175**

Arabian man, sterling, by Aikin Lambert Co., 2-3/4" x 1-3/4", EX......**$325**

Automobile, figural, brass, German, 2" x 2-1/2", EX............................**$375**

Baby kissing mother, sterling, by Unger Bros., catalog #9918, 2-1/2" x 1-1/2", EX..............................**$300**

Baden Powell photo in frame, book shaped, vulcanite, 2" x 1-1/4", EX **$40**

Banner Cigar Company/eagle motif, multi-colored graphics, celluloid wrapped, by Whitehead & Hoag Co., 2-1/4" x 1-1/2", EX..............**$250**

"Bat woman" motif, sterling, by Wm. Kerr, catalog #1197, 2-1/2" x 1-1/2", EX..............................**$900**

Beaver lid/Dominion Coat of Arms, sterling, by Roden Bros., 2-1/2" x 1-1/2", EX..................**$200**

Book, figural, spine marked Bryant & May, vulcanite, 1-7/8" x 1-1/2", EX **$45**

Book-shaped, golf motif one side, cricket motif other side, vulcanite, 2" x 1-1/2", EX **$150**

Bowler Bros./Tadcaster Ale, multi-colored celluloid wrap, plated brass ends, 2-3/4" x 1-1/2", EX.............**$100**

BPOE, dropped forged elk head with enameled clock in antlers, glass eyes, sterling, by Fairchild & Johnson, 2-1/4" x 1-7/8", EX.....................**$225**

Bryant & May, book shaped, vulcanite, 1-7/8" x 1-1/2", EX.............**$35**

Bulldog emerging from doghouse, sterling, by R. Wallace & Sons, catalog #870, 2-5/8" x 1-3/4", EX **$400**

Burgyrus Company/steam shovel motif, b/w graphics, celluloid wrapped, plated brass ends, 2-1/2" x 1-1/2", EX..................................**$275**

Button hook, knife & safe combo, oval shaped, sterling with English hallmarks, 2-1/2" x 3/4", EX......**$300**

Candle in box, mother of pearl sides on nickel plate, spring lid release, hinged candle stand, 2-1/2" x 1-1/2", EX **$40**

Candle matches complete with matches, by Roche Bros., 3-1/8" x 1-5/8", EX..................................**$40**

Match safe, enameled with gold quartz stone on top of lid, 14k gold, 2-1/4" x 1-1/4", EX, **$7,500.**

Match safe, Anheuser Busch advertising, G. Silver with enameled "A" and star, 2-3/4" x 1-1/2", EX, **$300.**

Match safe, Indian tobacco pouch, figural, sterling with gold interior wash, by Gorham Mfg. Co., no manufacturing number, 2-9/16" x 1-5/8", EX, **$1,000.**

Match safe, burgee of the New York Yacht Club, figural, enameled on sterling, 2-3/8" x 1-5/8", EX, **$2,500.**

Match safe, geisha girl, figural, Japanese, brass, 2-5/8" x 1-1/2", EX, **$800.**

Match safe, Venus riding swan, with cigar cutter, sterling, by Frank M. Whiting, 2-7/8" x 1-1/2", EX, **$450.**

Centennial Match 1776-1876, litho tin, by Bryant & May, 1-1/2" x 2-1/4", EX **$75**

Charlie's Aunt, Dec 21st, 1895, sterling with English hallmarks, by Walker & Hall, 1-3/4" x 1-3/8", EX **$225**

Cigars, bunch of 4 marked Havana, nickel plated brass, 2-3/4" x 1-1/2", EX **$125**

Combination coin and stamp holder, pick and propelling pencil, engraved design, sterling with English hallmarks, by Wm. Neale, 2-1/2" x 1-1/2", EX **$225**

Devil motif, enameled top with "I am Capt. Price-Who the (devil image) are you?", sterling with English hallmarks, by J. Horton, 1-1/4" x 1-3/4", EX **$650**

Dog motif, enameled on sterling, by Carter, Howe Co., 1-5/8" x 2-5/8", EX **$800**

Egyptian/AAONMS motif, fez hat shaped, sterling, by Simons, Bro. & Co., 2-5/8" x 1-7/8", EX **$575**

Elephant standing with ivory tusks, figural, nickel plated brass, 2-1/8" x 1-5/8", EX **$150**

Farmhouse, figural, Japanese, brass, 1-1/2" x 2-1/2", EX **$800**

Ferris wheel/Columbus' image, made for 1893 Chicago World's Fair, brass, 2-7/8" x 1-1/2", EX **$100**

Fireman carrying child/"Good Wishes of FIreman's Fund Ins. Co.," sterling, by Shreve & Co., 2-3/8" x 1", EX **$600**

Fish/underwater scene, silver solder, by R. Wallace & Sons, catalog #097, 2-5/8" x 1-3/8", EX **$100**

Fishing creel, figural, brass, 2-1/2" x 1-1/2" x 3/4", EX **$125**

Flask, figural, top nickel plated brass, bottom glass, 2-3/4" x 1-3/8", EX **$110**

Floral motif with blue lapis strikers on each end, sterling, French hallmarks, 2-5/8" x 1-1/4", EX **$125**

Frog with bulging eyes, figural, patinated brass, Japanese, 2" x 1-3/4", EX **$400**

Gambling motif, old man smoking & playing cards, sterling, 2-1/2" x 1-5/8", EX **$375**

Gamewell Fire Alarm, insert type, by August Goertz Co., nickel plated

brass with red painted design, 2-3/4" x 1-1/2", EX **$375**

Gibson girl/salesman's sample, multicolored graphics, celluloid wrapped with plated brass ends, by Whitehead & Hoag Co., 2-3/4" x 1-1/2", EX **$275**

Goldstone, rectangular with rounded end, brass trim, 3" x 1-1/8", EX **$125**

Griffin motif, engraved, stamped "Hand Wrought," sterling with gold interior wash, by Gorham Mfg. Co., no manufacturing number, 2-3/4" x 1-5/8", EX **$400**

Gun with cigar cutter, figural, nickel plated, 4-1/2", EX **$425**

Happy/sad drinker, upright shows happy face, upside-down shows sad face, sterling, by Webster Company, 2-1/2" x 1-1/2", EX **$700**

Hood Rubber Company advertising on figural boot, gutta percha, 2-7/8" x 1-3/4", EX **$95**

Horse head, figural, sterling, by Howard Sterling Co., catalog #404, 1-1/8" x 2-3/4", EX **$400**

Horse with rider, country motif, nickel plated brass, crimped edges, 2-7/8" x 1-1/4", EX **$30**

Indian chief, sterling, by Unger Bros., 2-1/4" x 1-7/8", EX **$1,000**

Indian chief with single feather, sterling, by F. S. Gilbert, 2-1/2" x 1-1/2", EX **$375**

Irish symbols-Iberian harp, shamrock, etc., book shaped, bog oak, 2" x 1-1/2", EX **$65**

John Deere Plows advertising, nickel plated brass, by Whitehead & Hoag Co., 2-5/8" x 1-1/2", EX **$550**

Kid McCoy, boxing theme, b/w graphics, celluloid wrapped with nickel plated brass ends, by Whitehead & Hoag Co., 2-3/4" x 1-1/2", EX **$400**

King George V, figural, nickel plated brass, 2" x 1-5/8", EX **$375**

Knight in armor holding lance, castle background, sterling, 2-3/4" x 1-3/8", EX **$150**

Lacquered tin, top embossed "A. S. Stocker Patentee," vesta socket on lid, 1-9/16" x 2-5/16", EX **$75**

Lady urinating, risqué French type, enameled top and inside of lid, brass, 1-7/8" x 1-1/2", EX **$375**

'Leather package" with belt buckle design, lid opens at center exposing striker, silver plated, 2-3/4" x 1-1/2", EX **$150**

Leonardt & Co. pen points, book-shaped, gold lacquered tin, 2-1/8" x 2-5/8" x 3/4", EX **$85**

Lion motif, sterling, saw-tooth striker, 2-3/8" x 1-1/2", EX **$225**

Lisk Company advertising, multi-colored celluloid inserts, nickel plated brass ends, 2-3/4" x 1-1/2", EX **$200**

Louisiana Purchase, 1803-1903, copyrighted by I.G.K., brass, 2-3/8" x 1-1/4", EX **$100**

Malt-Nutrine/Anheuser Busch advertising, nickel plated brass, 2-7/8" x 1-3/4", EX **$150**

Maltese Cross & Baker Fabric Fire Hose advertising, gutta percha, by The Gutta Percha Company, 2-3/4" x 1-1/8", EX **$100**

McKinley for President, nickel plated brass, 2-7/8" x 1-1/2", EX......**$175**

Miller Brewing Co./F. Miller logo, nickel plated brass, 3" x 1-1/2", EX **$75**

Molassine Livestock Food, steer one side, multi-colored celluloid wrapped, nickel plated ends, 2-1/2" x 1-1/2", EX **$75**

Never-slip horseshoes, color graphics, celluloid wrapped, nickel plated ends, by Whitehead & Hoag Co., 2-3/4" x 1-1/2", EX....................**$150**

Order of Odd Fellows, insert type, nickel plated, 2-3/4" x 1-1/2", EX **$50**

Oriental Consistory 1909/Frank Roundy, nickel plated, by White-head & Hoag Co., 2-3/4" x 1-3/8", EX **$65**

Oriental, lady holding lantern with working compass, brass, 2-1/2" x 1-1/4", EX **$225**

Panama Exposition 1915, San Francisco/gun motif, nickel plated brass, by Wm. Schimper & Co., 2-3/4" x 1-1/2", EX **$40**

Pants/overalls, figural, pewter, patent Nov. 9, 1886, 2-7/8" x 1-1/4", EX **$75**

Pekinese dog applied to sterling with English hallmarks, by H.

Woodward & Co., 1-3/4" x 1-3/4", EX **$200**

Pool/billiards motif, sterling with English hallmarks, 1-1/2" diameter, EX **$800**

Pope Pius IX, figural, sterling, by Howard Sterling Co., 2-3/4" x 1-3/4", EX **$750**

Privy, figural, man with top hat inside, nickel plated, 2" x 3/4" x 1/2", EX **$150**

Queen Victoria, In Memorium, design outlined in gold gilt, book shaped, vulcanite, 2" x 1-1/2", EX **$55**

Rattlesnakes, intertwined, bold design, sterling, by Wm. Kerr, 2-3/4" x 1-5/8", EX **$800**

Red Man, fraternal, insert type, by August Goertz Co., nickel plated brass, 2-3/4" x 1-1/2", EX.............**$60**

Red Top Rye, original white and red highlights, thermoplastic, 2-7/8" x 1-1/8", EX **$100**

Rock Island Railroad, celluloid wrapped with nickel plated brass ends, by Whitehead & Hoag Co., 2-3/4" x 1-7/16", EX.................**$150**

Rugby ball, figural, sterling with English hallmarks, by Sampson Mordan, 2-1/8" x 1-1/2", EX....................**$750**

Saddle & polo mallet motif, quasi-figural, silver plate, 2-1/2" x 1-1/2", EX **$175**

Scallop, crab and mussel motif, silver plated, by Meriden Britannia Co., catalog #025, 2-5/8" x 1-1/2", EX **$325**

Scientific American newspaper, figural, sterling with enameled stamp, by Enos Richardson & Co., 2-3/8" x 1-1/8", EX **$550**

Shoe, figural, hob-nailed type, 800 silver, 1-3/8" x 2-1/8", EX..............**$300**

Skin-like motif, silver plated, by Pairpoint Mfg. Co., 2-1/2" x 1-1/2", EX **$125**

Teddy bears dancing/advertising, insert type, nickel plated brass, by August Goertz Co., 2-3/4" x 1-1/2", EX **$225**

Thorne's Whiskey, figural bottle with maze opening, sterling with English hallmarks, 2 x 1-1/4", EX..........**$400**

Tiger lady, sterling, by Gorham Mfg. Co., manufacturing #B3612, 2-3/4" x 1-1/2" EX **$600**

Unity patented cigar cutter, sterling with English hallmarks, by Horton Allday, 2" x 1-3/8", EX **$135**

Venus Rising, G. silver, 2-5/8" x 1-5/8", EX **$65**

Victoria Jubilee 1837-1887 with image of Queen Victoria, nickel plated, 2-1/2" x 1-3/8", EX **$60**

Washington/HMMBA sterling, by Gorham Mfg. Co., manufacturing #MDS, 2-1/2" x 1-5/8", EX **$250**

MEDICAL AND PHARMACEUTICAL ITEMS

History: Modern medicine and medical instruments are well documented. Some instruments are virtually unchanged since their invention; others have changed drastically.

The concept of sterilization phased out decorative handles. Handles on early instruments, which were often carved, were made of materials such as mother-of-pearl, ebony, and ivory. Today's sleek instruments are not as desirable to collectors.

Pharmaceutical items include those things commonly found in a drugstore and used to store or prepare medications.

Advertising

Button, Cloverine Salve Authorized Agent, celluloid, product described in detail, tiny white clover buds on green stems, blue, red, or white rim inscriptions **$45**

Diecut, Johnson & Johnson talcum powder, cardboard litho, baby on back playing with talc container, string hanger, C-7.5, 8-1/8" x 14-1/8"................................**$575**

Trade card, Kidd's Cough Syrup, diecut cardboard, Victorian woman and product advertising, 13" x 7-1/2" **$110**

Amputation knife, Civil War era **$135**

Apothecary chest

Chinese, old black paint, mortised case, shaped aprons with inset panels on sides, six dovetailed drawers with old painted red character labels, ring pulls, and removable dividers, 16-1/2" w, 18" d, 26-1/2" h **$250**

Apothecary bottles, emerald green bottles, original labels and stoppers, price for set of four, 3" d, 7-1/2" h, **$300.**
Photo courtesy of David Rago Auctions, Inc.

Apothecary trade sign, oak, mortar and pestle, 19th century, 15" h, **$525.**
Photo courtesy of Pook & Pook, Inc.

Apothecary cabinet, 36 drawers, rosewood and mahogany, drawers have original lettered names on fronts, base moldings of later date, pine secondary wood, wooden knobs which appear to be mostly original, some losses to veneers and knobs, mid-19th century, 72" h, 57" w, 11" d, **$3,850.**
Photo courtesy of Green Valley Auctions.

Oriental, old reddish brown finish mortised case, 45 detailed drawers, some with divided interiors ring pulls, red and yellow painted labels on front, sq legs, shaped base aprons, restorations, 33" w, 17" d, 46" h **$815**

Apothecary jar, cov, hp dec in burgundy and gold, black lettering on white ground, stenciled signatures on bases "Pouchet Deroche, Paris," acorn-shaped finials, French, wear to gold, 10-3/8" h **$320**

Bifocal spectacles, by McAllister, Philadelphia, silver frame, horseshoe-shaped lenses, sliding temples **$375**

Blood pressure kit, orig manual, 1917 .... **$55**

Book

The Dental Art in Ancient Times, lecture at A.M.A. Meeting, Atlantic City, 1914, map of Atlantic City, New Jersey, and boardwalk layout, cuts of ancient artificial teeth and tools, Burroughs Welcome & Co., London, 216 pgs, 1914, 4" x 6-3/4" **$34**

The People's Common Sense Medical Adviser in Plain English, or Medicine Simplified, Pierce, illus, 100 pgs, 1889 .... **$19.95**

Broadside

Dr. Harding's Vegetable Medicines, top text reads "Dr. Harding's Vegetable Medicines; A Cure For Constipation, and Those Diseases...," text details various medicines, some folds, light foxing, minor edge chipping, ink notation on bottom border, mid-19th C, 18" x 9-3/4" **$150**

Drs. White & Oatman, top text reads "Stuttering or Stammering Permanently and Easily Cured!" text details accomplishments and details of cure, some folds, mid-19th C, 18" x 8-3/4" **$150**

Cabinet, emb tin insert front, wood cabinet

Munyon's Homeopathic Remedies, 41 orig dovetailed product drawers on back, most labeled, 24" x 18" x 7" **$1,750**

Dr. LeSure's Famous Remedies, 27" x 20-3/4" x 6-3/4" **$5,700**

Dr. Daniels Warranted Veterinary Medicines, orig finish, C.7.5, 28-5/8" x 21-1/2" x 7-3/4" **$2,900**

Pratts Veterinary Remedies, orig finish, stenciling, 30" x 17-1/4" x 7" **$2,200**

Dental cabinet, mahogany, superstructure with 3 doors, mirrored back, milk glass counter, 3 stacks of six small drawer, each above a deep drawer, tapered round fluted front legs, 49-3/4" w, 13-3/8" d, 58-3/4" h **$900**

Dispenser, Alka-Seltzer, blue and white, tin litho adv sign on front, chrome base, orig cobalt blue tumbler, C.8.5, 14-5/8" x 5" **$400**

Electro-medical induction coil, T. Hall, Boston, silvered coil and switches, mahogany base, pair of later handles, 10" h **$1,150**

Field surgeon's set, Lentz & Sons, Philadelphia, all metal instruments, including Rust's pattern bone saw, Liston knife, trephine, bone forceps, etc., metal case with canvas cover case, both marked "2nd Reg. N.G.P.," 10-1/2" w **$350**

Fleam

Two-blade, tortoiseshell on case .. **$60**

Three-blade **$45**

Forceps tooth key, removable bolster/claw, hatched handles, W & H Hutchinson, Sheffield, England, restorations, mid-19th C, 7-1/2" l ... **$690**

Hour glass, Tartanware, McDuff pattern, half hour, 9-1/2" h **$175**

Jar, orig stopper, Duff's Colic & Diarrhea Remedy, cylindrical glass, recessed reverse painted on glass label, ground stopper matches pattern at base, some minor staining, 10-1/2" h **$250**

Magic lantern slides, set of 195, c1915 .... **$200**

Medical case, Civil War era **$130**

Optician's trial set, Brown, Philadelphia, retailer's label, oak case, partial set, 21" w **$175**

Optometrist's sample case, mahogany, containing three trays of 20 spectacles each, chart in lid, 20" w **$690**

Photograph

Medical training type, students with skeletons **$80**

Medical training type, human skull **$250**

B.B. Thayer & Co. Apothecaries San Francisco Cal ointment jar, black transfer, near mint, **$90.**
Photo courtesy of American Bottle Auctions.

Prosthetic leg originally worn by soldier injured Feb. 7, 1865 at Hatcher's Run. The soldier had his right leg amputated below the knee at a hospital in Baltimore, Maryland, **$1,150.**
KP photo/Wisconsin Veterans Museum collection.

Wooden medicine chest used by Surgeon Ezra M. Rogers, 12th Wis. Inf. The wooden lid has hand-cut dovetail joints, iron bands on corners, two iron strap hinges secured with screws and a handle for carrying. The interior of chest has lift-out section with 20 holes for medicine bottles. The lower section is also divided to hold 24 bottles. Because the surgeon who owned the chest is identified, the value increases from about **$1,100** *to* **$1,850.**

KP photo/Wisconsin Veterans Museum collection.

Brass bleeder, engraved, floral dec, "GB" initials on side, orig case with "GB" and beehive on lid, case wear, first half 19th century, 4" l, 2-1/2" x 4-7/8" case, **$265.**

Photo courtesy of Green Valley Auctions.

Surgeon's kit used by Dr. James T. Reeve, 10th and 21st Wisconsin Infantry. It consists of a mahogany veneer case. Bottom has second compartment that lifts out, both padded in red velvet and shaped to hold the bone-handled instruments. Identified medical sets can fetch from **$3,000** *to* **$5,0000.**

KP Photo/Wisconsin Veterans Museum collection.

Unidentified doctor's office interior **$30**

Unidentified doctor with bag **$20**

Phrenological bust, plaster, Fowler, Wells & Co., Boston, labeled cranium, label on back, damaged, 9-1/2" h **$80**

Plugger, Goodman & Shurtler's Patent, mechanical gold foil, sprung, hinged mallet on ebonite body, interchangeable head, 8" l **$460**

Scarificator, brass, 16 blades, sgd "Kolb," European, early 19th C ... **$215**

Sign

Blackleg Veterinary Medicines, Parke, Davis & Co., diecut cardboard, two cowboys giving shot to calf, C.8++, 17-1/2" x 11-1/8" **$775**

C. F. Hussey Optometrist, zinc, double sided, polychrome and gilt dec, figural eyeglasses, name, and title in banner at base, imperfections, late 19th C, 41" l, 12-1/2" h **$2,550**

Spatula/knife, pearl handle, Remington **$200**

Surgical knife, from Civil War hospital, 5" l **$40**

Surgeon's kit, ebony handles, velvet lined case, Civil War era **$1,420**

Tin

Blue Ribbon Brand, American Hygienic Co., Baltimore, MD, yellow, white, and red litho with German Shepherd in center, C.8+, 1-7/8" x 2-1/4" x 5/16" **$925**

Cadette Tooth Powder, figural tin litho soldier, green cap and coat, full, C.8, 7-3/8" x 2-1/4" x 1-1/4" **$525**

F. W. Cough Drops, Geo Miller & Co., Phila, "Cured My Cough," detailed graphics, C.9, 8" x 5-1/8" x 5-1/8" **$1,400**

Patent Superior Liquid Latex, yellow and red, C.8.5+, 1-1/2" x 2" x 7/16" **$425**

Town and Country, Nelson Products, NY, C.8++, 1-5/8" x 2-1/8" x 5/16" **$1,750**

Tooth extractor, W. R. Goulding, New York, marked "Baker & Riley patented 1845," removable claw/bolster, cross-hatched handles, 6-3/4" l **$1,380**

Tooth key

Turned and hatched removable rosewood handle, turned crankshaft, adjustable circular bolster and claw, early 19th C, 6-1/2" l **$215**

Wrought-iron handle, cranked and curved octagonal shaft, circular bolster, 10 interchangeable claws, possibly French, 19th C, 5-3/4" l **$635**

Trade sign, optician's, figural spectacles, one red and one blue glass lens, orig mounting bracket, iron, zinc, America, 19th C, 21" l, 13-1/8" h **$1,450**

Trepan, burnished steel, sgd "Sir Henry a Paris," arrowhead perforator, ivory pivot, ebony handle, five elevators, 18th C, 10-1/4" l **$1,725**

MILITARIA

History: Wars have occurred throughout recorded history. Until the mid-19th century, soldiers often had to provide for their own needs, including supplying their own weapons. Even in the 20th century, a soldier's uniform and some of his gear are viewed as his personal property, even though issued by a military agency.

Conquering armed forces made a habit of acquiring souvenirs from their vanquished foes. They also brought their own uniforms and accessories home as badges of triumph and service.

Saving militaria may be one of the oldest collecting traditions. Militaria collectors tend to have their own special shows and view themselves outside the normal antiques channels. However, they haunt small indoor shows and flea markets in hopes of finding additional materials.

Reproduction Alert. Pay careful attention to Civil War and Nazi material.

Additional Resources:

Warman's® Civil War Collectibles, 2nd Ed., by John F. Graf, Krause Publications, Iola, WI.

Warman's® Civil War Collectibles Field Guide, by John F. Graf, Krause Publications, Iola, WI.

Revolutionary War

Account book, for the Privateer Ship *Chandler*, sailing from Salem, Massachusetts, 70 manuscript pages, names 23 different brigs, sloops, schooners and ships that were supplied during the course of the Revolutionary war, several named individuals, original calf, scattered foxing and toning, c1779-84 .... **$7,100**

Autograph, document sgd, promotion of First Lieutenant, by Benjamin Harrison, 1783, paper seal, 6" x 8" **$650**

Book
Anthony Haswell, Printer, Patriot, Ballader, J. Spargo, 35 plates, 293 pgs, 1925 .... **$30**
Yale and Her Honor Roll in the American Revolution, H. P. Johnston, privately printed, rebound, 357 pgs, 1888 .... **$40**

Broadsheet
Addressed to the Governor of Massachusetts, published in the *Boston Evening Post*, single folio sheet, double-sided, regarding disturbances in the Colonies, minor restorations, February 1, 1773, 18" x 11-1/2" **$1,880**

Raising troops, requiring all towns to provide full accounting of supplies, bounties and gratuities given any soldier as part of state's proportion of Continental Army, signed by John Hancock in type, originally sent to Tosfield, CT, Oct. 8th, 1779, 13" x 8-1/2" **$2,585**

Inaugural button, George Washington, copper, orig shank attached, American eagle with surrounding date and text design, Albert WI-1-A., c1789 .... **$2,000**

Map, Seat of War in New York, contained in Nathaniel Low's Almanack, printed by J. Gill, Boston, twenty-four pages, in original wrappers, shows positions of Washington and other troops, 1777 .... **$2,650**

Newspaper, *Thomas's MA Spy: or Worcester Gazette*, May 13th, volume 14, no. 681, folio, printed by Isaiah Thomas, masthead engraved by Paul Revere, four pages, some mentions of the events of the war, 1784, 18" x 11" **$550**

Ordnance report, sent by William Perkins to Samuel Adams as Lt. Governor of Massachusetts, cover letter and ledger sheets describing condition of heavy cannon carriages and platforms in Boston Harbor **$600**

Plaque, General (Mad Anthony) Wayne, America, carved ivory, round, relief carved three-quarter view bust length portrait, banner below inscribed with name, houses and foliage in background, age crack, conforming molded wood frame, late 18th/early 19th C, 3-7/8" d **$500**

Print
Perry's Victory on Lake Erie, Perry in rowboat, eight sailors in midst of battle, steel engraving from painting by Thomas Birch, engraved by A. Lawson, published by William Smith, Philadelphia, Eastlake frame, 24" x 31" **$295**
Washington's Dream, litho by Currier and Ives, New York, Washington, in uniform, sleeping in camp cabin, vignette dream of three women representing Liberty, Plenty, and Justice standing over America, stepping on crown of tyranny, framed, 1857, 25" x 19" **$775**

Snuff box, cov, gutta percha, round, relief scene of battle, ships, coastline, buildings, French inscription "Prise d'Yorck (Taking of Yorktown or Battle of Yorktown)," 1781, 2-7/8" d **$750**

French and Indian War

Marching order, letter addressed to Captain Josiah Thatcher, Yarmouth, his Majesty's Service, Boston, ordering Thatcher to march troops to Springfield to be mustered, sgd by J. Hoar, some fold weakness, June 24, 1761, 8" x 6-1/4" **$185**

Uniform button mold, brass, American, casts six round buttons with central raised letter "I" for infantry, one 25 mm, one 18 mm, four 14.5 mm, each with eyelet, wooden handles missing, 18th C, 9" l **$625**

War of 1812

Broadside, printed cavalry orders for the 2nd Brigade 1st Visis, and 7th Reg 2nd Brig 1st Divis, Edmund Fitzgerland Lt. Col. 7th Reg & Cavalry, one sheet, Aug. 18, 1814 .... **$375**

Cartridge box, leather, white cloth strap, very worn, missing plate **$70**

Flag, 13 stars, Naval, hand sewn, 60-1/2" x 110" **$1,100**

Military drum, large eagle painted on sides, red, and blue stripes, one drum head, 22" h, 17" d **$750**

Ship document, British, articles pertaining to private armed ship *Dart* and four carriage guns, six nine-pounders, four swivel guns lying in St. John, New Brunswick, designed to cruise against Americas, details prize division, chain of command, other shipboard administration, right section includes signatures and ratings of 44 seamen and officers as crew, some staining, edge chipping, foxing, and fold splitting, Whatman 1808 watermark, dated July 1813, 21" x 29" .. **$500**

Civil War

Autograph
Davis, Jefferson, partly printed check, Union & Planters Bank, Memphis cancelled, July 22, 1872, 2-1/2" x 8-1/4" **$1,100**
General Ambrose Burnside, clipped from document, sgd "Headquarters Defenses of Harper's Ferry, Oct 31, 1862, Respectfully forwarded A. E. Burnside, Major Gen'l Cond'g," 2-1/2" x 3-1/2" paper, mounted on slightly larger card **$100**

Book
The History of the First New Jersey Volunteers, Henry R. Pyne, Chaplain, Trenton, 1871, 350 pgs, glued-in GAR clippings, cover scuffed **$175**
The Seventy-Seventh Pennsylvania at Shiloh History of the Regiment, Harrisburg Publishing Co., Harrisburg, PA, 1908, 342 pgs **$100**

Painting, American Civil War encampment, watercolor on paper, late 19th century, 3-1/4" x 6-3/4"; 7-1/4" x 10-5/8" framed, **$120.**
Photo courtesy of Green Valley Auctions.

Civil War era American flag, 35 stars, inscribed "G.B. Mickle," 85" x 136", **$1,405.**
Photo courtesy of Pook & Pook, Inc.

Civil War powder flasks (pair), brass, 8", **$350-$400.**

The Underground Railroad. A Record of Facts, Authentic Narratives, Letters & etc., Narrating the Hardships Hair-breadth Escapes and Death Stuggles for the Slaves in their Efforts for Freedom as related by themselves and others, or witnessed by the author, William Still, revised edition, published by People's Publishing Co., Philadelphia, 1879, 878 pgs, deluxe paneled cloth binding, orig owner's name on 2nd fly-leaf, scuffing to spine and cov, some int. foxing **$435**

Broadside
Abraham Lincoln funeral, from Governor Joseph Gilmore of New Hampshire, giving profound and moving instructions to people of New Hampshire to observe and participate in day of mourning, "all of the churches within their jurisdiction to be tolled, and minute guns to be fired...drape their stores and dwelling houses with the appropriate emblems of that grief...," dated April 17th, 1865, 8" x 10"......... **$950**

Union, Condemning U.S. Grant for Battle of Shiloh, large folio, sold by Applegate & Co., Cincinnati, Ohio, recounting events leading up to battle and Grant's action during conflict, c1862, 17-1/2" x 11-1/2" **$750**

Union, recruiting, dated September 12, 1861, Saccarappa, Maine, "Attention Volunteers Seventy-five Men Must be enrolled At Once....," these troops attributed to served in Company C of the 12th ME Volunteers, 12-1/4" x 9-1/2" **$1,175**

Union, recruiting, for M'Call's Division, Reading (Pennsylvania), printed with globe form masthead with "our country" and U.S. flag, dated April 1st, 1862, 13-1/2" x 6" ...**$1,175**

Union Draft, proclaiming "War Meeting!," Hingham, Massachusetts, black printed on salmon colored paper, light wear, dated 1864, 18-1/2" x 12" **$1,000**

Cane, carved wood, 1-1/2" w x 3" h oval wood knob, relief carved and polychromed shaft with American flag, 24 Union army corps badges, worn red, white, blue, and green polychrome, 1-3/4" brass ferrule, made for veteran, c1880, 35-3/4" l **$350**

Canteen, bull's eye, orig woven cloth strap, pewter spout sgd "Hadden, Porter & Booth, Phila," 7-5/8" d **$325**

Cartridge box, cross belt and eagle plate, "Calhoune New York" maker's stamp on inner flap, tin liners, oval U.S. plate **$900**

Fife, rosewood, nickel silver ends, eight bands, orig dark finish, faint signature "W. Crosby, Boston," 17-1/2" l **$125**

Invitation and program sheet, Washington's Birthday Celebration, Fort Ethan Allen, VA, Feb 22, 1865, sgd Charles Barnes as Colonel, Commanding 2nd Brigade, 8" x 5"....... **$50**

Kepi, 13th Infantry soldier's **$850**

Letter, 4 pgs, datelined "Camp 42nd Ohio Reg't OV, Morganza, LA July 3rd 1864," sgd "Noble," hand written in ink, talks about camp movement, mosquitoes, thoughts of home, 4th of July celebration, 10" x 7-1/2" **$60**

Manual, "Rules, Regulations, Forms, and Suggestions, For The Instruction and Guidance of the 1st US Volunteer Calvary," prepared by James B. Swain, Colonel Commanding and lst Lt, 1st Cal, USA, printed by Baker & Goodwin, NY, 1863, 16vo, 96 pgs, paper wraps, some int. foxing, chipping to wraps **$275**

Manuscript page, titled "Morning Report of Sick and Wounded Horses in the 2nd NY Vet. Cav at Talladega, Alabama, July 20, 1865," sgd by Smyth Brill, Veterinary Surgeon, reverse with impressive drawing of eagle, 10" x 8" **$60**

Map, titled "Military May of the Middle & Southern States showing the Seat of War during the Great Rebellion of 1861," published by W. Schaus, NY, drawn and engraved by Schedler, litho by Sarony, 18 section map mounted on lien, 26-1/2" x 34-1/2", framed, light staining ... **$300**

Medal, Grand Army of the Republic, droop-winged eagle, enameled bar with colonel's device, orig Robert Stoll case, 5-1/4" l with faded ribbon **$215**

Newspaper, *Cincinnati Gazette*, fold lines and minor damage, group of 19 newspapers, for year of 1863 ...... **$150**

Painting, oil on canvas, Major James D. Keyser, sgd lower right "Wilkinson Philadelphia 1890," waist image wearing uniform with epaulettes and baldric, three medals including Mullis and GAR, 30" x 25", new frame, relined **$700**

Photograph, tintype, cased
Cavalryman, wearing shell jacket with gilt detail on collar and buttons, lightly tinted blue pants, holding cavalry saber, Colt pistol in belt, forage cap with "D2," sixth plate **$770**
Confederate, checked shirt, butternut colored coat, CDV mount **$110**

Infantryman, waist-up portrait, holding Hardee hat with feather, "K," and bugle insignia, wearing epaulettes, cartridge box, holding musket with bayonet, ninth plate **$550**

Soldiers in front of tent, very worn quarter plate tintype, gutta-percha case with relief scene of officers standing at table, scrolled border, minor edge chips......................**$470**

Presidential pardon, 2 pgs, Nov 8, 1865, for B. F. Morrison of Cass County, Georgia, pardon grants amnesty "for all offences by him committed arising from participation, direct or implied, in the said rebellion," Andrew Johnson metal stamp, ink sgd by Secretary of State William H. Seward, 18" x 11-1/2", folding and wrinkling..................................**$200**

Shaving mug, hp, US Civil War soldier holding American flag, name Jos. Davis in gold, 3-3/4" x 3-1/2" **$1,500**

Spurs, pr, brass, Confederate, Leech & Rigdon style, 4" h..................**$115**

Sword, belt rig, non-commissioned officer, NCO sword by Ames Mfg, Chicopee MA, marked on blade, also marked "US, GWC, 1864," marked "GKC" on guard, leather scabbard, NCO sword belt ring, eagle buckle, plated wreath, frog for NCO sword and hangers, some leather deterioration to belt and scabbard **$900**

Walking stick, carved wood, dog's head finial with silver collar inscribed "Thos. Thompson Co. H 106 Reg. Pa. Vols. Evacuation of York Town 1862," natural branch carved with dog, squirrel, leafy vine, and reeded and geometric devices, wear, 36-1/4" h..........**$775**

Indian War

Bayonet, Model 1873, 3-1/2" w blade **$80**

Belt buckle, Naval officer, brass, stamped "Horstman, Phila".......**$120**

Broadside, Ohio massacre, No. 4, 1791, printed in Boston, foxed, water stained, modern frame, 1792 .....**$900**

Spanish American War

Hat badge, infantry, brass, crossed krag rifles, 2" l..............................**$55**

Cartridge box, U.S. Army..........**$125**

Pinback button, "Remember the Maine," battleship scene, patent 1896 ....**$25**

Spy glass, pocket, brass, Naval, round holder, brown leather grip, 16" l **$110**

World War I

American flag, cloth, eight stars and five stripes, made by Prisoner of War, "Arlon Belgium Dec 11th, 1918" written on mat, framed, some losses, discoloration, 6-1/4" x 10-1/4" sight **$350**

Bayonet, British, MK II, No. 4, spike, scabbard......................................**$20**

Book, Morris Hall Bailey, Lieutenant, (J.G.) U.S.N.R.F. in Memoriam, no date or publisher, 60 pcs, 8vo, c1920 ....**$180**

Buckle, U.S. Balloon Corps, emb hot air balloon..................................**$75**

Flare pistol, Model 1918, French . **$100**

Gun sling, soft leather, for 03 Springfield, 1917..................................**$17.50**

Helmet, German, Pattern, painted gray/green, 1916............................**$80**

Overcoat, U.S. Army officers, Melton, olive drab, wool, double breasted, 10 bone buttons **$65**

World War I, British recruitment poster: "Britain Needs You At Once," St. George and the Dragon, lithograph with full margins, printed by Spottiswoode & Co., London, 31" x 20," sold with Titanic broadside from Boston Evening Telegram, Friday, April 19, 1912, four full pages, framed, **$375.**
Photo courtesy of David Rago Auctions, Inc.

Cartridge box and shoulder sling with two plates, Model 1855, .58 caliber, **$750-$1,150.**

Sword belt plate, Model 1851, Federal eagle, prewar linen waist belt, **$425-$500.**

Confederate wooden-drum canteen made like a wooden barrel with short staves at bottom and lid. Staves are held in place with an iron band on each end. Three iron loops held strap. A 3/4" hole was drilled in side with turned wooden mouthpiece, **$2,500.**
KP photo/Wisconsin Veterans Museum collection.

Miniature painting, watercolor on ivory, of George Washington, sgd "GW," American, 19th century, 3-3/8" h, **$1,170.**
Photo courtesy of Pook & Pook, Inc.

Miniature portrait, watercolor on ivory, young man wearing blue jacket, 3-1/4" x 2-1/4", **$468.**
Photo courtesy of Pook & Pook, Inc.

Miniature portrait, watercolor on ivory, gentleman, American School, mid-19th century, 3-1/4" h x 2-3/4" w, **$610.**
Photo courtesy of Pook & Pook, Inc.

Photograph, black and white, warship crashing thru waves, orig oak frame, large **$325**

Trench flashlight and note pad, German, black tin container, orig pad and pencil...................................... **$65**

Tunic and trousers, gabardine, pinback, Air Corps and U.S. discs **$75**

Watch fob, Federal Seal, U.S. officer **$15**

World War II

Armband, Japan, military police, red lettering, white cotton **$48**

Book

Baa Baa Black Sheep, Pappy Boyington, Marine Corps Pilot Ace with Flying Tigers, 400 pgs, 1958...... **$38**

Blood and Banquets, Fromm, 350 pgs, photos, 1942........................ **$30**

December 7th, 1941-The Day The Japanese Attacked Pearl Harbor, Prange, 509 pgs, 34 photo plates, 1988... **$38**

From Hell to Heaven-Memoirs From Patton's Third Army in WWII, McHugh, 1st ed, 1970 .. **$30**

Semper Fi, Mac-Living Memories of the US Marines in WWII, Berry, 403 pgs, photos........................... **$40**

Cane, Civilian Conservation Corps, fully carved, U-shaped horse-head handle, one piece, carved low relief of trees, bathing beauty, alligator, name of carver's friends, "Middle Creek Camp F34 Co. 997," finish removed around later added date, 1933, 30-3/4" l........... **$125**

Flag, New Zealand PT boat, printed on blue cotton **$55**

Flyers goggles, Japanese, boxed, gray fur lined cups, yellow lenses......... **$35**

Gas mask, German, canister style, rubber mask, canvas straps, carrying container **$80**

Helmet, Italian, steel, leather chip strap... **$100**

ID tag, U.S. Army, oval pattern, instruction envelope, chain **$25**

Manual, War Department, FM30-30, Military Intelligence, *Aircraft Recognition Pictorial Manual,* Bureau of Aeronautics, Washington, DC, 179 pgs, illus of US, Great Britain, German, Japanese, Italian, Russian, etc. plans, 1943, 6-1/4" x 10" **$40**

Telescope, Australian, MK 1, heavy leather case and carrying straps, 14" l **$45**

MINIATURE PAINTINGS

History: Prior to the advent of the photograph, miniature portraits and silhouettes were the principal way of preserving a person's image. Miniaturists were plentiful, and they often made more than one copy of a drawing. The extras were distributed to family and friends.

Miniaturists worked in watercolors and oil and on surfaces such as paper, vellum, porcelain, and ivory. The miniature paintings were often inserted into jewelry or mounted inside or on the lids of snuff boxes. The artists often supplemented commission work by painting popular figures of the times and copying important works of art.

After careful study, miniature paintings have been divided into schools, and numerous artists are now being researched. Many fine examples may be found in today's antiques marketplace.

Pencil and watercolor on paper, Brigadier General James Miller, Peterboro, New Hampshire, American School, oval frame, toning, sold with accompanying note giving brief history of General's career, early 19th C, 5-3/4" x 4-3/4" **$1,880**

Watercolor and gouache on ivory, two brown-haired, rosy-cheeked children, one wearing a pink dress and holding a tabby kitten in her lap, the other in a purple printed dress, holding a blue ribbon attached to the kitten, unsigned but attributed to Mrs. Moses B. Russell (American, 1809-54), molded giltwood frame, small areas of paint loss on clothing, 3-5/8" x 2-3/4" **$4,120**

Watercolor and pencil on paper

Lady in black, hair comb, reverse inscribed "painted May 12th 1834 by J Sears," oval eglomise mat, framed, scattered small abrasions, toning, 4" x 3-1/4" **$470**

Miss Stevens, Andover, MA, area, half-length profile likeness, precise outlines with delicate drawing, bright blue dress with lace offset, dark upswept hair with tortoiseshell comb, background of blue and orange flanked by black spandrels at corners, unsigned, attributed to Edwin Plummer (Massachusetts and Maine, 1802-1880), back inscribed in pencil "Stevens, lace, purple," and outline of woman's profile, later black and gilt frame, minor foxing, color loss, some pinpoints, 5" x 3-1/2" **$21,150**

Young man, brown coat, red vest, red paint, bevel edge pine frame, 6-1/4" w, 7-1/2" h......................**$350**

Watercolor, graphite and ink on paper

Bust-length profile portrait of young woman, Mary L. Amidon, Dudley, Massachusetts, indistinctly signed "Ten—s" on lower sleeve, sitter identified by ink inscription on reverse, mounted in embossed brass mat in poly-resin case, creases, small tear, 2-5/8" d **$775**

Watercolor on ivory

Bust length portrait of Elizabeth Freeman (1786-1815), gold brooch frame with seed pearl border, accompanied by three small notes: one note written in 1888 by her daughter Elizabeth Freeman Duren, concerning birthday gift of brooch to her daughter, another written by great-granddaughter stating it was painted about 1812, last written by friend of the family who mentions the brooch was given to her after she bought a portrait from the great-granddaughter, Bangor, Maine, c1812, 1-7/8" x 1-3/4" **$1,650**

Elizabeth Maderia, sgd "E. B. Taylor," reverse with locket of hair, engraved name and date, oval brass frame, fitted in leatherette case, 1934, 3-1/2" x 2-3/4" **$225**

Gentleman, Anglo/American School, engraved gold pendant frame, reverse centered with en grisaille dec ivory oval medallion depicting dove with ribbon and two hearts suspended in its beak above curved panel inscribed "one mind," surrounded by woven hair, glass cracked, late 18th C, 2" x 1-3/8" **$650**

Gentleman wearing spectacles, sgd "M. B. Katze," brass framed, fitted in leatherette case, 3-1/2" x 2-3/4" **$200**

Gustavis Tuckerman Jr., sgd and dated "Sacro Fratelli 1847" lower right, inscribed on paper within opening on reverse "Gustavis Tuckerman (Jr.,) Born Edgbaston, England, May 15th 1824, Died New York, February 12, 1897," painted in Palermo, Italy, 1847 by Sacro Fratelli, oval engine-turned gilt-metal frame within rect papier-mâché frame inlaid with abalone floral dec, 3" x 2-1/2" **$450**

James L. Small, Camden, Maine, unsigned, American School, mounted in oval metal locket case, cobalt blue and white enameled border, pen and ink inscriptions appear on paper backing including "1818," "TL 20 LWV," conjoined V and W and "1850," conjoined V and W and "1850" also incised into the interior of the frame, 19th C, 2-1/8" d **$1,650**

Julia Clarke Brewster (1796-1826), attributed to John Brewster Jr., painted in the Columbia or Hampton, Connecticut area, orig oval gilded copper locket case within orig red leather hinged case, c1820, 1-7/8" x 2-1/4" **$4,600**

Lady in burgundy, wearing lace bonnet, sgd "G. Harvey" lower right, hinged red leather case with ormolu mat, 3-1/2" x 2-3/4" **$725**

Military officer wearing a navy blue coat with crimson collar, white braid, and cross belt, silver breast plate, epaulettes, and buttons, unsigned, American School, oval format, ebonized wood frame, 2-3/4" x 2-1/4" **$1,100**

Mother and child Double portrait, dressed in white, blue trim, pearl tiara on mother, child playing with pocket watch, old German typed label on back identifies woman as "Marquise d'Huret-Gonzenbach," ebonized frame, 1803, 5-3/4" w, 6" h **$600**

Napoleonic portrait, tortoiseshell and brass frame, oval format, signature obscured, 3-1/4" x 2-1/2" **$725**

Nobleman in powdered wig, blue sash, medal, holding sheet of paper, oval brass frame, 2-3/4" h **$325**

Richard Wagner, illegible artist's signature, ivory frame, brass liner, nacre inlay, 3-7/8" x 3-1/2" **$250**

Semi-nude slave girl with two cajoling men, unsigned, Continental, giltwood frame, late 19th C, 5" x 3-7/8" **$750**

Woman with hair in braided ringlets, beaded cap, floral dress, laced bodice, cast brass frame with ram's head corners, 3" x 2-3/4" **$325**

Young blond military officer, green and red uniform with epaulettes, sgd "Haberle," oval brass frame with horn, small pc missing, 3-3/8" w, 4-1/2" h **$320**

Young boy, sgd "Jared Sparks Handerson, Baltimore" in pencil on reverse, American School, 19th C, oval format, 2-3/4" x 2-1/4" l **$620**

Young gentleman, black great coat, white waist coat, pleated shirt with stickpin and black neck cloth, unsigned, Anglo/American School, gilt-metal frame, aperture containing lock of braided hair, fitted leather case, 19th C, 2-3/4" x 2-1/4" **$950**

Young lady, attributed to Jacob Maentel, oval blue ground, lady in blue and white dress, orange ribbon on head covering, orig frame, 6" x 7-1/2" **$3,025**

Young woman with curled hair, attributed to Frederick Buck, wearing coral necklace, oval format, late 18th/early 19th C, 3" x 2-1/2" **$825**

Watercolor on paper

Believed to be Commodore Perry, brown curly hair and sideburns, dark blue naval officer's uniform, gold epaulettes, oval ground glued to blue backing, matted with old reeded frame with black paint, some flaking to gold, dark blue alligatored, 5" w, 7-1/8" h **$420**

Gentleman, oval aperture, unsigned, American School, framed, crease, minor foxing. 19th C, 4-1/2" d **$890**

Gentleman, reverse identified as "1825, Eleazar Graves, father of Laura Graves Lincoln," unsigned, attributed to Rufus Porter, America, grain painted frame, laid down, staining in margins, minor toning, c1792-1884, 5-3/4" x 4-3/4" **$445**

Miniature, slant front desk, Chippendale style, fall front, fitted int, two short and three long drawers, straight bracket feet, mid-19th century, 11" h, 8-3/4" w, 4-3/4" d, **$1,170.**
Photo courtesy of Pook & Pook, Inc.

Miniature, chest of drawers, late Georgian, mahogany, two over three drawers, applied cock beading, top has applied half-round molding, cut-out skirt and feet, pressed glass Lacey period knobs, one rear leg reattached, early 19th century, 17-3/4" h, 17-1/2" w, **$550.**
Photo courtesy of Green Valley Auctions.

Miniature, Chest of drawers, mahogany, rectangular top, four drawers, turned feet, Pennsylvania, mid-19th century, 9-1/4" h, 9" w, 5-1/4" d, **$1,055.**
Photo courtesy of Pook & Pook, Inc.

Gentleman, wearing black jacket, white vest and stock, seated before window on red upholstered chair before red drapery, penciled inscription "Herbert Lynesey squire Wier," on reverse, unsigned, Anglo/American, gilt gesso frame, minor foxing, 19th C, 5-1/2" x 4-3/8" **$360**

Lady in blue dress, white cap, brown ribbon, attributed to Edwin Plummer, Boston, c1841-46, oval eglomise mat, framed, laid down, small tear, minor toning, losses, repaint to mat, 4-1/8" x 3-1/2" **$765**

Woman wearing tortoiseshell comb, sitter identified on reverse as "Mrs. A. Saunders age 18 years," oval eglomise format, molded gilt frame, American School, toning, gilt loss on mat, c1840, 4-3/4" x 3-5/8" **$2,585**

Young brunette seated in lush interior, hair dressed with pearls, lace-trimmed gown and blue wrap, signed to left "J. Isabey," Continental, late 19th C, 6" x 4-7/8" gilt-metal frame, 3-1/8" x 4-1/4" h **$1,725**

Watercolor on porcelain, woman with classical profile, wearing scarf with pearl and gold brooch, brass frame, 4-3/8" h **$200**

MINIATURES

History: There are three sizes of miniatures: dollhouse scale (ranging from 1/2 to 1 inch), sample size, and child's size. Since most early material is in museums or extremely expensive, the most common examples in the marketplace today are from the 20th century.

Many mediums were used for miniatures: silver, copper, tin, wood, glass, and ivory. Even books were printed in miniature. Price ranges are broad, influenced by scarcity and quality of workmanship.

Miniature, blanket chest, walnut, lift lid, dovetailed case, single drawer, straight bracket feet. Pennsylvania, c1800, 6-3/4" h, 11" w, 4-1/2" d, **$1,055.**
Photo courtesy of Pook & Pook, Inc.

The collecting of miniatures dates back to the 18th century. It remains one of the world's leading hobbies.

Child or doll size

Bed, Arts & Crafts, rect headboard with two cartoon-like images of baby dolls, footboard with two sq-form cutouts, imperfections, 28-5/8" l, 16" w, 15-3/4" h **$230**

Blanket chest, six-board

America, pine, wire hinged top, dovetail and mortise and tenon constructed box, cavity with two compartments, natural surface, early 19th C, 9-3/4" l, 4-1/2" w, 6-3/4" h **$3,650**

America, poplar, dovetailed, sq nail construction, molded lid and base, turned feet, brass hinges, orig red covered by old mustard paint, early 19th C, 11" l, 6" w, 7-1/2" h ... **$4,400**

Lancaster County, Pennsylvania, dovetailed, bracket feet, molding at lid and bottom, till, red paint dec, old splits in lid, 16-3/4" l, 11" w, 12-1/2" h **$1,760**

New England, blue painted pine, rect hinged top with applied molded edge, dovetailed case, molded bracket base, wear, early 19th C, 20-3/4" l, 10-3/8" w, 9-5/8" h ... **$550**

Poplar, dovetailed, old thin red wash, applied moldings around lid and base with worn black paint, dated on back "Mar 6, 1827," restorations to hinge rail, feet missing, 15-3/4" l, 7-1/2" w, 7-3/4" h **$460**

Bookcase, hp, scalloped cornice over four open shelves, base with three drawers, Peter Hunt dec **$1,650**

Box on frame, America, grain painted, pine dome-top box with wire hinges, frame with vase and ring-turned legs, int. lined with floral patterned wallpaper, early 19th C, 7" w, 4" d, 5-3/4" h **$2,720**

Bucket, cov, turned wood, two drilled handles, turned lid, orig yellow paint on outside, orange on inside, white, red, black, and blue designs, some wear and varnish flaking, 4-1/2" w, 3-7/8" h **$150**

Buffet, carved wood, dark stained finish, two spindled shelves, lower section with two chip carved front doors, carved and stippled stylized floral dec on sides, Normandy, early 20th C, 9" w, 4-3/4" d, 13-3/4" h **$235**

Miniature tea service, Continental silver, four pcs, teapot, coffeepot, covered sugar, and oval footed tray, hallmarks on tray include Dutch, others unidentified, 19th century, 1-1/2" to 2-1/4" h, 4-5/8" x 5-3/4", **$330.**
Photo courtesy of Green Valley Auctions.

Miniature table and two chairs, sterling, American, oval top table with cabriole legs, chairs have pierced backs, mkd "Sterling" only, early 20th century, 1-1/4" and 2" h, 1-1/2" x 2-1/4", **$165.**
Photo courtesy of Green Valley Auctions.

Chair, arm, New England, carved maple, ball, vase, and ring turnings on banister back, stiles ending in ball finials, finely turned arms, legs, and stretchers, orig upholstered seat, mid-19th C, 7" w, 5-3/4" d, 13-1/2" h **$470**

Chair, side, worn orig light green paint, black striping, gold stenciling, polychrome floral dec, pr, 10-3/4" seat, 22" h **$625**

Chest of drawers

Biedermeier-style, fruitwood veneer, wire nail construction, three drawers, applied half turned pilasters painted black, capped with ormolu trim, tapered sq legs, old refinishing, green velvet lining in drawers, small brass pulls, 14" w, 7-1/2" d, 10-1/4" h **$550**

Carlisle, Cumberland County, Pennsylvania, softwood, paint dec, four drawers, sq nail construction, scrolled ribbon dec on front, wooden pulls, light brown grain paint dec, dark brown highlights to imitate burled walnut, 10" l, 5-1/2" d, 11-1/2" h **$990**

Cupboard, step-back

Middle Atlantic States, cherry, flat-molded cornice above cock-beaded case, two cupboard doors with raised panels, two shelves int., arched opening over projecting case with two short drawers with applied molding, two raised-panel cupboard doors, old red-stained surface, mid-19th C, 24" w, 11" d, 37-1/4" h **$1,725**

New England, stained, molded top overhangs case of two drawers opening to two-shelved int., stepped out board overhangs two drawers on legs, side shaping, orig surface, early 19th C, 24-1/2" w, 8-1/8" d, 33" h **$1,265**

Rocker, Empire style, mahogany, vase-shaped splat, rush seat, scrolled arms, 22" h **$225**

Settee, carved wood, dark stained finish, serpentine back, openwork spindled flowerheads and chip-carved and stippled stylized floral dec, hinged lid, Normandy, early 20th C, 7-5/8" l, 7-5/8" w, 4-1/4" h **$145**

Settle bench, PA, orig gold, copper, and silver fruit dec along crest and back slats, mustard yellow ground with areas of wear and touch-up, scrolled arms, plank seat with incised borders, eight turned legs, restoration, 24" l, 6-1/2" w, 6-1/2" h seat **$825**

Spiral staircase, mahogany, dark rosewood grained finials, rect base with demilune cut out in center, late 19th C, 17-5/8" w, 8-5/8" d, 22-1/8" h **$1,500**

Stool

Foot, pine, sq nail construction, D-shape cut-out legs, side skirt, orig natural wood finish with folky diamond and line inlaid wood on top, label "Stool belongs to Hannah C. Raymond," 7-1/2" l, 4-3/4" w, 4-1/2" h **$935**

Dec pine, round top, shaped legs, painted red with yellow and blue star, circular stenciled dec, America, repair, 19th C, 8-5/8" d, 5-1/2" h **$560**

Table, drop leaf, Sheraton, walnut, pine secondary wood, leaves with decoratively cut corners, one dovetailed drawer, turned legs, old finish, minor edge damage, hinges replaced, age crack on top, 23-1/2" l, 12-1/2" w, 10-3/4" l leaves, 19" h **$1,100**

Dollhouse accessories

Bird cage, brass, bird, stand, 7" h **$65**

Carpet sweeper, gilt, Victorian **$65**

Christmas tree, decorated **$50**

Coffeepot, brass **$25**

Cup and saucer, china, flower design, c1940 .... **$10**

Decanter, two matching tumblers, Venetian, c1920 .... **$35**

Fireplace, tin, Britannia metal fretwork, draped mantel, carved grate **$85**

Radio, Strombecker, c1930 .... **$35**

Refrigerator, Petite Princess **$75**

Silhouettes, Tynietoy, pr, c1930... **$25**

Telephone, wall, oak, speaker and bell, German, c1890 .... **$40**

Towel stand, golden oak, turned post **$45**

Umbrella stand, brass, ormolu, sq, emb palm fronds **$60**

Dollhouse furniture

Armoire, tin litho, purple and black **$35**

Bathroom, wood, painted white, Strombecker **$40**

Music box, Stella, disc, no. 571, double-comb movement, speed regulator, retailer plaque "Jacot & Sons," 39 Union Sq., New York, mahogany case, boxwood inlaid "Stella," carved front panel off oak leaves and branches, disc storage drawer, patent plaque dates Feb. 1897, 15 projectionless discs, 28" w, **$4,110.**
Photo courtesy of Skinner, Inc.

Buffet set, stenciled, three shelves, column supports, Biedermeier, 6" h **$400**

Chair, ormolu, ornate, pr, c1900, 3" h **$75**

Cradle, cast iron, painted green, 2" l **$40**

Desk, Chippendale style, slant front **$60**

Dining room, Edwardian style, dark red stain, extension table, chairs, marble top cupboard, grandfather clock, chandelier, candelabra, 5" h bisque shoulder head maid doll, table service for six, Gebruder Schneerass, Waltershausen, Thuringa, c1915 ....**$1,400**

Kitchen set, litho tin, Modern Kitchen, all parts and pieces, animals, and related items, orig box, Louis Marx **$250**

Living room, Empire-style, sofa, fainting couch, two side chairs, upholstered tapestry, matching drapery **$350**

Piano, grand, wood, eight keys, 5" h **$35**

Sewing table, golden oak, drawer, c1880 ....**$100**

Table, tin, painted brown, white top, floral design, 1-1/2" x 3/4" h, ornate **$30**

Tea cart, Petite Princess **$25**

Music box, lever wind, no. 43522, plays four overtures Zampa Aida, la Gazza Ladra and Va Pensiero, smooth brass bedplate, brass control panel, (later) engraved silvered tune programme and carrying handles, rosewood case with red int., inlaid front and lid, brass ebony and pewter arabesques in tulipwood borders, early bass tooth replacement, Nicole Freres, c1873, 22" w, cylinder 12" x 3-1/8", **$8,810.**
Photo courtesy of Skinner, Inc.

Vanity, Biedermeier **$90**

MUSIC BOXES

History: Music boxes, invented in Switzerland around 1825, encompass a broad array of forms, from small boxes to huge circus calliopes.

A cylinder box consists of a comb with teeth that vibrate when striking a pin in the cylinder. The music these boxes produce ranges from light tunes to opera and overtures.

The first disc music box was invented by Paul Lochmann of Leipzig, Germany, in 1886. It used an interchangeable steel disc with pierced holes bent to a point that hit the star-wheel as the disc revolved, and thus produced the tune. Discs were easily stamped out of metal, allowing a single music box to play an endless variety of tunes. Disc boxes reached the height of their popularity from 1890 to 1910, when the phonograph replaced them.

Music boxes also were incorporated in many items, e.g., clocks, sewing and jewelry boxes, steins, plates, toys, perfume bottles, and furniture.

Bremond, interchangeable cylinder, orchestral music, 12 19" cylinders **$82,500**

Music box, key wind, no. 16760, three overtures Semirramis, le Barbier de Seville and La Pie Voleuse, six-step cam, brass comb washers and instant stop, boxwood strung, figured rosewood case, hinged end flap, lid has trailing flowers and foliate scrolls inlaid, missing beading and old veneer repair to lid, Ducommun-Girod, 14-1/2" w, cylinder 8" x 2-1/2", **$16,450.**
Photo courtesy of Skinner, Inc.

Cellesta, single-comb ratchet-wind mechanism, walnut case with bone inlaid top and color print in lid, 16 discs, 8-1/4" disc **$980**

Cylinders

Lambert, common, c1900 ....**$225**

Lambert, recording of The Stars & Stripes, pink, 5" d **$2,000**

Criterion, matching cabinet, 15-1/2" disc **$5,200**

Lecoulture, D., plays four airs, plain case, 17" l, 8-1/4" cylinder **$1,100**

Manger, John, large cylinder type **$33,000**

Match striker, gilt cast metal figure of man holding his chamber pot out window, strike-plate activating two-air movement playing "Dixie" and "La Marsille," 9" h **$635**

Mermod Freres, interchangeable cylinder type, three cylinders

Orig finish case **$49,500**

Restored case **$5,500**

Olympia, No. 6566, 20-1/2" upright disc, twin-comb mechanism, disengaged coin slide, manual control, two-piece mahogany cabinet, side disc storage, 32 discs, sounding boards replaced, 70" h **$6,900**

Polychon, No. 27498, 15-1/2" disc, twin comb movement, coin slide, walnut case with bobbin turned corner columns, paneled and inlaid top, monochrome print in lid, disc storage drawer in plinth, 36 zinc disks, 24" w **$460**

Regina, Sublima, upright, coin-operated, sixteen 21" d disks, carved mahogany case, door with circular glazed center, 4 giltwood scrolled spandrels, fluted columns, molded pull-out door below with compartment for extra disks, molded base, 34-1/2" w, 64-3/4" h **$8,625**

Singing bird

Blue enameled case, ivory beak, moving wings and perch, lid with Alpine scene and floral spray, 3-3/4" w **$2,645**

Brass, moving head, circular base, 11" l₁ **$420**

Silver plated, serpentine front and sides, cast with views of country scenes, leather traveling case, bird detached and featherless, 4" w .. **$815**

Symphonion

Eroica, tall case clock, plays three disks simultaneously, 25 three-disc sets **$46,750**

Eroica, upright, walnut case, 18 three-disc sets, 81" h **$38,500**

Offset double combs, 9" disc .. **$1,650**

Theater, roll-to roll, wooden box, center-opening lithographed curtain and orchestra, full theater stage with audience, when turning slotted shafts on top, scenes of Snow White roll by, Dutch, c1880, 12" x 15" x 3-3/4", music box no longer functioning **$500**

MUSICAL INSTRUMENTS

History: From the first beat of the prehistoric drum to the very latest in electronic music makers, musical instruments have been popular modes of communication and relaxation.

The most popular antique instruments are violins, flutes, oboes, and other instruments associated with the classical music period of 1650 to 1900. Many of the modern instruments, such as trumpets, guitars, and drums, have value on the "used," rather than antiques market.

Collecting musical instruments is in its infancy. The field is growing very

rapidly. Investors and speculators have played a role since the 1930s, especially in early string instruments.

Additional Resources:

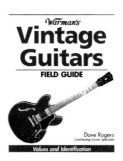

Warman's Vintage Guitar Field Guide, by Dave Rogers, Krause Publications, Iola, WI.

Banjo

Global, with case **$225**

Peerless, with case **$70**

Clarinet, with case

Henry Bouche **$675**

Selmer **$350**

Coronet, English, silver plated, stamped "F. Besson, Brevetee…," with case **$320**

Drum set, Gretsch, three pcs, aqua sides **$600**

Fife, American, Meacham & Co., Albany, maple, brass fittings, case **$320**

Flute, American

Gemeinhardt, with case **$125**

Peloubet, C., five keys, rosewood, round key covers **$550**

Phaff, John, Philadelphia, faintly stamped "J. Phaff…," eight keys, rosewood, silver fittings, period case, 19th C **$1,265**

Flute, English

Monzani, London, eight keys, head with turned reeding, silver fittings, round covered keys, 19th C **$200**

Rudall Carte & Co., London, silver, multiple stamps, hallmarks, case **$750**

Wrede, H., London, c1840, four keys, stained boxwood, ivory fittings, silver round cover keys, case **$320**

Guitar, archtop, D'Angelico, John, Model New York, irregular curl maple two-

This snare drum was used by Silas D. Taylor, 3rd Regiment, Wisconsin Voluntary. The band of the 3rd Wisconsin was broken up in 1862 in accord with the decision to eliminate regimental bands by the Federal Army, **$5,500.**
KP photo/Wisconsin Veterans Museum collection.

Mittenwald viola, with case, c1850, back length 15-3/16", **$470.**
Photo courtesy of Skinner, Inc.

piece back, medium curl sides, medium grain with cross-bracing top, medium curl neck, bound peghead with inlaid pearl D'Angelico logo, bound ebony fingerboard with split-block pearl inlay, stamped internally "D'Angelico, New York, 1808," 1947, 21-7/16" l back, 18-1/2" w bottom bout **$13,800**

Guitar, classical

Bazzolo, Thomas, three-piece rosewood back, similar sides, spruce top of fine grain fully bound, mahogany neck, ebony fingerboard, labeled "Thomas Bazzolo, Luthier #65C24, Lebanon, Connecticut, USA," and sgd, with case,1994, 18-15/16" l back, 14-1/8" w lower bout...... **$750**

Martin, C. F., Style D-35, three-piece Indian rosewood back, similar sides, spruce top of fine to medium grain, mahogany neck with bound ebony fingerboard, inlaid pearl eyes, stamped internally "CF Martin & Co., Nazareth, PA, Made in USA, D-35," 1975................. **$1,475**

Guitar, flat top, Gibson, flat top, orig case **$900**

Harp, Lyon & Healy, Chicago, No. 6563-15, maple, decorative painted foliage, seven pedals, 70-3/4" h **$7,200**

Mandolin, flat back, with case **$175**

Piano, Steinway and Sons, Style VII, sq grand, carved rosewood, c1879 .... **$1,380**

Organ

Band, Arthur Bursens, three-section, drums, symbols, and xylophone **$16,500**

Dance, Arburo, saxophone, accordion, drum, castanets, drums and symbols **$17,600**

Fairground, Limonaire, built in Germany, 1908, plays folding paper books **$24,750**

Recorder, Moeck **$135**

Trumpet, valve type

Buescher................................... **$125**

Sears & Roebuck........................ **$115**

Ukulele

Aloha Royal, with case **$120**

Giamnini, baritone, with case **$95**

Kkamakall, with case **$250**

Vibraphone **$350**

Viola, no inscription, with orig case, orig bow **$475**

Violin, German, labeled "Thomas Ranik, Lauten and Geigenmacher in

Breslau 1731," one-pc maple back, Lupot stamped bow, 19th C fitted rect leather case **$1,150**

Violin, Hungarian, medium curl two-piece back, similar ribs, medium curl scroll, fine grain top, red color varnish, labeled "Janos Spiegel, Budapest, 1907," 358 mm, with case, 14-1/16" l back....................... **$6,620**

Violin, Italian

Attributed to Andrea Postacchini, narrow curl one-piece back, irregular curl ribs, faint curl scroll, fine grain top, golden brown color varnish, labeled "Andreas Postacchini Amieie Filius Fecit Firmi Anno 1819, Opus 11?," 356 mm, with case, accompanied by bill of sale, 14" l back............................ **$17,250**

Bisiach, Leandro, strong medium curl two-piece back, strong narrow curl ribs and scroll, fine grain top, golden brown color varnish, labeled "Leandro Bisiach Da Milano, Fece L'Anno 1942," sgd, 356 mm, with case, undated numbered certificate, 14" l back............................. **$18,400**

Violin, Mittenwald, Klotz School, medium curl two-piece back, similar ribs and scroll, fine grain top, brown color varnish, unlabeled, 353 mm, with case, c1780, 13-7/8" l back **$2,415**

Violin bow, gold mounted

Ouchard, Emile, round stick stamped "Emile Ouchard" at butt, ebony frog with Parisian eye, plain gold adjuster, 63 grams **$4,025**

Seifert, Lothar, octagonal stick stamped "Lothar Seifert" at butt, ebony frog with Parisian eye, gold and ebony adjuster, 61 grams **$1,265**

Unstamped, octagonal stick, later frog engraved "A. Vigneron A Paris 1886," 59 grams **$1,485**

Violin bow, silver mounted

Hill, W. E., round stick stamped "W. E. Hill & Sons" at butt, ebony eye with Parisian eye, plain silver adjuster, 60 grams, baleen wrap **$2,530**

Nurnberger, Albert, octagonal stick stamped "Albert Nurnberger" at butt, "Saxony" under plain ebony frog, silver and ebony adjuster, 61 grams................................. **$1,265**

Violoncello

America, Settin, Joseph, strong narrow curl two-piece back, similar ribs and scroll, fine to medium grain top, golden brown color varnish, labeled "Joseph Settin Venetus, Fecit Anno Domani 1953," 748 mm, 29-7/16" l back **$8,100**

English, James and Henry Banks, narrow curl two-piece back, medium curl ribs, faint curl scroll, fine to medium grain top, red color varnish, sgd internally on table, "James and Henry Banks, Salisbury," c1800, 28-34" l back, 729 mm **$18,400**

German, irregular narrow curl two-piece back, similar ribs, narrow curl scroll, medium to wide grain top, orange color varnish, labeled "Erich Grunert, Penzberg Anno 1976," 756 mm, with case, 29-3/4" l back **$1,150**

Violoncello bow, nickel plated, round stick stamped "L. Bausch, Leipzig," 81 grams **$1,840**

Schumann upright piano and bench, pyramidal and keyed through-tenon, details, quarter-sawn oak case, case in good orig finish missing one castor, metal tag on back; piano 55" x 62" x 27-1/2"; bench 20" x 36" x 14", **$4,800.**
Photo courtesy of David Rago Auctions, Inc.

NAPKIN RINGS, FIGURAL

History: Gracious home dining during the Victorian era required a personal napkin ring for each household member. Figural napkin rings were first patented in 1869. During the remainder of the 19th century, most plating companies, including Cromwell, Eureka, Meriden, and Reed and Barton, manufactured figural rings, many copying and only slightly varying the designs of other companies.

Notes: Values are determined by the subject matter of the ring, the quality of the workmanship, and the condition. The following examples are all silver-plated.

Barking dog, unknown maker, barking dog jumping over fence, ring rests on back of dog, ring elaborately engraved with floral and basket weave dec, cartouche form panel incised "Leslie '93," scattered spots of wear or discoloration, 2-1/4" w, 2-3/4" h **$185**

Begging terrier, Hamilton, ring at back, central engraved foliate garland flanked by turned rings and ridged rim on ring, oval base dec with stars and bars, imp "Hamilton & Co., 01541," minor denting to rim of ring, 3" w, 2-1/2" h **$100**

Bird, Reed & Barton, rect platform with tapered sides with raised leaf and scroll dec, reeded ring topped by bird with outspread wings seated on ball, twisted cord and tassel descending from ball on one side of ring, imp "Mf'd. and Plated by Reed & Barton, no. 1310," 3-1/8" w, 3-1/4" h **$225**

Bird in fruit tree, Meriden, bird sitting in branches, ring engraved with birds in branches, circular base with fruit and leaves, imp "Rogers Smith & Co., Meriden, no. 247," minor wear to finish, 2-1/2" w, 3" h **$145**

Bird on branch, unknown maker, ring having circular base, raised flower and leaf dec, branch rising from base and following curve of ring, bird with wings spread sits atop branch, underside imp "1593," scattered spots of wear to finish, 2-1/2" w, 3-1/2" h **$375**

Birds and bud vase, Wilcox, ring resting on ftd pedestal, two birds with outstretched wings on ring on either side of central bud vase, flared rim, ring with beaded and ridged detail at edges, imp "Wilcox Silver Plate Co., no. 1899," very minor wear to finish, 2-1/2" w, 5-1/2" h **$165**

Boy with post, Meriden, boy holding post, shovel on ground beside him, ring with beaded rim details and central engraved band with foliage attached to one side of base, circular base, imp "Meriden Brittannia Company, no. 30," wear, 4" w, 3-1/4" h **$75**

Bud vase, Reed & Barton, circular base with raised fleur-de-lis motif, ring with floral-decorated rims, ewerform bud vase with flower inside curved handle, imp "Mf'd. & Plated by Reed & Barton, 1337," discoloration of finish at base of ewer, 2-1/2" w, 4-1/2" h **$175**

Butterfly and two fans, two Japanese style handled fans supporting ring, butterfly underneath ring, central plain band flanked by two raised curved bands with floral garland motif on ring, sq base with raised floral dec, four ball feet, imp "Meriden Brittannia Company, no. 208," minor wear to finish **$75**

Butterflies and leaf, unknown maker, ring resting on outspread wings of two butterflies resting on leaf, four ball feet, ring with central band and raised rims, floral motif, scattered spots of wear to finish, 2-1/2" w, 2-1/2" h **$225**

Chair, unknown maker, ring resting on seat of chair, ring with engraved panel and foliate swag, panel incised "M.A. Hall from Ed. V. Louise," scattered wear to finish, 1-3/4" x 4-1/2" h **$180**

Cherub

Rogers, ring resting on hips and legs of cherub, arms and head on top of ring, ring having central plain band flanked by bands, engraved floral dec on ridged ground, circular base, imp "Rogers & Bro., no. 224," 3" w, 4" h **$385**

Unknown maker, seated cherub leaning back against ring with floral dec rims, very minor nicking to rims of ring, 3-1/4" w, 1-3/4" h **$550**

Cherub with torch, Reed & Barton, cherub with fallen drape, one arm outstretched holding torch, leaning on pedestal and ring, ring with reeded rims, chased bird, and floral motif on center band, circular panel monogrammed "RGM," rect base, imp "Mf'd. & Plated by Reed & Barton, 1285," underside engraved "Aug. 27, 1888," minor loss to finish, 3" w, 4" h **$525**

Cow and tree, Meriden, oval ring supported by forked branches of tree, cow standing beside, engraved dec of birds on tree branches on ring, circular base, imp "Meriden Brittannia Company, no. 243," wear to finish, 1-3/4" w, 2-3/4" h **$100**

Crawling child, Rogers, crawling child beside ring, ring with pierced work scrolling dec on edges, imp "Wm. Rogers Mfg. Co., Hartford, Quadruple, 2254," 2-3/4" w, 1-3/4" h **$200**

Cupid and heart, Rogers, heart-form base with scallop dec at edge, seated cupid with one outstretched arm, arrow resting on base, scalloped dec ring supported by ftd pedestal, engraved "Rudolph, Hearts are Trumps," three ball feet, imp "Rogers & Bro., no. 435," discolored, 2-1/2" w, 2-1/2" h **$160**

Cupids in canoe, unknown maker, two cupids in canoe using arrows as oars, central ring with incised concentric rings, supporting bud vase with flared neck, canoe rests on two bracket feet, ring inscribed "Geo," wear to finish, 4-3/4" w, 3-1/4" h **$385**

Cupid, terrier and hearts, Reed & Barton, ring with turned rims supported on back of terrier, cupid facing outward, leaning on ring, two hearts atop ring, oval base with fern dec, imp "Mf'd. & Plated by Reed & Barton,

Combination napkin ring, open salt, pepper shaker, and butter pat, embossed florals, silver plate, marked "Tufts," **$175.**

1315," minor wear to finish, 2-1/4" w, 2-3/4" h **$750**

Dancing women, Pelton, central foliate engraved ring flanked by two women dancing with tambourines, cartouche form base, four ball feet, imp "Pelton Bros. Silver Plate Co., no. 17," slight nick to one side of ring, 2-1/2" w, 2-1/4" h **$100**

Dog and bird, Aurora, dog sitting on hind legs, looking at bird with wings raised seated on top of ring, beaded rim, foliate dec, and "Oscar" engraved on ring, imp "Aurora Silver Plate Co., no. 27," wear to finish, 3" w, 2-1/2" h **$95**

Dog and bud vase, Tufts, dog standing on hind legs, one front paw resting on scroll-engraved ring, vasiform bud vase at other side of ring, cartouche form base, imp "J.W. Tufts, Boston, no. 1582," minor spots of wear to finish, 3-3/4" w, 2-3/4" h **$285**

Elephant, unknown maker, ring flanked by elephant with raised trunk, raised dec of elephants on ring, considerable wear to finish, 3" w, 2" h **$130**

Eskimo, Meriden, hooded Eskimo holding pole, standing on ice floe, circular base, ring with central plain band flanked by bands of engraved floral dec on ridged ground, imp "Meriden Brittannia Company, no. 220," minor pitting to finish, 2-3/4" w, 2-1/2" h **$75**

Girl jumping rope, Wilcox, girl jumping rope, ring behind her resting on pierced scroll and floral motif support, ring with plain center band flanked by flared rims, engraved floral and foliate dec, large circular base with tapered sides, dec with flowers and birds, four feet, imp "Wilcox Silver Plate Co., no. 360," nicks to edges of ring, spots of wear to finish, 5" w, 4-1/2" h **$375**

Goat, standing goat figure at one side, ring decorated in engraved floral motif, wear, discoloration to finish, 2-1/2" w, 1-3/4" h **$95**

Greenaway girl, ring with engraved dec flanked by large Greenaway girl and lily flower, leaves on long upswept stems, one leaf broken off but present, scattered spots of wear to finish, 3-3/4" w, 7-1/8" h **$200**

Horse, unknown maker, horse rearing up on its hind legs, front hooves resting on scroll dec ring supported by ball, oval pierced scrollwork base,

wear to finish, 3-1/2" w, 2-1/2" h **$135**

Knights in armor, Simpson, Hall, Miller, central ring engraved with floral swags, flanked by figures of knights in armor, rect base, imp "Simpson, Hall, Miller & Co., no. 110," minor wear to finish, 2-1/8" w, 1-5/8" h **$215**

Lily pad, Acme, lily pads and flowers form base, stem forms loop handle and ring support, ring rests on ball, engraved wheat sheaf and sunburst dec on ring, imp "Acme Silver Company, Canada, no. 729," some loss to finish, 3-1/2" w, 2" h **$230**

Military band, unknown maker, ring supported by pedestal, flanked by three members of military band and flag bearer, circular base, four pad feet, scattered spots of wear to finish, crack in flag, 3-1/2" w, 3-1/4" h **$160**

Parrot, Rogers, parrot sitting on branch where ring is resting, ring with raised rings, engraved floral and geometric dec, imp on ring "Rogers & Bro., no. 228," denting to edge of ring, 3-1/2" w, 2-1/2" h **$185**

Peacock, Meriden, peacock standing on ring, engraved floral dec, rect panel inscribed "Charlie," imp "Meriden Britannia Company, no. 151," wear to finish, 2-1/4" w, 3-1/2" h **$400**

Phoenix birds, Simpson, Hall, Miller, ring resting on ftd pedestal, curved handle descending to two phoenix type birds on either side of ring, ring engraved with scrolling motif forming panel inscribed "Belle," imp "Simpson, Hall, Miller & Co.," 3-1/4" w, 4" h **$200**

Putto

Simpson, Hall, Miller, seated putto, ring at his back, ring engraved with owls in tree branches, octagonal base with raised scrolling dec, imp "Simpson, Hall, Miller & Co., no. 211," minor spots of wear to finish, 3" w, 2" h **$365**

Webster, putti seated at each end of cartouche form base, ring supported on wings, ring with flared rims and central band with engraved dec, imp "E.G. Webster & Bro., no. 170," denting to one edge of ring, 3" w, 2-1/2" h **$130**

Unknown maker, standing putto leaning back on ring with faintly engraved foliate dec, 3" w, 3" h **$420**

Putto, bird and wishbone, unknown maker, ring with engraved foliate spray resting on wishbone, flanked by songbird on one side and putto on other, minor wear to finish, 3" w, 2" h **$525**

Rampant lion, unknown maker, rampant lion at one side of ring with raised scrollwork rims, 2-1/2" w, 2" h **$265**

Recumbent lion, Meriden, floral dec ring resting on back of lion, rect base, imp on ring "Meriden Britannia Company, no. 152," small base nick, 2-1/2" w, 2-1/4" h **$145**

Squirrel with nut, unknown maker, squirrel alongside ring with scrolling rims, both sitting on branch, ring inscribed "Dudley," imp partially obscured, "143_," spotty wear to finish, 3-1/2" w, 2" h **$300**

Terrier, unknown maker, terrier at one side, front paws resting on ring with raised scrollwork rims and engraved scroll dec on band, no maker's mark, minor loss to finish, 2" w, 1-1/2" h **$180**

Terrier and bird, Reed & Barton, terrier barking at bird with outstretched wings atop ring, ring with turned rims with egg and dart type dec, fern dec on oval base, imp "Mf'd. & Plated by Reed & Barton, 1110," minor wear to finish, 3-1/4" w, 2" h **$250**

Turtles, unknown maker, plain oval ring resting on two fern leaves, flanked by two turtles, imp "75," 3-1/2" w, 2" h **$185**

Two boys

Meriden, two boys facing outward, supporting sq ring standing on corner in back-stretched hands, sq base with raised scrolling foliate dec, four ball feet, imp "Meriden Brittannia Company, no. 332," 3" w, 3" h **$200**

Middletown, boy leaning on each side of ring engraved with sunburst and scroll dec, imp "Middletown Plate Co., no. 87," wear to finish, 3" w, 2" h **$100**

Two cherubs, seated cherub on each side of barrel form ring on their backs, imp "Meriden Brittannia Company, no. 147," wear to finish, 2-3/4" w, 2-1/4" h **$100**

Two foxes, Meriden, two foxes holding birds on either side of ring with ridged rim, turned rings, and central engraved floral dec, panel engraved "Flora," imp "Meriden Silver Plate

Company, no. 217," 2-1/2" w, 2" h **$120**

NAUTICAL ITEMS

History: The seas have fascinated man since time began. The artifacts of sailors have been collected and treasured for years. Because of their environment, merchant and naval items, whether factory or handmade, must be of quality construction and long lasting. Many of these items are aesthetically appealing as well.

Account book, *Bark Arab*, showing purchases and sales from October 1853 to December 1856, 96 pgs, folio, New Bedford or Hawaii, label reads "purchased of John Kehew at his Navigation Store in New Bedford," Kehew's label mounted on front paste down, two volumes **$1,955**

Banner, carved and polychrome painted pine, "Don't Give Up The Ship!," American eagle, attributed to John Hales Bellamy, 26" x 8-1/2" **$24,150**

Book

Allyn, Captain Gurdon L., *Old Sailor's Story, or a Short Account of the Life, Adventures, and Voyages, The*, Norwich, 1879, 111 pgs, 8vo, orig flexible cloth wrappers **$316**

Bligh, William, *Dangerous Voyage of Captain Bligh, in an Open Boat, over 1200 Leagues of the Ocean, in the Year 1789*, Dublin, five full-page woodcut engraved illus, 180 pgs, small 12mo, 1818 ....**$345**

Dexter, Elisha, *Narrative of the Loss of the William and Joseph, of Martha's Vineyard*, Boston, five wood engraved plates, 54 pgs, 8vo, 1842.......................................**$1,370**

Box, cov, sailor made, walnut and ivory, rect, dovetail construction, hinged, top and sides with turned and carved pendant ring ivory handles ringed with red and black wax, kite-shaped carved ivory escutcheon, oral history relates that this box came from ship named "Carolus," which operated out of Boston, 19th C, 17-3/4" w, 9-1/4" d, 8-5/8" h.......................................**$1,765**

Broadside, issued as circular to mariners at Table Bay, Robben Island, advising of berthing procedures, 1827, 415 x 335 mm....................**$345**

Cane

Carved from single piece of tooth, 1-3/4" d x 2" h whale ivory handle, carved sailor's Turks-head knot, thin baleen spacer separates whalebone shaft, inlaid at top with four-pointed baleen fingers, white whalebone shaft, tapered with very slight natural bow, American, c1850, 32-7/8" l **$2,800**

Flat brass handle 1-3/4" d x 2/3" h, wide all metal black shaft fashioned with metal nubs all along length, when handle pulled off, hollow exposed to reveal watertight compartment to store nautical charts and documents, 3/4" brass ferrule, English, c1890, 36-1/2" l **$450**

Canoe paddle, painted deep red with black crescent moon and star, America, with stand, late 19th C, 60" l **$375**

Chronometer, Eggert & Son, New York, mahogany brass bound double lidded case, brass cased movement with engraved silver dial inscribed "Eggert & Son, NEW YORK, No 276," applied ivory plaque inscribed "Eggert & Son 276 New York," early 19th C, 7-3/4" h **$3,200**

Clock, brass, Seth Thomas, one-day lever-striking movement, circular case, domed bell mounted below

on wooden backboard, late 19th C, 10-1/2" h................................**$520**

Compass, lifeboat, 8" sq, 7-1/4" h, boxed, 20th C **$175**

Crew list, partly printed, two languages, *Jireh Swift*, lists 13 additional Hawaiian crew members, Lahaina, March 29, 1865 ....**$2,000**

Diorama, three-mast clipper, side-wheel paddle steamer, and smaller vessel, 17 men in black coats and top hats manning vessels, two painted lighthouses and dwelling in background, green-blue sky with white painted clouds, c1850, 40" l shadowbox................................**$6,500**

Figurehead, carved, Nantucket Island origin, c1830, 30" h **$12,000**

Fishing license, issued to sloop *Kial*, for cod fishing, issued in Newport, RI, some edge chipping, fold splitting, April 23, 1808, 16-1/2" x 10-1/2"....................**$165**

Hourglass, 19th C, 7" h...............**$550**

Inclinometer, brass, cased, bubble type, Kelvin Bottomley & Baird Ltd., 4-1/2" d..................................**$65**

Indenture, document indenturing William McGraa to Isaac Fisher as apprentice mariner for four years, details duties, payment schedule, May 19, 1813, signed by all parties, some foxing, edge chipping, 1810 watermark, 16" x 13-1/2" **$100**

Nautical, wooden model of Brigantine Flying Cloud, painted, "Built by Howard Moon, Hawkesbury, July 1925," three-masted model, black painted hull, green below water line, carved life boats and accoutrements, mounted on wooden base, imperfections, also includes two small framed articles: a letter from Popular Mechanics Magazine, *awarding the maker a bronze medal for "Excellence in Craftsmanship" in the 1927 Model Ship Competion, and the other contains a photo and printed image of the model, 24" h x 37" l,* **$880.**

Photo courtesy of Skinner, Inc.

Nautical, sailor's valentine, orig box, belonging to Samaul Clamer, a merchant marine from Elizabeth, New Jersey, on the USS Minneapolis, 9" d, **$3,500.**
Photo courtesy of David Rago Auctions, Inc.

Nautical, wooly ship portrait, English, 19th century, 13" x 18", **$735.**
Photo courtesy of Pook & Pook, Inc.

Nautical, watercolor ship portrait, sidewheeler attacking fort, American School, c1900, 17" x 24", **$2,340.**
Photo courtesy of Pook & Pook, Inc.

Nautical, ship's binnacle, Northwest Instrument Co., Seattle, WA, brass stand with two lanterns, plaque with Asian lettering, inscribed "No. 4004," break in one lantern, early 20th century, 42" h, **$395.**
Photo courtesy of Alderfer Auction Co.

Jewelry chest, sailor-carved walnut and whalebone, America, carved rosette, fan, lapped leaf, pendant, and other designs, front and side drawers, hinged lid opens to mirror which further opens to three oval frames with rope trim, box int. fitted with four compartments with carved lids, carved whalebone drawer and lid handles, 19th C, 18-1/4" l, 12-1/2" d, 10-3/8" h **$2,350**

Log book, Ship *Geneva*, George M. Tucker, Master, sailed from Boston, March 4, 1852 towards Richmond, later to San Francisco, then to Calcutta, back to Boston where she docked at Central Wharf on Aug. 13, 1853, worn spine, cover **$1,150**

Masthead, copper and brass, oil fired, complete with burner, 360 degrees, late 19th C, 16" h, 9-1/2" d **$200**

Membership certificate, certifying "...That Capt. Green Walden was by a majority of votes regularly admitted a member of the Portland Marine Society at a meeting held the 17th day of September 1839...," certificate dec with reserves depicting various marine scenes, toning, foxing, framed, 12-3/8" x 17-1/2" **$530**

Model, cased, Schooner Yacht *Laura*, carved and painted, fully rigged, painted metal sails, painted figures, metal and wood details, hull painted black, carved wood "water," America, imperfections, 19th C, 23-5/8" l, 12" w, 16-1/4" h **$1,550**

Oar, curly maple, well carved, thin broad end, good figure, 57-1/2" l **$420**

Painting, oil on canvas, framed
Sailing ship flying American flag, several fishing boats in rough seas, high cliffs in background, sgd "RJ Dawson 1882," 22-3/4" w x 14-3/4" h period gilt frame with wear, small areas of touch-up, 20" w x 12" h **$1,610**

Ships Before the Doges Palace, sgd "Ziller" lower left (Leopold Ziller), framed, strip lined, repaired punctures, retouch, surface grime, 21-1/4" x 32" **$3,525**

Two-Masted schooner *Masconnomet* in Marblehead Harbor, flying American flag, figures on pier in foreground, lighthouse in distance, unsigned, identified beneath image, craquelure, scattered retouch to background sky, 17" x 21" **$3,525**

Two-masted schooner off Vinalhaven, ME, sgd "Coombs" lower left, repaired tear, retouch to upper right sky, 22" x 36" **$4,250**

William, pictured off Dover with Dover Fort pictured under her bowsprit, sgd "R. B. Spencer" lower left, (Richard Barrett Spencer, c1840-74,) ship identified on bow, scattered retouch, lined, 36" x 22" **$6,450**

Quadrant, ebony, cased, marked "D Booth" and "New Zealand" **$330**

Sail maker's bench, long canvas cov bench, turned splayed legs, one end with compartments and pierced for tools, suspending two canvas pouches, two canvas sacks with sail maker's tools, America, 19th C, 77" l, 16" w, 15" h **$1,765**

Sailor's razor box, carved cherry, rect, heart-shaped handle, chip carved borders, incised sailing vessel on swivel top, 19th C, 10-3/4" l, 1-3/4" w, 1-1/2" h **$325**

Sailor's valentine, various exotic shells, "For My Love," very minor losses, 19th C, 9-5/8" octagonal segmented case **$750**

Sea chest, painted, green, lid painted with flags and pennants centered by Union Jack, name "William Bevan" **$2,760**

Ship anchor, cast, iron ring and chain, mounted on later iron brackets, corrosion, 54" w, 106" h **$825**

Ship bell, cast bronze
Raised linear bands, 14" d, 17" h **$560**
Weathered surface, raised "J. Warner & Sons, London, 1855," 13" d, 13-1/2" h **$1,175**

Ship billethead, scrolled foliate design, painted black, green and gilt highlights, minor loss on scroll, cracks, carved wood, 19th C, 24" l, 7-1/2" w **$715**

Ship billetheads, scrolled foliate design, weathered cracked surface, 19th C, carved wood, one 27-1/2" l x 5-1/2" w, second matching example 23" l x 7-1/4" w **$4,995**

Ship builder's half model, America, 19th C
Alternating laminated mahogany and other wood, mounted on walnut panel, 30" l, 6" h **$1,995**
Natural finished pine, black and gilt trim, loose stempost, 42" l, 10-5/8" h **$9,400**
Pine and other woods, mounted on pine panel, 37-1/2" l, 5" h **$1,300**

Ship license

Issued for ship *Aurora*, 303 tons, armed with 14 guns, two swivel guns, 20 muskets, 20 pistols, 20 cutlasses, 20 pikes, minor edge chipping, Nov. 4, 1912, 12-1/2" x 8" **$135**

Issued to the ship *Nancy* of Newfoundland, two guns weighing 222 tons, issued by High Admiral, masthead scene of allegorical figures and chip, scallop cut top, minor soiling, April 24, 1812, 18" x 11-1/2" .. **$450**

Shipping circular, concerning marine

papers lost, stolen, or taken by force on various ships, issued to port collector of Bristol, federal eagle watermark, some chipping, fold splitting, sgd by Clerk of Marine Records of the Treasury Dept, March 31, 1810, 15-1/2" x 9-1/2" **$35**

Ship wheel, various hardwoods,

turned spokes, iron reinforced center hub, 48" d **$350**

Stern board, Hesperus, New Eng-

land, rect form, rounded ends, chamfered edges, chiseled carved letters flanked by star, painted white on black ground, imperfections, 19th C, 7-3/4" h, 66" l **$980**

Telescope, silver plated, one draw,

Troughton & Simms, London, orig leather casing, inscription reads "Presented by the British Government, Captain Christopher Crowell, Master of the American Ship 'Highland Light' of Boston, in acknowledgment of his humanity and kindness to the Master and the Crew of the Barque 'Queen of Sheba' when he rescued from their waterlogged vessel, on the 16th, December 1861," damage to leather, mid-19th C, 32-3/4" l **$980**

Trump indicator, brass and copper,

ship's wheel, spinning center orb, 4-1/2" x 3-1/2" **$85**

Walking stick, wood, ivory knop, sil-

ver band on shaft engraved "U.S. Frigate Constitution 1797, J.L.S.," brass and iron tip, age cracks on ivory, wear, 35" l............................ **$1,295**

Watercolor on paper

Ship Portrait of the U.S.S. Constitution, unsigned, American School, taken from a ship's log, with Ruse & Turner's watermark, early 19th C, 9-1/2" h, 11-1/4" l **$1,000**

Study of steamboat on desolate river during winter, snow topped mountain in background, light shades of brown and blue, matted with gilt floral frame, minor surface wear, sgd "Mc E. Dun 1899," 14" h, 20" w **$300**

NETSUKES

History: The traditional Japanese kimono has no pockets. Daily necessities, such as money and tobacco supplies, were carried in leather pouches, or inros, which hung from a cord with a netsuke toggle. The word netsuke comes from "ne"—to root—and "tsuke"— to fasten.

Netsukes originated in the 14th century and initially were favored by the middle class. By the mid-18th century, all levels of Japanese society used them. Some of the most famous artists, e.g., Shuzan and Yamada Hojitsu, worked in the netsuke form.

Netsukes average from 1 to 2 inches in length and are made from wood, ivory, bone, ceramics, metal, horn, nutshells, etc. The subject matter is broad based, but always portrayed in a lighthearted, humorous manner. A netsuke must have smooth edges and balance in order to hang correctly on the sash.

Reproduction Alert. Recent reproductions are on the market. Many are carved from African ivory.

Notes: Value depends on artist, region, material, and skill of craftsmanship. Western collectors favor katabori, pieces which represent an identifiable object.

Antler, carved

Foreigner or monk holding trumpet pendant from his right hand, facing upward, hair curling on his back, stained details, himotoshi carved on back, unsigned, Japan, 18th or 19th C, 2-1/2" h **$1,275**

Kwanyu holding halberd in right hand, tugging his beard with his left hand, himotoshi on back, stained details, traces of red pigment on face and vestments, legs carved from separate piece and inserted, good patina and wear, Japan, hole drilled in left foot, small cavity on left leg, 18th C, 3" h.................. **$500**

Corozo nut, carved, basket of flowers, handle at center dividing flowers, small areas of openwork, bottom with attached metal ring himotoshi, Japan, crack along top, 19th C, 1-1/8" h **$125**

Nautical, spyglass, telescoping, brass and wood, late engraved "Cos, Plymouth Dock Imp'd Ship Telescope," 19th/early 20th century, 25-5/8"-33-1/4" l, **$350.**
Photo courtesy of Skinner, Inc.

Nautical, telescope, brass tabletop, English, mid-19th century, 35" l, 19" h, **$950.**
Photo courtesy of Pook & Pook, Inc.

Nautical table lamps, brass, made from lanterns, impressed mark "Perko, Perkins Marine Lamp Home Corp, Brooklyn, NY, USA," red glass lamps marked "Corning," 36" h, **$1,500.**
Photo courtesy of Alderfer Auction Co.

Nautical, Mediterranean port scene, oil on canvas, Frederick B. Serger (1889-1965), signed lower right, 24" x 36", **$1,295.**
Photo courtesy of David Rago Auctions, Inc.

Netsuke, wood carving, seated man with bowl over his face, signed, 1" h, **$250.**

Netsuke, Masatoshi, Japan, finely carved ebony, wild boar with its young, signed in oval reserve, contemporary, 1" x 2", **$1,700.**
Photo courtesy of David Rago Auctions, Inc.

Netsuke, Japanese Umimatsu, frog, Iuwami school, 1-1/4" h, **$650.**
Photo courtesy of Sloans & Kenyon Auctioneers and Appraisers.

Horn, carved, Hannya mask, sgd on back between himotoshi, stained detail, hole at top of head, Japan, 19th C, 2" h **$70**

Ivory, carved

Bearded man holding pumpkin over his left shoulder, flatly carved figure, good patina, worn details, himotoshi on back, unsigned, Japan, age cracks, 18th C, 2-7/8" h............**$320**

Boy carrying branch laden with precious things, puppy at left foot, sgd "Tomochikia," Japan, small crack on shoulder, 19th C, 1-1/2" l........**$700**

Boy holding rooster, stained details, himotoshi carved on back, Japan, c1900, 1-1/2" h..........................**$200**

Dutchman holding monkey in his arms, details lightly stained, himotoshi spaced wide apart, one hole on back, other carved under his cat, sgd "Takusai" on back, Japan, 18th C, 2-7/8" h..............................**$2,600**

Foo dog, single hole himotoshi, Japan, age cracks, 18th or 19th C, 1-5/8" h **$150**

Frog, sitting on rock with splashing water, turning to right, facing upwards, lightly stained details, himotoshi and sgd on base, mounted as ring with braided gold colored metal wire of varying shapes, Japan, 19th C, 2" h **$300**

Frog, stylized, comical, long thin body, elongated snout, inlaid eyes, himotoshi and signature on base, Japan, age cracks, 19th or 20th C, 3-1/8" h **$125**

Fukurokuju clipping his toenails, child on left side, stained detail, sgd "Gyokko" on rect on base, Japan, Meiji period, crack in face, 1-3/4" h **$460**

Goat, standing, head turned sharply to right, front leg slightly raised, arched back with cascading fleece,

left horn conforming to curve of neck, lightly stained, himotoshi carved on back, Japan, repairs to legs, details slightly worn, good patina, small age cracks, 18th C, 2-3/16" h **$5,200**

Horse, grazing, stained detail, himotoshi carved on back, unsigned, Japan, 18th or 19th C **$550**

Manju, rect, carved frog among persimmons and leaves, carved insect damage on leaves, himotoshi formed by interlacing branches, stained detail, Japan, Meiji period, 1-1/2" l....................................**$375**

Man and child with basket of fruit, himotoshi and signature carved on base, Japan, c1900, 1-5/8" h....**$200**

Octopus crawling out of large pot, himotoshi and signature on back, Gyokuzan, Japan, 19th C, 1-5/8" h **$300**

Okame, sitting position, stained hair and robe, himotoshi carved at her back, sgd, Japan, early 20th C **$200**

Oni carrying woman on back, stained detail, Japan, Meiji period, 2" h **$375**

Oni embracing drum with inlaid studs, inlaid metal eyes, signature on underside of drum, some staining detail, Japan, Meiji period, 1-1/2" l....................................**$1,265**

Rect, dragon among clouds, large holes forming himotoshi, Japan, 19th C, age cracks **$100**

Three blind men grappling with each other, himotoshi formed as part of design, slightly stained detail, sgd on base, Japan, normal age cracks, Meiji period, 1-1/2" l.............**$1,495**

Three men wrestling snake, unsigned, Japan, some losses, 19th C, 2-3/4" l **$250**

Tiger, recumbent, body curled to left, fierce expression, sinuous tail rest-

ing on back, inlaid eyes, himotoshi and sgd "Tomotada" on base, Japan, 19th C, 2-1/8" h **$400**

Turtle carrying young on its back, sgd on bottom, Japan, damage to back foot, early 20th C, 2" l **$100**

Two figures inside cavern, tengu above, single hole himotoshi, sgd on base, Japan, Meiji period, 1-1/2" h **$750**

Two happy sages, himotoshi carved on back, unsigned, Japan, 18th or 19th C, 2" h **$450**

Ivory and wood, carved, man and child, man with toy in left hand, sgd in small red tablet on base, Japan, Meiji period, 1-1/2" h.................**$320**

Porcelain, shishimai dancer, child holding lion mask above his head, painted over glaze enamels, himotoshi on back, Japan, possibly Kutani, Meiji period, small chip, 2-1/4" h **$125**

Staghorn, Manju, carved Kinko sennin on carp, 19th C, 2-1/2" d **$200**

Wood, carved

Crouched figure holding basket with peach, homotshi carved on base, good color and patina, Japan, details slightly worn, 19th C, 1" h **$200**

Foreigner, left arm twisted sharply behind his back, supporting child perched on right shoulder, right hand holding trumpet, himotoshi on back, lacquered, unsigned, Japan, areas of wear to lacquer, 18th C, 3-1/4" h **$1,400**

Fox wearing robe with long sleeves, pulling large laden sack, inlaid horn eyes, tail curling underneath to form himotoshi, sgd on base, stained with even brown patination, Japan, Meiji period, 2" l **$920**

NUTTING, WALLACE

History: Wallace Nutting (1861-1941) was America's most famous photographer of the early 20th century. A retired minister, Nutting took more than 50,000 pictures, keeping 10,000 of his best and destroying the rest. His popular and best-selling scenes included "Exterior Scenes," apple blossoms, country lanes, orchards, calm streams, and rural American countrysides; "Interior Scenes," usually featuring a colonial woman working near a hearth; and "Foreign Scenes," typically thatch-roofed cottages. Those pictures that were least popular in his day have become the rarest and most-highly collectible today and are classified as "Miscellaneous Unusual Scenes." This category encompasses such things as animals, architecturals, children, florals, men, seascapes, and snow scenes.

Nutting sold literally millions of his hand-colored platinotype pictures between 1900 and his death in 1941. Starting first in Southbury, Connecticut, and later moving his business to Framingham, Massachusetts, the peak of Wallace Nutting's picture production was 1915 to 1925. During this period, Nutting employed nearly 200 people, including colorists, darkroom staff, salesmen, and assorted office personnel. Wallace Nutting pictures proved to be a huge commercial success and hardly an American household was without one by 1925.

While attempting to seek out the finest and best early-American furniture as props for his colonial Interior Scenes, Nutting became an expert in American antiques. He published nearly 20 books in his lifetime, including his 10-volume State Beautiful series and various other books on furniture, photography, clocks, and his autobiography. He also contributed many photographs published in magazines and books other than his own.

Nutting also became widely known for his reproduction furniture. His furniture shop produced literally hundreds of different furniture forms: clocks, stools, chairs, settles, settees, tables, stands, desks, mirrors, beds, chests of drawers, cabinet pieces, and treenware.

The overall synergy of the Wallace Nutting name, pictures, books, and furniture, has made anything "Wallace Nutting" quite collectible.

Marks: Wallace Nutting furniture is clearly marked with his distinctive paper label, glued directly onto the piece, or with a block or script signature brand, which was literally branded into his furniture.

Notes: "Process Prints" are 1930s' machine-produced reprints of 12 of Nutting's most popular pictures. These have minimal value and can be detected by using a magnifying glass.

Adviser: Michael Ivankovich.

Books

American Windsors $85
Biography, 1936, 1st ed. $60
England Beautiful, 1st ed. $125
Furniture of the Pilgrim Century, 1st ed. $140
Furniture Treasury, Vol. I $125
Furniture Treasury, Vol. II.... $140
Furniture Treasury, Vol. III $115
Ireland Beautiful, 2nd ed. $45
Pathways of the Puritans $85
Social Life In Old New England $75

State Beautiful Series
Connecticut Beautiful, 1st ed. $75
Maine Beautiful, 1st ed. $45
Massachusetts Beautiful, 2nd ed. $45
New Hampshire Beautiful, 1st ed. $75
New York Beautiful, 1st ed., 1927, grade 3.5 .... $35
Pennsylvania Beautiful, 1st ed, 1924, grade 4.0 .... $40
Pennsylvania Beautiful, 2nd ed, 1935, grade 4.0 .... $40
Virginia Beautiful, 1st ed., sgd by Wallace Nutting, 1930 .... $60

Calendar
Exterior scene, 4-line verse by M.G.N. (possibly Mariet Griswald Nutting), complete calendar pad, orig mat and pen signature, grade 4.0, 1922, 5" x 9" period frame $125
Exterior scene, complete calendar pad, mkd "© Wallace Nutting No. Y 45," grade 3.75, 1939, 5-1/4" x 7-1/4" $45
Catalog, Wallace Nutting Reproduction Furniture, final edition, grade 4.0, 1937 .... $65

Furniture

Bed, low post, #809, mahogany, block branded signature, 38" h $250
Candle Stand, #17, Windsor, tripod base, punched brand, grade 4.0, 14" d, 25" h $550
Chair
#410, Windsor, comb back, arm, grade 3.5, 39" h $950
#420, Windsor, bow back, New England turnings, tapered legs, bulbous spindles, kniuckle arms, as found previously stripped condition $450
#440, Windsor, writing arm, Pennsylvania turnings, drawer beneath seat, block brand $2,145
#464, Carver, arm, script brand $550
#475, Flemish, arm, block brand $1,155
#490/#390, ladderback, two #490 arm chairs, two #390 side chairs, grade 3.75, price for set of four $600
Clock, #65, Goddard, tall case, mahogany, block and shell dec, block branded signature, provenance: purchased directly from Wallace Nutting Furniture Co., 1944, copies of orig purchase receipt, bill of lading, corres with Nutting Studio, all orig, 94" h **36,000**
Cupboard, #910, Sudbury Court, oak, two doors, two drawers, carved front and sides, inlay, double block branded signature, wear, 55" w, 54" w, x 22-1/2" d $5,500
High Chair, liftable food tray, New England turnings, orig light maple finish, block branded signature $2,310
Mirror, Larkspur, foreign scene with garden path leading past girl in flower garden, England, orig mat, pen signature, and title, grade 3.5, c1915-25, 10" x 12" image framed in 12" x 38" period mirror and frame $60
Settee, #515, triple bow back, ten legs, New England turnings, knuckle arms, 89" w, 18" d, unmarked, grade 4.0 .... $600
Stool, #169, rushed maple, branded block signature, replaced rush, 30" h $450
Table
#613, tavern, 36" w, 25-1/2" d, 27-1/2" h, paper label, grade 4.0 .... $750

Nutting, Wallace, table, tavern, ball turned legs and stretchers, paper label, 36" w, 25-1/2" d, 27-1/2" h, **$650.**

Nutting, Wallace, photo, hand colored, Garden of Larkspur, England, original mat, pen signature and title, 20" x 24" original frame with original backing paper, c1915-25, **$165.**

Nutting, Wallace, chair, Windsor, #410, comb back, early paper label, 39" h, **$850.**

Photos courtesy of Michael Ivankovich Auction Co., Inc.

#614b, trestle, maple, block branded signature, 42" w, 26" d, 30" h ...**$500**

#620, gateleg, maple drop leaf, Spanish feet, one drawer, block branded signature in drawer, noticeable tabletop wear, 48" d, 30" h **$600**

Greeting card

Easter, exterior scene, 7-line Easter Wishes verse, orig frame, c1915-25, grade 3.75, 4" x 9" **$60**

Mother's Day, foreign scene, English flower garden, thatch-roofed cottage above 4-line verse, mkd "© Wallace Nutting No. Y.81," grade 4.0, 4-1/2" x 5-1/2" **$30**

Ironwork, potato cooker, imp mark on handle **$1,500**

Picture, hand-colored photo, framed

A Barre Brook, orig mat, pen signature, and title, orig frame, orig backing paper mostly intact, grade 4.0, c1915-25, 22" x 15"............**$175**

A Birch Grove, orig mat, pen signature and title, new backing paper, grade 4.0, c1915-25, 15" x 13" period frame....................**$125**

A Bit of Sewing, Southbury, CT, orig mat, pen signature, and title, orig frame, orig baking paper mostly intact, grade 4.0, c1905-10, 13" x 10"....................**$175**

A Blue Luster Vase, "© WN" lower center on image, newer frame, grade 4.0, c1930-35 ....**$150**

A Chair for John, orig mat, pen signature, and title, older backing paper, grade 4.0, c1915-25, 17" x 14" orig frame **$100**

A Checkered Road, Pennsylvania, orig mat, pen signature and title, grade 3.75, c1930-35, 11" x 9" orig frame with new backing paper **$690**

A Colonial Stair, orig mat, pencil signature and title, new backing paper, grade 4.0, c1905-10, 10" x 16" orig frame **$195**

Affectionately Yours, orig mat, pen signature and title, no backing paper, grade 4.25, c1915-25, 14" x 11" orig frame...........................**$135**

A Favorite Corner, Vermont, remounted and re-signed, grade 3.0, c1915-25, 11" x 14" period frame **$50**

A Franconia Brook, NH, orig mat, pen signature and title, orig frame, orig backing paper, grade 4.0, c1915-25, 10" x 12" **$175**

A Garden Enclosed, orig mat, pencil signature and title, older/orig backing paper, slightly dark mat, grade 3.75, c1905-10, 12" x 16" orig frame **$295**

A May Drive, orig mat, pen signature, and title, orig frame, newer backing paper, grade 4.0, c1915-25, 17" x 14" **$195**

An Old Back Door, orig mat, pen signature and title, grade 3.75, slightly dark mat, c1915-25, 11" x 14" orig frame............................**$135**

An Old Time Romance, orig mat, pen signature and title, orig backing paper, grade 4.0, c1915-25, 17" x 14" orig frame **$120**

A Pilgrim Daughter, orig mat, pen signature and title, new backing paper, grade 3.5, c1915-25, 15" x 12" orig frame **$80**

A Springfield Curve, orig mat, pen signature and title, grade 3.25, c1915-25, 11" x 9" orig frame....**$35**

At Paul Revere's Tavern, orig mat, pen signature and title, new backing paper, grade 3.75, c1915-25, 15" x 13" period frame **$160**

A Warm Spring Day, orig mat, pen signature and title, no backing paper, grade 3.5, c1915-25, 30" x 22" orig frame..........................**$130**

A Woodland Cathedral, orig mat, pen signature and title, no backing paper, grade 3.0, cropped mat, c1915-25, 8" x 16" orig frame....**$45**

Block House Thru Blossoms, orig mat, pen signature, and title, grade 4.0, c1915-25, 16" x 13" orig frame **$115**

Blossomed Bordered, New England, exterior scene, orig mat, pen signature and title, orig frame with newer backing paper, grade 4.0, c1915-25, 17" x 14" **$185**

Blossom Point, orig mat, pen signature and title, (possibly by Wallace Nutting himself,) grade 3.5, c1915-25, 11" x 9" orig frame **$100**

Blow Me Down Bridge, New Hampshire, orig mat, pen signature, and title, no backing paper, grade 3.75, c1915-25, 14" x 17" orig frame **$165**

Brookside Blooms, orig mat, pen signature, and title, grade 3.75, c1915-25, 16" x 13" orig frame **$85**

Cape Cod Hollyhocks, orig mat, pen signature, and title, grade 3.5, c1915-25, 14" x 11" period frame with newer backing paper **$130**

Choosing a Bonnet, orig mat, pencil signature and title, old backing paper, dark mat, grade 3.0, c1905-10, 12" x 14" orig frame **$90**

Christmas Jelly, orig mat, pencil signature and title, newer backing paper, 3.0 grading, several minor white spots, c1915-25, 17" x 13" period frame **$45**

Comfort and a Cat, orig mat, pencil signature and title, new backing paper, grade 3.75, c1905-10, 7" x 14" orig frame **$225**

Decked as a Bride, Massachusetts, orig mat, pen signature, and title, orig frame with newer backing paper, grade 4.0, c1915-25, 14" x 11" **$175**

Dell Dale Road, Mystic, CT, orig mat, pen signature, and title, orig frame, no backing paper, grade 4.0, c1915-25, 14" x 11" **$185**

Dutch Knitting Lesson, orig pen signature lower left on image, orig backing paper, grade 4.0, c1930-35, 3" x 4" orig frame **$120**

Ellicott City, black and white, orig mat, pen signature and title, new backing paper, grade 4.0, c1930, 16" x 13" new frame **$500**

Five O'clock, England, orig mat, pen signature and title, orig backing paper, grade 4.0, c1915-25, 22" x 13" orig frame **$130**

Grandmother's Garden, orig mat, pen signature, and title, orig frame, no backing paper, grade 4.0, c1915-25, 12" x 10" **$235**

Hauling in the Nets, orig signature and title, orig backing paper, grade 4.0, c1905-10, 17" x 14" orig mahogany frame **$1,200**

Hollyhock Cottage, England, orig mat, pen signature, and title, orig backing paper, grade 4.0, c1915-25, 17" x 14" **$250**

Honeymoon Stroll, orig mat, pen signature and title, new backing paper, grade 3.75, c1915-25, 14" x 12" older frame **$50**

In Tenderleaf, orig mat, pen signature and title, no backing paper, grade 3.5, c1915-25, 12" x 16" orig frame **$25**

In Upland New England, orig mat, pencil signature and title, new backing paper, grade 4.0, c1905-10, 15" x 10" orig frame, ... **$80**

Joy Path, England, orig mat, pen signature and title, orig frame

with orig backing paper, grade 4.0, c1930-35, 9" x 11" **$175**

Justifiable Vanity, orig mat, pen signature, and title, orig Copyright label, grade 4.25, c1930-35, 9" x 10" orig frame with orig backing paper **$150**

Larkspur, orig frame, newer backing paper, grade 4.0, 11" x 14" **$200**

Life of the Golden Age, orig mat, pen signature and title, no backing paper, grade 4.25, c1915-25, 17" x 13" orig frame **$200**

Making a Summer Hat, orig mat, pen signature, and title, no backing paper, grade 3.75, c1915-25, 22" x 18" orig frame **$250**

Mountain Born, High Falls, NY, orig mat, pen signature and title, orig frame with orig backing paper, grade 4.0, c1930-35, 9" x 11" **$175**

Neighborhood News, orig mat, pen signature, and title, period frame, newer backing paper, slightly cropped mat, grade 3.75, c1915-25, 18" x 15" **$350**

Nuttinghame Blossoms, orig mat, pen signature, and title, newer backing paper, grade 3.5, c1915-25, 15" x 11" period frame **$175**

On the Slope, orig mat, pen signature and title, no backing paper, grade 3.5, c1915-25, 16" x 10" orig frame **$80**

Pine Pool, CT, orig mat, pen signature, and title, orig frame with older but not orig backing paper, c1915-25, 14" x 17" **$195**

Purity, Lake Mohonk, NY, exterior scene, orig mat, pen signature and title, orig frame with older (not orig) backing paper, grade 4.0, c1915-25, 12" x 20" **$195**

Stepping Heavenward, orig mat, pen signature and title, no backing paper, grade 4.5, c1930-35, 16" x 20" orig frame **$600**

Stepping Stones at Bolton Abbey, orig mat, pen signature and title, new backing paper, grade 3.75, c1915-25, 20" x 14" orig frame **$350**

Swirling Seas, close-framed, orig pen signature lower right on image, orig title lower left on image, title, no backing paper, grade 4.0, c1910-20, 40" x 20" orig frame **$100**

Tea for Two, Wentworth-Gardiner House, Portsmouth, NH, orig mat,

pen signature, and title, orig frame, newer backing paper, grade 4.0, c1915-25, 17" x 14" **$295**

Thanksgiving, Rhode Island, orig mat, pen signature, and title, grade 3.0, c1905-10, 7" x 9" period frame **$350**

The Great Wayside Oak, Sudbury, MA, orig mat, pen signature, and title, orig frame, newer backing paper, grade 4.0, c1915-25, 14" x 11" **$275**

The Hurrying Saranac, orig mat, pen signature and title, no backing paper, grade 4.0, c1915-25, 10" x 12" orig frame **$50**

The Langdon Door, Portsmouth, NH, orig mat, pencil signature and title, older backing paper, grade 3.5, cropped mat, c1905-10, 11" x 14" orig frame **$70**

The Maple Sugar Cupboard, orig mat, pen signature and title, new backing paper, grade 4.25, c1915-25, 20" x 16" orig frame **$130**

The Nashua Asleep, orig mat, pen signature and title, older backing paper, orig copyright label, grade 4.0, c1930-35, 16" x 13" orig frame **$150**

The Natural Bridge, orig mat, pen signature and title, new backing paper, grade 4.0, c1915-25, 9" x 12" orig frame **$90**

The Old Sugar Mill Florida, orig mat, pencil signature and title, new backing paper, grade 4.0, c1905-10, 10" x 12" period frame **$300**

The Saucy Bonnet, orig mat, pen signature and title, orig backing paper, grade 4.0, c1905, 14" x 9" orig frame **$190**

The Spinet Corner, orig mat, pen signature and title, no backing paper, grade 4.0, c1915-25, 14" x 11" orig frame **$90**

The Way It Begins, man in red jacket, orig mat, pencil signature and title, grade 3.25, c1905-10, 12" x 10" period mahogany frame **$250**

Untitled exterior, Connecticut, orig mat, pen signature and title, orig backing paper, grade 4.0, c1915-25, 9" x 7" orig frame **$35**

Untitled exterior, Heart of Maine, orig mat and pen signature, orig backing paper, grade 4.0, c1915-25, 7" x 9" orig frame **$35**

Untitled exterior, Massachusetts, orig mat, pen signature, no backing paper, grade 3.75, c1915-25, 7" x 9" orig frame **$50**

Untitled exterior, New Hampshire, orig backing paper, grade 4.0, c1930-35, 8" x 6-1/2" orig frame **$65**

Untitled girls at house, orig mat, pen signature, no backing paper, grade 4.0, c1915-25, 8" x 10" new frame **$45**

Untitled, Honeymoon Windings, MA, orig mat and pen signature, orig frame with orig backing paper, grade 4.0, c1930-35, 8" x 6-1/2" **$110**

Untitled interior, Massachusetts, possibly re-signed in pencil, new backing paper, grade 3.0, c1915-25, 10" x 8" orig frame **$25**

Untitled interior, New England, orig frame, newer backing paper, grade 4.0, c1915-25 .... **$25**

Untitled, snow scene, NH, A New Hampshire Roadside, orig mat, pen signature, orig frame with newer backing paper, grade 4.0, c1915-25, 9" x 7" **$475**

Upper Winooski, orig mat, pen signature and title, orig backing paper, grade 4.25, c1915-25, 16" x 10" orig frame **$175**

Where Grandma Was Wed, Woodbury, CT, orig mat, pencil signature and title, new backing paper, grade 4.0, c1915-25, 14" x 11" orig frame **$95**

With Fingers and Toes, black and white, orig mat, pencil signature and title, new backing paper, grade 4.0, c1905, 14" x 11" orig frame **$3,750**

Zinnias, copyright lower right on image, grade 3.0 with over mat, c1930-35, 14" x 18" older frame **$130**

Postcard, Topsfield, MA, black and white, "Parson-Capen House (1683), Topsfield Historical Society, Topsfield-Massachusetts, photograph by Wallace Nutting," grade 4.0, c1905-10, 3-1/2" x 5" period frame **$75**

Silhouettes

George and Martha Washington, 3" x 4" **$90**

Girl and Birdcage, copyright lower left, grade 4.0, c1927, 4" x 4" frame **$25**

Girl at Birdbath, grade 4.0, c1927, 4" x 4" new frame **$25**

Girl at Vanity Desk, 4" x 4" **$70**

Girl By Statue, small format, sgd "EJD" lower left and "©" lower center, new frame, grade 4.0, c1927 .... **$20**

Girl Holds Necklace, small format, sgd "© WN" lower left, new frame, grade 4.0, c1927 .... **$75**

Girl on Fence, new frame, new backing paper, grade 4.0, c1927, 4" x 4" **$20**

Girl Plays Piano, sgd "© WN" lower left, new frame, grade 4.0, c1927, ... **$45**

Girl Sews on Rocker, small format, sgd "WN" lower left, "EJD" (Ernest John Donnelly) lower right, new frame, grade 4.0, c1927 .... **$45**

Girl Sniffs Flowers, grade 4.0, c1927, 4" x 4" frame **$25**

Girl Reads Book, small format, sgd "© WN" lower left, new frame, grade 4.0, c1927 .... **$35**

Girl with Flowers, grade 4.0, c1927, 4" x 4" newer frame, ... **$30**

Hope and Josiah, c1927, medium format, grade 3.75, pr **$125**

Mary's Lamb, two handled mahogany pin tray, copyright lower left and "EJD" lower right, grade 4.0, c1927, 7" x 8" **$65**

WALLACE NUTTING-LIKE PHOTOGRAPHERS

History: Although Wallace Nutting was widely recognized as the country's leading producer of hand-colored photographs during the early 20th century, he was by no means the only photographer selling this style of picture. Throughout the country literally hundreds of regional photographers were selling hand-colored photographs from their home regions or travels. The subject matter of these photographers was comparable to Nutting's, including Interior, Exterior, Foreign, and Miscellaneous Unusual scenes.

Several photographers operated large businesses, and, although not as large or well known as Wallace Nutting, they sold a substantial volume of pictures which can still be readily found today. The vast majority of their work was photographed in their home regions and sold primarily to local residents or visiting tourists. It should come as little surprise that three of the major Wallace

Nutting-like photographers—David Davidson, Fred Thompson, and the Sawyer Art Co.—each had ties to Wallace Nutting.

Hundreds of other smaller local and regional photographers attempted to market hand-colored pictures comparable to Wallace Nutting's during the period of 1900 to the 1930s. Although quite attractive, most were not as appealing to the general public as Wallace Nutting pictures. However, as the price of Wallace Nutting pictures has escalated, the work of these lesser-known Wallace Nutting-like photographers have become increasingly collectible.

A partial listing of some of these minor Wallace Nutting-like photographers includes: Babcock; J. C. Bicknell; Blair; Ralph Blood (Portland, Maine); Bragg; Brehmer; Brooks; Burrowes; Busch; Carlock; Pedro Cacciola; Croft; Currier; Depue Brothers; Derek; Dowly; Eddy; May Farini (hand-colored colonial lithographs); George Forest; Gandara; Gardner (Nantucket, Bermuda, Florida); Gibson; Gideon; Gunn; Bessie Pease Gutmann (hand-colored colonial lithographs); Edward Guy; Harris; C. Hazen; Knoffe; Haynes (Yellowstone Park); Margaret Hennesey; Hodges; Homer; Krabel; Kattleman; La Bushe; Lake; Lamson (Portland, Maine); M. Lightstrum; Machering; Rossiler Mackinae; Merrill; Meyers; William Moehring; Moran; Murrey; Lyman Nelson; J. Robinson Neville (New England); Patterson; Own Perry; Phelps; Phinney; Reynolds; F. Robbins; Royce; Frederick Scheetz (Philadelphia, Pennsylvania);

Gutmann, Bessie Pease, Love's Blossom, *signed and titled lower center, 11" x 14" older frame, c1931,* **$95.**
Photo courtesy of Michael Ivankovich Auction Co., Inc.

Shelton, Standley (Colorado); Stott; Summers; Esther Svenson; Florence Thompson; Thomas Thompson; M. A. Trott; Sanford Tull; Underhill; Villar; Ward; Wilmot; Edith Wilson; and Wright.

Advisor: Michael Ivankovich.

Notes: The key determinants of value include the collectibility of the particular photographer, subject matter, condition, and size. Exterior Scenes are the most common.

Keep in mind that only the rarest pictures, in the best condition, will bring top prices. Discoloration and/or damage to the picture or matting can reduce value significantly.

David Davidson

Second to Nutting in overall production, Davidson worked primarily in the Rhode and Southern Massachusetts area. While a student at Brown University around 1900, Davidson learned the art of hand-colored photography from Wallace Nutting, who happened to be the Minister at Davidson's church. After Nutting moved to Southbury in 1905, Davidson graduated from Brown and started a successful photography business in Providence, Rhode Island, which he operated until his death in 1967.

A Winter Brook, Snow, orig mat, pen signature, and title, c1910-20, grade 4.0, 15" x 12" orig frame **$120**

Berkshire Sunset **$80**
Christmas Day **$160**
Driving Home The Cows **$120**
Ebbing Tide, orig mat, pen signature and title, grade 4.0, c1915-25, 11" x 14" orig frame **$80**
Heart's Desire **$30**
Her House In Order **$75**
Old Ironsides **$170**
On A News Hunt **$120**
Pine Lane, orig mat, pen signature, and title, pen signed lower left on image, cropped, grade 3.5, c1915-25, 13" x 16" period mahogany frame **$90**
San Juan Harbor, orig mat, pen signature, and title, orig backing paper, grade 4.0, c1915-25, 8" x 6-1/2" orig frame **$200**
The Enchanted Window, orig backing, mat discoloration, grade 3.75, c1915-25, 16" x 13" orig frame **$35**

The Village Prattlers, New England, grade 4.0, c1910-20, 13" x 16" orig frame **$50**
Untitled snow scene, orig mat, pen signature, illegible faded title, new backing paper, two Davidson labels preserved on back, grade 3.75, c1915-25, 7" x 5" orig frame **$60**
Weedland Brook, orig mat, pen signature, and title, orig backing paper, grade 4.5, c1930-35, 12" x 15" orig frame **$200**
Wisteria, New England, orig mat, pencil signature and title, older backing paper, grade 3.75, c1910-20, 13" x 16" orig frame **$90**

Sawyer

A father and son team, Charles H. Sawyer and Harold B. Sawyer, operated the very successful Sawyer Art Company from 1903 until the 1970s. Beginning in Maine, the Sawyer Art Company moved to Concord, New Hampshire, in 1920 to be closer to their primary market—New Hampshire's White Mountains. Charles H. Sawyer briefly worked for Nutting from 1902 to 1903 while living in southern Maine. Sawyer's production volume ranks third behind Wallace Nutting and David Davidson.

A Bridge of Gold, New England, evening exterior scene, orig map, pen signature, and title, orig backing paper, grade 3.75, c1915-25, 7" x 9" orig frame **$85**
A Rock Garden, Cape Cod, close-framed with orig white ink Sawyer signature lower right on image, newer backing paper, orig pen-signed titled, partial paper label, grade 4.0, c1930-35, 10" x 13" orig frame **$100**
At the Water's Edge, New England, orig mat, pen signature, and title, orig backing paper, orig Sawyer paper label, grade 4.0, c1915-25, 9" x 7" orig frame, ... **$75**
Echo Lake, Franconia Notch, orig mat, pen signature, and title, grade 3.0, c1915-25, 15" x 12" period frame **$50**
House, New England, country home with tall trees, close framed with orig black-ink Sawyer signature lower right, newer backing paper, preserved Sawyer back-stamp label, grade 4.0, 16" x 13" period ornate oval frame **$450**

Joseph Lincoln Garden, Cape Cod, close-framed, orig white ink signature lower right, orig backing paper, orig Sawyer triangular back-stamp and hand written title, grade 4.0, c1930-35, 7-1/2" x 9-1/2" orig frame, ... **$135**
Penobscot River at Bucksport, close-framed, orig white signature lower right on image, new backing paper, grade 4.0, c1930-35, 10" x 13" orig frame **$1,200**
Spanish Mission, close framed, preserved Sawyer paper label, grade 4.0, c1915-25, 7" x 5" newer frame **$60**
The Long Trail of Vermont, orig mat, pen signature, and title, orig backing paper, orig Sawyer paper label, grade 4.0, c1915-25, 16" x 12" orig frame **$100**
The Swimming Pool, orig mat, pen signature and title, no backing paper, grade 4.25, c1915-25, 16" x 20" orig frame **$165**
Veil of Tighannock, orig mat, pen signature and title, orig label on back, grade 4.25, c1915-25, 13" x 16" orig frame **$80**

Frederick Thompson

Frederick H. Thompson and Frederick M. Thompson, another father and son team, operated the Thompson Art Company (TACO) from 1908 to 1923, working primarily in the Portland, Maine, area. We know that Thompson and Nutting had collaborated because Thompson widely marketed an interior scene he had taken in Nutting's Southbury home. The production volume of the Thompson Art Company ranks fourth behind Nutting, Davidson, and Sawyer.

After Church, Mother and two children, orig mat, pencil signature and title, grade 3.75, c1910-20, 10" x 15" orig frame **$250**
Apple Tree Road, grade 3.75, c1910-15, 19" x 15" period frame **$50**
At the Close of Day, grade 4.0, c1910-15, 17" x 14" orig frame **$70**
Blossom Dale **$75**
Brook in Winter **$190**
Fireside Fancy Work **$140**
Golden Glow, New England, orig mat, pencil signature, and title, partial orig backing paper, grade 4.0, c1910-20, 8" x 16" orig frame **$60**

Thompson, Frederick, Roadside Brook, *hand colored photo, 20" x 16" original frame, original backing paper mostly intact, original Thompson stamp on back, slightly dark mat, c1910-15,* **$100.**

Sawyer, Charles, The Swimming Pool, *hand-colored photo, original mat, pen signature, and title, 16" x 20" original frame, c1915-25,* **$165.**

Photos courtesy of Michael Ivankovich Auction Co., Inc.

Payne, Elfin Gorge, New York, *hand-colored photo, original mat, pencil signature and title, 8" x 14" original frame, newer backing paper,* **$65.**

Miniature Exterior, mat stain, grade 3.5, c1910-20, 2" x 3" orig frame .. **$30**

Miniature interior, close framed, orig Thompson backstamp, hanging calendar missing, grade 3.75, c1915-25, 4" x 3" orig thin metal frame .. **$45**

Mirror, New England, Colonial interior scene, girl seated by fire, orig backing paper, grade 4.0, c1910-20, 3" x 2" image framed above 3-1/2" x 9" orig mahogany frame with mirror **$40**

Mother's Joy, orig mat, pencil signature, and title, grade 2.5, image silvering, c1910-20, 7" x 9" orig frame .. **$50**

Neath the Blossoms, orig mat, pencil signature and title, grade 4.0, c1910-15, 11" x 7" orig frame **$200**

Rivervale, orig mat, pencil signature and title, grade 4.0, c1910-20, 10" x 6" orig frame **$60**

Roadside Brook, orig Thompson stamp on back, grade 3.75, c1910-15, 20" x 16" orig frame **$100**

Snuffing the Candle, orig mat, pencil signature and title, new backing paper, grade 3.75, c1910-20, 7" x 9" orig frame **$30**

Sunset on the Suwanee **$45**

The Gossips **$80**

Untitled, girl by house, photocopy of Thompson Stamp on back on new backing paper, grade 4.0, c1910-15, 5" x 9" orig frame **$40**

Untitled seascape, Maine, orig mat, pencil signature, grade 4.0, c1910-15, 12" x 15" orig frame **$70**

Minor Wallace Nutting-Like Photographers

Generally speaking, prices for works by minor Wallace Nutting-like photographers would break down as follows: smaller pictures (5" x 7" to 10" x 12"), **$10-$75**; medium pictures (11" x 14" to 14" x 17"), **$50-$200**; larger pictures (larger than 14" x 17"), **$75-$200+**.

Barnhill, E. G., Florida, sgd lower left, unframed, grade 4.0, c1910-20, 10" x 13-1/2" **$30**

Bicknell, J. Carleton, closed framed exterior, orig "Bicknell Photos" label on orig backing paper, grade 4.0, c1915-25, 9" x 7" orig frame **$45**

Collier, Paul R., *Country House,* matted, sgd lower left on image, grade 4.0, c1920-30, 16" x 14" orig frame **$20**

Deane, Willis A, *The Flume,* orig mat, pencil signature and title, orig floral wallpaper backing, grade 4.0, c1920-25, 13" x 15" orig frame **$25**

Edson, Norman, *Mount Rainier,* close framed, orig white pen ink signature lower right, grade 4.25, c1920-30, 10" x 8" orig frame **$170**

Farini, *In Her Boudoir* **$30**

Gardiner, H. Marshall, *Bermuda,* orig mat, pencil signature and title, orig backing paper, grade 4.0, c1915-25, 9" x 7" orig frame **$120**

Garrison, J. M., *Tower Pine,* orig brown mat, pencil signature and title, grade 4.0, c1915-25, 20" x 1" orig frame **$40**

Gibson, *Orchard Blossoms,* orig mat, pencil signature and title, grade 4.0, 1915-25, 14" x 11" orig frame **$30**

Gutmann, Bessie Pease
Cover, *McCall's,* Bubbles print, sgd lower right, new over mat, grade 2.75, May, 1912, 12" x 15" new frame **$60**

Friendly Enemies, sgd and titled lower center, grade 4.0, c1937, 13" x 18" orig frame **$70**

To Love and Cherish, sgd lower left, titled lower center, grade 4.0, c1911, 13" x 18" orig frame **$275**

Harris, *Cocoanut Grove,* Florida, orig backing paper, grade 3.75, c1915-25, 13" x 10" orig frame.................... **$100**

MacAskill, Wallace R, *Margaier Valley,* Nova Scotia, Canada, grade 3.5, mat stains, foxing, c1915-25, 12" x 9-1/2" orig frame **$25**

Northend, Mary Harrod, *Cohassett Garden,* New England, new backing, grade 4.0, c1910-15, 15" x 12" new frame **$160**

Radel, F., *Buckwood Inn,* Shawnee on the Delaware, PA, orig mat, pen signature and title, orig Radel label, grade 3.75, c1910-20, 14" x 11" orig frame **$70**

Standley, Harry Landis, *Long's Peak Estates Park,* Colorado, orig mat, pencil signature and title, grade 4.0, c1915-25, 6" x 12" newer frame **$50**

Thompson, Florence, Sunset Clouds, Portland Harbor, schooners at dusk, orig mat, pencil signature and title, grade 4.0, c1910-20, 11" x 13" newer frame **$250**

Villar, After a Canter, orig mat, pencil signature and title, grade 4.0, c1915-25, 11" x 14" orig frame, orig backing paper.. **$200**

ORIENTAL RUGS

History: Oriental rugs or carpets date back to 3,000 B.C., but it was in the 16th century that they became prevalent. The rugs originated in the regions of Central Asia, Iran (Persia), Caucasus, and Anatolia. Early rugs can be classified into basic categories: Iranian, Caucasian, Turkoman, Turkish, and Chinese. Later India, Pakistan, and Iraq produced rugs in the Oriental style.

The pattern name is derived from the tribe that produced the rug, e.g., Iran is the source for Hamadan, Herez, Sarouk, and Tabriz.

Reproduction Alert.
Beware! There are repainted rugs on the market.

Notes: When evaluating an Oriental rug, age, design, color, weave, knots per square inch, and condition determine the final value. Silk rugs and prayer rugs bring higher prices than other types.

Afghan, dark blue and pale salmon, red ground, wear, minor edge damage, 7' 10" x 9' 2" **$350**

Afshar, South Persia, blue and burgundy borders, ivory ground, worn, second quarter 20th C, 3' 9" x 5' 4" **$120**

Agra, India, overall design of palmettes, rosettes, and flowering vines in rose, tan, light aubergine, ivory, olive, and blue-green on deep wine red field, wide blue-green border of similar design, small areas of wear, edges, and ends very slightly reduced and machine re-overcast, last quarter 19th C, 8' 6" x 6' 10" **$8,625**

Anatolian Kali, two columns of serrated diamonds in red, navy blue, gold, aubergine, and light and dark blue-green on dark brown field, tan eli-belinde motif border, ivory elems, cut and resewn, small repairs, last quarter 19th C, 13' 6" x 5' 9" **$420**

Armenian Karabagh, South Caucasus, three lightning medallions each inset with quatrefoil floral motifs, navy blue, royal blue, dark red, rose, camel, aubergine, and blue-green on midnight blue field, navy blue rosette border, small replied areas, corner repairs, dated 1911, 8' 10" x 3' 9" **$1,265**

Bahktiari, West Persia, mid/late 20th C

Garden pattern, polychrome colors, trees and peacocks, 5' 4" x 7' **$2,875**

Sq grid inset with various animal, bird, tree, and palmette motifs in midnight, slate, and sky blue, red, rose, camel, gold, ivory, and blue-green, red animal combat and palmette border, 12' 10" x 9' 4" **$1,175**

Baluch, Northeast Persia, column of 12 flowerheads flanked by stepped motifs in red, ivory, and brown on midnight blue field, wide red "boat" border, areas of wear, creases, last quarter 19th C, 6' x 3' 9" **$600**

Belooch, central rect with bands of wavy design, border of floral dec squares, old reweave, new sides, c1910, 3' 1" x 5' 3" **$300**

Bidjar, Northwest Persia, late 19th C

Central light blue medallion on red ground, dark blue floral border, some wear, 7' 2" x 4' 10", c1910 .... **$1,725**

Overall design with rows of rosettes, palmettes, and arabesque leaves, red, royal blue, gold, ivory, and blue-green on midnight blue field, red turtle border, areas of wear, small rewoven areas, 18' 2" x 12' **$9,990**

Bordjalou Kazak, Southwest Caucasus, prayer rug, rect prayer cartouche inset with concentric gabled sq medallion in navy blue, ivory, and light blue-green on red field, ivory border, small rewoven and replied areas, end fraying, third quarter 19th C, 4' 6" x 3' 7" **$2,235**

Erivan-Kazak, light abrash blue and red borders, medium blue ground, minor wear, 20th C, 5' 1" x 6' 7" **$550**

Ersari, West Turkestan, three columns of six octagonal gulli-gulls in midnight blue and navy blue, apricot and blue-green on red field, multicolored cruciform motif border, moth damage, small holes, several small patches and rewoven areas, last quarter 19th C, 10' 6" x 6' 10" **$1,100**

Feraghan Sarouk

Central black medallion with orange highlights, overall orange and black floral design, c1890, 3' 3" x 4' 9" **$1,150**

Central star-shaped medallion in dark blue and light blue on beige and red

Heriz rug, blue medallion on red field, ivory corners, c1930, 11' 5" x 8' 3", **$2,575.**
Photo courtesy of Pook & Pook, Inc.

Oriental throw rug, three medallions on red field, ivory border, c1900, 4' 10" x 3' 3", **$1,265.**
Photo courtesy of Pook & Pook, Inc.

Sejshour throw, floral pattern, mustard and navy border, c1900, 7' x 4' 2", **$2,760.**
Photo courtesy of Pook & Pook, Inc.

Tabriz rug, cream and rose red field, blue floral medallion, blue floral border,
$6,000.
Photo courtesy of David Rago Auctions, Inc.

*Caucasian throw, three medallions on red field, ivory border, c1910, 5' 1" x
3' 5",* **$1,150.**
Photo courtesy of Pook & Pook, Inc.

*Persian Kashan rug, cobalt, ivory and crimson central medallions, blue and white
vine scroll borders, 9' 5" x 13",* **$1,116.**
Photo courtesy of David Rago Auctions, Inc.

*Persian Kashan rug, dark blue and
cream center medallion, red floral
ground, elaborate floral border, post
WWII, 9' 10" x 13' 5",* **$840.**
Photo courtesy of David Rago Auctions, Inc.

*Persian rug, vine scroll and floral
medallion, crimson, cobalt blue,
and ivory, 163" x 118",* **$1,200.**
Photo courtesy of David Rago Auctions, Inc.

*Northwest Persian rug, red and ivory
star and diamond pattern surrounded
by polychrome geometric border, 5' 2"
x 8' 10",* **$350.**
Photo courtesy of David Rago Auctions, Inc.

ground, dark blue border, c1890, 3' 4" x 5'.................................**$980**

Hamadan, Northwest Persia, second quarter 20th C

Indented diamond medallion, matching spandrels, overall Herati design in midnight and navy blue, ivory, rose, and dark green on red field, midnight blue turtle border, 7' x 4' 8"...............................**$650**

Multiple ivory, blue, and tan borders, dark blue spandrels, ivory ground, wear, 4' 1" x 5' 8".............**$325**

Heriz, Northwest Persia

Azerbejan design, dark blue border, light rust ground, camel and green accents, 9' 4" x 12' 6"............**$6,620**

Dark blue border, ivory spandrels, burgundy ground, 9' 1" x 11' 1"...............................**$750**

Large gabled sq medallion with palmette pendants in midnight and navy blue, rose, camel, and blue-green on terra-cotta red field, large ivory spandrels, midnight blue rosette and serrated leaf border, areas of wear, end fraying, late 19th/early 20th C, 12' x 9' 2".............................**$2,585**

Large gabled sq medallion surrounded by floral motifs in midnight and royal blue, rose, tan, and dark blue-green on terra-cotta red field, stepped ivory spandrels, midnight blue "turtle" border, small spots of wear, end fraying, early 20th C, 11' 6" x 8'.............................**$1,300**

Light blue central medallion, overall floral ground in shades of red and blue, moth eaten in one corner, c1935, 8' 10" x 11' 9"...........**$900**

Three hooked diamond medallions in midnight blue, red, camel, dark brown, ivory, and blue-green on light tan field, ivory floral meander border, slight end fraying, very small edge and corner gouges, early 20th C, 9' 4" x 3' 5"............**$1,100**

Wide dark blue border, green and ivory spandrels, tomato red ground, 9' 8" x 12' 9"...........................**$7,475**

Jaf Kurd, Northwest Persia, bagface, diamond lattice of hooked diamonds in midnight and navy blue, red, gold, brown, rust, aubergine, and blue-green, aubergine border, slight brown corrosion, early 20th C, 2' 7" x 2' 7".............................**$530**

Karabagh, South Caucasus, last quarter 19th C

Bittersweet border, ivory ground, edge wear, small repairs, 3' 5" x 7'.............................**$2,175**

Ivory border, blue abrash ground, wear, 3' 10" x 7'.............**$500**

Prayer, dated, ivory, orange, and pale blue borders, black abrash ground, minor edge wear, 2' 1" x 4' 5".............................**$250**

Karaja, central medallion, red, dark blue, and light blue, floral borders, overall wear, c1920, 8' 2" x 10' 7".............................**$1,495**

Kashan, signature cartouche, midnight blue border, blue and ivory spandrels, deep burgundy ground, 7' 8" x 12' 8".............................**$1,495**

Konaghend, Northeast Caucasus, characteristic arabesque lattice in ivory, red, rose, royal blue, gold, and blue-green on black field, ivory border, some black corrosion, late 19th/early 20th C, 6' x 4' 3"..............**$1,295**

Kuba, Northeast Caucasus, three diamond medallions, each radiating four serrated motifs and four small diamonds in red, red-brown, navy blue, ivory, orange, and blue-green, abrashed midnight blue field, navy blue border, areas of minor wear, slight dye runs, black corrosion, some glue to back, late 19th/early 20th C, 4' 10" x 3' 6".............................**$1,000**

Kurd, Northwest Persia, column of five turkoman-style octagonal turret guls in red, sky blue, gold, aubergine-brown, olive, and blue-green, midnight blue field, dark red border, end fraying, early 20th C, 9' 5" x 3' 9".............................**$900**

Lenkoran, Southeast Caucasus, three large calyx medallions separated by two large rect medallions in red, navy blue, aubergine, ivory, apricot, light camel, and blue-green on dark brown field, ivory border, brown corrosion, even wear to center, creases, last quarter 19th C, 10' x 4' 4"...........**$715**

Lesghi, Northeast Caucasus, column of four Lesghi stars in red, sky blue, ivory, tan-gold, and blue-green on navy blue field, two ivory borders, even wear, slight end fraying, last quarter 19th C, 4' 10" x 3' 9".............................**$1,300**

Luri, Southwest Persia, large gabled and serrated sq medallions flanked

Soumak rug, flatweave, three cobalt blue and cerulean medallions against ivory and red ground, 5' 9" x 7' 5", **$600.**
Photo courtesy of David Rago Auctions, Inc.

Persian Shiraz rug, repeating diamond medallion, crimson ground, floral border on blue ground, c1970, 8' 3" x 11' 3", **$720.**
Photo courtesy of David Rago Auctions, Inc.

Shirvan throw, overall floral design, red field with navy and ivory borders, c1910, 5' 4" x 3' 3", $630.
Photo courtesy of Pook & Pook, Inc.

Oriental throw, Lori Pambok, three medallions on blue field, ivory border, late 19th century, 8' 2" x 3' 10", $4,025.
Photo courtesy of Pook & Pook, Inc.

by six large rosettes in red, navy blue, apricot, gold, and dark blue-green on midnight blue field, ivory border, even center wear, early 20th C, 7' x 4' 7" **$765**

Malayer, Northwest Persia, overall design of flowerheads and blossoming vines in red, ice blue, camel, and olive on abrashed royal blue field, ivory border, outer guard stripes partially missing from both ends, second quarter 20th C, 4' 10" x 3' 6" **$1,000**

Qashqai, Southwest Persia, large hooked hexagonal medallion inset with blossoming angular vines in red, navy blue, ivory, gold, brown, and blue-green, midnight blue field, brown border, slight wear to center, minor moth damage, small repair, late 19th/early 20th C, 6' 9" x 4' **$1,100**

Sarouk, West Persia, second quarter 20th C

Floral and checkered border with floral spandrels, pink, blues, and ivory on salmon ground, good sheen, 9' 1" x 12' 1" **$2,530**

Overall floral sprays in midnight, navy, and ice blue, red, gold, and light blue-green on rose field, narrow midnight blue floral border, 5' x 3' 4" **$500**

Seraband, Northwest Persia, staggered rows of small boteh in midnight blue, apricot, ivory, and blue-green on abrashed terra-cotta red field, three ivory and red floral meander borders, even wear to center, slight end fraying, early 20th C, 19' 6" x 7' 7" **$3,000**

Shiraz, East Caucasus, Caucasian type design, multiple borders, diagonal stripes in dark blue, red, ivory and gold, late 19th C, 3' x 5' **$460**

Shirvan, East Caucasus, late 19th C

Geometric and star designs in blue, burgundy, red, green, gold, and

Northwest Persian hall rug, red and ivory geometric motif on cobalt blue ground, red and ivory border, 4' 4" x 9' 7", $265.
Photo courtesy of David Rago Auctions, Inc.

ivory, wear and small splits, 3' 10" x 5' 6" **$920**

Three columns with stepped diamond and serrated diamond medallions in red, ivory, navy blue, black, gold, and abrashed blue-green on midnight blue field, narrow ivory border, slight moth damage, 9' 6" x 5 .... **$2,550**

Three medallions, shades of blue and red, minor border loss at ends, c1890, 5' 10" x 3' 6" **$950**

Soumak, Northeast Caucasus, four elongated diamond medallions flanked by half medallions in midnight blue, black, rose, red, and tan on maroon-brown field, black border, areas of slight wear, late 19th C, 9' 4" x 8' 6" **$2,475**

South Caucasian, column of eight radiating hexagonal medallions in navy blue, red, rust, gold, dark brown, and light blue-green on midnight blue field, narrow ivory rosette border, slight dye run in one corner, second quarter 20th C, 13' x 3' 8" **$1,175**

Tabriz, silk, tree of life, deer, and floral borders, shades of brown, overall wear, dry areas, missing one end border, c1890, 5' 11" x 4' 5" **$1,265**

Tekke Torba, West Turkestan, late 19th/early 20th C

Kejebe design in midnight blue, red, ivory, and dark brown on cochineal field, multiple borders of similar coloration, outer border partially missing from one end, 4' 2" x 1' 4" **$450**

Multiple borders, overall design, ivory, blue, orange, and red, brown/brown ground, minor pile wear, 7' 5" x 11' 9" **$1,150**

Ushak, West Anatolia, large crenellated hexagonal medallion and matching spandrels in tan-gold, ivory, and blue-green on red field, red rosette and flowering vine border, areas of wear, edge and end gouges, several patches and rewoven areas, late 19th C, 11' 10" x 8' 2" **$950**

Yomud Chuval, West Turkestan, nine Chuval guls in midnight blue, red, ivory, and blue-green on dark aubergine field, ivory border, plain aubergine elem, small spots of slight wear, re-overcast, last quarter 19th C, 3' 4" x 2' 3" **$825**

Plaques, Chinese hard stone, engraved writing, well-figured detail, 19th century, 5" x 3-3/8", 6-3/8" x 4-5/8", 8-1/2" x 4-1/8", price for set of three, **$525.**

Chinese vase, iron red porcelain, 18th century, 9" h, **$1,416.**
Photo courtesy of Sloans & Kenyon Auctioneers and Appraisers.

Plate, Chinese-style decoration, green enameled coiled dragon chasing flaming pearl, rose enamel border, Buddhist precious things, back signed in overglaze red "Tashiro," impressed square mark, Japan, c1900, 13-3/4" d, **$550.**

Chinese Kesi, wall hanging textile, woven with warriors on horseback, couched gold thread detail, silk border, 19th century, 74" x 37", **$800.**
Photo courtesy of David Rago Auctions, Inc.

Chinese, Étagère, hardwood, central cupboard covered by hinged doors, flanked by two drawers and open-work carvings, 20th century, 38-1/2" x 67" x 14-1/2" h, **$750.**
Photo courtesy of David Rago Auctions, Inc.

Pair of bronze candlesticks, deer form, each supporting candleholder on back, Chinese, 18th century, 10" h **$600.**

Chinese charger, porcelain, blue and white, birds and flowering decoration, 18th century, 12-3/4" h, **$750.**

Photo courtesy of Sloans & Kenyon Auctioneers and Appraisers.

Chinese fish bowl, porcelain, blue and crackle glaze, riverscape decoration, **$375.**

Photo courtesy of Sloans & Kenyon Auctioneers and Appraisers.

Chinese vases, porcelain, blue and white dragon, foliage, and mythical beast, **$600.**

Photo courtesy of Sloans & Kenyon Auctioneers and Appraisers.

ORIENTALIA

History: Orientalia is a term applied to objects made in the Orient, an area which encompasses the Far East, Asia, China, and Japan. The diversity of cultures produced a variety of objects and styles.

Additional Listings: Canton, Celadon, Cloisonné, Fitzhugh, Nanking, Netsukes, Rose Medallion, Japanese Prints, and other related categories.

Additional Resources:

Antique Trader® Oriental Antiques & Art, 2nd Ed., by Mark F. Moran & Sandra Andacht, Krause Publications, Iola WI.

Album, fan paintings, 11 works by various artists including, Ch'en Fang Ting, Hsu Lin Lu (b1916), Shao Ping Chang, Wu Hsi Tsai (1799-1870), Kuo Shang Hsien (1796-1820), Fei Shih Po, Wu Hua Yuan (1893-1972), Wang I Ting, Yang I, Wang I Ting, Hou Pi I (2) **$600**

Altar cabinet, Huang Hua Li wood, moon-shaped brasses, side flanges carved with Chih Lung dragons, Lung Chih fungus, and clouds, China, cracks to top, old repair to back feet, loss, 18th C, 35-1/2" w, 22" d, 34" h **$2,235**

Architectural element

Capitals, carved wood, foo dogs, gold lacquered surface, China, price for pr, 19th C, 22" l **$775**

Finial, bronze, figural dragon, patina with azurite areas, Khmer, 13th C, 4-3/4" h **$850**

Basin, bronze, low relief designs of stylized birds and trees, 18-character grass script poem on the base, Japan, 18th C or possibly earlier, 7" d **$300**

Bell, bronze, lid surmounted by two kneeling figures, iron mount with two apsara figures, Burma, 19th C, 19" h **$400**

Box, cov, lacquer, foliate form, maki-e of a woman with a fan, Raiden inlay, Japan, 19th C, 5" d **$2,115**

Bowl

Nephrite, white and pale green, incised and gilt character inscriptions with four character reign mark on base, Qing Dynasty, price for pr, 20th C, 6-1/2" d **$920**

Porcelain, dark blue ext. with gilt dragons, clouds, and pearls, white int., China, Ch'ien Lung six-character seal mark, 1736-95, 7-1/2" d **$600**

Brush pot, bamboo, carved in high relief with sages in forest, rosewood base, China, 18th C, 6" h **$1,300**

Buddha

Bodhisattva, carved stone, reclining figure, left hand supporting head, right hand resting on bent knee, peaceful expression, Chinese, possibly Tang Dynasty, 16" l, 6" h **$950**

Buddha Amida, lacquered wood, standing with his hands in "abeyance of fear" mudra, gold lacquered robes, eyes inlaid with crystal, Japan, 18th C, 17" h **$1,350**

Hardwood figure, seated on lotus throne, numerous coatings of lacquer, China, 18th C, 13" h **$425**

Buddhist bell, Japan, hammered brass with a lacquered design of a dragon and thunder meanders, late 19th/early 20th C, 14" d **$450**

Bust

Bronze, Quan Yin, Chinese, Sung or earlier period, losses, 7" h **$1,200**

Sandstone, head of divinity with jeweled crown, Eastern Thailand, Khmer period, 11th C, 13-1/2" h **$8,820**

Cabinet

Hung Mu wood, two drawers over single gate, moon-shaped brasses, China, 18th/19th C, 56-1/2" l, 20" d, 35" h **$1,560**

Two part, persimmon wood veneer, two long drawers over two smaller drawers each flanked by sq compartment, ornate iron mounts, Japan, early 20th C, 47-1/2" l, 17" d, 48" h **$1,530**

Cabinet on stand, black lacquer, cabinet with pair of doors, fitted int. of doors and pigeonholes, central painted oval portrait of a beauty, 27" h square base, cabriole legs, deco-

Chinese bottle vase, copper red porcelain, Qing dynasty, 18th century, 9-1/2" h, **$3,450.**

Photo courtesy of Sloans & Kenyon Auctioneers and Appraisers.

Korean, dragon jar, baluster form, collar neck, painted underglaze blue and iron-brown, dragon chasing flaming pearl among clouds, drilled base, Yi Dynasty, 19th century, 14-1/4" h, **$17,000.**

Photo courtesy of David Rago Auctions, Inc.

Chinese vase, blue and white bottle, porcelain, floral decoration, Guangxu six character underglaze mark, 16" h, **$2,360.**

Photo courtesy of Sloans & Kenyon Auctioneers and Appraisers.

rated all over with gilt scrollwork and foliage, Chinese Export, c1840, 23-1/2" w **$2,500**

Candlesticks, pr, bronze, deer form, each supporting candle holder on back, Chinese, 18th C, 10" h **$600**

Censer, bronze, modeled as caparisoned shishi playing with ball, parcel-gilt accents, Japan, 18th/19th C, 10" l **$1,410**

Chair, side, pr, Huang Hua Li wood with cane seats, China, 18th C or earlier **$18,800**

Charger, hawk design, sgd by member of Li family in red seal characters, China, 19th C, 18" d **$1,175**

Cup, Chinese, porcelain, engraved dragons under egg-yolk yellow color, six-character underglaze blue Kuang Hsu mark, possibly of the period, 1874-1908................................ **$200**

Deity, gilt bronze, sitting position, robes with chased dec, China, wear to gilding, 17th C, 8-1/2" h **$990**

Dish, Tou Tsai, scalloped edge, design of dragons and flowers in green on yellow ground, six-character Ch'ien Lung seal mark (1735-96), 5-1/4" d **$1,880**

Embroidery, on silk

Courtesan in elaborate costume holding pole with suspended basket of flowers, Chinese, 19th C, 28" x 20" **$345**

Crane by flowering tree, Japanese, Meiji period, 1867-1912, 17" x 13" **$320**

Fan, folding, China, 19th C

Ivory, shaped stays with numerous figures in garden scenes, fan painted with harbor scene, other vignettes of idyllic village scenes, black lacquer box with gilt butterflies and flowers **$490**

Wooden stays with black lacquer and gold dec, fan of paper dec with figures in silk and ivory, reverse magenta with three reserves of country scenes, gold and black lacquer case **$250**

Fan, folding, Japan, 19th C

All ivory stays dec with shibayama inlay of gold lacquer and semi-precious inlay of birds and flowers, orig box, 11-1/2" l **$4,025**

Carved ivory stays with shibayama inlay, one side dec with landscape, other with children watching fireworks **$775**

Figure

Carved and painted ivory and horn, maiden holding fan in left hand, basket of flowers in right hand, carved and pierced horn rock beside her with lantern sitting on top, head carved separately and pinned to shoulder, China, wear to paint surface, 19th C, 17-3/4" h **$990**

Carved quartz with mauve and white striations, green veining, longevity god or immortal, holding staff in left hand, ruyi scepter in right, fitted wood stand, China, 19th or 20th C, 5-5/8" h **$220**

Carved rose quartz, sitting puppy, head turned slightly to the left, possibly China, 20th C, 2-1/2" h, 2-7/8" d **$100**

Elephant, bronze, sgd on foot, Japan, Meiji period (1868-1911), 15" l **$500**

Goddess, carved stone, gray schist image of Kuan Yin, China, 20th C, 40" h **$285**

Fish bowl, porcelain, blue and white, design of phoenix in garden, scrolling at mouth, Ming period, probably Chia Ching period, 1522-1566, hairline **$1,175**

Flower vessel, bronze, tightly curled lotus leaf resembling small boat, attached lotus flowers, seed pod, and crabs crawling to top, carved wooden stand, sgd on base with rect reserve,

Chinese figure, Kilin, bronze, lying in curved position, some gold splashes, repaired dorsal fin, 19th century, 10" l, 5" h, **$925.**

Japanese cloisonné enamel vase, Meiji period, dragon on green ground, signed, 9-1/2" h, **$885.**
Photo courtesy of Sloans & Kenyon Auctioneers and Appraisers.

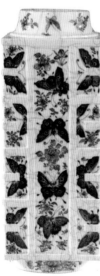

Chinese Cong vase, blue and white, porcelain, butterfly decoration, Qing dynasty, 18th century, 13" h, **$3,300.**
Photo courtesy of Sloans & Kenyon Auctioneers and Appraisers.

Japan, 19th C, 9-1/2" l, 3-1/2" h **$2,225**

Foo Dog, carved wood, surface lacquered in red and gold, China, 19th C, 11" l, 10-1/2" h **$600**

Gong, brass, dragons and tokugawa mons designs, Japan, early 20th C, 18" d **$325**

Guardian figure, standing figure of Nio, bronze, Japan, Meiji period (1868-1911), 9" h **$275**

Hanging scroll, ink and color on silk

Doves and blossoming rose bush, sgd, Japan, mounted on silk, 44-1/2" l, 20" w **$360**

Figure in boat amidst mountainous landscape, China, 37-1/2" h, 19-1/4" h **$360**

Scholar in boat, river landscape, China, 49" l, 25-3/4" w **$540**

Incense box, Komei-style, iron inlaid with gold and silver, Japan, Meiji period (1868-1911), 2" x 2" **$600**

Incense burner, bronze, decorative elements of elephants in handles, tripod base and finial, floral elements, inlaid glass and semi-precious stones, China, 18th C, 15" h **$1,530**

Inro, netsuke, ojime

Gold lacquer, four compartment, each side dec with hawk perched on railing, sgd "Igawa" lower right, 1-5/8" h carved ivory netsuke in form of shells, one with crab emerging from top, metal ojime with foo dog and peony, stylized signature on side, Japan, Meiji period, 3-1/4" h **$3,750**

Lacquer, three compartment, dragon amidst clouds, unsigned, 1-1/4" d carved wood manju netsuke of dragon with inlaid eyes, agate ojime bead, Japan, some wear and edge losses, crack on neck of netsuke, 19th C, 2-1/4" h, 2-1/8" w **$900**

Inro, Saya type, lacquer, four compartment, dec with Kwannon, moon behind her head, reverse dec with trees and waterfall, removable sheath having small cartouches with dragons, base sgd "Koma Koryu" with kakihan, Japan, slight losses, 19th C, 3-1/2" h **$1,265**

Jar, cov

Baluster, blue and white dec of village by water, foo dog finial, China, 19th C, 25" h **$2,350**

Blue and white, design of cranes, deer, and pine trees, carved hardwood cover, K'ang Hsi period (1662-1722), 11" h **$1,880**

Kogo, silver, chased and repousse dec of two phoenix birds among flowers, applied enamel highlights, silver lined interior sgd on underside, Japan, Meiji period, dent on inside of lid, 3-1/8" d **$1,725**

Libation cup, porcelain, applied Chi dragons in relief, two forming handle, underglaze enamels, Chinese, losses, 18th C, 2" h, 4-1/2" w **$115**

Officials' chairs, pr

Mortised construction, serpentine crests, carved back splats, paneled seats, sq legs, relief carved and scalloped aprons, old red wash, Chinese, restorations, 20" h seat, 43" h back **$650**

Huang Hua Li wood with cane seats, sq sections with inward tapering carving, China, Ming period, ex-James Hightower, 16th/17th C, 20-1/2" h seat, 47" h back, 24-1/2" w, 18-1/2" d **$99,500**

Okimono, ivory study of group of rats and lantern, horn inlay, 19th C, 3" l **$635**

Painting, oil on canvas, Chinese Export School, 19th Century, portrait of American clipper ship, gilt frame

The Almeda of Bath, Maine, lined, "Shanghai China 1878, May 8," scattered retouch, craquelure, 20" x 27" **$9,990**

The Charles B. Kenney of New York, handwritten inscription on the stretcher reads "Shanghai China 1878, May 8," lined, scattered retouch, craquelure, 20" x 27" **$9,400**

Painting table, Huang Hua Li Hunah back braces, China, Ming period, 16th/17th C, 70" l, 32-1/2" w, 34" h **$44,650**

Palace urn, bronze, elaborately dec with scenes of birds, foo dogs, foliage, large applied dragons, rich chocolate brown patina, Chinese, price for pr, c1900, 24" h **$750**

Panel, rosewood, deep relief carving of two peacocks on flowering tree, Chinese, early 20th C, 23" x 16" **$125**

Pitcher, Sumidagawa, monkeys, Japan, loss to one hand, early 20th C, 12" h **$400**

Plaque, bronze, relief dec of Kuan Yin surrounded by attending deities, extensive inscription on back, China, 19th C, 8" x 6" **$135**

Rank badges, pr, K'o ssu work, white egret rank, China, mounted as a tray, 19th C **$380**

Robe

Dragon, China, loose threads, late 19th/early 20th C.....................**$360**

Informal, woman's, black ground, floral embroidery, China, late 19th/early 20th C...........................**$360**

Sagemo, basket cup holder, celadon porcelain netsuke of karako, 19th C **$420**

Scepter, ju-i, carved boxwood, lotus pod with movable seeds and single leaf, sgd, Japan, 19th C, 13" l **$420**

Screen

Six panels, finely detailed Buddhist and Taoist figures, checkered silk border, black lacquered frame, Japanese, accompanied by "Certificate of Antiquity" dated 1971 addressed to US Customs by David Kidd and Y. Morimoto of "Three Dynasties," Ashiya City, Japan, minor losses, c1750, 94" x 18" **$1,450**

"Tagasode-byobu," two-fold, brocade with mounted ink, color, and gold leaf on paper panel showing kimono over rack and accessories, Japan, Meiji period (1868-1912), 67" h, 37" w **$10,755**

Sculpture, bronze

Crayfish, fully articulated, Japan, Meiji period (1868-1911), loose, 17" l...**$3,200**

Scene of bull and farmer, carved fitted wood base, sgd, Japan, Meiji period (1868-1911), 24" l.................**$1,300**

Seal case, four-compartment form with lacquer dec of warrior and courtier, crystal ojime, and netsuke sennin on horse, Japan, 19th C **$775**

Shanxi cupboard, gold and black Chinoiserie dec over dark red ground, mortised construction, paneled ends, two doors with brass hardware, removable int. shelf, wooden rod brackets, pieced restoration to moldings, touch-up, 57" w, 25-1/4" d, 69-1/4" h **$650**

Shrine

Black lacquer case, gilt standing image of Amida Buddha, Japan, 19th C, 7" h **$395**

Black lacquer, gold lacquered figure of Kshitagarba, inlaid eyes, Japan, 18th/19th C, 27" h **$3,200**

Lacquered, structured as temple building, triple roof; ornately carved with shishi, dragons, and flowers, surface lacquered in gold, red, brown, and black, engraved gilt copper metal mounts, Japan, Meiji period (1868-1911), 86" h **$1,250**

Stand, hardwood

Marble insert, round carved openwork sides, China, 19th C, light separation of joints, natural shrinkage, 39-3/4" h, 15" x 16-1/5" top **$520**

Rect, two wooden shelves, red marble insert on top, carved flower and tendrils around top frieze an openwork gallery, ball and claw feet, China, natural fissues in marble, 19th, 31-3/8" h, 16-5/8" x 12" top **$175**

Statues, pr, granite, two officials from spirit way, Korea, Yi period, 18th C or earlier, 53" h **$9,400**

Stool for two, Huang Hua Li wood, humpback stretchers, China, Ming to early Ch'ing dynasty, staining and cracking to top and legs, 40" w, 16" d, 19" h...**$9,400**

Stupa, bronze, four makala supports, stupa surmounted by four figures of Buddha, Nepal, 19th C, 6-1/2" h **$550**

Tankard, blue and white, scholar in garden scene, Continental silver mounts with Dutch export hallmarks, China, Transitional period, c1620, 8" h...**$3,985**

Table, pr, lacquered, Tzu Tan wood ornately carved with archaic scrolling, inlaid oval pale celadon jade plaques, carved resonance stones and archaic dragons, China, cracks to both tops of both, lacquer wear, 18th C, 47" l, 15-1/4" w, 33" h **$23,500**

Teapot

Globular, Fen tsai palette, design of flowers on brocaded blue ground, ju-i and stylized acanthus leaf borders, gilt accents, four-character seal mark within red square, China, 18th/19th C, 8-1/4" h **$13,000**

Silver, Hira Arare, globular, hailstone pattern, cov surmounted with pierced sphere finial, base marked,

Japanese Export, 16.65 oz, 7-1/2" h **$660**

Vase

Bronze, flared rim, paneled shoulder takers to base with flower petals, detailed peacock sits on flowering tree branch, peahen below, dark patina, peacock's crest missing, 42" h **$3,500**

Bronze, hexagonal body with designs of high relief dragons, Japan, late 19th C, 14" h **$600**

Bronze, relief dec of waves with dragon in round holding glass pearl, sgd "great Japan sei don sai," Japan, Meiji period, 15" h.................**$1,650**

Tsun-shape, Wu Tsai ware, birds and flowers dec, China, Transitional period, c1640, 20-1/2" h **$2,000**

Votive plaque, gilt copper and bronze, a central image of the Buddha surrounded by the wheel of law, Japan, late 19th/early 20th C, 7" d **$250**

Wine ewer, Hirado ware, form of Hoi tea, bag of wealth, underglaze blue, yellow, pale green, tan, and black accents, cover missing, 19th C, 6-1/4" h..**$750**

Chinese, Famille Jaune bottle vase, porcelain, grisaille peonies, yellow ground, Yung Qing Qang Qun eternal prosperity and enduring spring hallmark and motto of the Dowager Empress, 14-1/2" h, **$3,835.**
Photo courtesy of Sloans & Kenyon Auctioneers and Appraisers.

PAIRPOINT

History: The Pairpoint Manufacturing Co. was organized in 1880 as a silver-plating firm in New Bedford, Massachusetts. The company merged with Mount Washington Glass Co. in 1894 and became the Pairpoint Corporation. The new company produced specialty glass items, often accented with metal frames.

Pairpoint Corp. was sold in 1938 and Robert Gunderson became manager. He operated it as the Gunderson Glass Works until his death in 1952. From 1952 until the plant closed in 1956, operations were maintained under the name Gunderson-Pairpoint. Robert Bryden reopened the glass manufacturing business in 1970, moving it back to the New Bedford area.

China

Chocolate pot, cream ground, white floral dec, gold trim and scrolls, sgd "Pairpoint Limoges 2500 114," 10" h **$675**

Gravy boat and underplate, fancy white china with scrolls, Dresden multicolored flowers, elaborate handle, Limoges, two pcs **$175**

Plate, hp harbor scene, artist sgd "L. Tripp," fuchsia tinted rim, gold highlights, back sgd "Pairpoint Limoges," 7-3/8" d **$550**

Lamp, table

Candlestick type, urn-shaped tops, electric sockets, clear cut columns with diamond designs, octagonal base with fine leaf detail, relief cast signatures on bases "Quadruple Plate," price for pr, 18" h **$550**

Orange Poppy, reverse painted mold blown puffy shade, silvered base, imp "Pairpoint 3085," shade damaged and repaired, 21" h, 14" d **$1,500**

Reverse painted

Dome shade of harbor scene with sailboats in mauve, peach, blue, and gold, sgd "C. Durand," two sockets, wooden vasiform standard with brass mounts, minor nicks at top aperture, 21-3/4" h, 13-3/4" d **$1,645**

Shade dec with three floral and urn-form medallions separated by stylized circular medallions in pink,

blue, and gold against black ground, three sockets, trapped bubble colorless glass standard, hexagonal green stone base, 16-1/2" d **$3,290**

Metal

Lamp base

Patinated metal, quatrefoil wirework supporting shade, ribbed standard with applied foliate handles and feet, bronze patina on white metal, imp "Pairpoint Mfg Co.," "P" in diamond and "30031/2" on base, worn patina, 12" h, 8" d **$400**

Patinated metal, two-socket fixture, four-sided shaft and lobe base, bronze patina on white metal, imp "Pairpoint Mfg Co.," "P" in diamond, and "B3040" on base, patina wear, 15" h **$350**

Trophy, copper, two fancy handles, feather design, plaque inscribed "New Bedford Yacht Club Ocean Race won by Nutmeg for the fastest time, Aug. 5, 1909," base marked "Pairpoint Mfg Co.," "P" in diamond mark, numbered, 7" d, 8-1/2" h **$400**

PAPER EPHEMERA

History: Maurice Rickards, author of *Collecting Paper Ephemera*, suggests that ephemera are the "minor transient documents of everyday life," material destined for the wastebasket but never quite making it. This definition is more fitting than traditional dictionary definitions that emphasize time, e.g., "lasting a very short time." A driver's license, which is used for a year or longer, is as much a piece of ephemera as is a ticket to a sporting event or music concert. The transient nature of the object is the key.

Collecting ephemera has a long and distinguished history. Among the English pioneers were John Seldon (1584-1654), Samuel Pepys (1633-1703), and John Bagford (1650-1716). Large American collections can be found at historical societies and libraries across the country, and museums, e.g., Wadsworth Athenaeum, Hartford, Connecticut, and the Museum of the City of New York.

When used by collectors, "ephemera" usually means paper objects, e.g., billheads and letterheads, book-

plates, documents, labels, stocks and bonds, tickets, and valentines. However, more and more ephemera collectors are recognizing the transient nature of some three-dimensional material, e.g., advertising tins and pinback buttons. Today's specialized paper shows include dealers selling other types of ephemera in both two-and three-dimensional form.

Additional Listings: See Advertising, Catalogs, Comic Books, Photographs, and Sports Cards. Also see Calendars, Catalogs, Magazines, Newspapers, Postcards, and Sheet Music in *Warman's Americana & Collectibles*.

Additional Resources:

Warman's® Americana & Collectibles, 11th Ed., by Ellen T. Schroy, ed., Krause Publications, Iola, WI.

Calendars

1896, actors and actresses, one per month, sepia and white.............**$125**

1897, pansy, each page with different litho of a pansy, scalloped edges, printed in Bavaria, designed in England, 6" x 4-1/4" **$65**

1906, Christmas Belle, no calendar pad, 14" x 11" **$200**

1908, fish, adv for Spicer & Beasley, Smithshire, IL, 15" x 9" **$180**

1908, woman with red poppies, heavily emb, adv for J.I. Sawyel, General Merchandise, Smithshire, Illinois, full pad, 10" x 14" **$270**

1912, Calumet Baking Powder, adv for H. J. Coffey Grocers, LaKemp, Oklahoma, print titled "Firelight," by G. Sether **$220**

1918, Swifts Premium, for January, February, March, Haskell Coffin illus of "The Girl I Leave Behind Me,"

WWI soldier saying goodbye to pretty girl, 15" x 8-1/4" **$90**

1922, lady in car, Hayes Litho Co., Buffalo, NY, 15" x 20-1/2" **$100**

1926, Maxfield Parrish, Fountain of Pirene, orig 6" x 8" box, titled "Sunlit Road Calendar," Dodge Publishing Co., #5895 .... **$125**

1930, Love is Blind, antique cars, service station, 22-1/2" x 14" **$115**

1931, Midland Wood Products, Midland, Ontario, each page is different model home with floor plan on reverse, 9-3/4" x 5-1/2" **$35**

1951, Puzzling Pups, Kinghon, 10" x 17" **$60**

1952, Songbird Families, series 6, Betty Carnes, watercolors by Roger Tory Peterson, published by Barton-Cotton Co. **$12.75**

1960, Look for the Sign of Happy Motoring, Esso Gas; adv for R. Y. Foster, Johnson City, Tennessee, 14-3/4" x 8-1/2" **$48**

Checks

1863, State of Vermont Treasurer's Office, Rutland, state seal at left, brown on white, 2 cent US Internal Revenue bank check stamp, hand and punch canceled **$40**

1865, National Bank of Commerce, New York, issued by Central Railroad Co. of New Jersey, red on white design, orange 2 cent US Internal Revenue Documentary and Proprietary stamp **$20**

1869, First National Bank, New York, New York, bank building vignette, violet on white, orange 2 cent US Internal Revenue Documentary and Proprietary stamp **$15**

1871, Pennsylvania Academy of the Fine Arts, Philadelphia, Pennsylvania, Liberty, eagle, and shield, black on white **$35**

1875, First National Bank of Chicago, issued by the office of Downer & Bemis Brewing Co., vignette of brewery, horse drawn carriages and people in street scene, black printing, olive security paper **$45**

1875, Trenton Banking Co., Trenton, NJ, two vignettes, issued and canceled **$12**

1882, National Park Bank, New York, New York, blue 2 cent US Internal Revenue Documentary and Proprietary stamp at left, "Iron Cliffs Company" stamped in red above signature line, payable to Third National Bank for $30,000 .... **$20**

1898, Treasurer of Stanton Co., State of Nebraska, locomotive vignette at left, three horse heads at right, brown on sepia, hand stamp canceled **$30**

1903, Pittsburgh Brewing Co., Pittsburgh, Pennsylvania, pale blue, red, gold, and black round logo, hand written, payee endorsement on reverse **$6**

1911, First National Bank, Troutville, Virginia, vignette of bald eagle perched on rock, clutching arrows, olive branch, and US shield, black on orange, issued, canceled, printed by Kennedy Printing Co., Fredonia, Kansas **$10**

1924, Baker Loan & Trust Co., gray vignette of bank entrance **$7.50**

1957, Christmas Club, Anacostia National Bank, Washington, DC, Santa with open book, quill, ink bottle **$7.50**

Cigar box labels

Alfonso Rigos & Co. **$10**

Camel Brand Cigars, Arab man riding camel across desert **$18**

Elektra, red, gold, and white, pretty girl **$15**

Royal Banner, allegorical lion with flag **$15**

Documents

Appointment of administrator of estate, sgd by John Evans, Colonial Gov of Pennsylvania, dated March 24, 1704, wax seal, some fold weakness, 9-1/2" x 15" **$500**

Appointment of Gideon Mumford Deputy Postmaster at East Greenwich, Rhode Island, dated April 19, 1796, foxing, fold weakness, 12-1/2" x 7-1/2" **$75**

Bill of Exchange, written for Robert Robson, London, March 2, 1796, in Charleston, South Carolina, two pgs, concerns exchange for 160 pounds sterling, 8-1/2" x 7" **$50**

Calendar, "Who's Afraid of the Big Bad Wolf," cardboard top, calendar pad below, facsimile Disney signature, "Photo: United Artists," VF, 1933, 6-1/4" x 8", **$330.**
Photo courtesy of Hake's Auctions www.hakes.com.

Calendar, 1924 Edison Mazda Maxfield Parrish, "The Venetian Lamplighter," Southern Electric Company imprint, full month pad, 1924 cover sheet, 19" h x 8-1/2" w, **$440.**
Photo courtesy of Green Valley Auctions.

Program, Ringling Bros & Barnum & Bailey circus, 1955, full-color cover, **$15.**

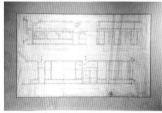

Elevation of building for Schlesinger and Mayer, Chicago, matted, several folds, minor discoloration, June 6, 1903, 20" x 33", **$2,820.**
Photo courtesy of David Rago Auctions, Inc.

Roseville pottery company stationery, original advertisements, unused letterhead and envelope, nine pieces total, **$120.**
Photo courtesy of David Rago Auctions, Inc.

Broadside advertising wallpaper stock, Cazenovia, New York, later wood frame, 14" x 11", **$325.**
Photo courtesy of Skinner, Inc.

Indenture

Vellum, John Penn and Edmund Physick, tract of land in Philadelphia, Pennsylvania, Dec. 27, 1799, framed, 13" x 27-1/2" **$130**

Vellum, between Samuel Jones and wife to John Stillwagon, tract of land in Philadelphia, Pennsylvania, May 10, 1757, sgd on reverse by Charles Brockden, Justice for Pennsylvania, folding, toning, foxing, 15-1/2" x 29" **$60**

Vellum, pre-printed royal seal, between Josiah Winter and wife to William Hambleton, tract of land in Solebury, Pennsylvania, bordering Delaware River, Nov. 9, 1770, folding, slight toning, foxing, 16" x 22" **$85**

Vellum, Jonathon Jones and wife to Samuel Norcross, tract of land in Gloucester Twp, New Jersey, July 23, 1792, small hand drawn map on reverse, sgd by Thomas Rodman, Burlington County Judge, folding, toning, foxing, ink stains, 21" x 24-1/2" **$50**

Legal deposition, involving litigation between Horace Day and Charles Goodyear, Aug. 29, 1851, concerning Indian rubber fabric, attached map of eastern US printed on Indian rubber fabric, reverse marked "Exhibit A4," damaged cover sheet, some soiling to sheets, 13" x 8" **$350**

Ship paper, issued by port of Charleston, South Carolina, for brig *Mary,* March 10, 1812, 8" x 11" **$80**

Greeting cards

Easter Greetings, raised satin fabric with two cloth flowers, red bow, gold lettering, fringed edges, hand writing on back **$25**

Get Well, dachshund, 1950s, 4-1/4" x 4-1/4" **$5**

Happy Birthday to a Sweet Daughter, Raggedy Ann, 4-1/2" x 6-1/2" **$15**

Hawaii Greetings, with orig handkerchief, 1942, 6" x 5" **$18**

Hearty Greeting, diecut, fold-out, emb red roses and dove, verse inside, scalloped edge, made in Germany, 3-1/4" x 4" **$25**

Hearty Greeting, male hand and female hand clasping wreath of ivy and forget-me-nots, front panel unfurls to paper card held in place with tasseled cord, "To Greet you and wish you a bright Christmas Day," with poem, published by Davidson Bros, London, printed in Saxony, c1900-10, 5-1/2" x 3-5/8" **$35**

Pinocchio and Gepetto, mechanical, 1930s...................................**$35**

Romeo and Juliet, diecut, 3-3/4" x 7-1/2" **$25**

Miscellaneous

Animal theater, box stage, three scenes, fourteen 4" animal characters, some damage to characters, c1850, 10-1/2" x 8" x 2" **$550**

Card set, Le Diable a Quatre, set of sixteen, four labeled "Tetes, Bras, Jambes, and Queue," full-figure depiction of men and women in various national costumes, orig decorative box, pink with gold trim, 4" x 6"................**$360**

Diary, Richard Tregaskis, *Guadal-Canal*, pictorial, 263 pgs, copyright 1945 ....**$12**

Folio, marbled brown and green folio, green ribbon ties, 3 pgs with twenty-one 4" h hp figures, twisted wire form bases, c1800, 12-1/2" x 19" folio **$500**

Ink blotter, Lancaster Iron Works, 8-1/2" x 3-1/2" **$8**

Ledger book, Schuylkill Navigation Co., from Aug. 13, 1816 to Feb. 11, 1830, 250 pgs, binding loose, pages dry, spine damage, 9" x 5" **$575**

Letterhead, Louisville & Nashville RR Co., typed message, 1913 ....**$6.50**

Mechanical paper figures, Cheerful Brothers and Sisters, boy and girl, fastened to counterbalance lever, mid 19th C, orig 7-1/4" x 10-3/4" box, missing small pcs of gold paper, top detached **$5,550**

Poster, Kennedy for President, Leadership for the US, red, white, blue, and black, two folds, 28" x 40" **$120**

Receipt, M. P. Norris Newspaper, Morristown, New Jersey, Nov 1, 1895 ....**$12**

Tobacco label, Watson & McGill Tobacco Co., multicolored stone litho, eagle, sailing ships, draped flags, topless woman, 1872 copyright, 14-1/8" x 7-1/4" **$90**

Postcards

Advertising

Austro Fiat, artist sgd "Wilrab," left side with Austrian ships on Danube

River, sailor and Fiat car, Fiat logo on back, 1920-30 .... **$48**

Munich Traffic Exhibition, Deutsche Verkehrsausstellung Muenchen, designed by Eugene O Sporer, man riding bicycle, first day cancellation, 1953 .... **$60**

Art Deco

Blacks, Aint's I yo Honey?, handwritten address, 1907...................... **$40**

Lady smoking cigarette, hand colored, French................................... **$32**

Taifun-Wheel, amusement park, sent to Wien, Austria, 1929 .... **$28**

Holiday

A Happy New Year 1908, heavily emb holly wreaths and snow, muted icy blue-gray, touch of red, icicles dangle at top, used............................ **$10**

A Merry Christmas, letters outlined in sandy glitter, covered with starlets, black and white, used, 1906 .... **$10**

Humor

Always After New Business, rooster chasing chicken, Lustercomics #151, Tichnor Bros, Inc., Boston, Massachusetts, 3-1/2" x 4-1/2" **$12.50**

"And Help Me to Forgive..." Mabel Lucie Attwell, #3696, copyright Valentine and Sons, Ltd., Dundee and London, 1900s, 3-1/2" x 4-1/2" . **$15**

"I Work and Worry, Scheme and Plan...," lustercomics #132, Tichnor Bros, Inc., Boston, Massachusetts, 3-1/2" x 4-1/2" **$12.50**

Let's Grow Old Together, Mabel Lucie Attwell, #3530, copyright Valentine and Sons, Ltd., Dundee and London, 1900s, 3-1/2" x 4-1/2" **$15**

Old Maid, Lustercomics #143, Tichnor Bros, Inc., Boston, MA, 3-1/2" x 4-1/2" **$12.50**

We're raising a big rumpus, Colourpicture Publication, Boston, Massachusetts, pre-1960................... **$5**

Leather

Disguise our bondage As we will, Tis woman, woman Rules us still, Tom Moore, postmarked Dec. 22, 1906, 5-3/8" x 3-1/4" **$45**

Look before you leap, There are two kinds of women, One that breaks you and one that makes you, hand written personnel message on front, postmarked April 1908, 5-3/8" x 3-1/4" **$45**

Political, John F. Kennedy, New York Democratic State Committee, unused, with five Kennedy for President buttons, 1960................................... **$80**

Real photo

Geisshuebel, Sauerbrunn, Austria, sent to Union Hotel, Singaore, black and white, 1902 .... **$110**

People digging for gold, black and white, printed in Germany, undivided back, c1910.................... **$36**

Zeynard's Lilliputian Troupe, black and white **$26**

Ship

Cunard *R.M.S. Lusitania-Mauretania*, New York harbor, Statue of Liberty at left, black and white illus, c1910 .... **$30**

U.S.S. Battleship Virginia, #6507, c1907 .... **$25**

Silk, WWI, butterfly design formed from flags of the Allies, c1917, 3-1/2" x 5-1/2".................................. **$95**

World War I, "And You? Sign in for War Bonds" WWI pilot, Germany, unused................................... **$32**

PAPIER-MÂCHÉ

History: Papier-mâché is a mixture of wood pulp, glue, resin, and fine sand, which is subjected to great pressure and then dried. The finished product is tough, durable, and heat resistant. Various finishing treatments are used, such as enameling, japanning, lacquering, mother-of-pearl inlaying, and painting.

During the Victorian era, papier-mâché articles such as boxes, trays, and tables were in high fashion. Banks, candy containers, masks, toys, and other children's articles were also made of papier-mâché.

Cigar Store Indian, painted, standing on wooden base, holding bundle of cigars in right hand, Indian pipe in decorated bag over left arm, Adams County, Pennsylvania, late 19th C, 8-3/4" l, 8-3/4" w, 42-1/2" h.................. **$7,150**

Doll, painted papier-mâché head, wooden arms and legs, stuffed cloth body, orig printed cotton dress, c1860 .... **$5,600**

Fan, demilune, scalloped border, turned wooden handle, one side painted with variety of ferns on ochre ground, black japanning on other side, Victorian, price for pr, late 19th C, 15-1/2" l.................................... **$250**

Hat stand, woman's head, painted facial features, sgd "Danjard, Paris," wearing later Amish straw hat, 19th C **$1,300**

Jewel box, painted lid top, fitted int., two doors enclosing small drawers, Victorian, minor restorations, mid-19th, 12" h, 10" w, 10" d **$520**

Lap desk, rect with bombe sides, sloped hinged lid with scalloped edge, painted and mother-of-pearl inlaid center with floral spray within gilt and inlay vines, opening to red velvet-lined writing surface fronted by fitted compartments, and storage, Victorian, late 19th C, 11-5/8" w, 9-1/4" d, 3-3/4" h............................... **$325**

Notebook, black lacquered ground, dec with floral arrangement, mother-of-pearl vines, hand painted accents, int. with notebook with some sketches, blank pages, 11-1/2" x 9-1/2" **$295**

Pip-squeak, rooster, orig paint, yellow, orange, and black, recovered wooden bellows, faint squeak, 4-1/4" h **$85**

Plate, painted cat, marked "Patented August 8, 1880," 12" d **$35**

Roly poly, clown, orig white and blue polychrome paint, green ribbon around neck, 4-1/8" h................... **$65**

Papier-mâché match safe with hinged lid, decorated with portrait of Kaiser Wilhelm II, metal push button latch, striker on bottom which shows considerable wear, commemorative piece from coronation, German, 1888, 2-1/2" x 1-7/16" x 9/16", **$250.**
Photo courtesy of Gamal Amer.

Snuffbox, round, lid painted with interior genre scene of family with baby, interior lid painted with title "Die Tanzpuppen," painted mark "StabwassersFabrik in Braunschweig," German, late 19th/early 20th C, 3-7/8" d...........**$460**

Table, tilt-top, hinged 20" d top painted with Continental city view, pedestal painted as stone tower, circular base with maritime scene, Victorian, stamped "J & B/Patent" for Jennens and Bethridge, Birmingham, England, 24" h...........**$7,475**

Tray, ovoid, ogee rim, painted black, hand painted center scene of children playing, thatched cottage, pigs, ducks, and hound, gold painted vine and butterfly surround, back imp "W. & P. Steele, 61 George Street, Edinburgh," Victorian, late 19th C, 32-1/4" w, 25" h...........**$1,765**

Perfume bottle, doll head, translucent white glass swirled with orange, teal, cobalt blue and gold flecks, child china head stopper, painted features, blonde hair, orange rayon neck ruff, c1920, 3" to top of stopper, $75.
Photo courtesy of McMasters Harris Auction Co.

Perfume bottle, cameo glass, ivory, circular lay-down type, cameo flowers, embossed flip lid, original stopper, Thomas Webb & Sons, 2-3/4" h, $1,700.
Photo courtesy of The Early Auction Company, LLC.

Tray and stand, English

Oval, 30" l, 24" w tray, black ground, large central scene with two scarlet-coated huntsmen, one standing, other seated on bobtail chestnut with black foal on a hill, border with gilt transfer printed guilloche border, Mark Knowles & Son maker, English Registry mark for 1864, burl hardwood 6-1/4" d, 18-3/4" h stand...........**$1,250**

Rect, 18-1/4" l, 14-1/8" w, black ground, large central scene of white haired gentleman on bobtail chestnut, five hunting dogs in open field, border gold painted with egg and dart design, 7-3/4" w, 4-1/4" d, 9" h mahogany stand...........**$1,100**

Traveling case, lady's, black lacquer and polychrome, hinged front doors dec with portraits of Queen Victoria and Prince Albert, hinged top and sides with scenes from English landscapes, sewing compartment with some orig accoutrements, two doors open to jewelry drawers, fourth drawer with foldout writing desk and ink bottle, Victorian, mid-19th C, 11" w, 9" d, 9-1/2" h...........**$1,150**

PERFUME, COLOGNE, AND SCENT BOTTLES

History: The second half of the 19th century was the golden age for decorative bottles made to hold scents. These bottles were made in a variety of shapes and sizes.

An atomizer is a perfume bottle with a spray mechanism. Cologne bottles usually are larger and have stoppers that also may be used as applicators. A perfume bottle has a stopper that often is elongated and designed to be an applicator.

Scent bottles are small bottles used to hold a scent or smelling salts. A vinaigrette is an ornamental box or bottle that has a perforated top and is used to hold aromatic vinegar or smelling salts. Fashionable women of the late 18th and 19th centuries carried them in purses or slipped them into gloves in case of a sudden fainting spell.

Cologne

Malachite, Ingrid Line, molded rose garden surrounds artistic medallions, Kurt Schlevogt, c1935, 6-1/2" h...........**$275**

Perfume

Enamel, pear shape, silvered metal lid with bale, green ground, two central cartouches of courting couples, Continental, late 18th/early 19th C, 3-1/4" l...........**$215**

Porcelain

Continental, underglaze blue crossed swords mark, leg-form, garter and pale blue shoe, flat metal lid, late 19th C, 2-1/2" l...........**$250**

Continental, swaddled infant shape, enamel detailing, silvertone domed lid, tapered base, late 18th/19th C, 3-1/4" l...........**$325**

Meissen, Germany, courting couple, ivy covered tree trunk, enamel and gilt detailing, orig stopper, late 19th C, 2-1/2" l...........**$635**

Silver gilt, shield shaped, collet-set heart-shaped opal applied to front, surrounded by applied ropetwist, green and yellow enamel dec, back engraved with leafy scrolls, conical screw-in stopper, Hungarian, 20th C, 1-3/4" l...........**$115**

Silver plate, Victorian, London, bud shape, engraved rim, all over repoussé reeding, glass int., 1885, 2-3/4" l...**$190**

Sterling silver

Birmingham, England, hinged heart-shaped case, domed lid, emb angel dec, gilt int. with heart-shaped green glass bottle, monogrammed, 2 troy oz, 1897, 3-1/4" l...........**$230**

Victorian, London, bud shape, engraved rim, body with all over repoussé reeding, glass int., 1885, 2-3/4" l...........**$175**

Scent

Silver, Japanese, tear shape, molded dragon dec on stippled ground, attached silver chains, approx 1 troy oz, late 19th/early 20th C, 3-5/8" l...........**$450**

Ivory, figural, woman holding basket of flowers in one hand, fan in other, polychrome dec, Japan, 3-3/4" h...........**$90**

Vinaigrette

English, silver

Marker's mark "JT," Birmingham, rect, foliate engraved lid, base with molded scroll rims, gilt interior with pierced and engraved dec, approx 1 troy oz, c1845, 1" w, 1-1/2" l ... **$290**

Tooled purse shape, gilded int., John Turner, Birmingham hallmarks, 1792, 7/8" l **$250**

Victorian, staghorn, mounted with thistle-cast lid, quatrefoil neck band, horn with guilloche strapping, short link chain, late 19th C, 2-1/2" l rough-textured horn **$350**

PEWTER

History: Pewter is a metal alloy consisting mostly of tin with small amounts of lead, copper, antimony, and bismuth added to make the shaping of products easier and to increase the hardness of the material. The metal can be cast, formed around a mold, spun, easily cut, and soldered to form a wide variety of utilitarian articles.

Pewter was known to the ancient Chinese, Egyptians, and Romans. England was the primary source of pewter for the American colonies for nearly 150 years until the American Revolution ended the embargo on raw tin, allowing the small American pewter industry to flourish until the Civil War.

Notes: The listings concentrate on the American and English pewter forms most often encountered by the collector.

Additional Resources:

Antique Trader® Metalwares Price Guide, 2nd Ed., by Kyle Husfloen, ed., and Mark Moran, contr. ed., Krause Publications, Iola, WI.

Basin

"Love," attributed to John Andrew Brunstrom, Philadelphia, PA, 1781-93, round, flared sides, single-reed brim, circular mark with facing birds and "LOVE," [Celia Jacobs 16], and "LONDON," minor wear, 10-1/8" d **$650**

Circular mark with facing birds and "LOVE," "LONDON," "X" and crown mark, [Celia Jacobs 16, 17], minor wear, 11-1/2" d **$2,250**

Circular mark with facing birds and "LOVE," "LONDON," and two "X" and crown marks, [Celia Jacobs 16, 17], minor wear, 12-5/8" d **$2,820**

Partial circular mark with facing birds and "LOVE," "LONDON," [Celia Jacobs 16, 17], and "X" and crown mark, 6-11/16" d **$650**

Partial circular mark with facing birds and "LOVE," [Celia Jacobs 16], and "LONDON," 8-1/8" d **$500**

Partial circular mark with facing birds [Celia Jacobs 16], and "LONDON," minor wear, 9-1/8" d **$530**

Basin, quart

Edward Danforth, Middletown and Hartford, Connecticut, 1788-94, circular form, flared sides, single reeded brim, small touch mark with lion and "ED" [Carl Jacobs 82], 7-7/8" d **$650**

Richard Austin, Boston, Massachusetts, round bowl, flared sides, single reed brim, touchmark with dove and lamb, "RICHARD AUSTIN" in shaped oval [Celia Jacobs 230], c1790-1810, 8" d **$750**

Beaker

Boardman & Hart, Hartford, Connecticut, tapered cylindrical body, incised bands, "BOARDMAN & HART" "N-YORK" touchmarks [Carl Jacobs 47], wear, scattered small dents and pitting, second quarter 19th C, 3-1/8" h **$200**

Samuel Danforth, Hartford, Connecticut, tapered cylindrical body, incised bands, "SD," eagle and dagger marks, [Carl Jacobs 105], 1795-1816, 5" h **$1,765**

Timothy Boardman, New York City, tapered cylindrical body, incised bands, molded base, "TB&Co" and "X" quality mark, [Carl Jacobs 49], 1822-24, 5-1/4" h **$900**

Teapot, S. Simpson, baluster form, domed lid, scroll handle, impressed mark, 8-1/2" h, American, mid-19th century, dented, **$225.**
Photo courtesy of Alderfer Auction Co.

Charger, ringed rim, three indistinct impressed marks, imp "AB," possibly English, scattered pitting and scratching, 16-1/2" d, **$320.**
Photo courtesy of Alderfer Auction Co.

Tankard, etched body, lid, pewter, German, **$365.**
Photo courtesy of Pook & Pook, Inc.

Bud vase, Secessionist style, orig green glass insert, peacock feather emb, stamped "WMF," 5" d, 10-1/2" h **$865**

Butter plate, American, unmarked, 6" d..**$70**

Candlesticks, pr, Freeman Porter, Westbrook, ME, baluster stem, molded round foot, circular mark with "F. PORTER WESTBROOK," and "No. 1," [Laughlin text II p. 110], imperfections, 1835-60, 6-1/4" h...............**$770**

Charger, Samuel Ellis, London, monogrammed on back "MH," wear, knife, scratches, small rim repairs, 16-3/8" d......................................**$350**

Coffeepot

Rufus Dunham, Westbrook, Maine, conical cover, flared cylindrical body, incised reeding, scrolled black painted handle, marked "R. DUNHAM," [Laughlin text II, p. 100], minor wear, 1837-82, 7-1/4" h **$500**

Issac C. Lewis, Meriden, Connecticut, tapered body, tooled rings around base and rim, worn black paint on scrolled ear handle, interior of base raised, additional touchmark scratched out, touchmark for I.C. Lewis on base, 1834-52, 10-1/2" h **$260**

Freeman Porter, Westbrook, Maine, ovoid, tooled ring at center, flared foot, and rim, domed lid, wafer finial, scrolled ear handle with later black paint, circular touchmark "F. Porter Westbrook No. 1," small hole at base of handle, restored dents, 1835-60, 11" h..........................**$320**

Communion chalice, unmarked American, handles removed, pr, 6-1/4" h....................................**$200**

Creamer, unmarked American, teapot shape, 5-7/8" h **$250**

Deep dish

"Love," attributed to John Andrew Brunstrom, Philadelphia, Pennsylvania, 1781-93, circular, single reed brim, circular mark with facing birds and "LOVE," [Celia Jacobs 16] and "LONDON," 13" d **$1,000**

Round, single reed brim, circular mark with facing birds and "LOVE," crown and "X" quality mark [Celia Jacobs 16, 17] and "LONDON"

stamped twice, minor wear, 11" d **$500**

Round, single reed brim, circular mark with facing birds and "LOVE," crown and "X" quality mark [Celia Jacobs 16, 17] and "LONDON" stamped twice, 13" d **$950**

S. Kilbourn, Baltimore, eagle mark, 11" d **$1,045**

Thomas Danforth III, Stepney (Rocky Hill), CT, circular form, rare eagle mark, [Laughlin 370], c1790, 6-1/8" d **$1,650**

Flagon, one quart, Thomas D. and Sherman Boardman, Hartford, Connecticut, disk finial, three domes, molded cover with "chair back" thumb piece above tapered cylindrical body with fillet, scroll handle with bud terminal, molded base, "TD & SB" in rectangle and "X" quality mark, [Celia Jacobs 150], c1815-20, 9" h..**$4,700**

Flagon, three quarts

Boardman & Hart, Hartford, Connecticut, domed cover with "chair back" thumb piece, tapered cylindrical form, molded fillet and base, double scrolled handle with bud terminal, "BOARDMAN & HART," "N-YORK" and two round eagle touchmarks, [Carl Jacobs 39, 47], c1825-30, 13" h....................**$3,100**

Thomas D. and Sherman Boardman, Hartford, Connecticut, urn finial, domed and molded cover with "chair back" thumb piece, tapered cylindrical body with molded fillet and molded base, double scroll handle with bud terminal, marked with "TD & SB," eagle, and "X" quality mark, [Celia Jacobs 64, 150], c1815-20,14" h **$4,000**

Inkwell, small circular lid, four quill holes surrounding wide flat circular base, replaced glass receptacle, 19th C, 1-3/4" **$225**

Ladle, plain pointed handle, touch mark "WH" in oval, 19th C, 13" l **$65**

Lamp

Plus brass and tin whale oil burner, Putnam touch, James Putnam, Madison, MA, some splits in rim of base, 5-3/4" h **$315**

Plus fluid burner, unmarked American, attributed to Meriden, reeded

detail on base, ear handle, light pitting, 7" h...................................**$110**

Plus burner, Yale and Curtis, New York 1 touch, matching fluid burner missing, snuffers and one brass tube loose, 8-1/2" h **$190**

Measure

Assembled set, bellied, English, minor damage, 2-3/8" to 8" h **$550**

John Warne, English, brass rim, battered, old repair, quart, 5-3/4" h **$100**

Mug

Jacob Whitmore, Middletown, Connecticut, flared cylindrical form with fillet, S-scroll handle with bud terminal, molded base, rare rose mark to interior base, round rose touch, [Laughlin 382], mug accompanied by 1997 note from John Carl Thomas commenting on its fine quality and marks, c1750-75, 5-7/8" h **$9,400**

Joseph Danforth Sr., Middletown, Connecticut, quart, flared cylindrical form with molded fillet, S-scroll handle with bud terminal, molded base, "ID" mark near rim and handle, [Celia Jacobs 164], minor wear, 1780-88, 6" h **$4,700**

Robert Palethorp, Jr., Philadelphia (1817-22), 4-1/8" h...............**$3,800**

Samuel Hamlin, Hartford, Connecticut, quart, flared cylindrical form, everted lip, molded fillet, S-scroll handle with bud terminal, molded base, shaped "SAMUEL HAMLIN" touch, [Carl Jacobs 158], minor wear and pitting, late 18th C, 5-7/8" h **$4,200**

Samuel Hamlin, Hartford, Connecticut, quart, tapered cylindrical form, everted lip, molded banding, S-scroll handle with bud terminal on molded base, shaped "SAMUEL HAMLIN" touch, [Carl Jacobs 158], minor wear, late 18th C, 5-7/8" h **$3,900**

Thomas D. and Sherman Boardman, Hartford, Connecticut, pint, tapered cylindrical form, medial incised banding, S-scroll handle with bud terminal, molded base, "TD & SB" touchmark in rectangle [Celia Jacobs 150], minor wear, small dent on base edge, c1815-20, 4-1/2" h **$1,530**

Unknown maker, Boston, Massachusetts, tapered cylindrical form, everted rim, molded band, scrolled strap handle with shell-like thumb grip, molded base, marked "CM" "S" and "CS" around rim, last half 18th C, 6-1/4" h **$7,100**

Pitcher

Continental, swirl design, hinged lid, angel touch, 6-1/2" h **$85**

Freeman Porter, Westbrook, ME, two quart, 6" h **$225**

Plate

Blakslee Barnes, Philadelphia, Pennsylvania, eagle touchmarks and "BB," [Carl Jacobs #15], knifemarks, dents, some edge damage, set of six, 1812-17, 7-7/8" d **$980**

Richard Austin, Boston, Massachusetts, circular, single reed brim, rare oval shaped touchmark with dove, lamb and "RICHARD AUSTIN," 1792-1817, 7-7/8" d **$250**

Thomas Badger Jr., Boston, Massachusetts, round, single reed brim, arched left facing eagle mark and "BOSTON," [Laughlin 309, 287a], normal wear, price for pr, 1787-1815, 7-7/8" d **$1,000**

Thomas Danforth III, circular, single reed brim, oval lion touchmark with "TI" initials and four hallmarks [Laughlin 363a and 365], normal wear, late 18th C, 7-7/8" d **$650**

John Skinner, Boston, Massachusetts, round, single reed brim and hammered booge, partial lion touchmark and four hallmarks, [Carl Jacobs 249], normal wear, 1760-90, 8" d **$825**

Gershom Jones, Providence, Rhode Island, circular, single reed brim, struck two lions in gateway touch marks, four small hallmarks, [Laughlin 339 and 340], normal wear, 1774-1809, 8-1/4" d **$1,200**

John Skinner, Boston, Massachusetts, round, hammered booge, left facing lion touchmarks, same owner's marks on all, [Laughlin 293], price for set of three, minor wear, 1760-90, 8-1/2" d **$1,880**

Thomas Danforth II, Middletown, Connecticut, round, smooth brim, hammered booge, two lion in gateway touches, four small hallmarks, and "X" quality mark [Carl Jacobs 113], c1760-70, 9-1/2" d **$3,175**

Platter, Townsend and Compton, London, pierced insert, marked "Cotterell," 28-3/4" l **$2,400**

Porringer

Thomas D. and Sherman Boardman, Hartford, Connecticut, round, boss bottom, flowered handle, "TD & SB" in rectangle touchmark [Laughlin 428], c1815-20, 3-1/4" d **$715**

Richard Lee or Richard Lee Jr. Springfield, Vermont or unknown maker, round basin form, boss bottom, openwork handle with crescents and hearts, raised reversed "R" mark on handle back, late 18th C, 3-1/4" d **$600**

Thomas D. and Sherman Boardman, Hartford, Connecticut, circular form, boss bottom, Old English handle, "TD & SB" in rectangle, touchmark [Laughlin 428], 1810-30, 4" d **$470**

William Calder, Providence, Rhode Island, round basin form, boss bottom, openwork handle with partial round eagle touchmark [Carl Jacobs 67], dents, pitting, 1817-56, 4-1/4" d **$360**

Gershom Jones, Providence, Rhode Island, round form, boss bottom, flowered handle, circular lion mark with "GI" initials on handle [Carl Jacobs 176], minor wear, 1774-1809, 4-1/4" d **$2,350**

Samuel Hamlin Jr., Providence, Rhode Island, circular basin form, boss bottom, flowered handle, round mark with eagle and anchor, [Laughlin plate XLIX, fig. 337], 4-1/2" d, 1801-56 ....**$1,100**

Gershom Jones, Providence, Rhode Island, round form, boss bottom, flowered handle, partial circular lion mark [Carl Jacobs 176 or 177], 1774-1809, 5" d **$2,115**

Thomas D. and Sherman Boardman, Hartford, CT, circular form, boss bottom, flowered handle, [Laughlin 428], 1810-30, 5-1/4" d **$900**

Samuel Hamlin Jr., Providence, RI, circular basin form, boss bottom, flowered handle, engraved "LAH"

monogram and date "1820" on bottom, round touchmark with eagle and anchor [Laughlin plate XLIX, fig. 337], 1801-56, 5-3/8" d **$1,550**

Soup plate, unmarked Continental, angel touch, 8-7/8" d **$75**

Sugar bowl, Ashril Griswold, Meriden, Connecticut, eagle touch, 6" h **$490**

Tablespoon, rattail handle, heart on back of bowl, marked "L. B.," (Luther Boardman, Massachusetts and Connecticut), set of six **$330**

Teapot

Roswell Gleason, Dorchester, Massachusetts, eagle touch, 6-3/4" h **$495**

Ashbil Griswold, Meriden, Connecticut, eagle touch, some battering and repairs, 6-3/4" h **$200**

Eben Smith, Beverly, Massachusetts, minor pitting and scratches, 1813-56, 7" h **$375**

PHONOGRAPHS

History: Early phonographs were commonly called "talking machines." Thomas A. Edison invented the first successful phonograph in 1877; other manufacturers followed with their variations.

Adviser: Lewis S. Walters.

Angelica, cylinder, duplex horns **$2,100**

Columbia

BN disc player **$1,000**

BQ cylinder player **$1,200**

HG cylinder player **$2,400**

Decca, Junior, portable, leather case and handle **$150**

Edison

Amberola 30 ....**$325**

Army-Navy, c. WW1 ....**$1,200**

Diamond Disc W-19 William & Mary **$500**

Excelsior, coin-op **$2,500**

Fireside-w/original horn **$900**

Gem, maroon, 2-4 minute reproducer **$1,700**

Opera, has moving mandrel & fixed reproducer **$2,500**

S-19 Diamond disc, floor model, oka case **$400**

Phonograph, Edison, Home, Model D, No. 39445 D, two and four-minute gearing, japanned bedplate, gilt and blue line dec, Edison transfer on oak case, no. 10 cygnet horn with transfers and crane, approx. 22 Blue Amberol and other cylinders, patent dates to 1907, 16″ w, **$700.**
Photo courtesy of Skinner, Inc.

Phonograph, Edison, oak case, **$350.**
Photo courtesy of Dotta Auction Co., Inc.

Phonograph, Delpheon, mahogany stained case, **$650.**

Standard, Model A, oak case w/metal horn...**$550**

Triumph w/cygney horn, mahogany case...**$2,500**

Graphone

12.5 oak case, metal horn, retailer's mark, cylinder...........................**$450**

15.0 oak case with columns on corners, nickel-plated platform, metal horn, stenciled cast-iron parts **$725**

Home Grand, oak case, nickel-plated works, #6 spring motor.........**$1,300**

Kalamazoo, Duplex, reproducer, original horns with decals, pat. date 1904 ....**$3,300**

Odeon Talking Machine Co., table model, crank wind, brass horn, straight tone arm........................**$500**

RCA-Victor, "45," bakelite record player...**$65**

Silvertone (Sears), two reproducers **$500**

Sonora

Gothic Deluxe, walnut case, triple spring, gold-plated parts, automatic stop and storage.......................**$400**

Luzerne, renaissance-style case w/ storage.....................................**$200**

Talk-O-Phone, Brooke, table model, oak case rope decorations, steel horn **$200**

Victor

Credenza, crank.......................**$1,100**

Monarch, table model, corner columns bell horn......................**$1,500**

School House...........................**$2,500**

Victor I, mahogany case, corner columns bell horn......................**$1,500**

Victor II, oak case, black bell horn **$1,200**

Victor II, oak case, smooth oak horn .... **$5,500+**

Victor III w/papier-maché horn **$1,400**

Victor V, oak case, corner columns, no horn.................................**$1,500**

Victor VI, oak case, no horn **$4,000**

PHOTOGRAPHS

History: A vintage print is a positive image developed from the original negative by the photographer or under the photographer's supervision at the time the negative is made. A non-vintage print is a print made from an original negative at a later date. It is quite common for a photographer to make prints from the same negative over several decades. Changes between the original and subsequent prints usually can be identified. Limited edition prints must be clearly labeled.

Additional Resources:

Stereo Views, An Illustrated History & Price Guide, 2nd Ed., by John Waldsmith, Krause Publications, Iola, WI.

Warman's® Civil War Collectibles, 2nd ed., by John F. Graf, Krause Publications, Iola, WI.

Album

"A Souvenir of the Harriman Alaska Expedition, volumes I and II," 251 photographs, more than 100 by Edward Curtin, additional images by Edward H. Harriman, C. Hart Merriam, G. K. Gilbert, D. G. Inverarity, and others, silver prints, various sizes to 6″ x 7-1/2″, several with handwritten credit and date in negative, others with copyright, album disbound and defective, title pages and map laid in, prints generally in excellent condition, 1899, pr **$21,850**

"Kodak," 104 photographs of Eastern and Midwestern U. S. by Wm Hoblitzell, prints document his train ride across country from Maryland to Missoula, Montana, unposed glimpses of trains and local stations, Missoulan bicyclists and Native-Americans on horseback, handwritten captions and/or dates on mount rectos, mounted four per page recto and verso, oblong 4to, gilt-lettered morocco, spine and edges worn, pgs loose, photographer's handstamp on front and rear pastdowns, ties missing, 1890-91 .... **$575**

Albumen print

Lincoln, Abraham.................... **$1,550**

View of the Oswego Harbor, arched top, title, photographer, and date printed on label affixed below image, 1869, 13" x 16-1/2" **$1,380**

Ambrotype, William Gannaway
Brownlow, known as Parson Brownlow, the fightin' preacher, half plate .. **$3,190**

Cabinet card

Early, Gen. Jabal A., sgd, 6-1/4" x 4-1/4" **$1,040**

Garfield, J.A., sgd, 6-1/2" x 4-1/4" **$1,495**

Lincoln, Abraham, lengthy inscription to Lucy Speed, 6-1/2" x 4-1/4" **$1,840**

Sitting Bull, D. F. Barry, titled, copyrighted, dated, and Barry's imprint on recto, Bismarck D. T. imprint on mount verso, 1885, 7" x 5"....**$1,495**

Wilde, Oscar, age 32, Alfred Ellis & Wallery imprint on mounts recto and verso, period German inscription handwritten on mount verso, 1892, 5" x 4" **$1,100**

CDV, carte de visite

Bill, Buffalo, long dark hair, wide lapel jacket, lighter overcoat with fur collar, light sepia color, 3-3/4" x 2-3/8", minor edge damage **$230**

Lee, Robert E., sgd, large bold signature, 3-3/4" x 2-1/2".............**$4,025**

Mott, Lucretia, bust portrait, backmark "H. C Phillips, Philadelphia, tax stamp manuscript canceled 2 cent playing card **$535**

Panorama, titled "Port Richmond, Philadelphia," blindstamp of William H. Rao, Philadelphia dock and railyard scene, 15" x 68" mounted on 21" x 74" card, oak frame ...**$500**

Sojourner Truth, seated, no backstamp.................... **$990**

Lincoln, Abraham, taken by Matthew Brady, 1864 .... **$1,045**

Mrs. Lincoln, portrait with spirit of Abe behind her, Wm Mumler's Boston imprint on mount verso, c1869 .... **$1,725**

Daguerreotype

Northern abolitionists, America, group of men believed to be five Northern abolitionists and a Southern politician, identified left to right as Joshua R. Giddings (1795-1864), John Adams Dix (1798-1879), John Alexander McClernand (1812-1900), Henry Alexander Wise (1806-1876), Levi Coffin (1789-1877), and John Parker Hale (1806-1873), quarter plate, 3-3/4" x 4-5/8" case, mounted in brass mat, black leather covered wood case with red velvet int., case with repaired spine, c1849, 2-1/2" x 3-1/2" plate ..**$5,000**

Daugerreotype Seated woman holding book, 1/4-plate, Root Gallery, 140 Chestnut St, Philadelphia, orig seal in leatherette case **$200**

Sell, John Todhunter, seated young child, tinted, sixth plate by M. A. Root, Philadelphia, stamped on matt, orig seal, some discoloration to mat, damaged leatherette case, c1840 .... **$475**

Store front, four-story brick building, signage on building, crates piled in front, man with top hat, unknown photographer, quarter-plate, image not sealed, plate marked "Chapman," leatherette case with some damage, c1850 .... **$4,775**

Unknown gentleman, sixth-plate image by Robert Cornelius, orig brass Cornelius frame with repeating diamond pattern, orig seal, affixed yellow paper label on reverse "Daguerreotype Miniatures by R. Cornelius, Eighth Street, above Chestnut, Philadelphia," minor oxidation to image, slight mineral deposits on glass, c1840 ......**$13,200**

Unknown gentleman, seated, sixth-plate image by W & F Langenheim, Philadelphia Exchange, re-sealed image, verdigris on mat, heavy tarnish halo at mat opening, leatherette case with photographer's name on pad, c1840 .... **$425**

Unknown woman, seated, sixth-plate image by W & F Langenheim, Philadelphia Exchange, re-sealed image, verdigris on mat, heavy tarnish halo at mat opening, leatherette case with photographer's name on pad, c1840 .... **$425**

Carte de visite of Tom Thumb, **$55-$65.**

Carte de visite, unidentified Union infantry captain, **$90-$105.**

Ambrotype, Ruby, 1/9-plate of Union corporal wearing slouch hat, **$225-$250.**

Double-cased, tintype of soldier and family, **$485-$515.**

Unknown woman, well dressed in dark taffeta dress, lace collar and cuffs, leather gloves, portrait brooch at neck, slight tint on cheeks, by Collins, 3rd & Chestnut St., Philadelphia, half-plate, orig seal, Collins paper label, full leatherette case, c1840-50.................................. **$450**

Magic lantern slides, group of 320 photographic images from 1920s and 1930s, Atlantic City views and events, yachting, fireboats, Mohonk (NY), Duluth (MN), etc. housed in four individual carrying cases, several slides cracked............................... **$230**

Photograph

Aspens, New Mexico, by Ansel Adams, sgd "Ansel Adams" in ink on mount, identified on label from Boston gallery on reverse, framed, 1958, 19-1/2" x 15-1/2"......... **$6,325**

First Annual Round-Up, sgd in plate "Doubleday Photo, Wichita, Kan, First Annual Round-Up," 47 cowboys, cowgirls, workers, some on horseback, tipping hats, buildings and fences in background with advertising signs, 1920, 33-3/4" l, 8" h, 35-1/2" l x 9-1/2" black frame with worn paint....................... **$550**

Portrait of Albert Einstein, by Lotte Jacobi, sgd "Lotte Jacobi" in pencil lower right, framed, c1938, 9-3/4" x 7".. **$1,265**

Portrait of Marc Chagall and His Daughter in His Studio, by Lotte Jacobi, sgd "Lotte Jacobi" in pencil lower right, 6-3/4" x 5-1/2", framed **$300**

Ten Mile Creek, detailed scene near mouth of Ten Mile Creek, Powder River, Montana, heard of cattle spread out in the valley, sev-eral cowboys on horseback, 20" l, 14-1/2" h, contemporary 21-1/8" l, 16" h frame **$350**

Silver print, sepia tones, by Edward S Curtis, shows Indians riding horses in single file, signature and "L.A." lower right, glued down to thin card backing, 14" x 17" orig brown and black frame, sold with book *Portraits from North American Indian Life*, by Coleman and McLuhan, 13-3/8" l, 10-3/8" h.................................. **$1,150**

Tintype

Civil War artilleryman, 9th plate, waist-up portrait, wearing artillery shell jacket, uncased **$115**

Civil War soldiers, 6th plate, 2 men, one with shell jacket, cavalry saber, and pistol cartridge on belt, other with NY depot style jacket....... **$320**

Unidentified Union soldier with rifle and bayonet, 1/6th plate **$360**

POLITICAL ITEMS

History: Since 1800, the American presidency has been a contest between two or more candidates. Initially, souvenirs were issued to celebrate victories. Items issued during a campaign to show support for a candidate were actively being distributed in the William Henry Harrison election of 1840.

There is a wide variety of campaign items—buttons, bandanas, tokens, pins, etc. The only limiting factor has been the promoter's imagination. The advent of television campaigning has reduced the quantity of individual items, and modern campaigns do not seem to have the variety of materials that were issued earlier.

Adviser: Theodore L. Hake. References by Ted Hake include: *The Encyclopedia of Political Buttons 1896-1972; Political Buttons Book II 1920-1972; Political Buttons Book III 1789-1916.* Each book pictures over 5,000 items and comes with free supplement Revised Prices 2004. Ordering details at www.hakes.com.

Additional Resources:

Warman's® Americana & Collectibles, 11th Ed., by Ellen T. Schroy, ed., Krause Publications, Iola, WI.

Arm band, Hoover, celluloid, back mkd "Whitehead + Hoag," 1-3/4" x 7-3/4" **$60**

Ashtray, Smoked glass, "Thanks To A Key Leader," facsimile signature "Dick Nixon," 1960, 3-1/2" sq................. **$20**

Badge

Inaugural, Harry Truman, brass bar pin 2" w, celluloid insert, "Inaugural Committee," medal with high relief reading "Inauguration Of President And Vice President/Truman-Barkley," gold ribbon text reads "1789-1949/41st Inaugural/Harry S. Truman/Alben W. Barkley/Jan 20th 1949," 1949, overall 7" l...........**$107**

Pencil and badge, "Roosevelt and Humanity," 2-1/2" celluloid-covered mechanical pencil suspended from bar pin, 6.5" chain housed in top of piece, metal case 1" **$62**

Portrait, cardboard, brass shell, Grant, stickpin hanger, eagle on rock with two stars, below shield with blue accent, star clusters, red enamel and brass shield stripes, clean cardboard photo at center, 1868, 2-1/2" t..**$840**

Bandana, George McGovern, red, white, and blue, map, red star on each state capitol, slogans surround map, 30" sq **$30**

Bank, T. Roosevelt, cast iron, 3-D bust of T. Roosevelt, inscribed "Teddy," gold paint, silver eyeglasses, small red accent on his Spanish-American War hat, 75% orig paint remains, c1898-1904, 5" h **$195**

Banner, Win with Windell L. Willkie, blue-tone photo, 12" x 12"............ **$50**

Bar pin, Hoover, brass lettering, white enamel dec, 3/4" l **$5**

Bookmark, Pres. Roosevelt, diecut aluminum, c1904, 2-14" l.............. **$75**

Brooch, Harrison, brass frame, front with elevated thick piece of glass with beveled edges over hand-colored scene on inserted paper, two tiny figures, red, white, and blue flag, log cabin, hard cider barrel, inscribed "Harrison & Reform," orig bar pin, 1840, 3/4" x 15/16" **$1,500**

Bust, hollow cast metal, Wm McKinley, black patina, reverse stamped "G. B. Haines & Co., Chicago," 7" h........ **$70**

Button

Button and beer mug, prohibition repeal Dec. 1933, "Happy Days Are Here Again," 1-1/4" mug with colored wax inside suspended from ribbon, 1-1/4" **$48**

"Fairbanks" name button, W&H backpaper, 1-1/4"........................ **$40**

FDR graphic, "Re-Elect Roosevelt," no paper as issued, Union bug on curl, glossy, 1936, 15/16" **$496**

JFK, "If I Were 21 I'd Vote For Kennedy," 1960, 3-1/2" **$50**

Nixon, "Elect Nixon," White House, "Not For Sale" sign in front of fountain, glossy, 1960, 4" **$320**

Special interest, "Coal Trade Sound Money Club," McKinley, 1896, W&H backpaper, 7/8" **$48**

Campaign poster

Hoover, Herbert, "Republican Candidate for President," 1932, triple matted in 22" x 27" frame, 17" x 22" **$75**

Johnson, Lyndon, red, white, and blue cardboard, for Senate election lost by LBJ to W, Lee O'Daniel, 1941, 11" x 14".. **$165**

Roosevelt, Franklin D., notation on bottom "Photo August 1944," 11" x 14-1/2".. **$35**

Car attachment, Willkie for President, diecut metal, attachment bracket at bottom, Donaldson Art Sign Co., Covington Kentucky, printed dark blue, red, creamy tan, varnish finish, 3-1/4" x 5"...................................... **$85**

Carte de viste, Lincoln family, stiff card, artist retouched sepia portrait of family gathered around Lincoln, holding book on lap, blank reverse, 2-1/2" x 4".. **$25**

Christmas card, Adlai E. Stevenson, with letter of authenticity from Hake's Americana and Collectibles, 1960s, 3-1/2" l signature, 4" x 5" **$45**

Reproduction Alert. The reproduction of campaign buttons is rampant. Many originated as promotional sets from companies such as American Oil, Art Fair/Art Forum, Crackerbarrel, Liberty Mint, Kimberly Clark and United States Boraxo. Most reproductions began life properly marked on the curl, i.e. the turned-under surface edge.

Look for evidence of disturbance on the curl where someone might try to scratch out the modern mark. Most of the backs of original buttons were bare metal or had a paper label. Beware of any button with a painted back. Finally, pinback buttons were first made in 1896, and nearly all made between 1896 and 1916 were celluloid covered. Any lithographed tin button from the election of 1916 or earlier is very likely a reproduction or fantasy item.

*Button, McKinley, celluloid, "McKinley Button" and "Made In The United States,"1896, lapel stud, 3/4", **$70.***
Photo courtesy of Hake's Auctions www.hakes.com.

*Pin, "V," FDR, "gold plated" on reverse, silver front luster, 1-15/16" tall, **$75.***
Photo courtesy of Hake's Auctions www.hakes.com.

*Jugate badge, Garfield and Arthur, mounted on original fabric rosette with streamer ribbons, brass shell, 1880, 1.5" tall, **$900.***
Photo courtesy of Hake's Auctions www.hakes.com.

Pin, inaugural, Wilson and Marshall, glossy cello and strong color, VF, "March 4, 1913," 1-3/4", $2,240.
Photo courtesy of Hake's Auctions www.hakes.com.

Jugate pin, Bryan and Kerns, no back paper, light surface wear, 1908, 1-1/4", $560.
Photo courtesy of Hake's Auctions www.hakes.com.

Jugate pin, McKinley and Roosevelt, couple of stain dots on right edge, Baldwin and Gleason, glossy and NM, 1-1/4", $175.
Photo courtesy of Hake's Auctions www.hakes.com.

Jugate, inaugural, Coolidge, original brass/glass compass, blue ribbon, Nodel Bros. NY backpaper, 1925, 1-14", 3/4" ribbon, $2,350.
Photo courtesy of Hake's Auctions www.hakes.com.

Coin, US one-cent coin, Liberty head on front, front stamped "Vote the Land Free," reverse lightly struck, date 1838, issued in 1848 for Martin Van Buren, 1-1/8" **$135**

Convention bandana, GOP, Fort Worth, Texas, red, bright white block printing, circle of repeated GOP elephant symbols within 1984 date at each corner, center Lone Star symbol surrounded by text and cowboy boot design, 11-1/2" sq folded, opens to 21-1/2" x 22" **$25**

Convention button, celluloid, 3" d

Carter, yellow, black lettering, Indiana Labor Coalition, name over outline of state of Indiana, 1976 .... **$25**

Reagan, green on white, sponsored by "The other Washington-Reagan Country," used at Rep. Convention-Dallas, Aug 1984 .... **$48**

Dinner program, Ford, slightly textured stiff paper folder, Feb. 15, 1974 annual Republican Douglas County dinner, Omaha Hilton Hotel Ballroom, front cover with black and white photo and id of Ford as Vice President, lists of "Our Republican Family" inside, 7-1/2" x 11" **$35**

Door stop, Teddy Roosevelt, brass-plated cast iron, Rough Rider outfit, patent date on reverse, 1899, 10-1/2" h **$185**

Drinking glass, FDR and Chicago Mayor, Chicago World's Fair, images and names on front, Chicago's Worlds Fair 1933 with two US flags on back, 1933, 2-1/2" d, 3/4" h" **$65**

Electoral ticket, linen-like fabric, black printed text, cream-colored ground, top reads "National American Fillimore and Donelson Ticket," various elector names, some as-made flaws, archival tape repair, 1856, 10-1/2" x 18" **$300**

Ferrotype pin

Grant, portrait with name, outer edge of diecut circular designs, vertical pin and clasp on back, 7/8" brass frame **$295**

Lincoln & Hamlin, portraits, slogan around front rim, circle of stars, rim hole, 1860, 5/8" **$750**

Goldbug, mechanical, McKinley, missing underside spring, orig luster traces, mint McKinley photo, Hobart photo VF, 1-5/8" w **$147**

Handout card, JFK for U.S. Senator, two sided, Massachusetts state and local candidates list, "Vote The Entire Democratic Ticket Including Your Senators, Representatives, and County Officers," back image of Furcolo and Kennedy, 1952, 3-3/4" x 5-3/4" **$72**

Hat, Theodore Roosevelt caricature, dark blue felt, stenciled large letters on front "Bull-Moose" under image of TR in tan Rough Rider hat, red bandanna, white eyeglasses and teeth, 1912, roll up brim 2" high in front, 3" h in back, 12" conical shape **$990**

Horse bridle rosettes, Cleveland and Stevenson, thick glass domes over real photo sepia portraits, gold and silver metal foil borders, silvered brass backs, attachment bar and cases stamped, "Pfluegs Patent U.S. & Canada," 1892, 1-3/4" d price for pr **$700**

Inaugural clothing button, Washington, brass, Linked States design, "GW" in center surrounded by slogan "Long Live The President," 13 oval linked chains with each surrounding initials of one of the original states, 1789, professionally replaced shank, 1-3/8" d **$4,000**

Inauguration program, Kennedy/Johnson, 64 pgs, orig envelope, 8-1/2" x 11" **$45**

Jugate button

Bryan-Stevenson, black and white photos accented by silver central area, surrounded by red, white, and blue stars and stripes, narrow silver rim, 7/8" d **$65**

Coolidge, Republican, back paper from Philadelphia Badge Co., 7/8" d **$65**

FDR-Wallace, litho with photos of both, 1940, 1" **$30**

Kennedy-Johnson, cello, black and white photos, top third with names in white lettering on red, bottom margin with blue arc inscribed in white "America's Men For The 60s," 4" **$70**

Nixon, inaugural, 1973, 2-1/4" d .. **$15**

Roosevelt, T. and Fairbanks, black and white portraits against red, white, and blue shield, Pulver, 1904, 1-1/4" **$265**

Stevenson, black printed names on yellow ribbon panel, red slogan above "Go Forward With Adlai Stevenson," 1952, 1-3/8" color portraits **$40**

Taft-Sherman, wreath, union bug imprint on back, 7/8" d **$65**

Jugate poster, McKinly/Hobart, paper, matted, framed, text below each image, Thyer & Jackson Stationary Co., Chicago, copyright 1896, 14" x 22" **$65**

Lapel stud

Cleveland, horseshoe, dark red fabric, name in white lettering, dark blue horseshoe, 3/4" **$30**

Harrison, diecut top hat, lapel stud, silver luster, 9/16" **$35**

William McKinley, black and white photo in center, dark blue and

bright red stars on cream rim **$20**

Letter opener, brass, Roosevelt, die-cut and raised FDR image handle, 1930s, 9" l **$45**

Mechanical pencil, Ritepoint, red, white, and blue, black and white photos of Stevenson and Sparkman at top, "Win with Adlai Stevenson and John Sparkman" in blue and red, 5-1/2" l **$35**

Mechanical pin, Taft, Presidential Chair, brass luster back and legs, silver luster seat cover "Who Shall Occupy It," small tab at bottom seat edge pulls and seat flies open to reveal sepia glossy paper real photo of Taft, 1908, 2" h **$175**

Medal

Buchanan, rebus, white metal, "Buchanan and Beckinridge 1856, The Union Must & Shall Be Preserved-United We Stand Divided We Fall," 1856 .... **$1,750**

Fremont, silver lustered white metal, high-relief portrait, "Col. John C. Fremont, Born Jan. 21st, 1813," die-maker's name "Anthony Pacquet" below neck, reverse with wreath and slogan "The Rocky mountains Echo Back Fremont-The People's Choice for 1856," with ribbon wrapped around wreath "Free Men/Soil," 2-3/8" d **$200**

Medalet, uncirculated, 1" d

Blaine and Logan, brass, front shows both men, reverse with shield at center "Union" on diagonal, surrounded by "The Republicans Have Ruled Since 1860 And With Blaine & Logan Are Good For Another Term," top rim hole, mint luster **$50**

Grant, copper, raised portrait and name on front, designer's name below his shoulder, reverse "Gen US Grant Our Next President May He In Wisdom Rule The Country He Has Saved," 1868, bright copper flashing worn **$85**

Harrison, 1" brass portrait, name, and 1841 on front, reverse with eagle with ribbons above and below, slogan "Got It Tip-Come It Tyler," **$40**

Button, Hoover, "Ok America," and "Play It Safe With Hoover," celluloid with high dome, high gloss, 1-3/4", **$1,640.**
Photo courtesy of Hake's Auctions www.hakes.com.

Stickpin, ferrotype with crescent-shaped cutouts, metallic red tin foil accents, brass frame 5/8", **$1,185.**
Photo courtesy of Hake's Auctions www.hakes.com.

Banner, gold foil miniature, FDR, eyelet at top, metallic red and blue, NM, c1940, 5-1/4" x 7-1/4", **$235.**
Photo courtesy of Hake's Auctions www.hakes.com.

Pin, Wilson, multicolor, W & H back-paper, glossy cello, NM, 1-1/4", $80.
Photo courtesy of Hake's Auctions www.hakes.com.

License die-cut, Landon and Knox, yellow petals on burgundy background, 4-1/2" x 6-3/4", $110.
Photo courtesy of Hake's Auctions www.hakes.com.

Jugate button, "The Old Guard Souvenir Designed By Dr. J.H. Rerich, LaGrange Ind. Republican National Committee. Worn in 1900 By (name of wearer)," minor surface wear, 1-1/2", $700.
Photo courtesy of Hake's Auctions www.hakes.com.

Mirror, pocket, Taft campaign, "It's Up To The Man On The Other Side To Put This Tried & Safe Man At The Head Of The Government," slight age tone to celluloid covering, 1912, 2-1/8" **$353**

Paperweight, William McKinley, solid brass bust, c1896, 2-1/2" x 3" **$60**

Pennant, inaugural, Eisenhower, brown felt, white letters, flesh-tone portrait, pale turquoise suit jacket, gray necktie, yellow-gold felt trim band and streamers, 1953, 12" x 29" **$30**

Pin, plastic, donkey's head, white, Adlai Stevenson printed in blue panel between ears, 7/8" **$15**

Pinback button

Bryan, colored portrait, silver background, brown and white shoulder areas, light flesh-tone coloring on face, unusual twisted wire orig pin, 1900, 1-1/4" **$70**

Goldwater, Go-Go Goldwater in '64, gold cello, black printing, small image of elephant as hyphen, tiny union printer symbol, 3-1/2" **$24**

Kennedy, All The Way With Kennedy For President, slogan in blue, white background, name in bright red, 1-3/4" **$75**

Kennedy, Youth for Kennedy, litho, curl reads "Green Duck, Chicago" 4" d **$150**

McKinley, black and white photo, gold trim diamond design flanked by red, white, and blue star and stripe motif, bright gold outer motif, 1896, 7/8" d **$30**

Roosevelt, T., Welcome TR, back paper from W. F. Miller Co., NY, 1-1/4" d **$100**

Stevenson, Adlai Likes Me, red, white and blue litho, 1" d **$20**

Truman, For President Harry S. Truman, black on cream, 1-1/4" d .. **$60**

Postcard, bright red, white, and blue flag design, emb white oval frame at center surrounding brown-tone image of Teddy Roosevelt, musical notes above "Yankee Doodle" and slogan "Glory to the Union," printed in Germany, undivided back, 3-1/2" x 5-1/2" **$35**

Press Badge, democratic convention, eagle hanger, text "Democratic

National Convention Baltimore 1912," pink ribbon, 1912, 4-1/2" t **$140**

Press photo, glossy sepia-tone, President Harding and young Douglas MacArthur, second unnamed individual in civilian clothes, authorization stamp by International Pres service, early 1920s, 6-1/2" x 8-1/2" **$25**

Print, Andrew Jackson, undated, "Andrew Jackson Seventh President of the United States," c1840, 10-3/4" x 13-1/2" stiff paper centered by 8-3/4" x 11" N Currier hand-colored print .. **$125**

Ribbon

Jugate, "The Plumed Knight 1884 Blaine/Logan," oval sepia photos, small crate design "40 Rounds U.S. (Logan's Corps)," missing corner tip, circular stain, 1884, 2-1/4" x 6-1/2" **$265**

Miniature, "Hancock/English" graphic, glossy fabric, jugate portraits, eagle, shield, sunbursts, flags, pin hole, trivial paper residue on reverse, 1880, 1-1/4" x 2-5/8" .. **$252**

Silk, Henry Clay "New York Delegation," bold image, tiny edge trim, pinholes, narrow crease, overall fine, 1844, 2-1/2" x 6-1/2" **$303**

Salt & pepper, campaign figural, removable head, text on uniform "We Like Ike," 1952, 3-3/4" t **$97**

Scarf, George McGovern, red, white, and blue repeat pattern of "For President George McGovern," also repeat pattern "Truth, Unity, Peace, Honesty, Togetherness," 13" x 58" **$30**

Snuff box, horn, ivory veneer on top, hinged lid, steel engraving paper portrait under glass, oval brass rim, John Quincy Adams, ivory has hairlines, minor scratching, c1825-1829, 1-5/8" w, 3-1/8" l, 7/8" d **$2,218**

Stickpin, prohibition, blue enamel, "Fisk and Brooks," 6-point brass star with banner, "Dare To Do Right," 1888 .... **$120**

Store display, I Like Ike Sunglasses, cardboard display, six pair of plastic sunglasses with elephants on either side and "Peace/Prosperity," orig generic box, 7-3/4" x 21" **$200**

Tintype

Lincoln, four levels of elevated ovals surrounding recessed center, accented by gold oval surrounding slightly domed glass, gutta-percha case, 3" h **$850**

Washington, possibly 1876 Centennial souvenir, 2-1/2" x 4" card with centered 1-1/4" x 1-3/4" x 2" tintype with octagonal edges **$150**

Watch fob, 1-3/4", brass, Bull Moose, raised moose image, "National Progressive Party New York State Convention, Syracuse, Sept 5 & 6, 1912," Bastian logo **$125**

Frame, ferrotype, Lincoln and Johnson, 32 stars on brass backing, Lincoln side is NM, Johnson side in Mint, "Pat. Apr. 2. 1861," 13/16" brass frame with suspension hole, **$3,250.**
Photo courtesy of Hake's Auctions www.hakes.com.

POSTERS

History: Posters were a critical and extremely effective method of mass communication, especially in the period before 1920. Enormous quantities were produced, helped in part by the propaganda role posters played in World War I.

Print runs of two million were not unknown. Posters were not meant to be saved; they usually were destroyed once they had served their purpose. The paradox of high production and low survival is one of the fascinating aspects of poster history.

The posters of the late 19th and early 20th centuries represent the pinnacle of American lithography. The advertising posters of firms such as Strobridge or Courier are true classics. Philadelphia was one center for the poster industry.

Europeans pioneered posters with high artistic and aesthetic content, and poster art still plays a key role in Europe. Many major artists of the 20th century designed posters.

Advertising

Clarenbach & Herder Ice Skate Manufacturers, Philadelphia, Pennsylvania, large scene of ice skaters on Schuylkill River, Waterworks in background, later archival backing, mid-19th C, 17-1/4" x 23" **$675**

Coffres-Forts Fichet, adv for French bank vaults, c1905, 68" x 23-1/2" **$2,760**

Cycles Clement, Arthur Foache, Bourgerie, Paris, c1900, 53-1/2" x 37" **$5,750**

Ferry's Seeds, full-color image of pretty young lass amid towering hollyhocks, light fold lines, restoration to edges, thin tears, 1925, 21" x 28" **$325**

Fire! Fire! Fire!, "Chicago Lost But J. Dearman of Knoxville, Penna. Continues to Roll Up, Bundle Up, and Box Up As Many Goods As Ever!" red and black, some replacement to border, Oct. 15, 1871, 22" x 27" **$225**

Maggi, Chocolat Menier, Firmin Bouissett, 1895, 54" x 38-1/4" **$4,140**

Richfield Gasoline, race driver in car, c1930, 39" x 53" **$1,100**

Royal Portable Typewriter, dark green detailed manual portable typewriter against leafed red and green ground, c1940, 24" x 36" **$285**

Waterman's Ideal Fountain Pen, paper, Uncle Sam at Treaty of Portsmouth, early 1900s, 41-1/2" x 19-1/2" **$950**

Art Nouveau

La Emeraude, Alphonse Mucha 1900, 26" x 11" **$9,775**

Leslie Carter, Alphonse Mucha, Strobridge, Cincinnati, 1908, 83" x 31-1/2" **$9,775**

Le Livre de Magda, Paul Berthon, Chaix, Paris, 1898, 25-1/4" x 19" **$2,300**

Les Eglantines, Paul Berthon, Chaix, Paris, 1900, 19-1/2" x 25-1/2" **$815**

Princezna Hyacintha, Alphonse Mucha, V. Neubert, Prague, 1911, 50-1/4" x 35-3/4" **$18,400**

Vi Slet Vsesokolsky & Lide Cesky! Alphonse Mucha, V. Neubert, Smichov, 1912, 66" x 32" **$14,950**

Exhibition

Bals Des Arts, Crane-Howard, Joseph W. Jicha, 1928, 37" x 23" **$2,990**

Kunst Im Handwerk, Vereinigte Druckerein und Kunstanstalten, Munich, Bruno Paul, 1901, 34-3/4" x 23-1/2" **$5,635**

Midas, Whatsoever He Touches Might Be Gold, Continental Litho, Cleveland, Joseph W. Jicha, 1927, 37-1/2" x 25" **$2,530**

Museum, Stedelijk, Roy Lichtenstein, 1967, framed **$200**

Magazine

The Chap Book, Stone & Kimball, Chicago, Claude Fayette Bragdon, c1895, 21" x 13-1/2" **$4,140**

The Idler, A. E. Forrest, J. M. Dent & Co, London, 1898, 29-3/4" x 20" **$690**

Movie and theatrical

A Good Man Is Hard To Find, Union Label, New York, Ben Shahn, expertly repaired tears in margins, 1948, 46" x 30-1/4" **$5,750**

Anatomy of a Murder, Columbia, Saul Bass design, 1959, 27" x 41" **$125**

A Trip To Chinatown, Dangerfield Printing Co., London, Beggarstaff Brothers, James Pryde and William Nicholson, 1894, 117" x 89-1/2" **$43,700**

Atlantic City, Republic, Constance Moore, Jerry Colonna in drag, by James Montgomery Flagg, 1941, 14" x 36" **$250**

Bad Boy, James Dunn and Louise Fazenda, Fox, 1934, 27" x 41" **$150**

Bringing Up Father, McManus, "Jiggs, Maggie, Dinty Moore-George McManus's cartoon comedy with music," early newspaper cartoon characters against New York skyline, c1915, 41" x 81" **$425**

Chaussures Caoutchouc, Marque "Au Coq," Gus Bofa (Gustav Blanchot), c1907, 53-1/4" x 37-1/4" **$3,220**

Poster, campaign, JFK, large b&w profile portrait, "A Time For Greatness," and "Kennedy For President," NM, 1960, 9-1/2" x 14", **$400.**
Photo courtesy of Hake's Auctions www.hakes.com.

Posters, U.S. Navy recruiting, color lithograph, "Your Country Needs You" and "Follow the Flag" (shown), 27" x 40-1/2", **$600.**
Photo courtesy of Sloans & Kenyon Auctioneers and Appraisers.

Poster, United Jewish Appeal, "Their Fight is Our Fight— Give Today," artwork by Fodor, Statue of Liberty background, mounted on linen, unframed, 22" x 14", **$763.**
Photo courtesy of Skinner, Inc.

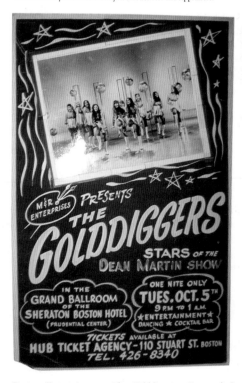

Poster, Entertainment, The Golddiggers, Stars of the Dean Martin Show, Boston, real photo of Golddiggers, blue and white ground, **$75.**
Photo courtesy of Gary Sohmers.

Dr. No, United Artist, Sean Connery, Ursula Andress, 1962, 27" x 41" **$325**

Goodbye Mr. Chips, Robert Donat and Greer Garson, MGM, 1939, 27" x 41" **$450**

Mule Train, Columbia Pictures, Gene Autry, Champion, full-color portraits, 1950, 27" x 41" **$150**

Music, Aspen Winter Jazz Concert, Roy Lichtenstein, 1967, framed.. **$200**

No No Nanette, Tony Gibbons, Theatre Mogador, Paris, European production of American musical, c1925, 15" x 22" **$375**

Smoldering Fires, Pauline Frederick and Laura La Plante, Universal, 1925, 14" x 22" **$125**

Political and patriotic

America Lets Us Worship As We Wish—Attend The Church Of Your Choice, for American Legion sponsored "Americanism Appreciation Month," full-color image of praying Uncle Sam, family at dinner table behind him, c1945, 20" x 26" **$275**

Confidence, large color portrait of Roosevelt over yacht at sea, "Election Day was our salvation/Franklin Roosevelt is the man/Our ship will reach her destination/Under his command…Bring this depression to an end…," c1933, 18" x 25" **$250**

Give Us The Faith And Courage of Our Forefathers, dark and somber image of Uncle Sam, Howard Chandler Christy, Recruiting Publicity Bureau, US Army, 1950, 35-1/4" x 24-3/4" **$1,265**

Kennedy for President, Leadership for the 60s, red, white, and blue, photo in center, some restoration, 1960, 42" x 27" **$2,530**

United Nations Day, blue and white U.N. banner waves over airbrushed stylized brown and yellow globe, minor edge crumple, 1947, 22" x 23" **$250**

Transportation

Air France—North Africa, Villemot, stylized imagery of mosques and minarets, lavenders, yellow, and blues against sky blue background, plane and Pegasus logo, c1950, 24" x 39" **$225**

A Subway Poster Pulls, Edward McKnight Kauffer, 1947, 45" x 30" **$7,475**

Europe, The SS *United States*, SS *America*, United States Lines, Lester Beall, 30" x 22" **$2,990**

Red Star Line, Antwerpen-Amerika, Henri Cassiers, Couleurs Berger & Wirth, Leipzig, 1899, 43-1/2" x 59-1/4" **$5,060**

Royal Mail Atlantis, Padden, tourists in Royal mail motor launch approaching harbor village, mountains in background, c1923, 25" x 38" **$675**

SS France, Bob Peak, launching of French ocean liner, champagne and confection in front of huge, nightlit bow of ship, 1961, 30" x 46" **$450**

Travel

Boston—New Haven Railroad, Nason, full color, stylized montage of Historic Boston by day and night, faint folio folds, c1938, 28" x 42" **$275**

Come to Ulster, Norman Wilkinson, sailboats and fishermen in front of lighthouse, full color, c1935, 50" x 40" **$450**

Hawaii—United Air Lines, Feher, stylized wahini, island behind her, full color, c1948, 25" x 40" **$650**

Paris, Paul Colin, doves floating above stylized Eiffel tower and Arc de Triumph, 1946, 24" x 39" **$600**

World War I

Call to Duty—Join the Army for Home and Country, Cammilli, recruiting image of Army bugler in front of unfurled banner, 1917, 30" x 40" **$325**

Follow the Flag—Enlist in the Navy, James Daugherty, sailor plants flag on shore, 1917, 27" x 41" **$600**

Gee!! I Wish I Were A Man I'd Join The Navy, Howard Chandler Christy, 1918, 41-1/4" x 27" **$1,955**

Give it Your Best, US Government Printing Office, Charles Coiner, red, white, and blue flag above slogan, 1942, 20" x 28" **$575**

Give Us The Faith And Courage of Our Forefathers, dark and somber image of Uncle Sam, Howard Chandler Christy, Recruiting Publicity Bureau, US Army, 1950, 35-1/4" x 24-3/4" **$1,265**

I Want You For The Navy, Howard Chandler Christy, Forbes, Boston, 1917, 41" x 26" **$1,265**

Keep Him Free, War Savings Stamps, bald eagle on edge of nest, Charles Livingston Bull, Ketterlinus, Philadelphia, 1918, 30" x 20" **$575**

Put Strength in the Final Blow, Buy War Bonds, Frank Brangwyn, Avenue Press, London, 1916, 60-1/2" x 40" **$815**

Save the Products of the Land, Eat More Fish, Charles Livingston Bull, Heywood Strasser & Voit, New York, c1918, 30" x 20-1/4" **$750**

The Spirit of America, nurse wrapped in American flag calling on people to join Red Cross, Howard Chandler Christy, Forbes, Boston, 1919, 30" x 20" **$1,150**

Treat 'Em Rough—Join The Tanks, A. Hutaf, window card, electric blue-black cat leaping over tanks in fiery battle, white border, c1917, 14" x 22" **$900**

Will You Supply Eyes For The Navy?, Gordon Grant, "Navy Ships Need Binoculars and Spy-Glasses… Tag Each Article with Your Name and Address, Mail to Hon. Franklin D. Roosevelt, Asst. Sec'y of Navy,…" image of Naval captain ready with blindfold on stormy deck, gun crew at ready behind him, 1918, 21" x 29" **$625**

PRINTS

History: Prints serve many purposes. They can be a reproduction of an artist's paintings, drawings, or designs, but often are an original art form. Finally, prints can be developed for mass appeal rather than primarily for aesthetic fulfillment. Much of the production of Currier & Ives fits this latter category. Currier & Ives concentrated on genre, urban, patriotic, and nostalgic scenes.

Additional Listings: See Nutting, Wallace.

*Print, Grant Wood, "In The Spring,"
lithograph, pencil signed lower right,
framed, 9" x 12", $4,650.*
Photo courtesy of David Rago Auctions, Inc.

Reproduction Alert. The reproduction of Maxfield Parrish prints is a continuing process. New reproductions look new, i.e., their surfaces are shiny and the paper crisp and often pure white. The color on older prints develops a mellowing patina. The paper often develops a light brown to dark brown tone, especially if it is acid-based or was placed against wooden boards in the back of a frame.

Size is one of the keys to spotting later reproductions. Learn the correct size for the earliest forms. Be alert to earlier examples that have been trimmed to fit into a frame. Check the dimensions before buying any print.

Carefully examine the edges within the print. Any fuzziness indicates a later copy. Also look at the print through a magnifying glass. If the colors separate into dots this indicates a later version.

Apply the same principles described above for authenticating all prints, especially those attributed to Currier & Ives. Remember, many prints were copied soon after their period introduction. As a result, reproductions can have many of the same aging characteristics as period prints.

Arms, John Taylor, *Rodez/The Tower of Notre Dame*, etching on paper, edition of 120 plus six trial proofs, sgd and dated "John Taylor Arms-1927" in pencil lower right, inscribed "Arms 1926" and "Rodez 1926" in the plate, 11-7/8" x 4-7/8", framed...**$230**

Atkins & Nightingale, publisher, J. Cartwright, engraver, *Georgetown and Federal City, or City of Washington*, etching with aquatint and hand coloring on paper, framed, few minor scattered stains, light toning, 1801, 16" x 23-1/4"................**$17,625**

Barlach, Ernest, *Fluchende Alt*, woodcut, sgd in pencil lower right, Ferdinand Roten Gallery, Baltimore, on back, 4" x 3"..........................**$920**

Barnet, Will, *Silent Seasons-Summer*, color litho, sgd, titled, and numbered 113/200 in pencil lower margin, 1975, 29" x 22-1/2"....................**$920**

Bearden, Romare, *Girl in the Garden*, color litho, sgd and numbered 29/150 in pencil, lower margin, 1979, 22-1/8" x 16-1/8"....................**$5,750**

Benson, Frank Weston, *Geese Alighting*, drypoint on paper, second of two published states, sgd "Frank W. Benson" in pencil lower left, dated in the plate lower left, numbered "44" in pencil lower right, framed, 1916, 9-3/4" x 8" plate size................**$1,035**

Benton, Thomas Hart, lithograph, sgd in pencil lower right, published by Associated American Artists, New York, edition of 250

Goin' Home, 1937, 9-1/2" x 12"
....**$1,840**

Missouri Farmyard, 1936, 10" x 16"
....**$2,070**

Old Man Reading, 1941, 10" x 12-1/8"....................................**$2,185**

Boileu, Philip, child, "The Associated Sunday Magazines" cover, Feb. 1, 1914, sgd lower right, grade 4.0, c1914, 16" x 20" frame..........**$45**

Boydell, John, publisher, image by Benjamin West, engraved by John Hall, *William Penn's Treaty with the Indians, When He Founded the Province of Pennsylvania in North America in 1681*, hand colored engraving, minor repairs to border, c1775, 18-1/2" x 23-1/2"..........**$1,450**

Brundel, Carl Alexander, *Return from the Fields*, color woodcut on cream wove paper, sgd and inscribed "orig Holzchnitt Hand-" in pencil, c1930, 12-1/2" x 15-3/4".............**$460**

Calder, Alexander, color litho

Composition with Mobile Forms, sgd in ink lower right, numbered 93/100 in pencil lower right, very pale time stain, 19-3/4" x 25-1/4"...................**$1,840**

Composition with Spirals, sgd in pencil lower right, 26" x 39"
....**$1,840**

Cassatt, Mary, color drypoint

Margot Wearing a Bonnet, c1902, 9" x 6"...**$1,840**

Sara Smiling, c1904, 7-1/4" x 5"
....**$1,725**

Chagall, Marc

De mauvais Sujets, color aquatint on Japon nacre, sgd and numbered 9/9 in pencil, printed by Lacourière and Frélaut, Paris, published by Les Bibliophiles de l'Union, Francaise, Paris, 1958, 13-5/8" x 10-1/2"
....**$5,060**

L'Avare qui a perdu son Trésor, aquatint and etching, sgd and numbered 49 in pencil, printed by Maurice Potin, Paris, published by Tériade, Paris, 1927-30, 11-3/4" x 9-5/8"....................................**$1,265**

L'Âne et le Chien, aquatint and etching, sgd and numbered 88/100 in pencil, printed by Maurice Potin, Paris, published by Tériade, Paris, 1927-30, 11-3/4" x 9-1/4"
....**$1,725**

Currier, Nathaniel, publisher, after Arthur Fitzwilliam Tait, *The Cares of a Family 1856*, lithograph with hand coloring heightened by gum Arabic on paper, identified in inscription in the matrix, Conningham, 814, matted, unframed, 22" x 28".........**$2,990**

Currier, Nathaniel, publisher, Frances Flora Palmer, lithographer, lithograph with hand coloring on paper, identified in inscription in matrix

American Farm Series No. One, Conningham 134, framed, 1853, 21-3/8" x 28-1/4"...................**$2,185**

American Forest Scene, Maple Sugaring, Conningham 157, label from Old Print Shop, New York on reverse, framed, 1856, 24-7/8" x 32-5/8"...............**$19,550**

American Winter Scene, Evening, Conningham 207, unframed, 1854, 20-3/4" x 27" **$8,625**

The American Clipper Ship, Witch of the Wave, undated, Conningham 115, framed, overall toning, scattered staining, fox marks, creases throughout, 13" x 16-1/2" **$865**

Currier and Ives, publishers

A Scene on the Susquehanna, C#5415, farm on one side of river, flock of sheep, damage to modern gilt frame, repaired tears, 21-1/4" w, 18-1/4" h **$175**

Fruit and Flowers No. 2, "Lith & Pub by N. Currier" lower left, "152 Nassau St. Cor. Of Spruce, NY" lower right, framed in 10" x 14" orig frame, grade 3.5, c1848, 8-1/2" x 12-1/2" print **$165**

Meeting of the Waters, orig wooden backing, grade 3.0, 14" x 10" orig frame **$75**

Scenery of the Upper Mississippi, An Indian Village, C#5422, trimmed, stained, matted, framed, 14" w, 10-1/4" h **$300**

Ensor, James, La Cathédrale, etching on imitation Japan paper, sgd and dated in pencil lower right, 1886, 9-1/2" x 7" **$7,475**

Fox, R. Atkinson

A Perfect Melody, pseudonym sgd "DeForest" lower right, title lower center, grade 4.0, c1920-25, 7" x 9" orig frame **$50**

Clipper Ship, grade 2.75, c1920-25, unsigned, 20" x 12" period frame, ... **$40**

Sunset Dreams, sgd "R. Atkinson Fox" lower right, "Copyright Borin Mfg Co., Chicago" lower left, grade 3.75, c1920-25, 18" x 10" orig frame **$370**

The Old Mill, unsigned, grade 4.0, c1920-25, 9" x 12" frame **$60**

Grimball, Meta M., The Loving Cup, sgd lower right, titled lower center, grade 3.0, unusual six-sided double over mat, c1909, 10" x 8" period frame **$165**

Hundertwasser, Friedensreich, Pacific Steamer, color woodcut on paper, dated, numbered and inscribed "989/999 ©…868A Auckland 3 March 1986" in ink lower left, sgd with vari-

ous chops lower right, framed, deckled edges, 1986, 20-1/2" x 15-3/4" image size **$2,875**

Hyde, Helen, Moon Bridge at Kameido, color woodcut on paper, sgd "Helen Hyde" in pencil lower right, monogram and clover seals lower left, numbered "67" in pencil lower left, inscribed "Copyright, 1914, by Helen Hyde" in the block lower left, framed, 13-1/4" x 8-7/8" **$460**

Icart, Louis, Sleeping Beauty, color etching and aquatint, sgd in pencil, artist's blindstamp, 1927, 14-3/4" x 18-1/2" **$1,495**

Kellogg & Co., hand-colored lithograph, Napoleon, four stages of life, Subaltern to Exile, yellow and orange painted frame, damage, 15" w, 13" h **$150**

Kent, Rockwell

Diver, wood engraving on paper, edition of 150, sgd "Rockwell Kent" in pencil lower right, 1931, 7-3/4" x 5-1/4" image size, framed, 3/8" margins or more **$1,120**

Resting, lithograph on paper, edition of 100, sgd "Rockwell Kent" in pencil lower right, 1929, 9-5/8" x 5-7/8" image size, framed, 3/8" margins or more **$1,175**

Knight, Dame Laura Knight, Gilding the Lily, etching and aquatint on paper, edition of 35, sgd "Laura Knight" in pencil lower right, 11-1/2" x 7-1/2" plate size, framed, margins over 1" **$750**

Lindenmuth, Tod, Low Tide, color woodcut on paper, sgd "Tod Lindenmuth" in pencil lower right, titled in pencil lower left, framed, 15" x 14" image size **$1,600**

Lindner, Richard, Man's Best Friend, color lithograph on paper, edition of 250, sgd "R. Lindner" in pencil lower right, numbered "31/250" in pencil lower left on Arches cream paper with watermark, unmatted, unframed, minor handling marks, nicks, creases, c1970, 27-3/4" x 21-1/2" sheet size **$530**

Marin, John, La Cathedral de Meaux, 1907, etching on Arches wove paper with watermark, sgd "…de J. Marin" in pencil lower center, sgd and dated within the plate, 8-1/2" x 6-1/8" plate size, matted, deckled edges on two sides **$350**

Print, Raphael Soyer, "Waitresses," lithograph, pencil signed lower right, and signed in the plate, framed with AAA label verso, 11-1/2" x 9-1/4" sight, **$800.**
Photo courtesy of David Rago Auctions, Inc.

Print, Gustave Baumann, "Fox River Farmyard," color, woodblock, soiled paper, dime-sized stain to lower margin, matted, pencil signed and dated, 1908, 6-3/4" x 8-3/4", **$3,000.**
Photo courtesy of David Rago Auctions, Inc.

Print, Frances H. Gearhart, "High Walled," color, woodblock, matted and framed, some folds to corner outside image, pencil titled and signed, 9-1/4" x 5-1/2", **$3,000.**
Photo courtesy of David Rago Auctions, Inc.

Marsh, Reginald

Tattoo-Shave-Haircut, etching and drypoint, tenth statc, 1932, 9-7/8" x 9-5/8"..................................**$9,775**

Three Girls on a Chicken, engraving, sgd in pencil lower right, second state of edition of 20, 1941, 8" x 9-3/4"....................................**$2,185**

Newell, J. P.

, lithographer and publisher, *Newport, R.I.*, identified in inscription in matrix, lithograph with hand-coloring on paper, framed, tear to margin upper right, toning, stains, foxing........................**$1,175**

Parrish, Maxfield

Chancellor and the King, grade 4.0, c1925, orig 9" x 12" frame **$65**

Dinky Bird, grade 4.0, c1915, 5" x 7" frame **$55**

Hilltop, framed in period 9" x 12" blue and gold frame, sgd lower left, titled lower center, "House of Art" lower right, grade 3.75, c1927, 6-1/4" x 10" **$195**

Lady Violetta in the Royal Kitchen, grade 4.0, c1925, 9" x 12" orig frame **$65**

Prince Codadad, orig 11" x 14" mat, orig blue and gold frame, "Copr P. F. Collier & Son" lower left, grade 4.0, c1906, 9" x 11" print..................**$70**

Rose Bower, unsigned, orig paper label preserved on back, grade 4.0, c1920-25, 10" x 15" period blue and gold frame....................................**$65**

Rubaiyat, "copyright 1917 C. A. Crane Cleveland" lower right, "Reinthal & Newman, New York" imp lower left, grade 4.0, c1917, 28-1/2" x 7" print in 33" x 11" orig brown and gold frame **$250**

Thy Templed Hills, "Original painting by Maxfield Parrish, of Cornish, NY, courtesy of Brown and Bigelow" lower center, grade 4.0, c1930, 5" x 7" period frame **$65**

Vegetables for the Meal, grade 4.0, c1925, 9" x 4" **$65**

Picasso, Pablo

Deux Femmes Nues, etching on paper, edition of 125, sgd and numbered "34/125 Picasso..." in ink beneath image, label from Goodspeed's Book Shop, Boston, on reverse, framed, scattered pale foxing, 1930, 12-1/4" x 8-7/8" plate size................................**$5,875**

La Guitare Sur la Table, etching with drypoint on paper, reprinted 1961, total edition of 70, stamped signature "Picasso" lower right, numbered "29/50" in pencil lower left, framed, 1922, 3-1/8" x 4-3/4" plate size................................**$1,100**

Pressler, Gene

, *Cinderella*, sgd lower right, titled, grade 4.0, c1920-25, 8" x 11" orig metal frame **$45**

Remington, Frederick

, *Indians in Canoe*, sgd lower left, grade 2.75, damaged mat, c1900, 16" x 12" period frame **$35**

Ripley, Aiden Lassell

, *Grouse on Pine Bough*, drypoint on paper, sgd "A Lassell Ripley" in pencil lower right, titled in pencil lower left, plate size, framed, unobtrusive mat toning, c1941, 8-3/4" x 11-7/8"..............**$1,100**

Roth, Ernest David

, *Florentine Roofs*, Florentine, etching on laid paper with "G" watermark, sgd and dated "Ernest D. Roth 1912" in pencil lower center, titled dated and inscribed "Trial Proof" in pencil lower left, matted, soiling, breaks to hinges, 10-1/2" x 10-3/8" **$315**

Schille, H.

, Publisher, American, 19th C, *Panorama of the Catskills*, large folio, lithograph printed in colors with panorama and numerous vignettes, c1870, 21" x 27" **$825**

Sloan, John

McSorley's Backroom, etching and drypoint, sgd, titled and inscribed "100 of 100," third state, 1916, 5-1/4" x 7" **$2,530**

Patience, sgd, titled, inscribed "100 proofs" in pencil, sgd by printer Ernest Roth, in pencil lower left, fourth state, 1925, 5" x 4" **$320**

Soyer, Raphael

, *Bust of a Girl*, lithograph in black, red and blue on paper, edition of 300, sgd "Raphael Soyer" in pencil lower right, numbered "86/300" in pencil lower left, image size 18-3/8" x 13-5/8", framed, over 1" margins **$210**

Spence, R. S.

, publisher, printed by William Robertson, New York, *American Hunting Scene*, four gentlemen with guns, dogs, and boat hunting waterfowl, hand colored lithograph, 22" x 28", framed, some foxing and waterstains at borders **$330**

Prang & Mayer

, publishers, J. F.A. Cole, delineator and lithographer, *New Bedford, Massachusetts*, identified in inscriptions in the matrix, hand coloring, framed, repaired tears and punctures, scattered fox marks, staining, light toning, 16" x 32" image size..**$865**

Toulouse-Lautrec, Henri

Carnival, color lithograph, fourth state, 1894, 9-7/8" x 6-1/2" **$3,450**

Étude de femme, lithograph, third state, published by Henry Floury, Paris, monogram in stone lower left, 1893, 10-1/2" x 8"..........**$1,265**

Ward, Lynd

, *Giant*, wood engraving on tissue-thin paper, sgd and dated in pencil, 1955, 15-7/8" x 6" **$920**

Warhol, Andy

, *Jimmy Carter III*, screenprint, sgd and numbered 14/100 in pencil, printed by Rupert Jasen Smith, New York, published by the Democratic National Committee, Washington, DC, 1977, 28-1/4" x 20-1/2" **$1,725**

Weidenaar, Reynold

, *Bridge Builders, Mackinac Straits*, mezzotint, trial proof, sgd and titled in pencil, 1956, 12-7/8" x 6-7/8" **$2,300**

Whistler, James A. M.

Annie, Seated, etching and drypoint on antique cream laid paper, second state, 1858, 5-1/8" x 3-3/4" **$2,070**

Fumette, etching on thin laid paper, fourth state, 1859, 6-3/8" x 4-1/4" **$1,380**

Le Veille aux Loques, etching and drypoint, third state, 1858, 8-1/8" x 5-7/8"..................................**$1,495**

Wood, Grant

, lithograph, published by Associated American Artists, New York, *Seed Time and Harvest*, sgd and dated in pencil, edition of 250, 1937, 7-3/8" x 12-1/8" **$4,830**

Zorn, Anders

, etching

The New Maid, sgd in pencil, sixth state, 1909, 11-3/4" x 8" **$1,265**

Two Butlers, sgd in pencil lower right, 1910, 6-1/4" x 4" **$1,035**

PRINTS, JAPANESE

History: Buying Japanese woodblock prints requires attention to detail and abundant knowledge of the subject. The quality of the impression (good, moderate, or weak), the color, and condition are critical. Various states and strikes of the same print cause prices to fluctuate. Knowing the proper publisher's and censor's seals is helpful in identifying an original print.

Most prints were copied and issued in popular versions. These represent the vast majority of the prints found in the marketplace today. These popular versions should be viewed solely as decorative since they have little monetary value.

A novice buyer should seek expert advice before buying. Talk with a specialized dealer, museum curator, or auction division head.

The following terms are used to describe sizes: chuban, 7-1/2 x 10 inches; hosoban, 6 x 12 inches; and oban, 10 x 15 inches. Tat-e is a vertical print; yoko-e a horizontal one.

Chikanobu, framed triptych of women by lake, good impression, somewhat faded, c1890..............................**$125**

Chinese, unidentified artist

Landscape, Blue and Green style, numerous seals, 18th/19th C, 35" x 19"..**$1,880**

Sino Japanese War Poster, fair to good impression, color, and condition, some tears, creases, soiling, losses, framed......................................**$120**

Goyo, *Portrait of a Beauty,* Dai-oban, excellent impression, toned and matted to within image.................**$1,100**

Harunobu, pillar print of woman carrying bucket, framed, very good impression, horizontal creases and tears..**$345**

Hasui

A Farmer with Wagon in View of Tall Pines and Mt. Fuji, fine color, impression, and condition.......**$650**

Nezu Shrine in Snow, excellent impression, color, and condition, framed..**$775**

Hiroshige, *An Island, Lake and Mountains in Rain,* from *Eight Views of Omi,* very good impression, color, and condition, some stains, not examined out of frame, c1850....**$360**

Hiroshige II, *Five Views of Edo,* set of five prints, very good impressions, color, and condition, one trimmed to image and laid down, others with soiling, stains, and creases, c1862..**$600**

Hiroshige III, *The Port of Yokohama with a Locomotive on a Stone Bridge and Western Steamships in the Harbor,* good impression and color, fading, toning, creases, and staining, framed, c1870.............**$825**

Hokusai, *Kajikazawa in Kai Province,* from *Thirty-six Views of Mt. Fuji,* good impression, color, and condition, some staining, soiling, and creases, 20th C...........................**$200**

Jaquolet, Paul, *An Elegant Chinese Lady Holding a Veil,* matted to image, very good impression, color, and condition, not examined out of frame...**$470**

Junichiro Sekino, portrait of actor Kichiemon, "il ne etat," printed signature and seal lower right within the image, pencil sgd, 13/50 in lower margin, 22" x 18".......................**$920**

Kasamatsu Shiro, *Pagoda in the Rain on a Spring Evening,* fine impression, color, and condition, upper right corner crease...........**$200**

Kunisada, *Ladies Gathering in Springtime for Music and Poetry,* triptych, good impression, color, and condition, with toning, fading, and stains, framed.............................**$150**

Kunisada II, scene from a legend, good impression, color, and condition, not examined out of frame, framed...**$215**

Kuniyoshi

A Courtesan in Elegant Kimono Holding a Pipe, excellent impression and color with visible wood grain, slight staining and holes...........**$190**

Ladies Feeding Carp from a Pleasure Boat, triptych, excellent impression, color, and condition, with some fading of the blue, c1840.................**$950**

Okiie Hashimoto, *Village in the Evening,* sgd in pencil in margin, dated, Hashi seal, good impression, framed, 17" x 21-1/2"..................**$250**

Toyokuni, perspective print of busy shopping area and temple grounds,

Hiroshige, Suruga Bank of OI River, Station 24, seal of Hoeido, signed Hiroshige ga – Nishiki-e, 1797-1858, 8-3/4" x 13-1/2", **$235.**
Photo courtesy of Sloans & Kenyon Auctioneers and Appraisers.

Hide Kawanishi, color woodblock print, harbor scene, signed in plate, 10-1/2" x 9-1/2", **$440.**
Photo courtesy of David Rago Auctions, Inc.

Utagawa Toyokuni III, color woodblock print, two courtesans, signed with artist's chop, framed, 19th century, 14" x 9", **$265.**
Photo courtesy of David Rago Auctions, Inc.

framed, good impression, faded, 1790s................................**$260**

Toyokuni II, *Two Courtesans*, good impression, faded, trimmed, small hole, stains, and creases, c1800..**$150**

Toyokuni III, Pentaptcyh of people in boat feeding goldfish, iris garden, framed, very good impression, missing leaf, somewhat faded...........**$230**

Utamaro, *Woman Washing Her Hair*, good impression, stained, rubbed, and faded, framed........**$725**

Utamaro II, three women in an interior, good impression, faded, soiled, c1811 ....**$175**

Yoshida Hiroshi, *Daibutsu Temple Gate*, signed in pencil, with Jizuri seal, excellent impression and color **$490**

PUZZLES

History: The jigsaw puzzle originated in the mid-18th century in Europe. John Spilsbury, a London mapmaker, was selling dissected-map jigsaw puzzles by the early 1760s. The first jigsaw puzzles in America were English and European imports aimed primarily at children.

Prior to the Civil War, several manufacturers, e.g., Samuel L. Hill, W. and S. B. Ives, and McLoughlin Brothers, included puzzles in their lines. However, it was the post-Civil War period that saw the jigsaw puzzle gain a strong foothold among American children.

In the late 1890s, puzzles designed specifically for adults first appeared. Both forms—adult and child—have existed side by side ever since.

Prior to the mid-1920s, the vast majority of jigsaw puzzles were cut out of wood for the adult market and composition material for the children's market. In the 1920s, the die-cut, cardboard jigsaw puzzle evolved and was the dominant medium in the 1930s.

Interest in jigsaw puzzles has cycled between peaks and valleys several times since 1933. Mini-revivals occurred during World War II and in the mid-1960s, when Springbok entered the American market. Internet auction sites are impacting the pricing of puzzles, raising some (Pars,

Pastimes, U-Nits, figure pieces), but holding the line or even reducing others (Straus, Victory, strip cut). As with all auctions, final prices tend to vary depending upon the time of year and the activity of at least two interested bidders.

Adviser: Bob Armstrong.

Notes: Prices listed here are for puzzles that are complete or restored, and in good condition. Most puzzles found in attics do not meet these standards. If evaluating an old puzzle, a discount of 50 percent should be calculated for moderate damage (one to two missing pieces, three to four broken knobs), with greater discounts for major damage or missing original box.

Cardboard, pre-1950
Consolidated Paper Box

A Dangerous Trail, 250 pcs, orig box, 1930s, 10-1/2" x 13-3/4" **$14**

Moonlight Beauty, 250 pcs, orig box, 1930s, 14" x 10-1/2" **$15**

Mutual Surprise, 250 pcs, orig box, 1930s, 10" x 13-1/2" **$14**

Milton Bradley

Grand Canyon, 200 pcs, orig box, 1933, 15" x 11-3/4" **$12**

Off the Norway Coast, 465 pcs, orig box, 1930s, 26-1/4" x 18-1/2" **$14**

Viking MFG

A Dutch Scene, 160 pcs, orig box, 1933, 13-3/4" x 10" **$15**

The Cardinal Portrait, 184 pcs, orig box, 1933, 13-3/4" x 10".............**$14**

Parker Brothers, plywood

Boston Tea Party, 200 pcs, orig box, 9" x 11-3/4" **$70**

Lovely Thatched Cottage, 525 pcs, replaced box, 22" x 16-1/4" **$170**

Drifting (courtship; pond), 300 pcs, orig box, exc. colors, 1909, 11-3/4" x 17-1/4" **$90**

Dutch Landing Place, 418 pcs, orig box, 1932, 25-3/4" x 9"............**$200**

Fisherfolk at Sunset, 402 pcs, orig box, 1930s, 20-3/4" x 16" **$165**

Summer Reflections, 755 pcs, orig box, 1930, 28" x 18-1/2"...........**$330**

The Awakening of Spring, 110 pcs, orig box, 1910s, 13-3/4" x 5-3/4"..**$45**

Thoroughbreds in Pasture, 307 pcs, replaced box, c1909, 16-1/2" x 10-1/2" **$125**

Joseph K. Strauss, plywood

Autumn Along the Seine, 100 pcs, orig box, 1930s, 9-1/2" x 6-3/4" **$15**

Trail of the Fox, plywood, 500 pcs, orig box, 1930s, 19-1/2" x 15-1/2" **$75**

The Hunt (hunting-fox), plywood, 500 pcs, replaced box, 1940-50, 16" x 19-3/4" **$65**

The Venetian Wedding (Venice), plywood, 300 pcs, replaced box, 1930s, 15-1/2" x 11-3/4"................**$45**

Wood and/or handcut, pre-1930

Ayer, Isabel/Camb, *The Shrine* (countryside; children), PuzzClub, solidwood, 495 pcs, orig box, 1914, 14" x 20-1/4" **$220**

Richardson, Margaret, *In the Meadow Lands,* solid wood, 192 pcs, replaced box, c1909, 11" x 7"........**$85**

Selchow & Righter/Picture, *Little Sweethearts* (children; Victorian), 247 pcs, orig box, 1910s, 14-1/2" x 9-3/4" **$75**

Tryawhile Puzzle co, Thc Blue Ribbons, plywood, 268 pcs, orig box, 1920/1930, 10" x 11-3/4"............**$100**

Unknown maker

A Winter Day, solid wood, 186 pcs, orig box, 1909, 11-3/4" x 7-3/4"..**$75**

Happiness, solid wood, 165 pcs, replaced box, 1909, 8-1/4" x 9-1/2" **$65**

Lincoln Training for Greatness, solid wood, 139 pcs, orig box, c1909, 7-1/2" x 11" **$50**

Rocky Portal, plywood, 233 pcs, orig box, 1910/20, 12" x 9-3/4" **$85**

Wood and/or handcut, 1930s-40s, plywood

Allen, P.J./Sparetime, *A Beautiful Garden,* 172 pcs, orig box, 1930s, 11-3/4" x 8-3/4"..............................**$35**

Browning, James/U-Nit, *Spirit of America* (state coach; settlers), 750

pcs, orig box, 1930, 24-1/2" x 16-1/4"
....**$320**

Cape Cod Puzzle Co., 1930s

A Good Story But A Bad Shot, 150 pcs, orig box, 10-1/2" x 7"..........**$25**

Freshening Breeze, 300 pcs, replaced, 11-3/4" x 13-3/4" **$60**

Capen, L./Master-Piece, *House and Garden*, 650 pcs, orig box, 1940/50, 19-3/4" x 15-3/4"........................**$150**

Chad Valley, *Lord Mayor's Coachman*, 500 pcs, orig box, 1930/40, 18" x 21"..**$85**

Crosby, A.T./Puzzler, *Mystic Lures of the Orient*, 19-3/4" x 15-3/4", 622 pcs, orig box, 1930s.....................**$140**

Foss, Horace E./Just-For-F Hunters Dream, 538 pcs, orig box, well cut; challenging, 1930s, 16" x 19-1/2"...**$130**

Hale, Cushman & Flint/Medi Girl at a Casement (Flemish; women), 601 pcs, 1930s, 15-1/4" x 17-1/4"......**$150**

Hamlen, H.E./Little Cut-Up, The Stirrup Cup, 411 pcs, orig box, 1930s, 16" x 12"..**$120**

Milton Bradley/Premier

Melody of Love, 301 pcs, orig box, 1930s, 15-3/4" x 11-1/2"..............**$90**

Washington at Valley Forge, 312 pcs, orig box, 1930s. 15-1/2" x 11-3/4" **$90**

Winsor, Mrs. Allen P., *Poppies and Delphinium*, 617 pcs, orig box, 1930s, 21" x 16"............................**$220**

Unknown

The Limit of Wind and Sail, 504 pcs, orig box, 1930/40, 20" x 16" **$150**

The Mill Pond Has Gone To Sleep, 665 pcs, replaced box, 1930s, 20" x 16-1/4"...**$100**

Wood and/or handcut, post 1950s, plywood

Browning, James/U-Nit, 1950s

Christening in the New Republic, 210 pcs, orig box, 13-1/2" x 9-3/4" **$60**

The Haywagon, 400 pcs, orig box, 18" x 13-3/4" **$130**

Scribner, Louise, 1950/60

Home For Christmas, 340 pcs, orig box, 13-3/4" x 9-1/2" **$85**

Meet Saeko, 186 pcs, orig box, 9-1/2" x 12" **$50**

Parker Brothers/Pastime, Fisherfolk at Sunset, plywood, 402 pcs, orig box, 1930s, 20-3/4" x 16" , **$165.**

Tuck/Zag-Zaw, In Disgrace, plywood, 520 pcs, orig box, 1930s, 19-1/2" x 13", **$200.**

Master Wooden Novelty, George Washington Enters, plywood, 557 pcs, orig box, 1930s, 19-3/4" x 15-3/4", **$125.**

Dance of the Nymphs, solid wood, 210 pcs, replaced box, c1909, 14" x 9-3/4", **$80.**

Bruin's Surprise, plywood, 500 pcs, replaced box, 1930s, 19-1/2" x 15-1/2", **$130.**

Puzzle Fan, 'Tis the Star-Spangled-Banner!, plywood, 400 pcs, 1960s, 17-1/4" x 13", **$120.**

L. Capen/Master-Piece, Ballet Dancers, plywood, 504 pcs, orig box, 1930s, 15-1/2" x 17-1/2", **$150.**

Charles L. Hart, The Fall, plywood, 237 pcs, replaced box, 1930s, **$50.**

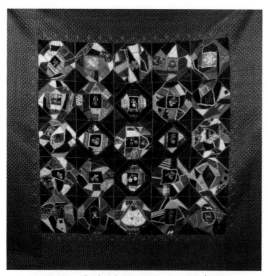

Crazy quilt, dated 1883, 74" x 72-1/4", **$475.**
Photo courtesy of Sloans & Kenyon Auctioneers and Appraisers.

Appliqué quilts, Rose Whig, scalloped border, c1850s, 82" x 83", **$590.**
Photo courtesy of Sloans & Kenyon Auctioneers and Appraisers.

QUILTS

History: Quilts have been passed down as family heirlooms for many generations. Each one is unique. The same pattern may have hundreds of variations in both color and design. The advent of the sewing machine increased, not decreased, the number of quilts made. Quilts are still being sewn today.

Notes: The key considerations for price are age, condition, aesthetic appeal, and design.

Appliqué

Eagle, red, green, and gold eagles, bordered nine block pattern, white ground, quilted in conforming eagle and geometric pattern, Missouri, 20th C, 83" x 77" **$2,350**

Flower Basket, red, green, and yellow calico, white ground, toning, minor staining, fabric wear, 77-1/2" x 67" **$885**

Grape vines, green and purple vines meandering between quilted stuffed grapes, hand quilted following pattern, minor stains, 66" x 82" **$800**

Nine blocks, each with large red flower, pink and yellow center, blue leaves and vines, red buds, border of blue quarter moons and red stars, white quilted ground, signed with embroidery "Polly Matthias (heart) Lug March 1837," 84" x 84" **$1,750**

Oak leaf, red and green printed fabric vine border, white ground, minor

stains, marker lines, late 19th C, 72" x 88" **$300**

Rose of Sharon, pieced scalloped border, red, green, pink, and yellow calico, white ground and backing, red binding, conforming floral pattern quilting, attributed to PA, c1840, 88" x 90" **$1,530**

Tulips

Bright pink and green tulips, white ground, figure eight quilting in border, white back, 80-1/2" x 92" **$300**

Pink and green tulips rising out of blue triangles, white ground with vining stem and leaf design quilted into it, white backing, 74-3/4" sq **$350**

Twenty medallion blocks, blue, green, and red flowers and berries, surrounded by red, and green vining, two with pots of flowers flanking central ground dated "1849" near top, hand quilted, light staining, some damage to appliqué, 82" x 88" **$1,380**

Vine and Blackberry, 16 white blocks, each with appliqued aqua vine with pendant blackberries, separated by aqua grid also forming border, white cotton backing with intricate quilting, America, minor stain, c1920, 82" x 86" **$4,000**

Appliqué and pieced

Album, red plaid separates squares with appliquéd polychrome prints, most are floral, some have deer or

birds, two have Eastern scenes with camels and elephants, inked signatures, stains, dates in the 1850s, 64" sq **$1,870**

Embroidered, appliquéd, pieced cotton, 16 white blocks separated by diagonal red grid, each with floral sprigs and blossoms in solid red, yellow, blue and green accented with wool yarn and cotton embroidered buds and leaves, white backing, New England, losses and fading, late 19th C, 80-1/2" x 90" **$1,410**

Nine floral medallions, red, yellow, and green, red and green sawtooth edging, hand quilted, feathering between medallions, scroll work along border, stains, 82" x 83" **$1,430**

Tulips, pink, purple, and orange, green leaves and borders, hand quilted with flowers, feathering, and diamonds, dark black and blue pencil lines, light green edging, 70" x 82" **$770**

Chintz

Printed, overall design of exotic birds drinking from urns hanging from trees, brown on white, printed gold, blue, green, and reddish-brown, brown floral baking, light stains, 94" x 116" **$1,450**

Crazy

Pieced, many embroideries, including chenille goldenrod, owl at center of pin-wheeled fabrics, 1891 .... **$4,500**

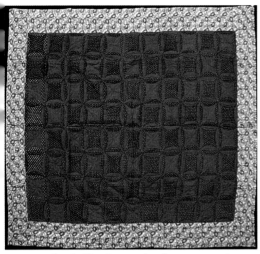

Pieced quilt, New Jersey, red and green geometric design, chintz border, mid-19th century, **$644.**
Photo courtesy of Pook & Pook, Inc.

Pieced quilt, Star-Of-Bethlehem quilt, American, c1840, 80" x 80", **$325.**
Photo courtesy of Sloans & Kenyon Auctioneers and Appraisers.

Pieced, velvet and satin multicolored fabrics, embroidered seams, many embroidered embellishments, appliquéd flowers, burgundy velvet border, gold cotton backing, wear to binding, 79-1/4" x 81" **$750**

Pieced

Basket, 16 baskets composed of solid white and yellow cotton triangles, white ground with double yellow borders, white cotton backing, quilted with feather medallions, diamond and undulating feather border, possibly Mennonite, c1900, 79" sq **$1,550**

Bow Tie, small green and red triangles, red zig zag border with green sawtooth edging, hand stitched four petal flower quilting, red edging, slight wear and facing, 74" sq **$1,575**

Broken Star, orange, yellow, green, red, brown, blue, and white printed calico patches, red and white calico Flying Geese border, PA, 19th C, 80" x 76" **$460**

Cathedral, multicolored diamonds within white circles, hand stitching, 90-1/4" x 105" **$425**

Chinese Lanterns, green, red, blue, yellow, and white printed calico and solid patches, blue and white ground, red border, diamond and rope quilting, PA, minor staining, late 19th C, 82" x 84" **$1,495**

Courthouse Steps, various silk colors, black border, highlighted by decorative embroidery, minor wear, late 19th C, 20" x 26-1/2" **$260**

Diamond blocks, bands of calico alternating with bands of diamond blocks, shades of brown on white ground, scattered staining on front, small hole in backing, 102" x 107" **$750**

Diamonds, polychrome calico bars forming concentric diamonds, white backing, white edge binding, quilting follows bars, 74" sq **$300**

Eagles and sunburst, central teal and red sunburst surrounded by four teal and red eagles and shields, bright yellow ground, leaf motifs in corners, border with band comprised of red and yellow triangles, red band, yellow outer band with red binding, floral motif quilted into yellow ground, pink and yellow broad bands backing, 76" x 81-1/2", some fading on back, small stain **$1,400**

Flower Basket in Diamond design, red, yellow, pink, and red calico, 1" tear, 20th C, 89" x 87" **$450**

Four petal flowers, two shades of light yellow and pale green, white ground, border of arches with buds, hand stitched, princess feather medallions, fancy scrolls, and interlacing lines quilting, scalloped edge, light stains, 84" sq **$495**

Irish Chain, pink, green, and peach calico, straight green and pink borders, brown calico backing, embroidered with red "B" in lower left hand corner, very minor staining, 6' 10" x 6' 11" **$225**

Log cabin

Silk, satin, and velvet, bright colors, four thin borders surround 20 large blocks, hand and machine stitched, small label attached says "Florida Quilt Heritage, #216 NQG #6, documented Florida quilt, Museum of Florida History," 58" x 74" **$320**

Thin multicolored strips paired with black strips, 70" x 69" **$1,400**

Martha Washington's Flower Garden, calicos and printed fabrics, predominately yellows, red and tan borders, hand stitched, minor wear, 66" x 86" **$300**

Moon and Stars, pieced wool, 49 full and three-quarter circles composed of four pie-shaped wedges, shades of rust and green, tan twill binding, woven wool backing, fading, stains, small holes, 83" x 96" **$770**

Nine Patch, various colors, red grid, hand and machine stitched, backed and bound with red and white printed fabric, minor fading, late 19th/early 20th C, 79" x 71" **$230**

Nine Patch variant

Chintz squares edged with triangles, floral printed border, hand stitched, diamond and floral quilting, orig

Appliqué quilt, Turkey Tracks, Sophie Campbell, 1930s, 80" x 83", **$475.**
Photo courtesy of Sloans & Kenyon Auctioneers and Appraisers.

Appliqué quilt, Turkey Red Princess Feather, c1900, 73" x 75-1/2", **$475.**
Photo courtesy of Sloans & Kenyon Auctioneers and Appraisers.

pencil marks, some stains, 82" x 83"...**$1,540**

Multicolored squares alternating with off-white, arranged diagonally in block and surrounded by red grid, sawtooth border, backed with white, red binding, minor imperfections, 81-1/2" x 75"...............................**$460**

Philadelphia Pavements, blue, red, orange, and white square printed and solid patches, orange and red banded borders with feather and floral fine quilting, PA, late 19th/ early 20th C, 84" x 80".....................................**$825**

Pineapple corner elements with birds, central medallion, golden yellow on red, white green borders, burnt orange calico backing, hand stitched, 92" sq..............................**$725**

Pineapple Log Cabin, pieced calico, border of four bands, two yellow, green, and pink, backed with brown figured print, bound with green, Mennonite, Washington, PA, c1880, 96" x 84" **$1,175**

Schoolhouse, red, orange, yellow, and tan buildings machine-stitched on white ground, several interesting quilting patterns, scallops, and zigzags on roofs, stars and geometric shapes in gable ends, birds and leaves on sashing, Midwest, late 19th C, 75-1/2" x 73-1/2"......................**$1,060**

Serrated Square, corresponding border, pink and green calico, shell and diamond quilting, 82" x 84"........**$320**

Spider Web, pink, red, blue, purple green, peach, and brown printed calico patches, wide purple calico border, diagonal line quilting, Mennonite, PA, some staining, late 19th C, 82" x 80"...**$825**

Starbursts with blocks and bars, multicolored starbursts, pink blocks and bars, complex quilting, reverse stamped "M. A. Darby," PA, scattered staining front and back, one star worn through, paper tag states c1865, 82" x 90"..**$350**

Star of Bethlehem, purple, green, red, blue, and pink calico, white ground, toning, minor staining, fabric wear, early 20th C, 82" x 73-1/2"...**$650**

Stars, eight-pointed green and pink calico stars, white calico ground, green and pink band on border with figure eight quilting, three broad pink bands on back, two small stains, 72-1/2" x 80" **$200**

Stars, 42 blocks of eight-point stars set on the diagonal in a variety of printed cotton fabrics separated by floral printed blocks, red, yellow, and black, triangle border, edged in same floral pattern, natural woven cotton backing, chevron and concentric diamond quilting stitches, America, minor stains, circa 1870, 80" x 90"
....**$1,765**

Windmill, yellow, red, green, and blue printed calico patches, wide red calico with swag quilting, PA, late 19th C, 86" x 76" **$690**

Pieced quilt, Fox and Geese, Sophie Campbell, c1930s, 73" x 88", **$535.**
Photo courtesy of Sloans & Kenyon Auctioneers and Appraisers.

Pieced quilt, Urn and Basket, signed and dated 1857, 79-1/2" x 78-3/4", **$530.**
Photo courtesy of Sloans & Kenyon Auctioneers and Appraisers.

Appliqué quilt, red and green calico flowers, orange background, 95" x 93", **$630.**
Photo courtesy of Pook & Pook, Inc.

RADIOS

History: The radio was invented more than 100 years ago. Marconi was the first to assemble and employ the transmission and reception instruments that permitted the sending of electric messages without the use of direct connections. Between 1905 and the end of World War I, many technical advances affected the "wireless," including the invention of the vacuum tube by DeForest. Technology continued its progress, and radios filled the entertainment needs of the average family in the 1920s.

Changes in design, style, and technology brought the radio from the black boxes of the 1920s to the stylish furniture pieces and console models of the 1930s and 1940s, to midget models of the 1950s, and finally to the high-tech radios of the 1980s.

Adviser: Lewis S. Walters.

Additional Resources:

Warman's® Americana & Collectibles, 11th Ed., by Ellen T. Schroy, ed., Krause Publications, Iola, WI.

Kolster, table model, type 6D, 1920s, **$100.**
Photo courtesy of Dotta Auction Co., Inc.

Admiral
33-35-37	$30
218 Leatherette	$40
909 All World	$85
Imperial	$45
Transistor 1960s	$15

Air King, Tombstone, Art Deco **$3,000**

Arvin
Hoppy w/lariatenna	$585
Mightymite #40	$30
Rhythm Baby #417	$275
Rhythm Maid	$215
Table 444	$100
522A	$65

Atwater Kent
Breadboard Style 9A	$55
Breadboard Style 10	$1,500
Breadboard Style 10C	$950
Breadboard Style 12	$1,200
Cathedral #80	$200
Dome #318	$150
Horn-Type R	$125
Table-Keil #55	$200

Bulova
Clock Radio 100	$25
Clock Radio 110	$25
Clock Radio 120	$30

Colonial, New World Radio **$1,000**

Columbia, Table Style Oak **$110**

Crosley
4-28 Battery Set	$120
10-135	$55
Ace V	$125
Bandbox	$80
Dashboard	$100
Gemchest	$425
Litfella	$175
Pup w/box	$375
Sheraton-Cathedral	$225
Showbox	$75
Sleigh	$125
Super Buddy Boy	$115

Dumont, RA346 Table, Fancy **$110**

Emerson
274 Brown Bakelite	$150
AU-190 Catalin Tombstone	$1,200
BT-245	$1,100

Freshman Masterpiece, three dial set, c1924, speaker not shown, **$95.**
Photo courtesy of Dotta Auction Co., Inc.

Dealer Sign-Porcelain	$150
Memento 570	$110
Mickey Mouse 409	$1,200
Mickey Mouse 411	$1,200
Patriot	$700
Portable 640	$30
Snow White	$1,200
Vanguard 888	$80

FADA
43	$250
53	$200
60W	$75
115 Bullet shape	$1,000
136	$1,000
252	$575
625 Rounded end-slide	$700
652 Butterscotch	$725
1000	$850
L56 Maroon & white	$2,600

Federal
58DX	$500
110	$550

General Electric
81, c1934	$150
400-410-411-414	$25
515-517 Clock radio	$30
K-126	$125
Tombstone	$225

Grebe
CR-8	$400
CR-9	$500
CR-12	$750
CR-18	$1,000
MU-1	$250
Service Manual	$50

Halicrafters
TW-200	$125
TW-600	$100

Majestic
92	$125
381	$225
Charlie McCarthy	$1,000
Treasure Chest	$150

Metrodyne
Super 7 c 1925	$265

Motorola
68X11Q, Art Deco	$75
Jet Plane	$25
Jewel Box	$80
M Logo	$25
Pixie	$65
Plastic Table c 1965	$35
Ranger 700	$30
Ranger-portable	$60

Olympic, radio/phonograph **$60**

Paragon
DA-2	$475
RD-5	$600

Philco
17-20-38 Cathedral	$290
37 table 2 Tone	$60

37-84 Cathedral **$125**
46-132 Table................................ **$20**
49 Boomerang.............................. **$750**
49 Transistone **$35**
52 Transistone **$40**
60 Cathedral................................ **$125**
551 c1928 .... **$165**
T-7 126 Transistor **$50**
T-1000 Clock Radio..................... **$80**

Radiobar
W/glasses & decanter.............. **$1,400**
Tumbler...................................... **$50**
Decanter.................................... **$75**

Radio Corporation of Amercia RCA
6X7 Table **$25**
8BT-7LE Portable **$35**
LaSiesta **$550**
Radiola 17 .... **$75**
Radiola 18 .... **$95**
Radiola 20 .... **$165**
Radiola 24 .... **$170**
Radiola 28 .... **$200**
Radiola 33 .... **$60**
World's Fair **$1,000**

Silvertone
1 Table **$75**
1582 Wood Cathederal............... **$200**
1955 Tombstone **$200**
9205 Plastic transistor **$45**
TFM-151 c 1960 .... **$50**
TR-63 c 1958.............................. **$125**
Clock Radio-plastic **$15**

Sparton
Blue Bird, Art Deco, original ... **$3,200**
Blue Bird, Art Deco, reproduction
.... **$100**

Stewart-Warner, table-slant...... **$150**

Stromberg Carlson, 636A console
.... **$125**

Westinghouse, WR-602 .... **$50**

Zenith
6D2615 table w/boomerang dial
.... **$95**
500 Transistor w/owl eye **$125**
500 D Transistor **$55**
750L w/leather case.................... **$40**
Trans-Oceanic............................. **$100**
Zephr-mulit-band........................ **$95**

RAILROAD ITEMS

History: Railroad collectors have existed for decades. The merger of the rail systems and the end of passenger service made many objects available to private collectors. The Pennsylvania Railroad sold its archives at public sale.

Notes: Railroad enthusiasts have organized into regional and local clubs. Join one if you're interested in this collectible field; your local hobby store can probably point you to the right person. The best pieces pass between collectors and rarely enter the general market.

Ashtray, Soo Line, ceramic, track and car design border, "Denver Wright Co." backstamp, 7" d **$25**

Badge pendant, gold luster finish thin metal rim holding color celluloid, showing steam engine during night run, lower center with red, white, and blue logo for Brotherhood of Locomotive Engineers, early 1900s
.... **$20**

Bond
Allegheny & Kinzua Railroad Co., NY & PA, $1000 first mortgage, 5 percent gold bond, train emerging from tunnel, green, Homer Lee Bank Note Co., 30 coupons attached
.... **$95**
Boston, Hartford & Erie Railroad Co., MA, $1,000 7 percent coupon bond, arched fancy "United States of America" over old steam train at station, Columbia, eagle, and shield, green, three printed revenue stamps, sgd by John S Eldridge, President, National Bank Note Co., 50 coupons attached **$125**
Chicago and North Western Railway Co., $1,000 second mortgage, 4-1/2% convertible income bond series A, vignette Wheel of Progress, olive, American Bank Note Co. **$35**
Cleveland, Cincinnati, Chicago & St. Louis Railway Co., $1,000 refunding and improvement, 4-1/2% mortgage bond, series E, vignette of two steam engines traveling thru tunnel, American Bank Note Co., 10 attached coupons...................... **$20**
West Shore RR, NY, $10,000 bond, brown and black, Hudson River panorama with trains, loading dock, steam ships, distant mountains, second vignette on reverse with bald eagle, canceled, American Bank Note Co............................. **$15**

Book
1900 Chicago Rock Island & Pacific History, Biographical Publishing Co., 756 pages, CRIP and representative employees, beautiful tooled and gilt engine dec cover, gilt edges, center signatures are loose **$260**
Southern Pacific Color Guide to Freight & Passenger Equipment, Vol. 1, Anthony Thompson, 128 pgs, hardcover **$30**
Western Maryland Diesel Locomotives, P. Salem, hardcover **$35**
Western Pacific Locomotives & Cars, Patrick C. Dorn, hardcover
.... **$35**

Booklet, *Quiz Jr Railroad Questions and Answers,* green and black, printed by Assoc. of American Railroads, 1955 .... **$10**

Brake gauge, Westinghouse, brass, two dial indicators, 140 lbs, 6-1/2" d
.... **$35**

Builders plate
Corps of Engineers U.S. Army 45-ton Diesel Electric Locomotive Manufactured by Vulcan Iron Works, cast bronze, dated 1941, 11" x 6"...... **$85**
Fairbanks-Morse, stainless steel, etched letters on enamel ground, serial #166-972, 1955, 17" x 8"
.... **$115**

Calendar
New York Central, illustration depicting travel in 1830 and 1920, timetables for various lines in margins, some minor losses, period oak frame, 1922, 18" x 30" **$265**
Soo Line, illus, Lake Louise Alberta by R. Atkinson Fox, later oak frame and mat, 1930, overall 34" x 29"
.... **$230**

Calendar plate, Pennsylvania Lines, after a painting by Grif Teller, framed, 1949, 30" x 23" **$35**

Check
Philadelphia & Erie RR Co., Pennsylvania, drawn on Phila National Bank, fancy script bank title, black on white, 1902
.... **$8.50**
Rocky Fork & Cooke City RR, Montana territory, fancy script bank title, hand stamped in blue above bank title, cut cancel, March 1899
.... **$18**

Cap
Agent, Soo Line, pill box style, embroidered "Agent" and "Soo Line," labeled "Marshall Field & Co. Chicago," size 7 .... **$50**
Brakeman's, open-weave crown, missing name plate, labeled "A. G. Meier & Co. Chicago," size 6-3/4......... **$35**
Railroad Conductors, labeled "A.G. Meier & CO. Chicago," size 7-1/4
.... **$95**

Crimper, railroad seal, nickel plate, dies marked "CNS & M. R. R. Co.," handle emb "Porter Safety Seal Co.," 7" l................**$115**

Cuspidor

Missouri Pacific Railroad, white porcelain on metal, black "MOPAC" lettering, minor loss, 7-1/2" d **$150**

Texas & Pacific Railroad, white porcelain on metal, blue lettering, minor loss, 8" d................**$260**

Date stamp, Atlantic Coast Line Railroad, c1940, Defiance Stamp Co., 4" h................**$35**

Depot clock, electric, oak case, hinged face, marked "Property of the Ball RR Time Service St. Paul, Minn," patent date 1908, 21" sq................**$210**

Depot sign, Rock Island System, reverse painted and mother of pearl, Chicago, Rock Island & Pacific 4-4-0 locomotive #476 pulling 11 cars, against tree-lined Midwest route, orig oak ogee frame with gilt liner, c1890, overall 50" x 22"................**$23,000**

Directory, *Soo Line Shippers Directory, Vol. III*, softcover, 644 pgs, gilt, ads, illus, two-pg Soo Line map, four color maps of Michigan, Minnesota, North Dakota, Wisconsin, 1918-19 ....**$60**

Fire bucket, Missouri, Kansas & Texas Railroad, orig red paint, stenciled "Fire," emb "MK&T," 12" h................**$60**

Flare and flag box, Gulf Mobile & Ohio, tin, stenciled letters, contains flag and fuses, 30" l................**$20**

Hollowware

Coffee pot, silver plate, Chicago & Eastern Illinois, 10-oz size, marked "Reed & Barton 086-H, C&E.I.RY. CO" on base, 7" h................**$265**

Coffee server, silvered, Nashville, Chattanooga & St. Louis, applied emb "N.C.& St. L" logo on front, gooseneck spout, long wood handle, backstamped "Reed & Barton 482-32 oz, N.C. & St. L" **$520**

Sauce tureen, silvered, Chicago Great Western Railway, two handles, lid. backstamped "C.G.W.R.R.–Reed & Barton," 8" l................**$125**

Sugar bowl, silvered, New York Central, imp "NYC" on hinged lid, 3-3/4" h **$50**

Teapot, silvered, Missouri Pacific & Iron Mountain, 10-oz size, front engraved "M.P.I.Mt.RY," backstamped "Missouri Pacific & Iron Mountain R. Wallace 03295," 4-1/2" h **$230**

Illustration, Great Northern Railway, orig illus for cover of travel brochure, scenic marvel of America, Glacier National Park, full-color gouache on paper, detailed study, c1920, 9-1/2" x 14", 1/2" margins **$315**

Jug, Baltimore & Ohio, stoneware, brown cone top, one gal, 11-1/2" **$210**

Kerosene can, Chicago & Northwestern, one gal, oxidized finish, emb "C&NRR," 13" h **$25**

Lantern

Adam & Westlake Co., Adlake Reliable, red 5-1/4" globe with P.R.R. stamped on top, Adlake #300 kero burner, orig wick **$75**

Conger Lantern Co., Twin-Bulb, battery operated, chromed, bulbs missing................**$15**

Dietz

Fitzall, Inspectors, clear globe etched "NYC Lines," raised "Dietz Fitzall NYUSA"................**$195**

Hi-Top, Vesta, clear globe, raised "US" and "Dietz Vesta" logo, bronze plated, rusted through kero pot **$48**

No. 999, NYC system, red Fresnel globe, Dietz convex kero burner, "NYCS" stamped on top **$95**

Letter opener, Southern Pacific, orig case, 7-3/4" l................**$30**

Locomotive nose plate, Frisco, black, heavy 1/8" stainless steel, 28" l **$1,150**

Map

Chicago, Iowa, and Nebraska Railroad, color litho, published by J. Sage & Sons, Buffalo, New York, some discoloration and losses, mounted on linen, 1859, 26" x 23" **$450**

Soo Line, Minneapolis, St. Paul, and Sault Ste. Marie RY, printed by Matthews, Northrup & Co. Buffalo, New York, c1890, 39" x 16" **$130**

Williams Telegraph and Railroad Map of the New England States, by Alexander Williams, published by Redding & Co. Boston, printed table of construction costs for area railroads, hand-colored state borders, separated folds with later linen backing, some toning, dated 1852, 32" x 30" **$60**

Name plate, Soo Line, cast aluminum, mounted on walnut back board, 24" l **$95**

Operation manual, New York Air Brake Co., 1909, 4-1/2" x 7" **$5**

Paperweight, Adlake Centennial, extruded aluminum, 1857-1957, 5" l **$40**

Pass, PRR, black and red on blue, 1940 ....**$5**

Photo

Chicago, Rock Island & Pacific, Rocky Mountains, orig frame, c1910, 7" mat, 53" x 23"................**$920**

Denver & Rio Grande Railroad Depot, Canyon of the Rio Las Animas, Colo, hand colored black and white print, printed logo and title, "Copyright 1900 by Detroit Photographic Co.," orig oak frame, stains in margin, overall 33-1/2" x 27-1/2" **$2,645**

Machinist Apprentices of the Chicago & Alton R.R., dated Sept. 5th 1908, depicting 34 apprentices posed on C & A R.R. locomotive #605, Stafford B. Cable photo, Bloomington, Illinois, orig frame and mat, 17" x 11" image size **$490**

Soo Line, Lake Louise, hand-colored black and white print, orig titled mat with Soo Line logo, orig oak frame, early 20th C, overall 25" x 21"................**$50**

Pinback button

Chesapeake & Ohio Railway Veteran Employees Assn, 21st annual meeting, Cincinnati Zoo, June 26, 1937 ....**$20**

Division 241, American Assn of Street & Electric Railway Employees of America, purple and pink membership button................**$20**

Reading Lines, red image, white logo, green rim, c1930s................**$20**

Poster, Greater Power, The New Haven Railroad, Latham Litho, Long Island City, Sascha Mauer, used to celebrate 50th anniversary and new locomotives, 41-1/2" x 27-1/2"................**$2,185**

Print, *Loco-Erie Watering*, etching, Reginald Marsh, sgd in pencil, 1929, 7" x 10" **$1,955**

Receipt

Baltimore and Ohio Assoc of Railways Surgeons, for membership dues, 1933................**$5**

Baltimore and Ohio Railroad, freight bill, for shingles, sgd by agent W. L. Gross, 1884 ....**$12**

Steam whistle, brass

Single chime, lever control, 1884 ....**$200**

Triple chime, manufactured by Crosby Steam, Gage & Valve Company, Boston, Pat. Jan. 30, 1877, 5-1/2" d, 12" h **$720**

Step ladder, ST.L.K & N-W Railroad, folding, wooden, four steps, stenciled "St.L.K&N W" and "Mail Car 103" **$270**

Step stool, Denver & Rio Grande Western RR, rubber no-skid top, 9" h **$260**

Stock certificate

Buffalo, Rochester and Pittsburgh Railway Co., New York, train at station at left, miners working at right, 100 shares, common, red-brown design, ornate border, Franklin Bank Note Co., New York **$30**

Cincinnati and Fort Wayne Railroad, Indiana, small train on left edge, common stock **$40**

Little Miami Railroad Co., Cincinnati, Ohio, vignette of Tom Thumb engine and cars with passengers and watchers, hole cancel, American Bank Note Co.................**$22.50**

Washington Railway & Electric Co., Washington, DC, vignette of trolley car in busy city, green, 100 shares, Western Bank Note Co., Chicago **$24**

Ticket

Niagara Gorge RR Co., Great Gorge Route, 1900, 2-1/4" x 1-5/16" **$12**

International Railway Co., Buffalo, New York, strip of five employees tickets, engraved title, Security Bank Note Co., Philadelphia, reverse with four digit number and "Not Good for Women or Children," 1903, 1-5/8" l, 11/16" w.............**$18**

Ticket cabinet, Soo Line, oak, locking tambour slant front, divided compartments for tickets, timetables, one drawer, stenciled "M.ST.P. & S.S.M.RY" on back, c1914, 21" x 35" x 16" **$460**

Timetable, 4" x 8-1/2"

Atlantic Coast, 1954 ....**$2.50**
Delaware & Hudson, 1951 ....**$2.50**
Lehigh Valley, 1951 ....**$3.50**
New York Central, 1946 ....**$2.50**
Santa Fe, 1959.............................**$2.50**
Seaboard, 1924-25..........................**$5**
Southern Pacific, 1912 ....**$4**

Tray, Soo Line, Montana Success, map of Soo Line Route, tin litho, 10-1/2" x 15"...**$200**

Wax sealer

American Exchange Co., El Paso, Ill, brass die with wood handle, 3" l **$150**

S.W. & B.V. RR, Agent-Bryan, Texas, one-piece brass die and handle, 2-1/2" l..**$550**

Toledo, Peoria & Western, Agent-El Paso, Ill, brass die, wood handle, 4" l..**$525**

RECORDS

History: With the advent of the more sophisticated recording materials, such as 33-1/3 RPM long-playing records, 8-track tapes, cassettes, and compact discs, earlier phonograph records became collectors' items. Most have little value. The higher-priced items are rare (limited-production) recordings. Condition is critical.

All records start with a master tape of an artist's or groups' performance. To make a record, a mastering agent would play the master tape and feed the sound to a cutting lathe which electronically transcribes the music into the grooves of a circular black lacquer disc, known as an acetate. The acetate was played to determine if the sound quality was correct, to listen for defects or timing errors, order of presentation, etc. The finished acetate was then sprayed with a metal film. Once the film dries, the acetate is peeled away, creating a new "master" with a raised groove pattern. Another metallic compound is sprayed on the new "master" and after this compound is removed, a "mother" disc is created. The "mother" disc is then coated with another metallic compound, and when that is removed, a "stamper" is made. Pertinent production information is often written on the stamper before it is pressed in the production process. Each two-sided record has two stampers, one for each side.

The material used for early 45s and LPs was polyvinyl chloride (PVC), and commonly called "vinyl." To make a record, hot PVC is pressed between the stampers using a compression molding process. Excess vinyl that is trimmed away after the pressing process is recycled. When this re-cycled material is reused, it may result in a record that looks grainy or pockmarked. Each stamper was good for about 1,000 pressings, then the whole process began again. Vinyl is still used for LPs, but polystyrene is now used for 45s. The production process for polystyrene is slightly different in that the base material is more liquid. Application of labels can be made directly to the polystyrene record, eliminating the label stamping process used with vinyl. To tell the difference between vinyl and styrene records, consider the following points:

Vinyl records are thicker and heavier.

7-inch vinyl 45s won't bend.

A label of one color with information "engraved" or spray painted in the center indicates a styrene record.

As with many types of antiques, a grading scale has been developed.

Mint (M): Perfect condition, no flaws, scratches, or scuffs in the grooves. The cardboard jacket will be crisp.

Near Mint (NM) or Mint-Minus (M-): The record will be close to perfect, with no marks in the grooves. The label will be clean, not marked, or scuffed. There will be no ring wear on the record or album cover.

Very Good Plus (VG+): Used for a record that has been played, but well taken care of. Slight scuffle or warps to the grooves is acceptable as long as it does not affect the sound. A faint ring wear discoloration is acceptable. The jacket may appear slightly worn, especially on the edges.

The records by Glenn Miller and his Orchestra, arguably the most recognizable of swing artists, are easy to find today—this four-record 78-RPM "Smart Set" features many of Miller's biggest hits, including "Pennsylvania 6-5000" and "Chattanooga Choo Choo," VG, **$10.**

Very Good (VG): Used to describe a record that has some pronounced defects, as does the cover. The record will still play well. This usually is the lowest grade acceptable to a serious collector. Most records listed in price guides are of this grade.

Good (G): This category of record will be playable, but probably will have loss to the sound quality. Careful inspection of a styrene record in this condition may allow the viewer to see white in the grooves. The cover might be marked or torn.

Poor or Fair (P, F): Record is damaged, may be difficult to play. The cover will be damaged condition, usually marked, dirty, or torn.

Notes: Most records, especially popular recordings, have a value of less than $3 per disc. The records listed here are classic recordings of their type and are in demand by collectors. Picture sleeves will generally increase values, and often have an independent value.

Additional Resources:

Goldmine™ Record Album Price Guide, 4th Ed., by Tim Neely, Krause Publications, Iola, WI.

Goldmine™ Price Guide to 45 RPM Records, 5th Ed., by Tim Neely, Krause Publications, Iola, WI.

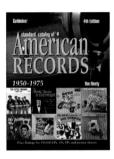

Standard Catalog of® American Records 1950-1975, 4th Ed., by Tim Neely, Krause Publications, Iola, WI.

Warman's® American Records, 2nd Ed., by Chuck Miller, Krause Publications, Iola, WI.

Warman's® Americana & Collectibles, 11th Ed., by Ellen T. Schroy, ed., Krause Publications, Iola, WI.

45s

The Bay City Rollers, Bell
45169, "Keep On Dancing"/"Alright," 1972 .... **$5-$10**
45618, "All of Me Loves All of You"/ "The Bump," 1974 .... **$7.50-$15**

Pat Boone, Mono 45s, Dot
15377, "Ain't That a Shame"/ "Tennessee Saturday Night," 1955 .... **$10-$20**
15443, "Tutti Frutti"/"I'll Be Home," 1956 .... **$10-$20**
15472, "I Almost Lost My Mind"/ "I'm in Love with You," 1956 .... **$10-$20**

15660, "April Love"/"When the Swallows Come Back to Capistrano," 1957 .... **$7.50-$15**
15955, "Twixt Twelve and Twenty"/"Rock Boll Weevil," 1959 .... **$7.50-$15**
15982, "Fools Hall of Fame"/"The Brightest Wishing Star," 1959 .... **$7.50-$15**
16209, "Moody River"/"A Thousand Years," 1961 .... **$7.50-$15**

David Bowie, RCA Victor
APBO-0001, "Time"/"The Prettiest Star," 1973 .... **$3-$6**
PB-10152, "Young Americans"/ "Knock on Wood," 1975 .... **$3-$6**
PB-10441, "Golden Years"/"Can You Hear Me," 1975 .... **$2-$4**

The Birds, Columbia
43271, "Mr. Tambourine Man"/ "I Knew I'd Want You," 1965 .... **$7.50-$15**
43578, "Eight Miles High"/"Why," 1966 .... **$6-$12**

The Captain and Tennille, Butterscotch Castle 001, "The Way I Want To Touch You"/"Disney Girls" (independent first pressing), 1974 ...... **$40-$80**

Creedence Clearwater Revival, Fantasy
617, "I Put A Spell On You"/"Walk on the Water," 1968 .... **$4-$8**
619, "Proud Mary"/"Born on the Bayou," 1969 .... **$3-$6**
637, "Travelin' Band"/"Who'll Stop The Rain," 1970 .... **$3-$6**

The 5th Dimension, Soul City
752, "I'll Be Loving You Forever"/ "Train, Keep On Moving," 1966 .... **$30-$60**
756, "Up-Up and Away"/"Which Way To Nowhere," 1967 .... **$4-$8**

Fleetwood Mac, Reprise 1345, "Rhiannon (Will You Ever Win)"/"Sugar Daddy," 1976 .... **$2-$4**

Michael Jackson, Epic
9-50742, "Don't Stop 'Til You Get Enough"/"I Can't Help It," 1979 .... **$2-$4**
34-03509, "Billie Jean"/"Can't Get Outta the Rain," 1983 .... **$2-$4**
34-78000, "Scream"/"Childhood," 1995 .... **$1.50-$3**
34-79656, "You Rock My World" (same on both sides), 2001 ..... **$1-$2**

Billy Joel, Family Productions 0900, "She's Got A Way"/"Everybody Loves You Now," 1971 .... **$12.50-$25**

Kenny Rogers, Carlton 454, Kenneth Rogers, "That Crazy Feeling"/

The Little Engine That Could, *narrated by Paul Wing, RCA Victor, NM,* **$40.**
Photo credit: Bozo record, Peter Muldavin collection; Little Nipper pressing.

Roy Orbison's picture sleeves are getting harder and harder to find. Here's one for his song "Crying" VG+ sleeve, **$30.**
Photo credit: From the collection of Val Shively.

Rare Ronettes album, LP, includes the tracks "Be My Baby," "Baby I Love You," and "Walkin' in the Rain," Good condition, **$200.**

"We'll Always Have Each Other," 1958 .... **$50-$100**

Blues

Jackie Brenston And His Delta Cats, 78s, Chess
1458, "Rocket 88"/"Come Back Where You Belong," 1949 .... **$150-$300**
1472, "Juiced"/"Independent Woman," 1951 .... **$100-$200**
Ida Cox, 78s, Paramount
12053, "Any Woman's Blues"/"Blue Monday Blues," 1923 .... **$60-$120**
12085," Mama Doo Shea Blues"/ "Worried Mama Blues," 1924 .... **$70-$140**
Lightnin' Hopkins, 45s, Jax
315, "No Good Woman"/"Been a Bad Man" (red vinyl), 1953 .... **$150-$300**
318, "Automobile"/"Organ Blues" (red vinyl), 1953 .... **$150-$300**
321, "Contrary Mary"/"I'm Begging You" (red vinyl), 1953 .... **$150-$300**
Papa Charlie Jackson, 78s, Paramount
12305, "Mama, Don't You Think I Know?"/"Hot Papa Blues," 1925 .... **$75-$150**
12320, "All I Want is a Spoonful"/ "Maxwell Street Blues," 1925 .... **$50-$100**
Blind Lemon Jefferson, 78s, Paramount
12347, "Booster Blues"/"Dry Southern Blues," 1926 .... **$500-$1,000**
12493, "Weary Dog Blues"/"Hot Dogs," 1926 .... **$500-$1,000**
12650, "Piney Woods Mama Blues"/ "Low Down Mojo Blues" (label has a portrait of Jefferson, record is designated as "Blind Lemon Jefferson Birthday Record"), 1928 .... **$750-$1,500**
B.B. King, 78s, Bullet
309, "Miss Martha King"/"When Your Baby Packs Up and Goes," 1949 .... **$500-$1,000**
315, "Got the Blues"/"Take a Swing with Me," 1949 .... **$350-$700**
Bessie Smith, 78s, Columbia
13007-D, "Far Away Blues"/"I'm Going Back to My Used To Be," 1924 .... **$60-$120**
14056-D, "Reckless Blues"/"Sobbin' Hearted Blues," 1925 .... **$80-$160**
Stevie Ray Vaughan And Double Trouble, LPs, Epic
BFE 38734, Texas Flood, 1983 .... **$5-$10**
FE 39304, Couldn't Stand the Weather, 1984 .... **$5-$10**

Children's

101 Dalmatians, (original motion picture soundtrack), LPs, Disneyland
ST-1908, mono, 1960 .... **$12.50-$25**
ST-4903, mono, gatefold cover with pop-up scene in center, 1963 .... **$75-$150**
ST-3931, mono, 1965 .... **$20-$40**
Ray Bolger, 78, Decca CU 102, "The Churkendoose," 1947 .... **$25-$50**
Betty Boop, 7-inch 78, Durotone R-81, Betty Boop in "Peter and Wendy"/ Betty Boop in "She Loves Him Not," 193? .... **$20-$40**
Bozo The Clown, 78s, Capitol
DAS-3046, Bozo Laughs, 1946 .... **$7.50-$15**
BBX65, Bozo and His Rocket Ship, 2 78s with book, 1947 .... **$10-$20**
DBS-84, Bozo Sings, 2 78s in gatefold sleeve, 1948 .... **$10-$20**
DBX-3076, Bozo on the Farm, 2 78s with book, 1950 .... **$10-$20**
The Electric Company, LP, Sesame Street 22052, The Electric Company, 1974 .... **$7.50-$15**
Goldilocks And The Three Bears, 78, Capitol DB-121, Goldilocks and the Three Bears, Margaret O'Brien, narrator, 1948 .... **$5-$10**
Little Nipper Series, 78-RPM records in folio, RCA Victor
Y-383, The Adventures Of Little Black Sambo, 1949 .... **$25-$50**
Y-385, Pinocchio, 1949 .... **$20-$40**
Y-397, Howdy Doody and the Air-O-Doodle, 1949........................ **$25-$50**
Y-414, Howdy Doody's Laughing Circus, 1949 .... **$20-$40**
Y-438, Winnie-the-Pooh No. 1, James Stewart, narrator, 1949 ...... **$30-$60**
Y-446, It's Howdy Doody Time, 1951 .... **$30-$60**

Country, LP

Eddy Arnold, LPs, RCA Victor
LPM-3753, Lonely Again, mono, 1967...................................... **$10-$20**
LSP-3753, same title, stereo, 1967 .... **$7.50-$15**
Gene Autry, 78, Banner 32349, "That Silver Haired Daddy of Mine"/ "Mississippi Valley Blues," 1931 .... **$35-$70**
The Carter Family, 78s
"Can the Circle Be Unbroken (By and By)"/"Glory to the Lamb"
(if on Perfect 13155, Oriola 8484, Banner 33465, Romeo 5484, Melotone 13432, or Conqueror 8529, value is equal), 1935 .... **$25-$50**

The Freewheelin' Bob Dylan, *with the "360 Sound" reference visible on original 1963 release, NM,* **$50.**

Stevie Ray Vaughan picture disc for his LP "Couldn't Stand the Weather," VG+ NM condition, **$100.**

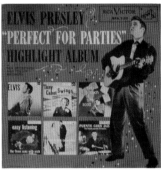

Although this six-song promotional EP contains only one Elvis Presley song, "Love Me," Presley introduces songs from several other artists, VG+, **$50.**

(if on Vocalion 03027, reissue), 1937
.... **$20-$40**
(if on OKeh 03027, reissue), 1940
.... **$15-$30**
(if on Columbia 37669, reissue), 1947
.... **$10-$20**
(if on Columbia 20268, reissue), 1948
.... **$10-$20**

Wilf Carter, 78s, Bluebird
4966, "My Swiss Moonlight Lullaby"/ "The Capture Of Albert Johnson," 1933 .... **$20-$40**
4600, "My Little Swiss and Me"/"I Long for Old Wyoming," 193??
.... **$15-$30**
4624, "Old Alberta Plains"/"Won't You Be the Same Old Pal," 193??
.... **$15-$30**

Johnny Cash, 45s, Sun
241, "I Walk The Line"/"Get Rhythm," 1956 .... **$20-$40**
283, "Ballad of a Teenage Queen"/"Big River," 1958 .... **$12.50-$25**

Patsy Cline, 45s, Decca
30221, "Walkin' After Midnight"/"A Poor Man's Roses (Or a Rich Man's Gold)," 1957 .... **$10-$20**
31317, "Crazy"/"Who Can I Count On," 1961 .... **$6-$12**

Billy "Crash" Craddock, 45, ABC Dot 17659, "Broken Down in Tiny Pieces"/"Shake It Easy," 1976 .... **$2-$4**

Vernon Dalhart, 78, Victor 19427, "The Prisoner's Song"/"Wreck of the Old '97" (A-side recorded for several different record companies), 1924
.... **$10-$20**

Dale Evans, 78, Majestic 11025, "Under a Texas Moon"/"His Hat Cost More Than Mine," 194?? ...... **$10-$20**

The Everly Brothers, 45s, Cadence
1315, "Bye Bye Love"/"I Wonder If I Care As Much," 1957
.... **$12.50-$25**

1337, "Wake Up Little Susie"/"Maybe Tomorrow," 1957 .... **$15-$30**

Merle Haggard, LPs, Capitol
ST 638, A Tribute to the Best Damn Fiddle Player in the World (Or, My Salute to Bob Wills), 1970
.... **$12.50-$25**

Emmylou Harris, 45, Jubilee 5679, "I'll Be Your Baby Tonight"/"I'll Never Fall In Love Again," 1969 ...... **$10-$20**

Homer And Jethro, LP, RCA Victor LPM-1560, The Worst of Homer and Jethro (RCA Victor LPM-1560), 1958
.... **$25-$50**

Waylon Jennings, 45s
Ramco 1997, "My World"/"Another Blue Day," 1968 .... **$6-$12**
RCA PB-10924, "Luckenbach, Texas (Back to the Basics of Love)"/"Belle of the Ball," 1977 .... **$2.50-$5**

Brenda Lee, 45, Decca 31309, "Fool #1"/"Anybody But Me," 1961
.... **$7.50-$15**

Jerry Lee Lewis, LP, Mercury SR-61366, Who's Gonna Play This Old Piano ... (Think About It Darlin'), 1972 .... **$7.50-$15**

Loretta Lynn, 45s, Zero
107, "I'm A Honky Tonk Girl"/ "Whispering Sea," 1960 . **$250-$500**
112, "The Darkest Day"/"Gonna Pack My Troubles," 1961 .... **$200-$400**

Willie Nelson, 45s
Belaire 107, "Night Life"/"Rainy Day Blues," 1963 .... **$15-$30**
(if pressed on colored vinyl), 1963
.... **$30-$60**
Sarg 260, "A Storm Has Just Begun"/ "When I Sing My Last Hillbilly Song," 196? .... **$25-$50**
Columbia 10176, "Blue Eyes Cryin' in the Rain"/"Bandera," 1975 .... **$2.50-$5**

Dolly Parton, 45s
Gold Band 1086, "Puppy Love"/"Girl Left Alone," 1959 .... **$300-$600**

Monument 982, "Dumb Blonde"/ "The Giving and the Taking," 1967
.... **$5-$10**
RCA Victor APBO-0145, "Jolene"/ "You're So Beautiful Tonight," 1973
.... **$2.50-$5**

The Sons Of The Pioneers, 78s, Decca
5047, "Tumbling Tumbleweeds"/ "Moonlight on the Prairie," 1934
.... **$15-$30**
5939, "Cool Water"/"So Long to the Red River Valley," 1941
.... **$12.50-$25**

Hank Williams, LPs
MGM E-168, Moanin' the Blues (10-inch LP), 1952 .... **$200-$400**
MGM PRO-912, Reflections of Those Who Loved Him (3 LPs) (promo-only box set), 1975
.... **$125-$250**

Jazz

Cannonball Adderly, Stereo LPs, Blue Note
BST-1595, Somethin' Else
(if deep groove pressed into label), 1959 .... **$50-$100**
(if West 63rd Street address on label), 1959 .... **$37.50-$75**
(if New York USA address on label), 1963 .... **$10-$20**

Louis Armstrong, 45s
Decca 29102, "Basin Street Blues" (Pt. 1)/(Pt. 2), 1954 .... **$7.50-$15**
Kapp 573, "Hello Dolly!"/"A Lot Of Lovin' To Do," 1964 .... **$3-$6**
(with picture sleeve, add), 1964*
.... **$5-$10**

Count Basie, 10-inch LPs
Clef MCG-120, Count Basie and His Orchestra Collates, 1953
.... **$100-$200**

EmArcy MG-26023, Jazz Royalty, 1954..................**$35-$70**

Art Blakey And The Jazz Messengers, Mono LPs
Blue Note BLP-1507, At the Café Bohemia, Volume 1
(if "deep groove" indentation on label), 1956......................**$75-$150**
(if regular version, Lexington Ave. address on label), 1956 ....**$50-$100**
Jubilee JLP-1049, Cu-Bop, 1958 ....**$40-$80**

Clifford Brown, Mono LPs
EmArcy MG-36005, Clifford Brown with Strings, 1955 ....**$60-$120**
Blue Note BLP-1526, Clifford Brown Memorial Album
(if deep groove indentation in label), 1956..................**$100-$200**
(if regular edition, Lexington Ave. address on label), 1956 ....**$75-$150**
(if "New York, U.S.A." address on label), 196?..................**$12.50-$25**
(if W. 63rd St. address on label), 196? ....**$25-$50**

Dave Brubeck, 45s
Fantasy 524, "Stardust"/"Lulu's Back in Town," 1953..................**$7.50-$15**
Columbia 41479, "Take Five"/"Blue Rondo A La Turk," 1960 ......**$6-$12**

Cab Calloway, 78s, Brunswick
6209, "Kickin' the Gong Around"/"Between the Devil and the Deep Blue Sea," 1931 ....**$7.50-$15**
6511, "Minnie the Moocher"/"Kickin' the Gong Around," 1931 ....**$10-$20**

John Coltrane, 45s
Impulse! 203, "Easy to Remember"/"Greensleeves," 1961 ....**$5-$10**
Prestige 267, "Stardust"/"Love Thy Neighbor," 1961 ....**$6-$12**

Miles Davis, 45s
Capitol F1221, "Venus de Milo"/"Darn That Dream," 1950 ......**$12.50-$25**
Columbia 42057, "It Ain't Necessarily So"/"All Blues," 1961..........**$6-$12**
42069, "I Loves You, Porgy"/"It Ain't Necessarily So," 1961..........**$6-$12**

Kenny Drew, 10-inch LPs
Blue Note BLP-5023, Introducing the Kenny Drew Trio, 1953 ....**$200-$400**
Norgran MGM-29, The Ideation of Kenny Drew, 1954 ....**$125-$250**

Duke Ellington, 45s
RCA Victor 47-2955, "The Sidewalks Of New York"/"Don't Get Around Much Anymore," 1949 ......**$10-$20**

Capitol F2458, "Satin Doll"/"Without A Song," 1953..................**$6-$12**

Ella Fitzgerald, Stereo LPs
Verve V6-4053, Clap Hands, Here Comes Charley, 1962........**$75-$150**
Atlantic SD 1631, Ella Loves Cole, 1972..................**$6-$12**

Stan Getz, 10-inch LPs
Savoy MG-9004, New Sounds in Modern Music, 1951..............**$150-$300**
Prestige PRLP-102, Stan Getz and the Tenor Sax Stars, 1951 ....**$100-$200**
Roost R-407, Jazz at Storyville, 1952 ....**$75-$150**

Billie Holiday, 10-inch LPs
Columbia CL 6129, Billie Holiday Sings, 1950..................**$100-$200**
Decca DL 5345, Lover Man, 1951 ....**$100-$200**

Ma Rainey, 10-inch LPs, Riverside
RLP-1003, Ma Rainey, Vol. 1, 1953 ....**$125-$250**
RLP-1016, Ma Rainey, Vol. 2, 1953 ....**$125-$250**
RLP-1045, Ma Rainey, Vol. 3, 1954 ....**$125-$250**

Rock

Paul Anka, 45s, ABC-Paramount
9831, "Diana"/"Don't Gamble with Love," 1957..................**$10-$20**
10082, "Puppy Love"/"Adam and Eve," 1960..................**$7.50-$15**

Annette, 45s, Buena Vista
349, "First Name Initial"/"My Heart Became of Age," 1959......**$7.50-$15**
414, "Teenage Wedding"/"Walkin' and Talkin'," 1962..................**$10-$20**
433, "Muscle Beach Party"/"I Dream About Frankie," 1964 ......**$7.50-$15**

Frankie Avalon, Stereo LPs, Chancellor
CHLXS 5004, Swingin' on a Rainbow, 1959..................**$25-$50**
CHLS 5027, You're Mine, 1962 ....**$20-$40**

Chuck Berry, 45s, Chess
1604, "Maybellene"/"Wee Wee Hours," 1955..................**$25-$50**
1626, "Roll Over Beethoven"/"Drifting Heart," 1956..................**$25-$50**
1671, "Rock & Roll Music"/"Blue Feeling," 1957..................**$15-$30**
1691, "Johnny B. Goode"/"Around and Around," 1958 ....**$15-$30**
1729, "Back in the U.S.A."/"Memphis Tennessee," 1959..................**$15-$30**

Chubby Checker, 45s, Parkway
804, "The Class"/"Schooldays, Oh Schooldays," 1959..............**$15-$30**

811, "The Twist"/"Toot" (first pressings, white label, blue print), 1960 ....**$15-$30**
811, "The Twist"/"Twistin' U.S.A.," 1961..................**$7.50-$15**
824, "Let's Twist Again"/"Everything's Gonna Be Alright," 1961 ....**$7.50-$15**

Dee Clark, Mono LPs, Abner
LP-2000, Dee Clark, 1959 ....**$60-$120**
LP-2002, How About That, 1960 ....**$40-$80**

Bo Diddley, LPs
Checker LP 1431, Bo Diddley, 1958 ....**$75-$150**
LP 2974, Have Guitar, Will Travel, 1960..................**$75-$150**
LP 2977, Bo Diddley Is a Gunslinger, 1961..................**$75-$150**

Fats Domino, 45s, Imperial
45-5058, "The Fat Man"/"Detroit City Blues" (blue-label "script" logo, pressed around 1952, counterfeits exist), 1950................**$1,000-$2,000**
45-5209, "How Long"/"Dreaming," 1952..................**$40-$80**
(if on red vinyl), 1952 ......**$150-$300**
X5369, "Poor Me"/"I Can't Go On," 1955..................**$12.50-$25**
X5407, "Blueberry Hill"/"Honey Chile" (black vinyl, red label), 1956 ....**$12.50-$25**
X5417, "Blue Monday"/"What's the Reason I'm Not Pleasing You," 1957 ....**$12.50-$25**

The Everly Brothers, 45s, Cadence
1337, "Wake Up Little Susie"/"Maybe Tomorrow," 1957 ....**$15-$30**
1348, "All I Have to Do Is Dream"/"Claudette," 1958 ....**$12.50-$25**

Fabian, 45s, Chancellor
1033, "Turn Me Loose"/"Stop Thief!," 1959..................**$10-$20**
1037, "Tiger"/"Mighty Cold (To a Warm, Warm Heart)," 1959 ....**$10-$20**

Bill Haley And His Comets, 7-inch EP, Decca ED 2168, Shake, Rattle and Roll (contains "Shake, Rattle and Roll"/"A.B.C. Boogie"/"(We're Gonna) Rock Around the Clock"/"Thirteen Women (And Only One Man in Town)," value is for record and jacket), 1954 ....**$60-$120**

Buddy Holly, 45s, Decca
29854, "Blue Days, Black Nights"/"Love Me" (with star under "Decca"), 1956 ....**$150-$300**
34034, "That'll Be the Day"/"Rock Around with Ollie Vee" (with

star under "Decca"), 1957 .... **$125-$250**

62074, "It Doesn't Matter Anymore"/ "Raining in My Heart," 1959 .... **$20-$40**

62134, "Peggy Sue Got Married"/ "Crying, Waiting, Hoping," 1959 .... **$30-$60**

62210, "True Love Ways"/"That Makes It Tough," 1960 .... **$25-$50**

Roy Orbison, Stereo LPs, Monument SM-14002, Lonely and Blue, 1961 .... **$300-$600**

SM-14007, Crying, 1962 .... **$300-$600**

SLP-18003, In Dreams (white-rainbow label), 1963 .... **$50-$100**

The Ronettes, 45s

Colpix 601, "I Want a Boy"/"Sweet Sixteen" (as "Ronnie and the Relatives"), 1961 .... **$50-$100**

Philles 116, "Be My Baby"/"Tedesco and Pittman," 1963 .... **$15-$30**

118, "Baby I Love You"/"Miss Joan and Mr. Sam," 1963 .... **$15-$30**

RELIGIOUS ITEMS

History: Objects used in worship or as expressions of man's belief in a superhuman power are collected by many people for many reasons.

This category includes icons, since they are religious mementos, usually paintings with a brass encasement. Collecting icons dates from the earliest period of Christianity. Most antique icons in today's market were made in the late 19th century.

Reproduction Alert. Icons are frequently reproduced.

Altar crucifix, wood frame overlaid with repoussé copper, cabochons, paste stones, verso with compartment for relic, 24" h **$550**

Architectural relief of saint, carved walnut, male figure holding pair of keys, standing in arched niche, traces of gilding, Continental, set into velvet framed open shadow box, late 17th/ early 18th C, 16-1/8" w, 25-5/8" h **$1,650**

Bronze

Amida in appeasement mudra, bronze, partial gilt, boxed, China, 19th C, 6" h **$2,820**

Amytaus, gilt bronze, China, 18th C, 8" h **$1,410**

Stone, bust, old tan color, 16-1/4" h, 12-1/4" w, 8" d **$415**

Wood, carved, standing image of Amida, ornate throne, halo at back, gilt surface, Japan, losses, 19th C, 21" h **$650**

Young features, crane at his feet, Chinese, slight wear to patina, 19th C **$850**

Buddha

Coral, carved, sitting position, base carved flat and with sedimentary inclusions, two-character signature, China, 18th or 19th C **$420**

Bust

Gilded metal Immaculate Heart of Mary and the Sacred Heart of Jesus, onyx pedestal with flared base, French, price for pr, c1920, 10-1/2" h **$320**

Veiled Madonna, hand painted porcelain, Royal Worcester, 1863, 11-1/2" h **$1,495**

Candlestick, Ciborium-form, silver plated, quatrefoil crown-form sconce, over cathedral-form stem with pointed arches and flying buttresses, square section standard, base with clipped corners and recumbent lion-form feet, conforming marble plinth base, Gothic Revival, C. Nisini, Rome, late 19th C, 38-1/2" h **$650**

Chalice and paten

Engraved and partial gilt sterling, French, c1920, 9" h **$815**

Heavy solid gilded silver, Gothic style, c1922, 9-1/4" h **$1,065**

Partial gilt sterling, c1920, 9-1/2" h **$700**

Sterling, c1920, 9" h **$435**

Chausable, Gothic Revival, silk, metallic embroidery, and stumpwork, cream silk ground, stitched central Gothic cross, centered by metal purl stumpwork Agnes Dei, flanked by scrolling gilt and gilt embroidered flowering vines, ending in metal spherule mounted grape bunches, metallic ribbon trim, late 19th C, 40-1/2" l **$600**

Corpus, carved wood, polychrome, gilt, detailed features, hand forged iron spike, European, some repainting, 18th C, 39" h, 23-1/4" w **$2,300**

Crucifix

Finely painted, overlaid with ornate repoussé, chased riza, Russian, 19th C, 14" h **$1,150**

Bible box, Queen Anne, walnut, lift lid, strap hinges, dovetailed case, bracket feet, Chester County, c1750, 7-3/4" h, 17-1/2" w, 13-3/4" d, **$1,290.**
Photo courtesy of Pook & Pook, Inc.

Madonna and child, oil on canvas, signed "A.T. Paterdeau(?)", round, carved gilt frame, portraits mounted in frame, prob. 18th century, 34" x 28", **$1,100.**
Photo courtesy of Wiederseim Associates, Inc.

Bust, parian, Jesus Christ, by Isaac Broome, hand incised, BROOME SCULP' 1876, 1876, 15-1/4" x 9", **$3,600.**
Photo courtesy of David Rago Auctions, Inc.

Finely carved, South German, 19th/20th C, 28" x 23" **$520**

Deity

Mahaka, bronze, deity standing on prostrated figure, double lotus base, polychrome highlights, Tibetan, 19th C, 6-3/8" h **$1,315**

Porcelain, seated on lotus pillow, Famille rose enamels, gilt body, Chinese, chips to petals on crown, old repairs around neck, 18th or 19th C, 4-1/2" h **$1,100**

Yamantaka Vajrabhairava, gilt bronze, buffalo-headed deity in yabyum with his consort, trampling prostrated figures and animals, sealed lotus base with Sanskrit inscription, Tibetan, 18th C, 7" h **$5,260**

Figure

Black Madonna and Child, Pattarino, 18-3/4" h **$3,450**

Christ on the Cross, carved and polychromed wood, clad in loin cloth, blood dripping down body, metal crown of thorns, metal halo inserts, nailed on cross with plaque marked INRI, raised on stepped square base with two carved miniature angels at feet, Spanish, Colonial, 14-1/2" h **$360**

Beaded altar flowers, polychrome, turquoise, white, gold and pink glass beads, 19th century, 19-1/2" x 9-1/2", **$590.**
Photo courtesy of Sloans & Kenyon Auctioneers and Appraisers.

Bible box, Queen Anne, walnut, lift lid, dovetailed case, straight bracket feet, Pennsylvania, c1750, 9-1/4" h, 18" w, 12" d, **$1,055.**
Photo courtesy of Pook & Pook, Inc.

Goddess, Chola-style, bronze, Indian, late 19th C, 7" h **$325**

Image of God of Literature, China, Ming period (1368-1644), bronze, 5-1/2" h **$500**

Lama, seated on double lotus throne, bronze, cold gold paste on the face, inscription on front, 7" h **$3,290**

Madonna and Child, Christ holding rosebud, delivering blessing, Pattarino, 16-1/2" h **$2,990**

Madonna and Child, carved and polychrome gilt wood, Baroque style, South German, 20th C, 21-1/2" h **$815**

Madonna and Child, fully carved in the round, base inscribed "Oberamergare," South German, c1930, 21-1/2" h **$500**

Madonna and Child, finely carved and polychromed, Baroque taste, German, 20th C, 22" h **$575**

Madonna and Child enthroned, Pattarino, 22" h **$3,795**

Madonna and Child, carved polychrome and gilt wood, South German, late 19th/early 20th, 25" h **$1,900**

Madonna and sleeping Christ, Pattarino, 14-1/2" h **$1,495**

Praying Madonna, Pattarino, 5-1/4" h **$435**

St. Christopher carrying Infant Christ, carved and polychrome, glass eyes, silver halo and crown, 20th C, 16" h **$700**

St. Thomas Aquinas, carved and polychrome gilt wood, Spanish-Colonial, 19th C, 12-1/4" **$750**

Wish Bestowing Avalokitesvara, gilt bronze, Korea, possible repair to the feet, 11th C, 15-1/2" **$5,875**

Funerary centerpiece, 45" x 31", beaded wire construction for casket top, French, c1890-1910.............**$300**

Icon, Buddhist, mandala of Yamantakra surrounded by wrathful deities of ancient Bon faith, Tibet, 18th C, 32" x 21" **$1,500**

Icon, Greek

Bishop Saint, carved and polychrome wood, Provincial, French, 17th C, 38" h **$460**

The Evangelist St. Mark, finely painted on gold leafed ground, c1700, 11" x 14"....................**$980**

The Mother of God, sgd by icongrapher lower right "Georgio Pandi," 18th C, 25-1/2" x 34".............**$865**

Icon, Russian

Mandylion (The Not Made By Hand Image), c1750, 10-1/2" x 12" **$835**

The Archangel Gabriel, gold leaf and incised ground, c1890, 22-3/4" x 12".................................**$750**

The Birth of John the Forerunner, c1700, 10" x 12" **$1,265**

The Kazan Mother of God, c1775, 10-1/2" x 12-1/2" **$1,495**

The Korsunskaya Mother of God, c1675-1725, 11" x 13"...........**$1,495**

The Lord Almighty, c1650, 11" x 9-1/4".................................**$3,220**

The Sign Mother of God, 32" x 19-1/2"....................................**$1,610**

Monstrance and lunette, 27-1/2" h Gothic-style gem set gilded silver and enamel monstrance on large sculpted circular base depicting four evangelists with their symbols, octagonal pillar with four sided shelter with column niches, each with saint, Gothic canopy, central exposition window set within open fretwork of scrolling grapevines resting on base set with horizontal row of guillouche enamel and four gilded silver bell drops, flanked by pair of Gothic shrines with spires, 16 individually sculpted saints, each set with champleve enamel, above window baldacchino set with intricate arches and spires, mounted with 82 rose cut garnets and four pearls, bezel surrounding central exposition set with 60 rose cut garnets, 19 diamonds, one synthetic diamond, 10 lbs 2 oz, engraved lunette with 2-1/2" d luna, Madrid, after 1935, custom padded case **$9,450**

Mosaic, Madonna and Child, more than 7,000 individually cut and placed colored stones, gilded frame,

Byzantine style, early 20th C, 24" x 30" **$2,990**

Painting, oil on board, Ernst Christian Pfannschmidt, German 1868-1941, Angels Mourning the Crucified Christ, sgd lower right, dated 1898, 16" x 12" **$2,070**

Painting, oil on canvas, Charles Bosseron Chambers, American, 1882-1964, Adoration of the Magi, sgd lower left, 32" x 26" **$6,900**

Pendant, 18k gold rope frame centering two reverse painted images of Virgin Mary holding infant Jesus **$265**

Plaque, Duomo from a Distance, pietra dura, showing roof of the Duomo in a distant landscape, with green and gold painted border, Italian, set in gold painted frame, late 19th/early 20th C, 5-1/4" x 4-1/8" **$275**

Processional candleholders, pr, metal, single light, trumpet shaped, eight trefoil ribs ending in scrolls, band of acanthus, guilloche and trefoil labrequins at waist, candle nozzle set into wood lined interior, Renaissance Revival, Venetian, lacking poles, late 19th C, 15-1/4" d, 19-1/2" l **$560**

Reliquary

Bronze, relics of cross, apostles, and several saints, 17-1/2" h **$1,610**

Cross-form, gilded, relic of true cross, 14-1/4" **$2,875**

Elaborately framed, 18 relics, 15" x 15" **$1,265**

Gilded filigree and enamel, French, 3-1/4" h **$300**

Ornate gilded filigree, relics of several saints and apostles, 12" h **$550**

Ornate gilded, paste stones and cabochons, relic of St. Catherine Laboure, 12-3/4" h **$700**

Rosary beads, 18k gold and platinum crucifix, Sloan & Co., black hardstone beads suspending two sided medal, yellow gold crucifix with platinum Christ, 43.1 dwt, hallmark, missing one bead, chain detached, provenance: from estate of Reverend Thomas Mary O'Leary (1875-1949), Bishop of Springfield.................. **$360**

Santos, carved wood, well dressed shepherd carrying lamb, tin flag, orig red, blue, and yellow paint, trace of gilt, wear, Spanish, 8-1/2" h **$200**

Still life, 25-3/4" x 29", mosaic, depicting fruit on a tabletop, Vatican Workshops, bearing paper label from the Mosaic Studios at San Pietro in the Vatican, artist name Cassio, early 20th C, 35-3/4" x 29" giltwood frame **$7,050**

Tabernacle, gilt bronze, removable dome lid for exposition, c1940, 31" h **$980**

Tantric crown, repoussè copper with parcel gilt, coral and turquoise inlays, Tibet or Nepal, 18th C or earlier, 10" h.. **$650**

Tapestry fragment, Madonna enthroned, flanked by saints, other biblical scenes, Continental, 17th/18th C, 118" x 81" **$6,465**

ROCK 'N' ROLL

History: Rock music can be traced back to early rhythm and blues. It progressed until it reached its golden age in the 1950s and 1960s. Most of the memorabilia issued during that period focused on individual singers and groups. The largest quantity of collectible material is connected to Elvis Presley and The Beatles.

In the 1980s, two areas—clothing and guitars—associated with key rock 'n' roll personalities received special collector attention. Sotheby's and Christie's East regularly feature rock 'n' roll memorabilia as part of their collectibles sales. At the moment, the market is highly speculative and driven by nostalgia.

It is important to identify memorabilia issued during the lifetime of an artist or performing group, as opposed to material issued after they died or disbanded. Objects of the latter type are identified as "fantasy" items and will never achieve the same degree of collectibility as period counterparts.

Reproduction Alert. Records, picture sleeves, and album jackets, especially for The Beatles, have been counterfeited. When compared to the original, sound may be inferior, as may be the printing on labels and picture jackets. Many pieces of memorabilia also have been reproduced, often with some change in size, color, and design.

Additional Resources:

Goldmine™ Record Album Price Guide, 4th Ed., by Tim Neely, Krause Publications, Iola, WI.

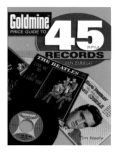

Goldmine™ Price Guide to 45 RPM Records, 5th Ed., by Tim Neely, Krause Publications, Iola, WI.

Standard Catalog of® American Records 1950-1975, 4th Ed., by Tim Neely, Krause Publications, Iola, WI.

Warman's® American Records, 2nd Ed., by Chuck Miller, Krause Publications, Iola, WI.

Rock and Roll, Beatles Daily Calendar, 1960s, **$135.**

Autograph, Elvis, poster, **$750.**
Photo courtesy of Gary Sohmers.

Poster, Bruce Springsteen, Liberty Hall, blue tone photo, March, 1974, **$750.**
Photo courtesy of Gary Sohmers.

Warman's® Americana & Collectibles, 11th Ed., by Ellen T. Schroy, ed., Krause Publications, Iola, WI.

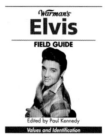

Warman's® Elvis Field Guide, by Paul Kennedy, ed., Krause Publications, Iola, WI.

Autograph, photo
Chuck Berry **$75**
Mick Jagger **$135**
Harry James **$35**
Madonna **$195**
Paul McCartney **$275**
Autograph, program, Wayne Newton, 1980s **$20**
Backstage pass, cloth
Aerosmith, Pump Tour '89, afternoon **$10**
Bon Jovi, NJ Guest **$7**
KISS, 10th anniversary, after show, unused **$7**
Cyndi Lauper, Crew '86-87 .... **$6**
Rolling Stones, American Tour '81 .... **$15**
Book, *The Beatles Authorized Biography,* McGraw-Hill, 32 glossy black and white photos, copyright 1968 .... **$25**
Christmas card, The Partridge Family, color photo of family opening presents, Christmas tree, facsimile signatures, matching red envelope, trimmed in dark gold, c1971, 5-3/4" x 8-1/2" **$15**
Counter display, Rolling Stones, "Made In The Shade," 1976, 3-D cardboard, bowed diecut, with four previ-

ous LP covers at left and "Rolling Stones & Tongue" logo on silver at top right, 21" x 19" **$250**
Drawing, pencil, 2-1/4" x 2-1/2" image of Jeremy the Bobb balancing on one foot, from Beatles Yellow Submarine, production notations, 1968, 12-1/2" x 16" sheet of animation paper **$150**
Drinking glass, Beatles, clear, images and text in black, 1960s, 6-1/2" h **$20**
Drumsticks
Alice in Chains **$25**
Black Crows, concerned used, logo **$20**
Iron Maiden, 1985 .... **$50**
Fan photo, 8" x 10"
Jackson Five, full color, 1970s **$10**
James Dean, black and white glossy, c1954 .... **$15**
Magazine
Lennon Photo Special, Sunshine Publications, copyright 1981, 8" x 11" **$15**
Life, Rock Stars at Home with Their Parents, Vol. 17, #13, Sept. 14, 1971 .... **$5**
Post, Mamas and Papas article, March 25, 1967 .... **$5**
The Rolling Stones Magazine, Straight Arrow Publishers, copyright 1975 .... **$10**
Newsletter, Rolling Stones Fan Club, four pgs, black and white, orig mailing envelope, 5" x 8" **$15**
Pinback button
Led Zeppelin, group logo in center, blue and white lettering: Summerfest At The Stadium Presents An Evening With Led Zeppelin, Sat, Aug. 6, 1977, Buffalo, NY, 3" d **$35**
Hey, Let's Twist, red lettering on white ground, striped peppermint candy design, c1961, 3-1/2" d **$20**
Portrait, Elvis Presley, by Ivan Jesse Curtain, wooden frame, 1960s **$125**
Poster
Beatles, four sheets, each with Richard Avedon stylized portrait, 1968, 79" x 29" **$1,840**
Family Dog, art by Victor Moscoso, second printing, Oct. 6-8, 1967 .... **$35**
Janis Joplin, Neon Rose, Matrix, San Francisco, Jan. 17-22, 1967, 13-3/4" x 20" **$75**

Press kit, KISS, Casablanca, custom folder, three-page bio, one-page press clipping, five 8" x 10" black and white photos, orig mailing envelope with no writing or postage, 1976 .... **$500**

Scarf, Beatles, glossy fabric, half corner design, marked "The Beatles/Copyright by Ramat & Co., Ltd./London, ECI," c1964, 25" sq **$160**

Sheet music

Jackson Five, *Mama's Pearl,* copyright 1971 Jobette Music Co. **$5**

Michael Jackson, *We're Almost There,* browntone photo cover, copyright 1974 Stone Diamond Corp **$5**

Ticket

Beatlefest '82-LA **$10**

Elvis, 9/88 .... **$75**

The Beatles Again Movie, 1976, 2-1/4" x 5-1/2" **$20**

Yardbirds/Doors, 1967 .... **$50**

Tour book

Depeche Mode, Devotional Tour 1993/94 .... **$10**

KISS, 10th anniversary, Vinnie V in makeup **$125**

Toy, Beatles car, battery operated tin, 1964 Ford Galaxie, vinyl Beatles-like group, "Los Yes-Yes" lithographed on hood, record inside car is bit garbled, but working, orig Rico (Spain) hangtag, orig box with insert, C.9 ..... **$850**

T-shirt, never worn

Bon Jovi, L, Slippery When Wet... **$25**

Deep Purple, L, Perfect Str...'85 .... **$25**

Rolling Stones, XL, Steel Wheels.. **$20**

Watch, Elvis Presley, dial with full-color illus of Elvis in elaborate white jumpsuit, blue background, copyright 1977 Boxcar Enterprises, Unique Time Co., orig blue vinyl straps, 1-1/4" d goldtone metal case **$45**

ROYCROFT

History: Elbert Hubbard founded the Roycrofters in East Aurora, New York, at the turn of the century. Considered a genius in his day, he was an author, lecturer, manufacturer, salesman, and philosopher.

Hubbard established a campus that included a printing plant where he published *The Philistine, The Fra,* and *The Roycrofter.* His most famous book was *A Message to Garcia,* published in 1899. His "community" also included a furniture manufacturing plant, a metal shop, and a leather shop.

Ali Baba bench, half-log top, flaring plank legs, keyed through tenon stretcher, carved orb and cross mark, minor loss to bark, orig finish, 42-1/2" l, 11" w, 20" h **$16,500**

Billfold, matching change purse, lady's, tooled leather, emb foliate motif, monongrammed "RK," orig mirror, pencil, and notepad, orb and cross mark, 3-1/2" x 6-3/4" **$425**

Bookcase, slab sides with keyed tenon construction, plate rail top, orig iron hardware, orb mark, refinished, 46" w, 16" d, 71" h **$9,775**

Bookends, pr, 4-1/8" w, 3-1/4" d, 5-1/4" h, model no. 309, hammered copper, rect, riveted center band suspending ring, dark brown patina, imp Roycroft orb, minor wear **$225**

Book

Old John Burroughs, by Elbert Hubbard, full levant, cover and inside covers incised and painted with blossoms, each hand made paper page with watercolor by Clara Schlegel and Richard Kruger, hand painted bookmark, 1901, 8" x 5-1/4" **$4,000**

So Here Then Is The Last Ride, by Robert Browning, half levant and marbleized paper, each page illuminated by Frances June Carmody, sgd and numbered, 1900, 8" x 5-3/4" **$650**

Box

"In" and "Out," from Roycroft Inn, one quarter-sawn oak, stenciled with letter "O," stamped "OF.336. S," other pine, stamped "P501," orig finish, branded orb and cross marks, 3-1/4" x 13" x 10" **$600**

Tooled leather and suede lined, lid emb with poppy medallion, orb and cross mark, some scuffs and wear to corners, 1-1/2" x 4" x 4" **$475**

Bowl, hammered copper, rolled rim, shouldered bowl, three point feet, red patina, imp mark, traces of brass wash, 10-1/4" d, 4-1/8" h **$450**

Bud vase, wall hanging, hammered copper, cut-out frame, 10-1/2" l .**$200**

Candle lamp, blue art glass, baluster form, flaring foot, stamped "Roycroft," electrified **$175**

Candle sconce, hammered copper, riveted strap holder, imp backplate, orig dark brown patina, orb and cross mark, few scratches, price for pr, 3-1/2" w, 10" h **$630**

Roycroft telephone hammered copper and Bakelite, inscribed "PROPERTY OF THE AMERICAN BELL TELEPHONE COMPANY," original wiring and patina, orb and cross mark, 12", **$8,100.**

Photo courtesy of David Rago Auctions, Inc.

Roycroft table lamp, designed and executed by Dard Hunter, gently sloping circular leaded-glass shade, stylized pattern of fruit and foliage in yellow and green slag glass, ceramic base modeled with salamanders, covered in matte green glaze, base marked "DH," from estate of Miriam Hubbard Roelofs, Elbert and Alice Hubbard's daughter, and the Salon room of the Roycroft Inn, 13" x 17-1/4", **$65,000.**

Photo courtesy of David Rago Auctions, Inc.

Roycroft side chair, four vertical backslats, Mackmurdo feet and replaced leather upholstered seat, original finish, orb and cross mark, 18" w, 17" d, 38" h, **$1,485.**

Photo courtesy of David Rago Auctions, Inc.

Roycroft bookends, pair, copper, original patina, poppy decoration, marked, early 20th century, 5-5/8" h x 5-1/4" w, **$330.**
Photo courtesy of Green Valley Auctions.

Roycroft bookcase, mahogany, 33rd degree single door with 16 panes, fixed shelves, shaped front and side posts, hammered copper escutcheon, knob pull, orig finish, carved orb and cross on door, good condition, 56-1/2" x 40" x 15", **$9,000.**
Photo courtesy of David Rago Auctions, Inc.

Candlesticks, pr
  Brass washed, good grain, Princess style, double shafts, faceted bases, stamped orb and cross mark, orig patina, 7-1/2" h......................**$650**
  Hammered copper, double light, wood grain pattern, orb and cross marks, 6" x 6-3/4"....................**$350**
  Hammered copper, triple light, curled bands, orig dark patina with some wear, orb and cross marks, 3" x 8-1/4"......................................**$500**

Chair, side, ladderback, three horizontal back slats, leather covered cushions, carved orb and cross mark, refinished, price for pr, 37" x 16-1/2" x 16-1/4".......................................**$460**

Chandelier, from Roycroft Inn, copper, triangular strap support base with cut-out hearts and three pendant fixtures, each with enameled amber glass shade dec in stylized floral motif, triangular ceiling plate, hanging chains, orb and cross mark, 14-1/2" w, 10-3/4" h..................**$1,955**

Desk lamp, Steuben blown glass lustered glass shade, hammered copper, shaft of four curled and riveted bands, stamped orb and cross mark, 14-3/4" h, 7" d...........................**$5,750**

Desk set, hammered copper, blotter corners, inkwell, letter holder, pen tray, perpetual calendar with cards, letter opener, orb and cross marks, orig dark patina...........................**$350**

Dresser, pine and oak, two small drawers over four long drawers, hammered iron hardware, paneled sides, orb and cross die-stamped on each pull, from Roycroft Inn, 62-3/4" x 45" x 21"...**$1,500**

Frame, hammered copper, emb with quatrefoils, orb and cross mark, and "Roycroft," orig dark patina, 8" x 5-3/4"...**$1,100**

Goody box, mahogany, wrought copper strap hardware, monogrammed "H," orig finish, carved orb and cross on top, 23" l, 13" d, 10" h.............**$630**

High chair, child's, tacked-on leather seat, hand carved name "Silas," orig finish, carved orb and cross front center, seat and tacks replaced, 42" x 16-1/2" x 21-1/2"..........................**$950**

Humidor, hammered copper, covered in brass wash, Trillium pattern, stamped orb and cross mark, minor wear to patina, 4-3/4" w, 5-3/4" h
....**$690**

Kitchen work table, mixed woods, tacked-on zinc counter over two lower shelves, orig finish, unsigned, from Roycroft Inn, 30" x 70" x 18-1/4"...................................**$2,700**

Lamp, boudoir, brass washed hammered copper base, base stamped with orb and cross mark, 10-1/2" d faceted mica shade, wear and flakes to mica...................................**$350**

Lamp, table

Hammered copper and mica, single socket, riveted heraldic shade, lined with band of mica, orig dark patina, orb and cross mark, 15" h, 10" d **$3,500**

Lime green and purple conical leaded slag glass shade, classical hammered copper base, riveted bands, ring pulls, three sockets, orb and cross mark, replaced cord, 23" h, 18" d **$35,000**

Magazine stand, arched tapering sides, three shelves, orb and cross mark, orig finish, 37-1/2" x 17-3/4" x 15-1/2"...................................**$5,550**

Marble bag, laced suede, large orb and cross mark tooled to front panel, 8" l...................................**$450**

Morris chair, shaped arms and posts, laced leather covered foam cushions, four slats under each arm, carved orb and cross mark on front stretcher, arms refinished, replaced leather and cushions, 39-1/2" x 29-1/2" x 38"........**$3,250**

Motto, orig Roycroft frame, matted, "Do Not Keep Your Kindness...," 17-1/4" x 12-1/2"...................................**$350**

Paper folio, six woodblock prints, Roycroft Inn pamphlet with photographs...................................**$750**

Smoking set, Trillium pattern, hammered copper, humidor, cigarette holder, cylindrical match holder, stacking ashtrays with matchbox holder, 14" x 9" rect tray.............**$500**

Sugar bowl, cov, china, hp by Bertha Hubbard, sgd "B. C. Hubbard".......**$200**

Tray, hexagonal, hammered copper, stitched border, two handles, orb and cross mark, orig dark patina, 14-3/4" d **$475**

Vase, hammered copper cylinder, emb with stylized quatrefoils on tall stems, stamped orb and cross mark and "KK" for Karl Kipp, patina cleaned some time ago, 7" h, 2-1/2" d **$1,600**

Russian caviar tub, silver, faux wood grain, vermeil reeded bands, locking cover, glass liner, 1860, 4" d, 10 oz, **$950.**
Photo courtesy of Sloans & Kenyon Auctioneers and Appraisers.

Russian icon, St. Nicholas, Moscow, silver-gilt Oklad, richly enameled halo, 1893, 12-1/2" x 10-1/4", **$1,200.**
Photo courtesy of Sloans & Kenyon Auctioneers and Appraisers.

Russian icon, Life of a Saint, tempera on wood, mosaic gold, 19th century, 11-3/4" x 8-1/2", **$295.**
Photo courtesy of Sloans & Kenyon Auctioneers and Appraisers.

Russian powder box, lift-off lid, lacquer, miniature of man and woman sitting with priest at a table, dark brown background, interior marked "O.F. Vishnyakov & Sons Workshop, Fedoskino Russia," 1882, 2-1/2" d, 1-1/4" h, **$300.**
Photo courtesy of Gamal Amer.

Russian cane, Moscow, silver and enamel champleve, 2-7/8" h x 7/8" d cylindrical handle, two shades of blue, green, red, and white on gold gilt background, Russian hallmarks for 84 zolotnicks, kokshnik marks for 1896-1907, maker marks "M.K." for Michael Koshov, black hardwood shaft, 1-1/4" burnished brass ferrule, 19th century, 35-7/8" l, **$3,250.**
Photo courtesy of Henry A. Taron.

Russian kovsh, silver-gilt and enamel, probably Moscow, typical shape, notched handle and band of trailing flowering branches in colors, 1895, 4-1/4" l, $675.

Photo courtesy of Sloans & Kenyon Auctioneers and Appraisers.

Russian icon, Mother of God, tempera on wood, 17th-18th century, 12" x 10", $200.

Photo courtesy of Sloans & Kenyon Auctioneers and Appraisers.

Russian silver, cigarette case, raised decoration of horse-drawn sleigh with figures, red stone cabochon on latch, gold wash interior, Russian standard marks, 4-3/4" l, 3-1/2" w, $250.

Photo courtesy of Alderfer Auction Co.

Russian icon, Madonna and Child, tempera on wood panel, 10-1/2" x 12" x 1-1/4", $375.

Photo courtesy of Sloans & Kenyon Auctioneers and Appraisers.

RUSSIAN ITEMS

History: During the late 19th and early 20th centuries, craftsmen skilled in lacquer, silver, and enamel wares worked in Russia. During the Czarist era (1880-1917), Fabergé, known for his exquisite enamel pieces, led a group of master craftsmen located primarily in Moscow. Fabergé also had an establishment in St. Petersburg and enjoyed the patronage of the Russian Imperial family and royalty and nobility throughout Europe.

Almost all enameling was done on silver. The artist and the government assayer sign pieces.

The Russian Revolution in 1917 brought an abrupt end to the century of Russian craftsmanship. The modern Soviet government has exported some inferior enamel and lacquer work, usually lacking in artistic merit. Modern pieces are not collectible.

Enamels

Blood cup, gilt and transfer dec, Imperial double headed eagle, cipher of Czar Nicholas II above date 1896, 4" h **$260**

Bonbonniere, orchid guillouche enamel on silver, cylindrical, cast silver bas-relief applied dec on cov and back, applied relief, monogram of Nicholas II set with precious stones, Henrik Wigstrom, workmaster, St. Petersburg, slight damage, 1908-17, 3-3/8" d, 2-3/16" h **$4,225**

Cane, 4-1/2" l x 3-1/4" tau handle dec with champleve style raised enamel, light blue, dark blue, green, white, and red, worn Russian hallmarks, heavy ebony shaft, 7/8" replaced brass ferrule, c1900, 35" l **$2,350**

Cigarette case, 84 standard, silver gilt, robin's egg blue enamel, feathered guillouche ground, opaque white enamel borders, diamond chips on clasp, gilt in., Ivan Britzin, St. Petersburg, small losses and chips to enamel, 1908-17, 3-1/2" l, 2-1/4" w **$1,200**

Coffee spoon, blue dot border in bowl, stylized polychrome enamel foliage, gilt stippled ground, twisted gilt stem, crown finial, G Tokmakov, c1890 .... **$300**

Cup, silver-gilt and cloisonné enamel, Antip Kuzmichev, Moscow, marked "Made for Tiffany & Co.," price for set of four, dated 1895, 3" w, 2-1/4" h **$4,025**

Egg, silver gilt and shaded enamel ware, two-pc construction, cabochon stone, maker's mark obliterated, ftd, 20th C, 3" h **$700**

Kovsh, silver, shaded enamel on moss green field, Pan Slavic style, hallmarked Moscow, Cyrillic "Faberge" under Imperial Warrant, 1907, 3" h **$2,875**

Matchbox holder, silver gilt and cloisonné, hallmarked Moscow, indistinguishable maker's mark, c1900, 2-1/4" l **$350**

Napkin ring, enameled green, blue, pink, brown, white, light blue and maroon, Maria Semenova, Moscow, c1890, 1-3/4" x 1" x 1-1/2" **$700**

Spoon
Round bowl, twisted handle ending in crown finial with enamel accents, obverse of bowl dec with hp portrait of woman surrounded by band of blue and green plique-a-jour in geometric design, illegible mark, 7-1/2" d **$1,760**
Silver-gilt and shaded enamel, back with colorful plumed bird on stippled ground, beaded border, Dmitri Nicholiaev, Moscow, c1900, 7-1/4" l **$865**

Sugar shovel, silver gilt and enamel, Antip Kuzmichev, Moscow, 1899, 4-3/4" l **$500**

Sugar tongs, silver gilt and cloisonné enamel, Moscow, indistinguishable maker's mark, 1899, 5-1/4" l **$250**

Vase, champleve enamel, central cartouche on both sides, one with stylized double headed eagle, other side with roosters, Slavonic inscription at base rim, hallmarked Moscow, Cyrillic "P. Ovchinnikov" under Imperial Warrant, dated 1874, 11-1/2" h **$5,750**

Icon

John the Forerunner, c1575, 10-3/4" x 13-1/2" **$8,625**

St. Nicholas, cast bronze and champleve enamel, 19th C, 9" x 10" **$635**

Saint Tikhon of Amathus, Moscow workshop, c1890, 35" x 28" **$2,990**

Six Days, c1600, 10-1/2" x 12" **$2,070**

The Apostle John and Prokhorus, 16th C, 15-1/2" x 23-1/2" **$16,100**

The Archangel Mikhail, 19th C, 12" x 14" **$2,645**

The Ascension of the Lord, 19th C, 14-1/4" x 17-1/2"........................**$920**

The Dormition, 19th C, 10" x 12" **$2,070**

The Entry Into Jerusalem, borders and background gilded and finely incised, c1890, 10-1/2" x 12-1/4" **$2,185**

The Eucharist, c1550-1600, inscribed "Peite Ot Neya Siya Est Krov Moya," 13-1/2" x 15-3/4"................**$13,800**

The Holy Great Martyr Catherine, 20th C, 12" x 14"..........................**$920**

The Holy Martyr Paraskeva, full-length figure, c1750, 32" x 13-1/2" **$4,370**

The Kazan Mother of God, faux enameled background and borders, c1890, 7" x 5-3/4"........................**$300**

The Lord Almighty, c1700, 10-1/4" x 12"...**$2,760**

The Lord Almighty, 18th or 19th C, 12-1/4" x 10-1/4".................**$1,725**

The Mystical (Last) Supper, 18th C, 17" x 12-1/2"..........................**$3,335**

The Not By Hands Made Image of Christ-The Holy Napkin, 10-1/2" x 12-1/4"...................................**$1,725**

The Passion, central panel with elaborate scene of Christ descending into Hades, 16 separate scenes, c1650, 12-1/2" x 15-1/4" **$1,725**

The Resurrection and Descent Into Hades, 1550-1600, attributed to Tver, 9-3/4" x 11-3/4".........**$10,350**

The Smolensk Mother of God, c1775-1825, 10-1/2" x 12-1/4" **$920**

The Smolensk Mother of God, 19th C, 9" x 7"........................**$1,035**

The Symbol of Faith, second half of 20th C, 28" x 23"...................**$1,955**

The Terrible Judgment, Strashnuiy Sud, second half 20th C, 31-1/2" x 22" **$2,645**

The Theodore Mother of God, overlaid with custom fitted silvered riza, attached gilded halos, late 18th C, 8-3/4" x 10-1/4".........**$1,350**

The Three Handed Mother of God, 19th C, 8-3/4" x 10-3/4" **$435**

The Tikhvin Mother of God, 18th C, 13-1/2" x 11-3/4"...................**$815**

The Tikhvin Mother of God, finely painted, overlaid with finely crafted riza, c1800-50, 9-3/4" x 11-1/2" **$1,380**

The Vladimir Mother of God, c1700-1750, 12-1/2" x 11"........**$1,725**

Metal

Bust, Tsar Alexander Mikhailovich, Cyrillic foundry mark "F. Shopeen," bronze, dated 1867, 10" h **$1,250**

Cross, Palekh or Mstera, recessed edges (kovcheg), painted in classic 16th C style, top with Holy Napkin and Angels, center crossbeam with Mary and Apostle John, center with crucified Christ with implements of the passion, base with skull of Adam, 19th C, 47" x 22".....................**$4,600**

Samovar

Cylindrical, front and rim stamped with profusion of awards, Kvana Kaprzina, Tula, c1905, 22" h **$575**

Cylindrical, orig bowl and undertray, 19th C, 14" h................**$400**

Cylindrical, paneled body, 19th C, 17-1/2" h.............................**$375**

Sculpture, bronze

Couple being driven in troika, deep brown patina, sgd in base in Cyrillic "Gratchev" (Vasilil Iakovelvich Gratchev, 1831-1905) and "Voerffel Foundry-St Petersburg," 12-1/4" l, 7" w, 7-1/2" h **$2,875**

Mounted Imperial soldier, dark brown patina, indistinguishably signed in Cyrillic on base, c1890, 18-1/2" x 16-1/2" h **$2,300**

Tray, painted and lacquered metal, troika scene, verso sgd in Cyrillic "Lukutin," beneath Imperial Warrant, 19th C, 13-1/2" x 10-1/2" **$690**

Miscellaneous

Box, lacquer and transfer printed papier-mâché, colorful foil backed transfer images of famous Russian scenes on lid, lock and key, price for pr, c1890, 6-1/2" x 4-1/2"..........**$460**

Card case, nephrite and gold, cabochon thumbpush, hallmarked St Petersburg 1908, standard 56, makers mark "A. A.," 3-1/2" l.............**$4,890**

Charger, carved in Pan Slavic style, borders carved relief inscription "To Her Imperial Highness Princess Yevheniya Maximiliyanova of Oldenburg," center with Imperial Russian coat of arms and Princess's coat of arms, relief carved "Housewarming from the Chertkov and Sverbeyev families 1887," verso with makers plaque in Cyrillic "F. Schilling, Moscow," 15" d **$850**

Purse, 14k yg, curved frame gypsy-set with 11 old mine-cut and old European-cut diamonds, approx. total wt. 3.00 cts, further set with gypsy-set oval sapphires and circular-cut rubies, mesh body, trace link chain, 95.2 dwt, Russian hallmarks **$200**

Stool, paint dec, geometric strapwork dec on top, turned tapered legs, early 20th C, 13-1/2" w, 9-1/4" d, 8-7/8" h **$125**

Porcelain

Cabinet plate, cobalt blue, green, and red central rosette, gilt ground, 9" d **$275**

Cup and saucer, blue glazed, honoring coronation of Nicholas II, M.S. Kuznetsov, 1878, 4-1/2" h **$250**

Dessert plate, floral rim, magenta ground, Islamic script, printed mark, I. E. Kuznetsov, set of six, 19th C **$265**

Plate, two soldiers, verso with underglaze Cyrillic P.S. beneath crown mark, 8-3/4" d....................**$750**

Portrait plate, Empress Elizabeth, Safronov, hairline, early 19th C, 8" d **$315**

Tankard, figural, Turk's head, marked "F. Gardner, Moscow," restored, 19th C, 8" h.....................**$1,210**

Tea service, 13 pcs, creamer, sugar, four cov cups, four saucers, two open cups, Kornilov Bros, c1910, 9" w x 5" h cov teapot......................**$2,415**

Vase, one green with medallion of Olga, other puce with medallion of Vladimir, all-over gilt foliate dec, Gardner, drilled, price for pr, 19th C, 8" h...**$250**

SALT AND PEPPER SHAKERS

History: Collecting salt and pepper shakers, whether late 19th-century glass forms or the contemporary figural and souvenir types, is becoming more and more popular. The supply and variety is practically unlimited; the price for most sets is within the budget of cost-conscious collectors. In addition, their size offers an opportunity to display a large collection in a relatively small space.

Specialty collections can be by type, form, or maker. Great glass artisans, such as Joseph Locke and Nicholas Kopp, designed salt and pepper shakers in the normal course of their work.

Additional Resources:

Warman's® Americana & Collectibles, 11th Ed., by Ellen T. Schroy, ed., Krause Publications, Iola, WI.

Warman's® Flea Market, 4th Ed., by Ellen T. Schroy, ed., Krause Publications, Iola, WI.

Spiffy Kitchen Collectibles, by Brian S. Alexander, Krause Publications, Iola, WI.

Art glass
(priced individually)
Cranberry, Inverted Thumbprint, sphere **$175**
Hobnail, sapphire blue, Hobbs, Brockunier & Co., one orig metal top, 2-3/4" h................................... **$95**
Mt. Washington
Egg shape, one with pink and blue daisies, other with red mums, 2-1/2" h.................................. **$120**
Egg shape, stemmed flower dec, 2-1/2" h..................................... **$65**
Pairpoint
Barrel shape, enameled flowers, 3" h
.... **$55**
Mold blown, faceted body, colored flowers, 3" h **$45**
Shell shape, colorless, two purple blossoms, spray of yellow daisies, green leaves................................ **$885**
Wave Crest, Erie Twist body, hp flowers, 2-1/2" h **$185**

Figural and souvenir types **(priced by set)**
Bride and groom, pigs, nodders, marked "Made in Japan," c1950
.... **$325**
Christmas, barrel shape, amethyst
.... **$165**
Ducks, sitting, glass, clear bodies, blue heads, sgd "Czechoslovakia," 2-1/2" h
.... **$45**
Egg shape, opaque white body, holly dec, 23 red raised enameled berries, Mt. Washington **$175**
Mammy and broom, orig "Norcrest Fine China Japan" foil labels, numbered H424, 4-1/4" h **$395**
Strawberries, flashed amberina glass strawberry-shaped shakers, white metal leaf caps, suspended from emb white metal fancy holder, sgd "Japan," c1921-41, 2-3/4" h strawberries, 5" h stand **$285**

Opalescent glass
(priced individually)
Argonaut Shell, blue.................... **$65**
Fluted Scrolls, vaseline................ **$65**
Seaweed, Hobbs, cranberry.......... **$60**
Windows, Hobbs, blue, pewter top
.... **$55**

Opaque glass
(priced individually)
Bulge Bottom, blue **$25**
Cathedral Panel, white **$20**
Creased Bale, pink...................... **$20**

Fleur-de-Lis Scrolling, custard **$20**
Heart, blue **$25**
Leaf Clover, blue **$20**
Little Shrimp, white...................... **$20**
Swirl Wide Diagonal, white........ **$20**

Pattern glass
(priced individually)
Block and Fan, colorless, 1891..... **$20**
Francesware, Hobbs, Brockunier Co., c1880, hobnail, frosted, amber stained
.... **$45**
Lobe, squatty **$120**
Tulip **$100**

Silver
Figural, Oriental street merchant pushing cart that contains salt and pepper shakers, toothpick container, hallmarked "90 HM," 5-1/4" l..... **$195**
Spratling, Mexico, domed forms on angular wooden bases, maker's marks, 3-1/2" h.................................... **$500**

SALTS, OPEN

History: When salt was first mined, the supply was limited and expensive. The necessity for a receptacle in which to serve the salt resulted in the first open salt, a crude, hand-carved, wooden trencher.

As time passed, salt receptacles were refined in style and materials. In the 1500s, both master and individual salts existed. By the 1700s, firms such as Meissen, Waterford, and Wedgwood were making glass, china, and porcelain salts. Leading glass manufacturers in the 1800s included Libbey, Mount Washington, New England, Smith Bros., Vallerysthal, Wave Crest, and Webb. Many outstanding silversmiths in England, France, and Germany also produced this form.

Open salts were the only means of serving salt until the appearance of the shaker in the late 1800s. The ease of procuring salt from a shaker greatly reduced the use of, and need for, the open salts.

Notes: Allan B. and Helen B. Smith have authored and published 10 books on open salts beginning with *One Thousand Individual Open Salts Illustrated* (1972) and ending with *1,334 Open Salts Illustrated: The Tenth Book* (1984). The numbers in parentheses refer to plate numbers in the Smiths' books. Another reference book that collectors refer to for salts was written by L. W. & D. B. Neal, *Pressed Glass Salt Dishes of the Lacy Period, 1825-50.*

Condiment sets with open salts

German silver, two castors, two salts, two salt spoons, Renaissance style with swan supports, marked ".800 fine," c1900 .... **$800**

Limoges, double salt and mustard, sgd "J. M. Limoges" (388) **$80**

Metal, coolie pulling rickshaw, salt, pepper, and mustard, blown glass liners, Oriental (461) **$360**

Quimper, double salt and mustard, white, blue, and green floral dec, sgd "Quimper" (388) **$120**

Early American glass

Blown molded, hat shape, brilliant cobalt blue, inward folded rim, rayed type IV base, rough pontil mark, Boston & Sandwich Glass Co., McKearin GIII-23, 1825-35, 2-1/4" h, 2-3/8" x 2-1/2" d rim, 2" d base **$650**

Pressed, lacy

Neal BF-1F, Basket of Flowers, fiery opalescent violet blue, four feet, Boston & Sandwich, unlisted color, extremely rare, slightly warped, small chips, 2" h, 1-3/4" x 3" **$1,100**

Neal BS-2, Beaded Scroll & Basket of Flowers, clambroth, Boston & Sandwich Glass Co., 1825-50, 2" h **$375**

Neal BS-2, Beaded Scroll & Basket of Flowers, colorless, Boston & Sandwich Glass Co., 1835-45, flakes on inner rim, 1-7/8" h, 1-7/8" x 3-1/8" **$135**

Neal BS-2, Beaded Scroll & Basket of Flowers, opalescent, Boston & Sandwich Glass Co., 1825-50, 2" h **$400**

Neal BS-3a, Beaded Scroll pattern, violet-blue, Boston & Sandwich Glass Co., edge cracks and chips, c1825-50, 2" h **$360**

Neal BT-2, Pittsburgh Steamboat, colorless, emb on stern, Stourbridge Flint Glass Works, minor rim flakes, 1-1830-45, 1/2" h, 1-7/8" x 3-5/8" **$825**

Neal BT-4D, Lafayet Steamboat, deep cobalt blue, mkd "B & S Glass Co." on stern, "Sandwich" in int. base, Boston & Sandwich Glass Co.,

minor inner rim flaking, 1830-45, 1-5/8" h, 1-7/8" x 3-5/8" **$2,750**

Neal CT-1, chariot, mottled silvery opaque blue, scallop and point rim, Boston & Sandwich Glass Co., rim corner chip, mold roughness, 1835-50, 1-3/4" h, 2-1/8" x 2-7/8" **$1,265**

Neal EE-3B, fiery opalescent, four feet, Boston & Sandwich Glass Co., near proof, chip on interior of one foot, 1835-45, 2-1/8" h, 2-1/8" x 3-1/4" **$615**

Neal JY-2, light green, scallop and point rim, emb "Jersey" under base, Jersey Glass Co., c1835-50, 2" h, 2-1/8" x 3 .... **$880**

Neal NE-6, light green, scallop and point rim, star under base, Jersey Glass Co. or New England Glass Co., two rim chips, 1835-50, 2" h, 2-1/8" x 2-7/8" **$245**

Neal OL 15, Beaded Strawberry Diamond, brilliant deep purple blue, high and low point rim, Boston & Sandwich Glass Co., 1830-50, 1-3/4" h **$495**

Neal OO-2, Octagon, oblong, colorless, c1825-50, 1-1/2" h **$195**

Neal OO-9, Octagon, oblong, colorless, flat rim, possibly New England, minor inner flake, 1835-50, 1-3/8" h **$210**

Neal OP-8, Oval Pedestal, amethyst tint, New England, imperfections, c1825-50, 1-7/8" h **$195**

Neal PO-1A, Peacock Eye, oval, colorless, serrated table ring, Boston & Sandwich Glass Co., unlisted color, 1830-50, 1-1/2" h **$275**

Neal PO-4, Peacock Eye, oval, dark blue, rayed base, Boston & Sandwich Glass Co., unlisted color, 1830-45, 1-3/8" h **$2,640**

Neal PO-5, Peacock Eye, oval, colorless, c1825-50, 1-1/2" h **$225**

Neal PR-1A, Peacock-Eye, round, violet-blue, Boston & Sandwich Glass Co., 1825-50, 1-1/2" h **$425**

Neal RP-9, Round Pedestal, colorless, imperfections, c1825-50, 1-1/2" h **$165**

Neal SC-5, Scroll, medium blue, c1825-50, 1-7/8" h **$365**

Neal SD-7, Strawberry Diamond, medium blue, Boston & Sandwich Glass Co., 1825-50, 2" h **$365**

Neal SL-1, Shell, red-amethyst, Boston & Sandwich Glass Co., minor

edge roughness, few base chips, c1825-50, 1-3/4" h **$650**

Neal SL-4, Shell pattern, dark amber, Pittsburgh area, edge chips, c1830, 1-3/4" h **$350**

Neal SL-11, Shell pattern, peacock blue, Boston & Sandwich Glass Co., 1825-50, 1-3/4" h **$295**

Salt and pepper shakers, pair of milk cans, cream, blue and red decoration, **$18.**

Salt and pepper, Mt. Washington, Burmese, ribbed pillar, pastel florals, Meridan silver plate caddy, 6-1/2" h, **$500.**
Photo courtesy of The Early Auction Company, LLC.

Silver salts, William IV, cauldron body, gilt int, gadrooned rim, scrolling feet, by E.J. and W. Barnard, London, 1834, **$325.**
Photo courtesy of Sloans & Kenyon Auctioneers and Appraisers.

Sampler, silk on linen, Elizabeth Lee Parsons, house and lawn over boy and girl within trailing floral and vine border, dated 1811, 12" x 11-3/4", **$1,150.**
Photo courtesy of Pook & Pook, Inc.

Needlework, silk on linen, alphabet, flowers, birds, deer, in orig hand-painted wallpaper surround, dated 1801, 10-1/2" h x 13" w, **$555.**
Photo courtesy of Pook & Pook, Inc.

Sampler, silk on linen, New Jersey, Eliza P. Sanger at the Newton Academy, dated 1805, Quaker, 20" x 21", **$1,380.**
Photo courtesy of Pook & Pook, Inc.

Neal SL-18, Shell pattern, raised scroll pedestal, colorless, Boston & Sandwich Glass Co., edge chips, small base cracks, 1825-50, 2-5/8" h ..**$715**

Figurals

Basket, coral colored glass, SP basket frame, salt with cut polished facets, 3" h, 2-3/4" d **$55**

Bucket, Bristol glass, turquoise, white, green, and brown enameled bird, butterfly and trees, SP rim and handle, 2-1/2" d, 1-5/8" h **$75**

Sea horse, Belleek, brilliant turquoise, white base, supports shell salt, first black mark (458) **$350**

Individual

Cameo, Daum Nancy, cameo glass, bucket form, two upright handles, frosted colorless ground, cameo etched and enameled black tree lined shore, distant ruins, gilt rim, sgd "Daum (cross) Nancy" in gilt on base, small rim chips, 1-3/8" h **$575**

Cut glass, cut ruby ovals, all-over dainty white enameled scrolls, clear ground, gold trim, scalloped top, 2" d, 1-1/2" h **$60**

Moser, cobalt blue, pedestal, gold bands, applied flowers sgd (380)..**$75**

Mount Washington, blue Johnny Jump-ups, cream ground, raised gold dots on rim **$135**

Pattern glass
Fine Rib, flint **$35**
Pineapple and Fan **$25**
Three Face **$40**

Purple slag, emb shell pattern, 3" d, 1-1/4" h.............................**$50**

Russian, colorless glass liner, gold finished metal, red and white enamel scallop design, Russian hallmarks, c1940, 1-1/4" h, 1-3/4" d **$110**

Sterling silver, Georg Jensen, Denmark, porringer (238) **$215**

Masters

Coin silver, made by Gorham for retailer Seth E. Brown, Boston, ftd, gold washed int., monogrammed, pair in fitted case, two coin silver spoons by Jones, Ball & Poor, pr, approx 4 troy oz **$375**

Cranberry, emb ribs, applied crystal ruffed rim, SP holder with emb lions heads, 3" d, 1-3/4" h **$160**

Cut glass, green cut to clear, SP holder, 2" d, 2" h.......................................**$115**

Green, light, dark green ruffled top, open pontil (449)..........................**$90**

Mocha, seaweed band, yellow ware ground, 2" h **$250**

Pattern glass
Barberry, pedestal **$40**
Basketweave, sleigh (397)..........**$100**
Portland, branches handle..........**$110**
Snail, ruby stained........................**$75**
Sunflower, pedestal **$40**

Pearlware
Rounded form, medium blue rim band, vertical ribbed dark brown slip dec on white ground, England, early 19th C, 2-1/2" d **$590**
Rounded form, dark brown banding, dark brown dendritic dec on rust

field, narrow green glazed reeded band, cracked, rim chip, early 19th C, 2-3/4" d **$590**

Pewter, pedestal, cobalt blue liner (349) **$65**

Redware, mottled brown alkaline glaze, c1850, 2-1/4" h **$75**

Sterling silver, Stieff Co., chased and emb all-over floral pattern, applied floral rim, three scrolled shell feet, pr, early 20th C, 6 troy oz, 1-3/4" h ...**$260**

Vaseline, applied crystal trim around middle, SP stand, 3" d, 2-1/4" h..**$125**

SAMPLERS

History: Samplers served many purposes. For a young child, they were a practice exercise and permanent reminder of stitches and patterns. For a young woman, they were a means to demonstrate skills in a "gentle" art and a way to record family genealogy. For the mature woman, they were a useful occupation and method of creating gifts or remembrances, e.g., mourning pieces.

Schools for young ladies of the early 19th century prided themselves on the needlework skills they taught. The Westtown School in Chester County, Pennsylvania, and the Young Ladies Seminary in Bethlehem, Pennsylvania, were two institutions. These schools changed their teaching as styles changed. Berlin work was introduced by the mid-19th century.

Examples of samplers date back to the 1700s. The earliest ones were

Needlework, silk on linen, Martha Willard Merritt, alphabet over trees, potted flowers, floral vine border, Boston, dated 181_, 20-1/2" x 16-1/2", **$645.**
Photo courtesy of Pook & Pook, Inc.

Sampler, silk on linen, Chester County, Pennsylvania, Quaker, initials, potted flowers, lovebirds, strawberry border, dated 1824, 11-1/2" x 11-1/2", **$760.**
Photo courtesy of Pook & Pook, Inc.

Needlework, silk on linen, Eleanor L. Coward, Young Ladies Seminary in Bethlehem, verse over school building, lawn, vine border, Pennsylvania, dated 1822, 20" h x 17" l, **$5,615.**
Photo courtesy of Pook & Pook, Inc.

long and narrow, usually done only with the alphabet and numerals. Later examples were square. At the end of the 19th century, the shape tended to be rectangular.

The same motifs were used throughout the country. The name of the person who stitched the piece is a key factor in determining the region.

Abigail A. Jenney, Plainfield, New Hampshire, three alphabets, trees, various devices, upper and lower borders, silk threads on linen ground, shades of green, yellow, and brown, 4-3/4" x 3-3/4" sight size, 6-3/4" x 5-3/4" frame, 1808 .... **$2,585**

Anne Armstrong, Aged 11 Years Clones 1810, geometric bands in red, pink, green, blue, brown, purple, and yellow, row of trees, alphabets, and vowels, linen ground, verse by "C. Quigley," minor stitch loss, framed, 1810, 19" w, 18-1/4" h **$1,265**

Ann Fuller, "Ann Eliza Fuller wrought in the 12th year of her age 1841," silk threads on linen ground, flowering border surrounding seven rows of alphabet examples, verse and signature, framed, 17" sq, fading, stains, 1841 .... **$300**

Caroline Wills, homespun linen, four alphabets, Roman numerals and house at base, "Paradise Tenant House," sgd "Caroline Elizabeth Wills," tiger maple frame, fading and discoloration, photo on back of maker, undated, 18-1/2" w, 20-3/4" h **$2,530**

Cynthia Taft, Uxbridge, Massachusetts, pink and green floral vine

encloses verse worked in pink linen above pictorial lower half with garden, trees, flowers, birds, and grass, pink, green, and red hues, good coloration and condition, reframed, minor imperfections, late 18th C, 10-5/8" w, 12" h **$4,115**

E. J., homespun linen, vase of flowers, sawtooth border, initialed "E. J. 1826," pulled and frayed edges, red painted frame, 1826, 4" w, 4-1/2" h **$2,090**

Elizabeth Thomas, homespun linen, alphabet and name, "Elizabeth Thomas, April 9, 1812," border by vine and floral motif, grain painted frame of yellow ground, red-brown highlights, 1812, 10-3/4" w, 12-3/4" h **$5,280**

Elizabeth Willits, each corner with different flower in soft pale blue, ivory, and gold, central vining wreath with tulip drop encircles verse, numbers, and "Maidencreek, Elizabeth Willits 1804" all done in dark brown, loosely woven linen ground, modern frame, minor stains, 1804, 13-1/4" x 14" **$2,970**

Fanny Chandler, Born December the 15 1803, silk threads on linen ground, rows of alphabets over pious verse, centered with house flanked by flowering trees and baskets of flowers, grid with the initials of family members, molded wood frame, fading, 1803, 15-1/2" x 19-1/2" **$825**

Frances Croll 1810, England or America, basket of flowers over alphabet panels above pious verse, surrounded by floral dec banner, worked in shades of red, blue, green, yellow, and blue threads, framed, fad-

ing, scattered staining, 1810, 16-3/8" x 12-3/4" **$825**

Genealogy, "Wrought by Charlotte Perkins AE t 12 Years Aug. 12 1819," attributed to ME, silk threads on linen ground, listing the vital statistics of Ezekiel Cushing and Frances (McCobb) Cushing and their six children, and Benjamin Perkins and Frances (Cushing) Perkins and their five children, beginning in 1752 and ending in 1808, lower reserve with monument and weeping willow commemorating the deaths of two family members, next to house, figure with sheep and dog, town across the river in the distance, all enclosed by border of flowers, foliage and a bowknot, unframed, toning, losses, stains, 1819, 24-1/4" x 21" **$2,585**

Homespun linen, alphabet at top, house scene with dog, bird, fruit, trees, and pump, red, green, blue, and brown, "Work in the year 1854," grain painted frame with yellow ochre ground, red-brown highlights, 1854, 17-1/2" w, 20-1/4" h **$4,620**

Isabella Lunds, work Aged 16 AD 1840, inspirational verse, attached buildings, trees, vines, floral and animal devices surrounded by stylized floral border, toning and fading, 1840, 26-3/4" x 32-1/4" **$2,470**

Lucenda Bingham, Massachusetts, silk threads on woven green and blue Linsey-Woolsey ground, three alphabet panels over pious verse over lettering reading "Lucenda Bingham aged 11 years 1809 born August the 3 1798," floral, star, bird, and

Store type, Chatillon's Improved Circular Spring Balance to Weigh 30 lbs by ounces, brass face, some wear, **$165.**

Health chart, trade stimulator type, black enamel base, tan and red top with chart, **$90.**

tree motifs enclosed in sawtooth border, framed, note on back of frame with family genealogy, several unobtrusive losses to background, 1809, 17-5/8" x 11-1/4" **$2,725**

Lydia Wood, sample Anno Domini 1799, stylized floral upper border above two alphabet panels over panel of flowering shrubs and birds, black, green, and pink silk threads, unframed, fading, toning, 1799, 15-1/4" x 10-1/2" **$715**

Mary B. Kimme, Massachusetts, "Wrought by Mary B Kimme---of Bolton 1823 (?) Aged 12 Years," verse and alphabets, house and floral symbols below, right-hand side appears to be unfinished, unframed, small areas of thread losses, some fabric loss to the linen ground, minor fading, 1823, 17-1/4" x 17-1/2" **$890**

Mary Jane Flint, aged 11 years, April 19, 1850, five alphabet panels, pictorial scene, Federal buildings, trees, bird and inspirational verse, framed, fading, toning, staining, 1850, 22-1/2" x 19-1/2" **$1,175**

Rebecca Myers, homespun linen, three alphabets, name at bottom, sawtooth border, veneered frame with minor paint dec, undated, 11-1/2" w, 14" h..**$1,100**

Sally Clark, Aged 8 Years 1801, inspirational verse flanked by stylized vases of flowers, upper borders above birds on branches, landscape with thatched roof cottages, framed, faded, 21" x 17", 1801 ....**$890**

Sawyer and Ryan families, border of vines and roses surrounding central image of two stylized trees, American, paper panels inscribed in ink with names of Ryan and Sawyer

Hanson, white enamel body, red and black logo, measures in pounds, **$40.**
Photo courtesy of Joseph P. Smalley, Jr.

families and dates from 1795 to 1816, 17" sq **$20,000**

SCALES

History: Prior to 1900, the simple balance scale was commonly used for measuring weights. Since then, scales have become more sophisticated in design and more accurate. There are a wide variety of styles and types, including beam, platform, postal, and pharmaceutical.

Advertising, Merchants Metal Spanish Tiles, Star Ventilator, Gothic Shingles, High Grade Roofing Plates, diecut multicolored tin litho, weighs up to 4 oz..................................**$400**

Apothecary, walnut, fitted ivory dec, 19-1/2" l, 15-3/4" h **$250**

Balance
Cast iron, orig red paint with black and yellow trim, nickel plated brass pans, marked "Henry Troemner, Phila. No. 5B, Baker's," 14" l.....**$120**
J. L. Brown & Co., 83 Fulton St., New York, circular pans, baluster turned cast iron stand, 26" h **$690**

Gold, Allender's Gold Scale, I. Wilson, New London, Connecticut, cast brass rocker balance, slots and platforms for 1, 2-1/2, 5, 10, and 20, additional weight and instructions in shaped paper box, mid-19th C, 9" l **$490**

Grain, chonodrometer, brass, Fairbanks, arm graduated for "lbs per bush," "lb & oz," and "% of lb," sliding weight, bucket, and suspension ring, 11" l...**$350**

Pamphlet, testimonials, Jones of Binghamton, New York, 32 pgs, illus price list of Jones Scales, cuts of canal weight-lock scale, universal, portable platform, postal, counter, rolling mill, lever, truss scales, etc., c1880, 3" x 5-1/2" **$55**

Platform, Peerless Junior, Peerless Weighing Machine Co., porcelainized steel, tiled platform, gold lettering, 63" h...**$350**

Pocket balance, steel, silvered pans, silver mounted shagreen case, engraved plaque, velvet-lined interior, two fitted circular weights and various others, 18th C, 5-1/2" w **$575**

Postal
Candlestick-style, gilt metal, British, for American market, circular pan with scrolled foliate borders, red enameled stem, trellis work and C-scrolls, rate table with eagle dec,

circular foot modeled in high relief with locomotive, steam clipper and farm implements interspersed with cornucopia, 1840s, 7-3/4" h **$275**

S. Mordan & Co., England, plates with blue and white Wedgwood jasper neoclassical roundels in ropetwist surround, rect base with three weights, 19th C, 4-1/2" h, 6-3/4" l **$350**

Store

"Computing Scale Co., Dayton, Ohio," 15-1/4" h, 17-1/2" w **$225**

Hanson Weightmaster, cast iron, gold case with ground, black lettering and indicator, 6" x 14" x 10" **$45**

SCRIMSHAW

History: Norman Flayderman defined scrimshaw as "the art of carving or otherwise fashioning useful or decorative articles as practiced primarily by whalemen, sailors, or others associated with nautical pursuits." Many collectors expand this to include the work of Eskimos and French POWs from the War of 1812.

Box, circular, engraved and stained, whaling scene, large whale surrounded by compass positions, late 19th C, 2-1/4" d, 2" h **$225**

Busk

Bone, scratch carved eagle, pinwheels, vining foliage, compass stars, and heart at top, black coloring with red in eagle's shield and one flower, small chip at top, 12-3/8" l **$550**

Wood, dec with eagle, shield, lovebirds, and ship under sail, heart and foliate devices, inscribed "GC & EW," dated 1840, 13-7/8" l **$345**

Cribbage board, carved walrus tusk

Carved in relief with Northwest fish and sea life, polychrome dec, late 19th C, 11" l **$360**

Carved on both sides, obverse, board in floral dec panel flanked by scenes of Northwest animals and fish, reverse with scenes of life in Northwest region, minor age splits, late 19th C, 23" l **$475**

Domino box, bone and wood, shoe form, pierced carved slide top with star and heart dec, domino playing pcs, Prisoner of War, cracks, minor

insect damage, 19th C, 6-7/8" l **$520**

Game box, bone, pierced carved box with geometric dec, three slide tops, compartmented int., backgammon and other playing pcs, traces of paint dec, Prisoner of War, repair, warping to tops, very minor losses, 19th C, 5-3/4" x 6-1/2" **$690**

Jagging wheel, dec with building flying American flag, berried vines, very minor losses, 19th C, 7-1/4" l **$520**

Obelisk, inlaid mahogany, inlaid with various exotic woods, abalone and ivory in geometric and star motifs, minor losses, minute cracks, 19th C, 13-3/8" h **$815**

Plaque, sailing ship, pencil inscription "Whale bone found in England by Mrs. Fred Rich," c1800, 14-1/2" l **$13,000**

Salt horn, engraved "John Snow March...1780 by S. H.," crosshatched borders enclosing reserve of ship, geometric, and foliate devices, insect damage, 5-1/2" l **$460**

Seam rubber, whalebone, geometric designs on handle, traces of orig paint, 19th C, 4" l **$850**

Snuff box, horn, architectural and marine motifs, dated "AD 1853" and "William Sandilands Plumber," English, 5" l **$950**

Swift, all whale bone and ivory, copper pegs, yarn ties, nicely turned detail, pincushion socket on top, age cracks, minor edge damage,

Reproduction Alert. The biggest problem in the field is fakes, although there are some clues to spotting them. A very hot needle will penetrate the plastics used in reproductions, but not the authentic material. Ivory will not generate static electricity when rubbed, plastic will. Patina is not a good indicator; it has been faked by applying tea or tobacco juice, and in other ingenious ways. Usually the depth of cutting in an old design will not be consistent since the ship rocked and tools dulled; however, skilled forgers have even copied this characteristic.

possible replaced section, 16" h **$900**

Walrus tusk

Reserves of animals, courting couples, ships under sail, memorials, sailors and armaments, later engraved brass presentation caps, "Presented by George M. Chase to Ike B. Dunlap Jan. 25th 1908," cracks, one restored, pr, 17-3/4" h **$2,530**

Walrus, dec with two eagles, lady, Indian, and vulture, age cracks, 19th C, 18-7/8" l **$1,840**

Watch hutch, bone, pierce carved floral and figural dec, brass backing, polychrome foliate highlights, Prisoner of War, custom-made case,

Scrimshaw ditty box, young woman, American ship, 19th century, 1-3/4" h x 4" w, **$820.**

Photo courtesy of Pook & Pook, Inc.

Scrimshaw whale tooth, six men in dory, 19th century, 4-1/2" h, **$760.**
Photo courtesy of Pook & Pook, Inc.

minor cracks, losses, repairs, 19th C, 11-7/8" h.....................................**$750**

Whale's tooth, 19th C

Dec with ship, woman resting on anchor holding flag, two potted plants, chips, minor cracks, 19th C, 4-3/8" l.....................................**$690**

Historic landmarks, dec on both sides, very minor cracks and chips, 6-5/8" h **$865**

Various ships under sail and young lady, cracks, 6-7/8" h.............**$1,380**

SEWING ITEMS

History: As recently as 50 years ago, a wide variety of sewing items were found in almost every home in America. Women of every economic and social status were skilled in sewing and dressmaking.

Iron or brass sewing birds, one of the interesting convenience items that developed, was used to hold cloth (in the bird's beak) while sewing. They could be attached to a table or shelf with a screw-type fixture. Later models included a pincushion.

Additional Resources:

Warman's® Americana & Collectibles, 11th Ed., by Ellen T. Schroy, ed., Krause Publications, Iola, WI.

Bodkins, whalebone and ivory, sealing wax inlaid scribe lines, minor losses, nine-pc set, 19th C **$400**

Book, *Fleisher's Knitting & Crocheting Manual,* S. B. & B. W. Fleisher, Inc., Philadelphia, Pennsylvania, 112 pgs, 21st edition, 1924, 7" x 9-1/2" **$15**

Catalog, E. Butterick & Co., New York, New York, 32 pgs, catalog for fall of women's clothing patterns, 1878, 7-1/2" x 10" **$38**

Folder, 8-3/4" x 14-1/4", Wm. R. Moore Dry Goods Co., Memphis, Tennessee, three pgs, heavy weight, "Guaranteed Fast Color No. 10 Batfast Suitings," 10 tipped-in blue Batfast Suiting swatches, c1937, 19-1/4" x 2" colored swatches tipped in **$28**

Etui, tapered ovoid agate case, ormolu mounts, hinged lid, fitted interior with scissors, knife, pen, ruler, needle, pincers, and spoon, Continental, late 18th/early 19th C, 3-1/2" l **$700**

Hand book, Davis Sewing Machine Co., Watertown, New York, *Centennial Hand Book Presented at the Great Exhibition,* 12 pgs, directions to get around at Exhibition, info on sewing machine, cabinets, etc. **$65**

Instruction book, *Singer Sewing Machines No. 99,* 32 pgs, c1910, 3-1/2" x 5-1/4"..............................**$16**

Magazine, *Home Needlework Magazine,* Florence Publishing Co., Florence, Massachusetts, 176 pgs, Vol. 1, No. 2, April, 1899..........................**$20**

Needle book, Rocket Gold Tipped Needles, cov illus of man and woman riding needle shaped like rocket, nighttime sky background, marked "Made in Japan," 1940s **$10**

Needle case, tri-color 18k gold, chase and engraved geometric and floral motifs, European hallmark **$320**

Pin cushion

Doughnut shape, brown and black cloth on one side, light blue and dark blue cloth on other side, purple hanging loop, 6" d, 1-1/2" h........**$85**

Eight-sided star, brown and red cloth on one side, purple and blue cloth on other side, black ribbon hanging loop, 4" d **$90**

Felt and yarn cushion strawberry mounted on pattern glass finial, Amish, Lancaster County, Pennsylvania, 9-1/2" h **$3,080**

Sewing bird shape, brown cloth, foliate pattern, 4" l, 1-1/2" w **$200**

Woolen, multicolored checkerboard pattern, black edges, brown velvet back, Amish, Centre County, Pennsylvania, price for pr, 6" sq **$165**

Sewing bird, ivory, four side-mounted spools, geometric and heart exotic wood inlay, inlay loss and replacements, 19th C, 4-1/8" l **$1,150**

Sewing box, bone and ebony inlaid, brass bound, Indo-Persian..........**$265**

Sewing box, wallpaper covered

Eight-sided, ftd, yellow wallpaper with maroon floral dec, green and blue cloth edging, sgd "Eli Myers, December 1885" in English and German, 5-1/2" d, 5" h **$3,850**

Round, nine paneled sides, dots and diamonds, orange, blue, green and white polychrome dec, under lid mkd "To Mother Ellin," 6" d, 5-1/2" h **$1,870**

Sewing box, wood

Inlaid hearts, arrows, diamonds, and circles, one dovetailed drawer, turned pull, worn pin cushion top, minor edge damage at corner, 5-1/2" w, 3-1/2" d, 3-1/4" h **$275**

Mahogany inlaid, hinged lid, center inlaid oval reserve with shell motif, ext. with inlaid borders and corners, int. lid centered with diamond motif, lift-out tray with several compartments, America, minor imperfections, 19th C, 12-1/4" w, 7-1/4" d, 5-5/8" h **$998**

Sewing egg, walrus ivory, unscrews to reveal ivory spool, thimble, and needle case, 19th C, 2-1/2" l **$920**

Spinning wheel

Upright, cherry, mellow refinishing, small ivory buttons, turned legs, tripod base, 9-1/2" d wheel, single flyer, 38" h **$350**

Upright, hardwoods, turned posts, iron fly wheel, ivory and ebonized wood details, old mellow refinishing, treadle with dec carving, old repair to cord belt, 34-1/2" h **$450**

Upright, hardwoods, turned posts, wood and wire fly wheel, small turned ivory pegs alternating with wheel spokes, traces of black paint on wheel, base, and legs, German, worm holes, some edge damage, one finial glued, two spokes damaged, 35" h **$295**

Stand, carved and turned walnut, round, four-tiered, graduated stand, pin cushion mounted on top, two rotating discs, each having six ivory spool holders, four ivory ball feet, New England, mid-19th C, 12-3/4" h **$300**

Tape loom, standing, floor type, turned wormy maple post, oak step down, cross bar base, loom pegged into post, replacements to loom and base, 39-1/2" h **$150**

Tape measure, advertising

General Electric Refrigerator, black and white beehive-style refrigerator on dark blue background, light blue rim, black and white name and text for local distributor on back **$20**

Kiwanis Club, blue and white celluloid canister printed on both sides, one side with international emblem, "We Build" on reverse **$15**

Lydia E. Pinkham, pale brown and white celluloid canister, sepia portrait of Lydia on one side, reverse with Vegetable Compound Blood Medicine tonics line **$25**

Parisian Novelty Co., celluloid canister printed in blue, white ground, both sides with text promoting celluloid novelties **$35**

Pillsbury's Family of Foods, celluloid canister, red, white, and blue flour sack printed on white, blue rim **$25**

Tape measure, figural, owl, metal, German **$45**

Thimble, brass, fancy band design **$15**

Thimble holder, fisherman holding large rod, beautifully detailed large fish on ground, bucket by fish, post in

*Sewing pin box, Royal Bayreuth, Tapestry, pink border roses, white and cream center roses, blue mark, gilt wear, early 20th century, 1-3/4" h x 2-1/2" x 4-1/2", **$131.***
Photo courtesy of Green Valley Auctions.

*Sewing flax spinning wheel, maple and oak, Virginia, turned legs and spindles, complete, minor repairs, mid-19th century, 20" d wheel, **$220.***
Photo courtesy of Green Valley Auctions.

Sewing scissor case, porcelain, scrollwork with light gilt highlights, gold filled mounts, gilt and mount wear, light denting, 19th century, 4-3/4" l, **$135.**
Photo courtesy of Green Valley Auctions.

Sewing clamp, carved ivory, two pin cushions, fabric wear, mid-19th century, 7" h, **$175.**
Photo courtesy of Green Valley Auctions.

front of fisherman, rect base, marked "Miller Silver Co. Silver Plate," 5-3/4" h **$350**

Thread and needle holder, turned wood, polychrome paint dec in yellow, red, and green banding, pin cushion on top with metal spool holders, opens to three compartments, 4" d, 7" h **$2,750**

Thread cabinet
Clarks, white lettering, four drawers, some damage to case **$100**
Dexter Fine Yarn, oak, four drawers, 18-3/4" h, 18-5/8" w, 16" d **$650**
Merrick's Spool Cotton, oak, cylindrical, curved glass, 18" d, 22" h **$725**
Willimantic, four drawers, ornate Eastlake style case, 14-1/4" h...**$550**

Yarn or cord winder, enameled steel and brass works, mahogany platform base, turned feet, signature plate "Goodbrand & Co. Ltd., Makers, Staleybridge," 28" w, 16-1/4" d, 29-1/2" h **$550**

SHAKER

History: The Shakers, so named because of a dance they used in worship, are one of the oldest communal organizations in the United States. Mother Ann Lee, who emigrated from England and established the first Shaker community near Albany, New York, in 1784, founded this religious group. The Shakers reached their peak in 1850, when there were 6,000 members.

Shakers lived celibate and self-sufficient lives. Their philosophy stressed cleanliness, order, simplicity, and economy. Highly inventive and motivated, the Shakers created many utilitarian household forms and objects. Their furniture reflected a striving for quality and purity in design.

In the early 19th century, the Shakers produced many items for commercial purposes. Chairmaking and the packaged herb and seed business thrived. In every endeavor and enterprise, the members followed Mother Ann's advice: "Put your hands to work and give your heart to God."

Apothecary cabinet, stained wood, rect, front fitted with 12 small drawers, molded white glazed porcelain handles, identification labels, drawer

sides inscribed with various content titles, New England, 19th C, 66" x 14" **$450**

Basket, finely woven splint, sq shape, two delicate bentwood handles, minor damage, traces of old red stain, 12" x 12" x 4-3/8" h..............**$360**

Blanket chest, New Lebanon, New York, hinged rect breadboard lift top, nail construction well, two long scratch beaded drawers, tapering cutout feet, all-over later grain paint to simulate exotic wood, old replaced pulls, surface imperfections, 1830-40, 40-1/2" w, 18-1/2" d, 36" h **$1,265**

Bonnet, dark brown palm and straw, black ribbons, Kentucky, 9" flounce **$395**

Book, *How the Shakers Cook & the Noted Cooks of the Country, Feature the Chefs and Their Cooking Recipes*, A. J. White, New York, New York, 50 pgs, bust of men illus, dusted, chips, 1889, 3-3/8" x 6-1/8" **$20**

Bottle, aqua, emb "Shaker Pickles," base labeled "Portland, Maine, E.D.P. & Co.," 9" h **$90**

Box, cov, bentwood
Finger construction, two fingers on base, one finger on lid, copper tacks, old green repaint, some wear on lid, 5-1/2" w, 3-1/2" d, 2-1/8" h **$850**
Finger construction, two fingers on base, one finger on lid, brass tacks, old green (black) repaint over traces of earlier green, minor wear, 6-1/8" w, 4" w, 2" h **$690**
Finger construction, two fingers on base, one finger on lid, copper tacks, reddish stain, 7-1/2" w, 5-1/8" d, 2-1/2" h **$320**
Finger construction, two fingers on base, one finger on lid, copper tacks, old blue paint, some wear, 9-1/2" w, 7" d, 3-3/4" h **$1,400**
Oval, Harvard lap, copper tacks, mellow natural finish, remnants of paper label on one end, 12" w, 8-3/8" d, 4-3/4" h **$440**
Oval, orig light green and cream paint sponged in leaf and feather patterned dec, seven fingers on side, one finger on lid, ex-Elgin, 20" w..................................**$26,000**

Carrier
Oval, maple, three lapped fingers, swing handle, copper tacks, number "5" impressed on base, clear

lacquer finish, 9-1/4" l, 6-3/4" w, 8" h **$425**

Round, single stapled finger, bentwood handle, some red stain remains, copy of old Currier & Ives hunting print in center, minor splits, 12-1/2" d, 1" h base, 6" h handle **$250**

Chair, dining, attributed to Canterbury, New Hampshire, birch and pine, concave rect back rail above turned stiles, four spindles, shaped seat, splayed turned tapering legs joined by stretchers, old red stain, missing right side stretcher, c1835, 17" h seat, 25" h back **$825**

Chair, side, maple and hickory, old brick red paint, pegged construction, back with three arched slats, high turned finials, turned and tapered posts with eight rungs each, old striped tape seats, minor variations in turnings, old pieced restoration to one leg, price for set of four, 16" h seat, 37-1/4" h back **$700**

Chest of drawers, pine, eight graduated dovetailed drawers arranged in two banks of four, turned pulls, six high feet with semi-curved cut-outs, old mellow refinish, replaced back boards, some pulls replaced, 63" w, 17-1/2" d, 39-1/2" h **$14,300**

Child's rocker, production, Mt. Lebanon, New York, incised "O" with decal on rocker, old varnished surface, replaced tape seat, minor imperfections, 1880-1930, 7-3/4" h seat, 24" h back **$3,300**

Cloak

Adult's, pink wool, labeled "The Dorothy Shakers, East Canterbury, New Hampshire," c1880-1920 .... **$1,195**

Child's, red wool, labeled "The Dorothy Shakers, East Canterbury, New Hampshire," c1880-1920 .... **$1,195**

Infant's, white wool, pink silk lining, shattering to lining, c1880-1920 .... **$595**

Dough scraper, wrought iron, 4-1/2" l **$40**

Dry sink, walnut, single double paneled door, shaped feet, Whitewater Shaker Meeting House **$5,500**

Flax wheel, various hardwoods, old dark brown finish, stamped "SR. AL," (Deacon Samuel Ring of Alfred, Maine 1784-1848), two pieces of distaff replaced, 33-1/2" h **$330**

Grain measure, bentwood, stencil label "Shaker Society, Sabbathday Lake, Me," minor edge damage, 7-1/2" d **$160**

Hanger, bentwood, chestnut, 24" w **$65**

Linen cupboard, painted poplar and pine, red, black sponged dec, Whitewater Shaker Meeting House **$21,000**

Mat, braided, plush velvet-like fabric, multiple colors and white, Canterbury, New Hampshire, 24" w **$80**

Recipe book, Laura Sarle, Canterbury, Shaker Village, New Hampshire, inscribed by author, recipes, brief autobiography, short play, housekeeping, records, knitting instructions, pen and ink on paper, mottled orange cardboard cover with black binding, wear to cover, few random annotations by later hand, 1883-87 .... **$5,520**

Rocker

#6, ladderback, old dark brown varnished surface, imp "6" on top slat, four arched back slats, elongated acorn shaped finials, later tan woven tape seat, curved arms with tapered rear posts, finely turned arm supports, splits at bottom of legs, restoration to one rocker, 15-1/2" h seat, 42" h back **$350**

#7, Mt. Lebanon, maple and birch, woven tape seat and back, shaped arms, domed caps, short acorn finials, imp "7" on upper slat, orig label remaining inside one runner, worn surface, 15-1/2" h seat, 42" h back **$500**

Small, Mt. Lebanon, black painted finish, small acorn finials, old woven tape back panel and seat, orig decal label inside one rocker, 14" h seat, 34" h back **$300**

Sewing box, cov, oval, pine lid with maple sides and lid rim, swing handle, five lapped fingers, int. lined with light blue padded silk, repair, wear, 15" l, 11-1/4" w, 11" h including upright handle **$1,880**

Shoe last, wooden, two with removable uppers, one with steel toe and heel, one with leather repair, Canterbury, New Hampshire, provenance: Lewis Noble Wiggins Shaker collection, price for set of four, 9" to 11" l **$150**

Table, maple, drop leaf, rect top, hinged rect leaves, single drawer, sq taper-

Shaker three finger oval box, 19th century, 4-1/4" h x 11-3/4" d, **$380.**
Photo courtesy of Pook & Pook, Inc.

Shaker herb bentwood box, pine top and base, maple sides, fingered, lift-off lid initialed "BC," mid-19th century, 3-1/2" l, 2" w, 1-1/2" h, **$250.**
Photo courtesy of Gamal Amer.

Shaker trinket box, bentwood, three-finger construction, old red wash surface, late 19th century, 6" l, 2" h, **$865.**
Photo courtesy of Pook & Pook, Inc.

Shaker miniature splint picnic hamper or purse, oval splint form, firm wrapped handle and hinged lids, 19th or 20th century, 6" x 5-3/4" x 3", **$530.**
Photo courtesy of David Rago Auctions, Inc.

ing legs, first half 19th C, 34-3/4" x 35-1/2" x 28" **$6,500**

Table swift, 25" h, maple, 19th C, 29-3/4" d extended **$230**

Tea table, attributed to Mt. Lebanon, NY, birch, circular tilt top with bull-nose edge, tilts on platform, tapering turned pedestal, tripod cabriole legs, pad feet, old refinish, c1830, 34-1/4" d, 26-3/4" h **$6,465**

Wash tub, New England, stave and lap fingered hoop construction, two handles, old red paint, imperfections, late 19th C, 24" d, 16-1/2" h **$460**

SHAVING MUGS

History: Shaving mugs, which hold the soap, brush, and hot water used to prepare a beard for shaving, come in a variety of materials including tin, silver, glass, and pottery. One style, which has separate compartments for water and soap, is the scuttle, so called because of its coal-scuttle shape.

Personalized shaving mugs were made exclusively for use in barbershops in the United Sates. They began being produced shortly after the Civil War and continued to be made into the 1930s.

Unlike shaving mugs that were used at home, these mugs were personalized with the owner's name, usually in gilt. The mug was kept in a rack at the barbershop, and it was used only when the owner came in for a shave. This was done for hygienic purposes, to keep from spreading a type of eczema known as barber's itch.

Shaving mug, Rockingham, divided int, medial molded floral band, unmarked, VG condition, second half 19th century, 4-1/2" h, 4-1/8" d rim, $65.

Photo courtesy of Green Valley Auctions.

The mugs were usually made on European porcelain blanks that often contained the mark of "Germany," "France," or "Austria" on the bottom. In later years, a few were made on American-made semi-vitreous blanks. Decorators who worked for major barber supply houses did the artwork on mugs. Occasionally the mark of the barber supply house is also stamped on the bottom of the mug.

After a short time, the mugs became more decorative, including hand-painted floral decorations, as well as birds, butterflies, and a wide variety of nature scenes, etc. These are classified today as "decorative" mugs.

Another category, "fraternal mugs," soon developed. These included the emblem of an organization the owner belonged to, along with his name emblazoned in gold above or below the illustration.

"Occupational mugs" were also very popular. These are mugs that contained a painting of something that illustrated the owner's occupation, such as a butcher, a bartender, or a plumber. The illustration might be a man working at his job, or perhaps the tools of his trade, or a product he made or sold.

Of all these mugs, occupationals are the most prized. Their worth is determined by several factors: rarity (some occupations are rarer than others), size of mug, and size of illustration (the bigger the better), quality of artwork, and condition—although rare mugs with cracks or chips can still be valuable if the damage does not affect the artwork on the mug. Generally speaking, a mug showing a man at work at his job is usually valued higher than that same occupation illustrated with only the tools or finished product.

The invention of the safety razor by King C. Gillette, issued to three and one-half million servicemen during World War I, brought about changes in personal grooming— men began to shave on their own, rather than visiting the barber shop to be shaved. As a result, the need for personalized shaving mugs declined.

Notes: Prices shown are for typical mugs that have no damage and show only moderate wear on the gilt name and decoration.

Fraternal

B.P.O.E., Elks, double emblem, Dr. title **$300**

F.O.E., Fraternal Order of Eagles, eagle holding F.O.E. plaque **$260**

IB of PM, International Brotherhood of Paper Makers, papermaking machine, clasped hands **$275**

I.O.M., International Order of Mechanics, ark ladder **$270**

Loyal Knights of America, eagle, flags, six-pointed star **$275**

Loyal Order of the Moose, gold circle with gray moose head, purple and green floral dec, gilt rim and base, marked "Germany" **$220**

United Mine Workers, clasped hands emblem flanked by crossed picks and shovels, floral dec, rose garland around top, marked "Germany" **$125**

Occupational

Electrician, hand-painted image of electrician wiring inside of electrical box, T & V Limoges, France, wear to gold lettering and trim, 3-5/8" d, 3-5/8" h **$2,500**

Express wagon, hp, man driving horse drawn wagon, word "Express" on side, floral springs, gold rim and name, 4" x 3-3/4" **$400**

Fabric store, colorful hp shop int., owner waiting on well-dressed woman, gold trim and name, 3-5/8" x 4-1/2" **$700**

General store, pork, flour, and whiskey barrels, Limoges, 4" x 4-3/4" **$650**

Hotel clerk, clerk at desk, guest signing register **$375**

House painter, detailed hand-painted image of man painting side of building, marked "Fred Dole" on bottom, light crack mark around top of handle, wear to gold lettering and trim, 3-1/2" d, 3-1/2" h **$350**

Hunting

Duck hunting, hp, duck hunter and dog in boat, 3-1/2" x 3-1/2" **$275**

Ducks, hp, two colorful ducks at water's edge, mkd "J. & C. Bavaria," 3-5/8" x 3-5/8" **$100**

Hunting dogs, hp, two hunting dogs, brown background, mkd "St Louis Electronic Grinding Co., Barber Supplies," some wear to gold trim,

Occupational shaving mug, service-man fixing boiler, inscribed "M.R. Goodall," 3-5/8" h, **$235.**
Photo courtesy of Pook & Pook, Inc.

Occupational shaving mug, bicy-clist on highwheeler, inscribed "P.J.," 3-4/8" h , **$700.**
Photo courtesy of Pook & Pook, Inc.

Occupational shaving mug, jockey racing horse and cart, inscribed "Geo. B. Wells," 3-5/8" h, **$305.**
Photo courtesy of Pook & Pook, Inc.

Occupational shaving mug, farmer with horse-drawn plow, field and farmhouse, inscribed "A.T. Butter-wick," 3-1/2" h, **$350.**
Photo courtesy of Pook & Pook, Inc.

Occupational shaving mug, fish-erman seated on rock, stream, inscribed "C.D. Fisher," 3-1/2" h, **$400.**
Photo courtesy of Pook & Pook, Inc.

Occupational shaving mug, teamster driving horse-drawn ice wagon, "Glen Willow Ice Company," inscribed "J.R. Hinkel," 3-5/8" h, **$645.**
Photo courtesy of Pook & Pook, Inc.

Occupational shaving mug, police-man, inscribed "H.D. Lewis," 3-5/8" h, **$265.**
Photo courtesy of Pook & Pook, Inc.

Occupational shaving mug, barber-shop scene, inscribed "Hunter Fran-cis," 3-1/2" h, **$645.**
Photo courtesy of Pook & Pook, Inc.

Occupational shaving mug, shoe store scene, inscribed "Chas. Lowenthal," 3-1/2" h, **$295.**
Photo courtesy of Pook & Pook, Inc.

Silhouette, hollow cut, "William S. Cowan M.D.," frame with envelope "West Chester, June 21" postmark, Pennsylvania, c1820-1830, 4-3/4" x 3-3/4", $322.
Photo courtesy of Pook & Pook, Inc.

Silhouette, family group, in gilt and black frame, prob. English, mid-19th century, 11-1/2" x 9-1/2" w, $400.
Photo courtesy of Wiederseim Associates, Inc.

Silhouette, bust, hollow cut, inscribed "Mrs. John Barker 1796 Phila.," with stamp "Museum," embossed under bustline, Charles Wilson Peale, 1796, image 4-1/2" x 3-1/2", $520.
Photo courtesy of Pook & Pook, Inc.

crack in ring handle, 4-1/8" x 3-3/4" **$120**

Rabbit hunting, hp, large rabbits in foreground, hunter walking thru snow, factory in background, 3-1/2" x 3-1/2" **$120**

Sportsman, hp, caught fish, fishing rod, shot gun, leafy sprigs, scene of men fishing in background, name in scroll, V D Austria, 3-5/8" x 3-5/8" **$130**

Ice man, hp, horse drawn Palmer's Ice Co. delivery wagon, rim and name in gold, T & V France, 3-1/2" x 3-1/2" **$825**

Mail wagon, hp, postal worker driving horse drawn mail wagon, German, repair to top rim on back, gold trim lines redone, 4" x 3-3/4" **$475**

Mover, detailed hand-painted image of two men in moving van, gold name and trim, Royal China Int'l, 3-7/8" d, 3-5/8" **$1,400**

Oil derrick, hp, detailed oil well scene, T & V France, 3-5/8" x 3-5/8" **$220**

Photographer, detailed hand-colored image of portrait photographer, marked "Webb Bros" in gold, wear to gold lettering and trim, 3-5/8" d, 3-1/2" h **$700**

Railroad, detailed hand-painted image of two railway workers on hand car, wear to gold lettering and trim, 3 1/2" d, 3-5/8" h **$650**

Shoemaker, hp, scene of shoemaker in shop, gilt foot and swags around name **$225**

Soda fountain, hp, serving clerk behind counter of soda fountain, well dressed woman sitting at counter on stool, name in gold, Germany, 3-3/4" x 3-5/8" **$2,500**

Surveyor, hp, detailed land surveying instrument in center, wear to gold name and trim, D & C, 3-1/2" x 3-5/8" **$550**

Tugboat, boat in water, crew and captain **$750**

Veteran, hp, US Civil War soldier holding American flag, name in gold, 3-3/4" x 3-1/2" **$1,500**

Writer, black desk inkwell with sander, pen, and brass handle **$350**

Other

Drape and flowers, purple drape, pot of flowers, gold name **$85**

Fish shape, scuttle, green and brown **$75**

Skull, white, gray, black, and cream, scuttle, marked "Bavaria" **$135**

SILHOUETTES

History: Silhouettes (shades) are shadow profiles produced by hollow cutting, mechanical tracing, or painting. They were popular in the 18th and 19th centuries.

The name came from Etienne de Silhouette, a French Minister of Finance, who cut "shades" as a pastime. In America, the Peale family was well known for the silhouettes they made.

Silhouette portraiture lost popularity with the introduction of the daguerreotype prior to the Civil War. In the 1920s and 1930s, a brief revival occurred when tourists to Atlantic City and Paris had their profiles cut as souvenirs.

Marks: An impressed stamp marked "PEALE" or "Peale Museum" identifies pieces made by the Peale family.

Boy

Boy under leafy branch, Hollow cut, very faint name underneath, worn gilt frame, fold lines with minor damage, 4-3/8" w, 5-3/4" h **$85**

Cutout, rosewood frame with worn gilt liner, 5" w, 5-3/4" h **$220**

Inked details, wrinkles, stains, partial typed label, pine frame, hollow cut, 4-3/4" w, 5-5/8" h **$200**

Boy and girl, full length, standing facing each other, hollow cut, gilt detail, bird's eye veneer ogee frame, 9-1/2" w, 7-5/8" h **$725**

Girl

Emily and Rosa, two girls playing, hand painted detailing, 1838, 7-1/2" x 10-1/4" **$600**

Girl with flower basket, jumping dog, titled "Miss Montague," 8-1/2" x 7-1/2" **$250**

Man

British officer, ink and watercolor on laid paper, red uniform jacket, gold epaulets and medal, sgd "de Mors," faint inscription on frame "Captain Robert Conig of His Majesty's 40th Regiment of Infantry...," orig gilt frame with damage, 5-3/4" w, 7-1/2" h **$230**

Cut-out, gold ink details in hair and coat, oval brass liner with convex glass, black painted frame, 5-1/2" h **$175**

Edward Brook, hollow cut, aged 16, wearing top hat, eglomise mat, period gilt frame, wear, repaint, stains, minor edge damage, 5-1/4" w, 5-7/8" h **$435**

Hollow cut, stenciled frock coat, eglomise glass mat with yellow painted designs, black velvet backing, black painted frame with traces of yellow on outer edge, 4-1/2" w, 5-1/2" h **$475**

Man identified in pencil as "Sir Walter Scott" writing at a table, Full length cut-out, attributed to Auguste Edoart, glued to page cut from book, hinged to mat, 12-5/8" w, 13-5/8" h frame, 8" w, 9-7/8" h **$320**

Man, inked hair, scarf, and labels, eglomisc mat, pcriod gilt framc, wear, stains, minor edge damage, 4-3/4" w, 5-5/8" h **$435**

Man, painted details, hair, scarf, and lapels, eglomise mat, period gilt frame, wear, repaint, stains, 4-3/4" w, 5-3/4" h **$350**

Man with floral motif around head, cut-work backed with black textile, old typed paper on back "Isaac Darlington, the famous Ice Cream Maker, whose farm overlooked the Brandywine above Jeffrey Bridge. This was cut by a traveling artist who held the scissors with his toes. Bought from Mr. Mark Darlington, May 10, 1927," orig frame, 5-3/4" w, 7-3/4" h **$1,430**

Man and Woman

Hollow cut, ink and watercolor details, framed together, sgd "Doyle," eglomise glass mat with two ovals, gilded frame, 10" w, 6-1/2" h **$425**

Hollow cut, man with high collar, woman with hair comb, black cloth backing, molded gold frame, some foxing of paper, price for pair, 5-1/4" w, 6" h **$440**

Hollow cut and painted, possibly work of William Chamberlain, bust length profile portraits, one of a young woman identified by inscription on reverse as "Pamelia DeWolf, sister of T. K. DeW, born July 16, 1794, D 1862," other young man identified on note as "T. W. DeWolf/Brother," hollow cut head and area below shoulder with black painted detailing of hair, vest, collar, and ruffles, deep blue vel-

vet, matted, molded giltwood frame, toning, stains, small tears, foxing, c1820, 3-1/8" x 2-1/8" **$775**

Man and wife, man with pigtail, wife with bonnet, laid paper, matching grain painted frames with gilt liners, stains, minor wear, 7-1/2" w, 7-1/2" h **$350**

Watercolor, pen and ink, gouache and silk on paper, hollow cut, half-length portraits of woman wearing comb in upswept hair, black dress, ruffled collar set off with blue ribbon, and man with blue vest, black jacket, holding red book, black silk lining, unsigned, indistinct penciled inscription on reverse of frame "Dudley, Oct.-1835," emb brass and wood frame, American School, pr, 19th C, 3-1/2" x 2-1/2" **$2,235**

Minister speaking from pulpit,

cut-out three-quarters length portrait, wearing spectacles, presentation note "Kings College Cam Apr 30 1836…," backing with notice for "Portrait, _ and Looking Glass Club…H. Flowers, carver and gilder…Southwark," bird's eye maple frame with worn gilt liner, 9-1/4" w, 11-1/4" h **$500**

Woman

Cut-out portrait of matronly woman wearing bonnet, penciled eyelash, reeded frame with black paint and punched brass rosettes, minor edge damage to frame, 3-3/4" w, 5-1/4" h **$220**

Lady with ornate hat, back marked "Mrs. Norman" and "Mrs. Norman, Henley on Thames," black lacquered case with gilded fittings, wear and stain, 4-7/8" w, 5-3/4" h **$200**

Mrs. Rosanna Lamb, full length, sgd and dated "Aug.st Edouart fecit 1842 Boston U.S.," cut-out paper figure laid down on paper, graphite, ink, and watercolor genre scene in background, sitter identified in note affixed to reverse, framed, toning, staining, 10" x 9-3/8" **$450**

Young woman, hollow cut, cut detail at collar, pencil inscription "Sarah Sage," stains, 5-3/8" w, 6-3/8" h **$200**

SILVER

History: The natural beauty of silver lends itself to the designs of artists and craftsmen. It has been mined and worked into an endless variety of useful and decorative items. Pure silver is too soft to be fashioned into strong, durable, and serviceable utensils. Therefore, a way was found to give silver the required degree of hardness by adding alloys of copper and nickel.

Silversmithing in America goes back to the early 17th century in Boston and New York and the early 18th century in Philadelphia. Boston artisans were influenced by the English styles, New Yorkers by the Dutch.

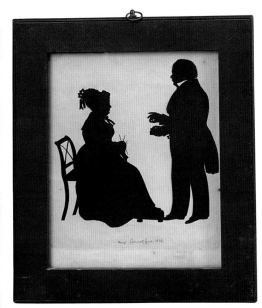

Silhouette, cut and pasted full length silhouette of a man and woman, "Aug. Edouart, fecit, 1838," Augustin Edouart, 1838, image 9-1/2" h x 7-1/2" w, **$935.**
Photo courtesy of Pook & Pook, Inc.

American coin silver sugar tongs, mkd "RM," early 19th century, 1.3 oz total wt., **$205.**
Photo courtesy of Pook & Pook, Inc.

American coin silver spoons, three serving and 10 teaspoons, Joseph Shoemaker, Philadelphia, c1800, approx. 10.6 oz total wt, **$468.**
Photo courtesy of Pook & Pook, Inc.

American, Dominick & Haff punch ladle, "Rococo," monogram and 1889 on reverse, late 19th century, 13" l, **$220.**
Photo courtesy of Green Valley Auctions.

American, Tiffany, vase, three handles, 44 troy oz, 6-1/4 PTS, 6" d, 8-1/2" h, **$1,800.**
Photo courtesy of David Rago Auctions, Inc.

Additional Resources:

Antique Trader® Metalwares Price Guide, 2nd Ed., by Kyle Husfloen, ed., and Mark Moran, contr. ed., Krause Publications, Iola, WI.

Warman's® Sterling Silver Flatware, by Mark F. Moran, Krause Publications, Iola, WI.

American, 1790-1840
Mostly coin

Coin silver is slightly less pure than sterling silver. Coin silver has 900 parts silver to 100 parts alloy. Sterling silver has 925 parts silver. American silversmiths followed the coin standards. Coin silver is also called Pure Coin, Dollar, Standard, or Premium.

Beaker, top and bottom molded rims, engraved, minor dents, Anthony Rasch, Philadelphia, 4 troy oz, 1807, 3" h, 3" d..................**$490**

Cake server, George C. Shreve, mark partially rubbed, shaped blade engraved with harbor scene within foliate cartouche, unfurling flag, engine-turned ground, fitted case, 3 troy oz, late 19th C, 9-1/8" l........**$200**

Coffee spoon, John David Jr., Philadelphia, PA, made for Cooch family, monogrammed, one with damage, dents, wear, price for set of eight, 4 troy oz, 1795-99, 5-1/4" l.........**$1,035**

Creamer, ewer form, beaded detailing, marked "RH," 6" h....................**$2,750**

Cup, scroll handle, geometric banding at top and bottom, engraved

sun motif, inscribed "Awarded by the S.C.A.S. (Southern Central Agriculture Society) & Mechanical Ins of Georgia, Oct 19th, 1852, for the best half dozen pair of Brogan Shoes," marked "Pure Silver Coin, J. E. Caldwell & Co., Phila," 2-1/2" h..**$1,320**

Dessert spoon, William Hollingshead, Philadelphia, Pennsylvania, marked "WH" in shaped stamp, twice on each handle, engraved "KIS," wear to bowls, imperfections, price for set of five, 9 troy oz, 1754-85 ....**$490**

Ewer, ftd, repoussé vintage dec, vine form handle extending round shoulder and around base of both pieces, engraved, minor dents, William F. Ladd, New York City, 1828-45, 12" h..**$1,200**

Goblet, Simon Chaundron, Philadelphia, Pennsylvania, marked "Chaundron" in banner, floriform, raised flutes at base of bowls, applied foliate band on bases, price for pr, 16 troy oz, 1812-15, 6-1/2" h and 6-3/4" h................**$3,750**

Jug, J. B. Jones & Co. makers, inverted pear-shaped body, scroll handle and stepped neck, round stepped foot, name engraved under spout, 12 troy oz, 2nd quarter 19th C, 7" h..**$700**

Mug, John L. Westervelt, Newburgh, New York maker, cylindrical, fine beading to foot and rim, scroll handle, central cartouche engraved with name and dated 1863, engraved Greek key border, allover engine turned ground, 6 troy oz, mid-19th C, 4" h..**$200**

Pitcher, bulbous, molded rim above engraved band, body with all-over repoussé strawberries and vines, weighted circular foot with emb dec, inscription on front and foot, mid-19th C, 8" h **$290**

Salt, oval form, four hoofed feet, repoussé floral and wreath dec at knees, gold wash bowls, minor dents, Ball, Black & Co., New York City, 1851-76, 7 troy oz, pr, 1-1/2" x 3-1/2"..**$290**

Snuff box, stamped "PP," flattened ovoid form, bottom inscribed "I trust this triffle in thy mind will favor find, 1791," imperfections, 1-1/2" x 3-1/2" x 2-5/8", 2 troy oz **$1,100**

Soup ladle, Simon Chaundron, Philadelphia, Pennsylvania, marked "Chaundron" in banner, English crest dec, 10 troy oz, 1812-15, 14-1/2" l **$920**

Sugar bowl, cov, Gorham, squat baluster, stepped foot, wide band of engine-turning, one plain and one engraved cartouche, two serpentine handles, domed lid with flower form finial, 17 troy oz, minor dents, mid-19th C, 8" h **$175**

Tablespoon, front tips, back engraved, bowl with emb scallop shell below short drop handle, minor dents, wear, Samuel Edwards, Boston, 2 troy oz, 1705-62, 8" l................................**$635**

Tea service, unmarked, 9-1/2" h teapot with hinged lid, creamer, cov sugar, lids with floriform knob finials attached to circle of ribbing, above round form bowl with shaped shoulders having vertical ribbing on lower half of body, raised on round stepped bases, four ball feet, applied tooled banding at neck, shoulder, and base, foliate devices attached to hollow strap handles and spout, 60 troy oz, 19th C..**$885**

American, 1840-1920
Mostly sterling

There are two possible sources for the origin of the word *sterling*. The first is that it is a corruption of the name Easterling. Easterlings were German silversmiths who came to England in the Middle Ages. The second is that it is named for the sterling (little star) used to mark much of the early English silver.

Sterling is 92.5 percent per silver. Copper comprises most of the remaining alloy. American manufacturers began to switch to the sterling standard about the time of the Civil War.

Basket, Whiting Mfg. Co., reticulated, sides with scrolls and diapering, scroll rim, three scroll feet, fluted base, monogrammed, 11 troy oz, late 19th C, 9" d, 3" h.........................**$460**

Bowl, Arthur Stone, Gardner, Massachusetts, chased decoration on bowl, circular stepped foot, imp mark with initial "H," 5" d, 3-1/4" h **$1,410**

Bread plate, Reed & Barton, banded dec, monogrammed, marked "Sterling 700," set of 12, 50 troy oz, 6-1/2" d..**$450**

Butter chip, Gorham, gadrooned border, engraved dragon with crown, monogram for Henredon Family, price for eight-pc set, 3" d..........**$150**

Cake plate, A. G. Schultz & Co., repousse, Baltimore, early 20th C **$160**

Castor, S. Kirk & Sons, Baltimore, Egyptian Revival, urn form, domed lid with repoussé leaves, bud form finial, body with three cast loop handles, all-over repoussé foliates, three cast sphinx feet, monogram, 4 troy oz, 1861-1868, 5-3/4" h **$690**

Center bowl, Frank W. Smith Silver Co., Inc., retailed by Bigelow, Kennard & Co., ovoid, engraved with quilted style pattern, edges reticulated with engraved leafy scrolls, edge with wide cast border of rocaille shells and C-scrolls, monogrammed center, 31 troy oz, late 19th C, 14-1/2" d..........**$1,840**

Challis, presentation, engraved "Award by the G. & A.A. Society to W. F. Fannin for the best collection of Southern made Plows, Oct 1852," inscription flanked by repoussé wheat sheaves, reverse side with repoussé plow, 7" h, 3-1/2" d at rim **$1,650**

Charger, Gorham, bicentennial commemorative, 155/250, special vermeil edition, 1972, cased....................**$300**

Cigarette case, Reed & Barton, 1" w 14k yg band running entire length and reverse, hinged gate stamped "14kt" and "Sterling R & B," 4.79 troy oz, 4-1/2" h.................................**$300**

Coffee set, Gorham, coffeepot, creamer, cov sugar, 16" tray, 73.05 troy oz..**$550**

Compote, Bigelow, Kennard & Co., Etruscan-style, bowl with central roundel of classical man holding grapes, seated woman with baby, dog, beaded surround, engraved anthemion and flowerheads, short stem with single rib to center, trumpet foot, plain flattened loop handles, applied Greek key rim, 22 troy oz, late 19th C, 8-3/4" d, 4-1/2" h **$700**

Dish, Howard & Co., quatrefoil form, filigree sides in fleur-de-lis pattern, applied ornamentation on rim of "C" and "S" scrolls and shells, marked "Howard & Co., New York, Sterling, 1903," 15 troy oz, 8" l.................**$300**

Dresser set, International Silver Co., Meriden, CT, cut glass powder jar, hair receiver, three dresser jars, all with sterling lids, pair of cut glass perfume bottles with silver mounted stoppers, hair brush, two clothes brushes, mirror, nail buffer, shoe-

American, sterling, presentation pitcher, squat ovoid, short spout, scroll handle, applied acanthus bands, engraved with presentation inscription dated 1889, 34 troy oz, 1886, 6-1/2" h, **$500.**

Photo courtesy of Skinner, Inc.

American, sterling serving spoon, overlapping stylized apple stem, gold-washed bowl, Tiffany & Co., Art Deco first half 20th century, 4 troy oz, 9-5/8" l, **$470.**

Photo courtesy of Skinner, Inc.

American, serving bowl, Tiffany & Co., Art Deco, footed, marked "23356," approximately 47.10 oz, 12-1/2" d, 4-1/4" h, **$1,150.**
Photo courtesy of Pook & Pook, Inc.

American, pitcher, bearing touch of James Thomson, New York, c1835, 39.5 oz total wt, 13-1/2" h, **$1,040.**
Photo courtesy of Pook & Pook, Inc.

American, water pitcher, presentation type, Tiffany & Co., 1875-91 mark, baluster body, repoussè and chased with Bacchanal couple, medallions framed by scrolling grape vines and acanthus leaf tips, centering presentation tablet inscription "Monmouth Park, July 12th 1879, Three Quarter Dash, Gentlemen Riders Won By Mr. W. C. Sanford's, Brg. Kadi by Lexington, Owner," wrapped anthemion-form handle rising from bacchanal mask, 38 oz 4 dwts., 8-3/4" h, **$5,350.**
Photo courtesy of Sloans & Kenyon Auctioneers and Appraisers.

horn, and nail file, all with engraved and banded rims, monograms, early 20th C **$920**

Fish knives, Gorham, Providence, Aesthetic Movement, blades with ornate monograms and bright cut foliates, mixed metal Japanese-style Kozuka handles with molded dec, price for set of 12, late 19th C **$2,300**

Flask

Ovoid, emb foliates on textured ground, domed lid with attached chain, approx two troy oz, late 19th/early 20th C, 4-1/4" l **$175**

Rect, Clarence Vanderbilt, New York, overall textured finish, reeded circular screw cap, approx 10 troy oz, c1909-35, 9" h **$260**

Fruit bowl, Dominick & Haff, retailed by Shreve, Crump & Low, fluted int., wide reticulated edge with realistically modeled chrysanthemums and daisies, 21 troy oz, late 19th/early 20th C, 12-1/2" d **$1,150**

Goblet, Whiting, monogrammed "R" **$120**

Ice cream slice, George W. Shiebler & Co., hammered finish, handle with Roman style male medallion on end, engraved bands of classical style designs, gold washed blade with further classical style engraving, medallion to lower right, central horizontal band of further small medallions, monogrammed on back of handle, 6 troy oz, late 19th C, 10" l **$4,025**

Ice water pitcher

Jaccard & Co., emb and chased dec, 1870, 12-1/2" h **$210**

Rogers Smith & Co., tilting, pitcher stand, goblet, and tumbler all dec with emb scenic bands of walrus hunters in icy water, enameled lined pitcher, c1872, 16-3/4" h **$550**

Jug, Lewis E. Jenks, Boston, vasiform, shaped lid with cast bird finial, lid and body with all over repoussé foliates, central monogrammed cartouche, spreading circular foot, 17 troy oz, c1875, 10" h **$635**

Kettle-on-stand, bombe repoussé all-over with flowers and leaves on fine stippled ground, hinged cover with similar dec, floral finial, fixed handle, circular base with conforming dec on four paw feet issuing from foliage, marked "S. Kirk & So., #101,"

burner marked "JI sterling silver," 56 oz, c1903-24, 13" h **$2,500**

Mustard pot, S. Kirk & Son, Baltimore, vegetal finial, glass liner, 7 troy oz, mid-19th C, 4-1/2" d **$150**

Perfume flask, Dominick & Haff, tapered cylindrical, floral chased and emb at lid, neck, and base, wide band of horizontal fluting at center, monogrammed, 5 troy oz, 9" l **$490**

Platter, Dominick & Haff, oval, border repoussé with flowers and leaves on fine matted ground, monogrammed, 16 oz **$475**

Punch bowl, circular stand with shaped rim, interior gold washed, chased and repoussé with garlands, scallop-shells and swags, maker's mark "BSC" on base, 10-1/4" d, 6-1/8" h **$750**

Roast platter, Gorham, Greek key border, early 20th C, 20-5/8" l, 14-1/8" w **$750**

Salad serving set, spoon and fork, Chambord pattern, Reed & Barton, monogrammed, 5 oz, 6 dwt, 9" l **$200**

Salt, open, Black, Starr & Frost, Classical Revival style, ovoid body, hoof feet terminating in lion's heads, red glass liner, 8 troy oz, four-pc set, late 19th C, 3-1/4" l, 1-3/4" h **$450**

Salver, Whiting M.F.G. Co., center chased with crab caught in a fishing net, monogrammed MLI, planished rim, shaped feet, 20.35 oz, 9-3/4" d **$1,195**

Sauce ladle, Wood & Hughes, New York, scalloped bowl, beaded handle with portrait medallion of classical warrior, monogrammed on reverse, 1 troy oz, second half 19th C, 6-3/4" l **$320**

Serving dish, cov, Thomas Kirkpatrick, New York, oval, domed lid with beaded band, cast stag finial, emb key pattern and beading on underside of rim, base with similar dec, some loses, 59 troy oz, third quarter 19th C, 8-7/8" w, 11-5/8" l **$1,035**

Tazza, Howard & Co., vessel with wide reticulated band and applied scroll rim, center monogram, applied scroll base, reticulated foot, pr, 19 troy oz, dated 1898, 7-1/8" d, 2-1/2" h **$700**

Serving spoon and fork set, Tiffany & Co., gold wash **$360**

Soup ladle, Tiffany & Co., Palm pattern, monogrammed, 1871-91, 12-1/2" l, 8 troy oz **$360**

Tea and coffee service, gadrooned border, chased with floral sprays and arabesques, monogrammed A.P.A., 15" h hot water kettle on lampstand, coffeepot, teapot, creamer, cov sugar, double handled waste bowl, all marked; together with silver plate tray, 164.05 oz **$2,400**

Tea service

Ball, Black & Co., tapered ovoid teapot, cov sugar, helmet-shaped open creamer, each with applied profile medallion and anthemion engraving, pendant handles, monogrammed, 36 troy oz, third quarter 19th C **$2,185**

Gorham, made for Blanche M. Halle, Cleveland, Ohio, each pc stamped with her name, panels separated by ribs, dec with repoussé and chased trumpet urns of fruit, lids with carved ivory pineapple finials, 10-1/2" h teapot, 11-1/2" h coffeepot, creamer, cov double handled sugar, waste bowl, 18-1/2" x 30" tray, 276 troy oz **$4,675**

Gorham, Plymouth pattern, coffeepot, teapot, creamer, cov sugar, waste bowl, monogrammed, 55 troy oz, some dents to sugar lid **$875**

Shreve, Stanwood & Co., 16" h hot water urn on stand, creamer, cov sugar, open sugar, and 9" h teapot, ovoid, beaded detailing, lids with swan finials, domed stepped foot, urn with presentation inscription on side, burner and one sugar lid missing, 35 troy oz, 1860 ...... **$2,185**

Tea tray, Gorham, Providence, shaped molded rim, beaded band, pierced handles, monogrammed, 114 troy oz, 1912, 17-7/8" w, 25-3/4" l **$1,725**

Tete-a-tete, Gorham, Providence, 4" h teapot, creamer, open sugar, cone shape, ball finial, reeded handles, banded necks, gilt interiors, monogrammed, 16 troy oz, 1880 .... **$320**

Travel clock, Wm. Kerr & Co., plain rect case with rounded corners, eight-day movement, oct goldtone engine-turned face, black Roman numerals, silver surround with engine turning, engraved scrolls and floral sprays, monogrammed cover, late 19th C, 3-5/8" l, 3-1/8" w **$200**

Travel clock, Tiffany & Co. **$250**

Tray, Reed & Barton, Taunton, Massachusetts, rect, shaped molded rim with openwork and engraved band, monogrammed center, 24 troy oz, late 19th/early 20th C, 10-1/4" w, 14-1/4" l **$350**

Trophy pitcher, Whiting, New York, Harvard University, cylindrical, inverted rim, waisted body with inscription on front, circular base with molded scroll dec, 33 troy oz, c1892 .... **$1,380**

Vase

Gorham, flared draped rim, scalloped edge, bulbous base, pedestal foot, engraved scroll, foliage, and floral urn designs, figural accents, monogrammed central cartouche, marked "1083L, Sterling," 99 troy oz, 20-1/2" h **$3,850**

J. E. Caldwell & Co., tapered baluster form with engraved laurel wreath on each side, one with monogram, everted rim with engraved band of lines and circles, trumpet foot with similarly engraved band, 34 troy oz, late 19th/early 20th C, 15-3/4" h **$750**

Water pitcher

Dominick & Haff, New York, vasiform, molded rim, "S" scroll handle, molded base, 22 troy oz, 20th C, 9" h **$375**

Gorham, Providence, paneled vasiform, rim and base with beaded bands, handle with cast acanthus dec, octagonal molded base, monogrammed, 26 troy oz, 1885, 9-1/4" h **$635**

Continental

Generations have enjoyed silver created by Continental silversmiths. Expect to find well-executed forms with interesting elements. Most Continental silver is well marked.

Austria

Candlesticks, pr, Rococo-style, paneled baluster stem and socket, scrolled weighted base, removable bobeche, lacquered, late 19th C, 12-1/2" h **$690**

Casket, rect, lid with cast pear form finial, molded rim and foot, waisted body with silver mount on lock, 14 troy oz, mid/late 19th C, 3-3/8" w, 5-1/4" l **$575**

Order, traces of gilt, inscribed "HM 1929/30," marked, 1.30 oz, 1929-30, 6" l **$120**

Continental, Denmark, Georg Jenson, two sterling hand-hammered bowls, raised on leaf and ball feet, price for pr, 12 t.o., 5" d, 2-3/4" h, **$1,900.**
Photo courtesy of David Rago Auctions, Inc.

Continental, centerpiece, oval, foliate scroll and shell feet, sides pierced with guilloches, hung with ribbontied berried laurel swags between bands of vitruvian scrolls, pierced anthemion, open double scroll handles, fitted with silver-plated liner, crowned A, crowned P and crowned fleur-de-lis marks, 27 oz, 14" h, **$1,100.**
Photo courtesy of Sloans & Kenyon Auctioneers and Appraisers.

Continental, Denmark, Georg Jensen, demitasse spoons, sterling, set of six, **$225.**
Photo courtesy of David Rago Auctions, Inc.

Continental, Denmark, Georg Jensen, pitcher, No. 385, sterling, ivory handle, **$4,250.**
Photo courtesy of David Rago Auctions, Inc.

Continental

Asparagus server, reticulated handles topped by crowned lion's head, flowerheads and scrolls, standing figure, ending in cherub face above floral basket flanked by cherub herms over reticulation, blades reticulated with C-scrolls and engraved with flowers and further scrolls, monogrammed, 9 troy oz, late 19th C, 11-1/4" l **$230**

Beaker, silver gilt, tapering cylindrical form, circular gadrooned foot, upper body engraved with strapwork enclosing arabesques, base chased with two bands of bosses, 3.35 oz, 17th C **$3,850**

Candelabra, three-light, shaped sq lobed foot with scroll and floral rim rising to fluted stem applied with similar dec, two scrolling foliate branches, central fixed sconce, detachable bobeches, convertible to candlestick, engraved with monogram below crown, weighted base, 21-1/2" h **$900**

Condiment jar, formed as sedan chair, stamped with scrolls and cartouches of dancing couples, hinged lid with quadripartite finial, cobalt blue glass liner, restorations, 5 troy oz, late 19th/early 20th C, 4-3/4" h **$375**

Creamer, figural, horned cow, fly hinged lid, 19th C, 5-1/2" l, 4-1/4" h **$800**

Oil lamp, tapered ovoid form, chased overall with grapes and vines, associated pierced silvered metal shade, 29" h **$720**

Spoon, figural terminal, pear shaped bowl chased on obverse with armorial crest, inscribed "MIS Df HS, ANNO 1642, WER-ALTID LYKLIG," verso inscribed "A," marked, 1.80 oz, possibly 17th C, 6-1/4" l **$420**

Danish

Coffee service, Georg Jensen Silversmithy, 1933-44, Blossom pattern, 7-1/8" h coffee pot, mkd "no. 2B"; cream jug, mkd "no. 2A"; waste bowl, mkd "no. 2A"; 25.10 oz **$2,650**

Compote, round bowl over round stepped standard, base imp "Denmark 300" at bowl center, price for pr, 6-5/8" d, 5-3/8" h **$290**

Flatware service, Georg Jensen Silversmithy, post 1945, Acorn pattern, 12 each dinner forks, salad forks, oyster forks, dinner spoons, dessert spoons, cream soup spoons, demitasse spoons, dinner knives, butter knives; two serving spoons, one serving fork, 111 pcs, 119.55 oz **$7,200**

Low bowl, circular foot, imp Georg Jensen, "G830s," in beaded oval, signed in script, 7-5/8" d, 2-1/8" h **$1,645**

Water pitcher, tapered egg-shaped body, flared stem with beading to top, stepped foot, spout with curved reeding to underside, wooden handle with stylized floral terminal to top, 20th C, 9-3/4" h **$750**

Wine coaster, F. Hingelberg, molded rim, twisted wire sides, composition base, price for pr, 20th C, 4-3/4" d **$490**

Dutch

Bowl, .833 fine, Dutch export mark, repoussé, lobed, reserves with chased and emb country scenes, two pierced handles with putto to top, central flowers flanked by putto riding dolphins, 15 troy oz, 19th C, 14-1/4" l, 3" h **$460**

Box, .833 silver, rect, shaped lid with engraved nativity scene within foliates, base with two biblical scenes, banded sides with engraved foliates, 8 troy oz, late 19th C, 2-5/8" w, 5-1/2" l **$960**

Chatelaine, cast brooch with scene of putti with goddess, medallion mounted chains supporting two boxes, cylindrical container, pair of scissors, stylized crown, 9 troy oz, c1890, 12-1/8" l **$600**

Coffeepot, .833 fine, baluster form pot with all-over scroll and foliage repoussé, windmill vignette on one side, scroll cartouche topped by crown flanked by putto on other side, legs topped by crowned human masks, four ball and claw feet, turned wood handle set at right angle to ram-horned grotesque spout, flattened lid with vertical ribbing, rampant lion finial, 11 troy oz, late 19th C, 8" h **$800**

Pitcher, .833 line, baluster form, neck with band of fluting, repoussé to lower section of foliage, birds and putti, domed foot with vertical ribbing, spout with putto, beaded serpentine handle, lid with vertical reeding, repoussé and vegetal finial, base engraved "Esther Cleveland," 6 troy oz, descended in family of Grover Cleveland, late 19th C, 5-1/2" h **$260**

French, .950 fine

Coffeepot, pear-shaped, cast quadripartite scroll embellished serpentine spout and handle, heat stops, domed lid with flower form finial, 22 troy oz, third quarter 19th C, 9-1/4" h **$460**

Dish, cov, undertray, Paris, "C. P." maker's mark, cylindrical body with acanthus and flat leaf handles, rim with beading and flat leaf band, base with band of flat leaves, foot with band of laurel, lid with beaded edge, removable circular handle formed as cornucopia on leaf and flower base, fitted leather case, 30 troy oz, 1819-38 .... **$2,615**

Fish serving platter, oval, reeded rim, monogrammed, 66 troy oz, 27-3/4" l, 11-1/2" w **$1,265**

Serving dish, oval, two shell handles, vertical reeded border, 17 troy oz, third quarter 19th C, 11-3/4" l, 2-1/4" h **$490**

Sweetmeat dish, Odiot, Paris, maker, shell form vessel drawn by sea creatures, reins held by two putti, flanking central standing putto poised as Neptune, holding trident-form fork, shaped rect base cast as water, 65 troy oz, pr, late 19th/early 20th C, 5-1/2" l, 5" h **$2,100**

Tureen, cov, sprays of acorns and oak leaves to top, reeded rim, lid with flat leaf rim, stem with reeded shoulder, oval foot, flat leaf band, angular handles with flat leaf to bottom, stylized corn finial about flat leaf and lotus ground, third/ fourth quarter 19th C, 12-3/4" l, 10-1/2" h **$1,840**

German, .800 fine

Basket, shaped oval, paneled sides pierced with flowers, garlands, and scrolling foliage centering four vacant cartouches, center repoussé with flowers, foliage, and three putti at play, 15 oz, 8 dwt, 14" l **$200**

Beaker, cov, silver gilt, chased with swags and tasseled drapery, highlighted with matting, marked on cover and base, 8.95 oz, 18th C, 7-3/4" h **$2,400**

Box, rect, hinged lid, Roman chariot scene in relief, beaded edge, reeded sides with vine accents, marked "800 Germany," 5-1/4" x 3-1/4" x 1-1/2" **$200**

Bread tray, repoussé, cartouches of courtship scene, imp German hallmarks and "800," c1920, 15" x 10-1/2" **$920**

Kettle-on-stand, compressed circular with lobed sides, four hoof feet, detachable cover with wooden finial, central swing partial wooden handle, multi-scroll stand with border, 48 oz, 8 dwt, 16" h............**$325**

Sauceboat, shape of open-mouthed fish, emb and engraved scales, open back with molded rim, tail shape handle, supported by cast fins, glass eyes, 13 troy oz, late 19th/early 20th C, 10-3/4" l..................**$1,495**

Serving dish, Wilhelm T. Binder, rounded trefoil shape, three handles, repoussé leaf bud and line dec, scalloped, ribbed glass insert, imp "WTB, 800 fine," c1900, 12" d, 3-1/2" h.........................**$1,150**

Tankard, silver gilt, barrel embossed with strapwork enclosing male masks above dentilated band, double scroll handle, cover with baluster finial, marked on footrim and cover, 9.45 oz, 17th C, 5-1/4" h........**$5,750**

Wedding cup, figural, beaded figure with chased and emb skirt, cup chased and emb with scrolls and grotesques, 15 troy oz, 9" h.........**$1,955**

Italian

Asparagus tongs, F. Broggi, Milan, individual, plain, tapered form, set of six, 6 troy oz, 20th C, 5-1/4" l
....**$115**

Punch bowl, repoussé, bowl with band of flat leaves to base below further continuous hunt scene of men attacking various animals, domed foot with band of flat leaves below continuous hunt scene, removable liner, 146 troy oz, late 19th/early 20th C, 12-5/8" d, 10-1/2" h **$4,025**

Portuguese, .833 silver

Bowl, Oporto, molded scroll and shell rim, band of chased dec, molded circular foot, 14 troy oz, 20th C, 11-3/4" d **$230**

Chalice, domed lid with applied openwork foliate band, engraved bands and cruciform finial, bowl with engraved band with Latin inscription, applied gothic style openwork mounts, stem with beaded and engraved knop, stepped circular base, int. gilt, 31 troy oz, 12-1/2" h
....**$690**

Ewer, maker's mark "S&P," bulbous, molded shaped rim, body with chased stippled dec, emb foliate, scroll, and shell band, cast scroll handle, molded circular foot with

emb dec, 33 troy oz, late 19th/early 20th C, 11-3/4" h......................**$815**

Kettle-on-stand, maker's mark effaced, inverted pear form, domed lid with cased foliates and wood urn finial, upright handle with cast silver acanthus mounts, body with all-over chased and engraved foliates and scrolls, circular stand with four scroll legs and shell feet, chased and engraved burner with turned wood handle, 54 troy oz, second half 19th C, 14-1/4" h..............................**$920**

Salver, molded openwork scroll and foliate rim, bright cut foliate dec on face, three cast legs with shell feet, 25 troy oz, 11-5/8" d.................**$350**

Tray, maker's mark "GP," rect, openwork raised rim with molded grape dec, cast foliate handles, face with engraved dec, 85 troy oz, 20th C, 13-1/2" w, 22-5/8" l.................**$1,265**

Swedish

Hot water kettle on lampstand, maker's mark "AH," globular body with gadroon rim and cover, acorn finial, stand raised on s-scroll legs terminating in shell-form feet, marked on kettle base, cover and stand, base and stand with illegible English marks, 49.20 oz, 14-3/4" h........**$850**

English

From the 17th century to the mid-19th century, English silversmiths set the styles which inspired the rest of the world. The work from this period exhibits the highest degree of craftsmanship. English silver is actively collected in the American antiques marketplace.

Basting spoon, George I, London, Brittania Standard, rat tail/ Hanoverian pattern, back of terminal inscribed with crest, mkd on back of stem, maker's mark illegible, 5.80 oz, 1714, 13-3/4" l........................**$2,155**

Basket, J. R. Hennell maker, London, Victorian, reticulated foliate pattern, circular banding, shaped edge with bead and flat leaf rim, four scroll and cylinder feet with husk swags, glass liner, 21 troy oz, pr, 1884, 6" d, 3-1/2" h....................................**$1,725**

Bowl, W. Comyns & Sons maker, London, Edward VII, shallow bowl emb with shield-shaped panels, hand-hammered surface, low flower form foot, 7 troy oz, 1902, 5-1/4" d, 1-1/2" h
....**$435**

English, punch ladle, bearing marks of William Gibson and John Langman, London, c1899, 13" l; together with English silver punch ladle, c1789, bearing mark of "T.S." (Thos. Shephard), 13-1/2" l, **$500.**
Photo courtesy of Pook & Pook, Inc.

English, Georgian, basket, bearing the touch of Thomas Robins, c1804, 25.6 oz total wt, 13-1/4" l, **$1,955.**
Photo courtesy of Pook & Pook, Inc.

English, cup, Edward VII, London, hammered body, scroll strap handles, 1905, 6 oz, 8 dwt, 2-3/4" h, **$265.**
Photo courtesy of Sloans & Kenyon Auctioneers and Appraisers.

English, Georgian, tankard, touch of Hester Bateman, dome lid, scrolled handle, heart terminal, 1787-1788, 8" h, approx, 26.3 oz total wt, **$4,210.**
Photo courtesy of Pook & Pook, Inc.

Candelabra, pr, William Comyns & Son, Edward VII, silver gilt, in Neo-Classical taste, fluted domed base rising to fluted baluster stem hung with floral swags, removable branches with laurel leaf arms supporting candle sockets and vase shaped nozzles, each fully marked on exterior base and detachable nozzle, 232.05 oz, 1908-09, 19" h **$11,360**

Candlesticks, pr, Crichton Brothers, London, Charles II style, quadripartite shell-form base rising to smaller quadripartite shell-form drip pan, vase form standard rising above four open scrolls to fluted columnar sconce with shaped bobeche, each fully marked on base and underside of bobeche, stamped "Crichton Brothers, New York & London," 74.45 oz, 1909-10 .... **$3,700**

Castor, Hester Bateman, London, George III, urn form, engraved pierced lid with cast urn finial, engraved bands at shoulder, waist, and spreading circular foot, 2 troy oz, 1788, 5-3/4" h **$690**

Caudle cup, Samuel Wastell maker, London, William III, Brittania Standard, tapered cylindrical body with single applied molded band, cast ear-shaped handles, spreading domed foot, engraved on one side, heraldic device in rococo-style cartouche, 26 troy oz, 1704, 6" h, 10-1/2" l **$2,990**

Center bowl, Robert Garrard, London, George III, lobed ovoid body, two short scroll and acanthus handles, gadroon and shell border offset with two scroll details to each side, four cast paw feet topped by group of scrolls, 51 troy oz, 1811, 17" l, 5-1/2" h **$4,325**

Chamberstick, W. Comyns maker, London, Victorian, chased and emb with flowers and scrolls, removable bobeche, handle with monogrammed thumb-piece, 2 troy oz, 1888, 4" l, 1-3/4" h **$115**

Charger, Rebecca Emes and Edward Barnard, London, George IV, shaped edge, applied gadroon and shell border, engraved gartered heraldic device on rim, 29 troy oz, 1826, 11-3/4" d **$1,380**

Cigarette case, engine turned ext., monogram, 5.29 oz, c1944, 4-1/2" h **$70**

Coaster, "W.H.H." maker's mark, Birmingham, 1904, Edward VII, round, 4 troy oz, pr, inset to center with George III Irish 10-pence bank tokens dated 1905, 4-3/8" d **$115**

Coffeepot, William Grundy maker, London, George III, baluster, spreading foot, scroll handle with ivory heat stops, serpentine spout with rocaille shell to base, flat leaf to spout, engraved monogram within foliate rococo-style cartouche, domed hinged lid with spiral reeded egg-shaped finial, 60 troy oz, 1767, 14-1/2" h **$5,750**

Compote, Benjamin Smith maker, London, Victorian, bowl with shaped edge and vertical ribbing, everted rim with applied grapevine dec, tree-trunk form base with twining grapevine, 36 troy oz, 1845, 12-1/2" d, 7" h **$1,150**

Cream jug, Hester Bateman, London, George III, vasiform, chased beaded rim, body with repoussé farm scenes surrounding central cartouche, trumpet foot with spreading rim, 3 troy oz, restoration, 1782, 5-1/4" h **$225**

Cup, Samuel Godbeheve, Edward Wigan and J. Bolt makers, London, George III, baluster form, two handles, four drill holes in base, 11 troy oz, 1800, 5-5/8" h **$490**

Demitasse spoon, John Wren maker, London, George III, bright cut engraved stem, fluted bowl, 3 troy oz, set of six, 1791, 5" l **$260**

Dish cross, "BD" maker's mark (Burrage Davenport), London, George III, pierced shell form feet and plate supports, burner with gadrooned rim, 15 troy oz, 1772, 12" l **$1,265**

Egg cup frame, Henry Nutting maker, London, George III, reeded central handle, four ball feet, six associated Sheffield egg cups, five associated demitasse spoons, 18 troy oz, 1800 .... **$550**

Entree dish, cov, "BS" maker's mark, London, George IV, lid modified with later band of foliate repoussé and engraved with heraldic crest and monograms, base with gadroon and shell rim, removable leaf and shell handle, 67 troy oz, 1820, 12-1/8" l, 5-3/4" h **$1,725**

Epergne, "GJ DF" maker's mark, London, George V, central stem below navette-shaped reticulated basket with applied border, flanked by smaller removable baskets on scrolled arms, ovoid reticulated base with applied scroll and shell border, four scroll feet, 76 troy oz, 1913, 10-1/2" l, 11-3/4" h **$6,325**

Fish server, attributed to John Neville, London, George III, reticulated blade with scrolling foliage, stem end with shell, handle, engraved with gadrooned edge, central heraldic device, 4 troy oz, 1770, 11-1/4" l **$1,100**

Flatware service, partial, Spaulding-Gorham, London, George VI, six lunch forks, six salad forks, six dinner forks, 18 fish forks, six dinner knives, 18 fish knives, six butter knives, 18 place spoons, six soup spoons, 18 cream soup spoons, 21 teaspoons, 18 five o'clock teaspoons, six demitasse spoons, 12 ice tea spoons, monogrammed MMR, 18 George VI/Elizabeth II fruit knives, maker's mark CWF, 1952, 189 pcs, 221.75 oz, 1938 .... **$3,150**

Flower bowl, George III, Paul Storr, classical design based on Warwick vase, hallmarked London, 1808 .... **$4,700**

Goblet, maker's mark partially obscured (attributed to Henry Greenway), London, George II, beaded collar, tapered round funnel bowl, beaded trumpet foot, engraved coat of arms in roundel, 16 troy oz, pr, 1775, 6-1/2" h **$1,955**

Hot water kettle on stand, John Emes maker, London, George III, lid partially reeded with wood finial, pot with ovoid body partially reeded with gadrooned edging, on tapered circular foot, fluted tap, upright silver and wood handle, stand with gadrooned rim with burner and cover, flat leaf legs, four hairy paw feet with wooden ball supports, pot engraved with motted coat of arms, small heraldic device on pot lid, burner lid, and burner, 83 troy oz, 1807, 12" h **$2,100**

Jug, cov, "C. W." maker's mark, London, George III, later Victorian adaptations, stamped bands flanking convex band at rim, ovoid body with twisted reeding and fluting to lower section, central cartouche flanked by C-scrolls, serpentine handle, domed foot, short spout, domed hinged lid with Victorian hallmarks, twisted reeding, fluting

on urn finial, 18 troy oz, 1769, 7 3/4" h
.... **$400**

Marrow scoop, Richard Pargeter, London, George II, back engraved "BWM," mkd, 1.65 oz, 1737-38, 9" l
.... **$500**

Meat skewer, Thomas Whipham & Charles Wright, London, George III, tapering, plain loop terminal, engraved "V," mkd, 3.90 oz, 1761-62, 12-3/4" l **$210**

Mirror, "JR SJ" makers, London, Victorian, rect, curved top, reticulated with scrolls and flowers, mask center at base, grotesque beasts on either corner, beveled edge mirror, easel stand on back, 1887, 14-1/4" h, 10" d
.... **$980**

Muffineer, Charles Stuart Harris maker, Brittania standard marks, London, tapered paneled lid with engraving, baluster form finial, paneled baluster form, tiered foot, 14 troy oz, 1899, 8-1/2" h **$800**

Mug, Richard Beale, London, George II, cylindrical, cast "S" scroll handle, molded circular foot, engraved crest, 6 troy oz, 1731, 3-3/4" h **$980**

Mustard pot, attributed to William Barrett II, George III, circular, disk finial, reeded rim and base, reticulated sides with engraved foliates and urns, associated glass insert, 3 troy oz, 1827, 2-1/2" h **$290**

Porringer, cov, maker's mark II, London, William & Mary, tapered body, engraved armorial within baroque strapwork cartouche below cast scroll handles, raised cov with central fluted dec and baluster finial, mkd only on body, 10.80 oz, 1691, 4-3/4" d, 4" h
.... **$1,800**

Salt, open, Walker & Hall, Sheffield, Edward VII, cobalt blue glass liner, mkd, 1902-03, 4" l **$180**

Salver

John Tuite maker, London, George II, shaped molded rim offset with shells, central engraved coat of arms in rococo cartouche, four scrolled leaf feet, 32 troy oz, 1783, 12-3/8" d
.... **$2,185**

John Cotton & Thomas Head maker, London, George III, beaded and ribbed border, four beaded and ribbed feet, center engraved with mottoed coat of arms, 64 troy oz, 1813, 16-1/4" d **$3,750**

Mappin & Webb makers, London, shaped edge with bead shell border,

four scrolled feet, 60 troy oz, 1946, 17-1/4" d **$1,610**

Robert Abercomby maker, London, George II, shaped edge, engraved with wide band of florals, fruits, shells, scrolls, and diapered cartouches, four paw feet topped by shells, engraved central Chinoiserie-style coat of arms, 156 troy oz, 1750, 22-7/8" h **$4,320**

Sauceboats, pr, maker's mark "T. D. & S.," Birmingham, George III style, oval form, shaped borders, flying scroll handles, hoof feet with fluted shell headers, marked on bases, 15 oz, 1947, 7-1/4" l **$400**

Sauce ladle, Hester Bateman, London, George III, Old English pattern, mkd on back of terminal, 4.30 oz, 1790, 13" l **$450**

Sauce tureen, cov, George Smith and Thomas Hayter makers, London, George III, domed lid with urn finial, boat shaped body with ribbed rim, loop handles, pedestal foot, lid and body monogrammed, 33 troy oz, pr, 1804, 9-1/4" l, 5-1/2" h **$2,760**

Serving spoon, William Eley and William Fearn, London, George III, engraved crest, 3 oz, 6 dwt, 1818, 11-3/4" l **$175**

Soup tureen, cov, William Elliott maker, London, George III, gadrooned rim, acanthus handles, four paw feet terminating in shell and acanthus leaves, lid with two bands of gadrooning and ribbed removable handle, engraved coat of arms on body and lid, 136 troy oz, 1819, 14-1/2" l, 10-1/4" h **$7,475**

Spoon

Illegible marker's mark, London, Henry VIII, maidenhead terminal with traces of gilding, crowned leopard's head mark very worn, 1.00 oz, 1540-41, 6-1/8" l
.... **$5,750**

Elizabeth I, London, prick-dot engraved with initials "HRM" to back of bowls, lion Sejant Affronte terminal, traces of gilding, 2.90 oz, worn terminals, pr, 1589-90, 6-5/8" l **$5,750**

Standish, J. C. Vickery maker, London, Edward VII, rect, reeded border, two horizontal pen wells, two tapered inkwells with canted corners and hinged lids, central ovoid covered well, hinged lid fitted with eight-day clock, four ball and claw feet, some

English silver dessert dishes, pr, touch of William Burwash, cast grapevine rim, 3-1/4" h, 11" d, approx. 53.2 oz total wt, **$1,755.**
Photo courtesy of Pook & Pook, Inc.

English silver creamer, George III, faceted body, ribbed bandwork, basket weave rim, urn-form feet, by Charles Fox, London, 1810, 6 oz, 4 dwt, **$236.**
Photo courtesy of Sloans & Kenyon Auctioneers and Appraisers.

English silver berry spoons, touch of "S.H.," 1804-1805, 8-1/2" l, approx. 4.2 oz total wt, **$235.**
Photo courtesy of Pook & Pook, Inc.

English, Georgian silver, covered sugar, touch of Samuel Taylor, floral repoussé dec, 1762-1763, 5-1/4" h, 13.2 oz. total wt., **$645.**
Photo courtesy of Pook & Pook, Inc.

restoration needed, 32 troy oz, 1906, 11-3/8" l, 7-1/2" w **$2,100**

Sugar basket, Peter & Ann Bateman, London, 1798, George III, navette shape, molded banded rim and swing handle, engraved body with reticulated bands, banded oval foot, monogrammed, cobalt glass insert, 3 troy oz, 5-1/2" l, 3-1/2" w **$920**

Sugar bowl, Georgian, marks rubbed, beaded rim, ovoid body with ribbon-tied floral sprays and swags, roundels on each side, heraldic device, spiraled loop handles, trumpet foot with bands of bright cut engraving, 5 troy oz, 6" l, 5-3/8" h **$350**

Sugar tongs, Georgian, cast with shell, foliage, scrolls engraved with flowers, center vacant cartouche, 1 oz, 2 dwt **$95**

Sweetmeat dish, R. & S. Garrard maker, London, 1879, ovoid, flanked by male and female figure, auricular scroll and stylized shell handle, four periwinkle shell feet, 13 troy oz, 9-1/8" l, 5-5/8" w, 2-1/4" h **$1,495**

Tablespoon, William Eley, London, George IV, fiddle pattern, monogrammed, pr, 6 troy oz, 1826, 8-3/4" l **$200**

Tankard, John Longlands I maker, Newcastle, George III, tapered cylindrical form, plain body with engraved cartouche, serpentine handle with reticulated thumb-piece, gadrooned foot rim, slightly domed lid with gadrooned rim, engraved presentation inscription, lacquered, 26 troy oz, 1769, 7-3/4" h **$1,265**

Taperstick, London, octagonal base with urn-shaped stem rising from circular well to banded campana sconce, base engraved with crest, worn marks, maker's mark appears to be mark for Samuel Margas, 5.10 oz, possibly early 18th C, 4" h **$2,160**

Tazza, pr, two-tier, R. & S. Garrard, London, Victorian, in the Renaissance taste, domed base and baluster stem supporting two dishes pierced with shells and chased with interlaced strapwork, top dish engraved with crest, with an inscription reading "Presented to Viscount Cole BY THE TENANTRY OF THE ENNISKILLEN ESTATES, ON THE OCCASION OF HIS MARRIAGE 12th JULY 1869," both marked on underside of base and exterior base of smaller dish with maker's mark, duty mark, lion

passant, and date letter, 144.50 oz, 1864-65, 16" h **$9,000**

Teapot

Andrew Fogelberg & Stephen Gilbert, London, George III, oval form, chased with arabesques, floral garlands, cov surmounted with ivory finial, monogrammed, mkd, 14.25 oz, 1786-87, 10-1/2" l, 4-1/4" h **$550**

Attributed to Augustus Le Sage, London, 1771, George III, cylindrical, disc finial, wood ear handle, engraved antelope crest on lid and side, 13 troy oz, 5" h **$1,100**

George Smith & Thomas Hayter, London, George III, fluted ovoid, engraved domed lid, bone mushroom finial and handle, engraved foliates and central crest, 15 troy oz, restorations, 1796, 6-1/4" h **$525**

Teapot stand, Robert & David Hennell, London, Georgian, oval with beveled corners, molded rim engraved, face with engraved and bright cut foliate bands, central cartouche, four feet, 5 troy oz, 1795, 4-7/8" w, 7" l **$435**

Tea and coffee service, Rebecca Eames & Edward Barnard, London, George III, coffeepot with gadrooned pedestal, teapot, creamer, open sugar, sq bulbous form, emb lids with cast foliate finials, molded gadrooned rims, bodies with bands of spiral reeding, four ball feet, 73 troy oz, 1814-15, 8-3/4" h **$2,300**

Tea service

Crichton Bros. makers, London, George V, coffee and teapots, kettle on stand, creamer, open sugar, cov sugar, all with ovoid body, arcaded and ribbed banding, teapot and coffeepot with wooden handles topped with silver flat leaves, lion's head roundels, reamer and sugar with curved handles terminating in lion's head roundels, 174 troy oz, 1930, 9" h coffeepot, 16" h kettle on stand **$2,990**

Peter, Ann, and William Bateman makers, London, George III, ovoid teapot, helmet shaped cov creamer with angular handle, cov sugar with angular handles, all with partial vertical lobing, bands of bright cut engraving and engraved heraldic device, wooden pineapple finials, 33 troy oz, 1800, 7-3/4" h teapot **$1,495**

Tea urn, maker's mark "I. R.," London, lid with tapered egg-shaped finial, beaded tape with ivory handle, bead-

ed loop handles, four ball feet with stepped rect base and beaded edge, bright cut engraving throughout with husks, cartouches, and floral swags, 37 troy oz, 1778, 15" h **$2,100**

Tray, "EB" makers mark, London, George IV, rect, gadrooned border, handles with shells and leaves, four paw feet flanked by floral roundels and stylized wings, engraved all-over pattern of flowers and leaves, center with mottoed crest and later monogram, 120 troy oz, 1822, 25" l, 16-1/4" w **$2,760**

Trefid spoon, stem mkd with arm and sword emerging from crown mark, round terminal, traces of gilding, 3.75 oz, 1686-87, 10-1/8" l **$2,400**

Trump indicator, hallmarked Birmingham, round base, celluloid suit indicators suspended from pair of loops, 2-3/4" x 2-1/4" **$200**

Waxjack, attributed to Augustus Le Sage, London, George III, cast handles, attached snuffer, spindle with spirally reeded bud form finial, domed base with beaded rim, supported by three cast claw and ball feet, inscription on base, 4 troy oz, third quarter 18th C, 6-1/2" h **$980**

Wine coaster, Joseph and John Angel makers, London, Victorian, applied scroll and shell rim, reticulated sides, engraved to base with scrolls, shells, and central heraldic crest, pr, 1846, 5-3/4" d, 2-3/4" h **$5,465**

Irish

Fine examples of Irish silver are becoming popular with collectors.

Candlesticks, pr, George III/IV, Dublin, attributed to John Laughlin, Jr., larger gadrooned knob over gadrooned knob below partially vertically reeded stem with single horizontal beaded band, well with applied stylized wheat or grass fronds, domed gadrooned base, vertically reeded sconce, removable nozzle with gadrooned rim, small heraldic crest engraved on foot and nozzle, 49 troy oz **$7,475**

Caudle cup, cov, Dublin, marked for John Hamilton, domed lid topped by ovoid finial, body with single molded band, crabstock handles, lobed spreading foot, no date mark, 37 troy oz, pr, mid-18th C, 7-1/4" h **$5,175**

Cup, marked for John Letabliere, tapered cylindrical body with leaf cut card work, band of foliate engraving, domed spreading foot, scroll handles topped with flat leaves, engraved on one side with cartouche, no date marks, 44 troy oz, pr, mid-18th C, 4-7/8" h......................**$5,465**

Ladle, chased floral and scroll designs on silver bowl, Irish hallmarks and maker's mark for Phineas Garde, Corke, baleen handle, minor battering on rim, c1815, 7" l................**$320**

Salver, George II/III, Dublin, William Townsend maker, shaped molded border, engraved center with heraldic crest in rococo cartouche, three pad feet with scroll legs, 8 troy oz, 6-1/2" l......................**$1,100**

Snuffer tray, George III, Dublin, William Doyle maker, octagonal boat shape, base with bright cut engraved husk drops, heraldic crest within roundel flanked by leaves, sides reticulated with arcading, paterae, 4 troy oz, 1798......................**$700**

Scottish

Not to be outdone by their Irish and English neighbors, Scottish silversmiths also created fine objects.

Berry spoon, Edinburgh, George Fenwick maker, 1820......................**$75**

Punch ladle

Edinburgh, maker's mark "CD," 6 troy oz, 1789, 13-1/2" l................**$300**

Edinburgh, maker's mark "AH," ovoid bowl, twisted baleen handle, silver end cap, 1820, 14-1/2" l..........**$150**

Sheffield, English

Sheffield silver, or Old Sheffield Plate, has a fusion method of silver-plating that was used from the mid-18th century until the mid-1880s, when the process of electroplating silver was introduced.

Sheffield plating was discovered in 1743, when Thomas Boulsover of Sheffield, England, accidentally fused silver and copper. The process consisted of sandwiching a heavy sheet of copper between two thin sheets of silver. The result was a plated sheet of silver, which could be pressed or rolled to a desired thickness. All Sheffield articles are worked from these plated sheets.

Most of the silver-plated items found today marked "Sheffield" are not early Sheffield plate. They are later wares made in Sheffield, England.

Basket, S. Smith & Son, England, second oval, molded foliate rim, emb and reticulated sides, cast foliage handles, oval reticulated and engraved base, cobalt blue glass liner, half 19th C, 7-3/4" w, 13-3/4" l................**$460**

Biscuit box, oval, hinged lid, gadrooned trim, lion mask side handles, attached tray base on ball feet, late 19th C, 7" w, 7-1/2" h..........**$120**

Carving set, fork, knife, and steel, engraved image of Windsor Castle on knife blade, horn handles, silver plated crown finials, leathered case, late 19th C, 16-1/2" l................**$350**

Claret jug, cut glass body mounted at neck, hinged cover, baluster finial, multi-scroll foliate handle, c1935, 11" h................**$500**

Domed lid, engraved armorial whippet, oval handle, early 19th C, 22" h, 11" l................**$575**

Pitcher, finely chased quatrefoil medallions and feathering, Sheffield hallmarks for 1857 by John Fred Fenton, ivory insulators on handle, minor damage, 7-1/4" h................**$520**

Plate, circular, gadrooned rim, engraved Carlill crest, George III, price for pr, 9-3/4" d................**$175**

Platter and meat cover, oval tree platter, four ball feet, two wooden handles, gadrooned rim, armorials on both sides, dome cover with gadrooned rim, reeded handles, engraved armorials, 26" l..........**$2,750**

Serving dish, cov, England, rect, gadrooned rim and lid, cast branch and maple leaf handle, engraved coat of arms, first half 19th C, 11-1/2" l, 8-5/8" w................**$230**

Tantalus, England, central casket with two engraved hinged lids below handle, sides supporting two cut and pressed glass decanters, pedestal base supported by four column legs, late 19th/early 20th C, 5-3/4" w, 15" l................**$490**

Tray, kidney shape, gadrooned rim, pierced gallery of open lattice work, centered engraved lion crest, early 20th C, 18-1/2" x 7-1/2"................**$120**

Vegetable dish, cov, plated, shaped rect, applied grapevine, scroll, and foliage handle, monogrammed, 13" l......................**$250**

Wine bottle holder, wooden base, vintage detail, ivory casters, 16" l..........**$275**

Irish silver, coffee pot, pear-shaped, repousse gadrooning, mkd with fire in basket, hallmarked CT, c1770, 37 oz., 12-3/4" x 4-1/2", **$4,700.**

Photo courtesy of David Rago Auctions, Inc.

Sheffield, English reticulated silver basket, George V, quatrefoil bowl, pierced with foliate scrolls and four heart-shaped cartouches, beaded C-scroll and flower head rim, openwork shell and acanthus scroll feet, approx. 21 troy oz, maker's mark "WS," 1913, 12-3/8" w, **$590.**

Photo courtesy of Skinner, Inc.

Silver-plated Sabbath candlesticks, Polish, baluster-form stem, acanthus leaf base details, scrolling feet, Norblin & Co., GALW, Warszawa, late 19th century, pair, 11-1/2" h, **$295.**
Photo courtesy of Sloans & Kenyon Auctioneers and Appraisers.

Sheffield, silver-plated hot water kettle, urn finial, lion mask handles, applied shield plaque, spout mkd "TH," early 19th century, 13-1/2" h, **$380.**
Photo courtesy of Pook & Pook, Inc.

Silver, plated

Englishmen G. R. and H. Elkington are given credit for being the first to use the electrolytic method of plating silver in 1838.

An electroplated-silver article is completely shaped and formed from a base metal and then coated with a thin layer of silver. In the late 19th century, the base metal was Britannia, an alloy of tin, copper, and antimony. Other bases are copper and brass. Today, the base is nickel silver.

In 1847, Rogers Bros. of Hartford, Connecticut, introduced the electroplating process in America. By 1855, a number of firms were using the method to produce silver-plated items in large quantities.

The quality of the plating is important. Extensive polishing can cause the base metal to show through. The prices for plated-silver items are low, making them popular items with younger collectors.

Bacon warmer, George III style, rect, dentilated rim, turned wood handle, hinged cover with ivory finial, inscribed crest, 10-1/4" l **$250**

Bun warmer, oval, cover chased with flowers and foliage, beaded rim, paw feet, liner, two reeded handles, 12-1/2" l **$275**

Candelabra, pr, Continental, three-light, tapering stem issuing central urn-form candle-cup and two scrolling branches supporting wax pan and conforming candle-cup, oval foot with reeded border, vertical flutes, 12" h **$150**

Candle lamp shade, Tiffany Studios, Grapevine pattern, domed, pierced grapevine design, imp "Tiffany Studios New York," minor dents, price for four, 6-1/2" d, 2" d fitter rim, 3-3/8" h **$1,265**

Candlesticks, pr, Wurtembergishe Metallwarenfabrik, sq base applied with bow-tie garlands and foliage, rim with stylized leaves and beads rising to Corinthian column stems, detachable bobeches with beaded rims, 7-1/2" h **$375**

Claret jug, eagle-form, textured cranberry glass body with realistic silver plate head and feet, set with glass eyes, hinged at neck, clear draw handle, Continental, early 20th C, 9-1/2" h **$460**

Silver-plated epergne, Victorian style, English, rock-type base, applied standing fox, two tiers plated silver leaf-form bowls, upper frosted and cut glass bowl at top, various unidentified hallmarks, loss of one leaf under glass bowl, 19th or 20th century, 21-3/4" h, 10" d bowl, **$1,650.**
Photo courtesy of Green Valley Auctions.

Coffee urn and stand, ovoid body, spout over reeded legs, paw feet joined to X-form stretcher raised on bun feet, cover surmounted with leaf and scroll finial, unmarked, 16" h **$300**

Egg cup, England, stems formed as cast kangaroos resting in circular underplates, price for pr, early 20th C, 2-3/4" h **$100**

Epergne, three pale blue patterned glass vases with central reeded shaft, tripod base, winged sea horses supports, marked "HW & Co.," top insert missing, 13-1/2" h **$450**

Fish set, English, six forks, six knives with engraved blades, mother-of-pearl handles, wood case, late 19th C **$320**

Game platter, English, well and three-platter base with attached hot water pan, raised on four medallion-capped feet, associated domed cov with beaded bands and engraved wide border of entwined circlets, applied open handle surrounded by conforming engraved dec, body with engraved griffin, late 19th C, 16" h, 26-1/2" l **$700**

Garniture, ftd compote with repoussé floral and foliate bands, each side pc with conforming dec, Tiffany & Co., 6-1/4" h **$350**

Hot water urn, Sheffield, Georgian-style **$300**

Inkwell, England or America, fence form, central fence supporting two urn form candle sconces, ends with three stakes bearing square cut glass inkwells with silver plated lids, 20th C, 11-1/2" h **$195**

Lamp, table, paneled shade, conical base, openwork silverplate grape vine designs, five panels of green and white slag glass, cast leaf finial, engraved leaves on base, base marked "Made and Guaranteed by the MB Co. USA," electrified, five sockets, 20-1/2" h **$1,200**

Monteith cooler, attributed to England, oval, shaped rims and cast loop handles, price for pr, late 19th C, 7-3/4" w, 13" l **$815**

Punch cup, Lavigne, 1881 Rogers .**$25**

Sandwich box, English, rect, loop handle, hinged lid monogrammed, gilt int., leather carrying case, early 20th C, 5-3/4" h, 4-1/8" h **$80**

Snuffbox, English, foliate scroll engraved lid, set with central faceted purple stone, cowry shell body, late 19th C, 2-3/4" l **$300**

Tea and coffee service, Pairpoint, matching serving tray, 5 pcs **$350**

Tea set, 3 pc, matching serving tray, Victorian **$200**

Toast rack, England, oval, central ring handle above cast cricket ball, rack formed as crossed cricket bats, four ball feet, late 19th/early 20th C, 7" l, 2-5/8" w **$90**

Tray, Victorian, oval, field engraved with floral and diaper medallions flanked by foliage with foliate garlands at intervals, beaded and geometrical design border and handles, 32" l **$350**

Sheffield

Englishmen G. R. Elkington and H. Elkington are given credit for being the first to use the electrolytic method of plating silver in 1838.

Candlesticks, pr, ornate columns with composite capitals, pale blue blown glass hurricane shades with cut floral designs, 24" h **$425**

Entree dish, shaped rect, gadrooned rim, detachable handle with gadroon dec, 11" x 8" **$75**

Hot water urn, Philip Ashberry & Sons makers, urn-form body with flat leaf engraving at base, wide central band of engraved anthemion, round domed base with beaded rim, trumpet foot with band of guilloche centered by flowerheads and accented with husks, angular handles terminating in flat leaves, anthemion handle on top, domed lid with flat leaf engraving and foliage baluster finial, inner sleeve, early 19th C, 22-3/4" h **$750**

Sauceboat with underplate, rim applied with grapevines **$95**

Soup tureen, ovoid body with applied gadroon and shell border, two fluted handles with leaf terminals, four scroll and flat leaf feet, domed lid with reeded band, leaf-form finial, body and lid with let-in engraved heraldic device, fitted drop-in liner, restorations, rosing, early 19th C, 16" l, 10-3/4" h **$1,725**

Tankard, Hy Wilkinson & Co. makers, tapered cylindrical form, plain ear handle, gold washed int., fitted leather case, 10 troy oz, 5" h **$235**

Tea and coffee service, baluster shaped coffeepot, teapot, creamer, two handled open sugar, waste bowl, oval with canted corners, angular handles, 12-1/4" h kettle-on-stand **$425**

Sheffield, silver-plated salver, gadrooned edge, ball and claw feet, early 19th century, 12" d, **$410.**
Photo courtesy of Pook & Pook, Inc.

SILVER OVERLAY

History: Silver overlay is silver applied directly to a finished glass or porcelain object. The overlay is cut and decorated, usually by engraving, prior to being molded around the object.

Glass usually is of high quality and is either crystal or colored. Lenox used silver overlay on some porcelain pieces. Most designs are from the Art Nouveau and Art Deco periods.

Basket, deep cranberry body, all-over floral and lattice design, sterling handle, 5-1/2" l, 6" h **$600**

Decanter, molded, pinched oval bottle, surface bamboo dec overall, base disk imp "Yuan Shun/ Sterling," faceted crystal hollow stopper, 11-1/2" h **$375**

Flask, clear bottle shaped body, scrolling hallmarked silver, hinged cov, 5" h **$275**

Inkwell, bright green ground, rose, scroll, and lattice overlay, matching cov, monogram, 3-3/4" x 3" **$650**

Jug, colorless glass, tapered baluster form, star-cut base, silver cased applied draw handle, overlay of twining grapes and grape vines, plain cartouche beneath spout, stylized cobweb overlay below, Alvin Mfg. Co., late 19th/early 20th C, 9" h **$1,380**

Perfume bottle

Baluster, elongated neck, colorless glass, scrolling foliage overlay, central monogrammed cartouche, 5" h **$225**

Bulbed colorless glass bottle with engraved scrolled foliate silver overlay dec, initial "S" in cartouche,

Silver overlay, boudoir lamp, Heintz, silver overlay of daylilies on verdigris patina, topped by pierced flaring shade with new lining, no visible mark, 12" x 11", **$1,600.**
Photo courtesy of David Rago Auctions, Inc.

Silver overlay, table screen with colorless glass, demilune, two engraved patera roundel, acanthus scroll and husk overlay, bifurcate scroll to top, monogrammed, early 20th century, 8-1/4" h, **$320.**
Photo courtesy of Skinner, Inc.

Silver overlay, bottle, cordial, long neck, matching stopper, Art Nouveau-type foliate silver overlay, **$125.**

silver overlay on ball shaped glass stopper, Continental, wear, some loss to silver, 4" h **$75**

Tea set, Lenox porcelain body, Reed & Barton silver overlay, three-pc set, 8-3/4" h **$325**

Vase

Art Nouveau free-form irid blue body, applied silver overlay in iris pattern, 7" h **$1,100**

Art Nouveau ovoid cranberry glass body, flared rim supported by three applied clear glass handles, silver overlay on rim and body, waterlily and cattails design, marks obscured, minor losses to silver overlay, 13-3/4" h **$1,250**

Baluster porcelain body, cerulean blue ground, painted prunus stems, overlaid with silver detailing, silver neck and foot rims, Aesthetic Movement, French, late 19th C, 9-3/4" h **$470**

Bronze, sterling silver overlay of trees, verdigris patina, Heintz, 5" d, 12-1/4" h **$850**

Bulbous stick, translucent green glass body overlaid with embossed floral Alvin, 8" h **$450**

Vessel, Tiger Ware, bulbous stoneware body with ear handle, narrow neck mounted with strapwork engraved silver collar, engraved monogram "ISA" and date "1594," English, 6-1/8" h **$4,410**

SNUFF BOTTLES

History: Tobacco usage spread from America to Europe to China during the 17th century. Europeans and Chinese preferred to grind the dried leaves into a powder and sniff it into their nostrils. The elegant Europeans carried their boxes and took a pinch with their fingertips. The Chinese upper class, because of their lengthy fingernails, found this inconvenient and devised a bottle with a fitted stopper and attached spoon. These utilitarian objects soon became objets d'art.

Snuff bottles were fashioned from precious and semi-precious stones, glass, porcelain and pottery, wood, metals, and ivory. Glass and transparent-stone bottles often were enhanced further with delicate hand paintings, some done on the interior of the bottle.

Agate, carved

Amber, quatrefoil form, each side carved with bat and stylized ruyi design, Chinese, tiny chip and slight wear on rim, slight fissure on shoulder, 19th C, 2-1/4" h **$150**

Flat rect shape, carved sprig of peony, reverse dec with carved ruyi scepter, Chinese, 19th C, 2-3/8" h **$125**

Mottled brown, flattened round form, carved fisherman, reverse with cat looking up at a flying insect, red glass top, orig spoon, Chinese, 19th C, 2-1/2" h **$200**

Mottled gray, flattened oval form, well carved with three men mooring boat, flower, tree dec, Chinese, 19th C, 2-1/2" h **$575**

Amber, landscape and figures, caramel inclusions, conforming id, Chinese, late 19th C, 4" l **$1,265**

Celadon, light jade, flattened ovoid short neck, 2-1/4" h **$200**

Chrysoprase, flattened ovoid, light green, conforming stopper, 3" h **$215**

Cinnabar lacquer, ovoid, continual scene of scholars and boys in a pavilion landscape, dark red, conforming stopper, 3-1/4" h **$230**

Cloisonné, auspicious symbols among clouds, yellow ground, lappet base border, ruyi head neck border, conforming stopper with chrysanthemum design, Qianlong four-character mark **$185**

Coral, carved, tree trunk with foliage, carved flower stopper, China, stopper glued to bottle, 19th or 20th C, 2-1/2" h **$320**

Glass

Clear, flat rect shape, broad oval foot, stone stopper with eye design, Chinese, 19th C, 2-1/4" h **$125**

Interior painted with three horned goats by tree, verso with inscription, sgd "Ma Shaoxian," China, no stopper, 2-1/2" h **$480**

Opaque body, enameled peony blossoms, verso with two birds, three-characters on base, China, 3" h **$175**

Ivory, curved ivory carved with bulrushes and crocodiles, flatleaf cap with ball finial, pebbled gilt-metal lid with glass-inset neck, mounted with short neck chain, Indian, late 19th/early 20th C, 3-3/4" l **$300**

Jade, carved

Flattened oval form, carved sage and pine tree on one side, reverse with man sitting under willow tree, fish on line, Chinese, 19th C, 3" h **$435**

Oval, carved butterfly near flowering branch, amber inclusions on one side, Chinese, design incorporates natural fissure, 18th or 19th C, 2-3/8" h **$875**

Slender oval form, carved basket-weave dec, tiger's eye stopper, Chinese, dark inclusion at base, spoon broken, 18th C, 2-3/8" h **$450**

Lapis lazuli, ovoid, relief carved, figures beneath tree, Chinese, 4" h **$125**

Malachite, carved, gourd, Chinese, 3" h **$95**

Opal, carved sage seated before gourd, Ch'ing Dynasty, 3" h **$125**

Overlay glass, seven colors, one side with floral designs in two archaic-form vases, reverse with immortal attending a crane and deer, bats flying above, each side with animal mask and ring handles, green, blue, mauve, coral, brown, and yellow, on white ground, 19th C **$520**

Peking glass, Snowflake

Blue overlay, each side with prancing deer, head turned with a lingchi branch in mouth, 19th C, 2-1/2" h **$490**

Red overlay, flattened ovoid, one side with serpent and tortoise, other with frog sitting under lily pad, 2-1/4" h **$1,265**

Porcelain

Famille Rose dec, vasiform, Chinese, marked, 19th C, 2-1/2" h **$125**

Famille Rose dec, flattened round form, Chinese, marked, 19th C, 2-3/4" h **$125**

Famille Rose dec, raised molded dec, iron-red sacred fungus and bat mark, gilt foot rim, coral stopper, China, small chip, stopper glued to bottle, 18th or 19th C, 3-1/8" h . **$95**

Famille Verte dec, Chinese, cap loose, 19th C, 3-3/8" h **$115**

Famille Verte dec, Chinese, 19th C, 3-3/4" h **$150**

Gamboling lions among clouds, ruyi band on shoulder and base, carved wooden stopper and ivory spoon, gilt rims, iron-red Jiaqing four-character mark on base,

China, small chips, 19th C, 3-1/4" h **$320**

Rock crystal, carved dec of pine trees in mountainous landscape, inclusions of black crystalline in various lengths, carved coral stopper, Chinese, spoon missing, 19th C, 3-1/2" h **$375**

Rose quartz, flattened ovoid, relief carved leaves and vines, Chinese, 3" h **$45**

Stag horn, flattened ovoid, one side with inset ivory panel with two laughing figures, reserve with inset panel with gold archaic script, 2-1/8" h **$175**

Turquoise, high relief carving of children and prunus trees, China **$235**

SOAPSTONE

History: The mineral steatite, known as soapstone because of its greasy feel, has been used for carving figural groups and designs by the Chinese and others. Utilitarian pieces also were made. Soapstone pieces were very popular during the Victorian era.

Bookends, pr, carved, block form, fu lion resting on top, Chinese, 5" h **$300**

Candlesticks, pr, red tones, flowers and foliage, 5-1/8" h **$85**

Carving

Buddha, seated, praying, carved stone base, 9-1/4" h **$60**

Dog's head, old darkened color, America, chips, with stand, 19th C, 4" w, 4-1/2" d, 3-1/2" h **$420**

Even white color, servant kneeling before woman holding fan, China, 19th C, 3" h **$115**

Woman, standing, wearing robe, restoration, 12" h **$120**

Hot plate, 16" l, 8-1/2" w **$75**

Plaque, birds, trees, flowers, and rocks, 9-1/2" h **$125**

Sculpture, kneeling nude young woman, Canadian, 10-1/4" h, 4-1/2" w **$95**

Sealing stamp, carved dec, curved scroll, 5" h, 1" d **$95**

Toothpick holder, two containers with carved birds, animals, and leaves **$85**

Vase

Four openings, red tones, Chinese, c1900, 6-3/4" h, 9-1/2" l **$125**

Snuff bottle, Famille Rose, porcelain, Chinese, flattened ovoid form, carved musicians in relief, Qianlong mark, **$1,770.**

Photo courtesy of Sloans & Kenyon Auctioneers and Appraisers.

Snuff bottle, Famille Rose, porcelain, Chinese, Daoguang mark, iron red seal mark, **$1,298.**

Photo courtesy of Sloans & Kenyon Auctioneers and Appraisers.

Snuff bottle, Famille Verte, porcelain, Chinese, molded boy form, Qing dynasty, 4" h, **$355.**

Photo courtesy of Sloans & Kenyon Auctioneers and Appraisers.

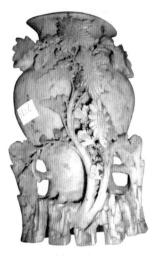

Soapstone vase, flat back, urn with cascading chrysanthemums, faux bamboo stand as base, $35.

Plate, Souvenir of St. Augustine, Florida, Old City Gates in center, vignettes of other sights around border, blue transfer decoration, marked "Usina Brothers King St, St Augustine, Fla, Staffordshire, England," $80.

Plate, Valley Forge, 1777-78, Washington's Headquarters in center, vignettes of other signs around border, blue transfer decoration, Rowland & Marcellus Co., Staffordshire, England, with poem by Gus Egolf, Dec. 19, 1910, Norristown, Pennsylvania, $95.

Carved peacock and chrysanthemums, 15-1/2" h **$495**

SOUVENIR AND COMMEMORATIVE CHINA AND GLASS

History: Souvenir, commemorative, and historical china and glass includes those items produced to celebrate special events, places, and people.

Collectors particularly favor China plates made by Rowland and Marcellus and Wedgwood. Rowland and Marcellus, Staffordshire, England, made a series of blue-and-white historic plates with a wide rolled edge. Scenes from the Philadelphia Centennial in 1876 through the 1939 New York World's Fair are depicted. In 1910, Wedgwood collaborated with Jones, McDuffee, and Stratton to produce a series of historic dessert-sized plates showing scenes of places throughout the United States.

Many localities issued plates, mugs, glasses, etc., for anniversary celebrations or to honor a local historical event. These items seem to have greater value when sold in the region in which they originated.

Commemorative glass includes several patterns of pressed glass that celebrate people or events. Historical glass includes campaign and memorial items.

Ashtray, New York City, china, blue and white transfer, Empire State Building, Statue of Liberty, Rockefeller Center, harbor scene, mkd "Fine Staffordshire Ware, Enco, National, Made in England" **$20**

Bust, Gillinder
Lincoln, frosted **$325**
Napoleon, frosted and clear **$295**

Creamer
New Academy, Truro, multicolored image on white medallion, cobalt blue ground, gold and white dec **$30**
Wadsworth Atheneum, Hartford, CT, multicolored image on white medallion, lustered ground, marked "Wheelock China, Austria," 2" h **$18**

Cup, Entrance to Soldier's Home, Leavenworth, Kansas, multicolored, beaded dec, marked "Germany," slight wear to gold dec, 2-1/2" h **$18**

Cup and saucer
Niagara Falls, cobalt blue ground, gold trim, scene of falls on saucer, marked "Made in Japan," matching wooden display stand, 1-1/4" h x 1-3/4" d, 3-1/2" d saucer **$20**
Souvenir of Edina, Missouri, white ground, rose dec, gold trim, marked "Japan," 2-1/2" h x 3-3/4" w cup, 5-1/2" w saucer **$20**
Washington and Lafayette, transfer print portraits on cup of George Washington and Lafayette, saucer with portrait titled "Washington His Country's Father," creamware, England, early 19th C, 1-3/4" h **$490**

Demitasse cup and saucer
My Old Kentucky Home, marked "Handpainted, Made in Japan, NICO," 2" h x 2" w cup, 4" d saucer **$15**
Souvenir of Chicago, Ill, Victorian man and woman on inside of cup, gold trim, marked "Crest O Gold, Sabin, Warranted 22K," 2" h x 2-1/2" w cup **$17.50**

Dish
Beauvoir House, Jefferson Davis House, Biloxi, Mississippi, marked "Made by Adams, England for the Jefferson Davis Shrine," 3-1/4" d **$20**
DeShong Memorial Art Gallery, Lester, Pennsylvania, yellow luster ground, marked "Made in Germany," wear to lettering and gold trim, 3-3/4" x 3-1/4" **$12**

Dish, cov, Remember the *Maine*, green opaque glass **$135**

Figure, souvenir of Atlantic City, two pigs having picture taken, green ground, marked "Germany" **$150**

Goblet
G.A.R., 1887, 21st Encampment **$100**
Mother, Ruby Thumbprint pattern **$35**

Mug, Souvenir of Blairsville, ruby stained, applied clear handle **$25**

Paperweight
Moses in Bulrushes, frosted center **$145**
Plymouth Rock, clear **$95**
Washington, George, round, frosted center **$295**

Pitcher, ironstone, shell molded oval form, wine-red ground, circular paneled sides enamel dec with landscape scenes, gilt trim, titled cartouche below spout "Senator Martin Wyck-off, of Warren County," imp mark "U Pottery," gilt wear, c1885, 10" h **$460**

Plate

Boston department stores, founders in border, blue transfer, white ground, Wedgwood, 9-3/4" d **$35**

Hogg, James Stephen, first native born governor of Texas, brown print, Vernon Kilns, marked "Designed for Daughters of the Republic of Texas" **$25**

Memorial, Garfield center, clear pressed glass, 10" d **$75**

Oklahoma, Agricultural and Mechanical College, Vernon Kilns, marked "Designed especially for Creech's Stillwater, Oklahoma" **$32**

Plymouth Rock, Plymouth, Massachusetts, brown and white, mkd "Old English Staffordshire Ware, Made in England, (Jonroth mark) (Adams mark) Imported Exclusively for Plymouth Rock Gift Shop, Plymouth, Mass" **$25**

Remember the *Maine*, Spanish-American war, c1900, 8-1/2" d **$240**

Sulphur Springs, Delaware, OH, light blue and black transfer, Staffordshire, New York retailer's label, chip on table ring, 10-1/2" d **$200**

Washington, Bellingham, green print, Vernon Kilns **$60**

Tile, Detroit Women's League, multi-colored irid glass, 4" d **$135**

Tumbler, etched

Lord's Prayer **$15**

Niagara Falls, Prospect Point, gold rim **$20**

SOUVENIR AND COMMEMORATIVE SPOONS

History: Souvenir and commemorative spoons have been issued for hundreds of years. Early American silversmiths engraved presentation spoons to honor historical personages or mark key events.

In 1881, Myron Kinsley patented a Niagara Falls spoon, and in 1884, Michael Gibney patented a new flatware design. M. W. Galt, Washington, D.C., issued commemora-

tive spoons for George and Martha Washington in 1889. From these beginnings, a collecting craze for souvenir and commemorative spoons developed in the late 19th and early 20th centuries.

Basiwgstoke, red, blue, and orange enameled shield, 5" l **$15**

Boulder, CO, name in bowl, Indian head handle **$40**

B. P. O. E. Elks #896, marked "Reed & Barton Klitzner RI," silverplate, 4-1/2" l **$15**

Cawston Ostrich Farms, marked "Sterling," 3-1/4" l **$15**

Denver, Colorado, sterling, gold washed bowl, acid etched pack mule, stem-end topped with winch with handle that turns, applied pick and shovel, stem entwined with rope, ending in bucket, opposed by modeled rock, 1 troy oz. late 19th C **$85**

Fort Dearborn, marked "Sterling, Hyman Berg," 1803-1857, 6" l **$20**

Golden Gate Bridge, San Francisco, California, marked "Holland 90" and hallmark, 5" l **$15**

Lancaster, city name engraved in bowl, sterling **$30**

Memorial Arch, Brooklyn, New York, round oak stove **$40**

Palm Springs, Aerial Tramway, SP, John Brown, marked "Antico" **$100**

Philadelphia, Independence Hall in bowl, SS **$45**

Prophet, veiled **$135**

Richmond, MO, SS **$30**

Royal Canadian Mounted Police, "Victoria, British Columbia" in bowl, marked "Made in Holland," 4-1/2" l **$30**

Stratford on Avon, yellow enameled shield, mkd "EPNS," 3-5/8" l **$15**

St. Paul, The Tower, Houses of Parliament, West Minister, each marked "L. E. P. A1" on back, set of four in orig box **$42**

Thousand Islands, fish handle, engraved bowl, SS, Watson **$45**

Vista House, Columbia River, Oregon, detailed handle, marked "Sterling" **$32**

SPORTS COLLECTIBLES

History: People have been saving sports-related equipment since the inception of sports. Some was passed

down from generation to generation for reuse; the rest was stored in dark spaces in closets, attics, and basements.

Two key trends brought collectors' attention to sports collectibles. First, decorators began using old sports items, especially in restaurant decor. Second, collectors began to discover the thrill of owning the "real" thing. Sports collectibles are more accessible than ever before because of online auctions and several houses that dedicate themselves to that segment of the hobby. Provenance is extremely important when investing in high-ticket sports collectibles. Being able to know the history of the object may greatly enhance the value, with a premium paid for items secured from the player or directly from their estate.

Additional Resources:

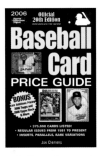

2006 Baseball Card Price Guide, by Joe Clemens, Krause Publications, Iola, WI.

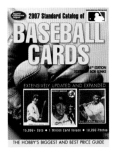

2007 Standard Catalog of Baseball Cards, by Bob Lemke, ed., Krause Publications, Iola, WI.

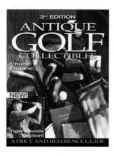

Antique Golf Collectibles, 3rd Ed., by Chuch Furjanic, Krause Publications, Iola, WI.

Standard Catalog of® Sports Memorabilia, 3rd Ed., by Bert Lehman, ed., Krause Publications, Iola, WI.

Tuff Stuff® 2006 Standard Catalog of® Football Cards, 9th Ed., by the price guide editors of *Tuff Stuff* magazine, Krause Publications, Iola, WI.

Baseball

Annual, *Official Baseball Annual,* Fawcett, color action photo of Los Angeles Dodgers Don Drysdale on cov, 1963 .... **$10**

Autograph

Brett, George, magazine page with full color photo in Kansas City Royals uniform, sgd on shoulder, c1980, 8" x 10-3/4" **$20**

Carew, Rod, four page folio segment from June 29, 1974, issue of *Sporting News*, bold signature, 11-1/2" x 14-1/2" **$30**

Coveleski, Stanley, Hall of Fame post-card, published for National Baseball Museum, Cooperstown, NY, showing player's bronze plaque, 1969, 3-1/2" x 5-1/2" **$30**

Spahn, Walter, glossy full-color photo, Milwaukee pitcher's uniform, c1953, 8" x 10" **$25**

Bank, All-Stars, bobbing head, painted composition figure, orig string tag, 1960s, 6-1/2" h **$50**

Baseball, autographed, sgd by members of team

American League All-Star Team, Foxx, Gehrig, DiMaggio, 1937 .... **$7,000**

Boston, Herman, Yastrzemski, 1964 .... **$250**

National League All-Star Team, Musial, 1955 .... **$600**

New York, Stengel, Kubek, Maris, Howard, Berra, Ford, 1960 ...... **$700**

Oakland, Martin, Henderson, 1981 .... **$200**

Baseball cap, autographed, game used

Bench, Johnny, 1970s Cincinnati Reds **$450**

Jackson, Bo, 1994 California Angels **$95**

Walker, Larry, 1995 Colorado Rockies **$165**

Baseball card, issued by Cracker Jack, Ty Cobb, Detroit Tigers Hall of Fame **$6,400**

Baseball glove

Ashburn, Richie **$45**

Berra, Yogi **$100**

Reese, Pee Wee **$65**

Bobbing head

New York, sq white base, professionally restored, 1961-63, 6-1/2" h **$65**

Painted composition figure, blue cap, painted white initial "M," white shirt trimmed in blue, gold tan trousers, holding yellow bat, mkd "Made In Japan," 3" x 3-1/2" x 6" orig box, 5-1/2" h **$40**

Dixie picture, Bob Feller, Cleveland Indians, four additional action photos on back, plus biography, 8" x 10" photo **$90**

Emblem, white plastic, on orig card

Pirates, black accents, c1950, 4" h **$12**

Reds, red accents, c1950, 4" h **$12**

Exhibit card, sepia tone, facsimile signature

Drysdale, Don, 3-3/8" x 5-3/8" **$25**

Premier baseball card/gum ball arcade vending machine, made by Oak Mfg., Co., Inc., red painted cast iron, 1950s, 13" x 13", **$575.**

Killebrew, Harmon, 3-3/8" x 5-3/8"
.... **$20**

Mayes, Willie, 3-3/8" x 5-3/8" **$35**

Mazeroski, Bill, 3-3/8" x 5-3/8" ... **$15**

Hartland figure, Roger Maris, 25th anniversary, orig 4" x 6" x 8-1/2" box, 7-1/2" h **$70**

Lunch box

Boston Red Sox, Ardee, vinyl, 1960s, 6-1/2" x 8-1/2" x 3-1/2" **$50**

Toronto Blue Jay's, Canadian issue, blue vinyl, late 1980s, 7" x 8-1/2" x 4" **$25**

Magazine

Baseball Monthly, Vol. 1, #4, June 1962 .... **$5**

Complete Baseball Magazine, Sports Life editors, summer issue, 1950 .... **$10**

Life, Aug. 1, black and white cover with close-up photo of Joe DiMaggio, 1949 .... **$15**

Men Your Goodyear Dealer's Magazine, Mickey Mantle cover, 1957 .... **$45**

Pennant, felt

Brooklyn Dodgers, Ebbert Field, blue, 1940s **$190**

Cooperstown, blue, multicolored Braves style Indian head, 1940s .. **$75**

Minnesota Twins A. L. Champs World Series, photo, 1965 .... **$125**

New York Yankees, photo "M&M Boys Last Year Together!", 1966 .... **$95**

Photograph, black and white stiff paper, Whiz Kids of 1950, The Fightin' Phillies, shows team lined up on field, holding hats and gloves, newspaper supplement, 10" x 35" **$90**

Pinback button

Go-Go Mets, dark orange on navy blue, image of youthful batter in oversized batting helmet, late 1960s, 3-1/2" d **$24**

Minnesota Twins, Western Division Champions, America League, 1987, red, white, and blue, 3-1/2" d **$12**

Ted Williams, black and white photo as youthful Boston Red Sox star, late 1930s, 1-3/4" d **$40**

York White Roses, blue and white celluloid figural baseball suspending blue and white fabric ribbons with miniature plastic baseball, 1940s, 1-1/4" d **$15**

Plate, Base Ball, Caught on the Fly, center transfer print, white glazed ground, c1850, 7-1/4" d **$920**

Pocket tin, Yankee Boy Plug Cut, Scotten, Dillion Co., tin litho, little boy slugger on shield shape, red and white

check background, 4-1/8" x 3-1/2" x 1-1/8" **$625**

Poster, 1930 Chicago Cubs, photo and facsimile signature of each player, adv Blue Ribbon Malt Co., contemporary frame, 11-1/2" x 38" **$250**

Presentation bat, red painted bat, polychrome Odd Fellows symbols, incised in gold "West Lynn 15-3 Kearsarge West Lynn 23 East Lynn 5 Presented by H. W. Eastham, July 21, 1900, Aug. 18, 1900," (MA), with stand, 34" l **$4,025**

Program

All-Star, Philadelphia, 1943 .... **$495**

All-Star, St. Louis, 1948 .... **$325**

New York Yankees, 1937 .... **$195**

New York Yankees, 1951 .... **$195**

World Series, 1950, at Philadelphia **$250**

Roster sheet, Pirates, 1927 .... **$175**

Score counter, six diecut openings, red and blue printing on white, blank back, c1890, 2" x 3-1/4" cardboard panels **$25**

Tab

Jerome "Dizzy" Dean, St. Louis Cards **$20**

Wally Berger, New York Giants **$15**

Window sign, Mike Higgins Savvy Skipper of the Red Sox, *Saturday Evening Post,* July 21, 1956, 10" x 13-1/2" **$30**

Yearbook

Famous Slugger, published by Hillerich & Bradsby Co., maker of Louisville Slugger bats, 1970, 4-1/2" x 6-1/2" **$10**

Los Angeles Dodgers, 1968, 8-1/2" x 11" **$15**

Mets, 1965, 8-1/2" x 11" **$20**

Basketball

Autograph, basketball

Archibald, Nate **$100**

Bird, Larry **$200**

Bradley, Bill **$150**

O'Brien, Larry **$125**

Autograph, photograph

McGuire, Dick, 8" x 10" **$20**

Phillip, Andy, 8" x 10" **$20**

Thurmond, Nate, 8" x 10" **$24**

Bobbing head, Seattle Supersonics, painted composition, orig sticker: American Sports Sales Ltd., Made in Korea, late 1970s, 7" h **$25**

Magazine, *Sports Illustrated,* Feb. 1949, Ralph Beard, Kentucky cover **$95**

Pencil holder, high gloss ceramics, All American basketball dribbler, flesh-

Scoreboard, "We/They," painted pine, American, round sheet metal scoreboard, adjustable metal indicators, painted black numerals on "We" side, dark red numerals on "They" side, mounted on red-painted, rectangular board, early 20th century, 14" x 12-1/2", $525.
Photo courtesy of Skinner, Inc.

Indian clubs, for ladies or children, narrow and lightweight, painted black red and green, no. 2, 17" l, $472.
Photo courtesy of Lang's Sporting Collectables.

*Golf trophy, metal, engraved "NYC,"
marble base, early 20th century,
6-1/2" h,* **$125.**

Photo courtesy of David Rago Auctions, Inc.

*Indian clubs, early, painted red,
green and black, no. 6, 1-1/2 or
2 lbs,* **$325.**

Photo courtesy of Lang's Sporting Collectables.

tone body parts, black hair and shoes,
pale blue shirt inscribed "Champ,"
white shorts, brown basketball hollowed out for pencils, 6-1/2" h, 4-1/4"
x 5-1/2" white base **$20**

Pin, Chicago Americans Tournament
Championship, brass, 1935 .... **$75**

Program

Basketball Hall of Fame Commemo-
ration Day Program, orig invitation,
1961 .... **$75**

NCAA Final Four Champion-
ship, Louisville, Kentucky, 1967
.... **$175**

World Series of Basketball, Harlem
Globetrotters and College All-
Americans, 1951 .... **$55**

Shoes, pr, game used, autographed

Drexler, Clyde, Avais **$225**

Sikma, Jack, Converse **$100**

Webber, Chris, Nikes **$550**

Souvenir book, *Los Angeles Lakers,* with two records, Jerry West and
Elgin Baylor on action cover **$75**

Ticket

NBA Finals Boston Celtics at Los
Angeles Lakers, 1963 .... **$95**

San Antonio Spurs ABA Phantom
Playoff, 1975, unused **$15**

St. Louis Hawks at San Francisco
Warriors, Dec. 17, 1963 .... **$50**

Yearbook

1961-62, Boston Celtics **$150**

1965-66, Boston Celtics **$85**

1969-70, Milwaukee Bucks **$40**

Boxing

Autograph

Baer, Max, 8" x 10" photo **$180**

Foreman, George, upper torso photo
in muscular pose, Humble, TX,
post office box address, black ink
signature, mailed fold creases,
8-1/2" x 11" letterhead **$35**

Badge, Larry Holmes, black and white
photo, red and black inscriptions,
1979 copyright Don King Produc-
tions, 4" d **$25**

Boxing gloves, 35 readable autographs **$380**

Cabinet card

Corbett, James F., dressed in suit, 4" x
6" **$375**

Ryan, Paddy, full boxing post, dark
brown border, 4" x 6" **$395**

Sullivan, John L., dark brown border,
"John L. Sullivan, Champion of the
World," 4" x 6" **$495**

Dinner program, Boxing Writers
Association, January 1968, 6-1/4" x 9"
.... **$20**

Figure, carved fruitwood, fully carved
figure throwing right jab, standing on
continuation of trunk with tree bark
intact, attributed to New Hampshire,
c1900, 8" w, 20-1/4" h **$1,955**

Letterhead, white stationery, printed
in blue on upper quarter for "International Boxing Club," bluetone photos
of Rocky Marciano-Champion, Joe
Walcott-Challenger, James D. Norris-
President, designates presentation
"For the Heavyweight Championship
of the World" schedule for Chicago
Stadium, Friday, April 10 (1953),
unused, 8-1/2" x 11" **$25**

Magazine

Foreman-Ali Zaire Fight, 52
pgs, Oct. 30, 1974, 8-1/2" x 11" l
.... **$35**

The Ring, cover photo of Emile
Griffith, March, 1965, 8-1/4" x 11"
.... **$10**

Plaque, carved pine, polychrome, figure of John L. Sullivan carved in
relief against landscape in horseshoe-
form, inscribed at base "J. L. Sullivan," old darkened crackled painted surface, New York, late 19th C,
12-1/2" w, 16-3/4" h **$2,185**

Football

Autograph, football

Bergey, Bill **$70**

Ditka, Mike **$125**

Flaherty, Ray **$150**

Green, Roy **$70**

Long, Howie **$75**

Autograph, helmet

Aikman, Troy, Dallas Cowboys
.... **$265**

Dawson, Len, Kansas City Chiefs
.... **$250**

Elway, John, Denver Broncos
.... **$275**

Autograph, photograph

Bradshaw, Terry, 8" x 10" **$40**

Brown, Jim, 8" x 10" **$30**

Thomas, Thurman, 8" x 10" **$25**

Bank, high gloss black finish ceramic,
helmet, orange stripes, white face,
orange and black decal "Northampton Area Senior High School/
Konkreet Kids," white sponsor decal
"First National Bank of Bath," c1960,
4-1/2" h **$20**

Cartoon, 14" x 19" orig sgd art in black
ink and pencil by cartoonist Williard

Mullin, blue pencil title "Theory vs Practice," blindfolded "All American Selector" attempting to select ideal college team and geographically correct, large center character "Pro Draft" who simply points to smiling footballer while deciding "Me For You," 1950s, 15" x 22" white art sheet **$125**

Drinking glass, National Football Clinic Banquet, Atlantic City, painted football passer, March 23-26, names of Dr. Harry G. Scott, Executive Director and Kenneth McFarland, banquet speaker, reverse lists staff of 14 university football coaches, 6-1/4" h, 3" d **$12**

Media guide, Philadelphia Stars, 1984, 5" x 7-1/2" paperback.........**$15**

Pennant, felt, A.F.L.

Boston Patriots, white on red, multicolored Patriot **$75**

Buffalo Bills, white on blue, pink buffaloes **$95**

Houston Oilers, white on light blue **$75**

Pinback button

Gustavus Homecoming, gold and black, cartoon art of Ole and Gus wearing football helmets while tugging at worm between them, 1929 ......**$15**

Hail to Pitt, blue on yellow, cartoon of football player using coal bucket to catch football, inscribed "Scuttle The Lions," c1940 ......**$15**

Philadelphia Eagles, green on white cello, orange suspended miniature football charm, c1950 ......**$15**

Program

Army vs. Duke, at the Polo Grounds, 1946......**$40**

Green Bay Packers, 1960......**$30**

Heisman Trophy, John David Crow, 1957......**$30**

Rose Bowl, USC vs. Ohio State, 1974 ......**$40**

Soda bottle or can, unopened

Baltimore Colts, RC Cola, late 1970s **$2**

Penn State Championship Season 1986, unopened Coke bottle, 9-1/2" h **$15**

Golf

Autograph, photo, sgd, Tiger Woods **$60**

Drinking glass, USGA Tournament, set of four, clear glass, green inscription "U.S.G.A 56th Open Championship" and "Oak Hill Country Club-Rochester, NY," images of golfers at 18th hole in brown and white, 5" h **$25**

Golf club cane, known as "Sunday Stick," 3" l x 3-1/2" h handle fashioned as early driver, ivory foot held in place with four ebony pins, faux lead weight, marked "Addington" on top of handle, orig owner's initials, two ivory and one ebony separators, oak shaft, 7/8" burnished brass and iron ferrule, c1890, 37-1/2" l **$1,075**

Magazine, *American Golfer*, June 1932 ......**$10**

Noisemaker, litho tin, full-color image of male golfer, marked "Germany" on handle, 1930s, 2-3/4" d, 6-1/2" l **$35**

Print, Charles Crombie, *The Rules of Golf Illustrated*, 24 humorous lithographs of golfers in medieval clothes, London, 1905 ......**$1,265**

Program, Fort Worth Open Golf Championship, Glen Garden Country Club, Ft. Worth, Texas, 1945......**$100**

Tournament badge

Henredon Classic, celluloid, 1987 ......**$12**

PGA Tour, diecut rigid plastic, 1999 ......**$7.50**

21st Bob Hope Desert Classic, Jan. 9-13, diecut rigid plastic, 1980 ......**$9.50**

Hockey

Autograph

Orr, Bobby, photograph, 8" x 10" **$50**

Smith, Clint, photograph, 8" x 10" **$12**

Thompson, Tiny, puck **$50**

Worsley, Gump, sgd 1968-69 Topps card......**$15**

Hockey stick, game used, autographed

Beliveau, Jean, 1960s CCM, cracked **$700**

Cashman, Wayne, Sherwood, uncracked **$175**

LeBlanc, J. B., Koho, cracked **$50**

Jersey, game used, Wayne Gretzky, Rangers, autographed **$415**

Magazine, *Sport Revue*, Quebec publication, Feb 1956, Bert Olmstead, Hall of Fame cov **$15**

Program, Boston Bruins, Sports News, 1937-38......**$250**

Stick, game used, autographed

Bondra, Peter, Sherwood **$90**

Photo, W.P.I. Football Team of 1893, Worcester, Mass., framed, **$177.**
Photo courtesy of Lang's Sporting Collectables.

Sled, painted, "Willie," brown ground, orange sides, c1900, 44" l, **$556.**
Photo courtesy of Pook & Pook, Inc.

Lindros, Eric, Bauer Supreme
.... **$295**

Tobacco tin, Puck Tobacco, Canadian, tin litho, detailed image of two hockey players on both sides, 4" d, 3-1/4" h.............................. **$190**

Tournament badge, 4" d, celluloid, World Hockey Tournament, Canada, red and white.............................. **$8.50**

Hunting

Badge, Western Cartridge Co., plant type, emb metal, pin back, 1-3/4" x 1-3/8".. **$100**

Book, *The World of the White-Tailed Deer*, Leonard Lee Rue III, J. B. Lippencott, 134 pgs, black and white illus, dj, 1962.............................. **$15**

Box, Peters High Velocity, two-pc cardboard shot gun shells, multicolored graphics, 25 16-gauge shells
.... **$250**

Calendar top, Winchester, paper, man atop rock ledge, hunting rams, artist sgd "Philip R. Goodwin," metal top rim, 20" x 14"...................... **$125**

Manual, *How To Be A Crack Shot*, Remington/Dupont, June 1936
.... **$20**

Print

"Life in the Woods-The Hunters Camp," published by Lyon & Co., printed by J. Rau, NY, five gentlemen in camp, two more fishing in lake, framed, some foxing, center line burn, water stains in borders, 22" x 28"...................................... **$150**

"Rabbit Catching-The Trap Sprung," lithographed by Currier and Ives, NY, two boys approaching box trap, winter setting, framed, some toning, water stains at borders, 10" x 13"
.... **$495**

Sign

Paul Jones Whiskey, game-hunting scene, orig gold gilt frame, 43" x 57"
.... **$750**

Remington UMC, diecut cardboard Oversized shell next to box of ammunition, 15" x 14"........................ **$200**

Nitro Club Shells, English Setter atop pile of Remington Shotgun Shells, 15-1/2" x 9"................................ **$100**

L. C. Smith Guns, paper, two setters pointing to prey, 14" x 14-3/4"
.... **$1,200**

Winchester, diecut, cardboard, stand-up, Indian Chief with Winchester shotgun in one hand, additional barrels in other hand, 24" x 60"
.... **$200**

Trophy, silverplate teapot, engraved in German "2nd Prize of the First Shooting Festival in Cincinnati held the 29th and 30th of September 1867 and won by Julius Lang," Eastlake style,

Watch fob, Savage Revolver, figural, metal.. **$110**

Olympics

Badge

Enamel on brass, Winter Olympics, Albertville, red and blue on white, colored Olympic rings, 1-3/4" x 2-1/4".. **$25**

Red, white, and blue celluloid, 1966 Central America Games, 4" d....**$10**

Brochure, Official Pictorial Souvenir, issued by organizing committee, Los Angeles, stiff paper covers, lightly emb soft green cover design with silver and gold accents, 64 black and white pages, 1932, 9-1/4" x 12-1/2"
.... **$40**

Cartoon, white art sheet centered by 6-1/4" x 12" orig art cartoon in black ink by Carl Hubenthal, Los Angeles Examiner, art and caption relate to first ever 7' high jump in Olympic trials by US athlete Charlie Dumas, 1956, 8-1/2" x 12-1/2"
.... **$45**

Key ring tag, metal, finished in pewter silver luster finish, official emblem for 1980 Lake Placid Winter Olympics, 2" x 2-1/2"............................ **$15**

Photo album, 1932 Summer Olympics hosted in Los Angeles, hard-

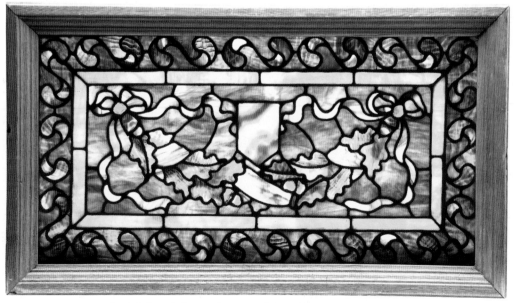

Leaded glass window, trophy center of crest, ribbons, acorns, red "jewels" and oak leaves, swirling leaves surround, unmarked, 16" x 28", **$8,400.**
Photo courtesy of David Rago Auctions, Inc.

cover, printed in Germany, 142 pgs of mounted photos, German text with results and statistics, orig dj, 10" x 12-1/2" **$95**

Poster, Lake Placid Winter Olympics, full color, copyright 1978 Amy Schneider, tightly curled, 22" x 30" **$20**

STAINED AND/OR LEADED GLASS PANELS

History: American architects in the second half of the 19th century and the early 20th century used stained- and leaded-glass panels as a chief decorative element. Skilled glass craftsmen assembled the designs, the best known being Louis C. Tiffany.

The panels are held together with soft lead cames or copper wraps. When purchasing a panel, protect your investment by checking the lead and making any necessary repairs.

Leaded

Door, bench leaded, clear glass, elongated with ornate part beveled glass inserts, 28" w, 78" h **$1,450**

Fire screen, leaded glass, tripartite, central square panel and two narrow side panels set with multicolored textured and bull's eye glass pieces, brass surround, griffin-form trestle feet, Renaissance Revival, late 19th/early 20th C, 32-3/4" h **$1,100**

Panel, rect, rippled, and opaque glass, turquoise, white, and avocado, clear glass ground, stylized flowering plant motif, six panels, c1910, 96" h, 20" w **$6,000**

Sketch for leaded glass window
Charcoal on paper, The Crucifixion, America, c1920, 26" d **$170**
Watercolor, garden scene, mother and child before Christ figure, sgd on mat "Louis Comfort Tiffany," 6-3/4" x 4-1/2" **$1,725**

Triptych, twining grapevines and grape clusters, green slag, textured purple and brown glass, amber border segments, textured colorless glass background, wood frame, cracks, 34-3/4" h, 17-3/4" w **$1,380**

Window
Crossed American flag and other fanciful flag, 44" x 33" **$875**
Henry Belcher, mosaic and chunk jewels, orig frame, 29" h, 93" l **$8,400**
Outside, bull's eye, beaded gilt-metal frame, octagonal surround, central

beveled colorless glass octagon, surrounded by beveled diamonds, price for pr, 17-3/4" d int., 19-1/4" d **$1,035**

Prairie School, zinc caming, clear, white, green, and violet slag glass, stylized lilies and tulips, set of five, few minor cracks in glass, 36" h, 16-1/4" d **$4,250**

Stained

Panel

Red, white, green, pink, and blue floral design, two layers of striated and fractured glass, green patinated bronze frame, stamped "Tiffany Studios New York" pr, 24" x 14" ..**$2,400**
Richard the Lion-Hearted on horseback, 1883, 26" x 21" **$675**

Transom window, arched form, amber, green, and red, later walnut frame, brass plaque, "Illinois Traction System Car Number 523," 59" x 17" **$260**

Window

Fruit and flower design, layered glass in ewer and some fruit, waffle texture ribbon, from west side Buffalo, New York, c1885 home, 36" w, 22" h **$4,200**
Over entry door type, blue and orange shield and geometric design, c1920, 61" l, 61-1/2" h **$490**
Rect, arched top, brown glass border, gold glass panels, central stain pained medallion of bush of classical male, sgd "Louis Shuys," scrolled leaf surround, late 19th/early 20th C, 35-1/8" w, 15-1/2" h **$425**

STEIFF

History: Margarete Steiff, GmbH, established in Germany in 1880, is known for very fine-quality stuffed animals and dolls, as well as other beautifully made collectible toys. It is still in business, and its products are highly respected.

The company's first products were wool-felt elephants made by Margaret Steiff. In a few years, the animal line was expanded to include a donkey, horse, pig, and camel.

By 1903, the company also was producing a jointed mohair teddy bear, whose production dramatically increased to more than 970,000 units in 1907. Margarete's nephews took over the company at this point.

Framed stained and leaded glass window decorated with flowers and leaves, blue and red jewels, 24" x 52", **$350.**
Photo courtesy of Joy Luke.

Pair of tall leaded glass windows, arrow motif in green, yellow, and gold-leaf on clear glass ground, orig zinc frames, Arthur Huen, 46" x 22" x 6", **$5,400.**
Photo courtesy of David Rago Auctions, Inc.

Two leaded glass windows, green leaves, pink berries, blue-green ground, mounted in window frames, 65" x 20", **$1,998.**
Photo courtesy of David Rago Auctions, Inc.

Steiff teddy bear, dark brown mohair, brown glass eyes, beige shaved muzzle, black floss nose and mouth, paws face down, beige shaved feet, beige felt pads on bottom of feet and paws, red leather collar with metal studs and two Steiff buttons, excelsior stuffed, button in left ear, paper chest tag, bare areas on tops of feet, aged leather collar and tag, hole in left foot pad, 10", $1,250.

Photo courtesy of McMasters Harris Auction Co.

Steiff teddy bear, black steel eyes, brown mouth, nose and claws, blank ear button, fully jointed, cream color felt pads, long arms, excelsior stuffing, minor fur loss on feet, poor left paw repair, c1905, 16" h, **$3,055.**

Photo courtesy of Skinner, Inc.

Newly designed animals were added: Molly and Bully, the dogs, and Fluffy, the cat. Pull toys and kites also were produced, as well as larger animals on which children could ride or play.

Marks: The bear's-head label became the symbol for the firm in about 1907, and the famous "Button in the Ear" round, metal trademark was added.

Notes: Become familiar with genuine Steiff products before purchasing an antique stuffed animal. Plush in old Steiff animals was mohair; trimmings usually were felt or velvet. Unscrupulous individuals have attached the familiar Steiff metal button to animals that are not Steiff.

Bear

Blond mohair

Ear button, blond mohair, shoe button eyes, vertically stitched nose, embroidered mouth and claws, long arms and body, large feet, non-functioning growler, 16" h, one hand pad recovered, stuffing compressed, minor fur loss, soil **$4,200**

Rattle, no button, black shoe button eyes, fully jointed, embroidered nose and mouth, overall wear, stains, rip on arm, working rattle, excelsior stuffing, no pad style, c1910, 5" h **$415**

Script ear button, glass eyes, embroidered nose, mouth, claws excelsior stuffed, fully jointed, felt feet pads have scattered moth holes, break at sides, mid-19th C, 30" h **$1,955**

Shoe button eyes, fully jointed, embroidered nose and claws, excelsior stuffing, c1905, 9-1/2" h, well-loved, loss to fur, stuffing, and fiber
.... **$710**

White mohair, fully jointed, long curly fur, embroidered brown nose, mouth, and claws, glass eyes, felt pads, excelsior stuffing, c1910, 20" h, slight fur loss on snout **$7,100**

Cinnamon mohair, swivel head, black shoe button eyes, cotton floss stitched nose with vertical stitching, stitched mouth, center seam body and head, no button in ear, orig felt pads on paws, 20" h **$9,500**

Golden mohair

One Hundredth Anniversary Bear, ear button, fully jointed, plastic eyes, black embroidered nose, mouth, and claws, peach felt pads, excelsior stuffing, certificate no. 3934, orig box, 17" h **$200**

Shoe button eyes, ear button, black embroidered nose and claws, mouth missing, black shoe button eyes, squeaker, fully jointed body, excelsior stuffing, original felt pads, one-inch fabric tear right front arm joint, very minor fur loss, overall soil, c1905, 14" h **$1,955**

Shoe button eyes, embroidered nose, mouth, and claws, fully jointed, excelsior stuffing, no pad arms, moth damage to foot pads, c1915, 8-1/2" h **$1,380**

Light apricot mohair, ear button, fully jointed, shoe button eyes, embroidered nose, mouth, and claws, excelsior stuffing, felt pads, fur loss, lower back and back of legs, slight moth damage on pads, c1905, 12-1/2" h **$1,610**

Light golden mohair, underscored ear button, black shoe button eyes, center seam, black embroidered nose, mouth, and claws, fully jointed, tan felt pads, holes in hand pads, c1905, 14" h **$4,890**

Bison, mohair, ear button, chest tag, post WWII, 9-1/2" l **$200**

Boxer, beige mohair coat, black trim, glass eyes, leather collar marked "Steiff," head turns, minor wear, straw stuffing, 16-1/2" l, 15-1/2" h **$165**

Boxer puppy, paper label "Daly," 4 1/4" h.. **$135**

Cat, pull toy, white mohair coat, gray stripes, glass eyes, worn pink ribbon with bell, pink felt ear linings, button, cast iron wheels, 14" l.............. **$1,980**

Cocker spaniel, sitting, glass eyes, ear button, chest tag, post WWII, 5-3/4" h.. **$125**

Cocker spaniel puppy, button, 4-3/4" h.. **$90**

Dalmatian puppy, paper label "Sarras," 4-1/4" h................................ **$145**

Dog, pull toy, orange and white mohair coat, glass eyes, steel frame, cast iron wheels, one ear missing, button in remaining ear, voice box does not work, 15-1/2" l, 14" h.................. **$280**

Frog, velveteen, glass eyes, green, sitting, button and chest tag, 3-3/4" l
.... **$125**

Goat, ear button, 6-1/2" h............. **$150**

Gussy, white and black kitten, glass eyes, ear button, chest tag, post WWII, 6-1/2" l............................. **$125**

Horse on wheels, ear button, glass eyes, white and brown, wear and breaks to fabric, on solid metal wheels, non-functioning pull-ring, c1930, 21" l, 17" h **$215**

Kanga and Roo, shaded mohair, glass eyes, swivel neck and arms, 21" h kangaroo, 4" h velveteen joey in pouch **$450**

Kangaroo and joey, both with glass eyes, embroidered nose, and mouth, ear button and tag, 20-3/4" h mohair mother, 4" h velveteen baby........**$395**

Koala, glass eyes, ear button, chest tag, post WWII, 7-1/2" h...................**$135**

Lion, pull toy, worn gold mohair coat, glass eyes, worn streaked mane incomplete, no tail, ring pull voice box, steel frame, sheet metal wheels with white rubber treads marked "Steiff," 21" l, 18" h.....................**$500**

Owl, Wittie, glass eyes, ear button, chest tag, post WWII, 4-1/2" h **$95**

Parakeet, Hansi, bright lime green and yellow, airbrushed black details, plastic eyes, button tag, chest tag, plastic beak and feet, 6-1/2" h **$115**

Rabbit, unmarked, wear, 9-1/2" h .**$220**

Soldier, slight moth damage, hat and equipment missing, c1913, 14" h **$460**

Turtle, Slo, plastic shell, glass eyes, ear button, chest tag, post WWII, 7" l...**$85**

Walrus, Paddy, plastic tusk, glass eyes, ear button, chest tag, post WWII, 6-1/2" l...**$145**

STEINS

History: Steins, mugs especially made to hold beer or ale, range in size from the smaller 3/10 and 1/4 liter to the larger 1, 1-1/2, 2, 3, 4, and 5 liters, and in rare cases to 8 liters. A liter is 1.05 liquid quarts.

Master steins or pouring steins hold three to five liters and are called krugs. Most steins are fitted with a metal-hinged lid with thumb lift. The earthenware character-type steins usually are German in origin.

Character

Beethoven, half liter, porcelain, lire on side of body and on porcelain inlaid lid, E. Bohne & Sohn **$570**

Frederick III, in uniform, 1/2 liter, porcelain, porcelain lid, Schierholz, chips on lid repaired, int. color yellowing **$1,735**

Monk, 1/3 liter, design by Frank Ringer, marked "J. Reinemann, Munchen" on underside of base, inlaid lid, 5" h **$580**

Pug dog, Mettlach, #2018, 1/2 liter, character, pug dog, inlaid lid...**$1,100**

Singing pig, 1/2 liter, porcelain, Schierholz, inlaid lid...........................**$580**

Skull, 1/3 liter, porcelain, large jaw, inlaid lid, E. Bohne & Sohn, pewter slightly bent **$550**

Faience

Thuringen, 1 liter, hp, floral design on front, purple trees on sides, pewter top rim and lid, pewter base ring, tight hairline on side, 18th C, 9-1/2" h **$1,155**

Glass

1 liter, blown, wedding type, hp floral design and verse, pewter lid with earlier date of 1779, pewter brass ring, c1850, 9-1/2" h............................**$925**

Amber, encased in fancy French pewter frame, ram's heads around stein, hinged top lid, 15-1/4" h, 6-1/2" d **$495**

Ivory, c1850-70

Battle scene, elaborately hand carved around entire body, scene with over 100 figures, silver top with repoussé fruit, figural knight finial, man in armor as figural handle, silver base, with cherub dec, touch marks, discoloation to ivory, 11-1/2" **$6,700**

Hunting scene, elaborately hand carved four men on horseback, 15 dogs, ivory lid with various animals carved around border, man blowing trumpet with dog as 3-1/2" h finial, crowned bare-breasted woman figural handle, dog's head thumb lift, left arm and trumpet missing, 13-1/2" h **$11,550**

Porcelain and pottery

Delft, 1/2 liter, elaborate scene of two people playing lawn tennis, porcelain inlaid lid of sail boat, marked "Delft, Germany" **$1,390**

Meissen, 1 liter, hp, scene of three people in forest, floral design around sides, porcelain lid with berry finial and painted flowers, closed hinge, cross swords and "S" mark, strap repoured, c1820, 7" h **$3,100**

Steiff Mickey Mouse doll, original neck string, no tag, no whiskers or tail, button in ear with fabric tag, MOP buttons on pants, light aging, 1930s, 7" h, **$1,000.**
Photo courtesy of Hake's Auctions www.hakes.com.

Steiff dog, sitting, mohair, brown glass eyes, black floss nose and mouth, three floss claws on feet, excelsior stuffed, Steiff button left ear tip, 8", **$500.**
Photo courtesy of McMasters Harris Auction Co.

Steiff teddy bear, brown glass eyes, swivel head, jointed arms and legs, 17-1/2" h, **$600.**
Photo courtesy of Joy Luke Auctions.

Mettlach

#1896, 1/4 liter, maiden on one side, cherub face on other, grape dec, pewter lift handle **$350**

#2007, 1/2 liter, etched, black cat, inlaid lid **$660**

#2057, 1/2 liter, etched, festive dancing scene, inlaid lid **$325**

#2580, 1/2 liter, etched, Die Kannenburg, conical inlay lid, knight in castle **$695**

#2755, 1/4 liter, cameo and etched, three scenes of people at table, Art Nouveau design between scenes, inlaid lid **$560**

Salt glaze

Blue and brown accent of man and woman drinking at table, thread relief blue accented vine design on back, orig pewter lid, mold mark #6, 11-1/2" h **$180**

Pouring type, imp "Fort Edward Brew Co." along base with blue accents, relief and blue accented man with cane on one side, man and woman reading on opposite side, heavy orig pewter lid, mold mark #3, 11-1/2" h **$1,100**

Relief and blue accented man and woman drinking at table, thread relief blue accented vine design on back, orig pewter lid, gargoyle thumb lift, mold mark #6, 13-1/2" h **$150**

Unknown maker, 1/4 liter, transfer and enameled, color, Ulmer Splatz!, The Bird from the City of Ulm, pewter lid **$115**

Regimental, 1/2 liter, porcelain

2 Schwer. Reit. Regt. Erzh. Fz, Ferd u. Osterr-Este Esk Landshut 1899-02, named to Friederich Schmidt, two side scenes, lion thumb lift, old tear on lid repaired, minor scruffs, 11-1/2" h **$675**

11 Armee Corps, Mainz 1899, names to Res. Doring, two side scenes, plain thumb lift, strap tear repaired, lines in lithophane, 10" h **$485**

123 Grenadier, Ulm 1908-10, named to Grenadier Schindler, four side scenes, roster, bird thumb lift, open blister on int. base, finial missing **$550**

Wood and pewter, Daubenkrug

1/2 liter, pewter scene of deer, vines and leaves on sides, pewter handle and lid, some separations to pewter, c1820, 6-1/2" h **$925**

1/3 liter, Floral design on sides, oval with crown on front, pewter handle and lid, splints in pewter and wood, 18th C, 5-1/2" h **$1,270**

STEVENGRAPHS

History: Thomas Stevens of Coventry, England, first manufactured woven silk designs in 1854. His first bookmark was produced in 1862, followed by the first Stevengraphs, perhaps in 1874, but definitely by 1879 when they were shown at the York Exhibition. The first portrait Stevengraphs (of Disraeli and Gladstone) were produced in 1886, and the first postcards incorporating the woven silk panels in 1904. Stevens offered many other items with silk panels, including valentines, fans, pincushions, and needle cases.

Stevengraphs are miniature silk pictures, matted in cardboard, and usually having a trade announcement or label affixed to the reverse. Other companies, notably W. H. Grant of Coventry, copied Stevens' technique. Their efforts should not be confused with Stevengraphs.

Collectors in the U.S. favor the Stevengraphs with American-related views, such as "Signing of the Declaration of Independence," "Columbus Leaving Spain," and "Landing of Columbus." Sports-related Stevengraphs such as "The First Innings" (baseball), and "The First Set" (tennis) are also popular, as well as portraits of Buffalo Bill, President and Mrs. Cleveland, George Washington, and President Harrison.

Postcards with very fancy embossing around the aperture in the mount almost always have Stevens' name printed on them. The two most popular embossed postcard series in the U.S. are "Ships" and "Hands across the Sea." The latter set incorporates two crossed flags and two hands shaking. Seventeen flag combinations have been found, but only seven are common. These series generally are not printed with Stevens' name. Stevens also produced silks that were used in cards made by the Alpha Publishing Co.

Stevens' bookmarks are longer than they are wide, have mitered corners at the bottom, and are finished with a tassel. Many times his silks were used as the top or bottom half of regular bookmarks.

Marks: Thomas Stevens' name appears on the mat of the early Stevengraphs, directly under the silk panel. Many of the later portraits and the larger silks (produced initially for calendars) have no identification on the front of the mat other than the phrase "woven in pure silk" and have no label on the back.

Bookmarks originally had Stevens' name woven into the foldover at the top of the silk, but soon the identification was woven into the fold-under mitered corners. Almost every Stevens' bookmark has such identification, except the ones woven at the World's Columbian Exposition in Chicago, 1892 to 1893.

Note: Prices are for pieces in mint or close-to-mint condition.

Bookmarks

Assassination, Abraham Lincoln **$395**

Centennial, USA, 1776-1876, General George Washington, The Father of Our Country, The First in Peace, The First in War, The First in the Hearts of Our Countrymen!, few small stains **$125**

Forget-Me-Not, Godden #441 .... **$350**

I Wish You a Merry Christmas and a Happy New Year **$85**

Lord Have Mercy **$400**

Mother and Child, evening prayers, 10-1/2" l, 2" w, 1-1/2" silk tassel **$400**

Stevengraph, Landing of Columbus, framed, **$350.**

Mourning, Blessed Are They Who Mourn, 9-1/2" l, 2" w, 2" silk tassel **$450**

My Dear Father, red, green, white, and purple....................**$200**

Prayer Book Set, five orig markers attached with small ivory button, cream-colored tape fastened to orig frame, Communion, Collect, Lesson I, Lesson II, Psalms, gold lettering, gold silk tassels, orig mount, c1880-85 ....**$3,400**

The Old Arm Chair, chair, full text, musical score, four color, 2" w, 11" l **$125**

The Star Spangled Banner, U.S. flag, full text and musical score of song, red tassel, seven color, no maker's mark, 2-1/2" w, 11" l **$185**

Postcard
RMS Arabic, Hands Across the Sea **$465**

RMS Elmina **$225**

RMS Franconia **$225**

RMS Iverina **$215**

USMS Philadelphia **$225**

Stevengraph
Betsy Making the First United States Flag, Anderson Bros., Paterson, New Jersey, 5" x 8-1/2"..........**$80**

Buffalo Bill, Nate Salsbury, Indian Chief, orig mat and frame, 8" x 7" **$500**

Chateau Frontenac Hotel, Quebec, silver filigree frame **$95**

Coventry, 7-1/4" x 13", framed..**$100**

Death of Nelson, 7-1/4" x 2-1/2" **$200**

Declaration of Independence **$375**

For Life or Death, fire engine rushing to burning house, orig mat and frame **$350**

Good Old Days, Royal Mail Coach, orig frame, 5-3/4" h, 8-1/2" l, ...**$200**

Kenilworth Castle, 7-1/4" x 13" framed....................**$120**

Landing of Columbus **$350**

Oxford, Cambridge, Are You Ready, orig frame, 5-3/4" h, 8-1/2" l **$300**

STRING HOLDERS

History: The string holder developed as a useful tool to assist the merchant or manufacturer who needed tangle-free string or twine to tie packages.

The early holders were made of cast iron, with some patents dating to the 1860s.

When the string holder moved into the household, lighter and more attractive forms developed, many made of chalkware. The string holder remained a key kitchen element until the early 1950s.

Reproduction Alert. As a result of the growing collector interest in string holders, some unscrupulous individuals are hollowing out the backs of 1950s figural-head wall plaques, drilling a hole through the mouth, and passing them off as string holders. A chef, Chinese man, Chinese woman, Indian, masked man, masked woman, and Siamese face are altered forms already found on the market.

Figural wall lamps from the 1950s and 1960s also are being altered. When the lamp hardware is removed, the base can be easily altered. Two forms that have been discovered are a pineapple face and an apple face, both lamp-base conversions.

Advertising
Chase & Sanborn's Coffee, tin, 13-3/4" x 10-1/4" sign, 4" d wire basket string holder insert, hanging chain....................**$825**

Dutch Boy Paints, diecut tin, Dutch Boy painting door frame, hanging bucket string holder, American Art Sign Co., 13-3/4" x 30" **$2,000**

Es-Ki-Mo Rubbers, tin, cutout center holds string spool, hanging boot moves up and down on sign, 17" x 19-3/4" h **$2,500**

Heinz, diecut tin, pickle, hanging, "57 Varieties," 17" x 14" **$1,650**

Figural
Ball of string, cast iron, figural, hinged, 6-1/2" x 5" h **$100**

Black man and woman, chalkware, matched pair....................**$275**

Bonzo, blue, chalkware, 6-1/2" h **$185**

Boy, top hat and pipe, chalkware, 9" h **$125**

Bride, ceramic, marked "Made in Japan," 6-1/4" h....................**$145**

Carrots, chalkware, 10" h **$225**

Cat, red rose on top of face, green bow under chin, chalkware **$165**

Chef, multicolored, chalkware, 7-1/4" h....................**$165**

Chipmunk, ceramic, 5-1/8" h ...**$135**

Dutch girl, chalkware, 7" h **$100**

Indian, chalkware, 10-1/4" h **$295**

Jester, chalkware, 7-1/4" h..........**$195**

Mammy, yellow blouse, blue apron, scissors in pocket, chalkware, 6-1/2" h **$385**

Mammy, white dress, ceramic, 6-1/2" h **$225**

Parrot, chalkware, 9-1/4" h **$235**

Pineapple, face, chalkware, 7" h .**$165**

Porter, chalkware, 6-1/2" h **$220**

Rose, red, green leaves, chalkware, 8" h **$175**

Shirley Temple, chalkware, 6-1/4" w, 6-3/4" h **$395**

Terrier, chalkware, gray and white, 8-1/2" h **$195**

Woody Woodpecker, chalkware, copyright Walter Lantz, 9-1/2" h.....**$345**

SWORDS

History: The first swords used in America came from Europe. The chief cities for sword manufacturing were Solingen in Germany, Klingenthal in France, and Hounslow and Shotley Bridge in England. Among the American importers of these foreign blades was Horstmann, whose name is found on many military weapons.

New England and Philadelphia were the early centers for American sword manufacturing. By the Franco-Prussian War, the Ames Manufacturing Company of Chicopee, Massachusetts, was exporting American swords to Europe.

Sword collectors concentrate on a variety of styles: commissioned vs. non-commissioned officers' swords, presentation swords, naval weapons, and from a specific military branch, such as cavalry or infantry. The type of sword helped identify a person's military rank and, depending on how he had it customized, his personality as well.

Following the invention of repeating firearms in the mid-19th century, the sword lost its functional importance as a combat weapon and became a military dress accessory.

Note: Condition is key to determining value.

Additional Resources:

Warman's® Civil War Collectibles, 2nd Ed., by John F. Graf, Krause Publications, Iola, WI.

Warman's® Civil War Collectibles Field Guide, by John F. Graf, Krause Publications, Iola, WI.

Sword

Artillery, Ames, 18-3/4" blade stamped with faint signature, U. S. and inspectors' markings, brass hilt with fish scale design, relief eagle, 25" l **$440**

Artillery officer's saber, 27-1/2" l curved blade, wide fuller, eagle head pommel and hilt show most of orig fire gilding, replaced wooden handle, early 19th C, 33" l **$330**

Calvary saber

Civil War, 35-3/4" blade stamped "Ames Mfg. Chicopee Mas, U.S.J.R. 1857," brass three-branch hilt with good patina, part of wire wrap and most of leather remains, iron scabbard, 41-1/2" l **$700**

Import blade with later date stamp of 1851, brass three branch hilt missing leather and wire wrapping, with scabbard, 41" l, 35-1/2" l **$220**

Model 1860, Emerson & Silver, Trenton, New Jersey, signature on ricasso, inspector's initials and 1863 on other side, brass three branch hilt with good patina, dark leather wrapped handle missing its wire, browned steel scabbard, 42-3/4" **$825**

Stamped "U. S. 1862," brass three branch hilt with leather and wire wrapped handle, steel scabbard, 1840, 43" l **$660**

European

Broadsword, 31" blade, 1-1/2" wide blade with floral motif, leather covered wooden grip, brass guard, brown pommel cap, provenance descended from Gen. George Meade family, early 19th C, some rusting, some dryness to leather, no scabbard, 36" l **$650**

Court type, 33-1/2" blade, thin triangular blade with floral etching, hand engraved steel cross guard, bone grip, provenance descended from Gen. George Meade family, some rusting, loss to grip, no scabbard or chain guard, early 19th C, 38-1/2" l **$350**

French, artillery saber, brass single branch hilt, wire and leather cov handle, 32" l curved blade with engraving along top edge, steel scabbard, drag reshaped, 40" l **$350**

Indonesian, long blade carved with figures, scrolling leaf motifs and script, handle carved with figures, bulbous pommel, wooden scabbard, 35" l **$300**

Infantry officer, Model 1850, Ames, 30-1/4" l etched and engraved blade with "Chicopee, Mass" address, cast hilt wash with open work, leather scabbard with brass bands and drag, engraved "Lt. Geo. Trembley, 174th N.Y.S.I.," 36-1/4" l **$1,980**

Japanese

Koto period, No dachi type, mokume grain, choji temper line, single mekugi ana, silver habaki, scabbard and hilt of negoro lacquer, 34" l blade **$5,600**

Officer

Import, Model 1832, artillery, French made, short sword with matching scabbard, blade marked with maker's cartouche **$395**

Import, 34" blade, sgd "Sargent & Son, Manufacturer to the East India Company," cast brass three-branch hilt with leaf designs, handle retains orig sharkskin and wire wrapping, 19th C, 40" l **$150**

Non-regulation, Civil War, 32" blade with fine etching including "U.S." eagle, and banner on opposite side, steel hilt with pierced "U.S." and detailed eagle with "E. Pluribus Unum," sharkskin cov grip with orig copper wire remaining, steel scabbard with minor pitting, 39" l **$1,200**

Russia, dress, Nicholas II, engraved in Cyrillic lettering on partial basket hilt, further engraved with device of nobility above monogram, leathered sheath, 38-1/4" h **$4,120**

Model 1832, Roman-style, Union artillery short sword, **$850-$1,000.**

Model 1850, Union, foot-officer's saber with leather scabbard, **$950-$1,900.**

TEA CADDIES

History: Tea once was a precious commodity and stored in special boxes or caddies. These containers were made to accommodate different teas and included a special cup for blending.

Around 1700, silver caddies appeared in England. Other materials, such as Sheffield plate, tin, wood, china, and pottery, also were used. Some tea caddies are very ornate.

Famille Rose, Mandarin palette, arched rect form, painted front, figures and pavilion reserve, c1780, 5-1/2" h.. **$550**

Ivory tusk, formed as section of tusk, silver-plated mountings, flat hinged top with foliate finial, engraved scrolls, beaded and waved rim bands, 19th C, 4-1/4" w, 5" h **$460**

Papier-mâché, Regency Chinoiserie-style, rect case with canted corners, ornately dec with figural reserves within flower blossoms bordered by wide bands of gilding, conforming hinged lid opening to int. fitted with two removable pewter tea canisters with dec chasing, 9-1/4" l, 6-3/4" d, 6" h... **$950**

Quillwork, hexagonal, inlaid mahogany frames, blue and gilt quillwork panels covered with glass, floral vintage and leaf designs with crown and "MC 1804," two int. lidded compartments, replaced foil lining, English, 8-3/8" l, 4-3/4" d, 5-1/4" h........ **$2,750**

Silver, lobed hexagonal form, lobed lid with filigree finial, all-over Eastern style bird and foliate enamel dec, mounted with semi-precious stones, gilt int., approx 17 troy oz, Europe, late 19th/early 20th C, 7" h **$500**

Treen, ovoid, fruitwood, missing finial and internal hasp, late 18th C, 5" h
.... **$1,400**

Wood

Burled veneer, satinwood banding, brass claw and ball feet and ring handles, lion face plates, paneled lid with raised medallion at center, divided interior with two cov containers and well for glass canister, restorations to one foot and back of lid, 12-1/4" w, 6-1/2" d, 7-3/4" h **$635**

Mahogany veneer, banded and string Rosewood, rect box, sloped sides, inlaid hinged lid and front with brass scrollwork, sides with flush handles, int. fitted with two hinged and inlaid lidded wells flanking area for mixing bowl, int. of lid with velvet ruching, Georgian-style, late 19th C, 12-1/4" w, 6-1/4" d, 6-1/2" h
.... **$450**

Tea caddy, mahogany, oblong octagonal form, veneered body with line inlay and monogrammed cartouche, ebonized accents, minor losses to moldings, 6" l, 4" d, 5" h, **$275.**
Photo courtesy of Alderfer Auction Co.

Tea caddy, Regency style, mahogany, sarcophagus form, concave sides, pendant lion head handles, floriform flattened feet, interior fitted with two lidded wells flanking well for mixing bowl, late 19th century, 7" h x 13-7/8" w x 9-1/2" d, **$350.**
Photo courtesy of Skinner, Inc.

Tea caddy, Georgian style, parquetry inlaid, wood diamond inlay on top, elongated triangular inlay to three sides, interior fitted with two foil-lined wells with inlaid lids, late 19th/early 20th century, 4-1/8" h x 7-7/8" w x 4-1/8" d, **$410.**
Photo courtesy of Skinner, Inc.

Teddy bear, German, jointed, mohair, c1910, 14" h, **$200.**
Photo courtesy of Wiederseim Associates, Inc.

Rosewood, ivory escutcheon, sarcophagus shape, two lidded, foil-lined wells, colorless glass mixing bowl, interior of lid lined with ruched velvet, flattened ball feet, Regency, early 19th C, 12-3/8" w, 8" h **$400**

TEDDY BEARS

History: Originally thought of as "Teddy's Bears," in reference to President Theodore Roosevelt, these stuffed toys are believed to have originated in Germany. The first ones to be made in the United States were produced about 1902.

Most of the earliest teddy bears had humps on their backs, elongated muzzles, and jointed limbs. The fabric used was generally mohair; the eyes were either glass with pin backs or black shoe buttons. The stuffing was usually excelsior. Kapok (for softer bears) and wood-wool (for firmer bears) also were used as stuffing materials.

Quality older bears often have elongated limbs, sometimes with curved arms, oversized feet, and felt paws. Noses and mouths are black and embroidered onto the fabric.

The earliest teddy bears are believed to have been made by the original Ideal Toy Corporation in America and by a German company, Margarete Steiff, GmbH. Bears made in the early 1900s by other companies can be difficult to identify because they

Teddy bear, black nose and mouth, amber glass eyes, fully jointed, excelsior stuffing, remnant oil cloth pads, spotty fur loss, cloth "Farnell Alpha" label on foot, England, late 1930s, 16" h, **$4,990.**

Photo courtesy of Skinner, Inc.

were all similar in appearance and most identifying tags or labels were lost during childhood play.

Notes: Teddy bears are rapidly increasing as collectibles and their prices are rising proportionally. As in other fields, desirability should depend upon appeal, quality, uniqueness, and condition. One modern bear already has been firmly accepted as a valuable collectible among its antique counterparts: the Steiff teddy put out in 1980 for the company's 100th anniversary. This is a reproduction of that company's first teddy and has a special box, signed certificate, and numbered ear tag; 11,000 of these were sold worldwide.

Blond mohair, fully jointed, shoe button eyes, black embroidered nose, mouth, and claws, felt pads, substantial hump, long arms and body, short legs, overall fur loss, some fiber damage, excelsior hard, 12" h **500**

Brown mohair, brown glass eyes, black cotton floss nose with horizontal stitching, floss mouth, hump on back, excelsior stuffing, brown leather collar with decorative metal studs, wheels mounted on metal housed in mohair covered legs, some mohair missing, 8" h **$325**

Ginger mohair, fully jointed, glass eyes, long arms, shaved muzzle, vertically stitched nose, felt pads, arrow ear button, Bing, excelsior stuffing, very slight fur loss, head disk broken through front of neck, c1907, 16" h **$2,300**

Ginger mohair, fully jointed, black steel eyes, black embroidered nose, mouth, and claws, beige felt pads, excelsior stuffing, American, patchy fur loss, felt damage, c1919, 16-1/2" h **$800**

Ginger mohair, fully jointed, black steel eyes, black embroidered nose, mouth, and claws, felt pads, Steiff, blank ear button, spotty fur loss, 10" h **$1,150**

Gold mohair, black shoe button eyes, black floss nose and mouth, jointed at shoulders and hips, head lifts off to reveal small bottle for perfume, Schuco, 5" h **$375**

Golden yellow mohair, fully jointed, glass eyes, brown still nose, embroidered mouth, excelsior stuffed, light

fur loss, felt pads damaged, probably American, c1920, 16" h **$260**

Light yellow short mohair pile, fully jointed, excelsior stuffing, black steel eyes, embroidered nose, mouth, and claws, felt pads, Ideal, spotty fur and fiber loss, pr, c1905, 10" h ... **$920**

Saffron rayon plush, fully jointed, excelsior stuffing, glass eyes, embroidered nose, mouth, and claws, felt pads, some fur loss, and fiber damage, c1930, 13-1/2" h **$115**

Unjointed gray mohair, replaced shoe button eyes, black floss nose, vertical stitching, eyes high on head, felt paw pads, mounted on unmarked cast iron wheels, brown leather collar, 8" h **$500**

Yellow mohair, fully jointed, glass eyes, embroidered nose and mouth, excelsior stuffing, felt pads, Schuco, moth damage, spotty fur loss, early 1920s, 12" h **$350**

TEXTILES

History: Textiles is the generic term for cloth or fabric items, especially anything woven or knitted. Antique textiles that have survived are usually those that were considered the "best" by their original owners, since these were the objects that were used and stored carefully by the housewife.

Textiles are collected for many reasons—to study fabrics, to understand the elegance of a historical period, for decorative purposes, or to use as was originally intended. The renewed interest in antique clothing has sparked a revived interest in period textiles of all forms.

Bedspread

Embroidered candlewick, by Eliza Spink, (1807-77), Auburn, NY, white on white embroidered dec, central cartouche with floral urn, medallion above name and date surrounded by grapevine border, further framed by grapevine and tulip border, central floral urn, 108" x 112", small holes, light staining, repairs **$1,840**

Printed cotton toile, New England, Cupid and several allegorical female figures in scenes of love, hand sewn, pieced and quilted in diamond pattern, backed with white homespun fabric, extended center panel, two

Needlework, silk on linen, prob. Chester County, Phoebe Davis, central cartouche, floral and vine border, potted tulips, birds, butterflies, figures, fruit tress, deer, etc, Pennsylvania, dated 1822, 19-3/4" x 21-1/2", **$3,045.**
Photo courtesy of Pook & Pook, Inc.

Hooked rug, American, yellow cat with green eyes, teal balls and blocked border, early 20th C, 26-1/2" x 32", **$635.**
Photo courtesy of Pook & Pook, Inc.

Needlework, silk on linen, Anna Wilfong, central verse, doves, butterflies, two buildings, lawn, dated 1825, 15-1/2" h x 17" w, **$880.**
Photo courtesy of Pook & Pook, Inc.

pillow gussets, side drops, scalloped border on three sides, white binding, minor repair to backing, late 18th/early 19th C, 109-1/2" l, 52-1/2" w center panel, 31-1/2" l side drops **$1,295**

Braided rug

Oval, multicolored, predominately pink, 28-1/2" l, 23" w **$200**

Round, blue green, and pink, 17-1/2" d **$180**

Round, multicolored, hooked star in center, small repair, 33" d **$660**

Round, shades of green, red, and blue, 36-1/2" d **$125**

Round, blue, red, and green, 39" d
.... **$190**

Child's seat, woven, flame stitch saw tooth pattern, green, pink, and black, 9-1/2" sq **$200**

Coverlet, damask, two pcs, red, blue, and green on white ground, rose and star design, marked "made for P. Matthias by W. H. Gernand Damask Coverlet Manufacturer Westminster Carroll County, MD, 1871," 89" x 90"
.... **$1,125**

Coverlet, E. Hausman, Trexlertown, rust and white, c1856 .... **$350**

Coverlet, jacquard, one pc, Bierderwand, broad loom

Mustard, dark salmon, and navy blue stripes on natural, corner block "William & Rachel Guthrie" with poppy, overall floral designs, tulip-like medallions, added fringe, 84" x 96".. **$385**

Natural, dark navy blue, burgundy, and olive, "Latest Improvent P. Warranted M. by H. Stager, Mount Joy" on edge, star medallion with tulip center, surrounded by rose branches, Greek key and rose branch border, corner block with bird in tree branch, worn areas, fringe loss, some edge damage, 69" x 77"
.... **$300**

Coverlet, jacquard, two pcs, Biederwand

Natural and navy blue, corner block "Daniel Lehr, Dalton, Wayne County, Ohio, 1847," leaf medallions, borders with backwards looking birds with tulips, minor stains and wear, some fringe loss, edge backed with blue cloth, 70" x 76".......... **$450**

Natural and soft salmon, tan, and gold, corner block "Made by W. Moore 1848," (Newark, OH), rose medallion, grape vine border, another small diamond border, minor wear, fringe loss, some edge damage, two halves don't line up at center seam, 78" x 86".............. **$250**

Natural, navy blue, and tomato red, corner block "H. Petry, Canton, Stark County, Ohio, 1840," floral medallions with borders of potted tulips, eagles with trees and stars, fringe loss, minor stains, small hole, stitched repairs, 70" x 72"........ **$425**

Natural, navy blue, red, and golden olive, corner block "T. M. Alexander, Wayne County, S.C.T. Ohio 1845," floral motif, lions and sunbursts, borders of backwards looking birds with roses, grape vines, and diamonds, few stains, fringe

loss, small hole, unbound top edge, 72" x 88" **$650**

Natural, navy blue, salmon red, and olive brown stripes, corner block with four oak leaves "Peter Hartman, Wooster, Ohio, 1843," connected mirror images of potted flowers, alternating with bunches of grapes, border with eagles with shields sitting on grapevines and roses, wear, few stains, some repair, fringe loss, 77" x 90"................. **$300**

Navy blue, red, and olive green stripes, natural ground, corner block labeled "Gabriel Rausher, May 10, Delaware, Ohio, 1854," floral medallions, two vining floral borders, bottom border has backward looking parrots, one rolled edge, minor wear and fringe loss, some stitched repairs, 58" x 86"
.... **$440**

Navy blue, tomato red, and mixed green and yellow stripes with natural, corner block with fancy tulip and "F. Yahraus, Knox County, Ohio 1864," stars with flower and star medallions, one border with backward looking birds and flowers, two borders with grape vines, wear, small repair, edge damage, 74" x 88"
.... **$500**

Tomato red and navy blue bands on foundation of natural threads individually dyed light blue, border labeled "1848 Wove by J.S. for F.L.T.," quatrefoil corner block with bird under tree, diamonds alternating with wavy leaves, double borders of berry vines, worn edges with traces of blue calico binding, 74" x 90"
.... **$385**

Coverlet, jacquard, two pcs, double weave

Blue and white, attributed to Duchess County, New York, unidentified weaver, Agriculture & Manufactures are the Foundations of our Independence, floral medallions bordered by buildings, American eagle flanked by Masonic columns, monkeys, and small human figures, some stains and edge damage, 78" x 82"................................**$865**

Blue and white, attributed to James Alexander (1770-1870), Orange County, New York, cotton and wool, woven in two lengths with an interior of six large floral medallions on polka dotted background, border designs of Independence Hall flanked by eagles with overhead stars, and eagles with Masonic compass and square and columns, name "PHEBE HULSE OCT. 14 1824" woven in corner blocks, minor toning, stains, second quarter 19th C, 94" x 79" **$3,410**

Blue and white, New York State, central star and floral medallions, side borders of birds, undulating grapevines, and pine trees, lower border with eagles and willow trees over name "DEWITT," corner blocks with flower in vase, flanked by "SA" and "C" over "N.Y. 1841," toning, 1841, 86" x 82"..........................**$500**

Dark tomato red, navy blue, and natural, unusual geometric overshot type pattern, minor fringe loss, 68" x 78"......................................**$425**

Natural, navy blue, and salmon, conch shell corner block for Samel Balantyne, Lafayette, Indiana, flowers in grid, borders of urns and pineapple with internal hearts, fringe missing some wear, edge damage, 1808-1861, 75" x 86"..........................**$365**

Natural, salmon, and navy blue, sunflower corner blocks, thistle medallions surrounded by roses, borders with grape vines, wear, minor stains, 72" x 78"......................**$600**

Natural, tomato red, and dark green, corner block with pinwheel and "Jas McLD" for James McLeran, Columbiana County, Ohio, flower and leaf medallions on speckled background, pots of strawberries on border, bound edges, few areas of wear, after 1848, 72" x 76" **$425**

White and dark navy blue, geometric pattern, pine tree borders, overall light stains, one edge rebound with blue calico, 76" x 84" **$220**

Coverlet, overshot

One piece, broadloom, intricate optical pattern, natural, purple, and cinnamon, 74" x 106"...............**$495**

Two piece, optical pattern, natural, pink-red, and navy blue, some fringe trimmed, 68" x 78" **$450**

Two piece, tightly woven, natural, navy blue, and dark red, added red fringe, 80" x 90" **$250**

Coverlet, single weave, two pc, brick red, navy blue, medium blue, and some green on natural, striped designs, tree borders, most orig fringe, small areas of moth damage, 75" x 93" **$300**

Coverlet, summer/winter, one pc, broad loom

Centennial, red, green, and navy blue stripes on natural, central medallion with star surrounded by flowers and eagles with shields in each corner, bound edge with checkered design, worn areas, fringe loss, 80" x 87"...**$125**

Hunter green and tomato red, central floral medallion surrounded by triangles, wide border with capitol building in center flanked by grape vines and flower urns, small stitched repair with minor damage at one of bound ends, 78" x 84" **$450**

Natural, medium green, blue, and tomato red, corner block "Ettinger and Co. Arronsburg, Centre Co., 1865," central acanthus leaf medallion with floral corners, multiple borders including stars, diamonds, and grape vines, minor stains, one end cut down and rebound, 78" x 81"..**$350**

Natural, navy blue, red, dark green, corner block "Made by J. Hausman in Lobachsville for John Bechtol 1842," minor wear and stains, 76" x 100"...**$400**

Natural, red, blue, and yellow stripes, corner block "Emanuel Ettinger, Aaronsburg, Centre Co. 1846," quatrefoil leaf medallions alternating with stars and diamonds, tulip border, 76" x 91" **$200**

Tomato red and natural, central sunburst surrounded by acorn and oak leaf wreath, eagle corners, wide floral borders with paisley scrolls in corners, minor stains, 76" sq **$230**

Draperies, Fortuny, large green fleur-de-lis patterns on taupe ground, early 20th C, four 19-1/4" w by 54" l panels, three 40" l by 54" l panels.........**$2,990**

Foot rest, braided, round, padded, hanging loop, multicolored, stuffed with rags, wear, 15" d **$110**

Fragment

Linen and cotton toile, red printed designs on natural white, George Washington guiding leopard drawn chariot, Franklin, Goddess of Liberty, and soldiers, old but not orig edge binding, stains, torn typewritten paper label stitched to front, 42" x 66"...**$320**

Crewel work, wool yarn, colorful bird perched in flowers, tree, edges with later stitching, minor stains, 52-1/4" x 49"..**$215**

Handkerchief, printed on cotton, Democratic Party, donkeys from Jefferson to Truman, 1949 ....**$230**

Hooked mat

Round, gray, brown, red, and blue turkey on pale green ground, multiple borders, 12" d **$160**

Sailing ship, labeled "Grefell Labrador Industries, Hand Made in Newfoundland & Labrador," minor edge damage, 8" x 8-3/4" **$200**

Hooked rug

Center dog, surrounded by hearts, elves, and geometric designs, multicolored, date "1921" woven into background, repairs, 42-1/2" x 39" **$2,530**

Center gray rabbit, flanked by red tulips in each corner on dark background, scalloped pink-lavender fabric border, 25" x 18" **$690**

Center lying dog, multicolored, hooked crazy quilt background, initialed "E.G.M.," 39" x 30" **$7,150**

Center reclining cat, multicolored, blue ground, black cloth border, 21" x 21-1/2" **$3,300**

Center running horse, surrounded by butterflies and birds, multicolored, 39" x 24" **$1,710**

Hooked rug, folk art, pastoral stetting, horse, early/mid 20th century, 2' 1" h x 3' 7" l, **$175.**
Photo courtesy of Pook & Pook, Inc.

Needlework picture, silk on linen, man rowing boat in pastoral setting, 18th century, 9" x 13-1/2", **$1,170.**
Photo courtesy of Pook & Pook, Inc.

Coverlet, Jacquard, blue and cream, two joined panels, floral and star design, bird and rose border, two corner blocks inscribed "MADE BY/ J. HARTMAN/MILTON/TOWN-SHIP/RICHMOND/COUNTY/ OHIO/1844," fringe on three sides, light browning and fringe losses, 66" h x 86" l, **$220.**
Photo courtesy of Green Valley Auctions.

Coverlet, Jacquard blue and white, floral pattern, eagles, "Lyman E. Bigelow, Jeferson, Co. N.Y. United We Stand, Divided We Fall," New York, 79" x 89", **$550.**
Photo courtesy of Pook & Pook, Inc.

Needlework, silk on linen, Quaker, R.C. Orphan Asylum, wreath, dated 1835, 9-1/4" h x 11-1/4" w, **$1,115.**
Photo courtesy of Pook & Pook, Inc.

Hooked rug, American, two deer, c1900, 37" x 52", **$1,037.**
Photo courtesy of Pook & Pook, Inc.

Hooked rug, New England, reindeer flanking apple trees, 75-1/2" x 39", **$1,380.**
Photo courtesy of Pook & Pook, Inc.

Central blue elephant with black legs, eye, ear, and trunk, multicolored, 35" x 20" **$1,320**

Central gray dog, flanked by salmon butterflies, red five-pointed stars, two pink sassafras leaves at top, red and green vine with leaves and flowers at bottom, multicolored scalloped border, 41" x 33" **$2,750**

Eagle motif, rope border, 54" x 37" **$1,000**

Full figure red and black Indian holding tomahawk, standing on rock dated 1917, light background, multicolored striped border, 36" x 20" **$5,775**

Geometric pattern, multicolored, cloth bound edges, 36" x 22" ... **$935**

Horse's head center, multicolored angled line borders, olive green corner blocks, burgundy, red, and brown center ground, mounted to stretcher, areas of loss and wear, 26" x 44-1/2" **$260**

Rect, center cat with whiskers, multicolored, border, cloth backing, 27" x 11-1/2" **$1,210**

Theorem type, basket of multicolored flowers, black ground, red scalloped border, 31-1/2" x 20" **$1,155**

Three stars surrounded by flowers and concentric diamonds, borders of diamonds and triangles, rect, multicolored, predominantly wool strips hooked onto burlap backing, America, minor imperfections, 19th C, 38-1/2" x 85" **$2,235**

Two central black horses, red background, blue, green, yellow, and red floral vines on top and bottom, vivid orange ground, white panel "M.H." in black script (Mary Hull,) other white panel "1897," later printed cloth backing, provenance: purchased from Hull family estate, Dover, York County, Pennsylvania, 40" x 28" **$7,700**

Welcome, semi-circle, Cape Cod origin **$1,750**

Mourning picture, framed, silk threads, silk ground, central weeping willow tree, tombstone, obelisk, church in far left ground, never embroidered with names, minor losses, deterioration of silk ground, 16-1/4" x 22" **$600**

Needlework picture

Densely chain and couch stitched allegorical scene of couple espied by nobleman and woman in castle, painted faces, accented with French knots, faux pearls, and gold metal chain, matted, 29-1/2" x 23-1/2" frame, England/ France, mid to late 19th C, 22-5/8" x 17" **$1,300**

Mrs. Saunders and Miss Beach's Academy, Dorchester, Massachusetts, silk threads on silk ground, flowers and fruit in urn, pen and ink inscriptions below reading "Wrought at Mrs. SAUNDER'S & Miss BEACHES Academy Dorchester 1807, by Miss June Withrington," stains, laid down, 1807, 8-1/2" x 7-3/8" **$780**

Silk threads on silk ground, watercolor highlights, shepherdess seated while inscribing the letters "TANCRED" on nearby tree, two sheep in foreground, distant mountain, in an oval enclosed by meandering flowering vine, by "Maria Billings M.E. and A. Sketchley's Boarding School, Poughkeepsie," unframed, thread loss, color runs, couple of tears, 13-5/8" x 13" **$775**

Wool embroidery, allegorical scene of man casting out young woman and boy, French knotted trees, painted silk ground, bird's eye maple frame, Victorian, late 19th C, 17-1/2" x 14-1/4" **$360**

Penny rug

Round discs, black background, yellow, blue, and red, 37" x 23" **$1,210**

Six-sided, appliquéd felt pennies, yellow birds, red berries on stems, green leaves, orange daisies with yellow centers, light background, decorative scalloped border, 57" x 32" **$2,100**

Pillow, beadwork, central demi-lune beaded panel, white, gray, pink, and blue floral scene, gray velvet ground, blue, gray, and maroon silk trim, late 19th C, 15" h, 14" l **$200**

Pocketbook, America, crewel embroidery, rect containing initials "ZS," various flowers and foliage in shades of red, yellow, green, and gold issuing from urn set against

black ground, green twill woven taped edging, blue glazed wool int. lining with two compartments, imperfections, 1740-90, 4-5/8" x 7-5/8" **$10,575**

Rag runner

Blue, rainbow stripes, yellow predominate, Pennsylvania, stains, 2' 10" x 10' 9" **$125**

Brown, tan, blue, and orange stripes, 3' 1" x 12' 11" **$85**

Show towel

Homespun, dark brown finely stitched urns of flowers, one urn is heart shaped, "Betz Huhn 1808," woven decorative bands with pulled work and fringe at end, one end is bound, 19" w, 62" l **$250**

Homespun, pink and two shades of blue cross-stitch needlework, urns of flowers, one with birds, hearts, diamond, and fretwork lines, "Elisabeth Schli 1810," fringed, few small holes, some repaired, 15-3/4" w, 54" l **$440**

Red, pale blue, pink, and yellow yarn crewel-work flowers, potted tree, dark blue cross-stitched "ER 1840," decorative woven bands, wear to yarn border, stitch loss, very minor stains, added fringe, 19-1/2" w, 58" l **$385**

Strong blue and dark pink crossstitch geometric design, "Susanna Johnson 1839," 14-1/2" w, 40" l **$200**

Table cloth, banquet size, damask, banded foliate border with panels of classical subjects, central Portland vase designs, Wedgwood, England, 20th C, 16' 6" **$235**

Table mat, braided

Oval, multicolored, 24" w, 41" l ... **$470**

Oval, tan, maroon, and pink, 21" w, 34-1/2" l **$275**

Round, brown and green, cloth backing, price for pr, 6-3/4" d **$220**

Round, purple, 15" d **$200**

Table runner, homespun linen, brown, white, and blue checkered pattern, frayed ends, price for pr, 19" l, 10-1/4" h **$440**

Tapestry, Aubusson-style, shore bird in landscape of trees and flowering plants, tears and repairs, 60" x 36" **$2,000**

TIFFANY

History: Louis Comfort Tiffany (1849-1934) established a glass house in 1878 primarily to make stained glass windows. In 1890, in order to utilize surplus materials at the plant, Tiffany began to design and produce "small glass," such as iridescent glass lampshades, vases, stemware, and tableware in the Art Nouveau manner. Commercial production began in 1896.

Tiffany developed a unique type of colored iridescent glass called Favrile, which differs from other art glass in that it was a composition of colored glass worked together while hot. The essential characteristic is that the ornamentation is found within the glass; Favrile was never further decorated. Different effects were achieved by varying the amount and position of colors.

Louis Tiffany and the artists in his studio also are well known for their fine work in other areas— bronzes, pottery, jewelry, silver, and enamels.

Marks: Most Tiffany wares are signed with the name "L. C. Tiffany" or the initials "L.C.T." Some pieces also are marked "Favrile," along with a number. A variety of other marks can be found, e.g., "Tiffany Studios" and "Louis C. Tiffany Furnaces."

See additional Tiffany listings in the glass section.

Bronze

Bookends, pr, Zodiac, dark brown and green patina, imp "Tiffany Studios New York 1091," 4-3/4" w, 6" h ...**$490**

Box, cov

Circular, enameled stylized spray flowers in irid gold, blue, and green, on bronze ground, script signature, "Louis C. Tiffany 9151," 2-1/2" h, 5" d **$24,000**

Etched metal grapevine pattern, imp "Tiffany Studios New York 816," three Favrile panels damaged, hinge detached, c1900, 6-1/2" l **$550**

Candelabra

Four bulbous cups with blown green Favrile glass on four curved arms, base with 16 green "jewel" inserts around platform base, imp "TG & D Co., Tiffany Studios New York D

Tiffany, gold dore candlesticks, circular candle cups on hexagonal platform, tapered stem, hexagonal base, stamped Tiffany Studios, New York, numbered 1235, c1902-1938, 12-1/2", **$1,525.**
Photo courtesy of Skinner, Inc.

Tiffany & Co., sterling silver nutmeg grater, cylindrical form, 1-5/8" h approx. 1.3 oz total wt, **$410.**
Photo courtesy of Pook & Pook, Inc.

Tiffany, desk lamp, bronze acid-etched, acanthus leaf motif, adjustable socket, fitted with Arabian-pattern gold and amber Favrile glass shade, shade etched "L.C.T.," base mkd "TIFFANY STUDIOS NEW YORK 637," 13" base, 4-1/2" x 6-3/4" shade, **$4,500.**
Photo courtesy of David Rago Auctions, Inc.

Tiffany, jewelry box, gilt parcel, Grape-vine pattern, caramel slag glass, orig velvet-lined compartments, TIFFANY STUDIOS NEW YORK 830, 3-1/4" x 9-1/2" x 6-1/2", **$1,645.**
Photo courtesy of David Rago Auctions, Inc.

Tiffany, bronze, picture frame, Zodiac pattern, verdris and bronze patina, mkd "Tiffany Studios New York 943," 7" x 8", **$1,300.**
Photo courtesy of David Rago Auctions, Inc.

Tiffany, metalwork box, rectangular, Zodiac pattern, bronze dore finish, impressed Tiffany Studios, New York 811, c1902-1938 1-1/2" h x 7" w, **$500.**
Photo courtesy of Skinner, Inc.

Tiffany, Favrile, vase, glass and metal flower form, opal glass insert w/green pulled feathers tipped in iridescent gold, "L. C. T.," bronze footed holder stamped "Tiffany Studios New York 1043," 14-1/2" h, **$1,800.**
Photo courtesy of The Early Auction Company, LLC.

887," corrosion, missing bobeches, 2-1/2" h **$2,100**

Two arms supporting cups with seven green and gold irid glass "jewels," brown and green patina, imp "Tiffany Studios New York," 9-1/8" h **$2,760**

Candlestick, tripod shaft, circular base, prong-set bobeche with flaring rim, orig dark verdigris patina, stamped "Tiffany Studios, New York, 1211," 8" d, 24" h **$4,315**

Cigar box, rect hinged box, Zodiac pattern, multicolored enameling to each medallion, partial cedar liner, base stamped "Tiffany Studios New York 1655," 6-1/2" l, 6" d, 2-1/2" h **$1,610**

Clock, mantle, Pine Needle pattern, sgd "Tiffany Studios New York, #2246," 9" w, 6" d, 13" h **$3,585**

Desk accessories, inkwell, pen holder, stamp box, ten Favrile panels, secret drawer hidden within central drawer, 8-3/4" l, 4-1/2" h **$23,000**

Desk box, Pine Needle pattern, polished, stamped Tiffany Studios mark and numbered "824," 7-3/4" d, 2-1/2" h

Caramel slag glass **$825**

Green slag glass **$1,000**

Frame, gilt, easel back, cast Heraldic pattern, lower recessed finished in patinated brown, imp mark "Louis C. Tiffany Furnaces Inc. 61," 10-1/4" w, 12" h.. **$1,035**

Glove box, Grapevine pattern, striated green slag glass inserts, ball feet, imp "Tiffany Studios, New York," 13-1/2" l, 4-1/2" d, 3-1/8" h.........**$980**

Lamp base, three sockets, hexagonal standard, circular base, base stamped "Tiffany Studios New York 534," 22" h.. **$3,820**

Letter opener, Grapevine pattern, green slag glass **$450**

Letter stand, etched metal grapevine pattern, Favrile panels, brown and mottled verdis gras patina, imp "Tiffany Studios New York, c1910, 6-1/2" l, 5-1/4" h **$1,100**

Magnifying glass, gilt bronze, rosette pattern on handle, imp "Tiffany Studios 1788," imperfections, 8-7/8" l **$750**

Paperweight, sphinx, orig patina, some gilt, stamped "Tiffany Studios New York," 1-1/2" h, 2-1/4" l **$275**

Pen tray, Grapevine pattern, green slag glass, numbered "1004" **$650**

Plate, ftd, relief arts and crafts block designs around rim, sgd "Tiffany Studios New York, 1744," 9-3/4" d, 1" h.. **$475**

Stand, circular top centered by medallion relief-decorated with classical figures, three ribbed legs, base accented with scroll and leaf dec, imp Tiffany & Co. mark, and numbered "0297," maker's "7725 M," one ornamental finial missing, 31-1/2" d **$1,175**

Thermometer, Grapevine pattern, beaded border, green patina, green slag glass, easel stand, imp "Tiffany Studios New York" on reverse, minor corrosion, 8-3/4" h.................... **$1,495**

Tray, circular with extended rim and handles, etched, enameled blue, pink, and green floral cloisonné dec on handles, imp "Louis C. Tiffany Furnaces Inc., Favrile 512" under handle, 9-7/8" d...................................... **$460**

Twine holder, Bookmark pattern, hexagonal form, hinged lid, reddish patina in lower recesses, imp "Tiffany Studios New York 905," minor spotting, 3" h **$1,035**

Lamps

Boudoir, dome shade, restored oviform base, irid gold glass dec with intricate intaglio carved green leaves, trailing budded vines, both sgd "L. C. Tiffany Favrile," shade also marked "5594L," 15-1/2" h.. **$9,775**

Candlestick, 2-1/2" aperture size, quilted blue shade with stretched rim, ribbed and swirled base fitted with green and white pulled feather standard, aperture rim nicks, 12" h, 7-1/2" d shade............................ **$2,235**

Desk, bronze, three gold irid ribbed lily shades, each inscribed "L.C.T.," bronze base stamped "Tiffany Studios New York 319," crack and hole in one shade, 13" h............................... **$2,500**

Floor, counterbalance, gold Doré finish, base stamped "Tiffany Studios New York 681," unsigned 9-3/4" d shade with four rows of fourteen panels, 52-1/2" h.................................. **$3,055**

Mantel lamp, slight octagonal form, cream colored glass rising to bulbed top, caramel and gold pulled petal design, fitted gilt bronze and wood base, 8" h **$1,150**

Table

Bronze, double branch, each branch with three irid glass shades, central bronze stem hollowed to one side to accept separate candle snuffer (missing), base imp "Tiffany Studios 10456" on each glass shade, sgd "LCT" minor roughness on base of shades, 22" w, 15-1/2" h **$12,500**

Crocus, four inverted clusters of spring green flowers with stems, mottled white ground, lower geometric border, stamped metal tag on shade rim, standard with three sockets, knob with seven cabochon jewels, base plate stamped "S216 437 Tiffany Studios New York," 24" h, 16" d.......................... **$18,800**

Dragonfly, conical shade, seven blue-bodied dragonflies with red eyes, caramel-gold colored ground with twenty-one oval gold jewels and Doré metalwork, shade stamped "Tiffany Studios New York 1495," three-socket standard base in turtle back design with verdigris Doré finish, base plate stamped "Tiffany Studios New York 587," 24" h, 20" d **$44,650**

Leaded glass globe shade, mottled green geometric slag glass segments progressively arranged, stamped "Tiffany Studios" on rim, four socket bronze standard, domed, stepped, circular base, stamped "Tiffany Studios New York 532" on base, 28-1/2" h, 22-1/2" d **$19,550**

Linenfold, 10 panels of pleated amber glass, doré metalwork, lower edge slightly lipped, stamped "Tiffany Studios New York 1957, PAT APPL'D FOR," three sockets, gold doré standard, base stamped "Tiffany Studios New York 533," 21-1/2" h, 15-5/8" d.............**$10,575**

Nautilus, adjustable shell-form shade of striated green and white leaded glass segments, supported on bronze standard and cushion base, raised leaf dec, reddish-brown patina, base imp "Tiffany Studios New York 25891" and "Tiffany Glass and Decorating Company" mark, c1892-1902, 12-1/2" h **$8,625**

Silver

After dinner coffeepot, elongated handle and spout, flip lid with leaf finial, ftd, sgd "Tiffany & Co.," 11" h **$300**

Bowl

Ftd, shaped edge with applied flowerhead and fern rim, stylized pad and paw feet with scrolled legs topped by acanthus leaves, center monogram, 1891-1902, 24 troy oz, 9-1/4" h, 4-1/4" h **$1,610**

Incised banding, everted rim, low domed foot, c1907-38, 11 troy oz, 5-3/4" d, 3" h **$200**

Scalloped rim, foot ring marked "Tiffany & Co., Makers Sterling 23844," 26 troy oz, 10-1/4" d................. **$660**

Bread basket, oval, molded rim, center monogram, 1925-47, approx 12 troy oz, 7" w, 10-3/4" l **$215**

Cake plate, circular, shaped rim with molded foliate edge, face with reticulated and engraved bands, domed circular foot with engraved and reticulated dec, center monogram, c1908-1947, approx 47 troy oz, 13-1/4" d **$1,955**

Candelabra, three-light, cornucopia shoulder and central sconce, flanked by reeded scroll candle arms and further cornucopia sconces, plain

columnar stem, foliate cornucopia and shell edge, round floral repoussé foot, removable beaded nozzles, sq base, 1902-07, 26 troy oz, 12-1/4" h **$1,150**

Cigarette case, rect, rounded corners, gold-washed ovoid push button clasp, gold-washed interior, engraved on front with name and date, suspended from silver link chain, c1907-38, 4 troy oz, 3-3/8" x 2-1/4" **$90**

Cocktail set, 6-3/8" h cocktail shaker, six 4-1/8" cordial glasses, tapered ovoid shaker with hammered surface, engraved initials and date in base, glasses with conical bowl, baluster stem, plain foot, monogrammed, c1875-91, 26 troy oz **$865**

Coffee and tea service, coffeepot, creamer, hot water pot on ftd warming stand, cov sugar, waste bowl, each pc chased with band of ivy leaves, circular bases with bracket form feet, pinecone finials, each stamped "Tiffany & Co., 550 Broadway Quality 925-1000, 1375-3139 MM," late 19th C, 171.47 troy oz, 14" h coffeepot **$7,475**

Dresser set, 10 pcs, three brushes, comb, covered jar, receiving jar, hand mirror, shoe horn, button hook, rect box, floral and scroll acid etched dec, gold-washed int. on jars and boxes, monogrammed, c1907-38, 23 troy oz **$1,850**

Flower basket, flattened bell shape, flared sides, engraved husk drops and floral swags, reticulated to rim in guilloche pattern, overhead handle engraved with further husks, oval foot, pr, 1907-38, 26 troy oz **$2,645**

Iced tea spoon, Bamboo pattern, molded bamboo form handles, set of four in Tiffany & Co. blue cloth bag in Tiffany box, mid-20th C, 8" l......**$175**

Kettle on stand, bulbous, domed lid, reeded bud finial, cast upright handle with leather mount, body with engraved band, circular stand with openwork skirt, three cast scroll legs with shell feet, 1916-47, 59 troy oz, 11-1/2" h................................**$1,495**

Ladle, Wave Edge, marked "Tiffany & Co., Sterling Pat 1884 M," 6 troy oz, 11" l..**$320**

Muffiner, urn form body with bat's wing fluting below applied stylized leaf banding, spiral reeded stem, sq base, screw-in domed lid with paneled ball finial, 1891-1902, 12 troy oz, 7-1/2" h......................................**$635**

Pitcher, repoussé, waisted baluster form, ear handle, short spout, chased and emb all over with flowers and leaves, 1891-1902, 32 troy oz, 8-1/2" h **$3,220**

Serving dish, crenelated banding, lid with ovoid handle flanked by anthemion, c1854-70, 41 troy oz, 11-1/8" l, 5-1/2" h **$1,150**

Strawberry set, 11 strawberry forks, one sugar sifter, all gilt, twisted openwork handles and strawberry finials, early 20th C **$1,800**

Stuffing spoon, Chrysanthemum pattern, monogrammed, 8 troy oz, 12-1/2" l......................................**$750**

Tray, ovoid, reticulated border, emb flowers and shells, sgd "Tiffany & Co.," monogrammed, 11" w **$500**

Tinware, ABC plate, alphabet embossed around rim, plain center, use wear, **$30.**

Tinware, wall sconce, punched decoration, radiating sun motif in center, cutwork edges and details, **$195.**

Vase, cov, flared rims, incised lines, stepped round bases, cov with wafers, elongated tear shaped finials, marked "Tiffany & Co. Makers, Sterling Silver," price for pr, 65 troy oz, 16-3/4" h **$2,55**

TINWARE

History: Beginning in the 1700s, many utilitarian household objects were made of tin. Because it is non-toxic, rust resistant, and fairly durable, tin can be used for storing food; and because it was cheap, tinware and tin-plated wares were in the price range of most people. It often was plated to iron to provide strength.

An early center of tinware manufacture in the United States was Berlin, Connecticut, but almost every small town and hamlet had its own tinsmith, tinner, or whitesmith. Tinsmiths used patterns to cut out the pieces, hammered and shaped them, and soldered the parts. If a piece was to be used with heat, a copper bottom was added because of the low melting point of tin. The industrial revolution brought about machine-made, mass-produced tinware pieces. The handmade era had ended by the late 19th century.

Additional Resources:

Antique Trader® Metalwares Price Guide, 2nd Ed., by Kyle Husfloen, ed., and Mark Moran, contr. ed., Krause Publications, Iola, WI.

Anniversary top hat, 19th C, 11" d, 5-3/4" h......................................**$1,150**

Candle lantern

Conical, removable base, circular handle, banded pierce work, Pennsylvania, 10" h, 5-7/8" d......................................**$5,390**

Round removable base, glass panels in sides, cone shaped top with crimped dec, ring carrier, price for

pr, one with pitted surface, 12" h **$400**

Candle mold

Three-tube, handle, 5" h, 4-1/4" w **$715**

12 tube, applied handle, hanger ring, two wick holders, 10" h, 6-1/4" l **$250**

12-tube, round, crimped pie plate top and base, C-shaped handle, 10" h, 6-1/2" d **$990**

72 tubes, sq, applied tin handles, both resoldered, 10-3/4" h......................................**$320**

12-tube, round, ring handle and base, 15-3/4" h, 6-1/4" d......................................**$1,650**

Candlestick

Adjustable push-up, scallop grip ring handle, round base, 6" h, 4-1/4" d **$330**

Push-up, scalloped base, adjustable, cone-form sand-filled base with rod for candle adjustment, attributed to William Smith, Dillsburg, York County, Pennsylvania, 18-1/4" h, 6" d **$3,740**

Triangular base, push-up, ring handle, remnants of japanned finish, 3-1/2" h, 5-3/8" w......................................**$580**

Cheese mold, pierced stylized geometric pattern, three tin conical feet, wire hanger, Pennsylvania, 3" h, 7-1/4" w **$2,420**

Coffeepot, conical, gooseneck spout, padded handle, finial, punched birds and flowers, made by William Resser, East Berlin, Adams County, Pennsylvania, early 20th C, 11" h, 8" w **$715**

Cookie cutter, hand made, 19th C

Crowing rooster, mounted on flat back plate with crimped edges, 6" h, 3" w, 1" d......................................**$330**

Eagle on nest, mounted on back plate with raised post for eye, 5-1/4" h, 4-1/2" w, 1" d **$165**

George Washington on his horse, illegible center stamp attributed to Germantown, Pennsylvania maker, 12-1/2" h, 10-1/2" l, 7/8" d......................................**$13,200**

Indian holding tomahawk, 7" h **$2,700**

Man and woman dancing, 8" h **$3,900**

Man in the moon, mounted on flat back plate, 4-3/4" h, 2-1/2" w, 7/8" w **$385**

Toleware, coffeepot, from Oliver Filley Tinsmiths, yellow bird and fruit decoration, inscribed on underside "H. Case, April 1824," Pennsylvania, paint loss, 11" h, **$1,725.**
Photo courtesy of Pook & Pook, Inc.

Toleware, tray, oval, double handles, hand-painted barroom scene with sailors and dancing woman, paint loss, discoloration, 14-1/2" d, 21-3/4" l, **$450.**
Photo courtesy of Alderfer Auction Co.

Toleware coffeepot, gooseneck spout, vibrant red, yellow, green floral dec, Pennsylvania, 19th century, 9-3/4" h, **$878.**
Photo courtesy of Pook & Pook, Inc.

Moose, mounted on back plate with crimped edges, 8" h, 10" l, 7/8" d **$1,210**

Parrot, mounted to flat back plate, 8" h, 4" w, 1" d **$1,100**

Standing rooster, mounted on flat back plate, 5-5/8" h, 4-3/4" w, 1" d **$1,320**

Swan, mounted to flat back plate, 6" h, 6-1/2" l, 1" d **$880**

Uncle Sam profile, mounted on flat back plate, unusually shaped handle with thumb rest, 8" h, 5" w, 1-1/8" d **$770**

Creamer, polychrome spray of yellow, green, and red flowers beneath spout, attributed to New York, minor paint loss, mid-19th C, 4" h **$200**

Doll-sized bathroom items, half bath with tub, pails, shower, stands, painted, 13 pcs **$300**

Dust pan, bell shaped, crimped molding, compass wheel and various stamps, anniversary type, wooden handle, 13-1/2" w, 16-1/2" l **$440**

Foot warmer

Punched panels with heart in circle design, mortised wooden frame with turned posts and incised lines, wire bale handle, refinished, 8-3/4" x 7-3/4" x 6" h **$315**

Punched panels with heart in circle design, mortised wooden frame with turned posts, old red stain, wire bale handle, traces of rust, penciled note inside, 9" x 7-1/2" x 5-5/8" h **$200**

Grater, pierced, tapered sides, reinforced back, 9-1/8" l, 4" w **$310**

Lamp

Grease, colorful glaze, 1-5/8" h **$165**

Petticoat, orig whale oil burner, orig black paint, 4" h **$65**

Skater's, light teal-green globe, 6-3/8" h **$225**

Lantern, hanging, old dark green repaint, rococo detail, six panes of glass with reverse painted dec, candle socket in base, attributed to Ohio, one pane with corner missing, 17-1/2" h **$420**

Mold

Heart shape, wire crimped rim, 7-3/4" w, 7" l, 1-3/4" d **$300**

Star shape, wire crimped rim, 9-1/2" w, 1-3/4" d **$385**

Quilt pattern

Compass wheel in plumed wreath, 9-3/4" d **$990**

Eight-sided star, central hole, 13-1/2" d **$275**

Six-sided star, central hole, names in pencil, 7-3/4" d **$200**

Spice box, dome lid, punched floral dec, molded banding, ring feet, leaf form hasp support, int. spice grater, three compartments **$1,320**

Tea bin, painted red, litho portrait of pretty young lady, stenciled gold dec, America, minor paint loss, price for pr, 19th C, 8-3/4" w, 8" d, 10" h **$750**

Tea kettle, swing handle, copper brackets, straight spout, base finial, 5" h, 5-1/2" h **$525**

Wall sconce

Oval, crimped and scalloped edges, 15" h, 9" w **$990**

Oval, scalloped edges, crimped edge reflector, 11" h, 6-3/4" w **$1,045**

Rect, crimped dec reflector, scalloped roof, crimped band on candleholder base, 12" h, 5" w **$880**

Rect, japanned black, half circle roof, candleholder base, 12-1/4" h, 3-3/4" w **$110**

Rect, scalloped roof, D-shaped base, 12" h, 4" w **$330**

Tapered back, crimped dec, 9" h, 3-1/2" w **$500**

Weather vane pattern

Running horse, 11" h, 15" l **$20**

Running horse, 11" h, 19-1/2" l **$385**

TINWARE, DECORATED

History: The art of decorating sheet iron, tin, and tin-coated sheet iron dates back to the mid-18th century. The Welsh called the practice pontypool; the French, tôle peinte. In America, the center for tin-decorated ware in the late 1700s was Berlin, Connecticut.

Several styles of decorating techniques were used: painting, japanning, and stenciling. Both professionals and itinerants did designs. English and Oriental motifs strongly influenced both form and design.

A special type of decoration was the punch work on unpainted tin practiced by the Pennsylvania tinsmiths.

Forms included coffeepots, spice boxes, and grease lamps.

Notes: Some record setting prices for decorated toleware were achieved during the auction of the collection of Eugene and Dorothy Elgin, at Conestoga Auction Company, Inc., in April of 2004. Those items are noted as "ex-Elgin."

Additional Resources:

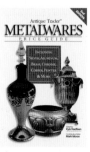

Antique Trader® Metalwares Price Guide, 2nd Ed., by Kyle Husfloen, ed., and Mark Moran, contr. ed., Krause Publications, Iola WI.

Box, cov, dome top, wire and turned wooden handle on lid, yellow scrolled foliate designs, box with red and white swags, yellow leaf embellishments, black ground, America, 19th C, 13-3/4" l, 8-3/4" d, 9" h **$765**

Bun tray, elliptical, pierced handles, off-white rim band dec with yellow, red, green-blue, green, and black flowers, asphaltum ground, crystallized in interior, America, paint losses, late 19th/early 20th C, 12-5/8" d, 3-5/8" h **$500**

Canister, cylindrical, red cherries, green leaves, white border, yellow stylized leaves and swag borders, lid centered with leaf dec, red japanned ground, minor scratches, 6-1/4" h **$400**

Chamberstick, applied handle, japanned ground, polychromed floral dec, yellow, red, green, and white, yellow banding, ex-Elgin, 6-1/4" d, 2" h **$22,000**

Coffeepot, cov

Gooseneck spout, dome top, japanned ground, central medallion, white, orange, red, green, blue, and yellow fruit, floral and foliate dec, ex-Elgin, 10-1/2" h, 6-1/4" d **$38,500**

Gooseneck spout, red ground, central medallion with floral motifs, yellow, black, blue, green, and tan, ex-Elgin, 10-1/2" h, 6-3/8" d, 9-1/2" w **$55,000**

Hooked spout, hinged lid, bands of red and yellow flanking bands of yellow flowers and foliage, asphaltum ground, America, paint wear, minor dents, late 18th/early 19th C, 10-3/4" h **$1,530**

Orig red and yellow pomegranate dec, yellow foliage, brown japanned ground worn and alligatored, orig construction with pieced triangle below handle, wear, 10-1/4" h **$1,495**

Cream pitcher, cov, applied handle, triangular spout, japanned base, yellow floral and band dec, red, yellow, green, and white highlights, ex-Elgin, 3" d, 4" h **$5,500**

Deed box, dome top

Orig dark brown japanning, white band on front panel, green leaves, red cherries, yellow border dec, wire bale handle, tin latch, slight wear, 6-3/4" w, 3-1/8" d, 3-5/8" h **$660**

Black ground, yellow swags and lines, front with fruit, yellow, and green foliate, wire bale handle, tin hasp, minor wear, mostly to lid edges, 8" w, 4" d, 4-3/4" h **$250**

Document box, dome top, brown japanning, red draped swags, yellow leaves, wavy lines, tin hasp, brass bale handle, int. lined with remnants of glue-on leaves, minor touch-up on front of lid and some edges, some wear, 11-1/2" w, 5" d, 6-1/4" h **$990**

Match holder, hanging, scalloped crimped edge, triangular pocket, black base, yellow, orange, and green floral banding, paint flaking, ex-Elgin, 4-3/4" w, 1-5/8" d, 7-1/2" h **$420**

Milk can, black japanning, stenciled red and gold stylized floral design, 8-1/2" h **$200**

Spice box, round, seven int. containers, worn orig brown japanning, gold stenciled labels, 7-1/4" d **$175**

Sugar bowl, cov, scrolled finial, japanned base, floral polychrome, yellow, green, red, and white band dec, ex-Elgin, 4" d, 3-3/4" h **$11,550**

Tea caddy, dark ground, worn stenciled bronze powder dec, int. lift-out tray fits over two lidded compartments, orig emb brass handle, minor damage, 8-1/4" l **$220**

Toy, dancing man with top hat, arm and leg movement, polychrome dec, wooden handle, 11-1/2" h...........**$615**

Tray

Eight-sided, black base painted red ground, polychrome floral design, leaves, yellow banding, wire rim edge, minor paint flaking, 8-3/4" l, 6-1/4" w.....................................**$990**

Eight-sided, japanned base, polychrome floral banding, crystallized center, yellow banding to sides with white, blue, yellow, orange, and red highlights, wire rim edge, ex-Elgin, 12-1/2" l, 8-3/4" w **$17,050**

Eight-sided, japanned base, crystallized center, yellow, blue, and green floral banding on white ground, wire rim edge, attributed to Adams County, Pennsylvania, ex-Elgin, 12-1/2" l, 8-3/4" w **$9,350**

Oblong, scalloped edge, polychrome paint dec, centered scene of three masted ship, possibly U.S. frigate *Independence,* in coastal waters, enclosed by gilt stenciled leaf and scroll borders, black ground, metal hanging rack, America, imperfections, early 19th C, 29-5/8" l, 24" w **$2,000**

Urn, cov

Slender stem, ovoid foot, gilt florals, birds, and butterflies, pr, 19th C, 13-1/4" h **$1,725**

Two handles, acorn finials, dec with floral sprays and birds, scalloped floral and repeating gilt leaf borders, weighted base, French, some paint loss, minor dents, pr, 19th C **$575**

TOBACCO JARS

History: A tobacco jar is a container for storing tobacco. Tobacco humidors were made of various materials and in many shapes, including figurals. The earliest jars date to the early 17th century; however, most examples seen in the antiques market today were made in the late 19th or early 20th centuries.

Bear with beehive, majolica, Continental, 6-1/2" h...................**$770**

Blackamoor, majolica, marked "DEP" in circle, some restoration, c1900, 6" h...**$330**

Black boy, red hat with tassel, majolica, repainted, nicks......................**$275**

Creamware, plum colored transfers on side, one titled "Success to the British Fleet," striped orange, blue, and yellow molding, domed lid, 9" h, 6" d......................................**$900**

Crystal, hammered copper top, Roman coin dec, sgd "Benedict Studios," 7" h **$250**

Dog's head, with pipe and green hat and collar, majolica **$375**

Dwarf in sack, terra cotta, multicolor dec, marked "JM3478," chips, wear, 8" h...**$255**

Indian, black, majolica, 5-1/2" h **$330**

Jasperware, raised white Indian chief on cov, Indian regalia on front, green ground..................................**$195**

Majolica, barrel shape, cobalt blue, green, gold, and brown, Doulton, Lambeth, England, #8481, artist's initials, 6" h....................................**$225**

Mandarin, papier-mâché.............**$95**

Man with pipe, large bow tie, with match holder and striker, rim chips, hairline **$165**

Man with top hat, majolica, Sarreguemines, hairline in base............**$165**

Moose, porcelain, Austrian..........**$200**

Owl, majolica, brown, yellow glass eyes, 11" h **$825**

Royal Winton, hp relief scene, marked "Royal Winton, England"............**$195**

Stoneware, applied Egyptian motif, brown ground, c1890, 5" d, 6" h... **$130**

Treenware, turned and painted poplar, lid with turned finial

Ftd base, incised banding, painted brown, spitting, chips, 4" d, 9-1/2" h **$600**

Finger grained paint dec on yellow base, brown highlights, 8" d, 8" h **$5,500**

Incised banding, red, black, and green polychrome dec, 5-3/4" d, 9-1/4" h **$2,475**

Incised banding, salmon base paint, black banding, 4-3/4" d, 7-1/4" h **$990**

Wave Crest, white opaque body, SP fittings, 5" sq **$450**

Wood, hand-carved walnut, knotty tree trunk, foreground of foliage, rabbit exiting his lair, flowering trumpet fine encircling vase, side inscribed "Viv Le Vin Lamour et le Tabac 1871," fitted lid with carved branch finial, 7" l, 6-1/2" h **$320**

TOOLS

History: Before the advent of the assembly line and mass production, practically everything required for living was handmade at home or by a local tradesman or craftsman. The cooper, the blacksmith, the cabinetmaker, and the carpenter all had their special tools.

Early examples of these hand tools are collected for their workmanship, ingenuity, place of manufacture, or design. Modern-day craftsman often search out and use old hand tools in order to authentically recreate the manufacture of an object.

Antique Trader® Tools Price Guide, by Kyle Husfloen, ed. and Clarence Blanchard, contr. ed., Krause Publications, Iola, WI.

Encyclopedia of Antique Tools & Machinery, by C.H. Wendel, Krause Publications, Iola, WI.

Tobacco jar, earthenware, green and orange mottled glaze, fox and chicken dec, late 19th century, 12-1/2", **$700.**
Photo courtesy of Pook & Pook, Inc.

Tobacco jars, Royal Doulton, Walton Ware, 1910; one depicting Battle of Hastings, 7-1/2" h; other street scene, 5-1/2" h, both cream-color earthenware ground, stamped marks, minor wear, **$365.**
Photo courtesy of David Rago Auctions, Inc.

Tobacco jar, cast spelter, fox head, c1900, 9-3/4", **$935.**
Photo courtesy of Pook & Pook, Inc.

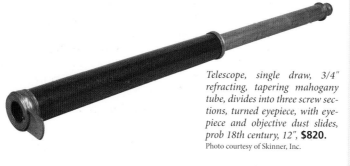

Telescope, single draw, 3/4" refracting, tapering mahogany tube, divides into three screw sections, turned eyepiece, with eyepiece and objective dust slides, prob 18th century, 12", $820.
Photo courtesy of Skinner, Inc.

Radius Octant, ebony, R.W.S. Stevens, bone scale divided 0-100, brass index arm, chipped vernier, mirror double pinhole sight, three shades, adjustable magnifier, bone plaque and two of three brass feet, 12" radius, $295.
Photo courtesy of Skinner, Inc.

Surveyor's quadrant, walnut, colonial, pewter scale, punched divisions, 0-45-0, alidade with rough compass, manuscript directional, read out and brass screw-thread clamp, likely Jeremiah Bennett, Bridgewater, Mass., 8-1/2" radius, $585.
Photo courtesy of Skinner, Inc.

Arithmometer, Burkhardt, black-enameled plate, eight slides, crank and sixteen digit display, oak case, German operating instructions, retail transfer of Carl H. Reuter, Philadelphia, 23" **$1,528**

Auger, E. C. Stearns, No. 4, adjustable, hollow, 70% japanning..................**$60**

Axe head, ship builder's, Campbell's, XXX, New Brunswick, 6" w **$55**

Balance, brass beam, solid arm, two trays, brass pillar with finial and lever adjustment, mahogany base, F. Attwood, Brimingham, 16" h **$235**

Bicycle wrench, Billings & Spencer Co., made for Pope Mfg. Co., patent Jan. 15th 1895, adjusting screw on side, 5-1/2" **$95**

Brace

P. S. & W., No. 1202, Samson patent ball bearing chuck, rosewood handle, 1895 patent date, 12" sweep **$40**

Stanley, No. 923-8, 8" sweep **$55**

Yankee, No. 2101-10, 10" sweep **$65**

Chamfer knife, cooper's, L. & I. J. White, laminated blade................**$65**

Chisel

Buck Bros., 3/8" bevel edge, cast steel **$45**

Stanley, No. 750, 5/8" bevel edge, mkd "Stanley, D., Made in USA," 9-1/4" l **$35**

Clapboard marker, Stanley, No. 88, 80% nickel remains **$25**

Compass, surveyor's type, 5-1/2" d compass card divided 0-90 in four quadrants, brass needle clamp, mahogany body, straight maple arm, two bubble levels, bone vernier w/screw thread adjustment, two horizontal sights, two vertical sights, George Leighton Whitehouse, Dover, NH, fitted green box, 14" l......**$2,350**

Doweling machine, Stanley, No. 77, 3/8" cutter **$375**

Draw knife

C. E. Jennings, pattern maker's type, black egg-shaped handles, 4" **$40**

Whitherby, Winstead, Connecticut, folding handles, 8".....................**$70**

Fret saw, Miller Falls Co., No. 2, deep throat, extra blades, orig box, 12" l **$175**

Hammer

Claw, Stanley, 7 oz, bell face **$25**

Magnetic tack, Stanley, No. 601, orig decal **$40**

Hand drill

Miller Falls, No. 353, ratchet, three-jaw chuck, solid steel frame, 11" l **$50**

North Bros., Yankee No. 1530A, right and left hand ratchet movement, remnants of orig decal, orig box **$175**

Jeweler's vice, Stevens Patent, c1900, 2" jaws **$175**

Jointer and raker gauge, Simonds, No. 342, adjustable **$30**

Nippers, W. Schollhorn, Bernard's patent, Pat. Oct 24, 90% nickel plating, 1899 .... **$25**

Nut wrench

Boos Tool Corp, Kansas City, Missouri, screw adjust, orig box, 6" l **$85**

Boston Wrench Co., Boston, Massachusetts, quick adjust nut, patent Oct. 2, 1906, 6" l **$195**

Octant, ebony, brass index arm, ivory vernier, double pinhole, three shades, finial and scale engraved SBR (Spencer, Browning & Co.), stained oak case, two printed labels, "John Kehew, Nautical Instrument Maker, 69 North Water St., New Bedford," 11" radius **$940**

Pipe wrench

Balin Tool Co., Los Angeles, California, patent no. 2210274, spring-loaded jaw, 10" **$165**

Eaton, Cole & Burnham, Franklin patent, July 20, 1886 .... **$135**

Plane

Preston & Sons, miniature, beech, 4" l **$95**

Record, No. 050, "Improved Combo," metallic, Sheffield, England, orig cutters, orig wood box, 9" l **$185**

Stanley, No. 3, made in USA logo, rosewood handle, c1950 .... **$100**

Stanley, No. 4, type 11, three patent dates cast in bed, dark rosewood handle **$115**

Stanley, No. 5, Jack, 1910 patent date cast in bed, dark rosewood handle, tall knob **$135**

Stanley, No. 9-1/2, block, adjustable throat and cutter **$40**

Stanley, No. 20, Circular, locking screw, '92 patent date on cutter **$225**

Stanley, No. 72, chamfer, cast cap screw, brass star-wheel date, rosewood handle and knob, 1886 patent date on cutter **$395**

Stanley, No. 271, router, 3" l **$65**

Pliers, W. Schollhorn, Bernard's patent, parallel jaws, top nippers, blued, 6-1/2" l **$25**

Protractor, brass sector rule, two quadrant arcs, Price, No. 726625, 24" **$294**

Putty knives, Stanley, Handyman, cocobolo handles, six-pc set, orig box **$95**

Ratchet brace, Stanley No. 2101, Yankee, 14" l **$75**

Rip saw, Henry Disston & Sons, No. 12, London Spring steel, four-screw apple wood handle with early wheat carving, 1896-1917 medallion, 28" l **$145**

Saw jointer, Atkins **$30**

Saw set, Stanley, No. 43, pistol-grip, orig box **$60**

Saw vise, Sears, Roebuck & Co., No. 4920, Dunlap, orig box, 11" l **$55**

Screwdriver, spiral ratchet, North Bros. Mfg. Co., Philadelphia

Yankee No. 30A, three orig straight bits, orig box **$50**

Yankee No. 35, one orig bit, 12" l **$35**

Ship caulking mallet, oak head, 15-1/2" l **$85**

Shipwright's slick, L. H. Watts, New York, 2-1/2" size, 22-1/2" l **$245**

Slide rule, boxwood, c1800, 24" l **$395**

Socket gouge, Zenith, 1/4", 12-1/2" l **$30**

Spoke pointer, Hargrave, Cincinnati Tool Co., No. 343, 90% enamel remains **$65**

Sweep gouge, J. B. Addis & Sons, No. 9, rosewood handle, 5/8" medium sweep **$30**

Swivel vice, North Bros., Yankee No. 1993, quick adjusting swivel base, cam-action lock, 2-3/4" jaws **$115**

Tap and die set, Greenfield No. AA-4, two-pc adjustable die screw plate **$45**

Yard rule, Stanley, No. 41, maple, 36" l **$45**

Wire gauge, Starrett Co., L. S., Athol, Massachusetts, No. 283, US standard, 3-1/2" l **$15**

Tools, work bench, W. P. Walters & Sons, original drawer and cast metal vice, tapped "W. P. Walters & Sons, Philadelphia," 31-1/2" x 21-1/2" x 42", **$400.**
Photo courtesy of David Rago Auctions, Inc.

Tramp art, picture frames, left: applied roundels and diamonds, $45; right: carved American eagle, stars, and laurel motif, $95.

Tramp art, spice box, hanging type, painted black, white porcelain knobs, six small drawers over one longer drawer, ornate carved crest, $250.

Tramp art, frame, crown of thorns, 26-1/2" x 31-1/2", $150.
Photo courtesy of David Rago Auctions, Inc.

TRAMP ART

History: Tramp art was an internationally practiced craft, brought to the United States by European immigrants. Its span of popularity was between the late 1860s to the 1940s. Made with simple tools—usually a pocketknife, and from scrap woods—non-reusable cigar box wood, and crate wood, this folk-art form can be seen in small boxes to large pieces of furniture. Usually identifiable by the composition of thin-layered pieces of wood with chip-carved edges assembled in built-up pyramids, circles, hearts, stars, etc. At times, pieces included velvet, porcelain buttons, brass tacks, glass knobs, shards of china, etc., that the craftsmen used to embellish his work. The pieces were predominantly stained or painted.

Collected as folk art, most of the work was attributed to anonymous makers. A premium is placed on the more whimsical artistic forms, pieces in original painted surfaces, or pieces verified to be from an identified maker.

Bank, secret access to coins, 6" h x 4" w x 4" d..**$335**

Box, cov

Hinged cover, dove, heart, and anchor dec, 4-1/4" w, 3" d, 1-3/4" h **$200**

Hinged top, cast brass pull, mounted pincushion on base, two concealed short drawers, painted blue and gold, c1890-1910, 14" l, 7-1/8" d, 8-1/4" h **$815**

Cabinet, building shape, two towers, steeple roofline, small shelves **$3,600**

Chest of drawers, scratch built from crates with four drawers, 10 layers deep, 40" h x 29" w x 20" d **$2,400**

Clock, mantel, red stain with drawers at base, 22" h x 14" w x 7" d........**$475**

Comb case, adorned with horseshoes, hearts, birds, two drawers and mirrors, 27" h x 17" w x 4" d............**$700**

Crucifix, wooden pedestal base, wooden carved figure, 16" h x 7" w x 4-1/2" d..**$195**

Document box, diamond designs, sgd and date, 14" h x 9-1/2" w x 9" d **$375**

Frame

Double opening frame with oval opening for photos, 14" h x 24" w **$325**

Horseshoe shape, light and dark wood, 13" h x 12" w..................**$465**

Photograph of maker, signed and dated "1906," 9" h, 6-3/4" w.....**$275**

Velvet panels and sq corners, 26" h x 24" w..**$350**

Jewelry box

Covered with hearts painted silver over gold, velvet lined, 6" h x 11" w x 6" d..**$595**

Large, dated "1898," metal lion pulls, 9" h x 11-1/2" w x 7" d **$300**

Lamp, table, double socket, 24" h, 10" w, 10" d..**$550**

Medicine cabinet, light and dark woods, 22" h x 18" w x 10" d **$675**

Miniature

Chair, crown of thorns, 8" h x 6" w x 5-1/2" d **$245**

Chest of drawers, made of cigar boxes, 14" h x 5" w x 4" d **$375**

Music box, velvet sides, 3" h x 7" w x 6" d..**$425**

Night stand, dark stain, drawer on top and cabinet on bottom, no losses, 37" h x 22" w x 14" d **$1,600**

Pedestal

Multi-level, six draws, 14-1/2" h x 12" w x 8" d..............................**$675**

Polychromed in green and black paint, 16" h x 7" w x 4-1/2" d **$950**

Plant stand, painted gold, heavily layered, 22" h x 11" w x 11" d **$675**

Pocket watch holder, ftd, 9" h x 6-1/2" w x 5-1/2" d **$375**

Sewing box, velvet pin cushion on top, 8-1/2" h x 11-1/2" w x 8-1/2" d **$265**

Vanity mirror, table top, heart on top and drawer, 26" h, 14" d, 10" d ...**$375**

Wall pocket

Painted with hearts and stars, pr, 14" h x 11" w x 7" d **$700**

Three pockets, hearts on crest, diamond and circle dec, trim and dec painted orig medium blue and goldenrod, 8" w, 3-1/2" d, 14" h......**$275**

VALENTINES

History: Early cards were handmade, often containing both handwritten verses and hand-drawn pictures. Many cards also were hand colored and contained cutwork.

Mass production of machine-made cards featuring chromolithography began after 1840. In 1847, Esther Howland of Worcester, Massachusetts, established a company to make valentines that were hand decorated with paper lace and other materials imported from England. They had a small "H" stamped in red in the top left corner. Howland's company eventually became the New England Valentine Company (N.E.V. Co.).

The company George C. Whitney and his brother founded after the Civil War dominated the market from the 1870s through the first decades of the 20th century. They bought out several competitors, one of which was the New England Valentine Company.

Lace paper was invented in 1834. The golden age of lacy cards took place between 1835 and 1860.

Embossed paper was used in England after 1800. Embossed lithographs and woodcuts developed between 1825 and 1840, and early examples were hand colored.

There was a big revival in the 1920s by large companies, like R. Tuck in England, which did lots of beautiful cards for its 75th Diamond Jubilee; 1925 saw changes in card production, especially for children with paper toys of all sorts, all very collectible now. Little girls were in short dresses, boys in short pants, which helps date that era of valentines. There was an endless variety of toy types of paper items, many companies created similar items and many stayed in production until World War II paper shortages stopped production both here and abroad.

Adviser: Evalene Pulati.

Animated, large
- Felix, half tone, German **$30**
- Jumping Jack, Tuck, 1900 .... **$75**

Bank of Love note, England, 1865
.... **$40**

Bank of Love note, Nister, 1914
.... **$25**

Charm string
- Brundage, three pcs..................... **$55**
- Four hearts, ribbon **$45**

Comic
- Sheet, McLoughlin Co., USA, 1915, 9" x 14" .... **$5-$7.50**
- Sheet, Park, London, 8" x 10" .... **$15-$20**
- Woodcut, Strong, USA, 1845 .... **$25**

Diecut foldout
- Brundage, flat, cardboard **$25**
- Cherubs, two pcs **$35**
- Clapsaddle, 1911.......................... **$35**

Documentary
- Passport, love, 1910 .... **$25**
- Wedding certificate, 1914 .... **$45**

English Fancy, from "Unrequited Love Series"
- Aquatint, couple, wedding, 8" x 10" **$135**
- Aquatint, girl and grandmother, 8" x 10".. **$95**

Engraved
- American, verse, 5" x 7" **$35**
- English, hand colored, 8" x 10" sheet .... **$65-$85**

Handmade
- Calligraphy, envelope, 1885 .... **$145**
- Cutwork, hearts, 1855, 6" x 6" **$250**
- Fraktur, cutwork, 1800 .... **$950**
- Pen and ink loveknot, 1820 .... **$275**
- Puzzle, purse, 1855, 14" x 14" **$500**
- Theorem, c1885, 9" x 14" **$400**
- Woven heart, hand, 1840 .... **$200**

Honeycomb
- American, kids, tunnel of love **$45**
- American, wide-eyed kids, 9" **$35**
- German, white and pink, 1914, 11" **$85**
- Simple, Beistle, 1920, 8" **$15**

Lace paper

American, B & J Cameo Style
- Large.. **$85**
- Small, 1865.................................. **$55**

American, layered
- McLoughlin Co., c1880 .... **$35**
- Cobweb center, c1855.................. **$250**

English, fancy
- 3" x 5", 1865 .... **$35**
- 5" x 7", 1855 .... **$75**
- 8" x 10", 1840 .... **$145**
- Hand layered, scraps, 1855 .... **$65**

Layered, in orig box
- 1875, Howland............................ **$75**
- 1910, McLoughlin Co................... **$45**

Folk art, scherenschnitte, Pennsylvania, 19th century, circular, heart cutouts, 6-3/4" d, **$575.**
Photo courtesy of Pook & Pook, Inc.

- Simple, small pc, 1875 .... **$35**
- Whitney, 1875, 5" x 7"................. **$45**

Novelty, American Fancy, c1900
- Mat, fancy corners, parchment, orig box, 5" x 7-1/2" **$45**
- Oblong, satin, celluloid, orig box, 16" x 10-1/2" **$65**
- Rect, panel with silk, celluloid, orig box, 7-1/2" x 10" **$65**
- Star shape, silk ruching, orig box, 10-1/2" x 10" **$65**

Pulldown, German
- Airplane, 1914, 8" x 14" **$175**
- Auto, 1910, 8" x 11" x 4".............**$175**
- Car and kids, 1920s **$35**
- Dollhouse, large, 1935................... **$45**
- Rowboat, small, honeycomb paper puff **$65**
- Seaplane, 1934, 8" x 9" **$75**
- Tall Ship, 8" x 16"....................... **$175**

Silk fringed
- Prang, double sided, 3" x 5" **$20**
- Triple layers, orig box................... **$45**

Standup novelty
- Cupid, orig box **$45**
- Hands, heart, without orig box **$35**
- Parchment, violin, large, boxed **$125**
- Parchment, violin, small, boxed **$85**

Weather vane, soldier, sheet iron, old black surface, late 19th century, 34-3/4" h, **$1,990.**
Photo courtesy of Pook & Pook, Inc.

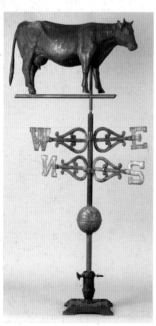

Weather vane, American, copper full body cow, solid brass head, original directionals, c1900, **$10,925.**
Photo courtesy of Pook & Pook, Inc.

WEATHER VANES

History: A weather vane indicates wind direction. The earliest known examples were found on late 17th-century structures in the Boston area. The vanes were handcrafted of wood, copper, or tin. By the last half of the 19th century, weather vanes adorned farms and houses throughout the nation. Mass-produced vanes of cast iron, copper, and sheet metal were sold through mail-order catalogs or at country stores.

The champion vane is the rooster—in fact, the name weathercock is synonymous with weather vane—but the styles and patterns are endless. Weathering can affect the same vane differently; for this reason, patina is a critical element in collectible vanes.

Reproduction Alert: Reproductions of early models exist, are being aged, and then sold as originals.

Allen, Ethan, molded and gilded copper, attributed to J. F. Fiske & Co. **$68,500**

Arrow
Copper, spire and belted ball finial, verdigris surface, no stand, dents, several bullet holes, 60" l, 29" h **$950**
Gilt copper, ball finial, weathered gilt surface, no stand, dents, 36" l, 16" h **$360**

Banner
Sheet copper scrolled banner with pierced "1921," cut-out bird perched on end, copper directionals, America, sq white painted wooden plinth, verdigris surface, minor imperfections, c1921, 31-1/4" l, 49-1/2" h **$2,350**
Sheet iron, iron ball finial on shaft above banner, heart and oval cut-outs, weathered black paint, stand, 15-3/4" l, 37" h **$1,645**

Bird and fish, molded metal, full bodied, bird flies with aid of propellers above fish, marble eyes, unpainted weathered gray surface, Illinois, tall stand, early 20th C, 18-1/2" w, 19" h **$1,150**

Cow, full bodied, molded metal **$1,475**

Deer, running, green patinated copper, hollow body, missing one antler, 19th C, 33" l **$32,000**

Eagle
Copper, full bodied, cast zinc feet, wooden base, one foot loose, arrow bent, 21" wing span, 18-1/2" h **$250**
Gilt copper, outstretched wings perched on belted sphere over arrow directional, old gilt-copper verdigris surface, no stand, small loss on arrow feather, 15-1/2" l, 14-3/4" w, 9-1/8" h **$1,100**
Spread-wing, on globe, 37" l arrow above directionals, mixed metal, verdigris, 45" h **$500**

Fire wagon, painted copper, two horses, driver, steam fire engine, iron supports on underside, red, black, and gold paint, attributed to I. W. Cushing & Sons, Waltham, MA, including stand, imperfections, late 19th C, 40" l, 29-1/4" h **$15,275**

Fish
Carved and painted wood, salmon orange, chamfered edge, tin reinforced carved bracket, Wakefield, MA, inscribed "this set on a cedar tree near our farm before the Civil War," with stand, 19th C, 27" l, 6" h **$1,150**
Carved wood, full bodied, tail wrapped with lead sheeting, tacked button eyes, Midwestern U.S., remnant of post, minor losses, with stand, late 19th C, 12-3/4" l, 3-1/4" h **$2,645**

Heart and feather, sheet iron, found in New York state, fine rust and overall pitting, with stand, late 18th C, 76-3/4" l, 13-1/4" h **$4,900**

Heron, molded copper **$39,950**

Horse
Prancing, molded copper, weathered gilt surface, vestiges of sizing, with stand, imperfections, 34" l, 25-1/2" h **$4,115**
Running, copper, verdigris patina, traces of gilt, America, includes copper sphere, no stand, dents, small seam separations, late 19th C, 17-3/4" h **$2,350**

Running, copper head, hollow molded full body, no stand, gilt wear, minor dent, 41-1/2" l, 21" h **$4,115**

Running, copper, painted, flattened full bodied, older darkened putty painted surface, traces of gilt, no stand, dents, bullet hole repairs, 32" l, 17" h.........................**$1,410**

Running, sheet iron, one side with gilt surface, other side gilt with black painted details, including stand, minor wear, late 19th/early 20th C, 38-1/4" l, 24-1/4" h..............**$3,100**

Running, zinc torso, copper ears, legs, and body, corrugated copper tail, attributed to J. Howard & Co., West Bridgewater, MA, old surface with vestiges of gilt, no stand, old repair on one leg, wear, minor dents, third quarter 19th C, 24" l, 18-1/2" h **$7,650**

Horse and jockey, copper, old yellow sizing surface, no stand, minor dents on ears and jockey's head, 31-1/2" l, 22-3/4" h...........................**$9,400**

Horse and rider, molded sheet iron, hollow body, orig mustard painted surface, wear, cracks.............**$6,465**

Quill, copper **$4,950**

Pig, molded copper, weathered dark verdigris surface, traces of gilt, stand, imperfections, late 19th C, 32" l, 20-1/4" h.........................**$32,300**

Plow, iron and bronze, old surface, no stand, 38-1/4" l, 13-1/2" h **$3,415**

Pointing hand, sheet iron and wood, two wood finials on iron shaft, hand and sunburst sheet iron motif, no stand, imperfections, 23" l, 35-1/4" h **$2,235**

Rooster

Cast iron, two pc cast iron body, sheet steel tail feathers, old red paint, good detail, on later notched wooden base needs re-welding, 24" w, 23" h **$6,670**

Molded copper, L. W. Cushing & Sons **$41,125**

Painted tin, silhouette, wood base, 16" w, 12-3/4" h **$1,380**

Ruby glass globe, spun wire with tail feather dec, 31-1/2" l **$220**

Sloop, gaff-rigged, molded copper, verdigris surface, America, no stand, early 20th C.........................**$4,415**

Stag, leaping

Molded copper, full body, attributed to A. I. Harris & Son, Waltham, MA, including stand, regilded old surface, 55-1/2" l, 41-5/8" h **$12,925**

Molded copper, old regilded surface, mounted on wooden stand, 21-1/2" l, 17-3/4" h...............**$5,290**

WOODENWARE

History: Many utilitarian household objects and farm implements were made of wood. Although they were subjected to heavy use, these implements were made of the strongest woods and well cared for by their owners. Today collectors and decorators treasure their worn lines and patina. Collectors often consider their hand-made wooden items as folk art, elevating what once might have been a common utilitarian item to a place of honor.

Apple tray, pine, dovetailed and sq nail construction, painted yellow ground, green stylized foliate motif, wood separation in base, 10" l, 10" w, 3-1/2" h..................................**$6,050**

Bag stamp, pine, relief carved tulip in heart-dec urn, PA, c1750, 5" h **$2,100**

Bank, rect, carved gardenia blossoms and leaves on top and sides, dark blue painted ground, 4-1/2" w, 3-13/16" d, 3-5/8" h..................................**$525**

Bas-relief carving

Basket of fruit, repaired, 6-1/8" l, 4-1/8" h **$435**

Woman holding bird, found in Iowa, 5" w, 6-3/4" h **$525**

Basket, carved freeform burl, America, 19th C, 10-3/4" l, 5-3/4" h.........**$1,120**

Bowl

Cigar box construction, ten paneled cut-out floral and circle designs, cigar label base, painted red ground, yellow, red, and green highlights to cut-outs, 7-1/4" d, 3-1/2" h......**$715**

Red paint on ext. rim, 18" d, 7" h **$1,380**

Bowl, burl

Early red paint, 9-3/8" d.........**$11,500**

Dark brown finish, raised band around rim, turned foot, age split, 22-3/4" d, 28-1/2" h.................**$200**

Wooden dough bowl, notched out handles, hanging hole one end, orig dry surface, second half 19th century, 4" h, 11-1/2" x 22", **$135.**
Photo courtesy of Green Valley Auctions.

Woden, wall pocket, walnut, carved female head and leaves, Victorian, 17" w, 22" h, **$195.**
Photo courtesy of Joy Luke Auctions.

Wooden, canister and cover, turned and painted wood, yellow and ochre grain decoration, early 19th century, 5-1/2" h x 6" w, **$3,680.**
Photo courtesy of Pook & Pook, Inc.

Wooden frame, mahogany, line inlaid sides, concentric circle carved corner blocks, Pennsylvania, c1840, 9-1/2" x 7-1/2" and 13-1/2" x 11-3/8", **$700.**
Photo courtesy of Pook & Pook, Inc.

Good figure, dark patina, turned rim and foot, 9" d, 2-1/2" h..........**$1,380**

Box, cov

Book shape, spruce, inland bands, star, crescent moon, hearts, and leaves, one end with sliding lid, minor alligatoring to varnish, short age cracks, 5-3/4" w, 4" d, 1-3/4" h **$200**

Oval, bentwood, single finger construction with opposite directions on lid and base, iron tacks, old dark green paint shows lighter under lid, minor wear to paint, 5-1/4" d, 3-3/8" h **$2,420**

Oval, bentwood, single finger on lid, overlapping seams on base, steel tacks, old medium blue paint, wear to lid, 8-1/4" w, 6-1/4" d, 4-1/4" h **$495**

Pine and poplar, orig red paint, applied molding on lid, dovetailed case, molded base, int. slotted for divider (missing), 12" w, 6-1/4" d, 5-3/4" h **$550**

Bucket, oak, slat, tapered, metal band, lid with porcelain finial, painted salmon, 9-1/2" d, 10-1/4" h..........**$880**

Busk, carved maple, engraved with Indian smoking pipe, chip-carved geometric compass designs, attributed to New England, stand, early 19th C, 12" h **$980**

Butter paddle, figured maple, open heart terminal...............**$2,500**

Candle mold, twenty-four pewter tubes, old brown paint with spattered white, sq cut nail construction, old edge chips and splits, 16" h, 21-1/2" l, 9-1/2" w **$590**

Canoe cup, cup with elongated bowl, carved beaver, New England, with stand, 19th C, 5-3/4" l, 2-1/4" h **$520**

Chandelier shaft, turned, acorn finial, painted in dry red and green, never used, 18th C, 20-1/2" l, 2-3/4" d **$385**

Compote, turned, orig painted dec, initials "M.H.D.H." on base, 6" h **$1,500**

Cookie board, walnut, 10" x 12"

Carved man and women in Victorian dress **$3,000**

Carved soldier holding sword, tent, American flag, drum, stack of cannon balls...............**$3,750**

Figure, carved and painted

Frog, pine, applied metal eyes, painted dark green, red mouth, 3-1/4" l, 2-1/4" w, 1-7/8" h...............**$495**

Seated Doberman with collar, shellacked, aged patina, 2-3/4" l, 1-1/4" w, 3-5/8" h...............**$495**

Standing bird, white gesso with red and black highlights, 2-3/4" l, 1" w, 3" h **$385**

Standing Scottie terrier, incised lines for fur, painted black, painted black paws, carved "C. S." for Carl Snavely, 4" l, 1-1/4" w, 3-1/2" h **$200**

Firkin

Staved construction, four wooden bands, hand forged iron bail handle, wooden stopper, painted red, America, minor wear, early 19th C, 9" d base, 7" h **$265**

Staved construction, green lapped bands, swing handle fastened with pegs, painted red, "Cassia" inscribed in white letters, matching cover, America, wear, mid-19th C, 12" d, 12-1/2" h **$530**

Flax wheel, upright type, mixed hardwoods, four turned legs, single treadle, double flyers with bobbins, single wheel at top with turned spokes, few replacements, 45" h **$250**

Foot stool, black lacquer, stenciled peach motif, splayed turned round legs, 12-5/8" l **$200**

Fruit, grouping of carved, gessoed, and polychromed fruits, grapes, apples, citrus, bananas, and cantaloupe, attributed to Adams County, PA **$6,050**

Fruit bowl, hardwood, sample-type, six-sided, dovetailed, pegged turned feet, painted yellow ground with brown highlighted grain painting, each panel with different graining, rag sponged interior with finger dot pattern, 9-1/2" w, 4" h **$2,860**

Herb drying rack, pine, old brown surface, mortised construction, later added old shoe feet, 29-1/2" w, 48-1/2" h...............**$115**

Jar, cov

Peaseware, bulbous, shaped finial, incised ring dec on lid and body, low foot, 3-1/2" d, 6" h **$325**

Treenware, fan shaped sponged vinegar dec in red over mustard, wide sloping rim and base, glued repair, edge damage on lid flange, age crack, 8-3/4" d, 9" h **$1,210**

Mask, carved

Divinity, pronounced teeth and eyes, painted white, yellow, red, black, and green, Nepal, 19th C, 14-1/2" l **$825**

Face painted red, early 20th C, 12" l **$715**

Wild boar, red, black, green, white, and orange, 11" l...............**$470**

Mortar and pestle, burl, flame graining, tapered sides, incised ring dec, lignum vitae pedestal, age splits, 7" h...............**$375**

Pantry box

Oval, cov, bentwood, orig red wash, single finger joint on lid, 11-3/4" h, 23-3/4" l...............**$575**

Round, painted black, top carved with central star within medallion and leafy border, cross hatch swags on side, int. lined with partial advertising lithographs, New England, minor imperfections, mid-19th C, 6-1/4" d, 2-1/4" h **$715**

Pewter rack, hanging, oak, dark finish, two shelves, stylized lion finials on tops, wire nail construction, English, 35" w, 3-3/4" d, 29-3/4" h **$150**

Picture frame

Painted pine, black half round frame, meandering fruited vine and plant border, finish alligatored, 19th C, 13-3/4" w, 17-5/8" h **$520**

Rect, reticulated scalloped edge, compass star corner rosettes, painted black, finish alligatored, 19th C, 19-5/16" w, 22" h **$550**

Stenciled and painted, rect, gold floral dec on black ground, remnants of paper label on reverse, 13-3/8" w, 15-1/2" h **$375**

Quilt rack, folding

Three sections, each fitted with three cross pcs mortised into frame, cast iron hinges, old putty colored paint, 108" w, 66" h **$120**

Two sections, pine, old natural finish, three cross pcs mortised into frame, 3/4" w, 64" h **$95**

Saffron canister, cov, Lehnware, painted, inscribed "2156/6," 4-7/8" h, chips **$300**

Salver, mahogany, molded pie-crust edge, America, staining, edge loss, 19th C, 10-3/4" d **$2,820**

World's Fairs, plate, Libbey, enameled, depicts Santa Maria, "World's Fair 1893" verbiage, acid stamped, "Libbey Cut Glass Company," 7-1/2" w, **$500.**
Photo courtesy of The Early Auction Company, LLC.

World's Fairs, Exposition Universelle at Internationale de Bruxelles, Paris, poster by Eugene Verneau, 1910, framed, 51" x 39-1/2", **$1,100.**
Photo courtesy of David Rago Auctions, Inc.

World's Fairs, Centennial Exhibition scarf, 1876 Philadelphia, American eagle above central image of Memorial Hall, four additional buildings on corner reserves, framed, good condition, late 19th century, 23" x 27", **$145.**
Photo courtesy of Green Valley Auctions.

Scoop, carved, America, 19th C, 9-3/4" l **$210**

Scrub box, wall type, pine, painted green, America, wear, 19th C, 7-1/2" w, 11-3/4" h **$715**

Shelf, hanging

Softwood, scalloped and scrolled cut-outs, painted black and red, 21-1/2" w, 7-1/2" d, 26-1/2" h ... **$1,650**

Walnut, four graduated shelves, rope suspended through hole in top of both side supports, 22" w, 6-3/4" d, 29-1/2" h **$990**

Shoe horn, tiger maple, carved clasped hand terminal, 1826 ... **$4,000**

Slate board, tiger maple frame, slate on both sides, 11-1/4" w, 4-1/2" h **$1,980**

Spoon rack, hanging, butternut or walnut, old faint blue-green graining on black ground, red bird's claw shaped dec, three racks hold six spoons each, pierced arch crest, triangular shaped scalloping across base, nailed splits, one scallop repaired, 10" w, 20" h **$300**

Sugar bucket, cov

Old blue-gray paint over earlier colors, tapered sides, copper tacks in staves, bottom painted green, arched bentwood handle, old chips on lid, 21" h **$490**

Stave construction, copper tacks, bent hickory wood handle, minor wear and edge chips, 13-3/4" h **$460**

Tobacco jar, cov, treenware, turned and painted poplar, round, finger grained paint dec on yellow base, brown highlights, 6-1/2" d, 7-1/2" h **$1,430**

Toddy ladle, carved, notched handle, round bowl, dark brown patina, America, wear, early 19th C, 14-1/4" l **$440**

Trencher, rect, canted sides, rough hewn from pine, good patina, 23" l, 10-3/4" w, 3-1/4" h **$65**

Trivet, pine, wire nails, cut-out feet and ends on apron, old robin's egg blue with red stripes, hand painted decoupaged print of Mt. Vernon on top, minor flaking, multiple nail holes in one area, 4-1/4" x 7-7/8" x 4-3/8" h **$350**

Wall shelf, bird's eye maple, carved, shaped and slightly bowed top shelf with incised front on pierced, shaped, scrolling supports, each with three circular bosses joined by incised medial bar, lower shaped shelf, old finish, New England, minor imperfections, mid-19th C, 38-1/2" l, 6-1/2" d, 16" h **$920**

WORLD'S FAIRS AND EXPOSITIONS

History: The Great Exhibition of 1851 in London marked the beginning of the World's Fair and Exposition movement. The fairs generally featured exhibitions from nations around the world displaying the best of their industrial and scientific achievements.

Many important technological advances have been introduced at world's fairs, including the airplane, telephone, and electric lights. Ice cream cones, hot dogs, and iced tea were first sold by vendors at fairs. Art movements often were closely connected to fairs, with the Paris Exhibition of 1900 generally considered to have assembled the best of the works of the Art Nouveau artists.

Centennial, 1876

Bank, still, cast iron, Independence Hall, 9" h x 7" w **$350**

Glass slipper, Gillinder, clear **$35**

Handkerchief, silk, dark golden background, black printed designs of Memorial Hall Art Gallery, Horticultural Hall, Machinery Hall, Agricultural Hall, Main Exhibition Building, large eagle and shield at top with "Fairmount Park, Philadelphia, 1776-1876" at bottom, stitched to cloth covered backing board, framed, small holes and staining, 29-1/2" x 33" **$435**

Medal, wooden, Main Building, 3" d **$60**

Scarf, Memorial Hall, Art Gallery colorful, 19" x 34" **$100**

New Orleans World's Industrial and Cotton Expo, 1885

Program, cover stamped "April 1885" **$45**

Columbian Exposition, 1893

Album, hardcover, gold emb "World's Fair Album of Chicago 1893," 5-3/4" x 9" **$50**

Cup, peachblow glass, double handles, ribbed, shading from pink to white, gilt dec "World's Fair-1893 Chicago," minor crack at handle, 2-1/2" h **$300**

Medal, brass luster finish white metal, bust portrait of Christopher Columbus on one side, other side "400th Anniversary of The Discovery of America," 1492-Oct-1892, 1-1/2" **$20**

Mug, salt glazed stoneware, imp, blue accents "World's Fair Chicago 1893," 4-3/4" h **$165**

Photo booklet **$25**

Souvenir spoon **$25**

Salt and pepper shakers, pr, lay down, verse, Mt. Washington, dated 1893, 2-1/2" l **$125**

Sugar bowl, open, peachblow, rose-colored walls, pronounced off-white ribs, satin finish, two applied opaque white glass handles, smooth pontil mark, made by Mt. Washington Glass Co., sold by Libbey Glass Co., signature with flourishes, 5-1/2" w, 2-3/4" h **$485**

Ticket **$30**

Watch case opener, Keystone Watch Case Co. **$15**

Pan American, 1901

Cigar case, hinged aluminum, 2-1/2" x 5-1/2" **$35**

Frying pan, pictures North and South America, 6" long **$75**

Medallion, bright luster brass, profile of buffalo between "Souvenir" and "1901," reverse marked "Pan-American Exposition/May-November Buffalo, NY" **$15**

Pinback button

Swifts Pig, multicolored plump pig seated in frying pan, tiny inscription "Pan-American Souvenir," black lettering "Swift's Premium Hams and Bacon-Swift & Co., U.S.A." **$25**

Temple of Music, multicolored art view of building exterior **$25**

Plate, frosted glass, three cats painted on dec, 7-1/2" d **$35**

Poster, Pan American Exposition, Buffalo, May 1-November 1, 1901, based on painting "Spirit of Niagara" by Evelyn Rumsey Carey, 47-1/2" x 24-3/4" **$12,650**

St. Louis, 1904

Match safe and cigar cutter, detailed drawing of Palace of Varied Industries on one side, picture of Gardens and Terraces of States on other, tarnished, 2-3/4" w, 1-1/2" h **$150**

Medal, silvered brass, 2-3/4" d **$60**

Photo album, eight pgs, 15 orig photos **$45**

Plate, scene in center, lacy border, 7-1/4" d **$25**

Souvenir mug, bronze, emb scene of Palace of Electricity, 6" h **$115**

Souvenir plate, Festival Hall, Cascade Gardens, 7" d **$55**

Stamp holder, aluminum, 1-1/8" x 1-3/8" **$35**

Tumbler, copper plated base, metal, shows Louisiana Purchase Monument, Cascades, Union Station and Liberal Arts Bldg, 4" h **$35**

Panama-Pacific, 1915

Pocket watch, official, silver plated, 2" **$300**

Postcard **$5**

Century of Progress, Chicago, 1933

Employee badge, round medallion with "A Century of Progress" around perimeter, "International Exposition Chicago 1933" and employee number below **$55**

Menu, Walgreens **$45**

Pinback button, New York Visitor, red, white, and blue **$20**

Playing cards, full deck, showing views of the fair, all different, black and white **$45**

Ring, adjustable, silvered brass, miniature exhibit building on blue enamel

background, inscribed "Chicago, 1934" **$25**

Souvenir key, bright silver luster brass, sponsored by Master Lock Co., "Master Laminated Padlocks Sold All Over the World," opposite side with miniature form image of exhibit buildings and "World's Fair 1933," tiny horseshoe and four-leaf clover, inscribed "Keep Me For Good Luck" **$28**

Toy wagon, red, white wheels, decal of Transportation Bldg in middle approx 3-1/2" l **$175**

Golden Gate, 1939

Bookmark, typical view, 4" l **$20**

Match book, orig matches, pictures Pacifica **$10**

Token, shows Sun Tower and Bridge, 1-1/8" d **$15**

New York, 1939

Bookmark, diecut and silvered thin brass spear page marker and letter opener, applied metal disk with blue and dark orange accents on silver luster "New York Worlds Fair, 1939," plus images of Trylon and Perisphere, 3-3/4" l **$20**

Folder, printed paper, blue, white, and orange, one side with three images of Borden's Elsie, Trylon, and Perisphere, reverse with blue and white printing, pictorial family endorsement, recipe, and text relating to Borden's Chateau cheese, August 1939 publication date, 6-1/4" x 12" **$20**

Pencil sharpener, Bakelite **$45**

Pocketknife, steel knife based on each side by pearl-like plastic panels, one with tiny blue Trylon and Perisphere, plus inscription "New York World's Fair 1939," two steel blades, 2" l **$40**

Ring, adjustable, silvered brass, inscribed "World's Fair" over "NY," flanked by numeral "19" on left, "39" on right **$25**

Souvenir spoon, Theme Building on front, "Pat. Pend., Wm. Rogers Mfg. Co.," 7" l **$25**

YARD-LONG PRINTS

History: In the early 1900s, many yard-long prints could be had for a few cents postage and a given number of wrappers or box tops. Others were premiums for renewing a subscription to a magazine or newspaper. A large number were advertising items created for a store or company and had calendars on the front or back. Many people believe that the only true yard-long print is 36 inches long and titled "A Yard of Kittens," etc. But lately collectors feel that any long and narrow print, horizontal or vertical, can be included in this category. It is a matter of personal opinion.

Values are listed for full-length prints in near-mint condition, nicely framed, and with original glass.

Reproduction Alert. Some prints are being reproduced. Know your dealer.

Notes: Numbers in parentheses below indicate C. G. and J. M. Rhoden and W. D. and M. J. Keagy, *Those Wonderful Yard-Long Prints and More*, Book 1 (1989), Book 2 (1992), Book 3 (1995), book number and page on which the item is illustrated, e.g. (3-52) refers to Book 3, page 52.

Animals

A Yard of Puppies, ten puppies playing, one with foot in feeding dish (Bk 1-50) **$450**

Ducklings, by W. M. Carey, baby ducks playing around a pool of water (Bk 3-22) **$400**

Our Feathered Pets, by Paul DeLongpre, twelve birds sitting on lattice work fence (Bk 3-19) **$400**

Spring is Here, by Cambril, The Gray Litho Co., New York (Bk 2-18), c1907 .... **$325**

Tug of War, seven kittens and seven puppies playing tug of war (Bk 2-28) **$400**

Twenty-one birds, sitting on a wire, (Bk 3-20), c1899 .... **$400**

Yard of Dogs, eight adult dogs, one with bird in mouth, one with bandage on head covering eye (Bk 2-21), copyright 1903 .... **$325**

Yard of Kittens, eleven kittens playing, one climbing on box (Bk 2-23) **$400**

Calendar

1905, Swift's Premium, four beautiful ladies showing four seasons (Bk 3-112) **$400**

1906, Pabst Extract, Indian, by C. W. Henning, "Hiawatha's Wooing" poem on back of print (Bk 2-101) **$575**

1907, Metropolitan Life Ins. Co., showing four stages of life (Bk 3-111) **$475**

1915, Seiz Good Shoes, lady and child on swing (Bk 2-102) **$575**

1917, by Knowles Hare Jr., lady in pink hat and dress (Bk 3-88) **$500**

1919, Clay, Robinson & Co., Live Stock Commission, advertising and picture of bull, Merry Monarch, on back (Bk 3-106) **$500**

1925, Seiz Good Shoes, lady with walking stick **$800**

Flowers and fruits

A Yard of Cherries, by Guy Bedford, (Bk 2-69), c1906 .... **$300**

A Yard of Chrysanthemums, by Maud Stumm (Bk 2-33) **$300**

A Yard of Wild Flowers, artist sgd in lower left corner (Bk 3-39) **$300**

Bridal Favors, by Mary E. Hart (Bk 2-65) **$300**

Dogwood and Violets, Paul DeLongpre, sgd (Bk 3-28) **$350**

Lilacs and Lillies, artist sgd in lower right corner (Bk 3-31) **$300**

Study of Sweet Peas, by Grace Barton Allen, (Bk 2-62), copyright 1900 .... **$300**

Yard of Assorted Fruit, basket of cherries, plate of fruit on book (Bk 2-73) **$300**

Long ladies

At the Gate, lady in pink by garden gate (Bk 3-82) **$500**

Beautiful lady, holding vase of red roses (Bk 3-93) **$500**

Beautiful lady, standing by table, holding open basket, vase of yellow roses on table (Bk 2-88) **$700**

Butterick Pattern Lady, copyright 1930 (Bk 3-42) **$600**

Indian Maiden, holding basket of flowers (Bk 3-89) **$500**

The Girl with the Laughing Eyes, by F. Carlyle, lady in long off-shoulder gown, holding paper lantern (Bk 2-92), copyright 1910 .... **$500**

The Girl with the Poppies, by B. Lichtman (Bk 3-125) **$500**

Wynette Lady, standing by large vase of yellow roses (Bk 3-80) **$500**

DEPRESSION GLASS REPRODUCTIONS

by Mark Chervenka

Detection Tips

Depression glass has been widely reproduced since the 1970s. Reproductions include rare patterns and colors such as Royal Lace in cobalt blue as well as everyday standards such as pink Cherry Blossom.

The most reliable way to catch reproductions is to compare details in the molded pattern. Unfortunately, there is no one single test that can be used across all the patterns, colors, and shapes. Eliminating the fakes is pretty much a piece-by-piece process, requiring comparisons to the originals you'll find in the following pages.

That said, here are some very broad rules of thumb about Depression glass reproductions.

• Almost all new pieces feel slick or greasy to the touch due to a high sodium content in the glass formula that attracts moisture and dust.

• Many pieces will not function for the purpose they were supposedly created. New spouts often don't pour correctly. Knobs and handles, like those on pitchers and butter dish lids, can be difficult to grasp.

• Color alone is not a good test of age. Colors change with the glass batch. The best test is to compare molded details.

• Some new glass has a strong vinegar-like odor.

It is very important to apply guidelines to only the particular piece of a pattern piece being discussed. For example, don't assume the test for tumblers is the same test you would use for shakers. Don't assume a particular test described for a piece in one pattern can be used for a similarly shaped piece in any other pattern.

There are many more reproductions than those listed in these pages. Pieces for this section were chosen because they are either so widespread almost everyone will encounter them or are very similar to originals and harder to detect. Patterns are listed alphabetically with the various shapes listed separately under the pattern name.

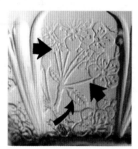

Pattern detail of a typical new cup. The blossoms don't touch the ends of the twigs, and the leaves do not appear natural.

Pattern detail of a typical original cup. Note that the blossoms and twigs touch, and the leaves look natural and realistic.

Cherry Blossom

Original: Jeanette Glass Co., 1930s.

Reproductions: Reproductions have been on the market since 1973. The majority of new pieces have been made in Japan, Taiwan, and China. New colors include pink, green, red, transparent blue, Delphite, cobalt blue, and a variety of iridized (carnival) finishes.

Reproduction Cherry Blossom has been made or is being made in the following known shapes:

berry bowls, 8-1/2" and 4-3/4"

butter dish, covered

cake plate (on three feet)

cereal bowl, 5-3/4"

child/toy sizes in cup, saucer, butter, sugar, and creamer

cup and saucer

pitcher, 36-ounce all over pattern (AOP), scalloped foot

plate, 9" dinner

shakers

platter, 13", divided

tray, 10-1/2", two-handled, sandwich

tumbler, all over pattern (AOP), scalloped foot

As a general rule, most Cherry Blossom reproductions can be identified by crudely shaped cherries and leaves. Old leaves have a realistic appearance with serrated (sawtooth) edges and veins that vary in length and thickness. New leaves commonly have perfectly straight and uniformly even veins that form V-shaped grooves. Original cherries usually give an illusion of a rounded three-dimensional ball-shaped figure; many new cherries appear to be only a flat circle. Differences between old and new patterns are generally greater in earlier 1970s reproductions than in more recent reproductions.

Most original Cherry Blossom in green glass fluoresces under long wave black light. This is not a positive test for age, though, because several green reproductions also fluoresce. This includes a new butter dish, new tumbler, new cup, and several other shapes. While a black light is useful, don't rely on it as your only test of age.

BUTTER DISH (COVERED)

Child/Toy Size: This is a fantasy item; no original child's butter dish was ever made. All pieces now on the market are new.

Full Size: There are at least two styles of reproductions. The 1970s reproduction has a very crude pattern in the base. A later reproduction has an improved pattern in the base, but the branch stops short of the rim. The original base has realistic leaves and cherries with a branch that extends from rim to rim.

All reproduction lids made so far have a smooth band separated from the rest of the lid by a single line. On old lids, the band is separated by two lines.

CUP

The pattern in old cups is very realistic. Each old twig ends in a blossom with the twig touching the blossom. In new cups, there is an obvious gap between the blossom and the twig. In old cups, the pattern fills almost the entire bottom; in new cups, the pattern is faint and weak. Leaves on old cups look like leaves; leaves on the new cups look like arrowheads or barbs.

Original lid has two lines around bottom rim of lid. Original base has realistic cherries and leaves; the branch touches both sides of the rim.

First reproduction base has unrealistic flat cherries and fishbone-type veins in leaves.

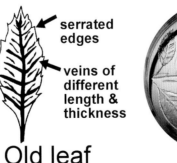

serrated edges

veins of different length & thickness

New leaves | Old leaf

Original Cherry Blossom leaves look real. They have irregular saw-tooth edges and both large and small veins. Reproduction leaves usually have smooth or feathery edges. New veins are generally straight-sided V-shaped grooves or regularly spaced lines.

Second reproduction base has improved pattern, but note that the branch stops short of the rim.

Nine cherries are visible in the pattern on bases of original AOP pitchers. Leaves and cherries are well molded and natural in appearance.

PITCHER

The all over pattern (AOP) scallop-foot pitcher has been reproduced since the 1970s. The easiest way to tell old from new pitchers is to turn the pitcher over and look at the design on the bottom. Now, count the cherries. Old pitchers have nine cherries; new pitchers have only seven cherries. The arrangement of leaves and cherries on the bases of new pitchers is poorly designed with lots of open space in the pattern. Leaves and cherries on the bases of original pitchers are realistic and the pattern covers almost the entire bottom.

The base of new AOP pitchers have crude leaves with unnatural V-shaped veins in leaves. Only seven cherries are visible in the base of new pitchers.

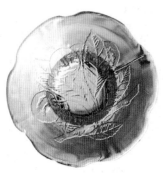

Original tumbler. The design in the foot is sharp and almost fills the entire base; the leaves and cherries are natural and realistic.

TUMBLER

Like the pitchers, new and old tumblers have been reproduced since the 1970s and can be distinguished by examining the base pattern. The pattern of cherries and leaves in the bases of original tumblers is sharp and well defined. The pattern nearly fills the entire concave space of original tumblers. There are at least two different reproductions of AOP tumblers. Both have very poorly molded details in their bases with the unrealistic cherries and leaves. In both new tumblers, the pattern is primarily in the center of the concave center with lots of open space between the pattern and the flat rim. You can also separate old and new tumblers by examining the molded horizontal lines running around the smooth band in the top rim. Old tumblers have three horizontal lines; new tumblers only one. The three molded lines on original tumblers are sharp and strong.

New tumbler, Style A. This style was introduced in the mid-1970s and continued to be made through the 1990s. The design in the foot has the typical new leaves and cherries. The pattern in the foot is mostly in the center with lots of open space around the edge of the foot.

New tumbler, Style B. The design on the foot is very weak and usually found in the very center only. This style was made in pink, green, and Delphite Blue. New Style B was made around 1980 and, when it first came out, H.M. Weatherman reported it in Price Trends 1981.

Floral (Poinsettia)

Original: Jeannette Glass Co., 1931 to 1935. Original colors include amber, crystal, delphite, green, pink, red, and yellow.

Reproductions: New shakers are appearing in cobalt blue, dark green, pink, and red. Shakers in cobalt blue, dark green, and red are obvious reproductions because those colors were never used in original production. The new pink shakers, however, are very close in color and pattern to the originals.

SHAKER

The quickest test for separating new and old shakers is to examine the molded glass threads. In old shakers, there is a 1/4" horizontal gap between the raised threads along the mold seam. No thread goes over the mold seam on old shakers. In the new shakers, threads are continuous, and there is no gap at the mold seam. New shakers also tend to have more glass at the bottom, but this can be hard to measure and may vary slightly. Checking the threads is a more reliable way to identify the new pieces.

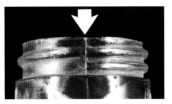

In new shakers, the threads run in an unbroken continuous line across the mold seam.

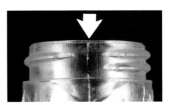

In old shakers, there is a 1/4" gap in the threads as they cross the mold seam.

Florentine #2 (Poppy #2)

Original: Hazel Atlas Glass Co., 1932 to 1935.

Reproductions: Cone-footed 7-1/2" pitcher and 4" footed tumbler. New colors include a blue that is often mistaken for the rarest original color, which is ice blue.

TUMBLER

The center of the bases in new tumblers (left) is plain without a pattern. The pattern is included in the bases of old tumblers (right).

PITCHER

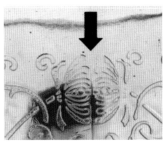

In the new pitcher, the pattern stops and starts at the mold seam under the pour spout.

In the old pitcher, the pattern is split by the mold seam under the pour spout.

The original Madrid pattern was renamed "Recollection" and marketed by Indiana Glass Co. Many new shapes are similar to the original 1930s Madrid, including the butter dish shown here in the new Recollection box.

Madrid

Original: Federal Glass Co., 1932 to 1939.

Reproductions: There are two groups of modern Madrid. In 1976, Federal changed the pattern name to Recollection and began making new pieces. The first new pieces of Recollection were easily identified because pieces were dated in the mold with the year "1976." But then, Federal Glass went bankrupt, and the rights to the design were acquired by Indiana Glass. Indiana Glass discontinued dating the glass and that has caused problems for collectors. So far, new pieces have been made in five colors: amber, blue, clear, pink, and teal. Teal, a greenish-blue, almost aqua color, is the only new color not originally made. The other four colors—amber, pink, blue, and clear—were all used for the 1930s Madrid.

The situation is further confused because Indiana Glass has also introduced many shapes never originally made, such as the cake stand, goblet, covered candy dish, and others. Don't mistake these items for rare or unlisted pieces just because you can't find them in a book.

Known shapes reproduced to date include: covered butter dish, dinner plate, grill plate, luncheon plate, creamer, open sugar, shaker, cup, saucer, goblet*, vase*, hurricane lamp*, pedestal covered candy dish*, footed cake stand*, footed fruit stand/dish*, 9-1/2" bowl, 10" oval vegetable bowl, 7" soup/cereal bowl, and candleholder. Items marked with an asterisk* are shapes never made in original 1930s Madrid.

New covered candy dish (left); new footed goblet (right). Neither shape was made in the original 1930s Madrid.

New shapes not made in original 1930s Madrid: A. "hurricane lamp" made by attaching candleholder to tumbler; B. tumbler; C. fruit stand made by joining candleholder to dinner plate; D. cake stand, same as C. but with flat edges.

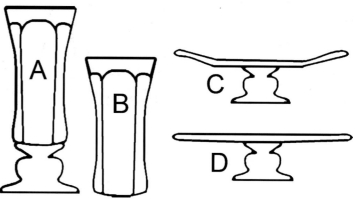

BUTTER DISH

Top: The mold seam in the knob on the new butter dish lid has a vertical mold seam.

Bottom: The mold seam on the old butter dish knob is horizontal.

CUP AND SUGAR BOWL

The easiest way to detect new cups and new sugars is to examine how their handles join the bodies. Looking at the inside of a sugar bowl or cup, the lower part of old handles (right) forms a tear drop shape. The same area in new handles form an oval (left).

CREAMER

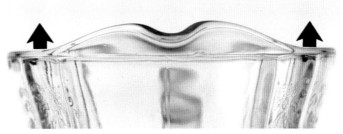

Spouts on new creamers rise above the top rim.

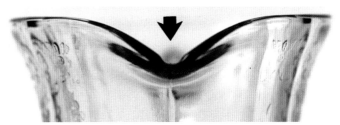

Spouts on old creamers dip below the top rim.

SHAKER

New **Old**

The new shaker is a squat barrel-shape. There are two styles of old shakers. Both old shakers are slender, vertical shapes: one is footed, the other has a flat bottom.

The easiest way to detect new cups and new sugars is to examine how their handles join the bodies. Looking at the inside of a sugar bowl or cup, the lower part of old handles (right) forms a teardrop shape. The same area in new handles form an oval.

Royal Lace

Original: Hazel Atlas, 1934 to 1941.

Reproductions: Cookie jar, 9 ounce tumbler, and 5 ounce juice glass. The majority of new tumblers are cobalt blue. Cookie jars are produced in a variety of colors.

New Royal Lace cookie jar.

COOKIE JAR

Pay particular attention to lids, as they are the most valuable part of the cookie jar. Genuine old jars are easier to find than old lids, so be alert for new lids on old jars. All old lids have a single mold seam that splits the lid in half. There is no mold seam on the new lids.

The bottom of the base of the new cookie jar is smooth and plain.

The bottom of the base of the old cookie jar has a molded circular plunger mark.

TUMBLER

The glass in the sides and bottoms of both sizes of new tumblers is generally about two to three times as thick as originals.

Bottoms of new 5 ounce juice glasses are plain with no pattern (right). Old 5 ounce juice glasses have a geometric design molded in the bottom (left).

Sharon (Cabbage Rose)

Original: Federal Glass Co., 1935 to 1939.

Reproductions: Includes covered butter dish, candy jar, cheese dish, shakers, and sugar and creamer.

Butter Dish

The best test for lids is to examine the knob. On old lids there is only about 1/4" between the bottom of the old knob and the top of the lid. It's very hard to get your fingers under the knob of an original lid. The gap under the knobs on new lids is about 1/2".

An original Sharon butter dish. New and old can be separated by the knob on the lid.

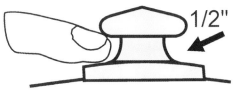

There is a much larger gap under the knobs of new lids. The gap under the knob in new lids is about 1/2". The space under the old knob is 1/4".

Candy Jar

The new Sharon candy jar (left) is very similar to the original (right).

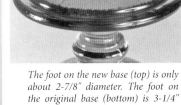

The foot on the new base (top) is only about 2-7/8" diameter. The foot on the original base (bottom) is 3-1/4" in diameter.

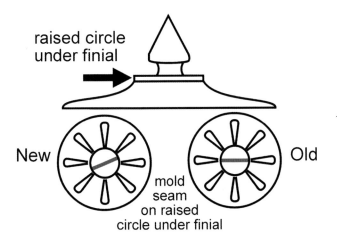

raised circle under finial

New   Old

mold seam on raised circle under finial

You can separate new and old lids by the location of the mold seam, shown in red, on the raised disc under the finial. When you look down at the circle from above, the mold seam on old lids is aligned with two raised ribs. The mold seam in the new lid appears between two raised ribs.

THUMBNAIL GUIDE

This thumbnail guide includes a selection of thumbnails from *Warman's Depression Glass, 4th edition*.

American Pioneer	Aurora	Beaded Block	Beaded Edge
Block Optic	Bubble	Candlewick	Cape Cod
Cherry Blossom	Christmas Candy	Cloverleaf	Colonial
Colonial Block	Colonial Fluted	Colony	Crocheted Crystal
Daisy	Diamond Quilted	Diana	Doric

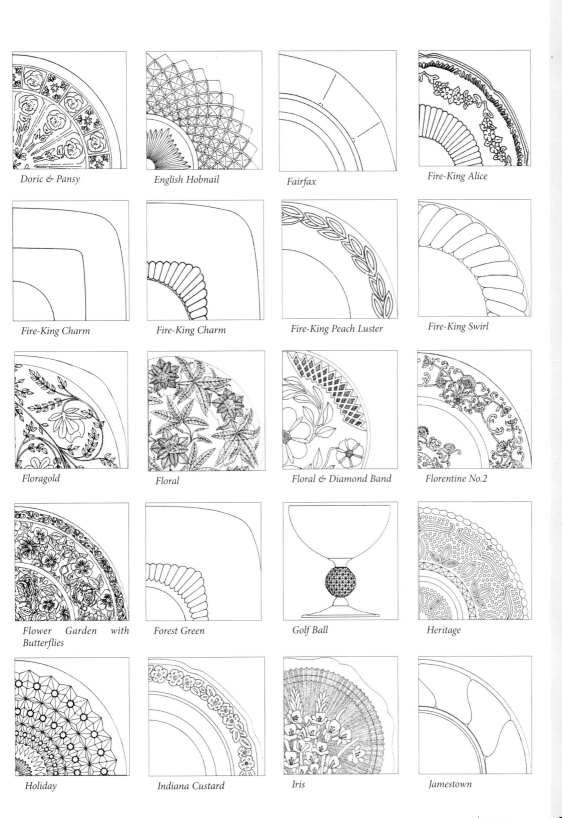

Doric & Pansy

English Hobnail

Fairfax

Fire-King Alice

Fire-King Charm

Fire-King Charm

Fire-King Peach Luster

Fire-King Swirl

Floragold

Floral

Floral & Diamond Band

Florentine No.2

Flower Garden with Butterflies

Forest Green

Golf Ball

Heritage

Holiday

Indiana Custard

Iris

Jamestown

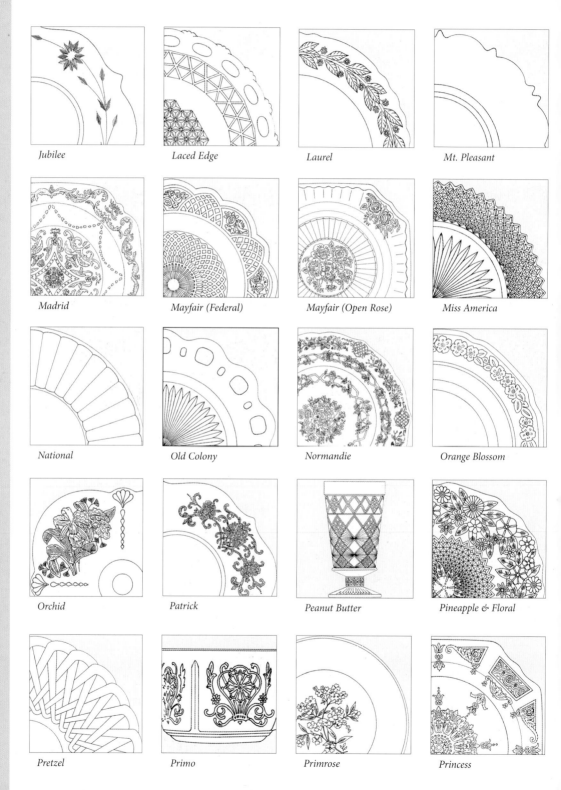

Jubilee	*Laced Edge*	*Laurel*	*Mt. Pleasant*
Madrid	*Mayfair (Federal)*	*Mayfair (Open Rose)*	*Miss America*
National	*Old Colony*	*Normandie*	*Orange Blossom*
Orchid	Patrick	Peanut Butter	Pineapple & Floral
Pretzel	Primo	Primrose	Princess

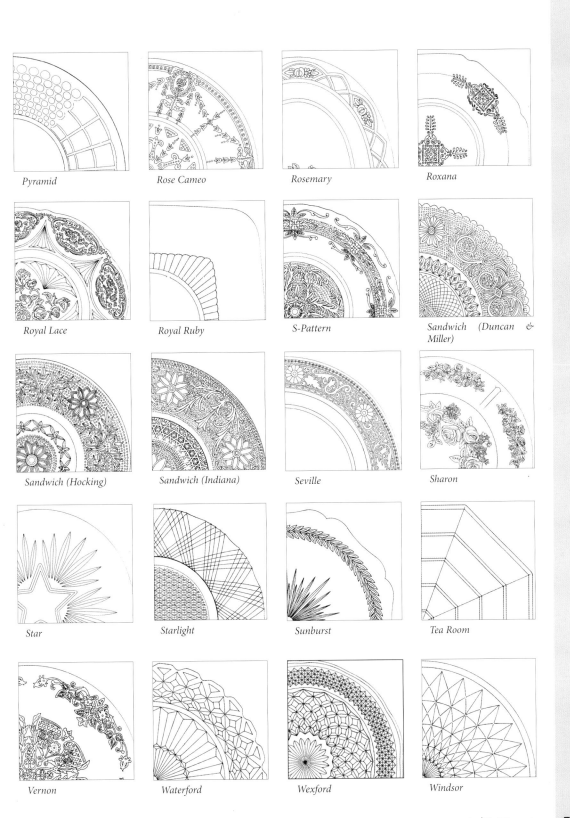

Pyramid

Rose Cameo

Rosemary

Roxana

Royal Lace

Royal Ruby

S-Pattern

Sandwich (Duncan & Miller)

Sandwich (Hocking)

Sandwich (Indiana)

Seville

Sharon

Star

Starlight

Sunburst

Tea Room

Vernon

Waterford

Wexford

Windsor

CERAMICS COLLECTING & CARE—POTTERY

by Suzanne Perrault
of the Perrault-Rago Gallery

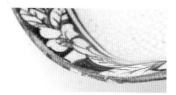

Damage such as chips and hairline cracks can be left alone, but if they jump out at you, repair might be a consideration.

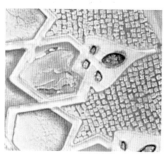

Signs of aging can be repaired, but you need to decide if the piece is financially or emotionally worth the investment.

Caution: Neither the author or publisher take any responsibility for damage that may occur from people cleaning their pottery by the methods reported herein.

Assuming that you, dear collectors, have been as a group amassing pottery for a good many years now, and assuming that that pottery had some age to begin with, chances are you've confronted the fact that you were either going to live with dirty and/or damaged ceramics, or were going to do something about it. You've thought of the dishwasher. You've considered Easy-Off oven cleaner. Do not despair. Help is on the way. Here's what I'd do:

Problem: You have a dirty vessel with vitrified (glossy) glaze, such as some porcelains, or Ohio wares such as Standard Glaze, Iris Glaze, etc.

Solution: Windex, then paws off.

Problem: You have a dirty vessel covered in a matte glaze, such as middle period Roseville, Rookwood Production, Grueby, etc.

Solution: Soak for several hours in very hot water, which will melt away greases, and a little drop of dishwashing liquid, which should help get rid of it. Move wares around during soaking (gently), and scrub (also gently) with a plastic brush or sponge. Rinse very well, dry with soft towel.

Problem: You have a vessel which was painted over by some demonic child with an artistic bent.

Solution: Find out what kind of paint. If it melts away in water, you're in luck. Let it soak, scrub, dry. If it's oil paint, you'll need to do something more drastic. Try spraying with Easy-Off oven cleaner and see what happens. It should start peeling off pretty cleanly. Once done, rinse, rinse, and rinse again, to remove every trace of chemical products. Buff dry. While it might sound abusive, do consider the alternative.

Problem: You have a candlestick or bud vase with wax on it.

Solution: Stop scratching and start melting. Put vessel or stick on a flat tray in your toaster oven at very low heat, like 100° or 150°. The wax should melt quickly. Wipe with paper towel.

Problem: You have a vase or tile with nicks to high points which bother you.

Solution: You can either a) accept the aging signs for what they are, and love it in spite of its defects or b) get it repaired. In this case, little nicks to high points should not require invasive surgery. The restorer, however, will easily charge you $100/hour, which may translate into $100/chip. Is the piece worth it?

Problem: You have a tile or vessel with a hairline crack or a chip. What to do?

Solution: Well, it depends. Did the imperfection occur during firing? If so, leave it be. It was most likely sold from the company or studio that way. If it happened post-manufacture, figure out if it is endangering the integrity of the piece. If it's just there and won't go anywhere, you might want to leave it alone. If, however, the damage is what jumps at you, and takes focus away from the piece, then you should have it repaired. The value of the piece often does not change significantly after restoration, but might make it easier to sell.

A FEW POINTS TO CONSIDER ABOUT RESTORATION:

• Restorers will charge you from $50-$150 per hour, which can translate into around $100 per chip. Do the math before sending your baby away.

• Figure out if you want a basic repair, or an invisible one. The former will fill in and stabilize, the latter do a blend with the rest of the piece, which will involve overspraying of the area, and in some cases, an overspraying of the entire piece. Would you be okay with a basic job by a lesser worker, or do you need top-of-the-line work by an artist?

• Most restorers, we have found, get the dreaded "Restorer's Disease." They start out friendly, quick, and cheap, and end up cranky, slow, and very expensive. We think it has something to do with all the chemicals they use.

• You can contact your local art museum for their referrals of restorers.

• Restorations have a finite shelf life, and will turn yellow with time, at which time they should be revamped.

• Some surfaces will take a bad restoration better than others. For example, a matte, sprayed-on glaze or one with much texture could hide a lot of sins. A smooth, shiny, light-colored glaze will show more faults.

Problem: You have a lamp base which was originally a vase. Do you keep it as such, or return it to its original condition?

Solution: If you love it and use it as a lamp, by all means leave it as such. If you are considering selling it, you may want to take it apart, as vases usually get higher prices than lamps do, even if drilled, even with a large rim belying the former presence of an oil font. Obviously, there are many exceptions to this rule, such as high-end makers like Tiffany, or lamps topped by fine and expensive shades.

When taking apart a drilled lamp, look for glaze around the drilled hole(s); the absence of which will indicate post-factory drilling. In this case, you should consider having the hole(s) filled in and restored.

Problem: You have a tile or panel, and wonder if you should have it framed.

Solution: By all means. You can't hurt it, and it is much better for your tile than mounting it in a spring-loaded plate rack. Framing is an excellent way to elevate a flat object to art status, and a great way to display it. Bring your tile to your local framer for a quick and inexpensive job, or contact one of the many carpenters who fabricate Arts & Crafts frames of quarter-sawn oak. For a list of those, pick up a copy of Style 1900 magazine (or www.style1900.com).

I've jotted down the ideas I thought would be most important, within my allocated space. I hope these tips will come in handy for you collectors of all things ceramic.

To frame or not to frame?

GLASS COLLECTING & CARE

by Ellen T. Schroy

Carnival Glass, Wishbone, Northwood, bowl, pie-crust edge, purple, 9-1/2", **$400.**

Amberina water pitcher, reverse diamond optic, applied reeded handle, polished pontil mark, late 19th/early 20th century, 7-1/4" h, **$155.**
Photo courtesy of Green Valley Auctions.

Loetz urn, iridescent blue body, oil spot pattern, two iridescent gold ribbed handles, 9" h, **$1,300.**
Photo courtesy of The Early Auction Company, LLC.

The world of antique glassware is as fascinating as ever. New discoveries of who made what and when continue to delight collectors. This segment of the marketplace continues to expand and disseminate knowledge because of ongoing scholarship. Museums such as Corning Glass and West Virginia Museum of American Glass have become leaders in the preservation of documentation relating to the glassware industry.

Remembering that glassware was created with high temperatures, many companies suffered terrible losses due to fires. Some rebounded and rebuilt, often glassblowers would travel to a new area or company after a disaster, taking along their formulas and techniques. Because glassware was one of the original American industries, there is a wealth of wonderful antique and collectible glassware available to collectors. Active participation in collector clubs in many aspects of the glassware market, such as carnival and depression glass, also allow collectors to learn more about this fascinating world.

The first glassware made is credited to the early Egyptians, but can be found in other cultures and civilizations. Glass became a good way to store and preserve food, something necessary before the days of refrigeration. Because glassware could be re-used and was trusted to be sanitary, millions of fruit jars, bottles, and other household items were made. As the glass industry geared up to make these mass-produced types of utilitarian items, many other factories, such as Fenton, Fostoria, and Heisey also decided it was a good time to encourage the American consumer to put more glassware on their tables. Early American Pattern Glass started the trend with beautiful stemware patterns.

The Depression-era glass manufacturers took this trend a step further in their desire to make affordable colorful glassware table settings. Add artists such as Louis Comfort Tiffany and his contemporaries, allowing the glassware industry to bloom with spectacular colors and textures. Companies such as Millersburg and Dugan took the techniques of pressing glass that the Early American Pattern Glass companies had perfected, added color, and finally iridescence to create their versions of carnival glass, which were early attempts to create inexpensive art glass for the masses.

This is an excellent time to buy antique glassware. Many dealers are finding new collectors not coming into the marketplace as fast as old collectors are disposing of their treasures. As with much of the antique marketplace, the high-end quality items are always in demand. The middle market is a little soft, and the low end of the market finds new collectors beginning to look at the market and trying to learn more. It's also a time when tray lots of wonderful vintage pieces of Early American Pattern Glass can be bought for excellent prices. Many of these pieces still have years of useful service in them and can safely be used to set a pretty table.

The very thing that often attracts collectors to glassware, the clarity, the brilliance, or the rich color, can be taken away in a few seconds if the piece is dropped. Antique glassware has been known to crack in cupboards without any warning because of temperature changes, or perhaps, a long hidden internal crack that decided it was time to let go. Because of this very fragile nature, care must be taken when handling and collecting antique glassware.

The use of cabinets with glass doors is one way to keep dust and pollutants from attacking the surface, but caution must be taken if there is lighting included in the cabinet. Excessive heating and/or exposure to lighting may cause some internal cracking. Exposure to strong ultra violet rays can also alter the chemical formula of glassware. Early American Pattern Glass is particulary prone to this problem when it has a high lead content. Long periods of exposure to strong sunlight may cause it to become purple in hue. Some collectors accept this as fine, a way for them to tell the glassware is old. Other collectors aren't so kind and prefer their glassware in as close to original condition as possible.

Opaque glass formulas, such as milk glass, and some of the agate formulas, are very susceptible to heat changes too. Actually it's the newer milk glass, circa 1950s and later, that's more prone to shattering with temperature changes. Apparently the glassblowers who first made milk glass added something to that formula that made it a little more durable. Westmoreland Glass Company offered a guarantee with several of their milk glass patterns and soon regretted the policy as many pieces were returned because of breakage as a result of temperature changes.

To be on the safe side, if purchasing antique glassware on a hot day, wrap it well and leave it cool down before washing it. The same is true for transporting glassware during cold temperatures. Wrap it well and then leave it wrapped and in a quiet state for several hours until it gradually warms up to room temperature.

Repairs to antique glassware can be made, but should be left to the professionals. Some old pieces of Early American Pattern Glass and Victorian Wares can be found with some interesting "make-do" repairs. However, glued on knobs, handles, etc., need to be properly done or the resulting repair shows and can detract from the whole look of a vintage piece. Small chips on the rim or foot of antique glassware can be professionally ground away. This type of professional repair can actually enhance the value of a piece as it will render it useful again. If considering making repairs to antique glassware, ask the restorer to see some examples of their work, discuss what kinds of techniques they would recommend and don't be timid about inquiring how much the work will cost.

Never ever put antique glassware in the dishwasher; the temperatures, chemicals, and rushing water may actually leave tiny surface scratches, something that can never be removed. Some depression-era glassware dealers have taken to the practice of removing aging gilt decoration as they feel its imperfect nature detracts from the beauty of the piece. Likewise, gilt decoration in excellent condition will add to the value of a piece, so check to see if the decoration appears to be original and not something that's been recently added. Because gilt and other enamel decorations were put onto the surface of the glassware after it was cooled and not re-fired, it is relatively easy to remove it. Modern craft paints and even stains are very good and are often used to touchup missing elements.

Carefully examine any decorated piece and compare the colors, texture, and technique to make sure it is original. If a piece of decorated glassware needs a good cleaning, start with as gentle a process as possible. Fill a plastic dishpan with lukewarm water, and then gently try washing the piece. If the surface dirt does not disappear, use Woolite or another gentle type of detergent first. A little experimentation on the back is a

Bride's basket, Hobbs' No. 323 Dew Drop pattern glass bowl, blue with frosted finish, Atkinson Silver Co. quadruple-plate frame, undetermined association, several flakes, late 19th century, 10-1/4" h, 10-1/2" d, **$100.**
Photo courtesy of Green Valley Auctions.

Beaded Block, ice blue vase, **$45.**

Pattern Glass, Jacob's Ladder celery, pale blue, **$55.**

Carnival Glass, Embroidered Mums, Northwood, bowl, blue electric, 9", **$600.**

Sugar shaker, Mount Washington, ovoid Burmese-colored body, enameled floral decoration, correct cap, 4-1/4" h, **$300.**
Photo courtesy of The Early Auction Company, LLC.

good idea. Using common household items, such as vinegar or ammonia, will also make antique glassware sparkle. Again, use a small amount, vinegar will help make it shine, no need to pickle it.

Make sure to carefully rinse and hand dry the object. Using a dishpan and carefully avoiding the faucets of a sink are of up-most importance as many a piece of antique glassware has fallen victim to a terrible clink as it hits the sink or plumbing fixtures. Putting an old towel into the bowl of the sink to eliminate hard surfaces may also be a good idea. Better yet, carefully dust antique glassware on a regular basis so that washing is limited.

If an accident should occur with a piece of antique glassware, carefully note any damage on your personal household inventory. This way, you'll be better informed when selling the piece and can honestly tell the next owner about its history. Some items, such as vintage cup plates, are often found in less-than-perfect condition. They were being made in some of the first mass-production settings and quality control wasn't as strict as it is today.

Some molds were simply under or over filled, causing gaps or extra bits of glass on the edges. Collectors often will calculate this type of manufacturing flaw into their valuation of a piece and many do not take too much off because of it. When collecting antique glassware, it's always good to remember that product was one of the first recycled materials known to the young American market. If imperfect pieces were created, they were often just smashed and returned to the cullet mixture where they would re-emerge as a beautiful piece of glassware.

Steuben shouldered vase, Rose Quartz body, 8-3/4" h, **$1,250.**
Photo courtesy of The Early Auction Company, LLC.

INDEX

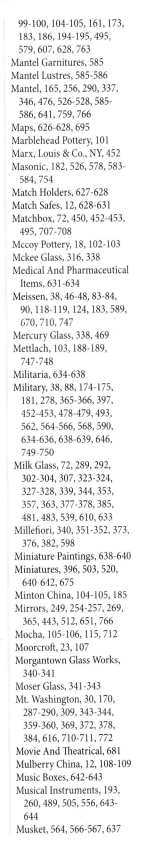

Turn to Collector Guides for Reliable Pricing

Depression Glass
Warman's® Companion
by Ellen T. Schroy
Tips for spotting fakes, reliable secondary market values, and 500 color photos for accurate identification of your glass appear in this handy collectors' companion.
5 x 8 • 272 pages
500 color photos

Item# Z0727 • $17.99

Carnival Glass
Warman's® Companion
by Ellen T. Schroy
The beauty and value of carnival glass is celebrated in 5,000 price listings for 250 classic and popular patterns, and the 650 stunning color photos included in this book.
Softcover • 5 x 8 • 272 pages
650 color photos

Item# Z0331 • $17.99

Warman's® Depression Glass
Identification and Price Guide
4th Edition
by Ellen T. Schroy
Provides the most specific identification process on the market, including current market values for more than 5,000 Depression glass items.
Softcover • 8-¼ x 10-⅞
288 pages • 500 color photos & line drawings
Item# WDG04 • $27.99

Warman's® Americana & Collectibles
Identification and Price Guide
11th Edition
by Ellen T. Schroy
Covers 240 popular Americana and collectibles categories, with collecting tips, historical information, reproduction and copycat information, detailed descriptions and up-to-date pricing.
Softcover • 7 x 10 • 544 pages
16-page color section
Item# WAMC11 • $18.99

Warman's® Flea Market Price Guide
4th Edition
Edited by Ellen T. Schroy
Offers more than 700 categories of hot collectibles, with descriptions and current pricing and practical advice on preparation, organization, and detecting fakes and forgeries. Includes a national flea market directory.
Softcover • 7 x 10 • 488 pages
1,000 b&w photos
8-page color section
Item# WFM4 • $21.99

Antique Trader® Guide to Fakes & Reproductions
4th Edition
by Mark Chervenka
Make sense of today's reproduction riddled collectibles market with the only guide to provide you with the tips, tools and 1,000 side-by-side color photos to spot telltale differences between the real deal, and fakes.
Softcover • 6 x 9 • 368 pages
1,000 color photos
Item# Z0723 • $24.99

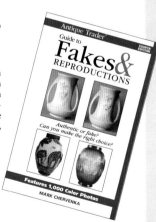